the ITF year 2004

The official yearbook of the International Tennis Federation

edited by mitzi ingram evans

The ITF Year Contributors

Writers

Stephen Bierley is the tennis correspondent of *The Guardian*, writes a weekly sports column on anything and everything, and also reports regularly on most sporting events ranging from the Olympics to night orienteering.

Tori Billington is the ITF Administrator for the Tennis Development programme and is responsible for a range of initiatives in developing countries including touring teams, junior circuits, coaches education, the supply of tennis equipment and the ITF School Tennis Initiative.

Chris Bowers is a freelance writer and broadcaster who has covered the global tennis circuit for more than 12 years. He has worked with the ITF in his capacity as executive director of the Tennis Radio Network, which provides radio reports from Davis Cup ties, he is the author of *The Book of Tennis* and *Davis Cup by BNP Paribas – The Year in Tennis 2004*, and has written and narrated a television series appearing in 2005 called The Book of Tennis Chronicles.

Isabelle Gemmel and **Neil Robinson** work in the ITF Seniors Department and are responsible for the running of the ITF Seniors Circuit and the ITF Seniors Individual World Championships and Team Competitions.

Richard Evans is the author of more than a dozen books on tennis, rugby and cricket, including the *ITF's Official History of the Davis Cup* He has commentated on Wimbledon for over 20 years for BBC Radio and writes a column for *Tennis Week*, New York and *Tennis Magazine*, Paris.

Craig Gabriel has been working in tennis for 25 years. He covers tennis for radio, television and the print media around the world, writes for several websites and has worked at four Olympic Games. He handles media operations and PR for tennis events that have included the Tennis Masters Cup and the World Doubles.

Sandra Harwitt is a freelance journalist covering tennis for the past 25 years. Among the over 30 prominent media outlets she has worked for through her career are: *The Miami Herald*, *The Philadelphia Inquirer*, *The New York Times*, *USA Today*, *The Australian*, *The Guardian*, *ESPN.com* and *Tennis Magazine*.

John Haylett has been a tennis writer for 25 years. He is the author of *The Illustrated Encyclopaedia of World Tennis (1989)* and is currently a staff writer for *Ace* magazine in Britain and editor of *British Tennis* magazine.

Stuart Miller is the ITF's Technical Manager. He is also Vice President of the International Society of Biomechanics in Sports, and has published academic research papers in tennis and other scientific subjects.

Eleanor Preston is a freelance tennis journalist and broadcaster. She reports on the men's and women's circuit and on junior events around the world for a number of UK publications and English language radio stations.

Ossian Shine is the Tennis Correspondent for Reuters international news agency. Author of *The Language of Tennis*, he has reported on the sport from around the globe for the past decade and writes a weekly column for Reuters.

Joanne Sirman is a member of the ITF Communications Department and editor of *ITFWorld magazine*. She coordinated the ITF's contribution to the annual *World of Tennis* for several years, and was responsible for the launch and first two editions of *The ITF Year*.

Photographers

Ron Angle, Sergio Carmona, Florian Eisele, Sergei Golovanov, Rien Hokken, Daniel Maurer, Fred Mullane, Susan Mullane, Paul Zimmer.

ISBN: 1-903013-25-9

Designed and produced by Domino 4, 01932 264550.

Contents

Page

Introduction

Welcome to the ITF Year by Francesco Ricci Bitti	1
ITF Board of Directors	4
ITF Office Holders	9
2005 ITF Calendar of Events	10

Section 1: The 2004 ITF World Champions

Biographies of Senior Champions	11
Biographies of Junior Champions	13
Biographies of Wheelchair Champions	14
ITF World Champions Roll of Honour	15

Section 2: ITF Team Competitions

Spain Make History in Seville by Ossian Shine	18
2004 Davis Cup by BNP Paribas Results	22
Russian Revolution Reaches Fed Cup by Sandra Harwitt	38
2004 Fed Cup Results	42
Defending Champions Triumph in Hopman Cup by Joanne Sirman	52
2004 Hyundai Hopman Cup Results	54

Section 3: Elite Tournaments

The Men's Year 2004 by Steve Bierley	56
The Women's Year 2004 by Richard Evans	60
Tennis Wins Gold in Athens by Craig Gabriel	64
Olympic Results: Athens 2004	68
2004 Australian Open Drawsheets	70
2004 Roland Garros Drawsheets	80
2004 Wimbledon Drawsheets	90
2004 US Open Drawsheets	100
2004 Tennis Masters Cup Results	110
2004 WTA Tour Championships Results	111
2004 Men's Professional Tournaments	112
2004 Women's Professional Tournaments	113

Section 4: ITF Tournaments

The ITF Men's Circuit 2004	116
ITF Men's Circuit 2004 Futures Results	118
ITF Men's Circuit 2004 Satellite Results	137
The ITF Women's Circuit 2004	140
ITF Women's Circuit 2004 Results	142

Section 5: ITF Development

Tennis Development in 2004 by Tori Billington	162
Marketing the Game	166
Monfils Shines as a Star of the Future by Eleanor Preston	168

Abbreviations used in this book:

A alternate	**SE** special exempt	**GD** Girls' Doubles
abn abandoned	**WC** wildcard	**WS** Women's Singles
d defeated	**w/o** walkover	**WD** Women's Doubles
def default	**(I)** Indoor	**MS** Men's Singles
LL lucky loser	**(O)** Outdoor	**MD** Men's Doubles
P protected ranking	**BS** Boys' Singles	**QS** Quad Singles
Q qualifier	**GS** Girls' Singles	**QD** Quad Doubles
ret retired	**BD** Boys' Doubles	

Contents (continued)

Section 5: ITF Development (continued)

	Page
ITF Junior World Rankings 2004 Points Explanation	172
ITF Junior World Rankings 2004	173
ITF Junior Circuit 2004 Results	174
World Junior Tennis Finals 2004	199
Junior Davis Cup by BNP Paribas Final 2004	201
Junior Fed Cup Final 2004	201
2004 Australian Open Junior Drawsheets	202
2004 Roland Garros Junior Drawsheets	206
2004 The Junior Championships, Wimbledon Drawsheets	210
2004 US Open Junior Drawsheets	214
The Wheelchair Tennis Year by Chris Bowers	218
NEC Wheelchair Tennis Tour 2004 Results	222
Invacare World Team Cup 2004	229
ITF Wheelchair Tennis World Rankings 2004	230
Paralympic Results: Athens 2004	231
The Seniors Year 2004 by Isabelle Gemmel and Neil Robinson	232
24th ITF Seniors and Super-Seniors World Individual Championships	236
2004 ITF Seniors and Super-Seniors World Team Championships	237
ITF Seniors World Rankings 2004	238
The Technical Year by Dr Stuart Miller	242

Section 6: Reference Section

The Greatest – Biographies of Leading Men	246
The Greatest – Biographies of Leading Women	270
Roll of Honour: Davis Cup	288
Roll of Honour: Fed Cup	296
Roll of Honour: Hopman Cup	300
Roll of Honour: Olympic Tennis Event	301
Roll of Honour: Australian Championships	305
Roll of Honour: French Championships	310
Roll of Honour: The Championships, Wimbledon	316
Roll of Honour: US Championships	322
Roll of Honour: The Grand Slam	331
Roll of Honour: Tennis Masters Cup	331
Roll of Honour: WTA Tour Championsips	332
Roll of Honour: ATP Tour World Championships	333
Roll of Honour: Grand Slam Cup	334
Roll of Honour: Australian Junior Championships	335
Roll of Honour: French Junior Championships	339
Roll of Honour: The Junior Championships, Wimbledon	342
Roll of Honour: US Junior Championships	344
Roll of Honour: World Junior Tennis	347
Roll of Honour: Junior Davis Cup and Junior Fed Cup	348
Roll of Honour: ITF Sunshine and Connolly Cups	352
Roll of Honour: Wheelchair Tennis Masters	354
Roll of Honour: World Team Cup	354
Roll of Honour: Paralympic Wheelchair Tennis Event	355
Roll of Honour: ITF Seniors and Super-Seniors World Individual Championships	357
Roll of Honour: ITF Seniors and Super-Seniors World Team Championships	367
Roll of Honour: Nations Senior Cup	373
National Associations	374
ITF Recognised Organisations	389
Official Tennis Championships Recognised by the ITF	390
International Tennis Hall of Fame Enshrinees	391
Obituaries	393
Country Abbreviations	395

Welcome to the ITF Year

By Francesco Ricci Bitti

The ITF Year 2004 proved to be one of the most compelling in memory with great stories from start to finish. From the Hopman Cup in January through the Davis Cup Final in December, this year captivated not only tennis fans but sports fans everywhere.

Roger Federer won almost everything of note in 2004, except Roland Garros and a longed-for Olympic medal. With three Grand Slams and the Tennis Masters Cup in his win column, Roger virtually lapped the next highest man, Andy Roddick, in both the race and entry rankings and dominated men's tennis more thoroughly than any man since the days of McEnroe and Borg. And that he achieved it with such professionalism and genuine good humour makes him a great representative of our sport. The ITF is honoured to have Roger Federer as our ITF Men's World Champion for 2004.

On the women's side, no one player dominated but one country, Russia, certainly did with seven players in the year-end top 15. Three different Russian women won Grand Slam titles – Anastasia Myskina at Roland Garros, Maria Sharapova at Wimbledon and Svetlana Kuznetsova at the US Open with Sharapova winning the season-ending WTA Tour Championships. Myskina reached the semis at the Olympic Tennis Event and led her country to its first Fed Cup title before an adoring hometown crowd. Myskina's consistency throughout the year plus her outstanding Fed Cup performance made her the ITF Women's World Champion for 2004.

Our congratulations go to Roger and Anastasia as well as to Bob and Mike Bryan, and Virginia Ruano Pascual and Paola Suarez who will repeat at ITF Doubles World Champions. The Bryans edged ahead based on their 2004 performance in Davis Cup and their victory in the Tennis Masters Cup while Ruano Pascual and Suarez, World Champions for the third consecutive year, continue to be the best doubles team in women's tennis.

Four of the most memorable weeks for me were the Olympic Tennis Event in August, the Paralympics in September, the Fed Cup Final in November and the Davis Cup by BNP Paribas Final in December. All provided the drama, the passion, that special magic that comes when you play for your country. We have seen that unique quality again and again in our international team competitions, from Juniors through to Super Seniors, and we prize it.

I will start with Davis Cup by BNP Paribas, enjoying another banner year from the first round to the Final. And what a Final it was. Some 27,200 people crowded into a temporary stadium within a stadium in Seville, covered by a temporary roof, to see Spain take on the United States. The sheer number of spectators was impressive and made more so by the knowledge that twice that number of tickets could easily have been sold. The tennis was top quality and the drama high and so was the sportsmanship. It was clear that, for both teams, the desire to win the Davis Cup was a dream and that made it as poignant to watch the Americans in defeat as it was joyous to witness the Spanish victory. We saw Rafael Nadal emerge as a full-fledged star and Carlos Moya cap his outstanding career with the victory that he wanted the most. We saw how very good the Bryan brothers are and how hard Andy Roddick and Mardy Fish were prepared to fight to win the prize. It was a memorable weekend.

It was good news all year for Davis Cup with a full complement of sponsorship. Thanks to our title sponsor, BNP Paribas, and to our international sponsors, Adecco, Fossil, Getronics, Hugo Boss, Kia Motors and NH Hotels. We are happy to announce that we have renewed our agreements with Adecco and with Wilson Sporting Goods and signed a new agreement with NTT as our official managed hosting partner. This success is in no small part due to outstanding attendance figures, tv ratings and website numbers as well as strong player participation and that incredible magic that is Davis Cup.

Fed Cup also had a strong year in 2004 but we look forward with great anticipation to 2005 when we will launch a new format and a new brand. With the support of the players and the WTA Tour, Fed Cup 2005 and beyond will be played in the home-and-away format that has proved so successful in Davis Cup over three weeks inside the calendar with the final being staged the week after the US Open. To celebrate the new beginning for Fed Cup, we have launched a vibrant new brand. Our confidence in Fed Cup for the future is very high and we look forward to a strong new start for Fed Cup.

Everyone at the ITF thought the Olympic Tennis Event in Athens was the best ever. The excellence of the field, the outstanding quality of the new purpose-built tennis centre and the enthusiastic crowds, that appeared after a sparse opening day, all contributed to a great event. But the drama on the court distinguished this year's Olympic Tennis Event from the others before it. Who will ever forget the golden glory of Justine Henin-Hardenne, whose truncated year had one moment of pure emotion? Who will ever forget the elation of Fernando Gonzalez and Nicolas Massu as they won the first ever gold medal for Chile, repeated on the following day as Massu won the singles gold as well? Or the delight of the Chinese women, Tian Tian Sun and Ting Li, winning a first tennis gold for their country? And these highs were sobered by the disappointed, almost tragic faces of the players who lost in the medal rounds and those, like Roger Federer and Andy Roddick, who wanted so much to do well in Athens and could not find a way to achieve it.

One new player who will be remembered from Athens was the effervescent Marcos Baghdatis of Cyprus, last year's ITF Junior World Champion. He has already begun to make his mark on the tour. The 2004 ITF Junior Boys World Champion Gael Monfils, like Baghdatis, is a strong contender for success on the tour. Monfils won the first three Grand Slams of the year and had a chance to equal Stefan

Edberg's feat of a Junior Grand Slam but fell just short of that hurdle. Nevertheless, the very talented Frenchman has signalled his arrival and we look forward to watching him as he develops over the coming years.

The 2004 ITF Junior Girls World Champion is Michaela Krajicek of the Netherlands, winner of the US Open Juniors. She finished the year ranked No. 1 and fought off a strong challenge from Katerina Bondarenko of Ukraine. The profile of the ITF Juniors Circuit continues to grow and that is as true of the Circuit as it is of the team competitions, Junior Davis Cup by BNP Paribas, Junior Fed Cup and the World Junior Tennis. This is a special year for Junior Tennis. We launched the Combined Ranking and that means that we will have a single World Champion this year, one for boys and one for girls. We also celebrated over a quarter of a century of competition and launched a book in its honour in June.

Junior Davis Cup by BNP Paribas and Junior Fed Cup found a new home in 2004 at the Real Club de Polo in Barcelona where the competition will be played until 2006. Fittingly the Spanish boys won the Junior Davis Cup title while the Argentine girls won the Junior Fed Cup crown. World Junior Tennis, the ITF's annual 14-and-under competition, was held again this year in Prostejov, Czech Republic for the sixth consecutive year and the excitement was high as the British boys and the Belarus girls lifted the trophy.

Two familiar faces will be the ITF Wheelchair World Champions for 2005, Esther Vergeer of the Netherlands and

Estadio Olimpico de Sevilla held a record-breaking 27,200 spectators

No. 1 for the third consecutive year. He won ten singles and five doubles titles in 2004 and won the silver medal in singles at the Paralympic Games, losing to Robin Ammerlaan of the Netherlands, and the bronze medal in doubles.

The Paralympic Games were also a major success, with over 30,000 spectators in the first three days alone watching wonderful tennis. Eight different nations were represented on the medal table, showing the growing depth of wheelchair tennis. Congratulations to the other gold medallists, Shingo Kunieda and Satoshi Saida of Japan in men's doubles, Peter Norfolk of Great Britain in Quad Singles, and Nick Taylor and David Wagner of the United States in Quad Doubles and to all

sponsors and thank them for their enthusiastic support of wheelchair tennis.

Another wheelchair tennis initiative that continues to grow is the Silver Fund, a development initiative in association with the Cruyff Foundation. The Silver Fund aims to bring the sport to areas of the world that would not normally have the means or the infrastructure to develop it. In 2004, the Cruyff Foundation increased its involvement to further develop junior programmes in wheelchair tennis including four international and 15 national junior wheelchair camps, Junior Masters, Junior Invacare World Team Cup and the development of a junior wheelchair ranking.

Junior and Wheelchair Tennis are just two of the departments that fall under Tennis Development overseeing the growth of tennis around the world. In 2004, over US $3.3 million was spent on the development of tennis worldwide with US$2 million being provide by the ITF and the rest by the Grand Slam tournaments.

The growth of interest in tennis in Asia was reflected by the appointment of Hichem Riani as the ITF Development Officer for West Asia. Both Oman and Myanmar hosted junior events in 2004 for the first time, Oman at the new Sultan Qaboos Sports Complex. Coaches education remains a top priority for our Tennis Development and in 2004, 44 courses were held including a memorable one in Amman in September.

The ITF Touring Teams have nurtured

> It was clear that, for both teams, the desire to win the Davis Cup was a dream and that made it as poignant to watch the Americans in defeat as it was joyous to witness the Spanish victory.

David Hall of Australia. Esther, World Champion for the fifth time, has dominated wheelchair tennis, holding the No. 1 ranking since 1999. She turned in a perfect record in both singles and doubles, winning 15 singles and 14 doubles titles including a Paralympics gold medal in both singles and doubles. David Hall, World Champion for the sixth time, finished as the year-end

the other medallist in Athens.

There were 120 tournaments on the NEC Wheelchair Tennis Tour this year and approximately $800,000 in prize money. Other principal competitions in wheelchair tennis include the NEC Wheelchair Masters, the Invacare World Team Cup and the Camozzi Doubles Masters. We appreciate the support of all of our the talent of many of today's top stars and continues its important work with 17 teams involving 152 players from 72 countries. Particularly successful was the girls team from Eastern Europe that included Madaline Gojnea of Romania, a finalist at the Roland Garros juniors, Katerina Bondarenko of Ukraine and Victoria Azarenka and Volha Havartsova, who won the Wimbledon junior singles and doubles respectively.

One other initiative managed by Tennis Development that was initiated through the ITF's Marketing the Game Programme is the International Tennis Number. This rating system, that reflects a player's general standard of play, had by midyear 22 nations who had adopted the ITF as its rating system or recognised the ITN alongside its existing system. The ITN On-Court Assessment, the ITN website and materials have all enhanced this great programme.

Also a part of Development is the Senior Tennis Department, a new name for the former Vets Department with Super-Seniors for the older age groups. The ITF Seniors World Team Competition and World Individual Championships were held at the Club Ali Bey Manavgat, Turkey in May while the ITF Super-Seniors World Individual and World Team Championships were held in Philadelphia, USA in September. A record 137 teams representing some 24 nations entered the Super-Seniors Team Championships while a record 723 individuals participated in the Individual Competition.

The Technical Department continues to set the standard for technical research in our sport. Some innovations in 2004 are the development of Tennis GUT, a software package that simulates the interaction between rackets, balls and surfaces, allowing the ITF to control the nature of the game and the expansion of the Court Surface Classification Scheme. Over 60 surfaces have obtained an ITF surface pace rating. The Department has also undertaken the ITF Survey of Nations, the most comprehensive survey of the global state of tennis with results due in 2005.

The ITF Professional Tennis Department not only takes care of our flagship events, Davis Cup by BNP Paribas, Fed Cup and Hopman Cup, but also looks after the ITF Men's and Women's Circuit events.

The ITF Men's and Women's Circuits provide entry level opportunities for professional players with the Men's Circuit offering 471 weeks of tournaments in 74 countries with total prize money of $4,900,000 and the Women's Circuit 349 events in 62 countries with total prize money of $7,110,000.

The big news in Professional Circuits, however, and a big step forward for the ITF in general is the introduction on the on-line entry system, IPIN. This innovation, developed by the ITF's Professional Circuits and Information and Communication Technology Departments, will revolutionise the running of the circuit. Over 3,000 players have already obtained their unique IPIN number. The ITF will become the sole entry authority for all men's and women's ITF Pro Circuit events in January 2005 while the online service is due to be launched in April. This is a great step for our sport and I am proud that the ITF has taken the lead in this technology.

Also, in 2004, the ITF launched seven new weblets including the new IPIN, Technical and Paralympic sites. Overall, the ITF has three standalone websites, itftennis.com with 13 weblets, daviscup.com and fedcup.com. Davis Cup and Fed Cup are reaching huge audiences while the ITF website and weblets are showing gratifying growth.

The ITF staged another a successful AGM this year in Barcelona, the final celebration of the centenary of the Catalan Tennis Federation. Some 90 nations and 280 delegates, partners and staff participated in this year's AGM and their dedication to their role in managing our sport is much appreciated. The new ITF logo was launched at the AGM and has been well received throughout the year.

Yannick Noah received the ITF's highest honour, the Philippe Chatrier Award, at the ITF World Champions Dinner in Paris in June. It was an emotional evening for all of us as he paid tribute to the former ITF President who had been so influential in Yannick's life.

As I look ahead to 2005, I cannot help but wonder how the important benchmarks of this year will affect the future. Will Roger Federer match his peerless 2004? Will the Russian women continue to dominate women's tennis and perhaps achieve a Russian Slam at the 2005 Australian Open and a repeat of Fed Cup success in next year's new format? Will the huge outpouring of love for Davis Cup shown by 27,200 people in Seville provide a catalyst for an even stronger competition in the coming years? Of course, I don't have the answers but my guess is that 2005 will provide even more wonderful moments for our sport and for the ITF.

Francesco Ricci Bitti with Olympic men's singles medallists

2005 ITF Calendar of Events

Davis Cup by BNP Paribas: World Group 1st Round: 4-6 March
World Group Quarterfinals: 15-17 July
World Group Semifinals: 23-25 September
World Group Final: 2-4 December

Fed Cup: World Group I 1st Round: 23-24 April
World Group I Semifinals: 9-10 July
World Group I Final: 17-18 September

Hyundai Hopman Cup: Perth, Australia: 1-8 January

Grand Slams: Australian Open: 17-30 January
Roland Garros: 23 May-5 June
Wimbledon: 20 June-3 July
US Open: 29 August-11 September

WTA Tour Championships presented by Porsche: Los Angeles, USA: 9-14 November

Tennis Masters Cup: Shanghai, China: 12-20 November

ITF Seniors World Team Championships: Perth, Australia: 27 March – 1 April

ITF Seniors World Individual Championships: Perth, Australia: 2-9 April

ITF World Champions Dinner: Paris, France: 31 May

ITF Annual General Meeting: Prague, Czech Republic: 15-17 June

Invacare World Team Cup (Wheelchair): Groningen, Netherlands: 20-26 June

World Junior Tennis Final (14&U): Prostejov, Czech Republic: 8-13 August

Junior Davis Cup by BNP Paribas/ Junior Fed Cup (16&U): Barcelona, Spain: 27 September – 2 October

ITF Super-Seniors World Team Championships: Antalya, Turkey: 17-22 October

14th ITF Worldwide Coaches Workshop: Antalya, Turkey: 17-23 October

ITF Super-Seniors World Individual Champs: Antalya, Turkey: 23-30 October

Camozzi Doubles Masters (Wheelchair): Brescia, Italy: 8-13 November

NEC Wheelchair Tennis Masters: Amersfoort, Netherlands: 15-20 November

Nations Senior Cup: Marbella, Spain: 7-9 July

The 2004 ITF World Champions

Every year, the ITF honours the players who have made the biggest impact on the tennis world in that season, naming a World Champion in senior, junior and wheelchair competition. On the following pages are the biographies of the 2004 recipients of the accolade, and the honours list of past winners.

The 2004 ITF World Champions will receive their awards at the ITF World Champions Dinner, an annual event which takes place in June during Roland Garros.

Roger Federer (SUI)

Federer is the undisputed No. 1, his World Champion status assured after winning three Grand Slam titles and a second successive Tennis Masters Cup crown. With a total of 11 titles in 2004, he equalled the record of Thomas Muster for the most titles in a season and surpassed the achievements of John McEnroe and Bjorn Borg in winning 13 straight finals.

The Swiss 23-year-old claimed his second Grand Slam title at the Australian Open in January and went on to successfully defend his Wimbledon crown, defeating Roddick in the decider. Federer scooped his third major of the year at the US Open becoming the first man since Mats Wilander in 1988 to win three of the four majors in a season. His 11th title came in Houston where he successfully defended his Tennis Masters Cup title.

On top of all this, he found time to represent his country. Federer took Switzerland to the quarterfinals of the Davis Cup by BNP Paribas, winning all four of his singles matches.

Perhaps the only significant blip in Federer's stunning year was his devastating second-round loss at the Olympics.

Date and place of birth: 8 August 1981, Basel, Switzerland
Residence: Oberwil, Switzerland
Height: 6'1"/1.85m
Weight: 177lbs/80kg
Plays: right handed
Coach: None

Highest Entry System singles ranking: 1 (first reached 2 February 2004)
Year-end Entry System singles ranking: 2004-1; 2003-2; 2002-6; 2001-13; 2000-29; 1999-64; 1998-302; 1997-T700.
2004 Grand Slam singles titles: Australian Open, Wimbledon, US Open
Other 2004 singles titles: Dubai, Indian Wells, Hamburg, Halle, Gstaad, Canadian Open, Bangkok, Tennis Masters Cup
Career Grand Slam singles titles: 4
Total other singles titles: 18
2004 singles win-loss record: 74-6
Career singles win-loss record: 314-119

Anastasia Myskina (RUS)

It was a tough year for naming the ITF Women's World Champion, but Anastasia Myskina, with the highest year-end ranking of the season's Grand Slam winners and as the architect of Russia's historic Fed Cup victory, edged out the competition.

The 23-year-old from Moscow opened the floodgates for Russian women when her Roland Garros triumph made her the first woman from her country ever to claim a Grand Slam title, overwhelming friend and countrywoman Elena Dementieva in an emotional final.

In addition to titles in Doha and on home soil at the Kremlin Cup, Myskina reached the semifinals of the Olympics and was just one game away from the gold medal match before losing a 5-1 lead to eventual champion Justine Henin-Hardenne. Myskina lost the bronze medal play-off to Alicia Molik.

Maybe it was narrowly missing out on a medal that spurred her on when it came to representing Russia in the Fed Cup Semifinals and Final. Myskina went 5-0 through the last two rounds, but it was a doubles victory, when she teamed with Vera Zvonareva to win the nail-biting decisive fifth rubber in the final, that gave Russia its first-ever Fed Cup title.

Date and place of birth: 8 July 1981, Moscow, Russia
Residence: Moscow, Russia
Height: 5'8"/1.74m
Weight: 130lbs/59kg
Plays: right handed
Coach: Jens Gerlach

Highest singles ranking: 2 (first reached 13 September 2004)
Year-end singles ranking: 2004-3; 2003-7; 2002-11; 2001-59; 2000-58; 1999-65; 1998-293; 1997-622; 1996-818; 1995-920
2004 Grand Slam singles titles: Roland Garros
Other 2004 singles titles: Doha, Moscow
Career Grand Slam singles titles: 1
Total other singles titles: 8
2004 singles win-loss record: 56-20
Career singles win-loss record: 186-106

The 2004 ITF World Champions (continued)

Bob Bryan (USA) and Mike Bryan (USA)

The Bryan twins are ITF World Doubles Champions for the second successive year thanks to their tour-best seven team titles and an outstanding performance representing the United States in Davis Cup by BNP Paribas. At the Australian Open the Californian duo reached their second straight Grand Slam final, but lost to defending champions Michael Llodra and Fabrice Santoro. Although there would be no further Grand Slam titles in 2004 the Bryans did win titles on all four surfaces and capped the year in Houston when they were the first team in almost 20 years to successfully defend a doubles season-ender. The Bryans played four Davis Cup rubbers in 2004 without dropping a set, a feat never previously achieved since the World Group was established in 1981. In USA's 3-2 loss to Spain in the final, it was the nation's indestructible twins who kept hopes alive until the Sunday, taking their career doubles record in the competition to 5-0.

Bob Bryan (USA)
Date and place of birth: 29 April 1978, Camarillo, California, USA
Residence: Camarillo, California, USA
Height: 6'4"/1.93m
Weight: 193lbs/87kg
Plays: left handed
Coach: Philip Farmer
Highest doubles entry system ranking: 1= (first reached 8 September 2003)
Year-end doubles entry system rankings: 2004-4=; 2003-2=; 2002-7; 2001-23; 2000-63; 1999-T64; 1998-T174; 1997-T635; 1996-T654; 1995-T1200

Mike Bryan (USA)
Date and place of birth: 29 April 1978, Camarillo, California, USA
Residence: Camarillo, California, USA
Height: 6'3"/1.91m
Weight: 185lbs/83kg
Plays: right handed
Coach: Philip Farmer
Highest doubles entry system ranking: 1= (first reached 8 September 2003)
Year-end doubles entry system rankings: 2004-4=; 2003-2=; 2002-7; 2001-23; 2000-63; 1999-T64; 1998-T174; 1997-T635; 1996-T654; 1995-T1200

2004 Grand Slam team titles: None
Other 2004 team titles: Adelaide, Memphis, Acapulco, Queen's, Los Angeles, Basle, Tennis Masters Cup.
Career Grand Slam team titles: 1
Total other team titles: 20
2004 team win-loss record: 64-17
Career team win-loss record: 257-131

Virginia Ruano Pascual (ESP) and Paola Suarez (ARG)

Roger Federer wasn't the only player who won three Grand Slam titles in 2004. Virginia Ruano Pascual and Paola Suarez teamed to victory in Melbourne, Paris and New York to finish the No. 1-ranked pair by a mile. They were the first female doubles team to win three majors in a year since Martina Hingis and Jana Novotna in 1998.

The Spanish-Argentine combination are ITF World Champions in doubles for a third successive year, having reached 11 finals in 2004 and taken six titles. Their third Grand Slam title of the year, in New York, booked their place in the record books as the first team in the Open Era to win three consecutive US Open titles.

Representing different countries, the pair went their separate ways for the Olympic Games, but both came home from Athens with medals. Ruano Pascual won the silver with Conchita Martinez, while Suarez teamed with Patricia Tarabini to win bronze.

Virginia Ruano Pascual (ESP)
Date and place of birth: 21 September 1973, Madrid, Spain
Residence: Madrid, Spain
Height: 5'6"/1.69m
Weight: 132lbs/60kg
Plays: right handed
Coach: brother, Juan Ramon Ruano
Highest doubles ranking: 1 (first reached 8 September 2003)
Year-end doubles rankings: 2004-1; 2003-2; 2002-2; 2001-7; 2000-10; 1999-44; 1998-27; 1997-90; 1996-115; 1995-T387; 1994-145; 1993-T212; 1992-97; 1991-124; 1990-184

Paola Suarez (ARG)
Date and place of birth: 23 June 1976, Pergamino, Argentina
Residence: Munro, Argentina
Height: 5'7"/1.70m
Weight: 141lbs/64 kg
Plays: right handed
Coach: Daniel Pereya
Highest doubles ranking: 1 (first reached 9 September 2002)
Year-end doubles rankings: 2004 – 2; 2003-1; 2002-1; 2001-5; 2000-7; 1999-40; 1998-23; 1997-53; 1996-83; 1995-224; 1994-T707; 1993-290; 1992-T248; 1991-T419

2004 Grand Slam team titles: Australian Open, Roland Garros, US Open
Other 2004 team titles: Indian Wells, Charleston, Luxembourg
Career Grand Slam team titles: 7
Total other team titles: 19
2004 team win-loss record: 56-11
Career team win-loss record: 262-79

Gael Monfils (FRA)

Michaella Krajicek (NED)

Outstanding is the word to describe Gael Monfils who captured three Grand Slam titles in 2004. The French boy was on course to emulate Edberg's 1983 Junior Grand Slam before a knee injury hampered his chances at the US Open.

The first black player since Zina Garrison in 1981 to become ITF Junior World Champion, Monfils only lost two matches on the ITF Junior Circuit in 2004. The amazing run of 30 victories began at the Australian Open where he defeated compatriot Josselin Ouanna to win the title. His winning streak also took in Roland Garros and Wimbledon titles. An injury shortly afterwards left him too short a recovery time to achieve the coveted win at the US Open.

Monfils also found the time to make a splash on the professional circuit when he qualified for the Paris Masters. Once in the main draw Monfils defeated former champion Thomas Enqvist, before giving Lleyton Hewitt a run for his money.

Date and place of birth: 01 September 1986, Paris, France
Residence: Paris, France
Height: 6'3"/1.92m
Weight: 168lbs/76kg
Plays: right handed
Coach: Thierry Champion
Highest ranking: 1 (first reached 2 February 2004)
Year end ranking: 2004-1; 2003-21 (singles); 2002-44 (singles)

2004 Grand Slam titles: Australian Open, Roland Garros, Wimbledon
Other 2004 singles titles: LTA International Junior Championships – Roehampton
2004 singles win-loss record: 31-2
Career singles win-loss record: 78-22

After finishing a close second to Kirsten Flipkens last year Michaella Krajicek fulfilled her promise and becomes the first Dutch player to receive the honour of ITF Junior World Champion.

The highlight of the 15-year-old's year was undoubtedly the US Open where she fought off match points in the semifinals before taking the title with victory over home favourite Jessica Kirkland. Krajicek also won the doubles with Marina Erakovic. Her reward was reaching the No. 1 position in the rankings for the first time on 13 September.

During the year Krajicek won three further singles titles and reached the semifinals at Wimbledon and the Italian Open. In the first year of the Junior Combined Ranking, doubles results are also vital. As well as the US Open doubles title, she also won Roland Garros (with Katerina Bohmova) and three more titles.

Despite her busy schedule she also found time to make her debut for Netherlands in Fed Cup, competing in the Europe/Africa Zone 1 in Greece.

Date and place of birth: 09 January 1989, Delft, Netherlands
Residence: Almere, Netherlands
Height: 5'9"/1.76m
Weight: 145lbs/65kg
Plays: right handed
Coach: Petr Krajicek (father)
Highest ranking: 1 (first reached 13 September 2004)
Year end rankings: 2004-1, 2003-2 (singles), 2002-59 (singles)

2004 Grand Slam titles: US Open
Other 2004 singles titles: International Bavarian Junior Challenge, LTA International Junior Championships – Roehampton, International Luxembourg Indoor Junior Championships
2004 singles win-loss record: 41-6
Career singles win-loss record: 116-16

The 2004 ITF World Champions (continued)

David Hall (AUS)

Having been ITF World Champion in 2003, Hall started 2004 in pole position but was chased to the year-end No. 1 ranking all the way by his nemesis Robin Ammerlaan. Throughout the season, Hall and Ammerlaan fought over the top spot, which changed hands between the pair six times. Hall collected ten singles titles in 2004, three of which were at Super Series tournaments.

At the Paralympic Games in Athens, Hall had been hoping to become the first man to win two singles gold medals after his triumph in Sydney 2000, but he was to be denied by Ammerlaan in the final. In addition to his silver medal in singles, Hall also made the podium in doubles, winning the bronze with countryman Anthony Bonaccurso.

Hall defeated Michael Jeremiasz in the final of the NEC Wheelchair Masters in October to clinch No. 1. The 34-year-old becomes year-end No. 1 and ITF World Champion for the sixth time in his career, having first done so in 1995.

Date and place of birth: 14 January 1970, Sydney, Australia
Residence: Rockdale, Australia
Weight: 143lbs/65kg
Plays: right handed
Coach: Rich Berman
Age began wheelchair tennis: 19

Highest singles ranking: 1 (first reached 17 October 1995)
Year-end singles ranking: 2004-1; 1003-1; 2002-1; 2001-2; 2000-1; 1999-3; 1998-1; 1997-2; 1996-4; 1995-1; 1994-2; 1993-9.
2004 Super Series singles titles: Australian Open, British Open, US Open
Other 2004 singles titles: Wheelchair Classic 8s, Nasdaq-100 Open, Sardinia Open, French Open, Belgian Open, Atlanta, NEC Wheelchair Masters.
Career Super Series singles titles: 17
Total other singles titles: 66
2004 singles win-loss record: 64-4
Career singles win-loss record: 586-103

Esther Vergeer (NED)

Vergeer cemented her place as the greatest women's wheelchair tennis player of all time in 2004 and for the fifth successive year is ITF World Champion. The 23-year-old had a staggering 62-0 singles record for the season, and has not been beaten since February 2003. That loss to Daniela Di Toro marks Vergeer's only defeat in the last four years.

The highlight of Vergeer's outstanding season was winning double gold at the Athens Paralympics, fulfilling a long-cherished dream to repeat what she achieved four years before in Sydney. This time around, Vergeer overwhelmed Sonja Peters in the singles gold medal match and teamed with Maaike Smit to win the top prize for Netherlands in the doubles.

Vergeer also led her country to a 17th triumph in the Invacare World Team Cup in June. She won a total of 15 singles titles in 2004, including three Super Series crowns. In doubles she was victorious 14 times.

Date and place of birth: 18 July, 1981, Woerden, Netherlands
Residence: Woerden, Netherlands
Weight: 147lbs/67kg
Plays: right handed
Coach: Aad Zwaan
Age began wheelchair tennis: 12

Highest singles ranking: 1 (first reached 6 April 1999)
Year-end singles ranking: 2004-1; 2003-1; 2002-1; 2001-1; 2000-1; 1999-2; 1998-2; 1997-14; 1996-21; 1995-48.
2004 Super Series singles titles: Australian Open, Japan Open, British Open.
Other 2004 singles titles: Wheelchair Classic 8s, Sydney International, Nasdaq-100, Florida Open, Kobe Open, DaimlerChrysler At-Risk Open, Dutch Open, Belgian Open, Swiss Open, Citta di Livorno, Athens Paralympic Games, Wheelchair Tennis Masters.
Career Super Series singles titles: 12
Total other singles titles: 67
2004 singles win-loss record: 62-0
Career singles win-loss record: 332-25

ITF World Champions Roll of Honour

ITF World Champions

	Men's Singles	Women's Singles
1978	Bjorn Borg (SWE)	Chris Evert (USA)
1979	Bjorn Borg (SWE)	Martina Navratilova (USA)
1980	Bjorn Borg (SWE)	Chris Evert (USA)
1981	John McEnroe (USA)	Chris Evert (USA)
1982	Jimmy Connors (USA)	Martina Navratilova (USA)
1983	John McEnroe (USA)	Martina Navratilova (USA)
1984	John McEnroe (USA)	Martina Navratilova (USA)
1985	Ivan Lendl (TCH)	Martina Navratilova (USA)
1986	Ivan Lendl (TCH)	Martina Navratilova (USA)
1987	Ivan Lendl (TCH)	Steffi Graf (GER)
1988	Mats Wilander (SWE)	Steffi Graf (GER)
1989	Boris Becker (GER)	Steffi Graf (GER)
1990	Ivan Lendl (TCH)	Steffi Graf (GER)
1991	Stefan Edberg (SWE)	Monica Seles (USA)
1992	Jim Courier (USA)	Monica Seles (USA)
1993	Pete Sampras (USA)	Steffi Graf (GER)
1994	Pete Sampras (USA)	Arantxa Sanchez-Vicario (ESP)
1995	Pete Sampras (USA)	Steffi Graf (GER)
1996	Pete Sampras (USA)	Steffi Graf (GER)
1997	Pete Sampras (USA)	Martina Hingis (SUI)
1998	Pete Sampras (USA)	Lindsay Davenport (USA)
1999	Andre Agassi (USA)	Martina Hingis (SUI)
2000	Gustavo Kuerten (BRA)	Martina Hingis (SUI)
2001	Lleyton Hewitt (AUS)	Jennifer Capriati (USA)
2002	Lleyton Hewitt (AUS)	Serena Williams (USA)
2003	Andy Roddick (USA)	Justine Henin-Hardenne (BEL)
2004	Roger Federer (SUI)	Anastasia Myskina (RUS)

	Men's Doubles	Women's Doubles
1996	Todd Woodbridge/Mark Woodforde (AUS)	Lindsay Davenport/Mary Joe Fernandez (USA)
1997	Todd Woodbridge/Mark Woodforde (AUS)	Lindsay Davenport (USA)/Jana Novotna (CZE)
1998	Jacco Eltingh/Paul Haarhuis (NED)	Lindsay Davenport (USA)/Natasha Zvereva (BLR)
1999	Mahesh Bhupathi/Leander Paes (IND)	Martina Hingis (SUI)/Anna Kournikova (RUS)
2000	Todd Woodbridge/Mark Woodforde (AUS)	Julie Halard-Decugis (FRA)/Ai Sugiyama (JPN)
2001	Jonas Bjorkman (SWE)/Todd Woodbridge (AUS)	Lisa Raymond (USA)/Rennae Stubbs (AUS)
2002	Mark Knowles (BAH)/Daniel Nestor (CAN)	Virginia Ruano Pascual (ESP)/Paola Suarez (ARG)
2003	Bob Bryan/Mike Bryan (USA)	Virginia Ruano Pascual (ESP)/Paola Suarez (ARG)
2004	Bob Bryan/Mike Bryan (USA)	Virginia Ruano Pascual (ESP)/Paola Suarez (ARG)

ITF Junior World Champions

	Boys' Singles	Girls' Singles
1978	Ivan Lendl (TCH)	Hana Mandlikova (TCH)
1979	Raul Viver (ECU)	Mary-Lou Piatek (USA)
1980	Thierry Tulasne (FRA)	Susan Mascarin (USA)
1981	Pat Cash (AUS)	Zina Garrison (USA)
1982	Guy Forget (FRA)	Gretchen Rush (USA)
1983	Stefan Edberg (SWE)	Pascale Paradis (FRA)
1984	Mark Kratzmann (AUS)	Gabriela Sabatini (ARG)
1985	Claudio Pistolesi (ITA)	Laura Garrone (ITA)
1986	Javier Sanchez (ESP)	Patricia Tarabini (ARG)
1987	Jason Stoltenberg (AUS)	Natalia Zvereva (URS)
1988	Nicolas Pereira (VEN)	Cristina Tessi (ARG)
1989	Nicklas Kulti (SWE)	Florencia Labat (ARG)
1990	Andrea Gaudenzi (ITA)	Karina Habsudova (TCH)

ITF World Champions Roll of Honour (continued)

1991	Thomas Enqvist (SWE)	Zdenka Malkova (TCH)
1992	Brian Dunn (USA)	Rossana De Los Rios (PAR)
1993	Marcelo Rios (CHI)	Nino Louarsabishvili (GEO)
1994	Federico Browne (ARG)	Martina Hingis (SUI)
1995	Mariano Zabaleta (ARG)	Anna Kournikova (RUS)
1996	Sebastien Grosjean (FRA)	Amelie Mauresmo (FRA)
1997	Arnaud Di Pasquale (FRA)	Cara Black (ZIM)
1998	Roger Federer (SUI)	Jelena Dokic (AUS)
1999	Kristian Pless (DEN)	Lina Krasnoroutskaia (RUS)
2000	Andy Roddick (USA)	Maria Emilia Salerni (ARG)
2001	Gilles Muller (LUX)	Svetlana Kuznetsova (RUS)
2002	Richard Gasquet (FRA)	Barbora Strycova (CZE)
2003	Marcos Baghdatis (CYP)	Kirsten Flipkens (BEL)

	Boys' Doubles	**Girls' Doubles**
1982	Fernando Perez (MEX)	Beth Herr (USA)
1983	Mark Kratzmann (AUS)	Larisa Savchenko (URS)
1984	Augustin Moreno (MEX)	Mercedes Paz (ARG)
1985	Petr Korda/Cyril Suk (TCH)	Mariana Perez-Roldan/Patricia Tarabini (ARG)
1986	Tomas Carbonell (ESP)	Leila Meskhi (URS)
1987	Jason Stoltenberg (AUS)	Natalia Medvedeva (URS)
1988	David Rikl/Tomas Zdrazila (TCH)	Jo-Anne Faull (AUS)
1989	Wayne Ferreira (RSA)	Andrea Strnadova (TCH)
1990	Marten Renstroem (SWE)	Karina Habsudova (TCH)
1991	Karim Alami (MAR)	Eva Martincova (TCH)
1992	Enrique Abaroa (MEX)	Laurence Courtois/Nancy Feber (BEL)
1993	Steven Downs (NZL)	Cristina Moros (USA)
1994	Benjamin Ellwood (AUS)	Martina Nedelkova (SVK)
1995	Kepler Orellana (VEN)	Ludmila Varmuzova (CZE)
1996	Sebastien Grosjean (FRA)	Michaela Pastikova/Jitka Schonfeldova (CZE)
1997	Nicolas Massu (CHI)	Cara Black (ZIM)/Irina Selyutina (KAZ)
1998	Jose De Armas (VEN)	Eva Dyrberg (DEN)
1999	Julien Benneteau/Nicolas Mahut (FRA)	Daniela Bedanova (CZE)
2000	Lee Childs/James Nelson (GBR)	Maria Emilia Salerni (ARG)
2001	Bruno Echagaray/Santiago Gonzalez (MEX)	Petra Cetkovska (CZE)
2002	Florin Mergea/Horia Tecau (ROM)	Elke Clijsters (BEL)
2003	Scott Oudsema (USA)	Andrea Hlavackova (CZE)

The Junior World Champion Singles and Doubles award was combined in 2004.

	Boys	**Girls**
2004	Gael Monfils (FRA)	Michaella Krajicek (NED)

ITF Wheelchair World Champions

	Men	**Women**
1991	Randy Snow (USA)	Chantal Vandierendonck (NED)
1992	Laurent Giammartini (FRA)	Monique van den Bosch (NED)
1993	Kai Schrameyer (GER)	Monique Kalkman (NED)
1994	Laurent Giammartini (FRA)	Monique Kalkman (NED)
1995	David Hall (AUS)	Monique Kalkman (NED)
1996	Ricky Molier (NED)	Chantal Vandierendonck (NED)
1997	Ricky Molier (NED)	Chantal Vandierendonck (NED)
1998	David Hall (AUS)	Daniela Di Toro (AUS)
1999	Stephen Welch (USA)	Daniela Di Toro (AUS)
2000	David Hall (AUS)	Esther Vergeer (NED)
2001	Ricky Molier (NED)	Esther Vergeer (NED)
2002	David Hall (AUS)	Esther Vergeer (NED)

| 2003 | David Hall (AUS) | Esther Vergeer (NED) |
| 2004 | David Hall (AUS) | Esther Vergeer (NED) |

The Philippe Chatrier Award
Named after former ITF President Philippe Chatrier and awarded for Contributions to the Game of Tennis.

1996	Stefan Edberg
1997	Chris Evert
1998	Rod Laver
1999	Nicola Pietrangeli
2000	Juan Antonio Samaranch
2001	NEC
2002	Jack Kramer
2003	Billie Jean King
2004	Yannick Noah (FRA)

Yannick Noah (FRA)

spain make history in seville

by ossian shine

The concept of mind over matter is a familiar one. But when the matter in question is slow, rich, energy-sapping Spanish clay, desire and determination – however resolute – more often than not proves futile.

The fact that the American Davis Cup team featured the world's fastest server in Andy Roddick didn't matter. And certainly, the Spaniards didn't mind. Over the course of three December days in Seville the Spanish team of Carlos Moya, Rafael Nadal, Tommy Robredo and Juan Carlos Ferrero combined with the cloying claycourt surface to suck the fire out of Roddick's serve and the breath out of the US bid for the Davis Cup.

Instead Spain won its second Davis Cup title, smashing records along the way. The 27,200 fans crammed into the specially-constructed stands at Seville's grandly-named Olympic Stadium was a record for a tennis crowd.

Nadal also entered the record books, becoming the youngest player to help a side win the men's team competition. Aged 18 years and 185 days, the teenager beat the record set by Australia's Pat Cash in 1983 by 30 days.

Carlos Moya (ESP)

"It is a moment I have been waiting for for many years," Moya smiled as tears glistened in his eyes. "An incredible way to win the Cup. The Davis Cup is my dream. I don't believe there is anything bigger than what I've lived through today,"

"What a great way to end the year," grinned the muscular youth. Nadal was no bit-part player. Selected over former world No. 1 Juan Carlos Ferrero for a precious singles spot, the youngster barely put a foot wrong in front of his frenzied fans, blowing away Roddick in his opening match to set Spain up for a famous victory.

But it fell to his friend and fellow Mallorcan Carlos Moya to clinch the victory. It could hardly have proved a more fitting finale. Moya, one of the most amiable men on the Tour, had been desperately disappointed four years earlier when a back injury forced him to watch from the sidelines as Spain won its maiden Cup in Barcelona.

Happy for the team but harbouring personal heartbreak, Moya vowed at the time that he would one day lift the famous trophy for Spain. He was good as his word, thumping Roddick in Sunday's first reverse singles to spark jubilation in the Seville stands.

"It is a moment I have been waiting for for many years," Moya smiled as tears glistened in his eyes. "An incredible way to win the Cup. The Davis Cup is my dream. I don't believe there is anything bigger than what I've lived through today," the former World No. 1 added as the enormity of his achievement sank in.

"I've thought about this so many times...you can't imagine how many, countless. I've even been dreaming, waking up in the middle of the night, thinking that I'm winning the deciding point. Since I was not in the 2000 team, this was my biggest goal, and my dream, and today it came true. I cannot ask for more."

With Spanish trumpeters tooting in the crowd and against a sea of red and yellow flags, Moya had teased and tormented the rampaging Roddick with an array of spins and angles.

The American, caked in red clay, had hurled himself all over the court throughout the contest but was simply unable to fend off his tormentor. Stoic and dignified in defeat, he had few answers. "Bottom line is they were just better than us," he shrugged. "You can say whatever you want, but they came out, they took care of business. They beat us. It's as simple as that."

While the US team went back to the drawing board, the whole of Spain was euphoric. The nation hailed the fulfilment of an old dream and the rise of a new star in Nadal.

Davis Cup Champions Spain

spain make history in seville
by ossian shine

"In sporting terms this is the biggest thing that could happen to me," a reflective Spanish captain Jordi Arrese said after the partying had subsided. "Even if we manage it again in the future, it will not be the same, the atmosphere and setting could not be repeated."

> "The key thing for us is that we have four number one players," beamed Juan Avendano, part of the three-man coaching team in charge of Spain.

The glorious weekend was capped for the Spaniards by the International Tennis Hall of Fame and the International Tennis Federation awarding Manuel Santana the 2004 Davis Cup Award of Excellence. ITF President Francesco Ricci Bitti and Agustin Pujol, President of Real Federacion Española de Tenis, made the presentation with Prince Felipe and Princess Letiza of Spain present on court. Santana won the award as he was deemed to represent the ideals and spirit of Davis Cup competition.

"In representing Spain for 14 years in Davis Cup competition, Manuel holds virtually every Davis Cup record for Spain," Ricci Bitti said in Seville. "His proven talent, leadership and love for our sport make him a most deserving recipient of this award."

If the Davis Cup final was all Spain, the United States had proved its mettle by reaching it. Without a Davis Cup title since 1995, the US blasted their way past a hapless Austria 5-0 in Uncasville, Connecticut in the opening round before sweeping past Sweden 4-1 in the quarterfinals.

The Swedes had earlier stunned 2003 champions Australia in February's first round 4-1, when both Thomas Enqvist and Jonas Bjorkman handily defused the Scud, Mark Philippoussis.

Philippoussis, Lleyton Hewitt and the rest of the Australian squad were left to grumble about insufficient rest and the lack of a first-round bye for the champions while Sweden prepared for its trip to Delray Beach.

If Australia had been tough, the Americans proved to be something else all together. Roddick, something of a talismanic figure for the American team, simply powered the US into the semifinals. He even broke his own world record serve during the tie, thumping a delivery measured at 244.57km/h.

While the US advanced impressively, Spain were cutting through the bottom half of the draw. A 3-2 win over the Czech Republic at the Brno Exhibition Center saw them through round one – Nadal winning the crucial fifth rubber of that tie.

Back on more familiar ground at the Plaza de Toros "Coliseo" de Palma de Mallorca, Moya and Ferrero made light work of the Dutch team with Nadal playing a doubles role as they romped through 4-1.

The irresistible Roger Federer was powerless to prevent France from ousting his Swiss team in the quarterfinals and the French lay in wait for Spain in the semis.

Again, the Spanish had the benefit of a home crowd, playing the tie at the Plaza de Toros of Alicante. In the event, it was Spain's unmatchable depth in claycourt tennis which guided them into the final after injury and exhaustion had upset their original plans.

The Spanish discarded Moya and Ferrero, both former French Open champions, for the reverse singles yet were still able to complete a 4-1 victory. Ferrero's absence was forced, after a blister on his hand left him barely able to pick up his racket. However, the decision to bring in Nadal in place of Moya, who had lost the longest match of his career against Paul-Henri Mathieu on the opening day, was more tactical than anything else. It was a tactical masterstroke and Nadal responded with a thrilling 64 61 62 victory over Arnaud Clement to give Spain an unassailable lead.

"The key thing for us is that we have four number one players," beamed Juan Avendano, part of the three-man coaching team in charge of Spain. "It makes it easy.

Rafael Nadal (ESP)

US Team Captain Patrick McEnroe with Andy Roddick

Perhaps one glorious tilt at the Davis Cup could lure Agassi back to the US fold. Certainly the Americans could do with his experience and baseline prowess.

The elite World Group had no monopoly on thrills, however. There was plenty of excitement around, provided none more so than by the Chileans. In a feat that would have made ancient alchemists green with envy, Chile's Fernando Gonzalez and Nicolas Massu turned sweat, tears and raw desire into solid gold at the Athens Olympic Games in August.

The small South American nation had waited more than 80 years for a gold medal at an Olympics and in an Athenian amphitheatre they won two in less than 24 hours.

Gonzalez and Massu bagged the nation's first in a memorable doubles marathon. Less than 24 hours later, the Chilean national anthem was being played again in Greece after Massu also clinched the gold in the men's singles.

The Chileans brought that sensational form to Davis Cup and in September returned to the top flight for the first time

Gone are the days when the US could claim to have great quality in depth, but they do still boast in Roddick one of the most explosive players in men's tennis. In its semifinal against Belarus, it was the spiky-haired speed server who led the way once again.

If we have one player who is not absolutely perfect we bring in someone who's equally good. That's what we saw in this tie."

Gone are the days when the US could claim to have great quality in depth, but they do still boast in Roddick one of the most explosive players in men's tennis. In its semifinal against Belarus, it was the spiky-haired speed server who led the way once again. He again broke his record for the world's fastest serve – this time with a 155mph (249kph) delivery – as the US triumphed 4-0.

Belarus had never won a World Group tie before 2004, and its journey to the semifinals put the small nation firmly on the map, especially after its historic first round victory over neighbouring Russia.

Roddick, Mardy Fish, the Bryan twins Mike and Bob and captain Patrick McEnroe had high hopes for December's final but it was not to be. The Americans did,

however, win a lot of fans in Seville with the dignified and decorous manner of their defeat. However, with the last American victory coming in 1995, this is the longest Davis Cup drought for the United States since before World War II.

Drastic times call for drastic measures and US captain McEnroe left Spain dreaming of being able to name Andre Agassi in his squad for next year. "For Andre, the door is always open," McEnroe smiled ruefully. "He's never completely shut the door, at least to me. As long as he's still out there competing at the level he's at, I'm going to keep asking."

Agassi stopped playing for the US four years ago to focus on Grand Slams, and it is now nine years since the Americans won the Davis Cup. "It's difficult to dominate for any country," McEnroe said. "But it's certainly too long for the US to not have won one," said McEnroe.

in 20 years with a 5-0 whitewash of Japan at Club Naval de Campo Las Salinas, Vina del Mar.

Already the South Americans are talking about challenging for the title in 2005. "There's no harm in dreaming," Chilean No. 2 Gonzalez said after beating the Japanese. "We have to hope we get drawn to play in Chile, because here we're not afraid of anyone. Obviously, it's very tough to win the Davis Cup but our team is good enough to do it."

In fact, Andres Fazio, President of the Chilean Tennis Federation, is already planning to construct a new stadium in the resort of Vina del Mar in case his team do manage to go all the way. "Our target is to play in the final of the Davis Cup and if we play at home I want us to have a worthy setting," he smiled.

Don't rule them out. In Davis Cup anything is possible – just ask Rafael Nadal.

2004 Davis Cup by BNP Paribas Results

World Group

First Round 6-8 February
Sweden defeated Australia 4-1, Adelaide, AUS; Hard (O): Thomas Enqvist (SWE) d. Mark Philippoussis (AUS) 63 64 62; Lleyton Hewitt (AUS) d. Robin Soderling (SWE) 64 63 61; Jonas Bjorkman/Joachim Johansson (SWE) d. Wayne Arthurs/Todd Woodbridge (AUS) 76(5) 64 26 67(4) 75; Jonas Bjorkman (SWE) d. Mark Philippoussis (AUS) 75 62 62; Thomas Enqvist (SWE) d. Wayne Arthurs (AUS) 76(8) 36 64. **USA defeated Austria 5-0, Uncasville, CT, USA; Hard (I):** Robby Ginepri (USA) d. Jurgen Melzer (AUT) 67(6) 46 64 64 62; Andy Roddick (USA) d. Stefan Koubek (AUT) 64 64 62; Bob Bryan/Mike Bryan (USA) d. Julian Knowle/Jurgen Melzer (AUT) 62 61 64; Andy Roddick (USA) d. Jurgen Melzer (AUT) 64 62; Robby Ginepri (USA) d. Stefan Koubek (AUT) 75 62. **Belarus defeated Russia 3-2, Minsk, BLR; Carpet (I):** Igor Andreev (RUS) d. Vladimir Voltchkov (BLR) 67(3) 76(4) 57 44 ret; Max Mirnyi (BLR) d. Marat Safin (RUS) 76(3) 76(5) 16 46 119; Marat Safin/Mikhail Youzhny (RUS) d. Max Mirnyi/Alexander Shvec (BLR) 64 75 76(4); Max Mirnyi (BLR) d. Igor Andreev (RUS) 63 64 64; Vladimir Voltchkov (BLR) d. Mikhail Youzhny (RUS) 75 62 64. **Argentina defeated Morocco 5-0, Agadir, MAR; Hard (I):** Guillermo Coria (ARG) d. Mounir El Aarej (MAR) 61 61 64; David Nalbandian (ARG) d. Hicham Arazi (MAR) 46 61 75 21 ret; Lucas Arnold/Agustin Calleri (ARG) d. Mehdi Tahiri/Mounir El Aarej (MAR) 61 64 62; Guillermo Coria (ARG) d. Mehdi Tahiri (MAR) 62 76(4); Agustin Calleri (ARG) d. Mounir El Aarej (MAR) 76(1) 36 61. **Switzerland defeated Romania 3-2, Bucharest, ROM; Clay (I):** Andrei Pavel (ROM) d. Michel Kratochvil (SUI) 64 63 57 64; Roger Federer (SUI) d. Victor Hanescu (ROM) 76(4) 63 61; Yves Allegro/Roger Federer (SUI) d. Andrei Pavel/Gabriel Trifu (ROM) 64 16 63 36 108; Roger Federer (SUI) d. Andrei Pavel (ROM) 63 62 75; Victor Hanescu (ROM) d. Stanislas Wawrinka (SUI) 63 67(3) 63. **France defeated Croatia 4-1, Metz, France; Clay (I):** Arnaud Clement (FRA) d. Mario Ancic (CRO) 64 63 63; Ivan Ljubicic (CRO) d. Thierry Ascione (FRA) 75 64 64; Nicolas Escude/Michael Llodra (FRA) d. Mario Ancic/Ivo Karlovic (CRO) 61 76(5) 63; Arnaud Clement (FRA) d. Ivan Ljubicic (CRO) 62 36 76(3) 64; Nicolas Escude (FRA) d. Ivo Karlovic (CRO) 76(5) 62. **Netherlands defeated Canada 4-1, Maastricht, NED; Clay (I):** Sjeng Schalken (NED) d. Frank Dancevic (CAN) 63 57 62 61; Martin Verkerk (NED) d. Simon Larose (CAN) 64 76(9) 46 63; Daniel Nestor/Frederic Niemeyer (CAN) d. Paul Haarhuis/Martin Verkerk (NED) 76(10) 10 ret; Martin Verkerk (NED) d. Frank Dancevic (CAN) 67(5) 62 75 63; Sjeng Schalken (NED) d. Simon Larose (CAN) 62 75. **Spain defeated Czech Republic 3-2, Brno, CZE; Carpet (I):** Jiri Novak (CZE) d. Rafael Nadal (ESP) 76(2) 63 76(3); Tommy Robredo (ESP) d. Radek Stepanek (CZE) 75 36 76(4) 76(7); Jiri Novak/Radek Stepanek (CZE) d. Rafael Nadal/Tommy Robredo (ESP) 64 76(6) 63; Feliciano Lopez (ESP) d. Tomas Berdych (CZE) 64 67(2) 63 62; Rafael Nadal (ESP) d. Radek Stepanek (CZE) 76(2) 76(4) 63.

Quarterfinals 9-11 April
USA defeated Sweden 3-2, Delray Beach, FL, USA; Hard (O): Jonas Bjorkman (SWE) d. Mardy Fish (USA) 46 63 62 75; Andy Roddick (USA) d. Thomas Enqvist (SWE) 64 75 62; Bob Bryan/Mike Bryan (USA) d. Jonas Bjorkman/Thomas Johansson (SWE) 63 64 64; Andy Roddick (USA) d. Jonas Bjorkman (SWE) 76(3) 64 60; Mardy Fish (USA) d. Thomas Johansson (SWE) 36 61 64. **Belarus defeated Argentina 5-0, Minsk, BLR; Carpet (I):** Vladimir Voltchkov (BLR) d. Agustin Calleri (ARG) 63 64 62; Max Mirnyi (BLR) d. Guillermo Canas (ARG) 62 62 62; Max Mirnyi/Vladimir Voltchkov (BLR) d. Lucas Arnold/Agustin Calleri (ARG) 63 64 61; Max Mirnyi (BLR) d. Lucas Arnold (ARG) 61 62; Vladimir Voltchkov (BLR) d. Juan Monaco (ARG) 36 63 63. **France defeated Switzerland 3-2, Prilly, SUI; Hard (I):** Roger Federer (SUI) d. Nicolas Escude (FRA) 62 64 64; Arnaud Clement (FRA) d. Ivo Heuberger (SUI) 63 63 62; Nicolas Escude/Michael Llodra (FRA) d. Yves Allegro/Roger Federer (SUI) 67(4) 63 76(5) 63; Roger Federer (SUI) d. Arnaud Clement (FRA) 62 75 64; Nicolas Escude (FRA) d. Michel Kratochvil (SUI) 76(3) 64 76(6). **Spain defeated Netherlands 4-1, Palma de Mallorca, ESP; Clay (O):** Carlos Moya (ESP) d. Martin Verkerk (NED) 62 75 64; Juan Carlos Ferrero (ESP) d. Raemon Sluiter (NED) 62 62 64; John Van Lottum/Martin Verkerk (NED) d. Rafael Nadal/Tommy Robredo (ESP) 36 26 63 62 62; Juan Carlos Ferrero (ESP) d. Martin Verkerk (NED) 64 67(5) 46 75 61; Carlos Moya (ESP) d. Sjeng Schalken (NED) 63 64.

Semifinals 24-26 September
USA defeated Belarus 4-0, Charleston, SC, USA; Hard (O): Andy Roddick (USA) d. Vladimir Voltchkov (BLR) 61 64 64; Mardy Fish (USA) d. Max Mirnyi (BLR) 75 62 36 63; Bob Bryan/Mike Bryan (USA) d. Max Mirnyi/Vladimir Voltchkov (BLR) 61 63 75; Andy Roddick (USA) d. Alexander Skrypko (BLR) 64 62; Mardy Fish (USA) v. Andrei Karatchenia (BLR) 30 abn. **Spain defeated France 4-1, Alicante, ESP; Clay (O):** Paul-Henri Mathieu (FRA) d. Carlos Moya (ESP) 63 36 26 63 63; Juan Carlos Ferrero (ESP) d. Fabrice Santoro (FRA) 63 61 16 63; Rafael Nadal/Tommy Robredo (ESP) d. Arnaud Clement/Michael Llodra (FRA) 76(4) 46 62 26 63; Rafael Nadal (ESP) d. Arnaud Clement (FRA) 64 61 62; Tommy Robredo (ESP) d. Paul-Henri Mathieu (FRA) 64 64.

Final 3-5 December
Spain defeated USA 3-2; Seville, ESP; Clay (O): Carlos Moya (ESP) d. Mardy Fish (USA) 64 62 63; Rafael Nadal (ESP) d. Andy Roddick (USA) 67(6) 62 76(6) 62; Bob Bryan/Mike Bryan (USA) d. Juan Carlos Ferrero/Tommy Robredo (ESP) 60 63 62; Carlos Moya (ESP) d. Andy Roddick (USA) 62 76(1) 76(5); Mardy Fish (USA) d. Tommy Robredo (ESP) 76(8) 62.

World Group Play-offs 24-26 September
Australia defeated Morocco 4-1, West Perth, AUS; Grass (O): Wayne Arthurs (AUS) d. Mounir El Aarej (MAR) 76(6) 64 63; Lleyton Hewitt (AUS) d. Mehdi Tahiri (MAR) 60 62 62; Wayne Arthurs/Todd Woodbridge (AUS) d. Mounir El Aarej/Mehdi Tahiri (MAR) 76(7) 76(2) 63; Mounir El Aarej (MAR) d. Todd Reid (AUS) 62 63; Todd Woodbridge (AUS) d. Mehdi Ziadi (MAR) 60 62. **Chile defeated Japan 5-0, Vina del Mar, CHI; Clay (O):** Nicolas Massu (CHI) d. Gouichi Motomura (JPN) 61 61 61; Fernando Gonzalez (CHI) d. Takao Suzuki (JPN) 64 62 76(1); Fernando Gonzalez/Nicolas Massu (CHI) d. Thomas Shimada/Takao Suzuki (JPN) 63 63 61; Hermes Gamonal (CHI) d. Takao Suzuki (JPN) 75 26 62; Fernando Gonzalez (CHI) d. Gouichi Motomura (JPN) 63 63. **Croatia defeated Belgium 3-2, Rijeka, CRO; Carpet (I):** Ivan Ljubicic (CRO) d. Gilles Elseneer (BEL) 76(6) 75 64; Mario Ancic (CRO) d. Olivier Rochus (BEL) 63 76(2) 61; Mario Ancic/Ivan Ljubicic (CRO) d. Dick Norman/Kristof Vliegen (BEL) 67(8) 64 67(1) 63 75; Olivier Rochus (BEL) d. Sasa Tuksar (CRO) 46 63 63; Gilles Elseneer (BEL) d. Mario Ancic (CRO) 76(4) 21 ret. **Czech Republic defeated Paraguay 5-0, Lambare, PAR; Clay (O):** Jiri Novak (CZE) d. Paulo Carvallo (PAR) 36 64 75 63; Tomas Berdych (CZE) d. Ramon Delgado (PAR) 36 46 63 62 64; Jiri Novak/Radek Stepanek (CZE) d. Paulo Carvallo/Ramon Delgado (PAR) 62 75 63; Radek Stepanek (CZE) d. Ramon Delgado (PAR) 64 62; Michal Tabara (CZE) d. Francisco Rodriguez (PAR) 63 61. **Slovak Republic defeated Germany 3-2, Bratislava, SVK; Hard (I):** Dominik Hrbaty (SVK) d. Florian Mayer (GER) 63 61 63; Tommy Haas (GER) d. Karol Beck (SVK) 67(2) 61 61 61; Tommy Haas/Alexander Waske (GER) d. Dominik Hrbaty/Karol Kucera (SVK) 63 63 36 46 63; Dominik Hrbaty (SVK) d. Tommy Haas (GER) 63 63 75; Karol Kucera (SVK) d. Florian Mayer (GER) 64 60 62. **Austria defeated Great Britain 3-2, Portschach, AUT; Clay (O):** Stefan Koubek (AUT) d. Tim Henman (GBR) 63 63 61; Greg Rusedski (GBR) d. Jurgen Melzer (AUT) 36 63 64 76(4); Julian Knowle/Alexander Peya (AUT) d. Tim Henman/Greg Rusedski (GBR) 64 16 62 61; Tim Henman (GBR) d. Jurgen Melzer (AUT) 06 62 76(4) 62; Stefan Koubek (AUT) d. Greg Rusedski (GBR) 76(2) 64 75. **Romania defeated Canada 4-1, Bucharest, ROM; Clay (O):** Andrei Pavel (ROM) d. Simon Larose (CAN) 75 63 62; Victor Hanescu (ROM) d. Frank Dancevic (CAN) 57 63 36 63 64; Daniel Nestor/Frederic Niemeyer (CAN) d. Victor Ionita/Florin Mergea (ROM) 64 64 26 62; Andrei Pavel (ROM) d. Frank Dancevic (CAN) 62 64 62; Victor Ionita (ROM) d. Simon Larose (CAN) 42 ret. **Russia defeated Thailand 5-0, Moscow, RUS; Clay (I):** Igor Andreev (RUS) d. Paradorn Srichaphan (THA) 75 62 64; Marat Safin (RUS) d. Danai Udomchoke (THA) 64 61 62; Marat Safin/Mikhail Youzhny (RUS) d. Sanchai Ratiwatana/Sonchat Ratiwatana (THA) 62 61 64; Nikolay Davydenko (RUS) d. Sonchat Ratiwatana (THA) 62 60; Mikhail Youzhny (RUS) d. Sanchai Ratiwatana (THA) 64 62.

Europe/Africa Zone Group I

First Round 6-8 February
Luxembourg defeated Finland 4-1, Esch/Alzette, LUX; Hard (I): Gilles Muller (LUX) d. Tuomas Ketola (FIN) 46 75 75 62; Jarkko Nieminen (FIN) d. Gilles Kremer (LUX) 62 61 64; Gilles Muller/Mike Scheidweiler (LUX) d. Tuomas Ketola/Jarkko Nieminen (FIN) 75 64 62; Gilles Muller (LUX) d. Jarkko Nieminen (FIN) 62 62 46 76(6); Gilles Kremer (LUX) d. Janne Ojala (FIN) 46 63 62. **Zimbabwe defeated Greece 3-2, Harare, ZIM; Hard (I):** Konstantinos Economidis (GRE) d. Kevin Ullyett (ZIM) 64 75 36 76(4); Wayne Black (ZIM) d. Vasilis Mazarakis (GRE) 63 63 64; Wayne Black/Kevin Ullyett (ZIM) d. Alexander Jakupovic/Vasilis Mazarakis (GRE) 64 62 61; Wayne Black (ZIM) d. Alexander Jakupovic (GRE) 64 62 75; Elefterios Alexiou (GRE) d. Genius Chidzikwe (ZIM) 63 46 63.

Second Round 9-11 April
Germany defeated Israel 5-0, Aachen-Alsdorf, GER; Hard (I): Rainer Schuettler (GER) d. Noam Okun (ISR) 62 62 61; Nicolas Kiefer (GER) d. Harel Levy (ISR) 62 75 63; Tommy Haas/Alexander Waske (GER) d. Jonathan Erlich/Andy Ram (ISR) 26 57 62 64 63; Rainer Schuettler (GER) d. Harel Levy (ISR) 63 76(5); Nicolas Kiefer (GER) d. Noam Okun (ISR) 62 67(2) 76(3). **Great Britain defeated Luxembourg 4-1, Esch/Alzette, LUX; Hard (I);** Gilles Muller (LUX) d. Arvind Parmar (GBR) 46 75 36 64 64; Tim Henman (GBR) d. Gilles Kremer (LUX) 63 63 62; Tim Henman/Greg Rusedski (GBR) d. Gilles Muller/Mike Scheidweiler (LUX) 64 76(7) 63; Tim Henman (GBR) d. Gilles Muller (LUX) 76(2) 62 61; Greg Rusedski (GBR) d. Mike Scheidweiler (LUX) 63 76(5). **Belgium defeated Zimbabwe 4-1, Tournai, BEL; Clay (I):** Wayne Black (ZIM) d. Olivier Rochus (BEL) 36 76(3) 63 36 62; Xavier Malisse (BEL) d. Genius Chidzikwe (ZIM) 60 61 63; Olivier Rochus/Kristof Vliegen (BEL) d. Wayne Black/Kevin Ullyett (ZIM) 76(4) 67(4) 64 62; Xavier Malisse (BEL) d. Wayne Black (ZIM) 46 26 63 76(6) 64; Christophe Rochus (BEL) d. Genius Chidzikwe (ZIM) 63 60. **Slovak Republic defeated South Africa 3-2, Johannesburg, RSA; Grass (O):** Karol Beck (SVK) d. Wayne Ferreira (RSA) 63 64 67(10) 62; Karol Kucera (SVK) d. Wesley Moodie (RSA) 64 76(4) 76(5); Dominik Hrbaty/Michal Mertinak (SVK) d. Jeff Coetzee/Chris Haggard (RSA) 75 75 76(5); Wayne Ferreira (RSA) d. Dominik Hrbaty (SVK) 64 62; Wesley Moodie (RSA) d. Michal Mertinak (SVK) 76(8) 76(3).

Belgium, Germany, Great Britain and Slovak Republic advance to World Group Play-offs on 24-26 September 2004.

Third Round/Play-off 24-26 September
Israel defeated Finland 3-2, Ramat Hasharon, ISR; Hard (O): Tuomas Ketola (FIN) d. Harel Levy (ISR) 64 64 63; Noam Okun (ISR) d. Jarkko Nieminen (FIN) 64 75 64; Jonathan Erlich/Andy Ram (ISR) d. Lassi Ketola/Tuomas Ketola (FIN) 61 61 61; Jarkko Nieminen (FIN) d. Andy Ram (ISR) 61 61 46 62; Noam Okun (ISR) d. Tuomas Ketola (FIN) 62 62 62. **South Africa defeated Greece 4-1, Pretoria, RSA; Hard (O):**

2004 Davis Cup by BNP Paribas Results (continued)

Wayne Ferreira (RSA) d. Vasilis Mazarakis (GRE) 63 57 75 62; Wesley Moodie (RSA) d. Konstantinos Economidis (GRE) 63 62 76(4); Jeff Coetzee/Rik De Voest (RSA) d. Konstantinos Economidis/Alexander Jakupovic (GRE) 76(6) 61 62; Konstantinos Economidis (GRE) d. Wayne Ferreira (RSA) 63 16 64; Wesley Moodie (RSA) d. Alexander Jakupovic (GRE) 63 64.

Finland and Greece relegated to Europe/Africa Zone Group II in 2005.

Americas Zone Group I

First Round   6-8 February
Paraguay defeated Venezuela 4-1, Caracas, VEN; Hard (O): Ramon Delgado (PAR) d. Jimy Szymanski (VEN) 64 61; Jose De Armas (VEN) d. Francisco Rodriguez (PAR) 26 62 46 62 61; Paulo Carvallo/Ramon Delgado (PAR) d. Jose De Armas/Jimy Szymanski (VEN) 36 76(4) 26 64 63; Ramon Delgado (PAR) d. Jose De Armas (VEN) 46 16 63 61 64; Francisco Rodriguez (PAR) d. Daniel Vallverdu (VEN) 75 63. **Chile defeated Peru 5-0, Lima, PER; Clay (O):** Fernando Gonzalez (CHI) d. Luis Horna (PER) 64 64 61; Nicolas Massu (CHI) d. Ivan Miranda (PER) 62 64 63; Adrian Garcia/Fernando Gonzalez (CHI) d. Luis Horna/Ivan Miranda (PER) 62 64 64; Hermes Gamonal (CHI) d. Diego Acuna (PER) 75 63; Adrian Garcia (CHI) d. Piero Demichelli (PER) 62 62.

Second Round   9-11 April
Paraguay defeated Brazil 3-2, Bahia, BRA; Clay (O): Francisco Rodriguez (PAR) d. Marcos Daniel (BRA) 64 16 26 64 119; Ramon Delgado (PAR) d. Julio Silva (BRA) 76(3) 64 61; Josh Goffi/Alexandre Simoni (BRA) d. Paulo Carvallo/Ramon Delgado (PAR) 64 46 63 64; Ramon Delgado (PAR) d. Alexandre Simoni (BRA) 61 76(6) 63; Julio Silva (BRA) d. Daniel Lopez (PAR) 61 30 ret. **Chile defeated Ecuador 5-0, Vina del Mar, CHI; Clay (O):** Nicolas Massu (CHI) d. Giovanni Lapentti (ECU) 63 62 62; Fernando Gonzalez (CHI) d. Nicolas Lapentti (ECU) 62 62 64; Fernando Gonzalez/Nicolas Massu (CHI) d. Giovanni Lapentti/Nicolas Lapentti (ECU) 61 62 75; Adrian Garcia (CHI) d. Carlos Avellan (ECU) 61 63; Paul Capdeville (CHI) d. Jhony De Leon (ECU) 63 63.

Chile and Paraguay advance to World Group Play-offs on 24-26 September 2004.

Second Round/Play-off   16-18 July
Venezuela defeated Brazil 3-2, Caracas, VEN; Hard (O): Jimy Szymanski (VEN) d. Diego Cubas (BRA) 46 60 76(5) 63; Kepler Orellana (VEN) d. Bruno Rosa (BRA) 62 63 64; Kepler Orellana/Jimy Szymanski (VEN) d. Raony Carvalho/Caio Zampieri (BRA) 61 62 61; Diego Cubas (BRA) d. Jhonathan Medina-Alvarez (VEN) 75 76(4); Caio Zampieri (BRA) d. Yohny Romero (VEN) 63 64. **Ecuador defeated Peru 4-1, Guayaquil, ECU; Hard (I):** Carlos Avellan (ECU) d. Matias Silva (PER) 62 64 62; Giovanni Lapentti (ECU) d. Mario-Alberto Cayo (PER) 62 60 60; Jhony De Leon/Giovanni Lapentti (ECU) d. Luis-Felipe Bellido/Matias Silva (PER) 62 63 61; Matias Silva (PER) d. Jhony De Leon (ECU) 63 36 61; Carlos Avellan (ECU) d. Juan-Carlos Rebaza-Lozano (PER) 62 60.

Third Round/Play-off   24-26 September
Peru defeated Brazil 4-1, Brasilia, BRA; Clay (O): Luis Horna (PER) d. Gabriel Pitta (BRA) 63 64 64; Ivan Miranda (PER) d. Ronaldo Carvalho (BRA) 76(6) 67(6) 46 63 61; Luis Horna/Ivan Miranda (PER) d. Ronaldo Carvalho/Gabriel Pitta (BRA) 62 62 63, Matias Silva (PER) d. Alessandro Camarco (BRA) 64 36 64, Leonardo Kirche (BRA) d. Mauricio Echavu (PER) 62 61.

Brazil relegated to Americas Zone Group II in 2005.

Asia/Oceania Zone Group I

First Round   6-8 February
Thailand defeated Pakistan 5-0, Nonthaburi, THA; Hard (I): Paradorn Srichaphan (THA) d. Nomi Qamar (PAK) 62 61 60; Danai Udomchoke (THA) d. Aqeel Khan (PAK) 61 61 62; Sanchai Ratiwatana/Sonchat Ratiwatana (THA) d. Aqeel Khan/Jalil Khan (PAK) 61 76(3) 62; Sonchat Ratiwatana (THA) d. Aqeel Khan (PAK) 64 64; Sanchai Ratiwatana (THA) d. Nomi Qamar (PAK) 62 60. **Uzbekistan defeated Chinese Taipei 4-1, Kaohsiung, TPE; Hard (O):** Vadim Kutsenko (UZB) d. Tai-Wei Liu (TPE) 60 61 61; Dmitri Mazur (UZB) d. Ti Chen (TPE) 62 64 64; Murad Inoyatov/Vadim Kutsenko (UZB) d. Wei-Jen Cheng/Wang-Cheng Hsieh (TPE) 62 36 63 63; Ti Chen (TPE) d. Sarvar Ikramov (UZB) 64 46 62; ...rad Inoyatov (UZB) d. Tai-Wei Liu (TPE) 63 61. **Japan defeated Indonesia 3-2, Jakarta, INA; Hard (O):** Takao Suzuki (JPN) d. Prima Simpatiaji ... 44 63 46 64; Febi Widhiyanto (INA) d. Gouichi Motomura (JPN) 46 63 62 36 75; Thomas Shimada/Takahiro Terachi (JPN) d. Hendri-Susilo

Pramono/Suwandi Suwandi (INA) 64 76(3) 61; Febi Widhiyanto (INA) d. Takahiro Terachi (JPN) 75 34 ret.; Gouichi Motomura (JPN) d. Prima Simpatiaji (INA) 57 26 64 62 63. **India defeated New Zealand 3-2, Invercargill, NZL; Carpet (I):** Simon Rea (NZL) d. Harsh Mankad (IND) 64 61 76(2); Leander Paes (IND) d. Mark Nielsen (NZL) 62 63 76(2); Mahesh Bhupathi/Leander Paes (IND) d. Mark Nielsen/Matthew Prentice (NZL) 63 64 76(4); Mark Nielsen (NZL) d. Vishal Punna (IND) 64 63 61; Leander Paes (IND) d. Simon Rea (NZL) 36 75 63 62.

Second Round 9-11 April
Thailand defeated Uzbekistan 4-1, Bangkok, THA; Hard (I): Danai Udomchoke (THA) d. Vadim Kutsenko (UZB) 76(4) 64 63; Paradorn Srichaphan (THA) d. Dmitri Mazur (UZB) 46 75 75 63; Sanchai Ratiwatana/Sonchat Ratiwatana (THA) d. Murad Inoyatov/Vadim Kutsenko (UZB) 62 62 67(2) 62; Sarvar Ikramov (UZB) d. Sonchat Ratiwatana (THA) 76(3) 60; Sanchai Ratiwatana (THA) d. Murad Inoyatov (UZB) 64 36 76(2). **Japan defeated India 3-2, Osaka, JPN; Hard (O):** Gouichi Motomura (JPN) d. Prakash Amritraj (IND) 46 61 62 64; Leander Paes (IND) d. Takao Suzuki (JPN) 63 75 36 64; Mahesh Bhupathi/Leander Paes (IND) d. Thomas Shimada/Takahiro Terachi (JPN) 61 63 46 75; Takao Suzuki (JPN) d. Prakash Amritraj (IND) 64 63 62; Gouichi Motomura (JPN) d. Leander Paes (IND) 64 63 76(4).

Japan and Thailand advance to World Group Play-offs on 24-26 September 2004.

Second Round/Play-off 9-11 April
Chinese Taipei defeated Pakistan 5-0, Kaohsiung, TPE; Hard (O): Yen-Hsun Lu (TPE) d. Asim Shafik (PAK) 60 61 60; Yeu-Tzuoo Wang (TPE) d. Aqeel Khan (PAK) 62 61 46 62; Yen-Hsun Lu/Yeu-Tzuoo Wang (TPE) d. Aqeel Khan/Asim Shafik (PAK) 62 61 64; Ti Chen (TPE) d. Shahzad Khan (PAK) 60 61; Tai-Wei Liu (TPE) d. Jalil Khan (PAK) 61 62. **Indonesia defeated New Zealand 5-0, Jakarta, INA; Hard (O):** Febi Widhiyanto (INA) d. Matthew Prentice (NZL) 63 62 64; Prima Simpatiaji (INA) d. Mark Nielsen (NZL) 75 67(7) 61 61; Suwandi Suwandi/Bonit Wiryawan (INA) d. Mark Nielsen/Lee Radovanovich (NZL) 61 61 76(3); Febi Widhiyanto (INA) d. William Ward (NZL) 64 63; Prima Simpatiaji (INA) d. Matthew Prentice (NZL) 64 76(2).

Third Round/Play-off 24-26 September
Pakistan defeated New Zealand 3-2, Islamabad, PAK; Clay (O): Mark Nielsen (NZL) d. Aqeel Khan (PAK) 60 62 62; Aisam Qureshi (PAK) d. Simon Rea (NZL) 63 64 67(6) 63; Aqeel Khan/Aisam Qureshi (PAK) d. Mark Nielsen/Simon Rea (NZL) 64 64 61; Mark Nielsen (NZL) d. Aisam Qureshi (PAK) 64 67(1) 62 57 64; Aqeel Khan (PAK) d. Simon Rea (NZL) 76(5) 26 36 63 62.

New Zealand relegated to Asia/Oceania Zone Group II in 2005.

Europe/Africa Zone Group II

First Round 9-11 April
Italy defeated Georgia 3-2, Cagliari, ITA; Clay (O): Alessio Di Mauro (ITA) d. Irakli Ushangishvili (GEO) 61 60 62; Irakli Labadze (GEO) d. Andreas Seppi (ITA) 64 75 16 26 62; Massimo Bertolini/Giorgio Galimberti (ITA) d. Lado Chikhladze/Irakli Labadze (GEO) 76(5) 75 64; Irakli Labadze (GEO) d. Giorgio Galimberti (ITA) 61 62 57 63; Andreas Seppi (ITA) d. Lado Chikhladze (GEO) 62 64 64. **Bulgaria defeated Egypt 5-0, Sofia, BUL; Carpet (I):** Ivaylo Traykov (BUL) d. Karim Maamoun (EGY) 62 63 64; Todor Enev (BUL) d. Mohamed Maamoun (EGY) 62 60 62; Todor Enev/Ivaylo Traykov (BUL) d. Amro Ghoneim/Karim Maamoun (EGY) 63 75 62; Ilia Kushev (BUL) d. Amro Ghoneim (EGY) 62 62; Yordan Kanev (BUL) d. Karim Maamoun (EGY) 76(1) 63. **Algeria defeated Denmark Walkover, Algiers, ALG; Clay (O). Poland defeated Slovenia 3-2, Portoroz, SLO; Clay (O):** Lukasz Kubot (POL) d. Luka Gregorc (SLO) 76(5) 76(2) 63; Mariusz Fyrstenberg/Marcin Matkowski (POL) d. Andrej Kracman/Bostjan Osabnik (SLO) 61 75 76(2); Marko Tkalec (SLO) d. Lukasz Kubot (POL) 61 76(2) 46 36 64; Mariusz Fyrstenberg (POL) d. Andrej Kracman (SLO) 75 06 62 63. **Portugal defeated Tunisia 3-2, Tunis, TUN; Hard (O):** Leonardo Tavares (POR) d. Heithem Abid (TUN) 76(5) 61 46 62; Malek Jaziri (TUN) d. Bernardo Mota (POR) 62 16 57 76(4) 86; Frederico Gil/Leonardo Tavares (POR) d. Heithem Abid/Malek Jaziri (TUN) 75 63 62; Frederico Gil (POR) d. Heithem Abid (TUN) 64 63 75; Malek Jaziri (TUN) d. Rui Machado (POR) 64 63. **Serbia & Montenegro defeated Latvia 5-0, Belgrade, SCG; Carpet (I):** Nenad Zimonjic (SCG) d. Andis Juska (LAT) 63 62 64; Janko Tipsarevic (SCG) d. Deniss Pavlovs (LAT) 60 60 63; Dejan Petrovic/Nenad Zimonjic (SCG) d. Deniss Pavlovs/Janis Skroderis (LAT) 64 60 63; Janko Tipsarevic (SCG) d. Andis Juska (LAT) 64 64; Novak Djokovic (SCG) d. Janis Skroderis (LAT) 62 62. **Hungary defeated Ireland 4-1, Dublin, IRL; Carpet (I):** Gergely Kisgyorgy (HUN) d. Peter Clarke (IRL) 64 64 64; Kornel Bardoczky (HUN) d. Kevin Sorensen (IRL) 36 57 64 76(5) 63; Kornel Bardoczky/Gergely Kisgyorgy (HUN) d. Eoin Collins/David Mullins (IRL) 46 61 75 16 64; Gyorgy Balazs (HUN) d. Peter Clarke (IRL) 63 61; Gergely Kisgyorgy (HUN) d. Kevin Sorensen (IRL) w/o. **Norway defeated Ukraine 3-2, Oslo, NOR; Hard (I):** Jan-Frode Andersen (NOR) d. Sergei Yaroshenko (UKR) 46 60 76(5) 62; Stian Boretti (NOR) d. Orest Tereshchuk (UKR) 16 63 64 62; Jan-Frode Andersen/Stian Boretti (NOR) d. Mikhail Filima/Orest Tereshchuk (UKR) 64 64 76(3); Mikhail Filima (UKR) d. Erling Tveit (NOR) 64 63; Sergei Yaroshenko (UKR) d. Frederik Sundsten (NOR) 63 63.

2004 Davis Cup by BNP Paribas Results (continued)

Second Round 16-18 July
Italy defeated Bulgaria 5-0, Teramo, ITA; Clay (O): Filippo Volandri (ITA) d. Ivaylo Traykov (BUL) 64 62 64; Potito Starace (ITA) d. Todor Enev (BUL) 61 62 63; Massimo Bertolini/Andreas Seppi (ITA) d. Yordan Kanev/Ilia Kushev (BUL) 64 60 61; Filippo Volandri (ITA) d. Ilia Kushev (BUL) 62 60; Andreas Seppi (ITA) d. Yordan Kanev (BUL) 62 75. **Poland defeated Algeria 4-1, Gdynia, POL; Clay (O):** Lukasz Kubot (POL) d. Abdel-Hak Hameurlaine (ALG) 61 76(3) 61; Lamine Ouahab (ALG) d. Marcin Matkowski (POL) 61 57 63 64; Mariusz Fyrstenberg/Marcin Matkowski (POL) d. Rachid Baba-Aissa/Abdel-Wahid Henni (ALG) 64 61 60; Lukasz Kubot (POL) d. Lamine Ouahab (ALG) 76(1) 63; Filip Urban (POL) d. Rachid Baba-Aissa (ALG) 76(6) 62. **Serbia & Montenegro defeated Portugal 5-0, Maia, POR; Clay (O):** Boris Pashanski (SCG) d. Leonardo Tavares (POR) 36 61 16 61 62; Janko Tipsarevic (SCG) d. Frederico Gil (POR) 62 64 61; Nikola Ciric/Dusan Vemic (SCG) d. Frederico Gil/Leonardo Tavares (POR) 16 67(5) 63 61 64; Dusan Vemic (SCG) d. Rui Machado (POR) 63 63; Boris Pashanski (SCG) d. Frederico Gil (POR) 67(3) 62 60. **Hungary defeated Norway 3-2, Szeged, HUN; Clay (O):** Kornel Bardoczky (HUN) d. Helge Koll-Frafjord (NOR) 62 61 61; Jan-Frode Andersen (NOR) d. Sebo Kiss (HUN) 64 64 36 64; Kornel Bardoczky/Gergely Kisgyorgy (HUN) d. Jan-Frode Andersen/Frederik Sundsten (NOR) 63 64 63; Jan-Frode Andersen (NOR) d. Kornel Bardoczky (HUN) 63 64 67(8) 46 63; Gyorgy Balazs (HUN) d. Helge Koll-Frafjord (NOR) 60 62 64.

Third Round 24-26 September
Italy defeated Poland 3-2, Livorno, ITA; Clay (O): Filippo Volandri (ITA) d. Michal Przysiezny (POL) 61 62 61, Potito Starace (ITA) d. Lukasz Kubot (POL) 64 63 64; Mariusz Fyrstenberg/Marcin Matkowski (POL) d. Massimo Bertolini/Andreas Seppi (ITA) 63 26 64 64; Lukasz Kubot (POL) d. Filippo Volandri (ITA) 36 64 61 67(4) 62; Potito Starace (ITA) d. Mariusz Fyrstenberg (POL) 26 63 46 63 75. **Serbia & Montenegro defeated Hungary 3-0, Szeged, HUN; Clay (O):** Boris Pashanski (SCG) d. Kornel Bardoczky (HUN) 67(5) 64 64 62; Janko Tipsarevic (SCG) d. Gyorgy Balazs (HUN) 61 64 62; Dusan Vemic/Nenad Zimonjic (SCG) d. Kornel Bardoczky/Gergely Kisgyorgy (HUN) 63 62 62; Kornel Bardoczky (HUN) v Janko Tipsarevic (SCG) not played; Gyorgy Balazs (HUN) v Boris Pashanski (SCG) not played.

Italy and Serbia & Montenegro promoted to Europe/Africa Zone Group I in 2005.

Play-off 16-18 July
Georgia defeated Egypt 3-2, Tbilisi, GEO; Clay (O): Irakli Ushangishvili (GEO) d. Karim Maamoun (EGY) 16 76(4) 64 75; Irakli Labadze (GEO) d. Mohamed Maamoun (EGY) 63 63 62; Lado Chikhladze/Irakli Labadze (GEO) d. Karim Maamoun/Mohamed Maamoun (EGY) 63 62 62; Omar Hedayet (EGY) d. Lado Chikhladze (GEO) 63 61; Mohamed Maamoun (EGY) d. David Kvernadze (GEO) 64 63. **Slovenia defeated Denmark Walkover. Latvia defeated Tunisia 3-2, Liepaja, LAT; Clay (O):** Malek Jaziri (TUN) d. Andis Juska (LAT) 64 63 64; Deniss Pavlovs (LAT) d. Heithem Abid (TUN) 60 46 64 75; Andis Juska/Deniss Pavlovs (LAT) d. Tarek Ben Soltane/Malek Jaziri (TUN) 63 61 61; Andis Juska (LAT) d. Heithem Abid (TUN) 60 60 64; Malek Jaziri (TUN) d. Adrians Zguns (LAT) 75 64. **Ukraine defeated Ireland 4-1, Donetsk, UKR; Hard (O):** Orest Tereshchuk (UKR) d. Conor Niland (IRL) 63 63 63; Kevin Sorensen (IRL) d. Sergei Yaroshenko (UKR) 61 64 46 62; Mikhail Filima/Orest Tereshchuk (UKR) d. John Doran/David Mullins (IRL) 76(3) 63 75; Orest Tereshchuk (UKR) d. Kevin Sorensen (IRL) 64 63 62; Dmytro Tolok (UKR) d. David Mullins (IRL) 75 64.

Denmark, Egypt, Ireland and Tunisia relegated to Europe/Africa Zone Group III in 2005.

Americas Zone Group II

First Round 6-8 February
Bahamas defeated Puerto Rico 3-2, Bayamon, PUR; Hard (I): Gabriel Montilla (PUR) d. Christopher Eldon (BAH) 64 26 64 64; Mark Merklein (BAH) d. Luis Haddock (PUR) 61 64 76(4); Mark Merklein/Bjorn Munroe (BAH) d. Gilberto Alvarez/Gabriel Montilla (PUR) 64 67(5) 63 76(3); Mark Merklein (BAH) d. Gabriel Montilla (PUR) 60 63 63; Ricardo Gonzalez (PUR) d. H'Cone Thompson (BAH) 64 75. **Mexico defeated Jamaica 4-1, Kingston, JAM; Hard (O):** Miguel Gallardo-Valles (MEX) d. Scott Willinsky (JAM) 64 64 61; Ryan Russell (JAM) d. Luis-Manuel Flores (MEX) 63 16 61 64; Daniel Langre/Victor Romero (MEX) d. Karl Hale/Ryan Russell (JAM) 62 61 60; Miguel Gallardo-Valles (MEX) d. Ryan Russell (JAM) 60 76(4) 75; Daniel Langre (MEX) d. Scott Willinsky (JAM) 46 64 75. **Uruguay defeated Haiti 3-2, Port-au-Prince, HAI; Clay (O):** Pablo Cuevas (URU) d. Iphton Louis (HAI) 64 60 63; Bertrand Madsen (HAI) d. Federico Sansonetti (URU) 62 63 76(1); Iphton Louis/Bertrand Madsen (HAI) d. Pablo Cuevas/Federico Sansonetti (URU) 64 64 76(5); Pablo Cuevas (URU) d. Bertrand Madsen (HAI) 76(6) 63 76(3); Federico Sansonetti (URU) d. Iphton Louis (HAI) 61 63 36 64. **Dominican Republic defeated Cuba 4-1, Havana, CUB; Hard (O):** Victor Estrella (DOM) d. Sandor Martinez-Breijo (CUB) 61 76(4) 64; Johnson Garcia (DOM) d. Ricardo Chile-Fonte (CUB) 36 76(3) 62 36 61; Ricardo Chile-Fonte/Sandor Martinez-Breijo (CUB) d. Victor Estrella/Johnson Garcia (DOM) 64 76(4) 46 76(3); Victor Estrella (DOM) d. Eddy Gonzalez (CUB) 26 64 06 64 64; Jose Bernard (DOM) d. Favel Antonio Freyre-Perdomo (CUB) 63 63.

Second Round 9-11 April
Mexico defeated Bahamas 5-0, Mexico City, MEX; Clay (O): Alejandro Hernandez (MEX) d. Christopher Eldon (BAH) 60 75 62; Miguel Gallardo-Valles (MEX) d. Bjorn Munroe (BAH) 62 61 63; Bruno Echagaray/Santiago Gonzalez (MEX) d. Christopher Eldon/Bjorn Munroe (BAH) 60 62 63; Miguel Gallardo-Valles (MEX) d. H'Cone Thompson (BAH) 60 60; Alejandro Hernandez (MEX) d. Bjorn Munroe (BAH) 62 76(2). **Dominican Republic defeated Uruguay 4-1, Santo Domingo, DOM; Hard (O):** Victor Estrella (DOM) d. Pablo Cuevas (URU) 64 63 75; Johnson Garcia (DOM) d. Marcel Felder (URU) 75 64 75; Victor Estrella/Johnson Garcia (DOM) d. Ricciardi Augusto/Marcel Felder (URU) 36 26 63 75 64; Michael-Ray Pallares (DOM) d. Federico Sansonetti (URU) 63 63; Pablo Cuevas (URU) d. Federico Rodriguez (DOM) 63 16 63.

Third Round 24-26 September
Mexico defeated Dominican Republic 5-0, Toluca, MEX; Clay (O): Alejandro Hernandez (MEX) d. Johnson Garcia (DOM) 64 64 64; Miguel Gallardo-Valles (MEX) d. Victor Estrella (DOM) 63 64 36 76(5); Bruno Echagaray/Santiago Gonzalez (MEX) d. Victor Estrella/Johnson Garcia (DOM) 62 63 76(4); Santiago Gonzalez (MEX) d. Johnson Garcia (DOM) 61 75; Alejandro Hernandez (MEX) d. Federico Rodriguez (DOM) 61 64.

Mexico promoted to Americas Zone Group I in 2005.

Play-off 9-11 April
Jamaica defeated Puerto Rico 3-2, Bayamon, PUR; Hard (O): Gabriel Montilla (PUR) d. Scott Willinsky (JAM) 63 76(6) 64; Luis Haddock (PUR) d. Ryan Russell (JAM) 75 63 62; Ryan Russell/Jermaine Smith (JAM) d. Gilberto Alvarez/Gabriel Montilla (PUR) 62 76(1) 63; Ryan Russell (JAM) d. Gabriel Montilla (PUR) 67(3) 63 60 62; Scott Willinsky (JAM) d. Juan-Oscar Rios (PUR) 26 76(5) 62 64. **Cuba defeated Haiti 3-2, La Habana, CUB; Hard (O):** Bertrand Madsen (HAI) d. Eddy Gonzalez (CUB) 75 62 63; Ricardo Chile-Fonte (CUB) d. Olivier Claude Sajous (HAI) 64 60 60; Ricardo Chile-Fonte/Sandor Martinez-Breijo (CUB) d. Iphton Louis/Bertrand Madsen (HAI) 64 63 63; Ricardo Chile-Fonte (CUB) d. Bertrand Madsen (HAI) 62 63 63; Olivier Claude Sajous (HAI) d. Edgar Hernandez (CUB) 57 76(6) 62.

Haiti and Puerto Rico relegated to Americas Zone Group III in 2005.

Asia/Oceania Zone Group II

First Round 6-8 February
Korea, Rep. defeated Malaysia 5-0, Kuala Lumpur, MAS, Hard (I): Hyung-Taik Lee (KOR) d. Dannio Yahya (MAS) 61 60 60; Hee-Seok Chung (KOR) d. Yew-Ming Si (MAS) 63 75 64; Hee-Seok Chung/Hyung-Taik Lee (KOR) d. Adam Jaya/Yew-Ming Si (MAS) 67(5) 62 64 63; Kyu-Tae Im (KOR) d. Adam Jaya (MAS) 75 64; Hyun-Woo Nam (KOR) d. Mohammed-Noor Noordin (MAS) 63 61. **Lebanon defeated Iran 3-2, Beirut, LIB; Carpet (I):** Will Farah-Lebar (LIB) d. Anoosha Shahgholi (IRI) 60 75 63; Patrick Chucri (LIB) d. Ashkan Shokoofi (IRI) 46 16 75 63 64; Patrick Chucri/Will Farah-Lebar (LIB) d. Anoosha Shahgholi/Ashkan Shokoofi (IRI) 63 64 62; Anoosha Shahgholi (IRI) d. Fady Youssef (LIB) 60 76(3); Ashkan Shokoofi (IRI) d. Wahib Maknieh (LIB) 63 67(5) 61. **China defeated Philippines 4-1, Manila, PHI; Clay (I):** Hao Lu (CHN) d. Johnny Arcilla (PHI) 75 26 61 76(3); Xin-Yuan Yu (CHN) d. Joseph Victorino (PHI) 61 62 61; Ran Xu/Xin-Yuan Yu (CHN) d. Adelo Abadia/Johnny Arcilla (PHI) 63 61 36 62; Johnny Arcilla (PHI) d. Jing-Yi Li (CHN) 62 75; Hao Lu (CHN) d. Joseph Victorino (PHI) 75 64. **Kuwait defeated Hong Kong, China 3-1, Causeway Bay, HKG; Carpet (I):** Mohammed Al Ghareeb (KUW) d. Michael Brown (HKG) 62 63 61; Musaad Al Jazzaf (KUW) d. Hiu-Tung Yu (HKG) 26 64 64 36 75; John Hui/Brian Hung (HKG) d. Abdullah Magdas/Ahmed Rabeea (KUW) 63 62 60; Mohammed Al Ghareeb (KUW) d. Hiu-Tung Yu (HKG) 64 64 62; Musaad Al Jazzaf (KUW) v. Michael Brown (HKG) not played.

Second Round 9-11 April
Korea, Rep. defeated Lebanon 5-0, Busan, KOR; Hard (O): Hee-Seok Chung (KOR) d. Will Farah-Lebar (LIB) 62 62 61; Young-Jun Kim (KOR) d. Patrick Chucri (LIB) 76(5) 76(4) 61; Hee-Seok Chung/Hyung-Taik Lee (KOR) d. Patrick Chucri/Will Farah-Lebar (LIB) 63 61 64; Woong-Sun Jun (KOR) d. Patrick Chucri (LIB) 64 75; Young-Jun Kim (KOR) d. Will Farah-Lebar (LIB) 62 64. **China defeated Kuwait 5-0, Nan Jing, CHN; Hard (O):** Ben-Qiang Zhu (CHN) d. Mohamed-Khaliq Siddiq (KUW) 60 64 75; Shao-Xuan Zeng (CHN) d. Mohammed Al Ghareeb (KUW) 76(5) 67(5) ret.; Shao-Xuan Zeng/Ben-Qiang Zhu (CHN) d. Abdullah Magdas/Mohamed-Khaliq Siddiq (KUW) 61 63 60; Xin-Yuan Yu (CHN) d. Abdullah Magdas (KUW) 64 63; Jing-Yi Li (CHN) d. Ahmed Rabeea (KUW) 60 63.

2004 Davis Cup by BNP Paribas Results (continued)

Third Round 24-26 September
China defeated Korea, Rep. 3-2, Nanjing, CHN; Hard (O): Hyung-Taik Lee (KOR) d. Ben-Qiang Zhu (CHN) 64 75 64; Yu Jr. Wang (CHN) d. Young-Jun Kim (KOR) 76(8) 36 46 63 62; Shao-Xuan Zeng/Ben-Qiang Zhu (CHN) d. Hee-Seok Chung/Hyung-Taik Lee (KOR) 46 36 76(4) 63 64; Hyung-Taik Lee (KOR) d. Yu Jr. Wang (CHN) 62 63 63; Ben-Qiang Zhu (CHN) d. Young-Jun Kim (KOR) 57 67(3) 61 75 63.

China promoted to Asia/Oceania Zone Group I in 2005.

Play-off 9-11 April
Iran defeated Malaysia 4-1, Tehran, IRI; Clay (O): Shahab Hassani-Nafez (IRI) d. Adam Jaya (MAS) 61 64 62; Ashkan Shokoofi (IRI) d. Yew-Ming Si (MAS) 46 67(2) 75 64 64; Adam Jaya/Yew-Ming Si (MAS) d. Ashkan Shokoofi/Farshad Talavar (IRI) 76(4) 63 75; Shahab Hassani-Nafez (IRI) d. Yew-Ming Si (MAS) 63 36 76(3) 62; Saeed Ahmandvand (IRI) d. Mohammed-Noor Noordin (MAS) 60 63. **Philippines defeated Hong Kong, China 4-1, Manila, PHI Clay (I):** Adelo Abadia (PHI) d. Hiu-Tung Yu (HKG) 62 61 63; Johnny Arcilla (PHI) d. Michael Brown (HKG) 26 61 62 64; Adelo Abadia/Johnny Arcilla (PHI) d. John Hui/Asif Ismail (HKG) 75 62 63; Patrick Tierro (PHI) d. Hiu-Tung Yu (HKG) 64 63; Michael Brown (HKG) d. Joseph Victorino (PHI) 36 63 10 ret.

Hong Kong, China and Malaysia relegated to Americas Zone Group III in 2005.

Europe/Africa Zone Group III – Venue I

Date:	12-16 May
Venue:	Windhoek, Namibia
Surface:	Hard (O)
Group A:	Cote D'Ivoire, Kenya, Turkey
Group B:	Ghana, Madagascar, Namibia

- **Group A 12 May Turkey defeated Kenya 3-0:** Haluk Akkoyun (TUR) d. Christian Vitulli (KEN) 64 60; Ergun Zorlu (TUR) d. Allan Cooper (KEN) 61 62; Haluk Akkoyun/Esat Tanik (TUR) d. Allan Cooper/Christian Vitulli (KEN) 75 63.

- **13 May Cote D'Ivoire defeated Kenya 3-0:** Charles Irie (CIV) d. Christian Vitulli (KEN) 64 60; Claude N'Goran (CIV) d. Allan Cooper (KEN) 61 63; Claude N'Goran/Nouhoun Sangare (CIV) d. Aldrin Ndinya/Christian Vitulli (KEN) 61 63.

- **14 May Cote D'Ivoire defeated Turkey 2-1:** Haluk Akkoyun (TUR) d. Charles Irie (CIV) 64 61; Claude N'Goran (CIV) d. Ergun Zorlu (TUR) 62 63; Claude N'Goran/Nouhoun Sangare (CIV) d. Haluk Akkoyun/Ergun Zorlu (TUR) 67(0) 76(9) 62.

- **Group B 12 May Namibia defeated Madagascar 3-0:** Jurgens Strydom (NAM) d. Donne-Dubert Radison (MAD) 67(6) 76(4) 61; Johan Theron (NAM) d. Jacob Rasolondrazana (MAD) 26 62 75; Henrico Du Plessis/Johan Theron (NAM) d. Harivony Andrianafetra/Jean-Marc Randriamanalina (MAD) 63 62.

- **13 May Ghana defeated Namibia 2-1:** Henry Adjei-Darko (GHA) d. Jurgens Strydom (NAM) 67(11) 76(5) 86; Gunther Darkey (GHA) d. Johan Theron (NAM) 64 40 ret.; Henrico Du Plessis/Jurgens Strydom (NAM) d. Gunther Darkey/Samuel-Etse Fumi (GHA) 64 36 63.

- **14 May Ghana defeated Madagascar 2-1:** Henry Adjei-Darko (GHA) d. Donne-Dubert Radison (MAD) 63 61; Jacob Rasolondrazana (MAD) d. Gunther Darkey (GHA) 75 64; Henry Adjei-Darko/Gunther Darkey (GHA) d. Harivony Andrianafetra/Jacob Rasolondrazana (MAD) 62 75.

- **Play-off for 1st-4th Positions:**
  Results carried forward: Cote D'Ivoire defeated Turkey 2-1; Ghana defeated Namibia 2-1
  15 May Cote D'Ivoire defeated Namibia 3-0: Charles Irie (CIV) d. Jurgens Strydom (NAM) 76(2) 62; Claude N'Goran (CIV) d. Johan Theron (NAM) 61 76(1); Claude N'Goran/Nouhoun Sangare (CIV) d. Henrico Du Plessis/Jurgens Strydom (NAM) 76(4) 75. **Ghana defeated Turkey 2-1:** Henry Adjei-Darko (GHA) d. Haluk Akkoyun (TUR) 63 60; Gunther Darkey (GHA) d. Ergun Zorlu (TUR) 61 61; Haluk Akkoyun/Esat Tanik (TUR) d. Samuel-Etse Fumi/Solomon Koomsom (GHA) 62 64.

USA's Bob and Mike Bryan undefeated in Davis Cup

2004 Davis Cup by BNP Paribas Results (continued)

- **16 May   Cote D'Ivoire defeated Ghana 2-1:** Nouhoun Sangare (CIV) d. Solomon Koomsom (GHA) 75 36 63; Charles Irie (CIV) d. Samuel-Etse Fumi (GHA) 76(5) 63; Henry Adjei-Darko/Gunther Darkey (GHA) d. Charles Irie/Claude N'Goran (CIV) 32 ret. **Turkey defeated Namibia 3-0:** Esat Tanik (TUR) d. Henrico Du Plessis (NAM) 75 61; Haluk Akkoyun (TUR) d. Jurgens Strydom (NAM) 62 63; Haluk Akkoyun/Esat Tanik (TUR) d. Henrico Du Plessis/Johan Theron (NAM) 64 64.

- **Play-off for 5th-6th Positions:**
  15 May   Kenya defeated Madagascar 3-0: Christian Vitulli (KEN) d. Donne-Dubert Radison (MAD) 76(1) 36 64; Allan Cooper (KEN) d. Jacob Rasolondrazana (MAD) 46 63 97; Allan Cooper/Christian Vitulli (KEN) d. Harivony Andrianafetra/Jean-Marc Randriamanalina (MAD) 61 64.

- **Final Positions:** 1. Cote D'Ivoire, 2. Ghana, 3. Turkey, 4. Namibia, 5. Kenya, 6. Madagascar.

Cote D'Ivoire and Ghana promoted to Europe/Africa Zone Group II in 2005.
Benin and Togo relegated to Europe/Africa Zone Group IV in 2005 (both teams withdrew from the competition).

Europe/Africa Zone Group III – Venue II

Date: 4-8 February
Venue: Kaunas, Lithuania
Surface: Carpet (I)
Group A: Cyprus, Estonia, Lithuania
Group B: Andorra, Iceland, Macedonia F.Y.R., Monaco

- **Group A   4 February   Lithuania defeated Cyprus 2-1:** Rolandas Murashka (LTU) d. Fotos Kallias (CYP) 61 64; Marcos Baghdatis (CYP) d. Aivaras Balzekas (LTU) 61 46 64; Paulius Jurkenas/Gvidas Sabeckis (LTU) d. Marcos Baghdatis/Demetrios Leontis (CYP) 63 63.

- **5 February   Cyprus defeated Estonia 2-1:** Alti Vahkal (EST) d. Fotos Kallias (CYP) 57 63 64; Marcos Baghdatis (CYP) d. Mait Kunnap (EST) 64 76(3); Marcos Baghdatis/Demetrios Leontis (CYP) d. Mait Kunnap/Alti Vahkal (EST) 57 64 1210.

- **6 February   Estonia defeated Lithuania 2-1:** Oskar Saarne (EST) d. Rolandas Murashka (LTU) 67(3) 64 64; Aivaras Balzekas (LTU) d. Mait Kunnap (EST) 75 36 97; Mait Kunnap/Alti VahkalL (EST) d. Rolandas Murashka/Gvidas Sabeckis (LTU) 64 63.

- **Group B   4 February   Macedonia, F.Y.R. defeated Iceland 3-0:** Predrag Rusevski (MKD) d. Raj Bonifacius (ISL) 64 64; Lazar Magdincev (MKD) d. Arnar Sigurdsson (ISL) 36 62 63; Lazar Magdincev/Predrag Rusevski (MKD) d. Raj Bonifacius/Arnar Sigurdsson (ISL) 61 75.
  Monaco defeated Andorra 3-0: Guillaume Couillard (MON) d. Kenneth Tuilier-Curco (AND) 61 61; Benjamin Balleret (MON) d. Joan Jimenez-Guerra (AND) 60 67(3) 62; Thomas Drouet/Emmanuel Heussner (MON) d. Paul Gerbaud-Farras/Marc Vilanova (AND) 61 64.

- **5 February   Macedonia, F.Y.R. defeated Andorra 2-1:** Predrag Rusevski (MKD) d. Kenneth Tuilier-Curco (AND) 63 63; Lazar Magdincev (MKD) d. Joan Jimenez-Guerra (AND) 62 64; Paul Gerbaud-Farras/Joan Jimenez-Guerra (AND) d. Dimitar Grabulovski/Kristijan Mitrovski (MKD) 76(4) 64. **Monaco defeated Iceland 2-1:** Guillaume Couillard (MON) d. Raj Bonifacius (ISL) 64 62; Benjamin Balleret (MON) d. Arnar Sigurdsson (ISL) 63 62; Raj Bonifacius/Arnar Sigurdsson (ISL) d. Thomas Drouet/Emmanuel Heussner (MON) 75 64.

- **6 February   Monaco defeated Macedonia, F.Y.R. 2-1:** Emmanuel Heussner (MON) d. Predrag Rusevski (MKD) 63 67(2) 75; Lazar Magdincev (MKD) d. Benjamin Balleret (MON) 64 67(3) 63; Guillaume Couillard/Emmanuel Heussner (MON) d. Lazar Magdincev/Predrag Rusevski (MKD) 46 76(8) 64. **Iceland defeated Andorra 3-0:** Raj Bonifacius (ISL) d. Kenneth Tuiler-Curco (AND) 62 57 97; Arnar Sigurdsson (ISL) d. Joan Jimenez-Guerra (AND) 61 62; Raj Bonifacius/Arnar Sigurdsson (ISL) d. Paul Gerbaud-Farras/Kenneth Tuiler-Curco (AND) 63 64.

- **Play-off for 1st-4th Positions:**
  Results carried forward: Estonia defeated Lithuania 2-1; Monaco defeated Macedonia, F.Y.R. 2-1
  7 February   Lithuania defeated Monaco 2-1: Gvidas Sabeckis (LTU) d. Guillaume Couillard (MON) 64 36 75; Aivaras Balzekas (LTU) d. Benjamin Balleret (MON) 64 76(5); Guillaume Couillard/Emmanuel Heussner (MON) d. Paulius Jurkenas/Gvidas Sabeckis (LTU) 26 75 1412.
  Estonia defeated Macedonia, F.Y.R. 2-1: Predrag Rusevski (MKD) d. Oskar Saarne (EST) 76(6) 64; Mait Kunnap (EST) d. Lazar Magdincev (MKD) 26 64 62; Mait Kunnap/Alti Vahkal (EST) d. Lazar Magdincev/Predrag Rusevski (MKD) 64 67(7) 75.

- **8 February Monaco defeated Estonia 3-0:** Emmanuel Heussner (MON) d. Oskar Saarne (EST) 67(8) 75 1311; Guillaume Couillard (MON) d. Mait Kunnap (EST) 63 76(3); Benjamin Balleret/Thomas Drouet (MON) d. Mait Kunnap/Alti Vakhal (EST) 67(1) 76(4) 10 ret. **Macedonia, F.Y.R. defeated Lithuania 2-1:** Rolandas Murashka (LTU) d. Predrag Rusevski (MKD) 64 62; Lazar Magdincev (MKD) d. Aivaras Balzekas(LTU) 64 76(3); Lazar Magdincev/Predrag Rusevski (MKD) d. Paulius Jurkenas/Rolandas Murashka (LTU) 46 75 108.

- **Play-off for 5th-7th Positions:**
  Result carried forward: Iceland defeated Andorra 3-0
  7 February Cyprus defeated Andorra 2-1: Paul Gerbaud-Farras (AND) d. Fotos Kallias (CYP) 76(6) 63; Marcos Baghdatis (CYP) d. Kenneth Tuilier-Curco (AND) 62 60; Marcos Baghdatis/Demetrios Leontis (CYP) d. Paul Gerbaud-Farras/Joan Jimenez-Guerra (AND) 67(5) 76(1) 62.

- **8 February Iceland defeated Cyprus 2-1:** Demetrios Leontis (CYP) d. Andri Jonsson (ISL) 63 64; Arnar Sigurdsson (ISL) d. Eleftherios Christou (CYP) 62 62; Jon-Axel Jonsson/Arnar Sigurdsson (ISL) d. Eleftherios Christou/Demetrios Leontis(CYP) 63 64.

- **Final Positions:** 1. Monaco, 2. Estonia, 3. Macedonia, F.Y.R., 4. Lithuania, 5. Iceland, 6. Cyprus, 7. Andorra.

Monaco and Estonia promoted to Europe/Africa Zone Group II in 2005.
Andorra relegated to Europe/Africa Zone Group IV in 2005.

Americas Zone Group III

Date: 4-8 February
Venue: Tegucigalpa, Honduras
Surface: Hard (O)
Group A: Bolivia, Colombia, Honduras, Panama
Group B: El Salvador, Netherlands Antilles, Trinidad & Tobago, US Virgin Islands

- **Group A 4 February Colombia defeated Honduras 3-0:** Michael Quintero (COL) d. Carlos Caceres (HON) 75 63; Alejandro Falla-Ramirez (COL) d. Franklin Garcia (HON) 62 63; Alejandro Falla-Ramirez/Carlos Salamanca (COL) d. Carlos Caceres/Pablo Hernandez (HON) 64 62. **Bolivia defeated Panama 3-0:** Carlos Alvarez (BOL) d. Chad Valdes (PAN) 63 75; Javier Taborga (BOL) d. Alberto Gonzalez (PAN) 64 64; Oscar Blacutt/Mauricio Estivariz (BOL) d. Juan-Pablo Herrera/David Lopez (PAN) 63 64.

- **5 February Colombia defeated Panama 3-0:** Michael Quintero (COL) d. Chad Valdes (PAN) 63 64; Alejandro Falla-Ramirez (COL) d. Alberto Gonzalez (PAN) 62 62; Alejandro Falla-Ramirez/Carlos Salamanca (COL) d. Juan-Pablo Herrera/David Lopez (PAN) 61 63. **Bolivia defeated Honduras 2-1:** Calton Alvarez (HON) d. Carlos Alvarez (BOL) 36 63 61; Javier Taborga (BOL) d. Carlos Caceres (HON) 62 63; Oscar Blacutt/Javier Taborga (BOL) d. Franklin Garcia/Pablo Hernandez (HON) 61 63.

- **6 February Colombia defeated Bolivia 3-0:** Michael Quintero (COL) d. Carlos Alvarez (BOL) 62 62; Alejandro Falla-Ramirez (COL) d. Javier Taborga (BOL) 64 64; Alejandro Falla-Ramirez/Carlos Salamanca (COL) d. Oscar Blacutt/Javier Taborga (BOL) 64 76(4). **Honduras defeated Panama 2-1:** Calton Alvarez (HON) d. Chad Valdes (PAN) 40 ret; Alberto Gonzalez (PAN) d. Carlos Caceres (HON) 63 62; Calton Alvarez/Franklin Garcia (HON) d. Alberto Gonzalez/Juan-Pablo Herrera(PAN) 75 60.

- **Group B 4 February Netherlands Antilles defeated Trinidad & Tobago 2-1:** Richard Brown (TRI) d. Pietr Boeckel (AHO) 64 60; Jean-Julien Rojer (AHO) d. Dexter Mahase (TRI) 61 62; Raoul Behr/Jean-Julien Rojer (AHO) d. Richard Brown/Jonathan Gomez (TRI) 64 63. **El Salvador defeated US Virgin Islands 3-0:** Jaime Cuellar (ESA) d. John Richards (ISV) 61 76(2); Rafael Arevalo Gonzalez (ESA) d. Eugene Highfield (ISV) 62 60; Rafael Arevalo Gonzalez/Jaime Cuellar (ESA) d. Kristopher Elien/Eugene Highfield (ISV) 62 61.

- **5 February Netherlands Antilles defeated US Virgin Islands 3-0:** Pietr Boeckel (AHO) d. Kristopher Elien (ISV) 36 62 63; Jean-Julien Rojer (AHO) d. Eugene Highfield (ISV) 64 61; Raoul Behr/Jean-Julien Rojer (AHO) d. Kristopher Elien/John Richards (ISV) 62 62. **El Salvador defeated Trinidad & Tobago 3-0:** Jaime Cuellar (ESA) d. Richard Brown (TRI) 61 61; Rafael Arevalo Gonzalez (ESA) d. Dexter Mahase (TRI) 60 62; Rafael Arevalo Gonzalez/Jaime Cuellar (ESA) d. Richard Brown/Jonathan Gomez (TRI) 61 76(4).

- **6 February Netherlands Antilles defeated El Salvador 2-1:** Jaime Cuellar (ESA) d. Pietr Boeckel (AHO) 62 61; Jean-Julien Rojer (AHO) d. Rafael Arevalo Gonzalez (ESA) 63 63; Raoul Behr/Jean-Julien Rojer (AHO) d. Rafael Arevalo Gonzalez/Jaime Cuellar (ESA) 62 64. **US Virgin Islands defeated Trinidad & Tobago 2-1:** Jonathan Gomez (TRI) d. Kristopher Elien (ISV) 75 64; Eugene Highfield (ISV) d. Richard Brown (TRI) 64 61; Eugene Highfield/John Richards (ISV) d. Jonathan Gomez/Dexter Mahase (TRI) 63 64.

2004 Davis Cup by BNP Paribas Results (continued)

- **Play-off for 1st-4th Positions:**
  Results carried forward: Colombia defeated Bolivia 3-0; Netherlands Antilles defeated El Salvador 2-1
  7 February Colombia defeated Netherlands Antilles 3-0: Michael Quintero (COL) d. Rasid Winklaar (AHO) 62 60; Alejandro Falla-Ramirez (COL) d. Jean-Julien Rojer (AHO) 61 64; Alejandro Falla-Ramirez/Carlos Salamanca (COL) d. Raoul Behr/Pietr Boeckel (AHO) 63 60. **El Salvador defeated Bolivia 2-1:** Jaime Cuellar (ESA) d. Oscar Blacutt (BOL) 76(5) 62; Rafael Arevalo Gonzalez (ESA) d. Javier Taborga (BOL) 63 76(5); Oscar Blacutt/Javier Taborga (BOL) d. Rafael Arevalo Gonzalez/Jaime Cuellar (ESA) 62 64.

- **8 February Colombia defeated El Salvador 3-0:** Pablo Gonzalez (COL) d. Jaime Cuellar (ESA) 75 61; Alejandro Falla-Ramirez (COL) d. Rafael Arevalo Gonzalez (ESA) 46 63 63; Michael Quintero/Carlos Salamanca (COL) d. Rafael Arevalo Gonzalez/Jaime Cuellar (ESA) 36 61 61. **Netherlands Antilles defeated Bolivia 2-1:** Carlos Alvarez (BOL) d. Rasid Winklaar (AHO) 60 64; Jean-Julien Rojer (AHO) d. Javier Taborga (BOL) 63 61; Raoul Behr/Jean-Julien Rojer (AHO) d. Oscar Blacutt/Javier Taborga (BOL) 75 67(2) 86.

- **Play-off for 5th-8th Positions:**
  Results carried forward: Honduras defeated Panama 2-1; US Virgin Islands defeated Trinidad & Tobago 2-1
  7 February Honduras defeated US Virgin Islands 3-0: Pablo Hernandez (HON) d. John Richards (ISV) 63 60; Calton Alvarez (HON) d. Eugene Highfield (ISV) 63 63; Carlos Caceres/Franklin Garcia (HON) d. Albert Richards/John Richards (ISV) 62 64. **Panama defeated Trinidad & Tobago 2-1:** Richard Brown (TRI) d. David Lopez (PAN) 61 57 86; Alberto Gonzalez (PAN) d. Dexter Mahase (TRI) 75 61; Alberto Gonzalez/David Lopez (PAN) d. Richard Brown/Dexter Mahase (TRI) 61 62.

- **8 February Honduras defeated Trinidad & Tobago 3-0:** Calton Alvarez (HON) d. Jonathan Gomez (TRI) 62 64; Carlos Caceres (HON) d. Dexter Mahase (TRI) 64 62; Franklin Garcia/Pablo Hernandez (HON) d. Jermille Danclar/Dexter Mahase (TRI) 62 64. **Panama defeated US Virgin Islands 2-1:** John Richards (ISV) d. David Lopez (PAN) 64 75; Alberto Gonzalez (PAN) d. Eugene Highfield (ISV) 60 61; Alberto Gonzalez/David Lopez (PAN) d. Eugene Highfield/John Richards (ISV) 63 62.

- **Final Positions:** 1. Colombia, 2. Netherlands Antilles, 3. El Salvador, 4. Bolivia, 5. Honduras, 6. Panama, 7. US Virgin Islands, 8. Trinidad & Tobago.

Colombia and Netherlands Antilles promoted to Americas Zone Group II in 2005.
US Virgin Islands and Trinidad & Tobago relegated to Americas Zone Group IV in 2005.

Asia/Oceania Zone Group III

Date:	7-11 April
Venue:	Ho Chi Minh City, Vietnam
Surface:	Hard (O)
Group A:	Kazakhstan, Oman, Qatar, Tajikistan
Group B:	Bahrain, Pacific Oceania, Syria, Vietnam

- **Group A 7 April Kazakhstan defeated Oman 3-0:** Dias Doskaraev (KAZ) d. Mohammed Al Nabhani (OMA) 61 61; Alexey Kedriouk (KAZ) d. Khalid Al Nabhani (OMA) 64 64; Alexey Kedriouk/Anton Tsymbalov (KAZ) d. Khalid Al Nabhani/Mohammed Al Nabhani (OMA) 61 62. **Tajikistan defeated Qatar 3-0:** Mansour Yakhyaev (TJK) d. Mohammed-Saadon Al Kawari (QAT) 64 16 64; Sergei Makashin (TJK) d. Sultan-Khalfan Al Alawi (QAT) 60 22 ret; Sergei Makashin/Mansour Yakhyaev (TJK) d. Mohammed-Saadon Al Kawari/Amir Ebrahim (QAT) 63 63.

- **8 April Kazakhstan defeated Tajikistan 3-0:** Dias Doskaraev (KAZ) d. Mansour Yakhyaev (TJK) 61 76(7); Alexey Kedriouk (KAZ) d. Sergei Makashin (TJK) 60 63; Alexey Kedriouk/Anton Tsymbalov (KAZ) d. Sergei Makashin/Mansour Yakhyaev (TJK) 61 60. **Qatar defeated Oman 3-0:** Mohammed-Saadon Al Kawari (QAT) d. Mohammed Al Nabhani (OMA) 63 63; Amir Ebrahim (QAT) d. Khalid Al Abhani (OMA) 75 36 62; Mohammed-Saadon Al Kawari/Abdallah Hassan (QAT) d. Khalid Al Nabhani/Mohammed Al Nabhani (OMA) 75 67(5) 63.

- **9 April Kazakhstan defeated Qatar 3-0:** Dias Doskaraev (KAZ) d. Mohammed-Saadon Al Kawari (QAT) 60 62; Alexey Kedriouk (KAZ) d. Amir Ebrahim (QAT) 60 64; Alexey Kedriouk/Anton Tsymbalov (KAZ) d. Mohammed-Saadon Al Kawari/Abdallah Hassan (QAT) 61 62. **Tajikistan defeated Oman 3-0:** Mansour Yakhyaev (TJK) d. Mohammed Al Nabhani (OMA) 62 46 62; Sergei Makashin (TJK) d. Khalid Al Nabhani (OMA) 61 61; Sergei Makashin/Mansour Yakhyaev (TJK) d. Mohammed Al Nabhani/Suleiman Al Rawahi (OMA) 64 67 86.

- **Group B 7 April Vietnam defeated Bahrain 2-1:** Abdul-Rahman Shehab (BRN) d. Quoc-Khanh Le (VIE) 62 61; Minh-Quan Do (VIE) d. Esam Abdul-Aal (BRN) 62 57 86; Chi-Khuong Huynh/Quoc-Khanh Le (VIE) d. Khaled Al Thawadi/Abdul-Rahman Shehab (BRN) 64 36 63. **Pacific Oceania defeated Syria 3-0:** Juan Sebastien Langton (POC) d. Laith Salim (SYR) 76(4) 61; Michael Leong (POC) d. Abraham Ibrahim (SYR) 61 64; Brett Baudinet/Juan Sebastien Langton (POC) d. Moufak Hafez/Hayan Marouf (SYR) 64 62.

- **8 April Vietnam defeated Syria 3-0:** Quang-Huy Ngo (VIE) d. Laith Salim (SYR) 64 61; Minh-Quan Do (VIE) d. Abraham Ibrahim (SYR) 63 61; Chi-Khuong Huynh/Quoc-Khanh Le (VIE) d. Moufak Hafez/Hayan Marouf (SYR) 63 63. **Pacific Oceania defeated Bahrain 3-0:** Juan Sebastien Langton (POC) d. Abdul-Rahman Shehab (BRN) 46 63 64; Michael Leong (POC) d. Khaled Al Thawadi (BRN) 60 60; Brett Baudinet/Juan Sebastien Langton (POC) d. Esam Abdul-Aal/Abdul-Karim Abdul-Redha (BRN) 61 64.

- **9 April Pacific Oceania defeated Vietnam 2-1:** Juan Sebastien Langton (POC) d. Quang-Huy Ngo (VIE) 63 64; Minh-Quan Do (VIE) d. Michael Leong (POC) 57 64 63; Brett Baudinet/Juan Sebastien Langton (POC) d. Chi-Khuong Huynh/Quoc-Khanh Le (VIE) 76(4) 76(6). **Bahrain defeated Syria 2-1:** Abdul-Rahman Shehab (BRN) d. Laith Salim (SYR) 61 62; Esam Abdul-Aal (BRN) d. Abraham Ibrahim (SYR) 63 64; Moufak Hafez/Hayan Marouf (SYR) d. Khaled Al Thawadi/Abdul-Rahman Shehab (BRN) 64 63.

- **Play-off for 1st-4th Positions:**
  Results carried forward: Kazakhstan defeated Tajikistan 3-0; Pacific Oceania defeated Vietnam 2-1
  10 April Kazakhstan defeated Vietnam 3-0: Dias Doskaraev (KAZ) d. Quoc-Khanh Le (VIE) 60 61; Alexey Kedriouk (KAZ) d. Minh-Quan Do (VIE) 64 62; Alexey Kedriouk/Anton Tsymbalov (KAZ) d. Minh-Quan Do/Quoc-Khanh Le (VIE) 63 61. **Pacific Oceania defeated Tajikistan 2-1:** Mansour Yakhyaev (TJK) d. Juan Sebastien Langton (POC) 62 76(5); Michael Leong (POC) d. Sergei Makashin (TJK) 61 76(5); Brett Baudinet/Juan Sebastien Langton (POC) d. Sergei Makashin/Mansour Yakhyaev (TJK) 64 76(6).

- **11 April Kazakhstan defeated Pacific Oceania 2-1:** Anton Tsymbalov (KAZ) d. Brett Baudinet (POC) 63 61; Michael Leong (POC) d. Dias Doskaraev (KAZ) 67(6) 22 ret; Alexey Kedriouk/Anton Tsymbalov (KAZ) d. Brett Baudinet/Juan Sebastien Langton (POC) 62 62. **Vietnam defeated Tajikistan 2-0:** Quang-Huy Ngo (VIE) d. Mansour Yakhyaev (TJK) 63 62; Minh-Quan Do (VIE) d. Sergei Makashin (TJK) 62 63; doubles not played.

- **Play-off for 5th-8th Positions:**
  Results carried forward: Qatar defeated Oman 3-0; Bahrain defeated Syria 2-1
  10 April Qatar defeated Syria 3-0: Mohammed-Saadon Al Kawari (QAT) d. Hayan Marouf (SYR) 63 75; Amir Ebrahim (QAT) d. Abraham Ibrahim (SYR) 64 64; Mohammed-Saadon Al Kawari/Abdallah Hassan (QAT) d. Moufak Hafez/Laith Salim (SYR) 64 64. **Bahrain defeated Oman 3-0:** Abdul-Rahman Shehab (BRN) d. Mohammed Al Nabhani (OMA) 57 64 64; Esam Abdul-Aal (BRN) d. Khalid Al Nabhani (OMA) 61 57 62; Abdul-Karim Abdul-Redha/Khaled Al Thawadi (BRN) d. Suleiman Al Rawahi/Saleh Al Zadjali (OMA) 60 63.

- **11 April Bahrain defeated Qatar 2-1:** Abdallah Hassan (QAT) d. Abdul-Rahman Shehab (BRN) 26 60 ret; Esam Abdul-Aal (BRN) d. Amir Ebrahim (QAT) 76(4) 61; Esam Abdul-Aal/Abdul-Rahman Shehab (BRN) d. Mohammed-Saadon Al Kawari/Abdallah Hassan (QAT) 62 26 86. **Oman defeated Syria 2-1:** Mohammed Al Nabhani (OMA) d. Moufak Hafez (SYR) 06 61 64; Hayan Marouf (SYR) d. Khalid Al Nabhani (OMA) 63 62; Khalid Al Nabhani/Mohammed Al Nabhani (OMA) d. Moufak Hafez/Laith Salim (SYR) 63 63.

- **Final Positions:** 1. Kazakhstan, 2. Pacific Oceania, 3. Vietnam, 4. Tajikistan, 5. Bahrain, 6. Qatar, 7. Oman, 8. Syria.

Kazakhstan and Pacific Oceania promoted to Asia/Oceania Zone Group II in 2005.
Oman and Syria relegated to Asia/Oceania Zone Group IV in 2005.

Europe/Africa Zone Group IV – Venue I

Date: 4-8 February
Venue: Dakar, Senegal
Surface: Hard (O)
Nations: Gabon, Mali, Nigeria, San Marino, Senegal

- **4 February Nigeria defeated Mali 3-0:** Abdul-Mumin Babalola (NGR) d. Madou Keita (MLI) 63 60; Jonathan Igbinovia (NGR) d. Mahamadou Diallo (MLI) 63 64; Jonathan Igbinovia/Sunday Maku (NGR) d. Amadou Diallo/Madou Keita (MLI) 62 63. **San Marino defeated Senegal 3-0:** Christian Rosti (SMR) d. Djadji Ka (SEN) 64 61; Domenico Vicini (SMR) d. Daouda Ndiaye (SEN) 63 62; William Forcellini/Domenico Vicini (SMR) d. Daouda Ndiaye/Mamadou Seye (SEN) 64 64.

2004 Davis Cup by BNP Paribas Results (continued)

- **5 February** **Nigeria defeated Gabon 3-0:** Abdul-Mumin Babalola (NGR) d. Yvan Nefane (GAB) 60 62; Jonathan Igbinovia (NGR) d. Brice Pendi (GAB) 60 60; Jonathan Igbinovia/Sunday Maku (NGR) d. Fabrice Nefane/Brice Pendi (GAB) 61 60. **Senegal defeated Mali 2-1:** Djadji Ka (SEN) d. Amadou Diallo (MLI) 75 63; Madou Keita (MLI) d. Daouda Ndiaye (SEN) 36 64 64; Youssou Berthe/Mamadou Seye (SEN) d. Mahamoud Diallo/Madou Keita (MLI) 61 36 63.

- **6 February** **Nigeria defeated San Marino 3-0:** Abdul-Mumin Babalola (NGR) d. Domenico Vicini (SMR) 76(3) 61; Jonathan Igbinovia (NGR) d. William Forcellini (SMR) 62 63; Jonathan Igbinovia/Sunday Maku (NGR) d. William Forcellini/Diego Zonzini (SMR) 60 64. **Mali defeated Gabon 3-0:** Madou Keita (MLI) d. Yvan Nefane (GAB) 63 64; Mahamoud Diallo (MLI) d. Brice Pendi (GAB) 46 61 62; Amadou Diallo/Madou Keita (MLI) d. Fabrice Nefane/Yvan Nefane (GAB) 61 61.

- **7 February** **San Marino defeated Mali 3-0:** Christian Rosti (SMR) d. Madou Keita (MLI) 64 62; Domenico Vicini (SMR) d. Mahamoud Diallo (MLI) 76(1) 76(6); William Forcellini/Christian Rosti (SMR) d. Amadou Diallo/Madou Keita (MLI) 64 62. **Senegal defeated Gabon 3-0:** Youssou Berthe (SEN) d. Fabrice Nefane (GAB) 63 62; Djadji Ka (SEN) d. Brice Pendi (GAB) 64 62; Youssou Berthe/Mamadou Seye (SEN) d. Fabrice Nefane/Yvan Nefane (GAB) 62 62.

- **8 February** **Nigeria defeated Senegal 3-0:** Abdul-Mumin Babalola (NGR) d. Youssou Berthe (SEN) 60 63; Jonathan Igbinovia (NGR) d. Djadji Ka (SEN) 63 61; Toyin Dairo/Sunday Maku (NGR) d. Daouda Ndiaye/Mamadou Seye (SEN) 63 64. **San Marino defeated Gabon 3-0:** Christian Rosti (SMR) d. Yvan Nefane (GAB) 64 61; Domenico Vicini (SMR) d. Fabrice Nefane (GAB) 61 75; William Forcellini/Christian Rosti (SMR) d. Fabrice Nefane/Yvan Nefane (GAB) 62 64.

- **Final Positions:** 1. Nigeria, 2. San Marino, 3. Senegal, 4. Mali, 5. Gabon.

Nigeria and San Marino promoted to Europe/Africa Zone Group III in 2005.

Europe/Africa Zone Group IV – Venue II

Date:	15-18 July
Venue:	Chisinau, Moldova
Surface:	Clay (O)
Group A:	Armenia, Botswana, Malta, Mauritius
Group B:	Bosnia/Herzegovina, Moldova, Rwanda, Uganda

- **Group A** **15 July** **Armenia defeated Mauritius 3-0:** Harutyun Sofyan (ARM) d. Rey Oliver (MRI) 61 61; Sargis Sargsian (ARM) d. Kamil Patel (MRI) 64 64; Tsolak Gevorgyan/Ara Harutyunyan (ARM) d. Alexandre Daruty/Simon Koenig (MRI) 64 16 63. **Botswana defeated Malta 2-1:** Bokang Setshogo (BOT) d. Marcus Delicata (MLT) 62 61; Phenyo Matong (BOT) d. Daniel Ceross (MLT) 64 64; Daniel Ceross/Marcus Delicata (MLT) d. Uyapo Nleya/Keneilwe Phuthego (BOT) 76(5) 60.

- **16 July** **Armenia defeated Botswana 3-0:** Harutyun Sofyan (ARM) d. Keneilwe Phuthego (BOT) 63 62; Sargis Sargsian (ARM) d. Uyapo Nleya (BOT) 60 61; Sargis Sargsian/Harutyun Sofyan (ARM) d. Uyapo Nleya/Bokang Setshogo (BOT) 60 61. **Armenia defeated Malta 3-0:** Ara Harutyunyan (ARM) d. Marcus Delicata (MLT) 61 62; Sargis Sargsian (ARM) d. Daniel Ceross (MLT) 61 61; Ara Harutyunyan/Harutyun Sofyan (ARM) d. Matthew Borg/Daniel Ceross (MLT) 61 61. **Mauritius defeated Botswana 2-1:** Bokang Setshogo (BOT) d. Simon Koenig (MRI) 61 63; Kamil Patel (MRI) d. Phenyo Matong (BOT) 63 62; Alexandre Daruty/Kamil Patel (MRI) d. Phenyo Matong/Uyapo Nleya (BOT) 61 60. **Mauritius defeated Malta 3-0:** Alexandre Daruty (MRI) d. Marcus Delicata (MLT) 60 60; Kamil Patel (MRI) d. Daniel Ceross (MLT) 61 62; Alexandre Daruty/Simon Koenig (MRI) d. Matthew Borg/Daniel Ceross (MLT) 63 67(5) 62.

- **Group B** **15 July** **Moldova defeated Uganda 3-0:** Andrei Ciumac (MDA) d. Godfrey Uzunga (UGA) 60 63; Andrei Gorban (MDA) d. Charles Yokwe (UGA) 60 60; Andrei Gorban/Denis Molcianov (MDA) d. Patrick Olobo/Charles Yokwe (UGA) 62 61. **Bosnia/Herzegovina defeated Rwanda 3-0:** Bojan Vujic (BIH) d. Jean Paul Nshimiyimana (RWA) 61 61; Aleksandar Maric (BIH) d. Jean-Claude Gasigwa (RWA) 63 63; Aleksandar Maric/Bojan Vujic (BIH) d. Jean-Claude Gasigwa/Eric Hagenimana (RWA) 64 62.

- **16 July** **Bosnia/Herzegovina defeated Moldova 2-1:** Bojan Vujic (BIH) d. Denis Molcianov (MDA) 36 20 ret.; Andrei Gorban (MDA) d. Ugljesa Ostojic (BIH) 61 64; Aleksandar Maric/Bojan Vujic (BIH) d. Andrei Ciumac/Andrei Gorban (MDA) 76(5) 36 62. **Moldova defeated Rwanda 3-0:** Andrei Ciumac (MDA) d. Eric Hagenimana (RWA) 36 64 64; Andrei Gorban (MDA) d. Jean-Claude Gasigwa (RWA) 60 60; Ilie Babinciuc/Andrei Ciumac (MDA) d. Eric Hagenimana/Jean Paul Nshimiyimana (RWA) 60 63. **Bosnia/Herzegovina defeated Uganda 3-0:**

Bojan Vujic (BIH) d. Godfrey Uzunga (UGA) 61 61; Ugljesa Ostojic (BIH) d. Charles Yokwe (UGA) 60 61; Aleksandar Maric/Bojan Vujic (BIH) d. Patrick Olobo/Godfrey Uzunga (UGA) 61 62. **Rwanda defeated Uganda 3-0:** Alain Hakizimana (RWA) d. Patrick Olobo (UGA) 61 64; Eric Hagenimana (RWA) d. Godfrey Uzunga (UGA) 36 63 62; Jean-Claude Gasigwa Alain Hakizimana (RWA) d. James Odongo/Patrick Olobo (UGA) 63 63.

- **Play-off for 1st-4th Positions:**
  Results carried forward: Armenia defeated Mauritius 3-0; Bosnia/Herzegovina defeated Moldova 2-1
  17 July   Armenia defeated Moldova 2-1: Andrei Ciumac (MDA) d. Harutyun Sofyan (ARM) 64 76(3); Sargis Sargsian (ARM) d. Andrei Gorban (MDA) 64 62; Sargis Sargsian/Harutyun Sofyan (ARM) d. Andrei Ciumac/Andrei Gorban (MDA) 63 63. **Bosnia/Herzegovina defeated Mauritius 3-0:** Bojan Vujic (BIH) d. Alexandre Daruty (MRI) 61 60; Ugljesa Ostojic (BIH) d. Kamil Patel (MRI) 64 63; Aleksandar Maric/Bojan Vujic (BIH) d. Alexandre Daruty/Simon Koenig (MRI) 61 61.

- **18 July   Bosnia/Herzegovina defeated Armenia 3-0:** Aleksandar Maric (BIH) d. Ara Harutyunyan (ARM) 60 61; Ugljesa Ostojic (BIH) d. Harutyun Sofyan (ARM) 62 61; Aleksandar Maric/Ugljesa Ostojic (BIH) d. Ara Harutyunyan/Harutyun Sofyan (ARM) 61 60. **Moldova defeated Mauritius 3-0:** Ilie Babinciuc (MDA) d. Alexandre Daruty (MRI) 60 60; Andrei Ciumac (MDA) d. Kamil Patel (MRI) 26 63 62; Ilie Babinciuc/Andrei Ciumac (MDA) d. Simon Koenig/Rey Oliver (MRI) 63 61.

- **Play-off for 5th-7th Positions:**
  Results carried forward: Botswana defeated Malta 2-1; Rwanda defeated Uganda 3-0
  17 July   Rwanda defeated Botswana 2-1: Eric Hagenimana (RWA) d. Bokang Setshogo (BOT) 36 63 62; Phenyo Matong (BOT) d. Jean-Claude Gasigwa (RWA) 64 62; Eric Hagenimana/Alain Hakizimana (RWA) d. Keneilwe Phuthego/Bokang Setshogo (BOT) 63 26 61. **Uganda defeated Malta 3-0:** James Odongo (UGA) d. Matthew Borg (MLT) 61 62; Patrick Olobo (UGA) d. Daniel Ceross (MLT) 62 61; Patrick Olobo/Charles Yokwe (UGA) d. Matthew Borg/Daniel Ceross (MLT) 62 62.

- **18 July   Botswana defeated Uganda 3-0:** Bokang Setshogo (BOT) d. James Odongo (UGA) 75 63; Phenyo Matong (BOT) d. Patrick Olobo (UGA) 62 63; Phenyo Matong/Bokang Setshogo (BOT) d. Patrick Olobo/Charles Yokwe (UGA) 76(5) 06 63. **Rwanda defeated Malta 2-1:** Eric Hagenimana (RWA) d. Marcus Delicata (MLT) 63 36 64; Jean-Claude Gasigwa (RWA) d. Daniel Ceross (MLT) 63 62; Daniel Ceross/Marcus Delicata (MLT) d. Alain Hakizimana/Jean Paul Nshimiyimana (RWA) 75 64.

- **Final Positions:** 1. Bosnia/Herzegovina, 2. Armenia, 3. Moldova, 4. Mauritius, 5. Rwanda, 6. Botswana, 7. Uganda, 8. Malta.

Armenia and Bosnia/Herzegovina promoted to Europe/Africa Zone Group III in 2005.

Americas Zone Group IV

Date: 7-11 April
Venue: San Jose, Costa Rica
Surface: Hard (O)
Nations: Barbados, Bermuda, Costa Rica, Guatemala, Eastern Caribbean, St. Lucia

- **7 April   St Lucia defeated Costa Rica 2-1:** Federico Chavarria (CRC) d. Kane Easter (LCA) 67 75 40 ret; Vernon Lewis (LCA) d. Juan-Carlos Gonzalez (CRC) 61 62; Vernon Lewis/Alberton Richelieu (LCA) d. Federico Chavarria/Marcos Salazar (CRC) 64 63. **Barbados defeated Bermuda 2-1:** Russell Moseley (BAR) d. Jovan Whitter (BER) 57 63 64; James Collieson (BER) d. Duane Williams (BAR) 61 75; Russell Moseley/Duane Williams (BAR) d. Janson Bascome/James Collieson (BER) 46 76(3) 62. **Guatemala defeated Eastern Caribbean 3-0:** Cristian Paiz (GUA) d. Dexter Christian (ECA) 61 26 61; Jacobo Chavez (GUA) d. Glynn James (ECA) 60 61; Daniel Chavez/Luis Perez-Chete (GUA) d. Hayden Ashton/Corey Huggins (ECA) 61 63.

- **8 April   Costa Rica defeated Bermuda 3-0:** Federico Chavarria (CRC) d. Gavin Manders (BER) 62 63; Juan-Carlos Gonzalez (CRC) d. James Collieson (BER) 63 16 64; Ignasi Roca/Marcos Salazar (CRC) d. Gavin Manders/Jovan Whitter (BER) 75 75. **Eastern Caribbean defeated Barbados 2-1:** Ryan Moseley (BAR) d. Dexter Christian (ECA) 64 63; Glynn James (ECA) d. Duane Williams (BAR) 61 61; Hayden Ashton/Glynn James (ECA) d. Russell Moseley/Ryan Moseley (BAR) 62 64. **Guatemala defeated St. Lucia 3-0:** Cristian Paiz (GUA) d. Alberton Richelieu (LCA) 75 75; Jacobo Chavez (GUA) d. Vernon Lewis (LCA) 60 64; Daniel Chavez/Luis Perez-Chete (GUA) d. Kane Easter/Alberton Richelieu (LCA) 61 61.

2004 Davis Cup by BNP Paribas Results (continued)

- **9 April Costa Rica defeated Eastern Caribbean 3-0:** Federico Chavarria (CRC) d. Corey Huggins (ECA) 64 63; Marco Salazar (CRC) d. Glynne James (ECA) 61 64; Ignasi Roca/Marco Salazar (CRC) d. Hayden Ashton/Corey Huggins (ECA) 64 10 ret. **Guatemala defeated Barbados 2-1:** Cristian Paiz (GUA) d. Ryan Moseley (BAR) 63 63; Russell Moseley (BAR) d. Jacobo Chavez (GUA) 62 61; Daniel Chavez/Luis Perez-Chete (GUA) d. Russell Moseley/Duane Williams (BAR) 64 64. **St. Lucia defeated Bermuda 3-0:** Kane Easter (LCA) d. Jenson Bascombe (BER) 62 62; Vernon Lewis (LCA) d. James Collieson (BER) 64 62; Kane Easter/Alberton Richelieu Jr. d. Gavin Manders/Jovan Whitter (BER) 62 61.

- **10 April Barbados defeated Costa Rica 3-0:** Damien Applewhaite (BAR) d. Federico Chavarria (CRC) 26 60 63; Russell Moseley (BAR) d. Marcos Salazar (CRC) 64 75; Ryan Moseley/Duane Williams (BAR) d. Federico Chavarria/Ignasi Roca (CRC) 76(3) 64. **Guatemala defeated Bermuda 3-0:** Luis Perez-Chete (GUA) d. Jovan Whitter (BER) 60 61; Cristian Paiz (GUA) d. James Collieson (BER) 63 63; Jacobo Chavez/Cristian Paiz (GUA) d. Gavin Manders/Jovan Whitter (BER) 62 61. **St. Lucia defeated Eastern Caribbean 3-0:** Kane Easter (LCA) d. Dexter Christian (ECA) 62 60; Vernon Lewis (LCA) d. Glynn James (ECA) 61 63; Trevor Hunte/Alberton Richelieu (LCA) d. Dexter Christian/Corey Huggins (ECA) 62 60.

- **11 April Guatemala defeated Costa Rica 3-0:** Luis Perez-Chete (GUA) d. Federico Chavarria (CRC) 36 61 75; Cristian Paiz (GUA) d. Juan-Carlos Gonzalez (CRC) 63 61; Jacobo Chavez/Luis Perez-Chete (GUA) d. Ignasi Roca/Marcos Salazar (CRC) 62 62. **Bermuda defeated Eastern Caribbean 2-1:** Gavin Manders (BER) d. Hayden Ashton (ECA) 60 76(3); Glynn James (ECA) d. James Collieson (BER) 75 16 64; James Collieson/Gavin Manders (BER) d. Hayden Ashton/Glynn James (ECA) 41 ret. **St. Lucia defeated Barbados 2-1:** Russell Moseley (BAR) d. Kane Easter (LCA) 61 62; Vernon Lewis (LCA) d. Duane Williams (BAR) 62 60; Kane Easter/Vernon Lewis (LCA) d. Russell Moseley/Duane Williams (BAR) 62 62.

- **Final Positions:** 1. Guatemala, 2. St. Lucia, 3. Barbados, 4. Costa Rica, 5. Bermuda, 6. Eastern Caribbean.

Guatemala and St. Lucia promoted to Americas Zone Group III in 2005.

Asia/Oceania Zone Group IV

Date:	7-11 April
Venue:	Amman, Jordan
Surface:	Hard (O)
Group A:	Brunei, Jordan, Saudi Arabia, Singapore, Turkmenistan, United Arab Emirates
Group B:	Bangladesh, Iraq, Kyrgyzstan, Myanmar, Sri Lanka

- **Group A 7 April United Arab Emirates defeated Brunei 3-0:** Mahmoud-Nader Al Balushi (UAE) d. Ian Chok (BRU) 60 64; Omar Bahrouzyan (UAE) d. Sie-Lu On (BRU) 60 62; Mahmoud-Nader Al Balushi/Omar Bahrouzyan (UAE) d. Nelson Cheong/Sie-Lu On (BRU) 60 60. **Saudi Arabia defeated Singapore 3-0:** Omar Al Thagib (KSA) d. Andrew Kam (SIN) 60 67(0) 64; Fahad Al Saad (KSA) d. Yuan-Xiong Hui (SIN) 63 64; Saleh Abdul Al Raajeh/Fahad Al Saad (KSA) d. Heryanta Dewandaka/Yuan-Xiong Hui (SIN) 46 64 64. **Jordan defeated Turkmenistan 2-1:** Ahmad Al Hadid (JOR) d. Dovran Chagylov (TKM) 60 63; Myalikkuli Mamedkuliev (TKM) d. Khaled Naffa (JOR) 46 64 64; Ahmad Al Hadid/Khaled Naffa (JOR) d. Dovran Chagylov/Myalikkuli Mamedkuliev (TKM) 62 62.

- **8 April Jordan defeated United Arab Emirates 2-1:** Ahmad Al Hadid (JOR) d. Mahmoud-Nader Al Balushi (UAE) 64 75; Khaled Naffa (JOR) d. Omar Bahrouzyan (UAE) 63 61; Mahmoud-Nader Al Balushi/Omar Bahrouzyan (UAE) d. Fabio Badra/Tareq Shkakwa (JOR) 62 63. **Singapore defeated Turkmenistan 3-0:** Andrew Kam (SIN) d. Stanislav Naydenov (TKM) 62 64; Yuan-Xiong Hui (SIN) d. Myalikkuli Mamedkuliev (TKM) 60 64; Alex Sun Gin Chew/Heryanta Dewandaka (SIN) d. Dovran Chagylov/Stanislav Naydenov (TKM) 76(2) 60. **Saudi Arabia defeated Brunei 3-0:** Omar Al Thagib (KSA) d. Ian Chok (BRU) 62 60; Fahad Al Saad (KSA) d. Sie-Lu On (BRU) 64 61; Saleh Abdul Al Raajeh/Omar Al Thagib (KSA) d. Ian Chok/Ismasufian Ibrahim (BRU) 61 62.

- **9 April United Arab Emirates defeated Saudi Arabia 3-0:** Mahmoud-Nader Al Balushi (UAE) d. Omar Al Thagib (KSA) 62 64; Omar Bahrouzyan (UAE) d. Fahad Al Saad (KSA) 64 64; Mahmoud-Nader Al Balushi/Omar Bahrouzyan (UAE) d. Fahad Al Saad/Omar Al Thagib (KSA) 26 62 63. **Singapore defeated Jordan 2-1:** Heryanta Dewandaka (SIN) d. Ahmad Al Hadid (JOR) 63 62; Khaled Naffa (JOR) d. Yuan-Xiong Hui (SIN) 76(6) 64; Heryanta Dewandaka/Yuan-Xiong Hui (SIN) d. Ahmad Al Hadid/Khaled Naffa (JOR) 63 61. **Brunei defeated Turkmenistan 2-1:** Ian Chok (BRU) d. Dovran Chagylov (TKM) 61 63; Myalikkuli Mamedkuliev (TKM) d. Sie-Lu On (BRU) 62 60; Ian Chok/Ismasufian Ibrahim (BRU) d. Myalikkuli Mamedkuliev/Stanislav Naydenov (TKM) 61 64.

- **10 April** **Jordan defeated Brunei 3-0:** Fabio Badra (JOR) d. Nelson Cheong (BRU) 60 60; Khaled Naffa (JOR) d. Ian Chok (BRU) 60 61; Fabio Badra/Khaled Naffa (JOR) d. Pa Ismasufian/Sie-Lu On (BRU) 64 63. **Singapore defeated United Arab Emirates 2-1:** Daniel Dewandaka (SIN) d. Mahmoud-Nader Al Balushi (UAE) 63 61; Omar Bahrouzyan (UAE) d. Yuan-Xiong Hui (SIN) 63 26 63; Daniel Dewandaka/Yuan-Xiong Hui (SIN) d. Mahmoud-Nader Al Balushi (UAE) 26 60 62. **Saudi Arabia defeated Turkmenistan 3-0:** Omar Al Thagib (KSA) d. Stanislav Naydenov (TKM) 60 61; Fahad Al Saad (KSA) d. Myalikkuli Mamedkuliev (TKM) 64 36 64; Majid Al Jaroudi/Saleh Abdul Al Raajeh (KSA) d. Dovran Chagylov/Stanislav Naydenov (TKM) 64 63.

- **11 April** **United Arab Emirates defeated Turkmenistan 2-1:** Mohmoud-Khalifa Al Balushi (UAE) d. Stanislav Naydenov (TKM) 60 60; Omar Bahrouzyan (UAE) d. Dovran Chagylov (TKM) 62 62; Dovran Chagylov/Stanislav Naydenov (TKM) d. Mohmoud-Khalifa Al Balushi/Mohammed-Saeed Al Merri (UAE) 62 75. **Singapore defeated Brunei 3-0:** Andrew Kam (SIN) d. Nelson Cheong (BRU) 61 61; Yuan-Xiong Hui (SIN) d. Ian Chok (BRU) 61 61; Alex Sun Gin Chew/Andrew Kam (SIN) d. Nelson Cheong/Sie-Lu On (BRU) 62 61. **Saudi Arabia defeated Jordan 2-1:** Omar Al Thagib (KSA) d. Ahmad Al Hadid (JOR) 60 76(1); Fahad Al Saad (KSA) d. Khaled Naffa (JOR) 63 62. Fabio Badra/Tarek Shkakwa (JOR) d. Majid Al Jaroudi/Saleh Abdul Al Raajeh (KSA) 64 62.

- **Final Positions:** 1. Saudi Arabia, 2. Singapore, 3. Jordan, 4. United Arab Emirates, 5. Brunei, 6. Turkmenistan.

- **Group B** **7 April** **Sri Lanka defeated Bangladesh 3-0:** Renouk Wijemanne (SRI) d. Sree Roy (BAN) 63 61; Franklyn Emmanuel (SRI) d. Shibu Lal (BAN) 60 64; Rohan De Silva/Rajeev Rajapakse (SRI) d. Alamgir Hossain/Shibu Lal (BAN) 76(9) 75. **Myanmar defeated Kyrgyzstan 2-1:** Boris Baichorov (KGZ) d. Zaw-Zaw Latt (MYA) 64 62; Tu Maw (MYA) d. Eduard Koifman (KGZ) 61 60; Zaw-Zaw Latt/Tu Maw (MYA) d. Temir Akkaziev/Boris Baichorov (KGZ) 61 64.

- **8 April** **Sri Lanka defeated Iraq 3-0:** Renouk Wijemanne (SRI) d. Nasir Hatam (IRQ) 61 60; Franklyn Emmanuel (SRI) d. Haidar Kadhim (IRQ) 60 61; Rohan De Silva/Rajeev Rajapakse (SRI) d. Haidar Kadhim/Hussain Rashid (IRQ) 64 62. **Bangladesh defeated Kyrgyzstan 3-0:** Sree Roy (BAN) d. Sergey Ni (KGZ) 63 61; Shibu Lal (BAN) d. Boris Baichorov (KGZ) 62 64; Shibu Lal/Sree Roy (BAN) d. Temir Akkaziev/Eduard Koifman (KGZ) 63 63.

- **9 April** **Sri Lanka defeated Myanmar 2-1:** Renouk Wijemanne (SRI) d. Zaw-Zaw Latt (MYA) 64 63; Tu Maw (MYA) d. Franklyn Emmanuel (SRI) 36 64 64; Rohan De Silva/Rajeev Rajapakse (SRI) d. Zaw-Zaw Latt/Tu Maw (MYA) 61 61. **Bangladesh defeated Iraq 3-0:** Sree Roy (BAN) d. Haidar Kadhim (IRQ) 60 62; Shibu Lal (BAN) d. Hussain Rashid (IRQ) 62 61; Shibu Lal/Sree Roy (BAN) d. Haidar Kadhim/Hussain Rashid (IRQ) 60 61.

- **10 April** **Kyrgyzstan defeated Iraq 2-1:** Boris Baichorov (KGZ) d. Akram Al Karim (IRQ) 62 36 63; Nasir Hatam (IRQ) d. Eduard Koifman (KGZ) 63 64; Temir Akkaziev/Boris Baichorov (KGZ) d. Nasir Hatam/Haidar Kadhim (IRQ) 75 63. **Bangladesh defeated Myanmar 2-1:** Sree Roy (BAN) d. Zaw-Zaw Latt (MYA) 75 62; Shibu Lal (BAN) d. Tu Maw (MYA) 62 63; Zaw-Zaw Latt/Min Min (MYA) d. Shibu Lal/Sree Roy (BAN) 75 76(5).

- **11 April** **Sri Lanka defeated Kyrgyzstan 3-0:** Renouk Wijemanne (SRI) d. Temir Akkaziev (KGZ) 60 63; Franklyn Emmanuel (SRI) d. Sergey Ni (KGZ) 64 62; Rohan De Silva/Rajeev Rajapakse (SRI) d. Temir Akkaziev/Sergey Ni (KGZ) 62 60. **Iraq defeated Myanmar 2-1:** Akram Al Karim (IRQ) d. Lyan-Sein Man (MYA) 63 36 75; Zaw-Zaw Latt (MYA) d. Hussain Rashid (IRQ) 61 62; Nasir Hatam/Haidar Kadhim (IRQ) d. Zaw-Zaw Latt/Min Min (MYA) 46 76(3) 119.

- **Final Positions:** 1. Sri Lanka, 2. Bangladesh, 3. Myanmar, 4. Kyrgyzstan, 5. Iraq.

Saudi Arabia and Sri Lanka promoted to Asia/Oceania Zone Group III in 2005.

russian revolution reaches fed cup
by sandra harwitt

Fed Cup Champions Russia

It's when events don't go exactly as planned on the way to the finish line that the world's attention is captured. And that's just what happened when Russia had a vigorous fight to win its first Fed Cup title 3-2 over the defending champion France in Moscow last November.

> "Here you are playing for your country and this is really important for me. I will always play for my country, no matter what," said Myskina

The victory left Russian heroine Anastasia Myskina, who brought in the three winning points by winning both of her singles, and teaming with Vera Zvonereva to score the doubles point as well, happier than she's ever been before in her career.

"All my friends are around me here and I'm definitely more happy here right now [than when I won the French Open in June]," Myskina said, with a broad smile on her face. "Here it is for the team and my country.

"Here you are playing for your country and this is really important for me. I will always play for my country, no matter what," the Russian No. 1 said.

Anastasia Myskina (RUS)

It also left Fed Cup Captain Shamil Tarpischev, who also led Russia to its first Davis Cup title, declaring this moment even more momentous by saying, "If you had to measure joy, I can tell you, definitely, that I feel more relieved and more fatigued from the Fed Cup win."

And it left Russia's first tennis fan, former President Boris Yeltsin, not only leading the packed stadium of fans in cheering for their team, but kissing and hugging the Russian players all weekend long. In fact, when the Russian's finally nailed down the victory, Yeltsin jumped from his seat, scrambled to the side of the court and was so anxious to greet the players, that with assistance of two guards, climbed over the side fence to celebrate.

Coming into the competition – the semifinal round took place during the week and the final during the weekend – Russia was considered a nearly untouchable force to be reckoned with. That certainly wasn't a surprising expectation considering the roster of the Russian team – French Open champion Anastasia Myskina was cast as the leading lady, while US Open winner Svetlana Kuznetsova was to be the invaluable supporting actress. The challenge seemed even more insurmountable for the teams from France, Spain and Austria because the Russian's had the added benefit of a home court advantage at the brand new Ice Stadium "Krylatskoe."

All the teams had distinctly different journeys to the semifinals, and there was no denying that the presence of Austria among the final four nations was the most surprising.

Austria moved into the quarterfinals to meet the United States after taking a 3-2 win over the Slovak Republic in the first round. The United States had little trouble taking out Slovenia 4-1 in the first round with an impressive squad that included Venus Williams, Martina Navratilova and Lisa Raymond.

But things went awry for the American's when they landed in the beautiful alpine town of Innsbruck for the quarterfinals without a major singles competitor on board, leaving Chanda Rubin, Lisa Raymond and Martina Navratilova in charge. In contrast, the Austrian's had their heavy-hitters Barbara Schett and Barbara Schwartz, who were ready to pull off a 4-1 upset. Only Rubin was able to come out of the quarterfinal with a win, taking the opening match against Schwartz in three sets.

russian revolution reaches fed cup

by sandra harwitt

Svetlana Kuznetsova (RUS)

Spain arrived in the semifinals by beating Switzerland 3-2 in the first round and Belgium 3-2 in the quarterfinals. Belgium, with the help of Kim Clijsters, was able to bypass Croatia 3-2 in the first round. But without either Clijsters or Justine Henin-Hardenne on tap Belgium was nudged out of contention in the quarters.

France stormed passed Germany 5-0 in the first round and then took out Italy in a close 3-2 quarterfinal showing. Italy earned its quarterfinal spot with a 3-1 win over the Czech Republic.

Showing themselves to be a dominant force all year long, Russia had an easy run to the semifinals by posting 4-1 wins over Australia and Argentina, respectively. Argentina moved into the quarters by taking out Japan 4-1 in the first round.

Initially, there were no surprises when the semifinals kept to form with both the Russian and French teams winning their ties over Austria and Spain, respectively, with impressive 5-0 victories. While it was expected that the Russian's would annihilate the Austrian contingent of Yvonne Meusburger and Patricia Wartusch – understanding they were not household names the Austrian's wore t-shirts around Moscow that were emblazoned with the words "I Am An Austrian" – most thought that the Spanish squad of Anabel Medina Garrigues, Maria Sanchez Lorenzo, Virginia Ruano Pascual and Marta Marrero would at least get on the scoreboard, but they couldn't even pull off winning a set.

To be honest, the French team that arrived in Russia – veteran Nathalie Dechy, teen Tatiana Golovin, Marion Bartoli and Emilie Loit – were considered to be understaffed without their stars, Amelie Mauresmo, who withdrew from the team a week earlier, and Mary Pierce, benched with a shoulder injury. But they hardly looked understaffed against Spain in the semifinals, or for that matter Russia in the final.

"It was not for us, the French did much better," said Miguel Margets, Spain's Fed Cup captain. "All I can say is, well played to the French team; we're going to have to keep learning to play on this kind of surface."

The only potential trouble Russia faced in the semifinals was when Myskina was challenged to three sets by Meusburger before settling in for a 36 63 61 win that provided Russian with an insurmountable 3-0 lead.

The Russian's doubles line-up was altered in the semifinals to substitute Kuznetsova to pair off with Elena Likhovtseva because Vera Zvonereva's grandmother had passed away earlier in the day.

If the past could be used as a yardstick in determining the outcome of the Fed Cup final, then history would definitely have favoured the French. In both of their previous journeys to the final; in 1997 with Yannick Noah at the helm and, in 2003, with Guy Forget in charge, the French came out as the champions. In contrast, the Russians had reached the final on four previous occasions [1988,1990,1999,2001] with no success.

But Forget, who accepted the underdog position of his squad, was also careful to caution that his team was not about to surrender And it can be said that underdogs or not, the French gave the

> "I was not thinking positive and it was my mistake not to change," said a down-trodden Kuznetsova. "I was over-hitting and that was my mistake"

> While not a noteworthy doubles performer, Tarpischev elected to give the responsibility of winning the Fed Cup to Myskina, a champion bristling with determination.

Russian squad a massive migraine all weekend long before stepping aside to let the favourites reap their reward.

"The Russian team, by far, on paper, are the favourites," Forget said. "There is no nation today, except for maybe the United States who could pretend that, on a ranking basis they have the better chance to win.

"Now I don't think we are that far behind. And the only goal for us is to go out on the court and try to play the best we can. If we don't succeed in that we have no chance at all. And if we do manage to play our best tennis from the first point to the last, which is already not easy, we have a little chance. But being a captain, and being optimistic and ambitious I'm going to make everything possible."

Dechy upset the apple cart first by showing that her team had no intention of backing down, upsetting an edgy Svetlana Kuznetsova 36 76(4) 86 to start France off with a 1-0 lead in the final.

"I knew she was going to go for all her shots all the time," Dechy said. "She has very powerful shots and from all around the court. But because I fought all the match, she got a little nervous."

Kuznetsova is a go-for-broke player on the court, a strategy that often lends itself to producing breathtaking winners, but is also a strategy capable of crippling a player. In the match against a steady as you go Dechy, Kuznetsova's 37 winners were a moot factor when compared against her astonishing 77 unforced errors in the two hour, 26 minute match.

"I was not thinking positive and it was my mistake not to change," said a down-trodden Kuznetsova. "I was over-hitting and that was my mistake. This is my game and I have to go for my shots, but I do need to try and make less errors. I'm very upset because I had chances in the match, but I missed them."

In the second match, Myskina was not about to let Golovin, a 16-year-old Fed Cup neophyte, get the best of her with history in the making. Myskina had Golovin nipping at her heels throughout their encounter, but experience told the tale when she turned back the Russian-born, French teen 64 76(5).

While Myskina came through with the win to end the first day tied at 1-1, Golovin, making her first visit to Russia since she left as a baby, sent a loud and clear message: she's got the game. Indeed, she started the year ranked No. 365 in the world and closed out the season at No. 26.

"I think I had very good preparation last year which is why I improved so much," Golovin said. "I still think there's much more I can do. There's so many things I still have to work on. But for me to be top 30, it's really exciting and has been a great year."

"I think physically I have to get stronger. In terms of my game, I have to get more aggressive. Right now, I think all the top players are playing from the baseline. But if you really want to be great, you have to be able move around the court, come in, change the pace."

When Sunday's reverse singles came along, Myskina put the Russians in position for a glorious victory by beating Dechy 63 64 to give her team a 2-1 lead. But Kuznetsova, who so brilliantly reigned over the US Open two months before, seemed catatonic while Golovin was nerveless in producing a 64 61 win to even the final at 2-2 and send the Russian team in disarray.

Tarpischev had a major decision in front of him in terms of what to do for the doubles. He could stick with his designated team of Elena Likhovtseva and Vera Zvonerva or he could switch his line-up. While not a noteworthy doubles performer, Tarpischev elected to give the responsibility of winning the Fed Cup to Myskina, a champion bristling with determination.

In terms of pure doubles strategy, the Myskina and Zvonereva pairing seemed out of sorts to the doubles prowess of Bartoli and Loit, who were only silenced by a few untimely errors in the first set. The bottom line was that the strength of Myskina's stature won the day, as it won the final, in a 76(5) 75 doubles victory that started the celebration – Russia were the Fed Cup champions.

French Captain Guy Forget with Nathalie Dechy

2004 Fed Cup Results

World Group

First Round 24-25 April
USA defeated Slovenia 4-1, Portoroz, SLO, Clay (O): Tina Pisnik (SLO) d. Lisa Raymond (USA) 75 75; Venus Williams (USA) d. Katerina Srebotnik (SLO) 61 62; Venus Williams (USA) d. Tina Pisnik (SLO) 63 61; Lisa Raymond (USA) d. Katerina Srebotnik (SLO) 57 63 64; Martina Navratilova/Lisa Raymond (USA) d. Tina Krizan/Katerina Srebotnik (SLO) 61 16 60. **Austria defeated Slovak Republic 3-2, St. Pölten, AUT, Clay (O):** Barbara Schett (AUT) d. Janette Husarova (SVK) 46 61 64; Barbara Schwartz (AUT) d. Ludmila Cervanova (SVK) 36 76(1) 62; Barbara Schett (AUT) d. Martina Sucha (SVK) 75 16 62; Janette Husarova (SVK) d. Sybille Bammer (AUT) 63 62; Ludmila Cervanova/Janette Husarova (SVK) d. Barbara Schwartz/Patricia Wartusch (AUT) 63 36 64. **Russia defeated Australia 4-1, Moscow, RUS, Carpet (I):** Anastasia Myskina (RUS) d. Samantha Stosur (AUS) 64 61; Svetlana Kuznetsova (RUS) d. Alicia Molik (AUS) 64 36 64; Alicia Molik (AUS) d. Anastasia Myskina (RUS) 63 63; Vera Zvonareva (RUS) d. Samantha Stosur (AUS) 62 63; Svetlana Kuznetsova/Elena Likhovtseva (RUS) d. Alicia Molik/Rennae Stubbs (AUS) 62 36 76(7). **Argentina defeated Japan 4-1, Buenos Aires, ARG, Clay (O):** Gisela Dulko (ARG) d. Ai Sugiyama (JPN) 63 64; Paola Suarez (ARG) d. Akiko Morigami (JPN) 64 60; Paola Suarez (ARG) d. Ai Sugiyama (JPN) 67(4) 63 76 ret.; Akiko Morigami (JPN) d. Gisela Dulko (ARG) 62 62; Mariana Diaz-Oliva/Patricia Tarabini (ARG) d. Shinobu Asagoe/Saori Obata (JPN) 76(4) 67(4) 62. **Italy defeated Czech Republic 3-1, Lecce, ITA, Clay (O):** Francesca Schiavone (ITA) d. Barbora Strycova (CZE) 57 61 60; Silvia Farina Elia (ITA) d. Klara Koukalova (CZE) 63 76(6); Barbora Strycova (CZE) d. Maria-Elena Camerin (ITA) 75 36 75; Francesca Schiavone (ITA) d. Klara Koukalova (CZE) 16 62 62. **France defeated Germany 5-0, Amiens, FRA Clay (I):** Nathalie Dechy (FRA) d. Anna-Lena Groenefeld (GER) 67(4) 61 64; Amelie Mauresmo (FRA) d. Barbara Rittner (GER) 61 62; Amelie Mauresmo (FRA) d. Anna-Lena Groenefeld (GER) 62 63; Emilie Loit (FRA) d. Julia Schruff (GER) 62 62; Nathalie Dechy/Amelie Mauresmo (FRA) d. Anna-Lena Groenefeld/Julia Schruff (GER) 62 60. **Spain defeated Switzerland 3-2, Los Belones, ESP, Clay (O):** Patty Schnyder (SUI) d. Marta Marrero (ESP) 36 76(6) 75; Conchita Martinez (ESP) d. Emmanuelle Gagliardi (SUI) 26 61 60; Conchita Martinez (ESP) d. Patty Schnyder (SUI) 63 64; Myriam Casanova (SUI) d. Marta Marrero (ESP) 67(4) 64 60; Conchita Martinez/Virginia Ruano Pascual (ESP) d. Myriam Casanova/Emmanuelle Gagliardi (SUI) 76(3) 62. **Belgium defeated Croatia 3-2, Bree, BEL, Clay (I):** Kim Clijsters (BEL) d. Jelena Kostanic (CRO) 61 46 61; Karolina Sprem (CRO) d. Kirsten Flipkens (BEL) 62 60; Kim Clijsters (BEL) d. Karolina Sprem (CRO) 61 63; Els Callens (BEL) d. Jelena Kostanic (CRO) 62 36 64; Darija Jurak/Iva Majoli (CRO) d. Elke Clijsters/Kirsten Flipkens (BEL) 64 61.

Quarterfinals 10 July
Austria defeated USA 4-1, Innsbruck, AUT; Clay (O): Chanda Rubin (USA) d. Barbara Schwartz (AUT) 61 57 64; Barbara Schett (AUT) d. Lisa Raymond (USA) 62 64; Barbara Schett (AUT) d. Chanda Rubin (USA) 63 62; Barbara Schwartz (AUT) d. Lisa Raymond (USA) 76(3) 46 108; Barbara Schett/Patricia Wartusch (AUT) d. Jill Craybas/Martina Navratilova (USA) 63 06 63. **Russia defeated Argentina 4-1, Buenos Aires, ARG; Clay (O):** Gisela Dulko (ARG) d. Svetlana Kuznetsova (RUS) 64 36 64; Anastasia Myskina (RUS) d. Natalia Gussoni (ARG) 63 60; Anastasia Myskina (RUS) d. Gisela Dulko (ARG) 61 75; Vera Zvonareva (RUS) d. Mariana Diaz-Oliva (ARG) 63 60; Svetlana Kuznetsova/Elena Likhovtseva (RUS) d. Gisela Dulko/Patricia Tarabini (ARG) 62 57 64. **France defeated Italy 3-2, Rimini, ITA; Clay (O):** Amelie Mauresmo (FRA) d. Silvia Farina Elia (ITA) 62 61; Mary Pierce (FRA) d. Francesca Schiavone (ITA) 63 64; Amelie Mauresmo (FRA) d. Francesca Schiavone (ITA) 76(2) 62; Silvia Farina Elia (ITA) d. Emilie Loit (FRA) 63 26 62; Tathiana Garbin/Roberta Vinci (ITA) d. Tatiana Golovin/Mary Pierce (FRA) 60 76(5). **Spain defeated Belgium 3-2, Jerez de la Frontera, ESP; Clay (O):** Kirsten Flipkens (BEL) d. Anabel Medina Garrigues (ESP) 76(5) 16 62; Els Callens (BEL) d. Virginia Ruano Pascual (ESP) 26 64 119; Anabel Medina Garrigues (ESP) d. Els Callens (BEL) 64 60; Maria Sanchez Lorenzo (ESP) d. Kirsten Flipkens (BEL) 63 64; Anabel Medina Garrigues/Virginia Ruano Pascual (ESP) d. Els Callens/Kirsten Flipkens (BEL) 63 62.

Semifinals 24-25 November
Russia defeated Austria 5-0, Moscow, RUS, Carpet (I): Svetlana Kuznetsova (RUS) d. Yvonne Meusburger (AUT) 61 61; Anastasia Myskina (RUS) d. Patricia Wartusch (AUT) 60 60; Anastasia Myskina (RUS) d. Yvonne Meusburger (AUT) 36 63 61; Svetlana Kuznetsova (RUS) d. Daniela Kix (AUT) 61 61; Svetlana Kuznetsova/Elena Likhovtseva (RUS) d. Yvonne Meusburger/Patricia Wartusch (AUT) 62 62. **France defeated Spain 5-0, Moscow, RUS, Carpet (I):** Tatiana Golovin (FRA) d. Anabel Medina Garrigues (ESP) 63 63; Nathalie Dechy (FRA) d. Maria Sanchez Lorenzo (ESP) 62 64; Nathalie Dechy (FRA) d. Anabel Medina Garrigues (ESP) 63 61; Tatiana Golovin (FRA) d. Marta Marrero (ESP) 63 64; Marion Bartoli/Emilie Loit (FRA) d. Marta Marrero/Virginia Ruano Pascual (ESP) 75 62.

Final 27-28 November
Russia defeated France 3-2, Moscow, RUS, Carpet (I): Nathalie Dechy (FRA) d. Svetlana Kuznetsova (RUS) 36 76(4) 86; Anastasia Myskina (RUS) d. Tatiana Golovin (FRA) 64 76(5); Anastasia Myskina (RUS) d. Nathalie Dechy (FRA) 63 64; Tatiana Golovin (FRA) d. Svetlana Kuznetsova (RUS) 64 61; Anastasia Myskina/Vera Zvonareva (RUS) d. Marion Bartoli/Emilie Loit (FRA) 76(5) 75.

World Group II Play-offs 10-11 July
Thailand defeated Australia 3-2, Bangkapi, THA; Hard (I): Suchanun Viratprasert (THA) d. Nicole Pratt (AUS) 62 16 61; Tamarine Tanasugarn (THA) d. Samantha Stosur (AUS) 57 62 86; Tamarine Tanasugarn (THA) d. Nicole Pratt (AUS) 16 64 61; Samantha Stosur (AUS) d. Napaporn Tongsalee (THA) 46 60 60; Lisa McShea/Christina Wheeler (AUS) d. Montinee Tangphong/Napaporn Tongsalee (THA) 46 63 75. **Croatia defeated Brazil 4-1, Sao Paulo, BRA; Clay (O):** Maria-Fernanda Alves (BRA) d. Ivana Abramovic (CRO) 63 60; Jelena Kostanic (CRO) d. Bruna Colosio (BRA) 60 61; Jelena Kostanic (CRO) d. Maria-Fernanda Alves (BRA) 64 61; Darija Jurak (CRO) d. Bruna Colosio (BRA) 62 57 75; Ivana Abramovic/Ivana Lisjak (CRO) d. Carla Tiene/Bruna Colosio (BRA) 64 62. **Czech Republic defeated Estonia 3-2, Tallinn, EST; Clay (O):** Margit Ruutel (EST) d. Klara Koukalova (CZE) 75 57 62; Barbora Strycova (CZE) d. Maret Ani (EST) 76(3) 57 86; Klara Koukalova (CZE) d. Maret Ani (EST) 75 64; Barbora Strycova (CZE) d. Margit Ruutel (EST) 64 64; Maret Ani/Margit Ruutel (EST) d. Michaela Pastikova/Lucie Safarova (CZE) 62 64. **Germany defeated Ukraine 3-2, Illichevsk, UKR; Clay (O):** Barbara Rittner (GER) d. Tatiana Perebiynis (UKR) 57 62 64; Juliana Fedak (UKR) d. Anna-Lena Groenefeld (GER) 26 62 62; Tatiana Perebiynis (UKR) d. Anna-Lena Groenefeld (GER) 46 64 119; Barbara Rittner (GER) d. Juliana Fedak (UKR) 63 46 64; Barbara Rittner/Jasmin Woehr (GER) d. Juliana Fedak/Tatiana Perebiynis (UKR) 36 64 63. **Japan defeated Bulgaria 3-2, Plovdiv, BUL; Clay (O):** Shinobu Asagoe (JPN) d. Tzvetana Pironkova (BUL) 76(6) 36 64, Desislava Topalova (BUL) d. Saori Obata (JPN) 75 30 ret.; Shinobu Asagoe (JPN) d. Desislava Topalova (BUL) 61 67(3) 64; Tzvetana Pironkova (BUL) d. Yuka Yoshida (JPN) 61 63; Shinobu Asagoe/Rika Fujiwara (JPN) d. Maria Geznenge/Svetlana Krivencheva (BUL) 63 62. **Slovak Republic defeated Belarus 4-0, Bratislava, SVK; Clay (O):** Lubomira Kurhajcova (SVK) d. Tatiana Uvarova (BLR) 62 61; Martina Sucha (SVK) d. Anastasia Yakimova (BLR) 60 62; Lubomira Kurhajcova (SVK) d. Tatiana Poutchek (BLR) 60 61; Henrieta Nagyova (SVK) d. Daria Kustava (BLR) 61 75; Lubomira Kurhajcova/Martina Sucha (SVK) v. Daria Kustava/Tatiana Poutchek (BLR) not played. **Indonesia defeated Slovenia 4-1, Jakarta, INA; Hard (O):** Angelique Widjaja (INA) d. Katerina Srebotnik (SLO) 64 63; Wynne Prakusya (INA) d. Tina Pisnik (SLO) 61 64; Angelique Widjaja (INA) d. Tina Pisnik (SLO) 64 57 61; Andreja Klepac (SLO) d. Liza Andriyani (INA) 76(2) 62; Wynne Prakusya/Angelique Widjaja (INA) d. Andreja Klepac/Tina Krizan (SLO) 62 62. **Switzerland defeated Canada 3-2, Dorval, CAN; Clay (O):** Myriam Casanova (SUI) d. Stephanie Dubois (CAN) 60 63; Timea Bacsinszky (SUI) d. Marie-Eve Pelletier (CAN) 63 64; Myriam Casanova (SUI) d. Marie-Eve Pelletier (CAN) 62 63; Aleksandra Wozniak (CAN) d. Timea Bacsinszky (SUI) 60 64; Melanie Marois/Marie-Eve Pelletier (CAN) d. Timea Bacsinszky/Martina Lautenschlager (SUI) 76(6) 76(8).

Americas Zone Group I

Date:	19-24 April
Venue:	Bahia, Brazil
Surface:	Clay (O)
Group A:	Brazil, Canada, Chile, Cuba, Uruguay
Group B:	Colombia, El Salvador, Mexico, Puerto Rico

- **Group A 20 April   Mexico defeated Colombia 3-0:** Marcela Arroyo (MEX) d. Andrea Giraldo (COL) 62 62; Daniela Munoz (MEX) d. Karen Castiblanco (COL) 63 62; Melissa Torres/Graciela Velez (MEX) d. Karen Castiblanco/Andrea Giraldo (COL) 60 62. **El Salvador defeated Puerto Rico 2-1:** Miriam Cruz (ESA) d. Bianca Gorbea (PUR) 61 63; Vilmarie Castellvi (PUR) d. Liz Cruz (ESA) 62 61; Liz Cruz/Marcela-Ivon Rodezno-Hernandez (ESA) d. Vilmarie Castellvi/Bianca Gorbea (PUR) 67(5) 76(4) 64.

- **21 April   Colombia defeated Puerto Rico 2-1:** Andrea Giraldo (COL) d. Maria Calbeto (PUR) 62 36 119; Vilmarie Castellvi (PUR) d. Karen Castiblanco (COL) 63 61; Karen Castiblanco/Andrea Giraldo (COL) d. Maria Calbeto/Vilmarie Castellvi (PUR) 63 57 63. **Mexico defeated El Salvador 3-0:** Marcela Arroyo (MEX) d. Miriam Cruz (ESA) 64 61; Daniela Munoz (MEX) d. Liz Cruz (ESA) 75 62; Melissa Torres/Graciela Velez (MEX) d. Liz Cruz/Marcela-Ivon Rodezno-Hernandez (ESA) 64 75.

- **22 April   El Salvador defeated Colombia 2-0:** Miriam Cruz (ESA) d. Andrea Giraldo (COL) 64 61; Liz Cruz (ESA) d. Karen Castiblanco (COL) 63 61. **Mexico defeated Puerto Rico 3-0:** Melissa Torres (MEX) d. Bianca Gorbea (PUR) 63 61; Daniela Munoz (MEX) d. Vilmarie Castellvi (PUR) 76(2) 62; Melissa Torres/Graciela Velez (MEX) d. Vilmarie Castellvi/Bianca Gorbea (PUR) 62 ret.

- **Final Positions:** 1. Mexico, 2. El Salvador, 3. Colombia, 4. Puerto Rico.

- **Group B 19 April   Canada defeated Cuba 3-0:** Aleksandra Wozniak (CAN) d. Yamile Fors-Guerra (CUB) 62 61; Marie-Eve Pelletier (CAN) d. Yanet Nunez-Mojarena (CUB) 60 63; Melanie Marois/Marie-Eve Pelletier (CAN) d. Yamile Fors-Guerra/Yanet Nunez-Mojarena (CUB) 63 62. **Chile defeated Uruguay 2-1:** Valentina Castro (CHI) d. Maria-Eugenia Roca (URU) 46 63 61; Ana-Lucia Migliarini De Leon (URU) d. Andrea Koch (CHI) 63 62; Valentina Castro/Andrea Koch (CHI) d. Camila Belassi/Ana-Lucia Migliarini De Leon (URU) 16 75 61.

2004 Fed Cup Results (continued)

- **20 April Brazil defeated Uruguay 3-0:** Carla Tiene (BRA) d. Maria-Eugenia Roca (URU) 62 63; Maria-Fernanda Alves (BRA) d. Ana-Lucia Migliarini De Leon (URU) 62 76(6); Maria-Fernanda Alves/Carla Tiene (BRA) d. Camila Belassi/Ana-Lucia Migliarini De Leon (URU) 61 61. **Cuba defeated Chile 2-1:** Yamile Fors-Guerra (CUB) d. Valentina Castro (CHI) 75 63; Andrea Koch (CHI) d. Yanet Nunez-Mojarena (CUB) 75 06 60; Yamile Fors-Guerra/Yanet Nunez-Mojarena (CUB) d. Valentina Castro/Andrea Koch (CHI) 61 61.

- **21 April Brazil defeated Chile 3-0:** Larissa Carvalho (BRA) d. Valentina Castro (CHI) 26 75 61; Maria-Fernanda Alves (BRA) d. Andrea Koch (CHI) 62 61; Maria-Fernanda Alves/Carla Tiene (BRA) d. Valentina Castro/Andrea Koch (CHI) 62 63. **Canada defeated Uruguay 3-0:** Aleksandra Wozniak (CAN) d. Camila Belassi (URU) 61 61; Marie-Eve Pelletier (CAN) d. Ana-Lucia Migliarini De Leon (URU) 64 46 63; Melanie Marois/Marie-Eve Pelletier (CAN) d. Camila Belassi/Ana-Lucia Migliarini De Leon (URU) 62 61.

- **22 April Canada defeated Brazil 2-1:** Aleksandra Wozniak (CAN) d. Carla Tiene (BRA) 63 63; Marie-Eve Pelletier (CAN) d. Maria-Fernanda Alves (BRA) 64 63; Maria-Fernanda Alves/Carla Tiene (BRA) d. Melanie Marois/Marie-Eve Pelletier (CAN) 62 62. **Cuba defeated Uruguay 2-1:** Yamile Fors-Guerra (CUB) d. Maria-Eugenia Roca (URU) 63 62; Ana-Lucia Migliarini De Leon (URU) d. Yanet Nunez-Mojarena (CUB) 61 62; Yamile Fors-Guerra/Yanet Nunez-Mojarena (CUB) d. Camila Belassi/Ana-Lucia Migliarini De Leon (URU) 62 61.

- **23 April Brazil defeated Cuba 2-0:** Carla Tiene (BRA) d. Yamile Fors-Guerra (CUB) 63 60; Maria-Fernanda Alves (BRA) d. Yanet Nunez-Mojarena (CUB) 64 64. **Canada defeated Chile 2-0:** Aleksandra Wozniak (CAN) d. Valentina Castro (CHI) 63 61; Marie-Eve Pelletier (CAN) d. Andrea Koch (CHI) 60 60.

- **Final Positions:** 1. Canada, 2. Brazil, 3. Cuba, 4. Chile, 5. Uruguay.

- **Promotion Play-off 24 April Brazil defeated Mexico 2-0:** Carla Tiene (BRA) d. Marcela Arroyo (MEX) 61 62; Maria-Fernanda Alves (BRA) d. Daniela Munoz (MEX) 60 61. **Canada defeated El Salvador 2-0:** Aleksandra Wozniak (CAN) d. Miriam Cruz (ESA) 60 60; Marie-Eve Pelletier (CAN) d. Liz Cruz (ESA) 62 64.

- **Relegation Play-off 24 April Uruguay defeated Colombia 2-0:** Maria-Eugenia Roca (URU) d. Gabriela Mejia (COL) 64 64; Ana-Lucia Migliarini De Leon (URU) d. Karen Castiblanco (COL) 60 61. **Puerto Rico defeated Chile 2-1:** Valentina Castro (CHI) d. Maria Calbeto (PUR) 62 61; Vilmarie Castellvi (PUR) d. Andrea Koch (CHI) 75 64; Kristina Brandi/Vilmarie Castellvi (PUR) d. Valentina Castro/Andrea Koch (CHI) 62 61.

Brazil and Canada advance to 2004 World Group II Play-offs on 10-11 July 2003.
Chile and Colombia relegated to Americas Zone Group II in 2005.

Asia/Oceania Zone Group I

Date:	19-26 April
Venue:	New Delhi, India
Surface:	Hard (O)
Group A:	China PR, Philippines, New Zealand, Thailand
Group B:	Chinese Taipei, India, Indonesia, Korea Rep., Uzbekistan

- **Group A 20 April Thailand defeated China 2-1:** Suchanun Viratprasert (THA) d. Shu-Jing Yang (CHN) 64 36 32 ret.; Tamarine Tanasugarn (THA) d. Wei-Juan Liu (CHN) 62 60; Jie Hao/Ying Yu (CHN) d. Montinee Tangphong/Napaporn Tongsalee (THA) 61 62. **New Zealand defeated Philippines 3-0:** Shelley Stephens (NZL) d. Anna-Patricia Santos (PHI) 61 60; Eden Marama (NZL) d. Czarina-Mae Arevalo (PHI) 36 75 60; Marina Erakovic/Paula Marama (NZL) d. Czarina-Mae Arevalo/Anna-Patricia Santos (PHI) 36 60 61.

- **21 April New Zealand defeated China 2-1:** Marina Erakovic (NZL) d. Wei-Juan Liu (CHN) 64 61; Jie Hao (CHN) d. Shelley Stephens (NZL) 76(6) 76(3); Eden Marama/Paula Marama (NZL) d. Shu-Jing Yang/Ying Yu (CHN) 64 60. **Thailand defeated Philippines 3-0:** Napaporn Tongsalee (THA) d. Anna-Patricia Santos (PHI) 61 61; Tamarine Tanasugarn (THA) d. Czarina-Mae Arevalo (PHI) 62 61; Montinee Tangphong/Suchanun Viratprasert (THA) d. Czarina-Mae Arevalo/Anna-Patricia Santos (PHI) 60 64.

- **22 April China defeated Philippines 3-0:** Shu-Jing Yang (CHN) d. Alyssa-Anne Labay (PHI) 60 60; Jie Hao (CHN) d. Czarina-Mae Arevalo (PHI) 61 75; Shu-Jing Yang/Ying Yu (CHN) d. Czarina-Mae Arevalo/Anna-Patricia Santos (PHI) 62 61. **Thailand defeated New Zealand 2-1:** Suchanun Viratprasert (THA) d. Marina Erakovic (NZL) 75 36 97; Tamarine Tanasugarn (THA) d. Eden Marama (NZL) 63 63; Paula Marama/Shelley Stephens (NZL) d. Montinee Tangphong/Napaporn Tongsalee (THA) 64 63.

- **Final Positions:** 1. Thailand, 2. New Zealand, 3. China, 4. Philippines.

- **Group B   19 April   India defeated Chinese Taipei 3-0:** Ankita Bhambri (IND) d. I-Ting Wang (TPE) 63 61; Sania Mirza (IND) d. Chia-Jung Chuang (TPE) 64 76(3); Manisha Malhotra/Sania Mirza (IND) d. I-Hsuan Hwang/Ting-Wen Wang (TPE) 75 61. **Indonesia defeated Uzbekistan 2-1:** Ivanna Isroilova (UZB) d. Sandy Gumulya (INA) 63 46 61; Wynne Prakusya (INA) d. Akgul Amanmuradova (UZB) 75 60; Wynne Prakusya/Angelique Widjaja (INA) d. Akgul Amanmuradova/Ivanna Isroilova (UZB) 63 76(5).

- **20 April   Chinese Taipei defeated Uzbekistan 2-1:** Ivanna Israilova (UZB) d. I-Hsuan Hwang (TPE) 46 63 75; Chia-Jung Chuang (TPE) d. Akgul Amanmuradova (UZB) 57 62 108; Chia-Jung Chuang/I-Ting Wang (TPE) d. Elina Arutyunova/Ivanna Israilova (UZB) 60 62. **India defeated Korea, Rep. 2-1:** Ankita Bhambri (IND) d. Kyung-Mi Chang (KOR) 61 46 62; Mi-Ra Jeon (KOR) d. Sania Mirza (IND) 64 62; Manisha Malhotra/Sania Mirza (IND) d. Yoon-Jeong Cho/Mi-Ra Jeon (KOR) 76(2) 75.

- **21 April   Indonesia defeated Chinese Taipei 3-0:** Sandy Gumulya (INA) d. I-Hsuan Hwang (TPE) 26 63 62; Wynne Prakusya (INA) d. Chia-Jung Chuang (TPE) 61 61; Wynne Prakusya/Angelique Widjaja (INA) d. I-Ting Wang/Ting-Wen Wang (TPE) 64 60. **Korea, Rep. defeated Uzbekistan 2-1:** Jin-Hee Kim (KOR) d. Vlada Ekshibarova (UZB) 62 64; Ivanna Israilova (UZB) d. Mi-Ra Jeon (KOR) 63 46 64; Kyung-Mi Chang/Yoon-Jeong Cho (KOR) d. Akgul Amanmuradova/Ivanna Israilova (UZB) 64 64.

- **22 April   Korea, Rep. defeated Chinese Taipei 3-0:** Jin-Hee Kim (KOR) d. I-Hsuan Hwang (TPE) 62 60; Mi-Ra Jeon (KOR) d. I-Ting Wang (TPE) 62 62; Kyung-Mi Chang/Yoon-Jeong Cho (KOR) d. I-Hsuan Hwang/I-Ting Wang (TPE) 63 76(2). **Indonesia defeated India 2-1:** Ankita Bhambri (IND) d. Sandy Gumulya (INA) 64 64; Wynne Prakusya (INA) d. Sania Mirza (IND) 75 64; Wynne Prakusya/Angelique Widjaja (INA) d. Manisha Malhotra/Sania Mirza (IND) 76(2) 63.

- **23 April   India defeated Uzbekistan 2-1:** Ivanna Israilova (UZB) d. Ankita Bhambri (IND) 64 64; Sania Mirza (IND) d. Akgul Amanmuradova (UZB) 64 62; Manisha Malhotra/Sania Mirza (IND) d. Vlada Ekshibarova/Ivanna Israilova (UZB) 76(19) 61. **Indonesia defeated Korea, Rep. 2-1:** Jin-Hee Kim (KOR) d. Sandy Gumulya (INA) 63 61; Wynne Prakusya (INA) d. Mi-Ra Jeon (KOR) 75 67(2) 64; Wynne Prakusya/Angelique Widjaja (INA) d. Kyung-Mi Chang/Yoon-Jeong Cho (KOR) 63 75.

- **Final Positions:** 1. Indonesia, 2. India, 3. Korea, Rep., 4. Chinese Taipei, 5. Uzbekistan.

- **Promotion Play-off   24 April   Thailand defeated India 2-0:** Suchanun Viratprasert (THA) d. Sania Mirza (IND) 76(3) 61; Tamarine Tanasugarn (THA) d. Rushmi Chakravarthi (IND) 60 61. **Indonesia defeated New Zealand 2-1:** Marina Erakovic (NZL) d. Wynne Prakusya (INA) 62 61; Angelique Widjaja (INA) d. Shelley Stephens (NZL) 60 63; Wynne Prakusya/Angelique Widjaja (INA) d. Eden Marama/Paula Marama (NZL) 46 76(5) 61.

- **Relegation Play-off   24 April   China, P.R. defeated Uzbekistan 2-1:** Shu-Jing Yang (CHN) d. Vlada Ekshibarova (UZB) 36 63 60; Ivanna Israilova (UZB) d. Jie Hao (CHN) 60 63; Shu-Jing Yang/Ying Yu (CHN) d. Akgul Amanmuradova/Ivanna Israilova (UZB) 75 63. **Chinese Taipei defeated Philippines 2-1:** I-Hsuan Hwang (TPE) d. Anna-Patricia Santos (PHI) 63 63; Czarina-Mae Arevalo (PHI) d. I-Ting Wang (TPE) 63 76(4); I-Hsuan Hwang/I-Ting Wang (TPE) d. Czarina-Mae Arevalo/Anna-Patricia Santos (PHI) 26 76(1) 1210.

Indonesia and Thailand advance to 2004 World Group II Play-offs.
Philippines and Uzbekistan relegated to Asia/Oceania Zone Group II in 2005.

Europe/Africa Zone Group I

Date: 19-24 April
Venue: Athens, Greece
Surface: Clay (O)
Group A: Lithuania, Serbia & Montenegro, Sweden
Group B: Israel, Netherlands, South Africa, Ukraine
Group C: Belarus, Denmark, Hungary
Group D: Bulgaria, Estonia, Greece, Poland

- **Group A   19 April   Sweden defeated Lithuania 3-0:** Hanna Nooni (SWE) d. Edita Liachoviciute (LTU) 61 60; Sofia Arvidsson (SWE) d. Lina Stanciute (LTU) 75 62; Sofia Arvidsson/Hanna Nooni (SWE) d. Edita Liachoviciute/Lina Stanciute (LTU) 60 75.

2004 Fed Cup Results (continued)

- **20 April   Serbia & Montenegro defeated Lithuania 3-0:** Jelena Jankovic (SCG) d. Edita Liachoviciute (LTU) 61 61; Jelena Dokic (SCG) d. Lina Stanciute (LTU) 60 64; Ana Timotic/Dragana Zaric (SCG) d. Edita Liachoviciute/Lina Stanciute (LTU) 75 63.

- **22 April   Serbia & Montenegro defeated Sweden 3-0:** Jelena Jankovic (SCG) d. Hanna Nooni (SWE) 36 75 63; Jelena Dokic (SCG) d. Sofia Arvidsson (SWE) 57 75 63; Jelena Jankovic/Ana Timotic (SCG) d. Michaela Johansson/Nadja Roma (SWE) 62 60.

- **Final Positions:** 1. Serbia & Montenegro, 2. Sweden, 3. Lithuania.

- **Group B   19 April   Israel defeated Netherlands 3-0:** Tzipi Obziler (ISR) d. Anouska Van Exel (NED) 75 64; Anna Smashnova-Pistolesi (ISR) d. Elise Tamaela (NED) 61 62; Tzipi Obziler/Anna Smashnova-Pistolesi (ISR) d. Michaella Krajicek/Anouska Van Exel (NED) 36 75 61.

- **20 April   Ukraine defeated South Africa 2-1:** Elena Tatarkova (UKR) d. Nicole Rencken (RSA) 64 61; Natalie Grandin (RSA) d. Yulia Beygelzimer (UKR) 75 75; Maria Koryttseva/Olga Savchuk (UKR) d. Natalie Grandin/Nicole Rencken (RSA) 60 61.

- **21 April   Israel defeated South Africa 2-1:** Tzipi Obziler (ISR) d. Chanelle Scheepers (RSA) 61 64; Anna Smashnova-Pistolesi (ISR) d. Nicole Rencken (RSA) 61 61; Natalie Grandin/Nicole Rencken (RSA) d. Shahar Peer/Anna Smashnova-Pistolesi (ISR) 61 63. **Ukraine defeated Netherlands 2-1:** Elena Tatarkova (UKR) d. Michaella Krajicek (NED) 62 63; Yulia Beygelzimer (UKR) d. Elise Tamaela (NED) 62 76(4); Tessy Van De Ven/Anouska Van Exel (NED) d. Maria Koryttseva/Olga Savchuk (UKR) 63 64.

- **22 April   Netherlands defeated South Africa 2-1:** Michaella Krajicek (NED) d. Chanelle Scheepers (RSA) 75 26 62; Elise Tamaela (NED) d. Natalie Grandin (RSA) 62 46 119; Nicole Rencken/Chanelle Scheepers (RSA) d. Tessy Van De Ven/Anouska Van Exel (NED) 63 62.

- **23 April   Ukraine defeated Israel 3-0:** Elena Tatarkova (UKR) d. Shahar Peer (ISR) 64 62; Yulia Beygelzimer (UKR) d. Tzipi Obziler (ISR) 63 61; Maria Koryttseva/Olga Savchuk (UKR) d. Shahar Peer/Anna Smashnova-Pistolesi (ISR) 44 ret.

- **Final Positions:** 1. Ukraine, 2. Israel, 3. Netherlands, 4. South Africa.

- **Group C   19 April   Belarus defeated Denmark 3-0:** Tatiana Uvarova (BLR) d. Maria Rasmussen (DEN) 61 61; Tatiana Poutchek (BLR) d. Karina Jacobsgaard (DEN) 62 62; Daria Kustava/Anastasia Yakimova (BLR) d. Mette Iversen/Karina Jacobsgaard (DEN) 61 64.

- **20 April   Hungary defeated Denmark 3-0:** Kyra Nagy (HUN) d. Mette Iversen (DEN) 60 62; Melinda Czink (HUN) d. Karina Jacobsgaard (DEN) 61 62; Melinda Czink/Katalin Marosi (HUN) d. Mette Iversen/Karina Jacobsgaard (DEN) 76(4) 36 86.

- **22 April   Belarus defeated Hungary 3-0:** Tatiana Uvarova (BLR) d. Kyra Nagy (HUN) 63 60; Anastasia Yakimova (BLR) d. Melinda Czink (HUN) 61 60; Daria Kustava/Tatiana Poutchek (BLR) d. Katalin Marosi/Kyra Nagy (HUN) 64 64.

- **Final Positions:** 1. Belarus, 2. Hungary, 3. Denmark.

- **Group D   19 April   Estonia defeated Bulgaria 2-1:** Maret Ani (EST) d. Tzvetana Pironkova (BUL) 26 60 63; Sesil Karatancheva (BUL) d. Kaia Kanepi (EST) 63 63; Maret Ani/Margit Ruutel (EST) d. Sesil Karatancheva/Maria Penkova (BUL) 75 36 64.

- **20 April   Poland defeated Greece 2-1:** Karolina Kosinska (POL) d. Christina Zachariadou (GRE) 75 61; Eleni Daniilidou (GRE) d. Joanna Sakowicz (POL) 61 64; Klaudia Jans/Alicia Rosolska (POL) d. Eleni Daniilidou/Christina Zachariadou (GRE) 46 64 64.

- **21 April   Estonia defeated Poland 2-1:** Karolina Kosinska (POL) d. Margit Ruutel (EST) 64 46 75; Maret Ani (EST) d. Joanna Sakowicz (POL) 75 61; Maret Ani/Kaia Kanepi (EST) d. Klaudia Jans/Alicia Rosolska (POL) 76(4) 61. **Bulgaria defeated Greece 2-1:** Tzvetana Pironkova (BUL) d. Asimina Kaplani (GRE) 60 61; Sesil Karatancheva (BUL) d. Eleni Daniilidou (GRE) 46 63 75; Asimina Kaplani/Christina Zachariadou (GRE) d. Maria Penkova/Tzvetana Pironkova (BUL) 36 63 75.

- **22 April   Bulgaria defeated Poland 2-1:** Tzvetana Pironkova (BUL) d. Karolina Kosinska (POL) 75 64; Sesil Karatancheva (BUL) d. Klaudia Jans (POL) 63 60; Karolina Kosinska/Alicia Rosolska (POL) d. Sesil Karatancheva/Maria Penkova (BUL) 36 76(1) 75.

- **23 April   Estonia defeated Greece 3-0:** Margit Ruutel (EST) d. Anna Gerassimou (GRE) 63 46 63; Maret Ani (EST) d. Asimina Kaplani (GRE) 61 63; Ilona Poljakova/Margit Ruutel (EST) d. Eleni Daniilidou/Christina Zachariadou (GRE) 63 46 61.

- **Final Positions:** 1. Estonia, 2. Bulgaria, 3. Poland, 4. Greece.

Tatiana Golovin (FRA)

2004 Fed Cup Results (continued)

- **Promotion Play-off 24 April Bulgaria defeated Serbia & Montenegro 2-1:** Jelena Jankovic (SCG) d. Tzvetana Pironkova (BUL) 64 61; Sesil Karatancheva (BUL) d. Jelena Dokic (SCG) w/o; Sesil Karatancheva/Maria Penkova (BUL) d. Ana Timotic/Dragana Zaric (SCG) 64 26 63. **Ukraine defeated Hungary 2-0:** Elena Tatarkova (UKR) d. Kyra Nagy (HUN) 75 62; Yulia Beygelzimer (UKR) d. Melinda Czink (HUN) 36 63 62. **Belarus defeated Sweden 2-1:** Tatiana Uvarova (BLR) d. Hanna Nooni (SWE) 75 64; Sofia Arvidsson (SWE) d. Anastasia Yakimova (BLR) 76(5) 63; Daria Kustava/Tatiana Poutchek (BLR) d. Sofia Arvidsson/Hanna Nooni (SWE) 62 62. **Estonia defeated Israel 2-1:** Maret Ani (EST) d. Tzipi Obziler (ISR) 57 62 64; Anna Smashnova-Pistolesi (ISR) d. Kaia Kanepi (EST) 60 60; Maret Ani/Kaia Kanepi (EST) d. Tzipi Obziler/Anna Smashnova-Pistolesi (ISR) 75 61.

- **Relegation Play-off 24 April Greece defeated Lithuania 2-0:** Christina Zachariadou (GRE) d. Edita Liachoviciute (LTU) 36 60 63; Eleni Daniilidou (GRE) d. Lina Stanciute (LTU) 62 62. **South Africa defeated Denmark 2-0:** Nicole Rencken (RSA) d. Maria Rasmussen (DEN) 64 60; Natalie Grandin (RSA) d. Karina Jacobsgaard (DEN) 64 62.

Belarus, Bulgaria, Estonia and Ukraine advance to 2004 World Group II Play-offs.
Lithuania relegated to Europe/Africa Zone Group II in 2005.

Americas Zone Group II

Date: 20-24 April
Venue: Bahia, Brazil
Surface: Clay (O)
Group A: Ecuador, Guatemala, Jamaica, Paraguay
Group B: Bolivia, Dominican Republic, Venezuela

- **Group A 20 April Paraguay defeated Ecuador 2-1;** Sarah Tami (PAR) d. Pamela Duran-Vinueza (ECU) 36 63 64; Larissa Schaerer (PAR) d. Estefania Balda (ECU) 62 64; Estefania Balda/Maria-Teresa Salame (ECU) d. Larissa Schaerer/Sarah Tami (PAR) 67(5) 60 64. **Jamaica defeated Guatemala 3-0:** Megan Moulton-Levy (JAM) d. Luisa-Elfride Lopez (GUA) 62 61; Alanna Broderick (JAM) d. Lucia Henkle-Gomez (GUA) 62 61; Alanna Broderick/Megan Moulton-Levy (JAM) d. Luisa-Elfride Lopez/Saira Sanchinelli (GUA) 60 64.

- **21 April Ecuador defeated Guatemala 3-0:** Pamela Duran-Vinueza (ECU) d. Luisa-Elfride Lopez (GUA) 61 64; Estefania Balda (ECU) d. Lucia Henkle-Gomez (GUA) 63 64; Estefania Balda/Maria-Teresa Salame (ECU) d. Luisa-Elfride Lopez/Saira Sanchinelli (GUA) 61 46 60. **Paraguay defeated Jamaica 3-0:** Sarah Tami (PAR) d. Megan Moulton-Levy (JAM) 16 62 62; Larissa Schaerer (PAR) d. Alanna Broderick (JAM) 62 62; Larissa Schaerer/Sarah Tami (PAR) d. Alanna Broderick/Megan Moulton-Levy (JAM) 36 61 75.

- **22 April Jamaica defeated Ecuador 2-1:** Megan Moulton-Levy (JAM) d. Pamela Duran-Vinueza (ECU) 60 61; Estefania Balda (ECU) d. Alanna Broderick (JAM) 61 64; Alanna Broderick/Megan Moulton-Levy (JAM) d. Estefania Balda/Maria-Teresa Salame (ECU) 64 76(2). **Paraguay defeated Guatemala 2-1:** Luisa-Elfride Lopez (GUA) d. Rossona Vega (PAR) 64 64; Larissa Schaerer (PAR) d. Lucia Henkle-Gomez (GUA) 61 62; Larissa Schaerer/Sarah Tami (PAR) d. Luisa-Elfride Lopez/Saira Sanchinelli (GUA) 63 75.

- **Final Positions:** 1. Paraguay, 2. Jamaica, 3. Ecuador, 4. Guatemala.

- **Group B 20 April Bolivia defeated Venezuela 2-1:** Paola Iovino (VEN) d. Monica Hoz De Vila (BOL) 61 63; Maria-Fernanda Alvarez (BOL) d. Mariana Muci (VEN) 64 61; Maria-Fernanda Alvarez/Monica Hoz De Vila (BOL) d. Avel-Romaly Coronado/Paola Iovino (VEN) 64 76(4).

- **21 April Bolivia defeated Dominican Republic 3-0:** Monica Hoz De Vila (BOL) d. Chandra Capozzi (DOM) 64 62; Maria-Fernanda Alvarez (BOL) d. Natalia Baez (DOM) 64 64; Maria Alejandra Claure/Monica Hoz De Vila (BOL) d. Natalia Baez/Chandra Capozzi (DOM) 16 60 86.

- **22 April Venezuela defeated Dominican Republic 2-0:** Paola Iovino (VEN) d. Natalia Baez (DOM) 60 61; Mariana Muci (VEN) d. Chandra Capozzi (DOM) 75 62.

- **Final Positions:** 1. Bolivia, 2. Venezuela, 3. Dominican Republic

- **Play-off for 6th-7th Position:**
23 April Guatemala defeated Dominican Republic 2-1: Chandra Capozzi (DOM) d. Karen Saravia (GUA) 61 67(1) 64; Luisa-Elfride Lopez (GUA) d. Natalia Baez (DOM) 63 36 62; Luisa-Elfride Lopez/Saira Sanchinelli (GUA) d. Natalia Baez/Chandra Capozzi (DOM) 76(7) 26 75.

- **Promotion Play-off 24 April Paraguay defeated Venezuela 2-1:** Paola Iovino (VEN) d. Sarah Tami (PAR) 64 67(6) 75; Larissa Schaerer (PAR) d. Mariana Muci (VEN) 62 62; Larissa Schaerer/Sarah Tami (PAR) d. Paola Iovino/Mariana Muci (VEN) 61 61. **Bolivia defeated Jamaica 2-1:** Megan Moulton-Levy (JAM) d. Monica Hoz De Vila (BOL) 60 61; Maria-Fernanda Alvarez (BOL) d. Alanna Broderick (JAM) 63 63; Maria-Fernanda Alvarez/Monica Hoz De Vila (BOL) d. Alanna Broderick/Megan Moulton-Levy (JAM) 57 60 63.

Bolivia and Paraguay promoted to Americas Zone Group I in 2005.

Asia/Oceania Zone Group II

Date: 21-24 April
Venue: New Delhi, India
Surface: Hard (O)
Nations: Kazakhstan, Pacific Oceania, Singapore, Syria, Turkmenistan

- **20 April Singapore defeated Turkmenistan 3-0:** Wei-Ping Lee (SIN) d. Ummarahmat Alisultanova (TKM) 61 62; Rui-Jing Wong (SIN) d. Jenneta Hallyewa (TKM) 60 63; Wei-Ping Lee/Rui-Jing Wong (SIN) d. Ummarahmat Alisultanova/Jenneta Hallyewa (TKM) 60 60. **Kazakhstan defeated Pacific Oceania 3-0:** Amina Rakhim (KAZ) d. Irene George (POC) 60 61; Madina Rakhim (KAZ) d. Gurianna Korinihona (POC) 62 60; Yekaterina Morozova/Amina Rakhim (KAZ) d. Angelita Detudamo/Gurianna Korinihona (POC) 61 62.

- **21 April Singapore defeated Syria 2-1:** Wei-Ping Lee (SIN) d. Hazar Sudki (SYR) 62 60; Rui-Jing Wong (SIN) d. Lara Al Samman (SYR) 60 61; Nivin Al Kozbari/Hazar Sudki (SYR) d. Yun-Ling Ng/Pei-Ling Tong (SIN) 76(5) 64. **Pacific Oceania defeated Turkmenistan 3-0:** Irene George (POC) d. Almira Hallyewa (TKM) 63 76(10); Gurianna Korinihona (POC) d. Janneta Hallyewa (TKM) 63 76(14); Angelita Detudamo/Irene George (POC) d. Veronika Babayan/Almira Hallyewa (TKM) 61 62.

- **22 April Pacific Oceania defeated Syria 3-0:** Irene George (POC) d. Hazar Sudki (SYR) 63 63; Gurianna Korinihona (POC) d. Lara Al Samman (SYR) 60 61; Angelita Detudamo/Gurianna Korinihona (POC) d. Nivin Al Kozbari/Lara Al Samman (SYR) 62 64. **Kazakhstan defeated Turkmenistan 3-0:** Yekaterina Morozova (KAZ) d. Ummarahmat Alisultanova (TKM) 61 60; Amina Rakhim (KAZ) d. Veronika Babayan (TKM) 62 61; Amina Rakhim/Madina Rakhim (KAZ) d. Ummarahmat Alisultanova/Veronika Babayan (TKM) 60 60.

- **23 April Singapore defeated Pacific Oceania 2-1:** Wei-Ping Lee (SIN) d. Irene George (POC) 63 63; Rui-Jing Wong (SIN) d. Gurianna Korinihona (POC) 62 60; Irene George/Gurianna Korinihona (POC) d. Yun-Ling Ng/Pei-Ling Tong (SIN) 63 60. **Kazakhstan defeated Syria 3-0:** Yekaterina Morozova (KAZ) d. Nivin Al Kozbari (SYR) 63 60; Madina Rakhim (KAZ) d. Lara Al Samman (SYR) 60 60; Yekaterina Morozova/Amina Rakhim (KAZ) d. Nivin Al Kozbari/Hazar Sudki (SYR) 60 60.

- **24 April Kazakhstan defeated Singapore 3-0:** Yekaterina Morozova (KAZ) d. Pei-Ling Tong (SIN) 60 63; Amina Rakhim (KAZ) d. Yun-Ling Ng (SIN) 61 60; Amina Rakhim/Madina Rakhim (KAZ) d. Wei-Ping Lee/Rui-Jing Wong (SIN) 57 61 61. **Syria defeated Turkmenistan 2-1:** Hazar Sudki (SYR) d. Ummarahmat Alisultanova (TKM) 61 64; Lara Al Samman (SYR) d. Janneta Hallyewa (TKM) 62 76(5); Ummarahmat Alisultanova/Veronika Babayan (TKM) d. Nivin Al Kozbari/Hazar Sudki (SYR) 76(0) 64.

- **Final Positions:** 1.Kazakhstan, 2.Singapore, 3.Pacific Oceania, 4.Syria, 5. Turkmenistan.

Kazakhstan and Singapore promoted to Asia/Oceania Zone Group I in 2005.

Europe/Africa Zone Group II

Date: 26 April–1 May
Venue: Marsa, Malta
Surface: Hard (O)
Group A: Egypt, Great Britain, Romania, Turkey
Group B: Finland, Georgia, Ireland, Latvia, Luxembourg

- **Group A 26 April Great Britain defeated Egypt 3-0:** Amanda Janes (GBR) d. Noha Mohsen (EGY) 62 62; Anne Keothavong (GBR) d. Yomna Farid (EGY) 60 61; Elena Baltacha/Jane O'Donoghue (GBR) d. Yomna Farid/Noha Mohsen (EGY) 60 63. **Romania defeated**

2004 Fed Cup Results (continued)

Turkey 3-0: Gabriela Niculescu (ROM) d. Cigdem Duru (TUR) 63 61; Simona Matei (ROM) d. Pemra Ozgen (TUR) 63 63; Gabriela Niculescu/Monica Niculescu (ROM) d. Cagla Buyukacay/Pemra Ozgen (TUR) 62 64.

- **27 April Great Britain defeated Turkey 3-0:** Elena Baltacha (GBR) d. Cigdem Duru (TUR) 61 60; Amanda Janes (GBR) d. Pemra Ozgen (TUR) 64 76(3); Elena Baltacha/Jane O'Donoghue (GBR) d. Cagla Buyukacay/Pemra Ozgen (TUR) 60 63.

- **28 April Turkey defeated Egypt 3-0:** Cigdem Duru (TUR) d. Noha Mohsen (EGY) 64 62; Pemra Ozgen (TUR) d. Yomna Farid (EGY) 62 63; Cigdem Duru/Pemra Ozgen (TUR) d. Aliaa Fakhry/Yomna Farid (EGY) 75 61.

- **29 April Great Britain defeated Romania 2-1:** Elena Baltacha (GBR) d. Monica Niculescu (ROM) 61 64; Anne Keothavong (GBR) d. Simona Matei (ROM) 36 63 60; Gabriela Niculescu/Monica Niculescu (ROM) d. Amanda Janes/Jane O'Donoghue (GBR) 76(6) 67(3) 60.

- **30 April Romania defeated Egypt 3-0:** Monica Niculescu (ROM) d. Aliaa Fakhry (EGY) 60 63; Simona Matei (ROM) d. Yomna Farid (EGY) 60 63; Gabriela Niculescu/Monica Niculescu (ROM) d. Aliaa Fakhry/Noha Mohsen (EGY) 60 60.

- **Final Positions:** 1. Great Britain, 2. Romania, 3. Turkey, 4. Egypt.

- **Group B 26 April Luxembourg defeated Latvia 2-1:** Anne Kremer (LUX) d. Liga Dekmeijere (LAT) 62 60; Claudine Schaul (LUX) d. Anzela Zguna (LAT) 63 63; Liga Dekmeijere/Irina Kuzmina (LAT) d. Mandy Minella/Claudine Schaul (LUX) 64 62. **Ireland defeated Georgia 3-0:** Yvonne Doyle (IRL) d. Sophia Melikishvili (GEO) 75 64; Kelly Liggan (IRL) d. Salome Devidze (GEO) 64 61; Yvonne Doyle/Karen Nugent (IRL) d. Salome Devidze/Tinatin Kavlashvili (GEO) 64 61.

- **27 April Luxembourg defeated Finland 3-0:** Anne Kremer (LUX) d. Essi Laine (FIN) 61 62; Claudine Schaul (LUX) d. Carina Bjornstrom (FIN) 61 63; Anne Kremer/Mandy Minella (LUX) d. Carina Bjornstrom/Essi Laine (FIN) 61 63. **Latvia defeated Georgia 2-1:** Sophia Melikishvili (GEO) d. Liga Dekmeijere (LAT) 36 64 62; Anzela Zguna (LAT) d. Salome Devidze (GEO) 63 76(2); Liga Dekmeijere/Irina Kuzmina (LAT) d. Salome Devidze/Tinatin Kavlashvili (GEO) 63 64.

- **28 April Luxembourg defeated Georgia 3-0:** Anne Kremer (LUX) d. Tinatin Kavlashvili (GEO) 62 60; Claudine Schaul (LUX) d. Salome Devidze (GEO) 63 63; Anne Kremer/Claudine Schaul (LUX) d. Salome Devidze/Tinatin Kavlashvili (GEO) 75 ret. **Ireland defeated Finland 3-0:** Yvonne Doyle (IRL) d. Essi Laine (FIN) 63 63; Kelly Liggan (IRL) d. Carina Bjornstrom (FIN) 61 61; Karen Nugent/Elsa O'Riain (IRL) d. Carina Bjornstrom/Essi Laine (FIN) 76(4) 60.

- **29 April Luxembourg defeated Ireland 2-1:** Anne Kremer (LUX) d. Yvonne Doyle (IRL) 64 64; Claudine Schaul (LUX) d. Kelly Liggan (IRL) 62 75; Yvonne Doyle/Karen Nugent (IRL) d. Anne Kremer/Mandy Minella (LUX) 46 64 62. **Latvia defeated Finland 2-1:** Liga Dekmeijere (LAT) d. Essi Laine (FIN) 75 63; Emma Laine (FIN) d. Anzela Zguna (LAT) 76(5) 61; Liga Dekmeijere/Irina Kuzmina (LAT) d. Carina Bjornstrom/Emma Laine (FIN) 64 62

- **30 April Ireland defeated Latvia 3-0:** Yvonne Doyle (IRL) d. Liga Derkmeijere (LAT) 75 64; Kelly Liggan (IRL) d. Anzela Zguna (LAT) 63 64; Karen Nugent/Elsa O'Riain (IRL) d. Irina Kuzmina/Irina Strigalova (LAT) 76(3) 63. **Georgia defeated Finland 2-1:** Sophia Melikishvili (GEO) d. Carina Bjornstrom (FIN) 61 61; Emma Laine (FIN) d. Salome Devidze (GEO) 63 64; Salome Devidze/Tinatin Kavlashvili (GEO) d. Emma Laine/Essi Laine (FIN) 63 64.

- **Final Positions:** 1. Luxembourg, 2. Ireland, 3. Latvia, 4. Georgia.

- **Relegation Play-off 1 May Finland defeated Turkey 3-0:** Essi Laine (FIN) d. Cigdem Duru (TUR) 36 64 63; Emma Laine (FIN) d. Pemra Ozgen (TUR) 62 60; Emma Laine/Essi Laine (FIN) d. Cigdem Duru/Pemra Ozgen (TUR) 64 62. **Georgia defeated Egypt 3-0:** Sophia Melikishvili (GEO) d. Aliaa Fakhry (EGY) 60 64; Salome Devidze (GEO) d. Yomna Farid (EGY) 61 64; Tinatin Kavlashvili/Sophia Melikishvili (GEO) d. Aliaa Fakhry/Yomna Farid (EGY) 64 63.

- **Promotion Play-off 1 May Great Britain defeated Ireland 2-0:** Elena Baltacha (GBR) d. Yvonne Doyle (IRL) 61 75; Anne Keothavong (GBR) d. Kelly Liggan (IRL) 62 36 22 ret. **Luxembourg defeated Romania 2-1:** Anne Kremer (LUX) d. Monica Niculescu (ROM) 60 75; Claudine Schaul (LUX) d. Simona Matei (ROM) 63 64; Gabriela Niculescu/Monica Niculescu (ROM) d. Mandy Minella/Lynn Philippe (LUX) 63 64.

Great Britain and Luxembourg promoted to Europe/Africa Zone Group I for 2005.
Portugal, Turkey and Egypt relegated to Europe/Africa Zone Group III.

Europe/Africa Zone Group III

Date: 26 April–1 May
Venue: Marsa, Malta
Surface: Hard (O)
Group A: Botswana, Kenya, Malta, Tunisia
Group B: Algeria, Bosnia-Herzegovina, Namibia, Norway

- **Group A 27 April Tunisia defeated Malta 2-1:** Lisa Camenzuli (MLT) d. Ines Zouabi (TUN) 61 60; Selima Sfar (TUN) d. Sarah Wetz (MLT) 60 60; Issem Essaies/Selima Sfar (TUN) d. Lisa Camenzuli/Rosanne Dimech (MLT) 64 76(7). **Botswana defeated Kenya 2-1:** Tapiwa Marobela (BOT) d. Evelyn Otula (KEN) 61 61; Wanjika Ngaruiya (KEN) d. Lesedi Ramocha (BOT) 63 61; Laone Botshoma/Tapiwa Marobela (BOT) d. Caroline Oduor/Evelyn Otula (KEN) 63 60.

- **28 April Tunisia defeated Kenya 3-0:** Ines Zouabi (TUN) d. Meera Kantaria (KEN) 62 63; Selima Sfar (TUN) d. Wanjika Ngaruiya (KEN) 60 60; Issem Essaies/Selima Frioui (TUN) d. Caroline Oduor/Evelyn Otula (KEN) 63 62. **Malta defeated Botswana 3-0:** Lisa Camenzuli (MLT) d. Laone Botshoma (BOT) 60 60; Rosanne Dimech (MLT) d. Tapiwa Marobela (BOT) 76(5) 16 60; Lisa Camenzuli/Sarah Wetz (MLT) d. Laone Botshoma/Tapiwa Marobela (BOT) 61 62.

- **29 April Tunisia defeated Botswana 2-1:** Tapiwa Marobela (BOT) d. Ines Zouabi (TUN) 61 64; Selima Sfar (TUN) d. Lesedi Ramocha (BOT) 61 61; Issem Essaies/Selima Sfar (TUN) d. Laone Botshoma/Tapiwa Marobela (BOT) 61 60. **Malta defeated Kenya 3-0:** Lisa Camenzuli (MLT) d. Meera Kantaria (KEN) 60 61; Sarah Wetz (MLT) d. Wanjika Ngaruiya (KEN) 60 63; Esther Muscat/Sarah Wetz (MLT) d. Caroline Oduor/Evelyn Otula (KEN) 63 64.

- **Final Positions:** 1. Tunisia, 2. Malta, 3. Botswana, 4. Kenya.

- **Group B 27 April Norway defeated Namibia 3-0:** Karoline Borgersen (NOR) d. Elna De Villiers (NAM) 63 63; Ina Sartz (NOR) d. Ajet Boonzaaier (NAM) 64 76(4); Karoline Borgersen/Ina Sartz (NOR) d. Ajet Boonzaaier/Eleien De Villiers (NAM) 61 60. **Algeria defeated Bosnia/Herzegovina 2-1:** Sana Ben Salah (ALG) d. Selma Babic (BIH) 60 75; Samia Medjahdi (ALG) d. Sanja Racic (BIH) 63 60; Selma Babic/Nadia Secerbegovic (BIH) d. Assia Halo/Sara Meghoufel (ALG) 62 61.

- **28 April Norway defeated Bosnia/Herzegovina 2-1:** Karoline Borgersen (NOR) d. Selma Babic (BIH) 62 63; Ina Sartz (NOR) d. Sanja Racic (BIH) 64 75; Selma Babic/Nadia Secerbegovic (BIH) d. Anette Aksdal/Idunn Hertzberg (NOR) 61 26 63. **Algeria defeated Namibia 3-0:** Sana Ben Salah (ALG) d. Elna De Villiers (NAM) 63 60; Samia Medjahdi (ALG) d. Ajet Boonzaaier (NAM) 62 76(6); Assia Halo/Sara Meghoufel (ALG) d. Ajet Boonzaaier/Elna De Villiers (NAM) 46 62 62.

- **29 April Norway defeated Algeria 2-1:** Karoline Borgersen (NOR) d. Sana Ben Salah (ALG) 26 76(5) 60; Samia Medjahdi (ALG) d. Ina Sartz (NOR) 60 75; Karoline Borgersen/Ina Sartz (NOR) d. Sana Ben Salah/Samia Medjahdi (ALG) 46 64 61. **Bosnia/Herzegovina defeated Namibia 2-1:** Selma Babic (BIH) d. Eleien De Villiers (NAM) 61 62; Ajet Boonzaaier (NAM) d. Sanja Racic (BIH) 75 67(3) 63; Selma Babic/Nadia Secerbegovic (BIH) d. Ajet Boonzaaier/Elna De Villiers (NAM) 76(5) 26 64.

- **Final Positions:** 1. Norway, 2. Algeria, 3. Bosnia/Herzegovinia, 4. Namibia.

- **Promotion Play-off 30 April Tunisia defeated Algeria 2-1:** Sana Ben Salah (ALG) d. Selima Frioui (TUN) 60 61; Selima Sfar (TUN) d. Samia Medjahdi (ALG) 75 62; Issem Essaies/Selima Sfar (TUN) d. Sana Ben Salah/Assia Halo (ALG) 62 62. **Norway defeated Malta 2-1:** Lisa Camenzuli (MLT) d. Karoline Borgersen (NOR) 64 67(3) 64; Ina Sartz (NOR) d. Rosanne Dimech (MLT) 63 46 62; Karoline Borgersen/Ina Sartz (NOR) d. Lisa Camenzuli/Rosanne Dimech (MLT) 75 64. **Botswana defeated Namibia 2-1:** Eleien De Villiers (NAM) d. Laone Botshoma (BOT) 61 61; Tapiwa Marobela (BOT) d. Elna De Villiers (NAM) 75 76(1); Tapiwa Marobela/Lesedi Ramocha (BOT) d. Ajet Boonzaaier/Elna De Villiers (NAM) 46 76(5) 75. **Bosnia/Herzegovina defeated Kenya 3-0:** Selma Babic (BIH) d. Evelyn Otula (KEN) 64 61; Sanja Racic (BIH) d. Caroline Oduor (KEN) 61 61; Selma Babic/Nadia Secerbegovic (BIH) d. Wanjika Ngaruiya/Evelyn Otula (KEN) 61 62.

Norway and Tunisia promoted to Europe/Africa Zone Group II for 2005.

defending champions triumph in hopman cup
another star-spangled victory in perth
by joanne sirman

The USA made history in the 16th Hyundai Hopman Cup, becoming the first nation to successfully defend its title, and the only country to win the trophy three times.

As James Blake and Lindsay Davenport savoured their success, there was good news for the tournament too. The ITF's official mixed team competition will stay at the Burswood Dome in Perth through 2007, which will come as a relief to the many men and women who consider the Hopman Cup the ideal way to start their seasons, before heading 2,300 miles east to Melbourne to compete in the first Grand Slam of the year.

Blake had been due to team up with Serena Williams in a repeat of their Cup-winning combination from the previous year, but the six-time Grand Slam winner had not recovered from her knee injury in time and was replaced by world No. 5 Lindsay Davenport. The American duo swept through their three round robin clashes without losing a rubber, with 3-0 scorelines against the Czech Republic, France and Russia.

Hyundai Hopman Cup Champions, USA

Davenport was in particularly impressive form, not dropping a set in her singles matches against 2003 ITF Junior World Champion Barbora Strycova 64 63, world No. 4 Amelie Mauresmo 64 64, and world No. 7 Anastasia Myskina 64 64. Blake had a tougher time, needing three sets before coming through against Jiri Novak and soon-to-be Australian Open runner-up Marat Safin.

The Americans' place in the final was not secure until they had beaten Russia in the final round robin match of Group A. The Russians had lost 2-1 to France but had defeated Czech Republic 2-1, Safin coming back against Jiri Novak 67 76 63 in a close match that foreshadowed his Melbourne heroics two weeks later. Against Blake however, it was Safin who was on the receiving end of a comeback, losing 67 76 64.

Australia finished top of Group B, Lleyton Hewitt and Alicia Molik winning all three of the home nation's encounters.

USA's Lindsay Davenport and James Blake

However Australia would be unable to compete in the final, as its 2004 Hopman Cup campaign was first aided and then ultimately stopped by injury.

After a 3-0 defeat of Hungary, the Aussies faced Belgium in a much-anticipated clash between Hewitt and new fiancée Kim Clijsters which drew in 8,564 spectators, setting a new attendance record for a single Hopman Cup session. The women's world No. 2 was teamed with Xavier Malisse, and the Belgians were considered equal favourites with Australia to win the tournament, having already defeated the Slovak Republic 3-0.

Belgium's title dreams fell apart though when a left ankle injury forced Clijsters to retire from the third set of her singles match against Molik and then concede a walkover in the mixed doubles, denying the crowd its Hewitt-Clijsters face-off. Belgium later withdrew from the event, leaving Australia's place in the final secure, even before its final round robin meeting with the Slovaks.

Now it was Australia's turn to be cut down by injury, the hosts losing 2-1 to the Slovak Republic after Molik suffered a recurrence of a foot problem and retired against Daniela Hantuchova leading 63 30. Hewitt defeated Karol Kucera 62 67 63 before the hosts gave a walkover in the doubles.

Despite the setback, Australia was still hopeful of being able to contest the final against the USA, but a day's rest and a doctor's consultation did not improve the situation for Molik. The Australian pair were bitterly disappointed to have to withdraw from the event and see their place in the final taken by the Slovaks, who had finished in second place in Group B.

Although the fans did not have the final they most wanted, they were still treated to a competitive decider. Davenport continued to play commanding tennis, overcoming Hantuchova 63 61 in her fourth straight-sets win of the event. Kucera responded with a two-hour-14-minute victory over Blake, but the Slovak's battling performance was not enough to stop the Americans winning the decisive doubles, where Blake rebounded from his loss to play a key role in a 62 63 defeat, giving USA a 2-1 triumph.

The 24-year-old Blake, by helping USA to its second successive Hopman Cup title, also became the first player to successfully defend the title. "As long as I keep getting invited, I'll keep on coming back," he said. "It's a wonderful way to start the year."

The crowds that had packed in for the final ensured that the record attendance of the Australia v Belgium session was matched, and helped the 2004 Hopman Cup to clock up a new record for total attendance, a staggering 82,126 people watching the eight days of action.

> "As long as I keep getting invited, I'll keep on coming back," Blake said. "It's a wonderful way to start the year."

2004 Hyundai Hopman Cup Results

Perth, Australia, 3-10 January 2004

Seeds:
1: USA: Serena Williams/James Blake
2. Australia: Alicia Molik/Lleyton Hewitt
3. Belgium: Kim Clijsters/Xavier Malisse
4. Russia: Anastasia Myskina/Fabrice Santoro

Unseeded:
Czech Republic: Barbora Strycova/Jiri Novak
France: Amelie Mauresmo/Fabrice Santoro
Slovak Republic: Daniela Hantuchova/Karol Kucera

Alternate:
Canada: Maureen Drake/Frank Dancevic
Hungary: Petra Mandula/Attila Savolt

Note: Super tiebreak was used for mixed doubles: if matches are tied at one set all, winner is first to ten.

Play-off
Hungary d. Canada 2-1: Petra Mandula (HUN) d. Maureen Drake (CAN) 63 62; Frank Dancevic (CAN) d. Attila Savolt (HUN) 64 63; Petra Mandula/Attila Savolt (HUN) d. Maureen Drake/Frank Dancevic (CAN) 36 61 10(3).

Group A
France d. Russia 2-1: Amelie Mauresmo (FRA) d. Anastasia Myskina (RUS) 62 76(2); Marat Safin (RUS) d. Fabrice Santoro (FRA) 63 63; Amelie Mauresmo/Fabrice Santoro (FRA) d. Anastasia Myskina/Marat Safin (RUS) 63 64.
USA d. Czech Republic 3-0: Lindsay Davenport (USA) d. Barbora Strycova (CZE) 64 63; James Blake (USA) d. Jiri Novak (CZE) 46 61 75; Lindsay Davenport/James Blake (USA) d. Barbora Strycova/Jiri Novak (CZE) 63 62.
USA d. France 3-0: Lindsay Davenport (USA) d. Amelie Mauresmo (FRA) 64 64; James Blake (USA) d. Fabrice Santoro (FRA) 63 64; Lindsay Davenport/James Blake (USA) d. Amelie Mauresmo/Fabrice Santoro (FRA) 75 61.
Russia d. Czech Republic 2-1: Anastasia Myskina (RUS) d. Barbora Strycova (CZE) 63 76(0); Marat Safin (RUS) d. Jiri Novak (CZE) 67(4) 76(6) 63; Barbora Strycova/Jiri Novak (CZE) d. Anastasia Myskina/Marat Safin (RUS) 36 76(1) 10(9).
USA d. Russia 3-0: Lindsay Davenport (USA) d. Anastasia Myskina (RUS) 64 64; James Blake (USA) d. Marat Safin (RUS) 67(4) 76(4) 64; Lindsay Davenport/James Blake (USA) d. Anastasia Myskina/Marat Safin (RUS) 75 64.
France d. Czech Republic 2-1: Amelie Mauresmo (FRA) d. Barbora Strycova (CZE) 63 64; Jiri Novak (CZE) d. Fabrice Santoro (FRA) 61 46 62; Amelie Mauresmo/Fabrice Santoro (FRA) d. Barbora Strycova/Jiri Novak (CZE) 63 64.

Group B
Australia d. Hungary 3-0: Alicia Molik (AUS) d. Petra Mandula (HUN) 46 76(5) 62; Lleyton Hewitt (AUS) d. Attila Savolt (HUN) 62 62; Alicia Molik/Lleyton Hewitt (AUS) d. Petra Mandula/Attila Savolt (HUN) 76(5) 61.
Belgium d. Slovak Republic 3-0: Kim Clijsters (BEL) d. Daniela Hantuchova (SVK) 61 62; Xavier Malisse (BEL) d. Karol Kucera (SVK) 62 16 61; Kim Clijsters/Xavier Malisse (BEL) d. Daniela Hantuchova/Karol Kucera (SVK) 62 64.
Slovak Republic d. Hungary 2-1: Petra Mandula (HUN) d. Daniela Hantuchova (SVK) 60 76(5); Karol Kucera (SVK) d. Attila Savolt (HUN) 63 75; Daniela Hantuchova/Karol Kucera (SVK) d. Petra Mandula/Attila Savolt (HUN) 63 61.
Australia d. Belgium 3-0: Alicia Molik (AUS) d. Kim Clijsters (BEL) 36 76(6) 23 ret.; Lleyton Hewitt (AUS) d. Xavier Malisse (BEL) 36 61 62; Alicia Molik/Lleyton Hewitt (AUS) d. Kim Clijsters/Xavier Malisse (BEL) w/o.
Slovak Republic d. Australia 2-1: Daniela Hantuchova (SVK) d. Alicia Molik (AUS) 36 03 ret.; Lleyton Hewitt (AUS) d. Karol Kucera (SVK) 62 67(8) 63; Daniela Hantuchova/Karol Kucera (SVK) d. Alicia Molik/Lleyton Hewitt (AUS) w/o.

Final
USA d. Slovak Republic 2-1: Lindsay Davenport (USA) d. Daniela Hantuchova (SVK) 63 61; Karol Kucera (SVK) d. James Blake (USA) 46 64 76(5); Lindsay Davenport/James Blake (USA) d. Daniela Hantuchova/Karol Kucera (SVK) 62 63.

Marat Safin (RUS)

ITF Team Competitions: 2004 Hyundai Hopman Cup

the men's year 2004

by steve bierley

Quite simply it was the year of Roger Federer. After he had won Wimbledon and the Masters Cup in 2003 his many fans and admirers throughout the world finally relaxed a little, comforted by the knowledge that this most talented of player on the men's circuit had made his mark. Now they are ecstatic.

Inconsistency had been the young Swiss player's major problem. Suddenly, and gloriously, he sloughed off the last vestiges of dithering and doubts to win three of the four slams, three Masters series events, and defended his end-of-season Masters Cup title in Houston, where for the second successive year he was undefeated. Not only was he the new No, 1, but demonstrably head and shoulders clear of his nearest rivals.

The only slam to elude him was the French, and as if to make up for his absence in the second week the Philippe Chatrier stadium staged a final overflowing with surprise, suspense, and intrigue. Even now it barely seems possible that Gaston Gaudio won and Guillermo Coria, the hottest of favourites lost the all-Argentine final. But more of that later.

It could be argued that Marat Safin did all the hard work for Federer at the beginning of the year in Melbourne. The huge Russian knocked out Andy Roddick, then the world No. 1, in the quarterfinals and Andre Agassi, the reigning champion, in semis, either of whom might have given the Swiss a sterner challenge in the final.

There was always the danger that Safin would be too exhausted, physically and, above all, mentally, to offer Federer a sustained challenge, having battled his way through three five-setters in his previous four matches, and in total spending eight hours longer on court than Federer over the fortnight. And so it proved, Safin losing 76 64 62 his second Australian Open final defeat in three years.

Federer, several notches below his best, became a little over anxious in his search for outright winners after edging the critical opening set, and the tennis was markedly patchy, as finals so often are. But few doubted that the best player had won the title, and not only the best, but also the most enjoyable to watch. He guaranteed his position as the new world No. 1, a place he held for the rest of the year, when he

Roger Federer (SUI)

Gaston Gaudio (ARG)

defeated Spain's Juan Carlos Ferrero in the semifinals.

It had been a little sad to see Agassi lose to Safin, after a wonderful run of 26 matches unbeaten at Melbourne Park, which encompassed three of his four slam victories in Australia. But here was evolution and revolution in the Southern Hemisphere summer, with game after game of rich excitement that hugely stimulated the television ratings, particularly in the evening and so-called "twilight" sessions. Because of this the 2005 men's final was moved to 7.30pm Australian eastern daylight saving time.

The spring transfer to the US hard courts was preceded by Federer losing his first match of the year, and one of only six in total, against Tim Henman in Rotterdam. However the world No. 1 immediately won his next tournament in Dubai, and then transferred this form to Indian Wells and the Pacific Life Open, the first Masters Series event of the year. The Swiss dropped just one set, against Andre Agassi in the semifinals, before crushing Henman, when it mattered most, in the final.

Miami, the Nasdaq-100 Open, had been won by an American in 11 of the previous 14 years, and this time, perhaps predictably it was the turn of Andy Roddick, who ended Agassi's three hold on the title. Roddick defeated Guillermo Coria in the final, underlining the Argentine's growing threat on all surfaces. He even reached a grass court final in the summer.

When Coria transferred to his favourite clay his victory in the TMS Monte Carlo marked him out as the early and outstanding favourite for the French title and as the gates of Roland Garros swung open in May he was still in pole position.

Few doubted that the best player had won the title, and not only the best, but also the most enjoyable to watch.

Elite Tournaments: The Men's Year 2004

57

the women's year 2004
by richard evans

When Maria Sharapova slumped to the floor of the Staples Center in relief and disbelief after beating a stricken Serena Williams in the final of the WTA Tour Championships in Los Angeles, the Russian teenager was bringing down the curtain on a bewildering year of shock, suspense and spectacular achievement.

For women's tennis, 2004 will go down as the year of the Russians. But it was so much more than that and it left so many unanswered questions. How soon will it take Justine Henin-Hardenne to recover her strength and get back to the top? Will we ever see her Belgian compatriot Kim Clijsters shake off the injuries that are threatening her career? Can Amelie Mauresmo do justice to her huge talent and win big? Will Serena Williams find a balance between tennis and show business? How about Venus – more titles or a slow fade into the world of business and design?

It is possible to pose all these questions and still not answer the one that so many fans were asking at the end of the year – how did Lindsay Davenport end up as No. 1? The answer lies in her ability to offset a failure to get even as far as a final in any of the four Grand Slams with a rampaging summer season in the US. A sudden flow of form saw her win in Stanford, San Diego, Los Angeles and Cincinnati while earlier success in Tokyo and Amelia Island was boosted at the end of the year by a seventh title in Filderstadt. Even that body of

Anastasia Myskina (RUS)

suddenness. As the players flew into Paris for Roland Garros, a quarter of the year's tennis had been played and only two Russians had won a title – Vera Zvonareva in Memphis and, in the barest hint of things to come, Anastasia Myskina over Svetlana Kuznetsova in Doha. It was hardly a forewarning of the Grand Slam grab that was to follow.

another year of Belgium trying to decide which of their two female tennis stars they loved best. Even though Henin-Hardenne went on to collect two more titles in Dubai and Indian Wells, it would only be a matter of time before we saw how the geography and the accent of the tour would change. It had been a false dawn.

However before everyone was reaching for their Russian dictionaries, Venus Williams was staging what began to look like a serious attempt to climb back to the top with a Tier I victory at the Family Circle Cup in Charleston, South Carolina and then, to the delight of Polish fans, another win in Warsaw. Sister Serena had also got into the act, winning the prestigious Nasdaq-100 Open on Key Biscayne. But, going into Paris, Amelie Mauresmo had the French all worked up again about her chances of winning Roland Garros by cleaning up two big Tier I titles, first in Berlin and then Rome where she outplayed Jennifer Capriati in the final after Jennifer had overcome Serena in the semis.

Mauresmo, however was not the only big name to feel the brunt of the Russian advance once Roland Garros got underway. After Elena Dementieva had left Amelie looking forlorn and outplayed in front of a stunned crowd on Court Philippe Chatrier, the Williams sisters suffered the indignity

> Perhaps the most extraordinary thing about the Russian takeover was its suddenness. As the players flew into Paris for Roland Garros, a quarter of the year's tennis had been played and only two Russians had won a title...

success would not have been enough if just one of Davenport's opponents had won more than one Slam but the Russians shared the goodies around amongst themselves. However by winning Wimbledon and the WTA Championships, Sharapova emerged as the pre-eminent figure in a confusing year.

Perhaps the most extraordinary thing about the Russian takeover was its

The year had begun with the usual suspects moving through the gears and collecting most of the titles on offer. Henin-Hardenne, who had warmed up with a win in Sydney, won the third Grand Slam title of her career at Melbourne Park by denying Clijsters her first yet again. But by the time Clijsters had fought her way through the opposition at the Gaz de France Indoors in Paris and then got her hands on the Proximus Diamonds in Antwerp, it seemed that this would be

Maria Sharapova (RUS)

the women's year 2004
by richard evans

of losing on the same day of a Grand Slam for the first time. Under leaden skies that dripped light rain at odd intervals during the proceedings, Serena, in fuschia, and Jennifer, in red, tried to add some colour to the drab day but only Capriati ended up looking happy. Serena had little explanation for a below par performance. "My forehand stayed at the hotel," she offered by way of explanation. Venus couldn't even manage anything as original after her 19-match winning streak on clay had been washed away in a blizzard of errors against Myskina.

In the semifinals, Myskina built on the confidence she had gained from her easy win over Venus by outplaying Capriati 62 62 while Dementieva hid her weakness on the serve to beat the surprise survivor Paolo Suarez with ease. But there was no hiding any deficiency when the two young Russians took the court for the French Open final. Myskina, hitting solidly from the baseline and moving with feline grace, was all business and Dementieva could do nothing to prevent the 22-year-old Muscovite from winning her first Slam by the unarguable score of 61 62.

England soon got a close up of what was going on when Sharapova came through to win the DFS Classic at Edgbaston with a three set victory over a French girl we will be hearing more of, Tatiana Golovin, and then the following week on the pristine grass of Devonshire Park, Eastbourne, Svetlana Kuznetsova earned the third WTA title of her career with a tough 26 76 64 victory over Daniela Hantuchova, whose form and health had taken an upturn since returning to the care of her British coach, Nigel Sears.

So Wimbledon began with two Russians having won both British grass court titles. And still the experts were talking about the Williams sisters, Capriati, Davenport and even Mauresmo as potential champions.

Russia's Elena Dementieva and Svetlana Kuznetsova

Two weeks later the Russian imprint on the year was no longer in doubt. Sharapova, the tall, leggy blonde who immediately had the paparazzi and the pop media making comparisons with the all-but retired Anna Kournikova, emerged as the youngest Wimbledon winner since Martina Hingis after a fortnight that proved she had both the skill and the temperament to handle the awesome task of winning the world's most prestigious championship.

Early on, worthy opponents such as Hantuchova and Amy Frazier (who had beaten Myskina in the previous round) were dismissed in straight sets. Then, when things started to get a little more difficult, Maria showed that she had the resilience to fight back from serious deficits to beat such experienced opponents as Ai Sugiyama by a score of 57 75 61 and then a former champion in Davenport by 26 76 61. Youth has its advantages but it takes more than young legs to finish off this kind of opposition 61 in the third.

Elsewhere in the draw, Capriati had crumpled in alarming fashion against Serena 61 61 and then in probably the best duel of the championships, the youngest Williams sister had clawed her way past Mauresmo 67 75 64 in a match that gripped the Centre Court with the power and athleticism displayed by both women.

In the final, Serena seemed to be suffering a hangover from the effort she had put in against the French woman because she was swept away in the first set 61 and could not even hold on to a 4-2 lead in the second. Just as she had against Davenport, Sharapova seemed quite unphased by the power or reputation of her opponent and fought her way back with some clinical volleying and brilliant backhand winners to level at 4-4 and then go on to complete her dream by a score of 61 64.

"What a talent!" enthused Martina Navratilova whose defeat in the mixed doubles meant that she had failed to beat Billie Jean King's record of 20 Wimbledon titles. "It is so obvious that she just loves to play. This is so important. Yes, she has a father behind her but it is she who wants to be out there and not because he wants her to be there."

Myskina, hitting solidly from the baseline and moving with feline grace, was all business and Dementieva could do nothing to prevent the 22-year-old Muscovite from winning her first Slam by the unarguable score of 61 62.

Davenport's winning burst during the newly organized US Open Series, which stretched through July to September and included decisive victories over Venus Williams as well as a couple of those Russians, Myskina and Zvonareva, was interrupted by an event that only finds its way onto the tennis calendar every four years – The Olympic Games.

Most of the players revel in the idea of mixing with some of the world's greatest athletes in such a historic atmosphere and no city could have provided more history than Athens. From a strictly tennis point of view, it gave Henin-Hardenne the chance to re-emerge from a period of illness to prove that she was still a force in the game by winning the Gold Medal with a decisive 63 63 victory over Mauresmo in the Olympic final. Alicia Molik, who was to make further strides later in the year, grabbed the opportunity to take the bronze by beating Myskina in the medal play-off.

Significantly for the hosts of the next Olympic Games as well as for tennis itself, the doubles gold medal went to Ting Li and Tian Tian Sun who defeated Conchita Martinez and Virginia Ruano Pascual 63 63 in the final after getting the better of Venus Williams and Chanda Rubin in the first round. Li and Sun gained so much confidence from their win that they became a force on the tour for the rest of the year, adding WTA titles in Bangkok and Guangzhou in their bid to foster the growing tennis boom in China.

Even though Davenport was making the US summer circuit her own, it was impossible to stop the Russians from getting in on the act and Elena Bovina popped up in New Haven to add yet another of their number to the winner's roster. Nevertheless, it seemed inconceivable that the US Open would provide another platform for their talents, given the potential of the Williams sisters to feed off the support of New York crowds; Davenport's great run of form; and Capriati's desire to add another Slam to her collection.

But numerous experts were proved wrong again as Davenport limped out of the tournament injured, ending her 23-match winning streak with a disappointing loss to Kuznetsova. In the other semifinal Dementieva defied the odds by reaching her second Grand Slam final of the year with a 60 26 76 victory over Capriati that had people biting their finger nails in Arthur Ashe Stadium as the drama built to a crescendo. Even by today's standards of heightened skill and ever increasing athleticism in the women's game, the young Russian and the veteran American produced some mind-blowing rallies that left both players gasping for air and bent over in exhaustion at their conclusion. The third set lasted 86 minutes and contained one rally of 49 strokes which only ended when Dementieva, finally drawn into the net, blew an overhead off a desperate Capriati lob.

One way or the other it was impossible to keep Capriati away from controversy at Flushing Meadows. In the quarterfinals, Capriati had beaten Serena Williams 26 64 64 after a series of umpiring howlers had done their best to ruin the match.

Unhappily for American audiences, not to mention CBS and their TV ratings, all this excitement and controversy created by the Williams sisters, Capriati and Davenport's resurgence in form had evaporated by the time finals day arrived, leaving everyone with the prospect of two more Russians in a Grand Slam final. After Roland Garros, the delightful Dementieva might have been forgiven for thinking it was her turn but Kuznetsova, no doubt heeding lessons about grabbing one's chances after playing alongside Navratilova when she first arrived on the tour, was not interested in a pecking order. Hitting her ground strokes with ferocious power, the 19-year-old became the least likely Slam winner of this improbable year with a 63 75 victory.

Big crowds in Moscow were more receptive to the idea of two Russians in the final when the Kremlin Cup came to town and Dementieva did not let them down – reaching a final once again. But again it was not enough. This time it was Myskina who sealed a great year by showing her fans how she had become Roland Garros champion all those months before.

Molik, building on her Olympic success, put down a marker for 2005 by beating Sharapova in the Zurich final and then going on to win Luxembourg. Sharapova herself had reminded everyone that she was still around by winning in Seoul and Tokyo and reaching the quarterfinal in Philadelphia before pulling out injured. As events unfolded, it seemed to be a precautionary move because it was quickly obvious that there was little wrong with the Wimbledon champion once the WTA Championships got underway in Los Angeles.

As if to leave no one in any doubt as to which of the Russians should be regarded as top of the heap, the 17-year-old swept past Kuznetsova and Zvonareva in the round robin stage and then came back strongly after losing the first set to beat Myskina 26 62 62 in the semifinal. Meanwhile Mauresmo was getting close again but not close enough in the other semifinal. The French player led Serena by a set and 3-1 before Williams picked up the tempo of her game and emerged from an intense struggle a winner by 46 76 64.

The ill luck that had dogged Serena at various moments during a frustrating year returned to haunt her in the final. Having dominated the first set, Serena began to feel the effects of a pulled stomach muscle and needed heavy strapping around the midriff before she could continue. Sharapova quickly leveled by taking the second set 62 but then became confused as so many relatively inexperienced players do when faced with an injured opponent. Even though she was serving at little more than half pace, Serena was able to exploit the Russian's hesitancy and surprise everyone by establishing a 4-0 third set lead. But more was beyond her. Gathering her wits about her, Sharapova went back on the attack and claimed her second major title of a fabulous year 46 62 64.

By winning the Australian, French and US Opens, Virginia Ruano Pascual and Paola Suarez were clearly the doubles team of the year and if they go on winning with this consistency could start breaking some records. The Spanish-Argentine combination now have seven Grand Slam titles and one can expect more.

Cara Black and Rennae Stubbs took the Wimbledon crown and, as an interesting footnote to the year, Black also banked $105,067 from mixed doubles play alone. With Beijing introducing a mixed doubles event when the men and women converged on the Chinese capital maybe this popular form of the game will now spread beyond the Slams.

> Virginia Ruano Pascual and Paola Suarez were clearly the doubles team of the year and if they go on winning with this consistency could start breaking some records.

tennis wins gold in athens

by craig gabriel

Athens was a picture of contrasts as majestic ruins highlighted by the Parthenon high atop of the Acropolis almost seemed to cast a watchful eye over a new and modern Olympic complex that housed an impressive tennis facility for the 28th Olympiad.

During those days in August the unrelenting sun burned down on the concrete tennis courts of the Olympic Tennis Centre raising the mercury to 30, 35, 40 degrees celsius. There was little escape as the trees and shrubs were not matured enough to provide much shaded relief.

But like the Olympic heroes of a bygone era, tennis' modern stars coped with the conditions in their chase for glory at the spiritual home of the Olympic Games. To be bestowed with the olive wreath and to feel a medal hanging around one's neck was something to treasure for a lifetime.

Many times in Athens tennis players were awarded more than their 15 minutes of fame as memories were imbedded for eternity. Small countries, big countries, countries that rarely tasted success, countries just overjoyed to have the chance to participate, all shared the spirit as every gamut of emotion overflowed. It was a coming together. In a sport as individualistic as tennis, players embraced their national teams under their country's flags. This was a celebration of sport.

Justine Henin-Hardenne (BEL)

exactly four hours and ended in the wee small hours.

"To be here and to compete for the medal and get the gold is unbelievable, it's a dream" said Massu who choked back tears of joy. "It is a big honour to be here. Of course it's the happiest day of my life as an athlete. To play tennis all week, to win a medal, to enter in the history of our country, I think it's a dream for anyone.

"For an athlete, it's already an honour to compete in the Olympics for your country, but to actually win two gold medals is something incredible. I cannot believe it."

The match ended on Massu's first match point when Fish sent a backhand wide. Most thought Massu would have

had come so close to the ultimate prize, gold, and failed. "It's definitely a week that I'll never forget," said Fish. "How many people can say they have played the Olympics and won a medal. It was a great week ranking wise and I mean, I got a medal. That's the coolest thing about it. The most disappointing thing is that I really wanted to hear the National Anthem. The Olympics is the biggest thing and a gold medal is the biggest prize in sports."

The day before was just as much of a fairy-tale story. Justine Henin-Hardenne, playing her first event since the French Open, sized up an overhead from Amelie Mauresmo on match point and with the French player way across the deuce side of the court the Belgian used the open court to smash the ball away for a winner and with it became the first Belgian to win an Olympic tennis singles gold medal. The 63 63 final lasted 78 minutes.

Henin-Hardenne was so stunned that she didn't know what to do, how to react and she wanted "time to realise what happened".

"If I say stupid things, forgive me tonight. I can tell you it's totally different from a Grand Slam," she said. "I cannot tell you if it's better or not because it's a different feeling. I think it's been a great atmosphere the whole week. I had good feelings the whole week. I didn't know if I was going to be able to play, and I won the gold medal. (I know) that a lot of players have to dream about winning an Olympic gold medal because it's a great moment in your career."

> In a sport as individualistic as tennis, players embraced their national teams under their country's flags. This was a celebration of sport.

Quite probably the Athens Games will be remembered as Chile's Games. In 1934 the South American nation was made a member of the International Olympic Committee. Exactly 70 years later it rejoiced as it won its first ever gold medal in any sport by winning the men's doubles and soon after added a second gold with the men's singles as well as a bronze.

In Sydney 2000, Nicolas Massu carried the flag at the Opening Ceremony. In Athens he won gold and was deliriously happy as he came back from two sets to one down to beat American Mardy Fish 63 36 26 63 64 in a match that went

been exhausted after playing close to four hours in that doubles final but he started the final almost like a steam train by opening up a 5-0 lead against Fish. The American did have his chances but rued the fact that he was not able to capitalise. Fish did however make his return and created that two sets to one lead.

He thought he had the match in his hands with a "pretty commanding lead", especially with Massu looking tired. But this is the Olympics and even if Massu kept appearing tired he never slowed down.

Fish was proud of the fact that he had won a silver medal but was gutted that he

Nicolas Massu (CHI)

tennis wins gold in athens
by craig gabriel

Henin-Hardenne said she didn't sleep that well the night before because of nerves. However, once she got into the match she was aggressive but at the same time patient. She came to the net, she served well and she was very consistent with her returning. Mauresmo was surprised at the way the Belgian played and realised very early there were problems ahead. She said: "She didn't give me much chance to develop my own game. Well done to her. I tip my hat off to her. She did well."

Growing up Henin-Hardenne dreamed of Grand Slams but on this balmy Athens night she changed her mind. "You feel like you are playing for the whole country, you

Chile's Nicolas Massu and Fernando Gonzalez

"You feel like you are playing for the whole country, you play for the colours of your country and that's something really different," said Henin-Hardenne. "When you are in a Grand Slam, you are alone. All the Belgian athletes were here also Jacques Rogge (IOC President), all the Belgian team was behind me. That's big support. You never have it in a Grand Slam. It's different."

play for the colours of your country and that's something really different," said Henin-Hardenne. "When you are in a Grand Slam, you are alone. All the Belgian athletes were here also Jacques Rogge (IOC President), all the Belgian team was behind me. That's big support. You never have it in a Grand Slam. It's different."

That penultimate day was truly one to remember. Earlier, Australian Alicia Molik was filled with emotion. Never one to cry in public, tears unashamedly rolled down her face. She had made a major inroad with her career and she had created a lifelong memory by becoming the first Australian to win an Olympic singles medal when she won bronze, defeating Anastasia Myskina 63 64 in 64 minutes.

"I'm not usually an emotional person," said Molik. "I cried after that. I cried right at the end and I think I reduced my team to tears as well. I guess it's a mixture of satisfaction, it's a mixture of relief, it's a mixture of rewards for hard work and the hours and difficult times that I've had. I guess the time I've dedicated to my sport and tennis, my profession. I love it so much so to finally get a reward is an incredible feeling."

Myskina was very flat. The Russian just couldn't muster up the energy after her tearful loss to Henin-Hardenne the night before when she served for the match at 5-1 and 5-3 in the final set. The Belgian

Mardy Fish (USA)

China's Ting Li and Tian-Tian Sun

Gonzalez and Massu had won the doubles gold medal after coming back from match point down to beat Nicolas Kiefer and Rainer Schuettler in an excruciatingly exciting match 62 46 36 76 64.

The women's doubles was another turn up for the record books. China has never come close to winning any Olympic tennis medal but in Athens they claimed the gold medal as Li Ting and Sun Tian Tian defeated second seeds Conchita Martinez and Virginia Ruano Pascual of Spain 63 63.

"It is unbelievable that we have this gold medal," said Sun. "It is a great honour for us to have the first gold medal for Olympic Games tennis for China."

Seventh seeds Paola Suarez and Patricia Tarabini from Argentina secured the bronze medal with a 63 63 win over Japan's Shinobu Asagoe and Ai Sugiyama.

These Games also marked the first

> "It is unbelievable that we have this gold medal," said Sun. "It is a great honour for us to have the first gold medal for Olympic Games tennis for China."

kept coming back and the rally on match point became the point of the Olympics. Caution was thrown out as they crunched backhands and forehands with the ball kissing the lines as the players appeared like gazelles sprinting after it.

Then, with half the court open, Henin-Hardenne got her chance and she rifled a glorious backhand down the line for a winner. After two hours 44 minutes it was all over 75 57 86.

The men's bronze medal play-off was as much of a cliffhanger. Fernando Gonzalez gave Chile the medal when he beat American Taylor Dent in three hours 25 minutes 64 26 1614. Gonzalez had match point midway through the third set but Dent forged back and then had two match points of his own at 1413 in the set. It was the second consecutive men's bronze match that ended 1614 as the night before in the men's doubles Mario Ancic and Ivan Ljubicic defeated Mahesh Bhupathi and Leander Paes 76 46 1614. So overwhelmed were the Croats that they started throwing their clothes into the crowd.

time that Martina Navratilova, at the age of 47, had become an Olympian. She and Lisa Raymond reached the quarterfinals.

Tennis was one of the first events to be sold out. Besides those already mentioned, so many more stars had turned out in droves to play – Roger Federer, Andy Roddick, Carlos Moya, Juan Carlos Ferrero, Tim Henman, Paradorn Srichaphan, and the dejection they felt at not winning a medal was worn on their sleeves. But a look back at tennis at these Games would not be complete without a very special mention of Greece's Eleni Daniilidou.

She didn't reach the medal round but in reaching the third round she brought great pride to her nation. Writhing on the court in agony with cramps, she dug deep into her psyche to find something special and reward a packed stadium that was overflowing with atmosphere to come back and beat Maggie Maleeva in the second round 26 64 64.

Daniilidou's performance was one of those great moments that celebrated the human spirit and in doing so celebrated tennis at the Olympic Games.

Left: Amelie Mauresmo (FRA)
Right: Alicia Molik (AUS)

Olympic Results: Athens 2004

Men's Singles
First Round: R. Federer (SUI) (1) d. N. Davydenko (RUS) 63 57 61; T. Berdych (CZE) d. F. Mayer (GER) 63 75; F. Santoro (FRA) d. F. Volandri (ITA) 62 61; T. Robredo (ESP) (15) d. L. Ouahab (ALG) (WC) 63 64; J. Johansson (SWE) d. P. Srichaphan (THA) (12) 62 63; I. Ljubicic (CRO) d. S. Sargsian (ARM) 63 64; D. Hrbaty (SVK) d. Y. El Aynaoui (MAR) 63 64; T. Dent (USA) d. F. Niemeyer (CAN) (A) 62 36 64; C. Moya (ESP) (3) d. T. Enqvist (SWE) 76(7) 67(8) 97; O. Rochus (BEL) d. M. Philippoussis (AUS) 36 60 61; A. Clement (FRA) d. N. Lapentti (ECU) (WC) 76(5) 62; I. Karlovic (CRO) d. A. Pavel (ROM) (13) 64 67(10) 62; N. Massu (CHI) (10) d. G. Kuerten (BRA) 63 57 64; V. Spadea (USA) d. J. Melzer (AUT) 60 61; A. Calleri (ARG) d. K. Beck (SVK) 26 63 86; I. Andreev (RUS) d. R. Schuettler (GER) (7) 67(5) 76(2) 62; J. Ferrero (ESP) (5) d. H. Arazi (MAR) 63 61; M. Fish (USA) d. J. Bjorkman (SWE) 76(6) 10 ret.; J. Nieminen (FIN) d. Y. Lu (TPE) (WC) 63 63; M. Mirnyi (BLR) d. J. Chela (ARG) (11) 36 76(0) 64; N. Kiefer (GER) (14) d. V. Voltchkov (BLR) (A) 62 64; M. Baghdatis (CYP) (WC) d. G. Carraz (FRA) 57 76(5) 75; M. Youzhny (RUS) d. X. Malisse (BEL) 62 62; J. Novak (CZE) d. T. Henman (GBR) (4) 63 63; S. Grosjean (FRA) (8) d. L. Horna (PER) 62 75; W. Arthurs (AUS) (WC) d. V. Hanescu (ROM) (WC) 64 76(4); F. Lopez (ESP) d. R. Soderling (SWE) 63 36 64; M. Safin (RUS) (9) d. K. Kucera (SVK) 60 64; F. Gonzalez (CHI) (16) d. K. Economidis (GRE) (WC) 76(6) 62; H. Lee (KOR) (WC) d. M. Zabaleta (ARG) 46 63 62; T. Haas (GER) d. M. Ancic (CRO) 61 75; A. Roddick (USA) (2) d. F. Saretta (BRA) 63 76(4).

Second Round: T. Berdych (CZE) d. R. Federer (SUI) (1) 46 75 75; T. Robredo (ESP) (15) d. F. Santoro (FRA) 16 63 64; I. Ljubicic (CRO) d. J. Johansson (SWE) 76(3) 64; T. Dent (USA) d. D. Hrbaty (SVK) 76(4) 63; C. Moya (ESP) (3) d. O. Rochus (BEL) 60 76(3); I. Karlovic (CRO) d. A. Clement (FRA) 76(4) 46 64; N. Massu (CHI) (10) d. V. Spadea (USA) 76(3) 62; I. Andreev (RUS) d. A. Calleri (ARG) w/o; M. Fish (USA) d. J. Ferrero (ESP) (5) 46 76(5) 64; M. Mirnyi (BLR) d. J. Nieminen (FIN) 63 64; N. Kiefer (GER) (14) d. M. Baghdatis (CYP) (WC) 62 36 63; M. Youzhny (RUS) d. J. Novak (CZE) 64 63; S. Grosjean (FRA) (8) d. W. Arthurs (AUS) (WC) 76(2) 63; F. Lopez (ESP) d. M. Safin (RUS) (9) 76(4) 63; F. Gonzalez (CHI) (16) d. H. Lee (KOR) (WC) 75 62; A. Roddick (USA) (2) d. T. Haas (GER) 46 63 97.

Third Round: T. Berdych (CZE) d. T. Robredo (ESP) (15) 76(2) 46 86; T. Dent (USA) d. I. Ljubicic (CRO) 64 64; C. Moya (ESP) (3) d. I. Karlovic (CRO) 46 76(3) 64; N. Massu (CHI) (10) d. I. Andreev (RUS) 63 67(4) 64; M. Fish (USA) d. M. Mirnyi (BLR) 63 46 61; M. Youzhny (RUS) d. N. Kiefer (GER) (14) 62 36 62; S. Grosjean (FRA) (8) d. F. Lopez (ESP) 67(4) 64 60; F. Gonzalez (CHI) (16) d. A. Roddick (USA) (2) 64 64.

Quarterfinals: T. Dent (USA) d. T. Berdych (CZE) 64 61; N. Massu (CHI) (10) d. C. Moya (ESP) (3) 62 75; M. Fish (USA) d. M. Youzhny (RUS) 63 64; F. Gonzalez (CHI) (16) d. S. Grosjean (FRA) (8) 62 26 64.

Semifinals: N. Massu (CHI) (10) d. T. Dent (USA) 76(5) 61; M. Fish (USA) d. F. Gonzalez (CHI) (16) 36 63 64.

Final (Gold/Silver): N. Massu (CHI) (10) d. M. Fish (USA) 63 36 26 63 64.

Play-off (Bronze): F. Gonzalez (CHI) (16) d. T. Dent (USA) 64 26 1614.

Men's Doubles
Semifinals: F. Gonzalez/N. Massu (CHI) d. M. Ancic/I. Ljubicic (CRO) (WC) 75 46 64; N. Kiefer/R. Schuettler (GER) d. M. Bhupathi/L. Paes (IND) (5) 62 63.

Final (Gold/Silver): F. Gonzalez/N. Massu (CHI) d. N. Kiefer/R. Schuettler (GER) 62 46 36 76(7) 64.

Play-Off (Bronze): M. Ancic/I. Ljubicic (CRO) (WC) d. M. Bhupathi/L. Paes (IND) 76(5) 46 1614.

Women's Singles
First Round: J. Henin-Hardenne (BEL) (1) d. B. Strycova (CZE) 63 64; M. Vento-Kabchi (VEN) d. A. Kremer (LUX) 63 64; N. Pratt (AUS) d. M. Casanova (SUI) 63 75; T. Garbin (ITA) d. A. Smashnova-Pistolesi (ISR) (13) 62 61; N. Petrova (RUS) (9) d. M. Sucha (SVK) 63 63; M. Pierce (FRA) d. A. Medina Garrigues (ESP) 63 75; M. Matevzic (SLO) d. S. Obata (JPN) 76(3) 75; V. Williams (USA) (6) d. M. Czink (HUN) 61 62; A. Myskina (RUS) (3) d. M. Serna (ESP) 60 61; K. Brandi (PUR) d. J. Kostanic (CRO) 75 61; E. Daniilidou (GRE) d. C. Castano (COL) (A) 62 61; M. Maleeva (BUL) (15) d. K. Koukalova (CZE) 61 64; F. Schiavone (ITA) (11) d. S. Asagoe (JPN) 63 76(4); Y. Cho (KOR) d. K. Kanepi (EST) (WC) 76(1) 61; F. Zuluaga (COL) d. J. Jankovic (SCG) 64 61; P. Suarez (ARG) (7) d. N. Dechy (FRA) 67(1) 76(5) 97; A. Sugiyama (JPN) (8) d. J. Zheng (CHN) 46 63 86; T. Perebiynis (UKR) (WC) d. D. Randriantefy (MAD) (WC) 63 64; A. Widjaja (INA) (WC) d. T. Tanasugarn (THA) 16 62 61; K. Sprem (CRO) (12) d. G. Dulko (ARG) 76(6) 75; S. Farina Elia (ITA) (14) d. S. Testud (FRA) 62 60; L. Raymond (USA) d. L. Kurhajcova (SVK) 64 46 63; K. Srebotnik (SLO) d. M. Sanchez Lorenzo (ESP) 63 06 64; A. Molik (AUS) d. E. Dementieva (RUS) (4) 46 60 63; S. Kuznetsova (RUS) (5) d. M. Diaz-Oliva (ARG) (WC) 63 63; A. Morigami (JPN) d. I. Benesova (CZE) 61 64; D. Hantuchova (SVK) d. C. Schaul (LUX) 61 61; P. Schnyder (SUI) (10) d. P. Mandula (HUN) 63 64; C. Rubin (USA) (16) d. S. Stosur (AUS) 62 67(8) 60; C. Black (ZIM) (WC) d. T. Pisnik (SLO) 63 57 64; M. Camerin (ITA) d. M. Jugic-Salkic (BIH) (WC) 64 63; A. Mauresmo (FRA) (2) d. C. Martinez (ESP) 61 64.

Second Round: J. Henin-Hardenne (BEL) (1) d. M. Vento-Kabchi (VEN) 62 61; N. Pratt (AUS) d. T. Garbin (ITA) 16 76(5) 62; M. Pierce (FRA) d. N. Petrova (RUS) (9) 62 61; V. Williams (USA) (6) d. M. Matevzic (SLO) 60 60; A. Myskina (RUS) (3) d. K. Brandi (PUR) 62 36 64; E. Daniilidou (GRE) d. M. Maleeva (BUL) (15) 26 64 64; F. Schiavone (ITA) (11) d. Y. Cho (KOR) 26 76(0) 64; A. Sugiyama (JPN) (8) d. T. Perebiynis (UKR) (WC) 75 64; K. Sprem (CRO) (12) d. A. Widjaja (INA) (WC) 63 61; L. Raymond (USA) d. S. Farina Elia (ITA) (14) 61 62; A. Molik (AUS) d. K. Srebotnik (SLO) 75 64; S. Kuznetsova (RUS) (5) d. A. Morigami (JPN) 76(5) 62; P. Schnyder (SUI) (10) d. D. Hantuchova (SVK) 36 61 64; C. Rubin (USA) (16) d. C. Black (ZIM) (WC) 64 36 63; A. Mauresmo (FRA) (2) d. M. Camerin (ITA) 60 61.

Third Round: J. Henin-Hardenne (BEL) (1) d. N. Pratt (AUS) 61 60; M. Pierce (FRA) d. V. Williams (USA) (6) 64 64; A. Myskina (RUS) (3) d. E. Daniilidou (GRE) 75 64; F. Schiavone (ITA) (11) d. F. Zuluaga (COL) 67(5) 61 63; A. Sugiyama (JPN) (8) d. K. Sprem (CRO) (12) 76(6) 61; A. Molik (AUS) d. L. Raymond (USA) 64 64; S. Kuznetsova (RUS) (5) d. P. Schnyder (SUI) (10) 63 63; A. Mauresmo (FRA) (2) d. C. Rubin (16) 63 61.

Quarterfinals: J. Henin-Hardenne (BEL) (1) d. M. Pierce (FRA) 64 64; A. Myskina (RUS) (3) d. F. Schiavone (ITA) (11) 61 62; A. Molik (AUS) d. A. Sugiyama (JPN) (8) 63 64; A. Mauresmo (FRA) (2) d. S. Kuznetsova (RUS) (5) 76(5) 46 62.

Semifinal: J. Henin-Hardenne (BEL) (1) d. A. Myskina (RUS) (3) 75 57 86; A. Mauresmo (FRA) (2) d. A. Molik (AUS) 76(8) 63.

Final (Gold/Silver): J. Henin-Hardenne (BEL) (1) d. A. Mauresmo (FRA) (2) 63 63.

Play-off (Bronze): A. Molik (AUS) d. A. Myskina (RUS) (3) 63 64.

Women's Doubles

Semifinals: T. Li/T. Sun (CHN) (8) d. P. Suarez/P. Tarabini (ARG) (7) 62 26 97; C. Martinez/V. Ruano Pascual (ESP) (2) d. S. Asagoe/A. Sugiyama (JPN) (5) 63 60.

Final (Gold/Silver): T. Li/T. Sun (CHN) (8) d. C. Martinez/V. Ruano Pascual (ESP) 63 63.

Play-Off (Bronze): P. Suarez/P. Tarabini (ARG) (7) d. S. Asagoe/A. Sugiyama (JPN) (5) 63 63.

Francesco Ricci Bitti and Eiichi Kawatei with Olympic women's doubles medallists

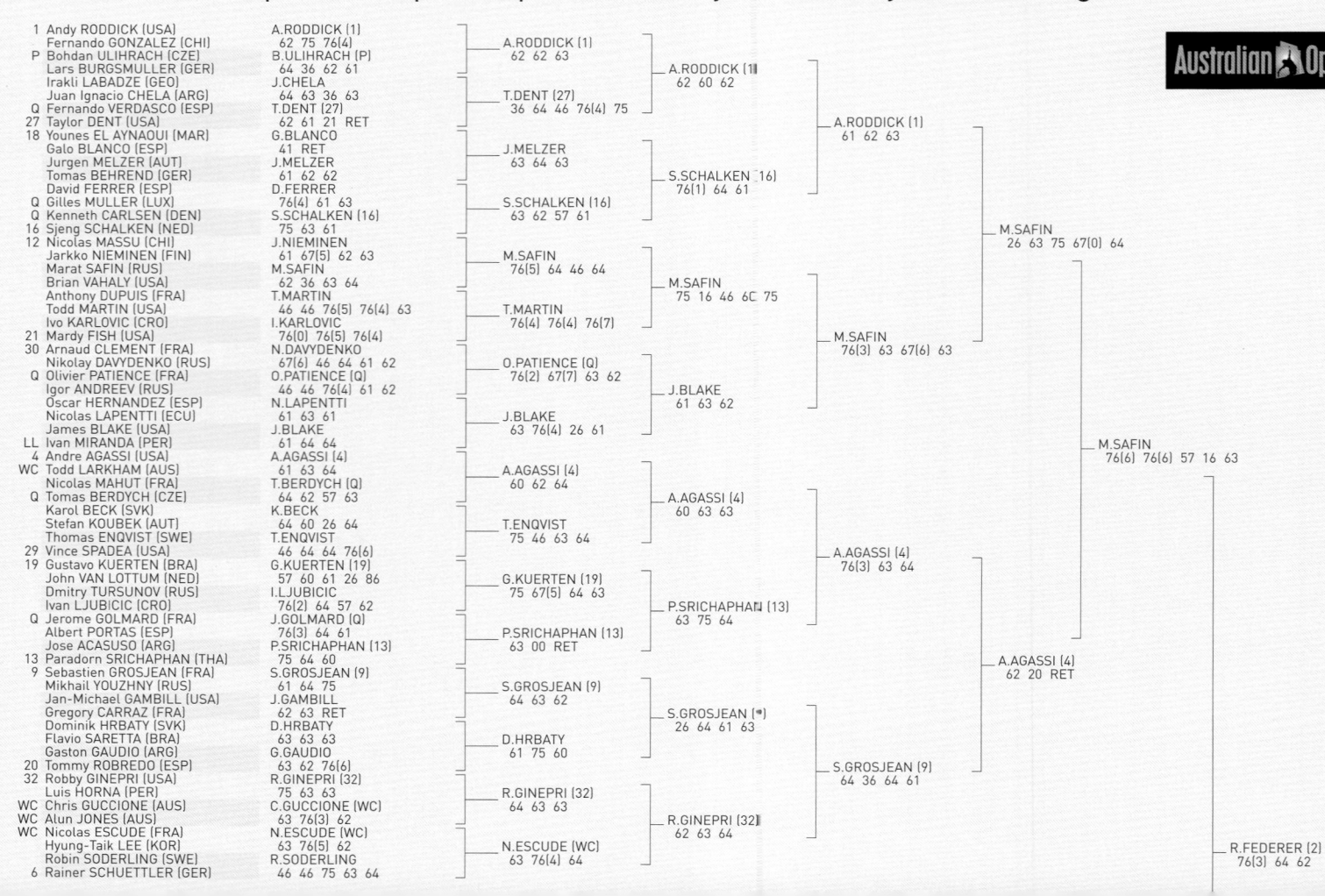

2004 Australian Open Championships, 19 January–1 February – Men's Singles

Final: R.FEDERER (2) def. M.SAFIN 7-6(3) 6-4 6-2

Quarter of Draw (Top Half)

1 Andy RODDICK (USA) def. Fernando GONZALEZ (CHI) 6-2 7-5 7-6(4)
P Bohdan ULIHRACH (CZE) def. Lars BURGSMULLER (GER) 6-4 3-6 6-2 6-1
Irakli LABADZE (GEO) lost to **J.CHELA** 6-4 6-3 3-6 6-3
Q Fernando VERDASCO (ESP) lost to **T.DENT (27)** 3-6 6-4 4-6 7-6(4) 7-5
27 Taylor DENT (USA)
Juan Ignacio CHELA (ARG)
18 Younes EL AYNAOUI (MAR) lost to **G.BLANCO (ESP)** 6-2 6-1 2-1 RET
Galo BLANCO (ESP)
Jurgen MELZER (AUT) — **J.MELZER** 4-1 RET
Tomas BEHREND (GER)
David FERRER (ESP) — **D.FERRER** 6-3 6-4 6-3
Kenneth CARLSEN (DEN) — **S.SCHALKEN (16)** 7-6(4) 6-1 6-3
Q Sjeng SCHALKEN (NED)
16 Sjeng SCHALKEN (NED) — **S.SCHALKEN** 6-3 6-2 5-7 6-1
12 Nicolas MASSU (CHI) — **J.NIEMINEN** 7-5 6-3 6-1
Jarkko NIEMINEN (FIN) — **J.NIEMINEN** 6-1 6-7(5) 6-2 6-3
Marat SAFIN (RUS) — **M.SAFIN** 6-2 3-6 6-3 6-4
Brian VAHALY (USA)
Anthony DUPUIS (FRA) — **T.MARTIN** 7-6(5) 7-6(4) 6-3
Todd MARTIN (USA)
Ivo KARLOVIC (CRO) — **I.KARLOVIC** 7-6(0) 7-6(5) 7-6(4)
21 Mardy FISH (USA) — **N.DAVYDENKO** 6-7(6) 4-6 6-4 6-1 6-2
30 Arnaud CLEMENT (FRA)
Nikolay DAVYDENKO (RUS)
Q Olivier PATIENCE (FRA) — **O.PATIENCE (Q)** 4-6 6-1 6-1 6-2
Igor ANDREEV (RUS)
Oscar HERNANDEZ (ESP) — **N.LAPENTTI** 6-1 6-3 6-1
Nicolas LAPENTTI (ECU)
James BLAKE (USA) — **J.BLAKE** 6-1 6-4 6-4
LL Ivan MIRANDA (PER)
4 Andre AGASSI (USA) — **A.AGASSI (4)** 6-1 6-3 6-4
WC Todd LARKHAM (AUS)
Tomas BERDYCH (CZE) — **T.BERDYCH (Q)** 6-4 6-2 5-7 6-3
Q Karol BECK (SVK) — **K.BECK** 6-4 6-0 2-6 6-4
Stefan KOUBEK (AUT) — **T.ENQVIST** 4-6 6-4 6-4 7-6(6)
Thomas ENQVIST (SWE)
29 Vince SPADEA (USA) — **G.KUERTEN (19)** 5-7 6-0 6-1 2-6 8-6
19 Gustavo KUERTEN (BRA)
John VAN LOTTUM (NED)
Dmitry TURSUNOV (RUS) — **I.LJUBICIC** 7-6(2) 6-4 5-7 6-2
Ivan LJUBICIC (CRO)
Q Jerome GOLMARD (FRA) — **J.GOLMARD (Q)** 7-6(3) 6-4 6-1
Jose ACASUSO (ARG)
13 Paradorn SRICHAPHAN (THA) — **P.SRICHAPHAN (13)** 6-3 0-0 RET
9 Sebastien GROSJEAN (FRA) — **S.GROSJEAN (9)** 6-1 6-4 7-5
Mikhail YOUZHNY (RUS)
Jan-Michael GAMBILL (USA) — **J.GAMBILL** 6-1 6-4 7-5
Gregory CARRAZ (FRA)
Dominik HRBATY (SVK) — **D.HRBATY** 6-2 6-3 RET
Flavio SARETTA (BRA)
Gaston GAUDIO (ARG) — **G.GAUDIO** 6-3 6-3
20 Tommy ROBREDO (ESP) — **R.GINEPRI (32)** 6-3 6-2 7-6(6)
32 Robby GINEPRI (USA)
Luis HORNA (PER)
WC Chris GUCCIONE (AUS) — **C.GUCCIONE (WC)** 6-3 7-6(3) 6-2
WC Alun JONES (AUS)
Nicolas ESCUDE (FRA) — **N.ESCUDE (WC)** 7-5 6-3 6-2
Hyung-Taik LEE (KOR)
WC Robin SODERLING (SWE) — **R.SODERLING** 7-6(5) 6-2
6 Rainer SCHUETTLER (GER) — 4-6 4-6 7-5 6-3 6-4

Round Results

- **A.RODDICK (1)** def. B.ULIHRACH (P) 6-2 6-2 6-3
- **T.DENT (27)** def. J.CHELA 6-4 6-3 3-6 6-3
- **A.RODDICK (1)** def. T.DENT (27) 3-6 6-4 4-6 7-6(4) 7-5
- **J.MELZER** def. G.BLANCO 6-3 6-4 6-3
- **S.SCHALKEN (16)** def. D.FERRER 6-3 6-2 5-7 6-1
- **S.SCHALKEN (16)** def. J.MELZER 7-6(4) 6-1 6-3
- **A.RODDICK (1)** def. S.SCHALKEN (16) 6-1 6-2 6-3
- **M.SAFIN** def. J.NIEMINEN 7-6(5) 6-4 4-6 6-4
- **T.MARTIN** def. I.KARLOVIC 7-6(4) 7-6(4) 7-6(7)
- **M.SAFIN** def. T.MARTIN 7-5 1-6 4-6 6-0 7-5
- **O.PATIENCE (Q)** def. N.DAVYDENKO 7-6(2) 6-7(7) 6-3 6-2
- **J.BLAKE** def. N.LAPENTTI 6-3 7-6(4) 2-6 6-1
- **J.BLAKE** def. O.PATIENCE 6-1 6-3 6-2
- **M.SAFIN** def. J.BLAKE 7-6(3) 6-3 6-7(6) 6-3
- **M.SAFIN** def. A.RODDICK (1) 2-6 6-3 7-5 6-7(0) 6-4
- **A.AGASSI (4)** def. T.BERDYCH (Q) 6-1 6-3 6-4
- **T.ENQVIST** def. K.BECK 6-4 6-0 2-6 6-4
- **A.AGASSI (4)** def. T.ENQVIST 6-0 6-2 6-4
- **I.LJUBICIC** def. G.KUERTEN (19) 7-5 6-7(5) 6-4 6-3
- **P.SRICHAPHAN (13)** def. J.GOLMARD (Q) 7-6(2) 6-4 5-7 6-2
- **P.SRICHAPHAN (13)** def. I.LJUBICIC 6-3 7-5 6-4
- **A.AGASSI (4)** def. P.SRICHAPHAN (13) 7-6(3) 6-3 6-4
- **S.GROSJEAN (9)** def. J.GAMBILL 6-4 6-3 6-2
- **D.HRBATY** def. G.GAUDIO 6-1 7-5 6-0
- **S.GROSJEAN (9)** def. D.HRBATY 2-6 6-4 6-1 6-3
- **R.GINEPRI (32)** def. C.GUCCIONE (WC) 6-4 6-3 6-3
- **N.ESCUDE (WC)** def. R.SODERLING 6-3 7-6(4) 6-4
- **R.GINEPRI (32)** def. N.ESCUDE (WC) 6-2 6-3 6-4
- **S.GROSJEAN (9)** def. R.GINEPRI (32) 6-4 3-6 6-1
- **A.AGASSI (4)** def. S.GROSJEAN (9) 6-2 2-0 RET
- **M.SAFIN** def. A.AGASSI (4) 7-6(6) 7-6(6) 5-7 1-6 6-3
- **R.FEDERER (2)** def. M.SAFIN 7-6(3) 6-4 6-2

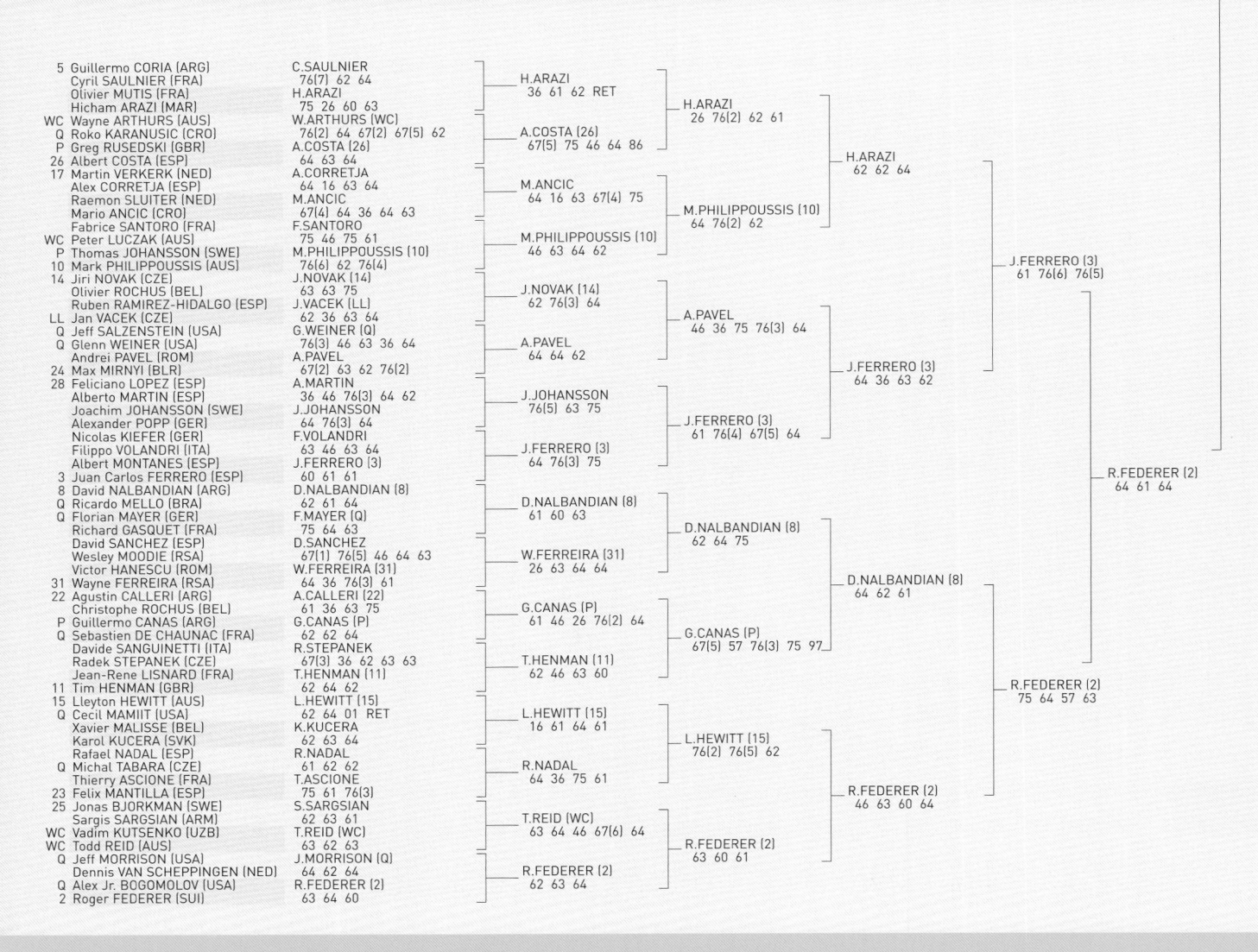

Elite Tournaments: 2004 Australian Open Drawsheets

Men's Singles — Bottom Half

Seed	Player	R1	R2	R3	R4	QF	SF	F
5	Guillermo CORIA [ARG]	C.SAULNIER 76(7) 62 64	H.ARAZI 36 61 62 RET	H.ARAZI 75 26 60 63	H.ARAZI 26 76(2) 62 61	H.ARAZI 62 62 64	J.FERRERO [3] 61 76(6) 76(5)	R.FEDERER [2] 64 61 64
	Cyril SAULNIER [FRA]							
	Olivier MUTIS [FRA]	H.ARAZI						
WC	Hicham ARAZI [MAR]							
WC	Wayne ARTHURS [AUS]	W.ARTHURS [WC] 76(2) 64 67(2) 67(5) 62	A.COSTA [26] 67(5) 75 46 64 86					
Q	Roko KARANUSIC [CRO]							
P	Greg RUSEDSKI [GBR]	A.COSTA [26] 64 63 64						
26	Albert COSTA [ESP]							
17	Martin VERKERK [NED]	A.CORRETJA 64 16 63 64	M.ANCIC 64 16 63 67(4) 75	M.PHILIPPOUSSIS [10] 64 76(2) 62				
	Alex CORRETJA [ESP]							
	Raemon SLUITER [NED]	M.ANCIC 67(4) 64 36 64 63						
	Mario ANCIC [CRO]							
	Fabrice SANTORO [FRA]	F.SANTORO 75 46 75 61	M.PHILIPPOUSSIS [10] 46 63 64 62					
WC	Peter LUCZAK [AUS]							
10	Mark PHILIPPOUSSIS [AUS]	M.PHILIPPOUSSIS [10] 76(6) 62 76(4)						
14	Jiri NOVAK [CZE]		J.NOVAK [14] 62 76(3) 64	J.FERRERO [3] 64 36 63 62	J.FERRERO [3] 64 36 63 62			
	Olivier ROCHUS [BEL]	J.NOVAK [14] 63 63 75						
LL	Ruben RAMIREZ-HIDALGO [ESP]							
	Jan VACEK [CZE]	J.VACEK [LL] 62 36 63 64	A.PAVEL 46 36 75 76(3) 64					
Q	Jeff SALZENSTEIN [USA]							
Q	Glenn WEINER [USA]	G.WEINER [Q] 76(3) 46 63 36 64						
	Andrei PAVEL [ROM]	A.PAVEL						
24	Max MIRNYI [BLR]	67(2) 63 62 76(2)	A.PAVEL 64 64 62	J.FERRERO [3] 61 76(4) 67(5) 64				
	Feliciano LOPEZ [ESP]							
28	Alberto MARTIN [ESP]	A.MARTIN 36 46 76(3) 64 62	J.JOHANSSON 76(5) 63 75					
	Joachim JOHANSSON [SWE]							
	Alexander POPP [GER]	J.JOHANSSON 64 76(3) 64						
	Nicolas KIEFER [GER]							
	Filippo VOLANDRI [ITA]	F.VOLANDRI 63 46 63 64	J.FERRERO [3] 64 76(3) 75					
	Albert MONTANES [ESP]							
3	Juan Carlos FERRERO [ESP]	J.FERRERO [3] 60 61 61						
8	David NALBANDIAN [ARG]		D.NALBANDIAN [8] 61 60 63	D.NALBANDIAN [8] 62 64 75	D.NALBANDIAN [8] 64 62 61	R.FEDERER [2] 75 64 57 63		
Q	Ricardo MELLO [BRA]	D.NALBANDIAN [8] 62 61 64						
	Florian MAYER [GER]							
Q	Richard GASQUET [FRA]	F.MAYER [Q] 75 64 63	W.FERREIRA [31] 26 63 64 64					
	David SANCHEZ [ESP]							
	Wesley MOODIE [RSA]	D.SANCHEZ 67(1) 76(5) 46 64 63						
31	Wayne FERREIRA [RSA]							
22	Agustin CALLERI [ARG]	W.FERREIRA [31] 64 36 76(3) 61	G.CANAS [P] 61 46 26 76(2) 64	G.CANAS [P] 67(5) 57 76(3) 75 97				
	Christophe ROCHUS [BEL]							
P	Guillermo CANAS [ARG]	G.CANAS [P] 61 36 63 61						
Q	Sebastien DE CHAUNAC [FRA]							
	Davide SANGUINETTI [ITA]	R.STEPANEK 62 62 64	T.HENMAN [11] 62 46 63 60					
	Radek STEPANEK [CZE]							
	Jean-Rene LISNARD [FRA]	T.HENMAN [11] 67(3) 36 62 63						
11	Tim HENMAN [GBR]							
15	Lleyton HEWITT [AUS]	L.HEWITT [15] 62 64 62	L.HEWITT [15] 16 61 64 61	L.HEWITT [15] 76(2) 76(5) 62	R.FEDERER [2] 46 63 60 64			
Q	Cecil MAMIIT [USA]							
	Xavier MALISSE [BEL]	K.KUCERA 62 64 01 RET						
	Karol KUCERA [SVK]							
	Rafael NADAL [ESP]	R.NADAL 62 63 64	R.NADAL 64 36 75 61					
Q	Michal TABARA [CZE]							
	Thierry ASCIONE [FRA]	T.ASCIONE 61 62 62						
23	Felix MANTILLA [ESP]							
	Jonas BJORKMAN [SWE]	S.SARGSIAN 75 61 76(3)	T.REID [WC] 63 64 46 67(6) 64	R.FEDERER [2] 62 63 64				
25	Sargis SARGSIAN [ARM]							
	Vadim KUTSENKO [UZB]	T.REID [WC] 62 63 61						
WC	Todd REID [AUS]							
WC	Jeff MORRISON [USA]	J.MORRISON [Q] 64 62 64	R.FEDERER [2] 63 64 60					
	Dennis VAN SCHEPPINGEN [NED]							
Q	Alex Jr. BOGOMOLOV [USA]	R.FEDERER [2] 63 62 63						
2	Roger FEDERER [SUI]							

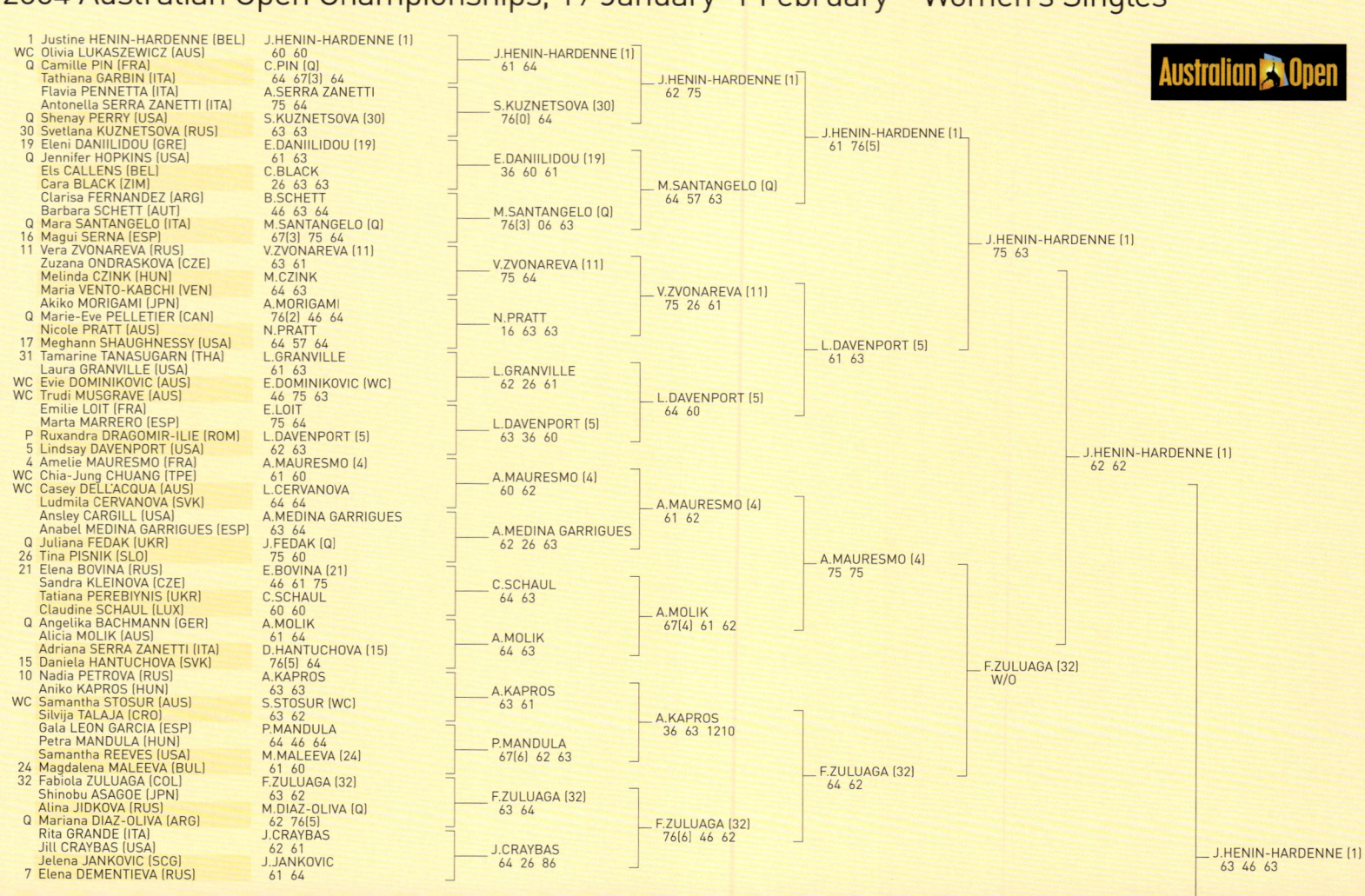

2004 Australian Open Championships, 19 January–1 February – Women's Singles

Top Half

Seed	Player	R1	R2	R3	R4	QF	SF	F
1	Justine HENIN-HARDENNE [BEL]	J.HENIN-HARDENNE [1] 60 60	J.HENIN-HARDENNE [1] 61 64	J.HENIN-HARDENNE [1] 62 75	J.HENIN-HARDENNE [1] 61 76(5)	J.HENIN-HARDENNE [1] 75 63	J.HENIN-HARDENNE [1] 62 62	J.HENIN-HARDENNE [1] 63 46 63
WC	Olivia LUKASZEWICZ [AUS]							
Q	Camille PIN [Q]	C.PIN [Q] 64 67(3) 64						
	Tathiana GARBIN [ITA]							
	Flavia PENNETTA [ITA]	A.SERRA ZANETTI 75 64	S.KUZNETSOVA [30] 76(0) 64					
	Antonella SERRA ZANETTI [ITA]							
Q	Shenay PERRY [USA]	S.KUZNETSOVA [30] 63 63						
30	Svetlana KUZNETSOVA [RUS]							
19	Eleni DANIILIDOU [GRE]	E.DANIILIDOU [19] 61 63	E.DANIILIDOU [19] 36 60 61	M.SANTANGELO [Q] 64 57 63				
	Jennifer HOPKINS [USA]							
	Els CALLENS [BEL]	C.BLACK 26 63 63						
	Cara BLACK [ZIM]							
	Clarisa FERNANDEZ [ARG]	B.SCHETT 46 63 64	M.SANTANGELO [Q] 76(3) 06 63					
	Barbara SCHETT [AUT]							
Q	Mara SANTANGELO [Q]	M.SANTANGELO [Q] 67(3) 75 64						
16	Magui SERNA [ESP]							
11	Vera ZVONAREVA [RUS]	V.ZVONAREVA [11] 63 61	V.ZVONAREVA [11] 75 64	V.ZVONAREVA [11] 75 26 61	L.DAVENPORT [5] 61 63			
	Zuzana ONDRASKOVA [CZE]							
	Melinda CZINK [HUN]	M.CZINK 64 63						
	Maria VENTO-KABCHI [VEN]							
	Akiko MORIGAMI [JPN]	A.MORIGAMI 76(2) 46 64	N.PRATT 16 63 63					
Q	Marie-Eve PELLETIER [CAN]							
17	Nicole PRATT [AUS]	N.PRATT 64 57 64						
	Meghann SHAUGHNESSY [USA]							
31	Tamarine TANASUGARN [THA]	L.GRANVILLE 61 63	L.GRANVILLE 62 26 61	L.DAVENPORT [5] 64 60				
	Laura GRANVILLE [USA]							
WC	Evie DOMINIKOVIC [WC]	E.DOMINIKOVIC [WC] 46 75 63						
WC	Trudi MUSGRAVE [AUS]							
	Emilie LOIT [FRA]	E.LOIT 75 64	L.DAVENPORT [5] 63 36 60					
	Marta MARRERO [ESP]							
P	Ruxandra DRAGOMIR-ILIE [ROM]	L.DAVENPORT [5] 62 63						
5	Lindsay DAVENPORT [USA]							

Bottom Half

Seed	Player	R1	R2	R3	R4	QF	SF	F
4	Amelie MAURESMO [FRA]	A.MAURESMO [4] 61 60	A.MAURESMO [4] 60 62	A.MAURESMO [4] 61 62	A.MAURESMO [4] 75 75	F.ZULUAGA [32] W/O		
WC	Chia-Jung CHUANG [TPE]							
WC	Casey DELLACQUA [AUS]	L.CERVANOVA 64 64						
	Ludmila CERVANOVA [SVK]							
	Anabel MEDINA GARRIGUES [ESP]	A.MEDINA GARRIGUES 63 64	A.MEDINA GARRIGUES 62 26 63					
	Ansley CARGILL [USA]							
Q	Juliana FEDAK [UKR]	J.FEDAK [Q] 75 60						
26	Tina PISNIK [SLO]							
21	Elena BOVINA [RUS]	E.BOVINA [21] 46 61 75	C.SCHAUL 64 63	A.MOLIK 67(4) 61 62				
	Sandra KLEINOVA [CZE]							
	Tatiana PEREBIYNIS [UKR]	C.SCHAUL 60 60						
Q	Claudine SCHAUL [LUX]							
Q	Angelika BACHMANN [GER]	A.MOLIK 61 64	A.MOLIK 64 63					
	Alicia MOLIK [AUS]							
15	Adriana SERRA ZANETTI [ITA]	D.HANTUCHOVA [15] 76(5) 64						
10	Daniela HANTUCHOVA [SVK]							
	Nadia PETROVA [RUS]	A.KAPROS 63 63	A.KAPROS 63 61	A.KAPROS 36 63 1210	F.ZULUAGA [32] 64 62			
	Aniko KAPROS [HUN]							
WC	Samantha STOSUR [AUS]	S.STOSUR [WC] 63 62						
	Silvija TALAJA [CRO]							
	Gala LEON GARCIA [ESP]	P.MANDULA 64 46 64	P.MANDULA 67(6) 62 63					
	Petra MANDULA [HUN]							
	Samantha REEVES [USA]	M.MALEEVA [24] 61 60						
24	Magdalena MALEEVA [BUL]							
32	Fabiola ZULUAGA [COL]	F.ZULUAGA [32] 63 62	F.ZULUAGA [32] 63 64	F.ZULUAGA [32] 76(6) 46 62				
	Shinobu ASAGOE [JPN]							
Q	Mariana DIAZ-OLIVA [ARG]	M.DIAZ-OLIVA [Q] 62 76(5)						
	Rita GRANDE [ITA]							
	Jill CRAYBAS [USA]	J.CRAYBAS 62 61	J.CRAYBAS 64 26 86					
	Jelena JANKOVIC [SCG]							
7	Elena DEMENTIEVA [RUS]	J.JANKOVIC 61 64						

Champion: J.HENIN-HARDENNE [1] 63 46 63

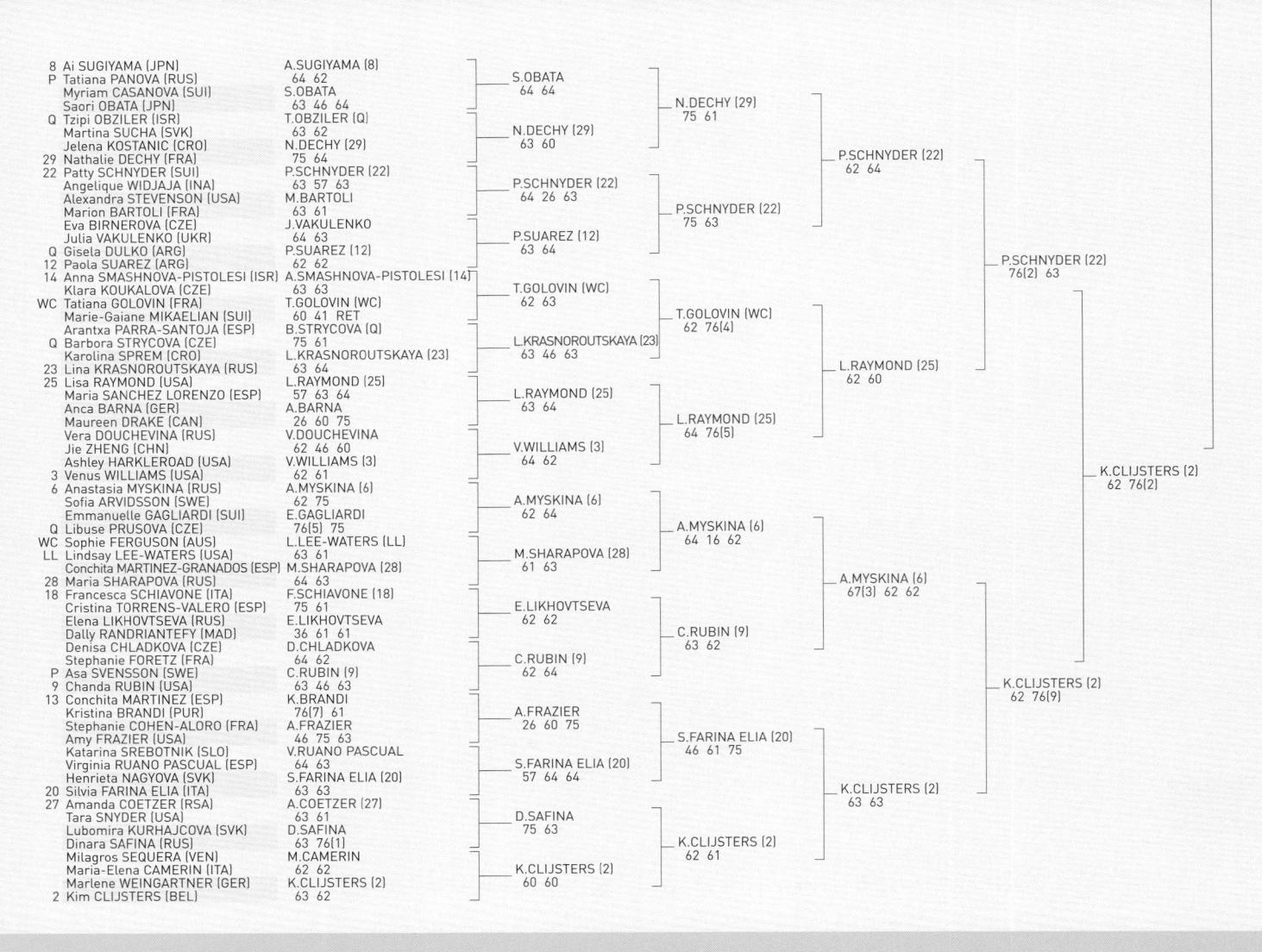

Elite Tournaments: 2004 Australian Open Drawsheets

Women's Singles Draw (partial)

Seed/Status	Player	R1	R2	R3	R4	QF
8	Ai SUGIYAMA (JPN)	A.SUGIYAMA (8) 64 62	S.OBATA 64 64	N.DECHY [29] 75 61	P.SCHNYDER [22] 62 64	P.SCHNYDER [22] 76(2) 63
P	Tatiana PANOVA (RUS)					
	Myriam CASANOVA (SUI)	S.OBATA 63 46 64				
	Saori OBATA (JPN)					
Q	Tzipi OBZILER (ISR)	T.OBZILER (Q) 63 62	N.DECHY [29] 63 60			
	Martina SUCHA (SVK)					
	Jelena KOSTANIC (CRO)	N.DECHY [29] 75 64				
29	Nathalie DECHY (FRA)					
22	Patty SCHNYDER (SUI)	P.SCHNYDER [22] 63 57 63	P.SCHNYDER [22] 64 26 63	P.SUAREZ [12] 75 63		
	Angelique WIDJAJA (INA)					
	Alexandra STEVENSON (USA)	M.BARTOLI 63 61	J.VAKULENKO 64 63			
	Marion BARTOLI (FRA)					
	Eva BIRNEROVA (CZE)	J.VAKULENKO 64 63				
	Julia VAKULENKO (UKR)					
	Gisela DULKO (ARG)	P.SUAREZ [12] 62 62	P.SUAREZ [12] 63 64			
12	Paola SUAREZ (ARG)					
14	Anna SMASHNOVA-PISTOLESI (ISR)	A.SMASHNOVA-PISTOLESI [14] 63 63	T.GOLOVIN (WC) 62 63	T.GOLOVIN (WC) 62 76(4)	L.RAYMOND [25] 62 60	
	Kiara KOUKALOVA (CZE)					
WC	Tatiana GOLOVIN (FRA)	T.GOLOVIN (WC) 60 41 RET				
	Marie-Gaiane MIKAELIAN (SUI)					
Q	Arantxa PARRA-SANTOJA (ESP)	B.STRYCOVA (Q) 75 61	L.KRASNOROUTSKAYA [23] 63 46 63			
	Barbora STRYCOVA (CZE)					
	Karolina SPREM (CRO)	L.KRASNOROUTSKAYA [23] 63 64				
23	Lina KRASNOROUTSKAYA (RUS)					
25	Lisa RAYMOND (USA)	L.RAYMOND [25] 57 63 64	L.RAYMOND [25] 63 64	L.RAYMOND [25] 64 76(5)		
	Maria SANCHEZ LORENZO (ESP)					
	Anca BARNA (GER)	A.BARNA 26 60 75	V.DOUCHEVINA 62 46 60			
	Maureen DRAKE (CAN)					
	Vera DOUCHEVINA (RUS)	V.DOUCHEVINA 62 46 60				
3	Jie ZHENG (CHN)					
	Venus WILLIAMS (USA)	V.WILLIAMS [3] 62 61	V.WILLIAMS [3] 64 62	A.MYSKINA [6] 62 61	A.MYSKINA [6] 64 16 62	A.MYSKINA [6] 67(3) 62 62
	Ashley HARKLEROAD (USA)					
6	Anastasia MYSKINA (RUS)	A.MYSKINA [6] 62 75				
	Sofia ARVIDSSON (SWE)					
	Emmanuelle GAGLIARDI (SUI)	E.GAGLIARDI 76(5) 75	M.SHARAPOVA [28] 61 63	M.SHARAPOVA [28] 64 63		
Q	Libuse PRUSOVA (CZE)					
WC	Sophie FERGUSON (AUS)	L.LEE-WATERS (LL) 63 61				
LL	Lindsay LEE-WATERS (USA)					
28	Maria SHARAPOVA (RUS)	M.SHARAPOVA [28] 64 63				
18	Francesca SCHIAVONE (ITA)	F.SCHIAVONE 75 61	E.LIKHOVTSEVA 62 62	E.LIKHOVTSEVA 62 62	C.RUBIN [9] 63 62	C.RUBIN [9] 63 62
	Cristina TORRENS-VALERO (ESP)					
	Elena LIKHOVTSEVA (RUS)	E.LIKHOVTSEVA 36 61 61				
	Dally RANDRIANTEFY (MAD)					
	Denisa CHLADKOVA (CZE)	D.CHLADKOVA 64 62	C.RUBIN [9] 62 64			
	Stephanie FORETZ (FRA)					
P	Asa SVENSSON (SWE)	K.BRANDI 76(7) 61				
9	Chanda RUBIN (USA)					
13	Conchita MARTINEZ (ESP)	A.FRAZIER 46 75 63	A.FRAZIER 26 60 75	S.FARINA ELIA [20] 46 61 75	S.FARINA ELIA [20] 46 61 75	K.CLIJSTERS [2] 63 63
	Kristina BRANDI (PUR)					
	Stephanie COHEN-ALORO (FRA)					
	Amy FRAZIER (USA)					
	Katarina SREBOTNIK (SLO)	V.RUANO PASCUAL 64 63	S.FARINA ELIA [20] 63 63			
	Virginia RUANO PASCUAL (ESP)					
	Henrieta NAGYOVA (SVK)	S.FARINA ELIA [20] 57 64 64				
20	Silvia FARINA ELIA (ITA)					
27	Amanda COETZER (RSA)	A.COETZER [27] 63 61	D.SAFINA 75 63	D.SAFINA 63 61	K.CLIJSTERS [2] 62 61	K.CLIJSTERS [2] 62 76(2)
	Tara SNYDER (USA)					
	Lubomira KURHAJCOVA (SVK)	D.SAFINA 63 76(1)				
	Dinara SAFINA (RUS)					
	Milagros SEQUERA (VEN)	M.CAMERIN 62 62	K.CLIJSTERS [2] 60 60			
	Marie-Elena CAMERIN (ITA)					
2	Kim CLIJSTERS (BEL)	K.CLIJSTERS [2] 63 62				

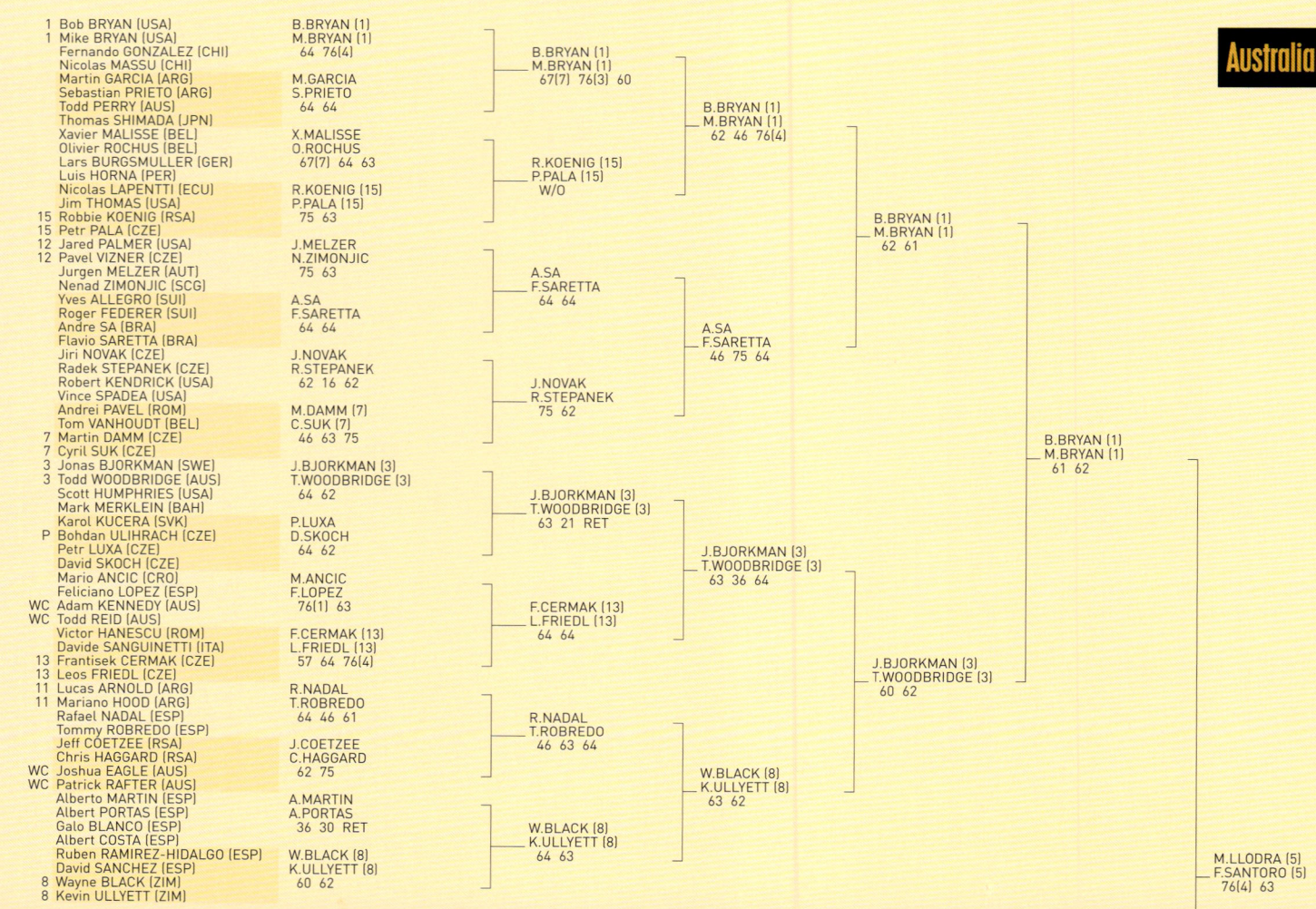

2004 Australian Open Championships, 19 January–1 February – Men's Doubles

1 Bob BRYAN (USA)
1 Mike BRYAN (USA)
   Fernando GONZALEZ (CHI)
   Nicolas MASSU (CHI)
   Martin GARCIA (ARG)
   Sebastian PRIETO (ARG)
   Todd PERRY (AUS)
   Thomas SHIMADA (JPN)
   Xavier MALISSE (BEL)
   Olivier ROCHUS (BEL)
   Lars BURGSMULLER (GER)
   Luis HORNA (PER)
   Nicolas LAPENTTI (ECU)
   Jim THOMAS (USA)
15 Robbie KOENIG (RSA)
15 Petr PALA (CZE)
12 Jared PALMER (USA)
12 Pavel VIZNER (CZE)
   Jurgen MELZER (AUT)
   Nenad ZIMONJIC (SCG)
   Yves ALLEGRO (SUI)
   Roger FEDERER (SUI)
   Andre SA (BRA)
   Flavio SARETTA (BRA)
   Jiri NOVAK (CZE)
   Radek STEPANEK (CZE)
   Robert KENDRICK (USA)
   Vince SPADEA (USA)
   Andrei PAVEL (ROM)
   Tom VANHOUDT (BEL)
7 Martin DAMM (CZE)
7 Cyril SUK (CZE)
3 Jonas BJORKMAN (SWE)
3 Todd WOODBRIDGE (AUS)
   Scott HUMPHRIES (USA)
   Mark MERKLEIN (BAH)
   Karol KUCERA (SVK)
P Bohdan ULIHRACH (CZE)
   Petr LUXA (CZE)
   David SKOCH (CZE)
   Mario ANCIC (CRO)
   Feliciano LOPEZ (ESP)
WC Adam KENNEDY (AUS)
WC Todd REID (AUS)
   Victor HANESCU (ROM)
   Davide SANGUINETTI (ITA)
13 Frantisek CERMAK (CZE)
13 Leos FRIEDL (CZE)
11 Lucas ARNOLD (ARG)
11 Mariano HOOD (ARG)
   Rafael NADAL (ESP)
   Tommy ROBREDO (ESP)
WC Jeff COETZEE (RSA)
WC Chris HAGGARD (RSA)
   Joshua EAGLE (AUS)
   Patrick RAFTER (AUS)
   Alberto MARTIN (ESP)
   Albert PORTAS (ESP)
   Galo BLANCO (ESP)
   Albert COSTA (ESP)
   Ruben RAMIREZ-HIDALGO (ESP)
   David SANCHEZ (ESP)
8 Wayne BLACK (ZIM)
8 Kevin ULLYETT (ZIM)

Round 1:
B.BRYAN [1] / M.BRYAN [1] 64 76(4)
M.GARCIA / S.PRIETO 64 64
X.MALISSE / O.ROCHUS 67(7) 64 63
R.KOENIG [15] / P.PALA [15] W/O
J.MELZER / N.ZIMONJIC 75 63
A.SA / F.SARETTA 64 64
J.NOVAK / R.STEPANEK 62 16 62
M.DAMM [7] / C.SUK [7] 46 63 75
J.BJORKMAN [3] / T.WOODBRIDGE [3] 64 62
P.LUXA / D.SKOCH 64 62
M.ANCIC / F.LOPEZ 76(1) 63
F.CERMAK [13] / L.FRIEDL [13] 57 64 76(4)
R.NADAL / T.ROBREDO 64 46 61
J.COETZEE / C.HAGGARD 62 75
A.MARTIN / A.PORTAS 36 30 RET
W.BLACK [8] / K.ULLYETT [8] 64 63

Round 2:
B.BRYAN [1] / M.BRYAN [1] 67(7) 76(3) 60
R.KOENIG [15] / P.PALA [15] 75 63
A.SA / F.SARETTA 64 64
J.NOVAK / R.STEPANEK 75 62
J.BJORKMAN [3] / T.WOODBRIDGE [3] 63 21 RET
F.CERMAK [13] / L.FRIEDL [13] 64 64
R.NADAL / T.ROBREDO 46 63 64
W.BLACK [8] / K.ULLYETT [8] 63 62

Round 3:
B.BRYAN [1] / M.BRYAN [1] 62 46 76(4)
A.SA / F.SARETTA 46 75 64
J.BJORKMAN [3] / T.WOODBRIDGE [3] 63 36 64
W.BLACK [8] / K.ULLYETT [8] 64 63

Quarterfinals:
B.BRYAN [1] / M.BRYAN [1] 62 61
J.BJORKMAN [3] / T.WOODBRIDGE [3] 60 62

Semifinal:
B.BRYAN [1] / M.BRYAN [1] 61 62

Final:
M.LLODRA [5] / F.SANTORO [5] 76(4) 63

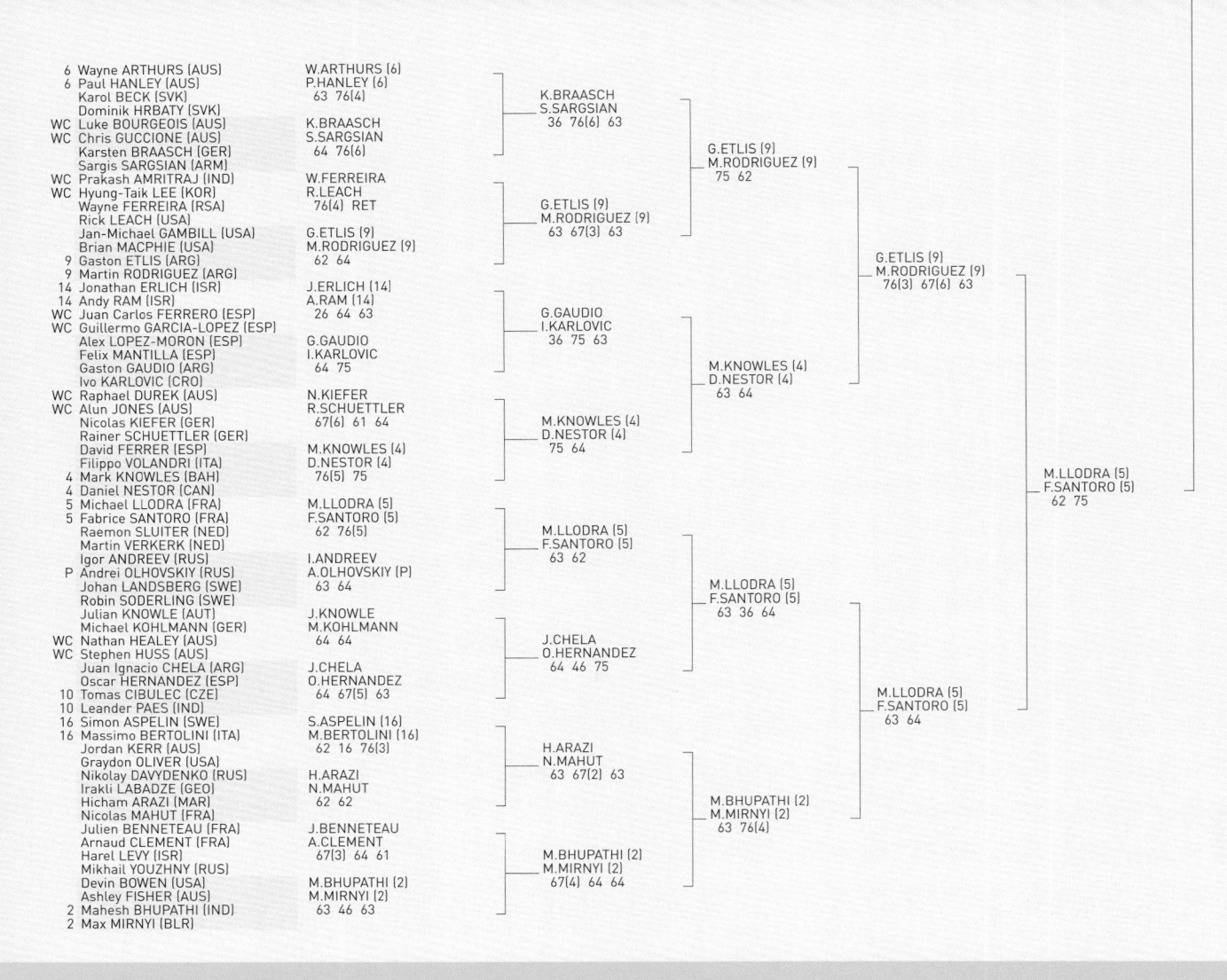

2004 Australian Open – Men's Doubles Draw (partial)

```
6  Wayne ARTHURS [AUS]     ┐
6  Paul HANLEY [AUS]       ├ W.ARTHURS [6]
   Karol BECK [SVK]        │ P.HANLEY [6]
   Dominik HRBATY [SVK]    ┘ 63 76(4)                    ┐
WC Luke BOURGEOIS [AUS]    ┐                             ├ K.BRAASCH
WC Chris GUCCIONE [AUS]    ├ K.BRAASCH                   │ S.SARGSIAN
   Karsten BRAASCH [GER]   │ S.SARGSIAN                  │ 36 76(6) 63
   Sargis SARGSIAN [ARM]   ┘ 64 76(6)                    ┘                           ┐
WC Prakash AMRITRAJ [IND]  ┐                             ┐                           │
WC Hyung-Taik LEE [KOR]    ├ W.FERREIRA                  │                           │
   Wayne FERREIRA [RSA]    │ R.LEACH                     ├ G.ETLIS [9]               │
   Rick LEACH [USA]        ┘ 76(4) RET                   │ M.RODRIGUEZ [9]           │
   Jan-Michael GAMBILL[USA]┐                             │ 63 67(3) 63               │
   Brian MACPHIE [USA]     ├ G.ETLIS [9]                 │                           ├ G.ETLIS [9]
9  Gaston ETLIS [ARG]      │ M.RODRIGUEZ [9]             ┘                           │ M.RODRIGUEZ [9]
9  Martin RODRIGUEZ [ARG]  ┘ 62 64                                                   │ 76(3) 67(6) 63
14 Jonathan ERLICH [ISR]   ┐                             ┐                           │
14 Andy RAM [ISR]          ├ J.ERLICH [14]               │                           │
WC Juan Carlos FERRERO[ESP]│ A.RAM [14]                  ├ G.GAUDIO                  │
   Alex LOPEZ-MORON [ESP]  ┘ 26 64 63                    │ I.KARLOVIC                │
   Guillermo GARCIA-LOPEZ[ESP]┐                          │ 36 75 63                  │
   Felix MANTILLA [ESP]    ├ G.GAUDIO                    ┘                           ┘
   Gaston GAUDIO [ARG]     │ I.KARLOVIC
   Ivo KARLOVIC [CRO]      ┘ 64 75                                                                  ┐
WC Raphael DUREK [AUS]     ┐                             ┐                                          │
WC Alun JONES [AUS]        ├ N.KIEFER                    │                                          │
   Nicolas KIEFER [GER]    │ R.SCHUETTLER                ├ M.KNOWLES [4]                            │
   Rainer SCHUETTLER [GER] ┘ 67(6) 61 64                 │ D.NESTOR [4]                             │
   David FERRER [ESP]      ┐                             │ 75 64                                    │
   Filippo VOLANDRI [ITA]  ├ M.KNOWLES [4]               ┘                                          ├ M.LLODRA [5]
4  Mark KNOWLES [BAH]      │ D.NESTOR [4]                                                           │ F.SANTORO
4  Daniel NESTOR [CAN]     ┘ 76(5) 75                                                               │ 62 75
5  Michael LLODRA [FRA]    ┐                             ┐                           ┐              │
5  Fabrice SANTORO [FRA]   ├ M.LLODRA [5]                │                           │              │
   Raemon SLUITER [NED]    │ F.SANTORO [5]               ├ M.LLODRA [5]              │              │
   Martin VERKERK [NED]    ┘ 62 76(5)                    │ F.SANTORO [5]             │              │
   Igor ANDREEV [RUS]      ┐                             │ 63 62                     │              │
P  Andrei OLHOVSKIY [RUS]  ├ I.ANDREEV                   ┘                           ├ M.LLODRA [5] │
   Johan LANDSBERG [SWE]   │ A.OLHOVSKIY [P]                                         │ F.SANTORO [5]│
   Robin SODERLING [SWE]   ┘ 63 64                                                   │ 63 64        │
   Julian KNOWLE [AUT]     ┐                             ┐                           │              │
   Michael KOHLMANN [GER]  ├ J.KNOWLE                    │                           │              │
WC Nathan HEALEY [AUS]     │ M.KOHLMANN                  ├ J.CHELA                   │              │
WC Stephen HUSS [AUS]      ┘ 64 64                       │ O.HERNANDEZ               │              │
   Juan Ignacio CHELA [ARG]┐                             │ 64 46 75                  │              │
   Oscar HERNANDEZ [ESP]   ├ J.CHELA                     ┘                           ┘              │
10 Tomas CIBULEC [CZE]     │ O.HERNANDEZ                                                            │
10 Leander PAES [IND]      ┘ 64 67(5) 63                                                            │
16 Simon ASPELIN [SWE]     ┐                             ┐                                          │
16 Massimo BERTOLINI [ITA] ├ S.ASPELIN [16]              │                                          │
   Jordan KERR [AUS]       │ M.BERTOLINI [16]            ├ H.ARAZI                                  │
   Graydon OLIVER [USA]    ┘ 62 16 76(3)                 │ N.MAHUT                                  │
   Nikolay DAVYDENKO [RUS] ┐                             │ 63 67(2) 63                              │
   Irakli LABADZE [GEO]    ├ H.ARAZI                     ┘                                          │
   Hicham ARAZI [MAR]      │ N.MAHUT                                                                ┘
   Nicolas MAHUT [FRA]     ┘ 62 62
   Julien BENNETEAU [FRA]  ┐                             ┐
   Arnaud CLEMENT [FRA]    ├ J.BENNETEAU                 │
   Harel LEVY [ISR]        │ A.CLEMENT                   ├ M.BHUPATHI [2]
   Mikhail YOUZHNY [RUS]   ┘ 67(3) 64 61                 │ M.MIRNYI [2]
   Devin BOWEN [USA]       ┐                             │ 63 76(4)
   Ashley FISHER [AUS]     ├ M.BHUPATHI [2]              ┘
2  Mahesh BHUPATHI [IND]   │ M.MIRNYI [2]
2  Max MIRNYI [BLR]        ┘ 67(4) 64 64
```

Final: M.LLODRA [5] / F.SANTORO [5] def. G.ETLIS [9] / M.RODRIGUEZ [9]   62 75

Elite Tournaments: 2004 Australian Open Drawsheets — 75

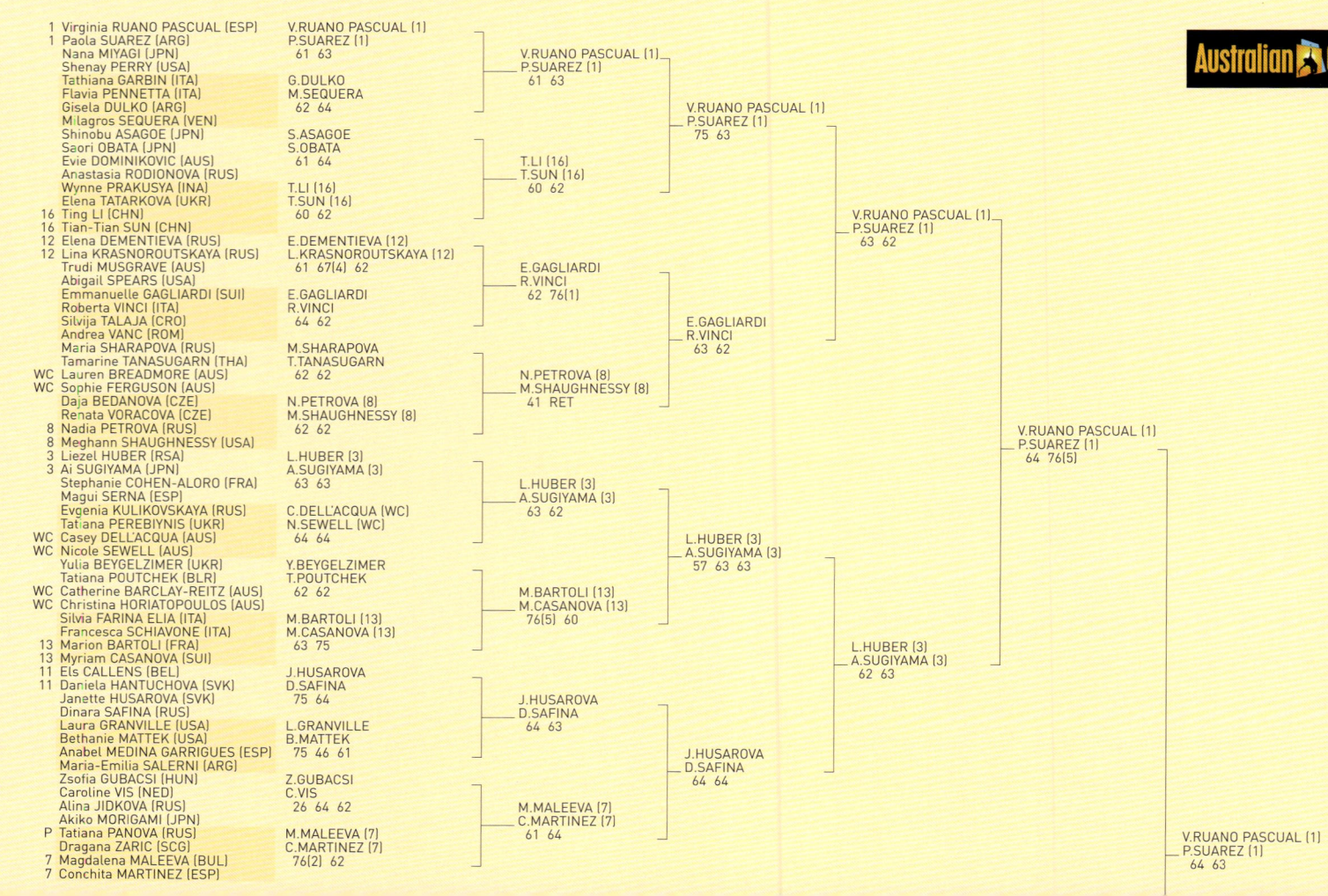

2004 Australian Open Championships, 19 January–1 February – Women's Doubles

```
 1  Virginia RUANO PASCUAL [ESP]  ┐
 1  Paola SUAREZ [ARG]             ├ V.RUANO PASCUAL [1]     ┐
    Nana MIYAGI [JPN]              ┘ P.SUAREZ [1]            │
    Shenay PERRY [USA]             ┐ 61 63                   │
    Tathiana GARBIN [ITA]          ├ G.DULKO                 ├ V.RUANO PASCUAL [1]   ┐
    Flavia PENNETTA [ITA]          ┘ M.SEQUERA               │ P.SUAREZ [1]          │
    Gisela DULKO [ARG]             ┐ 62 64                   │ 75 63                 │
    Milagros SEQUERA [VEN]         ┤                         │                       │
    Shinobu ASAGOE [JPN]           ┐ S.ASAGOE                ┘                       │
    Saori OBATA [JPN]              ├ S.OBATA                 ┐                       │
    Evie DOMINIKOVIC [AUS]         ┘ 61 64                   │                       │
    Anastasia RODIONOVA [RUS]      ┐                         ├ T.LI [16]             │
    Wynne PRAKUSYA [INA]           ┤ T.LI [16]               │ T.SUN [16]            │
    Elena TATARKOVA [UKR]          ┐ T.SUN [16]              │ 60 62                 │
16  Ting LI [CHN]                  ┘ 60 62                   ┘                       ├ V.RUANO PASCUAL [1]
16  Tian-Tian SUN [CHN]            ┐                                                 │ P.SUAREZ [1]
12  Elena DEMENTIEVA [RUS]         ├ E.DEMENTIEVA [12]       ┐                       │ 63 62
12  Lina KRASNOROUTSKAYA [RUS]     ┘ L.KRASNOROUTSKAYA [12]  │                       │
    Trudi MUSGRAVE [AUS]           ┐ 61 67(4) 62             ├ E.GAGLIARDI           │
    Abigail SPEARS [USA]           ┤                         │ R.VINCI               │
    Emmanuelle GAGLIARDI [SUI]     ┐ E.GAGLIARDI             │ 63 62                 │
    Roberta VINCI [ITA]            ├ R.VINCI                 │                       │
    Silvija TALAJA [CRO]           ┘ 64 62                   ┘                       │
    Andrea VANC [ROM]              ┐                                                 │
    Maria SHARAPOVA [RUS]          ┤ M.SHARAPOVA             ┐                       │
    Tamarine TANASUGARN [THA]      ┐ T.TANASUGARN            │                       │
WC  Lauren BREADMORE [AUS]         ┘ 62 62                   ├ N.PETROVA [8]         │
WC  Sophie FERGUSON [AUS]          ┐                         │ M.SHAUGHNESSY [8]     │
 8  Daja BEDANOVA [CZE]            ┤ N.PETROVA [8]           │ 41 RET                │
 8  Nadia PETROVA [RUS]            ┐ M.SHAUGHNESSY [8]       │                       │
    Meghann SHAUGHNESSY [USA]      ┘ 62 62                   ┘                       │
 3  Liezel HUBER [RSA]             ┐                                                 │
 3  Ai SUGIYAMA [JPN]              ├ L.HUBER [3]             ┐                       │
    Stephanie COHEN-ALORO [FRA]    ┘ A.SUGIYAMA [3]          │                       │
    Magui SERNA [ESP]              ┐ 63 63                   ├ L.HUBER [3]           │
    Evgenia KULIKOVSKAYA [RUS]     ┤                         │ A.SUGIYAMA [3]        │
    Tatiana PEREBIYNIS [UKR]       ┐ C.DELLACQUA [WC]        │ 57 63 63              │
WC  Nicole SEWELL [AUS]            ├ N.SEWELL [WC]           │                       │
WC  Casey DELLACQUA [AUS]          ┘ 64 64                   ┘                       ├ L.HUBER [3]
WC  Yulia BEYGELZIMER [UKR]        ┐                                                 │ A.SUGIYAMA [3]
WC  Tatiana POUTCHEK [BLR]         ┤ Y.BEYGELZIMER           ┐                       │ 62 63
WC  Catherine BARCLAY-REITZ [AUS]  ┐ T.POUTCHEK              │                       │
WC  Christina HORIATOPOULOS [AUS]  ┘ 62 62                   ├ M.BARTOLI [13]        │
    Silvia FARINA ELIA [ITA]       ┐                         │ M.CASANOVA [13]       │
    Francesca SCHIAVONE [ITA]      ┤ M.BARTOLI [13]          │ 76(5) 60              │
13  Marion BARTOLI [FRA]           ┐ M.CASANOVA [13]         │                       │
13  Myriam CASANOVA [SUI]          ┘ 63 75                   ┘                       │
11  Els CALLENS [BEL]              ┐                                                 │
11  Daniela HANTUCHOVA [SVK]       ├ J.HUSAROVA              ┐                       │
    Janette HUSAROVA [SVK]         ┘ D.SAFINA                │                       │
    Dinara SAFINA [RUS]            ┐ 75 64                   ├ J.HUSAROVA            │
    Laura GRANVILLE [USA]          ┤                         │ D.SAFINA              │
    Bethanie MATTEK [USA]          ┐ L.GRANVILLE             │ 64 63                 │
    Anabel MEDINA GARRIGUES [ESP]  ├ B.MATTEK                │                       │
    Maria-Emilia SALERNI [ARG]     ┘ 75 46 61                ┘                       │
    Zsofia GUBACSI [HUN]           ┐                                                 │
    Caroline VIS [NED]             ┤ Z.GUBACSI               ┐                       │
    Alina JIDKOVA [RUS]            ┐ C.VIS                   │                       │
    Akiko MORIGAMI [JPN]           ┘ 26 64 62                ├ M.MALEEVA [7]         │
P   Tatiana PANOVA [RUS]           ┐                         │ C.MARTINEZ [7]        │
    Dragana ZARIC [SCG]            ┤ M.MALEEVA [7]           │ 61 64                 │
 7  Magdalena MALEEVA [BUL]        ┐ C.MARTINEZ [7]          │                       │
 7  Conchita MARTINEZ [ESP]        ┘ 76(2) 62                ┘                       ┘
```

V.RUANO PASCUAL [1]
P.SUAREZ [1]
64 76(5)

V.RUANO PASCUAL [1]
P.SUAREZ [1]
64 63

76

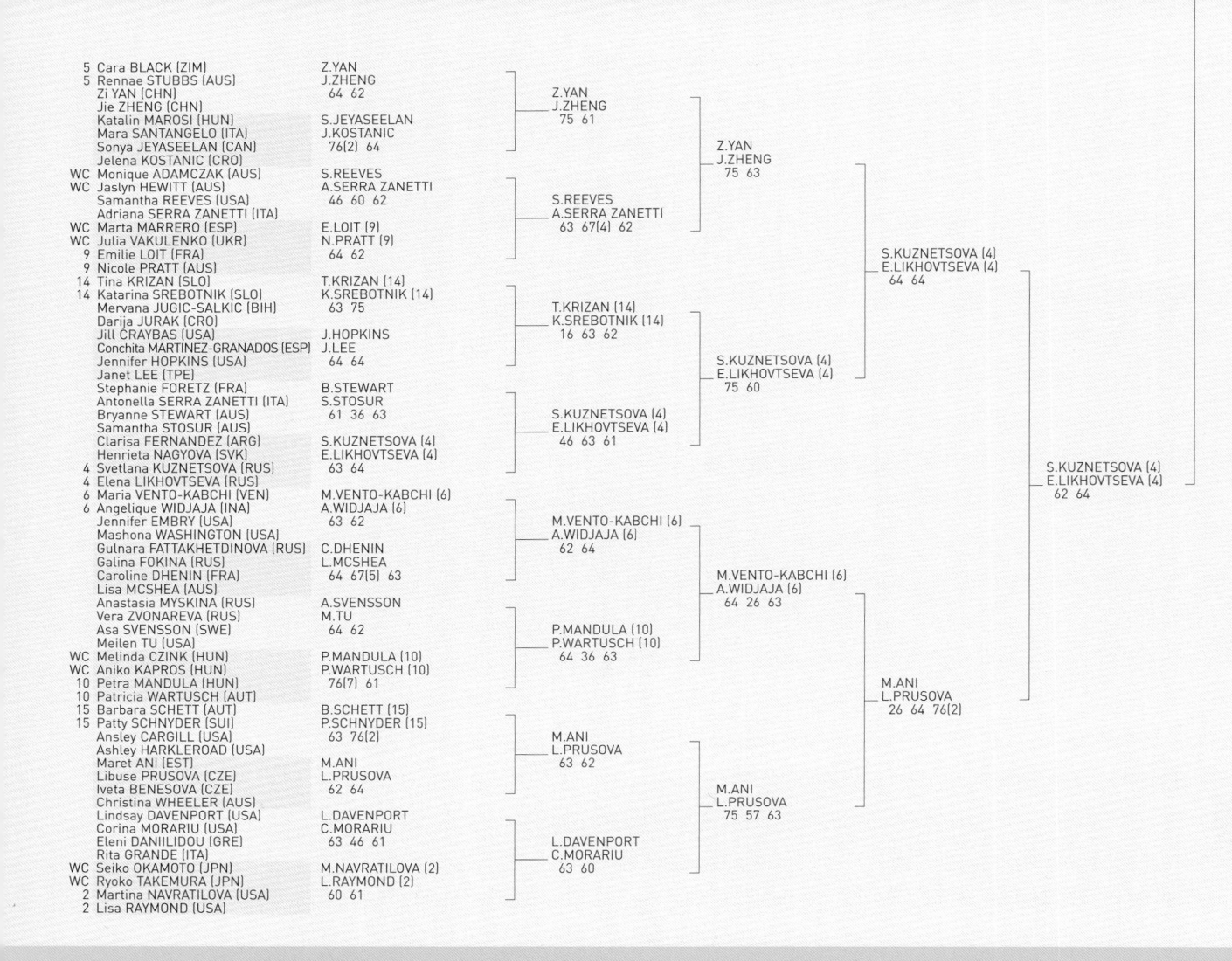

Elite Tournaments: 2004 Australian Open Drawsheets

Women's Doubles Draw (partial)

Final (this section): S.KUZNETSOVA [4] / E.LIKHOVTSEVA def. — 62 64

Bracket results

- Z.YAN / J.ZHENG def. S.REEVES / A.SERRA ZANETTI — 75 63
- S.KUZNETSOVA [4] / E.LIKHOVTSEVA [4] def. T.KRIZAN [14] / K.SREBOTNIK [14] — 75 60
- M.VENTO-KABCHI [6] / A.WIDJAJA [6] def. P.MANDULA [10] / P.WARTUSCH [10] — 64 26 63
- M.ANI / L.PRUSOVA def. L.DAVENPORT / C.MORARIU — 26 64 76(2)

Round results

- Z.YAN / J.ZHENG def. S.JEYASEELAN / J.KOSTANIC — 64 62
  - Z.YAN / J.ZHENG def. Katalin MAROSI / Mara SANTANGELO — (bye/result)
  - S.JEYASEELAN / J.KOSTANIC def. Sonya JEYASEELAN / Jelena KOSTANIC — 76(2) 64
- S.REEVES / A.SERRA ZANETTI def. Monique ADAMCZAK / Jaslyn HEWITT — 46 60 62
  - S.REEVES / A.SERRA ZANETTI def. Samantha REEVES / Adriana SERRA ZANETTI — 63 67(4) 62
  - E.LOIT [9] / N.PRATT [9] def. Marta MARRERO / Julia VAKULENKO — 64 62
- T.KRIZAN [14] / K.SREBOTNIK [14] def. Emilie LOIT / Nicole PRATT — 16 63 62
  - T.KRIZAN [14] / K.SREBOTNIK [14] def. Tina KRIZAN / Katarina SREBOTNIK — 63 75
  - J.HOPKINS / J.LEE def. Mervana JUGIC-SALKIC / Darija JURAK — 64 64
- B.STEWART / S.STOSUR def. Conchita MARTINEZ-GRANADOS / Jill CRAYBAS — Jennifer HOPKINS / Janet LEE — 61 36 63
  - S.KUZNETSOVA [4] / E.LIKHOVTSEVA [4] def. Stephanie FORETZ / Antonella SERRA ZANETTI — 46 63 61
  - Clarisa FERNANDEZ / Henrieta NAGYOVA — (Bryanne STEWART / Samantha STOSUR)
  - S.KUZNETSOVA [4] / E.LIKHOVTSEVA [4] — Svetlana KUZNETSOVA / Elena LIKHOVTSEVA — 63 64
- M.VENTO-KABCHI [6] / A.WIDJAJA [6] def. Maria VENTO-KABCHI / Angelique WIDJAJA — 63 62
  - C.DHENIN / L.MCSHEA def. Jennifer EMBRY / Mashona WASHINGTON — 64 67(5) 63
  - Gulnara FATTAKHETDINOVA / Galina FOKINA
  - A.SVENSSON / M.TU def. Caroline DHENIN / Lisa MCSHEA — 64 62
  - Anastasia MYSKINA / Vera ZVONAREVA
  - Asa SVENSSON / Meilen TU
- P.MANDULA [10] / P.WARTUSCH [10] def. Melinda CZINK / Aniko KAPROS — 76(7) 61
  - Petra MANDULA / Patricia WARTUSCH
  - B.SCHETT [15] / P.SCHNYDER [15] def. Barbara SCHETT / Patty SCHNYDER — 63 76(2)
  - Ansley CARGILL / Ashley HARKLEROAD
- M.ANI / L.PRUSOVA def. Maret ANI / Libuse PRUSOVA — 63 62
  - Iveta BENESOVA / Christina WHEELER
  - L.DAVENPORT / C.MORARIU def. Lindsay DAVENPORT / Corina MORARIU — 63 60
  - Eleni DANIILIDOU / Rita GRANDE
- M.NAVRATILOVA [2] / L.RAYMOND [2] def. Seiko OKAMOTO / Ryoko TAKEMURA — 60 61
  - Martina NAVRATILOVA / Lisa RAYMOND

Seeds / Players (left column)

- 5 Cara BLACK [ZIM]
- 5 Rennae STUBBS [AUS]
-   Zi YAN [CHN]
-   Jie ZHENG [CHN]
-   Katalin MAROSI [HUN]
-   Mara SANTANGELO [ITA]
-   Sonya JEYASEELAN [CAN]
-   Jelena KOSTANIC [CRO]
- WC Monique ADAMCZAK [AUS]
- WC Jaslyn HEWITT [AUS]
-   Samantha REEVES [USA]
-   Adriana SERRA ZANETTI [ITA]
- WC Marta MARRERO [ESP]
- WC Julia VAKULENKO [UKR]
- 9 Emilie LOIT [FRA]
- 9 Nicole PRATT [AUS]
- 14 Tina KRIZAN [SLO]
- 14 Katarina SREBOTNIK [SLO]
-   Mervana JUGIC-SALKIC [BIH]
-   Darija JURAK [CRO]
-   Conchita MARTINEZ-GRANADOS [ESP]
-   Jill CRAYBAS [USA]
-   Jennifer HOPKINS [USA]
-   Janet LEE [TPE]
-   Stephanie FORETZ [FRA]
-   Antonella SERRA ZANETTI [ITA]
-   Bryanne STEWART [AUS]
-   Samantha STOSUR [AUS]
-   Clarisa FERNANDEZ [ARG]
-   Henrieta NAGYOVA [SVK]
- 4 Svetlana KUZNETSOVA [RUS]
- 4 Elena LIKHOVTSEVA [RUS]
- 6 Maria VENTO-KABCHI [VEN]
- 6 Angelique WIDJAJA [INA]
-   Jennifer EMBRY [USA]
-   Mashona WASHINGTON [USA]
-   Gulnara FATTAKHETDINOVA [RUS]
-   Galina FOKINA [RUS]
-   Caroline DHENIN [FRA]
-   Lisa MCSHEA [AUS]
-   Anastasia MYSKINA [RUS]
-   Vera ZVONAREVA [RUS]
-   Asa SVENSSON [SWE]
-   Meilen TU [USA]
- WC Melinda CZINK [HUN]
- WC Aniko KAPROS [HUN]
- 10 Petra MANDULA [HUN]
- 10 Patricia WARTUSCH [AUT]
- 15 Barbara SCHETT [AUT]
- 15 Patty SCHNYDER [SUI]
-   Ansley CARGILL [USA]
-   Ashley HARKLEROAD [USA]
-   Maret ANI [EST]
-   Libuse PRUSOVA [CZE]
-   Iveta BENESOVA [CZE]
-   Christina WHEELER [AUS]
-   Lindsay DAVENPORT [USA]
-   Corina MORARIU [USA]
-   Eleni DANIILIDOU [GRE]
-   Rita GRANDE [ITA]
- WC Seiko OKAMOTO [JPN]
- WC Ryoko TAKEMURA [JPN]
- 2 Martina NAVRATILOVA [USA]
- 2 Lisa RAYMOND [USA]

2004 Australian Open Championships, 19 January–1 February – Mixed Doubles

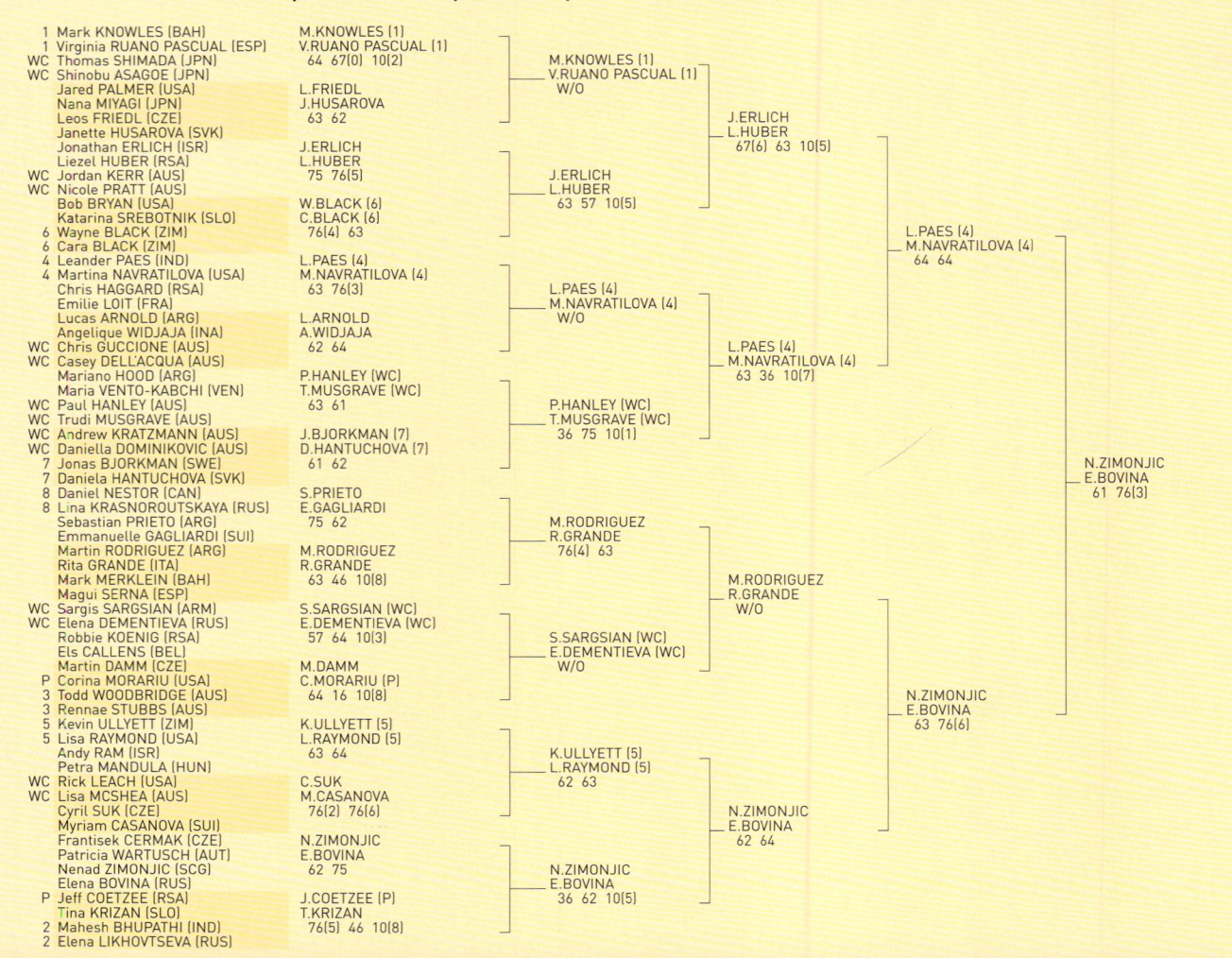

Final: N. ZIMONJIC / E. BOVINA def. L. PAES / M. NAVRATILOVA 6-1 7-6(3)

Top Half

- 1 Mark KNOWLES (BAH) / Virginia RUANO PASCUAL (ESP) [1]
- WC Thomas SHIMADA (JPN) / Shinobu ASAGOE (JPN)
  - M. KNOWLES / V. RUANO PASCUAL [1] 6-4 6-7(0) 10(2)
- Jared PALMER (USA) / Nana MIYAGI (JPN)
- WC Leos FRIEDL (CZE) / Janette HUSAROVA (SVK)
  - L. FRIEDL / J. HUSAROVA 6-3 6-2
    - M. KNOWLES [1] / V. RUANO PASCUAL [1] W/O
- Jonathan ERLICH (ISR) / Liezel HUBER (RSA)
- WC Jordan KERR (AUS) / Nicole PRATT (AUS)
  - J. ERLICH / L. HUBER 7-5 7-6(5)
- Bob BRYAN (USA) / Katarina SREBOTNIK (SLO)
- 6 Wayne BLACK (ZIM) / Cara BLACK (ZIM)
  - W. BLACK [6] / C. BLACK [6] 7-6(4) 6-3
    - J. ERLICH / L. HUBER 6-3 5-7 10(5)
      - J. ERLICH / L. HUBER 6-7(6) 6-3 10(5)
- 4 Leander PAES (IND) / Martina NAVRATILOVA (USA)
- Chris HAGGARD (RSA) / Emilie LOIT (FRA)
  - L. PAES [4] / M. NAVRATILOVA [4] 6-3 7-6(3)
- Lucas ARNOLD (ARG) / Angelique WIDJAJA (INA)
- WC Chris GUCCIONE (AUS) / Casey DELLACQUA (AUS)
  - L. ARNOLD / A. WIDJAJA 6-2 6-4
    - L. PAES [4] / M. NAVRATILOVA [4] W/O
- Mariano HOOD (ARG) / Maria VENTO-KABCHI (VEN)
- WC Paul HANLEY (AUS) / Trudi MUSGRAVE (AUS)
  - P. HANLEY (WC) / T. MUSGRAVE (WC) 3-6 7-5 10(1)
- WC Andrew KRATZMANN (AUS) / Daniella DOMINIKOVIC (AUS)
- 7 Jonas BJORKMAN (SWE) / Daniela HANTUCHOVA (SVK)
  - J. BJORKMAN [7] / D. HANTUCHOVA [7] 6-1 6-2
    - L. PAES [4] / M. NAVRATILOVA [4] 6-3 3-6 10(7)
      - L. PAES [4] / M. NAVRATILOVA [4] 6-4 6-4

Bottom Half

- 8 Daniel NESTOR (CAN) / Lina KRASNOROUTSKAYA (RUS)
- Sebastian PRIETO (ARG) / Emmanuelle GAGLIARDI (SUI)
  - S. PRIETO / E. GAGLIARDI 7-5 6-2
- Rita GRANDE (ITA) / Mark MERKLEIN (BAH)
- WC Magui SERNA (ESP) / Martin RODRIGUEZ (ARG)
  - M. RODRIGUEZ / R. GRANDE 7-6(4) 6-3
    - M. RODRIGUEZ / R. GRANDE 6-3 4-6 10(8)
- WC Sargis SARGSIAN (ARM) / Elena DEMENTIEVA (RUS)
- WC Robbie KOENIG (RSA) / Els CALLENS (BEL)
  - S. SARGSIAN (WC) / E. DEMENTIEVA (WC) 5-7 6-4 10(3)
- Martin DAMM (CZE) / Corina MORARIU (USA) [P]
- 3 Todd WOODBRIDGE (AUS) / Rennae STUBBS (AUS)
  - M. DAMM / C. MORARIU [P] 6-4 1-6 10(8)
    - M. RODRIGUEZ / R. GRANDE W/O
      - N. ZIMONJIC / E. BOVINA 6-3 7-6(6)
- 5 Kevin ULLYETT (ZIM) / Lisa RAYMOND (USA)
- Andy RAM (ISR) / Petra MANDULA (HUN)
  - K. ULLYETT [5] / L. RAYMOND [5] 6-2 6-3
- WC Rick LEACH (USA) / Lisa McSHEA (AUS)
- WC Cyril SUK (CZE) / Myriam CASANOVA (SUI)
  - C. SUK / M. CASANOVA 7-6(2) 7-6(6)
    - K. ULLYETT [5] / L. RAYMOND [5] 6-3 6-4
- Frantisek CERMAK (CZE) / Patricia WARTUSCH (AUT)
- Nenad ZIMONJIC (SCG) / Elena BOVINA (RUS)
  - N. ZIMONJIC / E. BOVINA 6-2 7-5
- P Jeff COETZEE (RSA) / Tina KRIZAN (SLO)
- 2 Mahesh BHUPATHI (IND) / Elena LIKHOVTSEVA (RUS)
  - J. COETZEE (P) / T. KRIZAN 7-6(5) 4-6 10(8)
    - N. ZIMONJIC / E. BOVINA 3-6 6-2 10(5)
      - N. ZIMONJIC / E. BOVINA 6-2 6-4

Australian Open Champion
Justine Henin-Hardenne (BEL)

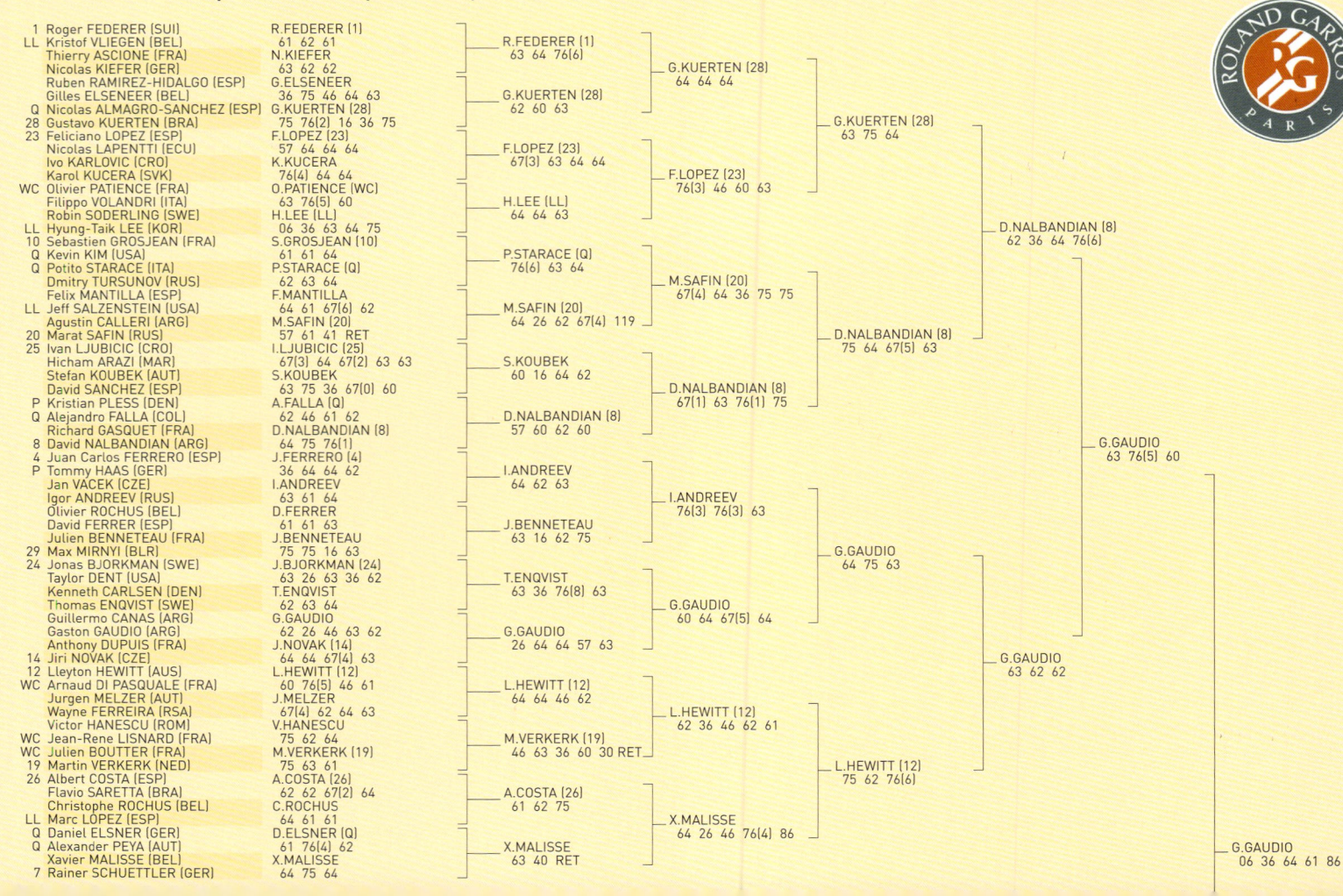

2004 French Open Championships Roland Garros, 24 May–6 June – Men's Singles

Winner: G. GAUDIO def. G. Coria-style opponent (final score shown): G.GAUDIO 0‑6 3‑6 6‑4 6‑1 8‑6

First Round / Draw

1 Roger FEDERER (SUI) — R.FEDERER [1] 6‑1 6‑2 6‑1
LL Kristof VLIEGEN (BEL)
   Thierry ASCIONE (FRA) — N.KIEFER 6‑3 6‑2 6‑2
   Nicolas KIEFER (GER)
   Ruben RAMIREZ-HIDALGO (ESP) — G.ELSENEER 3‑6 7‑5 4‑6 6‑4 6‑3
Q Gilles ELSENEER (BEL)
Q Nicolas ALMAGRO-SANCHEZ (ESP) — G.KUERTEN [28] 7‑5 7‑6(2) 1‑6 3‑6 7‑5
28 Gustavo KUERTEN (BRA)

23 Feliciano LOPEZ (ESP) — F.LOPEZ [23] 5‑7 6‑4 6‑4 6‑4
   Nicolas LAPENTTI (ECU)
   Ivo KARLOVIC (CRO) — K.KUCERA 7‑6(4) 6‑4 6‑4
   Karol KUCERA (SVK)
WC Olivier PATIENCE (FRA) — O.PATIENCE (WC) 6‑3 7‑6(5) 6‑0
   Filippo VOLANDRI (ITA)
   Hyung-Taik LEE (KOR) — H.LEE (LL) 6‑4 6‑4 6‑3
LL Robin SODERLING (SWE)
10 Sebastien GROSJEAN (FRA) — S.GROSJEAN [10] 0‑6 3‑6 6‑3 6‑4 7‑5

Q Kevin KIM (USA) — P.STARACE (Q) 6‑1 6‑1 6‑4
Q Potito STARACE (ITA)
   Dmitry TURSUNOV (RUS) — F.MANTILLA 6‑2 6‑3 6‑4
   Felix MANTILLA (ESP)
LL Jeff SALZENSTEIN (USA) — M.SAFIN [20] 6‑4 6‑1 6‑7(6) 6‑2
   Agustin CALLERI (ARG)
20 Marat SAFIN (RUS) — 5‑7 6‑1 4‑1 RET
25 Ivan LJUBICIC (CRO) — I.LJUBICIC [25] 6‑7(3) 6‑1 6‑4 6‑7(2) 6‑3
   Hicham ARAZI (MAR)
   Stefan KOUBEK (AUT) — S.KOUBEK 6‑0 1‑6 6‑4 6‑2
P Kristian PLESS (DEN)
P Alejandro FALLA (COL) — A.FALLA (Q) 6‑2 4‑6 6‑1 6‑2
   Richard GASQUET (FRA)
8 David NALBANDIAN (ARG) — D.NALBANDIAN [8] 6‑4 7‑5 7‑6(1)
4 Juan Carlos FERRERO (ESP) — J.FERRERO [4] 7‑6(1)
P Tommy HAAS (GER) — 3‑6 6‑4 6‑4 6‑2

   Jan VACEK (CZE) — I.ANDREEV 6‑3 6‑1 6‑4
   Igor ANDREEV (RUS)
   Olivier ROCHUS (BEL) — D.FERRER 6‑1 6‑1 6‑3
   David FERRER (ESP)
29 Julien BENNETEAU (FRA) — J.BENNETEAU 7‑5 7‑5 1‑6 6‑3
24 Max MIRNYI (BLR)
24 Jonas BJORKMAN (SWE) — J.BJORKMAN [24] 6‑3 2‑6 6‑3 3‑6 6‑2
   Taylor DENT (USA)
   Kenneth CARLSEN (DEN) — T.ENQVIST 6‑3 7‑6(8) 6‑3
   Thomas ENQVIST (SWE)
   Guillermo CANAS (ARG) — G.GAUDIO 6‑2 6‑3 6‑4
   Gaston GAUDIO (ARG)

   Anthony DUPUIS (FRA) — J.NOVAK 6‑2 2‑6 4‑6 6‑3 6‑2
14 Jiri NOVAK (CZE)
12 Lleyton HEWITT (AUS) — L.HEWITT [12] 6‑4 6‑4 6‑7(4) 6‑3
WC Arnaud DI PASQUALE (FRA)
   Jurgen MELZER (AUT) — J.MELZER 6‑0 7‑6(5) 4‑6 6‑1
   Wayne FERREIRA (RSA)
   Victor HANESCU (ROM) — V.HANESCU 6‑7(4) 6‑2 6‑4 6‑3
WC Jean-Rene LISNARD (FRA)
WC Julien BOUTTER (FRA) — M.VERKERK [19] 7‑5 6‑2 6‑4
19 Martin VERKERK (NED)
26 Albert COSTA (ESP) — A.COSTA [26] 6‑2 6‑2 6‑7(2) 6‑4
   Flavio SARETTA (BRA)
   Christophe ROCHUS (BEL) — C.ROCHUS 6‑2 7‑5
LL Marc LOPEZ (ESP)
Q Daniel ELSNER (GER) — D.ELSNER (Q) 6‑4 6‑1 6‑1
Q Alexander PEYA (AUT)
   Xavier MALISSE (BEL) — X.MALISSE 6‑1 7‑6(4) 6‑2
7 Rainer SCHUETTLER (GER) — 6‑4 7‑5

Bracket Progression

- R.FEDERER [1] 6‑3 6‑4 7‑6(6) def. N.KIEFER
- G.KUERTEN [28] 6‑4 6‑4 6‑4 def. G.ELSENEER
- G.KUERTEN [28] 6‑2 6‑0 6‑3 def. R.FEDERER
- F.LOPEZ [23] 7‑6(3) 4‑6 6‑0 6‑3 def. H.LEE (LL)
- P.STARACE (Q) 7‑6(6) 6‑3 6‑4 def. S.GROSJEAN [10]
- M.SAFIN [20] 6‑7(4) 6‑4 3‑6 7‑5 7‑5 def. P.STARACE
- D.NALBANDIAN [8] 6‑7(1) 6‑3 7‑6(1) 7‑5 def. S.KOUBEK
- G.KUERTEN [28] 6‑3 7‑5 8‑4 ... (round continues)
- F.LOPEZ [23] 7‑6(3) ...
- M.SAFIN [20] 6‑7(4) 6‑4 3‑6 7‑5 7‑5
- D.NALBANDIAN [8] 7‑5 6‑4 6‑7(5) 6‑3
- I.ANDREEV 7‑6(3) 6‑3 def. J.BENNETEAU
- G.GAUDIO 6‑0 6‑4 6‑7(5) 6‑4 def. T.ENQVIST
- L.HEWITT [12] 6‑2 3‑6 4‑6 6‑2 6‑1 def. M.VERKERK
- X.MALISSE 6‑4 2‑6 4‑6 7‑6(4) 8‑6 def. A.COSTA
- D.NALBANDIAN [8] 6‑2 3‑6 6‑4 7‑6(6) def. G.KUERTEN
- G.GAUDIO 6‑3 6‑2 6‑2 def. I.ANDREEV
- L.HEWITT [12] 7‑5 6‑2 7‑6(6) def. X.MALISSE
- G.GAUDIO 6‑4 7‑5 6‑3 def. L.HEWITT
- G.GAUDIO 6‑3 7‑6(5) 6‑0 def. D.NALBANDIAN

Final: G.GAUDIO 0‑6 3‑6 6‑4 6‑1 8‑6

2004 Roland Garros Draw (Section)

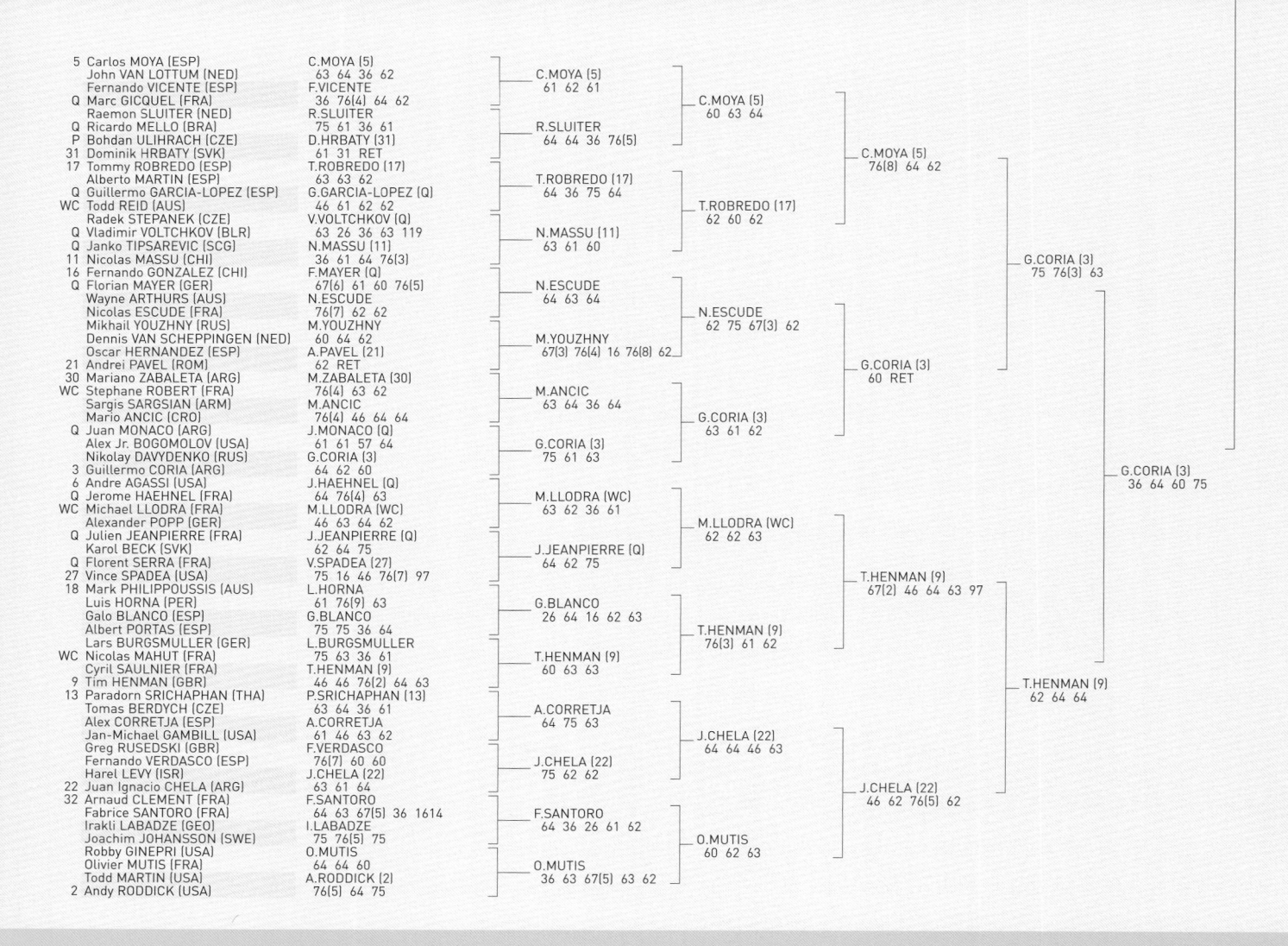

Elite Tournaments: 2004 Roland Garros Drawsheets — p. 81

Bracket Results

- 5 Carlos MOYA (ESP) — C.MOYA (5) 6 3 6 4 3 6 6 2
- John VAN LOTTUM (NED)
- Q Marc GICQUEL (FRA) — F.VICENTE 6 1 6 2 6 1
- Fernando VICENTE (ESP)
  - → C.MOYA (5) 6 0 6 3 6 4
- Q Raemon SLUITER (NED) — R.SLUITER 3 6 7 6(4) 6 4 6 2
- Q Ricardo MELLO (BRA)
- P Bohdan ULIHRACH (CZE) — D.HRBATY (31) 7 5 6 1 3 6 6 1
- 31 Dominik HRBATY (SVK)
  - → R.SLUITER 6 4 6 4 3 6 7 6(5)
- 17 Tommy ROBREDO (ESP) — T.ROBREDO (17) 6 1 3 1 RET
- Alberto MARTIN (ESP)
    - ⇒ C.MOYA (5) 7 6(8) 6 4 6 2
- Q Guillermo GARCIA-LOPEZ (ESP) — G.GARCIA-LOPEZ (Q) 6 3 6 3 6 2
- WC Todd REID (AUS)
  - → T.ROBREDO (17) 4 6 6 1 6 2 6 2
- Radek STEPANEK (CZE) — V.VOLTCHKOV (Q) 6 4 3 6 7 5 6 4
- Q Vladimir VOLTCHKOV (BLR)
    - → T.ROBREDO (17) 6 3 2 6 3 6 6 3 11 9
- Q Janko TIPSAREVIC (SCG) — N.MASSU (11) 6 3 6 1 6 0
- 11 Nicolas MASSU (CHI)
      - ⇒ G.CORIA (3) 7 5 7 6(3) 6 3
- 16 Fernando GONZALEZ (CHI) — F.MAYER (Q) 3 6 6 1 6 4 7 6(3)
- Q Florian MAYER (GER)
  - → N.ESCUDE 6 7(7) 6 1 6 0 7 6(5)
- Wayne ARTHURS (AUS) — N.ESCUDE 6 4 6 3 6 4
- Nicolas ESCUDE (FRA)
    - → N.ESCUDE 6 2 7 5 7 6(3) 6 2
- Dennis VAN SCHEPPINGEN (NED) — M.YOUZHNY 6 0 6 4 6 2
- Mikhail YOUZHNY (RUS)
  - → M.YOUZHNY 7 6(3) 7 6(4) 1 6 7 6(8) 6 2
- Oscar HERNANDEZ (ESP) — A.PAVEL (21) 6 2 RET
- 21 Andrei PAVEL (ROM)
      - → G.CORIA (3) 6 0 RET
- 30 Mariano ZABALETA (ARG) — M.ZABALETA (30) 7 6(4) 6 3 6 2
- WC Stephane ROBERT (FRA)
  - → M.ANCIC 7 6(4) 4 6 6 4 6 4
- Sargis SARGSIAN (ARM) — M.ANCIC 6 3 6 4 3 6 6 4
- Mario ANCIC (CRO)
    - → G.CORIA (3) 6 3 6 1 6 2
- Q Juan MONACO (ARG) — J.MONACO (Q) 6 1 6 1 5 7 6 4
- Alex Jr. BOGOMOLOV (USA)
  - → G.CORIA (3) 7 5 6 1 6 3
- Nikolay DAVYDENKO (RUS) — G.CORIA (3) 6 4 6 2 6 0
- 3 Guillermo CORIA (ARG)
        - ⇒ G.CORIA (3) 3 6 6 4 6 0 7 5
- 6 Andre AGASSI (USA) — J.HAEHNEL (Q) 6 4 7 6(4) 6 3
- Q Jerome HAEHNEL (FRA)
  - → M.LLODRA (WC) 6 3 6 2 3 6 6 1
- WC Michael LLODRA (FRA) — M.LLODRA (WC) 4 6 6 3 6 4 6 2
- Alexander POPP (GER)
    - → M.LLODRA (WC) 6 2 6 2 6 3
- Q Julien JEANPIERRE (FRA) — J.JEANPIERRE (Q) 6 2 6 4 7 5
- Karol BECK (SVK)
  - → J.JEANPIERRE (Q) 6 4 6 2 7 5
- Q Florent SERRA (FRA) — V.SPADEA (27) 7 5 1 6 4 6 7 6(7) 9 7
- 27 Vince SPADEA (USA)
      - ⇒ T.HENMAN (9) 6 7(2) 4 6 6 4 6 3 9 7
- 18 Mark PHILIPPOUSSIS (AUS) — L.HORNA 6 1 7 6(9) 6 3
- Luis HORNA (PER)
  - → G.BLANCO 2 6 6 4 1 6 6 2 6 3
- Albert PORTAS (ESP) — G.BLANCO 7 5 7 5 3 6 6 4
- Galo BLANCO (ESP)
    - → T.HENMAN (9) 7 6(3) 6 1 6 2
- Lars BURGSMULLER (GER) — L.BURGSMULLER 7 5 3 6 3 6 6 1
- WC Cyril SAULNIER (FRA)
  - → T.HENMAN (9) 6 0 6 3 6 3
- Nicolas MAHUT (FRA) — P.SRICHAPHAN (13) 4 6 4 6 7 6(2) 6 4 6 3
- 9 Tim HENMAN (GBR)
          - → T.HENMAN (9) 6 2 6 4 6 4
- 13 Paradorn SRICHAPHAN (THA) — T.BERDYCH (CZE) 6 3 6 4 3 6 6 1
- Tomas BERDYCH (CZE)
  - → A.CORRETJA 6 4 7 5 6 3
- Alex CORRETJA (ESP) — A.CORRETJA 6 1 4 6 6 3 6 2
- Jan-Michael GAMBILL (USA)
    - → J.CHELA (22) 6 4 6 4 4 6 6 3
- Greg RUSEDSKI (GBR) — F.VERDASCO 7 6(7) 7 6 0 6 0
- Fernando VERDASCO (ESP)
  - → J.CHELA (22) 7 5 6 2 6 2
- Harel LEVY (ISR) — J.CHELA (22) 6 3 6 1 6 4
- 22 Juan Ignacio CHELA (ARG)
      - ⇒ J.CHELA (22) 4 6 6 2 7 6(5) 6 2
- 32 Arnaud CLEMENT (FRA) — F.SANTORO 6 4 3 6 2 6 6 1 6 2
- Fabrice SANTORO (FRA)
  - → F.SANTORO 6 4 6 3 6 7(5) 3 6 16 14
- Irakli LABADZE (GEO) — I.LABADZE 7 5 7 6(5) 7 5
- Joachim JOHANSSON (SWE)
    - → O.MUTIS 6 0 6 2 6 3
- Robby GINEPRI (USA) — O.MUTIS 6 4 6 4 6 0
- Olivier MUTIS (FRA)
  - → O.MUTIS 3 6 6 3 6 7(5) 6 3 6 2
- Todd MARTIN (USA) — A.RODDICK (2) 7 6(5) 6 4 7 5
- 2 Andy RODDICK (USA)

Final shown in this section: G.CORIA (3) def. T.HENMAN (9) 3 6 6 4 6 0 7 5

2004 French Open Championships Roland Garros, 24 May–6 June – Women's Singles

Seed	Player	R1	R2	R3	R4	QF	SF	F
1	Justine HENIN-HARDENNE (BEL)	J.HENIN-HARDENNE [1] 64 64						
WC	Sandrine TESTUD (FRA)		T.GARBIN 61 62					
	Tathiana GARBIN (ITA)	T.GARBIN 75 64						
	Conchita MARTINEZ-GRANADOS (ESP)			J.ZHENG 57 7611 62				
	Dally RANDRIANTEFY (MAD)		J.ZHENG 64 61					
	Jie ZHENG (CHN)				P.SUAREZ [14] 64 75			
31	Emilie LOIT (FRA)	E.LOIT [31] 61 57 64						
24	Jelena DOKIC (SCG)		T.PEREBIYNIS 61 63					
	Tatiana PEREBIYNIS (UKR)	T.PEREBIYNIS 64 64						
P	Ashley HARKLEROAD (USA)			P.SUAREZ [14] 63 63				
	Mariana DIAZ-OLIVA (ARG)	A.HARKLEROAD 64 61						
	Vera DOUCHEVINA (RUS)		V.DOUCHEVINA 61 57 64					
	Saori OBATA (JPN)	V.DOUCHEVINA 62 61						
	Milagros SEQUERA (VEN)					P.SUAREZ [14] 61 63		
14	Paola SUAREZ (ARG)	P.SUAREZ [14] 61 57 64						
	Vera ZVONAREVA (RUS)		V.ZVONAREVA [10] 63 64					
10	Zuzana KUCOVA (SVK)	V.ZVONAREVA [10] 60 62						
Q	Magui SERNA (ESP)			V.ZVONAREVA [10] 57 61 64				
	Akiko MORIGAMI (JPN)	M.SERNA 63 36 86						
	Rita GRANDE (ITA)	R.GRANDE 76(7) 61						
	Henrieta NAGYOVA (SVK)		M.SHARAPOVA [18] 63 60					
P	Barbara SCHWARTZ (AUT)	M.SHARAPOVA [18] 62 60						
18	Maria SHARAPOVA (RUS)			M.SHARAPOVA [18] 63 76(3)				
27	Eleni DANIILIDOU (GRE)	M.WEINGARTNER 63 63						
	Marlene WEINGARTNER (GER)		M.WEINGARTNER 46 64 64					
	Amy FRAZIER (USA)	M.CAMERIN 63 62						
	Maria-Elena CAMERIN (ITA)				M.SHARAPOVA [18] 63 61			
Q	Juliana FEDAK (UKR)	J.FEDAK (Q) 63 61						
	Mara SANTANGELO (ITA)		N.PETROVA [8] 60 61					
	Catalina CASTANO (COL)	N.PETROVA [8] 62 63						
8	Nadia PETROVA (RUS)			M.WEINGARTNER 63 62				
	Amelie MAURESMO (FRA)	A.MAURESMO [3] 63 63						
3	Ludmila CERVANOVA (SVK)		A.MAURESMO [3] 60 46 61					
	Jill CRAYBAS (USA)	A.MEDINA GARRIGUES 62 61						
	Anabel MEDINA GARRIGUES (ESP)			A.MAURESMO [3] 63 62				
	Julia VAKULENKO (UKR)	A.PARRA-SANTONJA 75 62						
	Arantxa PARRA-SANTONJA (ESP)		A.PARRA-SANTONJA 64 60					
	Lubomira KURHAJCOVA (SVK)	L.RAYMOND [28] 06 75 63						
28	Lisa RAYMOND (USA)				A.MAURESMO [3] 62 61			
21	Magdalena MALEEVA (BUL)	M.MALEEVA [21] 62 62						
	Anca BARNA (GER)		M.MALEEVA [21] 75 67(3) 75					
WC	Christina WHEELER (AUS)	M.MARRERO 62 46 97						
	Marta MARRERO (ESP)			M.SHAUGHNESSY 63 76(3)				
	Samantha REEVES (USA)	M.SHAUGHNESSY 63 36 97						
	Meghann SHAUGHNESSY (USA)		S.FARINA ELIA [15] 64 63					
	Jelena JANKOVIC (SCG)	S.FARINA ELIA [15] 46 60 62						
15	Silvia FARINA ELIA (ITA)			E.DEMENTIEVA [9] 61 75				
9	Elena DEMENTIEVA (RUS)	E.DEMENTIEVA [9] 76(4) 16 64						
	Mervana JUGIC-SALKIC (BIH)		E.DEMENTIEVA [9] 62 62					
	Nicole PRATT (AUS)	N.PRATT 64 62						
	Tina PISNIK (SLO)				E.DEMENTIEVA [9] 06 76(2) 01 RET			
	Klara KOUKALOVA (CZE)	K.KOUKALOVA 76(4) 76(2)						
	Tatiana GOLOVIN (FRA)		A.SMASHNOVA-PISTOLESI [19] 61 75					
	Flavia PENNETTA (ITA)	A.SMASHNOVA-PISTOLESI [19] 61 64						
19	Anna SMASHNOVA-PISTOLESI (ISR)			M.IRVIN (Q) 76(5) 62				
32	Dinara SAFINA (RUS)	D.SAFINA [32] 75 67(4) 63						
Q	Julia SCHRUFF (GER)		M.IRVIN (Q) 62 60					
Q	Marissa IRVIN (USA)	M.IRVIN (Q)						
	Maria SANCHEZ LORENZO (ESP)			L.DAVENPORT [5] 61 64				
	Sanda MAMIC (CRO)	M.SANCHEZ LORENZO 64 75						
WC	Virginie PICHET (FRA)		L.DAVENPORT [5] 64 61					
5	Lindsay DAVENPORT (USA)	L.DAVENPORT [5] 64 62						

Semifinals / Final:
- P.SUAREZ [14] def. M.SHARAPOVA [18] 63 61
- E.DEMENTIEVA [9] def. A.MAURESMO [3] 64 63
- E.DEMENTIEVA [9] def. P.SUAREZ [14] 60 75
- A.MYSKINA [6] def. E.DEMENTIEVA [9] 61 62

Elite Tournaments: 2004 Roland Garros Drawsheets

Women's Singles Draw (partial)

```
6  Anastasia MYSKINA (RUS)    A.MYSKINA [6]
   Alicia MOLIK (AUS)          46 63 64      A.MYSKINA [6]
   Barbora STRYCOVA (CZE)     B.STRYCOVA     60 64
   Els CALLENS (BEL)           63 62                        A.MYSKINA [6]
   Denisa CHLADKOVA (CZE)     D.CHLADKOVA                   63 76(3)
WC Kelly McCAIN (USA)          64 63         D.CHLADKOVA
29 Petra MANDULA (HUN)        P.MANDULA [29] 62 63
   Severine BELTRAME (FRA)     57 64 61                                   A.MYSKINA [6]
   Karolina SPREM (CRO)       M.CASANOVA                                  16 64 86
22 Myriam CASANOVA (SUI)       75 62         M.CASANOVA
   Maria VENTO-KABCHI (VEN)   M.VENTO-KABCHI 64 26 63
   Lindsay LEE-WATERS (USA)    64 62                        S.KUZNETSOVA [11]
Q  Barbara RITTNER (GER)      B.RITTNER [Q]                 36 63 64
Q  Barbara SCHETT (AUT)        63 63         S.KUZNETSOVA [11]
   Lubomira BACHEVA (BUL)     S.KUZNETSOVA [11] 61 64
11 Svetlana KUZNETSOVA (RUS)   60 76(2)                                                 A.MYSKINA [6]
LL Tzipi OBZILER (ISR)        S.PERRY [Q]                                               63 64
Q  Shenay PERRY (USA)          64 63         K.SREBOTNIK
   Katerina SREBOTNIK (SLO)   K.SREBOTNIK    64 63
   Cara BLACK (ZIM)            63 63                        F.ZULUAGA [23]
   Elena LIKHOVTSEVA (RUS)    E.LIKHOVTSEVA                 57 62 63
   Alina JIDKOVA (RUS)         62 16 75      F.ZULUAGA [23]
   Martina SUCHA (SVK)        F.ZULUAGA [23] 75 57 61
23 Fabiola ZULUAGA (COL)       62 61                                     V.WILLIAMS [4]
30 Mary PIERCE (FRA)          M.PIERCE [30]                              61 76(3)
   Claudine SCHAUL (LUX)       62 63         M.PIERCE [30]
   Laura GRANVILLE (USA)      G.LEON GARCIA  61 61
   Gala LEON GARCIA (ESP)      64 61                        V.WILLIAMS [4]
   Jelena KOSTANIC (CRO)      J.KOSTANIC                    63 61
WC Camille PIN (FRA)           62 63         V.WILLIAMS [4]
   Tamarine TANASUGARN (THA)  V.WILLIAMS [4]  63 63
4  Venus WILLIAMS (USA)        62 64                                                    J.CAPRIATI [7]
7  Jennifer CAPRIATI (USA)    J.CAPRIATI [7]                                            63 26 63
   Yulia BEYGELZIMER (UKR)     62 46 64      J.CAPRIATI [7]
LL Eva BIRNEROVA (CZE)        K.PESCHKE [Q]  75 63
Q  Kveta PESCHKE (CZE)         76(5) 60                     J.CAPRIATI [7]
   Anna-Lena GROENEFELD (GER) A.GROENEFELD                  62 36 64
   Samantha STOSUR (AUS)       62 60         E.BOVINA [25]
Q  Roberta VINCI (ITA)        E.BOVINA [25]  32 RET
25 Elena BOVINA (RUS)          75 61                                     F.SCHIAVONE [17]
17 Francesca SCHIAVONE (ITA)  F.SCHIAVONE [17]                           62 63
   Stephanie COHEN-ALORO (FRA) 61 62         F.SCHIAVONE [17]
   Kristina BRANDI (PUR)      V.RAZZANO [WC] 61 46 63
WC Virginie RAZZANO (FRA)      63 76(4)                     V.RUANO PASCUAL
   Virginia RUANO PASCUAL (ESP) V.RUANO PASCUAL             67(4) 62 61
   Marion BARTOLI (FRA)        64 62         V.RUANO PASCUAL
12 Ai SUGIYAMA (JPN)          A.SUGIYAMA [12] 64 63
16 Patty SCHNYDER (SUI)       P.SCHNYDER [16]                                          S.WILLIAMS [2]
   Aniko KAPROS (HUN)          64 61                                                   63 61
   Shinobu ASAGOE (JPN)       S.ASAGOE       S.ASAGOE
   Daniela HANTUCHOVA (SVK)    61 63         75 36 64
   Gisela DULKO (ARG)         G.DULKO                       S.ASAGOE
WC Martina NAVRATILOVA (USA)   61 63         G.DULKO        75 46 64
Q  Teryn ASHLEY (USA)         C.MARTINEZ [20] 64 75
20 Conchita MARTINEZ (ESP)     62 64                                     S.WILLIAMS [2]
WC Stephanie FORETZ (FRA)     S.FORETZ [WC]                              60 64
   Nathalie DECHY (FRA)        16 75 61      S.TALAJA
   Silvija TALAJA (CRO)       S.TALAJA       26 76(8) 62
   Emmanuelle GAGLIARDI (SUI)  63 64                        S.WILLIAMS [2]
   Marie-Gaiane MIKAELIAN (SUI) M.KIRILENKO                 46 62 64
   Maria KIRILENKO (RUS)       75 76(5)      S.WILLIAMS [2]
   Iveta BENESOVA (CZE)       S.WILLIAMS [2] 62 62
2  Serena WILLIAMS (USA)       62 62
```

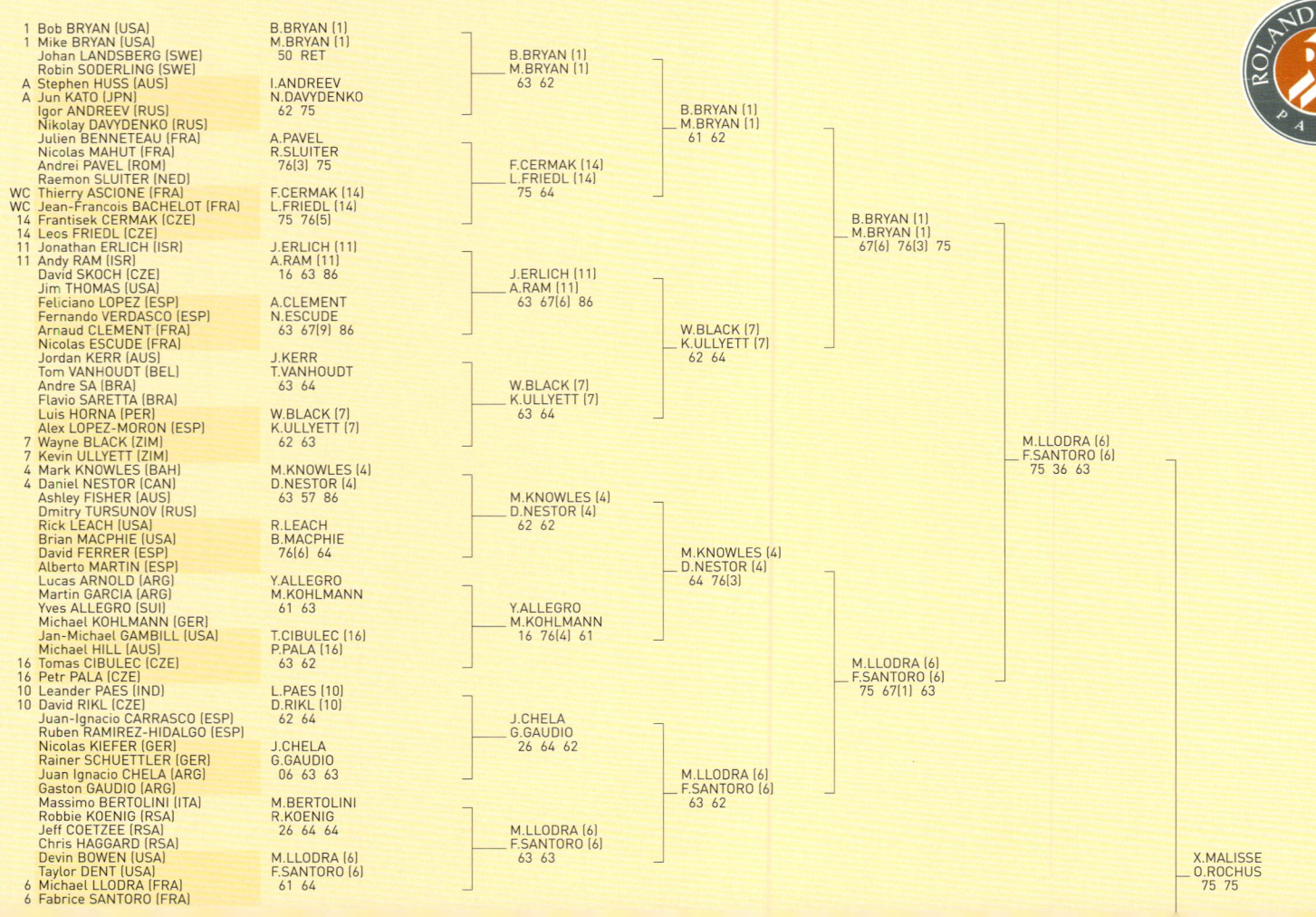

2004 French Open Championships Roland Garros, 24 May–6 June – Men's Doubles

```
 1  Bob BRYAN [USA]              B.BRYAN [1]
 1  Mike BRYAN [USA]             M.BRYAN [1]
    Johan LANDSBERG [SWE]        50 RET
    Robin SÖDERLING [SWE]                          B.BRYAN [1]
 A  Stephen HUSS [AUS]           I.ANDREEV         M.BRYAN [1]
 A  Jun KATO [JPN]               N.DAVYDENKO       63 62
    Igor ANDREEV [RUS]           62 75
    Nikolay DAVYDENKO [RUS]                                          B.BRYAN [1]
    Julien BENNETEAU [FRA]       A.PAVEL                             M.BRYAN [1]
    Nicolas MAHUT [FRA]          R.SLUITER                           61 62
    Andrei PAVEL [ROM]           76(3) 75
    Raemon SLUITER [NED]                           F.CERMAK [14]
 WC Thierry ASCIONE [FRA]        F.CERMAK [14]    L.FRIEDL [14]
 WC Jean-Francois BACHELOT [FRA] L.FRIEDL [14]    75 64
 14 Frantisek CERMAK [CZE]       75 76(5)
 14 Leos FRIEDL [CZE]                                                                 B.BRYAN [1]
 11 Jonathan ERLICH [ISR]                                                             M.BRYAN [1]
 11 Andy RAM [ISR]               J.ERLICH [11]                                        67(6) 76(3) 75
    David SKOCH [CZE]            A.RAM [11]
    Jim THOMAS [USA]             16 63 86
    Feliciano LOPEZ [ESP]                          J.ERLICH [11]
    Fernando VERDASCO [ESP]      A.CLEMENT         A.RAM [11]
    Arnaud CLEMENT [FRA]         N.ESCUDE          63 67(6) 86
    Nicolas ESCUDE [FRA]         63 67(9) 86
    Jordan KERR [AUS]                                                W.BLACK [7]
    Tom VANHOUDT [BEL]           J.KERR                              K.ULLYETT [7]
    Andre SA [BRA]               T.VANHOUDT                          62 64
    Flavio SARETTA [BRA]         63 64
    Luis HORNA [PER]                               W.BLACK [7]
    Alex LOPEZ-MORON [ESP]       W.BLACK [7]       K.ULLYETT [7]
  7 Wayne BLACK [ZIM]            K.ULLYETT [7]     63 64
  7 Kevin ULLYETT [ZIM]          62 63
  4 Mark KNOWLES [BAH]                                                                                M.LLODRA [6]
  4 Daniel NESTOR [CAN]          M.KNOWLES [4]                                                        F.SANTORO [6]
    Ashley FISHER [AUS]          D.NESTOR [4]                                                         75 36 63
    Dmitry TURSUNOV [RUS]        63 57 86
    Rick LEACH [USA]                               M.KNOWLES [4]
    Brian MACPHIE [USA]          R.LEACH           D.NESTOR [4]
    David FERRER [ESP]           B.MACPHIE         62 62
    Alberto MARTIN [ESP]         76(6) 64
    Lucas ARNOLD [ARG]                                               M.KNOWLES [4]
    Martin GARCIA [ARG]          Y.ALLEGRO                           D.NESTOR [4]
    Yves ALLEGRO [SUI]           M.KOHLMANN                          64 76(3)
    Michael KOHLMANN [GER]       61 63
    Jan-Michael GAMBILL [USA]                      T.CIBULEC [16]
    Michael HILL [AUS]           T.CIBULEC [16]    P.PALA [16]
 16 Tomas CIBULEC [CZE]          P.PALA [16]       63 62
 16 Petr PALA [CZE]              63 62                                                M.LLODRA [6]
 10 Leander PAES [IND]                                                                F.SANTORO [6]
 10 David RIKL [CZE]             L.PAES [10]                                          75 67(11) 63
    Juan-Ignacio CARRASCO [ESP]  D.RIKL [10]
    Ruben RAMIREZ-HIDALGO [ESP]  62 64
    Nicolas KIEFER [GER]                           J.CHELA
    Rainer SCHUETTLER [GER]      J.CHELA           G.GAUDIO
    Juan Ignacio CHELA [ARG]     G.GAUDIO          26 64 62
    Gaston GAUDIO [ARG]          06 63 63
    Massimo BERTOLINI [ITA]                                          M.LLODRA [6]
    Robbie KOENIG [RSA]          M.BERTOLINI                         F.SANTORO [6]
    Jeff COETZEE [RSA]           R.KOENIG                            63 62
    Chris HAGGARD [RSA]          26 64 64
    Devin BOWEN [USA]                              M.LLODRA [6]
    Taylor DENT [USA]            M.LLODRA [6]      F.SANTORO [6]
  6 Michael LLODRA [FRA]         F.SANTORO [6]     63 63
  6 Fabrice SANTORO [FRA]        61 64
```

X.MALISSE
O.ROCHUS
75 75

2004 Roland Garros — Men's Doubles Draw (partial)

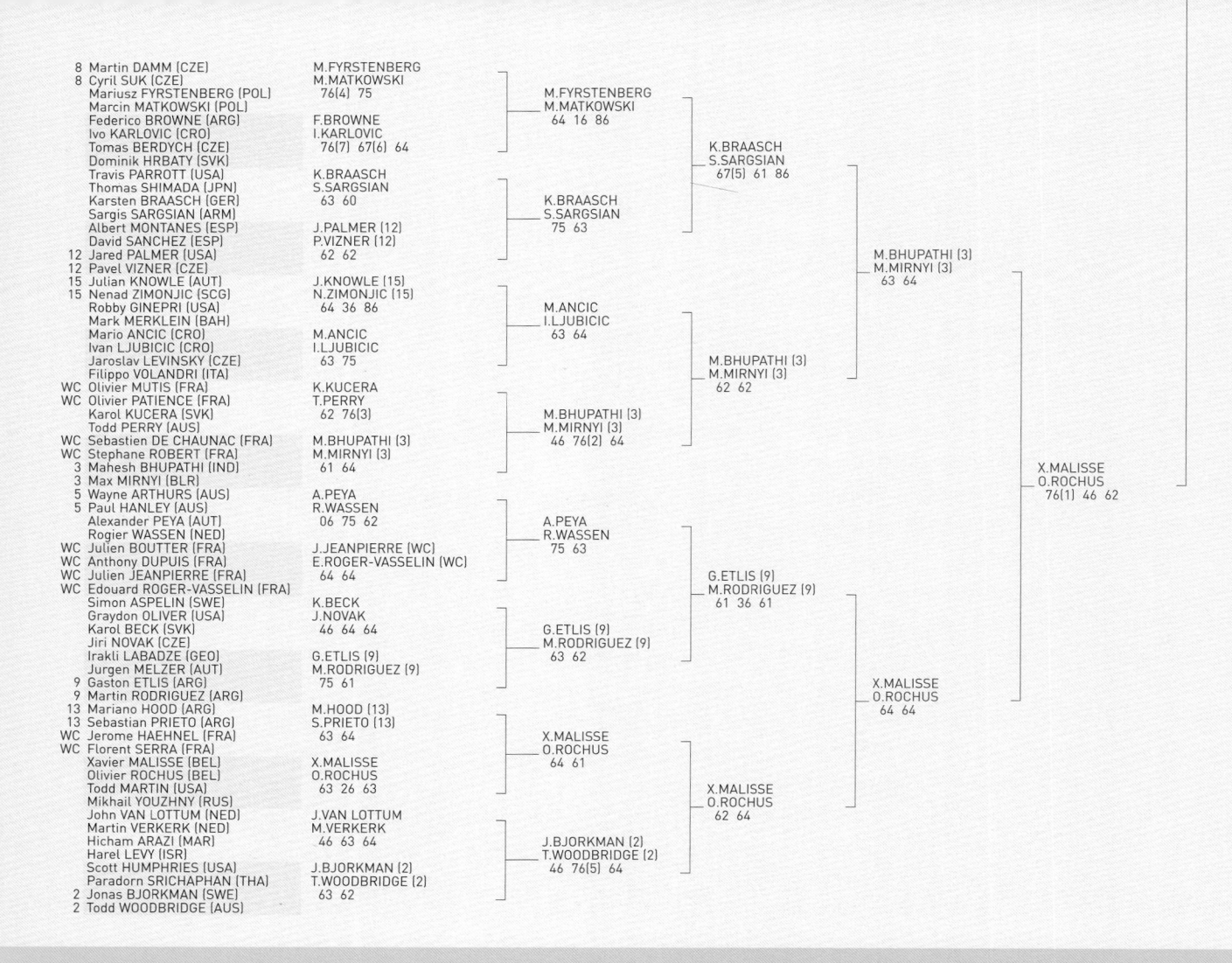

```
 8  Martin DAMM [CZE]          ┐
 8  Cyril SUK [CZE]             ├ M.FYRSTENBERG
    Mariusz FYRSTENBERG [POL]   │ M.MATKOWSKI
    Marcin MATKOWSKI [POL]     ─┘ 76(4) 75
    Federico BROWNE [ARG]      ┐
    Ivo KARLOVIC [CRO]          ├ F.BROWNE
    Tomas BERDYCH [CZE]         │ I.KARLOVIC
    Dominik HRBATY [SVK]       ─┘ 76(7) 67(6) 64      ┐
    Travis PARROTT [USA]       ┐                       ├ K.BRAASCH
    Thomas SHIMADA [JPN]        ├ K.BRAASCH            │ S.SARGSIAN
    Karsten BRAASCH [GER]       │ S.SARGSIAN          ─┘ 67(5) 61 86
    Sargis SARGSIAN [ARM]      ─┘ 63 60
    Albert MONTANES [ESP]      ┐
12  Jared PALMER [USA]          ├ J.PALMER [12]
12  David SANCHEZ [ESP]         │ P.VIZNER [12]
    Pavel VIZNER [CZE]         ─┘ 62 62                                ┐
15  Julian KNOWLE [AUT]        ┐                                        │
15  Nenad ZIMONJIC [SCG]        ├ J.KNOWLE [15]                         │
    Robby GINEPRI [USA]         │ N.ZIMONJIC [15]                      │
    Mark MERKLEIN [BAH]        ─┘ 64 36 86             ┐               │
    Mario ANCIC [CRO]          ┐                        ├ M.ANCIC       │
    Ivan LJUBICIC [CRO]         ├ M.ANCIC               │ I.LJUBICIC   │
    Jaroslav LEVINSKY [CZE]     │ I.LJUBICIC           ─┘ 63 64         ├ M.BHUPATHI [3]
    Filippo VOLANDRI [ITA]     ─┘ 63 75                                │ M.MIRNYI [3]
WC  Olivier PATIENCE [FRA]     ┐                                        │ 63 64
    Karol KUCERA [SVK]          ├ K.KUCERA
    Todd PERRY [AUS]            │ T.PERRY
    Sebastien DE CHAUNAC [FRA] ─┘ 62 76(3)             ┐
WC  Stephane ROBERT [FRA]      ┐                        ├ M.BHUPATHI [3]
 3  Mahesh BHUPATHI [IND]       ├ M.BHUPATHI [3]        │ M.MIRNYI [3]
 3  Max MIRNYI [BLR]            │ M.MIRNYI [3]         ─┘ 62 62
 5  Wayne ARTHURS [AUS]        ─┘ 61 64
 5  Paul HANLEY [AUS]          ┐
    Alexander PEYA [AUT]        ├ A.PEYA
    Roger WASSEN [NED]          │ R.WASSEN
WC  Julien BOUTTER [FRA]       ─┘ 06 75 62
WC  Anthony DUPUIS [FRA]       ┐
WC  Julien JEANPIERRE [FRA]     ├ J.JEANPIERRE [WC]
WC  Edouard ROGER-VASSELIN [FRA]│ E.ROGER-VASSELIN [WC]
    Simon ASPELIN [SWE]        ─┘ 64 64                ┐
    Graydon OLIVER [USA]       ┐                        ├ G.ETLIS [9]
    Karol BECK [SVK]            ├ K.BECK                │ M.RODRIGUEZ [9]
    Jiri NOVAK [CZE]            │ J.NOVAK              ─┘ 61 36 61
    Irakli LABADZE [GEO]       ─┘ 46 64 64
    Jurgen MELZER [AUT]        ┐
 9  Gaston ETLIS [ARG]          ├ G.ETLIS [9]
 9  Martin RODRIGUEZ [ARG]      │ M.RODRIGUEZ [9]
    Mariano HOOD [ARG]         ─┘ 75 61                                ┐
13  Sebastian PRIETO [ARG]     ┐                                        │
13  Jerome HAEHNEL [FRA]        ├ M.HOOD [13]                           │
WC  Florent SERRA [FRA]         │ S.PRIETO [13]                        │
    Xavier MALISSE [BEL]       ─┘ 63 64                ┐               │
    Olivier ROCHUS [BEL]       ┐                        ├ X.MALISSE     ├ X.MALISSE
    Todd MARTIN [USA]           ├ X.MALISSE             │ O.ROCHUS      │ O.ROCHUS
    Mikhail YOUZHNY [RUS]       │ O.ROCHUS             ─┘ 64 61         │ 64 64
    John VAN LOTTUM [NED]      ─┘ 63 26 63                              │
    Martin VERKERK [NED]       ┐                                        │
    Hicham ARAZI [MAR]          ├ J.VAN LOTTUM                         │
    Harel LEVY [ISR]            │ M.VERKERK                            │
    Scott HUMPHRIES [USA]      ─┘ 46 63 64             ┐               │
    Paradorn SRICHAPHAN [THA]  ┐                        ├ J.BJORKMAN [2]│
 2  Jonas BJORKMAN [SWE]        ├ J.BJORKMAN [2]        │ T.WOODBRIDGE [2]
 2  Todd WOODBRIDGE [AUS]       │ T.WOODBRIDGE [2]     ─┘ 46 76(5) 64
                                ─┘ 63 62
```

Final: X.MALISSE / O.ROCHUS 76(1) 46 62

Elite Tournaments: 2004 Roland Garros Drawsheets — 85

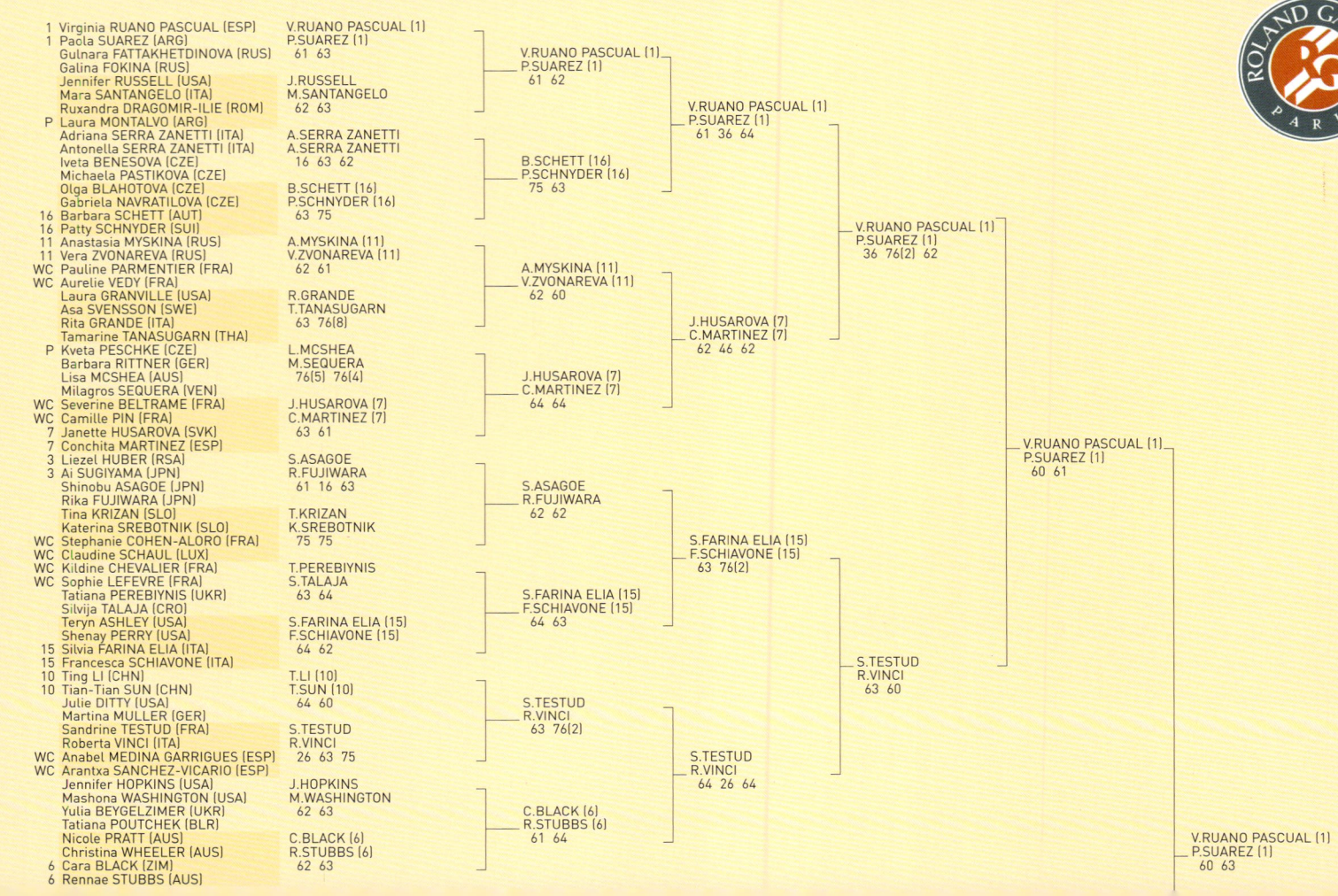

2004 French Open Championships Roland Garros, 24 May–6 June – Women's Doubles

Seed	Player 1 / Player 2	R1	R2	R3	QF	SF	F
1	Virginia RUANO PASCUAL (ESP) / Paola SUAREZ (ARG)	V.RUANO PASCUAL [1] / P.SUAREZ [1] 6 1 6 3	V.RUANO PASCUAL [1] / P.SUAREZ [1] 6 1 6 2	V.RUANO PASCUAL [1] / P.SUAREZ [1] 6 1 3 6 6 4	V.RUANO PASCUAL [1] / P.SUAREZ [1] 3 6 7 6(2) 6 2	V.RUANO PASCUAL [1] / P.SUAREZ [1] 6 0 6 1	V.RUANO PASCUAL [1] / P.SUAREZ [1] 6 0 6 3
	Gulnara FATTAKHETDINOVA (RUS) / Galina FOKINA (RUS)						
	Jennifer RUSSELL (USA) / Mara SANTANGELO (ITA)	J.RUSSELL / M.SANTANGELO 6 2 6 3					
P	Laura MONTALVO (ARG) / Ruxandra DRAGOMIR-ILIE (ROM)						
	Adriana SERRA ZANETTI (ITA) / Antonella SERRA ZANETTI (ITA)	A.SERRA ZANETTI / A.SERRA ZANETTI 1 6 6 3 6 2	B.SCHETT [16] / P.SCHNYDER [16] 7 5 6 3				
	Iveta BENESOVA (CZE) / Michaela PASTIKOVA (CZE)						
16	Olga BLAHOTOVA (CZE) / Gabriela NAVRATILOVA (CZE)	B.SCHETT [16] / P.SCHNYDER [16] 6 3 7 5					
16	Barbara SCHETT (AUT) / Patty SCHNYDER (SUI)						
11	Anastasia MYSKINA (RUS) / Vera ZVONAREVA (RUS)	A.MYSKINA [11] / V.ZVONAREVA [11] 6 2 6 1	A.MYSKINA [11] / V.ZVONAREVA [11] 6 2 6 0	J.HUSAROVA [7] / C.MARTINEZ [7] 6 2 4 6 6 2			
WC	Pauline PARMENTIER (FRA) / Aurelie VEDY (FRA)						
WC	Laura GRANVILLE (USA) / Asa SVENSSON (SWE)	R.GRANDE / T.TANASUGARN 6 3 7 6(8)					
	Tamarine TANASUGARN (THA) / Rita GRANDE (ITA)						
P	Kveta PESCHKE (CZE) / Barbara RITTNER (GER)	L.MCSHEA / M.SEQUERA 7 6(5) 7 6(4)	J.HUSAROVA [7] / C.MARTINEZ [7] 6 4 6 4				
	Lisa MCSHEA (AUS) / Milagros SEQUERA (VEN)						
WC	Severine BELTRAME (FRA) / Camille PIN (FRA)	J.HUSAROVA [7] / C.MARTINEZ [7] 6 3 6 1					
7	Janette HUSAROVA (SVK) / Conchita MARTINEZ (ESP)						
3	Liezel HUBER (RSA) / Ai SUGIYAMA (JPN)	S.ASAGOE / R.FUJIWARA 6 1 1 6 6 3	S.ASAGOE / R.FUJIWARA 6 2 6 2	S.FARINA ELIA [15] / F.SCHIAVONE [15] 6 3 7 6(2)	S.FARINA ELIA [15] / F.SCHIAVONE [15]		
3	Shinobu ASAGOE (JPN) / Rika FUJIWARA (JPN)						
	Tina KRIZAN (ISLO) / Katerina SREBOTNIK (SLO)	T.KRIZAN / K.SREBOTNIK 7 5 7 5					
WC	Stephanie COHEN-ALORO (FRA) / Claudine SCHAUL (LUX)						
WC	Kildine CHEVALIER (FRA) / Sophie LEFEVRE (FRA)	T.PEREBIYNIS / S.TALAJA 6 3 6 4	S.FARINA ELIA [15] / F.SCHIAVONE [15] 6 4 6 3				
WC	Tatiana PEREBIYNIS (UKR) / Silvija TALAJA (CRO)						
	Teryn ASHLEY (USA) / Shenay PERRY (USA)	S.FARINA ELIA [15] / F.SCHIAVONE [15] 6 4 6 2					
15	Silvia FARINA ELIA (ITA) / Francesca SCHIAVONE (ITA)						
10	Ting LI (CHN) / Tian-Tian SUN (CHN)	T.LI [10] / T.SUN [10] 6 4 6 0	S.TESTUD / R.VINCI 6 3 7 6(2)	S.TESTUD / R.VINCI 6 4 2 6 6 4	S.TESTUD / R.VINCI 6 3 6 0		
10	Julie DITTY (USA) / Martina MULLER (GER)						
	Sandrine TESTUD (FRA) / Roberta VINCI (ITA)	S.TESTUD / R.VINCI 2 6 6 3 7 5					
WC	Anabel MEDINA GARRIGUES (ESP) / Arantxa SANCHEZ-VICARIO (ESP)						
WC	Jennifer HOPKINS (USA) / Mashona WASHINGTON (USA)	J.HOPKINS / M.WASHINGTON 6 2 6 3	C.BLACK [6] / R.STUBBS [6] 6 1 6 4				
	Yulia BEYGELZIMER (UKR) / Tatiana POUTCHEK (BLR)						
	Nicole PRATT (AUS) / Christina WHEELER (AUS)	C.BLACK [6] / R.STUBBS [6] 6 2 6 3					
6	Cara BLACK (ZIM) / Rennae STUBBS (AUS)						

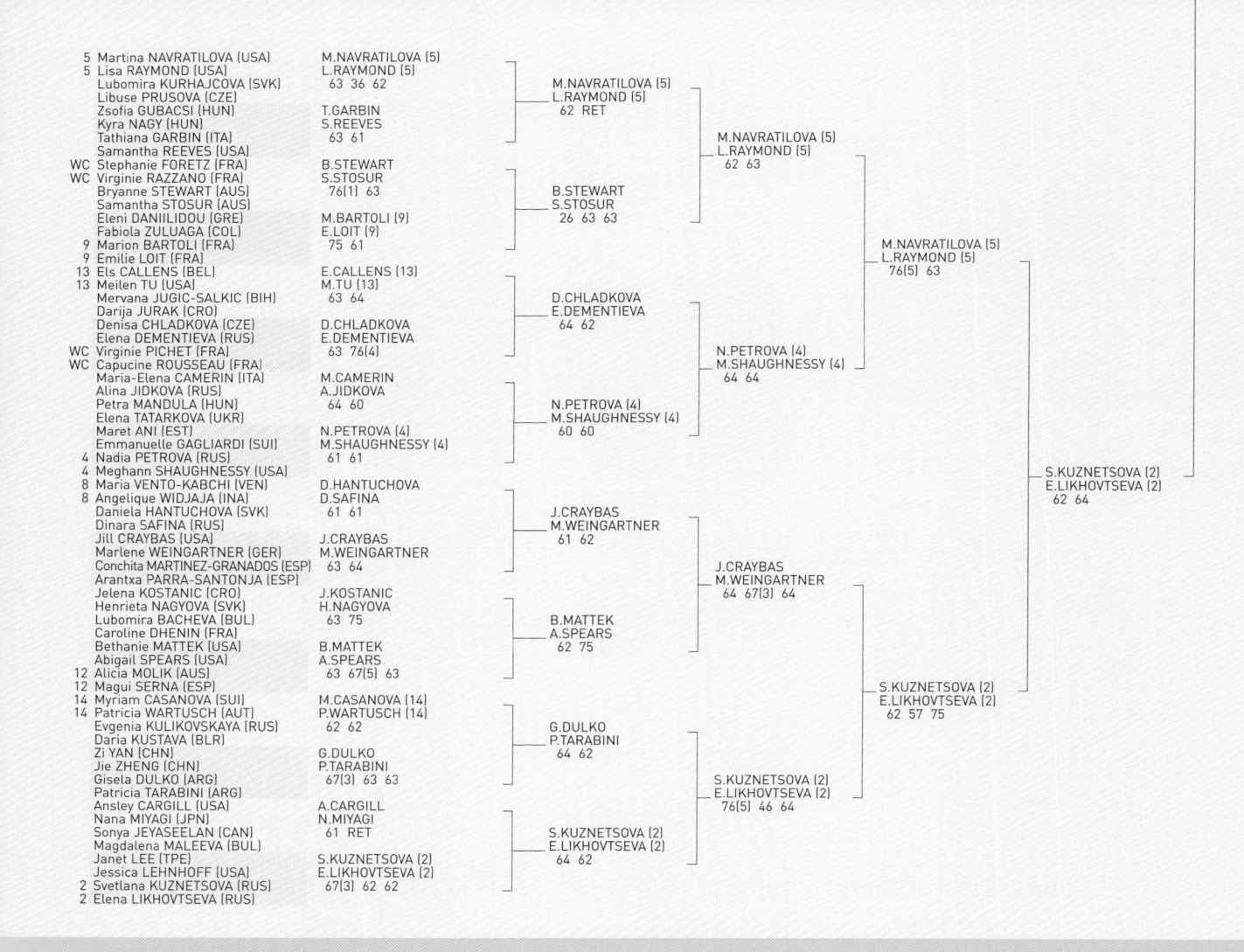

2004 Roland Garros – Women's Doubles Draw (partial)

Final (shown): S. KUZNETSOVA / E. LIKHOVTSEVA [2] def. M. NAVRATILOVA / L. RAYMOND [5] 6-2 6-4

Semifinal / Quarterfinal results

- M. NAVRATILOVA / L. RAYMOND [5] def. N. PETROVA / M. SHAUGHNESSY [4] 7-6(5) 6-3
- S. KUZNETSOVA / E. LIKHOVTSEVA [2] def. J. CRAYBAS / M. WEINGARTNER 6-2 5-7 7-5

Round of 16

- M. NAVRATILOVA / L. RAYMOND [5] def. B. STEWART / S. STOSUR 6-2 6-3
- N. PETROVA / M. SHAUGHNESSY [4] def. D. CHLADKOVA / E. DEMENTIEVA 6-4 6-4
- J. CRAYBAS / M. WEINGARTNER def. B. MATTEK / A. SPEARS 6-4 6-7(3) 6-4
- S. KUZNETSOVA / E. LIKHOVTSEVA [2] def. G. DULKO / P. TARABINI 7-6(5) 4-6 6-4

Second Round

- M. NAVRATILOVA / L. RAYMOND [5] def. T. GARBIN / S. REEVES 6-2 RET
- B. STEWART / S. STOSUR def. M. BARTOLI / E. LOIT [9] 2-6 6-3 6-3
- D. CHLADKOVA / E. DEMENTIEVA def. E. CALLENS [13] / M. TU 6-3 6-4
- N. PETROVA [4] / M. SHAUGHNESSY def. M. CAMERIN / A. JIDKOVA 6-4 6-0
- J. CRAYBAS / M. WEINGARTNER def. D. HANTUCHOVA / D. SAFINA 6-1 6-1
- B. MATTEK / A. SPEARS def. J. KOSTANIC / H. NAGYOVA 6-3 7-5
- G. DULKO / P. TARABINI def. M. CASANOVA / P. WARTUSCH [14] 6-2 6-2
- S. KUZNETSOVA / E. LIKHOVTSEVA [2] def. A. CARGILL / N. MIYAGI 6-1 RET

First Round

- M. NAVRATILOVA / L. RAYMOND [5] def. Martina NAVRATILOVA (USA) / Lisa RAYMOND (USA) 6-3 3-6 6-2
  (opponents: Lubomira KURHAJCOVA (SVK) / Libuse PRUSOVA (CZE))
- T. GARBIN (ITA) / S. REEVES (USA) def. Zsofia GUBACSI (HUN) / Kyra NAGY (HUN) 6-3 6-1
- B. STEWART / S. STOSUR (AUS) def. WC Stephanie FORETZ (FRA) / Samantha REEVES (USA) 7-6(1) 6-3
  (WC Bryanne STEWART (AUS) / Samantha STOSUR (AUS))
- M. BARTOLI / E. LOIT [9] def. Eleni DANIILIDOU (GRE) / Fabiola ZULUAGA (COL) 7-5 6-1
  (Marion BARTOLI (FRA) / Emilie LOIT (FRA))
- E. CALLENS [13] / M. TU def. Els CALLENS (BEL) / Mellen TU (USA) — 6-3 6-4
  (vs. Mervana JUGIC-SALKIC (BIH) / Darija JURAK (CRO))
- D. CHLADKOVA / E. DEMENTIEVA def. Denisa CHLADKOVA (CZE) / Elena DEMENTIEVA (RUS) 6-3 7-6(4)
  (vs. WC Virginie PICHET (FRA) / Capucine ROUSSEAU (FRA))
- M. CAMERIN / A. JIDKOVA def. WC Maria-Elena CAMERIN (ITA) / Alina JIDKOVA (RUS) 6-4 6-0
  (vs. Petra MANDULA (HUN) / Elena TATARKOVA (UKR))
- N. PETROVA [4] / M. SHAUGHNESSY def. Maret ANI (EST) / Emmanuelle GAGLIARDI (SUI) 6-1 6-1
  (Nadia PETROVA (RUS) / Meghann SHAUGHNESSY (USA))
- D. HANTUCHOVA / D. SAFINA [8] def. Maria VENTO-KABCHI (VEN) / Angelique WIDJAJA (INA) 6-1 6-1
  (Daniela HANTUCHOVA (SVK) / Dinara SAFINA (RUS))
- J. CRAYBAS / M. WEINGARTNER def. Jill CRAYBAS (USA) / Marlene WEINGARTNER (GER) 6-3 6-4
  (vs. Conchita MARTINEZ-GRANADOS (ESP) / Arantxa PARRA-SANTONJA (ESP))
- J. KOSTANIC / H. NAGYOVA def. Jelena KOSTANIC (CRO) / Henrieta NAGYOVA (SVK) 6-3 7-5
  (vs. Lubomira BACHEVA (BUL) / Caroline DHENIN (FRA))
- B. MATTEK / A. SPEARS def. Bethanie MATTEK (USA) / Abigail SPEARS (USA) 6-3 6-7(5) 6-3
  (vs. 12 Alicia MOLIK (AUS) / Magui SERNA (ESP))
- M. CASANOVA / P. WARTUSCH [14] def. 14 Myriam CASANOVA (SUI) / Patricia WARTUSCH (AUT) 6-2 6-2
  (vs. Evgenia KULIKOVSKAYA (RUS) / Daria KUSTAVA (BLR))
- G. DULKO / P. TARABINI def. Zi YAN (CHN) / Jie ZHENG (CHN) 6-7(3) 6-3 6-3
  (Gisela DULKO (ARG) / Patricia TARABINI (ARG))
- A. CARGILL / N. MIYAGI def. Ansley CARGILL (USA) / Nana MIYAGI (JPN) 6-1 RET
  (vs. Sonya JEYASEELAN (CAN) / Magdalena MALEEVA (BUL))
- S. KUZNETSOVA [2] / E. LIKHOVTSEVA [2] def. Janet LEE (TPE) / Jessica LEHNHOFF (USA) 6-7(3) 6-2 6-2
  (Svetlana KUZNETSOVA (RUS) / Elena LIKHOVTSEVA (RUS))

Elite Tournaments: 2004 Roland Garros Drawsheets — 87

2003 French Open Championships Roland Garros, 24 May–6 June – Mixed Doubles

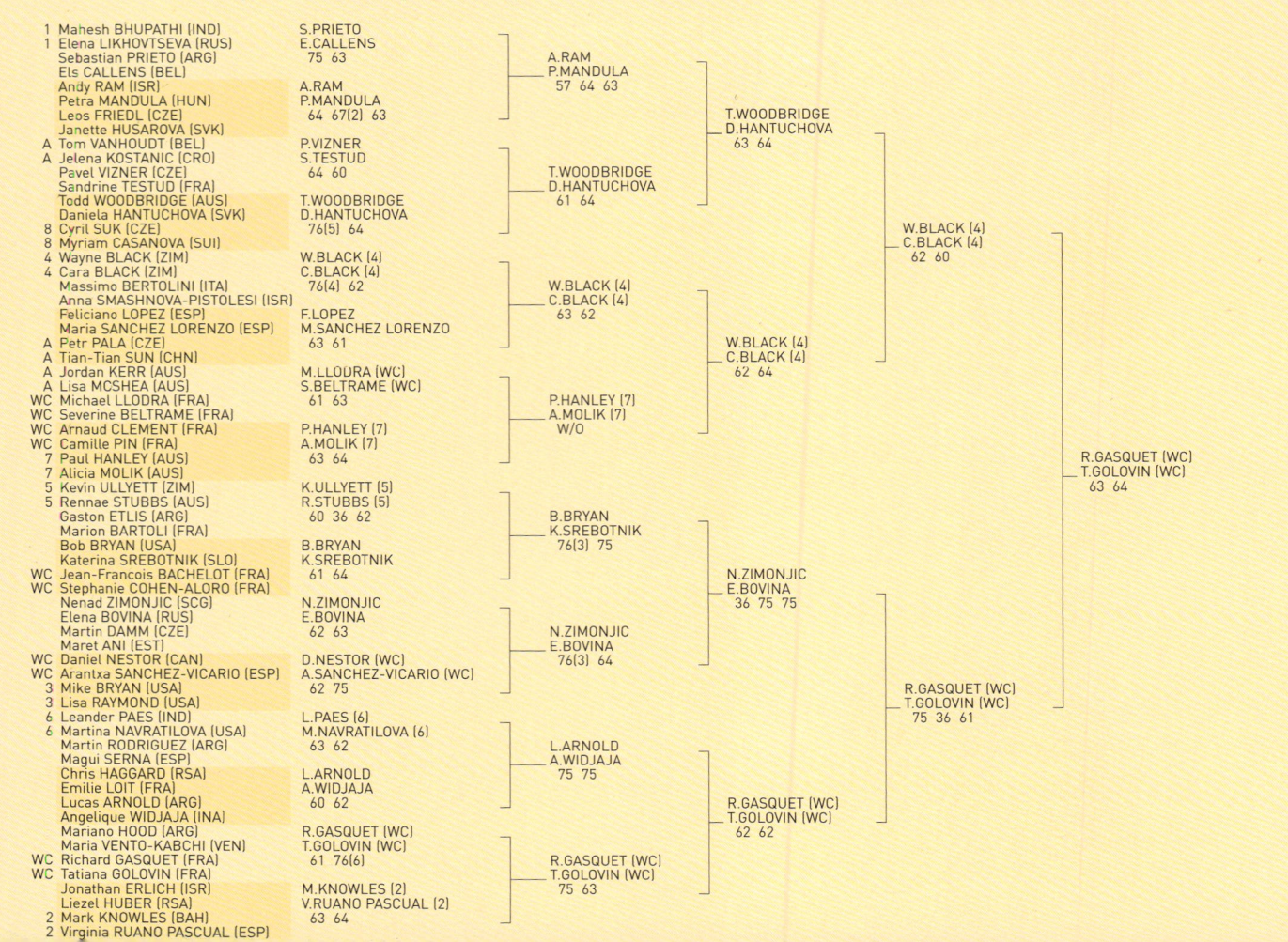

Winners: R. Gasquet (WC) / T. Golovin (WC)

First Round

- 1 Mahesh BHUPATHI (IND) / Elena LIKHOVTSEVA (RUS)
-    Sebastian PRIETO (ARG) / Els CALLENS (BEL) — S. Prieto / E. Callens 7-5 6-3
-    Andy RAM (ISR) / Petra MANDULA (HUN)
-    Leos FRIEDL (CZE) / Janette HUSAROVA (SVK) — A. Ram / P. Mandula 6-4 6(7)-2 6-3
- A Tom VANHOUDT (BEL) / Jelena KOSTANIC (CRO)
-    Pavel VIZNER (CZE) / Sandrine TESTUD (FRA) — P. Vizner / S. Testud 6-4 6-0
-    Todd WOODBRIDGE (AUS) / Daniela HANTUCHOVA (SVK)
- 8 Cyril SUK (CZE) / Myriam CASANOVA (SUI) — T. Woodbridge / D. Hantuchova 7-6(5) 6-4
- 4 Wayne BLACK (ZIM) / Cara BLACK (ZIM)
-    Massimo BERTOLINI (ITA) / Anna SMASHNOVA-PISTOLESI (ISR) — W. Black / C. Black 7-6(4) 6-2
-    Feliciano LOPEZ (ESP) / Maria SANCHEZ LORENZO (ESP)
-    Petr PALA (CZE) / Tian-Tian SUN (CHN) — F. Lopez / M. Sanchez Lorenzo 6-3 6-1
- A Jordan KERR (AUS) / Lisa MCSHEA (AUS)
- WC Michael LLODRA (FRA) / Severine BELTRAME (FRA) — M. Llodra / S. Beltrame 6-1 6-3
- WC Arnaud CLEMENT (FRA) / Camille PIN (FRA)
- 7 Paul HANLEY (AUS) / Alicia MOLIK (AUS) — P. Hanley / A. Molik W/O
- 5 Kevin ULLYETT (ZIM) / Rennae STUBBS (AUS)
-    Gaston ETLIS (ARG) / Marion BARTOLI (FRA) — K. Ullyett / R. Stubbs 6-0 3-6 6-2
-    Bob BRYAN (USA) / Katerina SREBOTNIK (SLO)
- WC Jean-François BACHELOT (FRA) / Stephanie COHEN-ALORO (FRA) — B. Bryan / K. Srebotnik 7-6(3) 7-5
- WC Nenad ZIMONJIC (SCG) / Elena BOVINA (RUS)
-    Martin DAMM (CZE) / Maret ANI (EST) — N. Zimonjic / E. Bovina 6-1 6-4
- WC Daniel NESTOR (CAN) / Arantxa SANCHEZ-VICARIO (ESP)
-    Mike BRYAN (USA) / Lisa RAYMOND (USA) — A. Sanchez-Vicario / D. Nestor 6-2 7-5
- 6 Leander PAES (IND) / Martina NAVRATILOVA (USA)
-    Martin RODRIGUEZ (ARG) / Magui SERNA (ESP) — L. Paes / M. Navratilova 6-3 6-2
-    Chris HAGGARD (RSA) / Lucas ARNOLD (ARG)
-    Emilie LOIT (FRA) / Angelique WIDJAJA (INA) — L. Arnold / A. Widjaja 6-0 6-2
- WC Mariano HOOD (ARG) / Maria VENTO-KABCHI (VEN)
- WC Richard GASQUET (FRA) / Tatiana GOLOVIN (FRA) — R. Gasquet / T. Golovin 6-1 7-6(6)
-    Jonathan ERLICH (ISR) / Liezel HUBER (RSA)
- 2 Mark KNOWLES (BAH) / Virginia RUANO PASCUAL (ESP) — M. Knowles / V. Ruano Pascual 6-3 6-4

Second Round

- T. Woodbridge / D. Hantuchova 6-3 6-4
- W. Black / C. Black 6-3 6-2
- P. Hanley / A. Molik 6-3 6-4
- B. Bryan / K. Srebotnik 6-1 6-4
- N. Zimonjic / E. Bovina 6-2 6-3
- L. Arnold / A. Widjaja 7-5 7-5
- R. Gasquet / T. Golovin 6-1 7-6(6)

Quarterfinals

- T. Woodbridge / D. Hantuchova 6-1 6-4
- W. Black / C. Black 6-2 6-4
- N. Zimonjic / E. Bovina 3-6 7-5 7-5
- R. Gasquet / T. Golovin 6-2 6-2

Semifinals

- W. Black / C. Black 6-2 6-0
- R. Gasquet / T. Golovin 7-5 3-6 6-1

Final

- R. Gasquet / T. Golovin 6-3 6-4

Roland Garros Champion Gaston Gaudio (ARG)

2004 Wimbledon Championships, 21 June–4 July – Women's Singles

Seed/Status	Player	R1	R2	R3	R4	QF	SF	F
1	Serena WILLIAMS (USA)	S.WILLIAMS [1] 6 3 6 1	S.WILLIAMS [1] 6 0 6 4	S.WILLIAMS [1] 6 4 6 0	S.WILLIAMS [1] 6 2 6 1	S.WILLIAMS [1] 6 1 6 1	S.WILLIAMS [1] 6 7(4) 7 5 6 4	M.SHARAPOVA [13] 6 1 6 4
	Jie ZHENG (CHN)							
Q	Stephanie FORETZ (FRA)	S.FORETZ (Q) 6 1 6 3						
	Stephanie COHEN-ALORO (FRA)							
WC	Jane O'DONOGHUE (GBR)	J.O'DONOGHUE (WC) 2 6 6 3 6 3	M.SERNA 6 3 6 3					
	Lindsay LEE-WATERS (USA)							
	Magui SERNA (ESP)	M.SERNA 6 4 6 2						
30	Eleni DANIILIDOU (GRE)							
18	Francesca SCHIAVONE (ITA)	F.SCHIAVONE [18] 6 4 7 6(4) 6 3	T.GOLOVIN 6 1 6 0	T.GOLOVIN 6 3 2 6 6 3				
	Myriam CASANOVA (SUI)							
	Tatiana GOLOVIN (FRA)	T.GOLOVIN 6 4 7 6(4)						
	Alina JIDKOVA (RUS)							
	Emmanuelle GAGLIARDI (SUI)	E.GAGLIARDI 3 3 RET	E.GAGLIARDI 2 6 7 6(4) 6 2					
	Tara SNYDER (USA)							
WC	Patty SCHNYDER (SUI)	P.SCHNYDER [15] (WC) 6 4 6 1						
15	Akiko MORIGAMI (JPN)							
10	Nadia PETROVA (RUS)	N.PETROVA [10] 6 3 2 6 6 4	N.PETROVA [10] 3 6 6 2	N.PETROVA [10] 7 6(5) 6 2	J.CAPRIATI [7] 6 4 6 4			
	Flavia PENNETTA (ITA)							
	Maria VENTO-KABCHI (VEN)	M.VENTO-KABCHI 6 1 6 0						
	Martina SUCHA (SVK)							
	Tatiana PEREBIYNIS (UKR)	T.PEREBIYNIS 6 3 6 2	T.PEREBIYNIS 6 2 7 5					
	Christina WHEELER (AUS)							
Q	Milagros SEQUERA (VEN)	M.SEQUERA 6 4 7 6(6)						
22	Corchita MARTINEZ (ESP)							
25	Nathalie DECHY (FRA)	N.DECHY [25] 6 3 6 4	N.DECHY [25] 6 1 6 1	J.CAPRIATI [7] 7 5 6 1				
	Anabel MEDINA GARRIGUES (ESP)							
LL	Maria SANCHEZ LORENZO (ESP)	M.SANCHEZ LORENZO 6 4 6 4						
	Kate O'BRIEN (GBR)							
	Marta MARRERO (ESP)	E.BALTACHA (WC) 6 1 6 3	J.CAPRIATI [7] 6 2 6 2					
WC	Elena BALTACHA (GBR)							
7	Jennifer CAPRIATI (USA)	J.CAPRIATI [7] 6 2 6 2						
4	Amelie MAURESMO (FRA)	A.MAURESMO [4] 6 3 6 3	A.MAURESMO [4] 6 1 6 4	A.MAURESMO [4] 7 5 6 3	A.MAURESMO [4] 6 0 5 7 6 1			
	Jelena KOSTANIC (CRO)							
Q	Julia VAKULENKO (UKR)	J.HOPKINS (Q) 7 6(5) 6 2						
	Jennifer HOPKINS (USA)							
	Barbara SCHETT (AUT)	L.CERVANOVA 3 6 6 4 6 4	L.CERVANOVA 6 4 6 3					
	Ludmila CERVANOVA (SVK)							
26	Lisa RAYMOND (USA)	L.RAYMOND [26] 6 3 7 6(4)						
	Shinobu ASAGOE (JPN)							
24	Mary PIERCE (FRA)	V.RUANO PASCUAL 6 2 7 5	V.RUANO PASCUAL 6 4 6 4	S.FARINA ELIA [14] 2 6 6 4 7 5				
	Virginia RUANO PASCUAL (ESP)							
	Lina KRASNOROUTSKAYA (RUS)	H.NAGYOVA 3 6 6 4 6 3						
	Henrieta NAGYOVA (SVK)							
	Barbora STRYCOVA (CZE)	S.TALAJA 6 3 6 4	S.FARINA ELIA [14] 6 3 6 3					
	Silvija TALAJA (CRO)							
14	Silvia FARINA ELIA (ITA)	S.FARINA ELIA [14] 6 0 6 4						
	Shuai PENG (CHN)							
9	Paola SUAREZ (ARG)	P.SUAREZ [9] 6 2 6 4	P.SUAREZ [9] 6 2 6 2	P.SUAREZ [9] 6 1 4 6 6 0	P.SUAREZ [9] 4 6 6 0 6 2			
	Shenay PERRY (USA)							
	Ashley HARKLEROAD (USA)	E.CALLENS 6 3 5 7 6 4						
	Els CALLENS (BEL)							
Q	Tian-Tian SUN (CHN)	T.SUN (Q) 2 6 6 0 6 2	A.KREMER (P) 6 3 7 5					
	Tathiana GARBIN (ITA)							
P	Anne KREMER (LUX)	A.KREMER (P) 6 3 7 5						
19	Fabiola ZULUAGA (COL)							
29	Dinara SAFINA (RUS)	A.PARRA-SANTONJA 6 0 2 0 RET	R.GRANDE 5 7 6 2 6 3	R.GRANDE 6 4 4 6 6 3				
	Arantxa PARRA-SANTONJA (ESP)							
	Rita GRANDE (ITA)	R.GRANDE 7 5 7 5						
	Mara SANTANGELO (ITA)							
	Gala LEON GARCIA (ESP)	E.LIKHOVTSEVA 6 2 6 2	V.RAZZANO (Q) 6 1 6 2					
	Elena LIKHOVTSEVA (RUS)							
Q	Virginie RAZZANO (FRA)	V.RAZZANO (Q) 7 6(4) 3 6 6 4						
8	Svetlana KUZNETSOVA (RUS)							

Elite Tournaments: 2004 Wimbledon Drawsheets

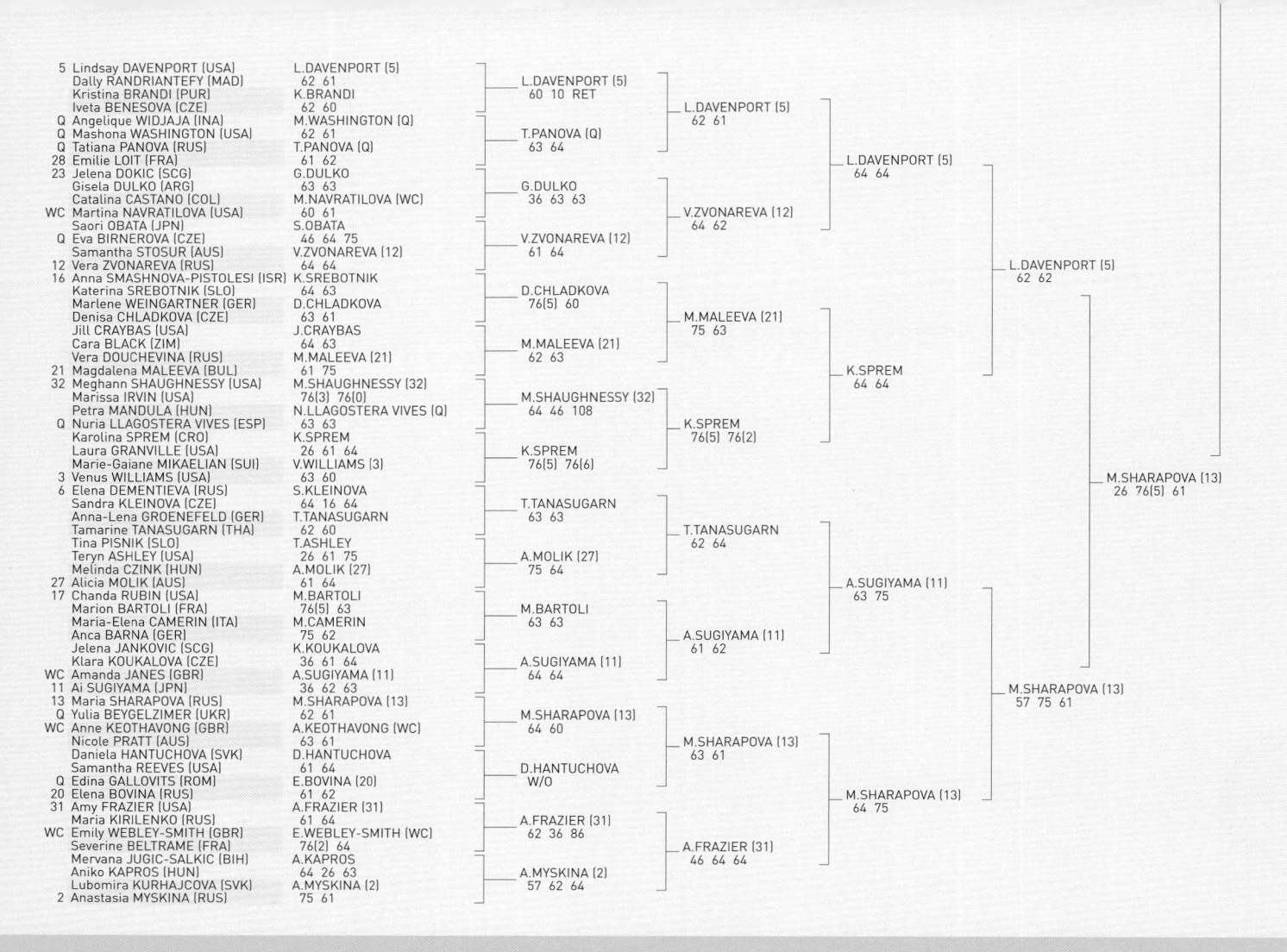

Ladies' Singles (bottom half)

Final of quarter: M.SHARAPOVA [13] def. L.DAVENPORT [5] 2-6 7-6(5) 6-1

Round of 16
- L.DAVENPORT [5] def. V.ZVONAREVA [12] 6-2 6-2
- K.SPREM def. M.MALEEVA [21] 6-4 6-4
- A.SUGIYAMA [11] def. T.TANASUGARN 6-3 7-5
- M.SHARAPOVA [13] def. A.FRAZIER [31] 6-4 7-5

Third round
- L.DAVENPORT [5] def. T.PANOVA (Q) 6-4 6-4
- V.ZVONAREVA [12] def. G.DULKO 6-4 6-2
- M.MALEEVA [21] def. D.CHLADKOVA 7-5 6-3
- K.SPREM def. M.SHAUGHNESSY [32] 7-6(5) 7-6(2)
- T.TANASUGARN def. V.WILLIAMS [3] 6-2 6-4
- A.SUGIYAMA [11] def. M.BARTOLI 6-1 6-2
- M.SHARAPOVA [13] def. D.HANTUCHOVA 6-3 6-1
- A.FRAZIER [31] def. A.MYSKINA [2] 4-6 6-4 6-4

Second round
- L.DAVENPORT [5] 6-0 1-0 RET
- T.PANOVA (Q) 6-3 6-4
- G.DULKO 3-6 6-3 6-3
- V.ZVONAREVA [12] 6-1 6-4
- D.CHLADKOVA 7-6(5) 6-0
- M.MALEEVA [21] 6-2 6-3
- M.SHAUGHNESSY [32] 6-4 4-6 10-8
- K.SPREM 7-6(5) 7-6(6)
- T.TANASUGARN 6-3 6-3
- A.MOLIK [27] 7-5 6-4
- M.BARTOLI 7-6(5) 6-3
- A.SUGIYAMA [11] 6-4 6-4
- M.SHARAPOVA [13] 6-4 6-0
- D.HANTUCHOVA W/O
- A.FRAZIER [31] 6-2 3-6 8-6
- A.MYSKINA [2] 5-7 6-2 7-6(4)

First round
- L.DAVENPORT [5] 6-2 6-1
- K.BRANDI 6-2 6-0
- M.WASHINGTON (Q) 6-2 6-1
- T.PANOVA (Q) 6-1 6-2
- G.DULKO 6-3 6-3
- M.NAVRATILOVA (WC) 6-0 6-1
- S.OBATA 4-6 6-4 7-5
- V.ZVONAREVA [12] 6-1 6-4
- K.SREBOTNIK 6-4 6-3
- D.CHLADKOVA 6-3 6-1
- J.CRAYBAS 6-4 6-3
- M.MALEEVA [21] 6-2 6-3
- V.DOUCHEVINA 6-1 7-5
- M.SHAUGHNESSY [32] 7-6(3) 7-6(0)
- N.LLAGOSTERA VIVES (Q) 6-3 6-3
- K.SPREM 2-6 6-1 6-4
- V.WILLIAMS [3] 6-3 6-0
- S.KLEINOVA 6-4 1-6 6-4
- E.DEMENTIEVA (RUS) -
- T.TANASUGARN 6-2 6-0
- T.ASHLEY 2-6 6-1 7-5
- A.MOLIK [27] 6-1 6-4
- M.BARTOLI 7-6(5) 6-3
- M.CAMERIN 7-5 6-2
- K.KOUKALOVA 3-6 6-1 6-4
- A.SUGIYAMA [11] 3-6 6-2 6-3
- M.SHARAPOVA [13] 6-2 6-1
- A.KEOTHAVONG (WC) 6-3 6-1
- D.HANTUCHOVA 6-1 6-4
- E.BOVINA [20] 6-1 6-2
- A.FRAZIER [31] 6-1 6-4
- E.WEBLEY-SMITH (WC) 7-6(2) 6-4
- A.KAPROS 6-4 2-6 6-3
- A.MYSKINA [2] 7-5 6-1

Players
5 Lindsay DAVENPORT (USA)
Dally RANDRIANTEFY (MAD)
Kristina BRANDI (PUR)
Iveta BENESOVA (CZE)
Q Angelique WIDJAJA (INA)
Q Mashona WASHINGTON (USA)
Q Tatiana PANOVA (RUS)
28 Emilie LOIT (FRA)
23 Jelena DOKIC (SCG)
Gisela DULKO (ARG)
Catalina CASTANO (COL)
WC Martina NAVRATILOVA (USA)
Saori OBATA (JPN)
Q Eva BIRNEROVA (CZE)
Samantha STOSUR (AUS)
12 Vera ZVONAREVA (RUS)
16 Anna SMASHNOVA-PISTOLESI (ISR)
Katerina SREBOTNIK (SLO)
Marlene WEINGARTNER (GER)
Denisa CHLADKOVA (CZE)
Jill CRAYBAS (USA)
Cara BLACK (ZIM)
Vera DOUCHEVINA (RUS)
21 Magdalena MALEEVA (BUL)
32 Meghann SHAUGHNESSY (USA)
Marissa IRVIN (USA)
Q Petra MANDULA (HUN)
Nuria LLAGOSTERA VIVES (ESP)
Karolina SPREM (CRO)
Laura GRANVILLE (USA)
Marie-Gaiane MIKAELIAN (SUI)
3 Venus WILLIAMS (USA)
6 Elena DEMENTIEVA (RUS)
Sandra KLEINOVA (CZE)
Anna-Lena GROENEFELD (GER)
Tamarine TANASUGARN (THA)
Tina PISNIK (SLO)
Teryn ASHLEY (USA)
Melinda CZINK (HUN)
27 Alicia MOLIK (AUS)
17 Chanda RUBIN (USA)
Marion BARTOLI (FRA)
Maria-Elena CAMERIN (ITA)
Anca BARNA (GER)
Jelena JANKOVIC (SCG)
Klara KOUKALOVA (CZE)
WC Amanda JANES (GBR)
11 Ai SUGIYAMA (JPN)
13 Maria SHARAPOVA (RUS)
Yulia BEYGELZIMER (UKR)
WC Anne KEOTHAVONG (GBR)
Nicole PRATT (AUS)
Daniela HANTUCHOVA (SVK)
Samantha REEVES (USA)
20 Elena BOVINA (RUS)
31 Amy FRAZIER (USA)
Maria KIRILENKO (RUS)
WC Emily WEBLEY-SMITH (GBR)
Severine BELTRAME (FRA)
Mervana JUGIC-SALKIC (BIH)
Aniko KAPROS (HUN)
Lubomira KURHAJCOVA (SVK)
2 Anastasia MYSKINA (RUS)

93

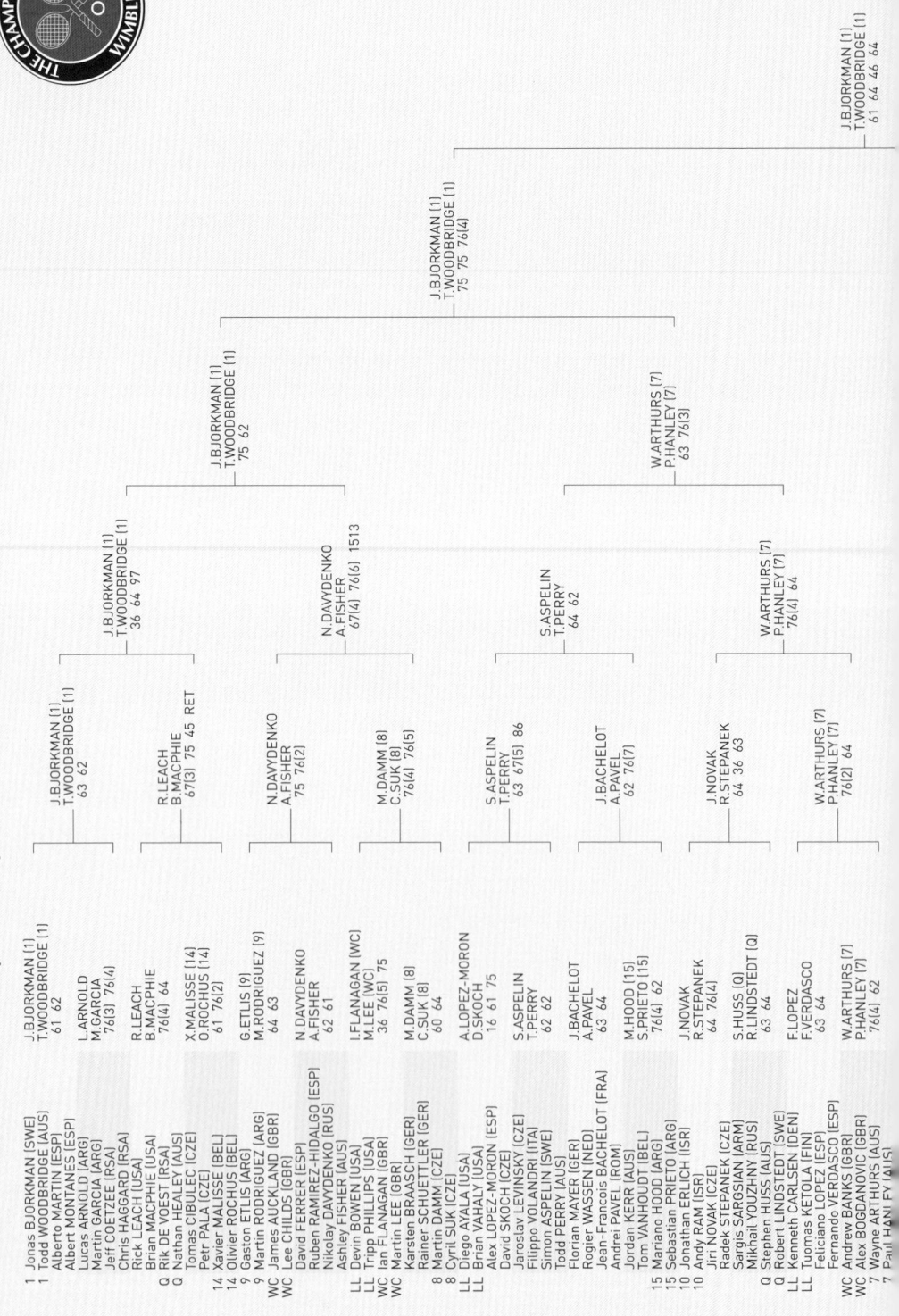

2004 Wimbledon Championships, 21 June–4 July – Men's Doubles

1 Jonas BJORKMAN (SWE)
1 Todd WOODBRIDGE (AUS)
Alberto MARTIN (ESP)
Albert MONTANES (ESP)
Lucas ARNOLD (ARG)
Martin GARCIA (ARG)
Jeff COETZEE (RSA)
Chris HAGGARD (RSA)
Rick LEACH (USA)
Brian MACPHIE (USA)
Q Rik DE VOEST (RSA)
Q Nathan HEALEY (AUS)
Tomas CIBULEC (CZE)
Petr PALA (CZE)
14 Xavier MALISSE (BEL)
14 Olivier ROCHUS (BEL)
9 Gaston ETLIS (ARG)
9 Martin RODRIGUEZ (ARG)
WC James AUCKLAND (GBR)
WC Lee CHILDS (GBR)
David FERRER (ESP)
Ruben RAMIREZ-HIDALGO (ESP)
Nikolay DAVYDENKO (RUS)
Ashley FISHER (AUS)
LL Devin BOWEN (USA)
LL Tripp PHILLIPS (USA)
WC Ian FLANAGAN (GBR)
WC Martin LEE (GBR)
Karsten BRAASCH (GER)
Rainer SCHUETTLER (GER)
8 Martin DAMM (CZE)
8 Cyril SUK (CZE)
LL Diego AYALA (USA)
LL Brian VAHALY (USA)
Alex LOPEZ-MORON (ESP)
David SKOCH (CZE)
Jaroslav LEVINSKY (CZE)
Filippo VOLANDRI (ITA)
Simon ASPELIN (SWE)
Todd PERRY (AUS)
Florian MAYER (GER)
Rogier WASSEN (NED)
Jean-Francois BACHELOT (FRA)
Andrei PAVEL (ROM)
Jordan KERR (AUS)
Tom VANHOUDT (BEL)
15 Mariano HOOD (ARG)
15 Sebastian PRIETO (ARG)
10 Jonathan ERLICH (ISR)
10 Andy RAM (ISR)
Jiri NOVAK (CZE)
Radek STEPANEK (CZE)
Sargis SARGSIAN (ARM)
Mikhail YOUZHNY (RUS)
Q Stephen HUSS (AUS)
Q Robert LINDSTEDT (SWE)
LL Kenneth CARLSEN (DEN)
LL Tuomas KETOLA (FIN)
Feliciano LOPEZ (ESP)
Fernando VERDASCO (ESP)
WC Andrew BANKS (GBR)
WC Alex BOGDANOVIC (GBR)
7 Wayne ARTHURS (AUS)
7 Paul HANLEY (AUS)

J.BJORKMAN (1) / T.WOODBRIDGE (1) 61 62
L.ARNOLD / M.GARCIA 76(3) 76(4)
R.LEACH / B.MACPHIE 76(4) 64
X.MALISSE (14) / O.ROCHUS (14) 61 76(2)
G.ETLIS (9) / M.RODRIGUEZ (9) 64 63
N.DAVYDENKO / A.FISHER 62 61
I.FLANAGAN (WC) / M.LEE (WC) 36 76(5) 75
M.DAMM (8) / C.SUK (8) 60 64
A.LOPEZ-MORON / D.SKOCH 16 61 75
S.ASPELIN / T.PERRY 62 62
J.BACHELOT / A.PAVEL 63 64
M.HOOD (15) / S.PRIETO (15) 76(4) 62
J.NOVAK / R.STEPANEK 64 76(4)
S.HUSS (Q) / R.LINDSTEDT (Q) 63 64
F.LOPEZ / F.VERDASCO 63 64
W.ARTHURS (7) / P.HANLEY (7) 76(4) 62

J.BJORKMAN (1) / T.WOODBRIDGE (1) 63 62
R.LEACH / B.MACPHIE 67(3) 75 45 RET
N.DAVYDENKO / A.FISHER 75 76(2)
M.DAMM (8) / C.SUK (8) 76(4) 76(5)
S.ASPELIN / T.PERRY 63 67(5) 86
J.BACHELOT / A.PAVEL 62 76(7)
J.NOVAK / R.STEPANEK 64 36 63
W.ARTHURS (7) / P.HANLEY (7) 76(2) 64

J.BJORKMAN (1) / T.WOODBRIDGE (1) 36 64 97
N.DAVYDENKO / A.FISHER 67(4) 76(6) 1513
S.ASPELIN / T.PERRY 64 62
W.ARTHURS (7) / P.HANLEY (7) 76(4) 64

J.BJORKMAN (1) / T.WOODBRIDGE (1) 75 62
W.ARTHURS (7) / P.HANLEY (7) 63 76(3)

J.BJORKMAN (1) / T.WOODBRIDGE (1) 75 75 76(4)

J.BJORKMAN (1) / T.WOODBRIDGE (1) 61 64 46 64

Elite Tournaments: 2004 Wimbledon Drawsheets

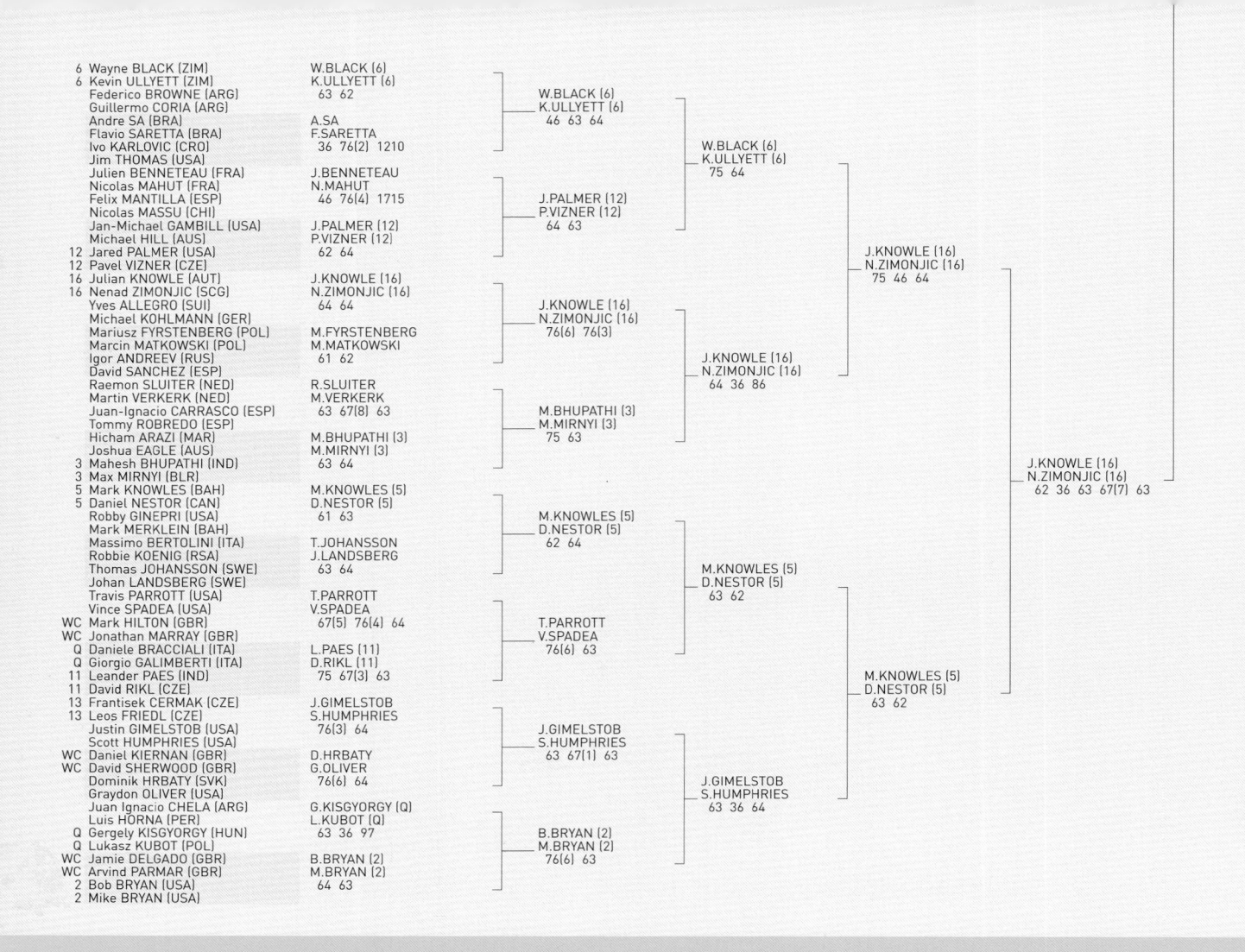

Men's Doubles Draw (partial)

Final shown on this half:
J.KNOWLE / N.ZIMONJIC [16] def. M.KNOWLES / D.NESTOR [5]
6-2 3-6 6-3 6-7(7) 6-3

Bracket results

- W.BLACK / K.ULLYETT [6] def. J.PALMER / P.VIZNER [12] — 7-5 6-4
- J.KNOWLE / N.ZIMONJIC [16] def. M.BHUPATHI / M.MIRNYI [3] — 6-4 3-6 8-6
- J.KNOWLE / N.ZIMONJIC [16] def. W.BLACK / K.ULLYETT [6] — 7-5 4-6 6-4
- M.KNOWLES / D.NESTOR [5] def. J.GIMELSTOB / S.HUMPHRIES — 6-3 6-2
- M.KNOWLES / D.NESTOR [5] — 6-3 6-2
- J.GIMELSTOB / S.HUMPHRIES def. B.BRYAN / M.BRYAN [2] — 6-3 3-6 6-4

Round of 16 / earlier round results

- W.BLACK / K.ULLYETT [6] d. A.SA / F.SARETTA — 3-6 7-6(2) 12-10
- J.PALMER / P.VIZNER [12] d. J.BENNETEAU / N.MAHUT — 4-6 7-6(4) 17-15
- J.PALMER / P.VIZNER [12] — 6-2 6-4
- J.KNOWLE / N.ZIMONJIC [16] d. M.FYRSTENBERG / M.MATKOWSKI — 6-4 6-4
- M.BHUPATHI / M.MIRNYI [3] d. R.SLUITER / M.VERKERK — 6-3 6-7(8) 6-3
- M.BHUPATHI / M.MIRNYI [3] — 6-3 6-4
- M.KNOWLES / D.NESTOR [5] d. M.MIRNYI — 6-1 6-3
- M.KNOWLES / D.NESTOR [5] d. T.JOHANSSON / J.LANDSBERG — 6-2 6-4
- T.PARROTT / V.SPADEA d. (opponent) — 6-7(5) 7-6(4) 6-4
- J.GIMELSTOB / S.HUMPHRIES d. L.PAES / D.RIKL [11] — 7-5 6-7(3) 6-3
- J.GIMELSTOB / S.HUMPHRIES d. D.HRBATY / G.OLIVER — 7-6(3) 6-4
- B.BRYAN / M.BRYAN [2] d. G.KISGYORGY / L.KUBOT — 6-3 3-6 9-7
- B.BRYAN / M.BRYAN [2] — 7-6(6) 6-3 / 6-4 6-3

Players (first round)

6 Wayne BLACK [ZIM]
6 Kevin ULLYETT [ZIM]
   Federico BROWNE [ARG]
   Guillermo CORIA [ARG]
   Andre SA [BRA]
   Flavio SARETTA [BRA]
   Ivo KARLOVIC [CRO]
   Jim THOMAS [USA]
   Julien BENNETEAU [FRA]
   Nicolas MAHUT [FRA]
   Felix MANTILLA [ESP]
   Nicolas MASSU [CHI]
   Jan-Michael GAMBILL [USA]
12 Michael HILL [AUS]
12 Jared PALMER [USA]
16 Pavel VIZNER [CZE]
16 Julian KNOWLE [AUT]
16 Nenad ZIMONJIC [SCG]
   Yves ALLEGRO [SUI]
   Michael KOHLMANN [GER]
   Mariusz FYRSTENBERG [POL]
   Marcin MATKOWSKI [POL]
   Igor ANDREEV [RUS]
   David SANCHEZ [ESP]
   Raemon SLUITER [NED]
   Martin VERKERK [NED]
   Juan-Ignacio CARRASCO [ESP]
   Tommy ROBREDO [ESP]
   Hicham ARAZI [MAR]
3 Joshua EAGLE [AUS]
3 Mahesh BHUPATHI [IND]
3 Max MIRNYI [BLR]
5 Mark KNOWLES [BAH]
5 Daniel NESTOR [CAN]
   Robby GINEPRI [USA]
   Mark MERKLEIN [BAH]
   Massimo BERTOLINI [ITA]
   Robbie KOENIG [RSA]
   Thomas JOHANSSON [SWE]
   Johan LANDSBERG [SWE]
WC Travis PARROTT [USA]
WC Vince SPADEA [USA]
WC Mark HILTON [GBR]
WC Jonathan MURRAY [GBR]
Q Daniele BRACCIALI [ITA]
Q Giorgio GALIMBERTI [ITA]
11 Leander PAES [IND]
11 David RIKL [CZE]
13 Frantisek CERMAK [CZE]
13 Leos FRIEDL [CZE]
   Justin GIMELSTOB [USA]
   Scott HUMPHRIES [USA]
WC Daniel KIERNAN [GBR]
WC David SHERWOOD [GBR]
   Dominik HRBATY [SVK]
   Graydon OLIVER [USA]
   Juan Ignacio CHELA [ARG]
   Luis HORNA [PER]
Q Gergely KISGYORGY [HUN]
Q Lukasz KUBOT [POL]
WC Jamie DELGADO [GBR]
WC Arvind PARMAR [GBR]
2 Bob BRYAN [USA]
2 Mike BRYAN [USA]

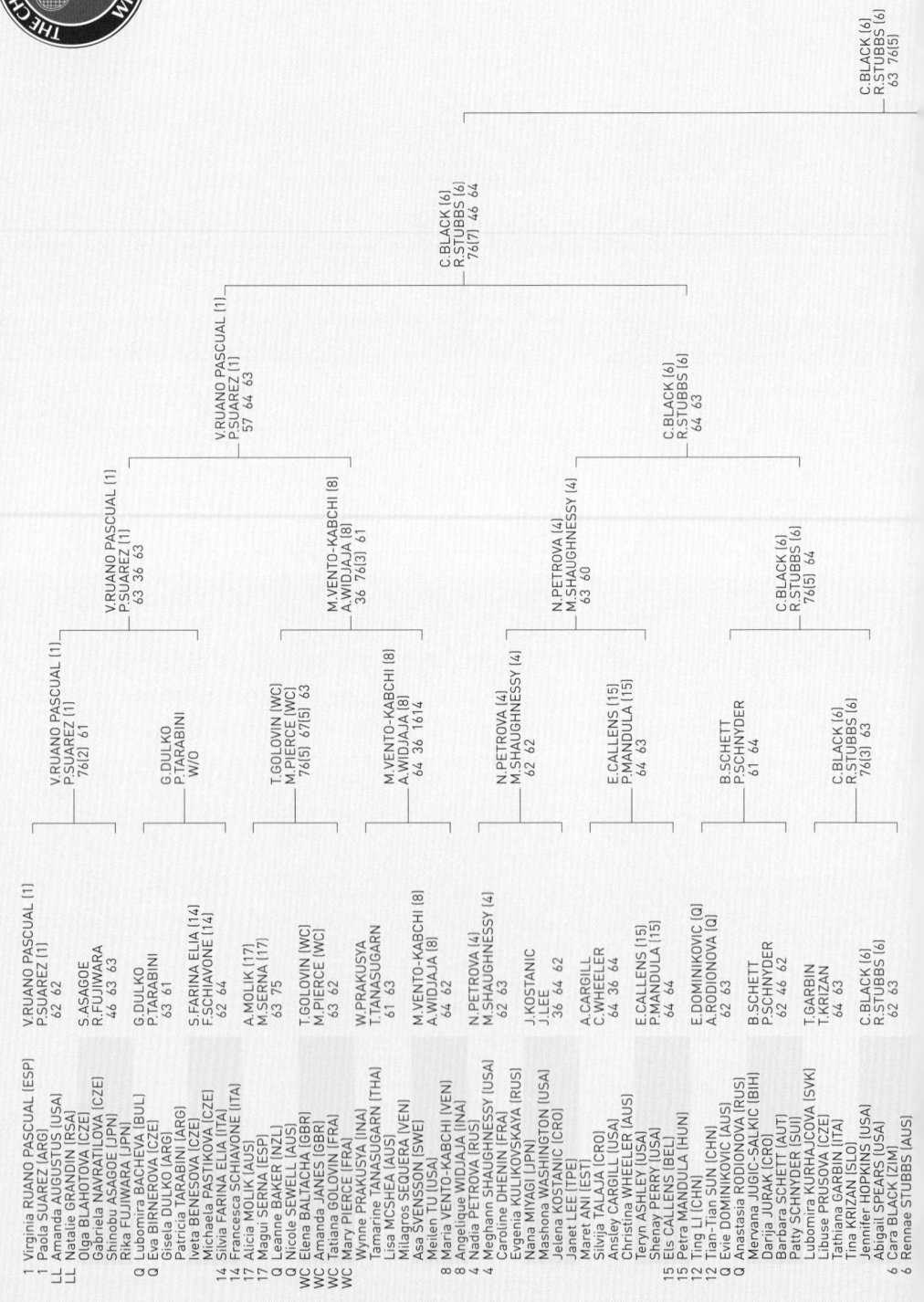

2004 Wimbledon Championships, 21 June–4 July – Women's Doubles

First Round

1. Virginia RUANO PASCUAL (ESP) / Paola SUAREZ (ARG) [1]
   LL Amanda AUGUSTUS (USA) / Natalie GRANDIN (RSA)
   Olga BLAHOTOVA (CZE) / Gabriela NAVRATILOVA (CZE)
   Shinobu ASAGOE (JPN) / Rika FUJIWARA (JPN)
Q Lubomira BACHEVA (BUL) / Eva BIRNEROVA (CZE)
Q Gisela DULKO (ARG) / Patricia TARABINI (ARG)
   Iveta BENESOVA (CZE) / Michaela PASTIKOVA (CZE)
14 Silvia FARINA ELIA (ITA) / Francesca SCHIAVONE (ITA)
17 Alicia MOLIK (AUS) / Magui SERNA (ESP)
Q Leanne BAKER (NZL) / Nicole SEWELL (AUS)
WC Elena BALTACHA (GBR) / Amanda JANES (GBR)
WC Tatiana GOLOVIN (FRA) / Mary PIERCE (FRA)
WC Wynne PRAKUSYA (INA) / Tamarine TANASUGARN (THA)
   Lisa MCSHEA (AUS) / Milagros SEQUERA (VEN)
   Asa SVENSSON (SWE) / Meilen TU (USA)
8 Maria VENTO-KABCHI (VEN) / Angelique WIDJAJA (INA)
4 Nadia PETROVA (RUS) / Meghann SHAUGHNESSY (USA)
   Caroline DHENIN (FRA) / Evgenia KULIKOVSKAYA (RUS)
   Nana MIYAGI (JPN) / Mashona WASHINGTON (USA)
   Jelena KOSTANIC (CRO) / Janet LEE (TPE)
   Maret ANI (EST) / Silvija TALAJA (CRO)
   Ansley CARGILL (USA) / Christina WHEELER (AUS)
   Teryn ASHLEY (USA) / Shenay PERRY (USA)
15 Els CALLENS (BEL) / Petra MANDULA (HUN)
12 Ting LI (CHN) / Tian-Tian SUN (CHN)
Q Evie DOMINIKOVIC (AUS) / Anastasia RODIONOVA (RUS)
   Mervana JUGIC-SALKIC (BIH) / Darija JURAK (CRO)
   Barbara SCHETT (AUT) / Patty SCHNYDER (SUI)
   Lubuse PRUSOVA (CZE) / Lubomira KURHAJCOVA (SVK)
   Tathiana GARBIN (ITA) / Tina KRIZAN (SLO)
   Jennifer HOPKINS (USA) / Abigail SPEARS (USA)
6 Cara BLACK (ZIM) / Rennae STUBBS (AUS)

Second Round

V.RUANO PASCUAL / P.SUAREZ [1] 62 62
S.ASAGOE / R.FUJIWARA 46 63 63
G.DULKO / P.TARABINI 63 61
S.FARINA ELIA / F.SCHIAVONE [14] 62 64
A.MOLIK / M.SERNA [17] 63 75
T.GOLOVIN / M.PIERCE [WC] 63 62
W.PRAKUSYA / T.TANASUGARN 61 63
M.VENTO-KABCHI / A.WIDJAJA [8] 64 62
N.PETROVA / M.SHAUGHNESSY [4] 62 63
J.KOSTANIC / J.LEE 36 64 62
A.CARGILL / C.WHEELER 64 36 64
E.CALLENS / P.MANDULA [15] 64 64
E.DOMINIKOVIC / A.RODIONOVA [Q] 62 64
B.SCHETT / P.SCHNYDER 62 46 62
T.GARBIN / T.KRIZAN 64 63
C.BLACK / R.STUBBS [6] 62 63

Third Round

V.RUANO PASCUAL / P.SUAREZ [1] 76(2) 61
G.DULKO / P.TARABINI W/O
T.GOLOVIN / M.PIERCE [WC] 76(5) 67(5) 63
M.VENTO-KABCHI / A.WIDJAJA [8] 64 36 1614
N.PETROVA / M.SHAUGHNESSY [4] 62 63
E.CALLENS / P.MANDULA [15] 64 63
B.SCHETT / P.SCHNYDER 61 64
C.BLACK / R.STUBBS [6] 76(3) 63

Quarterfinals

V.RUANO PASCUAL / P.SUAREZ [1] 63 63
M.VENTO-KABCHI / A.WIDJAJA [8] 36 76(3) 61
N.PETROVA / M.SHAUGHNESSY [4] 63 60
C.BLACK / R.STUBBS [6] 76(5) 64

Semifinals

V.RUANO PASCUAL / P.SUAREZ [1] 57 64 63
C.BLACK / R.STUBBS [6] 64 63

Final

C.BLACK / R.STUBBS [6] 76(7) 46 64

Champions

C.BLACK / R.STUBBS [6] 63 76(5)

Elite Tournaments: 2004 Wimbledon Drawsheets

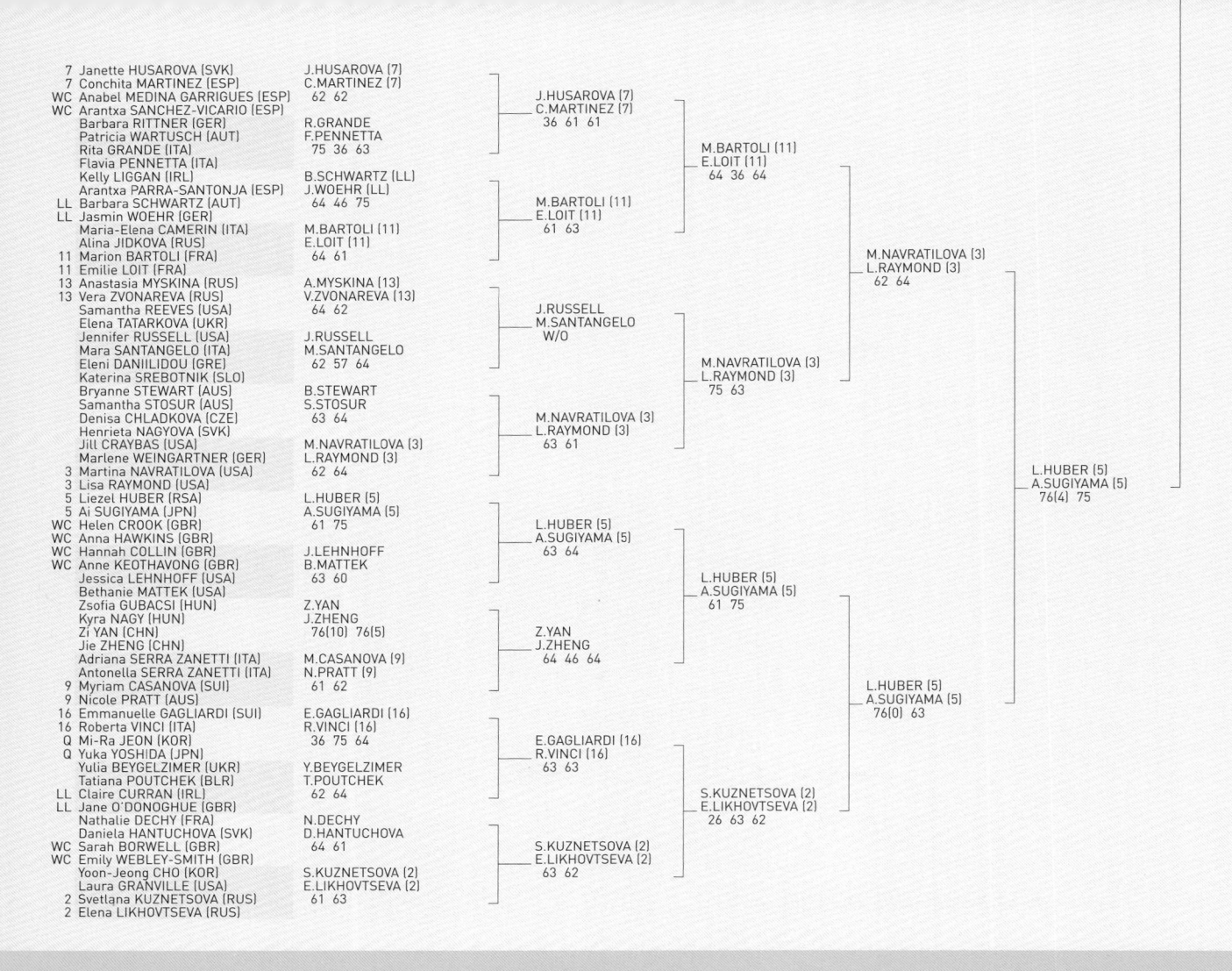

Women's Doubles (partial draw)

Seed	Player 1	Player 2	R1	R2	R3	QF
7	Janette HUSAROVA (SVK)		J.HUSAROVA			
7	Conchita MARTINEZ (ESP)		C.MARTINEZ	J.HUSAROVA		
WC	Anabel MEDINA GARRIGUES (ESP)		62 62	C.MARTINEZ		
WC	Arantxa SANCHEZ-VICARIO (ESP)		R.GRANDE	36 61 61		
	Barbara RITTNER (GER)		F.PENNETTA			
	Patricia WARTUSCH (AUT)		75 36 63		M.BARTOLI [11]	
	Rita GRANDE (ITA)				E.LOIT [11]	
	Flavia PENNETTA (ITA)		B.SCHWARTZ (LL)		64 36 64	
LL	Kelly LIGGAN (IRL)		J.WOEHR (LL)	M.BARTOLI [11]		
LL	Arantxa PARRA-SANTONJA (ESP)		64 46 75	E.LOIT [11]		
LL	Barbara SCHWARTZ (AUT)			61 63		
	Jasmin WOEHR (GER)		M.BARTOLI [11]			M.NAVRATILOVA [3]
	Maria-Elena CAMERIN (ITA)		E.LOIT [11]			L.RAYMOND [3]
11	Alina JIDKOVA (RUS)		64 61			62 64
11	Marion BARTOLI (FRA)					
	Emilie LOIT (FRA)		A.MYSKINA [13]			
13	Anastasia MYSKINA (RUS)		V.ZVONAREVA [13]	J.RUSSELL		
13	Vera ZVONAREVA (RUS)		64 62	M.SANTANGELO		
	Samantha REEVES (USA)			W/O		
	Elena TATARKOVA (UKR)		J.RUSSELL		M.NAVRATILOVA [3]	
	Jennifer RUSSELL (USA)		M.SANTANGELO		L.RAYMOND [3]	
	Mara SANTANGELO (ITA)		62 57 64		75 63	
	Eleni DANIILIDOU (GRE)					
	Katerina SREBOTNIK (SLO)		B.STEWART			
	Bryanne STEWART (AUS)		S.STOSUR	M.NAVRATILOVA [3]		
	Samantha STOSUR (AUS)		63 64	L.RAYMOND [3]		
	Denisa CHLADKOVA (CZE)			63 61		
	Henrieta NAGYOVA (SVK)		M.NAVRATILOVA [3]			
	Jill CRAYBAS (USA)		L.RAYMOND [3]			
	Marlene WEINGARTNER (GER)		62 64			
3	Martina NAVRATILOVA (USA)					L.HUBER [5]
3	Lisa RAYMOND (USA)		L.HUBER [5]			A.SUGIYAMA [5]
5	Liezel HUBER (RSA)		A.SUGIYAMA [5]	L.HUBER [5]		76(0) 63
5	Ai SUGIYAMA (JPN)		61 75	A.SUGIYAMA [5]		
WC	Anna HAWKINS (GBR)			63 64		
WC	Helen CROOK (GBR)		J.LEHNHOFF		L.HUBER [5]	
WC	Hannah COLLIN (GBR)		B.MATTEK		A.SUGIYAMA [5]	
WC	Anne KEOTHAVONG (GBR)		63 60		61 75	
	Jessica LEHNHOFF (USA)					
	Bethanie MATTEK (USA)		Z.YAN			
	Zsofia GUBACSI (HUN)		J.ZHENG	Z.YAN		
	Kyra NAGY (HUN)		76(10) 76(5)	J.ZHENG		
	Zi YAN (CHN)			64 46 64		
	Jie ZHENG (CHN)		M.CASANOVA [9]			
	Adriana SERRA ZANETTI (ITA)		N.PRATT [9]			
	Antonella SERRA ZANETTI (ITA)		61 62			S.KUZNETSOVA [2]
9	Myriam CASANOVA (SUI)					E.LIKHOVTSEVA [2]
9	Nicole PRATT (AUS)		E.GAGLIARDI [16]			26 63 62
16	Emmanuelle GAGLIARDI (SUI)		R.VINCI [16]	E.GAGLIARDI [16]		
16	Roberta VINCI (ITA)		36 75 64	R.VINCI [16]		
Q	Mi-Ra JEON (KOR)			63 63		
Q	Yuka YOSHIDA (JPN)		Y.BEYGELZIMER		S.KUZNETSOVA [2]	
	Yulia BEYGELZIMER (UKR)		T.POUTCHEK		E.LIKHOVTSEVA [2]	
	Tatiana POUTCHEK (BLR)		62 64		63 62	
LL	Claire CURRAN (IRL)					
LL	Jane O'DONOGHUE (GBR)		N.DECHY			
	Nathalie DECHY (FRA)		D.HANTUCHOVA	S.KUZNETSOVA [2]		
	Daniela HANTUCHOVA (SVK)		64 61	E.LIKHOVTSEVA [2]		
WC	Sarah BORWELL (GBR)			63 62		
WC	Emily WEBLEY-SMITH (GBR)		S.KUZNETSOVA [2]			
	Yoon-Jeong CHO (KOR)		E.LIKHOVTSEVA [2]			
	Laura GRANVILLE (USA)		63 63			
2	Svetlana KUZNETSOVA (RUS)					
2	Elena LIKHOVTSEVA (RUS)					

Final (shown): L.HUBER [5] / A.SUGIYAMA [5] def. 76(4) 75

2004 Wimbledon Championships, 21 June–4 July – Mixed Doubles

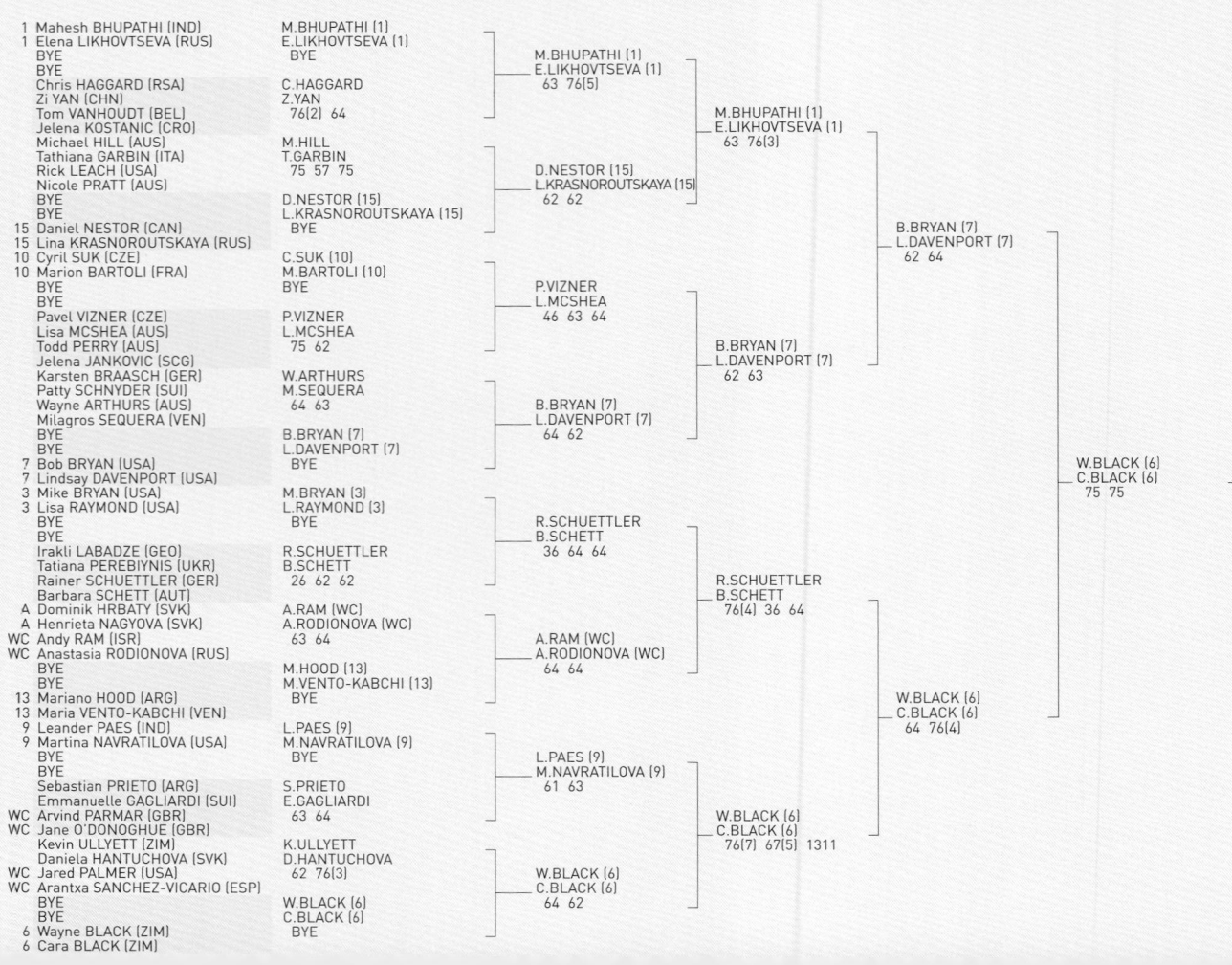

Winners: W. Black / C. Black [6] — 3 6 7 6(8) 6 4

First Round

- 1 Mahesh BHUPATHI (IND) / Elena LIKHOVTSEVA (RUS) [1] — BYE
- Chris HAGGARD (RSA) / Z. YAN (CHN) def. Tom VANHOUDT (BEL) / Jelena KOSTANIC (CRO) 7 6(2) 6 4
- Michael HILL (AUS) / Tathiana GARBIN (ITA) def. Rick LEACH (USA) / Nicole PRATT (AUS) 7 5 5 7 7 5
- 15 Daniel NESTOR (CAN) / Lina KRASNOROUTSKAYA (RUS) — BYE
- 10 Cyril SUK (CZE) / Marion BARTOLI (FRA) — BYE
- Pavel VIZNER (CZE) / Lisa MCSHEA (AUS) def. Todd PERRY (AUS) / Jelena JANKOVIC (SCG) 7 5 6 2
- Karsten BRAASCH (GER) / Patty SCHNYDER (SUI) def. Wayne ARTHURS (AUS) / Milagros SEQUERA (VEN) 6 4 6 3
- 7 Bob BRYAN (USA) / Lindsay DAVENPORT (USA) — BYE
- 3 Mike BRYAN (USA) / Lisa RAYMOND (USA) — BYE
- Irakli LABADZE (GEO) / Tatiana PEREBIYNIS (UKR) def. Rainer SCHUETTLER (GER) / Barbara SCHETT (AUT) 2 6 6 2 6 2
- A Dominik HRBATY (SVK) / Henrieta NAGYOVA (SVK) def. Andy RAM (ISR) / Anastasia RODIONOVA (RUS) 6 3 6 4
- 13 Mariano HOOD (ARG) / Maria VENTO-KABCHI (VEN) — BYE
- 9 Leander PAES (IND) / Martina NAVRATILOVA (USA) — BYE
- Sebastian PRIETO (ARG) / Emmanuelle GAGLIARDI (SUI) def. Arvind PARMAR (GBR) / Jane O'DONOGHUE (GBR) 6 3 6 4
- Kevin ULLYETT (ZIM) / Daniela HANTUCHOVA (SVK) def. Jared PALMER (USA) / Arantxa SANCHEZ-VICARIO (ESP) 6 2 7 6(3)
- 6 Wayne BLACK (ZIM) / Cara BLACK (ZIM) — BYE

Second Round

- M. BHUPATHI / E. LIKHOVTSEVA [1] def. C. HAGGARD / Z. YAN 6 3 7 6(3)
- D. NESTOR / L. KRASNOROUTSKAYA [15] def. M. HILL / T. GARBIN 6 2 6 2
- P. VIZNER / L. MCSHEA def. C. SUK / M. BARTOLI [10] 4 6 6 3 6 4
- B. BRYAN / L. DAVENPORT [7] def. K. BRAASCH / P. SCHNYDER 6 4 6 2
- R. SCHUETTLER / B. SCHETT def. M. BRYAN / L. RAYMOND [3] / I. LABADZE / T. PEREBIYNIS 3 6 6 4 6 4
- A. RAM / A. RODIONOVA (WC) def. D. HRBATY / H. NAGYOVA 6 4 6 4
- L. PAES / M. NAVRATILOVA [9] def. M. HOOD / M. VENTO-KABCHI [13] 6 1 6 3
- W. BLACK / C. BLACK [6] def. K. ULLYETT / D. HANTUCHOVA 6 4 6 2

Third Round

- M. BHUPATHI / E. LIKHOVTSEVA [1] def. D. NESTOR / L. KRASNOROUTSKAYA [15]
- B. BRYAN / L. DAVENPORT [7] def. P. VIZNER / L. MCSHEA 6 2 6 3
- R. SCHUETTLER / B. SCHETT def. A. RAM / A. RODIONOVA 7 6(4) 3 6 6 4
- W. BLACK / C. BLACK [6] def. L. PAES / M. NAVRATILOVA [9] 7 6(7) 6 7(5) 13 11

Quarterfinals

- B. BRYAN / L. DAVENPORT [7] def. M. BHUPATHI / E. LIKHOVTSEVA [1] 6 2 6 4
- W. BLACK / C. BLACK [6] def. R. SCHUETTLER / B. SCHETT 6 4 7 6(4)

Semifinal

- W. BLACK / C. BLACK [6] def. B. BRYAN / L. DAVENPORT [7] 7 5 7 5

Final

- **W. BLACK / C. BLACK [6]** 3 6 7 6(8) 6 4

Elite Tournaments: 2004 Wimbledon Drawsheets

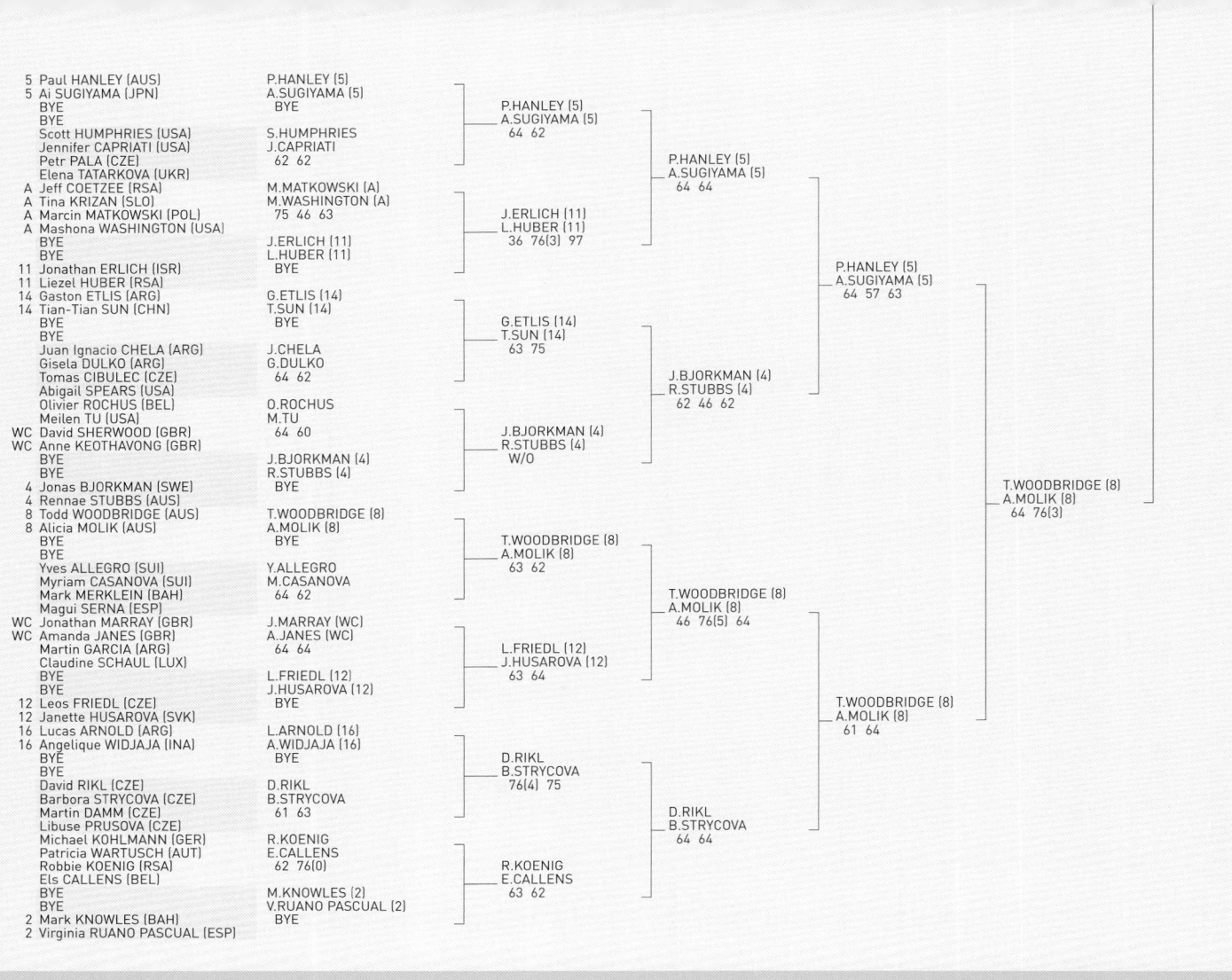

Mixed Doubles Draw (partial)

Final shown: T.WOODBRIDGE [8] / A.MOLIK [8] def. P.HANLEY [5] / A.SUGIYAMA [5] 6-4 7-6(3)

Semifinal bracket

P.HANLEY [5] / A.SUGIYAMA [5] def. J.BJORKMAN [4] / R.STUBBS [4] 6-4 5-7 6-3

T.WOODBRIDGE [8] / A.MOLIK [8] def. D.RIKL / B.STRYCOVA 6-1 6-4

Quarterfinals

- P.HANLEY [5] / A.SUGIYAMA [5] def. J.ERLICH [11] / L.HUBER [11] 6-4 6-4
- J.BJORKMAN [4] / R.STUBBS [4] def. G.ETLIS [14] / T.SUN [14] 6-2 4-6 6-2
- T.WOODBRIDGE [8] / A.MOLIK [8] def. L.FRIEDL [12] / J.HUSAROVA [12] 4-6 7-6(5) 6-4
- D.RIKL / B.STRYCOVA def. R.KOENIG / E.CALLENS 6-4 6-4

Round of 16

- P.HANLEY [5] / A.SUGIYAMA [5] def. S.HUMPHRIES / J.CAPRIATI 6-2 6-2
- J.ERLICH [11] / L.HUBER [11] def. M.MATKOWSKI (A) / M.WASHINGTON (A) 7-5 4-6 6-3
- G.ETLIS [14] / T.SUN [14] def. J.CHELA / G.DULKO 6-3 7-5
- J.BJORKMAN [4] / R.STUBBS [4] def. O.ROCHUS / M.TU W/O
- T.WOODBRIDGE [8] / A.MOLIK [8] def. Y.ALLEGRO / M.CASANOVA 6-3 6-2
- L.FRIEDL [12] / J.HUSAROVA [12] def. J.MARRAY (WC) / A.JANES (WC) 6-4 6-4
- D.RIKL / B.STRYCOVA def. L.ARNOLD [16] / A.WIDJAJA [16] 7-6(4) 7-5
- R.KOENIG / E.CALLENS def. M.KNOWLES [2] / V.RUANO PASCUAL [2] 6-2 7-6(0)

First round entries

- 5 Paul HANLEY (AUS) / Ai SUGIYAMA (JPN) — BYE
- Scott HUMPHRIES (USA) / Jennifer CAPRIATI (USA)
- Petr PALA (CZE) / Elena TATARKOVA (UKR)
- A Jeff COETZEE (RSA) / Tina KRIZAN (SLO)
- A Marcin MATKOWSKI (POL) / Mashona WASHINGTON (USA) — BYE
- 11 Jonathan ERLICH (ISR) / Liezel HUBER (RSA)
- 14 Gaston ETLIS (ARG) / Tian-Tian SUN (CHN) — BYE
- Juan Ignacio CHELA (ARG) / Gisela DULKO (ARG)
- Tomas CIBULEC (CZE) / Abigail SPEARS (USA)
- Olivier ROCHUS (BEL) / Meilen TU (USA)
- WC David SHERWOOD (GBR) / Anne KEOTHAVONG (GBR)
- 4 Jonas BJORKMAN (SWE) / Rennae STUBBS (AUS)
- 8 Todd WOODBRIDGE (AUS) / Alicia MOLIK (AUS) — BYE
- Yves ALLEGRO (SUI) / Myriam CASANOVA (SUI)
- Mark MERKLEIN (BAH) / Magui SERNA (ESP)
- WC Jonathan MARRAY (GBR) / Amanda JANES (GBR)
- WC Martin GARCIA (ARG) / Claudine SCHAUL (LUX) — BYE
- 12 Leos FRIEDL (CZE) / Janette HUSAROVA (SVK)
- 16 Lucas ARNOLD (ARG) / Angelique WIDJAJA (INA) — BYE
- David RIKL (CZE) / Barbora STRYCOVA (CZE)
- Martin DAMM (CZE) / Libuse PRUSOVA (CZE)
- Michael KOHLMANN (GER) / Patricia WARTUSCH (AUT)
- Robbie KOENIG (RSA) / Els CALLENS (BEL) — BYE
- 2 Mark KNOWLES (BAH) / Virginia RUANO PASCUAL (ESP) — BYE

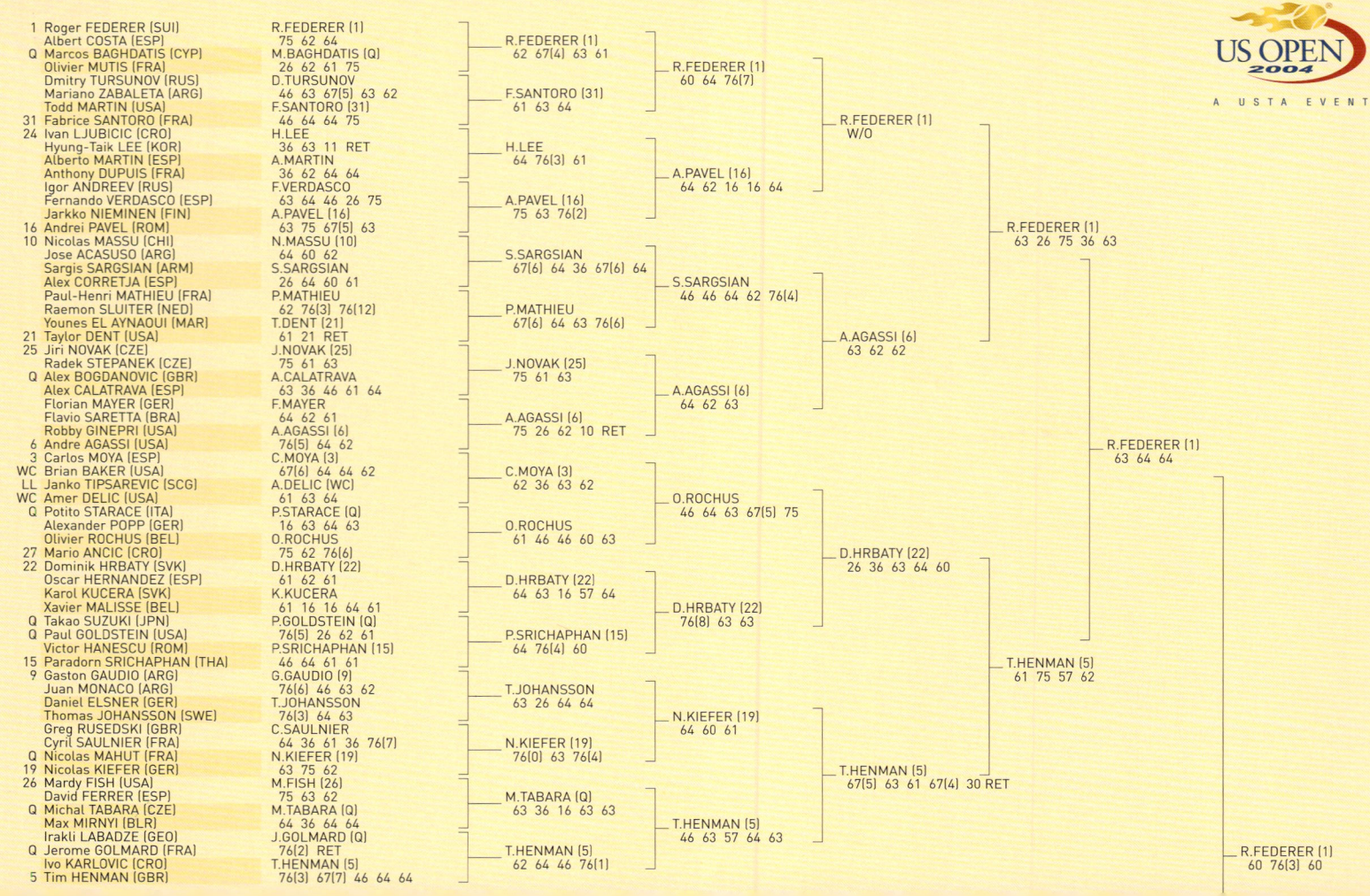

2004 US Open Championships, 30 August–12 September – Men's Singles

Final: R. FEDERER (1) def. — 6-0 7-6(3) 6-0

Draw

First round / Second round / Third round / Fourth round / Quarterfinals / Semifinals / Final

- 1 Roger FEDERER (SUI) — R.FEDERER [1] 75 62 64
- Albert COSTA (ESP)
  - R.FEDERER [1] 62 67(4) 63 61
- Q Marcos BAGHDATIS (CYP) — M.BAGHDATIS (Q) 26 62 61 75
- Olivier MUTIS (FRA)
  - R.FEDERER [1] 60 64 76(7)
- Dmitry TURSUNOV (RUS) — D.TURSUNOV 46 63 67(5) 63 62
- Mariano ZABALETA (ARG)
  - F.SANTORO [31] 61 63 64
- 31 Fabrice SANTORO (FRA) — F.SANTORO [31] 46 64 64 75
- Todd MARTIN (USA)
  - R.FEDERER [1] W/O
- 24 Ivan LJUBICIC (CRO) — H.LEE 36 63 11 RET
- Hyung-Taik LEE (KOR)
  - H.LEE 64 76(3) 61
- Alberto MARTIN (ESP) — A.MARTIN 36 62 64 64
- Anthony DUPUIS (FRA)
  - A.PAVEL [16] 64 62 16 16 64
- Fernando VERDASCO (ESP) — F.VERDASCO 63 64 46 26 75
- Igor ANDREEV (RUS)
  - A.PAVEL [16] 75 63 76(2)
- 16 Andrei PAVEL (ROM) — A.PAVEL [16] 63 75 67(5) 63
- Jarkko NIEMINEN (FIN)
  - R.FEDERER [1] 63 26 75 36 63
- 10 Nicolas MASSU (CHI) — N.MASSU [10] 64 60 62
- Jose ACASUSO (ARG)
  - S.SARGSIAN 26 64 60 61
- Sargis SARGSIAN (ARM) — S.SARGSIAN 67(6) 64 36 67(6) 64
- Alex CORRETJA (ESP)
  - S.SARGSIAN 46 46 64 62 76(4)
- Paul-Henri MATHIEU (FRA) — P.MATHIEU 62 76(3) 76(12)
- Raemon SLUITER (NED)
  - P.MATHIEU 67(6) 64 63 76(6)
- Younes EL AYNAOUI (MAR) — T.DENT [21] 61 21 RET
- 21 Taylor DENT (USA)
  - J.NOVAK [25] 75 61 63
- 25 Jiri NOVAK (CZE) — J.NOVAK [25]
- Radek STEPANEK (CZE)
  - A.AGASSI [6] 63 62 62
- Q Alex BOGDANOVIC (GBR) — A.CALATRAVA 63 36 46 61 64
- Alex CALATRAVA (ESP)
  - A.AGASSI [6] 64 62 63
- Florian MAYER (GER) — F.MAYER 64 62 61
- Flavio SARETTA (BRA)
  - A.AGASSI [6] 75 26 62 10 RET
- Robby GINEPRI (USA) — A.AGASSI [6] 76(5) 64 62
- 6 Andre AGASSI (USA)
  - A.AGASSI [6] 63 62 62
- 3 Carlos MOYA (ESP) — C.MOYA [3] 62 36 63 62
- WC Brian BAKER (USA)
  - C.MOYA [3]
- LL Janko TIPSAREVIC (SCG) — A.DELIC (WC) 67(6) 64 64 62
- WC Amer DELIC (USA)
  - O.ROCHUS 46 46 60 63
- Q Potito STARACE (ITA) — P.STARACE (Q) 61 63 64
- Alexander POPP (GER)
  - O.ROCHUS 61 46 46 60 63
- Olivier ROCHUS (BEL) — O.ROCHUS 16 63 64 63
- Mario ANCIC (CRO)
  - O.ROCHUS 46 64 63 67(5) 75
- 27 Dominik HRBATY (SVK) — D.HRBATY [22] 75 62 76(6)
- Oscar HERNANDEZ (ESP)
  - D.HRBATY [22] 64 63 16 57 64
- 22 Karol KUCERA (SVK) — K.KUCERA 61 16 16 64 61
- Xavier MALISSE (BEL)
  - D.HRBATY [22] 76(8) 63 63
- Takao SUZUKI (JPN) — P.GOLDSTEIN (Q) 76(5) 26 62 61
- Q Paul GOLDSTEIN (USA)
  - P.SRICHAPHAN [15] 64 76(4) 60
- Victor HANESCU (ROM) — P.SRICHAPHAN [15] 46 64 61 61
- 15 Paradorn SRICHAPHAN (THA)
  - T.JOHANSSON 63 26 64 64
- 9 Gaston GAUDIO (ARG) — G.GAUDIO [9] 76(6) 46 63 62
- Juan MONACO (ARG)
  - T.JOHANSSON 76(3) 64 63
- Daniel ELSNER (GER) — T.JOHANSSON 76(3) 64 63
- Thomas JOHANSSON (SWE)
  - N.KIEFER [19] 64 60 61
- Greg RUSEDSKI (GBR) — C.SAULNIER 64 36 61 36 76(7)
- Cyril SAULNIER (FRA)
  - N.KIEFER [19] 76(0) 63 76(4)
- Q Nicolas MAHUT (FRA) — N.KIEFER [19] 63 75 62
- 19 Nicolas KIEFER (GER)
  - T.HENMAN [5] 67(5) 63 61 67(4) 30 RET
- 26 Mardy FISH (USA) — M.FISH [26] 75 63 62
- David FERRER (ESP)
  - M.TABARA (Q) 63 36 16 63 63
- Q Michal TABARA (CZE) — M.TABARA (Q) 64 36 64 64
- Max MIRNYI (BLR)
  - T.HENMAN [5] 46 63 57 64 63
- Q Jerome GOLMARD (FRA) — J.GOLMARD (Q) 76(2) RET
- Ivo KARLOVIC (CRO)
  - T.HENMAN [5] 62 64 46 76(11)
- 5 Tim HENMAN (GBR) — T.HENMAN [5] 76(3) 67(7) 46 64 64

R.FEDERER [1] def. — 60 76(3) 60

	Player
8	David NALBANDIAN (ARG)
	Dennis VAN SCHEPPINGEN (NED)
	Albert MONTANES (ESP)
	Mikhail YOUZHNY (RUS)
	Jeff MORRISON (USA)
Q	Tuomas KETOLA (FIN)
	Tomas BERDYCH (CZE)
32	Jonas BJORKMAN (SWE)
17	Juan Ignacio CHELA (ARG)
Q	Ricardo MELLO (BRA)
WC	Wayne ODESNIK (USA)
	David SANCHEZ (ESP)
	Tommy HAAS (GER)
	Davide SANGUINETTI (ITA)
	Olivier PATIENCE (FRA)
12	Sebastien GROSJEAN (FRA)
14	Fernando GONZALEZ (CHI)
	Robin SODERLING (SWE)
	Nikolay DAVYDENKO (RUS)
	Mark PHILIPPOUSSIS (AUS)
	Karol BECK (SVK)
	Thierry ASCIONE (FRA)
P	Kristian PLESS (DEN)
20	Gustavo KUERTEN (BRA)
30	Feliciano LOPEZ (ESP)
P	Arnaud DI PASQUALE (FRA)
Q	Philipp KOHLSCHREIBER (GER)
	Julien BENNETEAU (FRA)
	Hicham ARAZI (MAR)
	Kenneth CARLSEN (DEN)
	Wayne FERREIRA (RSA)
4	Lleyton HEWITT (AUS)
7	Juan Carlos FERRERO (ESP)
Q	Tomas ZIB (CZE)
	Stefan KOUBEK (AUT)
WC	Alex Jr. BOGOMOLOV (USA)
WC	Rajeev RAM (USA)
	Jan-Michael GAMBILL (USA)
	Yen-Hsun LU (TPE)
28	Joachim JOHANSSON (SWE)
23	Vince SPADEA (USA)
	Luis HORNA (PER)
	Jurgen MELZER (AUT)
	Gregory CARRAZ (FRA)
	Michael LLODRA (FRA)
	Gilles ELSENEER (BEL)
Q	Andreas SEPPI (ITA)
11	Rainer SCHUETTLER (GER)
13	Marat SAFIN (RUS)
	Thomas ENQVIST (SWE)
Q	Alexander PEYA (AUT)
WC	Bobby REYNOLDS (USA)
	Wayne ARTHURS (AUS)
	Arnaud CLEMENT (FRA)
Q	Danai UDOMCHOKE (THA)
18	Tommy ROBREDO (ESP)
29	Guillermo CANAS (ARG)
LL	Kristof VLIEGEN (BEL)
WC	K.J. HIPPENSTEEL (USA)
	Filippo VOLANDRI (ITA)
Q	Ivo HEUBERGER (SUI)
	Rafael NADAL (ESP)
WC	Scoville JENKINS (USA)
2	Andy RODDICK (USA)

D.NALBANDIAN (8) 64 76(5) 63
M.YOUZHNY 61 63 62
T.KETOLA (Q) 61 36 63 76(8)
T.BERDYCH 63 26 62 16 63
R.MELLO (Q) 62 76(1) 26 26 62
D.SANCHEZ 46 76(7) 62 63
T.HAAS 61 57 62 36 62
S.GROSJEAN (12) 75 67(6) 62 61
R.SODERLING 64 76(3) 67(4) 61
N.DAVYDENKO 16 63 36 76(5) 41 RET
K.BECK 63 76(4) 64
K.PLESS (P) 64 36 61 76(4)
F.LOPEZ (30) 76(4) 63 62
P.KOHLSCHREIBER (Q) 61 61 64
H.ARAZI 64 76(5) 67(7) 36 63
L.HEWITT (4) 61 75 64
J.FERRERO (7) 46 75 76(6) 67(4) 63
S.KOUBEK 63 64 16 26 63
J.GAMBILL 63 62 36 64
J.JOHANSSON (28) 63 61 63
V.SPADEA (23) 67(3) 62 64 64
J.MELZER 75 60 46 63
M.LLODRA 26 76(2) 76(5) 62
A.SEPPI (Q) 36 46 76(5) 76(1) 61
T.ENQVIST 76(5) 64 36 63
A.PEYA (Q) 26 63 63 67(3) 64
A.CLEMENT 64 67(5) 63 63
T.ROBREDO (18) 64 75 64
G.CANAS (29) 63 46 75 61
F.VOLANDRI 63 64 62
R.NADAL 60 63 46 26 63
A.RODDICK (2) 60 62 62

M.YOUZHNY 67(4) 64 75 26 64
T.BERDYCH 63 76(1) 63
R.MELLO (Q) 61 61 63
T.HAAS 64 64 16 61
N.DAVYDENKO 61 26 75 64
K.BECK 61 76(3) 75
F.LOPEZ (30) 75 75 67(5) 16 62
L.HEWITT (4) 76(7) 61 62
S.KOUBEK 76(2) 46 67(6) 62 63
J.JOHANSSON (28) 64 75 75
J.MELZER 63 46 36 63 64
M.LLODRA 60 63 36 63
A.PEYA (Q) 16 63 63 62
T.ROBREDO (18) 63 63 36 64
G.CANAS (29) 64 75 61
A.RODDICK (2) 60 63 64

T.BERDYCH 26 61 63 46 61
T.HAAS 62 63 75
K.BECK 63 46 36 61 64
L.HEWITT (4) 61 64 62
J.JOHANSSON (28) 67(2) 76(1) 61 63
M.LLODRA 63 62 75
T.ROBREDO (18) 63 63 62
A.RODDICK (2) 61 63 63

T.HAAS 76(6) 61 75
L.HEWITT (4) 64 62 62
J.JOHANSSON (28) 62 63 62
A.RODDICK (2) 63 62 64

L.HEWITT (4) 62 62 62
J.JOHANSSON (28) 64 64 36 26 64

L.HEWITT (4) 64 75 63

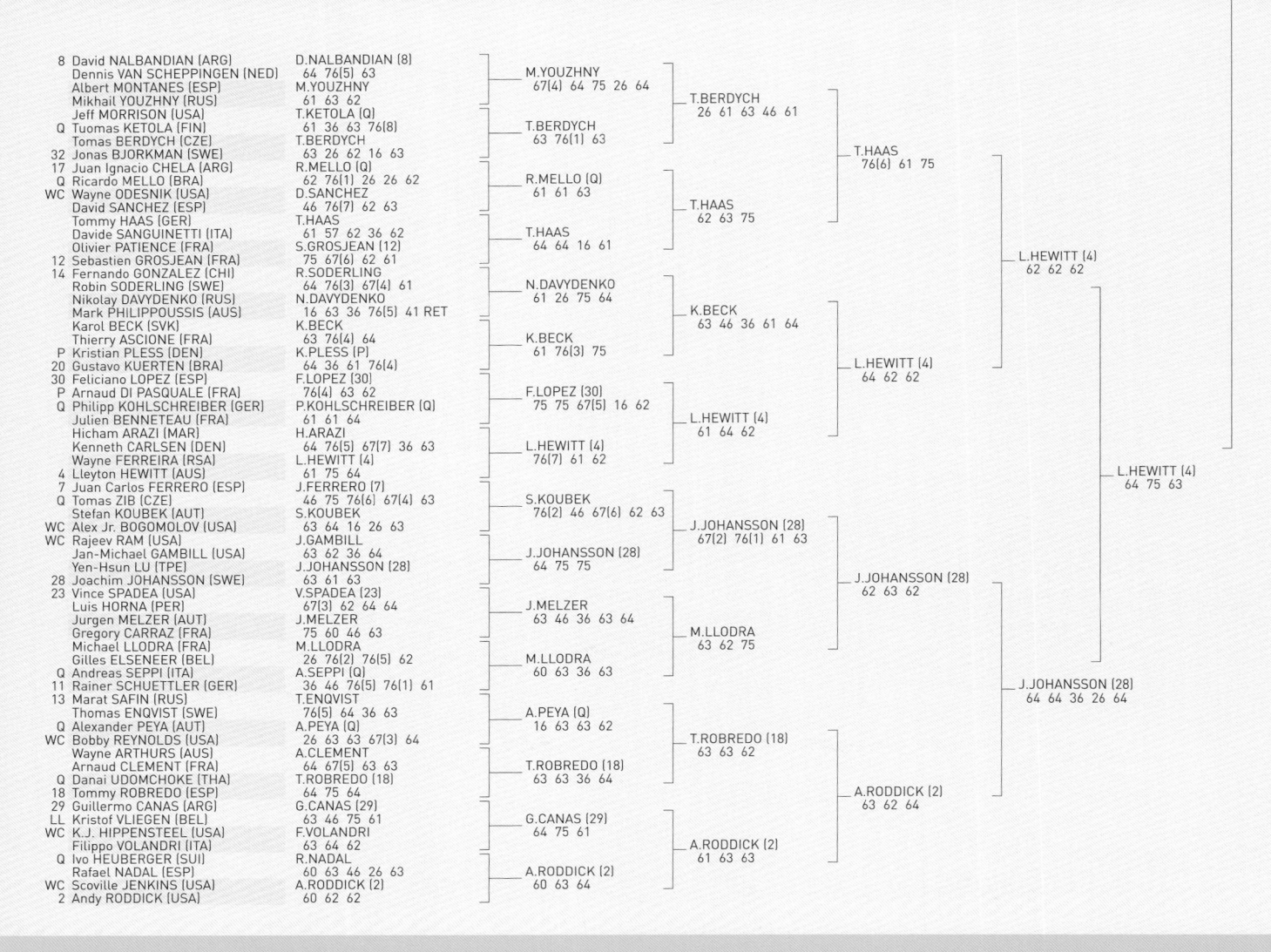

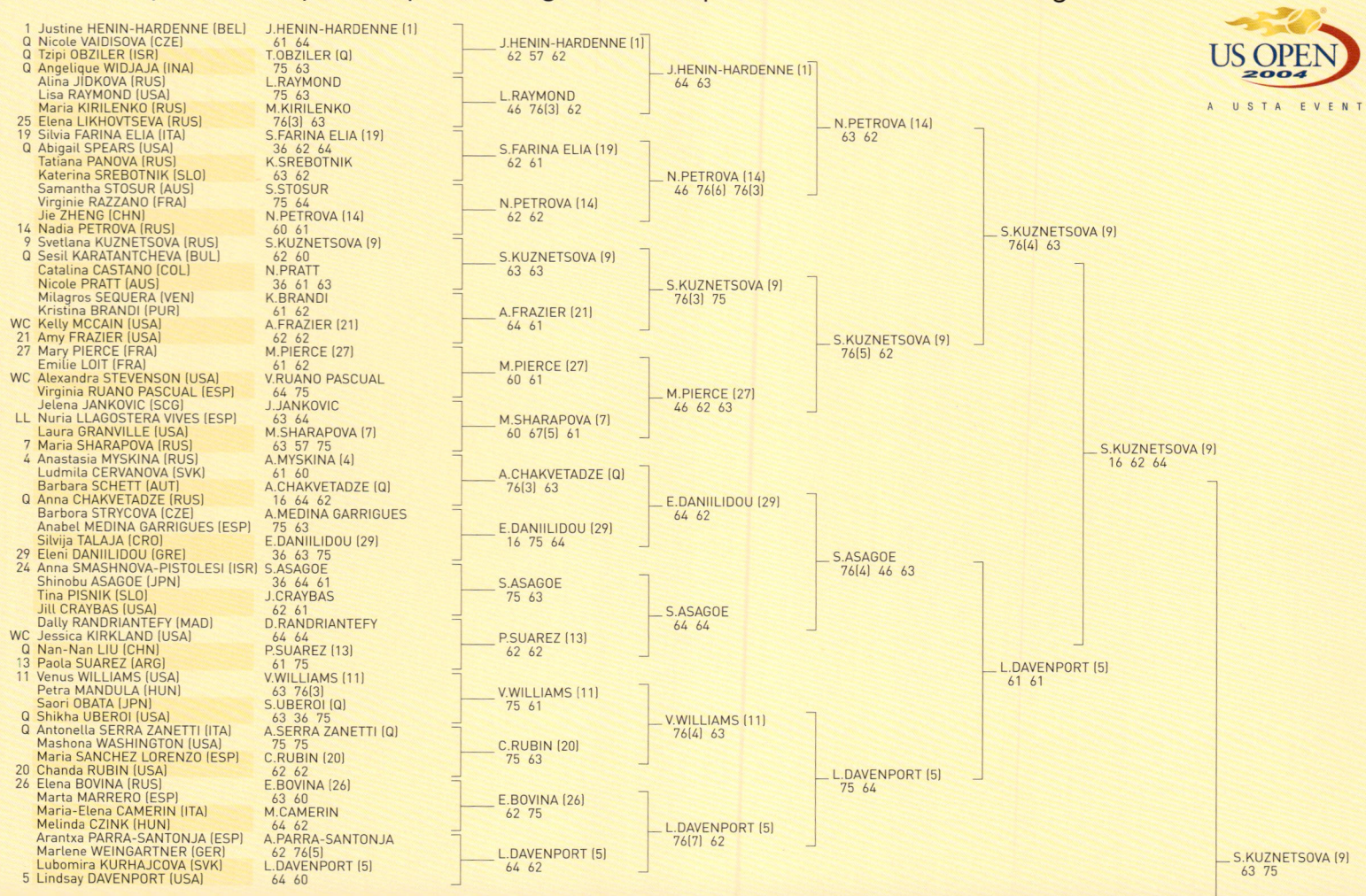

2004 US Open Championships, 30 August–12 September – Women's Singles

First Round

1 Justine HENIN-HARDENNE (BEL)
Q Nicole VAIDISOVA (CZE)
Q Tzipi OBZILER (ISR)
Q Angelique WIDJAJA (INA)
  Alina JIDKOVA (RUS)
  Lisa RAYMOND (USA)
  Maria KIRILENKO (RUS)
25 Elena LIKHOVTSEVA (RUS)
19 Silvia FARINA ELIA (ITA)
  Tatiana PANOVA (RUS)
  Katerina SREBOTNIK (SLO)
  Abigail SPEARS (USA)
  Samantha STOSUR (AUS)
  Virginie RAZZANO (FRA)
  Jie ZHENG (CHN)
14 Nadia PETROVA (RUS)
9 Svetlana KUZNETSOVA (RUS)
Q Sesil KARATANTCHEVA (BUL)
  Catalina CASTANO (COL)
  Nicole PRATT (AUS)
  Milagros SEQUERA (VEN)
  Kristina BRANDI (PUR)
WC Kelly McCAIN (USA)
21 Amy FRAZIER (USA)
27 Mary PIERCE (FRA)
  Emilie LOIT (FRA)
WC Alexandra STEVENSON (USA)
  Virginia RUANO PASCUAL (ESP)
  Jelena JANKOVIC (SCG)
LL Nuria LLAGOSTERA VIVES (ESP)
  Laura GRANVILLE (USA)
7 Maria SHARAPOVA (RUS)
4 Anastasia MYSKINA (RUS)
  Ludmila CERVANOVA (SVK)
  Barbora SCHETT (AUT)
Q Anna CHAKVETADZE (RUS)
  Anabel MEDINA GARRIGUES (ESP)
  Silvija TALAJA (CRO)
29 Eleni DANIILIDOU (GRE)
24 Anna SMASHNOVA-PISTOLESI (ISR)
  Tina PISNIK (SLO)
  Shinobu ASAGOE (JPN)
  Jill CRAYBAS (USA)
WC Jessica KIRKLAND (USA)
  Daily RANDRIANTEFY (MAD)
13 Paola SUAREZ (ARG)
11 Venus WILLIAMS (USA)
  Petra MANDULA (HUN)
  Nan-Nan LIU (CHN)
Q Saori OBATA (JPN)
Q Shikha UBEROI (USA)
  Antonella SERRA ZANETTI (ITA)
  Mashona WASHINGTON (USA)
20 Maria SANCHEZ LORENZO (ESP)
  Chanda RUBIN (USA)
26 Elena BOVINA (RUS)
  Marta MARRERO (ESP)
  Maria-Elena CAMERIN (ITA)
  Melinda CZINK (HUN)
  Arantxa PARRA-SANTONJA (ESP)
  Marlene WEINGARTNER (GER)
  Lubomira KURHAJCOVA (SVK)
5 Lindsay DAVENPORT (USA)

J.HENIN-HARDENNE [1] 61 64
T.OBZILER (Q) 75 63
L.RAYMOND 46 76(3) 62
M.KIRILENKO 75 63
S.FARINA ELIA [19] 76(3) 63
K.SREBOTNIK 36 62 64
S.STOSUR 63 62
N.PETROVA [14] 75 64
S.KUZNETSOVA [9] 60 61
N.PRATT 62 60
K.BRANDI 36 61 63
A.FRAZIER [21] 61 62
M.PIERCE [27] 64 61
V.RUANO PASCUAL 61 62
J.JANKOVIC 64 75
M.SHARAPOVA [7] 63 64
A.CHAKVETADZE (Q) 63 57 75
A.MEDINA GARRIGUES 61 60
E.DANIILIDOU [29] 75 63
S.ASAGOE 36 63 75
J.CRAYBAS 36 64 61
D.RANDRIANTEFY 62 61
P.SUAREZ [13] 64 64
V.WILLIAMS [11] 61 75
A.SERRA ZANETTI (Q) 63 76(3)
C.RUBIN [20] 75 75
E.BOVINA [26] 62 62
M.CAMERIN 63 60
A.PARRA-SANTONJA 64 62
L.DAVENPORT [5] 62 76(5)

Second Round

J.HENIN-HARDENNE [1] 62 57 62
L.RAYMOND 46 76(3) 62
S.FARINA ELIA [19] 62 61
N.PETROVA [14] 62 62
S.KUZNETSOVA [9] 63 63
A.FRAZIER [21] 64 61
M.PIERCE [27] 60 61
M.SHARAPOVA [7] 60 67(5) 61
A.CHAKVETADZE (Q) 76(3) 63
E.DANIILIDOU [29] 16 75 64
S.ASAGOE 75 63
P.SUAREZ [13] 62 62
V.WILLIAMS [11] 75 61
C.RUBIN [20] 75 63
E.BOVINA [26] 62 75
L.DAVENPORT [5] 64 62

Third Round

J.HENIN-HARDENNE [1] 64 63
N.PETROVA [14] 46 76(6) 76(3)
S.KUZNETSOVA [9] 76(3) 75
M.PIERCE [27] 46 62 63
E.DANIILIDOU [29] 64 62
S.ASAGOE 64 64
V.WILLIAMS [11] 76(4) 63
L.DAVENPORT [5] 76(7) 62

Fourth Round

N.PETROVA [14] 63 62
S.KUZNETSOVA [9] 76(5) 62
S.ASAGOE 76(4) 46 63
L.DAVENPORT [5] 75 64

Quarterfinals

S.KUZNETSOVA [9] 76(4) 63
L.DAVENPORT [5] 61 61

Semifinal

S.KUZNETSOVA [9] 16 62 64

Final

S.KUZNETSOVA [9] 63 75

Elite Tournaments: 2004 US Open Drawsheets

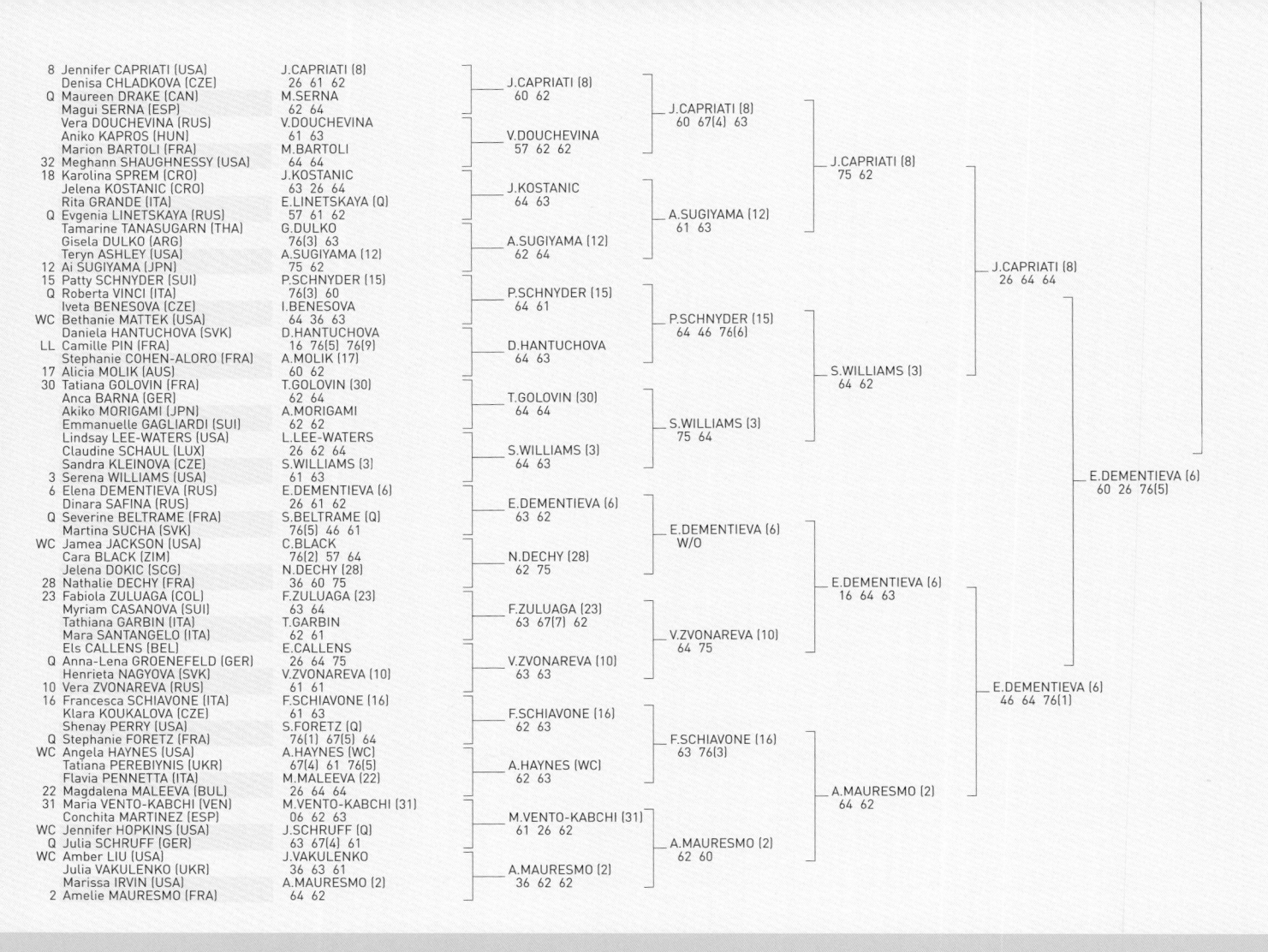

Bottom Half

Round 1 / Round 2 / Round 3 / Round 4 / Quarterfinal / Semifinal

Seed	Player	R1 Score
8	Jennifer CAPRIATI (USA)	J.CAPRIATI [8] 60 62
	Denisa CHLADKOVA (CZE)	
Q	Maureen DRAKE (CAN)	M.SERNA 62 64
	Magui SERNA (ESP)	
	Vera DOUCHEVINA (RUS)	V.DOUCHEVINA 57 62 62
	Aniko KAPROS (HUN)	
32	Marion BARTOLI (FRA)	M.BARTOLI 61 63
	Meghann SHAUGHNESSY (USA)	
18	Karolina SPREM (CRO)	J.KOSTANIC 64 64
	Jelena KOSTANIC (CRO)	
Q	Rita GRANDE (ITA)	E.LINETSKAYA 63 26 64
	Evgenia LINETSKAYA (RUS)	
	Tamarine TANASUGARN (THA)	G.DULKO 57 61 62
	Gisela DULKO (ARG)	
12	Teryn ASHLEY (USA)	A.SUGIYAMA 76(3) 63
	Ai SUGIYAMA (JPN)	
15	Patty SCHNYDER (SUI)	P.SCHNYDER 75 62
	Roberta VINCI (ITA)	
WC	Iveta BENESOVA (CZE)	I.BENESOVA 76(3) 60
	Bethanie MATTEK (USA)	
LL	Daniela HANTUCHOVA (SVK)	D.HANTUCHOVA 64 36 63
17	Camille PIN (FRA)	A.MOLIK 16 76(5) 76(9)
	Stephanie COHEN-ALORO (FRA)	
30	Alicia MOLIK (AUS)	T.GOLOVIN 60 62
	Tatiana GOLOVIN (FRA)	
	Anca BARNA (GER)	A.MORIGAMI 62 64
	Akiko MORIGAMI (JPN)	
	Emmanuelle GAGLIARDI (SUI)	L.LEE-WATERS 62 62
	Lindsay LEE-WATERS (USA)	
	Claudine SCHAUL (LUX)	S.WILLIAMS 26 62 64
	Sandra KLEINOVA (CZE)	
3	Serena WILLIAMS (USA)	61 63
6	Elena DEMENTIEVA (RUS)	E.DEMENTIEVA [6] 26 61 62
	Dinara SAFINA (RUS)	
Q	Severine BELTRAME (FRA)	S.BELTRAME 76(5) 46 61
	Martina SUCHA (SVK)	
WC	Jamea JACKSON (USA)	C.BLACK 76(2) 57 64
	Cara BLACK (ZIM)	
	Jelena DOKIC (SCG)	N.DECHY 36 60 75
28	Nathalie DECHY (FRA)	
23	Fabiola ZULUAGA (COL)	F.ZULUAGA 63 67(7) 62
	Myriam CASANOVA (SUI)	
	Tathiana GARBIN (ITA)	T.GARBIN 62 61
	Mara SANTANGELO (ITA)	
	Els CALLENS (BEL)	E.CALLENS 26 64 75
Q	Anna-Lena GROENEFELD (GER)	
10	Henrieta NAGYOVA (SVK)	V.ZVONAREVA 61 61
	Vera ZVONAREVA (RUS)	
16	Francesca SCHIAVONE (ITA)	F.SCHIAVONE 61 63
	Klara KOUKALOVA (CZE)	
Q	Shenay PERRY (USA)	S.FORETZ 76(1) 67(5) 64
	Stephanie FORETZ (FRA)	
WC	Angela HAYNES (USA)	A.HAYNES 67(4) 61 76(5)
	Tatiana PEREBYNIS (UKR)	
22	Magdalena MALEEVA (BUL)	M.MALEEVA 26 64 64
	Flavia PENNETTA (ITA)	
31	Maria VENTO-KABCHI (VEN)	M.VENTO-KABCHI 06 62 63
	Conchita MARTINEZ (ESP)	
WC	Jennifer HOPKINS (USA)	J.SCHRUFF 63 67(4) 61
Q	Julia SCHRUFF (GER)	
WC	Amber LIU (USA)	J.VAKULENKO 36 63 61
	Julia VAKULENKO (UKR)	
	Marissa IRVIN (USA)	A.MAURESMO 64 62
2	Amelie MAURESMO (FRA)	

Round Results

Round 2:
- J.CAPRIATI [8] 60 62
- V.DOUCHEVINA 57 62 62
- J.KOSTANIC 64 63
- A.SUGIYAMA [12] 62 64
- P.SCHNYDER [15] 64 61
- D.HANTUCHOVA 64 63
- T.GOLOVIN [30] 64 64
- S.WILLIAMS [3] 64 63
- E.DEMENTIEVA [6] 63 62
- N.DECHY [28] 62 75
- F.ZULUAGA [23] 63 67(7) 62
- V.ZVONAREVA [10] 63 63
- F.SCHIAVONE [16] 62 63
- A.HAYNES (WC) 62 63
- M.VENTO-KABCHI [31] 61 26 62
- A.MAURESMO [2] 36 62 62

Round 3:
- J.CAPRIATI [8] 60 67(4) 63
- A.SUGIYAMA [12] 61 63
- P.SCHNYDER [15] 64 46 76(6)
- S.WILLIAMS [3] 75 64
- E.DEMENTIEVA [6] W/O
- V.ZVONAREVA [10] 64 75
- F.SCHIAVONE [16] 63 76(3)
- A.MAURESMO [2] 64 62

Round 4:
- J.CAPRIATI [8] 75 62
- S.WILLIAMS [3] 64 62
- E.DEMENTIEVA [6] 16 64 63
- A.MAURESMO [2] 64 62

Quarterfinal:
- J.CAPRIATI [8] 26 64 64
- E.DEMENTIEVA [6] 46 64 76(1)

Semifinal:
- E.DEMENTIEVA [6] 60 26 76(5)

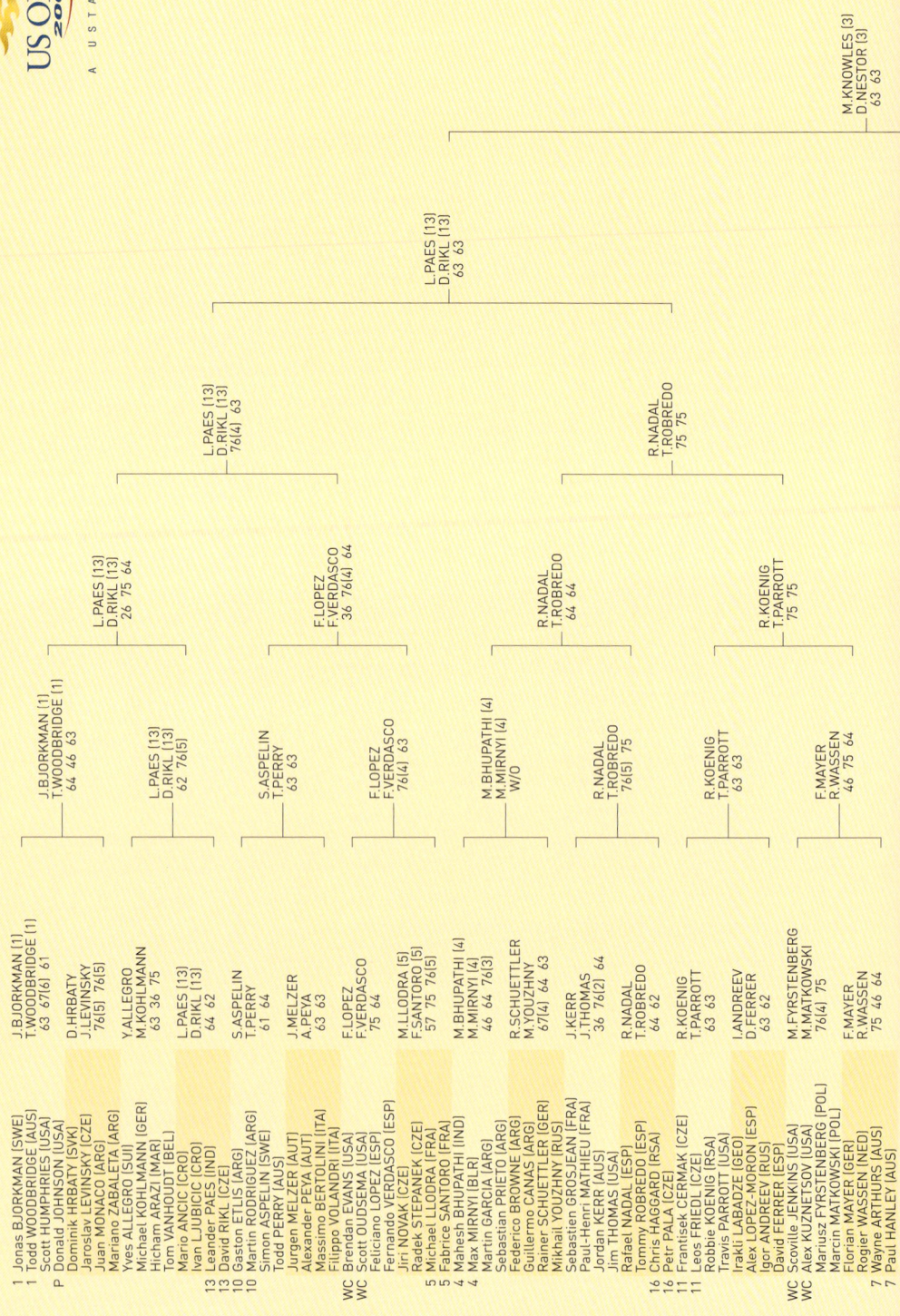

2004 US Open Championships, 30 August–12 September – Men's Doubles

Final: M. KNOWLES [3] / D. NESTOR [3] def. L. PAES [13] / D. RIKL [13] 6-3 6-3

Draw

- 1 J. BJORKMAN [1] (SWE) / T. WOODBRIDGE [1] (AUS)
  - Scott HUMPHRIES (USA) / Donald JOHNSON (USA) → J. BJORKMAN [1] / T. WOODBRIDGE [1] 6-4 4-6 6-1
- P Dominik HRBATY (SVK) / Jaroslav LEVINSKY (CZE) → D. HRBATY / J. LEVINSKY 7-6(5) 7-6(5)
  - Juan MONACO (ARG) / Mariano ZABALETA (ARG)
- Yves ALLEGRO (SUI) / Michael KOHLMANN (GER) → Y. ALLEGRO / M. KOHLMANN 6-3 3-6 7-5
  - Hicham ARAZI (MAR) / Tom VANHOUDT (BEL)
- 13 Mario ANCIC (CRO) / Ivan LJUBICIC (CRO)
- 13 Leander PAES (IND) / David RIKL (CZE) → L. PAES [13] / D. RIKL [13] 6-4 6-2
- 10 Gaston ETLIS (ARG) / Martin RODRIGUEZ (ARG)
- 10 Simon ASPELIN (SWE) / Todd PERRY (AUS) → S. ASPELIN / T. PERRY 6-1 6-4
- Jurgen MELZER (AUT) / Alexander PEYA (AUT) → J. MELZER / A. PEYA 6-3 6-3
  - Massimo BERTOLINI (ITA) / Filippo VOLANDRI (ITA)
- WC Brendan EVANS (USA) / Scott OUDSEMA (USA)
- WC Feliciano LOPEZ (ESP) / Fernando VERDASCO (ESP) → F. LOPEZ / F. VERDASCO 7-5 6-4
- Jiri NOVAK (CZE) / Radek STEPANEK (CZE)
- 5 Michael LLODRA (FRA) / Fabrice SANTORO (FRA) → M. LLODRA [5] / F. SANTORO [5] 5-7 7-5 7-6(5)
- 4 Mahesh BHUPATHI (IND) / Max MIRNYI (BLR)
- Martin GARCIA (ARG) / Sebastian PRIETO (ARG) → M. BHUPATHI [4] / M. MIRNYI [4] 4-6 6-4 7-6(3)
  - Federico BROWNE (ARG) / Guillermo CANAS (ARG)
- Rainer SCHUETTLER (GER) / Mikhail YOUZHNY (RUS) → R. SCHUETTLER / M. YOUZHNY 6-7(4) 6-4 6-3
  - Sebastien GROSJEAN (FRA) / Paul-Henri MATHIEU (FRA)
- Jordan KERR (AUS) / Jim THOMAS (USA) → J. KERR / J. THOMAS 3-6 7-6(2) 6-4
  - Rafael NADAL (ESP) / Tommy ROBREDO (ESP) → R. NADAL / T. ROBREDO 7-6(5) 7-5
- 16 Chris HAGGARD (RSA) / Petr PALA (CZE) → 6-4 6-2
- 16 Frantisek CERMAK (CZE) / Leos FRIEDL (CZE)
- 11 Robbie KOENIG (RSA) / Travis PARROTT (USA) → R. KOENIG / T. PARROTT 6-3 6-3
- 11 Irakli LABADZE (GEO) / Alex LOPEZ-MORON (ESP)
- Igor ANDREEV (RUS) / David FERRER (ESP) → I. ANDREEV / D. FERRER 6-3 6-2
- WC Scoville JENKINS (USA) / Alex KUZNETSOV (USA)
- WC Mariusz FYRSTENBERG (POL) / Marcin MATKOWSKI (POL) → M. FYRSTENBERG / M. MATKOWSKI 7-6(4) 7-5
- Florian MAYER (GER) / Rogier WASSEN (NED) → F. MAYER / R. WASSEN 4-6 7-5 6-4
- 7 Wayne ARTHURS (AUS) / Paul HANLEY (AUS)

Round results

- J. BJORKMAN [1] / T. WOODBRIDGE [1] def. D. HRBATY / J. LEVINSKY
- L. PAES [13] / D. RIKL [13] def. Y. ALLEGRO / M. KOHLMANN 6-2 7-6(5)
- L. PAES [13] / D. RIKL [13] def. J. BJORKMAN [1] / T. WOODBRIDGE [1] 2-6 7-5 6-4
- F. LOPEZ / F. VERDASCO def. S. ASPELIN / T. PERRY 3-6 7-6(4) 6-4
- L. PAES [13] / D. RIKL [13] def. F. LOPEZ / F. VERDASCO 7-6(4) 6-3
- M. BHUPATHI [4] / M. MIRNYI [4] def. R. SCHUETTLER / M. YOUZHNY W/O
- R. NADAL / T. ROBREDO def. M. BHUPATHI [4] / M. MIRNYI [4] 6-4 6-4
- R. KOENIG / T. PARROTT def. F. MAYER / R. WASSEN 7-5 7-5
- R. NADAL / T. ROBREDO def. R. KOENIG / T. PARROTT 7-5 7-5
- L. PAES [13] / D. RIKL [13] def. R. NADAL / T. ROBREDO
- M. KNOWLES [3] / D. NESTOR [3] def. L. PAES [13] / D. RIKL [13] 6-3 6-3

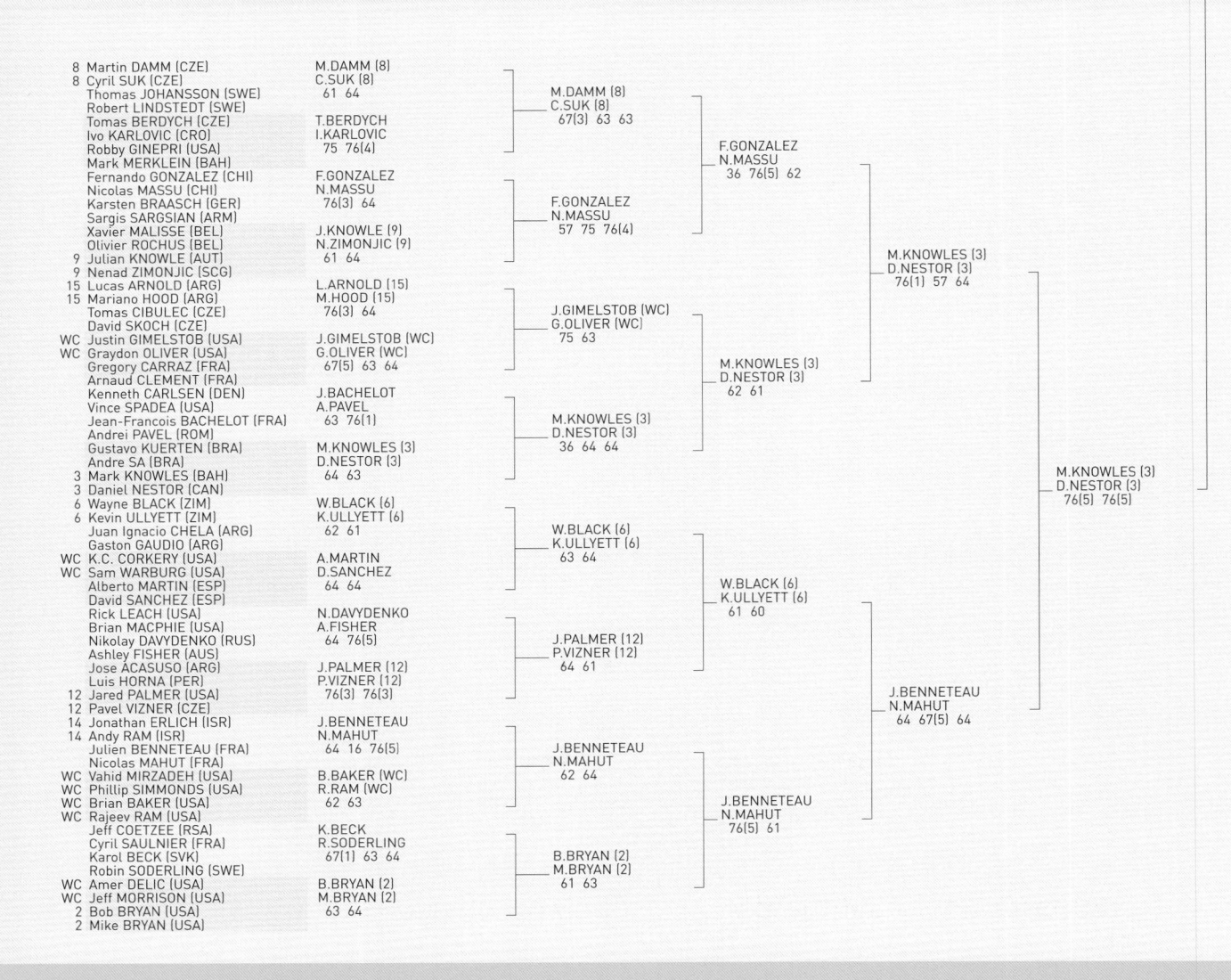

2004 US Open Doubles Draw (partial)

Final section shown

M.KNOWLES / D.NESTOR (3) — 76(5) 76(5)

- M.KNOWLES / D.NESTOR (3) — 76(1) 57 64
  - F.GONZALEZ / N.MASSU — 36 76(5) 62
    - M.DAMM / C.SUK (8) — 67(3) 63 63
      - M.DAMM (8) / C.SUK (8) — 61 64
        - 8 Martin DAMM (CZE)
        - 8 Cyril SUK (CZE)
      - T.BERDYCH / I.KARLOVIC — 75 76(4)
        - Thomas JOHANSSON (SWE)
        - Robert LINDSTEDT (SWE)
        - Tomas BERDYCH (CZE)
        - Ivo KARLOVIC (CRO)
    - F.GONZALEZ / N.MASSU — 57 75 76(4)
      - F.GONZALEZ / N.MASSU — 76(3) 64
        - Robby GINEPRI (USA)
        - Mark MERKLEIN (BAH)
        - Fernando GONZALEZ (CHI)
        - Nicolas MASSU (CHI)
      - J.KNOWLE / N.ZIMONJIC (9) — 61 64
        - Karsten BRAASCH (GER)
        - Sargis SARGSIAN (ARM)
        - 9 Xavier MALISSE (BEL)
        - 9 Olivier ROCHUS (BEL)
        - Julian KNOWLE (AUT)
        - Nenad ZIMONJIC (SCG)
  - M.KNOWLES / D.NESTOR (3) — 62 61
    - J.GIMELSTOB / G.OLIVER (WC) — 75 63
      - L.ARNOLD / M.HOOD (15) — 76(3) 64
        - 15 Lucas ARNOLD (ARG)
        - 15 Mariano HOOD (ARG)
        - Tomas CIBULEC (CZE)
        - David SKOCH (CZE)
      - J.GIMELSTOB (WC) / G.OLIVER (WC) — 67(5) 63 64
        - WC Justin GIMELSTOB (USA)
        - WC Graydon OLIVER (USA)
        - Gregory CARRAZ (FRA)
        - Arnaud CLEMENT (FRA)
    - M.KNOWLES / D.NESTOR (3) — 36 64 64
      - J.BACHELOT / A.PAVEL — 63 76(1)
        - Kenneth CARLSEN (DEN)
        - Vince SPADEA (USA)
        - Jean-Francois BACHELOT (FRA)
        - Andrei PAVEL (ROM)
      - M.KNOWLES (3) / D.NESTOR (3) — 64 63
        - Gustavo KUERTEN (BRA)
        - Andre SA (BRA)
        - 3 Mark KNOWLES (BAH)
        - 3 Daniel NESTOR (CAN)

- J.BENNETEAU / N.MAHUT — 64 67(5) 64
  - W.BLACK / K.ULLYETT (6) — 61 60
    - W.BLACK (6) / K.ULLYETT (6) — 63 64
      - 6 Wayne BLACK (ZIM)
      - 6 Kevin ULLYETT (ZIM)
      - Juan Ignacio CHELA (ARG)
      - Gaston GAUDIO (ARG)
    - A.MARTIN / D.SANCHEZ — 62 61
      - WC K.C. CORKERY (USA)
      - WC Sam WARBURG (USA)
      - Alberto MARTIN (ESP)
      - David SANCHEZ (ESP)
  - J.PALMER / P.VIZNER (12) — 64 61
    - N.DAVYDENKO / A.FISHER — 64 76(5)
      - Rick LEACH (USA)
      - Brian MACPHIE (USA)
      - Nikolay DAVYDENKO (RUS)
      - Ashley FISHER (AUS)
    - J.PALMER (12) / P.VIZNER (12) — 76(3) 76(3)
      - Jose ACASUSO (ARG)
      - Luis HORNA (PER)
      - 12 Jared PALMER (USA)
      - 12 Pavel VIZNER (CZE)

- J.BENNETEAU / N.MAHUT — 76(5) 61
  - J.BENNETEAU / N.MAHUT — 62 64
    - J.BENNETEAU / N.MAHUT — 64 16 76(5)
      - 14 Jonathan ERLICH (ISR)
      - 14 Andy RAM (ISR)
      - Julien BENNETEAU (FRA)
      - Nicolas MAHUT (FRA)
    - B.BAKER (WC) / R.RAM (WC) — 62 63
      - WC Vahid MIRZADEH (USA)
      - WC Phillip SIMMONDS (USA)
      - WC Brian BAKER (USA)
      - WC Rajeev RAM (USA)
  - B.BRYAN (2) / M.BRYAN (2) — 61 63
    - K.BECK / R.SODERLING — 67(1) 63 64
      - Jeff COETZEE (RSA)
      - Cyril SAULNIER (FRA)
      - Karol BECK (SVK)
      - Robin SODERLING (SWE)
    - B.BRYAN (2) / M.BRYAN (2) — 63 64
      - WC Amer DELIC (USA)
      - WC Jeff MORRISON (USA)
      - 2 Bob BRYAN (USA)
      - 2 Mike BRYAN (USA)

Elite Tournaments: 2004 US Open Drawsheets — 105

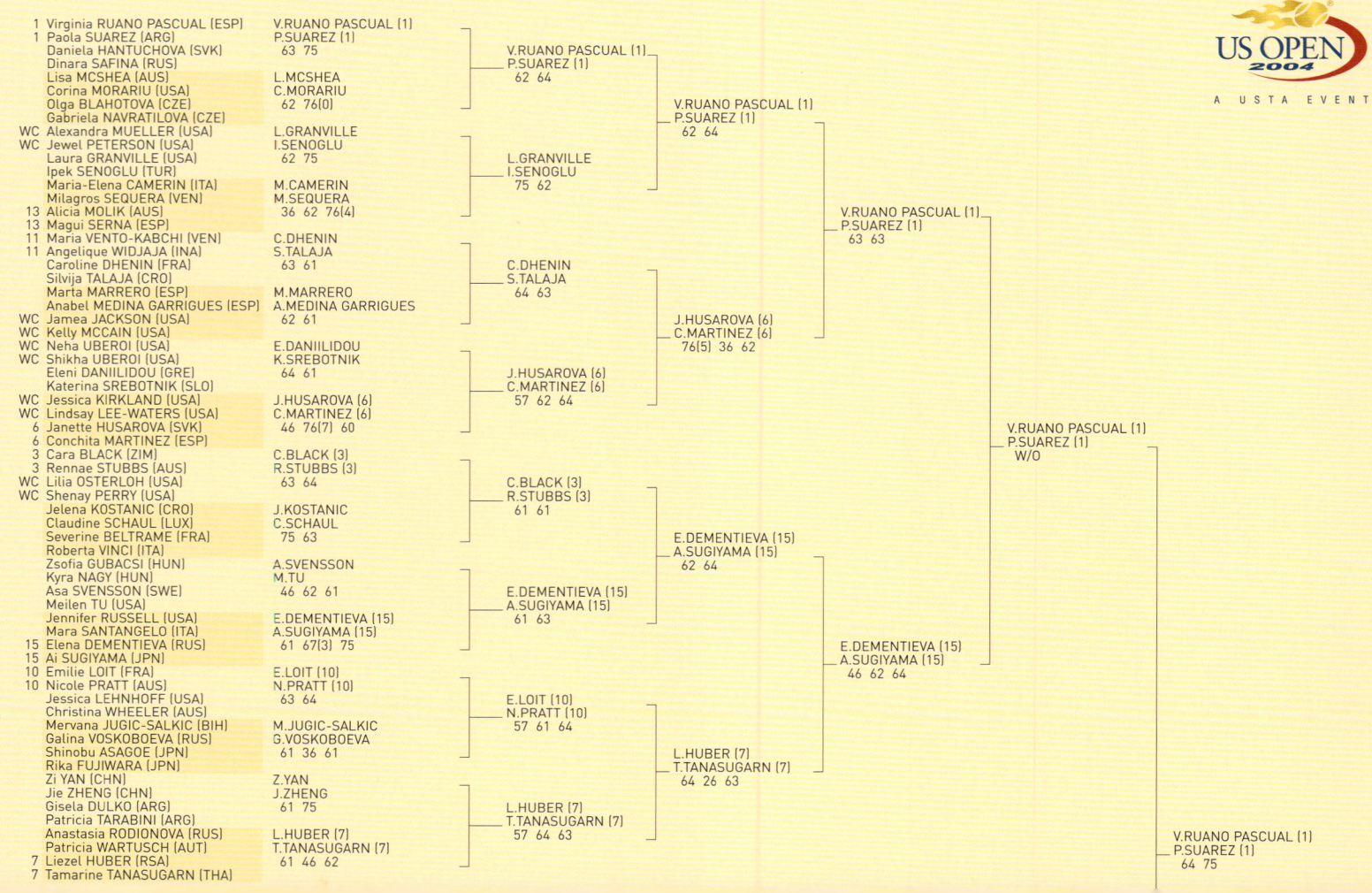

2004 US Open Championships, 30 August–12 September – Women's Doubles

```
 1 Virginia RUANO PASCUAL (ESP) ┐
 1 Paola SUAREZ (ARG)           ├ V.RUANO PASCUAL [1] ┐
   Daniela HANTUCHOVA (SVK)     ┘ P.SUAREZ [1]        │
   Dinara SAFINA (RUS)            6 3 7 5             │
   Lisa MCSHEA (AUS)            ┐                     ├ V.RUANO PASCUAL [1] ┐
   Corina MORARIU (USA)         ├ L.MCSHEA            ┘ P.SUAREZ [1]        │
   Olga BLAHOTOVA (CZE)         ┘ C.MORARIU             6 2 6 4             │
   Gabriela NAVRATILOVA (CZE)     6 2 7 6(0)                                │
WC Alexandra MUELLER (USA)      ┐                                           │
WC Jewel PETERSON (USA)         ├ L.GRANVILLE         ┐                     ├ V.RUANO PASCUAL [1] ┐
   Laura GRANVILLE (USA)        ┘ I.SENOGLU           ├ L.GRANVILLE         ┘ P.SUAREZ [1]        │
   Ipek SENOGLU (TUR)             6 2 7 5             │ I.SENOGLU             6 3 6 3             │
   Maria-Elena CAMERIN (ITA)    ┐                     │ 7 5 6 2                                   │
   Milagros SEQUERA (VEN)       ├ M.CAMERIN           ┘                                           │
13 Alicia MOLIK (AUS)           ┘ M.SEQUERA                                                       │
13 Magui SERNA (ESP)              3 6 6 2 7 6(4)                                                  │
11 Maria VENTO-KABCHI (VEN)     ┐                                                                 │
11 Angelique WIDJAJA (INA)      ├ C.DHENIN            ┐                                           │
   Caroline DHENIN (FRA)        ┘ S.TALAJA            │                                           │
   Silvija TALAJA (CRO)           6 3 6 1             ├ C.DHENIN            ┐                     │
   Marta MARRERO (ESP)          ┐                     │ S.TALAJA            │                     │
   Anabel MEDINA GARRIGUES (ESP)├ M.MARRERO           ┘ 6 4 6 3             │                     │
WC Jamea JACKSON (USA)          ┘ A.MEDINA GARRIGUES                        │                     │
WC Kelly MCCAIN (USA)             6 2 6 1                                   ├ J.HUSAROVA [6]      ┘
WC Neha UBEROI (USA)            ┐                                           │ C.MARTINEZ [6]
WC Shikha UBEROI (USA)          ├ E.DANIILIDOU        ┐                     │ 7 6(5) 3 6 6 2
   Eleni DANIILIDOU (GRE)       ┘ K.SREBOTNIK         │                     │
   Katerina SREBOTNIK (SLO)       6 4 6 1             ├ J.HUSAROVA [6]      ┘
WC Jessica KIRKLAND (USA)       ┐                     │ C.MARTINEZ [6]
   Lindsay LEE-WATERS (USA)     ├ J.HUSAROVA [6]      ┘ 5 7 6 2 6 4
 6 Janette HUSAROVA (SVK)       ┘ C.MARTINEZ [6]
 6 Conchita MARTINEZ (ESP)        4 6 7 6(7) 6 0

 3 Cara BLACK (ZIM)             ┐
 3 Rennae STUBBS (AUS)          ├ C.BLACK [3]         ┐
WC Lilia OSTERLOH (USA)         ┘ R.STUBBS [3]        │
WC Shenay PERRY (USA)             6 3 6 4             ├ E.DEMENTIEVA [15]   ┐
   Jelena KOSTANIC (CRO)        ┐                     │ A.SUGIYAMA [15]     │
   Claudine SCHAUL (LUX)        ├ J.KOSTANIC          ┘ 6 1 6 1             │
   Severine BELTRAME (FRA)      ┘ C.SCHAUL                                  │
   Roberta VINCI (ITA)            7 5 6 3                                   ├ E.DEMENTIEVA [15]   ┐
   Zsofia GUBACSI (HUN)         ┐                                           │ A.SUGIYAMA [15]     │
   Kyra NAGY (HUN)              ├ A.SVENSSON          ┐                     │ 6 2 6 4             │
   Asa SVENSSON (SWE)           ┘ M.TU                │                     │                     │
   Meilen TU (USA)                4 6 6 2 6 1         ├ E.DEMENTIEVA [15]   ┘                     │
   Jennifer RUSSELL (USA)       ┐                     │ A.SUGIYAMA [15]                           │
   Mara SANTANGELO (ITA)        ├ E.DEMENTIEVA [15]   ┘ 6 1 6 3                                   ├ E.DEMENTIEVA [15] ┐
15 Elena DEMENTIEVA (RUS)       ┘ A.SUGIYAMA [15]                                                 │ A.SUGIYAMA [15]   │
15 Ai SUGIYAMA (JPN)              6 1 6 7(3) 7 5                                                  │ 4 6 6 2 6 4       │
10 Emilie LOIT (FRA)            ┐                                                                 │                   │
10 Nicole PRATT (AUS)           ├ E.LOIT [10]         ┐                                           │                   │
   Jessica LEHNHOFF (USA)       ┘ N.PRATT [10]        │                                           │                   │
   Christina WHEELER (AUS)        6 3 6 4             ├ E.LOIT [10]         ┐                     │                   │
   Mervana JUGIC-SALKIC (BIH)   ┐                     │ N.PRATT [10]        │                     │                   │
   Galina VOSKOBOEVA (RUS)      ├ M.JUGIC-SALKIC      ┘ 5 7 6 1 6 4         │                     │                   │
   Shinobu ASAGOE (JPN)         ┘ G.VOSKOBOEVA                              ├ L.HUBER [7]         ┘                   │
   Rika FUJIWARA (JPN)            6 1 3 6 6 1                               │ T.TANASUGARN [7]                        │
   Zi YAN (CHN)                 ┐                                           │ 6 4 2 6 6 3                             │
   Jie ZHENG (CHN)              ├ Z.YAN               ┐                     │                                         │
   Gisela DULKO (ARG)           ┘ J.ZHENG             │                     │                                         │
   Patricia TARABINI (ARG)        6 1 7 5             ├ L.HUBER [7]         ┘                                         │
   Anastasia RODIONOVA (RUS)    ┐                     │ T.TANASUGARN [7]                                              │
   Patricia WARTUSCH (AUT)      ├ L.HUBER [7]         ┘ 5 7 6 4 6 3                                                   │
 7 Liezel HUBER (RSA)           ┘ T.TANASUGARN [7]                                                                    │
 7 Tamarine TANASUGARN (THA)      6 1 4 6 6 2                                                                         │
                                                                                                                      │
                                                       V.RUANO PASCUAL [1] ┐                                          │
                                                       P.SUAREZ [1]        ├ V.RUANO PASCUAL [1] ─────────────────────┘
                                                       W/O                 │ P.SUAREZ [1]
                                                                           ┘ 6 4 7 5
```

US OPEN 2004 — A USTA EVENT

Elite Tournaments: 2004 US Open Drawsheets

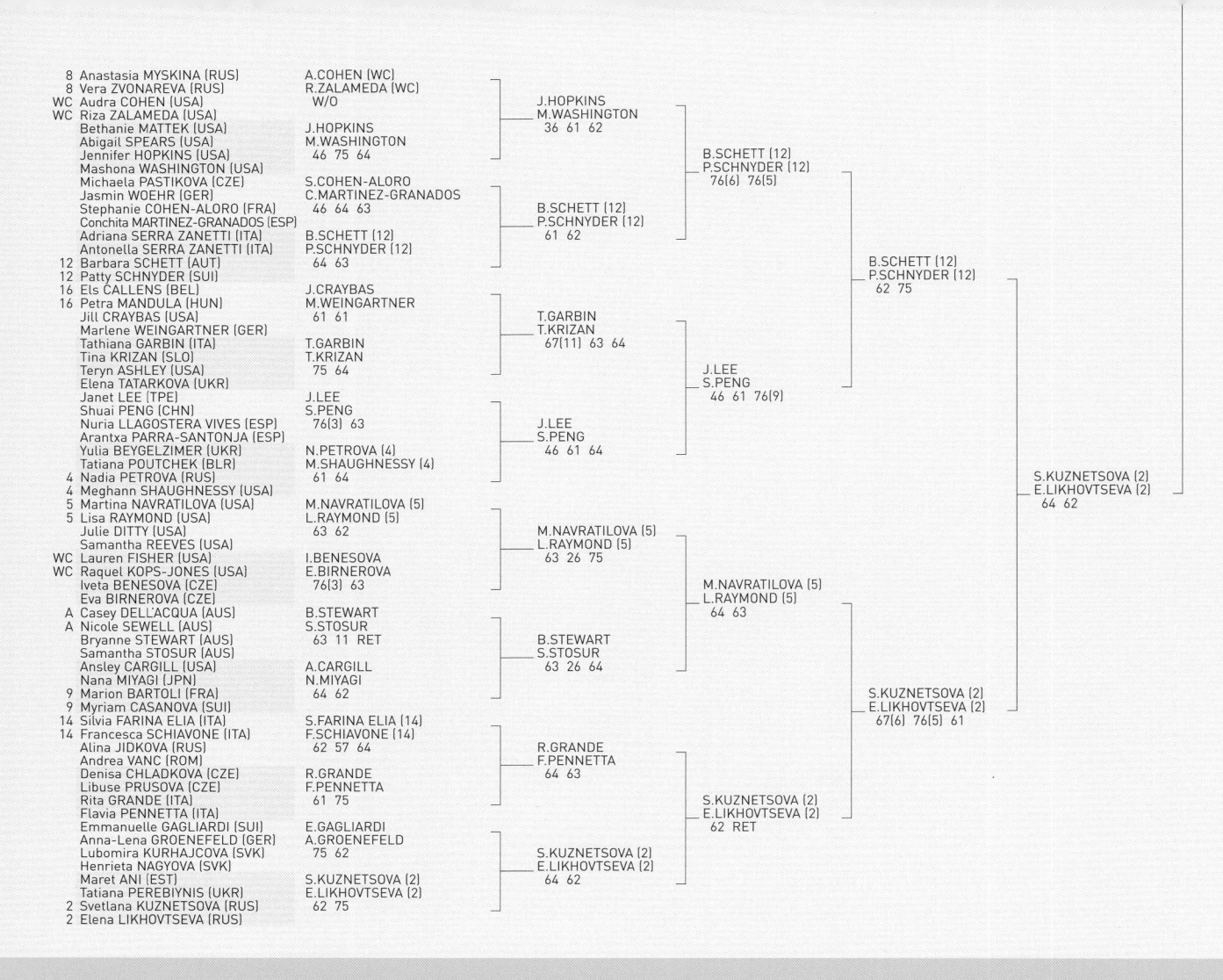

Doubles Draw (partial)

Final: S.KUZNETSOVA [2] / E.LIKHOVTSEVA [2] def. B.SCHETT [12] / P.SCHNYDER [12] 6-4 6-2

Top Half

- J.HOPKINS / M.WASHINGTON
- 8 Anastasia MYSKINA (RUS) / Vera ZVONAREVA (RUS)
- WC A.COHEN / R.ZALAMEDA — w/o
- WC Audra COHEN (USA) / Riza ZALAMEDA (USA)
- J.HOPKINS / M.WASHINGTON 4-6 7-5 6-4
- Bethanie MATTEK (USA) / Abigail SPEARS (USA)
- Jennifer HOPKINS (USA) / Mashona WASHINGTON (USA)
- S.COHEN-ALORO / C.MARTINEZ-GRANADOS 4-6 6-4 6-3
- Michaela PASTIKOVA (CZE) / Jasmin WOEHR (GER)
- Stephanie COHEN-ALORO (FRA) / Conchita MARTINEZ-GRANADOS (ESP)
- B.SCHETT [12] / P.SCHNYDER [12] 6-1 6-2
- 12 Adriana SERRA ZANETTI (ITA) / Antonella SERRA ZANETTI (ITA)
- 12 Barbara SCHETT (AUT) / Patty SCHNYDER (SUI)

B.SCHETT [12] / P.SCHNYDER [12] 7-6(6) 7-6(5)

- 16 Els CALLENS (BEL) / Petra MANDULA (HUN)
- 16 Jill CRAYBAS (USA) / Marlene WEINGARTNER (GER)
- J.CRAYBAS / M.WEINGARTNER 6-1 6-1
- Tathiana GARBIN (ITA) / Tina KRIZAN (SLO)
- T.GARBIN / T.KRIZAN 7-5 6-4
- Teryn ASHLEY (USA) / Elena TATARKOVA (UKR)
- T.GARBIN / T.KRIZAN 6-7(11) 6-3 6-4

J.LEE / S.PENG 4-6 6-1 7-6(9)

- Janet LEE (TPE) / Shuai PENG (CHN)
- J.LEE / S.PENG 7-6(3) 6-3
- Nuria LLAGOSTERA VIVES (ESP) / Arantxa PARRA-SANTONJA (ESP)
- J.LEE / S.PENG 4-6 6-1 6-4
- 4 Yulia BEYGELZIMER (UKR) / Tatiana POUTCHEK (BLR)
- 4 Nadia PETROVA (RUS) / Meghan SHAUGHNESSY (USA)
- N.PETROVA / M.SHAUGHNESSY 6-1 6-4

Bottom Half

M.NAVRATILOVA [5] / L.RAYMOND [5] 6-4 6-3

- 5 Martina NAVRATILOVA (USA) / Lisa RAYMOND (USA)
- M.NAVRATILOVA / L.RAYMOND 6-3 6-2
- Julie DITTY (USA) / Samantha REEVES (USA)
- M.NAVRATILOVA / L.RAYMOND 6-3 2-6 7-5
- WC Lauren FISHER (USA) / Raquel KOPS-JONES (USA)
- WC Iveta BENESOVA (CZE) / Eva BIRNEROVA (CZE)
- I.BENESOVA / E.BIRNEROVA 7-6(3) 6-3
- A Casey DELL'ACQUA (AUS) / Nicole SEWELL (AUS)
- B.STEWART / S.STOSUR 6-3 1-1 RET
- A Bryanne STEWART (AUS) / Samantha STOSUR (AUS)
- B.STEWART / S.STOSUR 6-3 2-6 6-4
- Ansley CARGILL (USA) / Nana MIYAGI (JPN)
- A.CARGILL / N.MIYAGI 6-4 6-2

S.KUZNETSOVA [2] / E.LIKHOVTSEVA [2] 6-7(6) 7-6(5) 6-1

- 9 Marion BARTOLI (FRA) / Myriam CASANOVA (SUI)
- 14 Silvia FARINA ELIA (ITA) / Francesca SCHIAVONE (ITA)
- S.FARINA ELIA [14] / F.SCHIAVONE [14] 6-2 5-7 6-4
- 14 Alina JIDKOVA (RUS) / Andrea VANC (ROM)
- R.GRANDE / F.PENNETTA 6-4 6-3
- Denisa CHLADKOVA (CZE) / Libuse PRUSOVA (CZE)
- R.GRANDE / F.PENNETTA 6-1 7-5
- Rita GRANDE (ITA) / Flavia PENNETTA (ITA)

S.KUZNETSOVA [2] / E.LIKHOVTSEVA [2] 6-2 RET

- Emmanuelle GAGLIARDI (SUI) / Anna-Lena GROENEFELD (GER)
- E.GAGLIARDI / A.GROENEFELD 7-5 6-2
- Lubomira KURHAJCOVA (SVK) / Henrieta NAGYOVA (SVK)
- S.KUZNETSOVA [2] / E.LIKHOVTSEVA [2] 6-4 6-2
- Maret ANI (EST) / Tatiana PEREBIYNIS (UKR)
- S.KUZNETSOVA [2] / E.LIKHOVTSEVA [2] 6-2 7-5
- 2 Svetlana KUZNETSOVA (RUS) / Elena LIKHOVTSEVA (RUS)

2004 US Open Championships, 30 August–12 September – Mixed Doubles

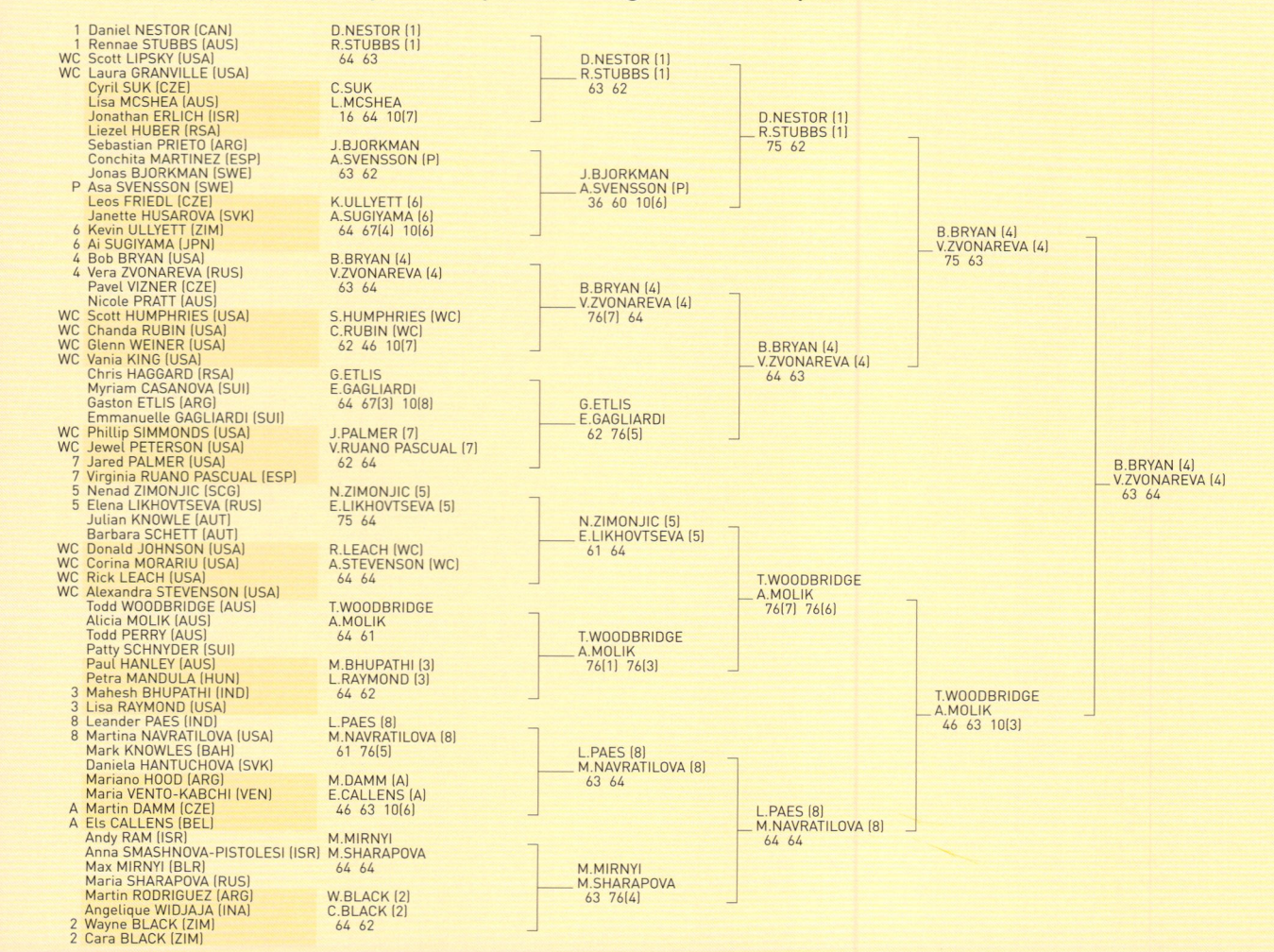

Champions: B. BRYAN / V. ZVONAREVA (4) — defeated T. WOODBRIDGE / A. MOLIK 6-3 6-4

Draw

Quarter 1 (Top)

- 1 Daniel NESTOR (CAN) / Rennae STUBBS (AUS) [1]
- WC Scott LIPSKY (USA) / WC Laura GRANVILLE (USA)
  - D. NESTOR / R. STUBBS [1] 6-4 6-3
- Cyril SUK (CZE) / Lisa McSHEA (AUS)
- WC Jonathan ERLICH (ISR) / Liezel HUBER (RSA)
  - C. SUK / L. McSHEA 1-6 6-4 10-[7]
    - D. NESTOR / R. STUBBS [1] 6-3 6-2

- Sebastian PRIETO (ARG) / Conchita MARTINEZ (ESP)
- P Jonas BJORKMAN (SWE) / Asa SVENSSON (SWE)
  - J. BJORKMAN / A. SVENSSON (P) 6-3 6-2
- Leos FRIEDL (CZE) / Janette HUSAROVA (SVK)
- 6 Kevin ULLYETT (ZIM) / Ai SUGIYAMA (JPN)
  - K. ULLYETT / A. SUGIYAMA [6] 6-4 6-7(4) 10-[6]
    - J. BJORKMAN / A. SVENSSON (P) 3-6 6-0 10-[6]
      - D. NESTOR / R. STUBBS [1] 7-5 6-2

Quarter 2

- 4 Bob BRYAN (USA) / Vera ZVONAREVA (RUS)
- Pavel VIZNER (CZE) / Nicole PRATT (AUS)
  - B. BRYAN / V. ZVONAREVA [4] 6-3 6-4
- WC Scott HUMPHRIES (USA) / WC Chanda RUBIN (USA)
- WC Glenn WEINER (USA) / WC Vania KING (USA)
  - S. HUMPHRIES / C. RUBIN (WC) 6-2 4-6 10-[7]
    - B. BRYAN / V. ZVONAREVA [4] 7-6(7) 6-4

- Chris HAGGARD (RSA) / Myriam CASANOVA (SUI)
- Gaston ETLIS (ARG) / Emmanuelle GAGLIARDI (SUI)
  - G. ETLIS / E. GAGLIARDI 6-4 6-7(3) 10-[8]
- WC Phillip SIMMONDS (USA) / WC Jewel PETERSON (USA)
- 7 Jared PALMER (USA) / Virginia RUANO PASCUAL (ESP)
  - J. PALMER / V. RUANO PASCUAL [7] 6-2 6-4
    - G. ETLIS / E. GAGLIARDI 6-2 7-6(5)
      - B. BRYAN / V. ZVONAREVA [4] 6-4 6-3

        B. BRYAN / V. ZVONAREVA [4] 7-5 6-3

Quarter 3

- 5 Nenad ZIMONJIC (SCG) / Elena LIKHOVTSEVA (RUS)
- Julian KNOWLE (AUT) / Barbara SCHETT (AUT)
  - N. ZIMONJIC / E. LIKHOVTSEVA [5] 7-5 6-4
- WC Donald JOHNSON (USA) / Corina MORARIU (USA)
- WC Rick LEACH (USA) / WC Alexandra STEVENSON (USA)
  - R. LEACH / A. STEVENSON (WC) 6-1 6-4
    - N. ZIMONJIC / E. LIKHOVTSEVA [5] 6-1 6-4

- WC Todd WOODBRIDGE (AUS) / Alicia MOLIK (AUS)
- Todd PERRY (AUS) / Patty SCHNYDER (SUI)
  - T. WOODBRIDGE / A. MOLIK 6-4 6-1
- Paul HANLEY (AUS) / Petra MANDULA (HUN)
- 3 Mahesh BHUPATHI (IND) / Lisa RAYMOND (USA)
  - M. BHUPATHI / L. RAYMOND [3] 6-4 6-2
    - T. WOODBRIDGE / A. MOLIK 7-6(1) 7-6(3)
      - T. WOODBRIDGE / A. MOLIK 7-6(7) 7-6(6)

Quarter 4 (Bottom)

- 8 Leander PAES (IND) / Martina NAVRATILOVA (USA)
- Mark KNOWLES (BAH) / Daniela HANTUCHOVA (SVK)
  - L. PAES / M. NAVRATILOVA [8] 6-1 7-6(5)
- A Mariano HOOD (ARG) / Maria VENTO-KABCHI (VEN)
- A Martin DAMM (CZE) / Els CALLENS (BEL)
  - M. DAMM / E. CALLENS (A) 4-6 6-3 10-[6]
    - L. PAES / M. NAVRATILOVA [8] 6-3 6-4
      - T. WOODBRIDGE / A. MOLIK 4-6 6-3 10-[3]

- Andy RAM (ISR) / Anna SMASHNOVA-PISTOLESI (ISR)
- Max MIRNYI (BLR) / Maria SHARAPOVA (RUS)
  - M. MIRNYI / M. SHARAPOVA 6-4 6-4
- Martin RODRIGUEZ (ARG) / Angelique WIDJAJA (INA)
- 2 Wayne BLACK (ZIM) / Cara BLACK (ZIM)
  - W. BLACK / C. BLACK [2] 6-4 6-2
    - M. MIRNYI / M. SHARAPOVA 6-3 7-6(4)
      - L. PAES / M. NAVRATILOVA [8] 6-4 6-4

US OPEN 2004 — A USTA EVENT

DecoTurf® is the proud supplier of tennis surfaces to:

2004 Olympic Games

2004 U.S. Open

2004 NCAA Men's Championship

Doesn't your facility deserve the best?
Demand DecoTurf!

1.978.623.9980 or www.decoturf.com

DecoTurf®
Tennis Surface of Champions

2004 Tennis Masters Cup Results

West Side Tennis Club, Houston, Texas, USA, 15-21 November

Seeded Players
1. Roger Federer (SUI)
2. Andy Roddick (USA)
3. Lleyton Hewitt (AUS)
4. Marat Safin (RUS)
5. Carlos Moya (ESP)
6. Guillermo Coria (ARG)
7. Tim Henman (GBR)
8. Gaston Gaudio (ARG)

Alternate
1. Guillermo Canas (ARG)

Round Robin

Red Group:
Roger Federer (SUI) d. Gaston Gaudio (ARG) 61 76(4)
Lleyton Hewitt (AUS) d. Carlos Moya (ESP) 67(5) 62 64
Carlos Moya (ESP) d. Gaston Gaudio (ARG) 63 64
Roger Federer (SUI) d. Lleyton Hewitt (AUS) 63 64
Roger Federer (SUI) d. Carlos Moya (ESP) 63 36 63
Lleyton Hewitt (AUS) d. Gaston Gaudio (ARG) 62 61

Blue Group:
Marat Safin (RUS) d. Guillermo Coria (ARG) 61 64
Andy Roddick (USA) d. Tim Henman (GBR) 75 76(6)
Tim Henman (GBR) d. Guillermo Coria (ARG) 62 62
Andy Roddick (USA) d. Marat Safin (RUS) 76(7) 76(4)
Andy Roddick (USA) d. Guillermo Coria (ARG) 76(4) 63
Marat Safin (RUS) d. Tim Henman (GBR) 62 76(2)

Final Standings
Red Group: 1. Roger Federer (SUI), 2. Lleyton Hewitt (AUS), 3. Carlos Moya (ESP), 4. Gaston Gaudio (ARG)
Blue Group: 1. Andy Roddick (USA), 2. Marat Safin (RUS), 3. Tim Henman (GBR), 4. Guillermo Coria (ARG)

Semifinals
Lleyton Hewitt (AUS) d. Andy Roddick (USA) 63 62
Roger Federer (SUI) d. Marat Safin (RUS) 63 76(18)

Final
Roger Federer (SUI) d. Lleyton Hewitt (AUS) 63 62

Doubles Final:
Bob Bryan/Mike Bryan (USA) d. Wayne Black/Kevin Ullyett (ZIM) 46 75 64 62

Tim Henman (GBR)

2004 WTA Tour Championships Results

Staples Center, Los Angeles, California, USA 9-14 November

Seeded Players
1. Lindsay Davenport (USA)
2. Amelie Mauresmo (FRA)
3. Anastasia Myskina (RUS)
4. Svetlana Kuznetsova (RUS)
5. Elene Dementieva (RUS)
6. Maria Sharapova (RUS)
7. Serena Williams (USA)
8. Vera Zvonareva (RUS)

Round Robin

Red Group:
Anastasia Myskina (RUS) d. Lindsay Davenport (USA) 76(5) 64
Lindsay Davenport (USA) d. Elena Dementieva (RUS) 60 61
Lindsay Davenport (USA) d. Serena Williams (USA) 36 75 61
Anastasia Myskina (RUS) d. Elena Dementieva (RUS) 63 63
Serena Williams (USA) d. Anastasia Myskina (RUS) 46 63 64
Serena Williams (USA) d. Elena Dementieva (RUS) 76(3) 75

Blue Group:
Amelie Mauresmo (FRA) d. Svetlana Kuznetsova (RUS) 63 62
Amelie Mauresmo (FRA) d. Maria Sharapova (RUS) 75 64
Amelie Mauresmo (FRA) d. Vera Zvonareva (RUS) 61 60
Maria Sharapova (RUS) d. Svetlana Kuznetsova (RUS) 61 64
Svetlana Kuznetsova (RUS) d. Vera Zvonareva (RUS) 62 64
Maria Sharapova (RUS) d. Vera Zvonareva (RUS) 64 75

Final Standings
Red Group: 1. Anastasia Myskina (RUS), 2. Serena Williams (USA), 3. Lindsay Davenport (USA), 4. Elena Dementieva (RUS)
Blue Group: 1. Amelie Mauresmo (FRA), 2. Maria Sharapova (RUS), 3. Svetlana Kuznetsova (RUS), 4. Vera Zvonareva (RUS)

Semifinals
Maria Sharapova (RUS) d. Anastasia Myskina (RUS) 26 62 62
Serena Williams (USA) d. Amelie Mauresmo (FRA) 46 76(2) 64

Final
Maria Sharapova (RUS) d. Serena Williams (USA) 46 62 64

Doubles Final:
Nadia Petrova (RUS)/Meghann Shaughnessy (USA) d. Cara Black (ZIM)/Rennae Stubbs (AUS) 75 62

Serena Williams (USA)

2004 Women's Professional Tournaments (continued)

Date	Tournament	Surface	Singles Final	Doubles Winners
26 Jul	San Diego	Hard	L. Davenport (USA) (4) d. A. Myskina (RUS) (3) 61 61	C. Black (ZIM)/R. Stubbs (AUS) (2)
2 Aug	Montreal	Hard	A. Mauresmo (FRA) (2) d. E. Likhovtseva (RUS) 61 60	S. Asagoe/A. Sugiyama (JPN) (5)
2 Aug	Stockholm	Hard	A. Molik (AUS) (3) d. T. Perebiynis (UKR) 61 61	A. Molik (AUS)/B. Schett (AUT) (1)
9 Aug	Sopot	Clay	F. Pennetta (ITA) (9) d. K. Koukalova (CZE) (11) 75 36 63	N. Llagostera Vives/M. Marrero (ESP)
9 Aug	Vancouver	Hard	N. Vaidisova (Q) (CZE) d. L. Granville (USA) (4) 26 64 62	B. Mattek/A. Spears (USA) (3)
16 Aug	**Olympics, Athens**	**Hard**	**J. Henin-Hardenne (BEL) (1) d. A. Mauresmo (FRA) (2) 63 63**	**T. Li/T. Sun (CHN) (8)**
16 Aug	Cincinnati	Hard	L. Davenport (USA) (1) d. V. Zvonareva (RUS) (2) 63 62	J. Craybas (USA)/M. Weingartner (GER) (3)
23 Aug	New Haven	Hard	E. Bovina (RUS) (7) d. N. Dechy (FRA) (8) 62 26 75	N. Petrova (RUS)/M. Shaughnessy (USA) (2)
23 Aug	Forest Hills	Hard	E. Likhovtseva (RUS) (1) d. I. Benesova (CZE) (4) 62 62	No doubles event
30 Aug	**US Open**	**Hard**	**S. Kuznetsova (RUS) (9) d. E. Dementieva (6) 63 75**	**V. Ruano Pascual (ESP)/P. Suarez (ARG) (1)**
13 Sep	Bali	Hard	S. Kuznestova (RUS) (2) d. M. Weingartner (GER) 61 64	A. Myskina (RUS)/A. Sugiyama (JPN) (1)
20 Sep	Shanghai	Hard	S. Williams (USA) (1) d. S. Kuznetsova (RUS) (2) 46 75 64	E. Gagliardi (SUI)/D. Safina (RUS)
27 Sep	Seoul	Hard	M. Sharapova (RUS) (1) d. M. Domachowska (POL) 61 61	Y. Cho/M. Jeon (KOR)
27 Sep	Guangzhou	Hard	N. Li (CHN) (Q) d. M. Sucha (SVK) 63 64	T. Li/T. Sun (CHN) (2)
27 Sep	Hasselt	Hard	E. Dementieva (RUS) (1) d. E. Bovina (BEL) (3) 06 60 64	J. Russell (USA)/M. Santangelo (ITA)
4 Oct	Filderstadt	Hard	L. Davenport (USA) (2) d. A. Mauresmo (FRA) (1) 62 ret.	C. Black (ZIM)/R. Stubbs (AUS) (1)
4 Oct	Tokyo	Hard	M. Sharapova (RUS) (1) d. M. Washington (USA) 60 61	S. Asagoe (JPN)/K. Srebotnik (SLO) (1)
11 Oct	Moscow	Carpet	A. Myskina (RUS) (1) d. E. Dementieva (RUS) (5) 75 60	A. Myskina/V. Zvonareva (RUS) (4)
11 Oct	Tashkent	Hard	N. Vaidisova (CZE) d. V. Razzano (FRA) (9) 57 63 62	Ad. Serra Zanetti/Am. Serra Zanetti (ITA) (4)
18 Oct	Zurich	Hard	A. Molik (AUS) d. M. Sharapova (RUS) (4) 46 62 63	C. Black (ZIM)/R. Stubbs (AUS) (2)
25 Oct	Linz	Hard	A. Mauresmo (FRA) (1) d. E. Bovina (RUS) (9) 62 60	J. Husarova (SVK)/E. Likhovtseva (RUS) (1)
25 Oct	Luxembourg	Hard	A. Molik (AUS) (2) d. D. Safina (RUS) 63 64	V. Ruano Pascual (ESP)/P. Suarez (ARG) (1)
1 Nov	Philadelphia	Hard	A. Mauresmo (FRA) (1) d. V. Zvonareva (RUS) (6) 36 62 62	A. Molik (AUS)/L. Raymond (USA) (3)
1 Nov	Quebec City	Hard	M. Sucha (SVK) d. A. Spears (USA) (Q) 75 36 62	C. Gullickson (USA/M. Salerni (ARG)
8 Nov	WTA Championships	Hard	M. Sharapova (RUS) (6) d. S. Williams (USA) (7) 46 62 64	N. Petrova (RUS)/M. Shaughnessy (USA)
22 Nov	**Fed Cup Final**	**Carpet**	**Russia d. France 3-2**	

The Definition of
Plexipave®

Wells, CA, U.S.A
Gaungzhou, China
Marbella, Spain
, China
Stockholm, Sweden
Abu Dhabi, U.A.E.

(kən·sis′tent)

consistent *adj.* **1.** Possessing unfailing qualities; Dependable; Reliable **2.** That which is even and uniform; Unfaltering **3. Plexicushion Tennis Court Surfaces**
(see also: www.plexipave.com)

Plexipave®
Sport Surfacing Systems

1-978-623-9980 • 1-800-225-1141 • www.plexipave.com

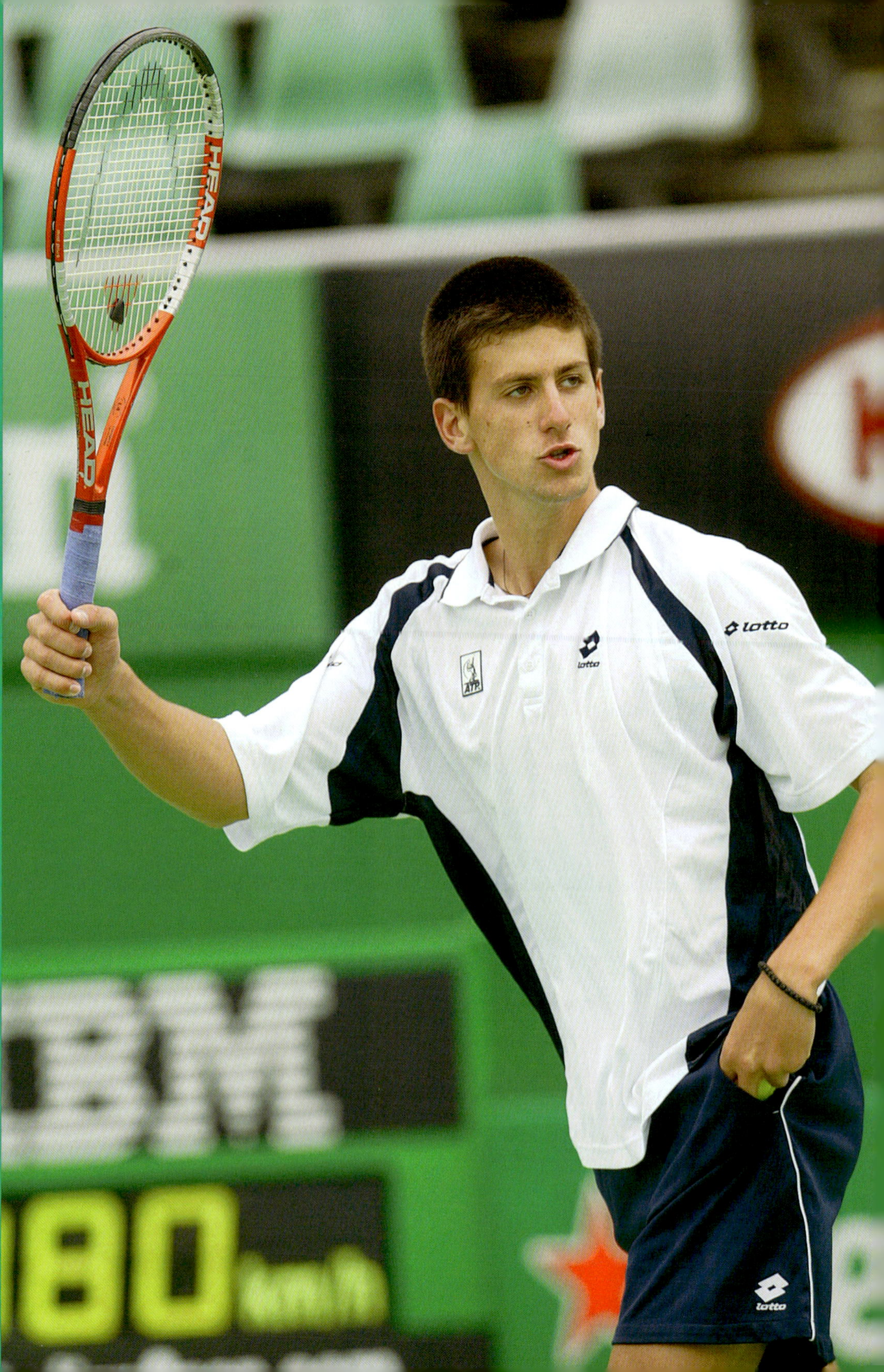
HEAD
HEAD
lotto
lotto
ATP
lotto

ITF Men's Circuit 2004

The total available prize money for ITF Men's Circuit in 2004 was US$4,900,000, just short of the $5 million landmark, which could well be achieved in 2005.

Men's Circuit events are categorised into two levels of individual weeklong Futures tournaments offering prize money of $10,000 and $15,000 and four-week Satellite Circuits offering prize money of $25,000, $50,000 and $75,000.

The single week Futures tournaments are scheduled as a minimum of three consecutive weeks of $10,000 tournaments or two consecutive weeks of $15,000 tournaments. Satellite Circuits are comprised of four Satellite legs, the final leg of which is called the Masters tournament, with each leg of the Satellite offering a minimum of $6,250 in prize money.

In continuation of the trend for the number of ITF Men's Circuit Tournaments to increase year on year, in 2004, no less than 355 weeks of Futures Tournaments and 116 weeks of Satellite Circuits took place, representing a combined total of 471 weeks of playing opportunities.

The number of countries hosting tournaments, up to 74 from the previous year's figure of 67, was most encouraging. First time hosts included Saudi Arabia with two $15,000 plus hospitality Futures and Lebanon with two $15,000 Futures tournaments, all of which were very successfully staged and ensured that the spread of competitive opportunities available to players in Asia was broadened further.

Europe continued to boast the highest number of tournaments with a total of 258 weeks, offering a total of $2,580,000 in prize money. Asia/Oceania also managed significant improvement with 81 tournaments and increased prize money of just under $100,000 to a total of $850,000. North/Central America remained stable at a healthy 56 tournaments and $655,000 in prize money, while South America and Africa with 51 weeks and 25 weeks respectively increased tournament numbers and prize money available.

Throughout the year many players, 263 to be precise, achieved success at either a Futures Tournament or during one week of a Satellite Circuit. A total of 28 players captured a Futures title and finished on top after a week of a Satellite. Spain topped the chart of most players to have won a Futures Tournament, with 24 success stories. Hector Ruiz-Cadenas, a 21-year old from Spain climbed an incredible 973 places to number 427 in the 2004 year end rankings, while USA's Tres Davis improved on his 2003 position of 1400 by some 918 spots, finishing the year at 482.

Other players worthy of note include Victor Ionita, a 21-year old Romanian, who dominated his national tournaments capturing all seven Futures titles in a four-month period. Argentina's Cristian Villagran collected five titles in South America, three in his own country, while Jean-Julien Rojer, from Curacao, Netherlands Antilles, won five tournaments throughout Central America.

Yet another 21-year old, Australian Marc Kimmich won all four weeks of the Australian 2 Satellite Circuit, while three players, Italy's Daniele Giorgini, Germany's Simon Greul and Pakistan's Aqeel Khan managed to win three legs of a Circuit.

As in previous years, the ITF Pro Circuit department worked closely with the ITF Development Department, assisting a number of countries to stage professional tournaments, through the Grand Slam Development Fund. Such funding ensured an even balance of tournaments within each region and also ensured that players were able to compete without the need to travel excessively in the hunt for playing opportunities.

Agreement was reached during 2004 for the ITF to expand its role as the centralised point for player entries. The need for an efficient, automated computer system in order to manage the needs of almost 10,000 male and female players, competing in over 750 ITF Pro Circuit tournaments annually, led to the concept of the IPIN (International Player Identification Number) and the development of an automated Online Service. The service, due to be launched in April 2005, will allow all players competing in ITF Pro Circuit tournaments to enter and withdraw via the internet and, in addition, provide players with easy access to important calendar updates and other information relating to the Circuit.

The USTA and Tennis Europe will undertake new roles as the first point of contact for players and tournament directors and will have responsibility for calendar coordination in their country/region.

The Regional Associations and National Associations have all played their part in publicising the project, which we trust will be a great success next year. For more information regarding IPIN, visit www.itftennis.com/ipin

Novak Djokovic (SCG) won two Futures tournaments and two Challengers in 2004

ITF Men's Circuit 2004 Futures Results

- **NUSSLOCH** (GER) ($10,000) 5-11 JANUARY – **Singles:** Yuri Schukin (RUS) d. Philipp Marx (GER) 67(3) 64 64.
  Doubles: Yuri Schukin/Dmitri Vlasov (RUS) d. Lado Chikhladze (GEO)/Aleksey Malajko (GER) 75 63.

- **DUBAI** (UAE) ($15,000) 12-18 JANUARY – **Singles:** Adam Chadaj (POL) d. Jacob Adaktusson (SWE) 63 76(2).
  Doubles: Ivo Klec (GER)/Jaroslav Levinsky (CZE) d. Julien Jeanpierre/Edouard Roger-Vasselin (FRA) 64 75.

- **SAN SALVADOR** (ESA) ($10,000) 12-18 JANUARY – **Singles:** Brian Dabul (ARG) d. Alejandro Fabbri (ARG) 63 75.
  Doubles: Diego Hartfield/Gustavo Marcaccio (ARG) d. Lucas Engel/Marcio Torres (BRA) 60 62.

- **STUTTGART** (GER) ($10,000) 12-18 JANUARY – **Singles:** Lukasz Kubot (POL) d. Jerome Haehnel (FRA) 76(4) 63.
  Doubles: Jens Knippschild (GER)/Robert Lindstedt (SWE) d. Dmitri Vlasov (RUS)/Lovro Zovko (CRO) 67(5) 63 63.

- **TAMPA, FL** (USA) ($10,000) 12-18 JANUARY – **Singles:** Brian Baker (USA) d. Todd Widom (USA) 63 64.
  Doubles: Brian Baker/Rajeev Ram (USA) d. Huntley Montgomery/Tripp Phillips (USA) 63 36 62.

- **DEAUVILLE** (FRA) ($10,000) 19-25 JANUARY – **Singles:** Jean-Christophe Faurel (FRA) d. Marc Gicquel (FRA) 75 26 76(5).
  Doubles: Marc Gicquel/Jean-Baptiste Perlant (FRA) d. Elefterios Alexiou/Alexander Jakupovic (GRE) 61 16 63.

- **DOHA** (QAT) ($15,000) 19-25 JANUARY – **Singles:** Marco Chiudinelli (SUI) d. Uros Vico (ITA) 62 64.
  Doubles: Philipp Petzschner/Lars Uebel (GER) d. Karim Maamoun/Mohamed Maamoun (EGY) 46 63 64.

- **GUATEMALA** (GUA) ($10,000) 19-25 JANUARY – **Singles:** Herbert Wiltschnig (AUT) d. Jean-Julien Rojer (AHO) 63 64.
  Doubles: Carlos Berlocq (ARG)/Miguel Gallardo-Valles (MEX) d. Brian Dabul/Ignacio Gonzalez-King (ARG) 67(2) 76(3) 76(5).

- **KISSIMMEE, FL** (USA) ($10,000) 19-25 JANUARY – **Singles:** Federico Luzzi (ITA) d. Andres Pedroso (USA) 63 64.
  Doubles: Tripp Phillips/Ryan Sachire (USA) d. Scott Lipsky/David Martin (USA) 64 16 63.

- **OBERHACHING** (GER) ($10,000) 19-25 JANUARY – **Singles:** Lukasz Kubot (POL) d. Mounir El Aarej (MAR) 76(8) 61.
  Doubles: Frederik Nielsen/Rasmus Norby (DEN) d. Lukasz Kubot (POL)/Igor Zelenay (SVK) 64 67(6) 60.

- **FEUCHEROLLES** (FRA) ($10,000+H) 26 JANUARY-1 FEBRUARY – **Singles:** Marc Gicquel (FRA) d. Julien Jeanpierre (FRA) 36 62 76(4).
  Doubles: Jean-Michel Pequery/Nicolas Tourte (FRA) d. Stephane Huet/Eric Prodon (FRA) 76(6) 64.

- **KEY BISCAYNE, FL** (USA) ($10,000) 26 JANUARY-1 FEBRUARY – **Singles:** Federico Luzzi (ITA) d. Lesley Joseph (USA) 76(4) 63.
  Doubles: Scott Lipsky/David Martin (USA) d. Marcus Fluitt/Lesley Joseph (USA) 62 62.

- **MANAMA** (BRN) ($15,000) 26 JANUARY-1 FEBRUARY – **Singles:** Uros Vico (ITA) d. Richard Bloomfield (GBR) 63 61.
  Doubles: Marco Chiudinelli (SUI)/Uros Vico (ITA) d. James Auckland (GBR)/Rameez Junaid (AUS) 64 61.

- **SAN JOSE** (CRC) ($10,000) 26 JANUARY-1 FEBRUARY – **Singles:** Stefan Wauters (BEL) d. Jean-Julien Rojer (AHO) 76(6) 63.
  Doubles: Carlos Berlocq (ARG)/Stefan Wauters (BEL) d. Lucas Engel/Marcio Torres (BRA) 76(5) 36 64.

- **BRESSUIRE** (FRA) ($10,000+H) 2-8 FEBRUARY – **Singles:** Marc Gicquel (FRA) d. Jerome Haehnel (FRA) 36 63 62.
  Doubles: Issam Jallali/Malek Jaziri (TUN) d. Eric Butorac (USA)/Petar Popovic (SCG) 61 76(5).

- **MURCIA** (ESP) ($10,000) 2-8 FEBRUARY – **Singles:** German Puentes-Alcaniz (ESP) d. Daniel Gimeno-Traver (ESP) 63 16 63.
  Doubles: Ion Moldovan/Gabriel Moraru (ROM) d. David Marrero-Santana/German Puentes-Alcaniz (ESP) 64 63.

- **ALGUEZARES** (ESP) ($10,000) 9-15 FEBRUARY – **Singles:** Nicolas Almagro-Sanchez (ESP) d. Gabriel Moraru (ROM) 36 64 63.
  Doubles: Nicolas Almagro-Sanchez/Roberto Menendez-Ferre (ESP) d. Marc Fornell-Mestres/Marcel Granollers-Pujol (ESP) 75 64.

- **BROWNSVILLE, TX** (USA) ($15,000) 16-22 FEBRUARY – **Singles:** Andres Pedroso (USA) d. Michael Quintero (COL) 61 36 64.
  Doubles: Tres Davis/Eric Nunez (USA) d. Clancy Shields/Luke Shields (USA) 63 63.

- **CALGARY** (CAN) ($15,000) 16-22 FEBRUARY – **Singles:** Jacob Adaktusson (SWE) d. Simon Greul (GER) 64 64.
  Doubles: Rajeev Ram/Ryan Sachire (USA) d. Ryan Haviland/K.J. Hippensteel (USA) 67(4) 76(7) 63.

- **SAN JAVIER** (ESP) ($10,000) 16-22 FEBRUARY – **Singles:** Santiago Ventura-Bertomeu (ESP) d. Marco Mirnegg (AUT) 62 62.
  Doubles: Ivan Navarro-Pastor/Santiago Ventura-Bertomeu (ESP) d. Salvador Navarro-Gutierrez/Gabriel Trujillo-Soler (ESP) 76(3) 61.

- **ZAGREB** (CRO) ($15,000) 16-22 FEBRUARY – **Singles:** Pavel Snobel (CZE) d. Jeroen Masson (BEL) 61 61.
  Doubles: Pavel Snobel/Martin Stepanek (CZE) d. Ivan Cerovic/Lovro Zovko (CRO) 67(3) 62 63.

- **BENIN CITY** (NGR) ($15,000) 23-29 FEBRUARY – **Singles:** Valentin Sanon (CIV) d. Guillaume Couillard (MON) 16 76(4) 76(4).
  Doubles: Diego Alvarez/Leonardo Azzaro (ITA) d. Jean-Kome Loglo/Komlavi Loglo (TOG) 64 63.

- **CARTAGENA** (ESP) ($10,000) 23-29 FEBRUARY – **Singles:** Didac Perez-Minarro (ESP) d. Jaroslav Pospisil (CZE) 63 76(0).
  Doubles: Ivan Navarro-Pastor/Santiago Ventura-Bertomeu (ESP) d. Marc Fornell-Mestres/Salvador Navarro-Gutierrez (ESP) 64 61.

- **EDMONTON** (CAN) ($15,000) 23-29 FEBRUARY – **Singles:** Rajeev Ram (USA) d. Juan-Pablo Brzezicki (ARG) 36 75 61.
  Doubles: Ryan Haviland/K.J. Hippensteel (USA) d. Paul Logtens/Matwe Middelkoop (NED) 63 46 76(5).

- **HARLINGEN, TX** (USA) ($15,000) 23-29 FEBRUARY – **Singles:** Nicolas Todero (ARG) d. Kepler Orellana (VEN) 62 63.
  Doubles: Scott Lipsky/David Martin (USA) d. Daniel Lustig (CZE)/Michal Przysiezny (POL) 63 62.

- **NEW DELHI** (IND) ($10,000+H) 23-29 FEBRUARY – **Singles:** Aisam Qureshi (PAK) d. Todor Enev (BUL) 63 64.
  Doubles: Mustafa Ghouse/Vishal Uppal (IND) d. Alexey Kedriouk (KAZ)/Orest Tereshchuk (UKR) 76(4) 64.

- **ZAGREB** (CRO) ($15,000) 23-29 FEBRUARY – **Singles:** Jean-Christophe Faurel (FRA) d. Francesco Aldi (ITA) 76(8) 63.
  Doubles: Lukas Dlouhy (CZE)/Branislav Sekac (SVK) d. Pavel Snobel/Martin Stepanek (CZE) 75 61.

- **BENIN CITY** (NGR) ($15,000) 1-7 MARCH – **Singles:** James Auckland (GBR) d. Diego Alvarez (ITA) 61 57 75.
  Doubles: Xavier Audouy (FRA)/Johar Mubarak Saeed (QAT) d. Jonathan Igbinovia/Sunday Maku (NGR) 76(5) 64.

- **BLENHEIM** (NZL) ($10,000) 1-7 MARCH – **Singles:** Domenic Marafiote (AUS) d. Herbert Wiltschnig (AUT) 46 60 76(2).
  Doubles: Kyu-Tae Im/Seung-Hoon Lee (KOR) d. Philip Gubenco (CAN)/Domenic Marafiote (AUS) 26 62 63.

- **CHENNAI** (IND) ($10,000) 1-6 MARCH – **Singles:** Dmitri Mazur (UZB) d. Filip Urban (POL) 76(3) 26 64.
  Doubles: Mustafa Ghouse/Vishal Uppal (IND) d. Filip Aniola/Filip Urban (POL) 64 46 63.

- **FARO** (POR) ($10,000) 1-7 MARCH – **Singles:** Guillermo Garcia-Lopez (ESP) d. Philipp Petzschner (GER) 63 62.
  Doubles: Christopher Kas/Philipp Petzschner (GER) d. Boris Borgula/Roman Kukal (SVK) 36 61 64.

- **FLORIANOPOLIS** (BRA) ($15,000) 1-7 MARCH – **Singles:** Bruno Soares (BRA) d. Franco Ferreiro (BRA) 62 61.
  Doubles: Marcelo Melo/Bruno Soares (BRA) d. Alexandre Bonatto/Franco Ferreiro (BRA) 36 75 63.

- **MCALLEN, TX** (USA) ($15,000) 1-7 MARCH – **Singles:** Nicolas Todero (ARG) d. Kepler Orellana (VEN) 62 62.
  Doubles: Raven Klaasen (RSA)/Nicolas Todero (ARG) d. Michael Kosta (USA)/Harsh Mankad (IND) 76(5) 62.

- **BURNIE, TAS** (AUS) ($15,000) 8-14 MARCH – **Singles:** Vasilis Mazarakis (GRE) d. Andrew Derer (AUS) 63 62.
  Doubles: Juan-Pablo Brzezicki (ARG)/Louis Vosloo (RSA) d. Jaymon Crabb/Peter Luczak (AUS) 36 61 10(14).

- **CALDAS NOVAS** (BRA) ($15,000) 8-14 MARCH – **Singles:** Bruno Soares (BRA) d. Ignacio Gonzalez-King (ARG) 63 75.
  Doubles: Marcelo Melo/Bruno Soares (BRA) d. Alessandro Camarco/Leonardo Kirche (BRA) 62 63.

- **CHETUMAL** (MEX) ($15,000) 8-14 MARCH – **Singles:** Oliver Marach (AUT) d. Marcelo Amador (MEX) 75 62.
  Doubles: Scott Lipsky/David Martin (USA) d. Jorge Haro (MEX)/Jean-Julien Rojer (AHO) 62 63.

- **HAMILTON** (NZL) ($10,000) 8-14 MARCH – **Singles:** Michihisa Onoda (JPN) d. Domenic Marafiote (AUS) 63 30 ret.
  Doubles: Sanchai Ratiwatana/Sonchat Ratiwatana (THA) d. Martin Slanar/Herbert Wiltschnig (AUT) 64 10 ret.

- **KOLKATA** (IND) ($10,000) 8-14 MARCH – **Singles:** Somdev Dev Varman (IND) d. Yordan Kanev (BUL) 64 62.
  Doubles: Mustafa Ghouse/Vishal Uppal (IND) d. Todor Enev/Yordan Kanev (BUL) 64 63.

ITF Men's Circuit 2004 Futures Results (continued)

- **LILLE** (FRA) ($15,000+H) 8-14 MARCH – **Singles:** Jean-Michel Pequery (FRA) d. Uros Vico (ITA) 64 64.
  Doubles: Jean-Francois Bachelot/Jean-Michel Pequery (FRA) d. Marc Gicquel/Edouard Roger-Vasselin (FRA) 76(4) 63.

- **ALBUFEIRA** (POR) ($10,000) 9-14 MARCH – **Singles:** Jeroen Masson (BEL) d. Ivo Minar (CZE) 62 63.
  Doubles: Juan-Ignacio Cerda (CHI)/Jasper Smit (NED) d. Frederico Gil/Leonardo Tavares (POR) 64 64.

- **DEVONPORT, TAS** (AUS) ($15,000) 15-21 MARCH – **Singles:** Rik De Voest (RSA) d. Juan-Pablo Brzezicki (ARG) 63 76(5).
  Doubles: Nathan Healey/Robert Smeets (AUS) d. Juan-Pablo Brzezicki (ARG)/Louis Vosloo (RSA) 64 76(5).

- **LAGOS** (POR) ($10,000) 15-21 MARCH – **Singles:** Jeroen Masson (BEL) d. Gilles Simon (FRA) 64 64.
  Doubles: Frederico Gil/Bernardo Mota (POR) d. Juan-Ignacio Cerda (CHI)/Jasper Smit (NED) 76(1) 61.

- **NORTH SHORE** (NZL) ($10,000) 15-21 MARCH – **Singles:** Takahiro Terachi (JPN) d. Naoki Arimoto (JPN) 62 63.
  Doubles: Kyu-Tae Im/Seung-Hoon Lee (KOR) d. Daniel King-Turner/Matthew Prentice (NZL) 62 36 64.

- **PENSACOLA, FL** (USA) ($15,000) 15-21 MARCH – **Singles:** Andres Pedroso (USA) d. Francisco Rodriguez (PAR) 75 46 61.
  Doubles: Cody Conley/Ryan Newport (USA) d. Rajeev Ram/Ryan Sachire (USA) 63 62.

- **POITIERS** (FRA) ($15,000+H) 15-21 MARCH – **Singles:** Uros Vico (ITA) d. Frank Dancevic (CAN) 76(6) 64.
  Doubles: Doug Bohaboy (USA)/Josh Goffi (BRA) d. Xavier Audouy/David Guez (FRA) 67(9) 62 60.

- **ATHENS** (GRE) ($15,000) 22-28 MARCH – **Singles:** Andrew Banks (GBR) d. Jeroen Masson (BEL) 62 67(7) 64.
  Doubles: Mark Hilton/Jonathan Marray (GBR) d. Tomasz Bednarek (POL)/Andres Dellatorre (ARG) 63 52 ret.

- **LITTLE ROCK, AR** (USA) ($15,000) 22-28 MARCH – **Singles:** Emin Agaev (AZE) d. Rajeev Ram (USA) 63 36 64.
  Doubles: Rajeev Ram/Ryan Sachire (USA) d. Daniel Homedes-Carballo/Gabriel Trujillo-Soler (ESP) 63 62.

- **NAUCALPAN** (MEX) ($15,000) 22-28 MARCH – **Singles:** Alejandro Hernandez (MEX) d. Miguel Gallardo-Valles (MEX) 64 64.
  Doubles: Miguel Gallardo-Valles/Alejandro Hernandez (MEX) d. Marcelo Amador/Federico Contreras (MEX) 76(1) 64.

- **FRASCATI** (ITA) ($10,000) 29 MARCH-4 APRIL – **Singles:** Daniele Giorgini (ITA) d. Santiago Ventura-Bertomeu (ESP) 76(4) 64.
  Doubles: Marcello Craca (GER)/Yuri Schukin (RUS) d. Daniele Giorgini/Giancarlo Petrazzuolo (ITA) 67(3) 63 64.

- **MOBILE, AL** (USA) ($15,000) 29 MARCH-4 APRIL – **Singles:** Robert Yim (USA) d. Yu Jr. Wang (CHN) 61 63.
  Doubles: Michael Kosta (USA)/Wesley Whitehouse (RSA) d. Esteban Carril-Caso/Gabriel Trujillo-Soler (ESP) 63 63.

- **SYROS** (GRE) ($15,000) 29 MARCH-4 APRIL – **Singles:** Lamine Ouahab (ALG) d. Pavel Snobel (CZE) 64 64.
  Doubles: Florin Mergea/Horia Tecau (ROM) d. Roman Michalik/Pavel Snobel (CZE) 75 36 63.

- **ANGERS** (FRA) ($15,000) 5-11 APRIL – **Singles:** Nicolas Devilder (FRA) d. Marc Gicquel (FRA) 26 63 64.
  Doubles: Xavier Audouy/Nicolas Tourte (FRA) d. Goran Tosic (SCG)/Igor Zelenay (SVK) 61 61.

- **MONZA** (ITA) ($10,000+H) 5-11 APRIL – **Singles:** Andres Dellatorre (ARG) d. Diego Moyano (ARG) 62 75.
  Doubles: Alessandro Da Col/Stefano Mocci (ITA) d. Dusan Karol/Jan Mertl (CZE) 63 63.

- **CREMONA** (ITA) ($10,000) 12-18 APRIL – **Singles:** Andrea Stoppini (ITA) d. Michael Lammer (SUI) 63 76(4).
  Doubles: David Marrero-Santana/Jose-Antonio Sanchez-De Luna (ESP) d. Fabio Colangelo/Alessandro Motti (ITA) 64 75.

- **GRASSE** (FRA) ($15,000) 12-18 APRIL – **Singles:** Gilles Simon (FRA) d. Marc Gicquel (FRA) 64 61.
  Doubles: Gilles Simon/Jo-Wilfried Tsonga (FRA) d. Gael Monfils/Josselin Ouanna (FRA) 75 62.

- **KARSHI** (UZB) ($15,000) 12-18 APRIL – **Singles:** Vadim Davletshin (RUS) d. Dmitri Vlasov (RUS) 75 16 63.
  Doubles: Ivan Cerovic (CRO)/Lazar Magdincev (MKD) d. Igor Kunitsyn/Dmitri Vlasov (RUS) 63 26 64.

- **KOFU** (JPN) ($10,000) 12-18 APRIL – **Singles:** Michihisa Onoda (JPN) d. Kentaro Masuda (JPN) 63 75.
  Doubles: Scott Lipsky/David Martin (USA) d. Mark Nielsen (NZL)/Michihisa Onoda (JPN) 26 75 76(6).

- **BERGAMO** (ITA) ($15,000) 19-25 APRIL – **Singles:** Lukas Dlouhy (CZE) d. Gael Monfils (FRA) 63 16 61.
  Doubles: Fabio Colangelo/Alessandro Motti (ITA) d. Victor Bruthans/Igor Zelenay (SVK) 64 61.

- **DOHA** (QAT) ($15,000) 19-25 APRIL – **Singles:** Jean-Michel Pequery (FRA) d. Ladislav Svarc (SVK) 63 63.
  Doubles: Florin Mergea/Horia Tecau (ROM) d. Frank Moser/Bernard Parun (GER) 61 62.

- **GULISTAN** (UZB) ($15,000) 19-25 APRIL – **Singles:** Igor Kunitsyn (RUS) d. Ivan Cerovic (CRO) 75 62.
  Doubles: Alexey Kedriouk (KAZ)/Vadim Kutsenko (UZB) d. Evgueni Smirnov/Dmitri Vlasov (RUS) 76(5) 63.

- **RIEMERLING** (GER) ($10,000) 19-25 APRIL – **Singles:** Jeroen Masson (BEL) d. Jan Mertl (CZE) 75 63.
  Doubles: Edwin Kempes/Melvyn Op Der Heijde (NED) d. Andreas Beck/Thorsten Popp (GER) 75 64.

- **SHIZUOKA** (JPN) ($10,000) 19-25 APRIL – **Singles:** Takahiro Terachi (JPN) d. Mark Nielsen (NZL) 62 61.
  Doubles: Matthew Prentice/Lee Radovanovich (NZL) d. Mark Nielsen (NZL)/Mirko Pehar (USA) 67(5) 63 64.

- **ALGIERS** (ALG) ($15,000) 26 APRIL-2 MAY – **Singles:** Jaroslav Pospisil (CZE) d. Slimane Saoudi (FRA) 46 64 20 ret.
  Doubles: Fabio Colangelo/Stefano Mocci (ITA) d. Roberto Menendez-Ferre (ESP)/Philipp Mullner (AUT) 64 62.

- **BOURNEMOUTH** (GBR) ($15,000) 26 APRIL-2 MAY – **Singles:** Gael Monfils (FRA) d. Alex Bogdanovic (GBR) 64 63.
  Doubles: James Auckland (GBR)/Thomas Blake (USA) d. Oliver Freelove/David Sherwood (GBR) 64 63.

- **BUENOS AIRES** (ARG) ($10,000) 26 APRIL-2 MAY – **Singles:** Cristian Villagran (ARG) d. Bo-Ram Cha (KOR) 63 63.
  Doubles: Lionel Noviski/Agustin Tarantino (ARG) d. Sebastian Decoud/Alejandro Fabbri (ARG) 61 60.

- **CIUDAD OBREGON** (MEX) ($10,000) 26 APRIL-2 MAY – **Singles:** Alejandro Hernandez (MEX) d. Bruno Echagaray (MEX) 75 60.
  Doubles: Lucas Engel/Marcelo Melo (BRA) d. Juan-Ignacio Cerda (CHI)/Jasper Smit (NED) 76(4) 64.

- **DOHA** (QAT) ($15,000) 26 APRIL-2 MAY – **Singles:** Jean-Michel Pequery (FRA) d. Ladislav Svarc (SVK) 60 67(4) 61.
  Doubles: Mustafa Ghouse/Harsh Mankad (IND) d. Rohan Bopanna (IND)/Jean-Michel Pequery (FRA) 61 ret.

- **ESSLINGEN** (GER) ($15,000) 26 APRIL-2 MAY – **Singles:** Tobias Summerer (GER) d. Melle Van Gemerden (NED) 75 76(5).
  Doubles: Marcello Craca/Sebastian Fitz (GER) d. Jakob Herm-Zahlava (GER)/Raven Klaasen (RSA) 75 64.

- **PADOVA** (ITA) ($10,000) 26 APRIL-2 MAY – **Singles:** Jose-Antonio Sanchez-De Luna (ESP) d. Steve Darcis (BEL) 63 67(6) 76(8).
  Doubles: Elefterios Alexiou/Alexander Jakupovic (GRE) d. Guillermo Carry/Andres Dellatorre (ARG) 76(3) 64.

- **TOKYO** (JPN) ($10,000) 26 APRIL-2 MAY – **Singles:** Satoshi Iwabuchi (JPN) d. David Martin (USA) 26 63 63.
  Doubles: Scott Lipsky/David Martin (USA) d. Mark Nielsen (NZL)/Michael Ryderstedt (SWE) 62 63.

- **BUCHAREST** (ROM) ($10,000) 3-9 MAY – **Singles:** Adrian Ungur (ROM) d. Adrian Cruciat (ROM) 62 64.
  Doubles: Adrian Barbu/Victor Ionita (ROM) d. Rainer Eitzinger (AUT)/Andrei Mlendea (ROM) 64 63.

- **BUENOS AIRES** (ARG) ($10,000) 3-9 MAY – **Singles:** Cristian Villagran (ARG) d. Carlos Berlocq (ARG) 64 62.
  Doubles: Juan Pablo Amado/Eduardo Schwank (ARG) d. Juan-Martin Aranguren/Sebastian Decoud (ARG) 61 76(6).

- **CALI** (COL) ($15,000) 3-9 MAY – **Singles:** Julio Silva (BRA) d. Michael Quintero (COL) 62 62.
  Doubles: Michael Quintero/Carlos Salamanca (COL) d. Diego Hartfield/Damian Patriarca (ARG) 75 64.

- **EDINBURGH** (GBR) ($15,000) 3-9 MAY – **Singles:** Eric Prodon (FRA) d. Daniel Munoz-De La Nava Rodriguez (ESP) 64 63.
  Doubles: Andrew Derer/Joseph Sirianni (AUS) d. Richard Brooks (GBR)/Santiago Ventura-Bertomeu (ESP) w/o.

- **GUADALAJARA** (MEX) ($10,000) 3-9 MAY – **Singles:** Alejandro Hernandez (MEX) d. Marcelo Melo (BRA) 61 63.
  Doubles: Marcelo Melo/Gabriel Pitta (BRA) d. Juan-Ignacio Cerda (CHI)/Jasper Smit (NED) 36 64 60.

- **JOUNIEH** (LIB) ($15,000) 3-9 MAY – **Singles:** Mattias Hellstrom (SWE) d. Victor Bruthans (SVK) 62 36 63.
  Doubles: Mustafa Ghouse/Harsh Mankad (IND) d. Florin Mergea/Horia Tecau (ROM) 63 57 76(1).

ITF Men's Circuit 2004 Futures Results (continued)

- **NAMANGAN** (UZB) ($15,000) 3-9 MAY – **Singles:** Jonathan Marray (GBR) d. Alexey Kedriouk (KAZ) 63 64.
  Doubles: Daniel Kiernan/Jonathan Marray (GBR) d. Alexey Kedriouk (KAZ)/Orest Tereshchuk (UKR) 64 63.

- **NEHEIM-HUSTEN** (GER) ($10,000) 3-9 MAY – Singles: Andis Juska (LAT) d. Andreas Beck (GER) 64 61.
  Doubles: Michal Przysiezny/Filip Urban (POL) d. Christopher Koderisch/Ulrich Tippenhauer (GER) 61 62.

- **REUS** (ESP) ($10,000) 3-9 MAY – **Singles:** Marcel Granollers-Pujol (ESP) d. Javier Genaro-Martinez (ESP) 63 63.
  Doubles: Carlos Rexach-Itoiz/Gabriel Trujillo-Soler (ESP) d. Diego Hipperdinger (ARG)/Jordi Marse-Vidri (ESP) 62 63.

- **SEOGWIPO** (KOR) ($15,000) 3-9 MAY – **Singles:** Gouichi Motomura (JPN) d. Joshua Goodall (GBR) 67(7) 64 61.
  Doubles: Kyu-Tae Im/Hyung-Taik Lee (KOR) d. Hee-Seok Chung/Hee-Sung Chung (KOR) 75 64.

- **SIDI FREDJ** (ALG) ($15,000) 3-9 MAY – **Singles:** Gilles Simon (FRA) d. David Guez (FRA) 62 60.
  Doubles: Dusan Karol/Jaroslav Pospisil (CZE) d. Noudjeim Hakimi/Abdel-Hak Hameurlaine (ALG) 64 60.

- **SZOLNOK** (HUN) ($10,000) 3-9 MAY – **Singles:** Novak Djokovic (SCG) d. Marko Tkalec (SLO) 64 62.
  Doubles: Gyorgy Balazs/Sebo Kiss (HUN) d. Alberto Brizzi (ITA)/Christian Grunes (GER) w/o.

- **VALDENGO** (ITA) ($10,000) 3-9 MAY – **Singles:** Andres Dellatorre (ARG) d. Jose-Antonio Sanchez-De Luna (ESP) 26 64 63.
  Doubles: Christopher Kas/Philipp Petzschner (GER) d. Giuseppe Menga/Massimo Ocera (ITA) 63 61.

- **VERO BEACH, FL** (USA) ($10,000) 3-9 MAY – **Singles:** Jose De Armas (VEN) d. Melvyn Op Der Heijde (NED) 67(4) 76(3) 63.
  Doubles: Scott Lipsky/David Martin (USA) d. Goran Dragicevic/Mirko Pehar (USA) 64 64.

- **ANDIJAN** (UZB) ($15,000) 10-16 MAY – **Singles:** Jonathan Marray (GBR) d. Aisam Qureshi (PAK) 76(3) 63.
  Doubles: Alexey Kedriouk (KAZ)/Orest Tereshchuk (UKR) d. Prakash Amritraj (IND)/Jean-Julien Rojer (AHO) 75 64.

- **BACAU** (ROM) ($10,000) 10-16 MAY – **Singles:** Rainer Eitzinger (AUT) d. Victor Crivoi (ROM) 26 64 76(1).
  Doubles: Adrian Barbu/Victor Ionita (ROM) d. Victor Crivoi/Andrei Mlendea (ROM) 76(4) 61.

- **BUENOS AIRES** (ARG) ($10,000) 10-16 MAY – **Singles:** Carlos Berlocq (ARG) d. Cristian Villagran (ARG) 64 62.
  Doubles: Carlos Berlocq/Antonio Pastorino (ARG) d. Diego Del Rio/Francisco Pozzi (ARG) 64 62.

- **GUANAJUATO** (MEX) ($10,000) 10-16 MAY – **Singles:** Tres Davis (USA) d. Juan-Ignacio Cerda (CHI) 63 61.
  Doubles: Bruno Echagaray/Jorge Haro (MEX) d. Marcelo Melo/Gabriel Pitta (BRA) def.

- **HODMEZOVASARHELY** (HUN) ($10,000) 10-16 MAY – **Singles:** Kornel Bardoczky (HUN) d. Melle Van Gemerden (NED) 75 63.
  Doubles: Kornel Bardoczky (HUN)/Gabriel Moraru (ROM) d. Zsolt Tatar (HUN)/Melle Van Gemerden (NED) 75 67(3) 63.

- **JOUNIEH** (LIB) ($15,000) 10-16 MAY – **Singles:** Florin Mergea (ROM) d. Augustin Gensse (FRA) 46 63 63.
  Doubles: Florin Mergea/Horia Tecau (ROM) d. Ivan Cerovic (CRO)/Alexander Jakupovic (GRE) 06 63 61.

- **ORANGE PARK, FL** (USA) ($10,000) 10-16 MAY – **Singles:** Melvyn Op Der Heijde (NED) d. Goran Dragicevic (USA) 64 60.
  Doubles: Levar Harper-Griffith/Chris Kwon (USA) d. Scott Melville/David Witt (USA) 75 63.

- **PAVIA** (ITA) ($10,000) 10-16 MAY – **Singles:** Andres Dellatorre (ARG) d. Jeroen Masson (BEL) 75 63.
  Doubles: Fabio Colangelo/Alessandro Da Col (ITA) d. Giancarlo Petrazzuolo/Frederico Torresi (ITA) 63 57 64.

- **PEREIRA** (COL) ($15,000) 10-16 MAY – **Singles:** Julio Silva (BRA) d. Leonardo Kirche (BRA) 62 61.
  Doubles: Lucas Engel/Andre Ghem (BRA) d. Julio Silva/Rogerio Silva (BRA) 64 63.

- **SEOGWIPO** (KOR) ($15,000) 10-16 MAY – **Singles:** Gouichi Motomura (JPN) d. Michihisa Onoda (JPN) 75 63.
  Doubles: Dong-Hyun Kim/Oh-Hee Kwon (KOR) d. Jae-Sung An/Kyu-Tae Im (KOR) 76(2) 62.

- **VIC** (ESP) ($10,000) 10-16 MAY – **Singles:** Ivan Navarro-Pastor (ESP) d. Javier Genaro-Martinez (ESP) 46 75 64.
  Doubles: Carlos Rexach-Itoiz/Gabriel Trujillo-Soler (ESP) d. Diego Hipperdinger (ARG)/Jordi Marse-Vidri (ESP) 75 62.

- **COATZACOALCOS** (MEX) ($10,000) 17-23 MAY – **Singles:** Eduardo Bohrer (BRA) d. Carlos Palencia (MEX) 62 36 61.
  Doubles: Marcelo Melo/Gabriel Pitta (BRA) d. Matt Behrmann/Troy Hahn (USA) 67(3) 64 63.

- **IASI** (ROM) ($10,000) 17-23 MAY – **Singles:** Victor Ionita (ROM) d. Francesco Piccari (ITA) 63 61.
  Doubles: Alessandro Piccari/Francesco Piccari (ITA) d. Emanuel Brighiu/Cosmin Cotet (ROM) 63 76(5).

- **LLEIDA** (ESP) ($10,000) 17-23 MAY – **Singles:** Jesse Huta-Galung (NED) d. Tomislav Peric (CRO) 76(3) 63.
  Doubles: Carlos Rexach-Itoiz/Gabriel Trujillo-Soler (ESP) d. Miguel-Angel Lopez-Jaen/Pablo Santos-Gonzalez (ESP) 75 75.

- **RIYADH** (KSA) ($15,000+H) 17-23 MAY – **Singles:** Horia Tecau (ROM) d. Thorsten Popp (GER) 64 26 63.
  Doubles: Jamie Delgado (GBR)/Leonardo Tavares (POR) d. Mustafa Ghouse (IND)/Jhonathan Medina-Alvarez (VEN) 62 36 63.

- **SARAJEVO** (BIH) ($10,000) 17-23 MAY – **Singles:** Vladimir Pavicevic (SCG) d. Ilija Bozoljac (SCG) 26 64 63.
  Doubles: Jakub Hasek/Josef Nesticky (CZE) d. Ilija Bozoljac/Vladimir Pavicevic (SCG) 64 64.

- **TAMPA, FL** (USA) ($10,000) 17-23 MAY – **Singles:** K.J. Hippensteel (USA) d. Brian Baker (USA) 16 76(5) 62.
  Doubles: Ryan Haviland/K.J. Hippensteel (USA) d. Huntley Montgomery/Ryan Sachire (USA) 36 64 62.

- **VERONA** (ITA) ($10,000) 17-23 MAY – **Singles:** Simone Bolelli (ITA) d. Alex Vittur (ITA) 61 76(4).
  Doubles: Simone Bolelli/Alberto Brizzi (ITA) d. Diego Alvarez (ITA)/Juan-Felipe Yanez (CHI) 63 62.

- **BALAGUER** (ESP) ($10,000) 24-30 MAY – **Singles:** Gabriel Trujillo-Soler (ESP) d. Mounir El Aarej (MAR) 76(1) 30 ret.
  Doubles: Miguel-Angel Lopez-Jaen/Pablo Santos-Gonzalez (ESP) d. Ivan Esguerdo-Andreu/Carlos Rexach-Itoiz (ESP) 63 63.

- **BRCKO DISTRICT** (BIH) ($10,000) 24-30 MAY – **Singles:** Ilija Bozoljac (SCG) d. Dominique Coene (BEL) 63 36 63.
  Doubles: Nikola Ciric/Goran Tosic (SCG) d. Juan-Martin Aranguren/Juan-Cruz Vesprini (ARG) 62 63.

- **BUCHAREST** (ROM) ($10,000) 24-30 MAY – **Singles:** Francesco Piccari (ITA) d. Vjekoslav Skenderovic (CRO) 62 64.
  Doubles: Philipp Mukhometov/Evgueni Smirnov (RUS) d. Artemon Apostu-Efremov/Teodor Bolanu (ROM) 46 63 75.

- **GDYNIA** (POL) ($10,000) 24-30 MAY – **Singles:** Adam Chadaj (POL) d. Solon Peppas (GRE) 64 60.
  Doubles: Maciej Dilaj/Andrzej Grusiecki (POL) d. Janis Skroderis/Nikita Svacko (LAT) 61 63.

- **MISKOLC** (HUN) ($10,000) 24-30 MAY – **Singles:** Ladislav Svarc (SVK) d. Martin Vacek (CZE) 64 64.
  Doubles: Filip Polasek/Ladislav Svarc (SVK) d. Xavier Audouy/Nicolas Tourte (FRA) 63 63.

- **MOST** (CZE) ($10,000) 24-30 MAY – **Singles:** Lukas Dlouhy (CZE) d. Jan Mertl (CZE) 63 64.
  Doubles: Ladislav Chramosta (CZE)/Igor Zelenay (SVK) d. Diego Junqueira/Damian Patriarca (ARG) 76(2) 46 61.

- **MUNAKATA** (JPN) ($15,000) 24-30 MAY – **Singles:** Young-Jun Kim (KOR) d. Gouichi Motomura (JPN) 76(6) 76(6).
  Doubles: Sanchai Ratiwatana/Sonchat Ratiwatana (THA) d. Naoki Arimoto/Atsuo Ogawa (JPN) 75 62.

- **RYHAID** (KSA) ($15,000+H) 24-30 MAY – **Singles:** Aisam Qureshi (PAK) d. Leonardo Tavares (POR) 64 67(5) 63.
  Doubles: Sebastian Fitz (GER)/Karim Maamoun (EGY) d. Mustafa Ghouse (IND)/Aisam Qureshi (PAK) 64 64.

- **TERAMO** (ITA) ($10,000) 24-30 MAY – **Singles:** Julio Silva (BRA) d. Frederico Torresi (ITA) 76(0) 64.
  Doubles: Alessandro Motti/Simone Vagnozzi (ITA) d. Rodrigo Monte/Marcio Torres (BRA) 30 ret.

- **CASTEL FRANCO VENETO** (ITA) ($10,000) 31 MAY-6 JUNE – **Singles:** Francesco Piccari (ITA) d. Matteo Colla (ITA) 36 76(2) 75.
  Doubles: Flavio Cipolla/Alessandro Motti (ITA) d. Julio Silva/Rogerio Silva (BRA) 64 61.

- **KARLOVY VARY** (CZE) ($10,000) 31 MAY-6 JUNE – **Singles:** Lukas Dlouhy (CZE) d. Jan Mertl (CZE) 63 62.
  Doubles: Daniel Lustig/Jan Mertl (CZE) d. Karel Luhan/Jiri Novy (CZE) 62 64.

- **KOSZALIN** (POL) ($10,000) 31 MAY-6 JUNE – **Singles:** Michal Przysiezny (POL) d. Sadik Kadir (AUS) 63 63.
  Doubles: Radoslav Nijaki/Dawid Olejniczak (POL) d. Dusan Karol (CZE)/Frederico Torresi (ITA) 63 67(4) 62.

ITF Men's Circuit 2004 Futures Results (continued)

- **KRANJ** (SLO) ($10,000) 31 MAY-6 JUNE – **Singles:** Carlos Berlocq (ARG) d. Marcos Daniel (BRA) 76(5) 61.
  Doubles: Andrej Kracman (SLO)/Benjamin Rufer (SUI) d. Carlos Berlocq (ARG)/Hector Ruiz-Cadenas (ESP) 64 64.

- **MESHREF** (KUW) ($15,000) 31 MAY-6 JUNE – **Singles:** Filip Prpic (SWE) d. Ivo Klec (GER) 63 63.
  Doubles: Rohan Bopanna/Mustafa Ghouse (IND) d. Sebastian Fitz/Frank Moser (GER) 46 64 63.

- **MONTERREY** (MEX) ($10,000) 31 MAY-6 JUNE – **Singles:** Alessandro Camarco (BRA) d. Alejandro Fabbri (ARG) 63 62.
  Doubles: Juan-Ignacio Cerda (CHI)/Rodrigo-Antonio Grilli (BRA) d. Matt Klinger (CAN)/Chris Letcher (AUS) 67(6) 63 64.

- **MUNAKATA** (JPN) ($15,000) 31 MAY-6 JUNE – **Singles:** Kyu-Tae Im (KOR) d. Michihisa Onoda (JPN) 46 76(5) 75.
  Doubles: Joji Miyao/Hiroyasu Sato (JPN) d. Kyu-Tae Im (KOR)/Michihisa Onoda (JPN) 64 36 75.

- **PITESI** (ROM) ($10,000) 31 MAY-6 JUNE – **Singles:** Victor Ionita (ROM) d. Gabriel Moraru (ROM) 75 76(2).
  Doubles: Adrian Barbu/Andrei Mlendea (ROM) d. Radu Barbu/Gabriel Moraru (ROM) 62 62.

- **PRIJEDOR** (BIH) ($10,000) 31 MAY-6 JUNE – **Singles:** Vladimir Pavicevic (SCG) d. Darko Madjarovski (SCG) 64 63.
  Doubles: Juan-Martin Aranguren/Lionel Noviski (ARG) d. Nikola Ciric/Goran Tosic (SCG) 64 63.

- **TENERIFE** (ESP) ($15,000) 31 MAY-6 JUNE – **Singles:** Komlavi Loglo (TOG) d. Jaymon Crabb (AUS) 46 64 64.
  Doubles: Javier Genaro-Martinez (ESP)/Komlavi Loglo (TOG) d. Ivan Esquerdo-Andreu/Daniel Munoz-De La Nava Rodriguez (ESP) 64 36 61.

- **CONSTANTA** (ROM) ($10,000) 7-13 JUNE – **Singles:** Gabriel Moraru (ROM) d. Victor Ionita (ROM) w/o.
  Doubles: Gabriel Moraru/Horia Tecau (ROM) d. David Luque-Velasco/Alberto Soriano-Maldonado (ESP) 61 76(5).

- **JABLONEC NAD NISOU** (CZE) ($10,000) 7-13 JUNE – **Singles:** Lukas Dlouhy (CZE) d. Pavel Snobel (CZE) 67(3) 75 62.
  Doubles: Daniel Lustig/Jan Mertl (CZE) d. Petr Kovacka/Jiri Vrbka (CZE) 64 62.

- **LA PALMA** (ESP) ($10,000) 7-13 JUNE – **Singles:** Bartolome Salva-Vidal (ESP) d. Daniel Munoz-De La Nava Rodriguez (ESP) 76(4) 26 64.
  Doubles: Daniel Monedero-Gonzalez/Daniel Munoz-De La Nava Rodriguez (ESP) d. Jose-Pablo Serna-Perez/Juan-Miguel Such-Perez (ESP) w/o.

- **MARIBOR** (SLO) ($10,000) 7-13 JUNE – **Singles:** Grega Zemlja (SLO) d. Carlos Berlocq (ARG) 67(1) 63 64.
  Doubles: Antonio Baldellou-Esteva/German Puentes-Alcaniz (ESP) d. Rok Jarc/Grega Zemlja (SLO) 62 61.

- **MESHREF** (KUW) ($15,000) 7-13 JUNE – **Singles:** Filip Prpic (SWE) d. Ivo Klec (GER) 76(3) 62.
  Doubles: Sebastian Fitz/Frank Moser (GER) d. Gouram Kostava (GEO)/Ramin Raziyani (IRI) 36 63 62.

- **S. FLORIANO** (ITA) ($10,000) 7-13 JUNE – **Singles:** Farrukh Dustov (UZB) d. Slimane Saoudi (FRA) 36 63 61.
  Doubles: Alessandro Motti/Giancarlo Petrazzuolo (ITA) d. Flavio Cipolla/Francesco Piccari (ITA) 64 64.

- **SOMBOR** (SCG) ($10,000) 7-13 JUNE – **Singles:** Philipp Mullner (AUT) d. Nikola Ciric (SCG) 46 75 62.
  Doubles: Nikola Ciric/Goran Tosic (SCG) d. Juan-Martin Aranguren/Lionel Noviski (ARG) 36 76(5) 63.

- **TORREON** (MEX) ($10,000) 7-13 JUNE – **Singles:** Alejandro Fabbri (ARG) d. Rodrigo-Antonio Grilli (BRA) 64 63.
  Doubles: Eduardo Bohrer/Andre Ghem (BRA) d. Rodrigo-Antonio Grilli (BRA)/Carlos Palencia (MEX) 36 61 76(1).

- **TUNIS** (TUN) ($10,000) 7-13 JUNE – **Singles:** Pablo Santos-Gonzalez (ESP) d. Stefano Mocci (ITA) 63 62.
  Doubles: Mattia Livraghi (ITA)/Karim Maamoun (EGY) d. Ruben Merchan-Huecas (ESP)/Stefano Mocci (ITA) 76(4) 61.

- **WARSAW** (POL) ($10,000) 7-13 JUNE – **Singles:** Dusan Karol (CZE) d. Kristian Pless (DEN) 63 64.
  Doubles: Sadik Kadir (AUS)/Dusan Karol (CZE) d. Filip Aniola/Filip Urban (POL) 76(4) 61.

- **YUBA CITY, CA** (USA) ($10,000) 7-13 JUNE – **Singles:** Scott Lipsky (USA) d. Marc Kimmich (AUS) 75 76(3).
  Doubles: Mark Hlawaty/Brad Weston (AUS) d. Scott Lipsky/David Martin (USA) 76(6) 75.

- **BASSANO DEL GRAPPA** (ITA) ($10,000) 14-20 JUNE – **Singles:** Matteo Colla (ITA) d. Andrea Stoppini (ITA) 63 62.
  Doubles: Alessandro Motti/Giancarlo Petrazzuolo (ITA) d. Alessandro Da Col/Francesco Piccari (ITA) 10 ret.

- **BELGRADE** (SCG) ($10,000) 14-20 JUNE – **Singles:** Nikola Ciric (SCG) d. Yordan Kanev (BUL) 64 67(1) 64.
  Doubles: Ilija Bozoljac/David Savic (SCG) d. Juan-Martin Aranguren/Lionel Noviski (ARG) 62 62.

- **BLOIS** (FRA) ($15,000+H) 14-20 JUNE – **Singles:** Mariano Albert-Ferrando (ESP) d. Carlos Berlocq (ARG) 63 62.
  Doubles: Brian Dabul/Diego Hartfield (ARG) d. Steve Darcis/Stefan Wauters (BEL) 75 64.

- **BUCHAREST** (ROM) ($10,000) 14-20 JUNE – **Singles:** Adrian Ungur (ROM) d. Vjekoslav Skenderovic (CRO) 63 64.
  Doubles: Adrian Cruciat (ROM)/Ferran Ventura-Martell (ESP) d. Catalin Gard/Andrei Mlendea (ROM) 76(6) 60.

- **KOPER** (SLO) ($10,000) 14-20 JUNE – **Singles:** Kamil Capkovic (SVK) d. Javier Garcia-Sintes (ESP) 67(5) 76(3) 64.
  Doubles: Antonio Baldellou-Esteva/German Puentes-Alcaniz (ESP) d. Filip Polasek (SVK)/Jiri Vencl (CZE) 62 75.

- **LANZAROTE** (ESP) ($15,000) 14-20 JUNE – **Singles:** Jo-Wilfried Tsonga (FRA) d. Daniel Munoz-De La Nava Rodriguez (ESP) 75 63.
  Doubles: Andrei Cherkasov (RUS)/Orest Tereshchuk (UKR) d. Jaymon Crabb/Brodie Stewart (AUS) 63 46 63.

- **MONTREAL** (CAN) ($10,000) 14-20 JUNE – **Singles:** Shannon Nettle (AUS) d. Thomas Blake (USA) 76(8) 75.
  Doubles: Huntley Montgomery/Ryan Sachire (USA) d. Dejan Cvetkovic (CAN)/Cary Franklin (USA) 63 67(6) 64.

- **SAVITAIPALE** (FIN) ($10,000) 14-20 JUNE – **Singles:** Petr Dezort (CZE) d. Daniel Klemetz (SWE) 63 76(5).
  Doubles: Frederik Nielsen/Rasmus Norby (DEN) d. Petr Dezort/Adam Vejmelka (CZE) 63 36 63.

- **SUNNYVALE, CA** (USA) ($10,000) 14-20 JUNE – **Singles:** Alejandro Fabbri (ARG) d. K.J. Hippensteel (USA) 64 63.
  Doubles: Ryan Haviland/K.J. Hippensteel (USA) d. Scott Lipsky/David Martin (USA) 76(7) 67(1) 63.

- **TUNIS** (TUN) ($10,000) 14-20 JUNE – **Singles:** Dimitri Lorin (FRA) d. Malek Jaziri (TUN) 06 60 76(3).
  Doubles: Oualid Jalali (TUN)/Alexey Kedriouk (KAZ) d. Cyril Baudin (FRA)/Valentin Sanon (CIV) 61 64.

- **ALKMAAR** (NED) ($15,000) 21-27 JUNE – **Singles:** Stefan Wauters (BEL) d. Vasilis Mazarakis (GRE) 36 64 62.
  Doubles: Diego Hartfield/Cristian Villagran (ARG) d. Jun Kato (JPN)/Jean-Julien Rojer (AHO) 62 63.

- **AUBURN, CA** (USA) ($10,000) 21-27 JUNE – **Singles:** Amer Delic (USA) d. K.J. Hippensteel (USA) 76(3) 63.
  Doubles: Lesley Joseph/Scott Lipsky (USA) d. Mark Hlawaty/Brad Weston (AUS) 64 76(4).

- **BELGRADE** (SCG) ($10,000) 21-27 JUNE – **Singles:** Frantisek Polyak (SVK) d. Ilia Kushev (BUL) 64 63.
  Doubles: Yordan Kanev/Ilia Kushev (BUL) d. Nikola Ciric/Goran Tosic (SCG) 67(8) 76(4) 60.

- **CESENA** (ITA) ($10,000) 21-27 JUNE – **Singles:** Matteo Colla (ITA) d. Farrukh Dustov (UZB) 64 64.
  Doubles: Christopher Kas (GER)/Frederico Torresi (ITA) d. Diego Junqueira (ARG)/Felipe Parada (CHI) 36 61 62.

- **DNIPROPETROVS'K** (UKR) ($10,000) 21-27 JUNE – **Singles:** Victor Bruthans (SVK) d. Sergiy Stakhovsky (UKR) 64 61.
  Doubles: Evgueni Smirnov/Dmitri Vlasov (RUS) d. Dmitry Gurichev (UKR)/Irakli Ushangishvili (GEO) 64 61.

- **FOCSANI** (ROM) ($10,000) 21-27 JUNE – **Singles:** Catalin Gard (ROM) d. Gabriel Moraru (ROM) 64 46 62.
  Doubles: Catalin Gard/Andrei Mlendea (ROM) d. Frederico Gil (POR)/Felipe Lemos (BRA) 62 61.

- **LACHINE** (CAN) ($10,000) 21-27 JUNE – **Singles:** Michael Russell (USA) d. Domenic Marafiote (AUS) 63 63.
  Doubles: Huntley Montgomery/Ryan Sachire (USA) d. Jonathan Igbinovia (NGR)/Nick Monroe (USA) 60 75.

- **LEUN** (GER) ($10,000) 21-27 JUNE – **Singles:** Kornel Bardoczky (HUN) d. Tobias Kamke (GER) 62 63.
  Doubles: Martin Slanar (AUT)/Pavel Snobel (CZE) d. Kornel Bardoczky (HUN)/Jan Mertl (CZE) 46 64 61.

- **MASPALOMAS** (ESP) ($10,000) 21-27 JUNE – **Singles:** Jacobo Diaz-Ruiz (ESP) d. Juan Giner (ESP) 63 75.
  Doubles: Jordi Marse-Vidri/Carlos Poch-Gradin (ESP) d. Roberto Menendez-Ferre/Rafael Moreno-Negrin (ESP) 67(4) 64 61.

- **TOULON** (FRA) ($15,000) 21-27 JUNE – **Singles:** Carlos Berlocq (ARG) d. Bruno Echagaray (MEX) 63 61.
  Doubles: Andrew Derer (AUS)/Filip Urban (POL) d. Xavier Audouy/Jonathan Hilaire (FRA) 63 46 63.

ITF Men's Circuit 2004 Futures Results (continued)

- **TUNIS** (TUN) ($10,000) 21-27 JUNE – **Singles:** Pablo Santos-Gonzalez (ESP) d. Oualid Jalali (TUN) 62 60.
  Doubles: Oualid Jalali (TUN)/Alexey Kedriouk (KAZ) d. Benjamin Balleret/Thomas Drouet (MON) w/o.

- **VIERUMAKI** (FIN) ($10,000) 21-27 JUNE – **Singles:** Andis Juska (LAT) d. Michael Ryderstedt (SWE) 64 62.
  Doubles: Frederik Nielsen/Rasmus Norby (DEN) d. Bart Beks/Rick Schalkers (NED) 76(2) 63.

- **BALS** (ROM) ($10,000) 28 JUNE-4 JULY – **Singles:** Victor Ionita (ROM) d. Gabriel Moraru (ROM) 62 76(4).
  Doubles: Gabriel Moraru/Horia Tecau (ROM) d. Juan-Martin Aranguren (ARG)/Dominique Coene (BEL) 60 46 62.

- **BUFFALO, NY** (USA) ($10,000) 28 JUNE-4 JULY – **Singles:** Michael Russell (USA) d. Jorge Aguilar (CHI) 63 60.
  Doubles: Goran Dragicevic/Mirko Pehar (USA) d. Dave Lingman/Philip Stolt (USA) 64 76(4).

- **CHICO, CA** (USA) ($10,000) 28 JUNE-4 JULY – **Singles:** Michael Yani (USA) d. Mark Hlawaty (AUS) 67(2) 76(8) 64.
  Doubles: Jason Cook/Lester Cook (USA) d. K.C. Corkery/Sam Warburg (USA) 75 76(5).

- **DONETSK** (UKR) ($10,000) 28 JUNE-4 JULY – **Singles:** Alexander Markin (RUS) d. Orest Tereshchuk (UKR) 64 61.
  Doubles: Mikhail Filima/Orest Tereshchuk (UKR) d. Alexander Markin/Sergei Pozdnev (RUS) 46 62 63.

- **FERRARA** (ITA) ($10,000) 28 JUNE-4 JULY – **Singles:** Alessandro Accardo (ITA) d. Francesco Piccari (ITA) w/o.
  Doubles: Diego Junqueira/Damian Patriarca (ARG) d. Massimo Ocera/Marco Pedrini (ITA) 61 62.

- **HELSINGOR** (DEN) ($10,000) 28 JUNE-4 JULY – **Singles:** Daniel Klemetz (SWE) d. Fotos Kallias (CYP) 46 76(4) 75.
  Doubles: Frederik Nielsen/Rasmus Norby (DEN) d. Johan Brunstrom/Alexander Hartman (SWE) 63 63.

- **HERRHUGOWAARD** (NED) ($15,000) 28 JUNE-4 JULY – **Singles:** Molle Van Gemerden (NED) d. Fred Jr. Hemmes (NED) 63 63.
  Doubles: Bart De Gier/Michel Koning (NED) d. Marc Ijzermann/Alexander Nonnekes (NED) 64 75.

- **KASSEL** (GER) ($15,000) 28 JUNE-4 JULY – **Singles:** Mounir El Aarej (MAR) d. Jan Minar (CZE) 62 64.
  Doubles: Filip Polasek/Ladislav Svarc (SVK) d. Lucas Engel (BRA)/Markus Schiller (GER) 64 62.

- **ONTARIO** (CAN) ($10,000) 28 JUNE-4 JULY – **Singles:** Takahiro Terachi (JPN) d. Todd Widom (USA) 64 26 64.
  Doubles: Matt Klinger (CAN)/Daniel Wendler (AUS) d. David Martin/Todd Widom (USA) w/o.

- **ALICANTE** (ESP) ($15,000) 5-11 JULY – **Singles:** Mariano Albert-Ferrando (ESP) d. Pablo Santos-Gonzalez (ESP) 36 62 64.
  Doubles: Antonio Baldellou-Esteva/German Puentes-Alcaniz (ESP) d. Mariano Albert-Ferrando/Ferran Ventura-Martell (ESP) 62 67(5) 61.

- **BOLOGNA** (ITA) ($10,000) 5-11 JULY – **Singles:** Simone Bolelli (ITA) d. Mattia Livraghi (ITA) 62 63.
  Doubles: Simone Bolelli/Alberto Brizzi (ITA) d. Ivan Dodig (BIH)/Michael Staniak (AUS) 76(4) 60.

- **BOURG-EN-BRESSE** (FRA) ($15,000+H) 5-11 JULY – **Singles:** Bertrand Contzler (FRA) d. Josselin Ouanna (FRA) 75 61.
  Doubles: Brian Dabul (ARG)/Lamine Ouahab (ALG) d. Diego Alvarez/Giuseppe Menga (ITA) 64 63.

- **CAMPINA** (ROM) ($10,000) 5-11 JULY – **Singles:** Adrian Cruciat (ROM) d. Victor Ionita (ROM) 62 06 42 ret.
  Doubles: Elefterios Alexiou/Theodoros Angelinos (GRE) d. Adrian Cruciat/Adrian Gavrila (ROM) 63 63.

- **DNEPROPETROVSK** (UKR) ($10,000) 5-11 JULY – **Singles:** Alexander Markin (RUS) d. Evgueni Smirnov (RUS) 62 63.
  Doubles: Alexander Markin/Sergei Pozdnev (RUS) d. Nikolai Dyachok/Alexander Yarmola (UKR) 30 ret.

- **FORCHHEIM** (GER) ($10,000) 5-11 JULY – **Singles:** Lars Uebel (GER) d. Philipp Hammer (GER) 64 60.
  Doubles: Peter Steinberger/Marcel Zimmermann (GER) d. Alexander Flock/Lars Uebel (GER) 75 20 ret.

- **HORSHOLM** (DEN) ($10,000) 5-11 JULY – **Singles:** Andis Juska (LAT) d. Johan Brunstrom (SWE) 67(3) 63 75.
  Doubles: Frederik Nielsen/Rasmus Norby (DEN) d. Andrea Arnaboldi (ITA)/Nicolas Tourte (FRA) 63 60.

- **PITTSBURGH, PA** (USA) ($10,000) 5-11 JULY – **Singles:** Michael Russell (USA) d. Kean Feeder (USA) 61 60.
  Doubles: Tres Davis/Ryan Sachire (USA) d. Goran Dragicevic/Mirko Pehar (USA) 63 64.

Cristian Villagran (ARG) won five Futures titles in South America

ITF Men's Circuit 2004 Futures Results (continued)

- **TELFS** (AUT) ($15,000) 5-10 JULY – **Singles:** Jan Mertl (CZE) d. Kamil Capkovic (SVK) 63 61.
  Doubles: Benedikt Dorsch (GER)/Stefan Wauters (BEL) d. Jan Mertl/Jiri Vencl (CZE) 63 75.

- **BUCHAREST** (ROM) ($10,000) 12-18 JULY – **Singles:** Adrian Cruciat (ROM) d. Adrian Ungur (ROM) 64 64.
  Doubles: Adrian Cruciat/Adrian Gavrila (ROM) d. Florin Mergea/Horia Tecau (ROM) 06 64 64.

- **ELCHE** (ESP) ($15,000) 12-18 JULY – **Singles:** Ivan Esquerdo-Andreu (ESP) d. Carlos Castellanos-Miguel (ESP) 36 64 63.
  Doubles: Ivan Esquerdo-Andreu/Marc Fornell-Mestres (ESP) d. Antonio Baldellou-Esteva/German Puentes-Alcaniz (ESP) 62 61.

- **KRAMSACH** (AUT) ($15,000) 12-17 JULY – **Singles:** Farrukh Dustov (UZB) d. Johannes Ager (AUT) 16 76(3) 61.
  Doubles: Johannes Ager/Marko Neunteibl (AUT) d. Cesar Ferrer-Victoria (ESP)/Darko Madjarovski (SCG) 62 36 62.

- **LYNGBY** (DEN) ($10,000) 12-18 JULY – **Singles:** Michael Ryderstedt (SWE) d. Timo Nieminen (FIN) 62 36 75.
  Doubles: Bart Beks (NED)/Stefano Ianni (ITA) d. Juri Barkov/Juho Paukku (FIN) 62 61.

- **PEORIA, IL** (USA) ($10,000) 12-18 JULY – **Singles:** Luis-Manuel Flores (MEX) d. Jesse Witten (USA) 76(2) 60.
  Doubles: Raphael Durek/Adam Feeney (AUS) d. Matt Cloer/Goran Dragicevic (USA) 75 75.

- **RABAT** (MAR) ($10,000) 12-18 JULY – **Singles:** Mehdi Tahiri (MAR) d. Jan Stancik (SVK) 26 64 63.
  Doubles: Massimo Bosa (ITA)/Benjamin Rufer (SUI) d. Mohcine Roudami (MAR)/Sherif Sabry (EGY) 63 62.

- **SAINT-GERVAIS** (FRA) ($15,000) 12-18 JULY – **Singles:** Bertrand Contzler (FRA) d. David Guez (FRA) 63 64.
  Doubles: Diego Alvarez (ITA)/Brian Dabul (ARG) d. Xavier Audouy/Nicolas Tourte (FRA) 36 63 75.

- **TRIER** (GER) ($15,000) 12-18 JULY – **Singles:** Eric Prodon (FRA) d. Steve Darcis (BEL) 63 63.
  Doubles: Michel Koning/Steven Korteling (NED) d. Felipe Parada (CHI)/Esteban Zanetti (ARG) 61 75.

- **AREZZO** (ITA) ($10,000) 19-25 JULY – **Singles:** Maximo Gonzalez (ARG) d. Stefano Ianni (ITA) 63 63.
  Doubles: Stefano Mocci/Giancarlo Petrazzuolo (ITA) d. Adam Chadaj (POL)/Maximo Gonzalez (ARG) 61 63.

- **BRASOV** (ROM) ($10,000) 19-25 JULY – **Singles:** Artemon Apostu-Efremov (ROM) d. Victor Crivoi (ROM) 64 76(3).
  Doubles: Catalin Gard/Andrei Mlendea (ROM) d. Adrian Barbu/Teodor Bolanu (ROM) 46 61 75.

- **GANDIA** (ESP) ($10,000) 19-25 JULY – **Singles:** Jacobo Diaz-Ruiz (ESP) d. Hector Ruiz-Cadenas (ESP) 64 75.
  Doubles: Ivan Esquerdo-Andreu/Marc Fornell-Mestres (ESP) d. Antonio Baldellou-Esteva/German Puentes-Alcaniz (ESP) 62 63.

- **JOPLIN, MO** (USA) ($10,000) 19-25 JULY – **Singles:** Jesse Witten (USA) d. Raphael Durek (AUS) 62 57 62.
  Doubles: K.C. Corkery/Jeremy Wurtzman (USA) d. Raphael Durek/Adam Feeney (AUS) 75 36 62.

- **LOHR AM MAIN** (GER) ($10,000) 19-25 JULY – **Singles:** Alexander Flock (GER) d. Lars Uebel (GER) 76(5) 64.
  Doubles: Jasper Smit (NED)/Lars Uebel (GER) d. Daniel Muller (GER)/Zoran Sevcenko (MKD) 63 75.

- **MARRAKECH** (MAR) ($10,000) 19-25 JULY – **Singles:** Frank Condor-Fernandez (ESP) d. Alessandro Accardo (ITA) 64 63.
  Doubles: Adam Thompson (NZL)/Martijn Van Haasteren (NED) d. Jordi Marse-Vidri/Carlos Rexach-Itoiz (ESP) 62 26 75.

- **AGADIR** (MAR) ($10,000) 26 JULY-1 AUGUST – **Singles:** David Guez (FRA) d. Mehdi Tahiri (MAR) 76(3) 64.
  Doubles: Alessandro Accardo/Fabio Colangelo (ITA) d. Jordi Gil-Fernandez/Roberto Lopez-Sanchez (ESP) 63 60.

- **ARAD** (ROM) ($10,000) 26 JULY-1 AUGUST – **Singles:** Victor Ionita (ROM) d. Artemon Apostu-Efremov (ROM) 63 64.
  Doubles: Catalin Gard/Andrei Mlendea (ROM) d. Karim Maamoun/Mohamed Maamoun (EGY) 36 64 76(4).

- **DENIA** (ESP) ($10,000) 26 JULY-1 AUGUST – **Singles:** Javier Genaro-Martinez (ESP) d. Jesse Huta-Galung (NED) 76(5) 26 75.
  Doubles: Antonio Baldellou-Esteva/German Puentes-Alcaniz (ESP) d. Bernat Mas-Avellaneda/Alejandro Vargas-Aboy (ESP) 76(10) 67(4) 61.

- **FOLIGNO** (ITA) ($10,000) 26 JULY-1 AUGUST – **Singles:** Ivan Cerovic (CRO) d. Giancarlo Petrazzuolo (ITA) 46 63 62.
  Doubles: Stefano Mocci/Giancarlo Petrazzuolo (ITA) d. Ismar Gorcic (BIH)/Stefano Ianni (ITA) 46 76(6) 75.

- **GODFREY, IL** (USA) ($10,000) 26 JULY-1 AUGUST – **Singles:** Rodrigo-Antonio Grilli (BRA) d. Tres Davis (USA) 46 76(3) 64.
  Doubles: Goran Dragicevic/Mirko Pehar (USA) d. Raphael Durek/Adam Feeney (AUS) 36 63 64.

- **LOME** (TOG) ($10,000) 26 JULY-1 AUGUST – **Singles:** Komlavi Loglo (TOG) d. Adam Thompson (NZL) 60 64.
  Doubles: Kwami Gakpo/Komlavi Loglo (TOG) d. Henry Adjei-Darko (GHA)/Nouhoun Sangare (CIV) 46 76(5) 64.

- **TALLINN** (EST) ($10,000) 26 JULY-1 AUGUST – **Singles:** Janne Ojala (FIN) d. Bart Beks (NED) 76(4) 63.
  Doubles: Johan Brunstrom/Alexander Hartman (SWE) d. Bart Beks (NED)/Mait Kunnap (EST) 76(6) 76(3).

- **DECATUR, IL** (USA) ($10,000) 2-8 AUGUST – **Singles:** Sam Warburg (USA) d. Tres Davis (USA) 64 62.
  Doubles: Trevor Spracklin/Michael Yani (USA) d. Raphael Durek/Adam Feeney (AUS) 75 63.

- **JAKARTA** (INA) ($10,000) 2-8 AUGUST – **Singles:** Seung-Hoon Lee (KOR) d. Oh-Hee Kwon (KOR) 36 64 76(2).
  Doubles: Hendri-Susilo Pramono/Febi Widhiyanto (INA) d. Whi Kim/Nick Monroe (USA) 62 64.

- **JURMALA** (LAT) ($10,000) 2-8 AUGUST – **Singles:** Radoslav Nijaki (POL) d. Janne Ojala (FIN) 61 62.
  Doubles: Bart Beks (NED)/Mait Kunnap (EST) d. Jasper Smit (NED)/Simon Stadler (GER) 64 57 76(3).

- **LAGOS** (NGR) ($10,000) 2-8 AUGUST – **Singles:** Henry Adjei-Darko (GHA) d. Roger Anderson (RSA) 36 62 63.
  Doubles: Romano Frantzen/Floris Kilian (NED) d. Henry Adjei-Darko (GHA)/Jonathan Igbinovia (NGR) 63 75.

- **SANTIAGO** (CHI) ($15,000) 2-8 AUGUST – **Singles:** Julio Peralta (CHI) d. Damian Patriarca (ARG) 62 61.
  Doubles: Juan-Martin Aranguren/Patricio Rudi (ARG) d. Rodolfo Daruich/Diego Junqueira (ARG) 16 63 63.

- **SEZZE** (ITA) ($10,000) 2-8 AUGUST – **Singles:** Giancarlo Petrazzuolo (ITA) d. Steven Korteling (NED) 76(4) 26 75.
  Doubles: Ismar Gorcic (BIH)/Giancarlo Petrazzuolo (ITA) d. Daniel Lustig (CZE)/Mikhail Vassiliev (RUS) 64 76(8).

- **TEHRAN** (IRI) ($15,000) 2-8 AUGUST – **Singles:** Michael Ryderstedt (SWE) d. Benjamin Balleret (MON) 64 62.
  Doubles: Benjamin Balleret (MON)/Clement Morel (FRA) d. Sarvar Ikramov/Murad Inoyatov (UZB) 61 61.

- **WREXHAM** (GBR) ($15,000) 2-8 AUGUST – **Singles:** David Sherwood (GBR) d. Mark Hilton (GBR) 76(5) 64.
  Doubles: Richard Bloomfield/Ken Skupski (GBR) d. Joshua Goodall/Miles Kasiri (GBR) 62 64.

- **XATIVA** (ESP) ($10,000) 2-8 AUGUST – **Singles:** Andrew Murray (GBR) d. Antonio Baldellou-Esteva (ESP) 62 64.
  Doubles: Jose-Manuel Garcia-Rodriguez/Arkaitz Manzarbeitia-Ugarte (ESP) d. Eduardo-Castro Magadan/Carlos Palencia (MEX) 63 63.

- **ZAJECAR** (SCG) ($10,000) 2-8 AUGUST – **Singles:** Vladimir Pavicevic (SCG) d. Nikola Ciric (SCG) 60 63.
  Doubles: Nikola Ciric/Goran Tosic (SCG) d. Ivan Dodig (BIH)/Vide Konjevod (CRO) 76(4) 63.

- **BUCHAREST** (ROM) ($10,000) 9-15 AUGUST – **Singles:** Victor Ionita (ROM) d. Adrian Ungur (ROM) 64 63.
  Doubles: Adrian Barbu/Victor Ionita (ROM) d. Marcos Conde-Jackson/Acaymo Medina-Rivero (ESP) 10 ret.

- **CACAK** (SCG) ($10,000) 9-15 AUGUST – **Singles:** Novak Djokovic (SCG) d. Flavio Cipolla (ITA) 64 63.
  Doubles: Novak Djokovic/Dejan Petrovic (SCG) d. Flavio Cipolla (ITA)/Alberto Soriano-Maldonado (ESP) 76(4) 62.

- **LONDON** (GBR) ($15,000) 9-15 AUGUST – **Singles:** Nicolas Tourte (FRA) d. James Auckland (GBR) 63 67(3) 61.
  Doubles: Richard Barker/William Barker (GBR) d. Richard Bloomfield/Ken Skupski (GBR) 63 61.

- **KENOSHA, WI** (USA) ($10,000) 9-15 AUGUST – **Singles:** Brian Wilson (USA) d. Ryan Newport (USA) 75 76(2).
  Doubles: Cody Conley/Ryan Newport (USA) d. Josh Cohen/Ry Tarpley (USA) 61 76(3).

- **LAGOS** (NGR) ($10,000) 9-15 AUGUST – **Singles:** Henry Adjei-Darko (GHA) d. Komlavi Loglo (TOG) 61 61.
  Doubles: Henry Adjei-Darko (GHA)/Jonathan Igbinovia (NGR) d. Romano Frantzen/Floris Kilian (NED) 67(10) 62 64.

- **L'AQUILA** (ITA) ($10,000) 9-15 AUGUST – **Singles:** Mathieu Montcourt (FRA) d. Andrei Goloubev (RUS) 62 61.
  Doubles: Fabio Colangelo/Federico Torresi (ITA) d. Stefano Mocci/Giancarlo Petrazzuolo (ITA) 64 76(6).

ITF Men's Circuit 2004 Futures Results (continued)

- **MAKASSAR** (INA) ($10,000) 9-15 AUGUST – **Singles:** Hee-Seok Chung (KOR) d. Suwandi Suwandi (INA) 76(6) 63.
  Doubles: Dong-Hyun Kim/Oh-Hee Kwon (KOR) d. Suwandi Suwandi/Bonit Wiryawan (INA) 75 67(5) 62.

- **SANTIAGO** (CHI) ($15,000) 9-15 AUGUST – **Singles:** Cristian Villagran (ARG) d. Julio Peralta (CHI) 64 64.
  Doubles: Damian Patriarca/Patricio Rudi (ARG) d. Hermes Gamonal/Miguel Miranda (CHI) 76(4) 75.

- **SERGIEV POSAD** (RUS) ($10,000) 9-15 AUGUST – **Singles:** Evgueni Smirnov (RUS) d. Denis Matsukevitch (RUS) 62 67(6) 76(5).
  Doubles: Philipp Mukhometov/Evgueni Smirnov (RUS) d. Denis Matsukevitch (RUS)/Eric Scherer (GER) 62 62.

- **TEHRAN** (IRI) ($15,000) 9-15 AUGUST – **Singles:** Michael Ryderstedt (SWE) d. Thorsten Popp (GER) 63 63.
  Doubles: Xavier Audouy/Charles Roche (FRA) d. Benjamin Balleret (MON)/Clement Morel (FRA) 64 61.

- **VIGO** (ESP) ($15,000) 9-15 AUGUST – **Singles:** Israel Matos-Gil (ESP) d. Frank Condor-Fernandez (ESP) 61 46 76(2).
  Doubles: Rui Machado (POR)/Martin Vilarrubi (URU) d. David Marrero-Santana/Carlos Rexach-Itoiz (ESP) 26 63 63.

- **VILNIUS** (LTU) ($10,000) 9-15 AUGUST – **Singles:** Javier Garcia-Sintes (ESP) d. Rolandas Murashka (LTU) 63 36 61.
  Doubles: Tomasz Bednarek (POL)/Javier Garcia-Sintes (ESP) d. Mait Kunnap (EST)/Janne Ojala (FIN) 61 64.

- **BOLZANO** (ITA) ($10,000) 16-22 AUGUST – **Singles:** Massimo Ocera (ITA) d. Dusan Karol (CZE) 46 64 63.
  Doubles: Maximo Gonzalez (ARG)/Federico Torresi (ITA) d. Flavio Cipolla/Alessandro Motti (ITA) 62 16 76(3).

- **CAKAVEC** (CRO) ($10,000) 16-22 AUGUST – **Singles:** Sasa Tuksar (CRO) d. Ferran Ventura-Martell (ESP) 61 64.
  Doubles: Ivan Cerovic/Kresimir Ritz (CRO) d. Sebo Kiss/Zsolt Tatar (HUN) 76(8) 64.

- **CALDAS NOVAS** (BRA) ($15,000) 16-22 AUGUST – **Singles:** Andre Ghem (BRA) d. Julio Silva (BRA) 62 75.
  Doubles: Daniel Melo/Marcelo Melo (BRA) d. Brian Dabul/Alejandro Fabbri (ARG) 64 62.

- **ENSCHEDE** (NED) ($15,000) 16-22 AUGUST – **Singles:** Ivo Klec (GER) d. Jeroen Masson (BEL) 63 61.
  Doubles: Jasper Smit (NED)/Stefan Wauters (BEL) d. Mounir El Aarej/Mehdi Tahiri (MAR) 64 76(4).

- **IRUN** (ESP) ($15,000) 16-22 AUGUST – **Singles:** Tomislav Peric (CRO) d. Ben-Qiang Zhu (CHN) 64 76(5).
  Doubles: Marcel Granollers-Pujol (ESP)/Valentin Sanon (CIV) d. Ivan Esquerdo-Andreu/Marc Fornell-Mestres (ESP) 62 60.

- **KRASNOARMEISK** (RUS) ($10,000) 16-22 AUGUST – **Singles:** Philipp Mukhometov (RUS) d. Konstantin Kravchuk (RUS) 26 63 62.
  Doubles: Philipp Mukhometov/Evgueni Smirnov (RUS) d. Denis Matsukevitch (RUS)/Eric Scherer (GER) 60 62.

- **NIS** (SCG) ($10,000) 16-22 AUGUST – **Singles:** Viktor Troicki (SCG) d. Alberto Soriano-Maldonado (ESP) 62 61.
  Doubles: Nikola Ciric/Goran Tosic (SCG) d. Rok Jarc/Grega Zemlja (SLO) 10 ret.

- **SEMARANG** (INA) ($10,000) 16-22 AUGUST – **Singles:** Seung-Hoon Lee (KOR) d. Takahiro Terachi (JPN) 61 36 64.
  Doubles: Ketut Arta/Eko Kurniawan (INA) d. Hendri-Susilo Pramono/Febi Widhiyanto (INA) 64 76(4).

- **TIRGU-MURES** (ROM) ($10,000) 16-22 AUGUST – **Singles:** Victor Ionita (ROM) d. Vjekoslav Skenderovic (CRO) 61 64.
  Doubles: Adrian Barbu/Victor Ionita (ROM) d. Ognian Kolev (AUS)/Mariano Pettigrosso (ARG) 62 76(6).

- **VILNIUS** (LTU) ($10,000) 16-22 AUGUST – **Singles:** Radoslav Nijaki (POL) d. Jedrzej Zarski (POL) 46 75 62.
  Doubles: Bart Beks (NED)/Mait Kunnap (EST) d. Marcin Maszczyk/Radoslav Nijaki (POL) 64 46 63.

- **ALPHEN AAN DEN RIJN** (NED) ($15,000) 23-29 AUGUST – **Singles:** Andreas Beck (GER) d. Stefan Wauters (BEL) 76(1) 62.
  Doubles: Francisco Costa (BRA)/Jeroen Masson (BEL) d. Dustin Brown (JAM)/Eric Kuijlen (NED) 61 76(3).

- **CLUB-NAPOCA** (ROM) ($10,000) 23-29 AUGUST – **Singles:** Victor Ionita (ROM) d. Vjekoslav Skenderovic (CRO) 62 62.
  Doubles: Adrian Cruciat/Adrian Gavrila (ROM) d. Vjekoslav Skenderovic (CRO)/Saurav Sukul (IND) 64 63.

- **FLORIANOPOLIS** (BRA) ($10,000+H) 23-29 AUGUST – **Singles:** Marcos Daniel (BRA) d. Julio Silva (BRA) 75 26 32 ret.
  Doubles: Marcos Daniel/Alexandre Simoni (BRA) d. Brian Dabul/Alejandro Fabbri (ARG) 63 76(3).

- **KRASNOARMEISK** (RUS) ($10,000) 23-29 AUGUST – **Singles:** Alexander Markin (RUS) d. Denis Matsukevitch (RUS) 62 62.
  Doubles: Sergei Demekhine/Alexander Pavlioutchenkov (RUS) d. Philipp Mukhometov/Evgueni Smirnov (RUS) 62 64.

- **MUNICH-UNTERFOEHRING** (GER) ($10,000) 23-29 AUGUST – **Singles:** Adam Chadaj (POL) d. Michael Lammer (SUI) 36 63 62.
  Doubles: Felipe Parada (CHI)/Jan Weinzierl (GER) d. Oliver Marach (AUT)/Mike Steinherr (GER) 67(10) 61 61.

- **POZNAN** (POL) ($10,000) 23-29 AUGUST – **Singles:** Maciej Dilaj (POL) d. David Novak (CZE) 36 63 75.
  Doubles: Filip Aniola/Filip Urban (POL) d. Tomasz Bednarek (POL)/Bart Beks (NED) 61 67(5) 63.

- **ROME** (ITA) ($10,000) 23-29 AUGUST – **Singles:** Andrew Murray (GBR) d. Dominique Coene (BEL) 60 63.
  Doubles: Maximo Gonzalez (ARG)/Claudio Grassi (ITA) d. Flavio Cipolla/Fabio Colangelo (ITA) 63 46 62.

- **SANTANDER** (ESP) ($15,000) 23-29 AUGUST – **Singles:** Mariano Albert-Ferrando (ESP) d. David Marrero-Santana (ESP) 63 36 76(7).
  Doubles: Marcel Granollers-Pujol (ESP)/Valentin Sanon (CIV) d. David Marrero-Santana/Pablo Santos-Gonzalez (ESP) w/o.

- **ZAGREB** (CRO) ($10,000) 23-29 AUGUST – **Singles:** Ivan Cerovic (CRO) d. Marin Bradaric (CRO) 67(8) 75 64.
  Doubles: Luka Kukulic/Marko Vukelic (CRO) d. Marin Cilic/Ante Nakic-Alfirevic (CRO) 63 63.

- **BUENOS AIRES** (ARG) ($10,000) 30 AUGUST-5 SEPTEMBER – **Singles:** Carlos Berlocq (ARG) d. Rodolfo Daruich (ARG) 61 61.
  Doubles: Brian Dabul/Damian Patriarca (ARG) d. Patricio Arquez/Emiliano Redondi (ARG) 75 61.

- **CHIETI** (ITA) ($10,000) 30 AUGUST-5 SEPTEMBER – **Singles:** Ivan Cerovic (CRO) d. Francesco Piccari (ITA) 57 75 63.
  Doubles: Daniele Giorgini/Stefano Mocci (ITA) d. Luca Bonati/Francesco Piccari (ITA) 75 46 62.

- **COLOMBO** (SRI) ($10,000) 30 AUGUST-5 SEPTEMBER – **Singles:** Chris Kwon (USA) d. Adam Vejmelka (CZE) 64 60.
  Doubles: Hsin-Han Lee/Tai-Wei Liu (TPE) d. Huai-En Chang/Wang-Cheng Hsieh (TPE) 61 63.

- **COMITAN** (MEX) ($10,000) 30 AUGUST-5 SEPTEMBER – **Singles:** Andrew Piotrowski (CAN) d. Bruno Echagaray (MEX) 76(6) 64.
  Doubles: Michael Kogan (ISR)/Victor Romero (MEX) d. Bruno Echagaray/Miguel Gallardo-Valles (MEX) 57 63 76(8).

- **CURITIBA** (BRA) ($10,000) 30 AUGUST-5 SEPTEMBER – **Singles:** Marcos Daniel (BRA) d. Lucas Engel (BRA) 64 64.
  Doubles: Julio Silva/Rogerio Silva (BRA) d. Daniel Melo/Marcelo Melo (BRA) 62 64.

- **GUAYAQUIL** (ECU) ($10,000) 30 AUGUST-5 SEPTEMBER – **Singles:** Eric Nunez (USA) d. Carlos Avellan (ECU) 63 62.
  Doubles: Levar Harper-Griffith (USA)/Jean-Julien Rojer (AHO) d. Matthew Hanlin (GBR)/Matt Klinger (CAN) w/o.

- **KASHIWA** (JPN) ($15,000) 30 AUGUST-5 SEPTEMBER – **Singles:** Satoshi Iwabuchi (JPN) d. Ti Chen (TPE) 64 62.
  Doubles: Minh Le (USA)/Mark Nielsen (NZL) d. Naoki Arimoto/Yasuo Miyazaki (JPN) 76(4) 57 64.

- **NUREMBERG-HERPERSDORF** (GER) ($10,000) 30 AUGUST-5 SEPTEMBER – **Singles:** Michael Lammer (SUI) d. Adam Chadaj (POL) 64 26 64.
  Doubles: Evgueni Korolev (RUS)/Alessandro Motti (ITA) d. Tom Dennhardt/Robert Jammer-Luhr (GER) 76(5) 61.

- **ORADEA** (ROM) ($10,000) 30 AUGUST-5 SEPTEMBER – **Singles:** Adrian Cruciat (ROM) d. Teodor-Dacian Craciun (ROM) 64 76(5).
  Doubles: Adrian Cruciat/Adrian Gavrila (ROM) d. Artemon Apostu-Efremov/Teodor-Dacian Craciun (ROM) 64 75.

- **OVIEDO** (ESP) ($15,000) 30 AUGUST-5 SEPTEMBER – **Singles:** Marc Fornell-Mestres (ESP) d. Carlos Cuadrado-Quero (ESP) 75 46 64.
  Doubles: Antonio Baldellou-Esteva/German Puentes-Alcaniz (ESP) d. David Marrero-Santana/Hector Ruiz-Cadenas (ESP) 64 60.

- **SZCZECIN** (POL) ($10,000) 30 AUGUST-5 SEPTEMBER – **Singles:** Javier Garcia-Sintes (ESP) d. Josselin Ouanna (FRA) 62 62.
  Doubles: Tomasz Bednarek (POL)/Javier Garcia-Sintes (ESP) d. Filip Aniola/Filip Urban (POL) 64 62.

- **ZILINA** (SVK) ($10,000) 30 AUGUST-5 SEPTEMBER – **Singles:** Rainer Eitzinger (AUT) d. Christian Magg (AUT) 63 61.
  Doubles: Tomas Janci/Michal Varsanyi (SVK) d. Kamil Capkovic (SVK)/Jan Mertl (CZE) 63 64.

- **BAGNERES DE BIGORRE** (FRA) ($15,000+H) 6-12 SEPTEMBER – **Singles:** Josselin Ouanna (FRA) d. Rodolphe Cadart (FRA) 75 76(4).
  Doubles: Xavier Audouy/Nicolas Tourte (FRA) d. David Guez/Jonathan Hilaire (FRA) 63 64.

ITF Men's Circuit 2004 Futures Results (continued)

- **BUENOS AIRES** (ARG) ($10,000) 6-12 SEPTEMBER – **Singles:** Cristian Villagran (ARG) d. Horacio Zeballos (ARG) 62 61.
  Doubles: Jorge Aguilar/Guillermo Hormazabal (CHI) d. Patricio Arquez/Emiliano Redondi (ARG) 36 62 63.

- **GUAYAQUIL** (ECU) ($10,000) 6-12 SEPTEMBER – **Singles:** Jean-Julien Rojer (AHO) d. Pablo Gonzalez (COL) 64 61.
  Doubles: Levar Harper-Griffith (USA)/Jean-Julien Rojer (AHO) d. Sebastian Decoud (ARG)/Pablo Gonzalez (COL) 26 75 63.

- **HYDERABAD** (IND) ($10,000) 6-12 SEPTEMBER – **Singles:** Aqeel Khan (PAK) d. Tai-Wei Liu (TPE) 67(5) 61 61.
  Doubles: Mustafa Ghouse/Ajay Ramaswami (IND) d. Chris Kwon (USA)/Tai-Wei Liu (TPE) 63 76(3).

- **KEMPTEN** (GER) ($10,000) 6-12 SEPTEMBER – **Singles:** Adam Chadaj (POL) d. Evgueni Korolev (RUS) 62 62.
  Doubles: Joaquin Lillo (CHI)/Armin Meixner (GER) d. Dustin Brown (JAM)/Sascha Hesse (GER) 64 36 64.

- **MADRID** (ESP) ($10,000) 6-12 SEPTEMBER – **Singles:** Juan-Luis Rascon-Lope (ESP) d. Eric Scherer (GER) 36 61 64.
  Doubles: Romano Frantzen/Floris Kilian (NED) d. Esteban Carril-Caso/Rafael Moreno-Negrin (ESP) 64 75.

- **MEXICO CITY** (MEX) ($10,000) 6-12 SEPTEMBER – **Singles:** Victor Romero (MEX) d. Santiago Gonzalez (MEX) 26 76(5) 76(8).
  Doubles: Santiago Gonzalez/Miguel Reyes-Varela (MEX) d. Juan-Manuel Elizondo/Oscar Zarzosa (MEX) 63 62.

- **PORTO ALEGRO** (BRA) ($10,000) 6-12 SEPTEMBER – **Singles:** Marcos Daniel (BRA) d. Thiago Alves (BRA) 64 62.
  Doubles: Thiago Alves/Francisco Costa (BRA) d. Alexandre Bonatto/Daniel Melo (BRA) 64 75.

- **SOPRON** (HUN) ($10,000) 6-12 SEPTEMBER – **Singles:** Marco Mirnegg (AUT) d. Marko Neunteibl (AUT) 63 67(4) 75.
  Doubles: Nikola Ciric/Goran Tosic (SCG) d. Filip Polasek/Frantisek Polyak (SVK) 61 62.

- **TOKYO** (JPN) ($15,000) 6-12 SEPTEMBER – **Singles:** Satoshi Iwabuchi (JPN) d. Michihisa Onoda (JPN) 61 46 64.
  Doubles: Minh Le (USA)/Mark Nielsen (NZL) d. Kentaro Masuda/Atsuo Ogawa (JPN) 62 63.

- **WROCLAW** (POL) ($10,000) 6-12 SEPTEMBER – **Singles:** Filip Urban (POL) d. Mathieu Montcourt (FRA) 76(3) 63.
  Doubles: Marcin Golab/Krzysztof Kwinta (POL) d. Piotr Olechowski/Dawid Olejniczak (POL) 76(4) 76(2).

- **BUENOS AIRES** (ARG) ($10,000) 13-19 SEPTEMBER – **Singles:** Brian Dabul (ARG) d. Diego Moyano (ARG) 76(1) 61.
  Doubles: Francisco Cabello/Diego Junqueira (ARG) d. Luciano Vitullo (ARG)/Daniel Wendler (AUS) 61 62.

- **CLAREMONT, CA** (USA) ($15,000) 13-19 SEPTEMBER – **Singles:** Bobby Reynolds (USA) d. Huntley Montgomery (USA) 46 62 63.
  Doubles: Nick Rainey/Brian Wilson (USA) d. Huntley Montgomery/Bobby Reynolds (USA) 64 64.

- **DELHI** (IND) ($10,000+H) 13-18 SEPTEMBER – **Singles:** Vijay Kannan (IND) d. Vinod Sridhar (IND) 75 63.
  Doubles: Mustafa Ghouse/Vishal Uppal (IND) d. Kai-Lung Chang/Wang-Cheng Hsieh (TPE) 76(3) 63.

- **FRIEDBERG** (GER) ($10,000) 13-19 SEPTEMBER – **Singles:** Evgueni Korolev (RUS) d. Marius Zay (GER) 62 62.
  Doubles: Tom Dennhardt/Oliver Markus (GER) d. Sergei Pozdnev/Nikolai Soloviev (RUS) 64 75.

- **GOTHENBURG** (SWE) ($15,000) 13-18 SEPTEMBER – **Singles:** Jacob Adaktusson (SWE) d. Frederik Nielsen (DEN) 57 62 61.
  Doubles: Martijn Van Haasteren/Boy Wijnmalen (NED) d. Rickard Holmstrom/Christian Johansson (SWE) 62 62.

- **GUAYAQUIL** (ECU) ($10,000) 13-19 SEPTEMBER – **Singles:** Sebastian Decoud (ARG) d. Eric Nunez (USA) 63 64.
  Doubles: Justin Slattery/Trevor Spracklin (USA) d. David Gonzalez/Jose Ycaza (ECU) 62 62.

- **MADRID** (ESP) ($15,000) 13-19 SEPTEMBER – **Singles:** Juan-Luis Rascon-Lope (ESP) d. Denis Gremelmayr (GER) 75 76(2).
  Doubles: Flavio Cipolla/Massimo Ocera (ITA) d. Tomislav Peric (CRO)/Juan-Miguel Such-Perez (ESP) 75 64.

- **MULHOUSE** (FRA) ($15,000+H) 13-19 SEPTEMBER – **Singles:** Nicolas Thomann (FRA) d. Gary Lugassy (FRA) 46 63 60.
  Doubles: Jonathan Marray/David Sherwood (GBR) d. Josselin Ouanna/Alexandre Sidorenko (FRA) 62 61.

- **PORTO TORRES** (ITA) ($15,000) 13-19 SEPTEMBER – **Singles:** Andrea Stoppini (ITA) d. Daniele Giorgini (ITA) 61 63.
  Doubles: Daniele Giorgini/Stefano Mocci (ITA) d. Andrea Stoppini/Matteo Volante (ITA) 63 64.

- **COSTA MESA, CA** (USA) ($15,000) 20-26 SEPTEMBER – **Singles:** Lesley Joseph (USA) d. Dennis Zivkovic (USA) 64 63.
  Doubles: Scott Lipsky/David Martin (USA) d. Mykyta Kryvonos/Dennis Zivkovic (USA) 75 63.

- **FORTALEZA** (BRA) ($10,000) 20-26 SEPTEMBER – **Singles:** Francisco Costa (BRA) d. Alexandre Bonatto (BRA) 64 36 63.
  Doubles: Eduardo Bohrer/Eduardo Portal (BRA) d. Alexandre Bonatto/Felipe Lemos (BRA) 62 76(4).

- **GOTHENBURG** (SWE) ($15,000) 20-25 SEPTEMBER – **Singles:** Johan Settergren (SWE) d. Stefano Ianni (ITA) 50 ret.
  Doubles: Fabio Colangelo/Stefano Ianni (ITA) d. Ervin Eleskovic/Pablo Figueroa (SWE) 76(3) 61.

- **LA PAZ** (BOL) ($15,000) 20-26 SEPTEMBER – **Singles:** Carlos Salamanca (COL) d. Gustavo Marcaccio (ARG) 32 ret.
  Doubles: Michael Quintero/Carlos Salamanca (COL) d. Guillermo Carry (ARG)/Leonardo Tavares (POR) 75 64.

- **MADRID** (ESP) ($15,000) 20-26 SEPTEMBER – **Singles:** Francisco Fogues-Domenech (ESP) d. Marco Mirnegg (AUT) 26 75 61.
  Doubles: Marcel Granollers-Pujol (ESP)/Komlavi Loglo (TOG) d. Marco Mirnegg/Marko Neunteibl (AUT) 64 60.

- **MOMBASA** (KEN) ($10,000) 20-26 SEPTEMBER – **Singles:** Roger Anderson (RSA) d. Mustafa Ghouse (IND) 36 61 60.
  Doubles: Andrew Anderson/Paul Anderson (RSA) d. Yassir Bouyahya/Kamil Filali (MAR) 61 63.

- **PLAISIR** (FRA) ($15,000+H) 20-26 SEPTEMBER – **Singles:** Julien Varlet (FRA) d. David Sherwood (GBR) 63 64.
  Doubles: Jean-Francois Bachelot/Jean-Michel Pequery (FRA) d. Marc Auradou/Arnaud Delgado (FRA) 62 60.

- **SELARGIUS** (ITA) ($15,000) 20-26 SEPTEMBER – **Singles:** Francesco Piccari (ITA) d. Alex Vittur (ITA) 63 64.
  Doubles: Daniele Giorgini/Stefano Mocci (ITA) d. Alessandro Piccari/Francesco Piccari (ITA) 63 67(4) 62.

- **BUDAPEST** (HUN) ($10,000) 27 SEPTEMBER-3 OCTOBER – **Singles:** Alejandro Vargas-Aboy (ESP) d. Peter Capkovic (SVK) 64 60.
  Doubles: Antonio Baldellou-Esteva/German Puentes-Alcaniz (ESP) d. Daniel Lustig (CZE)/Filip Polasek (SVK) 75 36 63.

- **CARACAS** (VEN) ($10,000) 27 SEPTEMBER-3 OCTOBER – **Singles:** Jean-Julien Rojer (AHO) d. Jhonathan Medina-Alvarez (VEN) 60 63.
  Doubles: Jean-Julien Rojer (AHO)/Marcio Torres (BRA) d. Alvaro Loyola/Felipe Parada (CHI) 62 67(6) 64.

- **EDINBURGH** (GBR) ($10,000) 27 SEPTEMBER-3 OCTOBER – **Singles:** David Sherwood (GBR) d. Tom Burn (GBR) 64 61.
  Doubles: Richard Bloomfield/Chris Lewis (GBR) d. Tom Burn/Jamie Murray (GBR) 64 61.

- **FORBACH** (FRA) ($10,000) 27 SEPTEMBER-3 OCTOBER – **Singles:** Kevin Sorensen (IRL) d. Josselin Ouanna (FRA) 63 64.
  Doubles: Philipp Hammer/Dominik Meffert (GER) d. Roman Kislianski (RUS)/Marc Saulle (FRA) 62 75.

- **IRVINE, CA** (USA) ($15,000) 27 SEPTEMBER-3 OCTOBER – **Singles:** Zbynek Mlynarik (AUT) d. Bruno Echagaray (MEX) 61 61.
  Doubles: Brendan Evans/Scott Oudsema (USA) d. Scott Lipsky/David Martin (USA) 76(7) 36 64.

- **KIGALI** (RWA) ($10,000) 27 SEPTEMBER-3 OCTOBER – **Singles:** Andrew Anderson (RSA) d. Matwe Middelkoop (NED) 63 76(3).
  Doubles: Matwe Middelkoop (NED)/Adam Thompson (NZL) d. Andrew Anderson/Paul Anderson (RSA) 62 26 64.

- **MARTOS** (ESP) ($15,000) 27 SEPTEMBER-3 OCTOBER – **Singles:** Marcel Granollers-Pujol (ESP) d. Tony Holzinger (GER) 63 64.
  Doubles: Miguel Perez-Puig-Domenech/Gabriel Trujillo-Soler (ESP) d. Adrian Cruciat (ROM)/Todor Enev (BUL) 63 76(4).

- **RECIFE** (BRA) ($10,000) 27 SEPTEMBER-3 OCTOBER – **Singles:** Alessandro Camarco (BRA) d. Marcelo Melo (BRA) 64 57 64.
  Doubles: Diego Cubas/Marcelo Melo (BRA) d. Eduardo Bohrer/Eduardo Portal (BRA) 76(6) 64.

- **SANTA CRUZ** (BOL) ($15,000) 27 SEPTEMBER-3 OCTOBER – **Singles:** Cristian Villagran (ARG) d. Leonardo Tavares (POR) 63 63.
  Doubles: Thiago Alves/Julio Silva (BRA) d. Juan-Martin Aranguren/Cristian Villagran (ARG) 63 57 60.

- **CARACAS** (VEN) ($10,000) 4-10 OCTOBER – **Singles:** Jean-Julien Rojer (AHO) d. Jose De Armas (VEN) 61 63.
  Doubles: Vincent Baudat (FRA)/Ryan Russell (JAM) d. Ricardo Chile-Fonte/Sandor Martinez-Breijo (CUB) 64 46 76(4).

- **EL EJIDO** (ESP) ($15,000) 4-10 OCTOBER – **Singles:** Tony Holzinger (GER) d. Dekel Valtzer (ISR) 46 62 62.
  Doubles: Adrian Cruciat (ROM)/Marcel Granollers-Pujol (ESP) d. Marc Rocafort-Dolz/Javier Ruiz-Gonzalez (ESP) 63 63.

ITF Men's Circuit 2004 Futures Results (continued)

- **GLASGOW** (GBR) ($10,000) 4-10 OCTOBER – **Singles:** Richard Bloomfield (GBR) d. David Sherwood (GBR) 67(4) 62 76(6).
  Doubles: Daniel Kiernan/David Sherwood (GBR) d. Richard Bloomfield/Chris Lewis (GBR) 64 64.

- **GUARULHOS** (BRA) ($10,000) 4-10 OCTOBER – **Singles:** Francisco Costa (BRA) d. Thiago Alves (BRA) 64 36 64.
  Doubles: Diego Cubas/Marcelo Melo (BRA) d. Eduardo Bohrer (BRA)/Pierre-Ludovic Duclos (CAN) 76(1) 64.

- **KAPOSVAR** (HUN) ($10,000) 4-10 OCTOBER – **Singles:** Alejandro Vargas-Aboy (ESP) d. Gyorgy Balazs (HUN) 26 76(5) 62.
  Doubles: Tomas Banczi/Peter Miklusicak (SVK) d. Daniel Lustig (CZE)/Filip Polasek (SVK) 57 64 76(5).

- **LAGOS** (NGR) ($15,000+H) 4-10 OCTOBER – **Singles:** Aisam Qureshi (PAK) d. Sebastian Fitz (GER) 26 76(7) 63.
  Doubles: Komlavi Loglo (TOG)/Valentin Sanon (CIV) d. Fabian Roetschi/Benjamin Rufer (SUI) 75 61.

- **LAGUNA NIGUEL, CA** (USA) ($15,000) 4-10 OCTOBER – **Singles:** Horia Tecau (ROM) d. Wayne Odesnik (USA) 63 62.
  Doubles: Mirko Pehar/Jeremy Wurtzman (USA) d. Justin Bower (RSA)/Brian Wilson (USA) 36 64 76(2).

- **MEDELLIN** (COL) ($15,000) 4-10 OCTOBER – **Singles:** Sebastian Decoud (ARG) d. Michael Quintero (COL) 64 75.
  Doubles: Lucas Engel/Andre Ghem (BRA) d. Jorge Aguilar/Guillermo Hormazabal (CHI) 76(2) 63.

- **NEVERS** (FRA) ($15,000+H) 4-10 OCTOBER – **Singles:** Bertrand Contzler (FRA) d. Jean-Francois Bachelot (FRA) 63 64.
  Doubles: Bertrand Contzler/Slimane Saoudi (FRA) d. Eric Butorac/Travis Rettenmaier (USA) 64 75.

- **TBILISI** (GEO) ($15,000) 4-10 OCTOBER – **Singles:** Michal Przysiezny (POL) d. Kirill Ivanov-Smolenski (RUS) 75 63.
  Doubles: Bart Beks (NED)/Mait Kunnap (EST) d. Kirill Ivanov-Smolenski/Philipp Mukhometov (RUS) 64 64.

- **TORREON** (MEX) ($10,000) 4-10 OCTOBER – **Singles:** Dawid Olejniczak (POL) d. Michael Kogan (ISR) 75 62.
  Doubles: Michael Kogan (ISR)/Victor Romero (MEX) d. Daniel Garza/Carlos Palencia (MEX) 61 62.

- **BOGOTA** (COL) ($15,000) 11-17 OCTOBER – **Singles:** Lukasz Kubot (POL) d. Julio Silva (BRA) 46 62 62.
  Doubles: Santiago Gonzalez/Alejandro Hernandez (MEX) d. Martin Alund/Diego Junqueira (ARG) 63 64.

- **CARACAS** (VEN) ($10,000) 11-17 OCTOBER – **Singles:** Jean-Julien Rojer (AHO) d. Jose De Armas (VEN) 64 62.
  Doubles: Nick Monroe (USA)/Marcio Torres (BRA) d. Whi Kim/Sukhwa Young (USA) 63 60.

- **CORDOBA** (ESP) ($10,000) 11-17 OCTOBER – **Singles:** Tomislav Peric (CRO) d. Esteban Carril-Caso (ESP) 76(4) 64.
  Doubles: Esteban Carril-Caso/Angel-Jose Martin-Arroyo (ESP) d. Sergio Contreras-Farinas (ESP)/Tony Holzinger (GER) 64 75.

- **LAGOS** (NGR) ($15,000+H) 11-17 OCTOBER – **Singles:** Sebastian Fitz (GER) d. Roger Anderson (RSA) 63 67(9) 63.
  Doubles: Roger Anderson (RSA)/Luka Gregorc (SLO) d. Juan-Ignacio Cerda (CHI)/Jasper Smit (NED) 63 62.

- **LUBBOCK, TX** (USA) ($15,000) 11-17 OCTOBER – **Singles:** Justin Bower (RSA) d. Zbynek Mlynarik (AUT) 64 63.
  Doubles: Julien Cassaigne (FRA)/Philip Gubenco (CAN) d. Lazar Magdincev (MKD)/Dudi Sela (ISR) 26 76(5) 64.

- **MONTERREY** (MEX) ($10,000) 11-17 OCTOBER – **Singles:** Michael Kogan (ISR) d. Zach Dailey (USA) 64 63.
  Doubles: Michael Kogan (ISR)/Victor Romero (MEX) d. David Brewer/Richard Irwin (GBR) 63 62.

- **SAINT-DIZIER** (FRA) ($10,000+H) 11-17 OCTOBER – **Singles:** Florin Mergea (ROM) d. Nicolas Thomann (FRA) 67(4) 76(6) 63.
  Doubles: Jean-Francois Bachelot (FRA)/Florin Mergea (ROM) d. Oualid Jalali (TUN)/Jamal Parker (USA) 62 63.

- **SUNDERLAND** (GBR) ($10,000) 11-17 OCTOBER – **Singles:** Alexander Flock (GER) d. David Sherwood (GBR) 62 63.
  Doubles: Daniel Kiernan/David Sherwood (GBR) d. Joshua Goodall/Miles Kasiri (GBR) 64 64.

- **TBILISI** (GEO) ($15,000) 11-17 OCTOBER – **Singles:** Javier Garcia-Sintes (ESP) d. Rainer Eitzinger (AUT) 63 62.
  Doubles: Bart Beks (NED)/Mait Kunnap (EST) d. Bastian Knittel/Peter Mayer-Tischer (GER) 67(4) 61 63.

- **ANTOFAGASTA** (CHI) ($10,000) 18-24 OCTOBER – **Singles:** Lionel Noviski (ARG) d. Oliver Marach (AUT) 26 64 62.
  Doubles: Oliver Marach/Marko Neunteibl (AUT) d. Paul Capdeville/Phillip Harboe (CHI) 62 60.

- **ARLINGTON, TX** (USA) ($15,000) 18-24 OCTOBER – **Singles:** Justin Bower (RSA) d. Alexander Hartman (SWE) 61 64.
  Doubles: Ti Chen (TPE)/Go Soeda (JPN) d. Scott Lipsky/Todd Widom (USA) 75 62.

- **BARCELONA** (ESP) ($10,000) 18-24 OCTOBER – **Singles:** Antonio Baldellou-Esteva (ESP) d. Marc Fornell-Mestres (ESP) 62 75.
  Doubles: Marc Fornell-Mestres/Mario Munoz-Bejarano (ESP) d. Gorka Fraile-Etxeberria/David Marrero-Santana (ESP) 64 46 64.

- **CAMPO GRANDE** (BRA) ($10,000) 18-24 OCTOBER – **Singles:** Thiago Alves (BRA) d. Julio Silva (BRA) 64 60.
  Doubles: Lucas Engel/Andre Ghem (BRA) d. Julio Silva/Rogerio Silva (BRA) 60 61.

- **LA HABANA** (CUB) ($10,000) 18-24 OCTOBER – **Singles:** Jean-Julien Rojer (AHO) d. Ricardo Chile-Fonte (CUB) 60 62.
  Doubles: Jean-Julien Rojer (AHO)/Marcio Torres (BRA) d. Ricardo Chile-Fonte/Sandor Martinez-Breijo (CUB) 76(2) 64.

- **LA ROCHE SUR YON** (FRA) ($15,000+H) 18-24 OCTOBER – **Singles:** Gilles Simon (FRA) d. Thorsten Popp (GER) 75 62.
  Doubles: Xavier Audouy/Jean-Francois Bachelot (FRA) d. Daniel Munoz-de la Nava (ESP)/Igor Zelenay (SVK) 36 61 62.

- **LAGOS** (NGR) ($15,000) 18-24 OCTOBER – **Singles:** Victor Bruthans (SVK) d. Sunil-Kumar Sipaeya (IND) 62 64.
  Doubles: Raven Klaasen (RSA)/Sunil-Kumar Sipaeya (IND) d. Henry Adjei-Darko (GHA)/Jonathan Igbinovia (NGR) 64 76(4).

- **AMERICANA** (BRA) ($10,000+H) 25-31 OCTOBER – **Singles:** Francisco Costa (BRA) d. Thiago Alves (BRA) 62 63.
  Doubles: Henrique Mello/Gabriel Pitta (BRA) d. Eduardo Bohrer/Eduardo Portal (BRA) 62 36 64.

- **BANGKOK** (THA) ($10,000) 25-31 OCTOBER – **Singles:** Konstantinos Economidis (GRE) d. Guillaume Legat (FRA) 62 64.
  Doubles: Konstantinos Economidis/Nikos Rovas (GRE) d. Joji Miyao/Atsuo Ogawa (JPN) 64 62.

- **BATON ROUGE, LA** (USA) ($15,000) 25-31 OCTOBER – **Singles:** Justin Bower (RSA) d. Ti Chen (TPE) 67(6) 64 64.
  Doubles: Michael Kogan (ISR)/Victor Romero (MEX) d. Julien Cassaigne (FRA)/Philip Gubenco (CAN) 63 61.

- **CIUDAD OBREGON, SONORA** (MEX) ($10,000) 25-31 OCTOBER – **Singles:** Santiago Gonzalez (MEX) d. Miguel Gallardo-Valles (MEX) 64 64.
  Doubles: Bruno Echagaray/Miguel Gallardo-Valles (MEX) d. Guillermo Carry (ARG)/Lauri Kiiski (FIN) 63 36 76(5).

- **LAGOS** (NGR) ($15,000) 25-31 OCTOBER – **Singles:** Jasper Smit (NED) d. Jonathan Igbinovia (NGR) 75 62.
  Doubles: Fabian Roetschi/Benjamin-David Rufer (SUI) d. Mustafa Ghouse (IND)/Raven Klaasen (RSA) 67(5) 63 63.

- **PRUHONICE** (CZE) ($10,000) 25-31 OCTOBER – **Singles:** Martin Stepanek (CZE) d. Ivan Cerovic (CRO) 76(8) 76(5).
  Doubles: Daniel Lustig/Jan Mertl (CZE) d. Martin Stepanek/Jiri Vrbka (CZE) 64 62.

- **RODEZ** (FRA) ($10,000+H) 25-31 OCTOBER – **Singles:** Gilles Simon (FRA) d. Nicolas Tourte (FRA) 76(8) 62.
  Doubles: Alessandro Motti (ITA)/Daniel Munoz-de la Nava (ESP) d. Gilles Simon/Cyril Spanelis (FRA) 62 62.

- **SANTIAGO** (CHI) ($15,000) 25-31 OCTOBER – **Singles:** Mariano Puerta (ARG) d. Diego Moyano (ARG) 61 61.
  Doubles: Maximo Gonzalez/Emiliano Redondi (ARG) d. Hermes Gamonal/Phillip Harboe (CHI) 63 57 62.

- **VILAFRANCA** (ESP) ($10,000) 25-31 OCTOBER – **Singles:** Didac Perez-Minarro (ESP) d. German Puentes-Alcaniz (ESP) 60 26 61.
  Doubles: Gorka Fraile-Etxeberria/David Marrero-Santana (ESP) d. Antonio Baldellou-Esteva/German Puentes-Alcaniz (ESP) 64 76(1).

- **WATERLOO** (BEL) ($15,000) 25-31 OCTOBER – **Singles:** Dominique Coene (BEL) d. Simone Bolelli (ITA) 62 63.
  Doubles: Darko Madjarovski (SCG)/Igor Zelenay (SVK) d. Michel Koning/Martijn Van Haasteren (NED) 64 76(3).

- **BANGKOK** (THA) ($10,000) 1-7 NOVEMBER – **Singles:** Denis Gremelmayr (GER) d. Ruben De Kleijn (NED) 64 60.
  Doubles: Mohammed Al Ghareeb (KUW)/Sunil-Kumar Sipaeya (IND) d. Minh Le (USA)/Hiroyasu Sato (JPN) 26 64 64.

- **CAMPINAS** (BRA) ($10,000) 1-7 NOVEMBER – **Singles:** Andre Ghem (BRA) d. Francisco Costa (BRA) 75 63.
  Doubles: Henrique Mello/Gabriel Pitta (BRA) d. Alexandre Bonatto/Henrique Pinto-Silva (BRA) 76(4) 63.

- **FRYDLANT NAD OSTRAVICI** (CZE) ($10,000) 1-7 NOVEMBER – Singles: Lukasz Kubot (POL) d. Jan Mertl (CZE) 63 61.
  Doubles: Daniel Lustig/Jan Mertl (CZE) d. Jan Riha/Pavel Riha (CZE) 61 36 64.

ITF Men's Circuit 2004 Futures Results (continued)

- **LEON, GUANAJUATO** (MEX) ($10,000) 1-7 NOVEMBER – **Singles:** Alejandro Hernandez (MEX) d. Miguel Gallardo-Valles (MEX) 75 64.
  Doubles: Daniel Langre/Victor Romero (MEX) d. Dawid Olejniczak/Piotr Szczepanik (POL) 76(4) 75.

- **SANT CUGAT** (ESP) ($10,000) 1-7 NOVEMBER – **Singles:** Javier Genaro-Martinez (ESP) d. Tomislav Peric (CRO) 76(3) 61.
  Doubles: Antonio Baldellou-Esteva/German Puentes-Alcaniz (ESP) d. Daniel Homedes-Carballo/Carlos Rexach-Itoiz (ESP) 76(5) 75.

- **SINT KATELIJNE WAVER** (BEL) ($15,000) 1-7 NOVEMBER – **Singles:** Jeroen Masson (BEL) d. Richard Bloomfield (GBR) 61 61.
  Doubles: Jeroen Masson/Stefan Wauters (BEL) d. Dominique Coene (BEL)/Djalmar Sistermans (NED) 36 61 63.

- **HROTOVICE** (CZE) ($10,000) 8-14 NOVEMBER – **Singles:** Jakub Hasek (CZE) d. Leos Friedl (CZE) 75 64.
  Doubles: Martin Stepanek/Jiri Vrbka (CZE) d. Daniel Lustig/Jan Mertl (CZE) 64 36 64.

- **JIANGMEN** (CHN) ($10,000) 8-14 NOVEMBER – **Singles:** Peng Sun (CHN) d. Melvyn Op Der Heijde (NED) 63 60.
  Doubles: Flavio Cipolla/Alessandro Motti (ITA) d. Ti Chen (TPE)/Shuon Madden (USA) 76(4) 61.

- **PATTAYA, CHOLBURI** (THA) ($10,000) 8-14 NOVEMBER – **Singles:** Young-Jun Kim (KOR) d. Denis Gremelmayr (GER) 63 31 ret.
  Doubles: David Martin (USA)/Matwe Middelkoop (NED) d. Martin Slanar/Herbert Wiltschnig (AUT) 36 64 75.

- **QUERETARO** (MEX) ($10,000) 8-14 NOVEMBER – **Singles:** Santiago Gonzalez (MEX) d. Zbynek Mlynarik (AUT) 62 76(5).
  Doubles: Nick Monroe/Jeremy Wurtzman (USA) d. Ricardo Chile-Fonte/Sandor Martinez-Breijo (CUB) 63 62.

- **SANTIAGO** (CHI) ($15,000) 8-14 NOVEMBER – **Singles:** Diego Hartfield (ARG) d. Marko Neunteibl (AUT) 63 67(7) 62.
  Doubles: Lionel Noviski/Damian Patriarca (ARG) d. Patricio Rudi (ARG)/Juan-Felipe Yanez (CHI) w/o.

- **SANTOS** (BRA) ($10,000) 8-14 NOVEMBER – **Singles:** Thiago Alves (BRA) d. Agustin Tarantino (ARG) 64 64.
  Doubles: Thiago Alves/Thomaz Bellucci (BRA) d. Pablo Cuevas (URU)/Agustin Tarantino (ARG) 63 36 64.

- **WAIKOLOA, HI** (USA) ($15,000) 8-14 NOVEMBER – **Singles:** Horia Tecau (ROM) d. Wayne Odesnik (USA) 64 64.
  Doubles: Brendan Evans/Scott Oudsema (USA) d. Scoville Jenkins/Phillip Simmonds (USA) 67(4) 76(2) 64.

- **BERRI** (AUS) ($15,000) 15-21 NOVEMBER – **Singles:** Chris Guccione (AUS) d. Robert Smeets (AUS) 64 64.
  Doubles: Mark Hlawaty/Brad Weston (AUS) d. Goran Kovacevic/Chris Letcher (AUS) 62 63.

- **BRASILIA** (BRA) ($10,000) 15-21 NOVEMBER – **Singles:** Thiago Alves (BRA) d. Marcelo Melo (BRA) 64 62.
  Doubles: Marcelo Melo/Antonio Prieto (BRA) d. Thiago Alves/Thomaz Bellucci (BRA) 63 36 63.

- **GABORONE** (BOT) ($10,000) 15-21 NOVEMBER – **Singles:** Kevin Anderson (RSA) d. Wesley Whitehouse (RSA) 67(1) 64 76(13).
  Doubles: Kevin Anderson/Stephen Mitchell (RSA) d. Benjamin Janse van Rensburg/Wesley Whitehouse (RSA) 76(1) 76(5).

- **GRAN CANARIA** (ESP) ($15,000) 15-21 NOVEMBER – **Singles:** Frank Condor-Fernandez (ESP) d. Daniel Munoz-de la Nava (ESP) 76(3) 36 64.
  Doubles: Daniel Munoz-de la Nava/Carlos Rexach-Itoiz (ESP) d. Antonio Baldellou-Esteva/German Puentes-Alcaniz (ESP) 63 76(6).

- **GUANGZHOU** (CHN) ($10,000) 15-21 NOVEMBER – **Singles:** Ben-Qiang Zhu (CHN) d. Kyu-Tae Im (KOR) 63 36 60.
  Doubles: Murad Inoyatov/Denis Istomin (UZB) d. Flavio Cipolla/Alessandro Motti (ITA) 30 ret.

- **HONOLULU, HI** (USA) ($15,000) 15-21 NOVEMBER – **Singles:** Brendan Evans (USA) d. Wayne Odesnik (USA) 67(5) 76(2) 76(4).
  Doubles: Alex Kuznetsov (USA)/Horia Tecau (ROM) d. Zack Fleishman/Wayne Odesnik (USA) w/o.

- **KISH ISLAND** (IRI) ($15,000) 15-21 NOVEMBER – **Singles:** Marco Mirnegg (AUT) d. Manuel Jorquera (ITA) 61 67(10) 61.
  Doubles: Juan-Ignacio Cerda (CHI)/Jasper Smit (NED) d. Manuel Jorquera (ITA)/Lamine Ouahab (ALG) w/o.

- **MONTEVIDEO** (URU) ($10,000) 15-21 NOVEMBER – **Singles:** Diego Junqueira (ARG) d. Antonio Pastorino (ARG) 60 46 75.
  Doubles: Jorge Aguilar/Felipe Parada (CHI) d. Francisco Cabello/Diego Junqueira (ARG) 61 46 76(4).

- **SFAX** (TUN) ($10,000) 15-21 NOVEMBER – **Singles:** Ilija Bozoljac (SCG) d. Malek Jaziri (TUN) 75 36 75.
  Doubles: Maciej Dilaj (POL)/Stefan Wiespeiner (AUT) d. Ilija Bozoljac/Viktor Troicki (SCG) 16 63 61.

- **GRAN CANARIA** (ESP) ($15,000) 22-28 NOVEMBER – **Singles:** Daniel Munoz-de la Nava (ESP) d. Rui Machado (POR) 57 76(7) 76(4).
  Doubles: David De Miguel-Lapiedra (ESP)/Rui Machado (POR) d. Dusan Karol (CZE)/Roberto Menendez-Ferre (ESP) 46 75 75.

- **JIANGMEN** (CHN) ($10,000) 22-28 NOVEMBER – **Singles:** Melvyn Op Der Heijde (NED) d. Ben-Qiang Zhu (CHN) 64 62.
  Doubles: Flavio Cipolla/Alessandro Motti (ITA) d. Yu Zhang/Ben-Qiang Zhu (CHN) 76(3) 62.

- **KISH ISLAND** (IRI) ($15,000) 22-28 NOVEMBER – **Singles:** Frantisek Cermak (CZE) d. Marco Mirnegg (AUT) 75 60.
  Doubles: Juan-Ignacio Cerda (CHI)/Jasper Smit (NED) d. Benedikt Dorsch (GER)/Marko Neunteibl (AUT) 76(3) 46 63.

- **MONASTIR** (TUN) ($10,000) 22-28 NOVEMBER – **Singles:** Bostjan Osabnik (SLO) d. Maciej Dilaj (POL) 62 63.
  Doubles: Bostjan Osabnik/Grega Zemlja (SLO) d. Maciej Dilaj/Piotr Dilaj (POL) 76(3) 63.

- **PRETORIA** (RSA) ($10,000) 22-28 NOVEMBER – **Singles:** Justin Bower (RSA) d. Kevin Anderson (RSA) 63 76(3).
  Doubles: Stephen Mitchell/Shaun Rudman (RSA) d. Thomas Liversage/W. P. Meyer (RSA) 64 62.

- **ROSARIO, SANTA FE** (ARG) ($10,000) 22-28 NOVEMBER – **Singles:** Maximo Gonzalez (ARG) d. Rodolfo Daruich (ARG) 26 62 63.
  Doubles: Emiliano Redondi/Patricio Rudi (ARG) d. Francisco Cabello/Maximo Gonzalez (ARG) 36 64 76(2).

- **DOHA** (QAT) ($10,000) 29 NOVEMBER-5 DECEMBER – **Singles:** Zbynek Mlynarik (AUT) d. Ilia Kushev (BUL) 46 61 63.
  Doubles: Artem Sitak/Dmitri Sitak (RUS) d. Jaco Mathew/Ravishankar Pathanjali (IND) 63 63.

- **MEGRINE** (TUN) ($10,000) 29 NOVEMBER-5 DECEMBER – **Singles:** Bostjan Osabnik (SLO) d. Ismar Gorcic (BIH) 76(1) 62.
  Doubles: Heithem Abid/Malek Jaziri (TUN) d. Bostjan Osabnik/Grega Zemlja (SLO) 76(3) 63.

- **PRETORIA** (RSA) ($10,000) 29 NOVEMBER-5 DECEMBER – **Singles:** Jakub Hasek (CZE) d. Stephen Mitchell (RSA) 42 ret.
  Doubles: Stephen Mitchell/Shaun Rudman (RSA) d. Andrew Anderson/Paul Anderson (RSA) 61 57 76(4).

- **DOHA** (QAT) ($10,000) 6-10 DECEMBER – **Singles:** Aleksander Vlaski (SCG) d. Melvyn Op der Heijde (NED) 62 60.
  Doubles: Artem Sitak/Dmitri Sitak (RUS) d. Yordan Kanev/Ilia Kushev (BUL) 76(5) 60.

- **ORENSE** (ESP) ($10,000) 6-12 DECEMBER – **Singles:** Andrew Murray (GBR) d. Andis Juska (LAT) 16 63 75.
  Doubles: Javier Foronda-Bolanos/Daniel Monedero-Gonzalez (ESP) d. Nicolas Renavand/Nicolas Tourte (FRA) 64 64.

- **DOHA** (QAT) ($10,000) 13-19 DECEMBER – **Singles:** Melvyn Op der Heijde (NED) d. Artem Sitak (RUS) 64 63.
  Doubles: Artem Sitak/Dmitri Sitak (RUS) d. Yordan Kanev/Ilia Kushev (BUL) w/o.

- **PONTEVEDRA** (ESP) ($10,000) 13-19 DECEMBER – **Singles:** Andrew Murray (GBR) d. Nicolas Tourte (FRA) 64 57 75.
  Doubles: Adrian Cruciat (ROM)/Komlavi Loglo (TOG) d. Petar Popovic (SCG)/Nicolas Tourte (FRA) 75 46 63.

ITF Men's Circuit 2004 Satellite Results

Circuit (US$ Value)	Start date	Singles winner(s) (pts)	Doubles winner(s) (pts)
Spain 1 ($25,000)	5 Jan	Daniel Gimeno-Traver (ESP) (33)	Ion Moldovan (ROM) (29), Gabriel Moraru (ROM) (29)
Australia 1 ($25,000+H)	2 Feb	Filip Prpic (SWE) (43)	Mark Hlawaty (AUS) (39), Marc Kimmich (AUS) (39)
Great Britain 1 ($50,000)	9 Feb	Jamie Delgado (GBR)	Mark Hilton (GBR) (46), Jonathan Marray (GBR), Jonathan Marray (GBR) (46), Michael Ryderstedt (SWE) (34)
Switzerland 1 ($25,000)	9 Feb	Tobias Summerer (GER) (33)	Alexander Flock (GER) (33), Frederik Nielsen (DEN) (33)
Israel 1 ($25,000)	23 Feb	Mohamed-Sekou Drame (FRA) (33)	Julien Cassaigne (FRA) (33), Levar Harper-Griffith (USA) (33)

ITF Men's Circuit 2004 Satellite Results (continued)

Event	Date	Winner	Finalists
Italy 1 ($25,000)	1 Mar	Eric Prodon (FRA) (33)	Daniele Giorgini (ITA) (36), Manuel Jorquera (ITA) (36)
Spain 2 ($25,000)	1 Mar	Daniel Gimeno-Traver (ESP) (33)	Marc Fornell-Mestres (ESP) (34), Ferran Ventura-Martell (ESP) (34)
Chile 1 ($25,000)	8 Mar	Damian Patriarca (ARG) (25)	Brian Dabul (ARG) (33), Damian Patriarca (ARG) (33)
Croatia 1 ($25,000)	8 Mar	Sasa Tuksar (CRO) (34)	Kornel Bardoczky (HUN) (33), Marco Mirnegg (AUT) (33)
Sweden 1 ($25,000)	29 Mar	Johan Settergren (SWE) (33)	Frederik Nielsen (DEN) (34)
Turkey 1 ($25,000)	12 Apr	Jose Checa-Calvo (ESP) (30)	Antonio Baldellou-Esteva (ESP) (35), German Puentes-Alcaniz (ESP) (35)
Bulgaria 1 ($25,000)	3 May	Johannes Ager (AUT)	Lazar Magdincev (MKD) (35), Ilia Kushev (BUL) (33), Predrag Rusevski (MKD) (35)
Ukraine 1 ($25,000)	17 May	Alexander Markin (RUS) (34)	Sergei Krotiouk (RUS) (34), Deniss Pavlovs (LAT) (34)
India 1 ($25,000+H)	7 Jun	Norikazu Sugiyama (JPN) (43)	Ajay Ramaswami (IND) (44), Vishal Uppal (IND) (44)
Turkey 2 ($25,000)	7 Jun	Alan Mackin (GBR) (36)	Vincent Baudat (FRA) (33), Marcio Torres (BRA) (33)
China 1 Satellite ($25,000)	5 Jul	Peng Sun (CHN) (33)	Xin-Yuan Yu (CHN) (33), Yu Zhang (CHN) (33)
Venezuela 1 Satellite ($25,000)	26 Jul	Shannon Nettle (AUS) (31)	Michal Ciszek (CAN) (28)
Pakistan ($25,000)	9 Aug	Aqeel Khan (PAK) (36)	Mirko Pehar (USA) (34), Toshiaki Sakai (JPN) (34)
Switzerland 2 ($25,000)	23 Aug	Kevin Sorensen (IRL) (33)	Jun Kato (JPN) (35), Fabian Roetschi (SUI) (35)
Portugal 1 Satellite ($25,000)	13 Sep	Rui Machado (POR) (33)	Julien Maes (FRA) (30), Michal Varsanyi (SVK) (30)
Australia 2 Satellite ($25,000+H)	20 Sep	Marc Kimmich (AUS) (46)	Adam Feeney (AUS) (41)
Italy 3 Satellite ($25,000)	27 Sep	Daniele Giorgini (ITA) (35)	Fabio Colangelo (ITA) (34), Daniele Giorgini (ITA) (34)
Germany 1 Satellite ($25,000)	4 Oct	Jakob Herm-Zahlava (GER) (33)	Christopher Kas (GER) (32)
Ecuador Satellite ($25,000)	25 Oct	Rainer Eitzinger (AUT) (33)	Sebastian Decoud (ARG) (33), Pablo Gonzalez (COL) (33)
Great Britain 2 ($25,000)	25 Oct	Mark Hilton (GBR) (33)	Lee Childs (GBR) (36), Daniel Kiernan (GBR) (36)
Italy 4 Satellite ($25,000)	25 Oct	Stefano Galvani (ITA) (34)	Stefano Galvani (ITA) (33), Federico Torresi (ITA) (33)
India 2 Satellite ($25,000+H)	8 Nov	Simon Greul (GER) (45)	Mustafa Ghouse (IND) (44), Vishal Uppal (IND) (44)
Israel 2 Satellite ($25,000)	8 Nov	Lazar Magdincev (MKD) (36)	Lazar Magdincev (MKD) (34), Denis Matsukevitch (RUS) (34)
Indonesia 1 Satellite ($25,000)	22 Nov	Alan Mackin (GBR) (33)	Hendri-Susilo Pramono (INA) (34), Febi Widhiyanto (INA) (34)

BIG BANGER
Strings for winners !

65 % of the ATP Top 100 play with Big Banger strings. Do you ?

40 % of the WTA Top 100 play with Big Banger strings. Do you ?

LUXILON SPORTS

Industriepark / Vosveld 11
B-2210 Antwerp, Belgium
Tel. ++32(0)3 326 33 88
Fax ++32(0)3 326 33 24
www.bigbanger.com

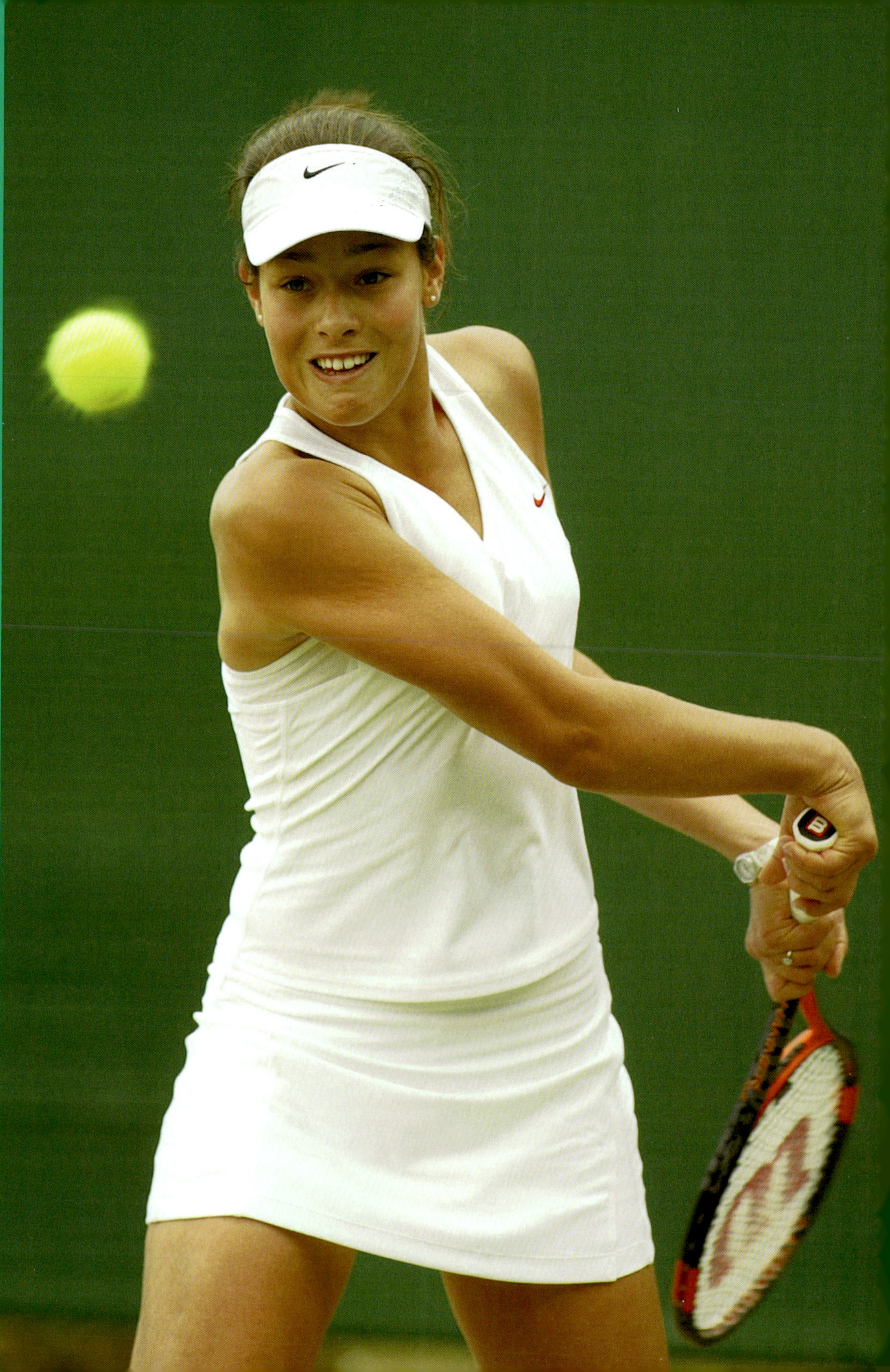

ITF Women's Circuit 2004

In 2004 the ITF Women's Circuit passed yet another landmark in its twenty-one year history. For the first time since 1983 and the inception of the Circuit the total available prize money was in excess of $7 million, an increase of almost $1 million on the previous year's total. The total prize money available is a direct result of the organisation of 349 tournaments in 62 countries.

Over the past 21 years the Circuit has maintained a continual increase in terms of the number of events on the calendar and the prize money available, and provides over 28,000 playing opportunities annually where female players acquire competitive experience together with earning the ranking points necessary for gaining acceptance into professional events. Women's Circuit events are categorised into four levels of individual weeklong tournaments offering total prize money of $10,000, $25,000, $50,000 and $75,000 and are eligible for WTA Computer Credit. The ITF Women's Circuit provides an essential bridge between Junior Circuit, the WTA Tour and the Grand Slams.

The global representation of Circuit tournaments shows that the majority of the events (195) take place in Europe. North America continues to provide many playing opportunities, with 44 tournaments taking place in the USA and Canada. In 2004 the growth of the Circuit continued in Africa where 17 tournaments were organised. A total of 64 events took place in Asia and Oceania with 29 tournaments taking place in South America and Central America.

Among those players who have achieved notable advancement on the rankings during 2004 are Nicole Vaidisova of the Czech Republic and Ana Ivanovic from Serbia & Montenegro. Although Nicole started the year unranked on the Professional Circuit, she placed eighth on the year-end ITF Junior World Rankings. As a consequence of her Junior year-end ranking Nicole qualified for the Junior Exempt Project and won her first selected event in Columbus, Ohio in February. This $25,000 event was a designated ITF/WTA Feed Up tournament and Nicole took the opportunity to participate in the WTA event in Acapulco scheduled in March. By doing well in Acapulco Nicole got off to a tremendous start to the year and, in addition to her Circuit title in the USA, she won two WTA Tour titles and ended the year 77 on the rankings. Her success can be attributed in part to taking advantage of and participating in the two major ITF Women's Circuit programmes, the Junior Exempt Project and the ITF/WTA Feed Up system. Ana Ivanovic, at seventeen years of age, won all five Circuit events entered and moved up an incredible 509 places on the rankings during the year to finish in 97 position. Other players who have achieved excellent results on the Circuit and deserve a mention are Sania Mirza from India, Hana Sromova and Lucie Hradecka of the Czech Republic and Na Li from China. Sania reached eight Circuit finals, winning six of them, whereas Hana and Lucie posted a 100% record in the six and five finals they reached respectively. Na Li was successful in five finals during the year, four of her triumphs coming in an incredible month long 20-match winning streak from 17 May to 14 June.

The Junior Exempt Project, which rewards the year-end top 10 female Junior players by given them direct acceptance into the Main Draw of three selected ITF $25,000, $50,000 and $75,000 events, continues to be successful and many of the players who have benefited from the Project now feature in the top 100 ranked players. Congratulations go to the following Junior Exempts in the 2004 programme all of whom reached either the semifinal or final rounds of at least one of their selected Junior Exempt tournaments; Kirsten Flipkens (BEL), Michaella Krajicek (NED), Alisa Kleybanova (RUS), Emma Laine (FIN), Katerina Bohmova (CZE), Nicole Vaidisova (CZE) and Vojislava Lukic (SCG).

By achieving success at their chosen events, as Nicole Vaidisova demonstrated, Junior Exempts can advance even further by taking advantage of the Feed Up system that offers the winner of selected $25,000 ITF Women's Circuit events the opportunity of securing a spot in the qualifying draw of a designated WTA Tour tournament. The winner of selected $50,000/$75,000 ITF Women's Circuit events has the opportunity of securing a spot in the main draw of a designated WTA Tour tournament.

The Women's Circuit aims to provide a balanced the calendar, giving players around the world the best access to tournaments upon which to build their careers.

In October 2004, the first phase of an initiative that will revolutionise the running of the ITF Pro Circuit, was launched. All players competing on the ITF Pro Circuit, will be allocated a unique number, known as the International Player Identification Number, or IPIN. The IPIN will make it possible to communicate more effectively with players via the internet and will improve the flow of information back to the ITF. The first system to take advantage of the IPIN will be a new Online Service which will allow all players to manage their ITF Pro Circuit entries via a specially designed website. For more information regarding IPIN, visit www.iftennis.com/ipin

Ana Ivanovic (SCG) won five ITF Women's Circuit events in 2004

ITF Women's Circuit 2004 Results

- **$10,000 DUBAI** (UAE) 12-18 JANUARY – **Singles:** Hana Sromova (CZE) d. Goulnara Fattakhetdinova (RUS) 46 75 63.
  Doubles: Goulnara Fattakhetdinova (RUS)/Hana Sromova (CZE) d. Daniella Klemenschits/Sandra Klemenschits (AUT) 63 46 64.

- **$10,000 HYDERABAD** (IND) 12-17 JANUARY – **Singles:** Sandy Gumulya (INA) d. Rushmi Chakravarthi (IND) 61 63.
  Doubles: Isha Lakhani/Meghaa Vakharia (IND) d. Rushmi Chakravarthi/Jayaram-Sai Jayalaksamy (IND) 75 57 63.

- **$10,000 TAMPA, FL** (USA) 12-18 JANUARY – **Singles:** Nan-Nan Liu (CHN) d. Kristen Schlukebir (USA) 63 61.
  Doubles: Alisa Kleybanova (RUS)/Mayumi Yamamoto (JPN) d. Milangela Morales/Sunitha Rao (USA) 62 64.

- **$10,000 BOCA RATON, FL** (USA) 19-25 JANUARY – **Singles:** Kelly McCain (USA) d. Nan-Nan Liu (CHN) 61 36 60.
  Doubles: Shuai Peng/Yan-Ze Xie (CHN) d. Allison Bradshaw/Julie Ditty (USA) 61 62.

- **$10,000 GRENOBLE** (FRA) 19-25 JANUARY – **Singles:** Martina Muller (GER) d. Aravane Rezai (FRA) 75 61.
  Doubles: Martina Muller/Stefanie Weis (GER) d. Antonia Matic (GER)/Lenka Tvaroskova (SVK) 62 61.

- **$10,000 HULL** (GBR) 19-25 JANUARY – **Singles:** Amanda Janes (GBR) d. Anna Bastrikova (RUS) 63 61.
  Doubles: Claire Curran (IRL)/Surina De Beer (RSA) d. Anna Bastrikova/Vasilisa Davydova (RUS) 60 64.

- **$10,000 MANAMA** (BRN) 19-25 JANUARY – **Singles:** Jennifer Schmidt (AUT) d. Frederica Piedade (POR) 64 63.
  Doubles: Raissa Gourevitch/Ekaterina Kozhokhina (RUS) d. Frederica Piedade (POR)/Christina Zachariadou (GRE) 64 64.

- **$10,000 NEW DELHI** (IND) 19-24 JANUARY – **Singles:** Montinee Tangphong (THA) d. Isha Lakhani (IND) 26 62 63.
  Doubles: Montinee Tangphong/Thassha Vitayaviroj (THA) d. Satomi Kinjo/Tomoyo Takagishi (JPN) 36 60 63.

- **$10,000 BOCA RATON, FL** (USA) 26 JANUARY-1 FEBRUARY – **Singles:** Sania Mirza (IND) d. Cory-Ann Avants (USA) 63 62.
  Doubles: Allison Bradshaw/Julie Ditty (USA) d. Natalia Dziamidzenka (BLR)/Sania Mirza (IND) 63 61.

- **$10,000 TIPTON** (GBR) 26 JANUARY-1 FEBRUARY – **Singles:** Emma Laine (FIN) d. Liana Balaci (ROM) 67(4) 62 63.
  Doubles: Rebecca Llewellyn/Melanie South (GBR) d. Klaudia Jans/Alicia Rosolska (POL) 26 61 64.

- **$25,000 BELFORT** (FRA) 26 JANUARY-1 FEBRUARY – **Singles:** Marta Domachowska (POL) d. Adriana Barna (GER) 36 60 60.
  Doubles: Olga Blahotova/Gabriela Navratilova (CZE) d. Kim Kilsdonk (NED)/Sophie Lefevre (FRA) 63 62.

- **$25,000 BERGAMO** (ITA) 26 JANUARY-1 FEBRUARY – **Singles:** Lucie Safarova (CZE) d. Iva Majoli (CRO) 36 76(1) 61.
  Doubles: Alberta Brianti (ITA)/Kildine Chevalier (FRA) d. Iva Majoli/Sanda Mamic (CRO) 64 64.

- **$50,000 WAIKOLOA, HI** (USA) 26 JANUARY-1 FEBRUARY – **Singles:** Melinda Czink (HUN) d. Maria-Emilia Salerni (ARG) 76(6) 62.
  Doubles: Gisela Dulko/Patricia Tarabini (ARG) d. Amanda Augustus (USA)/Natalie Grandin (RSA) 16 63 63.

- **$10,000 VALE DO LOBO** (POR) 2-8 FEBRUARY – **Singles:** Liana Balaci (ROM) d. Servane Delobelle (FRA) 62 64.
  Doubles: Kildine Chevalier (FRA)/Frederica Piedade (POR) d. Soledad Esperon/Flavia Mignola (ARG) 26 63 64.

- **$10,000 WELLINGTON** (NZL) 2-8 FEBRUARY – **Singles:** Cindy Watson (AUS) d. Lauren Breadmore (AUS) 64 61.
  Doubles: Shelley Stephens (NZL)/Kristen Van Elden (AUS) d. Emily Hewson/Nicole Kriz (AUS) 61 36 63.

- **$25,000 ROCKFORD, IL** (USA) 2-8 FEBRUARY – **Singles:** Lindsay Lee-Waters (USA) d. Gisela Dulko (ARG) 64 75.
  Doubles: Mariana Diaz-Oliva/Gisela Dulko (ARG) d. Leanne Baker (NZL)/Francesca Lubiani (ITA) 67(5) 63 61.

- **$75,000 ORTISEI** (ITA) 2-8 FEBRUARY – **Singles:** Iveta Benesova (CZE) d. Virag Nemeth (HUN) 63 61.
  Doubles: Olga Blahotova/Gabriela Navratilova (CZE) d. Lubomira Bacheva (BUL)/Angelika Roesch (GER) 61 63.

- **$10,000 ALBUFEIRA** (POR) 9-15 FEBRUARY – **Singles:** Monica Niculescu (ROM) d. Irina Kotkina (RUS) 61 36 60.
  Doubles: Zuzana Cerna/Vladmira Uhlirova (CZE) d. Kildine Chevalier (FRA)/Frederica Piedade (POR) 67(4) 64 75.

- **$10,000 MALLORCA** (ESP) 9-15 FEBRUARY – **Singles:** Laura Pous-Tio (ESP) d. Ana Timotic (SCG) 46 63 60.
  Doubles: Rosa-Maria Andres-Rodriguez (ESP)/Ana Timotic (SCG) d. Lourdes Dominguez-Lino/Laura Pous-Tio (ESP) 36 64 64.

- **$25,000 SUNDERLAND** (GBR) 9-15 FEBRUARY – **Singles:** Kaia Kanepi (EST) d. Anna Chakvetadze (RUS) 76(5) 60.
  Doubles: Claire Curran (IRL)/Kim Kilsdonk (NED) d. Helen Crook (GBR)/Martina Muller (GER) 64 36 63.

- **$25,000 WARSAW** (POL) 9-15 FEBRUARY – **Singles:** Marta Domachowska (POL) d. Angelique Kerber (GER) 76(5) 36 63.
  Doubles: Klaudia Jans/Alicia Rosolska (POL) d. Zsofia Gubacsi/Kyra Nagy (HUN) 64 63.

- **$75,000 MIDLAND, MI** (USA) 9-15 FEBRUARY – **Singles:** Jill Craybas (USA) d. Nicole Vaidisova (CZE) 62 64.
  Doubles: Sofia Arvidsson/Asa Svensson (SWE) d. Allison Baker/Tara Snyder (USA) 76(5) 62.

- **$10,000 CAPRIOLO** (ITA) 16-22 FEBRUARY – **Singles:** Emma Laine (FIN) d. Nika Ozegovic (CRO) 76(6) 67(4) 76(4).
  Doubles: Emma Laine/Essi Laine (FIN) d. Jolanda Mens (NED)/Stefanie Weis (GER) 63 63.

- **$10,000 MALLORCA** (ESP) 16-22 FEBRUARY – **Singles:** Ana Ivanovic (SCG) d. Ana Timotic (SCG) 61 61.

- **$10,000 PORTIMAO** (POR) 16-22 FEBRUARY – **Singles:** Monica Niculescu (ROM) d. Nadja Pavic (CRO) 64 76(3).
  Doubles: Soledad Esperon/Flavia Mignola (ARG) d. Florence Haring/Alexandra Mayrat (FRA) 61 61.

- **$25,000 COLUMBUS, OH** (USA) 16-22 FEBRUARY – **Singles:** Nicole Vaidisova (CZE) d. Shuai Peng (CHN) 76(2) 75.
  Doubles: Stanislava Hrozenska (SVK)/Lenka Nemeckova (CZE) d. Leanne Baker (NZL)/Francesca Lubiani (ITA) 76(3) 46 63.

- **$25,000 REDBRIDGE** (GBR) 16-22 FEBRUARY – **Singles:** Anna Chakvetadze (RUS) d. Virginie Pichet (FRA) 62 62.
  Doubles: Claire Curran (IRL)/Kim Kilsdonk (NED) d. Olga Blahotova/Gabriela Navratilova (CZE) 63 36 76(10).

- **$10,000 BENIN CITY** (NGR) 23-28 FEBRUARY – **Singles:** Chanelle Scheepers (RSA) d. Meghaa Vakharia (IND) 61 63.
  Doubles: Zuzana Cerna (CZE)/Franziska Etzel (GER) d. Chanelle Scheepers (RSA)/Jennifer Schmidt (AUT) 60 57 63.

- **$10,000 GRAN CANARIA** (ESP) 23-28 FEBRUARY – **Singles:** Laura Pous-Tio (ESP) d. Nuria Roig-Tost (ESP) 57 62 76(3).
  Doubles: Maria-Jose Argeri (ARG)/Leticia Sobral (BRA) d. Eszter Molnar (HUN)/Maria Wolfbrandt (SWE) 63 63.

- **$25,000 BENDIGO** (AUS) 23-28 FEBRUARY – **Singles:** Shahar Peer (ISR) d. Suchanun Viratprasert (THA) 64 75.
  Doubles: Casey Dell'Acqua/Nicole Sewell (AUS) d. Shahar Peer (ISR)/Wynne Prakusya (INA) 62 16 62.

- **$50,000 ST PAUL, MN** (USA) 23-28 FEBRUARY – **Singles:** Abigail Spears (USA) d. Jill Craybas (USA) 63 64.
  Doubles: Leanne Baker (NZL)/Francesca Lubiani (ITA) d. Jessica Lehnhoff (USA)/Trudi Musgrave (AUS) 67(3) 23 ret.

- **$10,000 BENIN CITY** (NGR) 1-7 MARCH – **Singles:** Chanelle Scheepers (RSA) d. Susanne Aigner (AUT) 61 46 64.
  Doubles: Alanna Broderick (JAM)/Chanelle Scheepers (RSA) d. Zuzana Cerna (CZE)/Franziska Etzel (GER) 62 62.

- **$10,000 BUCHEN** (GER) 1-7 MARCH – **Singles:** Amanda Janes (GBR) d. Eva Hrdinova (CZE) 63 62.
  Doubles: Lucie Hradecka/Eva Hrdinova (CZE) d. Elke Clijsters/Caroline Maes (BEL) 61 64.

- **$10,000 MELILLA** (ESP) 1-7 MARCH – **Singles:** Nina Bratchikova (RUS) d. Frederica Piedade (POR) 62 64.
  Doubles: Nina Bratchikova/Alla Kudryavtseva (RUS) d. Anastasia Dvornikova (RUS)/Irina Nossenko (UKR) 75 63.

- **$10,000 WARRNAMBOOL** (AUS) 1-7 MARCH – **Singles:** Casey Dell'Acqua (AUS) d. Nicole Sewell (AUS) 63 36 62.
  Doubles: Eden Marama/Paula Marama (NZL) d. Casey Dell'Acqua/Jaslyn Hewitt (AUS) 63 46 62.

- **$10,000 BENALLA** (AUS) 8-14 MARCH – **Singles:** Eden Marama (NZL) d. Cindy Watson (AUS) 63 46 64.
  Doubles: Eden Marama/Paula Marama (NZL) d. Lauren Breadmore (AUS)/Kaysie Smashey (USA) 75 61.

- **$10,000 ROMA** (ITA) 8-14 MARCH – **Singles:** Alberta Brianti (ITA) d. Tereza Veverkova (CZE) 64 46 62.
  Doubles: Alice Canepa/Emily Stellato (ITA) d. Daniella Klemenschits/Sandra Klemenschits (AUT) 63 26 64.

- **$10,000 AMIENS** (FRA) 15-21 MARCH – **Singles:** Vanessa Henke (GER) d. Virginie Razzano (FRA) 76(5) 64.
  Doubles: Caroline Maes (BEL)/Virginie Pichet (FRA) d. Florence Haring (FRA)/Natacha Randriantefy (MAD) 36 62 75.

ITF Women's Circuit 2004 Results (continued)

- **$10,000 RAMAT HASHARON** (ISR) 15-21 MARCH – **Singles:** Frederica Piedade (POR) d. Cheli Bargil (ISR) 46 61 60.
  Doubles: Iveta Gerlova (CZE)/Frederica Piedade (POR) d. Julia Gandia-Gomez/Gabriela Velasco-Andreu (ESP) 62 46 62.

- **$10,000 ROMA LANCIANI** (ITA) 15-21 MARCH – **Singles:** Lourdes Dominguez-Lino (ESP) d. Marta Fraga-Perez (ESP) 61 62.
  Doubles: Alice Canepa/Emily Stellato (ITA) d. Zuzana Hejdova (CZE)/Lenka Tvaroskova (SVK) 46 61 75.

- **$10,000 YARRAWONGA** (AUS) 15-21 MARCH – **Singles:** Paula Marama (NZL) d. Meng Yuan (CHN) w/o.
  Doubles: Beti Sekulovski/Cindy Watson (AUS) d. Emily Hewson/Nicole Kriz (AUS) 63 46 64.

- **$50,000 ORANGE, CA** (USA) 15-21 MARCH – **Singles:** Yulia Beygelzimer (UKR) d. Evgenia Linetskaya (RUS) 63 26 62.
  Doubles: Jennifer Hopkins/Abigail Spears (USA) d. Bryanne Stewart (AUS)/Mashona Washington (USA) 63 26 60.

- **$10,000 CAIRO** (EGY) 22-28 MARCH – **Singles:** Hana Sromova (CZE) d. Gabriela Velasco-Andreu (ESP) 63 61.
  Doubles: Eva Martincova/Hana Sromova (CZE) d. Raissa Gourevitch/Ekaterina Kozhokhina (RUS) 61 60.

- **$10,000 ALICANTE** (ESP) 22-28 MARCH – **Singles:** Romina Oprandi (ITA) d. Nuria Roig-Tost (ESP) 62 63.
  Doubles: Lourdes Dominguez-Lino (ESP)/Frederica Piedade (POR) d. Andrea Hlavackova/Jana Hlavackova (CZE) w/o.

- **$10,000 MONTERREY** (MEX) 22-28 MARCH – **Singles:** Alexandra Mueller (USA) d. Natalia Garbellotto (ARG) 57 61 64.
  Doubles: Katie Granson/Sarah Riske (USA) d. Stephanie Schaer (VEN)/Ayami Takase (JPN) 46 75 61.

- **$10,000 ROMA** (ITA) 22-28 MARCH – **Singles:** Alice Canepa (ITA) d. Margot Torre (ITA) 63 61.
  Doubles: Alice Canepa/Emily Stellato (ITA) d. Elisa Balsamo/Giulia Meruzzi (ITA) 76(0) 63.

- **$10,000 YARRAWONGA** (AUS) 22-28 MARCH – **Singles:** Emily Hewson (AUS) d. Kavitha Krishnamurthy (CAN) 67(4) 76(6) 63.
  Doubles: Emily Hewson/Nicole Kriz (AUS) d. Mirielle Dittmann/Kristen Van Elden (AUS) 63 62.

- **$25,000 ATHENS** (GRE) 22-28 MARCH – **Singles:** Virginie Pichet (FRA) d. Katerina Bohmova (CZE) 61 62.
  Doubles: Liga Dekmeijere (LAT)/Martina Muller (GER) d. Zsofia Gubacsi/Kyra Nagy (HUN) 62 16 64.

- **$25,000 REDDING, CA** (USA) 22-28 MARCH – **Singles:** Anne Keothavong (GBR) d. Mashona Washington (USA) 63 26 76(3).
  Doubles: Jennifer Hopkins/Mashona Washington (USA) d. Lilia Osterloh/Riza Zalameda (USA) 62 64.

- **$50,000 ST PETERSBURG** (RUS) 22-28 MARCH – **Singles:** Anastasia Yakimova (BLR) d. Emma Laine (FIN) 36 62 61.
  Doubles: Maria Goloviznina/Evgenia Kulikovskaya (RUS) d. Daria Kustava (BLR)/Elena Tatarkova (UKR) 75 61.

- **$10,000 CAIRO** (EGY) 29 MARCH-4 APRIL – **Singles:** Gaelle Widmer (SUI) d. Marina Shamayko (RUS) 36 64 76(5).
  Doubles: Raissa Gourevitch/Ekaterina Kozhokhina (RUS) d. Olena Antypina (UKR)/Lioudmila Nikoian (ARM) 62 60.

- **$10,000 CAVTAT** (CRO) 29 MARCH-4 APRIL – **Singles:** Lucie Hradecka (CZE) d. Lenka Tvaroskova (SVK) 75 60.
  Doubles: Nadja Pavic/Ivana Visic (CRO) d. Ljiljana Nanusevic (SCG)/Lenka Tvaroskova (SVK) 76(1) 76(6).

- **$10,000 MUMBAI** (IND) 29 MARCH-4 APRIL – **Singles:** Melanie South (GBR) d. Yan-Chong Chen (CHN) 64 64.
  Doubles: Shu-Jing Yang/Ying Yu (CHN) d. Yan Hua Dong/Jie Hao (CHN) 62 62.

- **$10,000 NAPOLI** (ITA) 29 MARCH-4 APRIL – **Singles:** Kirsten Flipkens (BEL) d. Mandy Minella (LUX) 57 63 61.
  Doubles: Elke Clijsters (BEL)/Mandy Minella (LUX) d. Michelle Gerards/Marielle Hoogland (NED) 61 60.

- **$10,000 OBREGON** (MEX) 29 MARCH-4 APRIL – **Singles:** Ayami Takase (JPN) d. Sarah Riske (USA) 76(5) 62.
  Doubles: Soledad Esperon/Flavia Mignola (ARG) d. Stephanie Schaer (VEN)/Ayami Takase (JPN) 26 64 64.

- **$10,000 PATRAS** (GRE) 29 MARCH-4 APRIL – **Singles:** Ekaterina Dzehalevich (BLR) d. Martina Muller (GER) 64 64.
  Doubles: Martina Muller (GER)/Vladmira Uhlirova (CZE) d. Chantal Coombs/Emily Webley-Smith (GBR) 76(7) 63.

- **$10,000 RABAT** (MAR) 29 MARCH-4 APRIL – **Singles:** Bahia Mouhtassine (MAR) d. Sania Mirza (IND) 62 75.
  Doubles: Maria-Fernanda Alves/Carla Tiene (BRA) d. Daniella Klemenschits/Sandra Klemenschits (AUT) 61 76(5).

- **$25,000 AUGUSTA, GA** (USA) 29 MARCH-4 APRIL – **Singles:** Tara Snyder (USA) d. Vilmarie Castellvi (PUR) 75 62.
  Doubles: Francesca Lubiani (ITA)/Mashona Washington (USA) d. Julie Ditty/Jessica Lehnhoff (USA) 61 63.

- **$10,000 CAIRO** (EGY) 5-11 APRIL – **Singles:** Hana Sromova (CZE) d. Annette Kolb (GER) w/o.
  Doubles: Simona Dobra/Hana Sromova (CZE) d. Helena Ejeson (SWE)/Annette Kolb (GER) w/o.

- **$10,000 MAKARSKA** (CRO) 5-11 APRIL – **Singles:** Lucia Krzelj (CRO) d. Mervana Jugic-Salkic (BIH) 62 75.
  Doubles: Martina Babakova (SVK)/Iveta Gerlova (CZE) d. Maria Penkova (BUL)/Lisa Tognetti (ITA) 61 64.

- **$10,000 NEW DELHI** (IND) 5-11 APRIL – **Singles:** Chia-Jung Chuang (TPE) d. Jie Hao (CHN) 63 61.
  Doubles: Shu-Jing Yang/Ying Yu (CHN) d. Chia-Jung Chuang (TPE)/Chin-Bee Khoo (MAS) 76(8) 21 ret.

- **$10,000 TORRE DEL GRECO** (ITA) 5-11 APRIL – **Singles:** Emma Laine (FIN) d. Chanelle Scheepers (RSA) 36 64 60.
  Doubles: Jolanda Mens (NED)/Chanelle Scheepers (RSA) d. Michelle Gerards/Marielle Hoogland (NED) 63 60.

- **$50,000 DINAN** (FRA) 5-11 APRIL – **Singles:** Timea Bacsinszky (SUI) d. Tzipi Obziler (ISR) 62 61.
  Doubles: Darija Jurak (CRO)/Galina Voskoboeva (RUS) d. Goulnara Fattakhetdinova/Anastasia Rodionova (RUS) 63 62.

- **$10,000 BOL** (CRO) 12-18 APRIL – **Singles:** Lucie Hradecka (CZE) d. Romina Oprandi (ITA) 64 63.
  Doubles: Anna Bastrikova/Alla Kudryavtseva (RUS) d. Viktoria Azarenka/Volha Havartsova (BLR) 64 61.

- **$10,000 MORELIA** (MEX) 12-18 APRIL – **Singles:** Natalia Garbellotto (ARG) d. Ipek Senoglu (TUR) 64 46 64.
  Doubles: Katie Granson/Sarah Riske (USA) d. Fernanda Caputi/Marcela Evangelista (BRA) 62 60.

- **$10,000 YAMAGUCHI** (JPN) 12-18 APRIL – **Singles:** So-Jung Kim (KOR) d. Chin-Wei Chan (TPE) 76(7) 62.
  Doubles: Chie Nagano/Keiko Taguchi (JPN) d. Hiroko Komori/Tomoko Sugano (JPN) 64 61.

- **$25,000 BIARRITZ** (FRA) 12-18 APRIL – **Singles:** Bahia Mouhtassine (MAR) d. Laura Pous-Tio (ESP) 64 76(4).
  Doubles: Maria Koryttseva/Elena Tatarkova (UKR) d. Alyona Bondarenko/Valeria Bondarenko (UKR) 75 60.

- **$25,000 HO CHI MINH CITY** (VIE) 12-18 APRIL – **Singles:** Suchanun Viratprasert (THA) d. Goulnara Fattakhetdinova (RUS) 64 60.
  Doubles: Rika Fujiwara/Aiko Nakamura (JPN) d. Olena Antypina (UKR)/Goulnara Fattakhetdinova (RUS) 63 63.

- **$25,000 JACKSON, MS** (USA) 12-18 APRIL – **Singles:** Evgenia Linetskaya (RUS) d. Alisa Kleybanova (RUS) 46 62 64.
  Doubles: Stephanie Dubois (CAN)/Alisa Kleybanova (RUS) d. Cory-Ann Avants/Kristen Schlukebir (USA) 62 63.

- **$10,000 HAMANAKO** (JPN) 19-25 APRIL – **Singles:** Tiffany Dabek (USA) d. Chin-Wei Chan (TPE) 62 63.
  Doubles: Hye-Mi Kim (KOR)/Keiko Taguchi (JPN) d. Chin-Wei Chan/Yi Chen (TPE) 61 61.

- **$10,000 HVAR** (CRO) 19-25 APRIL – **Singles:** Tereza Veverkova (CZE) d. Sandra Martinovic (BIH) 64 63.
  Doubles: Zuzana Cerna/Tereza Veverkova (CZE) d. Daniela Kix (AUT)/Sandra Martinovic (BIH) 46 64 76(5).

- **$25,000 BARI** (ITA) 19-25 APRIL – **Singles:** Alyona Bondarenko (UKR) d. Katerina Bondarenko (UKR) 26 62 64.
  Doubles: Rosa-Maria Andres-Rodriguez/Conchita Martinez-Granados (ESP) d. Martina Muller (GER)/Vladmira Uhlirova (CZE) 62 57 62.

- **$25,000 POZA RICA** (MEX) 19-25 APRIL – **Singles:** Jessica Kirkland (USA) d. Frederica Piedade (POR) 63 62.
  Doubles: Lourdes Dominguez-Lino (ESP)/Frederica Piedade (POR) d. Jorgelina Cravero (ARG)/Ipek Senoglu (TUR) 75 60.

- **$75,000 DOTHAN, AL** (USA) 19-25 APRIL – **Singles:** Shuai Peng (CHN) d. Evgenia Linetskaya (RUS) 62 61.
  Doubles: Lisa McShea (AUS)/Milagros Sequera (VEN) d. Shuai Peng/Yan-Ze Xie (CHN) 67(6) 64 62.

- **$10,000 BOURNEMOUTH** (GBR) 26 APRIL-2 MAY – **Singles:** Elke Clijsters (BEL) d. Melanie South (GBR) 36 61 62.
  Doubles: Jaslyn Hewitt (AUS)/Nicole Rencken (RSA) d. Raissa Gourevitch/Ekaterina Kozhokhina (RUS) 61 76(3).

- **$10,000 JAKARTA** (INA) 26 APRIL-1 MAY – **Singles:** So-Jung Kim (KOR) d. Liza Andriyani (INA) 62 62.
  Doubles: Septi Mende/Wukirasih Sawondari (INA) d. Kumiko Iijima/Mari Inoue (JPN) 62 63.

ITF Women's Circuit 2004 Results (continued)

- **$10,000 MOSTAR** (BIH) 26 APRIL-2 MAY – **Singles:** Diana Stojic (BIH) d. Adriana Basaric (BIH) 64 63.
  Doubles: Evie Dominikovic (AUS)/Nadja Pavic (CRO) d. Borka Majstorovic (SCG)/Nika Ozegovic (CRO) 64 61.

- **$25,000 COATZACOALCOS** (MEX) 26 APRIL-2 MAY – **Singles:** Jessica Kirkland (USA) d. Laura Pous-Tio (ESP) 60 64.
  Doubles: Soledad Esperon/Flavia Mignola (ARG) d. Lourdes Dominguez-Lino/Laura Pous-Tio (ESP) 60 61.

- **$25,000 TARANTO** (ITA) 26 APRIL-2 MAY – **Singles:** Martina Muller (GER) d. Nina Bratchikova (RUS) 63 62.
  Doubles: Daniella Klemenschits/Sandra Klemenschits (AUT) d. Stefanie Haidner/Patricia Wartusch (AUT) 62 61.

- **$50,000 GIFU** (JPN) 26 APRIL-2 MAY – **Singles:** Ana Ivanovic (SCG) d. Mi-Ra Jeon (KOR) 64 26 75.
  Doubles: Yoon-Jeong Cho/Mi-Ra Jeon (KOR) d. Chia-Jung Chuang (TPE)/Wynne Prakusya (INA) 76(4) 62.

- **$75,000 CAGNES SUR MER** (FRA) 26 APRIL-2 MAY – **Singles:** Severine Beltrame (FRA) d. Anna-Lena Groenefeld (GER) 64 64.
  Doubles: Lubomira Bacheva (BUL)/Eva Birnerova (CZE) d. Ruxandra Dragomir-Ilie (ROM)/Antonia Matic (GER) 46 76(4) 63.

- **$10,000 EDINBURGH** (GBR) 3-9 MAY – **Singles:** Ekaterina Kozhokhina (RUS) d. Elke Clijsters (BEL) 61 64.
  Doubles: Anna Hawkins (GBR)/Nicole Rencken (RSA) d. Raissa Gourevitch/Ekaterina Kozhokhina (RUS) 76(3) 62.

- **$10,000 JAKARTA** (INA) 3-9 MAY – **Singles:** Liza Andriyani (INA) d. Sandy Gumulya (INA) 63 62.
  Doubles: Septi Mende/Wukirasih Sawondari (INA) d. Liza Andriyani (INA)/Thassha Vitayaviroj (THA) 64 63.

- **$10,000 MERIDA** (MEX) 3-9 MAY – **Singles:** Andrea Benitez (ARG) d. Maria Wolfbrandt (SWE) 64 63.
  Doubles: Erika Clarke (MEX)/Anne Mall (USA) d. Andrea Benitez/Bettina Jozami (ARG) 75 75.

- **$10,000 TORTOSA** (ESP) 3-9 MAY – **Singles:** Marta Fraga-Perez (ESP) d. Claudia Jorda-Fernandez (ESP) 64 64.
  Doubles: Marta Fraga-Perez/Nuria Sanchez-Garcia (ESP) d. Estrella Cabeza-Candela/Katia Sabate-Orera (ESP) 46 64 64.

- **$10,000 WARSAW** (POL) 3-9 MAY – **Singles:** Danica Krstajic (SCG) d. Tereza Veverkova (CZE) 06 75 62.
  Doubles: Olga Brozda/Monika Schneider (POL) d. Natalia Bogdanova/Valeria Bondarenko (UKR) 26 64 62.

- **$25,000 CATANIA** (ITA) 3-9 MAY – **Singles:** Stephanie Foretz (FRA) d. Kathrin Woerle (GER) 64 67(2) 62.
  Doubles: Stephanie Foretz/Virginie Razzano (FRA) d. Maria Koryttseva (UKR)/Nadejda Ostrovskaya (BLR) 62 61.

- **$50,000 FUKUOKA** (JPN) 3-9 MAY – **Singles:** Ana Ivanovic (SCG) d. Jarmila Gajdosova (SVK) 62 67(4) 76(4).
  Doubles: Rika Fujiwara/Saori Obata (JPN) d. Monique Adamczak/Nicole Kriz (AUS) 62 64.

- **$50,000 RALEIGH, NC** (USA) 3-9 MAY – **Singles:** Marissa Irvin (USA) d. Mashona Washington (USA) 63 63.
  Doubles: Ansley Cargill (USA)/Christina Wheeler (AUS) d. Marie-Eve Pelletier (CAN)/Anouska Van Exel (NED) 64 64.

- **$10,000 ANTALYA** (TUR) 10-16 MAY – **Singles:** Andrea Petkovic (GER) d. Kateryna Avdiyenko (UKR) 63 64.
  Doubles: Pemra Ozgen (TUR)/Gabriela Velasco-Andreu (ESP) d. Kateryna Avdiyenko/Oxana Lyubtsova (UKR) 60 62.

- **$10,000 CASALE** (ITA) 10-16 MAY – **Singles:** Matea Mezak (CRO) d. Romina Oprandi (ITA) 20 ret.
  Doubles: Irina Smirnova (RUS)/Valentina Sulpizio (ITA) d. Martina Babakova (SVK)/Stefania Chieppa (ITA) 63 36 63.

- **$10,000 MONZON** (ESP) 10-16 MAY – **Singles:** Marta Fraga-Perez (ESP) d. Alienor Tricerri (SUI) 60 64.
  Doubles: Larissa Carvalho (BRA)/Neuza Silva (POR) d. Joana Cortez/Marina Tavares (BRA) 62 64.

- **$25,000 KARUIZAWA** (JPN) 10-16 MAY – **Singles:** Wynne Prakusya (INA) d. Sophie Ferguson (AUS) 16 63 61.
  Doubles: Rika Fujiwara (JPN)/Mi-Ra Jeon (KOR) d. Ryoko Fuda/Seiko Okamoto (JPN) 62 26 76(1).

- **$25,000 STOCKHOLM** (SWE) 10-16 MAY – **Singles:** Anastasia Rodionova (RUS) d. Anne Kremer (LUX) 76(5) 64.
  Doubles: Nadejda Ostrovskaya (BLR)/Dragana Zaric (SCG) d. Sofia Arvidsson/Hanna Nooni (SWE) 76(3) 63.

- **$50,000 CHARLOTTESVILLE, VA** (USA) 10-16 MAY – **Singles:** Marissa Irvin (USA) d. Jamea Jackson (USA) 63 76(5).
  Doubles: Erica Krauth (ARG)/Jessica Lehnhoff (USA) d. Vilmarie Castellvi (PUR)/Sunitha Rao (USA) 60 61.

- **$50,000 SAINT GAUDENS** (FRA) 10-16 MAY – **Singles:** Maria Kirilenko (RUS) d. Stephanie Foretz (FRA) 76(2) 63.
  Doubles: Ruxandra Dragomir-Ilie/Andrea Vanc (ROM) d. Marta Domachowska (POL)/Natalia Gussoni (ARG) 26 76(7) 64.

- **$10,000 ANTALYA** (TUR) 17-23 MAY – **Singles:** Ekaterina Makarova (RUS) d. Kateryna Avdiyenko (UKR) 63 63.
  Doubles: Pemra Ozgen (TUR)/Gabriela Velasco-Andreu (ESP) d. Kateryna Avdiyenko/Oxana Lyubtsova (UKR) 61 64.

- **$10,000 BUCHAREST** (ROM) 17-23 MAY – **Singles:** Monica Niculescu (ROM) d. Simona Matei (ROM) 62 62.
  Doubles: Gabriela Niculescu/Monica Niculescu (ROM) d. Lenore Lazaroiu/Andra Savu (ROM) 64 62.

- **$10,000 EL PASO, TX** (USA) 17-23 MAY – **Singles:** Cindy Watson (AUS) d. Angela Haynes (USA) 63 76(3).
  Doubles: Beau Jones/Anne Mall (USA) d. Asha Rolle/Tiya Rolle (USA) 61 75.

- **$10,000 GDYNIA** (POL) 17-23 MAY – **Singles:** Klaudia Jans (POL) d. Magdalena Kiszczynska (POL) 64 36 63.
  Doubles: Stefanie Weis (GER)/Maria Wolfbrandt (SWE) d. Natalia Bogdanova/Valeria Bondarenko (UKR) 36 63 75.

- **$10,000 SANTA CRUZ DE TENERIFE** (ESP) 17-23 MAY – **Singles:** Marta Fraga-Perez (ESP) d. Nuria Roig-Tost (ESP) 75 62.
  Doubles: Larissa Carvalho (BRA)/Anna Hawkins (GBR) d. Eva Hoch (AUT)/Martina Pavelec (GER) 26 61 76(4).

- **$10,000 ZADAR** (CRO) 17-23 MAY – **Singles:** Mandy Minella (LUX) d. Matea Mezak (CRO) 75 57 64.
  Doubles: Mandy Minella (LUX)/Lisa Tognetti (ITA) d. Martina Babakova/Michaela Michalkova (SVK) w/o.

- **$25,000 BEIJING** (CHN) 17-23 MAY – **Singles:** Na Li (CHN) d. Seiko Okamoto (JPN) 64 64.
  Doubles: Liga Dekmeijere (LAT)/Ipek Senoglu (TUR) d. Rui Du/Nan-Nan Liu (CHN) 46 64 76(1).

- **$25,000 CASERTA** (ITA) 17-23 MAY – **Singles:** Paula Garcia-Garcia-Doctor (ESP) d. Katerina Bohmova (CZE) 06 63 62.
  Doubles: Rosa-Maria Andres-Rodriguez (ESP)/Andrea Vanc (ROM) d. Giulia Casoni (ITA)/Vladmira Uhlirova (CZE) 61 46 64.

- **$10,000 BIOGRAD** (CRO) 24-30 MAY – **Singles:** Lucie Hradecka (CZE) d. Lisa Tognetti (ITA) 63 62.
  Doubles: Kika Hogendoorn (NED)/Bettina Pirker (AUT) d. Klara Jagosova/Eva Martincova (CZE) 62 61.

- **$10,000 CAMPOBASSO** (ITA) 24-30 MAY – **Singles:** Sania Mirza (IND) d. Magda Mihalache (ROM) 63 64.
  Doubles: Maria-Jose Argeri (ARG)/Leticia Sobral (BRA) d. Emilia Desiderio/Claudia Ivone (ITA) 60 61.

- **$10,000 HOUSTON, TX** (USA) 24-30 MAY – **Singles:** Cory-Ann Avants (USA) d. Varvara Lepchenko (USA) 61 64.
  Doubles: Bruna Colosio (BRA)/Anne Mall (USA) d. Angela Haynes/Asha Rolle (USA) 76(5) 64.

- **$10,000 ISTANBUL** (TUR) 24-30 MAY – **Singles:** Hana Sromova (CZE) d. Yevgenia Savransky (ISR) 64 61.
  Doubles: Iryna Kuryanovich (BLR)/Yevgenia Savransky (ISR) d. Hana Sromova (CZE)/Gabriela Velasco-Andreu (ESP) 63 64.

- **$10,000 LUCKNOW** (IND) 24-30 MAY – **Singles:** Rushmi Chakravarthi (IND) d. Ankita Bhambri (IND) 62 26 76(8).
  Doubles: Ankita Bhambri/Rushmi Chakravarthi (IND) d. Jayaram-Sai Jayalaksamy/Archana Venkataraman (IND) 64 61.

- **$10,000 OLECKO** (POL) 24-30 MAY – **Singles:** Ekaterina Dzehalevich (BLR) d. Olga Brozda (POL) 46 75 64.
  Doubles: Karolina Kosinska/Alicia Rosolska (POL) d. Iveta Gerlova (CZE)/Zuzana Zemenova (SVK) 64 63.

- **$10,000 ORADEA** (ROM) 24-30 MAY – **Singles:** Simona Matei (ROM) d. Petra Novotnikova (CZE) 63 64.
  Doubles: Ioana Gaspar/Lavinia Toader (ROM) d. Bianca Bonifate/Diana Gae (ROM) 26 61 62.

- **$25,000 SEOUL** (KOR) 24-30 MAY – **Singles:** Jin-Hee Kim (KOR) d. Su-Wei Hsieh (TPE) 62 64.
  Doubles: Jin-Young Choi/Mi-Ok Kim (KOR) d. Shiho Hisamatsu/Remi Tezuka (JPN) 46 61 61.

- **$25,000 TONGLIAO** (CHN) 24-30 MAY – **Singles:** Na Li (CHN) d. Bahia Mouhtassine (MAR) 64 26 76(5).
  Doubles: Liga Dekmeijere (LAT)/Ipek Senoglu (TUR) d. Anna Bastrikova/Nina Bratchikova (RUS) 75 76(5).

- **$10,000 CONSTANTA** (ROM) 31 MAY-6 JUNE – **Singles:** Sophia Melikishvili (GEO) d. Linda Smolenakova (SVK) 62 61.
  Doubles: Mihaela Buzarnescu/Gabriela Niculescu (ROM) d. Bianca Bonifate/Diana Gae (ROM) 64 63.

ITF Women's Circuit 2004 Results (continued)

- **$10,000 HILTON HEAD, SC** (USA) 31 MAY-6 JUNE – **Singles:** Melanie Marois (CAN) d. Natalia Dziamidzenka (BLR) 64 57 64.
  Doubles: Cory-Ann Avants/Varvara Lepchenko (USA) d. Tanner Cochran (USA)/Jaslyn Hewitt (AUS) 62 36 63.

- **$10,000 ISTANBUL** (TUR) 31 MAY-6 JUNE – **Singles:** Tinatin Kavlashvili (GEO) d. Iryna Kuryanovich (BLR) 62 16 63.
  Doubles: Tatia Mikadze/Nana Urotadze (GEO) d. Irina Buryachok (UKR)/Alexandra Kostikova (RUS) 61 62.

- **$10,000 NEW DELHI** (IND) 31 MAY-6 JUNE – **Singles:** Rushmi Chakravarthi (IND) d. Ankita Bhambri (IND) 64 64.
  Doubles: Sanaa Bhambri/Liza Pereira (IND) d. Ankita Bhambri/Rushmi Chakravarthi (IND) 67(5) 63 76(1).

- **$10,000 PALIC** (SCG) 31 MAY-6 JUNE – **Singles:** Eva Hrdinova (CZE) d. Andrea Popovic (SCG) 60 36 60.
  Doubles: Ana Cetnik/Ljiljana Nanusevic (SCG) d. Karolina Jovanovic/Natasa Zoric (SCG) w/o.

- **$25,000 CHANGWON** (KOR) 31 MAY-6 JUNE – **Singles:** Eun-Jeong Lee (KOR) d. Mi-Ok Kim (KOR) 67(1) 63 64.
  Doubles: Kyung-Mi Chang/Jin-Hee Kim (KOR) d. Ayami Takase/Tomoko Yonemura (JPN) 75 64.

- **$25,000 GALATINA** (ITA) 31 MAY-6 JUNE – **Singles:** Paula Garcia-Garcia-Doctor (ESP) d. Valentina Sassi (ITA) 61 36 62.
  Doubles: Giulia Casoni (ITA)/Vladmira Uhlirova (CZE) d. Nadejda Ostrovskaya (BLR)/Kathrin Woerle (GER) 64 60.

- **$25,000 SURBITON** (GBR) 31 MAY-6 JUNE – **Singles:** Akiko Morigami (JPN) d. Anna Chakvetadze (RUS) 64 16 61.
  Doubles: Leanne Baker (NZL)/Nicole Sewell (AUS) d. Surina De Beer (RSA)/Karen Nugent (IRL) 26 75 76(6).

- **$25,000 WULANHAOTE** (CHN) 31 MAY-6 JUNE – **Singles:** Na Li (CHN) d. Nan-Nan Liu (CHN) 60 60.
  Doubles: Chia-Jung Chuang (TPE)/Napaporn Tongsalee (THA) d. Rui Du/Nan-Nan Liu (CHN) 36 62 63.

- **$75,000 PROSTEJOV** (CZE) 31 MAY-6 JUNE – **Singles:** Shuai Peng (CHN) d. Zuzana Ondraskova (CZE) 61 63.
  Doubles: Libuse Prusova/Barbora Strycova (CZE) d. Shuai Peng/Yan-Ze Xie (CHN) 61 63.

- **$10,000 ALCOBACA** (POR) 7-13 JUNE – **Singles:** Neuza Silva (POR) d. Lucia Jimenez-Almendros (ESP) 75 57 61.
  Doubles: Alanna Broderick/Megan Moulton-Levy (JAM) d. Krizia Borgarello/Silvia Disderi (ITA) 75 61.

- **$10,000 PITESTI** (ROM) 7-13 JUNE – **Singles:** Mihaela Buzarnescu (ROM) d. Liana Balaci (ROM) 63 76(4).
  Doubles: Mihaela Buzarnescu/Gabriela Niculescu (ROM) d. Andrea Benitez (ARG)/Estefania Craciun (URU) 64 64.

- **$10,000 STARE SPLAVY** (CZE) 7-13 JUNE – **Singles:** Lucie Hradecka (CZE) d. Sabrina Jolk (GER) 61 76(3).
  Doubles: Blanka Kumbarova/Tereza Szafnerova (CZE) d. Jana Derkasova/Tereza Hladikova (CZE) 64 64.

- **$25,000 ALLENTOWN, PA** (USA) 7-13 JUNE – **Singles:** Diana Ospina (USA) d. Varvara Lepchenko (USA) 64 62.
  Doubles: Angela Haynes/Diana Ospina (USA) d. Cory-Ann Avants/Varvara Lepchenko (USA) 60 62.

- **$25,000 GRADO** (ITA) 7-13 JUNE – **Singles:** Nuria Llagostera Vives (ESP) d. Paula Garcia-Garcia-Doctor (ESP) 57 62 61.
  Doubles: Rosa-Maria Andres-Rodriguez (ESP)/Andrea Vanc (ROM) d. Klaudia Jans/Alicia Rosolska (POL) 62 62.

- **$25,000 HAMILTON** (CAN) 7-13 JUNE – **Singles:** Stephanie Dubois (CAN) d. Alexa Glatch (USA) 61 75.
  Doubles: Soledad Esperon/Flavia Mignola (ARG) d. Kaysie Smashey (USA)/Aneta Soukup (CAN) 76(4) 36 64.

- **$25,000 VADUZ** (LIE) 7-13 JUNE – **Singles:** Anastasia Rodionova (RUS) d. Yvonne Meusburger (AUT) 16 63 76(2).
  Doubles: Tatiana Poutchek (BLR)/Anastasia Rodionova (RUS) d. Kyra Nagy (HUN)/Maria Wolfbrandt (SWE) 63 64.

- **$50,000 BEIJING** (CHN) 7-13 JUNE – **Singles:** Na Li (CHN) d. Suchanun Viratprasert (THA) 62 64.
  Doubles: Chia-Jung Chuang (TPE)/Wynne Prakusya (INA) d. Liga Dekmeijere (LAT)/Ipek Senoglu (TUR) 63 61.

- **$50,000 MARSEILLE** (FRA) 7-13 JUNE – **Singles:** Anabel Medina Garrigues (ESP) d. Lubomira Kurhajcova (SVK) 57 63 63.
  Doubles: Shahar Peer (ISR)/Elena Vesnina (RUS) d. Kildine Chevalier (FRA)/Conchita Martinez-Granados (ESP) 61 61.

- **$10,000 BRASOV** (ROM) 14-20 JUNE – **Singles:** Mihaela Buzarnescu (ROM) d. Andrea Benitez (ARG) 63 75.
  Doubles: Corina Corduneanu/Alexandra Iacob (ROM) d. Lenore Lazaroiu/Raluca Olaru (ROM) 64 75.

- **$10,000 FORT WORTH, TX** (USA) 14-20 JUNE – **Singles:** Shikha Uberoi (USA) d. Neha Uberoi (USA) 61 62.
  Doubles: Vania King/Anne Mall (USA) d. Neha Uberoi/Shikha Uberoi (USA) 26 63 76(5).

- **$10,000 KEDZIERZYN KOZLE** (POL) 14-20 JUNE – **Singles:** Marta Lesniak (POL) d. Oksana Teplyakova (UKR) 62 64.
  Doubles: Iveta Gerlova/Sandra Zahlavova (CZE) d. Kateryna Avdiyenko/Oxana Lyubtsova (UKR) 63 61.

- **$10,000 MONT TREMBLANT** (CAN) 14-20 JUNE – **Singles:** Soledad Esperon (ARG) d. Stephanie Dubois (CAN) 63 64.
  Doubles: Soledad Esperon/Flavia Mignola (ARG) d. Kaysie Smashey (USA)/Aneta Soukup (CAN) 60 26 76(6).

- **$10,000 MONTEMOR-O-NOVO** (POR) 14-20 JUNE – **Singles:** Ana-Catarina Nogueira (POR) d. Lizaan Du Plessis (RSA) 62 63.
  Doubles: Frederica Piedade (POR)/Alienor Tricerri (SUI) d. Alanna Broderick/Megan Moulton-Levy (JAM) 64 63.

- **$10,000 PODGORICA** (SCG) 14-20 JUNE – **Singles:** Andrea Petkovic (GER) d. Danica Krstajic (SCG) 61 63.
  Doubles: Sofia Avakova (RUS)/Andrea Petkovic (GER) d. Ljiljana Nanusevic/Marta Simic (SCG) 63 ret.

- **$25,000 GORIZIA** (ITA) 14-20 JUNE – **Singles:** Vanina Garcia-Sokol (ARG) d. Martina Muller (GER) 61 64.
  Doubles: Ruxandra Dragomir-Ilie/Andrea Vanc (ROM) d. Martina Muller/Angelika Roesch (GER) 76(4) 62.

- **$25,000 LENZERHEIDE** (SUI) 14-20 JUNE – **Singles:** Katerina Bohmova (CZE) d. Julia Babilon (GER) 64 64.
  Doubles: Erica Krauth (ARG)/Aurelie Vedy (FRA) d. Joana Cortez/Marina Tavares (BRA) 62 64.

- **$10,000 ALKMAAR** (NED) 21-27 JUNE – **Singles:** Marta Lesniak (POL) d. Carly Gullickson (USA) 62 63.
  Doubles: Akgul Amanmuradova (UZB)/Kika Hogendoorn (NED) d. Kelly De Beer/Eva Pera (NED) 62 62.

- **$10,000 EDMOND, OK** (USA) 21-27 JUNE – **Singles:** Shikha Uberoi (USA) d. Anne Mall (USA) 62 64.
  Doubles: Heidi El Tabakh (EGY)/Anne Mall (USA) d. Kelly Anderson/Carine Vermeulen (RSA) 36 63 64.

- **$10,000 ORESTIADA** (GRE) 21-27 JUNE – **Singles:** Aurelie Vedy (FRA) d. Anna Koumantou (GRE) 61 61.
  Doubles: Mathilde Johansson/Aurelie Vedy (FRA) d. Belen Corbalan/Luciana Sarmenti (ARG) 60 60.

- **$10,000 PROTVINO** (RUS) 21-27 JUNE – **Singles:** Elena Tchalova (RUS) d. Vassilissa Bardina (RUS) 62 61.
  Doubles: Vassilissa Bardina/Julia Vorobieva (RUS) d. Maria Gugel (ISR)/Elena Tchalova (RUS) 63 62.

- **$25,000 BASTAD** (SWE) 21-27 JUNE – **Singles:** Lucie Safarova (CZE) d. Lenka Tvaroskova (SVK) 62 60.
  Doubles: Zuzana Hejdova (CZE)/Vanessa Henke (GER) d. Mirielle Dittmann (AUS)/Hanna Nooni (SWE) 26 62 63.

- **$25,000 FONTANAFREDDA** (ITA) 21-27 JUNE – **Singles:** Ludmila Skavronskaia (RUS) d. Conchita Martinez-Granados (ESP) 61 63.
  Doubles: Erica Krauth (ARG)/Katalin Marosi (HUN) d. Martina Muller (GER)/Vladmira Uhlirova (CZE) 26 63 62.

- **$25,000 INCHON** (KOR) 21-27 JUNE – **Singles:** Chia-Jung Chuang (TPE) d. Eun-Jeong Lee (KOR) 63 62.
  Doubles: Chin-Wei Chan/Su-Wei Hsieh (TPE) d. Jin-Young Choi/Mi-Ok Kim (KOR) 62 60.

- **$25,000 PERIGUEUX** (FRA) 21-27 JUNE – **Singles:** Maria-Fernanda Alves (BRA) d. Maria Wolfbrandt (SWE) 63 63.
  Doubles: Maria-Fernanda Alves (BRA)/Natalia Gussoni (ARG) d. Erica Biro (CAN)/Sarah Riske (USA) 61 62.

- **$10,000 BIBIONE** (ITA) 28 JUNE-4 JULY – **Singles:** Ana Jovanovic (SCG) d. Sabrina Jolk (GER) 63 63.
  Doubles: Emilia Desiderio/Valentina Sulpizio (ITA) d. Nadja Pavic (CRO)/Linda Smolenakova (SVK) 63 64.

- **$10,000 HEERHUGOWAARD** (NED) 28 JUNE-4 JULY – **Singles:** Sandra Martinovic (BIH) d. Aleksandra Srndovic (SWE) 62 61.
  Doubles: Aleksandra Srndovic (SWE)/Kristen Van Elden (AUS) d. Daniele Harmsen/Susanne Trik (NED) 61 62.

- **$10,000 INCHON** (KOR) 28 JUNE-4 JULY – **Singles:** Eun-Jeong Lee (KOR) d. Junri Namigata (JPN) 60 36 60.
  Doubles: Jin-A Lee/Soo-Mi Yoo (KOR) d. Maki Arai/Remi Tezuka (JPN) 62 46 64.

- **$10,000 KRASNOARMEISK** (RUS) 28 JUNE-4 JULY – **Singles:** Ekaterina Bychkova (RUS) d. Olga Panova (RUS) 62 63.
  Doubles: Ekaterina Bychkova/Vasilisa Davydova (RUS) d. Vassilissa Bardina/Julia Vorobieva (RUS) 76(4) 60.

ITF Women's Circuit 2004 Results (continued)

- **$10,000 SOUTH LAKE, TX** (USA) 28 JUNE-4 JULY – **Singles:** Nicole Leimbach (USA) d. Anda Perianu (ROM) 60 64.
  Doubles: Tamara Encina/Alison Ojeda (USA) d. Tetiana Luzhanska (UKR)/Paula Zabala-Alvarez (USA) 63 63.

- **$10,000 TLEMCEN** (ALG) 28 JUNE-4 JULY – **Singles:** Shelley Stephens (NZL) d. Joanne Akl (FRA) 64 61.
  Doubles: Joanne Akl (FRA)/Shelley Stephens (NZL) d. Karoline Borgersen (NOR)/Anna-Maria Miller (AUT) 61 60.

- **$25,000 MONT DE MARSAN** (FRA) 28 JUNE-4 JULY – **Singles:** Paula Garcia-Garcia-Doctor (ESP) d. Maria Kondratieva (RUS) 63 62.
  Doubles: Lourdes Dominguez-Lino/Paula Garcia-Garcia-Doctor (ESP) d. Nina Bratchikova (RUS)/Frederica Piedade (POR) 63 36 64.

- **$25,000 VAIHINGEN** (GER) 28 JUNE-4 JULY – **Singles:** Martina Muller (GER) d. Nathalie Vierin (ITA) 62 75.
  Doubles: Vanessa Henke (GER)/Anouska Van Exel (NED) d. Darija Jurak (CRO)/Maria Koryttseva (UKR) 64 75.

- **$50,000 LOS GATOS** (USA) 28 JUNE-4 JULY – **Singles:** Ludmila Skavronskaia (RUS) d. Maureen Drake (CAN) 76(0) 64.
  Doubles: Sofia Arvidsson (SWE)/Ipek Senoglu (TUR) d. Nana Miyagi (JPN)/Lilia Osterloh (USA) 61 26 64.

- **$75,000 ORBETELLO** (ITA) 28 JUNE-4 JULY – **Singles:** Catalina Castano (COL) d. Alyona Bondarenko (UKR) 26 62 63.
  Doubles: Alyona Bondarenko (UKR)/Galina Fokina (RUS) d. Juliana Fedak (UKR)/Andrea Vanc (ROM) 67(5) 62 75.

- **$10,000 FELIXSTOWE** (GBR) 5-11 JULY – **Singles:** Amanda Janes (GBR) d. Teodora Mircic (SCG) 62 61.
  Doubles: Hannah Collin/Anna Hawkins (GBR) d. Helen Crook/Karen Paterson (GBR) 64 64.

- **$10,000 GETXO** (ESP) 5-11 JULY – **Singles:** Tatiana Priachin (GER) d. Eloisa Compostizo-De Andres (ESP) 63 26 61.
  Doubles: Anna Font-Estrada/Carla Suarez-Navarro (ESP) d. Andrea Benitez (ARG)/Estefania Craciun (URU) 62 63.

- **$10,000 LE TOUQUET** (FRA) 5-11 JULY – **Singles:** Laurence Combes (FRA) d. Melanie Cohen (FRA) 60 63.
  Doubles: Janette Bejlkova (CZE)/Aneta Soukup (CAN) d. Zuzana Cerna (CZE)/Ekaterina Kirianova (RUS) 26 64 62.

- **$10,000 SEOUL** (KOR) 5-11 JULY – **Singles:** Eun-Jeong Lee (KOR) d. Jie Hao (CHN) 64 61.
  Doubles: Mi-Ok Kim/Jin-A Lee (KOR) d. Chin-Wei Chan/Yi Chen (TPE) 64 64.

- **$10,000 SIDI FREDJ** (ALG) 5-11 JULY – **Singles:** Shelley Stephens (NZL) d. Joanne Akl (FRA) 61 63.
  Doubles: Jayaram-Sai Jayalaksamy (IND)/Shelley Stephens (NZL) d. Jennifer Elie (USA)/Michaela Johansson (SWE) 63 61.

- **$25,000 COLLEGE PARK, MD** (USA) 5-11 JULY – **Singles:** Olga Poutchkova (BLR) d. Rossana Neffa-De Los Rios (PAR) 75 46 62.
  Doubles: Shiho Hisamatsu/Seiko Okamoto (JPN) d. Natalia Dziamidzenka (BLR)/Kaysie Smashey (USA) 76(5) 62.

- **$25,000 DARMSTADT** (GER) 5-11 JULY – **Singles:** Magda Mihalache (ROM) d. Asa Svensson (SWE) 61 36 75.
  Doubles: Vanessa Henke/Martina Muller (GER) d. Katarina Misic/Dragana Zaric (SCG) 61 75.

- **$25,000 TORUN** (POL) 5-11 JULY – **Singles:** Karolina Kosinska (POL) d. Magdalena Kiszczynska (POL) 46 75 61.
  Doubles: Kyra Nagy (HUN)/Gabriela Navratilova (CZE) d. Angelique Kerber (GER)/Marta Lesniak (POL) 64 76(2).

- **$50,000 CUNEO** (ITA) 5-11 JULY – **Singles:** Flavia Pennetta (ITA) d. Alice Canepa (ITA) 64 61.
  Doubles: Edina Gallovits (ROM)/Zsofia Gubacsi (HUN) d. Eva Hrdinova/Sandra Zahlavova (CZE) 75 63.

- **$10,000 BALTIMORE, MD** (USA) 12-18 JULY – **Singles:** Janet Bergman (USA) d. Tomoko Dokei (JPN) 67(2) 63 60.
  Doubles: Arpi Kojian (USA)/Nicole Melch (AUT) d. Anda Perianu (ROM)/Kelly Schmandt (USA) 76(5) 36 63.

- **$10,000 BRUSSELS** (BEL) 12-18 JULY – **Singles:** Michaella Krajicek (NED) d. Elisa Villa (ITA) 63 60.
  Doubles: Zuzana Cerna/Eva Hrdinova (CZE) d. Leslie Butkiewicz/Evelyne Van Hyfte (BEL) 76(3) 76(5).

- **$10,000 BUCHAREST** (ROM) 12-18 JULY – **Singles:** Petra Novotnikova (CZE) d. Gabriela Niculescu (ROM) 75 76(5).
  Doubles: Madalina Gojnea/Monica Niculescu (ROM) d. Liana Balaci (ROM)/Iris Ichim (USA) 64 61.

- **$10,000 LVIV** (UKR) 12-18 JULY – **Singles:** Zuzana Zemenova (SVK) d. Anna Sydorska (UKR) 75 64.
  Doubles: Valeria Bondarenko/Veronika Kapshay (UKR) d. Anna Sydorska/Oksana Teplyakova (UKR) 63 46 76(2).

Nicole Vaidisova (CZE)

ITF Women's Circuit 2004 Results (continued)

- **$10,000 MONTERONI** (ITA) 12-18 JULY – **Singles:** Alexia Virgili (ITA) d. Sandra Zahlavova (CZE) 64 64.
  Doubles: Valentina Sulpizio (ITA)/Sandra Zahlavova (CZE) d. Matea Mezak/Nadja Pavic (CRO) 75 46 76(5).

- **$25,000 CAMPOS DO JORDAO** (BRA) 12-18 JULY – **Singles:** Maria-Fernanda Alves (BRA) d. Katalin Marosi (HUN) 75 76(2).

- **$25,000 GARCHING** (GER) 12-18 JULY – **Singles:** Sanda Mamic (CRO) d. Maria Kondratieva (RUS) 63 16 62.
  Doubles: Erica Krauth (ARG)/Aurelie Vedy (FRA) d. Angelika Bachmann (GER)/Stanislava Hrozenska (SVK) 64 76(5).

- **$25,000 GUNMA** (JPN) 12-18 JULY – **Singles:** Rika Fujiwara (JPN) d. Ayami Takase (JPN) 61 62.
  Doubles: Mayumi Yamamoto/Tomoko Yonemura (JPN) d. Kaori Aoyama/Ayami Takase (JPN) 64 46 63.

- **$50,000 VITTEL** (FRA) 12-18 JULY – **Singles:** Nuria Llagostera Vives (ESP) d. Lubomira Bacheva (BUL) 62 64.
  Doubles: Severine Beltrame/Stephanie Cohen-Aloro (FRA) d. Maria Goloviznina (RUS)/Maria Wolfbrandt (SWE) 61 63.

- **$10,000 ANCONA** (ITA) 19-25 JULY – **Singles:** Sanja Ancic (CRO) d. Ekaterina Ivanova (RUS) 62 61.
  Doubles: Oana-Elena Golimbioschi (ROM)/Aurelie Vedy (FRA) d. Nadja Pavic (CRO)/Aleksandra Srndovic (SWE) 63 63.

- **$10,000 BALS** (ROM) 19-25 JULY – **Singles:** Simona Matei (ROM) d. Catalina Cristea (ROM) 61 62.
  Doubles: Petra Novotnikova (CZE)/Linda Smolenakova (SVK) d. Nadine Schlotterer (AUT)/Eva Valkova (CZE) 62 76(4).

- **$10,000 EVANSVILLE, IN** (USA) 19-25 JULY – **Singles:** Nicole Leimbach (USA) d. Anda Perianu (ROM) 63 61.
  Doubles: Kelly Schmandt/Aleke Tsoubanos (USA) d. Heidi El Tabakh (EGY)/Vania King (USA) 64 64.

- **$10,000 HORB** (GER) 19-25 JULY – **Singles:** Anna Foldenyi (HUN) d. Zuzana Zalabska (CZE) 64 67(7) 64.
  Doubles: Maria Arkhipova (RUS)/Yevgenia Savransky (ISR) d. Janette Bejlkova (CZE)/Meng Yuan (CHN) 64 63.

- **$10,000 ZWEVEGEM** (BEL) 19-25 JULY – **Singles:** Leslie Butkiewicz (BEL) d. Ekaterina Kirianova (RUS) 63 61.
  Doubles: Zuzana Cerna (CZE)/Aneta Soukup (CAN) d. Leslie Butkiewicz (BEL)/Shelley Stephens (NZL) 63 62.

- **$25,000 LES CONTAMINES** (FRA) 19-25 JULY – **Singles:** Hana Sromova (CZE) d. Evie Dominikovic (AUS) 64 61.
  Doubles: Caroline Dhenin (FRA)/Gabriela Navratilova (CZE) d. Evie Dominikovic (AUS)/Rita Kuti Kis (HUN) 64 63.

- **$50,000 INNSBRUCK** (AUT) 19-25 JULY – **Singles:** Kirsten Flipkens (BEL) d. Michaela Pastikova (CZE) 62 63.
  Doubles: Alyona Bondarenko (UKR)/Galina Fokina (RUS) d. Stanislava Hrozenska (SVK)/Lenka Nemeckova (CZE) 62 64.

- **$50,000 SCHENECTADY, NY** (USA) 19-25 JULY – **Singles:** Bethanie Mattek (USA) d. Maureen Drake (CAN) 63 61.
  Doubles: Casey Dell'Acqua/Nicole Sewell (AUS) d. Ansley Cargill/Julie Ditty (USA) 36 76(2) 62.

- **$10,000 BAD SAULGAU** (GER) 26 JULY-1 AUGUST – **Singles:** Greta Arn (GER) d. Tanja Ostertag (GER) 64 62.
  Doubles: Franziska Etzel/Christina Fitz (GER) d. Nicole Seitenbecher/Eveline Widiger (GER) 64 63.

- **$10,000 DUBLIN** (IRL) 26 JULY-1 AUGUST – **Singles:** Dubravka Cupac (AUS) d. Karen Nugent (IRL) 62 62.
  Doubles: Yvonne Doyle/Karen Nugent (IRL) d. Lizaan Du Plessis (RSA)/Rebecca Llewellyn (GBR) 64 36 62.

- **$10,000 ISTANBUL** (TUR) 26 JULY-1 AUGUST – **Singles:** Aurelie Vedy (FRA) d. Gabriela Velasco-Andreu (ESP) 60 76(5).
  Doubles: Vasilisa Davydova/Svetlana Mossiakova (RUS) d. Valeria Bondarenko (UKR)/Gabriela Velasco-Andreu (ESP) 63 63.

- **$10,000 PONTEVEDRA** (ESP) 26 JULY-1 AUGUST – **Singles:** Lucia Jimenez-Almendros (ESP) d. Estrella Cabeza-Candela (ESP) 67(3) 76(4) 76(2).
  Doubles: Frederica Piedade (POR)/Alienor Tricerri (SUI) d. Julianna Gates (USA)/Natasha Kersten (AUS) 75 64.

- **$10,000 ST. JOSEPH, MO** (USA) 26 JULY-1 AUGUST – **Singles:** Nicole Melch (AUT) d. Jessica Roland-Rosario (PUR) 64 63.
  Doubles: Jessica Roland-Rosario (PUR)/Kelly Schmandt (USA) d. Arpi Kojian (USA)/Nicole Melch (AUT) 46 63 76(2).

- **$25,000 PETANGE** (LUX) 26 JULY-1 AUGUST – **Singles:** Stanislava Hrozenska (SVK) d. Chanelle Scheepers (RSA) 67(10) 61 64.
  Doubles: Eva Fislova/Stanislava Hrozenska (SVK) d. Evie Dominikovic (AUS)/Goulnara Fattakhetdinova (RUS) 64 63.

- **$50,000 LEXINGTON, KY** (USA) 26 JULY-1 AUGUST – **Singles:** Camille Pin (FRA) d. Mi-Ra Jeon (KOR) 75 63.
  Doubles: Claire Curran (IRL)/Natalie Grandin (RSA) d. Casey Dell'Acqua/Nicole Sewell (AUS) 76(6) 64.

- **$75,000 MODENA** (ITA) 26 JULY-1 AUGUST – **Singles:** Anna-Lena Groenefeld (GER) d. Selima Sfar (TUN) 62 64.
  Doubles: Gabriela Navratilova/Michaela Pastikova (CZE) d. Lubomira Bacheva (BUL)/Eva Birnerova (CZE) 62 63.

- **$10,000 GDYNIA** (POL) 2-8 AUGUST – **Singles:** Karolina Kosinska (POL) d. Petra Cetkovska (CZE) 63 62.
  Doubles: Klaudia Jans/Alicia Rosolska (POL) d. Natalia Bogdanova/Valeria Bondarenko (UKR) 62 64.

- **$10,000 REBECQ** (BEL) 2-8 AUGUST – **Singles:** Liana Balaci (ROM) d. Antonela Voina (GER) 64 61.
  Doubles: Liana Balaci (ROM)/Antonela Voina (GER) d. Jessie De Vries/Debbrich Feys (BEL) 62 57 64.

- **$10,000 VIGO** (ESP) 2-8 AUGUST – **Singles:** Frederica Piedade (POR) d. Lucia Jimenez-Almendros (ESP) 61 63.
  Doubles: Andrea Benitez (ARG)/Estefania Craciun (URU) d. Sandra Volk (SLO)/Julia Vorobyeva (RUS) 75 64.

- **$10,000 WREXHAM** (GBR) 2-8 AUGUST – **Singles:** Sania Mirza (IND) d. Irina Bulykina (RUS) 16 64 61.
  Doubles: Eden Marama/Paula Marama (NZL) d. Rushmi Chakravarthi/Sania Mirza (IND) 76(4) 75.

- **$25,000 HECHINGEN** (GER) 2-8 AUGUST – **Singles:** Eva Hrdinova (CZE) d. Nathalie Vierin (ITA) 64 63.
  Doubles: Eva Fislova/Stanislava Hrozenska (SVK) d. Erica Krauth (ARG)/Jasmin Woehr (GER) 36 63 63.

- **$50,000 LOUISVILLE, KY** (USA) 2-8 AUGUST – **Singles:** Aiko Nakamura (JPN) d. Vilmarie Castellvi (PUR) 64 62.
  Doubles: Julie Ditty (USA)/Edina Gallovits (ROM) d. Claire Curran (IRL)/Natalie Grandin (RSA) 16 64 62.

- **$50,000 RIMINI** (ITA) 2-8 AUGUST – **Singles:** Juliana Fedak (UKR) d. Katerina Bohmova (CZE) 64 63.
  Doubles: Juliana Fedak/Maria Koryttseva (UKR) d. Rosa-Maria Andres-Rodriguez (ESP)/Andrea Vanc (ROM) 76(7) 63.

- **$10,000 CARACAS** (VEN) 9-15 AUGUST – **Singles:** Maria-Jose Argeri (ARG) d. Soledad Esperon (ARG) 64 62.
  Doubles: Maria-Jose Argeri (ARG)/Leticia Sobral (BRA) d. Marcela Evangelista/Carla Tiene (BRA) 64 63.

- **$10,000 COIMBRA** (POR) 9-15 AUGUST – **Singles:** Ana-Catarina Nogueira (POR) d. Irina Kotkina (RUS) 75 60.
  Doubles: Natalia Garbellotto (ARG)/Gabriela Velasco-Andreu (ESP) d. Alice Balducci (ITA)/Masa Zec-Peskiric (SLO) 64 61.

- **$10,000 KOKSIJDE** (BEL) 9-15 AUGUST – **Singles:** Michaella Krajicek (NED) d. Gaelle Widmer (SUI) 64 62.
  Doubles: Leslie Butkiewicz (BEL)/Shelley Stephens (NZL) d. Jessie De Vries/Debbrich Feys (BEL) 62 75.

- **$10,000 LONDON** (GBR) 9-15 AUGUST – **Singles:** Sania Mirza (IND) d. Jaslyn Hewitt (AUS) 46 61 60.
  Doubles: Rushmi Chakravarthi/Sania Mirza (IND) d. Anna Hawkins (GBR)/Nicole Rencken (RSA) 63 62.

- **$10,000 TARGU MURES** (ROM) 9-15 AUGUST – **Singles:** Ekaterina Makarova (RUS) d. Simona Matei (ROM) 61 61.
  Doubles: Gabriela Niculescu/Monica Niculescu (ROM) d. Simona Matei (ROM)/Barbara Pocza (HUN) 75 61.

- **$25,000 MARTINA FRANCA** (ITA) 9-15 AUGUST – **Singles:** Timea Bacsinszky (SUI) d. Bahia Mouhtassine (MAR) 64 64.
  Doubles: Aurelie Vedy (FRA)/Jasmin Woehr (GER) d. Nina Bratchikova (RUS)/Giulia Casoni (ITA) 61 36 76(6).

- **$10,000 COIMBRA** (POR) 16-22 AUGUST – **Singles:** Akgul Amanmuradova (UZB) d. Irina Kotkina (RUS) 62 63.
  Doubles: Akgul Amanmuradova (UZB)/Irina Kotkina (RUS) d. Sarah Raab (GER)/Sandra Volk (SLO) 26 61 61.

- **$10,000 COLOMBO** (SRI) 16-22 AUGUST – **Singles:** Yung-Jan Chan (TPE) d. Montinee Tangphong (THA) 61 61.
  Doubles: Rushmi Chakravarthi/Jayaram-Sai Jayalaksamy (IND) d. Yung-Jan Chan (TPE)/Minori Takemoto (JPN) 62 57 63.

- **$10,000 ENSCHEDE** (NED) 16-22 AUGUST – **Singles:** Antonela Voina (GER) d. Gaelle Widmer (SUI) 75 64.
  Doubles: Susanne Trik/Tessy Van de Ven (NED) d. Daniella Klemenschits/Sandra Klemenschits (AUT) 46 60 64.

- **$10,000 GUAYAQUIL** (ECU) 16-22 AUGUST – **Singles:** Jenifer Widjaja (BRA) d. Soledad Esperon (ARG) 63 62.
  Doubles: Maria-Jose Argeri (ARG)/Leticia Sobral (BRA) d. Marcela Evangelista/Carla Tiene (BRA) 63 61.

ITF Women's Circuit 2004 Results (continued)

- **$10,000 IASI** (ROM) 16-22 AUGUST – **Singles:** Monica Niculescu (ROM) d. Raluca Olaru (ROM) 76(5) 60.
  Doubles: Gabriela Niculescu/Monica Niculescu (ROM) d. Nadine Schlotterer (AUT)/Eva Valkova (CZE) 75 61.

- **$10,000 JESI** (ITA) 16-22 AUGUST – **Singles:** Rita Degli-Esposti (ITA) d. Petra Cetkovska (CZE) 63 62.
  Doubles: Stefania Chieppa/Valentina Sulpizio (ITA) d. Larissa Carvalho (BRA)/Elena Vianello (ITA) 63 75.

- **$10,000 KEDZIERZYN KOZLE** (POL) 16-22 AUGUST – **Singles:** Katalin Marosi (HUN) d. Veronika Raimrova (CZE) 64 46 62.
  Doubles: Katalin Marosi (HUN)/Marina Tavares (BRA) d. Iveta Gerlova/Sandra Zahlavova (CZE) 16 64 62.

- **$10,000 WESTENDE** (BEL) 16-22 AUGUST – **Singles:** Leslie Butkiewicz (BEL) d. Emma Laine (FIN) 76(4) 76(4).
  Doubles: Veronika Chvojkova (CZE)/Emma Laine (FIN) d. Janette Bejlkova (CZE)/Tatiana Malek (GER) 64 75.

- **$50,000 BRONX, NY** (USA) 16-22 AUGUST – **Singles:** Evgenia Linetskaya (RUS) d. Nuria Llagostera Vives (ESP) 46 63 64.
  Doubles: Na Li/Nan-Nan Liu (CHN) d. Jessica Lehnhoff (USA)/Christina Wheeler (AUS) 57 63 63.

- **$10,000 ALPHEN A/D RIJN** (NED) 23-29 AUGUST – **Singles:** Tessy Van de Ven (NED) d. Gaelle Widmer (SUI) 63 63.
  Doubles: Leslie Butkiewicz/Evelyne Van Hyfte (BEL) d. Daniella Klemenschits/Sandra Klemenschits (AUT) 75 63.

- **$10,000 BIELEFELD** (GER) 23-29 AUGUST – **Singles:** Kristina Barrois (GER) d. Nicole Seitenbecher (GER) 64 61.
  Doubles: Carmen Klaschka/Sabine Klaschka (GER) d. Christiane Hoppmann/Madita Suer (GER) 63 63.

- **$10,000 LA PAZ** (BOL) 23-29 AUGUST – **Singles:** Jenifer Widjaja (BRA) d. Andrea Koch (CHI) 36 64 60.
  Doubles: Maria-Jose Argeri (ARG)/Leticia Sobral (BRA) d. Marcela Evangelista/Carla Tiene (BRA) 61 63.

- **$10,000 MARIBOR** (SLO) 23-29 AUGUST – **Singles:** Masa Zec-Peskiric (SLO) d. Andreja Klepac (SLO) 62 75.
  Doubles: Alja Zec-Peskiric/Masa Zec-Peskiric (SLO) d. Lucie Kriegsmannova/Zuzana Zalabska (CZE) 63 63.

- **$10,000 TIMISOARA** (ROM) 23-29 AUGUST – **Singles:** Simona Matei (ROM) d. Yevgenia Savransky (ISR) 63 63.
  Doubles: Sorana Cirstea/Gabriela Niculescu (ROM) d. Lenore Lazaroiu/Raluca Olaru (ROM) 61 26 62.

- **$10,000 TRECASTAGNI** (ITA) 23-29 AUGUST – **Singles:** Andrea Benitez (ARG) d. Veronika Chvojkova (CZE) 64 46 63.
  Doubles: Andrea Benitez (ARG)/Estefania Craciun (URU) d. Veronika Chvojkova (CZE)/Emma Laine (FIN) 63 36 62.

- **$25,000 MOSCOW** (RUS) 23-29 AUGUST – **Singles:** Ekaterina Bychkova (RUS) d. Maria Kondratieva (RUS) 62 61.
  Doubles: Ekaterina Kosminskaya/Ekaterina Makarova (RUS) d. Renata Kucerkova (CZE)/Michaela Michalkova (SVK) 36 63 64.

- **$25,000 NEW DELHI** (IND) 23-29 AUGUST – **Singles:** Chia-Jung Chuang (TPE) d. Sania Mirza (IND) 75 64.
  Doubles: Chia-Jung Chuang/Su-Wei Hsieh (TPE) d. Akgul Amanmuradova (UZB)/Sania Mirza (IND) 76(8) 64.

- **$10,000 ARAD** (ROM) 30 AUGUST-5 SEPTEMBER – **Singles:** Liana Balaci (ROM) d. Barbara Pocza (HUN) 75 75.
  Doubles: Sorana Cirstea/Gabriela Niculescu (ROM) d. Yevgenia Savransky (ISR)/Sandra Zahlavova (CZE) 62 62.

- **$10,000 ASUNCION** (PAR) 30 AUGUST-5 SEPTEMBER – **Singles:** Jenifer Widjaja (BRA) d. Larissa Carvalho (BRA) 57 76(3) 63.
  Doubles: Bettina Jozami/Veronica Spiegel (ARG) d. Bruna Colosio (BRA)/Ana-Lucia Migliarini de Leon (URU) 75 64.

- **$10,000 KRANJSKA GORA** (SLO) 30 AUGUST-5 SEPTEMBER – **Singles:** Masa Zec-Peskiric (SLO) d. Diana Stojic (BIH) 64 63.
  Doubles: Polona Rebersak/Masa Zec-Peskiric (SLO) d. Janette Bejlkova (CZE)/Karolina Jovanovic (SCG) 76(4) 61.

- **$10,000 MEXICO CITY** (MEX) 30 AUGUST-5 SEPTEMBER – **Singles:** Julia Cohen (USA) d. Maria-Jose Lopez-Herrera (MEX) 64 64.
  Doubles: Lauren Barnikow/Mariana Correa (USA) d. Marcela Arroyo/Melissa Torres (MEX) 76(7) 75.

- **$10,000 MOLLERUSA** (ESP) 30 AUGUST-5 SEPTEMBER – **Singles:** Natalia Garbellotto (ARG) d. Lucia Jimenez-Almendros (ESP) 60 62.
  Doubles: Karina Jacobsgaard (DEN)/Emilie Trouche (FRA) d. Sabine Lisicki (GER)/Nelly Maillard (FRA) w/o.

- **$10,000 NEW DELHI** (IND) 30 AUGUST-5 SEPTEMBER – **Singles:** Rushmi Chakravarthi (IND) d. Jayaram-Sai Jayalaksamy (IND) 63 62.
  Doubles: Rushmi Chakravarthi/Jayaram-Sai Jayalaksamy (IND) d. Montinee Tangphong/Thassa Vitayaviroj (THA) w/o.

- **$10,000 SAITAMA** (JPN) 30 AUGUST-5 SEPTEMBER – **Singles:** Tomoko Yonemura (JPN) d. Maya Kato (JPN) 63 63.
  Doubles: Hye-Mi Kim (KOR)/Keiko Taguchi (JPN) d. Tomoko Taira/Akiko Yonemura (JPN) 64 60.

- **$10,000 WARSAW** (POL) 30 AUGUST-5 SEPTEMBER – **Singles:** Natalia Kolat (POL) d. Olga Brozda (POL) 64 46 63.
  Doubles: Klaudia Jans/Alicia Rosolska (POL) d. Martina Babakova (SVK)/Iveta Gerlova (CZE) 62 63.

- **$25,000 BALASHIKHA** (RUS) 30 AUGUST-5 SEPTEMBER – **Singles:** Yvonne Meusburger (AUT) d. Anastasia Yakimova (BLR) 63 67(2) 60.
  Doubles: Maria Goloviznina/Elena Vesnina (RUS) d. Olena Antypina (UKR)/Alla Kudryavtseva (RUS) 75 64.

- **$25,000 MESTRE** (ITA) 30 AUGUST-5 SEPTEMBER – **Singles:** Bahia Mouhtassine (MAR) d. Michelle Gerards (NED) 61 60.
  Doubles: Rosa-Maria Andres-Rodriguez/Lourdes Dominguez-Lino (ESP) d. Katalin Marosi (HUN)/Marina Tavares (BRA) 61 62.

- **$10,000 DURMERSHEIM** (GER) 6-12 SEPTEMBER – **Singles:** Lucie Hradecka (CZE) d. Petra Russegger (AUT) 60 57 76(1).
  Doubles: Janette Bejlkova/Petra Cetkovska (CZE) d. Carmen Klaschka/Imke Kusgen (GER) 63 76(4).

- **$10,000 PRESOV** (SVK) 6-12 SEPTEMBER – **Singles:** Miljana Adanko (HUN) d. Petra Novotnikova (CZE) 64 64.
  Doubles: Lucie Kriegsmannova/Zuzana Zalabska (CZE) d. Lenka Broosova/Lenka Dlhopolcova (SVK) 62 46 61.

- **$10,000 SANTIAGO** (CHI) 6-12 SEPTEMBER – **Singles:** Maria-Jose Argeri (ARG) d. Bettina Jozami (ARG) 64 75.
  Doubles: Maria-Jose Argeri (ARG)/Leticia Sobral (BRA) d. Bruna Colosio (BRA)/Ana-Lucia Migliarini de Leon (URU) 62 60.

- **$10,000 TBILISI** (GEO) 6-12 SEPTEMBER – **Singles:** Maria Kondratieva (RUS) d. Margalita Chakhnashvili (GEO) 75 64.
  Doubles: Kristina Grigorian (RUS)/Irina Kuzmina (LAT) d. Sophia Melikishvili (GEO)/Svetlana Mossiakova (RUS) 36 63 63.

- **$10,000 VICTORIA** (MEX) 6-12 SEPTEMBER – **Singles:** Melissa Torres (MEX) d. Tamara Encina (USA) 36 64 75.
  Doubles: Tamara Encina/Alison Ojeda (USA) d. Alicia Pillay (RSA)/Katarzyna Siwosz (POL) 64 36 61.

- **$25,000 IBARAKI** (JPN) 6-12 SEPTEMBER – **Singles:** Rika Fujiwara (JPN) d. Shiho Hisamatsu (JPN) 46 75 60.
  Doubles: Maki Arai/Remi Tezuka (JPN) d. Rika Fujiwara/Shiho Hisamatsu (JPN) 61 57 62.

- **$25,000 MADRID** (ESP) 6-12 SEPTEMBER – **Singles:** Hanna Nooni (SWE) d. Emma Laine (FIN) 64 63.
  Doubles: Emma Laine (FIN)/Hanna Nooni (SWE) d. Kildine Chevalier (FRA)/Marta Fraga-Perez (ESP) 63 76(3).

- **$50,000 FANO** (ITA) 6-12 SEPTEMBER – **Singles:** Ana Ivanovic (SCG) d. Delia Sescioreanu (ROM) 62 64.
  Doubles: Delia Sescioreanu/Andrea Vanc (ROM) d. Mervana Jugic-Salkic (BIH)/Darija Jurak (CRO) 75 16 62.

- **$75,000 DENAIN** (FRA) 6-12 SEPTEMBER – **Singles:** Anna-Lena Groenefeld (GER) d. Dally Randriantefy (MAD) 63 62.
  Doubles: Juliana Fedak (UKR)/Anna-Lena Groenefeld (GER) d. Lubomira Bacheva (BUL)/Michaela Pastikova (CZE) 16 61 62.

- **$10,000 BOGOTA** (COL) 13-19 SEPTEMBER – **Singles:** Estefania Balda (ECU) d. Maria-Belen Corbalan (ARG) 61 64.
  Doubles: Estefania Balda (ECU)/Karen Castiblanco (COL) d. Mariana Duque/Vicky Nunez-Fuentes (COL) 76(2) 75.

- **$10,000 KYOTO** (JPN) 13-19 SEPTEMBER – **Singles:** Haruka Inoue (JPN) d. Maika Ozaki (JPN) 64 61.
  Doubles: Natasha Kersten (AUS)/Eriko Mizuno (JPN) d. Maki Arai/Satomi Kinjo (JPN) 64 46 64.

- **$10,000 LLEIDA** (ESP) 13-19 SEPTEMBER – **Singles:** Elisa Villa (ITA) d. Adriana Gonzalez-Penas (ESP) 16 61 61.
  Doubles: Elena Vianello/Elisa Villa (ITA) d. Kildine Chevalier (FRA)/Neuza Silva (POR) 75 75.

- **$10,000 MANCHESTER** (GBR) 13-19 SEPTEMBER – **Singles:** Andrea Sieveke (GER) d. Katie O'Brien (GBR) 64 76(4).
  Doubles: Emma Laine/Essi Laine (FIN) d. Hannah Collin/Anna Hawkins (GBR) 64 64.

- **$10,000 MATAMOROS** (MEX) 13-19 SEPTEMBER – **Singles:** Story Tweedie-Yates (USA) d. Melissa Torres (MEX) 36 62 63.
  Doubles: Lauren Fisher/Aleke Tsoubanos (USA) d. Tamara Encina/Alison Ojeda (USA) 63 67(7) 76(5).

- **$25,000 ASHLAND, KY** (USA) 13-19 SEPTEMBER – **Singles:** Maria-Emilia Salerni (ARG) d. Kelly McCain (USA) 64 64.
  Doubles: Sandra Kloesel (GER)/Maria-Emilia Salerni (ARG) d. Cory-Ann Avants/Kristen Schlukebir (USA) 63 63.

ITF Women's Circuit 2004 Results (continued)

- **$25,000 BEIJING** (CHN) 13-19 SEPTEMBER – **Singles:** Jie Zheng (CHN) d. Na Li (CHN) 64 64.
  Doubles: Shu-Jing Yang/Ying Yu (CHN) d. Shan-Shan Li/Jie Zheng (CHN) 64 63.

- **$25,000 SOFIA** (BUL) 13-19 SEPTEMBER – **Singles:** Virag Nemeth (HUN) d. Zuzana Kucova (SVK) 51 ret.
  Doubles: Kyra Nagy/Virag Nemeth (HUN) d. Gabriela Niculescu (ROM)/Sandra Zahlavova (CZE) 26 62 75.

- **$25,000 TBILISI** (GEO) 13-19 SEPTEMBER – **Singles:** Olha Lazarchuk (UKR) d. Katarina Kachlikova (SVK) 62 62.
  Doubles: Daria Kustava (BLR)/Elena Vesnina (RUS) d. Maria Kondratieva/Ekaterina Kozhokhina (RUS) 62 64.

- **$75,000 BORDEAUX** (FRA) 13-19 SEPTEMBER – **Singles:** Virginie Razzano (FRA) d. Emilie Loit (FRA) 75 26 62.
  Doubles: Stephanie Cohen-Aloro (FRA)/Selima Sfar (TUN) d. Erica Krauth (ARG)/Jasmin Woehr (GER) 36 63 63.

- **$10,000 CIAMPINO** (ITA) 20-26 SEPTEMBER – **Singles:** Agnes Szavay (HUN) d. Stefania Boffa (SUI) 60 62.
  Doubles: Giulia Meruzzi/Verdiana Verardi (ITA) d. Raffaella Bindi/Frascensca Frappi (ITA) 06 64 62.

- **$10,000 HIROSHIMA** (JPN) 20-26 SEPTEMBER – **Singles:** Emily Hewson (AUS) d. Yurika Sema (JPN) 61 76(6).
  Doubles: Hye-Mi Kim (KOR)/Keiko Taguchi (JPN) d. Tomoko Dokei/Yukiko Yabe (JPN) 64 62.

- **$10,000 JAKARTA** (INA) 20-26 SEPTEMBER – **Singles:** Yung-Jan Chan (TPE) d. Sandy Gumulya (INA) 67(5) 62 61.
  Doubles: Yung-Jan Chan (TPE)/Pichittra Thongdach (THA) d. Liza Andriyani (INA)/Thassha Vitayaviroj (THA) 63 64.

- **$10,000 SAN SALVADOR** (ESA) 20-26 SEPTEMBER – **Singles:** Melissa Torres (MEX) d. Roxane Vaisemberg (BRA) 62 36 75.
  Doubles: Marcela Arroyo/Melissa Torres (MEX) d. Patricia Holzman (ARG)/Hilda Zuleta (ECU) 61 75.

- **$10,000 VOLOS** (GRE) 20-26 SEPTEMBER – **Singles:** Michaela Vogel (GER) d. Marielle Weihs (AUT) 36 60 64.
  Doubles: Eva Valkova/Sandra Zahlavova (CZE) d. Alice Balducci/Cristina Celani (ITA) 76(7) 61.

- **$25,000 JERSEY** (GBR) 20-26 SEPTEMBER – **Singles:** Emma Laine (FIN) d. Elena Baltacha (GBR) 36 62 61.
  Doubles: Emma Laine (FIN)/Kathrin Woerle (GER) d. Ipek Senoglu (TUR)/Anouska Van Exel (NED) 16 61 61.

- **$25,000 TUNICA RESORTS, MS** (USA) 20-26 SEPTEMBER – **Singles:** Kelly McCain (USA) d. Salome Devidze (GEO) 63 63.
  Doubles: Tetiana Luzhanska (UKR)/Aneta Soukup (CAN) d. Liga Dekmeijere (LAT)/Natalia Dziamidzenka (BLR) 62 61.

- **$50,000 BATUMI** (GEO) 20-26 SEPTEMBER – **Singles:** Ana Ivanovic (SCG) d. Anna Chakvetadze (RUS) 63 63.
  Doubles: Alyona Bondarenko (UKR)/Galina Fokina (RUS) d. Anna Bastrikova/Irina Kotkina (RUS) 62 62.

- **$50,000 BIELLA** (ITA) 20-26 SEPTEMBER – **Singles:** Kveta Peschke (CZE) d. Virginie Razzano (FRA) 61 61.
  Doubles: Erica Krauth (ARG)/Martina Muller (GER) d. Mervana Jugic-Salkic (BIH)/Darija Jurak (CRO) 62 63.

- **$50,000 JOUNIEH** (LIB) 20-26 SEPTEMBER – **Singles:** Nuria Llagostera Vives (ESP) d. Lourdes Dominguez-Lino (ESP) 26 60 64.
  Doubles: Petra Cetkovska/Hana Sromova (CZE) d. Nuria Llagostera Vives (ESP)/Frederica Piedade (POR) 64 62.

- **$75,000 ALBUQUERQUE, NM** (USA) 20-26 SEPTEMBER – **Singles:** Marissa Irvin (USA) d. Stephanie Dubois (CAN) 61 46 64.
  Doubles: Maureen Drake (CAN)/Carly Gullickson (USA) d. Stephanie Dubois (CAN)/Maria-Emilia Salerni (ARG) 63 76(6).

- **$10,000 BALIKPAPAN** (INA) 27 SEPTEMBER-3 OCTOBER – **Singles:** Napaporn Tongsalee (THA) d. Thassha Vitayaviroj (THA) 64 75.
  Doubles: Ayu-Fani Damayanti/Septi Mende (INA) d. Sandy Gumulya (INA)/Pichittra Thongdach (THA) 62 62.

- **$10,000 BENEVENTO** (ITA) 27 SEPTEMBER-3 OCTOBER – **Singles:** Giulia Meruzzi (ITA) d. Emily Stellato (ITA) 63 64.
  Doubles: Giulia Gabba/Karen Knapp (ITA) d. Martina Babakova (SVK)/Sandra Zahlavova (CZE) 62 01 ret.

- **$10,000 CLUJ NAPOCA** (ROM) 27 SEPTEMBER-3 OCTOBER – **Singles:** Madalina Gojnea (ROM) d. Oksana Teplyakova (UKR) 75 63.
  Doubles: Corina Corduneanu/Raluca Olaru (ROM) d. Veronika Raimrova (CZE)/Alexandra Sere (ROM) 46 60 64.

- **$25,000 BELGRADE** (SCG) 27 SEPTEMBER-3 OCTOBER – **Singles:** Virag Nemeth (HUN) d. Ekaterina Bychkova (RUS) 26 62 62.
  Doubles: Giulia Casoni (ITA)/Darija Jurak (CRO) d. Ekaterina Bychkova (RUS)/Nadejda Ostrovskaya (BLR) 60 62.

- **$25,000 CANBERRA** (AUS) 27 SEPTEMBER-3 OCTOBER – **Singles:** Jaslyn Hewitt (AUS) d. Evie Dominikovic (AUS) 16 63 75.
  Doubles: Daniella Dominikovic/Evie Dominikovic (AUS) d. Mirielle Dittmann/Cindy Watson (AUS) 63 61.

- **$25,000 OPORTO** (POR) 27 SEPTEMBER-3 OCTOBER – **Singles:** Nathalie Vierin (ITA) d. Michelle Gerards (NED) 36 75 63.
  Doubles: Yulia Beygelzimer (UKR)/Anouska Van Exel (NED) d. Sara Errani (ITA)/Joana Pangaio (POR) 75 60.

- **$25,000 PELHAM, AL** (USA) 27 SEPTEMBER-3 OCTOBER – **Singles:** Zuzana Zemenova (SVK) d. Olga Poutchkova (RUS) 46 64 60.
  Doubles: Liga Dekmeijere (LAT)/Natalia Dziamidzenka (BLR) d. Sarah Riske/Aleke Tsoubanos (USA) 63 61.

- **$50,000 TROY, AL** (USA) 27 SEPTEMBER-3 OCTOBER – **Singles:** Shenay Perry (USA) d. Maria-Emilia Salerni (ARG) 62 62.
  Doubles: Teryn Ashley/Laura Granville (USA) d. Bethanie Mattek/Shenay Perry (USA) 26 30 ret.

- **$10,000 DUBROVNIK** (CRO) 4-10 OCTOBER – **Singles:** Sanja Ancic (CRO) d. Lenka Dlhopolcova (SVK) 64 62.
  Doubles: Darija Jurak/Lucia Krzelj (CRO) d. Olga Brozda/Sylvia Niedbalo (POL) 46 62 64.

- **$10,000 PODGORICA** (SCG) 4-10 OCTOBER – **Singles:** Miljana Adanko (HUN) d. Dragana Zaric (SCG) 63 63.
  Doubles: Katarina Misic/Dragana Zaric (SCG) d. Janette Bejlkova (CZE)/Biliana Pavlova (BUL) 61 62.

- **$25,000 GLASGOW** (GBR) 4-10 OCTOBER – **Singles:** Margit Ruutel (EST) d. Sybille Bammer (AUT) 36 61 75.
  Doubles: Leanne Baker (NZL)/Francesca Lubiani (ITA) d. Claire Curran (IRL)/Ipek Senoglu (TUR) 63 57 64.

- **$25,000 JUAREZ** (MEX) 4-10 OCTOBER – **Singles:** Maria-Fernanda Alves (BRA) d. Maria-Jose Argeri (ARG) 75 63.
  Doubles: Maria-Fernanda Alves/Carla Tiene (BRA) d. Andrea Hlavackova/Jana Hlavackova (CZE) 64 60.

- **$25,000 LAFAYETTE, LA** (USA) 4-10 OCTOBER – **Singles:** Lina Stanciute (LTU) d. Karolina Kosinska (POL) 36 63 75.
  Doubles: Julie Ditty/Kristen Schlukebir (USA) d. Natalie Grandin (RSA)/Arpi Kojian (USA) 62 75.

- **$25,000 LAGOS** (NGR) 4-10 OCTOBER – **Singles:** Sania Mirza (IND) d. Tiffany Dabek (USA) 63 57 63.
  Doubles: Sania Mirza (IND)/Shelley Stephens (NZL) d. Surina De Beer/Chanelle Scheepers (RSA) 61 64.

- **$25,000 NANTES** (FRA) 4-10 OCTOBER – **Singles:** Leslie Butkiewicz (BEL) d. Rita Kuti Kis (HUN) 62 61.
  Doubles: Iryna Kuryanovich/Tatiana Uvarova (BLR) d. Greta Arn (GER)/Rita Kuti Kis (HUN) 64 46 76(5).

- **$75,000 GIRONA** (ESP) 4-10 OCTOBER – **Singles:** Marta Marrero (ESP) d. Dally Randriantefy (MAD) 36 76(6) 60.
  Doubles: Erica Krauth (ARG)/Jasmin Woehr (GER) d. Daniella Klemenschits/Sandra Klemenschits (AUT) 26 64 63.

- **$10,000 CAMPO GRANDE** (BRA) 11-17 OCTOBER – **Singles:** Joana Cortez (BRA) d. Estefania Craciun (URU) 61 61.
  Doubles: Estefania Balda (ECU)/Roxane Vaisemberg (BRA) d. Estefania Craciun (URU)/Ekaterina Dranets (RUS) 61 64.

- **$10,000 CASTEL GANDOLFO** (ITA) 11-17 OCTOBER – **Singles:** Aravane Rezai (FRA) d. Anna Floris (ITA) 36 62 75.
  Doubles: Raffaella Bindi/Frascensca Frappi (ITA) d. Nina Henkel (GER)/Aurelia Miseviciute (LTU) 64 36 60.

- **$10,000 DUBROVNIK** (CRO) 11-17 OCTOBER – **Singles:** Barbara Pocza (HUN) d. Sanja Ancic (CRO) 64 60.
  Doubles: Darija Jurak/Lucia Krzelj (CRO) d. Klara Jagosova (CZE)/Barbara Pocza (HUN) 63 46 63.

- **$10,000 HERCEG NOVI** (SCG) 11-17 OCTOBER – **Singles:** Dragana Zaric (SCG) d. Masa Zec-Peskiric (SLO) 67(4) 64 76(5).
  Doubles: Katarina Misic/Dragana Zaric (SCG) d. Alja Zec-Peskiric/Masa Zec-Peskiric (SLO) 61 62.

- **$25,000 JOUE LES TOURS** (FRA) 11-17 OCTOBER – **Singles:** Kveta Peschke (CZE) d. Dally Randriantefy (MAD) 63 62.
  Doubles: Kveta Peschke (CZE)/Angelika Roesch (GER) d. Stephanie Cohen-Aloro (FRA)/Selima Sfar (TUN) w/o.

- **$25,000 LAGOS** (NGR) 11-17 OCTOBER – **Singles:** Sania Mirza (IND) d. Chanelle Scheepers (RSA) 46 76(3) 75.
  Doubles: Surina De Beer/Chanelle Scheepers (RSA) d. Sania Mirza (IND)/Shelley Stephens (NZL) 60 60.

- **$25,000 MACKAY, QLD** (AUS) 11-17 OCTOBER – **Singles:** Evie Dominikovic (AUS) d. Sunitha Rao (USA) 75 63.
  Doubles: Daniella Dominikovic/Evie Dominikovic (AUS) d. Monique Adamczak/Nicole Kriz (AUS) w/o.

ITF Women's Circuit 2004 Results (continued)

- **$25,000 MEXICO CITY** (MEX) 11-17 OCTOBER – **Singles:** Frederica Piedade (POR) d. Melissa Torres (MEX) 75 62.
  Doubles: Olga Blahotova (CZE)/Kildine Chevalier (FRA) d. Larissa Carvalho/Jenifer Widjaja (BRA) 63 62.

- **$25,000 SUNDERLAND** (GBR) 11-17 OCTOBER – **Singles:** Tessy Van de Ven (NED) d. Margit Ruutel (EST) 46 60 63.
  Doubles: Elena Baltacha/Jane O'Donoghue (GBR) d. Eva Fislova/Stanislava Hrozenska (SVK) 61 46 62.

- **$50,000 ASHBURN, VA** (USA) 11-17 OCTOBER – **Singles:** Laura Granville (USA) d. Lucie Safarova (CZE) 64 62.
  Doubles: Kelly McCain/Kristen Schlukebir (USA) d. Ruxandra Dragomir-Ilie (ROM)/Samantha Reeves (USA) 62 62.

- **$10,000 AGUASCALIENTES** (MEX) 18-24 OCTOBER – **Singles:** Kildine Chevalier (FRA) d. Jorgelina Cravero (ARG) 63 64.
  Doubles: Marcela Arroyo/Melissa Torres (MEX) d. Jorgelina Cravero/Flavia Mignola (ARG) 63 62.

- **$10,000 BOLTON** (GBR) 18-24 OCTOBER – **Singles:** Tessy Van de Ven (NED) d. Karen Nugent (IRL) 62 64.
  Doubles: Sarah Borwell/Emily Webley-Smith (GBR) d. Hannah Collin/Anna Hawkins (GBR) 75 16 62.

- **$10,000 EVORA** (POR) 18-24 OCTOBER – **Singles:** Neuza Silva (POR) d. Laura Zelder (GER) 61 26 ret.
  Doubles: Danielle Steinberg/Efrat Zlotikamin (ISR) d. Kelly De Beer/Dorian Driessen (NED) 61 63.

- **$10,000 GOIANIA** (BRA) 18-24 OCTOBER – **Singles:** Maria-Jose Argeri (ARG) d. Estefania Balda (ECU) 62 64.
  Doubles: Maria-Jose Argeri (ARG)/Leticia Sobral (BRA) d. Joana Cortez/Marcela Evangelista (BRA) 63 63.

- **$10,000 LAGOS** (NGR) 18-24 OCTOBER – **Singles:** Tiffany Dabek (USA) d. Agnes Szatmari (ROM) 75 60.
  Doubles: Alanna Broderick (JAM)/Surina De Beer (RSA) d. Yevgenia Savransky (ISR)/Karin Schlapbach (SUI) 75 62.

- **$10,000 SETTIMO SAN PIETRO** (ITA) 18-24 OCTOBER – **Singles:** Aravane Rezai (FRA) d. Liana Balaci (ROM) 63 64.
  Doubles: Stefania Chieppa (ITA)/Sylvia Montero (FRA) d. Raffaella Bindi (ITA)/Sandra Zahlavova (CZE) 76(5) 36 62.

- **$25,000 HAIBARA** (JPN) 18-24 OCTOBER – **Singles:** Aiko Nakamura (JPN) d. Yuka Yoshida (JPN) 61 64.
  Doubles: Chin-Wei Chan/Yung-Jan Chan (TPE) d. Chia-Jung Chuang/Su-Wei Hsieh (TPE) 76(5) 46 76(3).

- **$25,000 ROCKHAMPTON** (AUS) 18-24 OCTOBER – **Singles:** Evie Dominikovic (AUS) d. Sunitha Rao (USA) 60 02 ret.
  Doubles: Daniella Dominikovic/Evie Dominikovic (AUS) d. Casey Dell'Acqua/Nicole Sewell (AUS) 75 62.

- **$25,000 SEVILLE** (ESP) 18-24 OCTOBER – **Singles:** Laura Pous-Tio (ESP) d. Kyra Nagy (HUN) 75 61.
  Doubles: Lourdes Dominguez-Lino/Laura Pous-Tio (ESP) d. Kyra Nagy/Virag Nemeth (HUN) 62 63.

- **$50,000 CARY, NC** (USA) 18-24 OCTOBER – **Singles:** Shenay Perry (USA) d. Kelly McCain (USA) 46 64 75.
  Doubles: Ruxandra Dragomir-Ilie (ROM)/Samantha Reeves (USA) d. Maureen Drake (CAN)/Nana Miyagi (JPN) 46 63 63.

- **$50,000 ST. RAPHAEL** (FRA) 18-24 OCTOBER – **Singles:** Barbora Strycova (CZE) d. Stephanie Cohen-Aloro (FRA) 61 62.
  Doubles: Stephanie Cohen-Aloro (FRA)/Selima Sfar (TUN) d. Barbora Strycova (CZE)/Galina Voskoboeva (RUS) 76(3) 26 64.

- **$10,000 FLORIANOPOLIS** (BRA) 25-31 OCTOBER – **Singles:** Larissa Carvalho (BRA) d. Maria-Jose Argeri (ARG) 26 62 75.
  Doubles: Maria-Jose Argeri (ARG)/Leticia Sobral (BRA) d. Larissa Carvalho/Jenifer Widjaja (BRA) 26 64 75.

- **$10,000 LAGOS** (NGR) 25-31 OCTOBER – **Singles:** Vasilisa Bardina (RUS) d. Jennifer Schmidt (AUT) 61 63.
  Doubles: Franziska Etzel (GER)/Jennifer Schmidt (AUT) d. Alanna Broderick (JAM)/Surina De Beer (RSA) 75 62.

- **$10,000 LOS MOCHIS** (MEX) 25-31 OCTOBER – **Singles:** Jorgelina Cravero (ARG) d. Micaela Moran (ARG) 62 61.
  Doubles: Jorgelina Cravero/Flavia Mignola (ARG) d. Valentina Castro (CHI)/Ana-Lucia Migliarini de Leon (URU) 62 36 75.

- **$10,000 PUNE** (IND) 25-31 OCTOBER – **Singles:** Akgul Amanmuradova (UZB) d. Rushmi Chakravarthi (IND) 60 76(5).
  Doubles: Akgul Amanmuradova (UZB)/Sai-Jayalakshmy Jayaram (IND) d. Wilawan Choptang/Thassha Vitayaviroj (THA) 63 46 63.

- **$10,000 QUARTU SANT ELENA** (ITA) 25-31 OCTOBER – **Singles:** Emily Stellato (ITA) d. Anna Floris (ITA) 26 63 64.
  Doubles: Anais Laurendon/Aurelie Vedy (FRA) d. Raffaella Bindi (ITA)/Sandra Zahlavova (CZE) 63 36 63.

- **$10,000 TAIPEI** (TPE) 25-31 OCTOBER – **Singles:** Yung-Jan Chan (TPE) d. Wen-Hsin Hsu (TPE) 75 63.
  Doubles: Hsin-Chieh Chang/Hsiao-Han Chao (TPE) d. Yung-Jan Chan/Szu-Yu Lin (TPE) 36 61 63.

- **$10,000 TOKYO** (JPN) 25-31 OCTOBER – **Singles:** Yurika Sema (JPN) d. Erika Takao (JPN) 36 76(4) 60.
  Doubles: Kumiko Iijima/Junri Namigata (JPN) d. Maki Arai/Akiko Yonemura (JPN) 63 61.

- **$25,000 ISTANBUL** (TUR) 25-31 OCTOBER – **Singles:** Virag Nemeth (HUN) d. Ipek Senoglu (TUR) 75 64.
  Doubles: Olena Antypina (UKR)/Hana Sromova (CZE) d. Ipek Senoglu (TUR)/Kathrin Woerle (GER) 67(5) 63 75.

- **$25,000 MINSK** (BLR) 25-31 OCTOBER – **Singles:** Olga Savchuk (UKR) d. Anastasia Yakimova (BLR) 64 64.
  Doubles: Daria Kustava/Anastasia Yakimova (BLR) d. Irina Bulykina (RUS)/Katarina Kachlikova (SVK) 64 60.

- **$50,000 SHENZHEN** (CHN) 25-31 OCTOBER – **Singles:** Na Li (CHN) d. Tian-Tian Sun (CHN) 63 46 62.
  Doubles: Zi Yan/Jie Zheng (CHN) d. Chia-Jung Chuang/Su-Wei Hsieh (TPE) 63 61.

- **$10,000 MALLORCA** (ESP) 1-7 NOVEMBER – **Singles:** Carla Suarez-Navarro (ESP) d. Petra Novotnikova (CZE) 62 36 61.
  Doubles: Estrella Cabeza-Candela/Adriana Gonzalez-Penas (ESP) d. Karina-Ildor Jacobsgaard/Hanne Skak-Jensen (DEN) 63 63.

- **$10,000 MANILA** (PHI) 1-7 NOVEMBER – **Singles:** Ye-Ra Lee (KOR) d. Hee-Sun Lyoo-Suh (KOR) 63 62.
  Doubles: Ayu-Fani Damayanti/Septi Mende (INA) d. Hae-Sung Kim/Ye-Ra Lee (KOR) 76(2) 16 60.

- **$10,000 ROMA CANOTTIERI** (ITA) 1-7 NOVEMBER – **Singles:** Sandra Zahlavova (CZE) d. Stefania Chieppa (ITA) 57 62 63.
  Doubles: Stefania Chieppa/Nicole Clerico (ITA) d. Valentina Sulpizio (ITA)/Sandra Zahlavova (CZE) 36 64 62.

- **$10,000 SALTA** (ARG) 1-7 NOVEMBER – **Singles:** Soledad Esperon (ARG) d. Andrea Benitez (ARG) 63 63.
  Doubles: Jorgelina Cravero/Soledad Esperon (ARG) d. Maria-Belen Corbalan/Luciana Sarmenti (ARG) 62 61.

- **$10,000 STOCKHOLM** (SWE) 1-7 NOVEMBER – **Singles:** Michaella Krajicek (NED) d. Anastasia Revzina (RUS) 61 62.
  Doubles: Michaella Krajicek/Jolanda Mens (NED) d. Sofia Avakova (RUS)/Irina Kuzmina (LAT) 62 63.

- **$25,000 MUMBAI** (IND) 1-7 NOVEMBER – **Singles:** Hana Sromova (CZE) d. Montinee Tangphong (THA) 62 61.
  Doubles: Akgul Amanmuradova (UZB)/Sai-Jayalakshmy Jayaram (IND) d. Maria Abramovic (CRO)/Hana Sromova (CZE) 46 64 64.

- **$25,000 ST. KATELIJINE-WAVER** (BEL) 1-7 NOVEMBER – **Singles:** Yvonne Meusburger (AUT) d. Selima Sfar (TUN) 64 63.
  Doubles: Virginie Pichet (FRA)/Selima Sfar (TUN) d. Eva Fislova/Stanislava Hrozenska (SVK) 61 76(2).

- **$25,000 SUTAMA** (JPN) 1-7 NOVEMBER – **Singles:** Natsumi Hamamura (JPN) d. Florence Haring (FRA) 36 63 75.
  Doubles: Kaori Aoyama/Ayami Takase (JPN) d. Tomoko Dokei/Yukiko Yabe (JPN) 64 63.

- **$50,000 SHENZHEN** (CHN) 1-7 NOVEMBER – **Singles:** Shuai Peng (CHN) d. Jie Zheng (CHN) 36 61 63.
  Doubles: Rika Fujiwara (JPN)/Elena Tatarkova (UKR) d. Zi Yan/Jie Zheng (CHN) 64 16 61.

- **$10,000 LE HAVRE** (FRA) 8-14 NOVEMBER – **Singles:** Mailyne Andrieux (FRA) d. Janette Bejlkova (CZE) 63 61.
  Doubles: Mailyne Andrieux/Kildine Chevalier (FRA) d. Maria Arkhipova (RUS)/Janette Bejlkova (CZE) 75 67(2) 64.

- **$10,000 MALLORCA** (ESP) 8-14 NOVEMBER – **Singles:** Masa Zec-Peskiric (SLO) d. Tatiana Priachin (GER) 64 63.
  Doubles: Alja Zec-Peskiric/Masa Zec-Peskiric (SLO) d. Karina-Ildor Jacobsgaard/Hanne Skak-Jensen (DEN) 60 26 63.

- **$10,000 MANILA** (PHI) 8-14 NOVEMBER – **Singles:** Ye-Ra Lee (KOR) d. Ayu-Fani Damayanti (INA) 60 10 ret.
  Doubles: Prim Buaklee/Nudnida Luangnam (THA) d. Ayu-Fani Damayanti/Septi Mende (INA) w/o.

- **$10,000 MEXICO CITY** (MEX) 8-14 NOVEMBER – **Singles:** Melissa Torres (MEX) d. Micaela Moran (ARG) 63 75.
  Doubles: Marcela Arroyo/Melissa Torres (MEX) d. Lorena Arias/Erika Clarke (MEX) 61 36 60.

- **$10,000 RAMAT HASHARON** (ISR) 8-14 NOVEMBER – **Singles:** Lenka Dlhopolcova (SVK) d. Yevgenia Savransky (ISR) 61 67(6) 60.
  Doubles: Tzipi Obziler/Danielle Steinberg (ISR) d. Pemra Ozgen (TUR)/Gabriela Velasco-Andreu (ESP) 75 63.

ITF Women's Circuit 2004 Results (continued)

- **$25,000 PORT PIRIE** (AUS) 8-14 NOVEMBER – **Singles:** Tiffany Welford (AUS) d. Meng Yuan (CHN) 57 62 75.
  Doubles: Casey Dell'Acqua (AUS)/Sunitha Rao (USA) d. Daniella Dominikovic/Evie Dominikovic (AUS) 46 63 76(6).

- **$50,000 PITTSBURGH, PA** (USA) 8-14 NOVEMBER – **Singles:** Shenay Perry (USA) d. Sofia Arvidsson (SWE) 62 61.
  Doubles: Teryn Ashley/Laura Granville (USA) d. Els Callens (BEL)/Samantha Stosur (AUS) 26 63 64.

- **$25,000 BARCELONA** (ESP) 15-21 NOVEMBER – **Singles:** Laura Pous-Tio (ESP) d. Tzvetana Pironkova (BUL) 46 75 62.
  Doubles: Lourdes Dominguez-Lino/Laura Pous-Tio (ESP) d. Nina Bratchikova/Ekaterina Kozhokhina (RUS) 64 76(4).

- **$25,000 NURIOOTPA** (AUS) 15-21 NOVEMBER – **Singles:** Evie Dominikovic (AUS) d. Yoon-Jeong Cho (KOR) 64 57 64.
  Doubles: Yoon-Jeong Cho/Jin-Hee Kim (KOR) d. Daniella Dominikovic/Evie Dominikovic (AUS) 75 62.

- **$25,000 PRUHONICE** (CZE) 15-21 NOVEMBER – **Singles:** Michaela Pastikova (CZE) d. Sandra Kloesel (GER) 63 62.
  Doubles: Gabriela Navratilova/Michaela Pastikova (CZE) d. Lucie Hradecka/Sandra Kleinova (CZE) 63 63.

- **$25,000 PUEBLA** (MEX) 15-21 NOVEMBER – **Singles:** Mariana Diaz-Oliva (ARG) d. Mathilde Johansson (FRA) 63 61.
  Doubles: Marcela Arroyo/Melissa Torres (MEX) d. Lorena Arias/Erika Clarke (MEX) 26 76(2) 60.

- **$50,000 DEAUVILLE** (FRA) 15-21 NOVEMBER – **Singles:** Kveta Peschke (CZE) d. Alyona Bondarenko (UKR) 60 63.
  Doubles: Virag Nemeth (HUN)/Tzipi Obziler (ISR) d. Vanessa Henke (GER)/Kveta Peschke (CZE) 64 61.

- **$50,000 TUCSON, AZ** (USA) 15-21 NOVEMBER – **Singles:** Jamea Jackson (USA) d. Stephanie Dubois (CAN) 76(5) 75.
  Doubles: Liga Dekmeijere (LAT)/Vladimira Uhlirova (CZE) d. Krysty Marcio/Jessica Nguyen (USA) 64 64.

- **$10,000 CAIRO** (EGY) 22-28 NOVEMBER – **Singles:** Julia Ustyuzhanina (UKR) d. Gabriela Niculescu (ROM) 64 64.
  Doubles: Petra Cetkovska (CZE)/Pauline Parmentier (FRA) d. Galina Fokina/Raissa Gourevitch (RUS) 64 62.

- **$10,000 FLORIANOPOLIS** (BRA) 22-28 NOVEMBER – **Singles:** Micaela Moran (ARG) d. Joana Cortez (BRA) 26 62 62.
  Doubles: Joana Cortez/Marcela Evangelista (BRA) d. Fernanda Hermenegildo (BRA)/Sarah Tami-Masi (PAR) 64 64.

- **$10,000 PRETORIA** (RSA) 22-28 NOVEMBER – **Singles:** Chanelle Scheepers (RSA) d. Lizaan Du Plessis (RSA) 61 63.
  Doubles: Karoline Borgersen (NOR)/Leonie Mekel (NED) d. Karin Schlapbach/Vanessa Wellauer (SUI) 62 64.

- **$25,000 MOUNT GAMBIER** (AUS) 22-28 NOVEMBER – **Singles:** Evie Dominikovic (AUS) d. Yoon-Jeong Cho (KOR) 75 63.
  Doubles: Chin-Wei Chan/Yung-Jan Chan (TPE) d. Ryoko Fuda (JPN)/Su-Wei Hsieh (TPE) 63 57 75.

- **$25,000 OPOLE** (POL) 22-28 NOVEMBER – **Singles:** Angelique Kerber (GER) d. Elena Tatarkova (UKR) 62 62.
  Doubles: Lucie Hradecka/Eva Hrdinova (CZE) d. Ekaterina Dzehalevich/Nadejda Ostrovskaya (BLR) 75 63.

- **$25,000 SAN LUIS POTOSI** (MEX) 22-28 NOVEMBER – **Singles:** Melinda Czink (HUN) d. Mariana Diaz-Oliva (ARG) 60 57 63.
  Doubles: Hannah Collin/Karen Paterson (GBR) d. Ivana Abramovic/Maria Abramovic (CRO) 64 26 62.

- **$75,000 POITIERS** (FRA) 22-28 NOVEMBER – **Singles:** Anastasia Yakimova (BLR) d. Marie-Gaiane Mikaelian (SUI) 75 62.
  Doubles: Stephanie Cohen-Aloro (FRA)/Selima Sfar (TUN) d. Gabriela Navratilova/Michaela Pastikova (CZE) 75 64.

- **$10,000 BANGKOK** (THA) 29 NOVEMBER-5 DECEMBER – **Singles:** Akgul Amanmuradova (UZB) d. Napaporn Tongsalee (THA) 62 63.
  Doubles: Akgul Amanmuradova (UZB)/Napaporn Tongsalee (THA) d. I-Hsuan Hwang (TPE)/Nudnida Luangnam (THA) 64 64.

- **$10,000 CAIRO** (EGY) 29 NOVEMBER-5 DECEMBER – **Singles:** Pauline Parmentier (FRA) d. Julia Ustyuzhanina (UKR) 61 61.
  Doubles: Katarina Misic/Dragana Zaric (SCG) d. Galina Fokina/Raissa Gourevitch (RUS) 75 64.

- **$10,000 PRETORIA** (RSA) 29 NOVEMBER-5 DECEMBER – **Singles:** Chanelle Scheepers (RSA) d. Karoline Borgersen (NOR) 61 63.
  Doubles: Melissa Berry (GBR)/Chanelle Scheepers (RSA) d. Karoline Borgersen (NOR)/Leonie Mekel (NED) 62 36 75.

- **$25,000 RAANANA** (ISR) 29 NOVEMBER-5 DECEMBER – **Singles:** Shahar Peer (ISR) d. Zsofia Gubacsi (HUN) 62 61.
  Doubles: Tzipi Obziler/Shahar Peer (ISR) d. Bahia Mouhtassine (MAR)/Ipek Senoglu (TUR) 63 60.

- **$50,000 PALM BEACH GARDENS** (USA) 29 NOVEMBER-5 DECEMBER – **Singles:** Sesil Karatantcheva (BUL) d. Sania Mirza (IND) 36 62 75.
  Doubles: Liga Dekmeijere (LAT)/Nana Miyagi (JPN) d. Kelly McCain/Kaysie Smashey (USA) 63 62.

- **$10,000 CAIRO 6** (EGY) 6-12 DECEMBER – **Singles:** Galina Fokina (RUS) d. Pauline Parmentier (FRA) 64 63.
  Doubles: Katarina Misic/Dragana Zaric (SCG) d. Galina Fokina/Raissa Gourevitch (RUS) 62 62.

- **$10,000 JAKARTA 4** (INA) 6-12 DECEMBER – **Singles:** Sandy Gumulya (INA) d. Ayu-Fani Damayanti (INA) 63 60.
  Doubles: Ayu-Fani Damayanti/Septi Mende (INA) d. Mi Lyoo (KOR)/Julia Vorobieva (RUS) 46 60 75.

- **$10,000 KOLKATA** (IND) 6-12 DECEMBER – **Singles:** Ankita Bhambri (IND) d. Wilawan Choptang (THA) 63 75.
  Doubles: Wilawan Choptang (THA)/Shruti Dhawan (IND) d. Ankita Bhambri/Sanaa Bhambri (IND) 62 75.

- **$10,000 GURGAON** (IND) 13-19 DECEMBER – **Singles:** Rushmi Chakravarthi (IND) d. Ankita Bhambri (IND) 67(5) 76(2) 64.
  Doubles: Rushmi Chakravarthi/Sai-Jayalakshmy Jayaram (IND) d. Ankita Bhambri/Sanaa Bhambri (IND) 26 62 64.

- **$10,000 JAKARTA 5** (INA) 13-19 DECEMBER – **Singles:** Julia Vorobieva (RUS) d. Yoo-Mi Jung (KOR) 36 61 63.
  Doubles: Mi Lyoo (KOR)/Julia Vorobieva (RUS) d. Kyung-Mi Chang/Ye-Ra Lee (KOR) 63 63.

- **$25,000 VALASSKE MEZIRICI** (CZE) 13-19 DECEMBER – **Singles:** Libuse Prusova (CZE) d. Lucie Safarova (CZE) 76(7) 64.
  Doubles: Daniella Klemenschits/Sandra Klemenschits (AUT) d. Lucie Hradecka/Eva Hrdinova (CZE) w/o.

- **$50,000 BERGAMO** (ITA) 13-19 DECEMBER – **Singles:** Michaella Krajicek (NED) d. Ekaterina Bychkova (RUS) 64 63.
  Doubles: Giulia Casoni/Francesca Lubiani (ITA) d. Lenka Nemeckova (CZE)/Julia Schruff (GER) 62 63.

tennis development in 2004

by tori billington

In 2004, the budgeted spending on ITF Development Programme activities was US$3.32 million, with US$2 million being provided by the ITF and US$1.32 million by the Grand Slam nations, bringing the total funding since 1986, when Grand Slam Development Fund first began, to just under US$53 million.

The aim of the programme is to raise the level of tennis worldwide and increase the number of countries competing in mainstream international tennis, and to do this the ITF Development Department works with more than 150 national associations from developing tennis nations on a range of initiatives from the grass roots level to participation at Grand Slams. The following report is a summary of activities in 2004 and highlights some of the success stories and new ventures this year.

In 2004, there were nine full-time Development Officers – the eyes and ears of the ITF Development Programme. Their role is to advise and assist national associations on their tennis activities, conduct coaches' courses and player training camps, coordinate regional competitions as well as talent scout and provide vital assessments of ITF funded initiatives across the globe. In 2004, the Development Officers visited 120 different countries and each spent on average 25 weeks on the road.

In June of 2004, the ITF appointed Hichem Riani as the ITF Development Officer for West Asia. Riani, formerly Technical Director and Davis Cup Captain for the Tunisian Tennis Federation, is based in Qatar and covers the Middle East. For Riani, like Achille Takpa who took over as ITF Development Officer for West & Central Africa at the end of 2003 and is based in Benin, it has been a frantic year of travelling, establishing working relationships with key national association members and building up a picture of the current activity as well as the potential within their respective regions.

One of their main areas of activity is coaches' education and it is encouraging to see an increasing number of ITF member nations working with us to put in place their own certification programme. In 2004, 44 courses were held including 12 x Level 1 and 19 x Level 2 courses. One of the most memorable courses took place in Amman in September 2004. Being unable to run a course in either Iraq or Palestine in the current climate, the ITF with the help of the Jordan Tennis Federation (JTF) ran a Level I Course at the JTF national tennis centre in Amman and coaches from Palestine and Iraq travelled by road to attend the nine-day course which was conducted in Arabic.

Regional Workshops were also held in each continent to enable coaches that have already undertaken the Level 1 and Level 2 courses to update their knowledge with presentations from top international speakers on the latest tennis coaching and sports science findings. One of the highlights was the 10th ITF South American Coaches Workshop organised in conjunction with COSAT and the Asociacion Paraguaya de Tenis, which saw more than 160 coaches from all over South America gather in Asunción for five days of presentations. Other Regional Workshops took place in the Dominican Republic, Malta, India and South Africa.

As well as courses, coaches worldwide are now able to keep themselves informed by visiting the new ITF coaching weblet (www.itftennis.com/coaching), which was launched in July 2004. The weblet contains information on the ITF Coach Education programme, upcoming courses, access to the latest issue of Coaching & Sport Science Review and ITF publications as well as a resource centre with information on injury prevention, ethics and tennis academies.

Lack of access to basic tennis equipment is still a problem facing developing nations and as such the ITF through its Equipment Distribution Programme provides ITF branded equipment (rackets, balls, strings), free of charge, for use by national associations. During 2004, 110 national associations benefited from the ITF equipment with the following quantities being distributed throughout the year:

- Rackets: 8497
- Balls: 242,435 or 20,203 dozen
- Mini-tennis nets: 983
- Strings: 1427 x 200m reels
- Coaching books: 16,102

ITF Equipment Distribution Programme in Mali

Inauguration of three new tennis courts in Oman

Junior Wimbledon Champion Katerina Bondarenko (UKR)

tennis development in 2004
by tori billington

Like equipment, many national associations do not have their own national tennis centre and instead have to rent private facilities. As a result facility grants are available to help these national associations build their own centre. While being only a small percentage of the overall building cost, the ITF grant often acts as an endorsement and catalyst to enable associations to attract other funding whether from the government or private sector. In 2004, five national associations were awarded facility grants and started the important process of building their own headquarters. In May 2004, with the help of an ITF facility grant, the Oman Tennis Association completed a four-court facility at the Sultan Qaboos Sports Complex. Following the success of this facility, the Oman Tennis Association secured additional funding from the ministry to build a further three courts giving them a venue large enough to host for the first time the ITF Asian 13 & U Championships – Zone 4 (West Asia) in December 2004.

These Championships were just one of 24 regional junior events (18, 16 and 14 & under) that took place with ITF Development Programme financial assistance as well as technical assistance from the ITF Development Officers. The competitions provide the opportunity for the players from each country to test themselves against the best in their region.

In Africa, events are organised at the 13 & Under level in Southern, East, West and Central Africa. Three-day training camps are followed by two tournaments using feed-in consolation, giving competitors the maximum possible matches and the chance for accompanying national coaches to work together and exchange ideas. The events also give the chance for ITF Development Officers to gauge the level of play, and talented players are often offered the chance to attend an ITF Training Camp later in the year or awarded a scholarship to attend the ITF/SATA African Training Centre. The African Training Centre is based in Pretoria, South Africa with players training at the High Performance Centre at the University of Pretoria while continuing their education at local schools. In 2004, 21 players attended the ITF Centre on a full-time basis with 37 players and four coaches attending on a part-time basis.

But the largest annual event of the year is of course the ITF/CAT African Junior Championships. This year's Championships took place at the Smash Tennis Academy in Cairo with the Egyptian Tennis Federation hosting the event for the third time in the event's 27-year history. Twenty-one African countries received direct acceptance into the event along with an ITF Team made up of players that had won through regional qualifying competitions earlier in the year for the weaker countries in West/Central Africa and East/Southern Africa. In all a total of 158 competitors made the trip to Cairo for individual and team competitions at the 14, 16 and 18 & under level. The home crowd were not disappointed when Egypt's Mohammed Safwat took the boys' U14 title, and Magy Nader Aziz winning the girls' U18 title. Morocco took the boys' U18 title and girls' U16 title, and Tunisia took the boys' U16 title and girls' U14 title, highlighting the strength of tennis in North Africa at the moment.

In Asia, the year started with the ITF 14 & Under Asian Championships (Zone 2) which was hosted by the Myanmar Tennis Federation (TFM) in January. The two-week event was not only the first ITF event to be organised by the TFM but also the first international tennis event to be held in the country for 30 years. The Championships attracted a great deal of support from the government and welcomed teams from Bhutan, Laos, Malaysia, Maldives, Mongolia, Nepal, Pakistan and Sri Lanka.

A large proportion of competitors in these 14 & under events have come through ITF funded School Tennis Initiative (STI) and Performance Tennis Initiative (PTI) programmes. PM Thar of Myanmar and B Munkhbaatar of Mongolia (winner and runner up respectively in the Asian Zone 2 event) are cases in point, highlighting that ITF initiated programmes are beginning to show results. Now operating in more than 80 countries, the STI programme gives children their first taste of tennis and since its inception in

ITF Touring Team won Girls' Singles and Doubles titles at Wimbledon

> A large proportion of competitors in the 14 & under Asian Championships have come through ITF funded School Tennis Initiative and Performance Tennis Initiative programmes.

> "The joint objective of the ITF Development Programme and Olympic Solidarity is to promote our sport, from grass roots to the elite level; to give nations like Cyprus the chance to develop the game and give talent a chance to shine on the international stage."

1996 more than three million have benefited from regular mini-tennis lessons and taken part in local mini-tennis competitions through the STI programme.

In the Pacific Oceania Region, the STI and PTI programmes are supported by ANZ Bank. In 1993 the original goal of the ANZ Bank mini-tennis programme was to give children a taste of tennis and at the same time to help coaches turn their hobby of teaching tennis into a career. Today the programme operates in 14 Pacific countries with 110 schools and 30,000 children taking part. Andrew Mailtorok of Vanuatu and Samuel Tesimu of Solomon Islands both started out playing in ANZ mini-tennis programmes and, having progressed through the ITF Training Centre in Fiji, are now studying in the USA on tennis scholarships.

Based on performances at regional competitions, players have the opportunity to win a place on an ITF Touring Team to play higher-level events outside their region, with the ITF coach and expenses during the tour financed by the Development Programme. For Michael Clarke of Trinidad and Andres Bucaro of Guatemala, the year started with a trip to South America to compete in COSAT 14 & under events as part of the ITF Central American and Caribbean Team. Despite being a step up in level, the boys performed well reaching doubles finals in Chile and Brazil. Later in the year they got another chance to test themselves, not only against the best South American 14 & unders but also players from Asia, Africa and Europe as they travelled to Paris along with 51 other players and 11 coaches to take part on one of five ITF funded 14 & under Teams in Europe.

The ITF Touring Team programme is probably the ITF's most well known development initiative. Paradorn Srichaphan (Thailand), Gustavo Kuerten (Brazil), Cara Black (Zimbabwe), Eleni Daniilidou (Greece) and this year's Olympic Gold medallist Nicolas Massu (Chile) have all been ITF Touring Team members in the past. In 2004 there were 17 ITF Touring Teams involving 152 players from 72 different countries. The flagship Team is undoubtedly the ITF 18 & under Team which plays an eight-week series of Grade 1 and Grade A events including junior Roland Garros and junior Wimbledon. This year's team consisted of 18 players from 15 different countries but despite the diversity of nations, the team was to be dominated by the performances of one region – the girls from Eastern Europe. Madalina Gojnea of Romania was a finalist at Roland Garros while at Wimbledon, Katerina Bondarenko of Ukraine won the singles title with the Belarussian duo of Viktoria Azarenka and Volha Havartsova winning the doubles event, making it an impressive four doubles titles during their 8-week tour.

Finally in an Olympic year, it is only fitting to acknowledge the continued support the ITF and its member nations receive from Olympic Solidarity (OS). OS is the part of the International Olympic Committee that distributes television income from the Olympic Games to National Olympic Committees and since the reintroduction of tennis into the Olympic family at Seoul in 1988, the ITF, through the Development Department, has collaborated closely with OS on a variety of programmes designed to grown tennis around the world. Coaches' education is the main area of activity and over the last four years, 50% of the 200 coaches' courses organised by the ITF have been funded through Olympic Solidarity. In addition from 2001–2004, a total of 22 players from 20 countries have benefited from OS Training Scholarships in preparation for the Athens and Beijing Games, including former ITF Team-member and last year's ITF Junior World Champion Marcos Baghdatis of Cyprus.

"The joint objective of the ITF Development Programme and Olympic Solidarity is to promote our sport, from grass roots to the elite level; to give nations like Cyprus the chance to develop the game and give talent an opportunity to shine on the international stage," comments Dave Miley, ITF Executive Director of Tennis Development. "We look forward to working together with OS and our respective member nations on more projects over the next Olympic quadrennial."

For more details on Development activities please visit the new ITF Development Programme weblet, www.itftennis.com/development.

ITF Central American, Caribbean and African 14 & Under team in Europe

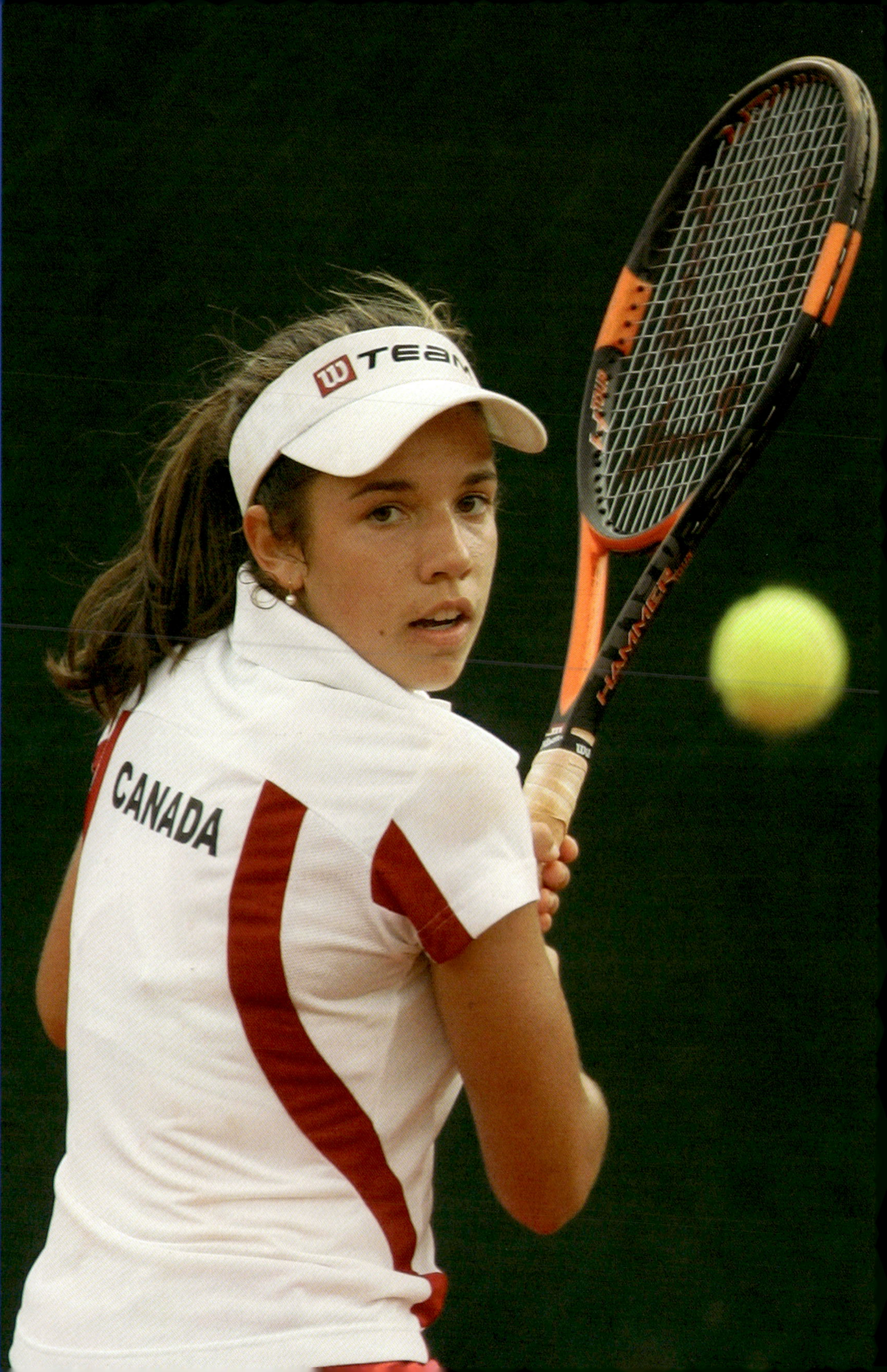
TEAM
CANADA
HAMMER

Marketing the Game

A Marketing the Game Summit was held in Windsor, UK in 2000, attended by representatives of all constituencies of the game and the established tennis nations. It was agreed to launch a number of projects to increase interest and participation in tennis, and task forces were formed, headed by an ITF cross-departmental working group. Projects have included a Joint Marketing Campaign, where ITF matched funds provided by other partners, for example Tennis Europe's "Fill the Stands – See Tennis Live" campaign. A Schools Tennis Website was created and is now available for nations to use and adapt to their home market. An individual rating system, now known as the International Tennis Number (ITN) has been successfully launched in 25 countries and an Intro to Tennis project is underway.

Team Identification

In 2001, the ITF's AGM unanimously approved the concept of Team Identification as a way to improve enjoyment for TV audiences and mirror the patriotism of the spectators. The project was designed to bring the ITF's international team competitions including the flagship events, Davis Cup and Fed Cup, into line with other international sports, requiring that players be dressed in a consistent manner, reflecting their national team colours.

The project was introduced in 2002 on a voluntary basis and is now mandatory in the Davis Cup and Fed Cup World Groups, and in the Finals of Junior Davis Cup and Junior Fed Cup, and World Junior Tennis.

The long-term ideal would be for full team uniform, as in Ryder Cup, for example, and wearing of both team colours and country name is already mandatory for the Junior events. However, due to sponsorship agreements with individual players, there is at present an element of compromise in Davis Cup and Fed Cup, with either national colours or country name being acceptable. A mixture of the two options one player in team colours the other with country name only or two players wearing colours not sufficiently identical is not visually appealing and efforts will continue to streamline the team colours option.

International Tennis Number (ITN)

Following the launch of the ITN in January 2003, the ITF has continued to work with ITF member nations to help increase tennis participation in their countries. The ITN Manual was completed in early January 2004 and is now available in PDF format on the new ITN weblet (www.itftennis.com/itn) along with all the other supporting ITN material. The new weblet provides nations with all the tools needed to implement the ITN on a national and club level as well as showcasing the latest news from participating ITN nations from around the globe.

An ITN On Court Assessment has also been developed and was launched at the ITF AGM in 2003 on a trial basis. This is an objective method of initially rating recreational players who do not play competitions on a regular basis. A flash programme demonstration of the On Court Assessment is also available on the ITN weblet along with a booklet in English, French and Spanish. To support the On Court Assessment and running alongside the official ITN website is an additional website, www.oncourtassessment.com, where coaches are encouraged to register as assessors and enter assessment results of all their players. Players can then log in and start charting their own development and improvement over time. It also allows players to compare their scores to other players on a local, national and international basis as well as print out their own ITN Certificate.

To date 25 countries have officially launched the ITN on a national basis with coaches in 47 countries using the On Court Assessment website to enter scores. To continue to promote the ITN and educate new nations, an ITN e-mail newsletter is now also produced on a monthly basis, and distributed to coaches, players, clubs, tournament administrators, key media, manufacturers, commercial contacts and all regional and national associations.

Intro to Tennis project

The Intro to Tennis project, started in 2003, aims to look closely at how tennis is currently being introduced to juniors and adults worldwide and ways in which it could be done more effectively. Following on from work already started in 2003, an Intro to Tennis Taskforce meeting to discuss these topics took place in February 2004, attended by coaches and representatives from national associations as well as manufacturers of tennis equipment.

Work has begun on a number of different projects including the production in English and Spanish of DVDs and tennis manuals on adult tennis (originally produced in French by the French Tennis Federation). In addition the ITF, in consultation with manufacturers, has carried out extensive research into the specifications of the various types of modified balls currently on the market that are used for introductory tennis. Research is also taking place to determine which colour of modified ball is best suited for adult beginner play. From January 2005, a ball approval scheme for all types of introductory tennis balls will operate.

A number of additional projects have been identified for further research in 2005. These include promoting the health benefits of tennis and also a "games based" teaching methodology for introducing adults and children to tennis, in an effort to attract and retain more people in the game.

Canada's Sharon Fichman competing in Junior Fed Cup

monfils shines as a star of the future

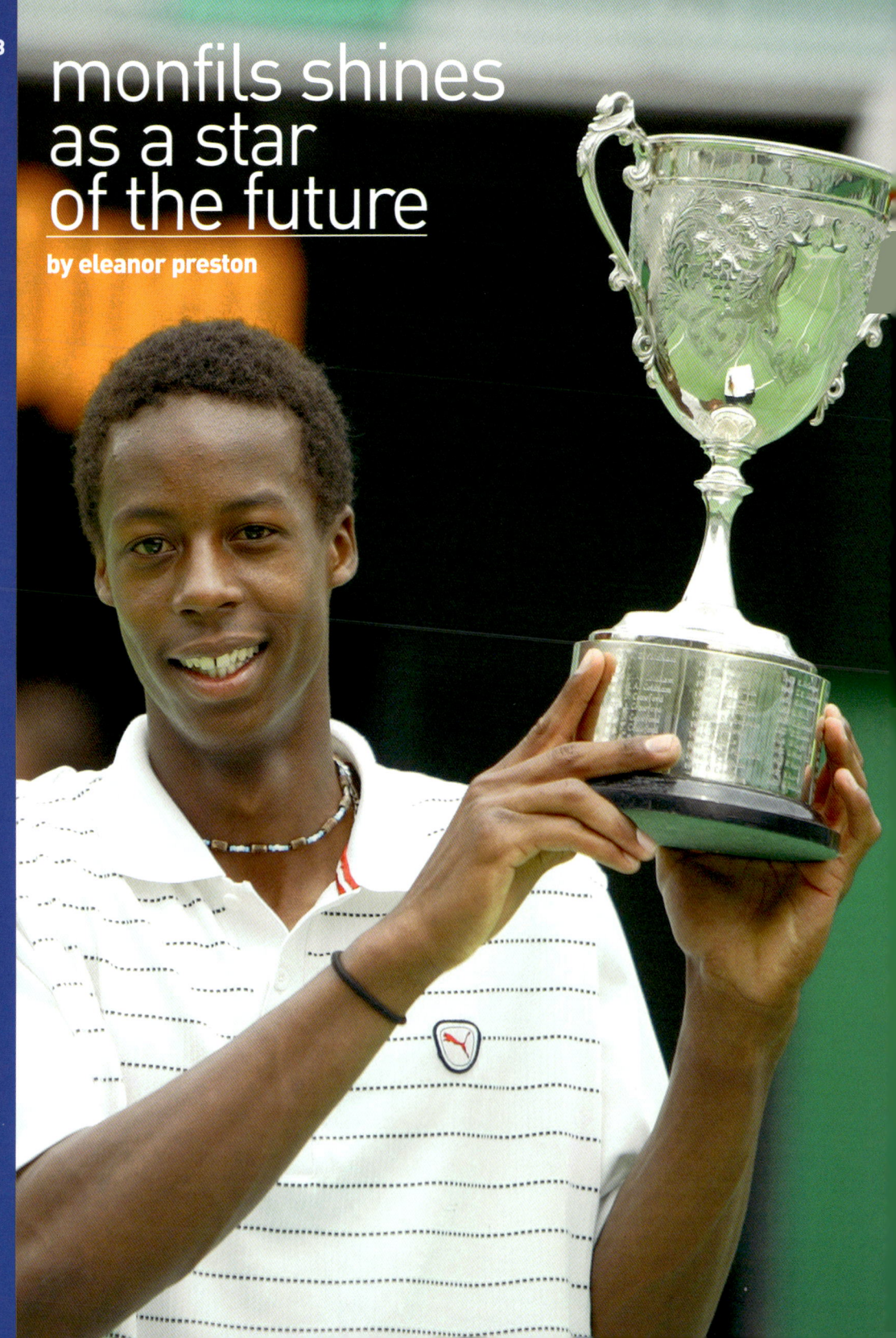

by eleanor preston

In every era there is one tennis player who is, for one reason or another, just that little bit better than everyone else. At various times in recent decades, the likes of Pete Sampras, Roger Federer, Steffi Graf, Serena Williams have all proved it – each generation has a star that, for a time at least, shines more brightly than all the others.

On the ITF Junior Circuit in 2004, French teenager Gael Monfils was positively incandescent.

He took the first three grand slams of the year and went unbeaten in the juniors until the US Open in August and, but for an ill-timed knee injury over the summer, might well have become the first boy since Stefan Edberg in 1983 to lift all four in a season. He won the race to finish the year as World No.1 so comfortably that he ended up with more than twice as many ranking points as the World No. 2, Eduardo Schwank (ARG), in the final reckoning.

Monfils enjoyed the sort of year that players of any age would dream about and it rather eclipsed the notable achievements of several other fledgling talents. The Netherlands' Michaella Krajicek ended the year (the first using the Combined Singles and Doubles Ranking system) as girls' World No. 1 after a string of sparkling performances in both singles and doubles, climaxing with her double US Open victory in September; Shahar Peer, Sesil Karatancheva and Katerina Bondarenko all won grand slam singles titles and the latter snapped menacingly at Krajicek's heels at No. 2 in the year-end rankings; 17-year-old Scot Andrew Murray gave much-maligned British tennis a boost by taking the boys' title in Flushing Meadows while American duo Brendan Evans and Scott Oudsema continued to excel in doubles. Yet as attention-grabbing as all those performances (and more) were, somehow it was hard to take your eyes off Monfils.

He began his odyssey in Melbourne, at the junior Australian Open, where he was as shy and self-effacing off the court as he was

Michaella Krajicek (NED)

dominant and certain on it. After playing and losing four consecutive finals going back to December 2003's USTA Winter Championships, Monfils beat his friend, training partner and room-mate Josselyn Ouanna 60 63 in the biggest final of all.

After that match he spoke in a voice that barely rose above a whisper, in hesitant English, and revealed how nervous he had been, yet his words hinted at the steel that lay beneath the diffident exterior, a strength of character that would come to the fore more and more as the season wore on.

"I forgot that he was my friend when we were on the court," said Monfils of Ouanna. "It's a bit sad that the scoreline wasn't very close but I am not sad that he lost because it's a match and that's sport. I made finals before and lost but I won the biggest one, and that will give me lots of confidence."

He turned out to be right about that one. Monfils and his coaches plotted his course to mix experience at senior level with a big push in the juniors, though it only became clear at Roland Garros just how big that push was going to be. There, under the pressure of playing in the venue where he trains and where the French crowd and media ratchet up the levels of expectation, Monfils proved beyond doubt that he had that special mix of talent, composure and athleticism that elevates the truly special players above the pack.

After looking less than convincing earlier in the tournament, Monfils romped through a 62 62 win over the USA's Alex Kuznetsov in the final.

"It's my reward for hard work with my coaches," he said after that match, to a room packed with French journalists, TV cameras and photographers. His voice was louder, his words more emphatic than they had been in Melbourne, as though the role of superstar was growing on him.

"I already won in Australia, so it proves that it's not luck and that I'm confirming what I'm able to do. I personally do not put pressure on myself but I have to believe in what I'm doing. There's no reason why I shouldn't play well in the main draw now because I'm one of the best juniors. It's possible if I work hard. Maybe in two or three years maybe I will be able to hold the men's trophy."

Few would bet against it, especially after Monfils romped through the draw at Wimbledon to give himself a shot at his third major of a year that was barely half-way through. 18-year-old Briton Miles Kasiri stood between Monfils and the title, having battled his way through a handful of

> "I forgot that he was my friend when we were on the court," said Monfils of Ouanna. "It's a bit sad that the scoreline wasn't very close but I am not sad that he lost because it's a match and that's sport."

Gael Monfils (FRA)

monfils shines as a star of the future
by eleanor preston

seeds to get there. Kasiri, playing his first junior final, acquitted himself admirably in front of his home crowd and had set-points in the first set and for neutral observers his efforts illuminated another of Monfils' qualities – his fighting spirit.

to watch. "I'm obviously disappointed that I lost because I know that I had a lot of chances in the first set and in the second set I was up in the tiebreak," said Kasiri. "It was so close. There's like one or two points that would have made the whole difference

> Sesil Karatancheva seems intent on bringing happiness too, if only from her lively, voluble press conferences... "I don't think I'm a star but it depends how you define a star," she laughed.

Kasiri brought the best out of Monfils but in the end France's finest battled to a 75 76 and was greeted by a chorus of La Marseillaise from the small but noisy band of French supporters on Court No.3.

"It was good to have them there and I thank them for their help," said Monfils, who joined in the fun by conducting their impromptu choir. "Before every final you are nervous and at first I felt so nervous that I could not play my game but also Miles played very well."

Kasiri had been unseeded on paper but it was clear from his bullish comments afterwards that he considers himself one of the match. That gives me confidence because he hasn't lost a match this year and he's won all three Grand Slams so far, so he's obviously a very good player. I know if I was to play him again, I would go on court believing I could win."

The prospect of anyone managing that against Monfils became more realistic after he was struck down with a knee injury just after his Wimbledon win and six weeks before the start of the US Open. He arrived in New York playing down his chances of matching Edberg's 21-year-old record of achieving the calendar Grand Slam and much to his own – and many neutrals' – disappointment, he was proved right. After limping past first Remko De Rijke of the Netherlands and then American Phillip Simmonds, Monfils was ambushed 64 62 by 18-year-old Viktor Troicki of Serbia & Montenegro.

Troicki's handiwork may have ended Monfils' dream but it did offer the chance for someone else to grab a little of the spotlight that had been trained on the French teenager all year. Murray proved more than able to step in, beating Ukrainian Sergiy Stakhovsky 64 62 in the final after a blistering run.

"I just couldn't believe I had won," said Murray, who missed much of the first half of the year with a nagging knee injury. "To win a junior Grand Slam after being out of tennis for so long is a big thing for me because I've only been playing again for two and a half, three months. I think when I was out injured, it made me mentally stronger because before, everything had been given to me, everything was really easy. But after that, obviously it was really difficult to come back from an injury. I got physically stronger as well because I did a lot of work on my upper body while I was out. That's helped me the last few weeks."

Murray's win certainly catapulted him into the public eye in the UK. He returned home to find a gaggle of photographers at the airport and reams of newsprint dedicated to his achievement in becoming the first ever British US Open champion. He was suddenly being mentioned in the same breath as his mentor, men's US Open semifinalist Tim Henman, who had been a supportive voice in Murray's ear throughout the tournament.

"To be compared to someone who's been in the Top 10 for six or seven years is great fun," said Murray after his win. "Just now I'm nowhere near as good as Tim. Obviously, I'm just at the bottom of the ladder and I need to try and work my way up. I think I can do it."

Winning a junior grand slam is a good place to start, as Shahar Peer of Israel found out in Melbourne at the start of the year. Peer beat 14-year-old Czech Nicole Vaidisova 61 64 in the Australian Open girls' final and was under no illusions about how significant her victory might turn out to be for her future career. "It is a big moment."

Shahar Peer (ISR)

Sesil Karatantcheva (BUL)

"I didn't really play well during the match but she played really, really bad, and she would say that herself," said 17-year-old Peer after the match. "That is the difference between being a Grand Slam champion and just making the final. You are both excited and nervous but I managed to get past that."

Peer also showed she has an understanding of the wider impact of a sport like tennis, and how much pleasure it can bring even in troubled times. "I'm very proud to have won this title for Israel, for the people, especially with all the bad things that are going on there," said Peer. "I hope it will bring some happiness."

Sesil Karatancheva seems intent on bringing happiness too, if only from her lively, voluble press conferences. The charming, funny, US-trained 15-year-old from Bulgaria was humble after winning the girls' title 64 60 at Roland Garros over Romania's Madalina Gojnea. "I don't think I'm a star but it depends how you define a star," she laughed.

It was a tough act for 17-year-old Katerina Bondarenko to follow in the Wimbledon final. Wisely, the Ukrainian's stuck to letting her racket do the talking and it was in eloquent enough form to help her beat Ana Ivanovic of Serbia & Montenegro 64 67 62 to win her first grand slam title.

It was a first junior Grand Slam title for Krajicek at Flushing Meadows, though not her first trip to the final. In 2003 the then 14-year-old had been in tears after losing to Kirsten Flipkens in the final and suffering the double agony of seeing the World No.1 ranking slip from her grasp as well. A year on an older, fitter and more battle hardened Krajicek returned to win the title courtesy of a 61 61 victory over American Jessica Kirkland in the final, having saved match-points in the semis. It was the sort of resilient performance of which her brother Richard (the 1996 Wimbledon men's champion) would have been proud.

"Last year I was really disappointed I lost the final, even though I did well to get there, and this year I'm really happy I won," said the younger Krajicek. "I think I was a lot of more comfortable in the final because I was going with the feeling that I already did this last year, so I don't have to be nervous. I think that was important for me."

Kirkland got some compensation for her defeat by winning the Orange Bowl singles title in December with a 62 60 win over Russia's Alla Kudryavtseva in the final. Thomas Neilly made it a clean sweep for USA in the Florida season finale for the first time in 20 years when he beat fellow American Donald Young 64 75 to take the boys' title.

The most outstanding performances in doubles came from Oudsema and Evans. They took the boys' doubles title at the Australian Open with a clinical 61 61 win over Australian wildcards David Galic and David Jeflea and used that as a springboard for another impressive year. The Americans took their second grand slam doubles title of the year at Wimbledon with a 64 64 win over Robin Haase (NED) and Viktor Troicki (SCG).

Two major titles became three at the US Open, when the Americans scored a 46 61 62 victory over Germans Andreas Beck and Sebastian Rieschick in the final. Krajicek won the doubles title in New York after teaming up with New Zealand's Marina Erakovic to beat Romanians Monica Niculescu and Madalina Gojnea 76 60, to add to her Roland Garros doubles title with Czech Katerina Bohmova.

In the season's team competitions, Great Britain capped off a good year for its juniors by winning the World Junior Tennis 14 & under boys' title with a win over the Czech Republic in Prostejov. Spain's 16 & under youngsters matched the achievements of their Davis Cup by BNP Paribas-winning men by taking the Junior Davis Cup by BNP Paribas with a win over the Czechs in Barcelona.

> "I think I was a lot of more comfortable in the final because I was going with the feeling that I already did this last year, so I don't have to be nervous. I think that was important for me," said Krajicek.

In girls' team events Belarus beat Austria to take the World Junior Tennis title, while Argentina edged out Canada in the Junior Fed Cup.

It's hard not to be impressed by all those who found enough precocious self-belief to make good on their talent and take home junior titles during 2004, but it's even harder not to regard Monfils' achievements as something very special indeed.

In a year full of stars, the boy who started the year a shy, wide-eyed unknown and ended it as a legend-in-the-making shone just a little brighter than the rest.

ITF Junior World Rankings 2004 Points Explanation

The ITF Junior Circuit is a world-wide points-linked circuit of 304 tournaments, including six continental championships and two team competitions in 112 countries under the management of the International Tennis Federation. There are ten separate points categories covering the three types of events. The best six singles results and one quarter of the best six doubles results from tournaments (Grade A and 1-5), continental championships (Grade B1-B3) and team competitions (Grade C) count towards a player's Junior Ranking. To qualify for a final year-end ranking a player must have competed in at least six events, including at least three Grade A tournaments and at least three outside his or her own home country.

Tournaments and Continental Championships

Singles

Grade	A	1	2	3	4	5	B1	B2	B3
Winner	250	150	100	60	40	30	180	120	80
Runner-up	180	100	75	45	30	20	120	80	50
Semifinalists	120	80	50	30	20	15	80	60	30
Quarterfinalists	80	60	30	20	15	10	60	40	15
Losers in last 16	50	30	20	15	10	5	30	25	5
Losers in last 32	30	20	-	-	-	-	20	10	-

Doubles

Grade	A	1	2	3	4	5	B1	B2	B3
Winners	180	100	75	50	30	20	120	80	50
Runners-up	120	75	50	30	20	15	80	60	30
Semifinalists	80	50	30	20	15	10	60	40	15
Quarterfinalists	50	30	20	15	10	5	30	25	5
Losers in last 16	30	20	-	-	-	-	20	10	-

Grade A Super Series Bonus Points

	Singles	Doubles
Winner of three or more Grade A events	250	180

Grand Slam Bonus Points

	Singles	Doubles
Winner	250	180

Qualifying players losing in the first round of the main draw will receive 25 ranking points
Players losing in the final round of qualifying will receive 20 ranking points

Grade C Team Competition – Regional Qualifying

	No. 1 Singles Player Win	No. 2 Singles Player Win	Doubles Win Each Player
Final	80	60	60
Semifinal	60	40	40
Quarterfinal	40	20	20

Points are to be given to a player for one result only (their best) in the competition.
Only players from the best eight teams will be considered for the allocation of World Ranking Points.

ITF Junior World Rankings 2004

End of year positions

Only those players who qualifed for a year-end ranking are listed. The minimum requirements for this were having played six events, three of which were outside their own country and three of which were Group A status.

Boys

1. Gael Monfils (FRA)
2. Eduardo Schwank (ARG)
3. Brendan Evans (USA)
4. Woong-Sun Jun (KOR)
5. Sun-Yong Kim (KOR)
6. Mihail Zverev (GER)
7. Pablo Andujar-Alba (ESP)
8. Scott Oudsema (USA)
9. Lukas Lacko (SVK)
10. Rafael Arevalo Gonzalez (ESA)
11. Chu-Huan Yi (TPE)
12. Viktor Troicki (SCG)
13. Donald Young (USA)
14. Coen Van Keulen (NED)
15. Fabio Fognini (ITA)
16. Jeremy Chardy (FRA)
17. Guillermo Alcaide-Justell (ESP)
18. Igor Sijsling (NED)
19. Timothy Neilly (USA)
20. Sergei Bubka (UKR)

Girls

1. Michaella Krajicek (NED)
2. Katerina Bondarenko (UKR)
3. Shahar Peer (ISR)
4. Viktoria Azarenka (BLR)
5. Yung-Jan Chan (TPE)
6. Monica Niculescu (ROM)
7. Marina Erakovic (NZL)
8. Olga Govortsova (BLR)
9. Irina Kotkina (RUS)
10. Wen-Hsin Hsu (TPE)
11. Julia Cohen (USA)
12. Agnes Szavay (HUN)
13. Timea Bacsinszky (SUI)
14. Dominika Cibulkova (SVK)
15. Aleksandra Wozniak (CAN)
16. Caroline Wozniacki (DEN)
17. Madalina Gojnea (ROM)
18. Alla Kudryavtseva (RUS)
19. Alisa Kleybanova (RUS)
20. Pichittra Thongdach (THA)

USA's Brendan Evans and Scott Oudsema won three Junior Grand Slam doubles titles in 2004

ITF Junior Circuit 2004 Results

- **TLALNEPANTLA** (MEX) (Grade A) 29 DECEMBER-4 JANUARY – **GS:** Julia Cohen (USA) d. Maraike Biglmaier (GER) 62 61. **GD:** Marina Erakovic (NZL)/Bibiane Schoofs (NED) d. Yung-Jan Chan (TPE)/Aleksandra Wozniak (CAN) 64 64. **BS:** Phillip Simmonds (USA) d. Coen Van Keulen (NED) 64 62. **BD:** Timothy Neilly/Phillip Simmonds (USA) d. Brendan Evans/Scott Oudsema (USA) 76(2) 76(2).

- **STOCKHOLM** (SWE) (Grade 4) 1-6 JANUARY – **GS:** Regina Kulikova (RUS) d. Nadja Roma (SWE) 64 75. **GD:** Johanna Larsson/Nadja Roma (SWE) d. Charlotte Harbom/Camilla Lundberg (SWE) 62 61. **BS:** Daniel Kumlin (SWE) d. Andrew Kennaugh (GBR) 63 76 (6). **BD:** Christian Bergh/Fredrik Sletting Johnsen (NOR) d. Daniel Kumlin/Jon Sigurdsson (SWE) 63 46 62.

- **WINNEBA** (GHA) (Grade 4) 3-7 JANUARY – **GS:** Alice Izomor (NGR) d. Emma Cudsoe (GHA) 76(3) 75. **GD:** Hannah Eke/Alice Izomor (NGR) d. Kate Coleman/Emma Cudsoe (GHA) 62 64. **BS:** Salifu Mohammed (GHA) d. Madou Keita (MLI) 75 60. **BD:** Eric Ato Baba/Salifu Mohammed (GHA) d. Myles Blake (GBR)/Michael Leong (SOL) 75 75.

- **SAN JOSE** (CRC) (Grade 1) 5-10 JANUARY – **GS:** Volha Havartsova (BLR) d. Sanja Ancic (CRO) 62 67(4) 61. **GD:** Viktoria Azarenka/Volha Havartsova (BLR) d. Josipa Bek/Mirna Marinovic (CRO) 60 64. **BS:** Guillermo Alcaide-Justell (ESP) d. Phillip Simmonds (USA) 75 62. **BD:** Juan Pablo Amado (ARG)/Pablo Andujar-Alba (ESP) d. Antal Van Der Duim/Coen Van Keulen (NED) 46 62 75.

- **DHAKA** (BAN) (Grade 4) 5-9 JANUARY – **GS:** Soon-Mi Seo (KOR) d. Punam Reddy (IND) 75 64. **GD:** Hae-Youm Bae/Soon-Mi Seo (KOR) d. Punam Reddy/Sandri Gangothri (IND) 63 76(2) 60. **BS:** Navdeep Singh (IND) d. Faris Khatib (GBR) 62 61. **BD:** Chris Eaton/Faris Khatib (GBR) d. Seong-Woo Lee/Hyung Joon Lim (KOR) 63 63.

- **VASTERAS** (SWE) (Grade 4) 7-12 JANUARY – **GS:** Regina Kulikova (RUS) d. Anastassia Petoukhova (RUS) 67(6) 64 62. **GD:** Ia Appelberg (SWE)/Alise Vaidere (LAT) d. Sousan Massi/Cora Vasilescu (SWE) 61 61. **BS:** Alexander Olsson (SWE) d. Andrew Kennaugh (GBR) 63 64. **BD:** Robin Fahgen/Christian Rojmar (SWE) d. Andrew Kennaugh/Anthony Peter Scragg (GBR) 64 36 63.

- **LOME** (TOG) (Grade 4) 9-13 JANUARY – **GS:** Alice Izomor (NGR) d. Emma Cudsoe (GHA) 62 36 62. **GD:** Hannah Eke/Alice Izomor (NGR) d. Ernestina Atiso/Sarah Plange (GHA) 63 62. **BS:** Salifu Mohammed (GHA) d. Loic Didavi (BEN) 62 64. **BD:** Loic Didavi/Jean Segodo (BEN) d. Julien Dubail (BEL)/Mahar Zeidan (FRA) 76(3) 67(6) 63.

- **TRARALGON, VIC** (AUS) (Grade 2) 9-14 JANUARY – **GS:** Timea Bacsinszky (SUI) d. Angelique Kerber (GER) 64 64. **GD:** Angelique Kerber (GER)/Marta Lesniak (POL) d. Mari Andersson (SWE)/Timea Bacsinszky (SUI) 62 60. **BS:** Mihail Zverev (GER) d. Fabio Fognini (ITA) 60 63. **BD:** Julian Reister/Mihail Zverev (GER) d. Nejc Podkrajsek/Grega Zemlja (SLO) 64 76(5).

- **CAUSEWAY BAY** (HKG) (Grade 5) 12-18 JANUARY – **GS:** Seul-Ki Chin (KOR) d. Yoon Young Jeong (KOR) 60 64. **GD:** Seul-Ki Chin/Yoon Young Jeong (KOR) d. Wing Yau Venise Chan (HKG)/Natalie Solevski (AUS) 64 61. **BS:** Martin Sayer (HKG) d. Xiao-Peng Lai (HKG) 61 62. **BD:** Jeong Woo Choe/Dong-Joon Park (KOR) d. Ryan Cheung/Martin Sayer (HKG) 64 62.

- **CARACAS** (VEN) (Grade 1) 12-18 JANUARY – **GS:** Jenifer Widjaja (BRA) d. Dominika Cibulkova (SVK) 64 12 ret. **GD:** Josipa Bek (CRO)/Fernanda Hermenegildo (BRA) d. Amanda Avedissian (USA)/Agnes Szatmari (ROM) 61 61. **BS:** Jamie Baker (GBR) d. Thomaz Bellucci (BRA) 64 67(7) 50. **BD:** Keith Meisner/Jamie Murray (GBR) d. Luka Ocvirk (SLO)/Antonio Veic (CRO) 75 63.

- **RAJSHAHI** (BAN) (Grade 3) 12-16 JANUARY – **GS:** Kartiki-Vijay Bhat (IND) d. Punam Reddy (IND) 62 76(12). **GD:** Ya-Wan Lee/Yu-Ting Lin (TPE) d. Dilyara Saidkhodjayeva (UZB)/Tjasa Smrekar (SLO) 75 62. **BS:** Faris Khatib (GBR) d. Huai-En Chang (TPE) 75 63. **BD:** Jeevan Nedunchezian/Sanam Singh (IND) d. Anshuman Dutta/Rupesh Roy (IND) 62 64.

- **BERGHEIM** (AUT) (Grade 4) 12-17 JANUARY – **GS:** Josanne Van Bennekom (NED) d. Aude Vermoezen (BEL) 16 63 62. **GD:** Agnieszka Radwanska/Ueszula Radwanska (POL) d. Tatiana Malek/Miriam Steinhilber (GER) 64 60. **BS:** Dominic Inglot (GBR) d. Jan Marek (CZE) 61 62. **BD:** Matthias Huthmair/Clemens Neidl (AUT) d. Andreas Haider-Maurer/Christoph Hodl (AUT) 67(10) 64 62.

- **GLEN WAVERLEY, VIC** (AUS) (Grade 1) 18-24 JANUARY – **GS:** Ana Ivanovic (SCG) d. Shahar Peer (ISR) 61 62. **GD:** Veronika Chvojkova/Nicole Vaidisova (CZE) d. Ana Ivanovic (SCG)/Alla Kudryavtseva (RUS) 62 64. **BS:** Mihail Zverev (GER) d. Gael Monfils (FRA) 75 26 63. **BD:** Brendan Evans/Scott Oudsema (USA) d. Miles Kasiri (GBR)/Aljoscha Thron (GER) 76(4) 63.

- **DHAKA** (BAN) (Grade 3) 19-23 JANUARY – **GS:** Soon-Mi Seo (KOR) d. Madura Ranganathan (IND) 16 61 61. **GD:** Ya-Wan Lee/Yu-Ting Lin (TPE) d. Elina Arutyunova (UZB)/Jung-Yoon Shin (KOR) 60 60. **BS:** Rupesh Roy (IND) d. Faris Khatib (GBR) 63 63. **BD:** Anshuman Dutta/Rupesh Roy (IND) d. Jeevan Nedunchezian/Sanam Singh (IND) 62 ret.

- **BARRANQUILLA** (COL) (Grade 1) 19-25 JANUARY – **GS:** Estefania Balda (ECU) d. Julia Cohen (USA) 62 63. **GD:** Marina Cossou (FRA)/Ana Jerman (SLO) d. Barbara Costa/Ana-Clara Duarte (BRA) 63 64. **BS:** Eduardo Schwank (ARG) d. Guillermo Alcaide-Justell (ESP) 67(4) 62 64. **BD:** Keith Meisner/Jamie Murray (GBR) d. Matias Sacconi/Eduardo Schwank (ARG) 63 62.

- **BRATISLAVA** (SVK) (Grade 2) 19-25 JANUARY – **GS:** Eugenia Grebeniuk (RUS) d. Evgeniya Rodina (RUS) 62 46 75. **GD:** Lenka Broosova (SVK)/Agnes Szavay (HUN) d. Nikola Frankova/Katerina Kramperova (CZE) 62 46 64. **BS:** Kamil Capkovic (SVK) d. Zacharias Katsigiannakis (GRE) 76(4) 62. **BD:** Kamil Capkovic/Peter Miklusicak (SVK) d. Nick Cavaday/Dominic Inglot (GBR) 76(4) 64.

- **HAMBURG** (GER) (Grade 4) 20-25 JANUARY – **GS:** Josanne Van Bennekom (NED) d. Sabine Lisicki (GER) 76(4) 64. **GD:** Sabine Lisicki (GER)/Claudia Smolders (BEL) d. Natalie Fehse (GER)/Melanie Klaffner (AUT) 64 61. **BS:** Dominic Muller (GER) d. Otto Lenhart (GER) 64 60. **BD:** Andreas Eichenberger (SUI)/Roman Herold (GER) d. Andrew Kennaugh/Anthony Peter Scragg (GBR) 62 76(5).

- **PREROV** (CZE) (Grade 1) 26 JANUARY-1 FEBRUARY – **GS:** Agnes Szavay (HUN) d. Tatiana Malek (GER) 61 64. **GD:** Gabriela Niculescu/Monica Niculescu (ROM) d. Tatiana Malek/Andrea Petkovic (GER) 64 60. **BS:** Kamil Capkovic (SVK) d. Dominic Muller (GER) 75 61. **BD:** Kamil Capkovic/Peter Miklusicak (SVK) d. David Klier/Philipp Piyamangkol (GER) 75 61.

- **MELBOURNE** (AUS) (Grade A) 26 JANUARY-1 FEBRUARY – **GS:** Shahar Peer (ISR) d. Nicole Vaidisova (CZE) 61 64. **GD:** Yung-Jan Chan (TPE)/Sheng-Nan Sun (CHN) d. Veronika Chvojkova/Nicole Vaidisova (CZE) 75 63. **BS:** Gael Monfils (FRA) d. Josselin Ouanna (FRA) 60 63. **BD:** Brendan Evans/Scott Oudsema (USA) d. David Galic/David Jeflea (AUS) 61 61.

- **CUENCA** (ECU) (Grade 2) 26 JANUARY-1 FEBRUARY – **GS:** Krysty Marcio (USA) d. Ana Jerman (SLO) 64 64. **GD:** Liset Brito (CHI)/Florencia Molinero (ARG) d. Maria-Fernanda Alvarez (BOL)/Estefania Balda (ECU) 76(4) 76(5). **BS:** Eduardo Schwank (ARG) d. Thomaz Bellucci (BRA) 67(5) 64 64. **BD:** Renan Delsin/Andre Miele (BRA) d. Leandro Burmeister/Luis-Henrique Grangeiro (BRA) 61 64.

- **KOLKATA** (IND) (Grade 3) 26-31 JANUARY – **GS:** I-Hsuan Hwang (TPE) d. Pichittra Thongdach (THA) 64 63. **GD:** Pichittra Thongdach (THA)/Yanina Wickmayer (BEL) d. Vandana Murali/Madura Ranganathan (IND) 63 64. **BS:** Rupesh Roy (IND) d. Xiao-Peng Lai (HKG) 64 64. **BD:** Anshuman Dutta/Rupesh Roy (IND) d. Xiao-Peng Lai/Martin Sayer (HKG) 61 63.

- **LEUGGERN** (SUI) (Grade 5) 26 JANUARY-1 FEBRUARY – **GS:** Nina Jauch (SUI) d. Martina Lautenschlager (SUI) 64 64. **GD:** Vanessa Kretsch/Paola Sprovieri (GER) d. Tatiana Cutrona/Julie Stas (BEL) 63 76(4). **BS:** Moritz Baumann (GER) d. Alexander Sadecky (SUI) 75 61. **BD:** Moritz Baumann (GER)/Alexander Sadecky (SUI) d. Felix Grabs/Kevin Lampert (GER) 76(1) 63.

- **ABU DHABI** (UAE) (Grade 5) 27-31 JANUARY – **GS:** Chantal Beetham (CAN) d. Wing Yau Venise Chan (HKG) 75 75. **GD:** Fatma Alnabhani (OMA)/Wing Yau Venise Chan (HKG) d. Kasumi Hattori/Kumiko Shirakawa (JPN) 76(6) 36 64. **BS:** Anas Fattar (MAR) d. Ahmed Rabeea (KUW) 36 62 63. **BD:** Abdullah Magdas/Ahmed Rabeea (KUW) d. Nikita Dudar/Andrei Levine (RUS) 61 61.

- **WREXHAM** (GBR) (Grade 4) 1-5 FEBRUARY – **GS:** Claire Peterzan (GBR) d. Hannah Grady (GBR) 62 63. **GD:** Amber Silverstone/Anna Smith (GBR) d. Hannah Grady/Jessica Weeks (GBR) 16 62 63. **BS:** Maxime Authom (BEL) d. Scott Dickson (GBR) 64 61. **BD:** James Feaver/Max Jones (GBR) d. Maxime Authom (BEL)/Herbert Weirather (AUT) 64 62.

- **NEW DELHI** (IND) (Grade 2) 2-7 FEBRUARY – **GS:** I-Hsuan Hwang (TPE) d. Pichittra Thongdach (THA) 36 64 64. **GD:** Vandana Murali/Madura Ranganathan (IND) d. Pichittra Thongdach (THA)/Yanina Wickmayer (BEL) 64 64. **BS:** Tushar Liberhan (IND) d. Divij Sharan (IND) 06 75 75. **BD:** Tushar Liberhan/Divij Sharan (IND) d. Jeevan Nedunchezian/Sanam Singh (IND) 75 64.

- **QUITO** (ECU) (Grade 2) 2-8 FEBRUARY – **GS:** Ana Jerman (SLO) d. Jenifer Widjaja (BRA) 63 16 75. **GD:** Liset Brito (CHI)/Florencia Molinero (ARG) d. Ana-Clara Duarte/Roxane Vaisemberg (BRA) 36 63 64. **BS:** Eduardo Schwank (ARG) d. Franco Skugor (CRO) 76(1) 62. **BD:** Frederico Marques (POR)/Eduardo Schwank (ARG) d. Julio-Cesar Campozano/Lorenzo Cava (ECU) 75 64.

- **KUNGOTA** (SLO) (Grade 5) 4-8 FEBRUARY – **GS:** Mateja Horvat (CRO) d. Timna Ticic (CRO) 62 61. **GD:** Maja Kambic/Polona Rebersak (SLO) d. Maja Sujica (CRO)/Natasa Zoric (SCG) w/o. **BS:** Mikhail Vassiliev (RUS) d. Boris Conkic (SCG) 76(11) 67(4) 61. **BD:** Boris Conkic/Sasa Stojisavljevic (SCG) d. Beka Komakhidze/Gregory Muzil (RUS) 63 36 64.

- **AUCKLAND** (NZL) (Grade 4) 7-12 FEBRUARY – **GS:** Jessica Hoath (AUS) d. Ellen Barry (NZL) 76(1) 61. **GD:** Lucy Cole/Shona Lee (NZL) d. Akiko Minami (JPN)/Natalie Solevski (AUS) 64 62. **BS:** Ji-Seob Im (KOR) d. Steven Goh (AUS) 26 64 64. **BD:** Martin Colenbrander (NZL)/Steven Goh (AUS) d. Young-Deok Cho/Ji-Seob Im (KOR) 62 63.

ITF Junior Circuit 2004 Results (continued)

- **LA PAZ** (BOL) (Grade 2) 9-15 FEBRUARY – **GS:** Florencia Molinero (ARG) d. Teodora Mircic (SCG) 61 75(1). **GD:** Maria-Fernanda Alvarez (BOL)/Liset Brito (CHI) d. Florencia Molinero (ARG)/Agnes Szatmari (ROM) 61 62. **BS:** Franco Skugor (CRO) d. Mykyta Kryvonos (USA) 64 62. **BD:** Ante Nakic-Alfirevic/Franco Skugor (CRO) d. Celso Ribeiro/Rodrigo Starling (BRA) w/o.

- **RUNGSTED KYST** (DEN) (Grade 4) 9-14 FEBRUARY – **GS:** Caroline Wozniacki (DEN) d. Gluay Kampookaew (DEN) 75 64. **GD:** Hanne Skak Jensen/Caroline Wozniacki (DEN) d. Nadja Laas Hansen/Gluay Kampookaew (DEN) 64 61. **BS:** Leander Van Der Vaart (NED) d. Martin Pedersen (DEN) 62 76. **BD:** Martin Pedersen/Joakim-Bay Simonsen (DEN) d. Christian Bergh/Fredrik Sletting Johnsen (NOR) 75 64.

- **CHANDIGARH** (IND) (Grade 3) 9-14 FEBRUARY – **GS:** Pichittra Thongdach (THA) d. I-Hsuan Hwang (TPE) 63 61. **GD:** Pichittra Thongdach (THA)/Yanina Wickmayer (BEL) d. Yana Nemerovski (ISR)/Jung-Yoon Shin (KOR) 63 61. **BS:** Navdeep Singh (IND) d. Jeevan Nedunchezian (IND) 62 06 64. **BD:** Jeevan Nedunchezian/Navdeep Singh (IND) d. Sumit Prakash Gupta/Rupesh Roy (IND) 61 46 64.

- **FRYDLANT NAD OSTRAVICI** (CZE) (Grade 4) 11-15 FEBRUARY – **GS:** Jana Juricova (SVK) d. Hannah Grady (GBR) 63 63. **GD:** Hana Birnerova/Veronika Dostalova (CZE) d. Pavlina Glosova/Lenka Svobodova (CZE) 60 76(2). **BS:** Jan Marek (CZE) d. Mateusz Kowalczyk (POL) 64 62. **BD:** David Klier (GER)/Jiri Pechr (CZE) d. Mateusz Kowalczyk/Dawid Piatkowski (POL) 26 75 63.

- **CHRISTCHURCH** (NZL) (Grade 4) 14-18 FEBRUARY – **GS:** Shayna McDowell (AUS) d. Tammi Patterson (AUS) 63 64. **GD:** Shayna McDowell/Tammi Patterson (AUS) d. Kairangi Vano/Lisa Wilkinson (NZL) 64 63. **BS:** Steven Goh (AUS) d. Ji-Seob Im (KOR) 64 62. **BD:** Steven Goh/Patrick Nicholls (AUS) d. Martin Colenbrander (NZL)/Matt Symons (AUS) 64 64.

- **COLOMBO** (SRI) (Grade 5) 16-22 FEBRUARY – **GS:** Jung-Yoon Shin (KOR) d. Asha Nanda Kumar (IND) 61 61. **GD:** Asha Nanda Kumar (IND)/Jung-Yoon Shin (KOR) d. Shivika Burman/Sanjana Kapur (IND) 67(1) 63 76(6). **BS:** Kaushik Raju (IND) d. Ju Yeong Im (KOR) 62 63. **BD:** Kaushik Raju (IND)/Amrit Rupasinghe (SRI) d. Manu Bajpai (IND)/Peerapach Tupwong (THA) 61 75.

- **SANTIAGO** (CHI) (Grade 2) 16-22 FEBRUARY – **GS:** Evgeniya Rodina (RUS) d. Regina Kulikova (RUS) 64 76(5). **GD:** Regina Kulikova/Evgeniya Rodina (RUS) d. Ali Van Horne (USA)/Stephanie Wetmore (CAN) 63 63. **BS:** Juan-Martin Del Potro (ARG) d. Luis-Felipe Bellido (PER) 62 57 63. **BD:** Juan-Martin Del Potro/Leonardo Mayer (ARG) d. Piero Luisi/David Navarrete (VEN) 64 46 64.

- **HELSINKI** (FIN) (Grade 4) 16-21 FEBRUARY – **GS:** Gajane Vage (EST) d. Nina Munch-Soegaard (USA) 75 75. **GD:** Irina Sotnikova/Alise Vaidere (LAT) d. Liene Linina (LAT)/Gajane Vage (EST) 64 63. **BS:** Juho Paukku (FIN) d. Georgy Morgoev (RUS) 64 63. **BD:** Karl Berthen/Juho Paukku (FIN) d. Martin Kildahl/Carl Sundberg (NOR) 64 62.

- **KAOHSIUNG** (TPE) (Grade 4) 17-22 FEBRUARY – **GS:** I-Hsuan Hwang (TPE) d. Erika Sema (JPN) 63 63. **GD:** Shao-Yuan Kao/Szu-Yu Lin (TPE) d. Lu-Ling Chen/I-Hsuan Hwang (TPE) 63 60. **BS:** Chu-Huan Yi (TPE) d. Huai-En Chang (TPE) 64 64. **BD:** Chu-Huan Yi/Yen-Sheng Yu (TPE) d. Huai-En Chang/Chia-Chu Lien (TPE) 63 64.

- **ALMERE** (NED) (Grade 4) 18-21 FEBRUARY – **GS:** Marrit Boonstra (NED) d. Natalie Fehse (GER) 63 64. **GD:** Hannah Grady/Claire Peterzan (GBR) d. Desiree Bastianon/Claudia Smolders (BEL) 62 64. **BS:** Pavel Chekhov (RUS) d. Frederic De Fays (BEL) 46 63 63. **BD:** Maxime Authom/Frederic De Fays (BEL) d. Thiemo De Bakker/Mark De Jong (NED) 62 57 63.

- **ADELAIDE, SA** (AUS) (Grade 4) 23-28 FEBRUARY – **GS:** Ayumi Morita (JPN) d. Shayna McDowell (AUS) 63 61. **GD:** Emiko Ito/Ayumi Morita (JPN) d. Shayna McDowell/Tammi Patterson (AUS) 60 75. **BS:** Chris Eaton (GBR) d. Kento Takeuchi (JPN) 76(4) 46 64. **BD:** Ryan Biancardi/Stefan Sorani (AUS) d. Adam Hubble/Ryan Thomas (AUS) 63 36 62.

- **SARAWAK** (MAS) (Grade 3) 23-29 FEBRUARY – **GS:** Tapiwa Marobela (BOT) d. Erika Sema (JPN) 62 61. **GD:** Shao-Yuan Kao/Jung Liao (TPE) d. Tapiwa Marobela (BOT)/Ghizela Schutte (RSA) 62 76(1). **BS:** Chu-Huan Yi (TPE) d. Charl Wolmarans (RSA) 75 61. **BD:** Chu-Huan Yi/Yen-Sheng Yu (TPE) d. Derek Drabble (RSA)/Richard Ruckelshausen (AUT) 64 76(6).

- **MONTEVIDEO** (URU) (Grade 2) 23-29 FEBRUARY – **GS:** Florencia Molinero (ARG) d. Evgeniya Rodina (RUS) 75 60. **GD:** Maria Irigoyen/Bettina Jozami (ARG) d. Teliana Pereira (BRA)/Barbara Pinterova (SVK) 63 62. **BS:** Pablo Cuevas (URU) d. Bryan Koniecko (USA) 60 63. **BD:** Andrea Arnaboldi (ITA)/Michael Johnson (USA) d. Pablo Cuevas/Diego Ksiazenicki (URU) 76(6) 26 64.

- **OSLO** (NOR) (Grade 4) 24-28 FEBRUARY – **GS:** Caroline Wozniacki (DEN) d. Gluay Kampookaew (DEN) 63 63. **GD:** Yanina Wickmayer (BEL)/Caroline Wozniacki (DEN) d. Sabrina Allaut/Antonia Föhse (GER) 16 63 64. **BS:** Jamie Murray (GBR) d. Fredrik Sletting Johnsen (NOR) 63 62. **BD:** Martin Kildahl/Carl Sundberg (NOR) d. Graham Dyce/Jamie Murray (GBR) 64 64.

- **NURNBERG** (GER) (Grade 2) 25-29 FEBRUARY – **GS:** Michaella Krajicek (NED) d. Agnes Szavay (HUN) 63 63. **GD:** Tatiana Malek/Andrea Petkovic (GER) d. Jana Juricova/Magdalena Rybarikova (SVK) 64 46 63. **BS:** Daniel Brands (GER) d. Juho Paukku (FIN) 64 62. **BD:** Robin Haase/Igor Sijsling (NED) d. Jan Marek/Jiri Pechr (CZE) 64 64.

- **MAR DEL PLATA** (ARG) (Grade 2) 1-7 MARCH – **GS:** Bettina Jozami (ARG) d. Ekaterina Shulaeva (CAN) 62 63. **GD:** Andrea Benitez/Bettina Jozami (ARG) d. Estefania Balda (ECU)/Estefania Craciun (URU) 62 61. **BS:** Juan Pablo Amado (ARG) d. Juan-Martin Del Potro (ARG) 62 61. **BD:** Juan-Martin Del Potro (ARG)/David Navarrete (VEN) d. Juan Pablo Amado/Francisco Pozzi (ARG) 62 61.

- **IZHEVSK** (RUS) (Grade 3) 1-7 MARCH – **GS:** Yaroslava Shvedova (RUS) d. Marina Shamayko (RUS) 75 63. **GD:** Marina Shamayko/Yaroslava Shvedova (RUS) d. Nina Maglatyuk/Elena Vesnina (RUS) 75 64. **BS:** Alexandra Nedovesov (UKR) d. Pavel Chekhov (RUS) 36 76(10) 76(7). **BD:** Ernest Erkeev (RUS)/Alexandra Nedovesov (UKR) d. Alexei Kravtsov/Mikhail Pavlov (RUS) 75 64.

- **JALAN BERAKAS** (BRU) (Grade 4) 1-7 MARCH – **GS:** Erika Sema (JPN) d. Ghizela Schutte (RSA) 75 60. **GD:** Erika Sema/Yurika Sema (JPN) d. Tapiwa Marobela (BOT)/Ghizela Schutte (RSA) 75 62. **BS:** Richard Ruckelshausen (AUT) d. Takanobu Fujii (JPN) 75 75. **BD:** Takanobu Fujii (JPN)/Kaushik Raju (IND) d. Anthony Tan/Ayrton Wibowo (INA) 63 76(4).

- **WOLLONGONG, NSW** (AUS) (Grade 4) 1-6 MARCH – **GS:** A. Morita (JPN) v. M. Brycki (AUS) not played. **GD:** Emiko Ito/Ayumi Morita (JPN) d. Elle Carney/Tiarne Ettingshausen (AUS) 61 61. **BS:** P. Jozwik (AUS) v. T. Habsuda (AUS) not played. **BD:** Ryan Biancardi/Stefan Sorani (AUS) d. Tomas Habsuda (AUS)/James Pilbro (NZL) 75 63.

- **ANNABA** (ALG) (Grade 5) 1-5 MARCH – **GS:** Sara Meghoufel (ALG) d. Maja Kambic (SLO) 63 75. **GD:** Christina Dienstl/Rebekka Seipel (AUT) d. Maja Kambic/Anja Poglajen (SLO) 62 62. **BS:** Anas Fattar (MAR) d. Pavel Tartasyuk (UKR) 61 64. **BD:** Anas Fattar/Hicham Laalej (MAR) d. Mehdi Bouabane (ALG)/Wael Kilani (TUN) 61 67(1) 76(4).

- **KRAMFORS** (SWE) (Grade 3) 2-7 MARCH – **GS:** Caroline Wozniacki (DEN) d. Sorana Mihaela Cirstea (ROM) 46 62 61. **GD:** Sorana Mihaela Cirstea (ROM)/Hewenfei Li (CHN) d. Malgorzata Silka (POL)/Caroline Wozniacki (DEN) 60 62. **BS:** Jamie Murray (GBR) d. Dominic Inglot (GBR) 16 76(4) 64. **BD:** Andy Chirita (SWE)/Jamie Murray (GBR) d. Mateusz Kowalczyk/Pawel Syrewicz (POL) w/o.

- **SIAULIAI** (LTU) (Grade 4) 3-7 MARCH – **GS:** Ksenia Tokareva (UKR) d. Maria Mosolova (RUS) 61 64. **GD:** Elena Boyartchik/Aleksandra Malyarikova (BLR) d. Maya Gaverova/Euguenia Pachkova (RUS) 64 26 76(5). **BS:** Vasco Antunes (POR) d. Salvijus Davalga (LTU) 63 64. **BD:** Andris Antonovs/Pjotrs Necajevs (LAT) d. Mikk Irdoja (EST)/Dzems Vinkis (LAT) w/o.

- **ASUNCION** (PAR) (Grade 1) 8-14 MARCH – **GS:** Irina Kotkina (RUS) d. Aleksandra Wozniak (CAN) 76(0) 64. **GD:** Liset Brito (CHI)/Florencia Molinero (ARG) d. Maraike Biglmaier (GER)/Magdalena Kiszczynska (POL) 76(5) 67(3) 64. **BS:** Lukas Lacko (SVK) d. Eduardo Schwank (ARG) 64 63. **BD:** Frederico Marques (POR)/Eduardo Schwank (ARG) d. Fabio Fognini (ITA)/Daniel Vallverdu (VEN) w/o.

- **JALISCO** (MEX) (Grade 5) 8-13 MARCH – **GS:** Ana-Cecilia Olivos (MEX) d. Caitlin Whoriskey (USA) 36 64 64. **GD:** Thalia Diaz Barriga/Ana-Cecilia Olivos (MEX) d. Xenia Schneider (GER)/Sarah Svoboda (USA) 60 61. **BS:** Salvador De La Torre (MEX) d. Miguel Reyes-Varela (MEX) 63 26 63. **BD:** Miguel Reyes-Varela/Eduardo Salas (MEX) d. Marc Dwyer (USA)/Mike Motyka (SVK) w/o.

- **KRAMFORS** (SWE) (Grade 4) 8-13 MARCH – **GS:** Caroline Wozniacki (DEN) d. Nadja Laas Hansen (DEN) 60 63. **GD:** Sorana Mihaela Cirstea (ROM)/Melanie Klaffner (AUT) d. Maria Ring/Wiveca Swarting (SWE) 62 64. **BS:** Marco Sattanino (ITA) d. Andreas Haider-Maurer (AUT) 16 64 76(3). **BD:** Christian Bergh/Bastian Harbo (NOR) d. Botond Godry (HUN)/Sebstian Rogaczewski (DEN) w/o.

- **ORAN** (ALG) (Grade 5) 8-12 MARCH – **GS:** Chantal Beetham (CAN) d. Jana Levchenko (UKR) 64 16 62. **GD:** Rebekka Seipel (AUT)/Justine Sutherland (RSA) d. Maja Kambic/Petra Pajalic (SLO) 62 76(4). **BS:** Anas Fattar (MAR) d. Mahar Zeidan (FRA) 76(8) 46 61. **BD:** Wael Kilani/Slah Mbarek (TUN) d. Emanuel Brighiu/Alexandru Victor Caliciu (ROM) 67(7) 64 64.

- **JAKARTA** (INA) (Grade 2) 9-14 MARCH – **GS:** Wen-Hsin Hsu (TPE) d. Pichittra Thongdach (THA) 64 75. **GD:** Septi Mende/Maya Rosa (INA) d. Tatiana Malek (GER)/Stefanie Rath (AUT) 63 63. **BS:** Sunu Wahya Trijati (INA) d. Luka Ocvirk (SLO) 63 63. **BD:** Takanobu Fujii (JPN)/Xiao-Peng Lai (HKG) d. Weerapat Doakmaiklee (THA)/Sunu Wahya Trijati (INA) 64 62.

- **SAO PAULO** (BRA) (Grade A) 15-21 MARCH – **GS:** Alisa Kleybanova (RUS) d. Agnes Szavay (HUN) 61 75. **GD:** Alisa Kleybanova/Irina Kotkina (RUS) d. Jana Juricova/Magdalena Rybarikova (SVK) 61 61. **BS:** Eduardo Schwank (ARG) d. Pablo Andujar-Alba (ESP) 75 63. **BD:** Lukas Lacko/Peter Miklusicak (SVK) d. Rafael Arevalo Gonzalez (ESA)/Vahid Mirzadeh (USA) 61 61.

ITF Junior Circuit 2004 Results (continued)

- **KUALA LUMPUR** (MAS) (Grade 1) 15-20 MARCH – **GS:** Yung-Jan Chan (TPE) d. Wen-Hsin Hsu (TPE) 62 62. **GD:** Yung-Jan Chan (TPE)/Thassha Vitayaviroj (THA) d. Septi Mende/Maya Rosa (INA) 75 62. **BS:** Tom Rushby (GBR) d. Joel Kerley (AUS) 61 62. **BD:** Lachlan Ferguson/Joel Kerley (AUS) d. Karan Rastogi (IND)/Donald Young (USA) 67(4) 62 63.

- **ALGIERS** (ALG) (Grade 4) 15-19 MARCH – **GS:** Chantal Beetham (CAN) d. Claudia Sanua (RSA) 62 61. **GD:** Claudia Sanua/Justine Sutherland (RSA) d. Maja Kambic/Petra Pajalic (SLO) 75 75. **BS:** Alexandr Dolgopolov (UKR) d. Pavel Tartasyuk (UKR) 63 26 62. **BD:** Alexandr Dolgopolov/Pavel Tartasyuk (UKR) d. Myalikkuli Mamedkuliev (TKM)/Rainer Nachbauer (AUT) 62 64.

- **LA LIBERTAD** (ESA) (Grade 4) 15-20 MARCH – **GS:** Valerie Tetreault (CAN) d. Dasha Cherkasova (USA) 62 61. **GD:** Dasha Cherkasova/Denise Dy (USA) d. Thalia Diaz Barriga (MEX)/Christy Striplin (USA) 61 61. **BS:** Matt Bruch (USA) d. Markus Fugate (USA) 16 64 64. **BD:** Marek Czerwinski/Maciek Sykut (USA) d. Matt Bruch/Markus Fugate (USA) 63 75.

- **PORTO ALEGRE** (BRA) (Grade 1) 22-28 MARCH – **GS:** Irina Kotkina (RUS) d. Aleksandra Wozniak (CAN) 63 63. **GD:** Maria-Fernanda Alvarez (BOL)/Ana Jerman (SLO) d. Marina Erakovic (NZL)/Bibiane Schoofs (NED) 64 63. **BS:** Eduardo Schwank (ARG) d. Mykyta Kryvonos (USA) 63 63. **BD:** Rafael Arevalo Gonzalez (ESA)/Vahid Mirzadeh (USA) d. Bruno Rosa (BRA)/Aljoscha Thron (GER) 62 36 63.

- **CHOLBURI** (THA) (Grade 1) 22-28 MARCH – **GS:** Yung-Jan Chan (TPE) d. Tara Iyer (IND) 36 62 63. **GD:** Yung-Jan Chan (TPE)/Pichitrra Thongdach (THA) d. Wan-Ting Liu/Shuai Zhang (CHN) 61 63. **BS:** Sun-Yong Jr. Kim (KOR) d. Woong-Sun Jun (KOR) 62 61. **BD:** Woong-Sun Jun/Sun-Yong Jr. Kim (KOR) d. Karan Rastogi (IND)/William Ward (NZL) 61 63.

- **SAN JOSE** (CRC) (Grade 3) 22-27 MARCH – **GS:** Valerie Tetreault (CAN) d. Melissa Percy (GBR) 61 63. **GD:** Lyndsay Burdette (USA)/Melissa Percy (GBR) d. Dasha Cherkasova/Denise Dy (USA) 62 63. **BS:** Peter Polansky (CAN) d. Fabrice Martin (FRA) 76(4) 63. **BD:** Henry Estrella (DOM)/Fabrice Martin (FRA) d. Johnny Hamui (MEX)/Roberto Maytin (VEN) 63 64.

- **CHISINAU** (MDA) (Grade 4) 23-28 MARCH – **GS:** Anastasia Pavliuchenkova (RUS) d. Ksenia Tokareva (UKR) 76(4) 63. **GD:** Mihaela Buzarnescu/Lenore Lazaroiu (ROM) d. Yelena Kulikova/Anastasia Pavliuchenkova (RUS) 36 64 62. **BS:** Denis Molcianov (MDA) d. Alexandr Zotov (BLR) 62 62. **BD:** Denis Molcianov (MDA)/Dmitry Novikov (BLR) d. Ionut Mihai Beleleu/Mihai Nichifor (ROM) 63 16 62.

- **MONASTIR** (TUN) (Grade 4) 24-28 MARCH – **GS:** Alexandra Kulikova (RUS) d. Amina Rakhim (KAZ) 64 62. **GD:** Hana Birnerova/Eva Kadlecova (CZE) d. Michaela Ince (GBR)/Alexandra Kulikova (RUS) 62 64. **BS:** Max Jones (GBR) d. Hakim Rezgui (TUN) 64 62. **BD:** Maxime Authom/Frederic De Fays (BEL) d. David Cardoso/Joao Coelho (POR) 67(6) 62 64.

- **MANILA** (PHI) (Grade 1) 29 MARCH-4 APRIL – **GS:** Yung-Jan Chan (TPE) d. Wen-Hsin Hsu (TPE) 46 64 62. **GD:** Yung-Jan Chan/Wen-Hsin Hsu (TPE) d. Megumi Fukui/Yurika Sema (JPN) 76(3) 36 63. **BS:** Tom Rushby (GBR) d. Tushar Liberhan (IND) 64 76(8). **BD:** Lachlan Ferguson/Joel Kerley (AUS) d. Antal Van Der Duim/Coen Van Keulen (NED) 75 57 22 ret.

- **MENDOZA** (ARG) (Grade 5) 29 MARCH-4 APRIL – **GS:** Virginia Bigliardi (ARG) d. Marai Jose Vallasciani (ARG) 60 61. **GD:** Virginia Bigliardi/Pamela Russo (ARG) d. Lucia Betti/Ainara Miro (ARG) w/o. **BS:** Julian Morosi (ARG) d. Demian Gschwend (ARG) 64 62. **BD:** Demian Gschwend/Nicolas Jara-lozano (ARG) d. Gerardo Azcurra/Martin Montalbetti (ARG) 61 64.

- **CURUNDU** (PAN) (Grade 4) 29 MARCH-4 APRIL – **GS:** Jessica Sweeting (BAH) d. Bianca Gorbea (PUR) 64 63. **GD:** Andrea Brenes (CRC)/Jessica Sweeting (BAH) d. Bianca Gorbea/Natalia Guevara (PUR) 62 61. **BS:** Ryan Sweeting (BAH) d. Henry Estrella (DOM) 76(2) 61. **BD:** Kei Nishikori/Genki Tomita (JPN) d. Henry Estrella (DOM)/Alberto Gonzalez (PAN) 75 57 76(2).

- **UMAG** (CRO) (Grade 1) 30 MARCH-4 APRIL – **GS:** Monica Niculescu (ROM) d. Masa Zec-Peskiric (SLO) 63 62. **GD:** Gabriela Niculescu/Monica Niculescu (ROM) d. Veronika Chvojkova (CZE)/Michaella Krajicek (NED) 26 76(9) 61. **BS:** Andrea Arnaboldi (ITA) d. Vilim Visak (CRO) 75 64. **BD:** Viktor Troicki (SCG)/Vilim Visak (CRO) d. Daniel Muller/Andreas Weber (GER) 36 63 62.

- **SFAX** (TUN) (Grade 4) 30 MARCH-3 APRIL – **GS:** Amina Rakhim (KAZ) d. Barbora Hodinarova (CZE) 62 64. **GD:** Tatiana Cutrona (BEL)/Maite Molling (LUX) d. Magdalena Ekert (POL)/Ornella Gentile (BEL) 46 76(5) 62. **BS:** Frederic De Fays (BEL) d. Paris Gemouchidis (GRE) 57 64 64. **BD:** James Feaver/Max Jones (GBR) d. Michal Konecny/Jiri Kosler (CZE) 76(2) 46 64.

- **ASUNCION** (PAR) (Grade 4) 5-11 APRIL – **GS:** Ana-Clara Duarte (BRA) d. Teresa Oberti (ARG) 62 62. **GD:** Teresa Oberti/Pamela Russo (ARG) d. Vanesa Furlanetto/Marai Jose Vallasciani (ARG) 62 62. **BS:** Emiliano Massa (ARG) d. Sebastian Fontana (ARG) 60 60. **BD:** Claudio Coronel/Enzo Pigola (PAR) d. Cesar Bracho/Juan-Carlos Ramirez (PAR) 62 75.

- **CAP D'AIL** (FRA) (Grade 2) 5-11 APRIL – **GS:** Alexia Virgili (ITA) d. Monica Niculescu (ROM) 62 63. **GD:** Estrella Cabeza-Candela/Adriana Gonzalez-Penas (ESP) d. Hannah Grady/Claire Peterzan (GBR) 64 62. **BS:** Niels Desein (BEL) d. Andrei Goloubev (RUS) 64 64. **BD:** Guillermo Alcaide-Justell (ESP)/Sergei Bubka (UKR) d. Paterne Mamata (FRA)/Roberto Velilla-Jerez (ESP) 63 62.

- **CAIRO** (EGY) (Grade 3) 6-10 APRIL – **GS:** Magy Aziz (EGY) d. Fatima-Zahra El Allami (MAR) 36 75 63. **GD:** Desiree Bastianon/Claudia Smolders (BEL) d. Eva Fernandez-Brugues (ESP)/Julie Stas (BEL) 46 64 64. **BS:** Mehdi Ziadi (MAR) d. Kevin Anderson (RSA) 63 36 76(3). **BD:** Kevin Anderson/Thomas Liversage (RSA) d. Mohcine Roudami/Mehdi Ziadi (MAR) 46 75 63.

- **BAT YAM** (ISR) (Grade 4) 6-10 APRIL – **GS:** Anastasia Pivovarova (RUS) d. Yana Nemerovski (ISR) 63 63. **GD:** Yana Nemerovski/Efrat Zlotikamin (ISR) d. Nadine Fahoum/Julia Glushko (ISR) 63 62. **BS:** Lior Barbash (ISR) d. Liran Levy (ISR) 62 61. **BD:** Lior Barbash/Sahar Shimiel (ISR) d. Ravid Hezi/Amir Weintraub (ISR) 75 61.

- **NAGOYA** (JPN) (Grade 1) 6-11 APRIL – **GS:** So-Jung Kim (KOR) d. Ayumi Morita (JPN) 61 62. **GD:** So-Jung Kim/Ye-Ra Lee (KOR) d. Erika Sema/Yurika Sema (JPN) 76(4) 57 61. **BS:** Sun-Yong Kim (KOR) d. Coen Van Keulen (NED) 61 64. **BD:** Remko De Rijke (NED)/David Galic (AUS) d. Tristan Farron-Mahon (IRL)/Bogdan Leonte (ROM) 76(5) 63.

- **FLORENCE** (ITA) (Grade 2) 7-12 APRIL – **GS:** Karen Knapp (ITA) d. Bibiane Schoofs (NED) 46 62 63. **GD:** Giulia Gabba/Verdiana Verardi (ITA) d. Bibiane Schoofs/Nicole Thijssen (NED) 75 64. **BS:** Miles Kasiri (GBR) d. Robin Haase (NED) 63 62. **BD:** Robin Haase/Igor Sijsling (NED) d. Daniel Muller/Andreas Weber (GER) 64 16 64.

- **SANTIAGO** (CHI) (Grade 5) 12-18 APRIL – **GS:** Mabel Rodriguez (CHI) d. Catalina Arancibia (CHI) 63 75. **GD:** Catalina Arancibia/Fernanda Martinez (CHI) d. Javiera Colignon/Gabriela Roux (CHI) 62 60. **BS:** Maximiliano Picon (CHI) d. Jorge Villanueva (BOL) 62 64. **BD:** Diego Ortuzar/Maximiliano Picon (CHI) d. Pedro Graber/Hans Podlipnick (CHI) 64 62.

- **CAIRO** (EGY) (Grade B2) 12-17 APRIL – **GS:** Magy Aziz (EGY) d. Ola Abou Zekri (EGY) 62 61. **GD:** Magy Aziz (EGY)/Tapiwa Marobela (BOT) d. Ola Abou Zekri/Nihal Saleh (EGY) 62 60. **BS:** Mehdi Ziadi (MAR) d. Kevin Anderson (RSA) 75 76(6). **BD:** Kevin Anderson/Thomas Liversage (RSA) d. Mohcine Roudami/Mehdi Ziadi (MAR) 61 63.

- **PORT OF SPAIN** (TRI) (Grade 4) 12-17 APRIL – **GS:** Marina Cossou (FRA) d. Charlotte Douwma (FRA) 06 62 63. **GD:** Melissa Percy (GBR)/Christy Striplin (USA) d. Olivia Bennett (TRI)/Andrea Brenes (CRC) 61 76(4). **BS:** Markus Fugate (USA) d. Alex Clayton (USA) 64 76(4). **BD:** Alex Clayton/Markus Fugate (USA) d. David Lopez (PAN)/Ryan Sweeting (BAH) 62 75.

- **MIRAMAS** (FRA) (Grade 2) 12-18 APRIL – **GS:** Sheng-Nan Sun (CHN) d. Eugenia Grebeniuk (RUS) 46 61 60. **GD:** Gabriela Niculescu/Monica Niculescu (ROM) d. Ekaterina Kirianova/Marina Shamayko (RUS) 60 61. **BS:** Viktor Troicki (SCG) d. Guillermo Alcaide-Justell (ESP) 75 75. **BD:** Evgeny Kirillov/Alexander Krasnoroutsky (RUS) d. Jérémy Chardy/Fabrice Martin (FRA) 64 64.

- **SEOUL** (KOR) (Grade 4) 12-16 APRIL – **GS:** Mi Lyoo (KOR) d. Seul-Ki Chin (KOR) 64 64. **GD:** Hee Ju Kim/Hee-Sun Lyoo-Suh (KOR) d. Hae-Youm Bae/Sung-A Hong (KOR) 63 75. **BS:** Sun-Yong Kim (KOR) d. Woong-Sun Jun (KOR) 46 64 63. **BD:** Min Hyeok Jo/Doo Hyun Lee (KOR) d. Ju Yeong Im/Sun-Yong Kim (KOR) 75 46 76(5).

- **HAIFA** (ISR) (Grade 4) 13-17 APRIL – **GS:** Ia Jikia (GEO) d. Anastasia Pivovarova (RUS) 64 67(5) 64. **GD:** Yana Nemerovski/Efrat Zlotikamin (ISR) d. Ia Jikia (GEO)/Anastasia Pivovarova (RUS) 36 63 75. **BS:** Amir Weintraub (ISR) d. Lior Barbash (ISR) 76(6) 60. **BD:** Ravid Hezi/Amir Weintraub (ISR) d. Ron Halabi/Alexei Milner (ISR) 64 62.

- **MOSTAR** (BIH) (Grade 5) 14-18 APRIL – **GS:** Iva Velkovska (MKD) d. Diana Nakic (SLO) 64 64. **GD:** Ivana Milutinovic (SCG)/Iva Velkovska (MKD) d. Vanessa Kretsch/Paola Sprovieri (GER) 62 36 63. **BS:** Zoran Golubovic (SLO) d. Serkan-Akin Dilek (TUR) 46 76(3) 61. **BD:** Serkan-Akin Dilek/Ilhan Mutlu (TUR) d. Tomislav Poljak/Luka Zaninovic (CRO) 26 63 62.

- **ST FRANCOIS** (GUD) (Grade 4) 19-24 APRIL – **GS:** Marina Cossou (FRA) d. Courtney Clayton (USA) 63 63. **GD:** Marah Calvo (PUR)/Caitlin Whoriskey (USA) d. Marina Cossou/Charlotte Douwma (FRA) 62 64. **BS:** Ryan Sweeting (BAH) d. Genki Tomita (JPN) 36 60 75. **BD:** Jean-Yves Aubone/Alex Stone (USA) d. Gregory Gumbs/Boris Obama (FRA) 62 63.

- **BEAULIEU SUR MER** (FRA) (Grade 1) 19-25 APRIL – **GS:** Monica Niculescu (ROM) d. Mailyne Andrieux (FRA) 62 62. **GD:** Gabriela Niculescu/Monica Niculescu (ROM) d. Ekaterina Kirianova/Irina Kotkina (RUS) 75 61. **BS:** Fabio Fognini (ITA) d. Jérémy Chardy (FRA) 64 75. **BD:** Guillermo Alcaide-Justell (ESP)/Sergei Bubka (UKR) d. Jamie Baker/Miles Kasiri (GBR) 62 ret.

ITF Junior Circuit 2004 Results (continued)

- **BEER SHEVA** (ISR) (Grade 4) 20-24 APRIL – **GS:** Ia Jikia (GEO) d. Anastasia Pivovarova (RUS) 62 62. **GD:** Ia Jikia (GEO)/Anastasia Pivovarova (RUS) d. Keren Shlomo/Margarita Spicin (ISR) 63 64. **BS:** Victor Kulick (ISR) d. Lior Barbash (ISR) 64 75. **BD:** Lior Barbash/Sahar Shimiel (ISR) d. Ravid Hezi/Amir Weintraub (ISR) 64 64.

- **PIESTANY** (SVK) (Grade 2) 21-25 APRIL – **GS:** Yaroslava Shvedova (RUS) d. Magdalena Rybarikova (SVK) 75 75. **GD:** Michaela Babicova/Magdalena Rybarikova (SVK) d. Barbora Hodinarova (CZE)/Alexandra Kulikova (RUS) 61 63. **BS:** Lukas Lacko (SVK) d. Peter Miklusicak (SVK) 64 63. **BD:** Vaclav Kucera/Jan Marek (CZE) d. Mirko Zapletal/Filip Zeman (CZE) 63 75.

- **BURLINGTON, ON** (CAN) (Grade 5) 26 APRIL-2 MAY – **GS:** Melanie Gloria (CAN) d. Valerie Tetreault (CAN) 64 63. **GD:** Tania Rice/Valerie Tetreault (CAN) d. Marie Pier Huet/Monica Lalewicz (CAN) 75 62. **BS:** Peter Polansky (CAN) d. Robert Rotaru (CAN) 63 76(6). **BD:** Vladimiros Mavropoulos-Stoliarenko (GRE)/Kirill Sinitsyn (RUS) d. Peter Polansky/John Taylor (CAN) 76(6) 76(5).

- **ALICANTE** (ESP) (Grade 4) 26 APRIL-1 MAY – **GS:** Antonia Föhse (GER) d. Teresa Ferrer-Lopez-Cuervo (ESP) 76(5) 62. **GD:** Natalia Orlova/Kristina Ufimtseva (RUS) d. Sabrina Allaut/Antonia Föhse (GER) w/o. **BS:** Pablo Andujar-Alba (ESP) d. Jorge Montesinos-Perales (ESP) 63 67(9) 64. **BD:** Pablo Andujar-Alba/Jorge Montesinos-Perales (ESP) d. Paris Gemouchidis (GRE)/Tomas Habsuda (AUS) 62 62.

- **ST MICHAEL** (BAR) (Grade 4) 26 APRIL-1 MAY – **GS:** Christy Striplin (USA) d. Lyndsay Burdette (USA) 64 64. **GD:** Lyndsay Burdette (USA)/Melissa Percy (GBR) d. Ashley Spicer/Christy Striplin (USA) 61 61. **BS:** Markus Fugate (USA) d. Alex Clayton (USA) 63 16 63. **BD:** Alex Clayton/Markus Fugate (USA) d. Marc Alexander Doumba (GAB)/David Grund (CZE) 62 63.

- **SALSOMAGGIORE** (ITA) (Grade 2) 26 APRIL-2 MAY – **GS:** Viktoria Azarenka (BLR) d. Volha Havartsova (BLR) 75 20 ret. **GD:** Ekaterina Kosminskaya/Ekaterina Makarova (RUS) d. Giulia Gabba/Verdiana Verardi (ITA) 16 62 62. **BS:** Andrei Goloubev (RUS) d. Robin Haase (NED) 61 62. **BD:** Kevin Anderson/David North (RSA) d. Robin Haase/Igor Sijsling (NED) 62 46 76(1).

- **ST MARIE** (MRN) (Grade 5) 26 APRIL-1 MAY – **GS:** Marina Cossou (FRA) d. Charlotte Douwma (FRA) 76 61. **GD:** Marina Cossou/Charlotte Douwma (FRA) d. Latrell Reed (USA)/Jo-Ann Van Aerde (SUR) w/o. **BS:** Laurent Rochette (FRA) d. Boris Obama (FRA) 76 76. **BD:** Samuel Banford (GUI)/Xavier Mounigua (FRA) d. Robin Coq/Alan Ferres (FRA) 62 62.

- **PRATO** (ITA) (Grade 2) 3-8 MAY – **GS:** Verdiana Verardi (ITA) d. Karen Knapp (ITA) 36 61 62. **BS:** Alexandra Nedovesov (UKR) d. Matteo Marrai (ITA) 63 57 62.

- **MAMAIA** (ROM) (Grade 4) 4-9 MAY – **GS:** Lenore Lazaroiu (ROM) d. Mihaela Buzarnescu (ROM) 76(3) 62. **GD:** Mihaela Buzarnescu/Diana Gae (ROM) d. Laura-Joana Andrei/Andrada Dinu (ROM) 75 64. **BS:** Emanuel Brighiu (ROM) d. Mihai Nichifor (ROM) 75 36 61. **BD:** Bogdan Leonte/Mihai Nichifor (ROM) d. Igor Khrushch/Vladyslav Klimenko (UKR) 76(5) 16 64.

- **ST POLTEN** (AUT) (Grade 2) 10-16 MAY – **GS:** Nikola Frankova (CZE) d. Tamira Paszek (AUT) 64 64. **GD:** Teodora Mircic (SCG)/Irena Pavlovic (FRA) d. Nikola Frankova/Katerina Kramperova (CZE) 75 46 64. **BS:** Dusan Lojda (CZE) d. Philipp Piyamangkol (GER) 46 64 63. **BD:** Jamie Murray (GBR)/David North (RSA) d. Alexander Gjesten/Martin Pedersen (DEN) 61 76.

- **SANTA CROCE** (ITA) (Grade 1) 10-16 MAY – **GS:** Sesil Karatantcheva (BUL) d. Nicole Vaidisova (CZE) 75 62. **GD:** Viktoria Azarenka/Volha Havartsova (BLR) d. Katerina Bondarenko (UKR)/Madalina Gojnea (ROM) 75 63. **BS:** Woong-Sun Jun (KOR) d. Matteo Marrai (ITA) 75 63. **BD:** Stefan Kilchhofer (SUI)/Denis Molcianov (MDA) d. Rafael Arevalo Gonzalez (ESA)/Thomaz Bellucci (BRA) 63 43 ret.

- **SAMARA** (RUS) (Grade 3) 10-16 MAY – **GS:** Natalia Rakhmanina (RUS) d. Anastasia Pavliuchenkova (RUS) 62 61. **GD:** Yaroslava Shvedova/Elena Tchalova (RUS) d. Anastasia Pavliuchenkova/Anastasia Pivovarova (RUS) 62 75. **BS:** Mikhail Pavlov (RUS) d. Mikhail Koukouchkine (RUS) 61 36 64. **BD:** Andrei Averin/Alexei Filonov (RUS) d. Alexander Panasik/Alexandr Zotov (BLR) 63 76(5).

- **ROUSSALKA** (BUL) (Grade 5) 11-16 MAY – **GS:** Margarita Vasileva (BUL) d. Elitsa Kostova (BUL) 76(4) 26 61. **GD:** Elitsa Kostova (BUL)/Ivana Milutinovic (SCG) d. Ina Sireteanu/Gabriela Stepa (MDA) 75 75. **BS:** Emanuel Brighiu (ROM) d. Dimitar Dimov (BUL) 62 64. **BD:** Emanuel Brighiu/Alexandru Victor Caliciu (ROM) d. Igor Khrushch/Vladyslav Klimenko (UKR) 63 62.

- **SANTIAGO** (CHI) (Grade 5) 17-23 MAY – **GS:** Mabel Rodriguez (CHI) d. Gabriela Roux (CHI) 75 61. **GD:** Candelaria Rizzuto/Pamela Russo (ARG) d. Valeria Guajardo/Fernanda Martinez (CHI) 16 63 63. **BS:** Maximiliano Picon (CHI) d. Gerardo Azcurra (ARG) 61 67(5) 75. **BD:** Leandro Osorio/Guillermo Rivera (CHI) d. Diego Ortuzar/Maximiliano Picon (CHI) 64 64.

US Open Champion Andrew Murray (GBR)

ITF Junior Circuit 2004 Results (continued)

- **MILAN** (ITA) (Grade A) 17-23 MAY – **GS:** Sesil Karatantcheva (BUL) d. Viktoria Azarenka (BLR) 57 62 61. **GD:** Viktoria Azarenka/Volha Havartsova (BLR) d. Marina Erakovic (NZL)/Sesil Karatantcheva (BUL) 26 62 63. **BS:** Sebastian Rieschick (GER) d. Juan-Martin Del Potro (ARG) 62 75. **BD:** Brendan Evans/Scott Oudsema (USA) d. Karan Rastogi (IND)/Chu-Huan Yi (TPE) 62 64.

- **ISTANBUL** (TUR) (Grade 5) 17-23 MAY – **GS:** Lutphia Velieva (BUL) d. Elitsa Kostova (BUL) 57 61 60. **GD:** Gozde Unkaya (TUR)/Huliya Velieva (BUL) d. Ina Sireteanu/Gabriela Stepa (MDA) 64 60. **BS:** Serkan-Akin Dilek (TUR) d. David Simon (AUT) 61 26 62. **BD:** David Simon (AUT)/Eren Turkmenler (TUR) d. Sami Beceren/Orcun Seyrek (TUR) 64 26 64.

- **PODGORICA** (SCG) (Grade 4) 17-21 MAY – **GS:** Alexandra Panova (RUS) d. Olga Panova (RUS) 63 75. **GD:** Alexandra Panova/Olga Panova (RUS) d. Suncica Strkic (BIH)/Natasa Zoric (SCG) 76(2) 64. **BS:** Sasa Stojisavljevic (SCG) d. Sinisa Markovic (BIH) 63 60. **BD:** Boris Conkic/Sasa Stojisavljevic (SCG) d. Ivan Djurdjevic/Branko Kuzmanovic (SCG) 75 62.

- **VILLACH** (AUT) (Grade 2) 18-22 MAY – **GS:** Alexandra Karavaeva (RUS) d. Polona Rebersak (SLO) 63 60. **GD:** Daniella Dominikovic/Natalie Tanevska (AUS) d. Alexandra Karavaeva (RUS)/Amina Rakhim (KAZ) 36 63 63. **BS:** Marin Cilic (CRO) d. Dusan Lojda (CZE) 63 63. **BD:** David Galic/David Jeflea (AUS) d. Andreas Haider-Maurer/Christoph Hodl (AUT) 60 76(8).

- **TOGLIATTI** (RUS) (Grade 4) 18-23 MAY – **GS:** Yaroslava Shvedova (RUS) d. Natalia Orlova (RUS) 61 62. **GD:** Natalia Rakhmanina/Yaroslava Shvedova (RUS) d. Oleksandra Belova (UKR)/Tatiana Kotelnikova (RUS) 63 63. **BS:** Artur Chernov (RUS) d. Valeri Rudnev (RUS) 60 64. **BD:** Pavel Charnushin (BLR)/Roman Kislianski (RUS) d. Artur Chernov/Valeri Rudnev (RUS) 36 64 62.

- **LOVERVAL** (BEL) (Grade 1) 24-29 MAY – **GS:** Volha Havartsova (BLR) d. Katerina Bondarenko (UKR) 63 61. **GD:** Stephanie Dubois (CAN)/Yasmin Schnack (USA) d. Ekaterina Kosminskaya/Alla Kudryavtseva (RUS) 75 63. **BS:** Scoville Jenkins (USA) d. Mykyta Kryvonos (USA) 67(2) 76(4) 60. **BD:** Karan Rastogi (IND)/Chu-Huan Yi (TPE) d. Tushar Liberhan/Divij Sharan (IND) 63 63.

- **TALLINN** (EST) (Grade 4) 24-29 MAY – **GS:** Ieva Irbe (LAT) d. Tatsiana Kapshai (BLR) 62 76(10). **GD:** Nadja Roma/Sandra Roma (SWE) d. Agnes Liepina/Irina Sotnikova (LAT) 75 62. **BS:** Ernests Gulbis (LAT) d. Almog Mashiach (ISR) 61 76(5). **BD:** Sven Kasper/Jurgen Zopp (EST) d. Martin Kildahl/Carl Sundberg (NOR) 36 75 64.

- **BUDAPEST** (HUN) (Grade 4) 26-30 MAY – **GS:** Dominice Ripoll (GER) d. Stephanie Herz (NED) 62 61. **GD:** Dominice Ripoll (GER)/Roxane Vaisemberg (BRA) d. Biljana Gajic (SWE)/Maya Plachkova (BUL) 75 64. **BS:** Dimitar Kutrovsky (BUL) d. Boris Conkic (SCG) 63 63. **BD:** Ionut Mihai Beleleu/Mihai Nichifor (ROM) d. Daniel Danilovic (SWE)/Thomas Kromann (DEN) w/o.

- **PARIS** (FRA) (Grade A) 30 MAY-6 JUNE – **GS:** Sesil Karatantcheva (BUL) d. Madalina Gojnea (ROM) 64 60. **GD:** Katerina Bohmova (CZE)/Michaella Krajicek (NED) d. Irina Kotkina/Yaroslava Shvedova (RUS) 63 62. **BS:** Gael Monfils (FRA) d. Alex Kuznetsov (USA) 62 62. **BD:** Pablo Andujar-Alba/Marcel Granollers-Pujol (ESP) d. Alex Kuznetsov (USA)/Mihail Zverev (GER) 63 62.

- **TASHKENT** (UZB) (Grade 3) 31 MAY-5 JUNE – **GS:** Xeniya Palkina (KGZ) d. Ia Jikia (GEO) 26 76(6) 75. **GD:** Elina Arutyunova (UZB)/Olesia Nazarova (RUS) d. Yekaterina Morozova (KAZ)/Xeniya Palkina (KGZ) 64 46 64. **BS:** Denis Istomin (UZB) d. Serguei Tarasevitch (BLR) 62 60. **BD:** Shanp-Wei Liao/Dai Chiao Lin (TPE) d. Myles Blake (GBR)/Serguei Tarasevitch (BLR) 50 ret.

- **TANGER** (MAR) (Grade 5) 31 MAY-5 JUNE – **GS:** Zineb Hilali (MAR) d. Ali Van Horne (USA) 36 61 63. **GD:** Ana Beltran-Trigueros/Sandra Del Rey-Guardiola (ESP) d. Vitalia Diatchenko (RUS)/Tegan Edwards (RSA) 76(5) 36 62. **BS:** Reda El Amrani (MAR) d. Ali El Alaoui (MAR) 64 26 76(3). **BD:** Reda El Amrani/Younes Rachidi (MAR) d. Ryan Biancardi (AUS)/Billy Timu (CAN) 64 61.

- **TALLINN** (EST) (Grade 4) 1-6 JUNE – **GS:** Nadja Roma (SWE) d. Marina Yudanov (SWE) 60 62. **GD:** Nadja Roma/Marina Yudanov (SWE) d. Sandra Hribar/Caroline Larsson (SWE) 63 63. **BS:** Dmitry Novikov (BLR) d. Vladimir Ivanov (EST) 46 76(4) 76(3). **BD:** Mikk Irdoja/Jaak Poldma (EST) d. Vladimir Ivanov (EST)/Dmitry Novikov (BLR) 64 43 ret.

- **BUDAPEST** (HUN) (Grade 2) 2-6 JUNE – **GS:** Anna Korzeniak (POL) d. Barbora Hodinarova (CZE) 67(4) 64 62. **BS:** Dusan Lojda (CZE) d. Jiri Skoloudik (CZE) 57 62 62.

- **TAMPICO** (MEX) (Grade 5) 7-13 JUNE – **GS:** Alejandra Guerra (MEX) d. Maria-Paulina Gamboa (MEX). **GD:** Maria-Paulina Gamboa/Alejandra Guerra (MEX) d. Ashley Spicer (USA)/Tatiany Tangerino (BRA) 62 63. **BS:** Jamie Hunt (USA) d. Nelson Rodriguez-Garza (MEX) 61 61. **BD:** Jeff Dadamo/Jamie Hunt (USA) d. Nathaniel Schnugg/Wil Spencer (USA) 63 62.

- **MOSCOW** (RUS) (Grade 3) 7-13 JUNE – **GS:** Olga Panova (RUS) d. Maria Zharkova (RUS) 61 62. **GD:** Maria Gugel (ISR)/Elena Tchalova (RUS) d. Natalia Rakhmanina/Maria Zharkova (RUS) 63 60. **BS:** Mikhail Pavlov (RUS) d. Artur Chernov (RUS) 16 64 64. **BD:** Alexei Filonov/Mikhail Koukouchkine (RUS) d. Denis Molcianov (MDA)/Dmitry Novikov (BLR) 61 64.

- **RABAT** (MAR) (Grade 3) 7-12 JUNE – **GS:** Maria-Fernanda Alvarez (BOL) d. Urska Klemenc (SLO) 46 75 64. **GD:** Claudia Sanua (RSA)/Ali Van Horne (USA) d. Goele Lemmens/Yanina Wickmayer (BEL) 75 46 60. **BS:** Kei Nishikori (JPN) d. Alexandr Dolgopolov (UKR) 26 75 62. **BD:** Alexandr Dolgopolov/Pavel Tartasyuk (UKR) d. Dariusz Kuligowski (GER)/Kristofer Wachter (AUT) 64 60.

- **OFFENBACH** (GER) (Grade 1) 8-12 JUNE – **GS:** Viktoria Azarenka (BLR) d. Volha Havartsova (BLR) 75 61. **GD:** Viktoria Azarenka/Volha Havartsova (BLR) d. Ekaterina Kirianova/Yaroslava Shvedova (RUS) 61 60. **BS:** Dominic Muller (GER) d. Kevin Anderson (RSA) 76(4) 36 61. **BD:** David Galic/David Jeflea (AUS) d. Jiri Pechr/Jiri Skoloudik (CZE) 61 62.

- **NAMANGAN** (UZB) (Grade 3) 8-12 JUNE – **GS:** Ia Jikia (GEO) d. Yulia Parasyuk (RUS) 63 61. **GD:** Vlada Ekshibarova (UZB)/Ia Jikia (GEO) d. Elina Arutyunova (UZB)/Olesia Nazarova (RUS) 62 61. **BS:** Serguei Tarasevitch (BLR) d. Dai Chiao Lin (TPE) 62 62. **BD:** Jitin Bishnoi (IND)/Ervand Gasparyan (RUS) d. Akmal Sharipov/Vaja Uzakov (UZB) 62 26 76(5).

- **DONETSK** (UKR) (Grade 5) 8-13 JUNE – **GS:** Yelena Kulikova (RUS) d. Anastasia Kharchenko (UKR) 76(5) 67(4) 62. **GD:** Valeria Dandik (CAN)/Anastasiya Dubova (UKR) d. Yana Akoulova (UKR)/Julia Helbet (MDA) 63 64. **BS:** Artem Smirnov (UKR) d. Vladislav Bondarenko (UKR) 67(5) 61 63. **BD:** Dmitry Brichek/Dmytro Petrov (UKR) d. Ilia Marchenko/Sergey Rudenko (UKR) 76(2) 46 61.

- **CARIARI** (CRC) (Grade 5) 14-19 JUNE – **GS:** Sarah Aulombard (FRA) d. Ashley Spicer (USA) 62 63. **GD:** Olivia Bennett (TRI)/Andrea Brenes (CRC) d. Ashley Spicer (USA)/Tatiany Tangerino (BRA) 63 63. **BS:** Jamie Hunt (USA) d. Wil Spencer (USA) 76(5) 63. **BD:** Jeff Dadamo/Jamie Hunt (USA) d. Kellen Damico/Dennis Lajola (USA) 67(4) 63 62.

- **BISHKEK** (KGZ) (Grade 5) 14-19 JUNE – **GS:** Dilyara Saidkhodjayeva (UZB) d. Xeniya Palkina (KGZ) 63 63. **GD:** Xeniya Palkina (KGZ)/Dilyara Saidkhodjayeva (UZB) d. Kunykei Koichumananova (KGZ)/Diana Narzukulova (UZB) 63 76(0). **BS:** Akmal Sharipov (UZB) d. Stas Zhuravski (RUS) 61 62. **BD:** Talgat Baygulov (UZB)/Jitin Bishnoi (IND) d. Vladislav Shegai/Jamolkhon Umarov (UZB) 36 62 63.

- **MOHAMMEDIA** (MAR) (Grade 2) 14-19 JUNE – **GS:** Maria-Fernanda Alvarez (BOL) d. Roxane Vaisemberg (BRA) 61 64. **GD:** Antonia Föhse (GER)/Roxane Vaisemberg (BRA) d. Maria-Fernanda Alvarez (BOL)/Chantal Beetham (CAN) 62 75. **BS:** Gianluca Naso (ITA) d. Sherif Sabry (EGY) 36 63 60. **BD:** Reda El Amrani/Anas Fattar (MAR) d. Emanuel Brighiu/Alexandru Victor Caliciu (ROM) 64 76(3).

- **PHILADELPHIA, PA** (USA) (Grade 3) 14-19 JUNE – **GS:** Alexa Glatch (USA) d. Lyndsay Burdette (USA) 62 61. **GD:** Lyndsay Burdette/Alexa Glatch (USA) d. Julia Koulbitskaya (USA)/Olga Poutchkova (BLR) 64 46 64. **BS:** Markus Fugate (USA) d. Jesse Levine (USA) 64 75. **BD:** Marek Czerwinski/Maciek Sykut (USA) d. Chris Chirico (USA)/Johnny Hamui (MEX) 76(5) 61.

- **DONETSK** (UKR) (Grade 4) 15-20 JUNE – **GS:** Ia Jikia (GEO) d. Kristina Antoniychuk (UKR) 60 61. **GD:** Ia Jikia/Sofia Kvatsabaia (GEO) d. Anett Lenart/Yevgenia Nudga (UKR) 64 62. **BS:** Dmytro Tolok (UKR) d. Vladislav Bondarenko (UKR) 76(5) 63. **BD:** Dmitry Brichek/Dmytro Petrov (UKR) d. Ernest Erkeev/Georgy Morgoev (RUS) 63 63.

- **HALLE** (GER) (Grade 3) 16-19 JUNE – **GS:** Marina Erakovic (NZL) d. Shana Claes-(BEL) 61 61. **GD:** Wan-Ting Liu/Shuai Zhang (CHN) d. Teodora Mircic (SCG)/Irena Pavlovic (FRA) 63 76(3). **BS:** Martin Fischer (AUT) d. Aljoscha Thron (GER) 76(6) 64. **BD:** Kevin Anderson (RSA)/Salifu Mohammed (GHA) d. Philipp Oswald/Herbert Weirather (AUT) 64 76(2).

- **GDYNIA** (POL) (Grade 4) 16-20 JUNE – **GS:** Agnieszka Radwanska (POL) d. Maria Spenceley (GBR) 75 75. **GD:** Agnieszka Radwanska/Ueszula Radwanska (POL) d. Ieva Irbe (LAT)/Maria Spenceley (GBR) 62 62. **BS:** Grzegorz Panfil (POL) d. Przemyslaw Stec (POL) 63 62. **BD:** Mateusz Kowalczyk/Michal Walkow (POL) d. Kacper Owsian/Przemyslaw Stec (POL) 64 62.

- **LONDON** (GBR) (Grade 1) 20-25 JUNE – **GS:** Michaella Krajicek (NED) d. Marina Erakovic (NZL) 64 64. **GD:** Marina Erakovic (NZL)/Michaella Krajicek (NED) d. Katerina Bondarenko (UKR)/Madalina Gojnea (ROM) 41 41. **BS:** Gael Monfils (FRA) d. Andrew Murray (GBR) 75 63. **BD:** Alex Kuznetsov (USA)/Mihail Zverev (GER) d. Brendan Evans/Scott Oudsema (USA) 64 36 64.

- **LA HABANA** (CUB) (Grade 5) 21-26 JUNE – **GS:** Abbie Probert (GBR) d. Lumay Diaz Hernandez (CUB) 60 62. **GD:** Lumay Diaz Hernandez/Elsa Serrano-Eduards (CUB) d. Sarah Aulombard (FRA)/Andrea Brenes (CRC) 63 64. **BS:** Favel Antonio Freyre-Perdomo (CUB) d. Roman Recarte (VEN) 26 64 75. **BD:** Marcos Fernandez/Favel Antonio Freyre-Perdomo (CUB) d. Luis Gonzales (PER)/Roman Recarte (VEN) 64 61.

ITF Junior Circuit 2004 Results (continued)

- **KIEV** (UKR) (Grade 3) 21-27 JUNE – **GS:** Ia Jikia (GEO) d. Yevgenia Stupak (UKR) 46 61 61. **GD:** Olga Duko/Tatsiana Kapshai (BLR) d. Yana Akoulova/Yevgenia Stupak (UKR) 76(6) 63. **BS:** Mikhail Pavlov (RUS) d. Mikhail Koukouchkine (RUS) 62 63. **BD:** Dawid Piatkowski (POL)/Serguei Tarasevitch (BLR) d. Alexei Evstratenkov/Alexander Vasin (RUS) 62 62.

- **CASABLANCA** (MAR) (Grade 2) 21-27 JUNE – **GS:** Mailyne Andrieux (FRA) d. Vesna Manasieva (RUS) 26 64 63. **GD:** Maria-Fernanda Alvarez (BOL)/Roxane Vaisemberg (BRA) d. Mailyne Andrieux/Charlotte Douwma (FRA) 67(6) 62 60. **BS:** Reda El Amrani (MAR) d. Alexandr Dolgopolov (UKR) 62 64. **BD:** Ryan Sweeting (BAH)/Billy Timu (CAN) d. Cesare Gallo (ITA)/Luka Ocvirk (SLO) 63 26 64.

- **BANDUNG** (INA) (Grade 4) 22-27 JUNE – **GS:** Lavinia Tananta (INA) d. Joana Febri (INA) 57 64 76(2). **GD:** Golda Rubina/Lavinia Tananta (INA) d. Dian Mayasari/Patricia Soesilo (INA) 76(4) 61. **BS:** Elbert Sie (INA) d. Kento Takeuchi (JPN) 26 75 60. **BD:** Elbert Sie (INA)/Stefan Sorani (AUS) d. Ryo Sekiguchi/Kento Takeuchi (JPN) 75 36 63.

- **LAUTOKA** (FIJ) (Grade 4) 26-30 JUNE – **GS:** Ayumi Morita (JPN) d. Erika Sema (JPN) 60 61. **GD:** Emiko Ito/Ayumi Morita (JPN) d. Maya Kato/Erika Sema (JPN) 75 60. **BS:** Michael Look (AUS) d. Patrick Nicholls (AUS) 64 62. **BD:** Patrick Nicholls/Matt Symons (AUS) d. Dejan Bodrozic (AUS)/Brock Mustard (NZL) 64 64.

- **LONDON** (GBR) (Grade A) 26 JUNE-4 JULY – **GS:** Katerina Bondarenko (UKR) d. Ana Ivanovic (SCG) 64 67(2) 62. **GD:** Viktoria Azarenka/Volha Havartsova (BLR) d. Marina Erakovic (NZL)/Monica Niculescu (ROM) 64 36 64. **BS:** Gael Monfils (FRA) d. Miles Kasiri (GBR) 75 76(6). **BD:** Brendan Evans/Scott Oudsema (USA) d. Robin Haase (NED)/Viktor Troicki (SCG) 64 64.

- **NASSAU** (BAH) (Grade 5) 28 JUNE-4 JULY – **GS:** Jessica Sweeting (BAH) d. Abbie Probert (GBR) 62 62. **GD:** Kir Kemuel Kemp (USA)/Abbie Probert (GBR) d. Sarah Aulombard (FRA)/Jessica Sweeting (BAH) 62 06 64. **BS:** Jose Luis Muguruza (ARU) d. Peter Aarts (USA) 76(2) 62. **BD:** Peter Aarts/Calvin Kemp (USA) d. Bradley Cox (USA)/Johnny Hamui (MEX) 61 64.

- **AARHUS** (DEN) (Grade 5) 28 JUNE-4 JULY – **GS:** Julia Goerges (GER) d. Nadja Laas Hansen (DEN) 63 62. **GD:** Julia Goerges/Mariella Greschik (GER) d. Nadja Laas Hansen/Gluay Kampookaew (DEN) 26 63 64. **BS:** Thomas Kromann (DEN) d. Sebstian Rogaczewski (DEN) 60 60. **BD:** Thomas Kromann/Joakim-Bay Simonsen (DEN) d. Rasmus Moller/Steen Vester (DEN) 63 63.

- **SOCHI** (RUS) (Grade 5) 28 JUNE-4 JULY – **GS:** Irina Kuzmenko (RUS) d. Yulia Parasyuk (RUS) 75 62. **GD:** Daria Babushkina/Ksenia Bukina (RUS) d. Julia Kharevich/Elizaveta Tochilovskaya (RUS) w/o. **BS:** Ervand Gasparyan (RUS) d. Roman Kislianski (RUS) 61 61. **BD:** Ervand Gasparyan/Beka Komakhidze (RUS) d. Victor Kozin/Andrei Plotniy (RUS) 64 63.

- **BRUCHKOEBEL** (GER) (Grade 4) 29 JUNE-3 JULY – **GS:** Anne Schaefer (GER) d. Katerina Vankova (CZE) 36 63 62. **GD:** Judith Konig/Alison Rauh (GER) d. Diana Nakic/Alja Zec Peskiric (SLO) 61 57 64. **BS:** Frank Wintermantel (GER) d. Denes Lukacs (HUN) 62 36 76(3). **BD:** Tobias Wernet/Frank Wintermantel (GER) d. Gerald Kamitz (AUT)/Leo Rosenberg (USA) 64 64.

- **CASTRICUM** (NED) (Grade 2) 29 JUNE-4 JULY – **GS:** Olga Savchuk (UKR) d. Sorana Mihaela Cirstea (ROM) 64 62. **GD:** Lisanne Balk (NED)/Olga Savchuk (UKR) d. Marrit Boonstra (NED)/Anna Tatishvili (GEO) 62 36 64. **BS:** Martin Pedersen (DEN) d. Markus Fugate (USA) 64 76(1). **BD:** Marin Cilic/Filip Siladi (CRO) d. Thiemo De Bakker (NED)/Cedric Roelant (BEL) 63 76(4).

- **JAKARTA** (INA) (Grade 4) 29 JUNE-4 JULY – **GS:** Mia Sacca (INA) d. Lu-Ling Chen (TPE) 46 61 62. **GD:** Denise Harijanto/Maya Rosa (INA) d. Golda Rubina/Lavinia Tananta (INA) 75 63. **BS:** Ryo Sekiguchi (JPN) d. Nick Lindahl (AUS) 63 61. **BD:** Elbert Sie (INA)/Stefan Sorani (AUS) d. Hsu-Chun Huang/Tung Han Lee (TPE) 63 ret.

- **TUNIS** (TUN) (Grade 3) 30 JUNE-4 JULY – **GS:** Laurene Fayol (FRA) d. Louise Doutrelant (FRA) 62 46 76(6). **GD:** Magy Aziz (EGY)/Tapiwa Marobela (BOT) d. Chantal Beetham (CAN)/Fadzai Mawisire (ZIM) 36 62 64. **BS:** Hakim Rezgui (TUN) d. Aly El Sherbini (EGY) 75 62. **BD:** Loic Didavi (BEN)/Bradwin Williams (RSA) d. Wael Kilani/Hakim Rezgui (TUN) 63 62.

- **AUCKLAND** (NZL) (Grade 4) 2-7 JULY – **GS:** Shayna McDowell (AUS) d. Ayumi Morita (JPN) 64 76(5). **GD:** Emiko Ito/Erika Sema (JPN) d. Machiko Shigefuji/Natsumi Yokota (JPN) 57 63 61. **BS:** Michael Look (AUS) d. James Lemke (AUS) 62 62. **BD:** Ryan Andrews/Samuel Groth (AUS) d. Brydan Klein/Michael Look (AUS) 63 36 60.

- **HANNIBAL** (TUN) (Grade 4) 5-10 JULY – **GS:** Magy Aziz (EGY) d. Stella Menna (ITA) 60 63. **GD:** Chantal Beetham (CAN)/Fadzai Mawisire (ZIM) d. Magy Aziz (EGY)/Tapiwa Marobela (BOT) 64 36 63. **BS:** Abdullah Magdas (KUW) d. Loic Didavi (BEN) 64 46 76. **BD:** Wael Kilani/Hakim Rezgui (TUN) d. Loic Didavi (BEN)/Bradwin Williams (RSA).

- **ST PETERSBURG** (RUS) (Grade 4) 5-11 JULY – **GS:** Olga Panova (RUS) d. Xeniya Palkina (KGZ) 60 62. **GD:** Alexandra Panova/Olga Panova (RUS) d. Ekaterina Krylova/Natalia Orlova (RUS) 64 61. **BS:** Mikhail Koukouchkine (RUS) d. Dmitry Novikov (BLR) 16 61 62. **BD:** Ervand Gasparyan/Beka Komakhidze (RUS) d. Achim Ceban (MDA)/Dmitry Novikov (BLR) 64 61.

- **SONGKHLA** (THA) (Grade 5) 5-10 JULY – **GS:** Punjaporn Ditthim (THA) d. Penporn Chantawannop (THA) 57 75 62. **GD:** Wing Yau Venise Chan (HKG)/Waratchaya Wongteanchai (THA) d. Mai Iwasaki/Chiaki Okadaue (JPN) 57 62 62. **BS:** Peerachat Chaiyapan (THA) d. Peraklat Siriluethaiwattana (THA) 26 63 75. **BD:** Kirati Siributwong/Peraklat Siriluethaiwattana (THA) d. Peerachat Chaiyapan/Chalermsak Sansaneh (THA) 64 64.

- **KAUNAS** (LTU) (Grade 5) 5-9 JULY – **GS:** Nadja Roma (SWE) d. Irina Cybina (LTU) 64 61. **GD:** Diana Eriksson/Nadja Roma (SWE) d. Anete Bandere/Irina Sotnikova (LAT) 61 26 64. **BS:** Edgars Manusis (LAT) d. Salvijus Davalga (LTU) 67(1) 64 63. **BD:** Aleksei Bessonov/Pavel Katliarou (BLR) d. Taavi Jogi/Jurgen Zopp (EST) 76(3) 63.

- **CURACAO** (AHO) (Grade 4) 5-10 JULY – **GS:** Sarah Aulombard (FRA) d. Valeria Pulido (MEX) 61 60. **GD:** Sarah Aulombard (FRA)/Johanna Morrison (AUS) d. Natalia Baez (DOM)/Anna Novo (VEN) 62 41 ret. **BS:** Jose Luis Muguruza (ARU) d. Jamie Hunt (USA) 64 64. **BD:** Jose Luis Muguruza (ARU)/Roman Recarte (VEN) d. Jamie Hunt/Conor Pollock (USA) 61 36 62.

- **EDINBURGH** (GBR) (Grade 4) 5-10 JULY – **GS:** Julia Bone (GBR) d. Samantha Murray (GBR) 63 63. **GD:** Julia Bone (GBR)/Mariella Greschik (GER) d. Rachael Hall/Natasha Marks (GBR) 61 63. **BS:** Jamie Murray (GBR) d. Myles A Blake (GBR) 26 76(3) 62. **BD:** Edward Corrie/Scott Dickson (GBR) d. Graham Dyce/David Rice (GBR) 61 63.

- **ESSEN** (GER) (Grade 1) 6-11 JULY – **GS:** Elena Tchalova (RUS) d. Sorana Mihaela Cirstea (ROM) 63 62. **GD:** Nikola Frankova (CZE)/Korina Perkovic (GER) d. Lenka Broosova (SVK)/Katerina Kramperova (CZE) 62 61. **BS:** Igor Sijsling (NED) d. Philipp Piyamangkol (GER) 63 61. **BD:** Peter Lucassen/Igor Sijsling (NED) d. Marin Cilic/Tonci Peric (CRO) 60 60.

- **LEIDSCHENDAM** (NED) (Grade 4) 6-11 JULY – **GS:** Noemi Scharle (FRA) d. Julia Goerges (GER) 62 60. **GD:** Desiree Bastianon/Claudia Smolders (BEL) d. Marlot Meddens/Melissa Ravestein (NED) 64 63. **BS:** Thiemo De Bakker (NED) d. Maximiliano Picon (CHI) 61 75. **BD:** Thiemo De Bakker/Mark De Jong (NED) d. Ravid Hezi/Victor Kulick (ISR) 46 62 62.

- **DARWIN, NT** (AUS) (Grade 3) 9-13 JULY – **GS:** Ayumi Morita (JPN) d. Erika Sema (JPN) 67(2) 60 63. **GD:** Emiko Ito/Maya Kato (JPN) d. Michelle Brycki/Shayna McDowell (AUS) 63 62. **BD:** Ryan Andrew (USA)/Samuel Groth (AUS) d. Dejan Bodrozic/Jeremy White (AUS) 46 63 64.

- **ORANJESTAD** (ARU) (Grade 4) 12-17 JULY – **GS:** Valeria Pulido (MEX) d. Marah Calvo (PUR) 62 75. **GD:** Jo-Ann Van Aerde (SUR)/Stephania Velazquez (ARU) d. Natalia Baez (DOM)/Anna Novo (VEN) 76(5) 75. **BS:** Jose Luis Muguruza (ARU) d. Luis Diaz-Barriga (MEX) 60 61. **BD:** Jose Luis Muguruza (ARU)/Roman Recarte (VEN) d. Clay Donato (CAN)/Jose Moncada (HON) 67(6) ret.

- **VANCOUVER** (CAN) (Grade 5) 12-20 JULY – **GS:** Jillian O'Neill (CAN) d. Marie Pier Huet (CAN) 63 60. **GD:** Marie Pier Huet/Jillian O'Neill (CAN) d. Leyla Morzan/Kristen Yoon (CAN) 61 62. **BS:** Peter Polansky (CAN) d. Graeme Kassautzki (CAN) 67(3) 63 62. **BD:** Graeme Kassautzki/Peter Polansky (CAN) d. Dennis Lajola (USA)/Guillaume St Maurice (CAN) 64 16 61.

- **BERLIN** (GER) (Grade 4) 12-17 JULY – **GS:** Sara Errani (ITA) d. Daniela Pernetova (CZE) 62 61. **GD:** Sabine Lisicki/Dominice Ripoll (GER) d. Alena Bayarchyk (BLR)/Florence De Vrye (BEL) 64 63. **BS:** Dmitry Novikov (BLR) d. Paris Gemouchidis (GRE) 75 62. **BD:** Frederic De Fays (BEL)/Cesare Gallo (ITA) d. Andreas Eichenberger/Patrick Eichenberger (SUI) 63 62.

- **BANGKOK** (THA) (Grade 5) 12-18 JULY – **GS:** Varanya Vijuksanaboon (THA) d. Porntip Mulsap (THA) 62 60. **GD:** Wing-Yau "Venise" Chan (HKG)/Waratchaya Wongteanchai (THA) d. Kamonthip Saovana/Chatsuda Thimjapo (THA) w/o. **BS:** Kirati Siributwong (THA) d. Peerachat Chaiyapan (THA) 64 75. **BD:** Weerapat Doakmaiklee/Kirati Siributwong (THA) d. Sho Aida/Takeru Yamamoto (JPN) 62 63.

- **MARSA** (MLT) (Grade 5) 12-17 JULY – **GS:** Barbora Zvatorova (CZE) d. Jelena Jetcheva (MLT) 60 60. **BS:** Jeremy Swyngedouw (BEL) d. Marko Ballok (HUN) 76 63. **BD:** Jeremy Swyngedouw (BEL)/Seiya Toyota (JPN) d. Attila Balazs/Alexisz Kacamakisz (HUN) 61 36 64.

- **WINCHESTER** (GBR) (Grade 4) 12-17 JULY – **GS:** Alexandra Kulikova (RUS) d. Katy Williams (GBR) 64 61. **GD:** Judith Konig/Alison Rauh (GER) d. Gemma Bisson/Jenna Webster (GBR) 63 61. **BS:** Max Jones (GBR) d. Anthony Peter Scragg (GBR) 75 63. **BD:** Anthony Peter Scragg/Edward Seator (GBR) d. George Carpeni/James Langford (GBR) 75 63.

ITF Junior Circuit 2004 Results (continued)

- **HELSINKI** (FIN) (Grade 5) 12-17 JULY – **GS:** Jekaterina Jeritsheva (EST) d. Katarina Tuohimaa (FIN) 62 61. **GD:** Julia Kharevich/Elizaveta Tochilovskaya (RUS) d. Mayya Pitenina/Kristina Ufimtseva (RUS) 61 76(4). **BS:** Richards Emulins (LAT) d. Toomas Jurikivi (EST) 16 62 76(3). **BD:** Nikolai Chernov/Igor Rud (RUS) d. Vegard Veskimagi/Jurgen Zopp (EST) 63 16 61.

- **HILLEGOM** (NED) (Grade 4) 13-18 JULY – **GS:** Noémie Scharle (FRA) d. Anastasia Revzina (RUS) 60 62. **GD:** Melissa Ravestein/Steffi Weterings (NED) d. Alexandra Poorta/Anouk Tigu (NED) 57 62 63. **BS:** Thiemo De Bakker (NED) d. Yannick Mertens (BEL) 26 76(3) 62. **BD:** Ravid Hezi/Victor Kulick (ISR) d. Thomas De Jong (NED)/Michal Nevrela (CZE) 61 64.

- **WELS** (AUT) (Grade 1) 14-18 JULY – **GS:** Marta Lesniak (POL) d. Karin Knapp (ITA) 63 26 75. **GD:** Nikola Frankova/Katerina Kramperova (CZE) d. Eugenia Grebenyuk/Elena Tchalova (RUS) 46 63 40 ret. **BS:** Steven Moneke (GER) d. Andreas Haider-Maurer (AUT) 63 36 76(5). **BD:** Bryan Koniecko (USA)/Dimitar Kutrovsky (BUL) d. Luka Ocvirk (SLO)/Antonio Veic (CRO) 63 64.

- **DARWIN, NT** (AUS) (Grade 3) 14-18 JULY – **GS:** Ayumi Morita (JPN) d. Erika Sema (JPN) 61 60. **GD:** Ayumi Morita/Erika Sema (JPN) d. Ellen Barry/Brittany Teei (NZL) 63 60. **BS:** Michael Look (AUS) d. Carsten Ball (USA) 62 75. **BD:** Joshua Crowe (AUS)/Haydn Lewis (BAR) d. Michael Look/Kenneth Prajoga (AUS) 76(2) 75.

- **PRAHA** (CZE) (Grade 4) 14-18 JULY – **GS:** Martina Ondrackova (CZE) d. Klaudia Malenovska (SVK) 63 64. **GD:** Katerina Vankova/Dana Vondrova (CZE) d. Michaela Pochakova/Patricia Veresova (SVK) 76(5) 64. **BS:** Vladislav Bondarenko (UKR) d. Filip Zeman (CZE) 75 63. **BD:** Roman Jebavy/Michal Kozerovsky (CZE) d. Miloslav Mecir/Marek Semjan (SVK) 76(2) 46 75.

- **ASTANA CITY** (KAZ) (Grade 5) 18-24 JULY – **GS:** Xenia Palkina (KGZ) d. Amina Rakhim (KAZ) 64 26 64. **GD:** Mariya Kovaleva/Yekaterina Morozova (KAZ) d. Maria Melihova (MDA)/Xenia Palkina (KGZ) 64 76(10). **BS:** Stanislav Buykov (KAZ) d. Talgat Baygulov (UZB) 46 63 63. **BD:** Arsen Asanov/Vladislav Shegai (UZB) d. Talgat Baygulov/Alexey Nomozov (UZB) 46 63 62.

- **KLOSTERS** (SUI) (Grade B1) 19-25 JULY – **GS:** Katerina Bohmova (CZE) d. Timea Bacsinszky (SUI) 62 60. **GD:** Madalina Gojnea/Monica Niculescu (ROM) d. Timea Bacsinszky (SUI)/Lisa Sabino (ITA) 26 64 61. **BS:** Tomeu Salva (ESP) d. Igor Sijsling (NED) 61 76(5). **BD:** Martin Fischer/Philipp Oswald (AUT) d. Niels Desein/Cedric Roelant (BEL) 46 62 63.

- **GIZA** (EGY) (Grade 3) 19-25 JULY – **GS:** Magy Aziz (EGY) d. Bianca Bonifate (ROM) 62 75. **GD:** Laura Ioana Andrei/Bianca Bonifate (ROM) d. Maya Gaverova/Maria Miziouk (RUS) 64 64. **BS:** Reda El Amrani (MAR) d. Chris Eaton (GBR) 75 62. **BD:** Omar Altmann (GER)/Ali El Sherbini (EGY) d. Reda El Amrani/Amas Fattar (MAR) 64 62.

- **COBH** (IRL) (Grade 5) 19-23 JULY – **GS:** Deborah Armstrong (GBR) d. Phillipa Reakes (GBR) 64 46 60. **GD:** Fiona Gallagher/Andrea Maughan (IRL) d. Deborah Armstrong/Natasha Marks (GBR) 36 76(2) 75. **BS:** Eoin Heavey (IRL) d. Graeme Hood (GBR) 64 67 61. **BD:** Graeme Hood/Christopher Llewellyn (GBR) d. Marc Baghdadi (FRA)/Eoin Heavey (IRL) 64 64.

- **SANTO DOMINGO** (DOM) (Grade 4) 19-24 JULY – **GS:** Valeria Pulido (MEX) d. Briggitte Marcovich (VEN) 62 26 62. **GD:** Liset Brito (ESA)/Jade Curtis (GBR) d. Andrea Brenes (CRC)/Carla Tamborini (USA) 40 40. **BS:** Luis Diaz-Barriga (MEX) d. Jesse Levine (USA) ret. **BD:** Luis Diaz-Barriga (MEX)/Henry Estrella (DOM) d. Augusto Alvarado (PAN)/Santiago Gruter (ESA) 14 41 41.

- **PRETORIA** (RSA) (Grade 2) 20-25 JULY – **GS:** Alexa Glatch (USA) d. Wen-Hsin Hsu (TPE) 64 63. **GD:** Wen-Hsin Hsu/I-Hsuan Hwang (TPE) d. Alexa Glatch (USA)/Else Potgieter (RSA) 75 62. **BS:** Thomas Liversage (RSA) d. Myles Blake (GBR) 62 61. **BD:** Kevin Anderson (RSA)/Salifu Mohammed (GHA) d. Christiaan Coetzee/Charl Wolmarans (RSA) 63 61.

- **PLZEN** (CZE) (Grade 3) 21-25 JULY – **GS:** Andrea Hlavackova (CZE) d. Daniela Pernetova (CZE) 63 63. **GD:** Tereza Hladikova/Martina Ondrackova (CZE) d. Daniela Pernetova/Katerina Vankova (CZE) 75 61. **BS:** David Klier (GER) d. Jiri Pechr (CZE) 60 63. **BD:** Andreas Haider-Maurer/Christoph Hodl (AUT) d. David Klier (GER)/Jiri Pechr (CZE) 64 62.

- **SANTIAGO** (CHI) (Grade 5) 26 JULY-1 AUGUST – **GS:** Soledad Podlipnik (CHI) d. Fernanda Da Valle (ARG) 36 64 64. **GD:** Giannina Minieri/Paulina Ojeda (CHI) d. Candelaria Rizzuto/Pamela Russo (ARG) 76(4) 61. **BS:** Pedro Graber (CHI) d. Borja Malo (CHI) 63 62. **BD:** Pedro Graber/Hans Podlipnick (CHI) d. Leandro Osorio/Guillermo Rivera (CHI) 64 16 75.

- **LUXEMBOURG** (LUX) (Grade 2) 26-31 JULY – **GS:** Nina Henkel (GER) d. Vanessa Pinto (GER) 61 41 ret. **GD:** Kristina Antoniychuk (UKR)/Ana Veselinovic (SCG) d. Marlot Meddens/Melissa Ravestein (NED) 63 46 63. **BS:** Benedict Halbroth (GER) d. Frederic De Fays (BEL) 63 63. **BD:** Petar Jelenic (CRO)/Ivan Sergeev (UKR) d. Frederic De Fays (BEL)/Michal Konecny (CZE) 75 76(3).

- **KINGSTON** (JAM) (Grade 4) 26-31 JULY – **GS:** Jade Curtis (GBR) d. Francesca Kinsella (GBR) 63 61. **GD:** Thalia Diaz Barriga/Ana-Cecilia Olivos (MEX) d. Carla Tamborini (USA)/Jo-Ann Van Aerde (SUR) 62 62. **BS:** Jose Luis Muguruza (ARU) d. Maciek Sykut (USA) 62 76(2). **BD:** Marek Czerwinski/Maciek Sykut (USA) d. Luis Diaz-Barriga (MEX)/Jose Luis Muguruza (ARU) 67(3) 76(10) ret.

- **DUBLIN** (IRL) (Grade 5) 26-30 JULY – **GS:** Deborah Armstrong (GBR) d. Alicia Dennison (GBR) 63 62. **GD:** Laura Burns/Joanna Craven (GBR) d. Charlotte Headon/Andrea Maughan (IRL) 67 63 64. **BS:** Edward Allinson (GBR) d. James Clusky (IRL) 64 75. **BD:** Morgan Dunne/Eoin Heavey (IRL) d. Sean Galpin/Bruce Wagstaff (GBR) 62 62.

- **HELIOPOLIS** (EGY) (Grade 3) 26 JULY-1 AUGUST – **GS:** Maria Miziouk (RUS) d. Ola Abou Zekri (EGY) 67(2) 60 62. **GD:** Magy Aziz (EGY)/Chantal Beetham (CAN) d. Laura Ioana Andrei/Bianca Bonifate (ROM) 64 64. **BS:** Abdullah Magdas (KUW) d. Reda El Amrani (MAR) 63 64. **BD:** Omar Altmann (GER)/Ali El Sherbini (EGY) d. Wael Kilani/Hakim Rezgui (TUN) 46 63 64.

- **PRETORIA** (RSA) (Grade 2) 27 JULY-1 AUGUST – **GS:** Alexa Glatch (USA) d. Irena Pavlovic (FRA) 60 62. **GD:** Irena Pavlovic (FRA)/Punam Reddy (IND) d. Wen-Hsin Hsu/I-Hsuan Hwang (TPE) 64 76(4). **BS:** Kevin Anderson (RSA) d. Myles Blake (GBR) 61 62. **BD:** Kevin Anderson (RSA)/Salifu Mohammed (GHA) d. Christian Vitulli (KEN)/Bradwin Williams (RSA) 76(3) 46 63.

- **MADRID** (ESP) (Grade 4) 28-31 JULY – **GS:** Julia Goerges (GER) d. Maite Gabarrus-Alonso (ESP) 62 64. **GD:** Teresa Ferrer-Lopez-Cuervo/Maite Gabarrus-Alonso (ESP) d. Julia Goerges/Saskia Monien (GER) 62 76(4). **BS:** Jorge Hernando-Ruano (ESP) d. Joao Coelho (POR) 61 63. **BD:** Artur Romanowski (POL)/Amarit Sanchez-Thammakrong (ESP) d. Jesus Martinez-Mozo/Borja Roldan-Miguel (ESP) 46 63 62.

- **PEMBROKE** (BER) (Grade 5) 2-7 AUGUST – **GS:** Jo-Ann Van Aerde (SUR) v. Susana Luque (CHI) not played; **GD:** Susana Luque (CHI)/Jo-Ann Van Aerde (SUR) d. Ashley Finnegan/Danielle Mills (USA) 62 36 62. **BS:** Gavin Maders (BER) v. Weston Wendt (USA) not played; **BD:** Gavin Manders (BER)/Ricardo Velasquez (ARU) d. Kirk De Silva (VIN)/Corey Huggins (ECA) 76(6) 62.

- **NAUCALPAN** (MEX) (Grade 3) 2-8 AUGUST – **GS:** Veronica Li (USA) d. Liset Brito (ESA) 61 75. **GD:** Liset Brito (ESA)/Jade Curtis (GBR) d. Andrea Brenes (CRC)/Jessica Sweeting (BAH) 61 63. **BS:** Ryan Sweeting (BAH) d. Luis Diaz-Barriga (MEX) 62 62. **BD:** Luis Diaz-Barriga/Miguel Reyes-Varela (MEX) d. Sergio Rojas/Jose Carlos Rosas Tolentino (PER) 64 64.

- **LEIRIA** (POR) (Grade 4) 3-7 AUGUST – **GS:** Kristina Antoniychuk (UKR) d. Melanie Gloria (CAN) 75 63. **GD:** Kristina Antoniychuk (UKR)/Maria Mosolova (RUS) d. Anna Movsisyan (ARM)/Kristina Ufimtseva (RUS) 64 62. **BS:** Joao Ferreira (POR) d. Diogo Mota (POR) 63 64. **BD:** Goncalo Falcao/Martim Manoel (POR) d. Joao Ferreira/Jose-Ricardo Nunes (POR) 63 63.

- **MASERU** (LES) (Grade 4) 3-7 AUGUST – **GS:** Kate McDade (RSA) d. Hanneri De Klerck (RSA) 46 61 61. **GD:** Elne Barnard/Justine Sutherland (RSA) d. Kate McDade/Else Potgieter (RSA) 75 16 64. **BS:** Myles Blake (GBR) d. Kevin Kerr (RSA) 64 62. **BD:** Christian Vitulli (KEN)/Bradwin Williams (RSA) d. Brad Brinkhause Williams/Charl Wolmarans (RSA) 46 61 64.

- **DOMZALE** (SLO) (Grade 3) 4-8 AUGUST – **GS:** Mihaela Buzarnescu (ROM) d. Raluca Olaru (ROM) 62 64. **GD:** Mihaela Buzarnescu/Raluca Olaru (ROM) d. Aleksandra Lukic/Diana Nakic (SLO) 64 64. **BS:** Petar Jelenic (CRO) d. Zoran Golubovic (SLO) 61 62. **BD:** Zoran Golubovic/Blaz Kavcic (SLO) d. Emanuel Brighiu/Alexandru Victor Caliciu (ROM) 61 67(3) 63.

- **NOTTINGHAM** (GBR) (Grade 5) 8-12 AUGUST – **GS:** Samantha Murray (GBR) d. Georgie Stoop (GBR) 75 64. **GD:** Catherine Green/Anna Smith (GBR) d. Sophia Marks/Holly Richards (GBR) 75 75. **BS:** Scott Dickson (GBR) d. Christopher Llewellyn (GBR) 61 61. **BD:** Edward Corrie/Scott Dickson (GBR) d. James Feaver/Graeme Hood (GBR) 61 75.

- **DAMASCUS** (SYR) (Grade 4) 9-14 AUGUST – **GS:** Wing-Yau "Venise" Chan (HKG) d. Rana El Derwy (EGY) 61 61. **GD:** Wing-Yau "Venise" Chan (HKG)/Rana El Derwy (EGY) d. Lara Al Samman (SYR)/Manushak Khanyan (ARM) 63 75. **BS:** Alexandre Lacroix (FRA) d. Marc Abdelnour (SYR) 61 26 61. **BD:** Marc Abdelnour/Nawar Baram (SYR) d. Magdi Salim/Yashar Sheet (SYR) 76(4) 64.

- **GENEVA** (SUI) (Grade 5) 9-14 AUGUST – **GS:** Elitsa Kostova (BUL) d. Judith Konig (GER) 63 61. **GD:** Judith Konig/Alison Rauh (GER) d. Justina Derungs (SUI)/Stephanie Vogt (LIE) 64 61. **BS:** Pirmin Haenle (GER) d. Tobias Wernet (GER) 61 63. **BD:** Pascal Krauth/Tobias Wernet (GER) d. Julian Dehn (GER)/David Simon (AUT) 67(5) 75 63.

- **IBAGUE-TOLIMA** (COL) (Grade 5) 9-15 AUGUST – **GS:** Andrea Giraldo (COL) d. Karina Kedzo (VEN) 62 76(1). **GD:** Daniela Castillo/Catalina Robles (COL) d. Andrea Ferrari/Karina Kedzo (VEN) 63 75. **BS:** Thomas Estrada (COL) d. Edgar Rodriguez (COL) 46 64 64. **BD:** Juan-Andres Gomez/Jose Zunino (ECU) d. Alejandro Gonzalez/Sergio Velez (COL) 75 36 61.

ITF Junior Circuit 2004 Results (continued)

- **GABORONE** (BOT) (Grade 4) 9-13 AUGUST – **GS:** Kate McDade (RSA) d. Else Potgieter (RSA) 75 60. **GD:** Kate McDade/Else Potgieter (RSA) d. Lisa Levenburg/Marne Roos (RSA) 67(2) 64 61. **BS:** Christiaan Coetzee (RSA) d. Christian Vitulli (KEN) 26 62 76(6). **BD:** Christian Vitulli (KEN)/Bradwin Williams (RSA) d. Christiaan Coetzee/Derek Drabble (RSA) 26 63 76(5).

- **SAN JOSE** (CRC) (Grade B3) 9-14 AUGUST – **GS:** Valeria Pulido (MEX) d. Ana-Cecilia Olivos (MEX) 63 75. **GD:** Liset Brito (ESA)/Ana-Cecilia Olivos (MEX) d. Andrea Brenes (CRC)/Jessica Sweeting (BAH) 62 62. **BS:** Jose Luis Muguruza (ARU) d. Ryan Sweeting (BAH) 62 61. **BD:** Luis Diaz-Barriga/Miguel Reyes-Varela (MEX) d. Henry Estrella (DOM)/Jose Luis Muguruza (ARU) 61 67(5) 75.

- **LEIDSCHENDAM** (NED) (Grade 4) 10-15 AUGUST – **GS:** Melissa Ravestein (NED) d. Ellen Linsenbolz (GER) 63 75. **GD:** Marlot Meddens/Melissa Ravestein (NED) d. Inga Beermann/Tracy Castillo (GER) 46 62 75. **BS:** Thiemo De Bakker (NED) d. Leander Van der Vaart (NED) 76(1) 76(3). **BD:** Kevin Lampert/Frank Wintermantel (GER) d. Nikolas Holzen/Branco Weber (GER) 63 75.

- **PORTO** (POR) (Grade 4) 10-16 AUGUST – **GS:** Sara Errani (ITA) d. Kristina Antoniychuk (UKR) 67(10) 76(2) 61. **GD:** Kristina Antoniychuk (UKR)/Maria Mosolova (RUS) d. Melanie Gloria (CAN)/Kristina Ufimtseva (RUS) 67(5) 75 60. **BS:** Joao Ferreira (POR) d. Nuno Jacinto (POR) 64 63. **BD:** Goncalo Falcao/Martim Manoel (POR) d. Joao Ferreira/Jose-Ricardo Nunes (POR) 75 46 62.

- **BALS** (ROM) (Grade 5) 11-15 AUGUST – **GS:** Raluca Olaru (ROM) d. Antia Ghiorghiu (ROM) 61 62. **GD:** Andrada Dinu/Raluca Olaru (ROM) d. Ortansa Danciu/Stanca Muresan (ROM) 60 36 64. **BS:** Emanuel Brighiu (ROM) d. Victor Stanica (ROM) 26 64 64. **BD:** Emanuel Brighiu/Alexandru Victor Caliciu (ROM) d. Mihai Nichifor/Victor Stanica (ROM) 64 66 ret.

- **ZABRZE** (POL) (Grade 4) 11-15 AUGUST – **GS:** Agnieszka Radwanska (POL) d. Ueszula Radwanska (POL) 64 64. **GD:** Agnieszka Radwanska/Ueszula Radwanska (POL) d. Alena Bayarchyk/Ketsjaryna Zheltova (BLR) 61 64. **BS:** Pawel Syrewicz (POL) d. Grzegorz Panfil (POL) 75 62. **BD:** Mateusz Kowalczyk/Grzegorz Panfil (POL) d. Peter Paulenka/Peter Plsicik (SVK) 61 62.

- **MARIBOR** (SLO) (Grade 4) 11-15 AUGUST – **GS:** Polona Rebersak (SLO) d. Alja Zec Peskiric (SLO) 63 62. **GD:** Maja Kambic/Polona Rebersak (SLO) d. Aleksandra Lukic/Tadeja Majeric (SLO) 63 67(4) 60. **BS:** Kristofer Wachter (AUT) d. Sasa Bende (SLO) 61 62. **BD:** Miloslav Mecir/Marek Semjan (SVK) d. Tomislav Poljak/Luka Zaninovic (CRO) 64 62.

- **WINDHOEK** (NAM) (Grade 4) 15-19 AUGUST – **GS:** Else Potgieter (RSA) d. Chane Hines (RSA) 63 63. **GD:** Elne Barnard/Justine Sutherland (RSA) d. Tegan Edwards/Else Potgieter (RSA) 62 64. **BS:** Jurgens Strydom (NAM) d. Kevin Kerr (RSA) 76(4) 75. **BD:** Christian Vitulli (KEN)/Bradwin Williams (RSA) d. Derek Drabble/Kevin Kerr (RSA) 46 60 61.

- **ALMATY CITY** (KAZ) (Grade 4) 16-21 AUGUST – **GS:** Dilyara Saidkhodjayeva (UZB) d. Amina Rakhim (KAZ) 63 63. **GD:** Mariya Kovaleva/Yekaterina Morozova (KAZ) d. Daria Bykodarova (RUS)/Dilyara Saidkhodjayeva (UZB) 61 62. **BS:** Akmal Sharipov (UZB) d. Vladislav Shegai (UZB) 61 60. **BD:** Akmal Sharipov/Vladislav Shegai (UZB) d. Stanislav Buykov/Maxim Filippov (KAZ) 76 75.

- **CASTRIES** (LCA) (Grade 5) 16-22 AUGUST – **GS:** Arielle Von Strolley (JAM) d. Victoria Brook (GBR) 64 60. **GD:** Ashley Finnegan (USA)/Yolande Leacock (TRI) d. Victoria Brook (GBR)/Arielle Von Strolley (JAM) 61 75. **BS:** Dominic Pagon (JAM) d. Nathan Rosenfeld (USA) 62 06 75. **BD:** Roy-Paul Bottse (AHO)/Devan McCartney (BAR) d. Dominic Pagon (JAM)/Nathan Rosenfeld (USA) w/o.

- **CAMPO DE MARTE** (GUA) (Grade 4) 16-21 AUGUST – **GS:** Valeria Pulido (MEX) d. Liset Brito (ESA) 75 63. **GD:** Carla Tamborini (USA)/Nazari Urbina (MEX) d. Maria-Paulina Gamboa/Valeria Pulido (MEX) 64 62. **BS:** Israel Morales (GUA) d. Alberto Gonzalez (PAN) 75 36 76(3). **BD:** Jose-Maria Herrera/Miguel Reyes-Varela (MEX) d. Johnny Hamui/Gustavo Loza (MEX) 75 64.

- **CALI** (COL) (Grade 5) 16-22 AUGUST – **GS:** Andrea Giraldo (COL) d. Karen-Natalia Martinez-Bernal (COL) 62 61. **GD:** Carolina Gutierrez/Juanita Munoz (COL) d. Juliana Alzate/Gabriela Mejia (COL) 64 63. **BS:** Jose Roberto Velasco (BOL) d. Thomas Estrada (COL) 76(3) 62. **BD:** Luis Arboleda/Thomas Estrada (COL) d. Diego-Fernando Motivar/Edgar Rodriguez (COL) 76(4) 63.

- **CAIRO** (EGY) (Grade 4) 17-22 AUGUST – **GS:** Ola Abou Zekri (EGY) d. Rana El Derwy (EGY) 63 62. **BS:** Abdullah Magdas (KUW) d. Marawan Osama (EGY) 61 61. **BD:** Omar Altmann (GER)/Ali El Sherbini (EGY) d. Hassan Abdel Fatah/Marawan Osama (EGY) 67(6) 61 63.

- **ST KATELIJNE WAVER** (BEL) (Grade 3) 17-22 AUGUST – **GS:** Desiree Bastianon (BEL) d. Aude Vermoezen (BEL) 76(3) 60. **GD:** Desiree Bastianon/Ornella Gentile (BEL) d. Marlot Meddens/Melissa Ravestein (NED) 62 63. **BS:** Niels Desein (BEL) d. Pavel Chekhov (RUS) 62 64. **BD:** Kevin Lampert/Frank Wintermantel (GER) d. Benedict Halbroth/Tobias Wernet (GER) 64 64.

US Open Champion Michaella Krajicek (NED)

ITF Junior Circuit 2004 Results (continued)

- **VILA DO CONDE** (POR) (Grade 3) 17-22 AUGUST – **GS:** Anastasia Petoukhova (RUS) d. Kristina Antoniychuk (UKR) 62 26 62. **GD:** Kristina Antoniychuk (UKR)/Maria Mosolova (RUS) d. Anastasia Petoukhova/Anastasia Revzina (RUS) 75 46 61. **BS:** Joao Ferreira (POR) d. Frederico Marques (POR) 76(4) 57 62. **BD:** Vasco Antunes/Frederico Marques (POR) d. Joao Ferreira/Jose-Ricardo Nunes (POR) 64 46 76(2).

- **BISHKEK** (KGZ) (Grade 4) 18-22 AUGUST – **GS:** Xenia Palkina (KGZ) d. Diana Narzukulova (UZB) 64 61. **GD:** Maria Melihova (MDA)/Xenia Palkina (KGZ) d. Farida Karaeva (UKR)/Diana Narzukulova (UZB) 61 75. **BS:** Alexy Tsyrenov (RUS) d. Alexander Selezner (KGZ) 36 63 64. **BD:** Jitin Bishnoi/Kinshuk Sharma (IND) d. Andrei Plotniy/Alexy Tsyrenov (RUS) 63 76(5).

- **WARSAW** (POL) (Grade 4) 18-22 AUGUST – **GS:** Anastasia Pavlyuchenkova (RUS) d. Ueszula Radwanska (POL) 64 26 64. **GD:** Alena Bayarchyk (BLR)/Anastasia Pavlyuchenkova (RUS) d. Barbara Sobasziewicz/Magdalena Tokarska (POL) 75 63. **BS:** Piotr Olechowski (POL) d. Dariusz Lipka (POL) 63 60. **BD:** Dariusz Lipka/Artur Romanowski (POL) d. Tomasz Krzyszkowski/Mateusz Skorek (POL) 61 75.

- **BRATISLAVA** (SVK) (Grade 4) 18-22 AUGUST – **GS:** Lenka Wienerova (SVK) d. Klaudia Boczova (SVK) 75 63. **GD:** Hana Birnerova (CZE)/Nikola Vajdova (SVK) d. Monika Kochanova/Lenka Wienerova (SVK) 63 64. **BS:** Zoran Golubovic (SLO) d. Marek Semjan (SVK) 61 64. **BD:** Martin Kamenik/Michal Konecny (CZE) d. Jiri Kosler/Filip Zeman (CZE) 63 63.

- **STOBREC-SPLIT** (CRO) (Grade 5) 21-25 AUGUST – **GS:** Tereza Mrdeza (CRO) d. Selma Salkovic (CRO) 63 61. **GD:** Anja Poglajen/Patricia Vollmeier (SLO) d. Vedrana Pelivan (CRO)/Suncica Strkic (BIH) 60 62. **BS:** Luka Zaninovic (CRO) d. Vedran Siljegovic (CRO) 57 75 64. **BD:** Luka Curavic/Duje Janjic (CRO) d. Nikola Mektic/Vedran Siljegovic (CRO) 63 64.

- **LAUTOKA** (FIJ) (Grade B2) 22-26 AUGUST – **GS:** Olivia Lukaszewicz (AUS) d. Michelle Brycki (AUS) 61 61. **GD:** Daniella Dominikovic/Natalie Tanevska (AUS) d. Tyra Calderwood/Marija Mirkovic (AUS) 40 41. **BS:** G. D. Jones (NZL) d. Steven Goh (AUS) 62 62. **BD:** Andrew Coelho/Todd Ley (AUS) d. Brydan Klein/Joel Lindner (AUS) 54(5) 53.

- **CLERMONT-FERRAND** (FRA) (Grade 4) 23-29 AUGUST – **GS:** Laurene Fayol (FRA) d. Aude Vermoezen (BEL) 63 06 63. **GD:** Manon Garcia/Manon Noe (FRA) d. Aude Vermoezen/Yanina Wickmayer (BEL) 26 62 76(4). **BS:** Boris Obama (FRA) d. Jonathan Dahan (FRA) 61 61. **BD:** Wael Kilani/Hakim Rezgui (TUN) d. Michiel Antheunis/Ruben Bemelmans (BEL) 60 63.

- **CIUDAD MERLIOT** (ESA) (Grade 4) 23-28 AUGUST – **GS:** Liset Brito (ESA) d. Carla Tamborini (USA) 60 60. **GD:** Liset Brito/Cecilia Lainez (ESA) d. Analy Guzman/Andrea Weedon (GUA) 76(5) 36 62. **BS:** Alberto Gonzalez (PAN) d. Sergio Rojas (PER) 64 64. **BD:** Alberto Gonzalez (PAN)/Jose-Maria Herrera (MEX) d. Sergio Rojas (PER)/Nathan Rosenfeld (USA) 76(5) 64.

- **CORFU** (GRE) (Grade 5) 23-29 AUGUST – **GS:** Anna Gerassimou (GRE) d. Tatiana Cutrona (BEL) 61 62. **GD:** Tatiana Cutrona (BEL)/Valeriya Kirichenko (RUS) d. Jordane Dobbins (GBR)/Anna Gerassimou (GRE) w/o. **BS:** Paris Gemouchidis (GRE) d. Evthemlos Karaliolios (NED) 62 62. **BD:** Paris Gemouchidis (GRE)/Dimitrios Loucareas (USA) d. Polychronis Goros (GRE)/David Grund (CZE) 61 63.

- **KRAMFORS** (SWE) (Grade 5) 23-29 AUGUST – **GS:** Mona Mansour (SWE) d. Annette Pohjalainen (FIN) 62 16 64. **GD:** Sandra Hribar/Caroline Larsson (SWE) d. Farida Karaeva (UKR)/Gayane Sarkisson (SWE) 36 76(4) 64. **BS:** Marc Baghdadi (FRA) d. Andreas Karlsson (SWE) 64 64. **BD:** Andreas Karlsson/Nicklas Szymanski (SWE) d. Bjorn Buskqvist/Sebastian Carlsson (SWE) 64 64.

- **TASKHENT** (UZB) (Grade 4) 23-28 AUGUST – **GS:** Yana Kireeva (RUS) d. Vlada Ekshibarova (UZB) 61 63. **GD:** Elina Hasanova (AZE)/Yulia Parasyuk (RUS) d. Yana Kireeva (RUS)/Eleonora Sitdjemileva (UZB) 63 61. **BS:** Akmal Sharipov (UZB) d. Stas Zhuravski (RUS) 63 63. **BD:** Anshuman Dutta/Sumit Prakash Gupta (IND) d. Arsen Asanov/Vladislav Shegai (UZB) 62 61.

- **ESTADO COJEDES** (VEN) (Grade 5) 23-28 AUGUST – **GS:** Briggitte Marcovich (VEN) d. Sarai Torres (VEN) 61 64. **GD:** Briggitte Marcovich/Jessica Palma (VEN) d. Ahinara Ramos/Natasha Vieira (VEN) 57 52 ret. **BS:** Roman Recarte (VEN) d. Roberto Maytin (VEN) 63 76(4). **BD:** Borja Malo/Diego Ortuzar (CHI) d. Edgar Rodriguez (COL)/Jose Roberto Velasco (BOL) 76(3) 62.

- **MANASQUAN, NJ** (USA) (Grade 3) 23-29 AUGUST – **GS:** Lauren Albanese (USA) d. Michaela Johansson (SWE) 36 63 61. **GD:** Kimberly Couts/Kristy Frilling (USA) d. Irina Matiychyk (UKR)/Kristen McVitty (USA) 63 61. **BS:** Jesse Levine (USA) d. Tim Smyczek (USA) 62 63. **BD:** Alexandr Dolgopolov (UKR)/Billy Timu (CAN) d. Michael Shabaz/Tim Smyczek (USA) 64 64.

- **MINSK** (BLR) (Grade 5) 25-29 AUGUST – **GS:** Ketsjaryna Zheltova (BLR) d. Ksenia Milevskaya (BLR) 75 46 63. **GD:** Volha Duko/Tatsiana Kapshai (BLR) d. Yevgenia Nudga (UKR)/Maria Zharkova (RUS) 75 63. **BS:** Andrei Karatchenia (BLR) d. Kiryl Harbatsiuk (BLR) 60 60. **BD:** Dmitry Novikov/Yahor Puntus (BLR) d. Andrei Karatchenia/Pavel Katliarou (BLR) 64 63.

- **MISKOLC** (HUN) (Grade 3) 25-29 AUGUST – **GS:** Lenka Broosova (SVK) d. Klaudia Boczova (SVK) 16 75 61. **GD:** Katerina Vankova (CZE)/Patricia Veresova (SVK) d. Abbie Probert (GBR)/Ksenia Tokareva (UKR) 63 63. **BS:** Victor Stanica (ROM) d. Filip Siladi (CRO) 62 61. **BD:** Thiemo De Bakker/Leander Van der Vaart (NED) d. Pavel Chekhov/Valeri Rudnev (RUS) 63 64.

- **TEHRAN** (IRI) (Grade 5) 30 AUGUST-4 SEPTEMBER – **BS:** Omid Souri (IRI) d. Nirvick Mohinta (IND) 63 57 63. **BD:** Saber Rostampoor/Omid Souri (IRI) d. Mohamed Al Nuaimi (UAE)/Nirvick Mohinta (IND) 62 61.

- **QUEBEC** (CAN) (Grade 1) 30 AUGUST-4 SEPTEMBER – **GS:** Shahar Peer (ISR) d. Monica Niculescu (ROM) 75 62. **GD:** Marina Erakovic (NZL)/Michaella Krajicek (NED) d. Katerina Bondarenko (UKR)/Yung-Jan Chan (TPE) 63 36 62. **BS:** Rafael Arevalo Gonzalez (ESA) d. Alexandr Dolgopolov (UKR) 60 61. **BD:** Timothy Neilly/Tim Smyczek (USA) d. Pablo Andujar-Alba (ESP)/Niels Desein (BEL) 63 36 75.

- **FERGANA** (UZB) (Grade 4) 30 AUGUST-4 SEPTEMBER – **GS:** Alexandra Kichutkin (ISR) d. Yana Kireeva (RUS) 62 16 63. **GD:** Alexandra Kichutkin/Keren Shlomo (ISR) d. Yekaterina Morozova (KAZ)/Nigora Sirojiddinova (UZB) 61 63. **BS:** Vaja Uzakov (UZB) d. Ervand Gasparyan (RUS) 75 64. **BD:** Alexey Nomozov/Vaja Uzakov (UZB) d. Jamolkhon Umarov (UZB)/Stas Zhuravski (RUS) 64 64.

- **JURMALA** (LAT) (Grade 5) 30 AUGUST-4 SEPTEMBER – **GS:** Irina Strigalova (LAT) d. Irina Sotnikova (LAT) 61 61. **GD:** Irina Sotnikova/Irina Strigalova (LAT) d. Anete Bandere/Alise Razina (LAT) 62 61. **BS:** Vladimir Ivanov (EST) d. Anton Bobytskyy (UKR) 62 63. **BD:** Karlis Lejnieks/Pjotrs Necajevs (LAT) d. Vladimir Ivanov (EST)/Victor Kozin (RUS) 61 62.

- **VALENCIA** (VEN) (Grade 5) 30 AUGUST-4 SEPTEMBER – **GS:** Briggitte Marcovich (VEN) d. Jessica Palma (VEN) 64 63. **GD:** Oriana Escalante/Mariaryeni Gutierrez (VEN) d. Valeria Dandik (CAN)/Jessica Labarte (VEN) 75 06 63. **BS:** Roman Recarte (VEN) d. Roberto Maytin (VEN) 76(5) 75. **BD:** Roberto Maytin/Roman Recarte (VEN) d. Borja Malo/Diego Ortuzar (CHI) 26 62 62.

- **SKOPJE** (MKD) (Grade 5) 31 AUGUST-4 SEPTEMBER – **GS:** Elitsa Kostova (BUL) d. Ina Hadziselimovic (CRO) 61 60. **GD:** Ira Aleksova (MKD)/Elitsa Kostova (BUL) d. Viktoria Bakardzhieva (BUL)/Kristina Pejkovic (AUS) 26 63 75. **BS:** Paris Gemouchidis (GRE) d. Danail Tarpov (BUL) 52 ret. **BD:** Stefan Nikolic/Milos Romic (SCG) d. David Grund (CZE)/Ilhan Mutlu (TUR) w/o.

- **CANTABRIA** (ESP) (Grade 5) 1-4 SEPTEMBER – **GS:** Edelyn Balanga (PHI) d. Sara Celma-Boix (ESP) 61 62. **GD:** Marta Oliva-Lopez/Belen Perez-de Juan (ESP) d. Sara Celma-Boix/Clara Schummacher (ESP) 46 62 63. **BS:** Agustin Boje-Ordonez (ESP) d. Andrei Karatchenia (BLR) 57 62 61. **BD:** Juan Beaus-Barquin/Abel Rincon-Vasquez (ESP) d. Jorge Hernando-Ruano/Hugo Taracido-Loureiro (ESP) 64 64.

- **TIMISOARA** (ROM) (Grade 4) 1-5 SEPTEMBER – **GS:** Alexandra Dulgheru (ROM) d. Raluca Olaru (ROM) 63 64. **GD:** Laura Ioana Andrei/Raluca Olaru (ROM) d. Andrada Dinu/Alexandra Dulgheru (ROM) 46 75 64. **BS:** Victor Stanica (ROM) d. Petru Luncanu (ROM) 76(5) 63. **BD:** Ionut Mihai Beleleu/Mihai Nichifor (ROM) d. Emanuel Brighiu/Alexandru Victor Caliciu (ROM) 76(3) 36 62.

- **HYOGO** (JPN) (Grade 5) 1-5 SEPTEMBER – **GS:** Yurina Koshino (JPN) d. Misa Kinoshita (JPN) 75 64. **GD:** Mika Kawai/Yurina Koshino (JPN) d. Mai Iwasaki/Ai Yamamoto (JPN) 64 62. **BS:** Sho Aida (JPN) d. Shinta Fujii (JPN) 61 64. **BD:** Shinta Fujii/Yuichi Sugita (JPN) d. Ryo Sekiguchi/Yuichi Yoshioka (JPN) 16 62 75.

- **BLED** (SLO) (Grade 5) 1-5 SEPTEMBER – **GS:** Diana Nakic (SLO) d. Taja Mohorcic (SLO) 76(3) 64. **GD:** Vana Sutalo/Sandra Zmak (CRO) d. Taja Mohorcic/Alja Zec Peskiric (SLO) 63 26 61. **BS:** Sasa Bende (SLO) d. Tadej Turk (SLO) 75 62. **BD:** Gal Brzin/Iztok Kukec (SLO) d. Ales Svigelj/Matej Zlatkovic (SLO) 60 63.

- **BUDAPEST** (HUN) (Grade 5) 1-5 SEPTEMBER – **GS:** Csilla Borsanyi (HUN) d. Vivien Laszloffy (HUN) 63 62. **GD:** Orsolya Kovacs/Edit Suhajda (HUN) d. Lucia Batta/Dora Somossy (HUN) 36 76(2) 62. **BS:** Dmytro Petrov (UKR) d. Sebastian Farkas (HUN) 61 36 63. **BD:** Dmitry Brichek/Dmytro Petrov (UKR) d. Roman Jebavy (CZE)/Miloslav Mecir (SVK) 62 64.

- **QUEEN'S, NY** (USA) (Grade A) 5-12 SEPTEMBER – **GS:** Michaella Krajicek (NED) d. Jessica Kirkland (USA) 61 61. **GD:** Marina Erakovic (NZL)/Michaella Krajicek (NED) d. Madalina Gojnea/Monica Niculescu (ROM) 76(4) 60. **BS:** Andrew Murray (GBR) d. Sergiy Stakhovsky (UKR) 64 62. **BD:** Brendan Evans/Scott Oudsema (USA) d. Andreas Beck/Sebastian Rieschick (GER) 46 61 62.

- **NICOSIA** (CYP) (Grade 4) 6-11 SEPTEMBER – **GS:** Sousan Massi (SWE) d. Barbora Zvatorova (CZE) w/o. **GD:** Melanie Klaffner (AUT)/Sousan Massi (SWE) d. Maria Ring/Wiveca Swarting (SWE) 64 62. **BS:** Mirko Zapletal (CZE) d. Alexander Gjesten (DEN) 64 64. **BD:** David Grund/Mirko Zapletal (CZE) d. Pavel Katliarou/Alexander Panasik (BLR) w/o.

ITF Junior Circuit 2004 Results (continued)

- **CARACAS** (VEN) (Grade 5) 6-11 SEPTEMBER – **GS:** Briggitte Marcovich (VEN) d. Mariaryeni Gutierrez (VEN) 63 62. **GD:** Briggitte Marcovich/Jessica Palma (VEN) d. Chandra Capozzi (DOM)/Natasha Vieira (VEN) 76(4) 26 64. **BS:** Roman Recarte (VEN) d. Roberto Maytin (VEN) 76(3) 61. **BD:** Alejandro Gonzalez/Edgar Rodriguez (COL) d. Miguel Cicenia/Jhonny Figueroa (VEN) 26 61 76(8).

- **COLOMBO** (SRI) (Grade 5) 6-12 SEPTEMBER – **GS:** Preethi Subramaniam (IND) d. Lia Tapper (AUS) 75 26 62. **GD:** Tzu Chen Hsu/Su-Han Yang (TPE) d. Jing-Chi Lin/Chieh Ju Wang (TPE) 16 60 75. **BS:** Oshada Wijemanne (SRI) d. Hsin-Han Lee (TPE) 61 16 60. **BD:** Franklyn Emmanuel/Oshada Wijemanne (SRI) d. Hsin-Han Lee/Yao-Cheng Wang (TPE) 36 63 64.

- **BEIRUT** (LIB) (Grade 5) 6-12 SEPTEMBER – **GS:** Maha Berti (EGY) d. Lara Al Samman (SYR) 61 60. **GD:** Maha Berti (EGY)/Leen Irani (JOR) d. Dima Al Saadi (SYR)/Fatma Alnabhani (OMA) 64 63. **BS:** Marc Abdelnour (SYR) d. Bassam Beidas (LIB) 63 63. **BD:** Marc Abdelnour/Nawar Baram (SYR) d. Georgio Bedran/Bassam Beidas (LIB) 63 64.

- **RIGA** (LAT) (Grade 5) 6-11 SEPTEMBER – **GS:** Alise Vaidere (LAT) d. Yelena Kulikova (RUS) 75 61. **GD:** Ieva Irbe/Alise Razina (LAT) d. Irina Khatsko (UKR)/Alina Zimina (RUS) 62 76(3). **BS:** Karlis Lejnieks (LAT) d. Mikk Irdoja (EST) 62 16 63. **BD:** Anton Bobytskyy/Artem Smirnov (UKR) d. Andris Antonovs/Richards Emulins (LAT) 64 63.

- **PONTEVEDRA** (ESP) (Grade 5) 7-12 SEPTEMBER – **GS:** Ana Beltran-Trigueros (ESP) d. Leticia Costas-Moreira (ESP) 63 62. **GD:** Sara Celma-Boix/Clara Schummacher (ESP) d. Anna Boixander/Sonia Corominas-Plaja (ESP) 61 61. **BS:** Eoin Heavey (IRL) d. Andrei Karatchenia (BLR) 26 75 75. **BD:** Eoin Heavey (IRL)/Andrei Karatchenia (BLR) d. Agustin Boje-Ordonez/Abel Rincon-Vasquez (ESP) 64 63.

- **HYOGO** (JPN) (Grade 5) 8-12 SEPTEMBER – **GS:** Yurina Koshino (JPN) d. Naoko Ueshima (JPN) 61 46 62. **GD:** Yumi Nakano/Ai Yamamoto (JPN) d. Mao Matsuo/Teina Todaka (JPN) 64 64. **BS:** Yuichi Sugita (JPN) d. Kento Takeuchi (JPN) 46 75 76(5). **BD:** Sho Aida/Yuichi Sugita (JPN) d. Lachlan Reed (AUS)/Ryo Sekiguchi (JPN) 63 46 75.

- **HASKOVO** (BUL) (Grade 5) 8-12 SEPTEMBER – **GS:** Margarita Vasileva (BUL) d. Radoslava Radeva (BUL) 63 63. **GD:** Fani Chifchieva/Maya Plachkova (BUL) d. Lora Stancheva/Tania Stoimanova (BUL) 46 64 60. **BS:** Victor Stanica (ROM) d. Dimitar Kutrovsky (BUL) w/o. **BD:** Roman Jebavy/Michal Konecny (CZE) d. Stefan Arsovski/Dimitar Labudovik (MKD) 62 64.

- **CHENNAI** (IND) (Grade 5) 13-18 SEPTEMBER – **GS:** Sandhya Nagraj (IND) d. Sandri Gangothri (IND) 63 62. **GD:** Vandana Murali/Sandhya Nagraj (IND) d. Ashmitha Easwaramurthi/Pooja Kommireddi (IND) 30 ret. **BS:** Jeevan Nedunchezhiyan (IND) d. Prateek Shantharaju (IND) 62 60. **BD:** Anantha Bhaskar/Jeevan Nedunchezhiyan (IND) d. Parival Rathnasawamy/Prateek Shantharaju (IND) 63 64.

- **CAIRO** (EGY) (Grade 5) 13-19 SEPTEMBER – **GS:** Noémie Scharle (FRA) d. Charlotte Soubrie (FRA) 61 61. **GD:** Charlotte Rodier/Charlotte Soubrie (FRA) d. Rana El Derwy (EGY)/Noémie Scharle (FRA) 76(1) 62. **BS:** Vladislav Bondarenko (UKR) d. Mahmoud Kamel (EGY) 61 64. **BD:** Mahmoud Ezz/Shereif Hegazy (EGY) d. Vladislav Bondarenko/Andrey Tolstenko (UKR) 64 46 64.

- **COLOMBO** (SRI) (Grade 5) 13-19 SEPTEMBER – **GS:** Lia Tapper (AUS) d. Preethi Subramaniam (IND) 64 75. **GD:** Jessica Moore/Lia Tapper (AUS) d. Jing-Chi Lin/Su-Han Yang (TPE) 64 64. **BS:** Hsin-Han Lee (TPE) d. Amrit Rupasinghe (SRI) 57 62 76(3). **BD:** Franklyn Emmanuel/Oshada Wijemanne (SRI) d. Peraklat Siriluethaiwattana/Kittipong Wachiramanowong (THA) 63 63.

- **LEXINGTON, KY** (USA) (Grade 1) 13-19 SEPTEMBER – **GS:** Aleksandra Wozniak (CAN) d. Marina Erakovic (NZL) 75 62. **GD:** Madalina Gojnea/Monica Niculescu (ROM) d. Magdalena Kiszczynska (POL)/Evgeniya Rodina (RUS) 61 63. **BS:** Tim Smyczek (USA) d. Petar Jelenic (CRO) 75 51 ret. **BD:** Viktor Troicki (SCG)/Chu-Huan Yi (TPE) d. Mikhail Pavlov (RUS)/Serguei Tarasevitch (BLR) 62 63.

- **PANCEVO** (SCG) (Grade 3) 13-19 SEPTEMBER – **GS:** Ekaterina Makarova (RUS) d. Olga Panova (RUS) 64 60. **GD:** Alexandra Dulgheru/Raluca Olaru (ROM) d. Kristina Antoniychuk (UKR)/Ana Veselinovic (SCG) 64 75. **BS:** Ivan Sergeev (UKR) d. Jochen Schottler (GER) 64 76(5). **BD:** Jochen Schottler (GER)/Kristofer Wachter (AUT) d. Slavko Bjelica/Branko Kuzmanovic (SCG) 62 61.

- **SHYMKENT CITY** (KAZ) (Grade 5) 13-18 SEPTEMBER – **GS:** Amina Rakhim (KAZ) d. Mariya Kovaleva (KAZ) 67(3) 63 60. **GD:** Maria Melihova (MDA)/Amina Rakhim (KAZ) d. Mariya Kovaleva/Yekaterina Morozova (KAZ) 75 06 64. **BS:** Stanislav Buykov (KAZ) d. Alexander Selezner (KGZ) 63 62. **BD:** Andrey Boldarev/Alexey Nomozov (UZB) d. Maxim Filippov (KAZ)/Vaja Uzakov (UZB) 26 62 62.

- **MOSTAR** (BIH) (Grade 5) 14-18 SEPTEMBER – **GS:** Selma Babic (BIH) d. Petra Martic (CRO) 76(1) 63. **GD:** Tereza Mrdeza (CRO)/Suncica Strkic (BIH) d. Caterina Marusic (ITA)/Mika Urbancic (SLO) 60 62. **BS:** Sinisa Markovic (BIH) d. Nikola Mektic (CRO) 62 36 64. **BD:** Tibor Simic/Igor Skoric (CRO) d. Josip Juric/Boran Poljancic (CRO) 64 06 64.

- **SOFIA** (BUL) (Grade 5) 15-19 SEPTEMBER – **GS:** Elitsa Kostova (BUL) d. Lutphia Velieva (BUL) 64 60. **GD:** Huliya Velieva/Lutphia Velieva (BUL) d. Ioana Bara/Nicoleta Bara (ROM) 60 64. **BS:** Paul-Mihai Puscasu (ROM) d. Alexander Kotsyuk (UKR) 63 26 63. **BD:** Arthur Basin (ISR)/Roman Tudoreanu (MDA) d. Sergey Belov (RUS)/Vladimir Dembinski (ROM) 61 16 63.

- **BEIJING** (CHN) (Grade 5) 15-19 SEPTEMBER – **GS:** Yi-Fan Xu (CHN) d. Jing Zhou (CHN) 64 63. **GD:** Shuang Wu/Jing Zhou (CHN) d. Xin-Xin Jin/Jin-Yi Liu (CHN) 63 63. **BS:** Munetoshi Kumagae (JPN) d. Junchao Xu (CHN) 36 64 62. **BD:** Yang Bai/Yang Li (CHN) d. Guo-Bin Cen (CHN)/Tetta Oyama (JPN) ret.

- **PRAGUE** (CZE) (Grade 2) 15-19 SEPTEMBER – **GS:** Sorana Cirstea (ROM) d. Nikola Frankova (CZE) 75 46 76(2). **GD:** Agnieszka Radwanska/Ueszula Radwanska (POL) d. Gabriela Bergmanova/Eva Kadlecova (CZE) 36 60 75. **BS:** Pavol Cervenak (SVK) d. Pawel Syrewicz (POL) 61 64. **BD:** Pavel Chekhov/Valeri Rudnev (RUS) d. Stanislav Burian/Mirko Zapletal (CZE) 64 64.

- **MUMBAI** (IND) (Grade 4) 20-25 SEPTEMBER – **GS:** Punam Reddy (IND) d. Sandhya Nagraj (IND) 64 61. **GD:** Vandana Murali/Sandhya Nagraj (IND) d. Sandri Gangothri/Punam Reddy (IND) 63 61. **BS:** Vivek Shokeen (IND) d. Rohan Gide (IND) 76(5) 64. **BD:** Anshuman Dutta/Sumit Prakash Gupta (IND) d. Rohan Gide/Tejesvi Rao (IND) 62 46 63.

- **CAIRO** (EGY) (Grade 5) 20-26 SEPTEMBER – **GS:** Noémie Scharle (FRA) d. Ola Abou Zekri (EGY) 64 63. **BS:** Mahmoud Kamel (EGY) d. Vladislav Bondarenko (UKR) w/o. **BD:** Ali El Sherbini/Mahmoud Kamel (EGY) d. Mohamed El Nagdy/Ahmed Monir (EGY) 62 64.

- **NOVI SAD** (SCG) (Grade 2) 20-25 SEPTEMBER – **GS:** Anastasia Poltoratskaya (RUS) d. Olga Panova (RUS) 64 36 63. **GD:** Tatsiana Kapshai (BLR)/Anastasia Poltoratskaya (RUS) d. Klaudia Boczova (SVK)/Anastasia Pivovarova (RUS) w/o. **BS:** Thiemo De Bakker (NED) d. Ante Nakic-Alfirevic (CRO) 26 64 64. **BD:** Ionut Mihai Beleleu/Mihai Nichifor (ROM) d. Emanuel Brighiu/Alexandru Victor Caliciu (ROM) 63 63.

- **VIÑA DEL MAR** (CHI) (Grade 4) 20-26 SEPTEMBER – **GS:** Catalina Arancibia (CHI) d. Celina Grisi (BOL) 62 26 61. **GD:** Manuela Esposito/Dolores Pazo (ARG) d. Denise Kirbuikain/Pamela Russo (ARG) 62 61. **BS:** Augustin Echarte (ARG) d. Pedro Graber (CHI) 62 36 61. **BD:** Pedro Graber/Daniel Tobar (CHI) d. Martin Di Mella/Augustin Echarte (ARG) 64 76(4).

- **ATLANTA, GA** (USA) (Grade 4) 21-26 SEPTEMBER – **GS:** Megan Alexander (USA) d. Melissa Mang (USA) 63 75. **GD:** Megan Alexander/Sarah Lancaster (USA) d. Jelena Durisic (SLO)/Maria Mokh (RUS) 63 61. **BS:** Donald Young (USA) d. Miguel Reyes-Varela (MEX) 61 61. **BD:** Calvin Kemp/Donald Young (USA) d. Kellen Damico/Nathaniel Schnugg (USA) 36 61 62.

- **HUZHOU** (CHN) (Grade 5) 22-26 SEPTEMBER – **GS:** Jing Ren (CHN) d. Fang Liu (CHN) 63 63. **GD:** Ying Qian/Yi Yang (CHN) d. Xin-Yun Han/Fang Liu (CHN) 64 46 64. **BS:** Junchao Xu (CHN) d. Chen Yu Wu (CHN) 62 63. **BD:** Li Qian/Jing-Xing Yu (CHN) d. Ronald Chow/Tsz-Chun Gilbert Wong (HKG) 64 67(7) 63.

- **ASHGABAT** (TKM) (Grade 5) 22-26 SEPTEMBER – **GS:** Nigora Sirojiddinova (UZB) d. Yulia Zelenskaya (KAZ) 62 64. **GD:** Nigora Sirojiddinova (UZB)/Yulia Zelenskaya (KAZ) d. Leila Alisultanova (TKM)/Nonna Safarova (KAZ) 61 63. **BS:** Vadim Zinchenko (RUS) d. Stanislav Naydenov (TKM) 75 06 60. **BD:** Serdarguly Mamedkuliyev/Stanislav Naydenov (TKM) d. Anton Krasnov (TKM)/Vadim Zinchenko (RUS) 76(2) 76(6).

- **MANILA** (PHI) (Grade 5) 27 SEPTEMBER-3 OCTOBER – **GS:** Ayumi Okuma (JPN) d. Anja-Vanessa Peter (GER) 64 60. **GD:** Ayumi Okuma/Natsumi Yokota (JPN) d. Jing-Chi Lin/Chieh Ju Wang (TPE) 26 75 63. **BS:** Martin Sayer (HKG) d. Nico-Riego De Dios (PHI) 63 64. **BD:** Xiao-Peng Lai/Martin Sayer (HKG) d. Ralph Barte/Kyle Joshua Dandan (PHI) 76(5) 63.

- **GURGAON** (IND) (Grade 4) 27 SEPTEMBER-2 OCTOBER – **GS:** Sandhya Nagraj (IND) d. Preethi Subramaniam (IND) 63 63. **GD:** Vandana Murali/Sandhya Nagraj (IND) d. Shweta Kakhandi/Preethi Subramaniam (IND) 76(5) 46 64. **BS:** Vivek Shokeen (IND) d. Rohan Gide (IND) 61 75. **BD:** Anshuman Dutta/Sumit Prakash Gupta (IND) d. Rohan Gide/Tejesvi Rao (IND) 46 63 60.

- **KARACHI** (PAK) (Grade 5) 27 SEPTEMBER-3 OCTOBER – **GS:** Chit Su Yee (MYA) d. Amitha Arudpragasam (SRI) 36 64 75. **GD:** Amitha Arudpragasam (SRI)/Chit Su Yee (MYA) d. Inayat Khosla/Ayesha Talwar (IND) 63 36 61. **BS:** Kirati Siributwong (THA) d. Gursher Singh Harika (IND) 60 60. **BD:** Kirati Siributwong/Peerakit Siributwong (THA) d. Jitin Bishnoi/Kinshuk Sharma (IND) 64 64.

- **SANTIAGO** (CHI) (Grade 4) 27 SEPTEMBER-3 OCTOBER – **GS:** Catalina Arancibia (CHI) d. Fernanda Davalle (ARG) 62 64. **GD:** Paulina Jorquera (CHI)/Denise Kirbuikain (ARG) d. Manuela Esposito/Maria Pazo (ARG) 16 76(8) 64. **BS:** Augustin Echarte (ARG) d. Martin Di Mella (ARG) 61 64. **BD:** Alejandro Breve/Daniel Tobar (CHI) d. Sebastian Aguilar/Marcos Linconir (CHI) 62 61.

ITF Junior Circuit 2004 Results (continued)

- **TULSA, OK** (USA) (Grade B1) 28 SEPTEMBER-3 OCTOBER – **GS:** Andrea Remynse (USA) d. Jennifer-Lee Heinser (USA) 64 61. **GD:** Jennifer-Lee Heinser/Elizabeth Plotkin (USA) d. Megan Alexander/Sarah Lancaster (USA) 64 76(2). **BS:** Donald Young (USA) d. Jamie Hunt (USA) 63 62. **BD:** Jesse Levine/Michael Shabaz (USA) d. Bryan Koniecko (USA)/Jose Moncada (HON) 67(1) 63 60.

- **MIJAS** (ESP) (Grade 5) 30 SEPTEMBER-3 OCTOBER – **GS:** Mariella Greschik (GER) d. Ana Beltran-Trigueros (ESP) 63 62. **GD:** Annette Pohjalainen (FIN)/Maria-Antonia Vives-Barquiel (ESP) d. Tatiana Teterina/Ketsjaryna Zheltova (BLR) 76(5) 76(7). **BS:** Thomas Fabbiano (ITA) d. Pavel Katliarou (BLR) 62 61. **BD:** Thomas Fabbiano (ITA)/Andrei Karatchenia (BLR) d. Goncalo Falcao/Martim Manoel (POR) 67(4) 62 75.

- **PORTO SEGURO** (BRA) (Grade 5) 4-10 OCTOBER – **GS:** Justina Derungs (SUI) d. Stephanie Vieira (BRA) 76(6) 63. **GD:** Karina Chiarelli/Bruna Paes (BRA) d. Rebecca Neves/Stephanie Vieira (BRA) 06 62 76(4). **BS:** Luis-Henrique Grangeiro (BRA) d. Andre Moreira (BRA) 61 62. **BD:** Luis-Henrique Grangeiro/Andre Moreira (BRA) d. Vitor Requiao/Bruno Scacallossi (BRA) 75 62.

- **MANILA** (PHI) (Grade 5) 4-10 OCTOBER – **GS:** Veronica Li (USA) d. Anja-Vanessa Peter (GER) 62 64. **GD:** Seul-Ki Chin/Ju Eun Kim (KOR) d. Tzu Chen Hsu/Jing-Chi Lin (TPE) 63 26 61. **BS:** Kyle Joshua Dandan (PHI) d. Huai-En Chang (TPE) 62 75. **BD:** Min Fu Ko/Chia-Chu Lien (TPE) d. Ralph Barte/Kyle Joshua Dandan (PHI) 62 62.

- **KARACHI** (PAK) (Grade 5) 4-10 OCTOBER – **GS:** Inayat Khosla (IND) d. Ayesha Talwar (IND) 61 60. **GD:** Amitha Arudpragasam (SRI)/Chit Su Yee (MYA) d. Inayat Khosla/Ayesha Talwar (IND) 63 63. **BS:** Jitin Bishnoi (IND) d. Yasir Khan (PAK) 63 61. **BD:** Jitin Bishnoi/Kinshuk Sharma (IND) d. Gursher Singh Harika (IND)/Peerakit Siributwong (THA) 64 61.

- **ALICANTE** (ESP) (Grade 5) 5-9 OCTOBER – **GS:** Beatriz Garcia-Vidagany (ESP) d. Anastasiya Solomko (KAZ) 63 61. **GD:** Melissa Cabrera-Handt (ESP)/Anastasia Kontratevidi (GRE) d. Inna Cherpunaya/Anastassia Zvereva (RUS) 64 57 60. **BS:** Thomas Fabbiano (ITA) d. Agustin Boje-Ordonez (ESP) 64 60. **BD:** Goncalo Falcao/Martim Manoel (POR) d. Thomas Fabbiano (ITA)/Andrei Karatchenia (BLR) 63 62.

- **MALI LOSINJ** (CRO) (Grade 4) 6-10 OCTOBER – **GS:** Ivana Maroh (CRO) d. Diana Nakic (SLO) 64 64. **GD:** Taja Mohorcic/Petra Pajalic (SLO) d. Tadeja Majeric (SLO)/Petra Martic (CRO) 46 63 64. **BS:** Denis Bejtulahi (SCG) d. Slavko Bjelica (SCG) 46 75 62. **BD:** Mario Jukic/Mikhail Karpol (CRO) d. Nikola Mektic/Tibor Simic (CRO) 61 67(5) 64.

- **ONTARIO** (CAN) (Grade 4) 11-16 OCTOBER – **GS:** Valerie Tetreault (CAN) d. Ekaterina Shulaeva (CAN) 64 63. **GD:** Monica Lalewicz/Ekaterina Shulaeva (CAN) d. Jillian O'Neill (CAN)/Ashley Spicer (USA) 67(7) 62 76(0). **BS:** Erik Chvojka (CAN) d. Milan Pokrajac (CAN) 76(3) 26 64. **BD:** Mariusz Adamski (POL)/Edward Ted Kelly (USA) d. Alexandre Labrosse/Guillaume St Maurice (CAN) 61 64.

- **CAUSEWAY BAY** (HKG) (Grade 4) 11-16 OCTOBER – **GS:** Ling Zhang (CHN) d. He-Wen-Fei Li (CHN) 62 64. **GD:** Lu-Ling Chen (TPE)/Veronica Li (USA) d. Anthea Look (HKG)/Ling Zhang (CHN) 76(3) 64. **BS:** Jason Jung (USA) d. Junchao Xu (CHN) 76(4) 46 64. **BD:** John Smith/Andrew Thomas (AUS) d. Christopher Rungkat/Anthony Tan (INA) 62 62.

- **LONDRINA** (BRA) (Grade 5) 11-17 OCTOBER – **GS:** Karina Chiarelli (BRA) d. Liege Vieira (BRA) 63 61. **BS:** Leonardo Mayer (ARG) d. Luis-Henrique Grangeiro (BRA) 62 57 62.

- **OSAKA** (JPN) (Grade A) 11-17 OCTOBER – **GS:** Caroline Wozniacki (DEN) d. Dominika Cibulkova (SVK) 63 60. **GD:** Megumi Fukui/Kaoru Maezawa (JPN) d. Michelle Brycki/Shayna McDowell (AUS) 63 26 64. **BS:** Woong-Sun Jun (KOR) d. Sun-Yong Kim (KOR) 61 76(4). **BD:** Woong-Sun Jun/Sun-Yong Kim (KOR) d. Myles Blake (GBR)/Abdullah Magdas (KUW) 64 46 64.

- **DOHA** (QAT) (Grade 5) 11-15 OCTOBER – **GS:** Samantha Murray (GBR) d. Julia Bone (GBR) 62 62. **GD:** Sona Novakova/Zora Vlckova (CZE) d. Julia Bone/Samantha Murray (GBR) 67(5) 75 64. **BS:** Christopher Llewellyn (GBR) d. Cristian Hodel (ROM) 64 76(7). **BD:** Iain Atkinson/Edward Corrie (GBR) d. Radoslaw Dektar (CAN)/Christopher Llewellyn (GBR) 61 62.

- **FORT WORTH, TX** (USA) (Grade 4) 12-17 OCTOBER – **GS:** Megan Alexander (USA) d. Lauren Albanese (USA) 63 63. **GD:** Megan Alexander/Sarah Lancaster (USA) d. Kristy Frilling (USA)/Georgia Rose (GBR) 61 62. **BS:** Carsten Ball (USA) d. Clint Bowles (USA) 62 64. **BD:** Carsten Ball/Conor Pollock (USA) d. Kellen Damico/Nathaniel Schnugg (USA) 63 63.

- **COPENHAGEN** (DEN) (Grade 4) 12-16 OCTOBER – **GS:** Johanna Larsson (SWE) d. Natalie Fehse (GER) 63 64. **GD:** Diana Eriksson/Johanna Larsson (SWE) d. Marija Mirkovic (AUS)/Anastasia Pavlyuchenkova (RUS) 62 67(6) 61. **BS:** Alexandr Zotov (BLR) d. David Rice (GBR) 67(3) 76(6) 62. **BD:** Andreas Karlsson/Nicklas Szymanski (SWE) d. Daniel Danilovic/Fredric Sandberg (SWE) 64 60.

- **DUBAI** (UAE) (Grade 4) 18-23 OCTOBER – **GS:** Julia Bone (GBR) d. Aliaa Fakhry (EGY) 61 76(4). **GD:** Sona Novakova/Zora Vlckova (CZE) d. Shivika Burman (IND)/Irina Matiychyk (UKR) 62 60. **BS:** Edward Corrie (GBR) d. Stanislav Buykov (KAZ) 76(5) 61. **BD:** Ivan Galic (AUT)/Cristian Hodel (ROM) d. Stanislav Buykov/Maxim Filippov (KAZ) 64 67(8) 64.

- **MONTREAL** (CAN) (Grade 3) 18-23 OCTOBER – **GS:** Melanie Gloria (CAN) d. Valerie Tetreault (CAN) 63 26 76(3). **GD:** Chantal Beetham/Valerie Tetreault (CAN) d. Monica Lalewicz/Ekaterina Shulaeva (CAN) 63 62. **BS:** Erik Chvojka (CAN) d. Peter Polansky (CAN) 62 62. **BD:** Erik Chvojka/Peter Polansky (CAN) d. Jonathon Boym (USA)/Vladimiros Mavropoulos-Stoliarenko (GRE) 64 63.

- **KOLDING** (DEN) (Grade 4) 18-22 OCTOBER – **GS:** Ksenia Pervak (RUS) d. Anastasia Pivovarova (RUS) 64 62. **GD:** Natalie Fehse (GER)/Melanie Klaffner (AUT) d. Anouk Tigu/Kim Van der Horst (NED) 63 75. **BS:** Alexandr Zotov (BLR) d. Igor Lakhno (UKR) 46 76(4) 61. **BD:** Mauro Piras/Lennart Samuelson (GER) d. Alexander Panasik/Alexandr Zotov (BLR) 76(3) 16 64.

- **NONTHABURI** (THA) (Grade 2) 18-24 OCTOBER – **GS:** Nudnida Luangnam (THA) d. Nungnadda Wannasuk (THA) 64 46 64. **GD:** Barbora Hodinarova/Katerina Kramperova (CZE) d. Barbara Pinterova (SVK)/Anastasia Poltoratskaya (RUS) 63 76(3). **BS:** Sergei Bubka (UKR) d. Martin Kamenik (CZE) 63 61. **BD:** Weerapat Doakmaiklee/Kirati Siributwong (THA) d. Syrym Abdukhalikov (KAZ)/Tristan Farron-Mahon (IRL) 64 62.

- **EL PASO, TX** (USA) (Grade 5) 18-24 OCTOBER – **GS:** Lyndsay Burdette (USA) d. Lauren Dossor (GBR) 63 75. **GD:** Marah Calvo (PUR)/Caitlin Whoriskey (USA) d. Maria Anisimova (RUS)/Kirsten Flower (USA) 63 62. **BS:** Spencer Vegosen (USA) d. Rook Schellenberg (USA) 36 63 61. **BD:** Spencer Vegosen/Michael Venus (USA) d. Danila Arsenov (RUS)/Serguei Boulanov (USA) 64 62.

- **ANDORRA LA VELLA** (AND) (Grade 5) 25-30 OCTOBER – **BS:** Tobias Wernet (GER) d. Dorian Descloix (FRA) 62 62. **BD:** Dean Jackson (GER)/Yury Shirshov (RUS) d. Pascal Krauth/Tobias Wernet (GER) 63 26 64.

- **VIERUMAKI** (FIN) (Grade 4) 25-29 OCTOBER – **GS:** Sara Errani (ITA) d. Elina Hasanova (AZE) 75 63. **GD:** Elina Hasanova (AZE)/Yelena Kulikova (RUS) d. Viktoria Agryutenkova/Maya Gaverova (RUS) 67(4) 62 64. **BS:** Eoin Heavey (IRL) d. Georgy Morgoev (RUS) 10 ret. **BD:** Anton Bobytskyy/Artem Smirnov (UKR) d. Teso Loytana/Mika Purho (FIN) 67(5) 63 63.

- **YANGON** (MYA) (Grade 5) 27-31 OCTOBER – **GS:** Wei-Ping Lee (SIN) d. Parichart Charoensukploypol (THA) 60 75. **GD:** Jawariah Noordin (MAS)/Chit Su Yee (MYA) d. Parichart Charoensukploypol/Hathaichanok Saenyaukhot (THA) 61 76(4). **BS:** Agung-Bagus Dewantoro (INA) d. Hsin-Han Lee (TPE) 64 76(4). **BD:** Faisal Aidil/Agung-Bagus Dewantoro (INA) d. Lopburi Nathasiri (THA)/Christopher Rungkat (INA) 61 61.

- **LEXINGTON, SC** (USA) (Grade 3) 2-7 NOVEMBER – **GS:** Elizabeth Plotkin (USA) d. Jennifer-Lee Heinser (USA) 62 57 63. **GD:** Jennifer-Lee Heinser/Elizabeth Plotkin (USA) d. Andrea Remynse/Keri Robison (USA) 61 46 64. **BS:** Michael Shabaz (USA) d. Roberto Maytin (VEN) 61 67(3) 64. **BD:** Spencer Vegosen/Michael Venus (USA) d. Jeff Dadamo/Okechi Womeodu (USA) 62 64.

- **HANOI** (VIE) (Grade 4) 2-7 NOVEMBER – **GS:** Wing-Yau "Venise" Chan (HKG) d. Thuy-Dung Nguyen (VIE) 61 63. **GD:** Wing-Yau "Venise" Chan (HKG)/Thuy-Dung Nguyen (VIE) d. Chia-Chian Lee/Chiao-Ya Shen (TPE) 63 62. **BS:** Martin Sayer (HKG) d. Xiao-Peng Lai (HKG) 61 60. **BD:** Xiao-Peng Lai/Martin Sayer (HKG) d. Kai Chieh Ma/Kai Chun Ma (TPE) 60 63.

- **CENTRAL JAVA** (INA) (Grade 4) 2-7 NOVEMBER – **GS:** Mia Sacca (INA) d. Dede-Tari Kusrini (INA) 61 61. **GD:** Golda Rubina/Lavinia Tananta (INA) d. Lutfiana Aris Budiharto/Vivien Silvany-Tony (INA) 62 64. **BS:** Elbert Sie (INA) d. Sandy Purnomo (INA) 76(4) 60. **BD:** Jonathan Amdanu/Christopher Rungkat (INA) d. Elbert Sie/Anthony Tan (INA) 63 61.

- **TAMPERE** (FIN) (Grade 4) 2-6 NOVEMBER – **GS:** Anastasia Pavlyuchenkova (RUS) d. Elina Hasanova (AZE) 63 61. **GD:** Sara Errani/Stella Menna (ITA) d. Yelena Kulikova/Anastasia Pavlyuchenkova (RUS) 64 63. **BS:** Thomas Kromann (DEN) d. Pirmin Haenle (GER) 46 64 75. **BD:** Thomas Kromann/Joakim-Bay Simonsen (DEN) d. Anton Bobytskyy/Artem Smirnov (UKR) w/o.

- **BOCA RATON, FL** (USA) (Grade 4) 9-14 NOVEMBER – **GS:** Yasmin Schnack (USA) d. Kimberly Couts (USA) 64 46 62. **GD:** Keri Robison/Yasmin Schnack (USA) d. Lyndsay Burdette/Mallory Burdette (USA) 61 62. **BS:** Alberto Gonzalez (PAN) d. Jean-Yves Aubone (USA) 67(3) 75 64. **BD:** Jonathan Boym (USA)/Vladimiros Mavropoulos-Stoliarenko (GRE) d. Attila Bucko (SCG)/Davey Sandgren (USA) 61 64.

- **SURABAYA** (INA) (Grade 4) 9-14 NOVEMBER – **GS:** Lavinia Tananta (INA) d. Dian Mayasari (INA) 36 63 63. **GD:** Nancy Metriya/Patricia Soesilo (INA) d. Jessy Rompies/Mia Sacca (INA) 67(1) 61 64. **BS:** Elbert Sie (INA) d. David Rice (GBR) 61 60. **BD:** Chris Mayanto/Sandy Purnomo (INA) d. David Rice/Darren Walsh (GBR) 64 63.

ITF Junior Circuit 2004 Results (continued)

- **SANTA CRUZ** (BOL) (Grade 5) 12-21 NOVEMBER – **GS:** Maria-Irene Squillaci-Sandoval (BOL) d. Briggitte Marcovich (VEN) 61 60. **GD:** Jessica Aguilera/Maria-Irene Squillaci-Sandoval (BOL) d. Briggitte Marcovich (VEN)/Nataly Yoo (USA) 62 75. **BS:** Daniel Lopez (PAR) d. Camillo Munoz (CHI) 61 63. **BD:** Filippo Baronti/Joaquin Guillier (CHI) d. Fabricio Morales/Justino Morales (MEX) 64 64.

- **ESCH/ALZETTE** (LUX) (Grade 1) 15-20 NOVEMBER – **GS:** Michaella Krajicek (NED) d. Caroline Wozniacki (DEN) 46 62 62. **GD:** Michaella Krajicek/Bibiane Schoofs (NED) d. Marrit Boonstra/Nicole Thyssen (NED) 62 26 61. **BS:** Lukas Lacko (SVK) d. Jochen Schottler (GER) 61 64. **BD:** Evgeny Kirillov/Alexander Krasnorutskiy (RUS) d. Sergei Bubka (UKR)/Tristan Farron-Mahon (IRL) 75 63.

- **TAIWAN** (TPE) (Grade 5) 15-20 NOVEMBER – **GS:** Yu-Ting Lin (TPE) d. Huai-Chi Huang (TPE) 62 63. **GD:** Jing-Chi Lin/Su-Han Yang (TPE) d. Yu-Lin Tai/Wen-Ling Wang (TPE) 64 63. **BS:** Huai-En Chang (TPE) d. Ting Lung Chang-Chien (TPE) 61 61. **BD:** Ting Lung Chang-Chien/Tung Han Lee (TPE) d. Min Fu Ko/Hsin-Han Lee (TPE) 64 36 63.

- **NONTHABURI** (THA) (Grade 4) 15-21 NOVEMBER – **GS:** Ye-Ra Lee (KOR) d. Anja-Vanessa Peter (GER) 61 61. **GD:** Ye-Ra Lee (KOR)/Porntip Mulsap (THA) d. Martina Lautenschlager/Stefanie Vogele (SUI) 62 61. **BS:** Robin Roshardt (SUI) d. Weerapat Doakmaiklee (THA) 62 46 62. **BD:** Robin Roshardt/Alexander Sadecky (SUI) d. Brydan Klein/Matt Symons (AUS) 76(4) 63.

- **MERIDA** (MEX) (Grade 1) 22-27 NOVEMBER – **GS:** Katerina Bondarenko (UKR) d. Andrea Remynse (USA) 64 61. **GD:** Elizabeth Kobak/Yasmin Schnack (USA) d. Jennifer-Lee Heinser/Elizabeth Plotkin (USA) 64 60. **BS:** Pablo Andujar-Alba (ESP) d. Spencer Vegosen (USA) 62 62. **BD:** Pablo Andujar-Alba (ESP)/Miguel Reyes-Varela (MEX) d. Jesse Levine/Michael Shabaz (USA) w/o.

- **LIMA** (PER) (Grade 5) 22-28 NOVEMBER – **GS:** Briggitte Marcovich (VEN) d. Rebecca Neves (BRA) 62 61. **GD:** Alejandra Meza Cuadra/Melissa Valenzuela (PER) d. Amanda Bambaren (PER)/Rebecca Neves (BRA) 62 63. **BS:** Jose Zunino (ECU) d. Oscar Machuca (ECU) 63 61. **BD:** Diego Machuca/Oscar Machuca (ECU) d. Michel Monteiro/Gustavo Schaefer (BRA) 62 62.

- **SARAWAK** (MAS) (Grade 3) 24-29 NOVEMBER – **GS:** Ye-Ra Lee (KOR) d. Stefanie Vogele (SUI) 60 61. **GD:** Irina Matiychyk (UKR)/Madura Ranganathan (IND) d. Ellen Barry (NZL)/Anastasia Poltoratskaya (RUS) 64 76(4). **BS:** Robin Roshardt (SUI) d. Martin Sayer (HKG) 64 36 63. **BD:** Xiao-Peng Lai/Martin Sayer (HKG) d. Brad Brinkhause Williams/Charl Wolmarans (RSA) 10 ret.

- **GUAYAQUIL** (ECU) (Grade 5) 29 NOVEMBER-5 DECEMBER – **BS:** Jose Zunino (ECU) d. Gabriel Garcia (ECU) 62 57 76(0). **BD:** Juan-Andres Gomez/Jose Zunino (ECU) d. Diego Machuca/Oscar Machuca (ECU) 62 26 63.

- **BRADENTON, FL** (USA) (Grade 1) 29 NOVEMBER-5 DECEMBER – **GS:** Monica Niculescu (ROM) d. Dominika Cibulkova (SVK) 61 60. **GD:** Mihaela Buzarnescu/Sorana-Mihaela Cirstea (ROM) d. Marina Erakovic (NZL)/Monica Niculescu (ROM) 64 36 64. **BS:** Jeremy Chardy (FRA) d. David Navarrete (VEN) 61 64. **BD:** Jesse Levine/Michael Shabaz (USA) d. Alexandr Dolgopolov (UKR)/Billy Timu (CAN) 63 57 76(2).

- **NAIROBI** (KEN) (Grade 4) 30 NOVEMBER-4 DECEMBER – **GS:** Fadzai Mawisire (ZIM) d. Lisa Levenberg (RSA) 62 63. **GD:** Suzelle Davin (NAM)/Fadzai Mawisire (ZIM) d. Walaa Elsir (SUD)/Lisa Levenberg (RSA) 36 63 64. **BS:** Christian Vitulli (KEN) d. Bokang Setshogo (BOT) 63 46 61. **BD:** Jurgens Strydom (NAM)/Christian Vitulli (KEN) d. Arlen Domoney/Vuk Milicevic (RSA) 62 63.

- **KUALA LUMPUR** (MAS) (Grade 3) 1-5 DECEMBER – **GS:** Stefanie Vogele (SUI) d. Antonia Fohse (GER) 63 57 63. **GD:** Shao-Yuan Kao (TPE)/He-Wen-Fei Li (CHN) d. Ellen Barry (NZL)/Anastasia Poltoratskaya (RUS) 63 63. **BS:** Weerapat Doakmaiklee (THA) d. Alexander Sadecky (SUI) 63 61. **BD:** Alexei Filonov/Valeri Rudnev (RUS) d. Alexander Sadecky (SUI)/Kento Takeuchi (JPN) 75 56 def.

- **ADDIS ABABA** (ETH) (Grade 4) 6-10 DECEMBER – **GS:** Xenia Samoilova (AUT) d. Nicole Rottmann (AUT) 61 61. **GD:** Suzelle Davin (NAM)/Fadzai Mawisire (ZIM) d. Nicole Rottmann/Xenia Samoilova (AUT) 75 75. **BS:** Christian Vitulli (KEN) d. Jurgens Strydom (NAM) 64 75. **BD:** Jurgens Strydom (NAM)/Christian Vitulli (KEN) d. Ned Boone (GBR)/Lukas Weinhandl (AUT) 60 63.

- **MIAMI, FL** (USA) (Grade 4) 6-10 DECEMBER – **GS:** Corinna Dentoni (ITA) d. Karina Porushkevich (USA) 64 61. **GD:** Corinna Dentoni/Erica Zanchetta (ITA) d. Emmy Fritz-Krockow/Karina Porushkevich (USA) w/o. **BS:** Wael Kilani (TUN) d. Graeme Kassautzki (CAN) 46 75 64. **BD:** Nathaniel Schnugg/Michael Sroczynski (USA) d. Roy-Paul Bottse (AHO)/Mikk Irdoja (EST) 46 62 76(5).

- **KEY BISCAYNE, FL** (USA) (Grade 1) 6-12 DECEMBER – **GS:** Jessica Kirkland (USA) d. Mary Gambale (USA) 61 62. **GD:** Vania King/Yasmin Schnack (USA) d. Marina Erakovic (NZL)/Monica Niculescu (ROM) 63 75. **BS:** Mihail Zverev (GER) d. Sun-Yong Kim (KOR) 64 46 64. **BD:** Marc Spicijaric (USA)/Mihail Zverev (GER) d. Rafael Arevalo Gonzalez (ESA)/Sun-Yong Kim (KOR) 62 61.

- **PERTH** (AUS) (Grade 5) 7-12 DECEMBER – **GS:** Jenny Swift (AUS) d. Aimi Koga (JPN) 64 75. **GD:** Mai Iwasaki/Machiko Shigefuji (JPN) d. Kristina Pejkovic (AUS)/Brittany Teei (NZL) 64 64. **BS:** Joshua Crowe (AUS) d. Lachlan Reed (AUS) 76(2) 62. **BD:** Brydan Klein/Joel Lindner (AUS) d. Joshua Crowe/Jason Lee (AUS) 67(8) 64 63.

- **KEY BISCAYNE, FL.** (USA) (Grade A) 13-19 DECEMBER – **GS:** Jessica Kirkland (USA) d. Alla Kudryavtseva (RUS) 63 62. **GD:** Marina Erakovic (NZL)/Monica Niculescu (ROM) d. Vania King/Yasmin Schnack (USA) 60 63. **BS:** Timothy Neilly (USA) d. Donald Young (USA) 64 75. **BD:** Piero Luisi/David Navarrete (VEN) d. Abdullah Magdas (KUW)/Martin Pedersen (DEN) 61 64.

- **SINGAPORE** (SIN) (Grade 5) 13-19 DECEMBER – **GS:** Irina Matiychyk (UKR) d. Aimi Koga (JPN) 61 64. **GD:** Irina Matiychyk (UKR)/Ling Zhang (CHN) d. Rumi Abe/Aimi Koga (JPN) 63 61. **BS:** Shuhei Uzawa (JPN) d. Agung-Bagus Dewantoro (INA) 61 60. **BD:** Christopher Rungkat (INA)/Shuhei Uzawa (JPN) d. Kitanoo Puthong (THA)/Muhd Ashaari Zainal (MAS) 61 60.

- **KAOHSIUNG** (TPE) (Grade B2) 14-18 DECEMBER – **GS:** Wen-Hsin Hsu (TPE) d. Yung-Jan Chan (TPE) 64 26 76(4). **GD:** Shao-Yuan Kao (TPE)/Jung-Yoon Shin (KOR) d. Yung-Jan Chan/Ching-Ching Tai (TPE) 36 61 61. **BS:** Chu-Huan Yi (TPE) d. Huai-En Chang (TPE) 64 64. **BD:** Jeevan Nedunchezhiyan/Sanam Singh (IND) d. Huai-En Chang/Chu-Huan Yi (TPE) 16 63 64.

- **SINT-KATELIJNE-WAVER** (BEL) (Grade 5) 26-31 DECEMBER – **GS:** Aude Vermoezen (BEL) d. Alexandra Kulikova (RUS) 75 62. **GD:** Marlot Meddens/Anouk Tigu (NED) d. Tiffany Cornelius (LUX)/Tatiana Cutrona (BEL) 52 ret. **BS:** Yannick Mertens (BEL) d. Maxime Authom (BEL) 76(5) 67(1) 62. **BD:** Maxime Authom/Frederic De Fays (BEL) d. Evthemlos Karaliolios (NED)/Jeremy Swyngedouw (BEL) 16 76(2) 64.

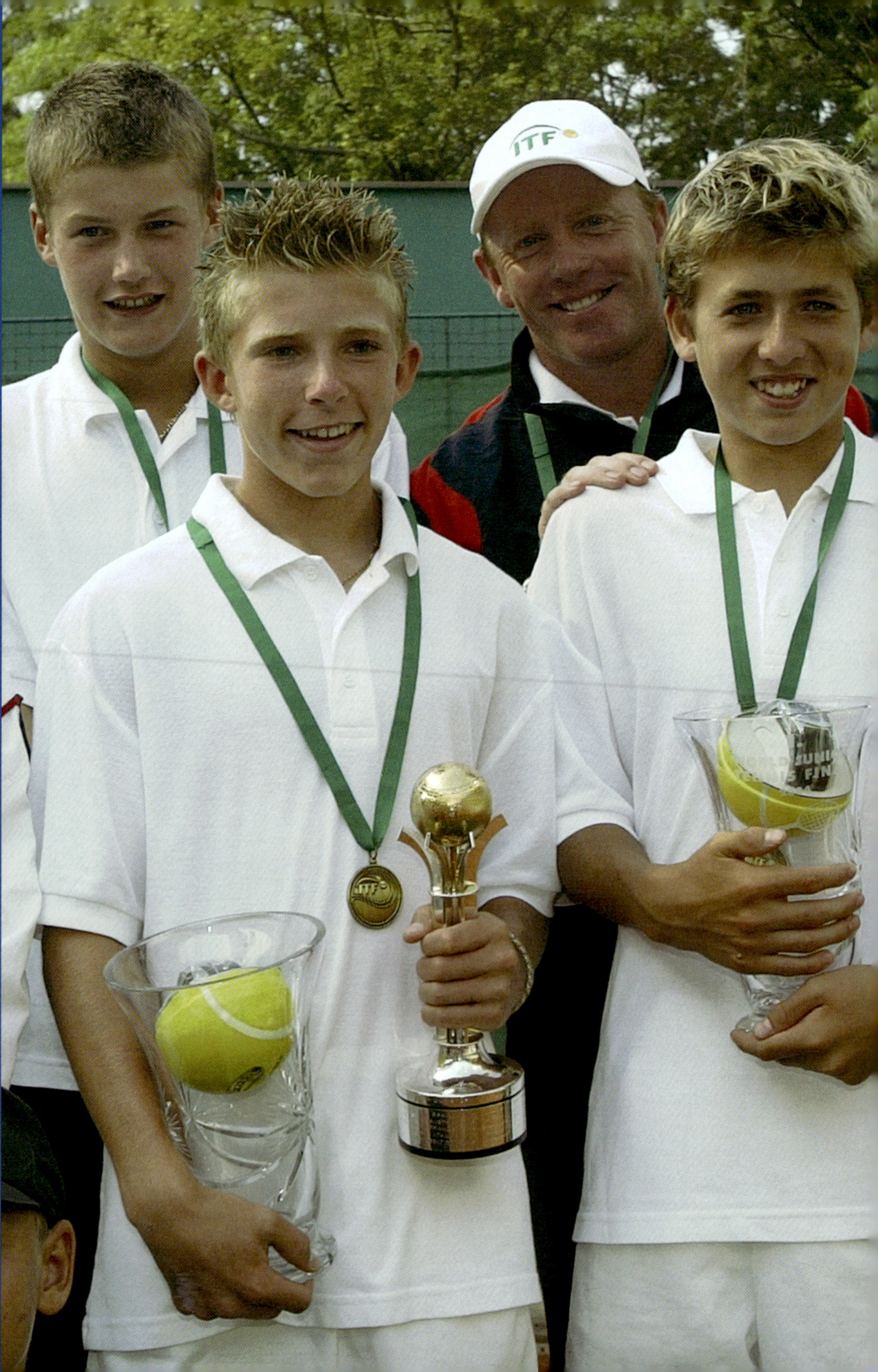
ITF

World Junior Tennis Finals 2004

ITF Junior Team Championships for boys and girls of 14 & Under

Prostejov, Czech Republic, 2-7 August 2004

BOYS' FINAL STANDINGS:
1. Great Britain, 2. Czech Republic, 3. Thailand, 4. Italy, 5. France, 6. Germany, 7. USA, 8. Croatia, 9. Australia, 10. Korea, 11. South Africa, 12. Argentina, 13. Brazil, 14. Mexico, 15. Venezuela, 16. Egypt.

Semifinals:
Great Britain d. Thailand 2-1: Lewis Barnes (GBR) d. Peerapach Tupwong (THA) 63 60; Daniel Cox (GBR) d. Kittipong Wachiramanowong (THA) 75 64; Peerakit Siributwong/Peerapach Tupwong (THA) d. Lewis Barnes/Daniel Evans (GBR) 76(5) 63. **Czech Republic d. Italy 3-0:** Jan Trocil (CZE) d. Davide Della Tommasina (ITA) 62 63; Emanuel Rehola (CZE) d. Daniele Piludu (ITA) 06 76(6) 62; Emanuel Rehola/Radim Urbanek (CZE) d. Erik Crepaldi/Davide Della Tommasina (ITA) 76(1) 46 64.

Final:
Great Britain d. Czech Republic 2-0: Lewis Barnes (GBR) d. Jan Trocil (CZE) 63 75; Daniel Cox (GBR) d. Emanuel Rehola (CZE) 75 76(1); doubles not played.

GIRLS' FINAL STANDINGS:
1. Belarus, 2. Austria, 3. Slovak Republic, 4. Czech Republic, 5. Russia, 6. Australia, 7. USA, 8. Mexico, 9. Japan, 10. Peru, 11. Indonesia, 12. Egypt, 13. Argentina, 14. Korea, 15. Italy, 16. Tunisia.

Semifinals:
Belarus d. Slovak Republic 2-1: Kristina Kucova (SVK) d. Ima Bohush (BLR) 60 75; Ksenia Milevskaya (BLR) d. Klaudia Boczova (SVK) 60 26 61; Ima Bohush/Ksenia Milevskaya (BLR) d. Martina Balagova/Klaudia Boczova (SVK) 75 61. **Austria d. Czech Republic 2-1:** Andrea Berkova (CZE) d. Melanie Klaffner (AUT) 75 61; Nikola Hofmanova (AUT) d. Petra Mokra (CZE) 76(5) 57 97; Nikola Hofmanova/Melanie Klaffner (AUT) d. Andrea Berkova/Petra Mokra (CZE) 67(2) 64 86.

Final:
Belarus d. Austria 2-1: Melanie Klaffner (AUT) d. Ima Bohush (BLR) 76(1) 75; Ksenia Milevskaya (BLR) d. Nikola Hofmanova (AUT) 61 75; Ima Bohush/Ksenia Milevskaya (BLR) d. Nikola Hofmanova/Melanie Klaffner (AUT) 60 61.

Above: Belarus Girls' team won the nation's first World Junior Tennis title
Left: Great Britain's winning Boys' team

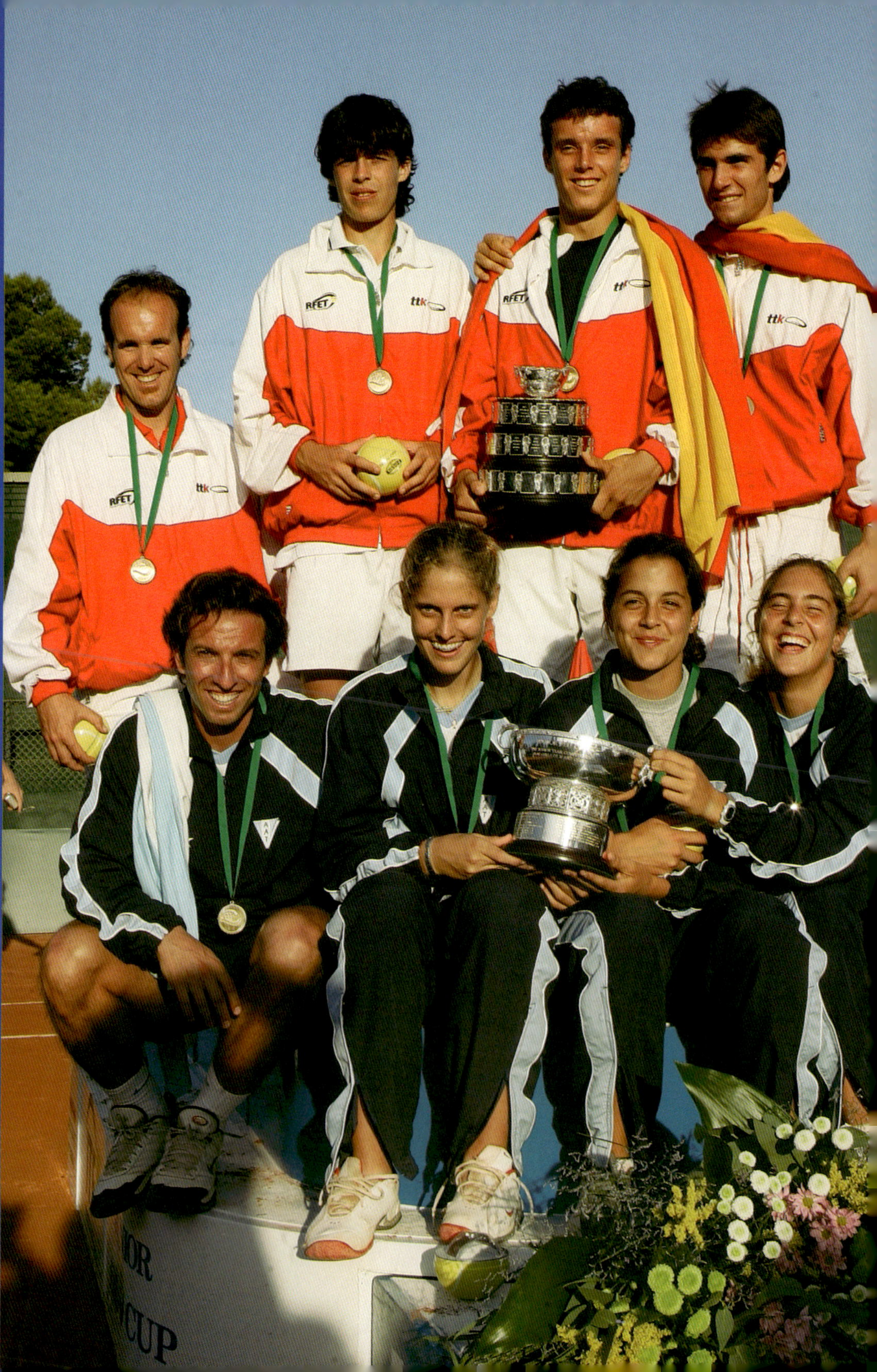
RFET
ttk

Junior Davis Cup by BNP Paribas Final 2004

ITF Junior Team Championships for boys of 16 & under; prior to 2002 the competition was known as the NEC World Youth Cup.

Barcelona, Spain, 28 September–3 October 2004

FINAL STANDINGS:
1. Spain, 2. Czech Republic, 3. Russia, 4. Croatia, 5. Argentina, 6. USA, 7. Australia, 8. India, 9. Tunisia, 10. Chinese Taipei, 11. Japan, 12. Germany, 13. Colombia, 14. France, 15. Morocco, 16. Venezuela.

Semifinals:
Spain d. Croatia 2-1: Roberto Bautista (ESP) d. Jurica Grubisic (CRO) 36 63 63; Marin Cilic (CRO) d. Pere Riba (ESP) 75 63; Roberto Bautista/Pere Riba (ESP) d. Marin Cilic/Mikhail Karpol (CRO) 61 75. **Czech Republic d. Russia 2-1:** Miroslav Navratil (CZE) d. Valery Rudnev (RUS) 61 76(3); Pavel Chekhov (RUS) d. Dusan Lojda (CZE) 63 75; Dusan Lojda/Miroslav Navratil (CZE) d. Pavel Chekhov/Valery Rudnev (RUS) 62 76(1).

Final:
Spain d. Czech Republic 2-1: Miroslav Navratil (CZE) d. Roberto Bautista (ESP) 61 64; Pere Riba (ESP) d. Dusan Lojda (CZE) 61 64; Roberto Bautista/Pere Riba (ESP) d. Dusan Lojda/Filip Zeman (CZE) 63 64.

Junior Fed Cup Final 2004

ITF Junior Team Championships for girls of 16 & under; prior to 2002 the competition was known as the NEC World Youth Cup.

FINAL STANDINGS:
1. Argentina, 2. Canada, 3. Netherlands, 4. Russia, 5. Czech Republic, 6. USA, 7. Croatia, 8. China, 9. Spain, 10. Brazil, 11. Denmark, 12. Morocco, 13. Chinese Taipei, 14. Chile, 15. Egypt, 16. Japan.

Semifinals:
Argentina d. Russia 2-1: Ekaterina Makarova (RUS) d. Betina Jozami (ARG) 57 75 60; Florencia Molinero (ARG) d. Ekaterina Kosminskaya (RUS) 36 60 63; Betina Jozami/Agustina Lepore (ARG) d. Ekaterina Kosminskaya/Ekaterina Makarova (RUS) 63 16 119. **Canada d. Netherlands 2-1:** Valerie Tetreault (CAN) d. Marrit Boonstra (NED) 16 61 64; Sharon Fichman (CAN) d. Bibiane Schoofs (NED) 61 64; Marrit Boonstra/Nicole Thijssen (NED) d. Tania Rice/Valerie Tetreault (CAN) 62 64.

Final:
Argentina d. Canada 2-0: Betina Jozami (ARG) d. Valerie Tetreault (CAN) 61 63; Florencia Molinero (ARG) d. Sharon Fichman (CAN) 36 64 62; doubles not played.

Spain Boys' and Argentina Girls' winning teams

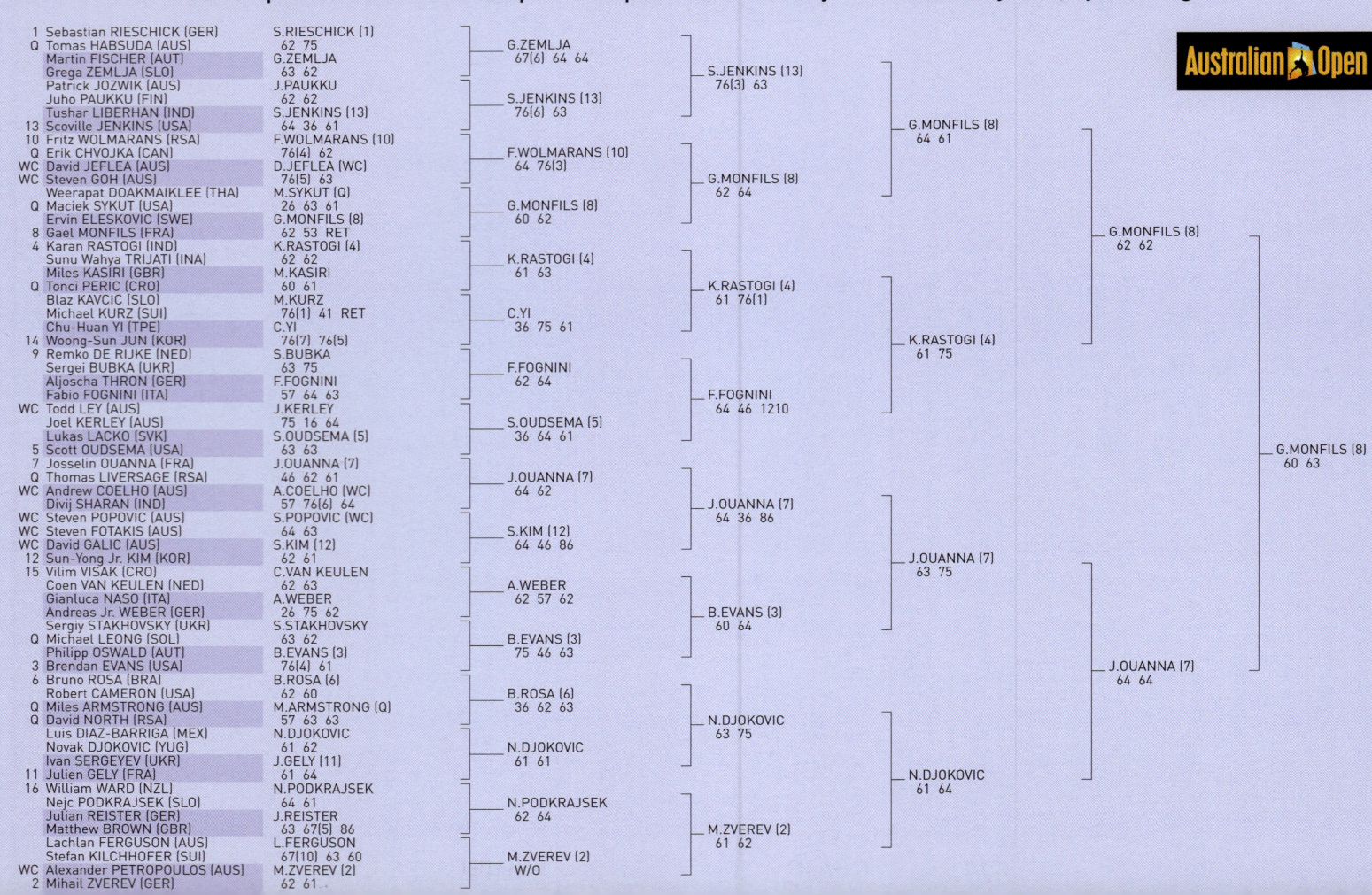

2004 Australian Open Junior Championships, 26 January–1 February – Boys' Singles

Seed	Player	R1	R2	R3	QF	SF	F
1	Sebastian RIESCHICK (GER)	S.RIESCHICK [1] 62 75					
Q	Tomas HABSUDA (AUS)	G.ZEMLJA 63 62	G.ZEMLJA 67(6) 64 64				
	Grega ZEMLJA (SLO)	J.PAUKKU 62 62		S.JENKINS [13] 76(3) 63			
Q	Juho PAUKKU (FIN)		S.JENKINS [13] 76(6) 63		G.MONFILS [8] 64 61		
	Tushar LIBERHAN (IND)	S.JENKINS [13] 64 36 61					
13	Scoville JENKINS (USA)	F.WOLMARANS [10] 76(4) 62	F.WOLMARANS [10] 64 76(3)				
10	Fritz WOLMARANS (RSA)	D.JEFLEA (WC) 76(5) 63				G.MONFILS [8] 62 62	
Q	Erik CHVOJKA (CAN)			G.MONFILS [8] 60 62			
WC	David JEFLEA (AUS)	M.SYKUT (Q) 26 63 61					
WC	Steven GOH (AUS)	G.MONFILS [8] 53 RET	G.MONFILS [8] 62 53 RET				
	Weerapat DOAKMAIKLEE (THA)				G.MONFILS [8] 62 64		
	Maciek SYKUT (USA)						
	Ervin ELESKOVIC (SWE)		K.RASTOGI [4] 61 63				
8	Gael MONFILS (FRA)	M.KASIRI 60 61					
4	Karan RASTOGI (IND)			K.RASTOGI [4] 61 76(1)			
	Sunu Wahya TRIJATI (INA)	M.KURZ 76(1) 41 RET					
	Miles KASIRI (GBR)		C.YI 36 75 61				
Q	Tonci PERIC (CRO)	C.YI			K.RASTOGI [4] 61 75		
	Blaz KAVCIC (SLO)	S.BUBKA 63 75					
	Michael KURZ (SUI)		F.FOGNINI 62 64			G.MONFILS [8] 60 63	
	Chu-Huan YI (TPE)			F.FOGNINI 64 46 1210			
14	Woong-Sun JUN (KOR)	F.FOGNINI 57 64 63					
9	Sergei BUBKA (UKR)	J.KERLEY 75 16 64	S.OUDSEMA [5] 36 64 61				
	Aljoscha THRON (GER)				F.FOGNINI		
	Fabio FOGNINI (ITA)						
WC	Todd LEY (AUS)	S.OUDSEMA [5] 63 63					
	Joel KERLEY (AUS)	J.OUANNA [7] 46 62 61					
	Lukas LACKO (SVK)		J.OUANNA [7] 64 62				
5	Scott OUDSEMA (USA)	A.COELHO (WC) 57 76(6) 64					
7	Josselin OUANNA (FRA)	S.POPOVIC (WC)		J.OUANNA [7] 64 36 86			
Q	Thomas LIVERSAGE (RSA)		S.KIM [12] 64 63				
WC	Andrew COELHO (AUS)				J.OUANNA [7] 63 75		
	Divij SHARAN (AUS)	S.KIM [12] 62 61					
WC	Steven POPOVIC (AUS)		C.VAN KEULEN 62 63				
WC	Steven FOTAKIS (AUS)					J.OUANNA [7] 64 64	
	David GALIC (AUS)	A.WEBER 26 75 62		S.KIM [12] 64 46 86			
12	Sun-Yong Jr. KIM (KOR)		A.WEBER 62 57 62				
	Vitim VISAK (CRO)						
	Coen VAN KEULEN (NED)			B.EVANS [3] 60 64			
	Gianluca NASO (ITA)	S.STAKHOVSKY (UKR) 63 62					
	Andreas Jr. WEBER (GER)		B.EVANS [3] 75 46 63				
Q	Sergiy STAKHOVSKY (UKR)	B.EVANS [3] 76(4) 61					
	Philipp OSWALD (AUT)				B.EVANS [3]		
	Michael LEONG (SOL)						
3	Brendan EVANS (USA)		B.ROSA (6) 36 62 63			N.DJOKOVIC 63 75	
6	Bruno ROSA (BRA)	B.ROSA (6) 62 60					
Q	Robert CAMERON (USA)	M.ARMSTRONG (Q) 57 63 63					
	Miles ARMSTRONG (AUS)		N.DJOKOVIC 61 62	B.ROSA (6)			
Q	David NORTH (RSA)	N.DJOKOVIC 61 61		N.DJOKOVIC			
	Luis DIAZ-BARRIGA (MEX)						
	Novak DJOKOVIC (YUG)				N.DJOKOVIC 61 64		
	Ivan SERGEYEV (UKR)	J.GELY [11] 61 64					
11	Julien GELY (FRA)		N.PODKRAJSEK 62 64				
	William WARD (NZL)	N.PODKRAJSEK 64 61					
16	Nejc PODKRAJSEK (SLO)	J.REISTER 63 67(5) 86		N.PODKRAJSEK			
	Julian REISTER (GER)		L.FERGUSON 67(10) 63 60				
	Matthew BROWN (GBR)	L.FERGUSON			M.ZVEREV [2] 61 62		
	Lachan FERGUSON (AUS)		M.ZVEREV [2] W/O				
	Stefan KILCHHOFER (AUS)						
Q	Alexander PETROPOULOS (AUS)	M.ZVEREV [2] 62 61					
2	Mihail ZVEREV (2)						

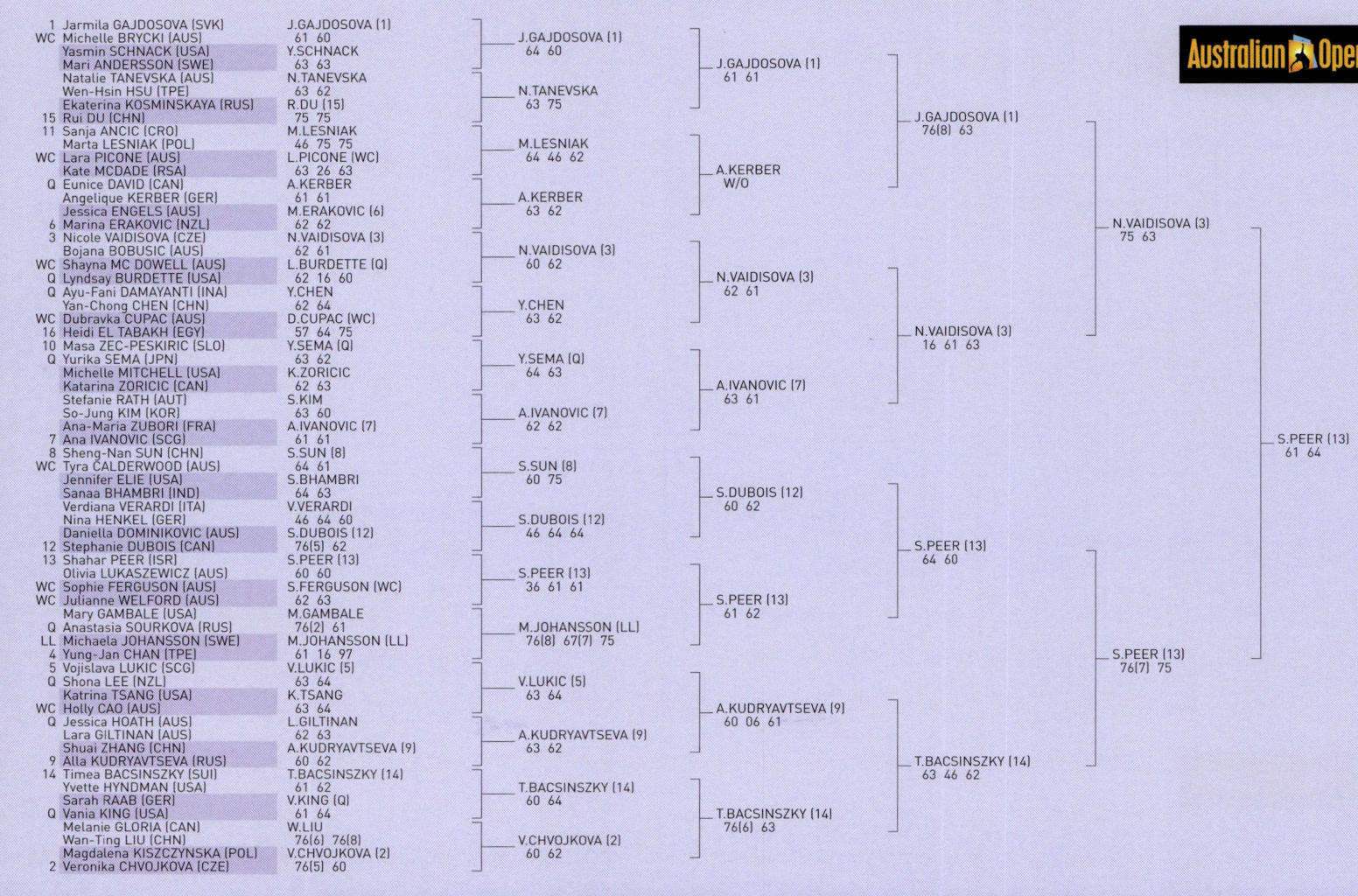

2004 Australian Open Junior Championships, 26 January–1 February – Girls' Singles

Winner: S. Peer (13) — def. N. Vaidisova (3) 6-1 6-4

First Round

Seed	Player	R1 Opponent	Score
1	Jarmila GAJDOSOVA (SVK)	Michelle BRYCKI (USA)	6-1 6-0
WC	Yasmin SCHNACK (USA)	Mari ANDERSSON (SWE)	6-3 6-3
	Natalie TANEVSKA (AUS)	Wen-Hsin HSU (TPE)	6-3 6-2
15	Ekaterina KOSMINSKAYA (RUS)	R. DU (CHN)	7-5 7-5
11	Sanja ANCIC (CRO)	Marta LESNIAK (POL)	4-6 7-5 7-5
WC	Lara PICONE (AUS)	Kate MCDADE (RSA)	6-3 2-6 6-3
Q	Eunice DAVID (CAN)	Angelique KERBER (GER)	6-1 6-1
6	Jessica ENGELS (AUS)	Marina ERAKOVIC (NZL)	6-2 6-2
3	Nicole VAIDISOVA (CZE)	Bojana BOBUSIC (AUS)	6-2 6-1
WC	Shayna MC DOWELL (AUS)	Lyndsay BURDETTE (USA)	6-2 1-6 6-0
Q	Ayu-Fani DAMAYANTI (INA)	Yan-Chong CHEN (CHN)	6-2 6-4
WC	Dubravka CUPAC (AUS)	Heidi EL TABAKH (EGY)	5-7 6-4 7-5
16	Masa ZEC-PESKIRIC (SLO)	Yurika SEMA (JPN)	6-3 6-2
Q	Michelle MITCHELL (USA)	Katarina ZORICIC (CAN)	6-2 6-3
	Stefanie RATH (AUT)	So-Jung KIM (KOR)	6-3 6-0
7	Ana IVANOVIC (SCG)	Ana-Maria ZUBORI (FRA)	6-1 6-1
WC	Tyra CALDERWOOD (AUS)	Sheng-Nan SUN (CHN)	6-4 6-1
8	Jennifer ELIE (USA)	Sanaa BHAMBRI (IND)	6-4 6-3
	Verdiana VERARDI (ITA)	Nina HENKEL (GER)	4-6 6-4 6-0
12	Stephanie DUBOIS (CAN)	Daniella DOMINIKOVIC (AUS)	7-6(5) 6-2
13	Shahar PEER (ISR)	Olivia LUKASZEWICZ (AUS)	6-0 6-0
WC	Sophie FERGUSON (AUS)	Julianne WELFORD (AUS)	6-2 6-3
WC	Mary GAMBALE (USA)	Anastasia SOURKOVA (RUS)	7-6(2) 6-1
LL	Michaela JOHANSSON (SWE)	Yung-Jan CHAN (TPE)	6-1 1-6 9-7
5	Vojislava LUKIC (SCG)	Shona LEE (NZL)	6-3 6-4
Q	Katrina TSANG (USA)	Holly CAO (AUS)	6-3 6-4
WC	Jessica HOATH (AUS)	Lara GILTINAN (AUS)	6-2 6-3
	Shuai ZHANG (CHN)	Alla KUDRYAVTSEVA (RUS)	6-0 6-2
9	Timea BACSINSZKY (SUI)	Yvette HYNDMAN (USA)	6-1 6-2
14	Sarah RAAB (GER)	V. KING (USA)	6-1 6-4
Q	Vania KING (USA)	Melanie GLORIA (CAN)	7-6(6) 7-6(8)
	Wan-Ting LIU (CHN)	Magdalena KISZCZYNSKA (POL)	7-6(5) 6-0
2	Veronika CHVOJKOVA (CZE)		

Second Round

- J. Gajdosova def. Y. Schnack 6-4 6-0
- N. Tanevska def. M. Lesniak 6-3 7-5
- M. Lesniak def. L. Picone 4-6 7-5 6-2
- A. Kerber def. M. Erakovic 6-3 6-2
- N. Vaidisova def. L. Burdette 6-2 6-1
- Y. Chen def. D. Cupac 6-3 6-2
- Y. Sema def. K. Zoricic 6-4 6-3
- A. Ivanovic def. S. Kim 6-2 6-2
- S. Sun def. S. Bhambri 6-0 7-5
- S. Dubois def. V. Verardi 4-6 6-4 6-0
- S. Peer def. S. Ferguson 3-6 6-1 6-1
- M. Johansson def. V. Lukic 7-6(8) 6-7(7) 7-5
- A. Kudryavtseva def. L. Giltinan 6-0 6-0 6-1
- T. Bacsinszky def. V. King 6-0 6-4
- V. Chvojkova def. W. Liu 6-0 6-2

Third Round

- J. Gajdosova def. N. Tanevska 6-1 6-1
- A. Kerber W/O
- N. Vaidisova def. Y. Chen 6-2 6-1
- A. Ivanovic def. Y. Sema 6-3 6-1
- S. Dubois def. S. Sun 6-0 6-2
- S. Peer def. M. Johansson 6-1 6-2
- A. Kudryavtseva def. T. Bacsinszky 6-0 0-6 6-1
- T. Bacsinszky def. V. Chvojkova 7-6(6) 6-3

Quarterfinals

- J. Gajdosova def. A. Kerber 7-6(8) 6-3
- N. Vaidisova def. A. Ivanovic 1-6 6-1 6-3
- S. Peer def. S. Dubois 6-4 6-0
- T. Bacsinszky def. A. Kudryavtseva 6-3 4-6 6-2

Semifinals

- N. Vaidisova def. J. Gajdosova 7-5 6-3
- S. Peer def. T. Bacsinszky 7-6(7) 7-5

Final

- **S. Peer (13) def. N. Vaidisova (3) 6-1 6-4**

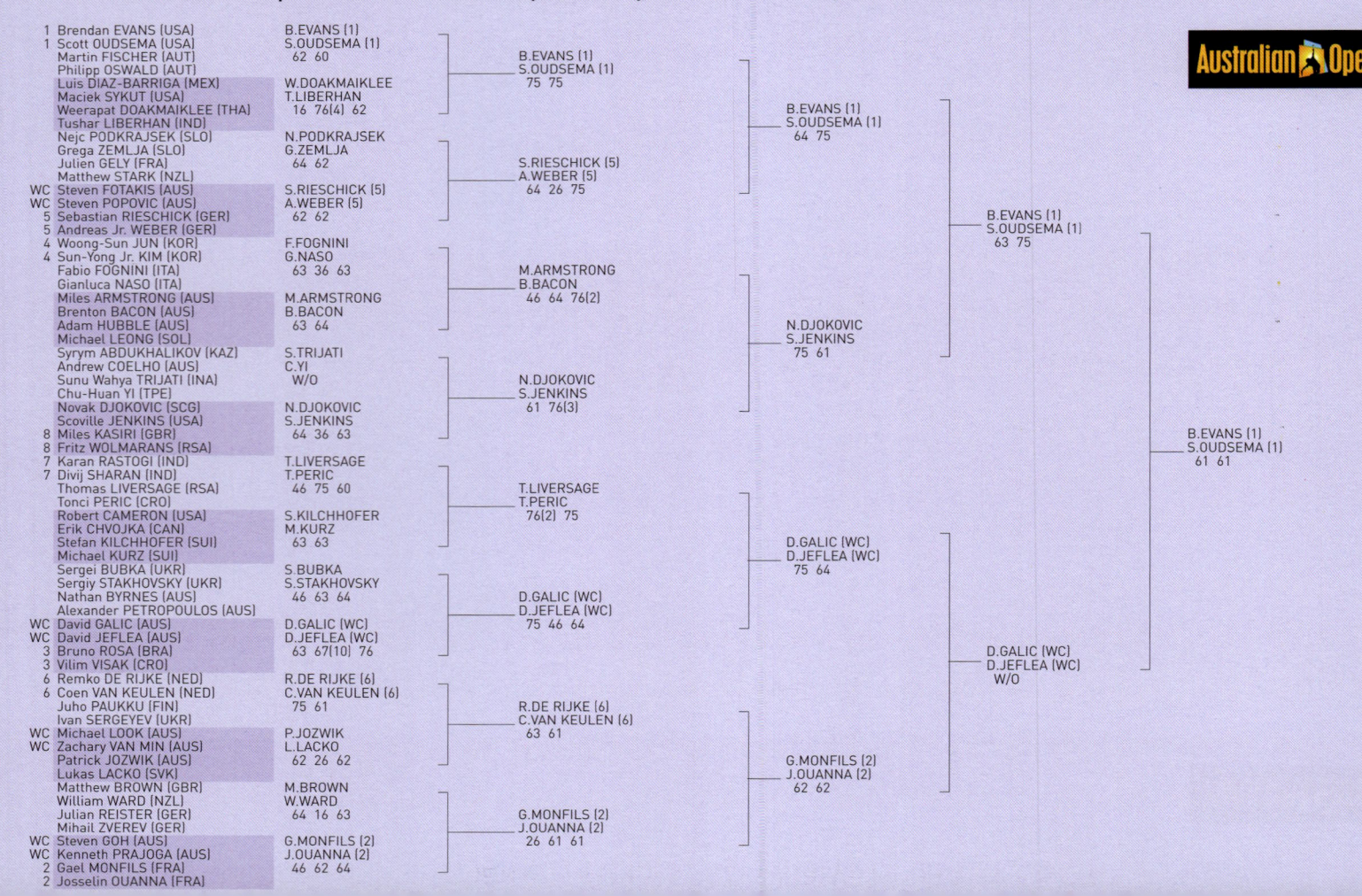

2004 Australian Open Junior Championships, 26 January–1 February – Boys' Doubles

Final: B. EVANS / S. OUDSEMA [1] def. D. GALIC / D. JEFLEA [WC] 6-1 6-1

First Round
- [1] B. Evans / S. Oudsema def. W. Doakmaiklee / T. Liberhan 6-2 6-0
- N. Podkrajsek / G. Zemlja def. M. Sykut / Weerapat Doakmaiklee 1-6 7-6(4) 6-2
- [5] S. Rieschick / A. Weber def. M. Stark / S. Popovic 6-2 6-2
- F. Fognini / G. Naso def. Sun-Yong Jr. Kim / Woong-Sun Jun 6-4 2-6 7-5
- [2] M. Armstrong / B. Bacon def. A. Hubble / M. Leong 6-3 6-4
- S. Trijati / C. Yi def. S. Abdukhalikov / A. Coelho w/o
- N. Djokovic / S. Jenkins def. M. Kasiri / S. Jenkins 6-4 3-6 6-3
- T. Liversage / T. Peric def. K. Rastogi / D. Sharan 4-6 7-5 6-0
- S. Kilchhofer / M. Kurz def. R. Cameron / E. Chvojka 6-3 6-3
- S. Bubka / S. Stakhovsky def. N. Byrnes / A. Petropoulos 4-6 6-3 6-4
- [WC] D. Galic / D. Jeflea def. [6] R. de Rijke / C. van Keulen 6-3 6-7(10) 7-6
- R. de Rijke / C. van Keulen def. J. Paukku / I. Sergeyev 7-5 6-1
- P. Jozwik / L. Lacko def. M. Look / Z. van Min 6-2 2-6 6-2
- M. Brown / W. Ward def. M. Ward / J. Reister 6-4 1-6 6-3
- [2] G. Monfils / J. Ouanna def. S. Goh / K. Prajoga 4-6 6-2 6-4

Second Round
- [1] B. Evans / S. Oudsema 7-5 7-5
- S. Rieschick / A. Weber 6-4 2-6 7-5
- M. Armstrong / B. Bacon 4-6 6-4 7-6(2)
- N. Djokovic / S. Jenkins 6-1 7-6(3)
- T. Liversage / T. Peric 7-6(2) 7-5
- D. Galic / D. Jeflea [WC] 7-5 4-6 6-4
- R. de Rijke / C. van Keulen [6] 6-3 6-1
- G. Monfils / J. Ouanna [2] 2-6 6-1 6-1

Quarterfinals
- [1] B. Evans / S. Oudsema 6-4 7-5
- N. Djokovic / S. Jenkins 7-5 6-1
- D. Galic / D. Jeflea [WC] 7-5 6-4
- G. Monfils / J. Ouanna [2] 6-2 6-2

Semifinals
- [1] B. Evans / S. Oudsema 6-3 7-5
- D. Galic / D. Jeflea [WC] w/o

Final
- [1] B. Evans / S. Oudsema 6-1 6-1

Draw Order

1. Brendan EVANS [USA] [1]
   Scott OUDSEMA [USA] [1]
   Martin FISCHER [AUT]
   Philipp OSWALD [AUT]
   Luis DÍAZ-BARRIGA [MEX]
   Maciek SYKUT [USA]
   Weerapat DOAKMAIKLEE [THA]
   Tushar LIBERHAN [IND]
   Nejc PODKRAJSEK [SLO]
   Grega ZEMLJA [SLO]
   Julien GELY [FRA]
   Matthew STARK [NZL]
   WC Steven FOTAKIS [AUS]
   WC Steven POPOVIC [AUS]
5. Sebastian RIESCHICK [GER] [5]
   Andreas Jr. WEBER [GER] [5]
4. Woong-Sun JUN [KOR]
   Sun-Yong Jr. KIM [KOR]
   Fabio FOGNINI [ITA]
   Gianluca NASO [ITA]
   Miles ARMSTRONG [AUS]
   Brenton BACON [AUS]
   Adam HUBBLE [AUS]
   Michael LEONG [SOL]
   Syrym ABDUKHALIKOV [KAZ]
   Andrew COELHO [AUS]
   Sunu Wahya TRIJATI [INA]
   Chu-Huan YI [TPE]
   Novak DJOKOVIC [SCG]
   Scoville JENKINS [USA]
8. Miles KASIRI [GBR]
   Fritz WOLMARANS [RSA]
7. Karan RASTOGI [IND]
   Divij SHARAN [IND]
   Thomas LIVERSAGE [RSA]
   Tonci PERIC [CRO]
   Robert CAMERON [USA]
   Erik CHVOJKA [CAN]
   Stefan KILCHHOFER [SUI]
   Michael KURZ [SUI]
   Sergei BUBKA [UKR]
   Sergiy STAKHOVSKY [UKR]
   Nathan BYRNES [AUS]
   Alexander PETROPOULOS [AUS]
   WC David GALIC [AUS]
   WC David JEFLEA [AUS]
3. Bruno ROSA [BRA]
3. Vilim VISAK [CRO]
6. Remko DE RIJKE [NED]
6. Coen VAN KEULEN [NED]
   Juho PAUKKU [FIN]
   Ivan SERGEYEV [UKR]
   WC Michael LOOK [AUS]
   WC Zachary VAN MIN [AUS]
   Patrick JOZWIK [AUS]
   Lukas LACKO [SVK]
   Matthew BROWN [GBR]
   William WARD [NZL]
   Julian REISTER [GER]
   Mihail ZVEREV [GER]
   WC Steven GOH [AUS]
   WC Kenneth PRAJOGA [AUS]
2. Gael MONFILS [FRA] [2]
2. Josselin OUANNA [FRA] [2]

2004 Australian Open Junior Championships, 26 January–1 February – Girls' Doubles

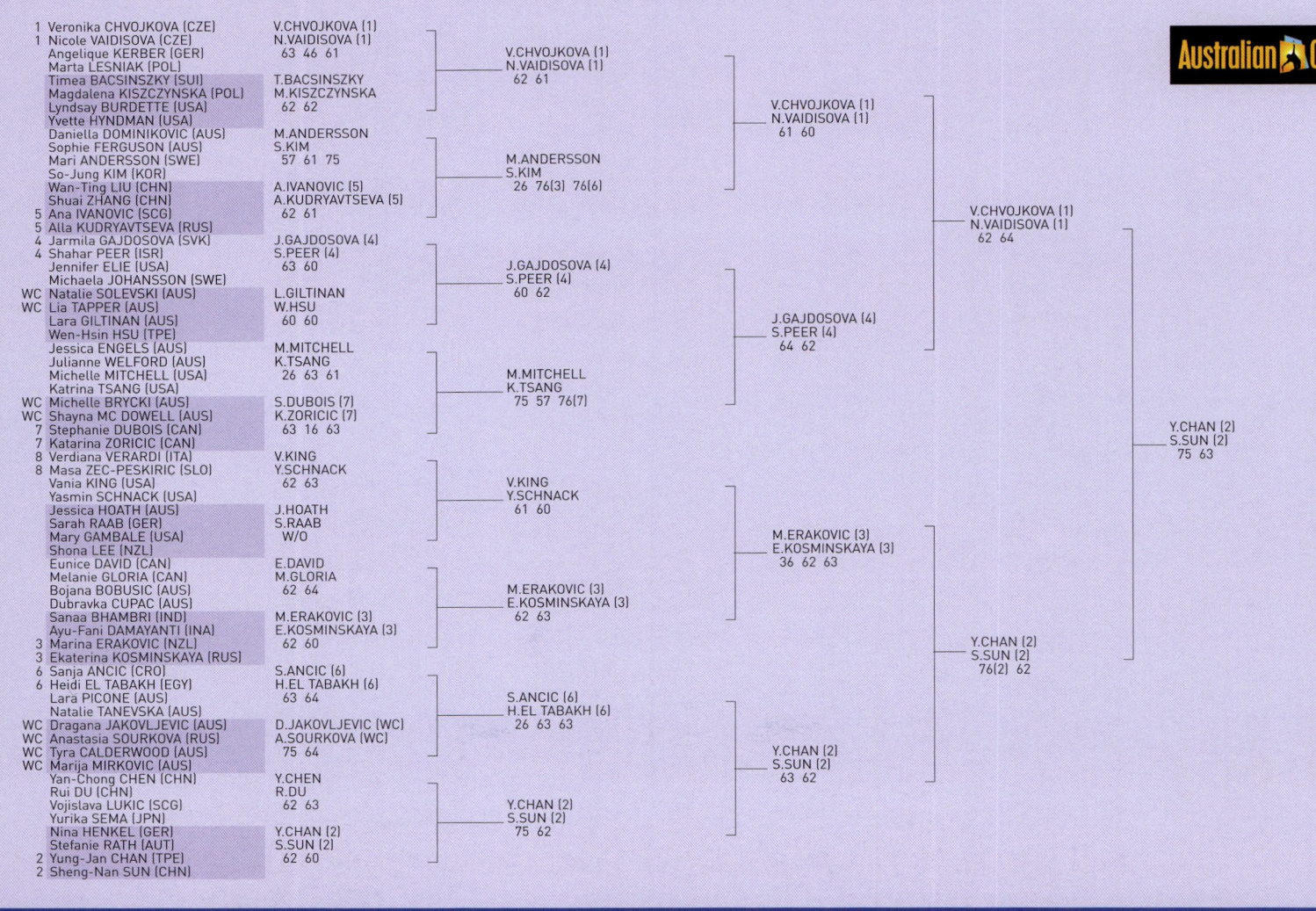

Draw

Final: V.CHVOJKOVA / N.VAIDISOVA [1] def. Y.CHAN / S.SUN [2] 7-5 6-3

First Round / Quarter 1 (top)

- [1] Veronika CHVOJKOVA (CZE) / Nicole VAIDISOVA (CZE) def. Angelique KERBER (GER) / Marta LESNIAK (POL) 6-3 4-6 6-1
- Timea BACSINSZKY (SUI) / Magdalena KISZCZYNSKA (POL) def. Lyndsay BURDETTE (USA) / Yvette HYNDMAN (USA) 6-2 6-2
  - V.CHVOJKOVA / N.VAIDISOVA [1] 6-2 6-1
- Daniela DOMNIKOVIC (AUS) / Sophie FERGUSON (AUS) def. Mari ANDERSSON (SWE) / So-Jung KIM (KOR) 5-7 6-1 7-5
- M.ANDERSSON / S.KIM def. Wan-Ting LIU (CHN) / Shuai ZHANG (CHN) 2-6 7-6(3) 7-6(6)
  - V.CHVOJKOVA / N.VAIDISOVA [1] 6-1 6-0
- [5] Ana IVANOVIC (SCG) / Alla KUDRYAVTSEVA (RUS) def. Jarmila GAJDOSOVA (SVK) / Shahar PEER (ISR) 6-2 6-1
  - J.GAJDOSOVA [4] / S.PEER [4] 6-3 6-0
- Jennifer ELIE (USA) / Michaela JOHANSSON (SWE) def. WC Natalie SOLEYSKI (AUS) / WC Lia TAPPER (AUS) 6-0 6-0
- Lara GILTINAN (AUS) / Wen-Hsin HSU (TPE) def. Jessica ENGELS (AUS) / Julianne WELFORD (AUS)
  - L.GILTINAN / W.HSU 6-0 6-0
  - J.GAJDOSOVA / S.PEER [4] 6-4 6-2

Quarter 2

- Michelle MITCHELL (USA) / Katrina TSANG (USA) def. WC Michelle BRYCKI (AUS) / WC Shayna MC DOWELL (AUS) 2-6 6-3 6-1
  - M.MITCHELL / K.TSANG 7-5 5-7 7-6(7)
- [7] Stephanie DUBOIS (CAN) / Katarina ZORICIC (CAN) def. Verdiana VERARDI (ITA) 6-3 1-6 6-3
- Vania KING (USA) / Yasmin SCHNACK (USA) def. [8] Masa ZEC-PESKIRIC (SLO) / Jessica HOATH (AUS) 6-2 6-3
  - V.KING / Y.SCHNACK 6-1 6-0
- Sarah RAAB (GER) / Mary GAMBALE (USA) w/o Shona LEE (NZL)
  - J.HOATH / S.RAAB w/o

Quarter 3

- Eunice DAVID (CAN) / Melanie GLORIA (CAN) def. Bojana BOBUSIC (AUS) / Dubravka CUPAC (AUS) 6-2 6-4
- [3] Marina ERAKOVIC (NZL) / Ekaterina KOSMINSKAYA (RUS) def. Sanaa BHAMBRI (IND) / Ayu-Fani DAMAYANTI (INA) 6-2 6-0
  - M.ERAKOVIC [3] / E.KOSMINSKAYA [3] 6-2 6-3
- [6] Sanja ANCIC (CRO) / Heidi EL TABAKH (EGY) def. Lara PICONE (AUS) / Natalie TANEVSKA (AUS) 6-3 6-4
  - S.ANCIC [6] / H.EL TABAKH [6] 2-6 6-3 6-3
  - M.ERAKOVIC [3] / E.KOSMINSKAYA [3] 3-6 6-2 6-3
- WC Dragana JAKOVLJEVIC (AUS) / WC Anastasia SOURKOVA (RUS) def. WC Tyra CALDERWOOD (AUS) / WC Marija MIRKOVIC (AUS)
  - D.JAKOVLJEVIC / A.SOURKOVA (WC) 7-5 6-4

Quarter 4

- Yan-Chong CHEN (CHN) / Rui DU (CHN) def. Vojislava LUKIC (SCG) / Yurika SEMA (JPN) 6-2 6-3
  - Y.CHEN / R.DU 6-2 6-3
- Nina HENKEL (GER) / Stefanie RATH (AUT) def. [2] Yung-Jan CHAN (TPE) / Sheng-Nan SUN (CHN) 6-2 6-0
  - Y.CHAN / S.SUN [2] 7-5 6-2
  - Y.CHAN / S.SUN [2] 6-3 6-2

Semifinals:
- V.CHVOJKOVA / N.VAIDISOVA [1] def. J.GAJDOSOVA / S.PEER [4] 6-2 6-4
- Y.CHAN / S.SUN [2] def. M.ERAKOVIC / E.KOSMINSKAYA [3] 7-6(2) 6-2

Final: V.CHVOJKOVA / N.VAIDISOVA [1] def. Y.CHAN / S.SUN [2] 7-5 6-3

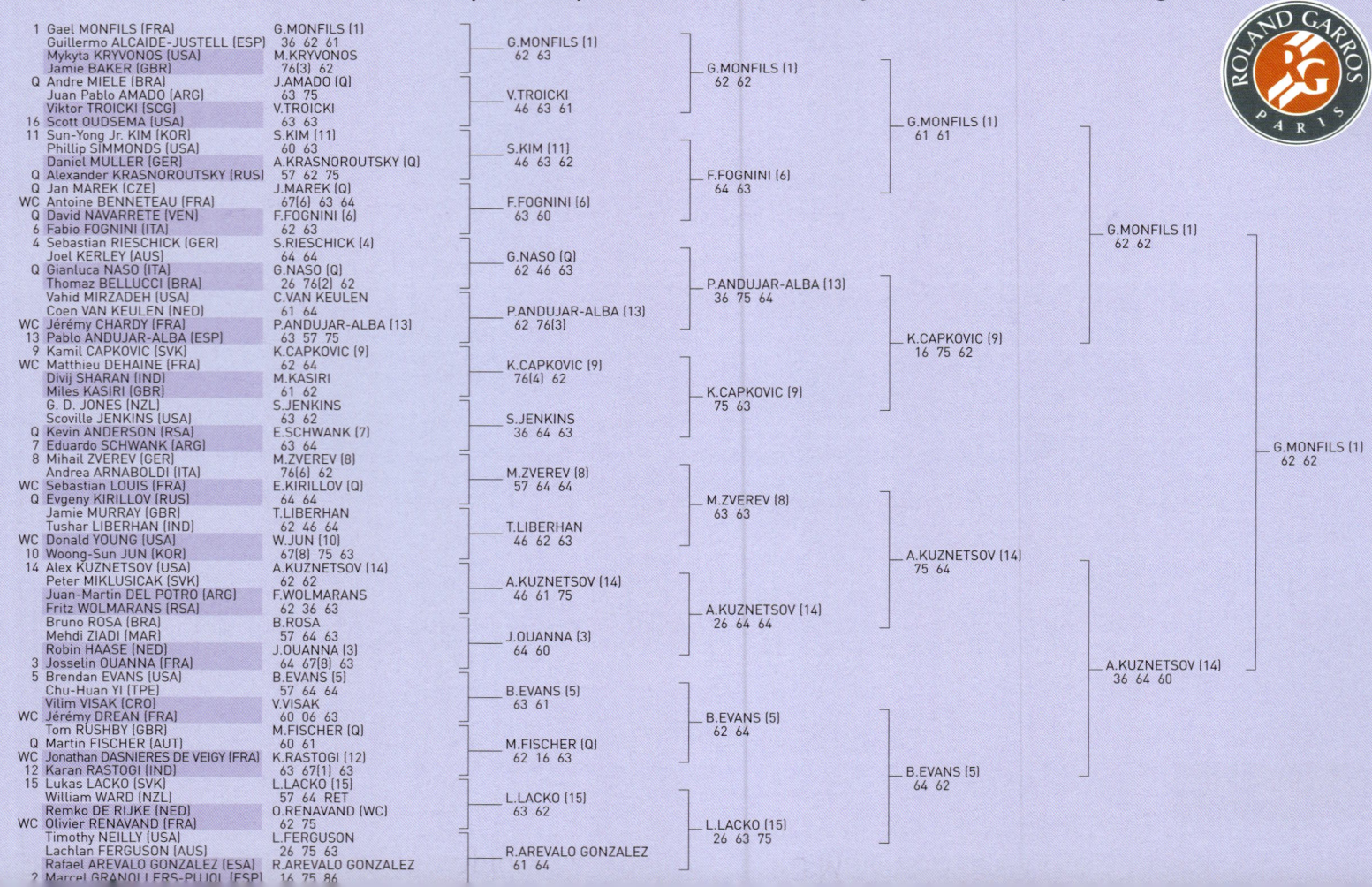

2004 International Junior Championships of France, 30 May–6 June – Boys' Singles

Winner: G. MONFILS [1] def. A. KUZNETSOV [14] 6-2 6-2

First Round

1. Gael MONFILS (FRA) [1] def. Guillermo ALCAIDE-JUSTELL (ESP) 6-3 6-2 6-1
- Mykyta KRYVONOS (USA) def. Jamie BAKER (GBR) 7-6(3) 6-2
- Q Juan Pablo AMADO (ARG) def. Andre MIELE (BRA) 6-3 7-5
- 16 Viktor TROICKI (SCG) def. Scott OUDSEMA (USA) 6-3 6-3
- 11 Sun-Yong Jr. KIM (KOR) def. Phillip SIMMONDS (USA) 6-0 6-3
- Q A. KRASNOROUTSKY (RUS) def. Daniel MULLER (GER) 5-7 6-2 7-5
- Q Jan MAREK (CZE) def. Alexander KRASNOROUTSKY (RUS) — J.MAREK (Q) 6-7(6) 6-3 6-4
- 6 Fabio FOGNINI (ITA) def. Antoine BENNETEAU (FRA) — F.FOGNINI [6] 6-2 6-3
- 4 Sebastian RIESCHICK (GER) def. David NAVARRETE (VEN) — S.RIESCHICK [4] 6-4 6-4
- Joel KERLEY (AUS)
- Gianluca NASO (ITA) def. G.NASO (Q) 6-2 4-6 6-3
- Thomaz BELLUCCI (BRA) 2-6 7-6(2) 6-2
- WC Vahid MIRZADEH (USA) — C.VAN KEULEN 6-1 6-4
- Coen VAN KEULEN (NED)
- 13 Pablo ANDUJAR-ALBA (ESP) — PANDUJAR-ALBA [13] 6-3 5-7 7-5
- WC Jérémy CHARDY (FRA)
- 9 Kamil CAPKOVIC (SVK) — K.CAPKOVIC [9] 6-2 6-4
- Matthieu DEHAINE (FRA) — M.KASIRI 6-1 6-2
- WC Divij SHARAN (IND)
- Miles KASIRI (GBR)
- G.D. JONES (NZL) — S.JENKINS 6-3 6-3
- Scoville JENKINS (USA)
- Q Kevin ANDERSON (RSA) — E.SCHWANK [7] 3-6 6-4 6-3
- 7 Eduardo SCHWANK (ARG)
- 8 Mihail ZVEREV (GER) — M.ZVEREV [8] 7-6(6) 6-2
- Andrea ARNABOLDI (ITA) — E.KIRILLOV (Q) 6-4 6-4
- WC Sebastian LOUIS (FRA)
- Q Evgeny KIRILLOV (RUS)
- Jamie MURRAY (GBR) — T.LIBERHAN 4-6 6-2 6-3
- Tushar LIBERHAN (IND)
- WC Donald YOUNG (USA) — W.JUN [10] 6-7(8) 7-5 6-3
- 10 Woong-Sun JUN (KOR)
- 14 Alex KUZNETSOV (USA) — A.KUZNETSOV [14] 6-2 6-2
- Peter MIKLUSICAK (SVK)
- Juan-Martin DEL POTRO (ARG) — F.WOLMARANS 6-2 3-6 6-3
- Fritz WOLMARANS (RSA)
- Bruno ROSA (BRA) — B.ROSA 5-7 6-4 6-3
- Mehdi ZIADI (MAR)
- Robin HAASE (NED) — J.OUANNA [3] 6-4 6-0
- 3 Josselin OUANNA (FRA)
- 5 Brendan EVANS (USA) — B.EVANS [5] 5-7 6-4 6-4
- Chu-Huan YI (TPE)
- WC Vilim VISAK (CRO) — V.VISAK 6-0 0-6 6-3
- Jérémy DREAN (FRA)
- Q Martin FISCHER (AUT) — M.FISCHER (Q) 4-0 6-1
- WC Jonathan DASNIÈRES DE VEIGY (FRA)
- 12 Karan RASTOGI (IND) — K.RASTOGI [12] 6-3 6-7(1) 6-3
- 15 Lukas LACKO (SVK) — L.LACKO [15] 5-7 6-4 RET
- William WARD (NZL)
- WC Remko DE RIJKE (NED) — O.RENAVAND (WC) 6-3 6-2
- Oliver RENAVAND (NED)
- Timothy NEILLY (USA) — L.FERGUSON 2-6 7-5
- Lachlan FERGUSON (AUS)
- Rafael AREVALO GONZALEZ (ESA) — R.AREVALO GONZALEZ 6-1 6-4
- 2 Marcel GRANOLLERS-PUJOL (ESP)

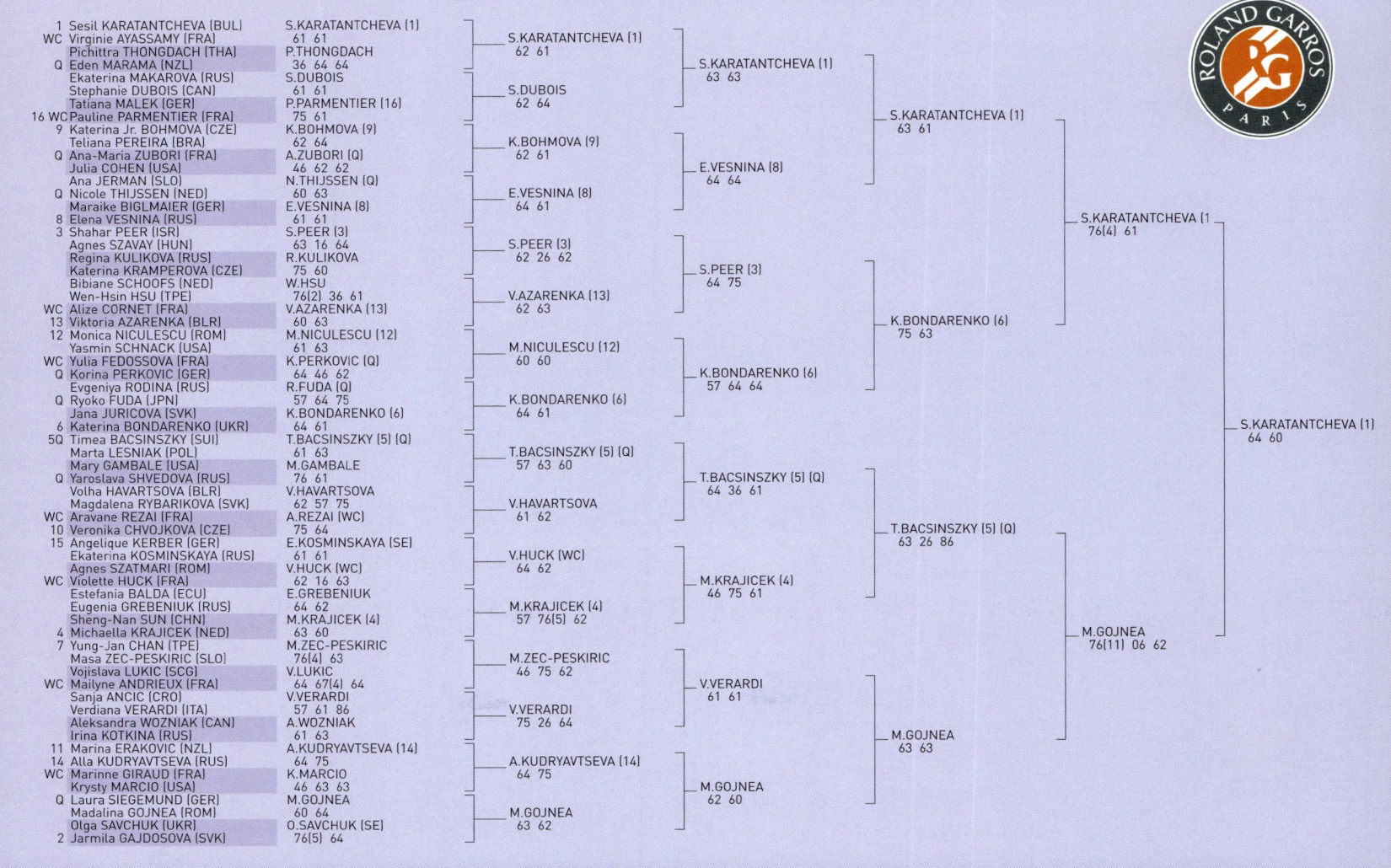

2004 International Junior Championships of France, 30 May–6 June – Girls' Singles

Winner: S. KARATANTCHEVA (1) 6-4 6-0

First Round

Seed	Player 1	Player 2	Score
1	S. KARATANTCHEVA (BUL)	Virginie AYASSAMY (FRA)	6-1 6-1
Q	Pichittra THONGDACH (THA)	Eden MARAMA (NZL)	3-6 6-4 6-4
	Ekaterina MAKAROVA (RUS)	Stephanie DUBOIS (CAN)	6-1 6-1
16 WC	Tatiana MALEK (GER)	Pauline PARMENTIER (FRA)	7-5 6-1
9	Katerina Jr. BOHMOVA (CZE)	Teliana PEREIRA (BRA)	6-2 6-4
	Ana-Maria ZUBORI (FRA)	Julia COHEN (USA)	4-6 6-2 6-2
Q	Ana JERMAN (SLO)	Nicole THIJSSEN (NED)	6-0 6-3
8	Elena VESNINA (RUS)	Maraike BIGLMAIER (GER)	6-1 6-1
3	Shahar PEER (ISR)	Agnes SZAVAY (HUN)	6-3 1-6 6-4
	Regina KULIKOVA (RUS)	Katerina KRAMPEROVA (CZE)	7-5 6-0
	Bibiane SCHOOFS (NED)	Wen-Hsin HSU (TPE)	7-6(2) 3-6 6-1
WC	Alizé CORNET (FRA)	Viktoria AZARENKA (BLR)	6-0 6-3
12	Monica NICULESCU (ROM)	Yasmin SCHNACK (USA)	6-1 6-3
WC	Yulia FEDOSSOVA (FRA)	Korina PERKOVIC (GER)	6-4 4-6 6-2
	Evgeniya RODINA (RUS)	Ryoko FUDA (JPN)	5-7 6-4 7-5
6	K. BONDARENKO (UKR)	Jana JURICOVA (SVK)	6-4 6-1
5 Q	T. BACSINSZKY (SUI)	Marta LESNIAK (POL)	6-1 6-3
	Mary GAMBALE (USA)	Yaroslava SHVEDOVA (RUS)	7-6 6-1
	Votha HAVARTSOVA (BLR)	Magdalena RYBARIKOVA (SVK)	6-2 5-7 7-5
WC	Aravane REZAI (FRA)	Veronika CHVOJKOVA (CZE)	7-5 6-4
10	Angelique KERBER (GER)	Ekaterina KOSMINSKAYA (RUS)	6-1 6-1
15	Agnes SZATMARI (ROM)	Violette HUCK (FRA)	6-2 1-6 6-3
WC	Estefania BALDA (ECU)	Eugenia GREBENIUK (RUS)	6-4 6-2
4	Michaella KRAJICEK (NED)	Sheng-Nan SUN (CHN)	6-3 6-0
7	Yung-Jan CHAN (TPE)	Masa ZEC-PESKIRIC (SLO)	7-6(4) 6-3
	V. LUKIC	Vojislava LUKIC (SCG)	
WC	Mailyne ANDRIEUX (FRA)	Verdiana VERARDI (ITA)	6-4 6-7(4) 6-4
	Sanja ANCIC (CRO)	Aleksandra WOZNIAK (CAN)	5-7 6-1 8-6
	Irina KOTKINA (RUS)	Marina ERAKOVIC (NZL)	6-1 6-3
11	Alla KUDRYAVTSEVA (RUS)	Marinne GIRAUD (FRA)	6-4 7-5
14 WC	Krysty MARCIO (USA)	K. MARCIO	4-6 6-3 6-3
	Madalina GOJNEA (ROM)	Laura SIEGEMUND (GER)	6-0 6-4
2	Olga SAVCHUK (UKR)	Jarmila GAJDOSOVA (SVK)	7-6(5) 6-4

Second Round Results

- S. KARATANTCHEVA (1) d. P. THONGDACH 6-2 6-1
- S. DUBOIS d. P. PARMENTIER (16) 6-2 6-4
- K. BOHMOVA (9) d. A. ZUBORI 6-2 6-1
- E. VESNINA (8) d. A. JERMAN 6-4 6-1
- S. PEER (3) d. R. KULIKOVA 6-2 2-6 6-2
- V. AZARENKA (13) d. B. SCHOOFS 6-2 6-3
- M. NICULESCU (12) d. K. PERKOVIC 6-0 6-0
- K. BONDARENKO (6) d. E. RODINA 6-4 6-1
- T. BACSINSZKY (5)Q d. M. GAMBALE 5-7 6-3 6-0
- V. HAVARTSOVA d. A. REZAI 6-1 6-2
- V. HUCK (WC) d. E. KOSMINSKAYA (10) 6-4 6-2
- M. KRAJICEK (4) d. E. GREBENIUK 5-7 7-6(5) 6-2
- M. ZEC-PESKIRIC d. V. LUKIC 4-6 7-5 6-2
- V. VERARDI d. A. WOZNIAK 7-5 2-6 6-4
- A. KUDRYAVTSEVA (14) d. I. KOTKINA 6-4 7-5
- M. GOJNEA d. O. SAVCHUK (2) 6-3 6-2

Third Round

- S. KARATANTCHEVA (1) d. S. DUBOIS 6-3 6-3
- E. VESNINA (8) d. K. BOHMOVA (9) 6-4 6-4
- S. PEER (3) d. V. AZARENKA (13) 6-2 6-3
- K. BONDARENKO (6) d. M. NICULESCU (12) 6-4 6-1
- T. BACSINSZKY (5)Q d. V. HAVARTSOVA 5-7 6-3 6-0
- M. KRAJICEK (4) d. V. HUCK (WC) 4-6 7-5 6-1
- V. VERARDI d. M. ZEC-PESKIRIC 4-6 7-5 6-2
- M. GOJNEA d. A. KUDRYAVTSEVA (14) 6-4 7-5

Quarterfinals

- S. KARATANTCHEVA (1) d. E. VESNINA (8) 6-3 6-1
- K. BONDARENKO (6) d. S. PEER (3) 6-4 7-5
- T. BACSINSZKY (5)Q d. M. KRAJICEK (4) 6-3 2-6 8-6
- M. GOJNEA d. V. VERARDI 6-3 6-3

Semifinals

- S. KARATANTCHEVA (1) d. K. BONDARENKO (6) 7-6(4) 6-1
- M. GOJNEA d. T. BACSINSZKY (5)Q 7-6(11) 0-6 6-2

Final

S. KARATANTCHEVA (1) d. M. GOJNEA 6-4 6-0

207

ITF Development: 2004 Roland Garros Junior Drawsheets

2004 International Junior Championships of France, 30 May-6 June – Boys' Doubles

```
1   Brendan EVANS [USA]              ┐
    Scott OUDSEMA [USA]              ├─ B.EVANS [1]
    Kevin ANDERSON [RSA]             ┐  S.OUDSEMA [1]
    Mehdi ZIADI [MAR]                ┘  61 64                      ┐
WC  Jérémy CHARDY [FRA]              ┐                             ├─ B.EVANS [1]
WC  Jérémy DREAN [FRA]               ├─ L.FERGUSON                 │  S.OUDSEMA [1]
    Lachlan FERGUSON [AUS]           ┐  J.KERLEY                   │  75 46 63
    Joel KERLEY [AUS]                ┘  62 64                      ┘                              ┐
    Daniel MULLER [GER]              ┐                                                            │
    Jamie MURRAY [GBR]               ├─ F.MARTIN [WC]              ┐                              │
WC  Fabrice MARTIN [FRA]             ┐  D.YOUNG [WC]               │                              │
WC  Donald YOUNG [USA]               ┘  64 75                      ├─ F.MARTIN [WC]               │
    Timothy NEILLY [USA]             ┐                             │  D.YOUNG [WC]                │
    Sebastian RIESCHICK [GER]        ├─ J.AMADO [6]                │  W/O                         │
6   Juan Pablo AMADO [ARG]           ┐  E.SCHWANK [6]              ┘                              ├─ B.EVANS [1]
6   Eduardo SCHWANK [ARG]            ┘  63 62                                                     │  S.OUDSEMA [1]
    Guillermo ALCAIDE-JUSTELL [ESP]  ┐                             ┐                              │  64 61
    Remko DE RIJKE [NED]             ├─ M.FISCHER                  │                              │
    Martin FISCHER [AUT]             ┐  P.OSWALD                   ├─ P.ANDUJAR-ALBA              │
    Philipp OSWALD [AUT]             ┘  61 61                      │  M.GRANOLLERS-PUJOL          │
WC  Antoine BENNETEAU [FRA]          ┐                             │  64 64                       │
WC  Sebastian LOUIS [FRA]            ├─ P.ANDUJAR-ALBA             │                              │
4   Pablo ANDUJAR-ALBA [ESP]         ┐  M.GRANOLLERS-PUJOL         ┘                              │
4   Marcel GRANOLLERS-PUJOL [ESP]    ┘  63 63                                                     │
    Robin HAASE [NED]                ┐                             ┐                              │
    Igor SIJSLING [NED]              ├─ E.KIRILLOV                 │                              │
    Evgeny KIRILLOV [RUS]            ┐  A.KRASNOROUTSKY            ├─ P.ANDUJAR-ALBA              │
    Alexander KRASNOROUTSKY [RUS]    ┘  64 36 63                   │  M.GRANOLLERS-PUJOL          │
    Fabio FOGNINI [ITA]              ┐                             │  16 75 64                    │
    Gianluca NASO [ITA]              ├─ R.AREVALO GONZALEZ [5]     │                              │
5   Rafael AREVALO GONZALEZ [ESA]    ┐  C.VAN KEULEN [5]           ┘                              │
5   Coen VAN KEULEN [NED]            ┘  62 46 62                                                  ┘
7   Alex KUZNETSOV [USA]             ┐                                                            ┐ P.ANDUJAR-ALBA
7   Mihail ZVEREV [GER]              ├─ A.KUZNETSOV [7]            ┐                              │ M.GRANOLLERS-PUJOL
    Juan-Martin DEL POTRO [ARG]      ┐  M.ZVEREV [7]               │                              │ 63 62
    Bruno ROSA [BRA]                 ┘  26 63 63                   ├─ A.KUZNETSOV [7]             │
    Mykyta KRYVONOS [USA]            ┐                             │  M.ZVEREV [7]                │
    Vahid MIRZADEH [USA]             ├─ M.KRYVONOS                 │  64 62                       │
    Thomaz BELLUCCI [BRA]            ┐  V.MIRZADEH                 │                              │
    Andre MIELE [BRA]                ┘  61 61                      ┘                              │
    Andrea ARNABOLDI [ITA]           ┐                             ┐                              ├─ A.KUZNETSOV [7]
    Miles KASIRI [GBR]               ├─ A.ARNABOLDI                │                              │  M.ZVEREV [7]
    Kamil CAPKOVIC [SVK]             ┐  M.KASIRI                   ├─ G.MONFILS [3]               │  76[5] 64
    Peter MIKLUSICAK [SVK]           ┘  64 61                      │  J.OUANNA [3]                │
    Jamie BAKER [GBR]                ┐                             │  63 63                       │
    Tom RUSHBY [GBR]                 ├─ G.MONFILS [3]              │                              │
3   Gael MONFILS [FRA]               ┐  J.OUANNA [3]               ┘                              │
3   Josselin OUANNA [FRA]            ┘  67[5] 75 63                                               │
    Karan RASTOGI [IND]              ┐                             ┐                              │
8   Lukas LACKO [SVK]                ├─ K.RASTOGI [8]              │                              │
8   Chu-Huan YI [TPE]                ┐  C.YI [8]                   ├─ P.SIMMONDS                  │
    David NAVARRETE [VEN]            ┘  67[4] 64 61                │  F.WOLMARANS                 │
    Philip SIMMONDS [USA]            ┐                             │  67[2] 76[6] 75              │
    Fritz WOLMARANS [RSA]            ├─ P.SIMMONDS                 │                              │
WC  Jonathan DASNIERES DE VEIGY [FRA]┐  F.WOLMARANS                ┘                              │
WC  Matthieu DEHAINE [FRA]           ┘  61 64                                                     │
    Tushar LIBERHAN [IND]            ┐                             ┐                              │
    Divij SHARAN [IND]               ├─ T.LIBERHAN                 │                              │
    Viktor TROICKI [SCG]             ┐  D.SHARAN                   ├─ T.LIBERHAN                  │
    Vilim VISAK [CRO]                ┘  16 63 RET                  │  D.SHARAN                    │
    G. D. JONES [NZL]                ┐                             │  64 62                       │
    William WARD [NZL]               ├─ W.JUN [2]                  │                              │
2   Woong-Sun JUN JUN [KOR]          ┐  S.KIM [2]                  ┘                              ┘
    S.KIM [2]                        ┘  63 63
```

2004 International Junior Championships of France, 30 May–6 June – Girls' Doubles

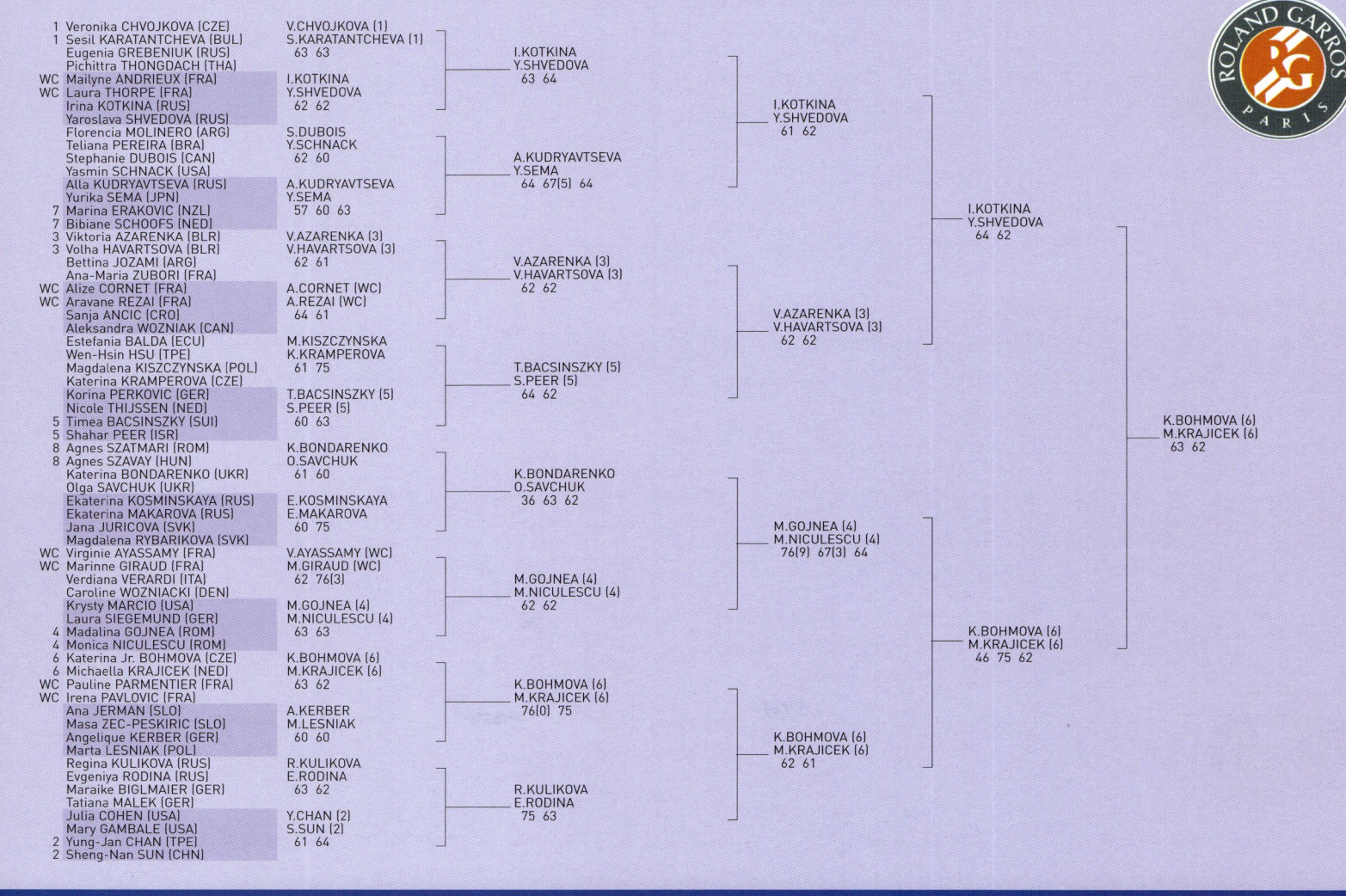

Round 1:

1. Veronika CHVOJKOVA (CZE) / Sesil KARATANTCHEVA (BUL) [1]
   - Eugenia GREBENIUK (RUS) / Pichittra THONGDACH (THA)
   - Result: V.CHVOJKOVA / S.KARATANTCHEVA [1] 63 63

WC. Mailyne ANDRIEUX (FRA) / Laura THORPE (FRA)
   - Irina KOTKINA (RUS) / Yaroslava SHVEDOVA (RUS)
   - Result: I.KOTKINA / Y.SHVEDOVA 62 62

- Florencia MOLINERO (ARG) / Teliana PEREIRA (BRA)
   - Stephanie DUBOIS (CAN) / Yasmin SCHNACK (USA)
   - Result: S.DUBOIS / Y.SCHNACK 62 60

- Alla KUDRYAVTSEVA (RUS) / Yurika SEMA (JPN)
   - Marina ERAKOVIC (NZL) / Bibiane SCHOOFS (NED)
   - Result: A.KUDRYAVTSEVA / Y.SEMA 64 67(5) 64

7. Viktoria AZARENKA (BLR) / Volha HAVARTSOVA (BLR) [3]
   - Bettina JOZAMI (ARG) / Ana-Maria ZUBORI (FRA)
   - Result: V.AZARENKA / V.HAVARTSOVA [3] 62 61

WC. Alize CORNET (FRA) / Aravane REZAI (FRA)
WC. Sanja ANCIC (CRO) / Aleksandra WOZNIAK (CAN)
   - Result: A.CORNET / A.REZAI [WC] 64 61

- Estefania BALDA (ECU) / Wen-Hsin HSU (TPE)
   - Magdalena KISZCZYNSKA (POL) / Katerina KRAMPEROVA (CZE)
   - Result: M.KISZCZYNSKA / K.KRAMPEROVA 61 75

- Korina PERKOVIC (GER) / Nicole THIJSSEN (NED)
   - Timea BACSINSZKY (SUI) / Shahar PEER (ISR) [5]
   - Result: T.BACSINSZKY / S.PEER [5] 64 62

8. Agnes SZATMARI (ROM) / Agnes SZAVAY (HUN)
   - Katerina BONDARENKO (UKR) / Olga SAVCHUK (UKR)
   - Result: K.BONDARENKO / O.SAVCHUK 61 60

- Ekaterina KOSMINSKAYA (RUS) / Ekaterina MAKAROVA (RUS)
   - Jana JURICOVA (SVK) / Magdalena RYBARIKOVA (SVK)
   - Result: E.KOSMINSKAYA / E.MAKAROVA 60 75

WC. Virginie AYASSAMY (FRA) / Marinne GIRAUD (FRA)
WC. Verdiana VERARDI (ITA) / Caroline WOZNIACKI (DEN)
   - Result: V.AYASSAMY / M.GIRAUD [WC] 62 76(3)

- Krysty MARCIO (USA) / Laura SIEGEMUND (GER)
4. Madalina GOJNEA (ROM) / Monica NICULESCU (ROM)
   - Result: M.GOJNEA / M.NICULESCU [4] 62 62

6. Katerina Jr. BOHMOVA (CZE) / Michaella KRAJICEK (NED)
   - Pauline PARMENTIER (FRA) / WC. Irena PAVLOVIC (FRA)
   - Result: K.BOHMOVA / M.KRAJICEK [6] 63 62

- Ana JERMAN (SLO) / Masa ZEC-PESKIRIC (SLO)
   - Angelique KERBER (GER) / Marta LESNIAK (POL)
   - Result: A.KERBER / M.LESNIAK 60 60

- Regina KULIKOVA (RUS) / Evgeniya RODINA (RUS)
   - Maraike BIGLMAIER (GER) / Tatiana MALEK (GER)
   - Result: R.KULIKOVA / E.RODINA 63 62

- Julia COHEN (USA) / Mary GAMBALE (USA)
2. Yung-Jan CHAN (TPE) / Sheng-Nan SUN (CHN)
   - Result: Y.CHAN / S.SUN [2] 61 64

Round 2:
- I.KOTKINA / Y.SHVEDOVA d. V.CHVOJKOVA / S.KARATANTCHEVA [1] 63 64
- A.KUDRYAVTSEVA / Y.SEMA d. S.DUBOIS / Y.SCHNACK
- V.AZARENKA / V.HAVARTSOVA [3] d. A.CORNET / A.REZAI [WC]
- T.BACSINSZKY / S.PEER [5] d. M.KISZCZYNSKA / K.KRAMPEROVA
- K.BONDARENKO / O.SAVCHUK d. E.KOSMINSKAYA / E.MAKAROVA 36 63 62
- M.GOJNEA / M.NICULESCU [4] d. V.AYASSAMY / M.GIRAUD [WC]
- K.BOHMOVA / M.KRAJICEK [6] d. A.KERBER / M.LESNIAK 76(0) 75
- R.KULIKOVA / E.RODINA d. Y.CHAN / S.SUN [2] 75 63

Quarterfinals:
- I.KOTKINA / Y.SHVEDOVA d. A.KUDRYAVTSEVA / Y.SEMA 61 62
- V.AZARENKA / V.HAVARTSOVA [3] d. T.BACSINSZKY / S.PEER [5] 62 62
- M.GOJNEA / M.NICULESCU [4] d. K.BONDARENKO / O.SAVCHUK 76(9) 67(3) 64
- K.BOHMOVA / M.KRAJICEK [6] d. R.KULIKOVA / E.RODINA 62 61

Semifinals:
- I.KOTKINA / Y.SHVEDOVA d. V.AZARENKA / V.HAVARTSOVA [3] 64 62
- K.BOHMOVA / M.KRAJICEK [6] d. M.GOJNEA / M.NICULESCU [4] 46 75 62

Final:
- K.BOHMOVA / M.KRAJICEK [6] d. I.KOTKINA / Y.SHVEDOVA 63 62

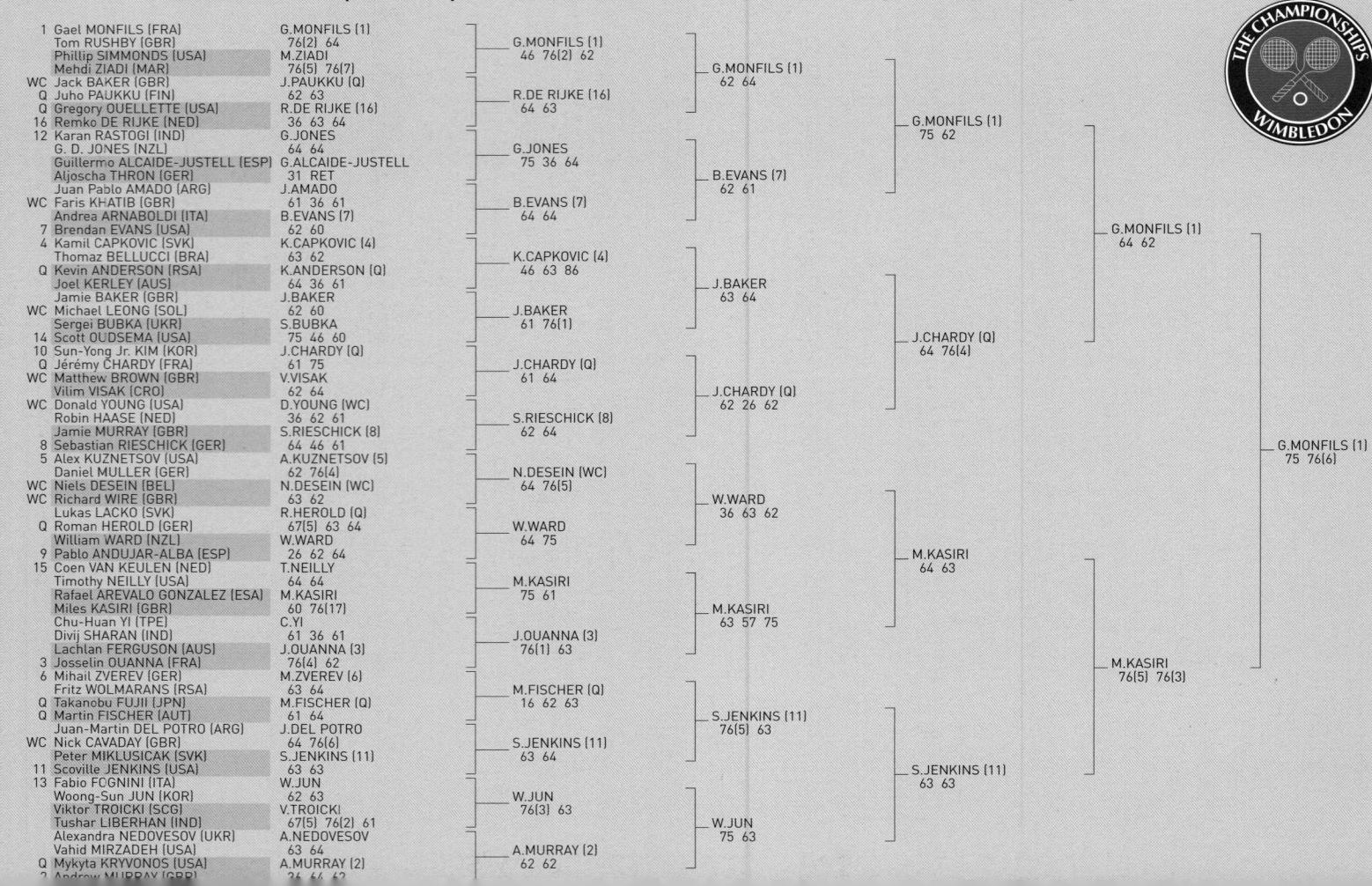

2004 The Junior Championships, Wimbledon, 26 June–4 July – Boys' Singles

Winner: G.MONFILS [1] — 7 5 7 6(6)

First Round

1 Gael MONFILS [FRA] [1] — 7 6(2) 6 2
   Tom RUSHBY [GBR]
   Phillip SIMMONDS [USA] — 7 6(5) 7 6(7)
   Mehdi ZIADI [MAR]
WC Jack BAKER [GBR]
Q Juho PAUKKU [FIN] — 6 2 6 3
Q Gregory OUELLETTE [USA]
16 Remko DE RIJKE [NED] — 3 6 6 3 6 4
12 Karan RASTOGI [IND]
   G. D. JONES [NZL] — 6 4 6 4
   Guillermo ALCAIDE-JUSTELL [ESP] — 3 1 RET
   Aljoscha THRON [GER]
   Juan Pablo AMADO [ARG] — J. AMADO
WC Faris KHATIB [GBR]
   Andrea ARNABOLDI [ITA] — 6 1 3 6 6 1
7 Brendan EVANS [USA] — 6 2 6 0
   Kamil CAPKOVIC [SVK]
4 Thomaz BELLUCCI [BRA] — 6 3 6 2
   Kevin ANDERSON [RSA]
Q Joel KERLEY [AUS] — K. ANDERSON [Q]
   Jamie BAKER [GBR] — 6 4 3 6 6 1
WC Michael LEONG [SOL] — J. BAKER — 6 2 6 0
   Sergei BUBKA [UKR] — S. BUBKA
14 Scott OUDSEMA [USA] — 7 5 4 6 6 0
10 Sun-Yong Jr. KIM [KOR]
Q Jérémy CHARDY [FRA] — 6 1 7 5
   Matthew BROWN [GBR] — V. VISAK
   Vilim VISAK [CRO] — 6 2 6 4
WC Donald YOUNG [WC] — D.YOUNG [WC]
   Robin HAASE [NED] — 3 6 6 2 6 1
   Jamie MURRAY [GBR]
8 Sebastian RIESCHICK [GER] — 6 4 4 6 6 1
5 Alex KUZNETSOV [USA]
   Niels DESEIN [BEL] — 6 2 7 6(5)
WC Daniel MÜLLER [GER]
   Lukas LACKO [SVK]
WC Richard WIRE [GBR] — 6 3 6 2
Q Roman HEROLD [GER] — 6 7(5) 6 3 6 4
9 Pablo ANDUJAR-ALBA [ESP] — 2 6 6 2 6 4
   William WARD [NZL] — W.WARD
   Coen VAN KEULEN [NED] — T. NEILLY
15 Timothy NEILLY [USA] — 6 4 6 4
   Rafael AREVALO GONZALEZ [ESA] — M.KASIRI
   Miles KASIRI [GBR] — 6 0 7 6(17)
   Chu-Huan YI [TPE] — C. YI
3 Lachlan FERGUSON [AUS] — 6 1 3 6 6 1
   Josselin OUANNA [FRA] — 7 6(4) 6 2
6 Mihail ZVEREV [GER]
   Fritz WOLMARANS [RSA] — 6 3 6 4
Q Takanobu FUJII [JPN]
   Martin FISCHER [AUT] — 6 1 6 4
   Juan-Martin DEL POTRO [ARG] — 6 4 7 6(6)
WC Nick CAVADAY [GBR] — S.JENKINS [11]
   Peter MIKLUSICAK [SVK]
11 Scoville JENKINS [USA] — 6 3 6 3
13 Fabio FOGNINI [ITA]
   Woong-Sun JUN [KOR] — 6 2 6 3
   Viktor TROICKI [SCG] — 6 7(5) 7 6(2) 6 1
   Tushar LIBERHAN [IND]
   Alexandra NEDOVESOV [UKR] — A.NEDOVESOV
Q Vahid MIRZADEH [USA] — 6 3 6 4
Q Mykyta KRYVONOS [UKR] — A.MURRAY [2]
   Andrew MURRAY [GBR] [2] — 6 2 6 2

Later Rounds

G.MONFILS [1] — 4 6 7 6(2) 6 2
R.DE RIJKE [16] — 6 4 6 3
G.JONES — 7 5 3 6 6 4
B.EVANS [7] — 6 4 6 4
K.CAPKOVIC [4] — 4 6 6 3 8 6
J.BAKER — 6 1 7 6(1)
J.CHARDY [Q] — 6 1 6 4
S.RIESCHICK [8] — 6 2 6 4
N.DESEIN [WC] — 6 4 7 6(5)
W.WARD — 6 4 7 5
M.KASIRI — 7 5 6 1
J.OUANNA [3] — 7 6(1) 6 3
M.FISCHER [Q] — 1 6 6 2 6 3
S.JENKINS [11] — 6 3 6 4
W.JUN — 7 6(3) 6 3
A.MURRAY [2] — 6 2 6 2

G.MONFILS [1] — 6 2 6 4
B.EVANS [7] — 6 2 6 1
J.BAKER — 6 3 6 4
J.CHARDY [Q] — 6 2 2 6 6 2
W.WARD — 3 6 6 3 6 2
M.KASIRI — 7 5 7 5
S.JENKINS [11] — 7 6(5) 6 3
W.JUN — 7 5 6 3

G.MONFILS [1] — 7 5 6 2
J.CHARDY [Q] — 6 4 7 6(4)
M.KASIRI — 6 4 6 3
S.JENKINS [11] — 6 3 6 3

G.MONFILS [1] — 6 4 6 2
M.KASIRI — 7 6(5) 7 6(3)

G.MONFILS [1] — 7 5 7 6(6)

2004 The Junior Championships, Wimbledon, 26 June–4 July – Girls' Singles

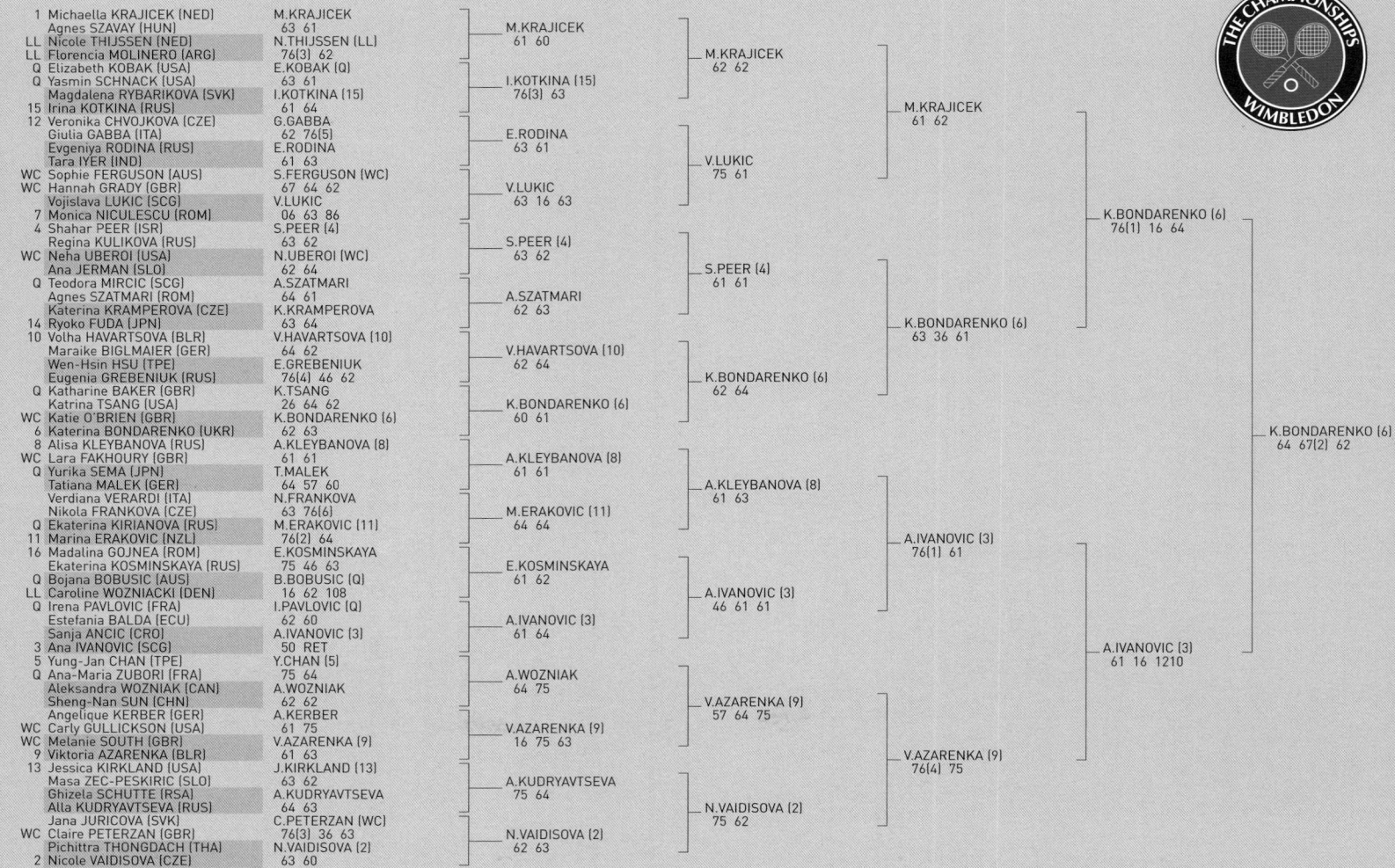

Winner: K. BONDARENKO (6) 6 4 6 7(2) 6 2

Final
K.BONDARENKO (6) def. A.IVANOVIC (3) 6 1 1 6 12 10

Semifinals
- K.BONDARENKO (6) def. M.KRAJICEK 7 6(1) 1 6 6 4
- A.IVANOVIC (3) def. V.AZARENKA (9) 7 6(4) 7 5

Quarterfinals
- M.KRAJICEK def. V.LUKIC 6 1 6 2
- K.BONDARENKO (6) def. S.PEER (4) 6 3 3 6 6 1
- A.IVANOVIC (3) def. A.KLEYBANOVA (8) 7 6(1) 6 1
- V.AZARENKA (9) def. N.VAIDISOVA (2) 7 5 6 2

Round of 16
- M.KRAJICEK def. I.KOTKINA (15) 6 2 6 2
- V.LUKIC def. E.RODINA 7 5 6 1
- S.PEER (4) def. A.SZATMARI 6 1 6 1
- K.BONDARENKO (6) def. V.HAVARTSOVA (10) 6 2 6 4
- A.KLEYBANOVA (8) def. M.ERAKOVIC (11) 6 1 6 3
- A.IVANOVIC (3) def. E.KOSMINSKAYA 4 6 6 1 6 1
- V.AZARENKA (9) def. A.WOZNIAK 5 7 6 4 7 5
- N.VAIDISOVA (2) def. A.KUDRYAVTSEVA 7 5 6 2

Round of 32
- M.KRAJICEK def. N.THIJSSEN (LL) 6 3 6 1
- I.KOTKINA (15) def. E.KOBAK (Q) 7 6(3) 6 2
- E.RODINA def. G.GABBA 6 3 6 1
- V.LUKIC def. S.FERGUSON (WC) 6 1 6 3
- S.PEER (4) def. N.UBEROI (WC) 6 3 6 2
- A.SZATMARI def. K.KRAMPEROVA 6 4 6 1
- V.HAVARTSOVA (10) def. E.GREBENIUK 6 4 6 2
- K.BONDARENKO (6) def. K.TSANG 6 0 6 1
- A.KLEYBANOVA (8) def. T.MALEK 6 1 6 1
- M.ERAKOVIC (11) def. N.FRANKOVA 7 6(2) 6 4
- E.KOSMINSKAYA def. B.BOBUSIC (Q) 7 5 4 6 6 3
- A.IVANOVIC (3) def. I.PAVLOVIC (Q) 6 2 6 0
- A.WOZNIAK def. Y.CHAN (5) 7 5 6 4
- V.AZARENKA (9) def. A.KERBER 6 1 7 5
- A.KUDRYAVTSEVA def. J.KIRKLAND (13) 6 1 6 3
- N.VAIDISOVA (2) def. C.PETERZAN (WC) 7 6(3) 3 6 6 3

Round of 64
1. Michaella KRAJICEK (NED) def. Agnes SZAVAY (HUN) 6 3 6 1
- LL Nicole THIJSSEN (NED) def. LL Florencia MOLINERO (ARG) 7 6(3) 6 2
- Q Elizabeth KOBAK (USA) def. Yasmin SCHNACK (USA) 6 3 6 1
- Q Magdalena RYBARIKOVA (SVK) def. 15 Irina KOTKINA (RUS) 6 1 6 4
- 12 Veronika CHVOJKOVA (CZE) def. Giulia GABBA (ITA) 6 2 7 6(5)
- Evgenya RODINA (RUS) def. Tara IYER (IND) 6 1 6 3
- WC Sophie FERGUSON (AUS) def. WC Hannah GRADY (GBR) 6 7 6 4 6 2
- Vojislava LUKIC (SCG) def. 7 Monica NICULESCU (ROM) 0 6 6 3 8 6
- 4 Shahar PEER (ISR) def. Regina KULIKOVA (RUS) 6 3 6 2
- WC Neha UBEROI (USA) def. Ana JERMAN (SLO) 6 2 6 4
- Q Teodora MIRCIC (SCG) def. Agnes SZATMARI (ROM) 6 4 6 1
- Katerina KRAMPEROVA (CZE) def. 14 Ryoko FUDA (JPN) 6 3 6 4
- 10 Volha HAVARTSOVA (BLR) def. Maraike BIGLMAIER (GER) 6 4 6 2
- Wen-Hsin HSU (TPE) def. Eugenia GREBENIUK (RUS) 7 6(4) 4 6 6 2
- Q Katharine BAKER (GBR) def. Katrina TSANG (USA) 2 6 6 4 6 2
- WC Katie O'BRIEN (GBR) def. 6 Kateryna BONDARENKO (UKR) 6 2 6 3
- 8 Alisa KLEYBANOVA (RUS) def. WC Lara FAKHOURY (GBR) 6 1 6 1
- Yurika SEMA (JPN) def. Tatiana MALEK (GER) 6 4 5 7 6 0
- Verdiana VERARDI (ITA) def. Nikola FRANKOVA (CZE) 7 6 3 6(6)
- 11 Marina ERAKOVIC (NZL) def. Ekaterina KIRIANOVA (RUS) 7 6(2) 6 4
- 16 Madalina GOJNEA (ROM) def. Ekaterina KOSMINSKAYA (RUS) 7 5 4 6 6 3
- LL Bojana BOBUSIC (AUS) def. Caroline WOZNIACKI (DEN) 1 6 6 2 10 8
- Q Irena PAVLOVIC (FRA) def. Estefania BALDA (ECU) 6 2 6 0
- Sanja ANCIC (CRO) def. 3 Ana IVANOVIC (SCG) 5 0 RET
- 5 Yung-Jan CHAN (TPE) def. Q Ana-Maria ZUBORI (FRA) 7 5 6 4
- Aleksandra WOZNIAK (CAN) def. Sheng-Nan SUN (CHN) 6 2 6 2
- Angelique KERBER (GER) def. WC Melanie SOUTH (GBR) 6 1 7 5
- 9 Viktoria AZARENKA (BLR) def. WC Carly GULLICKSON (USA) 6 1 6 3
- 13 Jessica KIRKLAND (USA) def. Masa ZEC-PESKIRIC (SLO) 6 3 6 2
- Alla KUDRYAVTSEVA (RUS) def. Ghizela SCHUTTE (RSA) 6 4 6 3
- C.PETERZAN (GBR) def. Jana JURICOVA (SVK) 7 6(3) 3 6 6 3
- 2 Nicole VAIDISOVA (CZE) def. Pichittra THONGDACH (THA) 6 3 6 0

2004 The Junior Championships, Wimbledon, 26 June–4 July – Boys' Doubles

Seed	First Round	Second Round	Quarter-finals	Semi-finals	Final
1	Alex KUZNETSOV [USA]	A.KUZNETSOV [1]			
1	Mihail ZVEREV [GER]	M.ZVEREV [1]	A.KUZNETSOV [1]		
	Tushar LIBERHAN [IND]	63 64	M.ZVEREV [1]		
	Divij SHARAN [IND]	T.NEILLY	61 76(3)		
	Tom RUSHBY [GBR]	P.SIMMONDS			
	Jamie BAKER [GBR]	64 64		R.HAASE	
	Timothy NEILLY [USA]	D.MULLER		V.TROICKI	
	Philip SIMMONDS [USA]	S.RIESCHICK	D.MULLER	76(3) 67(4) 14/12	
	Jeremy CHARDY [FRA]	36 76(4) 64	S.RIESCHICK		
	Fabrice MARTIN [FRA]	R.HAASE	36 62		
	Daniel MULLER [GER]	V.TROICKI			
	Sebastian RIESCHICK [GER]	64 67(4) 75	R.HAASE		
7	Robin HAASE [NED]	V.TROICKI	V.TROICKI		
7	Viktor TROICKI [SCG]	M.KRYVONOS	63 62		R.HAASE
	Scoville JENKINS [USA]	A.NEDOVESOV			V.TROICKI
	Miles KASIRI [GBR]	64 76(0)	M.KRYVONOS		63 63
	Woong-Sun JUN [KOR]	N.CAVADAY [WC]	A.NEDOVESOV		
3	Sun-Yong Jr. KIM [KOR]	R.WIRE [WC]	76(2) 75		
	Mykyta KRYVONOS [USA]	75 57 61		G.ALCAIDE-JUSTELL [6]	
	Alexandra NEDOVESOV [UKR]	L.FERGUSON		S.BUBKA [6]	
WC	Jack BAKER [GBR]	J.KERLEY	L.FERGUSON	62 67(6) 62	
WC	James LLOYD [GBR]	63 62	J.KERLEY		
WC	Nick CAVADAY [GBR]	G.ALCAIDE-JUSTELL [6]	26 63 63		
WC	Richard WIRE [GBR]	S.BUBKA [6]			
	Andrea ARNABOLDI [ITA]	63 64	G.ALCAIDE-JUSTELL [6]		
	Juan-Martin DEL POTRO [ARG]	K.CAPKOVIC [8]	S.BUBKA [6]		
	Lachlan FERGUSON [AUS]	L.LACKO [8]	76(3) 64		
	Joel KERLEY [AUS]	W/O			
	Peter MIKLUSICAK [SVK]	N.DESEIN	K.CAPKOVIC [8]		
	Vilim VISAK [CRO]	J.PAUKKU	L.LACKO [8]		
6	Guillermo ALCAIDE-JUSTELL [ESP]	62 63			
6	Sergei BUBKA [UKR]	M.BROWN [WC]		R.AREVALO GONZALEZ [4]	
	Kamil CAPKOVIC [SVK]	J.MURRAY [WC]	M.BROWN [WC]	C.VAN KEULEN [4]	
8	Lukas LACKO [SVK]	76(1) 67(5) 75	J.MURRAY [WC]	62 26 64	
8	Fabio FOGNINI [ITA]	R.AREVALO GONZALEZ [4]	36 63 64		
	Aljoscha THRON [GER]	C.VAN KEULEN [4]	R.AREVALO GONZALEZ [4]		
	Niels DESEIN [BEL]	64 64	C.VAN KEULEN [4]		
	Juho PAUKKU [FIN]	K.RASTOGI [5]			
	Takanobu FUJII [JPN]	C.YI [5]			B.EVANS [2]
	Sunu Wahya TRIJATI [INA]	67(6) 61 62	K.RASTOGI [5]		S.OUDSEMA [2]
WC	Matthew BROWN [GBR]	J.AMADO	C.YI [5]		64 64
WC	Jamie MURRAY [GBR]	V.MIRZADEH	61 63		
	Remko DE RIJKE [NED]	75 63		B.EVANS [2]	
	David GALIC [AUS]	D.INGLOT [WC]		S.OUDSEMA [2]	
	G. D. JONES [NZL]	F.KHATIB [WC]	D.INGLOT [WC]	63 36 64	
	William WARD [NZL]	67(4) 63 97	F.KHATIB [WC]		
4	Rafael AREVALO GONZALEZ [ESA]	B.EVANS [2]	67(4) 63 97		
4	Coen VAN KEULEN [NED]	S.OUDSEMA [2]			
5	Karan RASTOGI [IND]	61 63	B.EVANS [2]		
5	Chu-Huan YI [TPE]	B.EVANS [2]	S.OUDSEMA [2]		
	Martin FISCHER [AUT]	S.OUDSEMA [2]	62 62		
	Philipp OSWALD [AUT]	64 76(7)			
	Juan Pablo AMADO [ARG]				
	Vahid MIRZADEH [USA]				
	Thomaz BELLUCCI [BRA]				
	Mehdi ZIADI [MAR]				
WC	Dominic INGLOT [GBR]				
WC	Faris KHATIB [GBR]				
	Pablo ANDUJAR-ALBA [ESP]				
	Roman HEROLD [GER]				
	Kevin ANDERSON [RSA]				
	Gregory OUELLETTE [USA]				
2	Brendan EVANS [USA]				

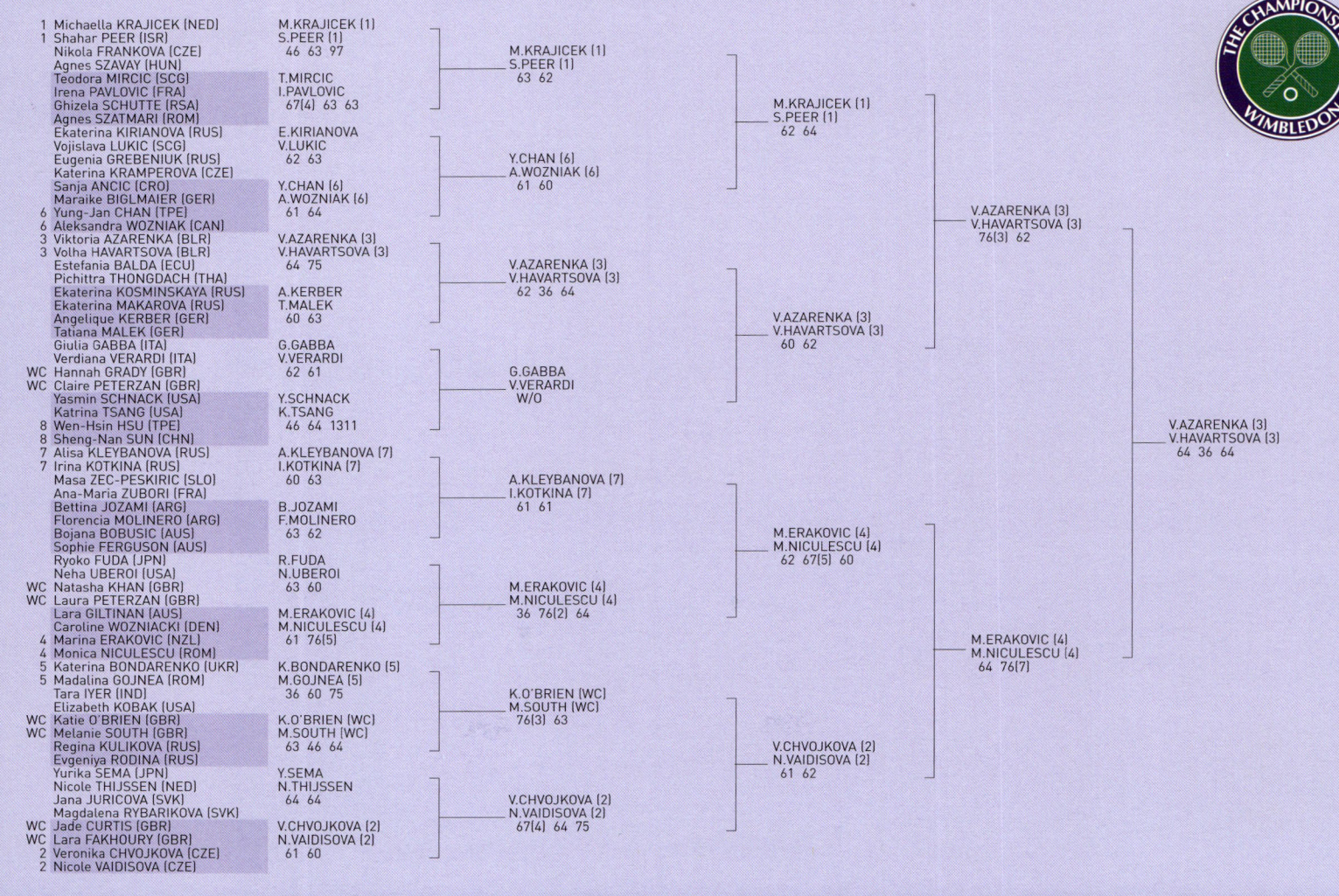

2004 The Junior Championships, Wimbledon, 28 June–6 July – Girls' Doubles

ITF Development: 2004 Wimbledon Junior Drawsheets

First Round

1. Michaela KRAJICEK (NED) / Shahar PEER (ISR) [1]
   Nikola FRANKOVA (CZE) / Agnes SZAVAY (HUN)
   — M.KRAJICEK [1] / S.PEER [1] 4-6 6-3 9-7

   Teodora MIRCIC (SCG) / Irena PAVLOVIC (FRA)
   Ghizela SZATMARI (ROM) / Agnes SZATMARI (ROM)
   — T.MIRCIC / I.PAVLOVIC 6-7(4) 6-3 6-3

   Ekaterina KIRIANOVA (RUS) / Vojislava LUKIC (SCG)
   Eugenia GREBENIUK (RUS) / Katerina KRAMPEROVA (CZE)
   — E.KIRIANOVA / V.LUKIC 6-2 6-3

   Sanja ANCIC (CRO) / Maraike BIGLMAIER (GER)
6. Aleksandra WOZNIAK (CAN) / Yung-Jan CHAN (TPE) [6]
   — Y.CHAN [6] / A.WOZNIAK [6] 6-1 6-0

3. Viktoria AZARENKA (BLR) / Volha HAVARTSOVA (BLR) [3]
   Estefania BALDA (ECU) / Pichittra THONGDACH (THA)
   — V.AZARENKA [3] / V.HAVARTSOVA [3] 6-4 7-5

   Ekaterina KOSMINSKAYA (RUS) / Ekaterina MAKAROVA (RUS)
   Angelique KERBER (GER) / Tatiana MALEK (GER)
   — A.KERBER / T.MALEK 6-0 6-3

   Giulia GABBA (ITA) / Verdiana VERARDI (ITA)
   WC Hannah GRADY (GBR) / Claire PETERZAN (GBR)
   — G.GABBA / V.VERARDI 6-2 6-1

   WC Yasmin SCHNACK (USA) / Katrina TSANG (USA)
8. Wen-Hsin HSU (TPE) / Sheng-Nan SUN (CHN)
   — Y.SCHNACK / K.TSANG 4-6 6-4 13-11

7. Alisa KLEYBANOVA (RUS) / Irina KOTKINA (RUS)
   Masa ZEC-PESKIRIC (SLO) / Ana-Maria ZUBORI (ARG)
   — A.KLEYBANOVA [7] / I.KOTKINA [7] 6-1 6-1

   Bettina JOZAMI (ARG) / Florencia MOLINERO (ARG)
   Bojana BOBUSIC (AUS) / Sophie FERGUSON (AUS)
   — B.JOZAMI / F.MOLINERO 6-3 6-2

   Ryoko FUDA (JPN) / Neha UBEROI (USA)
   WC Natasha KHAN (GBR) / Laura PETERZAN (GBR)
   — R.FUDA / N.UBEROI 6-3 6-0

   Lara GILTINAN (AUS) / Caroline WOZNIACKI (DEN)
4. Marina ERAKOVIC (NZL) / Monica NICULESCU (ROM)
   — M.ERAKOVIC [4] / M.NICULESCU [4] 3-6 7-6(2) 6-4

5. Katerina BONDARENKO (UKR) / Madalina GOJNEA (ROM)
   Tara IYER (IND) / Elizabeth KOBAK (USA)
   — K.BONDARENKO [5] / M.GOJNEA [5] 3-6 6-0 7-5

   WC Katie O'BRIEN (GBR) / Melanie SOUTH (GBR)
   Regina KULIKOVA (RUS) / Evgeniya RODINA (RUS)
   — K.O'BRIEN [WC] / M.SOUTH [WC] 6-3 4-6 6-4

   Yurika SEMA (JPN) / Nicole THIJSSEN (NED)
   Jana JURICOVA (SVK) / Magdalena RYBARIKOVA (SVK)
   — Y.SEMA / N.THIJSSEN 6-4 6-4

   WC Jade CURTIS (GBR) / Lara FAKHOURY (GBR)
2. Veronika CHVOJKOVA (CZE) / Nicole VAIDISOVA (CZE)
   — V.CHVOJKOVA [2] / N.VAIDISOVA [2] 6-1 6-0

Second Round

- M.KRAJICEK [1] / S.PEER [1] 6-3 6-2
- Y.CHAN [6] / A.WOZNIAK [6] 6-1 6-0
- V.AZARENKA [3] / V.HAVARTSOVA [3] 6-2 3-6 6-4
- G.GABBA / V.VERARDI w/o
- A.KLEYBANOVA [7] / I.KOTKINA [7] 6-1 6-1
- M.ERAKOVIC [4] / M.NICULESCU [4] 3-6 7-6(2) 6-4
- K.O'BRIEN [WC] / M.SOUTH [WC] 7-6(3) 6-3
- V.CHVOJKOVA [2] / N.VAIDISOVA [2] 6-7(4) 6-4 7-5

Quarterfinals

- M.KRAJICEK [1] / S.PEER [1] 6-2 6-4
- V.AZARENKA [3] / V.HAVARTSOVA [3] 6-0 6-2
- M.ERAKOVIC [4] / M.NICULESCU [4] 6-2 6-7(5) 6-0
- V.CHVOJKOVA [2] / N.VAIDISOVA [2] 6-1 6-2

Semifinals

- V.AZARENKA [3] / V.HAVARTSOVA [3] 7-6(3) 6-2
- M.ERAKOVIC [4] / M.NICULESCU [4] 6-4 7-6(7)

Final

V.AZARENKA [3] / V.HAVARTSOVA [3] 6-4 3-6 6-4

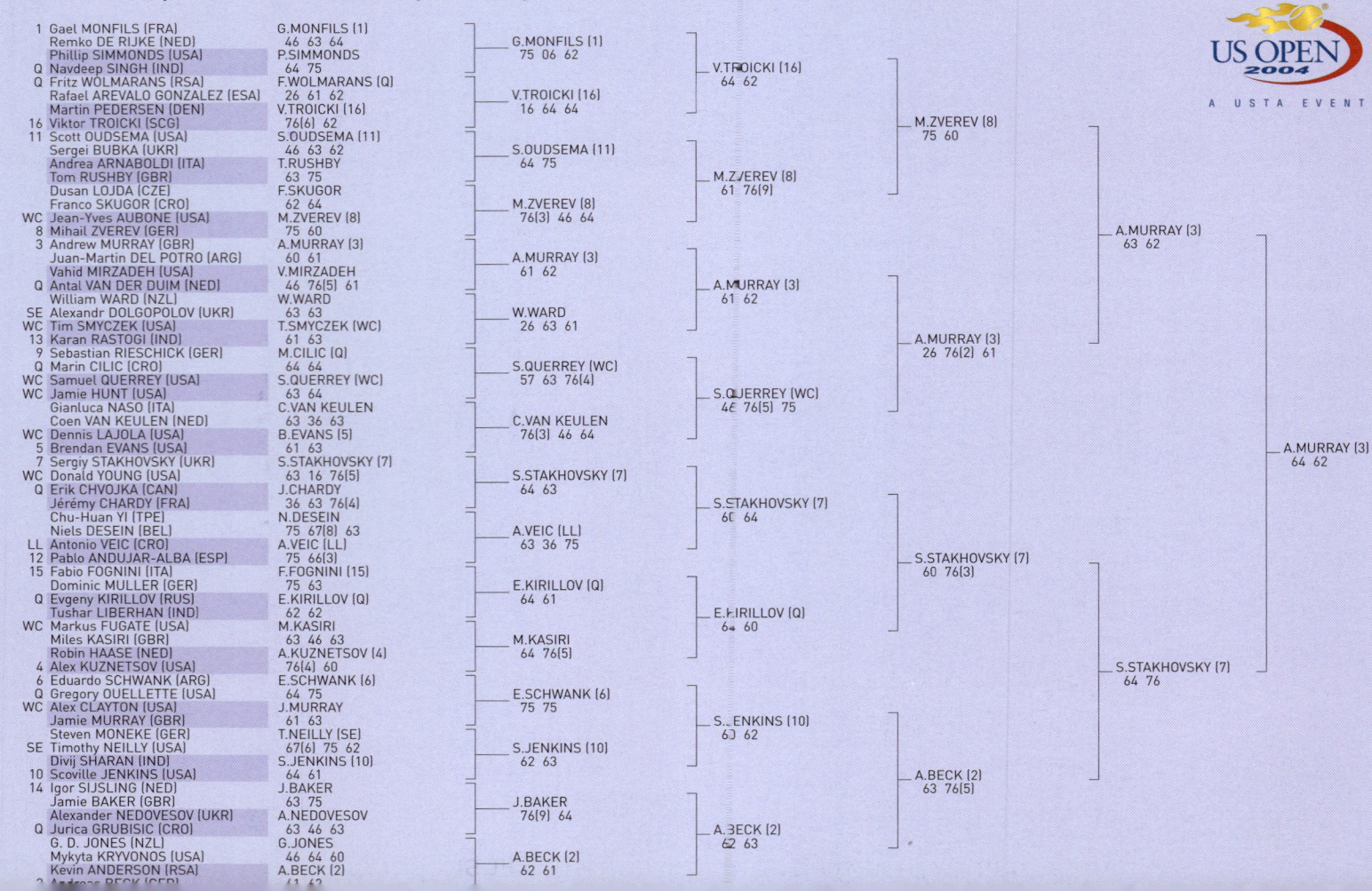

2004 US Open Junior Championships, 5–12 September – Boys' Singles

Round 1 / Round 2 / Round 3 / Quarterfinals / Semifinals / Final

- 1 Gael MONFILS [FRA]
-    Remko DE RIJKE [NED]
  - G.MONFILS [1] — 46 63 64
-    Phillip SIMMONDS [USA]
- Q Navdeep SINGH [IND]
  - P.SIMMONDS — 75 06 62
    - G.MONFILS [1] — 75 06 62
- Q Fritz WOLMARANS [RSA]
-    Rafael AREVALO GONZALEZ [ESA]
  - F.WOLMARANS [Q] — 64 75
-    Martin PEDERSEN [DEN]
- 16 Viktor TROICKI [SCG]
  - V.TROICKI [16] — 26 61 62
    - V.TROICKI [16] — 16 64 64
      - V.TROICKI [16] — 64 62
- 11 Scott OUDSEMA [USA]
-    Andrea ARNABOLDI [ITA]
  - S.OUDSEMA [11] — 76(6) 62
-    Tom RUSHBY [GBR]
-    Dusan LOJDA [CZE]
  - T.RUSHBY — 63 75
    - S.OUDSEMA [11] — 64 75
- WC Franco SKUGOR [CRO]
-    Jean-Yves AUBONE [USA]
  - F.SKUGOR — 62 64
- 8 Mihail ZVEREV [GER]
     - M.ZVEREV [8] — 75 60
       - M.ZVEREV [8] — 76(3) 46 64
         - M.ZVEREV [8] — 61 76(9)
           - M.ZVEREV [8] — 75 60
- 3 Andrew MURRAY [GBR]
-    Juan-Martin DEL POTRO [ARG]
  - A.MURRAY [3] — 60 61
-    Vahid MIRZADEH [USA]
- Q Antal VAN DER DUIM [NED]
  - V.MIRZADEH — 46 76(5) 61
    - A.MURRAY [3] — 61 62
-    William WARD [NZL]
- SE Alexandr DOLGOPOLOV [UKR]
  - W.WARD — 63 63
-    Tim SMYCZEK [USA]
- 13 Karan RASTOGI [IND]
  - T.SMYCZEK [WC] — 26 63 61
    - W.WARD — 61 63
      - A.MURRAY [3] — 26 76(2) 61
-    Sebastian RIESCHICK [GER]
- Q Marin CILIC [CRO]
  - M.CILIC [Q] — 61 63
-    Jamie HUNT [USA]
- 9 Samuel QUERREY [USA]
  - S.QUERREY [WC] — 64 64
    - S.QUERREY [WC] — 57 63 76(4)
-    Gianluca NASO [ITA]
- WC Coen VAN KEULEN [NED]
  - C.VAN KEULEN — 63 64
- 5 Dennis LAJOLA [USA]
  - B.EVANS [5] — 63 36 63
    - C.VAN KEULEN — 76(3) 46 64
      - S.QUERREY [WC] — 46 76(5) 75
- WC Brendan EVANS [USA]
- 7 Sergiy STAKHOVSKY [UKR]
  - S.STAKHOVSKY [7] — 61 63
-    Erik CHVOJKA [CAN]
-    Jérémy CHARDY [FRA]
  - J.CHARDY — 63 16 76(5)
    - S.STAKHOVSKY [7] — 64 63
-    Chu-Huan YI [TPE]
-    Niels DESEIN [BEL]
  - N.DESEIN — 36 63 76(4)
-    Antonio VEIC [CRO]
- LL Pablo ANDUJAR-ALBA [ESP]
  - A.VEIC [LL] — 75 67(8) 63
    - A.VEIC [LL] — 63 36 75
      - S.STAKHOVSKY [7] — 60 64
- 12 Fabio FOGNINI [ITA]
- 15 Dominic MULLER [GER]
  - F.FOGNINI [15] — 75 66(3)
- Q Evgeny KIRILLOV [RUS]
  - E.KIRILLOV [Q] — 75 63
-    Tushar LIBERHAN [IND]
- WC Markus FUGATE [USA]
- 4 Miles KASIRI [GBR]
  - M.KASIRI — 62 62
    - E.KIRILLOV [Q] — 64 61
-    Robin HAASE [NED]
-    Alex KUZNETSOV [USA]
  - A.KUZNETSOV [4] — 63 46 63
    - M.KASIRI — 64 76(5)
      - E.KIRILLOV [Q] — 6– 60
- 6 Eduardo SCHWANK [ARG]
-    Gregory OUELLETTE [USA]
  - E.SCHWANK [6] — 76(4) 60
-    Alex CLAYTON [USA]
-    Jamie MURRAY [GBR]
  - J.MURRAY — 64 75
    - E.SCHWANK [6] — 75 75
- SE Steven MONEKE [GER]
-    Timothy NEILLY [USA]
  - T.NEILLY [SE] — 61 63
- 10 Scoville JENKINS [USA]
-    Divij SHARAN [IND]
  - S.JENKINS [10] — 67(6) 75 62
    - S.JENKINS [10] — 62 63
      - S.JENKINS [10] — 63 62
- 14 Igor SIJSLING [NED]
-    Jamie BAKER [GBR]
  - J.BAKER — 63 75
-    Alexander NEDOVESOV [UKR]
- Q Jurica GRUBISIC [CRO]
  - A.NEDOVESOV — 63 46 63
    - J.BAKER — 76(9) 64
      - A.BECK [2] — 63 76(5)
- G. D. JONES [NZL]
-    Mykyta KRYVONOS [USA]
  - G.JONES — 46 64 60
-    Kevin ANDERSON [RSA]
- 2 Andreas BECK [GER]
  - A.BECK [2] — 61 62
    - A.BECK [2] — 62 63

Semifinals:
- A.MURRAY [3] — 63 62
- S.STAKHOVSKY [7] — 64 76

Final: A.MURRAY [3] — 64 62

2004 US Open Junior Championships, 5–12 September – Girls' Singles

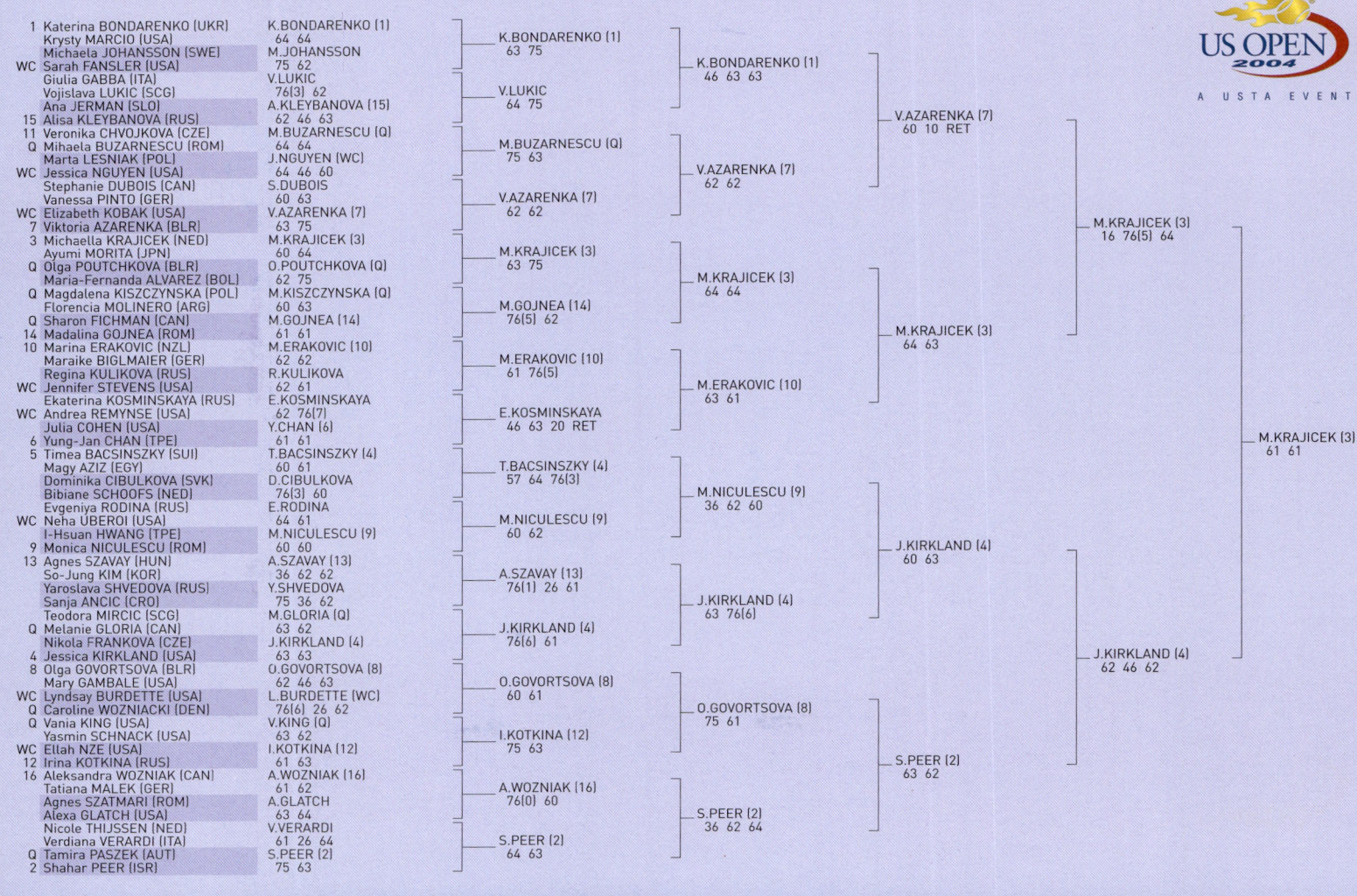

Winner: M. KRAJICEK [3] 6 1 6 1

First Round

1. Katerina BONDARENKO (UKR) [1] — 6 4 6 4
   Krysty MARCIO (USA)
WC Sarah FANSLER (USA) — 7 5 6 2
   Michaela JOHANSSON (SWE)
   Giulia GABBA (ITA) — 7 6(3) 6 2
   Vojislava LUKIC (SCG)
Q Ana JERMAN (SLO)
   15 Alisa KLEYBANOVA (RUS) — 6 2 4 6 6 3
11 Veronika CHVOJKOVA (CZE)
Q Mihaela BUZARNESCU (ROM) — 6 4 6 4
   Marta LESNIAK (POL)
WC Jessica NGUYEN (USA) — 6 4 4 6 6 0
   Stephanie DUBOIS (CAN)
   Vanessa PINTO (GER) — 6 0 6 3
   7 Viktoria AZARENKA (BLR)

3 Michaela KRAJICEK (NED) — 6 3 7 5
   Ayumi MORITA (JPN)
Q Olga POUTCHKOVA (BLR) — 6 0 6 4
   Maria-Fernanda ALVAREZ (BOL)
Q Magdalena KISZCZYNSKA (POL) — 6 2 7 5
   Florencia MOLINERO (ARG)
   14 Madalina GOJNEA (ROM) — 6 0 6 3
Q Sharon FICHMAN (CAN)
   10 Marina ERAKOVIC (NZL) — 6 1 6 1
   Maraike BIGLMAIER (GER)
   Regina KULIKOVA (RUS) — 6 2 6 1
Q Jennifer STEVENS (USA)
WC Ekaterina KOSMINSKAYA (RUS) — 6 2 7 6(7)
   Andrea REMYNSE (USA)

6 Yung-Jan CHAN (TPE) — 6 1 6 1
   Julia COHEN (USA)
   Magy AZIZ (EGY) — 6 0 6 1
   5 Timea BACSINSZKY (SUI)
   Dominika CIBULKOVA (SVK) — 7 6(3) 6 0
   Bibiane SCHOOFS (NED)
   Evgeniya RODINA (RUS) — 6 4 6 1
   Neha UBEROI (USA)
WC I-Hsuan HWANG (TPE) — 6 0 6 0
   9 Monica NICULESCU (ROM)
   13 Agnes SZAVAY (HUN) — 3 6 6 2 6 2
   So-Jung KIM (KOR)
   Yaroslava SHVEDOVA (RUS) — 7 5 3 6 6 2
   Sanja ANCIC (CRO)

Q Teodora MIRCIC (SCG) — 6 3 6 2
   Melanie GLORIA (CAN)
   Nikola FRANKOVA (CZE) — 7 6(6) 6 1
   4 Jessica KIRKLAND (USA)
8 Olga GOVORTSOVA (BLR) — 6 3 6 3
   Mary GAMBALE (USA)
WC Lyndsay BURDETTE (USA) — 7 6(1) 2 6 6 2
Q Caroline WOZNIACKI (DEN)
Q Vania KING (USA) — 6 3 6 2
   Yasmin SCHNACK (USA)
   12 Irina KOTKINA (RUS) — 6 1 6 3
   Ellah NZE (USA)

16 Aleksandra WOZNIAK (CAN) — 7 6(0) 6 0
   Tatiana MALEK (GER)
   Agnes SZATMARI (ROM) — 6 3 6 4
   Alexa GLATCH (USA)
   Nicole THIJSSEN (NED) — 6 1 2 6 6 4
   Verdiana VERARDI (ITA)
Q Tamira PASZEK (AUT) — 7 5 6 3
   2 Shahar PEER (ISR)

Second Round

K. BONDARENKO [1] 6 3 7 5
V. LUKIC 6 4 7 5
M. BUZARNESCU (Q) 7 5 6 3
V. AZARENKA [7] 6 2 6 2
M. KRAJICEK [3] 6 3 7 5
M. GOJNEA [14] 7 6(5) 6 2
M. ERAKOVIC [10] 6 1 7 6(5)
E. KOSMINSKAYA 6 2 7 6(7)
T. BACSINSZKY [4] 5 7 6 4 7 6(3)
M. NICULESCU [9] 6 0 6 2
A. SZAVAY [13] 7 6(1) 2 6 6 1
J. KIRKLAND [4] 7 6(6) 6 1
O. GOVORTSOVA [8] 6 0 6 1
I. KOTKINA [12] 7 5 6 3
A. WOZNIAK [16] 7 6(0) 6 0
S. PEER [2] 6 4 6 3

Third Round

K. BONDARENKO [1] 4 6 6 3 6 3
V. AZARENKA [7] 6 2 6 2
M. KRAJICEK [3] 6 4 6 4
M. ERAKOVIC [10] 6 3 6 1
M. NICULESCU [9] 3 6 6 2 6 0
J. KIRKLAND [4] 6 3 7 6(6)
O. GOVORTSOVA [8] 7 5 6 1
S. PEER [2] 3 6 6 2 6 4

Quarterfinals

V. AZARENKA [7] 6 0 1 0 RET
M. KRAJICEK [3] 6 4 6 3
J. KIRKLAND [4] 6 0 6 3
S. PEER [2] 6 3 6 2

Semifinals

M. KRAJICEK [3] 1 6 7 6(5) 6 4
J. KIRKLAND [4] 6 2 4 6 6 2

Final

M. KRAJICEK [3] 6 1 6 1

2004 US Open Junior Championships, 5–12 September – Boys' Doubles

Final
B. EVANS [1] / S. OUDSEMA [1] 4-6 6-1 6-2

Semifinals
- B. EVANS [1] / S. OUDSEMA [1] — 6-1 6⁷(4) 6-4
- A. BECK [5] / S. RIESCHICK [5] — 3-6 7-5 6-2

Quarterfinals
- B. EVANS [1] / S. OUDSEMA [1] — 4-6 6-4 6-3
- A. MURRAY / J. MURRAY — 6-3 6-4
- V. TROICKI [7] / C. YI [7] — 6-3 3-6 7⁶(8)
- A. BECK [5] / S. RIESCHICK [5] — 1-6 6-4 6-3

Round of 16
- B. EVANS [1] / S. OUDSEMA [1] — 4-6 6-3 6-2
- G. JONES / W. WARD — 3-6 6-3 6-4
- S. MONEKE / D. MULLER — 1-3 RET
- PANDUJAR-ALBA [3] / J. DEL POTRO [3] — 6-4 7⁶(11)
- A. MURRAY / J. MURRAY — 6-1 6-2
- V. MIRZADEH / P. SIMMONDS — 6-3 6-2
- R. HAASE [6] / I. SIJSLING [6] — 3-6 6-3
- V. TROICKI [7] / C. YI [7] — 6-2 6-3
- R. DE RIJKE / A. VAN DER DUIM — 6-4 6-4
- K. ANDERSON / F. WOLMARANS — 4-6 6-2 7-5
- S. JENKINS [4] / M. KRYVONOS [4] — 6-4 6-1
- A. BECK [5] / S. RIESCHICK [5] — 6-1 6-2
- S. BUBKA / M. KASIRI — 6-3 6-4
- T. NEILLY / T. SMYCZEK — 6-3 7⁶(1)
- A. KUZNETSOV [2] / M. ZVEREV [2] — 7⁶(6) 6-2

First Round (Entries)
1. Brendan EVANS (USA) / Scott OUDSEMA (USA) [1]
   Andrea ARNABOLDI (ITA) / Martin PEDERSEN (DEN)
   Dennis LAJOLA (USA) / Donald YOUNG (USA)
   WC Shan SONDHU (USA)
   WC Okechi WOMEODU (USA)
   Alex CLAYTON (USA) / Jamie HUNT (USA)
   G. D. JONES (NZL) / William WARD (NZL)
   Steven MONEKE (GER) / Dominic MULLER (GER)
8. Rafael AREVALO GONZALEZ (ESA) / Coen VAN KEULEN (NED)
8. Pablo ANDUJAR-ALBA (ESP) / Juan-Martin DEL POTRO (ARG) [3]
   Jérémy CHARDY (FRA) / Fabio FOGNINI (ITA)
   Andrew MURRAY (GBR) / Jamie MURRAY (GBR)
   Tushar LIBERHAN (IND) / Divij SHARAN (IND)
   Vahid MIRZADEH (USA) / Phillip SIMMONDS (USA)
   Dusan LOJDA (CZE) / Franco SKUGOR (CRO)
   Jurica GRUBISIC (CRO)
6. Antonio VEIC (CRO) / Robin HAASE (NED) / Igor SIJSLING (NED)
7. Viktor TROICKI (SCG) / Chu-Huan YI (TPE)
   WC Kelten DAMICO (USA) / Calvin KEMP (USA)
   Remko DE RIJKE (NED) / Antal VAN DER DUIM (NED)
   Jamie BAKER (GBR) / Tom RUSHBY (GBR)
   WC Dylan ARNOULD (USA) / Jesse LEVINE (USA)
   Kevin ANDERSON (RSA) / Fritz WOLMARANS (RSA)
   Erik CHVOJKA (CAN) / Navdeep SINGH (IND)
4. Scoville JENKINS (USA) / Mykyta KRYVONOS (USA)
5. Andreas BECK (GER) / Sebastian RIESCHICK (GER)
   Niels DESEIN (BEL) / Gianluca NASO (ITA)
   WC Samuel QUERREY (USA) / Spencer VEGOSEN (USA)
   WC Sergei BUBKA (UKR) / Miles KASIRI (GBR)
   Timothy NEILLY (USA) / Tim SMYCZEK (USA)
   Marin CILIC (CRO)
A Alexander NEDOVESOV (UKR)
A Robert CAMERON (USA)
A Gregory OUELLETTE (USA)
2. Alex KUZNETSOV (USA) / Mihail ZVEREV (GER)

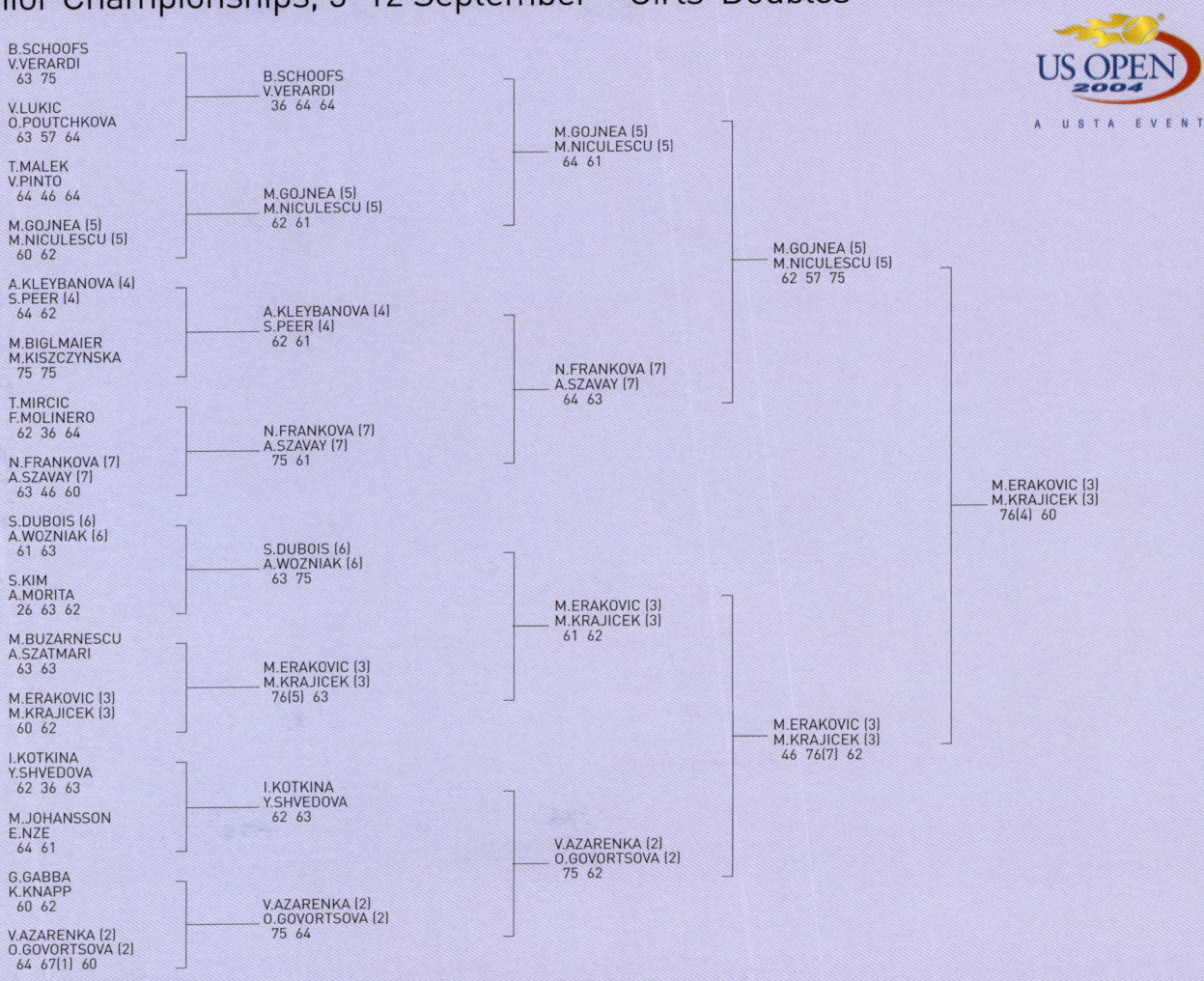

2004 US Open Junior Championships, 5-12 September – Girls' Doubles

Draw

- A I-Hsuan HWANG [TPE]
- A Roxane VAISEMBERG [BRA]
  - B.SCHOOFS / V.VERARDI 6 3 7 5
- Bibiane SCHOOFS [NED]
- Verdiana VERARDI [ITA]
  - B.SCHOOFS / V.VERARDI 3 6 6 4 6 4
- Mary GAMBALE [USA]
- Krysty MARCIO [USA]
  - V.LUKIC / O.POUTCHKOVA 6 3 5 7 6 4
- Vojislava LUKIC [SCG]
- Olga POUTCHKOVA [BLR]
- Tatiana MALEK [GER]
- Vanessa PINTO [GER]
  - T.MALEK / V.PINTO 6 4 4 6 6 4
- Sanja ANCIC [CRO]
- Nicole THIJSSEN [NED]
  - M.GOJNEA / M.NICULESCU [5] 6 4 6 1
- Sharon FICHMAN [CAN]
- Melanie GLORIA [CAN]
  - M.GOJNEA / M.NICULESCU [5] 6 0 6 2
- 5 Madalina GOJNEA [ROM]
- 5 Monica NICULESCU [ROM]
  - M.GOJNEA / M.NICULESCU [5] 6 2 6 1
- 4 Alisa KLEYBANOVA [RUS]
- 4 Shahar PEER [ISR]
  - A.KLEYBANOVA [4] / S.PEER [4] 6 4 6 2
- Andrea REMYNSE [USA]
- Jennifer STEVENS [USA]
  - A.KLEYBANOVA [4] / S.PEER [4] 6 2 6 1
- Ekaterina KOSMINSKAYA [RUS]
- Evgeniya RODINA [RUS]
  - M.BIGLMAIER / M.KISZCZYNSKA 7 5 7 5
- Maraike BIGLMAIER [GER]
- Magdalena KISZCZYNSKA [POL]
  - M.GOJNEA [5] / M.NICULESCU [5] 6 2 5 7 7 5
- Teodora MIRCIC [SCG]
- Florencia MOLINERO [ARG]
  - T.MIRCIC / F.MOLINERO 6 2 3 6 6 4
- Tamira PASZEK [AUT]
- Caroline WOZNIACKI [DEN]
  - N.FRANKOVA [7] / A.SZAVAY [7] 7 5 6 1
- WC Jessica KIRKLAND [USA]
- WC Alexandra MUELLER [USA]
  - N.FRANKOVA [7] / A.SZAVAY [7] 6 3 4 6 6 0
- 7 Nikola FRANKOVA [CZE]
- 7 Agnes SZAVAY [HUN]
  - N.FRANKOVA [7] / A.SZAVAY [7] 6 4 6 3
- 6 Stephanie DUBOIS [CAN]
- 6 Aleksandra WOZNIAK [CAN]
  - S.DUBOIS [6] / A.WOZNIAK [6] 6 3 7 5
- WC Vania KING [USA]
- WC Riza ZALAMEDA [USA]
  - S.DUBOIS [6] / A.WOZNIAK [6] 6 1 6 3
- Dominika CIBULKOVA [SVK]
- Mirna MARINOVIC [CRO]
  - S.KIM / A.MORITA 2 6 6 3 6 2
- So-Jung KIM [KOR]
- Ayumi MORITA [JPN]
  - M.ERAKOVIC [3] / M.KRAJICEK [3] 6 1 6 2
- Yasmin SCHNACK [USA]
- Katrina TSANG [USA]
  - M.BUZARNESCU / A.SZATMARI 6 3 6 3
- Mihaela BUZARNESCU [ROM]
- Agnes SZATMARI [ROM]
  - M.ERAKOVIC [3] / M.KRAJICEK [3] 7 6(5) 6 3
- WC Julia COHEN [USA]
- WC Yvette HYNDMAN [USA]
  - M.ERAKOVIC [3] / M.KRAJICEK [3] 6 0 6 2
- 3 Marina ERAKOVIC [NZL]
- 3 Michaella KRAJICEK [NED]
  - M.ERAKOVIC [3] / M.KRAJICEK [3] 4 6 7 6(7) 6 2
- 8 Timea BACSINSZKY [SUI]
- 8 Marta LESNIAK [POL]
  - I.KOTKINA / Y.SHVEDOVA 6 2 6 3
- Irina KOTKINA [RUS]
- Yaroslava SHVEDOVA [RUS]
  - I.KOTKINA / Y.SHVEDOVA 6 2 3 6 6 3
- Maria-Fernanda ALVAREZ [BOL]
- Ana JERMAN [SLO]
  - M.JOHANSSON / E.NZE 6 4 6 1
- Michaela JOHANSSON [SWE]
- Eliah NZE [USA]
  - V.AZARENKA [2] / O.GOVORTSOVA [2] 7 5 6 2
- Giulia GABBA [ITA]
- Karen KNAPP [ITA]
  - G.GABBA / K.KNAPP 6 0 6 2
- WC Sarah FANSLER [USA]
- WC Elizabeth KOBAK [USA]
  - V.AZARENKA [2] / O.GOVORTSOVA [2] 6 4 6 7(1) 6 0
- Lyndsay BURDETTE [USA]
- Alexa GLATCH [USA]
  - V.AZARENKA [2] / O.GOVORTSOVA [2] 7 5 6 4
- 2 Viktoria AZARENKA [BLR]
- 2 Olga GOVORTSOVA [BLR]

Final: M.ERAKOVIC [3] / M.KRAJICEK [3] 7 6(4) 6 0

217

ITF Development: 2004 US Open Drawsheets

the wheelchair tennis year

by chris bowers

The Paralympics were always going to be the highlight of wheelchair tennis in 2004, but few could have anticipated what a successful event it would be. Though wheelchair tennis moved from three Super Series events – the equivalent of the Grand Slams – to four in 2004, the Paralympics are the high point of the wheelchair tennis calendar, and all the top names of the sport turned out in Athens in September.

"Many of us felt that the Sydney Paralympics were so good that a high water mark had been set," said the ITF's Wheelchair Tennis Manager Ellen de Lange, "but Athens was in many ways as good, and in some people's eyes even better. It was an exceptional event which did a lot to boost the profile of wheelchair tennis."

Esther Vergeer's second double-gold medal haul – she won singles and doubles in both Sydney and Athens – was less of a surprise than Robin Ammerlaan's gold in the men's singles. Ammerlaan had seemed forever to be missing out on the biggest occasions to his great rival David Hall, but in the gold medal match he finally beat the Australian 62 61 in just 48 minutes to make it a clean sweep for the Netherlands in the singles.

David Hall (AUS)

> Esther Vergeer's second double-gold medal haul – she won singles and doubles in both Sydney and Athens – was less of a surprise than Robin Ammerlaan's gold in the men's singles.

"I wanted this medal for so long," said Ammerlaan, "and now I have got it. I played well [in the final], everything was going right, and I was able to hit a lot of lines. David also made some mistakes that he doesn't normally make."

Though Vergeer and Maaike Smit won the women's doubles, the event was a triumph for the Thai pair Sakhorn Khanthasit and Ratana Techameneewat, who took silver, with the Swiss pair Karin Erath-Suter and Sandra Kalt taking bronze.

The only blot on the Dutch landscape came in the men's doubles, where Ammerlaan and Eric Stuurman were beaten in a tight three-set semifinal by the French pair Michael Jeremiasz and Lahcen Majdi. Jeremiasz, who had won bronze in the singles, then claimed silver in doubles as the Japanese pair of Shingo Kunieda and Satoshi Saida took the gold medal, beating the Frenchmen 61 62 in the final.

While Kunieda and Saida were the first players from Japan to win a Paralympic gold medal, Peter Norfolk did the same for Great Britain when he beat the American David Wagner 63 62 to take gold in the quad event. Wagner took revenge in the doubles final winning gold, partnered by Nick Taylor (GBR), with victory over Norfolk and Mark Eccleston 64 61. Facing the media afterwards, Norfolk bit his gold medal and said: "Yes, it is real!"

Wheelchair tennis as a spectacle was made real for numerous television viewers round the world, with more coverage than ever before of the Athens Paralympics. And a survey of reactions from the Greek ballkids who worked at the Paralympic tennis event illustrates the sport's potential to inspire. Among the comments were:

- "I learned a lot during these games. If people want something they really can achieve it. The athletes were very friendly to us in contrast to the athletes of the Olympic games." – Katarina Païsiou
- "I truly believe wheelchair tennis is the most amazing sport of the Paralympics. The athletes are more ambitious, more passioned, and more heroes. Never give up!" – Sopianonouter Avareasin
- "I've tried wheelchair tennis and I still can't understand how they play so well. Wow! Excellent!" – Nikos Paulopoulos
- "It was the best experience of my life.

left: Esther Vergeer (NED)

the wheelchair tennis year

by chris bowers

"I feel lucky that they chose me to participate in the Paralympics." – Ksenia Parakeva

The highly successful Athens event crowned a year in which the wheelchair world once again expanded.

With the French Open staging its first exhibition event at Roland Garros, all four Grand Slam tournaments now offer wheelchair tennis in some form. The Roland Garros exhibition benefited from the world's top two players Hall and Vergeer, who were in Paris to receive their 2003 world champions trophies at the annual ITF Champions Dinner. Other exhibitions included one preceding the final of the ATP tournament in Buenos Aires, another came one evening at the ATP event in San Jose between matches involving Andy Roddick and Andre Agassi, and the South African Tennis Association staged one at the South Africa v Slovak Republic Davis Cup tie in Johannesburg. Indeed, such is the prestige wheelchair tennis has gained in America that the 2005 US Open will feature a fully-fledged wheelchair tournament in the second week at Flushing Meadows featuring the top eight entrants in the men's and women's rankings.

The addition of the Japan Open to the Super Series means there are now four top-level wheelchair tournaments on the

Robin Ammerlaan (NED)

eight-man NEC Wheelchair Masters, both Hall and Ammerlaan could have ended the year No 1. Ammerlaan fell in the semifinals to Jeremiasz, for whom 2004 was very much a breakthrough year, but that still meant Hall had to beat the Frenchman in the final to retain his year-end top ranking. He did so 62 64 to pip the Dutchman who had pipped him in Athens.

With Peter Norfolk injured it was David Wagner who took advantage of the Quad No. 1's absence by taking the Masters title.

The Invacare World Team Cup went south in 2004, New Zealand becoming the 12th different country – and the second in the southern hemisphere – to host the premier team event in wheelchair tennis, when it staged it in the south island city of

first four countries to benefit from assistance from the Silver Fund, the ITF's charitable initiative to boost wheelchair tennis in countries with immense potential but few resources for it to flourish. Indeed the expansion of the Silver Fund was one of the lesser publicised successes of the 2004 wheelchair year.

At the start of 2004 the Silver Fund had seen projects in four countries: Sri Lanka, South Africa, Romania and Bolivia. While work in those countries continued, by the end of the year the total number of countries benefiting from the three-year-old initiative had increased to ten, with full-scale projects in El Salvador, Indonesia, Colombia and India, and demonstration clinics held in Bulgaria and Moldova.

> Ammerlaan fell in the semifinals to Jeremiasz, for whom 2004 was very much a breakthrough year, but that still meant Hall had to beat the Frenchman in the final to retain his year-end top ranking. He did so 62 64 to pip the Dutchman who had pipped him in Athens.

NEC Tour (or five in a Paralympic year).

At the end of the year, the tour champions were once again Hall and Vergeer. The prolific Dutchwoman went through a year undefeated, in fact she ended 2004 having lost just once in five years, that to Dani di Toro who announced that 2004 would be her last as a competitor on the tour.

But the men's race to be world champion was much closer. Going into the

Christchurch. Like the Paralympics that were to follow, it proved a sweep for the Netherlands, who picked up the men's, women's and junior titles, with only Israel breaking up the Dutch dominance by taking the quad title for the third time. The event concluded with Invacare announcing a three-year extension to their sponsorship.

The World Team Cup was also notable for the presence of Sri Lanka, one of the

ITF Wheelchair Tennis Development Officer Mark Bullock said: "One of the most heartening sides of the Silver Fund has been the support it has been given by the leading wheelchair players. A number of them have been willing to be unpaid ambassadors for the programme, and many have donated kit and wheelchairs that they no longer use. Esther Vergeer donated a wheelchair to Sri Lanka, and Jayant Mistry got together 40 rackets and

ITF Development: The Wheelchair Tennis Year

Peter Norfolk (GBR)

eight chairs to take to India, the country his family came from. There is a real sense among the top players that they feel responsible for the growth and promotion of the game."

The enthusiasm generated by the introduction of wheelchair tennis has gone beyond just playing a sport. In Moldova, the ITF's demonstration of wheelchair tennis has led to a project for a wheelchair tennis club, which would not only be for wheelchair tennis but run by people with disabilities and part-funded by renting court time out to other players – both wheelchair and able-bodied.

Yet such enthusiasm can only be sustained where there is money to fund projects, and in 2004 the Silver Fund welcomed a new sponsor, NCDO from the Netherlands, which joins the pool of funders of which the Cruyff Foundation is the leading member. Ellen de Lange said: "It's terrific the support we are getting from the Netherlands, though in the interests of the sport we need to spread the net more widely and seek funding from sources in other countries."

Some funding can come from governments looking to alleviate the wreckage of wars and other violent conflicts. In Sri Lanka, for example, one of the Silver Fund's principal partners is the army, as a number of soldiers who cannot serve as front-line troops because of disabilities sustained in battle are able to keep fit and maintain their self-esteem by playing wheelchair tennis.

It remains to be seen how long it takes for a player from a Silver Fund project to break into the world's top 25. The presence of Sri Lanka at this year's Invacare World Team Cup was clearly a sign of progress, and if plans to use Silver Fund money in 2005 to take wheelchair tennis into China come to fruition, then the scope for someone to compete in the 2008 Beijing Paralympics is considerable.

But competition in international wheelchair tennis is becoming ever more intense, as the ITF's efforts to promote the sport continue. Mark Bullock said: "More and more mainstream coaches are becoming well versed in wheelchair tennis, to the point where being a tennis coach is increasingly about both able-bodied and wheelchair forms of the game."

Coaches workshops, junior programmes and camps continue to grow the sport, and an 18 & under wheelchair tennis competition is now part of Les Petits As, the 14 & under world tennis championships held every year in the French resort of Tarbes.

And wherever it is played, wheelchair tennis never loses its ability to impress. That was the value of the expanded coverage of the Athens Paralympics, so much so that two Greek ballkids felt motivated to stretch their English to its limits and write their own Wheelchair Tennis Song in recognition of the players they had served. The first verse goes:

There are some people who
  are flying like eagles
There are athletes who are
  fighting for singles
There are people who deserve
  our respect
And they must always be
  captains on the deck
They are working hard to
  develop their skills,
So they can break bones
  on chairs with wheels.
They are making their dreams come true
And they are the nicest people
  I could ever know.

Mark Bullock said: "More and more mainstream coaches are becoming well versed in wheelchair tennis, to the point where being a tennis coach is increasingly about both able-bodied and wheelchair forms of the game."

NEC Wheelchair Tennis Tour 2004 Results

- **NEW ZEALAND OPEN** (NZL) (CS3) ($5,000) 27-31 JANUARY – **WS:** Jiske Griffioen (NED) d. Korie Homan (NED) 61 63. **WD:** Yuka Chokyu/Helen Simard (CAN) d. Sharon Clark/Julia Dorsett (USA) 63 75. **MS:** Shingo Kunieda (JPN) d. Eric Stuurman (NED) 62 63. **MD:** Anthony Bonaccurso (AUS)/Peter Wikstrom (SWE) d. Maikel Scheffers/Ronald Vink (NED). **QS:** Bas Van Erp (NED) d. Nicholas Taylor (USA) 64 60. **QD:** Bas Van Erp/Monique De Beer (NED) d. Nicholas Taylor/Kevin Whalen (USA).

- **QUEENSLAND OPEN** (AUS) (CS3) 28 JANUARY-1 FEBRUARY – **WS:** Karin Suter-Erath (SUI) d. Kay Forshaw (GBR) 61 62. **MS:** Michael Jeremiasz (FRA) d. Ha-Gel Lee (KOR) 60 62. **MD:** Michael Jeremiasz/Lahcen Majdi (FRA) d. Miroslav Brychta (CZE)/Ha-Gel Lee (KOR) 75 64.

- **WHEELCHAIR CLASSIC 8'S AT AUSTRALIAN OPEN** (AUS) (CS2) 30 JANUARY-1 FEBRUARY – **WS:** Esther Vergeer (NED) d. Daniela Di Toro (AUS) 46 63 61. **WD:** Maaike Smit/Esther Vergeer (NED) d. Sonja Peters/Sharon Walraven (NED) 63 76(3). **MS:** David Hall (AUS) d. Robin Ammerlaan (NED) 64 75. **MD:** Robin Ammerlaan (NED)/Martin Legner (AUT) d. Tadeusz Kruszelnicki (POL)/Satoshi Saida (JPN) 63 63.

- **SYDNEY INTERNATIONAL** (AUS) (CS1) ($15,000) 4-8 FEBRUARY – **WS:** Esther Vergeer (NED) d. Daniela Di Toro (AUS) 62 63. **WD:** Maaike Smit/Esther Vergeer (NED) d. Florence Gravellier (FRA)/Janet Mcmorran (GBR) 63 60. **MS:** Robin Ammerlaan (NED) d. David Hall (AUS) 36 75 75. **MD:** Robin Ammerlaan (NED)/Martin Legner (AUT) d. Shingo Kunieda/Satoshi Saida (JPN) 62 62. **QS:** Peter Norfolk (GBR) d. Bas Van Erp (NED) 75 64. **QD:** Rick Draney/David Wagner (USA) d. Nicholas Taylor/Kevin Whalen (USA) 62 64.

- **AUSTRALIAN OPEN** (AUS) (SS) ($26,022) 11-15 FEBRUARY – **WS:** Esther Vergeer (NED) d. Sonja Peters (NED) 61 63. **WD:** Maaike Smit/Esther Vergeer (NED) d. Sharon Clark (USA)/Sonja Peters (NED) 63 62. **MS:** David Hall (AUS) d. Martin Legner (AUT) 61 61. **MD:** Robin Ammerlaan (NED)/Martin Legner (AUT) d. David Hall (AUS)/Michael Jeremiasz (FRA) 64 75. **QS:** Peter Norfolk (GBR) d. David Wagner (USA) 62 62. **QD:** Mark Eccleston (GBR)/David Wagner (USA) d. Roy Humphreys/Peter Norfolk (GBR) 75 76(4).

- **SION INDOOR** (SUI) (CS4) ($3,000) 26-29 FEBRUARY – **WS:** Britta Siegers (GER) d. Agnieszka Bartczak (POL) 61 60. **WD:** Armelle Fabre (FRA)/Britta Siegers (GER) d. Anna Alenas (SWE)/Eveline Hegi (SUI) w/o. **MS:** Jozef Felix (SVK) d. Lahcen Majdi (FRA) 64 76. **MD:** Miroslav Brychta (CZE)/Piotr Jaroszewski (POL) d. Laurent Fischer/Lahcen Majdi (FRA) 61 61.

- **TAIWAN LION'S CUP** (TPE) (CS4) ($5,000) 27-29 FEBRUARY – **WS:** Young-Suk Hong (KOR) d. Ratana Techamaneewat (THA) 62 61. **WD:** Young-Suk Hong/Myung-Hee Hwang (KOR) d. Christine Greer (GBR)/Ratana Techamaneewat (THA) 64 64. **MS:** Wittaya Peem-Mee (THA) d. Ryoichi To (JPN) 61 64. **MD:** John Greer (USA)/Dong-Ju Kwak (KOR) d. Satoshi Hamakado/Hiroyuki Takeda (JPN) 60 60.

- **YVELINES OPEN** (FRA) (CS3) 4-7 MARCH – **WS:** Jiske Griffioen (NED) d. Florence Gravellier (FRA) 46 75 63. **WD:** Jiske Griffioen (NED)/Britta Siegers (GER) d. Armelle Fabre/Florence Gravellier (FRA) 76 63. **MS:** Michael Jeremiasz (FRA) d. Peter Wikstrom (SWE) 63 76 75. **MD:** Michael Jeremiasz/Lahcen Majdi (FRA) d. Maikel Scheffers/Ronald Vink (NED) 61 62.

- **LES SYSTEMES ACCI** (CAN) (CS5) ($1,300) 5-7 MARCH – **MS:** Christoph Trachsel (CAN) d. Claude Brunet (CAN) 63 61. **MD:** Yan Mathieu/Frank Peter (CAN) d. Francois Lacourse/Georges Rousseau (CAN) 75 63.

- **BIEL-BIENNE INDOORS** (SUI) (CS3) ($8,500) 11-14 MARCH – **WS:** Jiske Griffioen (NED) d. Britta Siegers (GER) 60 60. **WD:** Jiske Griffioen (NED)/Britta Siegers (GER) d. Sandra Kalt/Karin Suter-Erath (SUI) 61 60. **MS:** Martin Legner (AUT) d. Stephen Welch (USA) 36 75 76. **MD:** Miroslav Brychta (CZE)/Martin Legner (AUT) d. Maikel Scheffers/Ronald Vink (NED) 62 46 63.

- **TASMANIAN WHEELCHAIR OPEN** (AUS) (CS5) ($500) 12-14 MARCH – **MS:** Ben Weekes (AUS) d. Jeff Hilton (AUS) 62 62.

- **LES INTERNATIONAUX SAVARIA** (CAN) (CS5) ($1,300) 13-14 MARCH – **MS:** Frank Peter (CAN) d. Mario Perron (CAN) w/o. **MD:** Yan Mathieu/Frank Peter (CAN) d. Jamie Lauzon/Christoph Trachsel (CAN) 64 60.

- **ALPI DEL MARE** (ITA) (CS3) ($8,000) 18-21 MARCH – **WS:** Jiske Griffioen (NED) d. Kimberly Blake (GBR) 63 63. **MS:** Kai Schrameyer (GER) d. Martin Legner (AUT) 61 63. **MD:** Jozef Felix (SVK)/Martin Legner (AUT) d. Maikel Scheffers/Ronald Vink (NED) 16 64 62.

- **USTA NATIONAL SOUTHWEST DESERT WHEELCHAIR CLASSICS** (USA) (CS4) ($5,000) 18-21 MARCH – **WS:** Kaitlyn Verfuerth (USA) d. Sharon Clark (USA) 63 67(5) 64. **WD:** Sharon Clark/Kaitlyn Verfuerth (USA) d. Kirsten Mohr/Nikki Saltzburg (USA) 36 60 60. **MS:** Larry Quintero (USA) d. Derek Bolton (USA) 60 62. **MD:** Derek Bolton/Larry Quintero (USA) d. Lee Hinson (USA)/Emilio Miramontes (MEX) 67(6) 61 63. **QS:** Sarah Hunter (CAN) d. Kevin Whalen (USA) 61 63. **QD:** Bryan Barten/David Wagner (USA) d. Kevin Whalen (USA)/Sarah Hunter (CAN) 75 26 62.

- **WAIKATO CHAMPIONSHIPS** (NZL) (CS5) ($1,200) 19-21 MARCH – **WS:** Jacqueline Courtier (NZL) d. Tiffiney Perry (NZL) 63 62. **MS:** Ben Weekes (AUS) d. Cameron Hastings (NZL) 61 63. **MD:** Dave Venter (NZL)/Ben Weekes (AUS) d. Robert Courtney/Cameron Hastings (NZL) 63 75.

- **GIRONA COSTA BRAVA OPEN** (ESP) (CS4) 25-28 MARCH – **WS:** Armelle Fabre (FRA) d. Lola Ochoa (ESP) 75 63. **WD:** Armelle Fabre (FRA)/Lola Ochoa (ESP) d. Ratana Techamaneewat (THA)/Mette Van Dongen (NED) 62 60. **MS:** Kai Schrameyer (GER) d. Peter Wikstrom (SWE) 63 63. **MD:** Miroslav Brychta (CZE)/Peter Wikstrom (SWE) d. Laszlo Farkas (HUN)/Kai Schrameyer (GER) 67(4) 64 63.

- **WINDSOR CLASSIC INDOOR GAMES** (CAN) (CS5) 26-28 MARCH – **WS:** Tami Saj (CAN) d. Sheri Roberts (CAN) 61 61. **MS:** Colin Mckeage (CAN) d. Frank Peter (CAN) 26 62 62. **MD:** Yan Mathieu/Frank Peter (CAN) d. Jamie Lauzon/Colin Mckeage (CAN) 64 64.

- **NASDAQ-100 OPEN** (USA) (CS1) 31 MARCH-3 APRIL – **WS:** Esther Vergeer (NED) d. Daniela Di Toro (AUS) 61 62. **WD:** Maaike Smit/Esther Vergeer (NED) d. Sharon Clark (USA)/Daniela Di Toro (AUS) 62 64. **MS:** David Hall (AUS) d. Robin Ammerlaan (NED) 64 64. **MD:** David Hall (AUS)/Shingo Kunieda (JPN) d. Robin Ammerlaan (NED)/Satoshi Saida (JPN) 26 64 60.

- **NORTH EAST WHEELCHAIR TENNIS TOURNAMENT** (GBR) (CS4) 1-4 APRIL – **WS:** Janet Mcmorran (GBR) d. Florence Gravellier (FRA) 63 76(6). **WD:** Kimberly Blake/Janet Mcmorran (GBR) d. Florence Gravellier (FRA)/Susan Paisley (GBR) 61 64. **MS:** Frederic Cazeaudumec (FRA) d. Lahcen Majdi (FRA) 63 26 62. **MD:** Frederic Cazeaudumec/Lahcen Majdi (FRA) d. David Gardner/Kevin Plowman (GBR) 62 64.

- **BANGKOK CUP** (THA) (CS5) ($1,000) 2-4 APRIL – **WS:** Roswan Nongnuch (THA) d. Choosri Inthanin (THA) 61 61. **WD:** Choosri Inthanin/Janhom Masayo (THA) d. Orathai Sudsom/Bang-On Suthani (THA) 63 64. **MS:** Wittaya Peem-Mee (THA) d. Sumrerng Kruamai (THA) 64 63. **MD:** Sumrerng Kruamai/Wittaya Peem-Mee (THA) d. Supparat Ponmingmad/Sunthorn Sridang (THA) 64 64.

- **PENSACOLA OPEN** (USA) (CS4) ($5,000) 2-4 APRIL – **MS:** Ronald Vink (NED) d. Lee Hinson (USA) 60 64. **MD:** Derek Bolton/Daniel Lachman (USA) d. Niclas Larsson (SWE)/Ronald Vink (NED) 64 64. **QS:** Kevin Whalen (USA) d. Hiroshi Toma (JPN) 57 64 61. **QD:** Sergio Garcia (MEX)/Hiroshi Toma (JPN) d. Rodrigo Acevedo/Pablo Araya (CHI) 63 63.

- **FLORIDA OPEN** (USA) (CS1) ($15,000) 7-11 APRIL – **WS:** Esther Vergeer (NED) d. Daniela Di Toro (AUS) 60 63. **WD:** Maaike Smit/Esther Vergeer (NED) d. Chiyoko Ohmae/Mie Yaosa (JPN) 60 62. **MS:** Robin Ammerlaan (NED) d. David Hall (AUS) 46 60 63. **MD:** Michael Jeremiasz (FRA)/Martin Legner (AUT) d. Shingo Kunieda/Satoshi Saida (JPN) 64 76(6). **QS:** Peter Norfolk (GBR) d. David Wagner (USA) 75 75. **QD:** Nicholas Taylor/David Wagner (USA) d. Mark Eccleston/Peter Norfolk (GBR) 60 64.

- **BRASILIA OPEN** (BRA) (CS2) ($12,000) 14-18 APRIL – **MS:** Michael Jeremiasz (FRA) d. Miroslav Brychta (CZE) 62 61. **MD:** Miroslav Brychta (CZE)/Michael Jeremiasz (FRA) d. Frederic Cazeaudumec (FRA)/Yan Mathieu (CAN) 61 61.

- **CAJUN CLASSIC** (USA) (CS2) ($12,000) 15-18 APRIL – **WS:** Sharon Walraven (NED) d. Mie Yaosa (JPN) 61 60. **WD:** Kay Forshaw (GBR)/Sharon Walraven (NED) d. Sharon Clark/Karin Korb (USA) 26 76(4) 76(6). **MS:** Jayant Mistry (GBR) d. Derek Bolton (USA) 63 64. **MD:** Simon Hatt/Jayant Mistry (GBR) d. Laszlo Farkas (HUN)/Lee Hinson (USA) 63 36 62. **QS:** David Wagner (USA) d. Sarah Hunter (CAN) 64 62. **QD:** David Wagner/Kevin Whalen (USA) d. David Jordan (USA)/Sarah Hunter (CAN) 46 63 62.

- **OPEN AMPHION-PUBLIER** (FRA) (CS4) 22-25 APRIL – **WS:** Janet Mcmorran (GBR) d. Sandra Kalt (SUI) 36 75 61. **WD:** Brigitte Ameryckx (BEL)/Sandra Kalt (SUI) d. Anna Alenas (SWE)/Janet Mcmorran (GBR) 61 60. **MS:** Lahcen Majdi (FRA) d. Serge Biron (FRA) 63 60. **MD:** Lahcen Majdi/Francois Xavier Morille (FRA) d. Serge Biron/Laurent Fischer (FRA) 36 61 64.

- **CHILEAN OPEN** (CHI) (CS3) ($6,000) 22-25 APRIL – **MS:** Miroslav Brychta (CZE) d. Niclas Larsson (SWE) 63 63. **MD:** Miroslav Brychta (CZE)/Oscar Diaz (ARG) d. Niclas Larsson (SWE)/Carlo Tresch (SUI) 61 62.

- **VICTORIAN HARDCOURT CHAMPIONSHIPS** (AUS) (CS5) 24-25 APRIL – **MS:** Anthony Bonaccurso (AUS) d. Ben Weekes (AUS) 26 76 61. **MD:** Anthony Bonaccurso/Daniela Di Toro (AUS) d. Andrew Browning/Michael Dobbie (AUS) 61 63.

- **ARGENTINA OPEN** (ARG) (CS5) ($5,000) 27-30 APRIL – **MS:** Niclas Larsson (SWE) d. Oscar Diaz (ARG) 61 64. **MD:** Oscar Diaz/Carlos Loza (ARG) d. Niclas Larsson (SWE)/Carlo Tresch (SUI) 75 60.

- **KOREA OPEN** (KOR) (CS2) ($12,000) 27-30 APRIL – **WS:** Sakhorn Khanthasit (THA) d. Sharon Walraven (NED) 64 62. **WD:** Young-Suk Hong (KOR)/Sakhorn Khanthasit (THA) d. Britta Siegers (GER)/Sharon Walraven (NED) 62 46 62. **MS:** Shingo Kunieda (JPN) d. Satoshi Saida (JPN) 63 26 62. **MD:** Shingo Kunieda/Satoshi Saida (JPN) d. John Greer (USA)/Ha-Gel Lee (KOR) 60 64.

NEC Wheelchair Tennis Tour 2004 Results (continued)

- **DAEGU OPEN** (KOR) (CS3) ($9,000) 4-7 MAY – **WS:** Sakhorn Khanthasit (THA) d. Sharon Walraven (NED) 67(4) 63 64. **WD:** Young-Suk Hong (KOR)/Sakhorn Khanthasit (THA) d. Christine Greer (GBR)/Myung-Hee Hwang (KOR) 61 62. **MS:** Ha-Gel Lee (KOR) d. John Greer (USA) 60 61. **MD:** John Greer (USA)/Ha-Gel Lee (KOR) d. Gi-Hyun Kim/Kyu-Seung Kim (KOR) 62 60.

- **JAPAN OPEN** (JPN) (SS) ($25,000) 11-16 MAY – **WS:** Esther Vergeer (NED) d. Daniela Di Toro (AUS) 60 64. **WD:** Jiske Griffioen/Esther Vergeer (NED) d. Sonja Peters/Sharon Walraven (NED) 60 60. **MS:** Robin Ammerlaan (NED) d. David Hall (AUS) 64 36 63. **MD:** David Hall (AUS)/Michael Jeremiasz (FRA) d. Shingo Kunieda/Satoshi Saida (JPN) 61 64. **QS:** Peter Norfolk (GBR) d. David Wagner (USA) 63 61. **QD:** David Wagner (USA)/Monique De Beer (NED) d. Peter Norfolk (GBR)/Sarah Hunter (CAN) 61 36 62.

- **ALBARELLA OPEN** (ITA) (CS4) 13-16 MAY – **MS:** Kai Schrameyer (GER) d. Martin Legner (AUT) 75 64. **MD:** Piotr Jaroszewski (POL)/Martin Legner (AUT) d. Laszlo Farkas (HUN)/Jozef Felix (SVK) 46 62 64.

- **JANA HUNSAKER MEMORIAL** (USA) (CS3) ($7,000) 13-16 MAY – **WS:** Florence Gravellier (FRA) d. Karin Korb (USA) 64 62. **MS:** Stephen Welch (USA) d. Jon Rydberg (USA) 63 62. **MD:** John Becker/Stephen Welch (USA) d. Frederic Cazeaudumec/Lahcen Majdi (FRA) 64 62.

- **CESENATICO OPEN** (ITA) (CS3) ($9,000) 19-22 MAY – **MS:** Kai Schrameyer (GER) d. Martin Legner (AUT) 63 67(5) 62. **MD:** Miroslav Brychta (CZE)/Martin Legner (AUT) d. Jozef Felix (SVK)/Piotr Jaroszewski (POL) 75 61.

- **KOBE OPEN** (JPN) (CS1) ($12,000) 19-23 MAY – **WS:** Esther Vergeer (NED) d. Daniela Di Toro (AUS) 61 62. **WD:** Jiske Griffioen/Esther Vergeer (NED) d. Daniela Di Toro (AUS)/Maaike Smit (NED) 62 61. **MS:** Robin Ammerlaan (NED) d. David Hall (AUS) 64 63. **MD:** Robin Ammerlaan (NED)/Jayant Mistry (GBR) d. David Hall (AUS)/Satoshi Saida (JPN) 76(2) 36 61. **QS:** Sarah Hunter (CAN) d. Monique De Beer (NED) 62 63. **QD:** Monique De Beer (NED)/Sarah Hunter (CAN) d. Roy Humphreys (GBR)/Sadahiro Kimura (JPN) 62 60.

- **ATLANTA OUTDOOR CHAMPIONSHIPS** (USA) (CS3) ($8,000) 20-23 MAY – **WS:** Sharon Clark (USA) d. Kaitlyn Verfuerth (USA) 61 46 62. **WD:** Sharon Clark/Kaitlyn Verfuerth (USA) d. Karin Korb (USA)/Helen Simard (CAN) 06 62 62. **MS:** Stephen Welch (USA) d. Jon Rydberg (USA) 46 62 61. **MD:** Larry Quintero/Stephen Welch (USA) d. Regis Harel/Lahcen Majdi (FRA) 63 63. **QS:** David Wagner (USA) d. Kevin Whalen (USA) 61 62. **QD:** David Wagner/Kevin Whalen (USA) d. David Jordan/Marc Mclean (USA) 62 61.

- **SARDINIA OPEN** (ITA) (CS2) ($12,000) 25-29 MAY – **WS:** Florence Gravellier (FRA) d. Britta Siegers (GER) 61 64. **WD:** Britta Siegers (GER)/Karin Suter-Erath (SUI) d. Armelle Fabre/Florence Gravellier (FRA) 62 63. **MS:** David Hall (AUS) d. Martin Legner (AUT) 62 63. **MD:** Miroslav Brychta (CZE)/Martin Legner (AUT) d. David Hall (AUS)/Kai Schrameyer (GER) 62 63.

- **USTA NATIONAL INDOOR ROHO GATEWAY CLASSIC** (USA) (CS1) ($15,000) 25-29 MAY – **WS:** Sharon Walraven (NED) d. Sonja Peters (NED) 63 46 76(4). **MS:** Michael Jeremiasz (FRA) d. Stephen Welch (USA) 76(2) 57 62. **MD:** Michael Jeremiasz/Lahcen Majdi (FRA) d. Simon Hatt/Jayant Mistry (GBR) 61 75. **QS:** David Wagner (USA) d. Nicholas Taylor (USA) 60 60. **QD:** Nicholas Taylor/David Wagner (USA) d. Bryan Barten/Kevin Whalen (USA) 63 61.

- **TOURNOI INDOORS BULLE** (SUI) (CS5) ($500) 28-30 MAY – **MS:** Daniel Pellegrina (SUI) d. Martin Erni (SUI) 63 46 63. **MD:** Martin Erni/Daniel Pellegrina (SUI) d. Pascal Chessel (FRA)/Konstantin Schmaeh (SUI) 62 62.

- **SZINVANET CUP** (HUN) (CS5) 28-30 MAY – **MS:** Jozef Felix (SVK) d. Laszlo Farkas (HUN) 75 46 76(1).

- **ISRAEL OPEN** (ISR) (CS3) ($5,000) 1-4 JUNE – **WS:** Ilanit Fridman (ISR) d. Natalie Liberman (ISR) 62 60. **MS:** Laszlo Farkas (HUN) d. Genadi Kohanov (ISR) 60 62. **MD:** Laszlo Farkas (HUN)/Bar-Hen Moshe (ISR) d. Genadi Kohanov/Andre Trantz (ISR) 64 60.

- **TROFEO DELLA MOLE** (ITA) (CS4) ($7,000) 2-6 JUNE – **MS:** Kai Schrameyer (GER) d. Daniel Pellegrina (SUI) 60 60. **MD:** Alberto Corradi (ITA)/Kai Schrameyer (GER) d. Mario Gatelli (ITA)/Daniel Pellegrina (SUI) 62 63.

- **9TH ANTIBES OPEN (FRA)** (CS5) ($1,500) 3-6 JUNE – **WS:** Arlette Racineux (FRA) d. Armelle Fabre (FRA) 64 62. **WD:** Christine Gontard/Arlette Racineux (FRA) d. Armelle Fabre/Christine Gardeau (FRA) 57 63 63. **MS:** Stefane Goudou (FRA) d. Francois Xavier Morille (FRA) 61 63. **MD:** Bernard Fasanelli/Laurent Giammartini (FRA) d. Stefane Goudou/Francois Xavier Morille (FRA) 16 63 62.

- **BIRKESDORF OPEN** (GER) (CS5) ($3,000) 4-6 JUNE – **WS:** Dorrie Timmermans Van Hall (NED) d. Mette Van Dongen (NED). **MS:** Steffen Sommerfeld (GER) d. Sven Hiller (GER) 62 62.

- **KPM CONSULT CZECH OPEN** (CZE) (CS2) ($15,000) 9-13 JUNE – **WS:** Jiske Griffioen (NED) d. Florence Gravellier (FRA) 75 61. **MS:** Robin Ammerlaan (NED) d. Peter Wikstrom (SWE) 63 62. **MD:** Robin Ammerlaan (NED)/Peter Wikstrom (SWE) d. Miroslav Brychta (CZE)/Martin Legner (AUT) 63 62.

- **FARWEST REGIONAL CHAMPIONSHIPS** (USA) (CS2) ($10,000) 10-13 JUNE – **WS:** Sharon Walraven (NED) d. Chiyoko Ohmae (JPN) 64 75. **MS:** Stephen Welch (USA) d. Jon Rydberg (USA) 62 62. **MD:** John Greer/Stephen Welch (USA) d. Richard Julian/Jon Rydberg (USA) 64 63. **QS:** Sarah Hunter (CAN) d. Brian Mcphate (CAN) 60 64.

- **CARINTHIAN OPEN** (AUT) (CS4) ($2,000) 10-13 JUNE – **MS:** Laszlo Farkas (HUN) d. Herbert Baumgartner (AUT) 75 46 75. **MD:** Manfred Sing (GER)/Karl Stefan (AUT) d. Laszlo Farkas/Csaba Prohaszka (HUN) 62 16 64.

- **TOURNOI HANDISPORT DE CAGNES SUR MER** (FRA) (CS5) ($1,500) 11-13 JUNE – **WS:** Armelle Fabre (FRA) d. Christine Gontard (FRA) 63 62. **MS:** Michael Jeremiasz (FRA) d. Frederic Cazeaudumec (FRA) 64 62. **MD:** Michael Jeremiasz/Denis Lechaplain (FRA) d. Frederic Cazeaudumec/Bernard Fasanelli (FRA) 62 46 61.

- **MUSIC CITY CLASSIC** (USA) (CS3) ($5,000) 11-13 JUNE – **MS:** Derek Bolton (USA) d. Larry Quintero (USA) 36 62 63. **MD:** Derek Bolton/Daniel Lachman (USA) d. Lahcen Majdi (FRA)/Larry Quintero (USA) 64 76(3). **QS:** David Jordan (USA) d. Troy Weise (USA) 62 63.

- **SARREGUEMINES HANDISPORT OPEN** (FRA) (CS4) 16-20 JUNE – **WS:** Armelle Fabre (FRA) d. Arlette Racineux (FRA) 63 63. **WD:** Muriel Ellissalde/Armelle Fabre (FRA) d. Christine Gontard/Arlette Racineux (FRA) 62 62. **MS:** Maikel Scheffers (NED) d. Frederic Cattaneo (FRA) 61 62. **MD:** Maikel Scheffers (NED)/Ralph Weisang (GER) d. Frederic Cattaneo/Regis Harel (FRA) 46 62 64.

- **SLOVAKIA OPEN** (SVK) (CS2) ($10,000) 17-20 JUNE – **WS:** Britta Siegers (GER) d. Janet Mcmorran (GBR) 46 64 62. **MS:** Robin Ammerlaan (NED) d. Martin Legner (AUT) 63 64. **MD:** Robin Ammerlaan (NED)/Martin Legner (AUT) d. Jozef Felix (SVK)/Tadeusz Kruszelnicki (POL) 62 61.

- **CANADIAN OPEN** (CAN) (CS2) ($11,500) 17-20 JUNE – **WS:** Sharon Walraven (NED) d. Sharon Clark (USA) 62 62. **MS:** Stephen Welch (USA) d. Jon Rydberg (USA) 64 61. **MD:** John Greer/Stephen Welch (USA) d. Lahcen Majdi (FRA)/Jon Rydberg (USA) 64 76 62. **QS:** Nicholas Taylor (USA) d. Sarah Hunter (CAN) 36 63 64.

- **MARTIGNY INDOOR** (SUI) (CS5) 18-20 JUNE – **MS:** Martin Erni (SUI) d. Konstantin Schmaeh (SUI) 64 64. **MD:** Martin Erni/Daniel Pellegrina (SUI) d. Pascal Chessel (FRA)/Konstantin Schmaeh (SUI) 60 60.

- **ORLEN POLISH OPEN** (POL) (CS2) ($12,000) 22-26 JUNE – **WS:** Britta Siegers (GER) d. Florence Gravellier (FRA) 16 64 64. **WD:** Florence Gravellier (FRA)/Britta Siegers (GER) d. Kimberly Blake/Janet Mcmorran (GBR) 64 60. **MS:** Tadeusz Kruszelnicki (POL) d. Martin Legner (AUT) 67(5) 75 60. **MD:** Tadeusz Kruszelnicki (POL)/Martin Legner (AUT) d. Miroslav Brychta (CZE)/Piotr Jaroszewski (POL) 61 61.

- **KIWANIS AMSTERDAM OPEN** (NED) (CS3) ($6,000) 24-27 JUNE – **WS:** Jiske Griffioen (NED) d. Maaike Smit (NED) 62 64. **MS:** Robin Ammerlaan (NED) d. Eric Stuurman (NED) 57 60 62.

- **CAPITAL CITY CLASSIC** (CAN) (CS4) 25-27 JUNE – **MS:** Colin Mckeage (CAN) d. John Greer (USA) 60 63. **MD:** Yan Mathieu/Frank Peter (CAN) d. Claude Brunet/Jeff Mcbride (CAN) 75 64.

- **FRENCH OPEN FIAT** (FRA) (CS1) ($16,000) 29 JUNE-4 JULY – **WS:** Sonja Peters (NED) d. Mie Yaosa (JPN) 36 63 76(1). **WD:** Britta Siegers (GER)/Mie Yaosa (JPN) d. Sonja Peters/Sharon Walraven (NED) 64 63. **MS:** David Hall (AUS) d. Michael Jeremiasz (FRA) 64 64. **MD:** David Hall (AUS)/Michael Jeremiasz (FRA) d. Maikel Scheffers/Ronald Vink (NED) 62 61. **QS:** Guiseppe Polidori (ITA) d. Bas Van Erp (NED) 63 64.

- **DAIMLERCHRYSLER AT-RISK OPEN** (NED) (CS4) ($8,000) 1-4 JULY – **WS:** Esther Vergeer (NED) d. Brigitte Ameryckx (BEL) 60 60. **WD:** Willemien Smits/Esther Vergeer (NED) d. Anna Alenas (SWE)/Katharina Kruger (GER) w/o. **MS:** Robin Ammerlaan (NED) d. Eric Stuurman (NED) 60 46 61. **MD:** Stefan Olsson (SWE)/Eric Stuurman (NED) d. Robin Ammerlaan/Piet Hermans (NED) 64 64.

- **BIRRHARD OPEN** (SUI) (CS4) ($3,000) 2-4 JULY – **WS:** Yuka Chokyu (CAN) d. Chiyoko Ohmae (JPN) 63 36 64. **MS:** Miroslav Brychta (CZE) d. Ralph Weisang (GER) 36 64 62. **MD:** Miroslav Brychta (CZE)/Stefan Krieghofer (AUT) d. Thomas Suter (SUI)/Ralph Weisang (GER) 62 61.

NEC Wheelchair Tennis Tour 2004 Results (continued)

- **DUTCH OPEN** (NED) (CS1) ($15,000) 6-11 JULY – **WS:** Esther Vergeer (NED) d. Sonja Peters (NED) 62 60. **WD:** Maaike Smit/Esther Vergeer (NED) d. Sonja Peters/Sharon Walraven (NED) 63 63. **MS:** Robin Ammerlaan (NED) d. David Hall (AUS) 63 63. **MD:** Satoshi Saida (JPN)/Stephen Welch (USA) d. Maikel Scheffers/Ronald Vink (NED) 64 63. **QS:** David Wagner (USA) d. Bas Van Erp (NED) 26 64 62. **QD:** Mark Eccleston (GBR)/David Wagner (USA) d. Roy Humphreys (GBR)/Shraga Weinberg (ISR) 61 63.

- **BELGIAN OPEN** (BEL) (CS2) ($15,000) 13-18 JULY – **WS:** Esther Vergeer (NED) d. Daniela Di Toro (AUS) 60 64. **WD:** Korie Homan/Esther Vergeer (NED) d. Sharon Clark/Kaitlyn Verfuerth (USA) 64 62. **MS:** David Hall (AUS) d. Satoshi Saida (JPN) 63 62. **MD:** Michael Jeremiasz/Lahcen Majdi (FRA) d. Tadeusz Kruszelnicki (POL)/Satoshi Saida (JPN) 26 64 75. **QS:** David Wagner (USA) d. Bas Van Erp (NED) 64 63.

- **BAVARIAN OPEN** (GER) (CS3) ($10,000) 15-18 JULY – **WS:** Sharon Walraven (NED) d. Britta Siegers (GER) 46 75 75. **MS:** Stephen Welch (USA) d. Martin Legner (AUT) 62 61. **MD:** Miroslav Brychta (CZE)/Martin Legner (AUT) d. Leonid Shevchik (RUS)/Stephen Welch (USA) 75 62.

- **BC CHAMPIONSHIPS** (CAN) (CS5) 16-18 JULY – **MS:** Colin Mckeage (CAN) d. Robinson Mendez (CHI) 75 75. **MD:** Tony Anderson (USA)/Phillip Rowe (CAN) d. Paul Johnson/Yan Mathieu (CAN) 62 62.

- **BRITISH OPEN** (GBR) (SS) ($12,000) 20-25 JULY – **WS:** Esther Vergeer (NED) d. Daniela Di Toro (AUS) 62 60. **WD:** Maaike Smit/Esther Vergeer (NED) d. Daniela Di Toro (AUS)/Britta Siegers (GER) 36 60 62. **MS:** David Hall (AUS) d. Michael Jeremiasz (FRA) 63 62. **MD:** Michael Jeremiasz (FRA)/Martin Legner (AUT) d. Jon Rydberg (USA)/Satoshi Saida (JPN) 62 36 75. **QS:** Bas Van Erp (NED) d. David Wagner (USA) 64 63. **QD:** Nicholas Taylor/David Wagner (USA) d. Bas Van Erp/Monique De Beer (NED) 67(4) 75 63.

- **MIDWEST REGIONAL CHAMPIONSHIPS** (USA) (CS3) ($7,000) 23-25 JULY – **WS:** Karin Korb (USA) d. Beth Arnoult (USA) 63 46 61. **MS:** Derek Bolton (USA) d. Frederic Cazeaudumec (FRA) 57 61 62. **MD:** Derek Bolton/Larry Quintero (USA) d. Frederic Cazeaudumec/Stefane Goudou (FRA) 75 64. **QS:** Chris Studwell (USA) d. David Jordan (USA) 61 62.

- **ROGERS AT&T OPEN AT STANLEY PARK** (CAN) (CS4) ($1,700) 23-25 JULY – **MS:** Colin Mckeage (CAN) d. Robinson Mendez (CHI) 61 62. **MD:** Tony Anderson (USA)/Phillip Rowe (CAN) d. Paul Johnson/Yan Mathieu (CAN) 64 46 63.

- **AUSTRIAN OPEN** (AUT) (CS1) ($15,000) 28 JULY-1 AUGUST – **WS:** Daniela Di Toro (AUS) d. Sharon Walraven (NED) 61 61. **MS:** Robin Ammerlaan (NED) d. Stephen Welch (USA) 62 61. **MD:** Martin Legner (AUT)/Stephen Welch (USA) d. Robin Ammerlaan/Ronald Vink (NED) 46 60 62.

- **BC INTERNATIONAL TENNIS FESTIVAL** (CAN) (CS4) ($1,000) 30 JULY-1 AUGUST – **MS:** Colin Mckeage (CAN) d. Tony Anderson (USA) 63 61. **MD:** Tony Anderson (USA)/Phillip Rowe (CAN) d. Jerome Bouvier/Colin Mckeage (CAN) 64 64.

- **SWISS OPEN** (SUI) (CS1) ($16,000) 3-8 AUGUST – **WS:** Esther Vergeer (NED) d. Florence Gravellier (FRA) 63 16 60. **WD:** Maaike Smit/Esther Vergeer (NED) d. Sandra Kalt/Karin Suter-Erath (SUI) 62 63. **MS:** Stephen Welch (USA) d. Michael Jeremiasz (FRA) 36 64 75. **MD:** Martin Legner (AUT)/Stephen Welch (USA) d. Eric Stuurman/Ronald Vink (NED) 26 60 62. **QS:** Nicholas Taylor (USA) d. David Wagner (USA) 64 76.

- **FLANDERS OPEN** (BEL) (CS3) ($7,500) 11-15 AUGUST – **WS:** Sharon Walraven (NED) d. Brigitte Ameryckx (BEL) 62 36 64. **WD:** Willemien Smits/Sharon Walraven (NED) d. Brigitte Ameryckx (BEL)/Monique De Beer (NED) 76 76. **MS:** Robin Ammerlaan (NED) d. Eric Stuurman (NED) 60 60. **MD:** Robin Ammerlaan/Eric Stuurman (NED) d. Anthony Bonaccurso (AUS)/Gert Vos (BEL) 61 63.

- **SSZ CUP** (CZE) (CS4) ($2,000) 13-15 AUGUST – **MS:** Miroslav Brychta (CZE) d. Laszlo Farkas (HUN) 61 63. **MD:** Miroslav Brychta/Michal Stefanu (CZE) d. Laszlo Farkas/Csaba Prohaszka (HUN) 64 64.

- **WROCLAW CUP** (POL) (CS4) ($5,000) 13-15 AUGUST – **WS:** Agnieszka Bartczak (POL) d. Lucyna Skorupinska (POL) 61 63. **MS:** Tadeusz Kruszelnicki (POL) d. Piotr Jaroszewski (POL) 60 64. **MD:** Piotr Jaroszewski/Tadeusz Kruszelnicki (POL) d. Albin Batycki/Jerzy Kulik (POL) 60 61.

- **NATIONS CAPITAL CHAMPIONSHIPS** (USA) (CS3) ($8,000) 20-22 AUGUST – **MS:** Derek Bolton (USA) d. Jon Rydberg (USA) 63 64. **MD:** Larry Quintero/Jon Rydberg (USA) d. Mauricio Pomme/Carlos Santos (BRA) 61 62.

- **SALZBURG OPEN** (AUT) (CS3) ($9,000) 26-29 AUGUST – **WS:** Karin Suter-Erath (SUI) d. Sandra Kalt (SUI) 62 75. **MS:** Martin Legner (AUT) d. Miroslav Brychta (CZE) 60 61. **MD:** Miroslav Brychta/Michal Stefanu (CZE) d. Herbert Baumgartner/Martin Legner (AUT) 64 62.

- **KANAGAWA OPEN** (JPN) (CS4) ($2,000) 26-29 AUGUST – **WS:** Yuko Okabe (JPN) d. Naomi Ishimoto (JPN) 61 ret. **WD:** Kanako Domori/Rieko Iida (JPN) d. Naomi Ishimoto/Yuko Okabe (JPN) w/o. **MS:** Ryoichi To (JPN) d. Hidekazu Nakano (JPN) 63 62. **MD:** Yoshiteru Hoshi/Toshiaki Yaosa (JPN) d. Hidekazu Nakano/Ryoichi To (JPN) 64 76(3). **QS:** Hiroshi Toma (JPN) d. Masao Takashima (JPN) 64 62.

- **ATH OPEN** (BEL) (CS3) ($7,500) 26-29 AUGUST – **WS:** Brigitte Ameryckx (BEL) d. Lola Ochoa (ESP) 61 63. **WD:** Brigitte Ameryckx/Nadege Carlier (BEL) d. Katharina Kruger (GER)/Slen Plas (BEL) 60 63. **MS:** Frederic Cazeaudumec (FRA) d. Anthony Bonaccurso (AUS) 62 61. **MD:** Frederic Cazeaudumec/Stefane Goudou (FRA) d. Anthony Bonaccurso (AUS)/Bernard Fasanelli (FRA) w/o.

- **PELLIKAAN WHEELS TOURNAMENT** (NED) (CS4) ($3,350) 27-29 AUGUST – **WS:** Aniek Van Koot (NED) d. Dorrie Timmermans van Hall (NED) 63 75. **MS:** Maikel Scheffers (NED) d. Ronald Vink (NED) 26 64 75. **MD:** Maikel Scheffers/Ronald Vink (NED) d. Berry Korst/Riens Raaij (NED) 60 61.

- **PACIFIC NORTHWEST SECTIONAL CHAMPS** (USA) (CS5) 27-29 AUGUST – **MS:** Phillip Rowe (CAN) d. Tony Anderson (USA) 46 61 64. **MD:** Tony Anderson (USA)/Phillip Rowe (CAN) d. R. Corbett/G. Proctor (USA) 63 63.

- **MALAYSIAN OPEN** (MAS) (CS4) ($5,000) 30 AUGUST-1 SEPTEMBER – **WS:** Mette Van Dongen (NED) d. Norisah Bahrom (MAS) 36 64 62. **WD:** Norisah Bahrom/Hamidah Hassan (MAS) d. Rosalie Turnbull (AUS)/Mette Van Dongen (NED) 62 61. **MS:** Lee Hinson (USA) d. Suwitchai Merngprom (THA) 26 62 63. **MD:** Suthi Khlongrua/Suwitchai Merngprom (THA) d. Warren Boggs (AUS)/Lee Hinson (USA) 60 61.

- **CITTA DI LIVORNO – O.S.D TROPHY** (ITA) (CS1) ($13,000) 31 AUGUST-5 SEPTEMBER – **WS:** Esther Vergeer (NED) d. Sharon Walraven (NED) 64 62. **WD:** Maaike Smit/Esther Vergeer (NED) d. Sonja Peters/Sharon Walraven (NED) 61 61. **MS:** Robin Ammerlaan (NED) d. Michael Jeremiasz (FRA) 36 61 64. **MD:** Michael Jeremiasz (FRA)/Jayant Mistry (GBR) d. Robin Ammerlaan/Eric Stuurman (NED) 63 61. **QS:** Guiseppe Polidori (ITA) d. Bas Van Erp (NED) 46 60 76(5).

- **SINGAPORE OPEN** (SIN) (CS4) ($3,000) 3-5 SEPTEMBER – **WS:** Norisah Bahrom (MAS) d. Miew Kuan Chung (SIN) 60 61. **MS:** Suwitchai Merngprom (THA) d. Suthi Khlongrua (THA) 62 63. **MD:** Suthi Khlongrua/Suwitchai Merngprom (THA) d. Lee Hinson (USA)/Zulkifli Mohammed-Ali (MAS) w/o.

- **JESOLO EURO BEACH CUP** (ITA) (CS2) ($13,000) 7-11 SEPTEMBER – **WS:** Korie Homan (NED) d. Daniela Di Toro (AUS) 62 63. **MS:** Martin Legner (AUT) d. Miroslav Brychta (CZE) 61 63. **MD:** Miroslav Brychta (CZE)/Martin Legner (AUT) d. Anthony Bonaccurso/Ben Weekes (AUS) 61 63.

- **SOUTHWEST REGIONAL CHAMPIONSHIPS** (USA) (CS3) ($1,800) 9-12 SEPTEMBER – **MS:** Derek Bolton (USA) d. Paul Walker (USA) 62 62.

- **SOUTH PACIFIC WHEELCHAIR TENNIS OPEN** (AUS) (CS5) ($3,000) 10-12 SEPTEMBER – **MS:** Lee Hinson (USA) d. Michael Esler (AUS) 61 76. **MD:** Errol Hyde/Chris Smith (AUS) d. Michael Esler/Jerry Markoja (AUS) 62 61.

- **SENDAI OPEN** (JPN) (CS4) 17-20 SEPTEMBER – **WS:** Yuko Okabe (JPN) d. Kanako Domori (JPN) 76 64. **WD:** Naomi Ishimoto/Norie Kawashima (JPN) d. Kanako Domori/Yuko Okabe (JPN) 63 67(6) 64. **MS:** Kazutaka Katou (JPN) d. Toshiaki Yaosa (JPN) 46 64 62. **MD:** Kazutaka Katou/Takashi Tsumagari (JPN) d. Kenichi Okawa/Yoshitaka Sano (JPN) 63 62.

- **ATHENS PARALYMPIC GAMES** (GRE) (CS1) 17-26 SEPTEMBER – **WS:** Esther Vergeer (NED) d. Sonja Peters (NED) 62 60. **WD:** Maaike Smit/Esther Vergeer (NED) d. Sakhorn Khanthasit/Ratana Techamaneewat (THA) 60 64. **MS:** Robin Ammerlaan (NED) d. David Hall (AUS) 62 61. **MD:** Shingo Kunieda/Satoshi Saida (JPN) d. Michael Jeremiasz/Lahcen Majdi (FRA) 61 62. **QS:** Peter Norfolk (GBR) d. David Wagner (USA) 63 62. **QD:** Nicholas Taylor/David Wagner (USA) d. Mark Eccleston/Peter Norfolk (GBR) 64 61.

- **ARAG GERMAN OPEN** (GER) (CS3) ($7,500) 22-26 SEPTEMBER – **WS:** Aniek Van Koot (NED) d. Dorrie Timmermans van Hall (NED) 62 60. **MS:** Frederic Cattaneo (FRA) d. Steffen Sommerfeld (GER) 75 61. **MD:** Steffen Sommerfeld/Ralph Weisang (GER) d. Sebastien Husser/Francois Xavier Morille (FRA) 61 64.

- **PTR/ROHO CHAMPIONSHIPS** (USA) (CS1) ($15,000) 22-26 SEPTEMBER – **WS:** Brigitte Ameryckx (BEL) d. Sarah Casteel (USA) 62 61. **MS:** Frederic Cazeaudumec (FRA) d. Maikel Scheffers (NED) 60 36 60. **MD:** Maikel Scheffers/Ronald Vink (NED) d. Frederic Cazeaudumec/Stefane Goudou (FRA) w/o. **QS:** Bryan Barten (USA) d. David Jordan (USA) 75 26 63. **QD:** Bryan Barten/Eric Daniels (USA) d. David Jordan/Marc Mclean (USA) 76(3) 63.

NEC Wheelchair Tennis Tour 2004 Results (continued)

- **OSAKA OPEN** (JPN) (CS4) ($2,000) 23-26 SEPTEMBER – **WS:** Yuko Okabe (JPN) d. Kanako Domori (JPN) 61 46 64. **WD:** Yuko Okabe/Ritsuko Sakamoto (JPN) d. Chie Ito/Keiko Nitta (JPN) 60 60. **MS:** Yoshinobu Fujimoto (JPN) d. Toshiaki Yaosa (JPN) 64 26 64. **MD:** Shinichi Nakamuta/Hiroyuki Takeda (JPN) d. Yoshinobu Fujimoto/Masaaki Taga (JPN) 16 64 76(3). **QS:** Shinsei Uchida (JPN) d. Kazumi Ohashi (JPN) 61 61. **QD:** Ryuji Kakinokihara/Sadahiro Kimura (JPN) d. Kazumi Ohashi/Shinsei Uchida (JPN) 64 63.

- **TAHOE DONNER INTERNATIONAL CHAMPIONSHIPS** (USA) (CS3) ($7,000) 7-10 OCTOBER – **MS:** Anthony Bonaccurso (AUS) d. Robinson Mendez (CHI) 62 60. **MD:** Anthony Bonaccurso (AUS)/Richard Julian (USA) d. Kriss Burwell/Mark Shepherd (USA) 61 60.

- **ATLANTA WHEELCHAIR TENNIS MASTERS SERIES** (USA) (CS2) ($50,000) 7-10 OCTOBER – **MS:** David Hall (AUS) d. Robin Ammerlaan (NED) 61 61. **MD:** Michael Jeremiasz (FRA)/Jayant Mistry (GBR) d. Robin Ammerlaan (NED)/David Hall (AUS) 76(9) 63. **QS:** David Wagner (USA) d. Peter Norfolk (GBR) 76(2) 76(3).

- **QUICKIE US OPEN** (USA) (SS) ($20,000) 12-17 OCTOBER – **WS:** Maaike Smit (NED) d. Daniela Di Toro (AUS) 75 26 75. **WD:** Jiske Griffioen/Maaike Smit (NED) d. Korie Homan/Sonja Peters (NED) 63 62. **MS:** David Hall (AUS) d. Robin Ammerlaan (NED) 63 36 61. **MD:** Robin Ammerlaan (NED)/David Hall (AUS) d. Michael Jeremiasz (FRA)/Jayant Mistry (GBR) 62 76(4). **QS:** Peter Norfolk (GBR) d. David Wagner (USA) 75 63. **QD:** Nicholas Taylor/David Wagner (USA) d. Peter Norfolk (GBR)/Sarah Hunter (CAN) 63 63.

- **OPEN DE GRENOBLE-LA TRONCHE** (FRA) (CS4) ($5,000) 14-17 OCTOBER – **WS:** Florence Gravellier (FRA) d. Katharina Kruger (GER) 62 60. **WD:** Muriel Ellisalde/Florence Gravellier (FRA) d. Christine Gontard/Arlette Racineux (FRA) 63 60. **MS:** Lahcen Majdi (FRA) d. Frederic Cazeaudumec (FRA) 63 76. **MD:** Frederic Cazeaudumec/Lahcen Majdi (FRA) d. Frederic Cattaneo/Stefane Goudou (FRA) 64 46 63.

- **VICTORIAN WHEELCHAIR OPEN** (AUS) (CS5) 16-17 OCTOBER – **MS:** Michael Esler (AUS) d. Justin Pryor (AUS) 64 62. **MD:** Errol Hyde/Justin Pryor (AUS) d. Ben Baker/Michael Esler (AUS) 62 62.

- **CAMOZZI WHEELCHAIR TENNIS DOUBLES MASTERS** (ITA) (CS1) ($40,000) 19-24 OCTOBER – **WD:** Jiske Griffioen/Korie Homan (NED) d. Brigitte Ameryckx (BEL)/Sharon Walraven (NED) 64 62. **MD:** Martin Legner (AUT)/Satoshi Saida (JPN) d. Michael Jeremiasz (FRA)/Jayant Mistry (GBR) 61 36 63. **QD:** Peter Norfolk (GBR)/Sarah Hunter (CAN) d. Guiseppe Polidori/Antonio Raffaele (ITA) 61 63.

- **PEACE CUP** (JPN) (CS3) ($4,000) 20-24 OCTOBER – **WS:** Mie Yaosa (JPN) d. Chiyoko Ohmae (JPN) 60 61. **WD:** Chiyoko Ohmae/Mie Yaosa (JPN) d. Kanako Domori (JPN)/Ju-Youn Park (KOR) 62 61. **MS:** Ha-Gel Lee (KOR) d. Kazutaka Katou (JPN) 62 60. **MD:** Ha-Gel Lee/Sang-Ho Oh (KOR) d. Yoshinobu Fujimoto/Masaaki Taga (JPN) 63 61. **QS:** Tzu-Hsuan Huang (TPE) d. Hiroshi Toma (JPN) 62 46 62. **QD:** Sadahiro Kimura/Hiroshi Toma (JPN) d. Kazumi Ohashi/Shinsei Uchida (JPN) w/o.

- **ESPORTA CARDIFF** (GBR) (CS5) 21-24 OCTOBER – **MS:** Matthew Faucher (GBR) d. James Robinson (GBR) 36 75 62. **MD:** Kevin Plowman/James Robinson (GBR) d. John Lambert/Keith Whiley (GBR) 61 61.

- **TOURNOI DE MONTFERMEIL** (FRA) (CS5) ($2,000) 22-24 OCTOBER – **WS:** Arlette Racineux (FRA) d. Muriel Ellisalde (FRA) 61 75. **WD:** Christine Gontard/Arlette Racineux (FRA) d. Muriel Ellisalde/Christine Schoenn-Anchling (FRA) 62 26 76. **MS:** Frederic Cattaneo (FRA) d. Francois Xavier Morille (FRA) 64 61. **MD:** Frederic Cattaneo/Regis Harel (FRA) d. Serge Biron/Pierre Fusade (FRA) 61 64.

- **KOREA CUP** (KOR) (CS4) ($2,000) 26-28 OCTOBER – **WS:** Young-Suk Hong (KOR) d. Myung-Hee Hwang (KOR) 64 61. **WD:** Young-Suk Hong/Myung-Hee Hwang (KOR) d. Young-Shil Cho/Ju-Youn Park (KOR) 61 61. **MS:** Ha-Gel Lee (KOR) d. Dong-Ju Kwak (KOR) 60 62. **MD:** Dong-Ju Kwak/Ha-Gel Lee (KOR) d. Gi-Hyun Kim/Ki-Chan Song (KOR) 63 64.

- **NEC WHEELCHAIR TENNIS MASTERS** (NED) (CS1) ($40,000) 26-31 OCTOBER – **WS:** Esther Vergeer (NED) d. Jiske Griffioen (NED) 62 60. **MS:** David Hall (AUS) d. Michael Jeremiasz (FRA) 62 64. **QS:** David Wagner (USA) d. Bas Van Erp (NED) 63 62.

- **CIS MARIN INDOOR** (SUI) (CS5) ($1,000) 29-31 OCTOBER – **MS:** Jozef Felix (SVK) d. Laurent Fischer (FRA) 64 60. **MD:** Laurent Fischer/Sebastien Husser (FRA) d. Martin Erni/Daniel Pellegrina (SUI) 62 46 63.

- **NOTTINGHAM INDOOR TOURNAMENT** (GBR) (CS2) ($6,000) 4-7 NOVEMBER – **WS:** Kay Forshaw (GBR) d. Aniek Van Koot (NED) 63 63. **WD:** Kay Forshaw (GBR)/Aniek Van Koot (NED) d. Kimberly Blake (GBR)/Armelle Fabre (FRA) 63 63. **MS:** Michael Jeremiasz (FRA) d. Jayant Mistry (GBR) 63 75. **MD:** Michael Jeremiasz (FRA)/Jayant Mistry (GBR) d. Lahcen Majdi (FRA)/James Robinson (GBR) 61 63. **QS:** Mark Eccleston (GBR) d. Roy Humphreys (GBR) 60 61.

- **NSW WHEELCHAIR TENNIS OPEN** (AUS) (CS5) ($2,300) 5-7 NOVEMBER – **MS:** Ben Weekes (AUS) d. Mick Connell (AUS) 57 64 62. **MD:** Mick Connell (AUS)/Lee Hinson (USA) d. Justin Pryor/Ben Weekes (AUS) 62 61.

- **HUNGARIAN OPEN** (HUN) (CS3) ($5,000) 24-27 NOVEMBER – **MS:** Tadeusz Kruszelnicki (POL) d. Jozef Felix (SVK) 61 63. **MD:** Jozef Felix (SVK)/Tadeusz Kruszelnicki (POL) d. Miroslav Brychta/Michal Stefanu (CZE) 60 63.

- **LA CLASSIQUE INTERNATIONALE OPHQ** (CAN) (CS3) ($10,000) 2-5 DECEMBER – **WS:** Florence Gravellier (FRA) d. Armelle Fabre (FRA) 64 63. **MS:** Frederic Cazeaudumec (FRA) d. Stefane Goudou (FRA) 61 61. **MD:** Frederic Cazeaudumec/Lahcen Majdi (FRA) d. Derek Bolton (USA)/Stefane Goudou (FRA) 62 76(2). **QS:** Sergio Garcia (MEX) d. Patrick Sappino (FRA) 57 75 63.

- **PRAGUECUP CZECH INDOOR** (CZE) (CS3) ($6,000) 2-5 DECEMBER – **WS:** Sandra Kalt (SUI) d. Brigitte Ameryckx (BEL) 63 16 76(4). **WD:** Brigitte Ameryckx (BEL)/Sandra Kalt (SUI) d. Agnieszka Bartczak (POL)/Ludmila Bubnova (RUS) 63 61. **MS:** Tadeusz Kruszelnicki (POL) d. Miroslav Brychta (CZE) 64 61. **MD:** Jozef Felix (SVK)/Tadeusz Kruszelnicki (POL) d. Miroslav Brychta (CZE)/Martin Legner (AUT) 36 64 63.

- **LESZNO CUP** (POL) (CS4) ($4,000) 6-9 DECEMBER – **WS:** Agnieszka Bartczak (POL) d. Ludmila Bubnova (RUS) 62 62. **MS:** Tadeusz Kruszelnicki (POL) d. Jozef Felix (SVK) w/o. **MD:** Jozef Felix (SVK)/Tadeusz Kruszelnicki (POL) d. Albin Batycki/Piotr Jaroszewski (POL) 60 61.

Invacare World Team Cup 2004

Christchurch, New Zealand, 20-25 January 2004

Men's World Group 1 final standings: 1. Netherlands, 2. Poland, 3. USA, 4. Australia, 5. France, 6. Sweden, 7. Japan, 8. Great Britain, 9. Austria, 10. Korea, 11. Czech Republic, 12. Spain, 13. Germany, 14. Brazil, 15. Italy, 16. Switzerland.

Final: Netherlands d. Poland 2-0: Robin Ammerlaan (NED) d. Tadeuz Kruszelnicki (POL) 64 62; Eric Stuurman (NED) d. Piotr Jaroszewski (POL) 61 60.

Men's World Group 2 final standings: 1. Slovak Republic, 2. Argentina, 3. Thailand, 4. Canada, 5. New Zealand, 6. Croatia, 7. Chinese Taipei, 8. Israel, 9. Chile, 10. Malaysia, 11. China, 12. Puerto Rico, 13. Sri Lanka.

Final: Slovak Republic d. Argentina 2-1: Carlos Loza (ARG) d. Marek Gergely (SVK) 76(2) 76(4); Josef Felix (SVK) d. Oscar Diaz (ARG) 76(6) 61; Josef Felix/Marek Gergely (SVK) d. Oscar Diaz/Carlos Loza (ARG) 64 46 76(13).

Women's final standings: 1. Netherlands, 2. Switzerland, 3. Australia, 4. Canada, 5. Japan, 6. New Zealand, 7. Thailand, 8. France, 9. USA, 10. Korea, 11. Malaysia, 12. Great Britain, 13. Spain.

Final: Netherlands d. Switzerland 2-0: Esther Vergeer (NED) d. Karin Suter-Erath (SUI) 61 60; Sonja Peters (NED) d. Sandra Kalt (SUI) 61 62.

Quad's final standings: 1. Israel, 2. Netherlands, 3. Japan, 4. USA, 5. Canada, 6. Italy, 7. Great Britain, 8. New Zealand.

Final: Israel d. Netherlands 2-1: Haim Lev (ISR) d. Monique De Beer (NED) 75 62; Bas Van Erp (NED) d. Shraga Weinberg (ISR) 46 62 76(2); Haim Lev/Shraga Weinberg (ISR) d. Monique De Beer/Bas Van Erp (NED) 57 76(4) 61.

Juniors' final standings: 1. Netherlands, 2. Australia, 3. Belgium, 4. USA, 5. Great Britain.

Final: Netherlands d. Australia 2-0: Korie Homan (NED) d. Michael Esler (AUS) 61 63; Aniek Van Koot (NED) d. Heath Davidson (AUS) 76(4) 62.

ITF Wheelchair Tennis World Rankings 2004

Men's Singles

Rank	Name	Points	Played
1	David Hall (AUS)	2372	16
2	Robin Ammerlaan (NED)	2360	20
3	Michael Jeremiasz (FRA)	1611	21
4	Stephen Welch (USA)	1326	19
5	Martin Legner (AUT)	1246	26
6	Satoshi Saida (JPN)	1027	14
7	Tadeusz Kruszelnicki (POL)	887	22
8	Frederic Cazeaudumec (FRA)	732	22
9	Peter Wikstrom (SWE)	727	12
10	Jayant Mistry (GBR)	717	19

Men's Doubles

Rank	Name	Points	Played
1	Michael Jeremiasz (FRA)	2126	22
2	Martin Legner (AUT)	2039	26
3	Robin Ammerlaan (NED)	1878	19
4	David Hall (AUS)	1804	14
5	Satoshi Saida (JPN)	1778	14
6	Shingo Kunieda (JPN)	1537	10
7	Jayant Mistry (GBR)	1516	15
8	Stephen Welch (USA)	1348	16
9	Ronald Vink (NED)	1189	18
10	Lahcen Majdi (FRA)	1121	25

Women's Singles

Rank	Name	Points	Played
1	Esther Vergeer (NED)	2006	15
2	Daniela di Toro (AUS)	1491	14
3	Sonja Peters (NED)	1315	14
4	Sharon Walraven (NED)	1085	20
5	Maaike Smit (NED)	1034	17
6	Jiske Griffioen (NED)	988	15
7	Florence Gravellier (FRA)	923	19
8	Britta Siegers (GER)	713	18
9	Sakhorn Khanthasit (THA)	702	9
10	Mie Yaosa (JPN)	630	15

Women's Doubles

Rank	Name	Points	Played
1	Esther Vergeer (NED)	1856	14
2	Maaike Smit (NED)	1853	16
3	Sonja Peters (NED)	1199	12
4	Jiske Griffioen (NED)	1153	14
5	Britta Siegers (GER)	1081	12
6	Sharon Walraven (NED)	1078	15
7	Daniela di Toro (AUS)	1013	12
8	Mie Yaosa (JPN)	941	15
9	Karin Suter-Erath (SUI)	940	10
10	Sakhorn Khanthasit (THA)	880	8

Quads Singles

Rank	Name	Points	Played
1	Peter Norfolk (GBR)	1044	7
2	David Wagner (USA)	853	14
3	Bas van Erp (NED)	619	9
4	Nicholas Taylor (USA)	548	11
5	Sarah Hunter (CAN)	526	16
6	Mark Eccleston (GBR)	459	10
7	Monique de Beer (NED)	369	11
8	David Jordan (USA)	303	13
9	Giuseppe Polidori (ITA)	275	4
10	Kevin Whalen (USA)	273	13

Quads Doubles

Rank	Name	Points	Played
1	David Wagner (USA)	974	13
2	Nicholas Taylor (USA)	831	10
3	Peter Norfolk (GBR)	652	6
4	Monique de Beer (NED)	618	9
5	Mark Eccleston (GBR)	613	6
6	Sarah Hunter (CAN)	603	12
7	Roy Humphreys (GBR)	468	9
8	Kevin Whalen (USA)	459	10
9	Bas van Erp (NED)	445	6
10	Bryan Barten (USA)	397	8

Paralympic Results: Athens 2004

Men's Singles
Quarterfinals: R. Ammerlaan (NED) (1) d. S. Saida (JPN) (6) 64 36 76(3); S. Welch (USA) (4) d. M. Legner (AUT) (5) 62 63; M. Jeremiasz (FRA) (3) d. T. Kruszelnicki (POL) (7) 75 61. D. Hall (AUS) (2) d. S. Kunieda (JPN) (8) 62 06 64.
Semifinals: R. Ammerlaan (NED) (1) d. S. Welch (USA) (4) 75 16 64; D. Hall (AUS) (2) d. M. Jeremiasz (FRA) (3) 61 61.
Final (Gold/Silver): R. Ammerlaan (NED) (1) d. D. Hall (AUS) (2) 62 61.
Play-off (Bronze): M. Jeremiasz (FRA) (3) d. S. Welch (USA) (4) 62 64.

Men's Doubles
Quarterfinals: S. Kunieda/S. Saida (JPN) (1) d. S. Hatt/J. Mistry (GBR) (5) 61 61; A. Bonaccurso/D. Hall (AUS) (6) d. J. Greer/S. Welch (USA) (4) 64 63; R. Ammerlaan/E. Stuurman (NED) (3) d. P. Jaroszewski/T. Kruszelnicki (POL) (7) 62 63; M. Jeremiasz/L. Majdi (FRA) (2) d. S. Olsson/P. Wikstrom (SWE) 61 62.
Semifinals: S. Kunieda/S. Saida (JPN) (1) d. A. Bonaccurso/D. Hall (AUS) (6) 46 64 76(6); M. Jeremiasz/L. Majdi (FRA) (2) d. R. Ammerlaan/E. Stuurman (NED) (3) 62 62.
Final (Gold/Silver): S. Kunieda/S. Saida (JPN) (1) d. M. Jeremiasz/L. Majdi (FRA) (2) 61 62.
Play-Off (Bronze): A. Bonaccurso/D. Hall (AUS) (6) d. R. Ammerlaan/E. Stuurman (NED) (3) 64 67(6) 64.

Women's Singles
Quarterfinals: E. Vergeer (NED) (1) d. S. Khanthasit (THA) (8) 63 61; F. Gravellier (FRA) (4) d. S. Kalt (SUI) 62 61; S. Peters (NED) (3) d. B. Siegers (GER) (7) 76(6) 63; D. Di Toro (AUS) (2) d. K. Forshaw (GBR) 76(1) 60.
Semifinals: E. Vergeer (NED) (1) d. F. Gravellier (FRA) (4) 63 61; S. Peters (NED) (3) d. D. Di Toro (AUS) (2) 75 46 63.
Final (Gold/Silver): E. Vergeer (NED) (1) d. S. Peters (NED) (3) 62 60.
Play-off (Bronze): D. Di Toro (AUS) (2) d. F. Gravellier (FRA) (4) 16 62 62.

Women's Doubles
Quarterfinals: M. Smit/E. Vergeer (NED) (1) d. A. Fabre/F. Gravellier (FRA) 62 63; C. Ohmae/M. Yaosa (JPN) (3) d. S. Clark/K. Verfuerth (USA) 75 63; S. Kalt/K. Suter-Erath (SUI) (4) d. Y.Hong/M. Hwang (KOR) 63 62; S. Khanthasit/R. Techamaneewat (THA) d. J. Griffioen/S. Peters (NED) (2) 62 63.
Semifinals: M. Smit/E. Vergeer (NED) (1) d. C. Ohmae/M. Yaosa (JPN) (3) 62 60; S. Khanthasit/R. Techamaneewat (THA) d. S. Kalt/K. Suter-Erath (SUI) (4) 75 60.
Final (Gold/Silver): M. Smit/E. Vergeer (NED) (1) d. S. Khanthasit/R. Techamaneewat (THA) 60 64.
Play-Off (Bronze): S. Kalt/K. Suter-Erath (SUI) (4) d. C. Ohmae/M. Yaosa (JPN) (3) 75 63.

Quad Singles
Quarterfinals: P. Norfolk (GBR) (1) d. S. Hunter (CAN) 63 75; B. Van Erp (NED) (3) d. M. Eccleston (GBR) 61 36 75; N. Taylor (USA) (4) d. M. De Beer (NED) 62 62; D. Wagner (USA) (2) d. S. Weinberg (ISR) 75 57 63.
Semifinals: P. Norfolk (GBR) (1) d. B. Van Erp (NED) (3) 62 63; D. Wagner (USA) (2) d. N. Taylor (USA) (4) 76(4) 75.
Final (Gold/Silver): P. Norfolk (GBR) (1) d. D. Wagner (USA) (2) 63 62.
Play-off (Bronze): B. Van Erp (NED) (3) d. N. Taylor (USA) (4) 64 76(8).

Quad Doubles
Quarterfinals: N. Taylor/D. Wagner (USA) (1) bye; S. Hunter/M. McPhate (CAN) d. M. Takashima/H. Toma (JPN) 63 60; M. De Beer/B. Van Erp (NED) d. G. Polidori/A. Raffaele (ITA) 63 61; M. Eccleston/P. Norfolk (GBR) (2) bye.
Semifinals: N. Taylor/D. Wagner (USA) (1) d. S. Hunter/M. McPhate (CAN) 60 63; M. Eccleston/P. Norfolk (GBR) (2) d. M. De Beer/B. Van Erp (NED) 26 75 61.
Final (Gold/Silver): N. Taylor/D. Wagner (USA) (1) d. M. Eccleston/P. Norfolk (GBR) (2) 64 61.
Play-Off (Bronze): M. De Beer/B. Van Erp (NED) d. S. Hunter/B. McPhate (CAN) 63 61.

the seniors year 2004

by isabelle gemmel and neil robinson

For those not in the know, the age of 35 may signal an end to a tennis career, but for the thousands who take part in the many events which make up the ITF Seniors tennis programme 35 is just the beginning.

A major change occurred for the over 35s in 2004, what had formerly been known as ITF Vets tennis was rebranded ITF Seniors tennis, to keep up with the ever growing international nature of the sport. The Seniors players may be older than their professional counterparts, but the competition for ranking points and World Championship titles is no less fierce.

Antalya, Turkey and Philadelphia, USA played host to the ITF Seniors and Super-Seniors World Team and Individual Championships in 2004 whilst a number of countries made their debuts on the ITF Seniors Circuit.

Following the success in Turkey of the World Team and Individual Championships for the older age categories in 2003, it was the turn of the 35 – 50 age groups to savour the delights of the Turkish Riviera. Club Ali Bey Manavgat, the 56-court venue near Antalya, hosted all eight Cups, the first time all of the team events have been held in one single venue.

An impressive 113 teams, representing 24 nations, participated in the events, which attracted many former professionals and past world champions.

Radovan Cizek (CZE)

The USA proved to be the strongest team in the Suzanne Lenglen Cup, beating the Netherlands 3-0 in the final. In what was the longest final of the Team Championships, the USA sealed victory over Netherlands in the Maria Esther Bueno after a marathon deciding doubles match. The US women added to their tally with victory over France in the Margaret Court Cup and the fourth, and only men's, title for the USA was captured in the Dubler Cup, the American men upsetting the form book by defeating top seeds Germany 3-0.

The wonderful surroundings of the Club Ali Bey Manavgat encouraged many of the team members to stay on to compete in the Seniors World Individual Championships the following week.

Two new names appeared on the rolls of honour for the men's 35 and men's 40 age categories: Sander Groen (NED) and Marcos Gorriz (ESP) picked up the title for their respective events. Mike Fedderly (USA) missed his chance to claim a hat-trick of titles after his success with the Dubler Cup team and a gold medal in the doubles event, when he lost in two close tiebreak sets against his compatriot Val Wilder in the men's 45 final.

There was no surprise in the men's 50 singles as top seed Radovan Cizek (CZE) defended his world crown, defeating Andrew Rae (AUS) in straight sets 63 61.

The two youngest women's age categories saw the seeding respected with wins for Lucie Zelinka (AUT) in the women's 35 singles and former tour player Klaartje Van Baarle (BEL) in the women's 40 singles.

Defending champion Patricia Medrado (BRA) lost her title in the women's 45 to Diane Fishburne (USA) in straight sets and another American created a surprise; unseeded Sherri Bronson proved too strong for Heidi Eisterlehner (GER) to win the women's 50 gold medal.

Various prestigious clubs in Philadelphia on the USA's east coast invited the world's over 55 players to compete in the Super-Seniors World Team and Individual Championships. With hundreds of years of history between them the Philadelphia Cricket Club, the Merion Cricket Club, the Germantown Cricket Club, as well as the smaller Cynwyd Club and Upper Dublin Racquet Club proved fitting venues for the ITF's flagship Super-Seniors events.

Home soil obviously proved helpful for USA as there were popular wins for USA teams in the Queens' Cup, Von Cramm Cup, Britannia Cup, Jack Crawford Cup and Gardnar Mulloy Cup. Two European teams managed to avert total US supremacy in the Men's Cups; Spain and France both scored 2-1 successes over the hosts to win the Austria Cup and Bitsy Grant Cup respectively.

The Althea Gibson and Maureen Connolly Cups will be heading down

Two new names appeared on the rolls of honour for the men's 35 and men's 40 age categories: Sander Groen (NED) and Marcos Gorriz (ESP)

The Italia Cup proved to be the only title that Germany was able to defend out of the five titles won at home the previous year. In one of the most hard fought and exciting finals of this year's Seniors World Team Championships, the Germans needed the final set of the doubles to secure victory over France 2-1.

Spain claimed its first title in the Tony Trabert Cup with a decisive 3-0 win over Austria, whilst Australia captured two of the team titles, overcoming the USA to win the Fred Perry Cup and causing an upset by defeating the German team to win the Young Cup.

Marcos Gorriz (ESP)

the seniors year 2004

by isabelle gemmel and neil robinson

under after Australia defeated the host nation in both finals. But the Aussies were not as successful against European opposition, losing out on the Alice Marble Cup to Great Britain and Kitty Godfree Cup to the French.

The entry numbers for the Super-Seniors World Individual Championships reached an all-time high; a record 720 players competed making it one of the biggest tennis events in history.

Playing at home was, like in the previous week, a great source of inspiration as American players captured 17 of the 24 singles and doubles titles available.

Whilst former professional Tomas Koch (BRA), secured the title for the youngest male players in the men's 55 singles event, Americans Alex Swetka and Fred Kovaleski proved that tennis can be enjoyable and fiercely competitive whatever your age as they won the men's 85 and men's 80 singles respectively.

Jimmy Parker (USA) earned his second world title in the singles, ten years after his first success in Buenos Aires, by fighting back to a 1 6 63 64 victory in the final of the Men's 60 Singles against Bruce Burns (AUS). USA's Jason Morton captured a fourth world title in the men's 75 event and another American, Gene Scott, won the men's 60 singles title in a tightly contested battle, defeating Peter Froelich (AUS) 57 63 63.

History was made at the ITF Super-Seniors World Individual Championships when USA's King and Yvonne Van Nostrand became the first husband and wife to claim singles titles at the same World Championships. Yvonne picked up the women's 70 title against Margaret Robinson (AUS) and then watched her husband win the men's 70 title in straight sets over Atushi Miyagi (JPN).

Heide Orth (GER) was the only player out of nine defending champions who managed to retain her title by beating her doubles partner, USA's Barbara Mueller in the final. It was her seventh World Championship title and her third in a row. Last year's World Champion Janine Lieffrig (RSA) was surpassed in the women's 65 final by Rosie Darmon (FRA). The same fate befell Carol Campling (AUS), who could not withstand the powerful game of first time winner Anne Guerrant (USA) in the women's 55 age category.

Louise Russ added two more titles for USA when she won both singles and doubles titles in the women's 75 category bringing the total US tally to nine singles and eight doubles titles.

While the World Championships are the principal focus of the year for many Seniors players, the ITF Seniors Circuit embraces another 140 events, all offering world ranking points, in over 40 countries on six continents and provides competitive opportunities almost every week of the year.

2004 saw a mixture of players dominating categories and the No.1 spot continuously changing hands, along with two significant events: Austria's Peter Pokorny's 95-match winning streak was ended and Bob Sherman was finally overtaken at the top of the men's 80 ranking.

Peter Adrigan (GER) was the player responsible for breaking Pokorny's run, which stretched back to August 2001. Although Pokorny got his revenge twice later in the year, it was USA's Jimmy Parker who ended up at the top of the men's 60 age category in a desperately close race.

American Sherman, ranked No.1 since December 2000, was thwarted in his attempt to reign in the men's 80s by compatriot Fred Kovaleski. Kovaleski, fresh out of the 75s, captured four Grade 1 titles, along with the World Championship

Klaarte Van Baarle (BEL)

Yvonne and King Van Nostrand (USA)

History was made at the ITF Super-Seniors World Individual Championships when USA's King and Yvonne Van Nostrand became the first husband and wife to claim singles titles at the same World Championships.

to steal the top spot without losing a match all year.

USA's Louise Russ and Alex Swetka were even more impressive; both players five Grade 1 titles to their World title successes to dominate the women's 75 and men's 85 rankings respectively with Russ remaining unbeaten and achieving a sweep of US titles on all four surfaces.

This latter feat was matched by Val Wilder in the men's 45 and Dorothy Matthiessen in the women's 65, resulting in both earning the No.1 ranking in their age category. Wilder's success in Antalya was crucial as Belgium's Pierre Godfroid also collected four Grade 1 titles while fellow American Matthiessen beat off the challenge of Nanda Fischer (GER), who swept three Grade 1 titles in the spring and early summer but had to miss the World Individual Championships through injury. Wilder also won three events in the men's 40 to finish well to the fore in the ranking behind Stefan Fasthoff (GER), whose three Grade 1 titles put him clearly ahead of his nearest rivals

Heide Orth outshone Wilder in this respect by ending the year top of two age categories. The German maintained her stranglehold on the No.1 spot in the women's 60 ranking as she collected three Grade 1 titles to go with her seventh world title, and in the women's 55 she took four Grade 1 titles in Europe to finish No. 1.

A three-way tussle ensued in the women's 50 from which Heidi Eisterlehner (GER), also now eligible for the 55 category, emerged triumphant. Her three Grade 1 victories just kept her ahead of Antalya champion Sherri Bronson and Eugenia Birukova (ITA). Bodo Nitsche's (GER) three Grade 1 titles allowed him to retain his top spot in the men's 65 throughout 2004 despite losing his world title to Gene Scott (USA), who won all three tournaments that he entered.

Mary Boswell (USA) also retained her No.1 spot in the women's 70. Her three Grade 1 titles were enough to overhaul compatriot Yvonne Van Nostrand. Yvonne's husband, King, made an immediate impact in the men's 70. Playing in this category for the first time, he was unbeaten, winning three Grade 1 titles to go with the world champion's crown. USA's Diane Fishburne suffered just one loss all year to ease to the top of the women's 45 list.

In total contrast, world champion Radovan Cizek (CZE) heads the men's 50, solely due to his world final victory over Andrew Rae (AUS), after the pair lifted seven Grade 1 titles between them. An even tighter contest took place in the men's 75; Jason Morton took the honours from Clem Hopp, due largely to winning in Philadelphia, where his fellow American was surprisingly defeated in the quarterfinals.

Italy's Giuseppe Marcora held on to pip his pursuers in the men's 55 ranking, while Nicolas Becerra (ARG) lead the way in the men's 35 in his first year as a senior after seeing off principal rival Hubert Karrasch (CAN) in the final of the last Grade 1 tournament of the year. Natascha Faschingbauer (GER) took the final European Grade 1 event in Mallorca to secure the women's 40 No.1 ranking while Renata Marcinkowska's (USA) consistent play saw her capture the year-end No.1 position in the women's 35 rankings for the consecutive second year.

The 2005 circuit will see further expansion as around 150 events appear on the calendar. Fiji, Sweden and Malta will host their first ITF Seniors tournaments and Belgium and New Zealand re-appear after a brief absence, further emphasizing the worldwide growth of the Seniors game.

Anne Guerront (USA)

24th ITF Seniors World Individual Championships

Antalya, Turkey, 9-16 May 2004

MEN
35 Singles – Final: Sander Groen (NED) d. Hubert Karrasch (CAN) 64 64.
35 Doubles – Final: Hubert Karrasch (CAN)/Pete Peterson (USA) d. Daniel Ahl/Chris Hearn (GBR) 06 64 76(2).
40 Singles – Final: Marcos Gorriz (ESP) d. Herve Bardot (FRA) 63 63.
40 Doubles – Final: Egan Adams/Tom Coulton (USA) d. Glenn Hamilton/Mark Stevens (AUS) 46 63 61.
45 Singles – Final: Val Wilder (USA) d. Mike Fedderly (USA) 76(6) 76(6).
45 Doubles – Final: Mike Fedderly(USA)/Paul Smith (NZL) d. Val Wilder/Van Winitsky (USA) 64 76(3).
50 Singles – Final: Radovan Cizek (CZE) d. Andrew Rae (AUS) 63 61.
50 Doubles – Final: Michael Collins/Andrew Rae (AUS) d. Ray Bray/Michael Phillips (AUS) 63 63.

WOMEN
35 Singles – Final: Lucie Zelinka (AUT) d. Renata Marcinkowska (USA) 64 62.
35 Doubles – Final: Karim Strohmeier (PER)/Lucie Zelinka (AUT) d. Mary Dailey/Renata Marcinkowska (USA) 26 63 64.
40 Singles – Final: Klaartje Van Baarle (BEL) d. Sylvie Mattel (FRA) 64 64.
40 Doubles – Final: Brenda Foster (AUS)/Sylvie Mattel (FRA) d. Mary Dailey/Diane Fishburne (USA) 63 75.
45 Singles – Final: Diane Fishburne (USA) d. Patricia Medrado (BRA) 76(2) 62.
45 Doubles – Final: Susana Villaverde (SUI)/Beatriz Villaverde (ARG) d. Jennifer Cerf/Terry Schweitzer (RSA) 62 61.
50 Singles – Final: Sherri Bronson (USA) d. Heidi Eisterlehner (GER) 75 63.
50 Doubles – Final: Lynette Mortimer/Susanne Walter (AUS) d. Heidi Eisterlehner/Monika Ohlendiek (GER) 67(2) 64 62.

24th ITF Super-Seniors World Individual Championships

Philadelphia, USA, 19-25 September 2004

MEN
55 Singles – Final: Tomas Koch (BRA) d. Bob Litwin (USA) w/o.
55 Doubles – Final: Neal Newman/Larry Turville (USA) d. Brian Marcus/Armistead Neely (USA) 64 75.
60 Singles – Final: Jimmy Parker (USA) d. Bruce Burns (AUS) 16 63 64.
60 Doubles – Final: Peter Adrigan/Hans-Joachim Ploetz (GER) d. Jimmy Parker/Jody Rush (USA) 63 36 75.
65 Singles – Final: Gene Scott (USA) d. Peter Froelich (AUS) 57 63 63.
65 Doubles – Final: Henry Leichtfried/George Sarantos(USA) d. Donald Biedinger/Rudy Hernando (USA) 64 16 61.
70 Singles – Final: King Van Nostrand (USA) d. Atsushi Miyagi (JPN) 60 63.
70 Doubles – Final: Richard Doss/John Powless (USA) d. Charles Devoe/Norman Fitz (USA) 67(6) 63 62.
75 Singles – Final: Jason Morton (USA) d. William Davis (USA) 61 60.
75 Doubles – Final: William Davis/Edward Kauder (USA) d. Morgan Macom/Bob Meyerdierks (USA) 75 63.
80 Singles – Final: Fred Kovaleski (USA) d. Robert Sherman (USA) 61 60.
80 Doubles – Final: Fred Kovaleski/Robert Sherman (USA) d. Jerry Joyce/Bob Seymour (USA) 64 62.
85 Singles – Final: Alex Swetka (USA) d. Federico Barboza (ARG) 61 62.
85 Doubles – Final: Irving Converse/Howard Kuntz (USA) d. Federico Barboza (ARG)/Jose Heighes (PER) 36 64 10(3).

WOMEN
55 Singles – Final: Anne Guerrant (USA) d. Carol Campling (AUS) 62 62.
55 Doubles – Final: Kerry Ballard/Elizabeth Craig-Allan (AUS) d. Carol Campling (AUS)/Frances Taylor (GBR) 63 64.
60 Singles – Final: Heide Orth (GER) d. Barbara Mueller (USA) 46 64 76(3).
60 Doubles – Final: Susan Hill/Jenny Waggott (GBR) d. Charleen Hillebrand/Suella Steel (USA) 62 76(5).
65 Singles – Final: Rosie Darmon (FRA) d. Janine Lieffrig (RSA) 62 62.
65 Doubles – Final: Janine Lieffrig/Audrey Van Coller (RSA) d. Nola Collins/Lesley Heumiller (AUS) 26 60 63.
70 Singles – Final: Yvonne Van Nostrand (USA) d. Margaret Robinson (AUS) 75 64.
70 Doubles – Final: Mary Boswell/Belmar Gunderson (USA) d. Lorice Forbes/Peg Hoysted (AUS) 64 63.
75 Singles – Final: Louise Russ (USA) d. Lucette Moreau(FRA) 63 36 10(8).
75 Doubles – Final: Louise Owen/Louise Russ (USA) d. Amelia Cury (BRA)/Lucette Moreau (FRA) 60 63.

2004 ITF Seniors World Team Championships

Turkey, 3-8 May 2004

- **ITALIA CUP (MEN'S 35) – ANTALYA (TUR); Final: Germany d. France 2-1:** Torben Theine (GER) d. Olivier Cayla (FRA) 75 62; Lionel Barthez (FRA) d. Damir Buljevic (GER) 60 20 ret; Torben Theine/Mathias Huning (GER) d. Lionel Barthez/Olivier Cayla (FRA) 67(5) 64 64.
- **TONY TRABERT CUP (MEN'S 40) – ANTALYA (TUR); Final: Spain d. Austria 3-0:** Miguel Puigdevall (ESP) d. Thomas Sperneder (AUT) 64 62; Marcos Gorriz (ESP) d. Manfred Hundstorfer (AUT) 63 61; Marcos Gorriz/Juan Pallares (ESP) d. Thomas Sperneder/Manfred Hundstorfer (AUT) w/o.
- **DUBLER CUP (MEN'S 45) – ANTALYA (TUR); Final: USA d. Germany 3-0:** Mike Fedderly (USA) d. Norbert Henn (GER) 61 75; Van Winitsky (USA) d. Manfred Jungnitsch (GER) 61 36 76(7); Sal Castillo/Mike Fedderly (USA) d. Manfred Jungnitsch/Norbert Henn (GER) w/o.
- **FRED PERRY CUP (MEN'S 50) – ANTALYA (TUR); Final: Australia d. USA 2-1:** John Peckskamp (USA) d. Michael Collins (AUS) 64 46 63; Andrew Rae (AUS) d. Oliver Scott (USA) 75 60; Michael Collins/Andrew Rae (AUS) d. John Peckskamp/Tom Smith (USA) 61 36 63.
- **SUZANNE LENGLEN CUP (WOMEN'S 35) – ANTALYA (TUR); Final: USA d. Netherlands 3-0:** Jennifer Dawson (USA) d. Eveline Hamers (NED) 61 46 76(7); Renata Marcinkowska (USA) d. Birgit van Ry-Pardoel (NED) 62 63; Christine Sheldon/Hyacinth Yorke (USA) d. Eveline Hamers/Birgit van Ry-Pardol (NED) w/o.
- **YOUNG CUP (WOMEN'S 40) – ANTALYA (TUR); Final: Australia d. Germany 2-1:** Kerrie Douglas (AUS) d. Carola Kintrup (GER) 63 61; Natascha Faschingbauer (GER) d. Brenda Foster (AUS) 61 61; Kerrie Douglas/Brenda Foster (AUS) d. Natascha Faschingbauer/Carola Kintrup (GER) 64 61.
- **MARGARET COURT CUP (WOMEN'S 45) – ANTALYA (TUR); Final: USA d. France 2-1:** Phyllis Zilm (USA) d. Betty Michel (FRA) 64 62; Diane Fishburne (USA) d. Catherine Suire (FRA) 64 75; Benedicte Le Grand/Catherine Suire (FRA) d. Carolyn Nichols/Susan Wright (USA) 61 57 76(5).
- **MARIA ESTHER BUENO CUP (WOMEN'S 50) – ANTALYA (TUR); Final: USA d. Netherlands 2-1:** Sherri Bronson (USA) d. Nora Blom (NED) 57 62 63; Elly Appel (NED) d. Mary Ginnard (USA) 60 36 75; Mary Ginnard/Christy Wing (USA) d. Elly Appel/Elly Krocke (NED) 46 75 63.

2004 ITF Super-Seniors World Team Championships

USA, 13-18 September

- **AUSTRIA CUP (MEN'S 55) – PHILADELPHIA (USA); Final: Spain d. USA 2-1:** Bob Litwin (USA) d. Jorge Camina (ESP) 76(4) 16 63; Jairo Velasco (ESP) d. Brian Cheney (USA) 76(4) 62; Jorge Camina/Jairo Velasco (ESP) d. Dan Bohannon/Peter Bronson (USA) 76(6) 64.
- **VON CRAMM CUP (MEN'S 60) – PHILADELPHIA (USA); Final: USA d. Germany 2-0:** Jody Rush (USA) d. Hans-Joachim Ploetz (GER) 63 63; Jimmy Parker (USA) d. Peter Adrigan (GER) 60 63.
- **BRITANNIA CUP (MEN'S 65) – PHILADELPHIA (USA); Final: USA d. Australia 2-0:** Rudy Hernando (USA) d. Peter Froelich (AUS) 64 62; Gene Scott (USA) d. Bob Howes (AUS) 64 16 61.
- **JACK CRAWFORD CUP (MEN'S 70) – PHILADELPHIA (USA); Final: USA d. Japan 3-0:** Jim Perley (USA) d. Seiki Tokuhiro (JPN) 62 60; King Van Nostrand d. Atsushi Miyagi (JPN) 61 30 ret.; Buddy Lomax/John Powless (USA) d. Kuno Miyagi/Seikei Mori (JPN) 63 62.
- **BITSY GRANT CUP (MEN'S 75) – PHILADELPHIA (USA); Final: France d. USA 2-1:** Jason Morton (USA) d. Edouard Cazetou (FRA) 76(3) 62; Alexandre Hirigoyen (FRA) d. Clem Hopp (USA) 76(5) 36 63; Edouard Cazetou/Alexandre Hirigoyen (FRA) d. Graydon Nichols/Jason Morton (USA) 16 62 64.
- **GARDNAR MULLOY CUP (MEN'S 80) – PHILADELPHIA (USA); Final: USA d. Australia 2-0:** Robert Sherman (USA) d. Frank Pitt (AUS) 75 57 63; Fred Kovaleski (USA) d. Neville Halligan (AUS) 61 61.
- **MAUREEN CONNOLLY CUP (WOMEN'S 55) – PHILADELPHIA (USA); Final: Australia d. USA 2-1:** Elizabeth Craig-Allan (AUS) d. Trish Faulkner (USA) 57 62 61; Anne Guerrant (USA) d. Carol Campling 64 64; Carol Campling/Elizabeth Craig-Allan (AUS) d. Trish Faulkner/Anne Guerrant (USA) 16 62 63.
- **ALICE MARBLE CUP (WOMEN'S 60) – PHILADELPHIA (USA); Final: Great Britain d. Australia 2-1:** Sue Hill (GBR) d. Heather McKay (AUS) 63 46 64; Lynne Nette (AUS) d. Frances Taylor (GBR) 61 76(5); Sue Hill/Frances Taylor (GBR) d. Dawn Martin/Margaret Wayte (AUS) 36 64 63.
- **KITTY GODFREE CUP (WOMEN'S 65) – PHILADELPHIA (USA); Final: France d. Australia 2-1:** Inger Delamare (FRA) d. Leslie Heumiller (AUS) 61 61; Rosie Darmon (FRA) d. Mary Gordon (AUS) 46 76(4) 62.
- **ALTHEA GIBSON CUP (WOMEN'S 70) – PHILADELPHIA (USA); Final: Australia d. USA 2-0:** Ann Fotheringham (AUS) d. Mary Boswell (USA) 75 63; Margaret Robinson (AUS) d. Yvonne Van Nostrand (USA) 63 36 63.
- **QUEENS' CUP (WOMEN'S 75) – PHILADELPHIA (USA); Final: USA d. Great Britain 3-0:** Louise Owen (USA) d. Ann Williams (GBR) 64 62; Louise Russ (USA) d. Betty Howard (GBR) 63 63; Dorothy Knode/Louise Owen (USA) d. Kay Davies/Mary Marsh (GBR) 64 76(3).

ITF Seniors World Rankings 2004

Men's 35

Rank	Name	Points	Played
1	Nicolas Becerra (ARG)	555	7
2	Hubert Karrasch (CAN)	440	7
3	Sean Karam (AUS)	420	3
4	Daniel Ahl (GBR)	400	5
5	Karoly Gyorgy (HUN)	330	3
6	Mark Furness (GBR)	330	4
7	Sandor Groen (NED)	320	2
8	Mario Tabares (USA)	305	3
9	Igor Tsirkun (RUS)	300	7
10	Pete Peterson (USA)	295	6

Men's 40

Rank	Name	Points	Played
1	Stefan Fasthoff (GER)	635	6
2	Marcos Gorriz (ESP)	520	3
3	Val Wilder (USA)	495	4
4	Manfred Hundstorfer (AUT)	450	4
5	Stefan Heckmanns (GER)	410	6
6	Glenn Erickson (USA)	405	5
7	Mark Stevens (AUS)	400	4
8	Alberto Kuhlmann (BRA)	390	4
9	Fernando De Marinis (BRA)	380	7
10	Alexandre Katz (BRA)	380	4

Men's 45

Rank	Name	Points	Played
1	Val Wilder (USA)	790	6
2	Pierre Godfroid (BEL)	720	9
3	Mike Fedderly (USA)	520	6
4	Zdenko Hoppe (CRO)	440	6
5	Roberto Lugones (ARG)	440	5
6	Luiz-Roberto Lobao (BRA)	415	6
7	Franz Schumann (GER)	405	5
8	Stephen Alger (GBR)	380	5
9	Mauricio Daza-Castano (BRA)	380	7
10	Van Winitsky (USA)	370	3

Men's 50

Rank	Name	Points	Played
1	Radovan Cizek (CZE)	790	5
2	Andrew Rae (AUS)	720	10
3	Roger Guedes (BRA)	540	6
4	Jozsef Pazmandi (HUN)	510	10
5	Mike Dawe (GBR)	435	8
6	Lubomir Petrov (BUL)	420	6
7	Roberto Yunis (CHI)	405	9
8	Alan Rasmussen (DEN)	390	3
9	Carlos Boidi (ARG)	380	4
10	Alfred Klammer (AUT)	370	8

Women's 35

Rank	Name	Points	Played
1	Renata Marcinkowska (USA)	460	5
2	Karim Strohmeier (PER)	450	3
3	Natalie Cutcliffe (AUS)	310	4
4	Luciene Muro (BRA)	300	2
5	Jennifer Dawson (USA)	265	4
6	Rene Simpson (CAN)	260	5
7	Isabelle Wild (GBR)	255	6
8	Lucie Zelinka (AUT)	250	1
9	Maria Goni (ARG)	240	2
10	Cristina Rossi (ARG)	210	2

Women's 40

Rank	Name	Points	Played
1	Natascha Faschingbauer (GER)	540	9
2	Barbara Koutna (CZE)	470	7
3	Ingrid Resch-Sommerauer (AUT)	420	4
4	Hana Burda (CZE)	380	3
5	Francesca Ciardi (ITA)	380	3
6	Brenda Foster (AUS)	375	4
7	Heike Frohlich (AUT)	365	8
8	Guillermina Occhipinti (ARG)	360	3
9	Kerrie Douglas (AUS)	350	4
10	Helen Dorricott (AUS)	320	3

Women's 45

Rank	Name	Points	Played
1	Diane Fishburne (USA)	670	5
2	Christine French (GBR)	570	5
3	Vladimira Andersson (SWE)	485	5
4	Gerda Pressing-Sigel (GER)	480	4
5	Julia Smutny (AUT)	470	6
6	Beatriz Villaverde (ARG)	420	4
7	Veronica Lima De Angelis (USA)	395	5
8	Carolyn Nichols (USA)	380	6
9	Patricia Barone (ITA)	370	4
10	Susan Wright (USA)	365	4

Women's 50

Rank	Name	Points	Played
1	Heidi Eisterlehner (GER)	720	5
2	Beatrice Chrystmann (BRA)	660	7
3	Sherri Bronson (USA)	640	7
4	Eugenia Birukova (ITA)	600	9
5	Tina Karwasky (USA)	480	3
6	Katalin Fagyas (HUN)	440	7
7	Paola Brizzi-Knoke (ITA)	405	5
8	Helen Worland (AUS)	400	7
9	Maria Geyer-Pichler (AUT)	390	3
10	Lyn Mortimer (AUS)	355	5

Men's 55

Rank	Name	Points	Played
1	Giuseppe Marcora (ITA)	560	6
2	Bob Litwin (USA)	530	5
3	Jorge Camina Borda (ESP)	495	4
4	Larry Turville (USA)	470	5
5	Terry Payton (AUS)	470	5
6	Vladimir Lacina (CZE)	470	9
7	Tomas Koch (BRA)	430	2
8	Peter Marklstorfer (GER)	420	7
9	Brian Cheney (USA)	410	4
10	Karl Cordin (AUT)	380	7

Women's 55

Rank	Name	Points	Played
1	Heide Orth (GER)	720	6
2	Anne Guerrant (USA)	705	4
3	Alena Klein (GER)	540	14
4	Sylvia Bauwens (GER)	510	8
5	Miriam Borali (ITA)	500	6
6	Sara Kelbert (BRA)	500	4
7	Diane Hill (GBR)	470	5
8	Carol Campling (AUS)	420	3
9	Luise Moser (AUT)	420	
10	Marjory Love (GBR)	380	5

Men's 60

Rank	Name	Points	Played
1	Jimmy Parker (USA)	730	5
2=	Peter Pokorny (AUT)	720	15
2=	Peter Adrigan (GER)	720	7
4	Leland Housman (USA)	440	4
5	Vittorio Monaco (ITA)	440	5
6	Hannes Futterknecht (AUT)	420	6
7	Michael Francis (GBE)	415	6
8	Leo Palacios (ARG)	395	8
9	Jackie Cooper (USA)	390	6
10	Murray French (AUS)	385	4

Women's 60

Rank	Name	Points	Played
1	Heide Orth (GER)	790	6
2	Adelaida Torrens Vallhonrat (ESP)	570	7
3	Renate Schroder (GER)	540	7
4	Frances Taylor (GBR)	540	7
5	Sofia Garaguly (AUT)	540	6
6	Suella Steel (USA)	510	5
7	Michele Bichon (FRA)	480	6
8	Maria Luisa Tinelli (ITA)	480	7
9	Charleen Hillebrand (USA)	450	5
10	Sylvie Galfard-Kirsten (FRA)	440	6

Men's 65

Rank	Name	Points	Played
1	Bodo Nitsche (GER)	720	9
2	Eugene Scott (USA)	620	3
3	Rudy Hernando (USA)	615	6
4	Ilio Santos (BRA)	540	7
5	Klaus-Jurgen Klein (GER)	540	15
6	Peter Froelich (AUS)	480	5
7	Gordon Davis (USA)	480	5
8	Eberhard Madlsperger (AUT)	455	7
9	Donald Shears (GBR)	455	7
10	Peter Kruck (AUT)	455	7

Women's 65

Rank	Name	Points	Played
1	Dorothy Matthiessen (USA)	720	7
2	Nanda Fischer (GER)	660	11
3	Renate Mayer-Zdralek (GER)	615	5
4	Marika Stock (GER)	510	8
5=	Elisabeth Van Bömmel (GER)	450	5
5=	Brigitte Jung (GER)	450	7
7	Rosie Darmon (FRA)	410	3
8	Doris Devries (USA)	360	5
9	Marielle Gallay (FRA)	350	4
10	Barbel Allendorf (GER)	335	7

Men's 70

Rank	Name	Points	Played
1	King Van Nostrand (USA)	790	7
2	Gunter Herrmann (GER)	720	7
3	John Powless (USA)	630	7
4	Hans Jell (AUT)	540	11
5	Dick Crawford (USA)	510	14
6	Lorne Main (CAN)	500	5
7	Buddy Lomax (USA)	480	6
8	Juan-Manuel Ruiz (ARG)	410	4
9	Martial Anais (FRA)	370	11
10	Max Byrne (AUS)	365	5

Women's 70

Rank	Name	Points	Played
1	Mary Boswell (USA)	660	7
2	Yvonne Van Nostrand (USA)	600	5
3	Clelia Mazzoleni (ITA)	570	4
4	Margaret Robinson (AUS)	480	3
5	Ada Cowan (USA)	480	5
6	Ilse Michael (GER)	470	5
7	Nancy Reed (USA)	340	3
8	Cynthia Smith (GBR)	310	6
9	Karin Lange (GER)	275	3
10	Joan Kingsley (USA)	275	4

ITF Seniors World Rankings 2004 (continued)

Men's 75

Rank	Name	Points	Played
1	Jason Morton (USA)	730	8
2	Clem Hopp (USA)	660	8
3	Guido Trevisan (ITA)	570	6
4	Jean Desmet (BEL)	540	14
5	Graydon Nichols (USA)	510	4
6	Raul Morganti (ARG)	465	5
7	William Davis (USA)	435	5
8	Adel Ismail (SUI)	400	5
9	Stanislav Hlavsa (CZE)	395	5
10	Heinz Joerger (GER)	385	5

Women's 75

Rank	Name	Points	Played
1	Louise Russ (USA)	790	8
2	Erzsebet Szentirmay (HUN)	540	4
3	Louise Owen (USA)	480	6
4	Ingeborg Zimmerlein (GER)	410	5
5	Ingeborg Haas (GER)	365	5
6	Renate Kittsteiner (GER)	335	5
7	Marianne Schulze (GER)	335	5
8	Rita Price (USA)	330	5
9	Nancy Stout (USA)	330	4
10	Bibine Belaustegiotia (MEX)	285	5

Men's 80

Rank	Name	Points	Played
1	Frederick Kovaleski (USA)	790	6
2	Oskar Jirkovsky (AUT)	660	5
3	Laszlo Lenart (HUN)	600	5
4	Robert Sherman (USA)	570	9
5	Robert Caruana (GBR)	530	5
6	Cees Marre (NED)	480	13
7	Bob Seymour (USA)	450	6
8	Neville Halligan (AUS)	440	4
9	Augusto Zwiefel (SUI)	425	4
10	Gianni Coi (ITA)	365	4

Men's 85

Rank	Name	Points	Played
1	Alex Swetka (USA)	790	8
2	Irving Converse (USA)	450	7
3	Howard William Kuntz (USA)	390	3
4	Dennis Hernaman (GBR)	270	2
5	Tom Whitlow (USA)	245	3
6=	Albert Ritzenberg (USA)	240	2
6=	Barrett Scallett (USA)	240	4
8	Franz Kornfeld (AUT)	210	2
9	Gerhard Tost (GER)	200	4
10	Robert Mix (USA)	195	3

Gene Scott (USA)

241

ITF Development: ITF Seniors World Rankings 2004

the technical year

by dr stuart miller

For the Technical Department, 2004 has seen significant progress in a number of areas, as existing programmes continue to expand, while several new projects have been started. Investment in the Technical Centre has helped to retain its position as the world's leading tennis-specific research and testing facility.

ITF Technical Centre

Fulfilment of the Technical Centre's mission to protect the nature of tennis by 'actively preserving the skills traditionally required to play the game, and, to encourage innovation and improvements which maintain the challenge of the game and make it more exciting to play and watch' requires it to be proactive. Thus, by undertaking research and testing programmes, and developing predictive models and simulations, the ITF will be an effective guardian of the technical and technological aspects of the game. This work is crucial in preventing a reactive approach to the regulation of tennis equipment, which history has shown to be potentially hazardous.

Development of the ITF wind tunnel – a unique device that measures the aerodynamic characteristics of tennis balls – has continued throughout 2004. Systematic testing of all approved brands of tennis ball is now under way.

Tennis strings under a microscope

measure the frictional and impact-absorbing characteristics of different shoe/surface combinations. The capability of measuring forces developed when pivoting was added, following which a successful validation was undertaken. A more realistic 'foot' and 'ankle' will be added in the near future.

Due to the significant influence of spin on the nature of tennis, an automated method of measuring ball spin is almost complete. This project will benchmark the spin-generating capacity of string, stringing systems and racket frames.

Ball testing

As the sole worldwide testing and approval centre for tennis balls that are used in tournament play according to the Rules of Tennis, the ITF Technical Centre conducted an expanded programme of testing in the last year:

1. Ball Approval. In 2003, over 200 brands of ball were approved for the 2004 calendar year, a record number for the 8th consecutive year. The Technical Centre published its annual official list of approved balls in January (the list is also available on the ITF web site). Ball approval testing for

> Due to the significant influence of spin on the nature of tennis, an automated method of measuring ball spin is almost complete. This project will benchmark the spin-generating capacity of string, stringing systems and racket frames.

Development of the racket power machine ("MYO") has also continued throughout 2004, with several improvements being made, including a modified gripping mechanism and automated analysis software. Further enhancements have been identified that will improve accuracy and reliability. Systematic analysis of the performance characteristics of tennis rackets is ongoing.

A third piece of equipment undergoing development in 2004 is the ITF Sports Shoe Tester, which will be used to

Version 1 of 'Tennis GUT', the Technical Centre's software package that quantifies the combined effects of all tennis equipment on the nature of tennis, will be completed at the end of 2004. This software will be a key tool that ensures that the ITF protects the nature of tennis.

The web-based global facilities guide is ongoing. This project aims to provide information on planning, construction and maintenance of tennis facilities, mainly to developing nations where such information does not exist. A meeting of an international working group took place in 2004, with the site anticipated to go live in 2005.

2005 has been ongoing since June, and a similar number of brands are expected to be approved.

2. Market testing. This continues to form a significant volume of the Technical Centre's ball testing programme. Continued cooperation with the ATP and WTA tours has resulted in a similar number of samples being received from tournaments in 2004 as compared to approval tests. The results of this testing will again be used to both form future ITF ball testing policy and strategy, and to provide feedback to the ball manufacturing industry and interested members of the ITF Foundation.

◀ *ITF racket power machine*

the technical year
by dr stuart miller

Further development of the testing and analysis processes have been undertaken to facilitate the increased volume of testing.

Quality assurance of testing standards forms a key part of the Technical Centre's philosophy. Following a British Standards Institute audit in March, the Technical Centre retained its ISO 9001:2000 quality assurance standard in 2004.

Court Surface Classification
The ITF Court Surface Classification Scheme continues to expand, with 63 surfaces now having an ITF classification. In 2004, one new laboratory was added to the list of facilities accredited by the ITF to perform surface classification pace testing. There are now five such centres, each of which is re-accredited every two years.

ITF Foundation
It is through the ITF Foundation that the Technical Centre enjoys an open and productive relationship with the tennis industry. In 2004 the ITF Foundation continued to grow, with Greenset, Luxilon and Tarkett Sports joining adidas, California Products, Dunlop Slazenger, Head/Penn and PTR as Supporting Level members, with a further 25 companies joining as General Level members. In June, the ITF hosted its annual meetings with members of the Foundation, which focussed on the racket, ball and court surfaces respectively. These meetings continue to provide the opportunity for the Technical Centre to communicate its activity to, and consult with, the industry as it moves forward. Such was the popularity of the court surfaces working group that a second meeting was held in December.

The main benefit of Foundation membership is exclusive access to the ITF attitude and participation survey. Research was conducted in 7 nations in 2004 at Davis Cup and Fed Cup ties. The countries were Belarus, Chile, Czech Republic, Italy, Japan, Netherlands and Russia. The data continues to be well received by Foundation members.

ITF Haines pendulum and high speed video of ball impacts

ITF Technical Commission
The Technical Commission has again been active throughout the year. Supplementing the membership with representatives from ITF Officiating and both the ATP and WTA tours facilitated a more complete discussion of technical issues, which has covered all areas of tennis equipment. In conjunction with the first meeting of 2004, a Technical Seminar was held, which brought together the ITF Technical Centre's external research partners. The second meeting was preceded by the third Technical Forum, at which experts from ITF member associations shared information and discussed technical issues.

ITF Sport Science and Medicine Commission
This commission, the name change of which from 'Sports Medical Commission' was approved by the ITF Board of Directors in October, is now managed by the Technical Department. Two meetings have taken place in 2004, which have generated significant progress in the understanding of science and medicine issues related to tennis. The commission is leading a key research project that aims to track injuries and injury trends in tennis, with the aim of minimising their frequency.

In summary, the Technical Department has again reinforced its role as the leading regulatory, research, testing and approval body for tennis equipment. In 2005, when several of the projects and initiatives described in this report come to fruition, considerable progress is expected towards understanding the ever-increasing influence of science on the game. The challenge of protecting the nature of tennis is a key role of the ITF, and one which the Technical Department has successfully met in 2004.

> The Technical Department has again reinforced its role as the leading regulatory, research, testing and approval body for tennis equipment.

Francesco Ricci Bitti with the late John Parsons

reference section

The greatest players, historic records, addresses of National Associations and other tennis organisations, obituaries.

The Greatest
Biographies of leading players

Written by John Haylett.

The Men

ANDRE AGASSI (USA)
One of six players who have won all four Grand Slam titles at least once. Has invented a new style of tennis, attacking from the baseline.

Born:	Las Vegas, USA, April 29, 1970.
Grand Slam titles:	Australian Open 1995, 2000-01, 2003. French Open 1999. Wimbledon 1992. US Open 1994, 1999.
Olympics:	Gold medal, singles, 1996.
Davis Cup winning teams:	USA 1990, 1992.

Agassi is the most exciting and charismatic tennis player of the current era. A powerhouse of energy and a vigorous shotmaker, he is one of only five men to take all four Grand Slam singles titles. He burst upon the scene in 1986 and became instantly recognisable, not only for his relentless go-for-broke baseline hitting, but also his flamboyant image.

He rapidly shot into the top five but it was five years before he won his first Grand Slam title. Having lost finals at the 1990 and 1991 Roland Garros, and 1990 US Open, and stated an avowed dislike of grass, Agassi surprised most experts by defeating Goran Ivanisevic in a pulsating five set final at Wimbledon in 1992. From then on he established himself as a leading contender, winning the 1994 US Open title. He developed a terrific rivalry with Pete Sampras, winning the final of the 1995 Australian Open and losing to him at the same stage at Flushing Meadows.

In 1997 he married the actress Brooke Shields and his form declined steeply – his ranking plummeted to 141 in the autumn and he was reduced to playing in Challenger events. But having engaged the former top ten player, Brad Gilbert, as his coach, Agassi rediscovered his enthusiasm for the game and achieved the finest sequence of his career. He defeated Andrei Medvedev in the final of the 1999 French Open then lost to Sampras in the Wimbledon final. He won the next two Slams, at Flushing Meadows and Melbourne, to claim an undisputed status as the world's top player at the age of 30. He captured the Australian Open title for a second consecutive year in 2001 and narrowly lost to Pete Sampras in the 2002 US Open Final. Agassi was forced to miss Melbourne in 2002 due to injury but returned to win his fourth title in 2003 to become the oldest Grand Slam Champion for nearly 31 years. Later in 2003 he became the oldest holder of the No. 1 Entry Ranking in the history of the rankings (since 1973) when he took over the top spot for the fifth time in his career. He married Steffi Graff in 2001, the couple have two children Jaden Gil (born October 01) and Jaz Elle (born October 2003).

ARTHUR ASHE (USA)
Style, elegance and consistency. The first black player to win a Grand Slam title. A great example for his sport and for his race.

Born:	Richmond, Virginia, USA, July 10, 1943.
Died:	New York, USA, February 6, 1993.
Grand Slam titles:	Australian Open 1970, Wimbledon 1975, US Open 1968. Two men's doubles titles.
Davis Cup winning teams:	USA 1968-70.

Ashe was the first and, to date, only African-American man to win any of the game's major titles, and such is the esteem in which he is held, when the new main stadium at Flushing Meadows was built in 1997 it was named after him. Born in the Deep South at a time when racial attitudes made it extremely difficult for any black player to make progress in tennis, Ashe overcame considerable obstacles to reach back-to-back Australian singles finals in 1966-67 while also serving in the US armed forces. He had a fast, accurate serve, impeccable volleys and a fine overhead, and he also had one of the best brains of any tennis player in history.

In 1968, the year the game went Open, he achieved the unique feat of winning both the US Nationals (an event confined to amateurs and registered players) at Boston and then the inaugural US Open at Forest Hills. As an amateur he was obliged to forfeit the prize money. He turned professional soon afterwards and would be one of the world's leading players for the next decade, winning the Australian Open in 1970 and Wimbledon in 1975. In the latter year he achieved the No. 1 ranking, and his Wimbledon final defeat of the holder, Jimmy Connors, by 61 61 57 64, was regarded as possibly the most astute and intelligent tactical display ever seen on the Centre Court. With clever changes of pace and spin, and slicing his serve wide to his opponent's double-handed backhand, Ashe bewildered the hitherto dominant Connors to claim a famous upset victory.

Ashe's style, elegance and consistency, coupled with his perceptive comments on the developing Open sport and his leadership of the fledgling Association of Tennis Professionals, made him a respected statesman of the game. Although he was almost 32 when he won Wimbledon he continued to play at a high level until 1979, when his career was terminated by a heart attack. Having represented the United States in the Davis Cup from 1963 to 1978, he assumed the captaincy for five years and led his country to victory in 1981 and 1982. Tragically, in 1988 he contracted AIDS through a blood transfusion and he died before his 50th birthday.

BORIS BECKER (GER)
Youngest player to win the men's singles title at Wimbledon and first unseeded champion.

Born:	Liemen, Germany, November 22, 1967.
Grand Slam titles:	Australian Open 1991, 1996. Wimbledon 1985-86, 1989. US Open 1989.
Olympics:	Gold medal, doubles: 1992.
Davis Cup winning teams:	Germany 1988-89.

Boris Becker, a big, powerful, redhead with battering-ram serves and crunching volleys, set three simultaneous records when he won Wimbledon at the age of 17 in 1985. He was the youngest-ever winner, the first unseeded champion and the first player from Germany to capture the world's premier grass court championship. In an astonishing display of courage and determination, Becker overcame the eighth-seeded South African, Kevin Curren, 63 67 76 64 in the final, literally hurling himself around the court. He become a great player, but he failed to achieve the domination of other champions like Laver, Borg and Sampras. There were two reasons for this: he had a suspect temperament, and occasionally imploded, as he did when losing to his compatriot, Michael Stich, in the 1991 Wimbledon final; and he lacked the patience to succeed on slower surfaces. He never won a professional singles title on clay.

Becker burst upon the world stage in 1984, when he reached the quarterfinals of the Australian Open as a 16-year-old. When he came to England for the grass court season in June 1985 he provided a portent of things to come by winning the title at Queen's Club, then came his momentous first Wimbledon triumph. Later that year he led West Germany (as it still was) to the final of the Davis Cup and beat both Edberg and Wilander, although he could not prevent Sweden winning the tie overall.

He retained his Wimbledon title in 1986 but the following year, in an astonishing upset, lost in the second round to a little-known Australian, Peter Doohan. But that was his only bad result in over a decade at the Championships. He contested three finals in a row against Edberg from 1988 to 1990, winning in 1989, the same year he overcame Ivan Lendl for his only US Open title. In 1991 came the surprise loss to Stich. There would be one further Wimbledon final (losing to Sampras in 1995) and one more Grand Slam title – the Australian in 1996, when he reached the No. 1 ranking for the only time in his career. But from the mid-1990s his form went into decline. He announced his retirement in 1997, but returned for another season in 1999. He reached the fourth round at Wimbledon but after a decisive loss to Patrick Rafter finally called it a day.

BJORN BORG (SWE)
Great athletic talent. Proved everybody wrong by winning, as a clay court specialist, five consecutive Wimbledon titles.

Born:	Sodertalje, Sweden, June 6, 1956.
Grand Slam titles:	French Open 1974-75, 1978-81. Wimbledon 1976-80.
Davis Cup winning team:	Sweden 1975.

Probably the best baseliner the world has ever seen, Bjorn Borg rewrote the coaching manuals by proving that it was possible to win consistently on grass without a conventional serve and volley game. Blessed with broad shoulders and tremendous upper body strength, Borg had a great serve, blistering topspin groundstrokes (double-handed on the backhand) and the ability to run down every shot. Whilst he was capable of playing the serve and volley, he relied chiefly on his superb fitness and great strength off the ground to win Wimbledon five years running – a feat unsurpassed since the abolition of the Challenge Round.

Selected to play for Sweden in the Davis Cup in 1972, when he was still only 15, Borg was a very young achiever. He won the Wimbledon junior title that year and 12 months later extended Britain's experienced Roger Taylor to a dramatic five set quarterfinal in the senior event. His dashing looks made him tennis's first ever teenybop heart-throb, idolised by an army of young girls who stormed the Centre Court and made him an icon comparable to contemporary pop stars like Donny Osmond and David Cassidy. Borg, who was basically shy, continued to make progress despite the attentions of his fans. In 1974 he became the youngest-ever winner of the French Open (at the time) and retained the title the following year, when he also led Sweden to its first ever triumph in the Davis Cup.

He won the first of his Wimbledon titles without dropping a set, and held onto it for four more years, despite a determined challenge from John McEnroe in the 1980 final, which has gone down in history as perhaps the best ever. But in 1981 McEnroe had his revenge, and Borg's motivation began to fade. He never managed to win the US Open, losing in four finals, and he did not play in Australia after his early years. But he lost only one match at Roland Garros after 1973, winning his sixth title there on his last appearance in 1981.

In 1982, in dispute with the authorities over the number of events he wished to play, he walked away from the game. He made an ill-judged comeback in the early 1990s, still using his by now obsolete wooden racket, but was unable to make any impression on a sport that had moved on during his decade away from the courts.

The Greatest – Men (continued)

JEAN BOROTRA (FRA)
The third best of the Four Musketeers by results, his flamboyant personality always making him a leader both on and off the court.

Born:	Arbonne, France, August 13, 1898.
Died:	Arbonne, France, July 17, 1994.
Grand Slam titles:	Australian 1928. French 1931. Wimbledon 1924, 1926. Eight men's doubles titles; four mixed doubles titles.
Davis Cup winning teams:	France 1927-32.

'The Bounding Basque', as Jean Borotra was known, was the most successful of the 'Four Musketeers' – a quartet of highly talented Frenchmen (the others were Henri Cochet, Rene Lacoste and Jacques Brugnon) who, along with the American, Bill Tilden, dominated men's tennis from the mid-1920s to the early 1930s. They won the Davis Cup for France for six consecutive years from 1927 to 1932 and between them gathered 18 Grand Slam singles titles.

Borotra, as Gallic as the actor Maurice Chevalier, was instantly recognisable not only for his trademark blue beret but also his explosive style of play. Although slight in physique he possessed extraordinary energy and would hurtle around the court, always eager to attack but equally capable of running down any drop shot or lob an opponent gave him. He was a consummate volleyer – a skill rewarded with a career total of 12 Grand Slam doubles and mixed doubles titles, and his backhand return of serve was a potent weapon. Not only was Borotra an exciting and entertaining player, but he was debonair and charming – an inveterate ladies' man who never missed an opportunity to kiss the hand of an attractive female spectator.

As a winner of all the major titles except the American, where he was runner-up in 1926, Borotra proved he could play well on all surfaces. But his unparalleled net game was particularly effective on wood, then the principal surface indoors. He won 11 British Covered Court singles championships – the last as late as 1949, when he was 53 years old – and four US Indoor singles titles. In the Davis Cup he represented France with huge distinction every year from 1923 to 1937 and again in 1947, compiling a 19-12 win-loss record in singles and 17-6 in doubles. Perhaps his greatest feat was retaining the Cup for France against the Americans in 1932. With the French leading 2-1 on rubbers in the Challenge Round, Borotra, then 33, lost the first two sets against Wilmer Allison and saved six match points before going on to triumph 16 36 64 62 75.

During World War II he served as a minister in the Vichy government. He was also president of the French Tennis Federation for many years. Borotra played more matches at Wimbledon than any other player (223 between 1922 and 1964) and took part in every International Club match between France and Great Britain from 1929 to 1985.

DONALD BUDGE (USA)
The first man to achieve the Grand Slam. One of the best backhands ever. His career was shortened by turning professional at 23.

Born:	Oakland, California, USA, June 13, 1915.
Died:	Scranton, Pennsylvania, USA, January 20, 2000.
Grand Slam titles:	Australian 1938. French 1938. Wimbledon 1937-38. United States 1937-38. Four men's doubles titles; four mixed doubles titles.
Davis Cup winning teams:	USA 1937-38.

Donald Budge had one of the shortest careers in major competition of any tennis champion, but in the space of two years he won six major singles titles, plus four men's doubles and four mixed doubles championships. Until his total domination of the 1938 season the concept of the Grand Slam was unheard of. The Grand Slam was originally a term borrowed from the game of bridge by American journalist Allison Danzig and now denotes the winning of all four of tennis's greatest titles, the Australian, French, Wimbledon and United States Championships, by the same player in the same calendar year. Only one other man (Rod Laver in 1962 and 1969) and three women – Maureen Connolly (1953), Margaret Court (1970) and Steffi Graf (1988) have followed in Budge's footsteps.

The son of a Scottish immigrant who played professional football for Paisley, Donald Budge was a strapping 6ft 2in redhead who had a commanding all-round game, with a ferocious service and one of the best backhands the sport has ever seen. He was first selected to the US Davis Cup team at the age of 20 in 1935, and in September 1936 he defeated Fred Perry, the world No. 1, to win the important Pacific Southwest tournament in Los Angeles. When Perry turned professional shortly afterwards Budge was ready to succeed him as the world's leading player.

In 1937 he won all three titles at Wimbledon – the singles, beating Germany's Gottfried von Cramm in straight sets, the men's doubles with fellow-American Gene Mako and the mixed with Alice Marble. The same month he beat von Cramm again in the deciding rubber of the Davis Cup Inter-Zone Final at Wimbledon. This was one of the greatest matches of all time. Budge won 68 57 64 62 86 from 1-4 down in the final set, and the Americans went on to take the Cup from Great Britain in the Challenge Round. In September of that year Budge won the triple crown at the US Championships. In 1938 he won the Australian title for the loss of one set, the French for the loss of three, Wimbledon without dropping any sets, and Forest Hills for the loss of one. He also retained all his doubles titles. After a successful US defence of the Davis Cup he signed a professional contract and swiftly conquered the pro game as well.

HENRI COCHET (FRA)

A master of strategy. Able to play inside the baseline with great anticipation, taking the ball early. Staged a great recovery against Bill Tilden to win the 1927 Wimbledon semifinal.

Born:	Lyon, France, December 14, 1901.
Died:	St Germain-en-Laye, France, April 1, 1987.
Grand Slam titles:	French 1926, 1928, 1930, 1932. Wimbledon 1927, 1929. United States 1928. Five men's doubles titles, three mixed doubles titles.
Olympics:	Silver medals, singles and doubles, 1924.
Davis Cup winning teams:	France 1927-32.

Henri Cochet was an extraordinarily talented player who defied the usual precepts of the game. He could create winners from seemingly impossible situations, taking the ball early, with fantastic volleys and half-volleys even when apparently out of position. Reluctant to work hard, he nevertheless relied on marvellous strategic ability and ease of shot to beat stronger and more technically orthodox opponents.

The Frenchman was a mainstay of his country's Davis Cup team, winning 10 consecutive Challenge Round rubbers after he and the other Musketeers (Jean Borotra, Rene Lacoste and Jacques Brugnon) captured the trophy for the first time from the United States in 1927. His victory over William Johnston at Forest Hills sealed the historic victory, and he continued the sequence with wins over John Hennessey, Bill Tilden (twice), George Lott (twice), Bunny Austin, Fred Perry and Wilmer Allison, plus doubles wins with Borotra and Brugnon.

He was also a highly successful performer in Grand Slam events, where his greatest triumph was probably at Wimbledon in 1927. In the semifinals he trailed Tilden by two sets to love and 1-5 in the third, yet managed to recover to win 26 46 75 64 63. He went on to defeat Borotra in the final. The following year he won the French and American titles and began a four year run as world No. 1. He won the French championship for the first time in 1922, when it was restricted to French nationals, and took the title four more times – in 1926 and 1928 (beating Lacoste in the final), in 1930 (over Tilden) and in 1932 (over Giorgio de Stefani). He was also runner-up the following year to Jack Crawford. At Wimbledon his victim in both winning finals (1927 and 1929) was Borotra. In the 1927 final Cochet made a thrilling recovery from 2-5 in the final set, saving six match points. He was runner-up in 1928 to Lacoste. He won the US title in 1928 against Francis Hunter and was losing finalist to Ellsworth Vines in 1932.

In 1933 France lost its grip on the Davis Cup despite Cochet's win over Austin in the fourth rubber, having earlier lost to Perry. After this he turned professional, but did not have a particularly successful career as a paid performer. In 1945 he was reinstated as an amateur.

JIMMY CONNORS (USA)

The greatest fighter of them all. Won the US Open at 31 and reached the semis there at 39. Won the three Grand Slam tournaments he played in 1974.

Born:	September 2, 1952, East St Louis, Illinois, USA.
Grand Slam titles:	Australian Open 1974. Wimbledon 1974, 1982. US Open 1974, 1976, 1978, 1982-83. Two men's doubles titles.

Jimmy Connors was one of four players – the others were Bjorn Borg, Ilie Nastase and John McEnroe – who were largely responsible for turning tennis from a minority sport into a huge, multi-million dollar entertainment industry in the late 1970s. He was a tremendously exciting player – feisty, jocular, controversial, hard-hitting, dogged and a marvel of longevity. He was a leading contender and a top box office attraction for a span of two decades.

Connors was a streetfighter who knew how to milk a crowd and orchestrate it into a frenzy of excitement as he waged winning battles against opponents who knew that he was capable of beating them from seemingly impossible positions. He was often uncouth and unsporting, but such was his charisma that audiences forgave his excesses and applauded his sheer guts and fighting qualities. His style was all-out attrition from the baseline. His serve was not a major weapon, and he could volley and smash efficiently, but it was his groundstrokes, especially his double-handed backhand, that were the hallmark of his success. It was a physically demanding mode of play that made his longevity as a top flight player all the more remarkable. He was very fast, able to cover the court so well that it was extremely difficult to put a winner past him. Even more remarkable was his loyalty to the Wilson T-2000 – a steel frame racket that he used from the late 1960s (when still a junior) into the 1980s, long after all other players had discarded it as unusable.

Connors' first major success was winning the Wimbledon doubles with Nastase in 1973, but after that he concentrated on singles. He won three of the four Grand Slam titles in 1974, overwhelming the 39-year-old Ken Rosewall in the finals at Wimbledon and Forest Hills, and might have taken the French as well had he not been barred because he was under contract to the World Team Tennis league. He holds the unique distinction of winning the US Open on three different surfaces – on grass in 1974, on clay in 1976 and on hard courts in 1978, 1982 and 1983. During his career he had many memorable battles against Borg, McEnroe and Ivan Lendl, and he reached the semifinals of the US Open at the age of 39 in 1991.

The Greatest – Men (continued)

JIM COURIER (USA)
Reached the finals of all four Slam tournaments and triumphed on vastly different surfaces to win the Australian and French twice.

Born:	Sanford, Florida, USA, August 17, 1970.
Grand Slam titles:	Australian Open 1992-93. French Open 1991-92.
Davis Cup winning teams:	USA 1992, 1995.

A rugged athlete with a brutally physical style, Jim Courier relied on his supreme fitness and relentless work ethic to reach the pinnacle of the game in the early 1990s. A product of the Nick Bollettieri Academy in Bradenton, Florida – breeding ground for such stars as Andre Agassi, Monica Seles and David Wheaton – Courier was an exponent of the powerhitting baseline style which virtually took over tennis. His chief weapons were his ferocious double-handed backhand and devastating inside-out forehand with which he would slug endless shots deep into his opponent's court. Courier toiled long hours on the practice court as a junior and became a feared adversary because his stamina and determination ensured that he could usually last longer than most other men in marathon baseline battles.

One of a batch of top American prospects to burst upon the scene in the late 1980s – others included Agassi, Wheaton, Pete Sampras and Michael Chang – Courier established an early ascendancy with his back-to-back French titles in 1991-92 and Australian victories in 1992-93. He achieved the No. 1 ranking in 1992 and looked set for a long reign, but after losing the 1993 finals at Roland Garros (to Sergi Bruguera) and Wimbledon (to Sampras) he went into a slow decline. He never won the US Open, having lost to Stefan Edberg in the 1991 final, and his loss to Cedric Pioline in the fourth round at Flushing Meadows in 1993 marked a turning point in his career from which he never recovered.

Somewhat of an individualist, Courier was admired for the way he refused to behave like a celebrity and his crowd-pleasing gestures. But at the 1993 ATP World Championships in Frankfurt he raised eyebrows by abandoning his trademark baseball cap and reading a novel during changeovers. From 1994 until his abrupt retirement in May 2000, Courier never again advanced beyond a Grand Slam quarterfinal and slid inexorably down the rankings. He would have become almost unnoticeable but for his continuing heroic exploits in the Davis Cup. He is the only American player to win two five set deciding rubbers – against Marat Safin in 1998 and against Greg Rusedski in 1999.

JACK CRAWFORD (AUS)
By winning the three major titles in 1933 and losing the final of the fourth, he first raised the concept of the Grand Slam in tennis.

Born:	Albury, New South Wales, Australia, March 22, 1908.
Died:	Cessnock, New South Wales, Australia, September 10, 1991.
Grand Slam titles:	Australian 1931-33, 1935. French 1933. Wimbledon 1933. Six men's doubles titles, five mixed doubles titles.

Jack Crawford came within one set of winning the Grand Slam five years before Donald Budge took the four major singles titles in 1938. He won the 1933 Australian, French and Wimbledon championships and advanced to the final at Forest Hills, where he faced Britain's Fred Perry. The Briton won the first set 63 but lost the next two 1113 46, so the Australian stood on the brink of an historic feat. But he had been suffering from asthma and insomnia, and his strength evaporated. Perry won the last two sets 60 61, denying Crawford an achievement which up until then had never been considered possible, far less given a name which, through Budge, would become the ultimate goal for any top class tennis player.

Crawford was a hugely admired player in his time, dubbed by one contemporary "the most popular Wimbledon winner in history". Impeccably sporting, he was regarded as a throwback to the pre-World War I era, not only in his attire – he always wore long-sleeved cricket shirts, buttoned at the wrist, but also his equipment – he used an old-fashioned flat-topped racket, and his style of play – from the back of the court, with fluent, accurate ground strokes rather than bludgeoning power. His hair was parted in the middle and he was every inch a courteous Edwardian gentleman. Between sets on a hot day he customarily revived himself by sipping hot tea.

His winning Wimbledon final against Ellsworth Vines in 1933 is regarded as one of the greatest of all time. Vines, a hard-hitting American in a peaked cap, renowned for his devastating serve, was expected to retain his title. But Crawford, for all his outdated characteristics, had the guile to beat him. He nullified the power of Vines's forehand by feeding him a succession of high-bouncing shots to the forehand side and then preventing Vines from getting into a groove by switching to low, sliced shots to his weaker backhand flank.

Crawford lost to Perry in the 1934 Australian final but gained his revenge the following year. He lost two further Australian finals to Adrian Quist in 1936 and 1940. He was easily beaten by Perry in the 1934 Wimbledon final. His only appearance for Australia in the Davis Cup Challenge Round resulted in defeats by both Perry and Bunny Austin in 1936.

JAROSLAV DROBNY (CZE/EGY/GBR)

Won Wimbledon at 33. An all-court player who was able to follow his lethal drop shot to the net. Like Jack Kramer and Ted Schroeder, his career was shortened by the war.

Born: Prague, Czechoslovakia, October 12, 1921.
Died: London, England, September 13, 2001.
Grand Slam titles: French 1951-52. Wimbledon 1954. One men's doubles title, one mixed doubles title.

Jaroslav Drobny is the most cosmopolitan of Grand Slam champions. He first competed as a representative of Czechoslovakia, then played under the flag of Bohemia-Moravia, a nation that existed briefly before World War II, then again as a Czech. He defected in 1949 and was for a while stateless, until he secured Egyptian nationality in 1950. In 1960, in time for his last appearance at Wimbledon, he achieved British citizenship.

Burly and bespectacled, he did not look like a top class athlete, but this enduring competitor was one of the world's leading tennis players for many years. He was also a top ice hockey player, representing Czechoslovakia in international competition.

Drobny learned his tennis on the clay courts of a club in Prague, where his father was the groundsman, but became one of the few European players of his generation who was able to translate his skills onto grass. A left-hander, he had a terrific service and smash but also possessed great touch and his clever court management, including a devastating drop shot, made him a feared opponent on all surfaces. He made his Wimbledon debut in 1938, at the age of 16, but his highly promising career was stalled for seven long years by World War II.

At Wimbledon in 1946 he scored a huge upset by defeating Jack Kramer, but lost to Australia's Geoff Brown in a straight-sets semifinal. He became a strong Wimbledon favourite and was involved in some of the tournament's most emotional matches – including a 93-game marathon against Budge Patty in 1953. He was runner-up twice – in 1949 and 1952, before winning the title in 1954 at the age of 32 with a four set victory over the 19-year-old Ken Rosewall in the longest final ever in terms of games – a 13 11 4 6 62 97 triumph in 2 hours, 37 minutes. It was his 11th attempt and was greeted by the crowd with as much enthusiasm as if a Briton had won.

He was also runner-up three times in the French Championships – in 1946, 1948 and 1950 – before winning the title in 1951 and 1952. He reached two semifinals at the US Championships, in 1947 and 1948, and won the French men's and mixed doubles in 1948. His Davis Cup career was confined to representing Czechoslovakia from 1946 to 1949, during which time the team reached the Inter-Zone final in 1947 and 1948.

STEFAN EDBERG (SWE)

His backhand volley was one of the best shots the game has ever seen. A five-set loss to Michael Chang in the 1989 Roland Garros final prevented him from winning all four Slam tournaments.

Born: Vastervik, Sweden, January 19, 1966.
Grand Slam titles: Australian Open 1985, 1987. Wimbledon 1988, 1990. US Open 1991-92. Three men's doubles titles.
Olympics: Gold medal, singles, 1984. Bronze medal, singles, 1988.
Davis Cup winning teams: Sweden 1984-85, 1994.

Stefan Edberg was the third of a triumvirate of Swedish players – the others were Bjorn Borg and Mats Wilander – to achieve the No. 1 ranking. He is the only man apart from John McEnroe to reach No. 1 at both singles and doubles, and he holds the record for consecutive appearances in the Grand Slam events – 54 between 1983 and 1996.

Unlike Borg and Wilander, he played a classic serve and volley game, with a style that was almost an anachronism in an era when power hitting from the baseline became the norm. He had a beautifully timed serve, elegant ground strokes, single-handed on the backhand, and the best net game of his generation. He was an exponent of chip and charge tactics to gain the net whenever possible. He could dispatch exquisitely angled volleys to all parts of the court and put away lobs with crunching smashes.

It was clear that he would become an outstanding player when, in 1983, he became the first boy since Earl Buccholz in 1958 to win a Grand Slam of major junior singles titles. Edberg wasted little time in beginning his collection of senior Grand Slam titles. At the age of 19 he captured the 1985 Australian Open – then played on grass in December – outplaying Wilander in straight sets in the final. Thirteen months later, in January 1987, he retained the title over that year's Wimbledon champion, Pat Cash. He was runner-up three more times in Melbourne.

He appeared in three consecutive Wimbledon finals against Boris Becker between 1988 and 1990, winning the first and third of these encounters. And at the US Open he triumphed in 1991 and 1992, winning the former final over Jim Courier 62 64 60 in one of the most perfect displays of aggressive tennis ever seen. When he retained the title against Pete Sampras while still only 26 it seemed that many more successes would come his way.

However, Edberg would reach only one more Grand Slam final – the 1993 Australian, where he lost to Courier. In his only French Open final, in 1989, he was frustrated by the dogged returning of Michael Chang. The final four years of his career saw a decline, although he could still delight audiences with his skills and impeccable sportsmanship. He was a staunch member of the Swedish Davis Cup team and in the victorious teams of 1984, 1985 and 1994.

The Greatest – Men (continued)

ROY EMERSON (AUS)

Took advantage of Lew Hoad, Ken Rosewall and Rod Laver turning professional; however 12 Slam titles is still a great achievement. Won all the Grand Slam tournaments at least twice.

Born:	Blackbutt, Queensland, Australia, November 3, 1936.
Grand Slam titles:	Australian 1961, 1963-67. French 1963, 1967. Wimbledon 1964-65. United States 1961, 1964. 16 men's doubles titles.
Davis Cup winning teams:	Australia 1959-62, 1964-67.

Although Roy Emerson's record of 12 Grand Slam singles titles was overtaken by Pete Sampras in 2000, the Australian's total of 28 major singles and doubles championships is still unsurpassed in the men's game. It is, however, important to note that his six Australian titles were won at a time when the tournament did not attract a similar quality of entry as the other three Slam events. Emerson was one of the greatest of a long line of superlative Australian players trained by the country's Davis Cup captain, Harry Hopman, in the 1950s and 1960s. A country boy reared on a dairy farm about 100 miles north of Brisbane, he developed exceptionally strong wrists by milking large numbers of cows every day. He was also an outstanding athlete, running the 100 yards in 10.6 seconds at the age of 14. But "Emmo" decided at an early age to concentrate on tennis, because he saw a greater future in it. That he became such a good player was due in no small part to the very high standard of fitness he maintained throughout his 20-year top class tennis career.

He was a gregarious fellow and partied as hard as he played, but he was always prepared for major events. He had an all-out attacking game with a vicious serve prefaced by a unique corkscrew wind-up, but he could adapt his game to survive on any surface, as proved by his two French championships. He won them in 1963, when he defeated Pierre Darmon in the final, and 1967, when he dethroned his compatriot Tony Roche.

In those days the other three Grand Slam titles were all played on grass. Emerson began his conquest of the major prizes in 1961, when he beat Rod Laver in both the Australian and American finals. After Laver turned professional in 1962 Emerson was almost unbeatable in his own country, winning the championship for the next five years. He also took back-to-back Wimbledons in 1964-65 and a further US title in 1964.

In 1967 he played on a record eighth winning Australian Davis Cup team, crushing his great rival Manuel Santana in the opening rubber of the Challenge Round. He resisted the temptation to turn professional until the eve of Open tennis in 1968, but by this time he was 30 and on the wane. Emerson continued to compete until 1973.

ROGER FEDERER (SUI)

Roger Federer is the rarest of tennis players – a genius who only comes along perhaps once in a generation. Although he is only 23, the Swiss player is already being mentioned in the same breath as Pete Sampras, John McEnroe and Rod Laver.

Born:	Basel, Switzerland, August 8, 1981.
Grand Slam titles:	Australian Open 2004. Wimbledon 2003-04. US Open 2004.

The great Laver says of Federer: "I would be honoured to even be compared with Roger. He is such an unbelievable talent and is capable of anything. Roger could be the greatest tennis player of all time." McEnroe is equally enthusiastic. "When he plays his best tennis there is no player that plays better than him," he says. "He's one of the best players that ever played, already."

Federer has a complete game and is equally awesome on all surfaces, having won titles on clay, hard courts, grass and carpet. His service, though not as fast as Andy Roddick's, is powerful and varied. His forehand is heavy and accurate, whilst his backhand, one-handed and struck with supreme elegance, is infinitely versatile, both in attack and defence. His volley and overhead are perfectly timed, and his movement, courtcraft and anticipation so good that opponents are often demoralised, such is his brilliance.

Federer was an outstanding junior, winning the boys' singles at Wimbledon in 1998, and in the same year he reached the quarterfinals of only his second ATP Tour event, at Toulouse. He was ranked inside the world's top 100 by mid-1999, improving 248 positions from the previous year. In 2000 he was in two ATP finals and was good enough to reach the semifinals at the Sydney Olympics, losing the bronze medal play-off to Arnaud di Pasquale. In 2001 he vaulted into the top 20, winning his first ATP title at Milan, leading Switzerland to an upset victory over the USA in the Davis Cup and stunning Sampras in the fourth round at Wimbledon. In 2002 he established himself in the top 10 and won his first Masters Series title, in Hamburg. But his Grand Slam hopes received a setback when he was beaten in the first round both at Roland Garros and Wimbledon. In winning his first Wimbledon title in 2003, Federer dropped only one set – to Mardy Fish in the third round. He reached No.2 that summer but, despite also winning the Masters Cup in Houston, was held off the top position by Roddick.

In 2004, however, Federer lifted himself to a position of complete domination. Having worked with Peter Lundgren since the start of his pro career, he played all year without a coach. He won three of the four Grand Slams, failing only in Paris where he was beaten by Gustavo Kuerten, and won a total of 11 titles (the most since Muster in 1995). He did not lose to any other player in the top 10 and at the end of the year had won 13 consecutive finals – an open era record. In the final of the Masters Cup he repeated his US Open final rout of Lleyton Hewitt, who could only say: "I don't think I've ever seen a guy play that well in my life."

NEALE FRASER (AUS)
The last player to win, in 1960, the US Championships without the loss of a set. Part of a Davis Cup winning team four times as a player, four times as a captain.

Born: Melbourne, Victoria, Australia, October 3, 1933.
Grand Slam titles: Wimbledon 1960. United States 1959-60. 11 men's doubles titles, five mixed doubles titles.
Davis Cup winning teams: Australia 1959-62.

Neale Fraser, a rugged left-hander who exemplified the sort of attacking, all-court player with a perfect serve and volley game that came out of the Harry Hopman champion production line in the 1950s and 1960s, is perhaps more closely associated with the Davis Cup than any other player. He was on four winning teams between 1959 and 1962, and captained the Australian side for a record 22 years from 1970 to 1992, receiving the trophy four times in this capacity (1973, 1977, 1983 and 1986). So it was entirely appropriate that when the ITF honoured a select number of distinguished players as Davis Cup Ambassadors on the competition's centenary in 1999, he was included.

Fraser was the son of a judge, and although his parents did not play tennis, he and his brother John were encouraged to take up the game because they lived near courts in the Melbourne suburb of South Yarra. He developed an almost unreturnable repertoire of serves – a hard flat one, a swinging slice and a vicious twister, which was especially effective against right-handers. It was this that enabled him to beat the reigning Wimbledon champion, Alex Olmedo, in Fraser's debut Challenge Round singles rubber against the United States at Forest Hills in 1959. He repeated this win in the final of the US Championships shortly afterwards, and retained the title the following year without dropping a set – the last man to do so.

At Wimbledon he was runner-up to fellow-Australian Ashley Cooper in 1958, then in 1960 he defeated another compatriot, Rod Laver, in the final. Fraser won no more big singles titles after that, although he and his brother John were both Wimbledon semifinalists in 1962. Unlike Cooper, Laver and all the other great Aussie champions, he never turned professional because he was employed in part-time jobs by Slazenger and tobacco company WD & HO Wills and preferred this financial security to the tough, roadshow existence of the contract pros in those days.

Fraser was even more successful in doubles than singles. He formed a highly effective partnership with Emerson that won eight Grand Slam titles, and he also acquired five major mixed doubles championships. An occasional competitor right up to the mid-1970s, he reached the Wimbledon doubles final in 1973 with John Cooper, younger brother of Ashley, with whom he won the US title in 1957.

PANCHO GONZALES (USA)
Along with Ken Rosewall, the best player never to have won Wimbledon. Played his best tennis as a professional.

Born: Los Angeles, USA, May 9, 1928.
Died: Las Vegas, USA, July 3, 1995.
Grand Slam titles: United States 1948-49. Two men's doubles titles.
Davis Cup winning team: USA 1949.

An imposing 6ft 2in tall Mexican-American who played with pantherish elegance and glowered menacingly at opponents, court officials and spectators, Ricardo 'Pancho' Gonzales had personality with a capital 'P' and bestrode the international scene like a colossus for nearly four decades. Regarded as one of the two finest players (along with Ken Rosewall) who never won Wimbledon, he was a contract professional in the pre-Open Era for most of his career and as such unable to take part in the major championships.

Originating in a large and poor family of Mexican immigrants in a tough district of Los Angeles, he was a problem child and his early life was tainted with delinquency. But when he took up tennis at 12 he developed a commanding game, with one of the purest service actions ever seen. Such was the quality of his stylish, aggressive method of play that he was good enough to win the US Championship at the age of 20, sweeping past Eric Sturgess 62 63 1412 in the final, and he retained the title by outlasting Wimbledon champion Ted Schroeder in five sets in 1949. In his one and only Wimbledon appearance as an amateur in the same year he lost in the fourth round to Geoff Brown but won the doubles with Frank Parker.

After helping the United States retain the Davis Cup he turned professional, though still only 21. For much of the next 18 years he dominated the pro tour, and when Open tennis arrived he was still a leading contender despite the fact he was 40. At Wimbledon in 1969 he won the longest match (in terms of games) ever played at the Championships, recovering from two sets down and saving seven match points against 25-year-old Charlie Pasarell, 2224 16 1614 63 119. Later that year he beat John Newcombe, Rosewall, Stan Smith and Arthur Ashe to win a big-money tournament in Las Vegas. In 1972, three months before his 44th birthday, he became the oldest winner of a tour-level event in Open history when he beat Georges Goven in the final at Des Moines, Iowa.

He was a top box-office draw not only for his enduring skills but also his explosive personality. At Queen's Club in 1972 he stormed off the court after shoving the female referee, Bea Seal, in a disagreement over a line call.

The Greatest – Men (continued)

LLEYTON HEWITT (AUS)

Two Grand Slam titles, two Masters Cup titles and a solid No. 1 position in the rankings at age 21. His athletic talent and his mental toughness make him a player who may stay at the top for a long time.

Born:	Adelaide, South Australia, February 24, 1981.
Grand Slam titles:	Wimbledon 2002. US Open 2001. One doubles title.
Davis Cup winning team:	Australia 1999, 2003.

Lleyton Hewitt is the modern tennis player par excellence: fiercely competitive, fast and hard-hitting baseliner. Although not physically intimidating, the Australian is so tenacious that he is always a formidable opponent. His aggressive, take-no-prisoners attitude has already brought him two Grand Slam singles titles, a share of the Davis Cup and two Tennis Masters Cup titles at the age of 21.

Hewitt burst onto the world scene at an early age. Having been primarily an Australian Rules footballer who took up tennis seriously only at 15, he qualified for the 1997 Australian Open before his 16th birthday. A year later he won the ATP event in his home city of Adelaide, the lowest ranked man (at 550) ever to win a tour title. He moved swiftly up the rankings, making a huge leap in 1999, reaching No. 22 by the end of that year. During the course of an impressive season he won at Delray Beach and reached three other ATP finals.

In 2000 Hewitt overtook Patrick Rafter to become the Australian No. 1 and secured four titles. He reached his first Grand Slam semifinal at the US Open. There was no let-up in 2001, when Hewitt surged to six titles, including the US Open and the Masters Cup at Sydney, en route to becoming the year-end No. 1. He took over the No. 1 Entry System ranking in November 2001 and held it for 75 weeks until Andre Agassi took over on 28 April 2003.

At the start of 2002 he was sidelined by chicken pox, then a virus precluded activity until the early spring. But he made up for lost time by winning at San Jose and Indian Wells. After winning Queen's for the third year running he blazed to the Wimbledon title. His US Open title defence ended in the semis at the hands of Agassi but then he held off a challenge from the American to claim the year-end No. 1 crown for the second consecutive year. His second Masters Cup title was the icing on the cake.

Hewitt announced his intention of dedicating the 2003 season to Grand Slams and Davis Cup. His performance in Davis Cup was faultless, the patriotic Australian remained unbeaten in six rubbers and his defeat of Juan Carlos Ferrero on the opening day of the final was vital to Australia's 28th Davis Cup victory. Hewitt's Grand Slam performances however were disappointing. He lost his Wimbledon Crown when he became the first defending champion in the open era to lose in the first round when he fell to qualifier Ivo Karlovic. His best result was a quarterfinal appearance at the US Open, losing to Ferrero in four sets. Regaining his form in 2004 Hewitt captured four titles, reached the final of the US Open and qualified for the year-end Tennis Masters Cup.

LEW HOAD (AUS)

Turning professional at 23 and problems with his back limited his successes. At his best he was probably the greatest player ever.

Born:	Sydney, New South Wales, Australia, November 23, 1934.
Died:	Fuengirola, Spain, July 3, 1994.
Grand Slam titles:	Australian 1956. French 1956. Wimbledon 1956-57. Eight men's doubles titles, one mixed doubles title.
Davis Cup winning teams:	Australia 1953, 1955-56.

At his best, Lew Hoad possibly played tennis better than any other man in history. This blond Adonis, whose striking good looks and muscular physique were matched by the breathtaking strength and command of his shots, would have been even more successful had he not been struck down by a cruel and chronic back injury when he was at the height of his powers. Like his compatriot Jack Crawford, Hoad came within one match of winning the Grand Slam. In 1956, already holding the Australian, French and Wimbledon titles, he faced his friend and Davis Cup partner, Ken Rosewall, in the final of the US Championship. Hoad lost a match of superlative quality in four sets and was thus denied the chance to become only the second man to hold all four majors at the same time.

Hoad was a flamboyant player, always preferring to attempt a big shot rather than play safe, and when his huge, aggressive game was on song he was irresistible. He and Rosewall emerged at the same time as Australia's Davis Cup heroes, brought in for the 1953 Challenge Round after Frank Sedgman and Ken McGregor had turned professional. They were trailing the USA 2-1 when Hoad won a dramatic five set rubber against US champion Tony Trabert and Rosewall clinched victory for Australia by defeating Wimbledon champion Vic Seixas.

Hoad and Rosewall, though sharply contrasting in appearance and playing styles, were known as 'The Twins' and were Australia's leading players for the next three years. They won three Grand Slam doubles together in 1953 and contested three Slam singles finals in 1956, with Hoad triumphing at Brisbane and Wimbledon. Before the final of the French he partied all night and got over his hangover by running all the way from his hotel in central Paris to Roland Garros, where he demolished Sven Davidson in straight sets.

Whereas Rosewall turned professional at the start of 1957, Hoad remained amateur and retained his Wimbledon title with a devastating display in the final against Ashley Cooper. After this he too signed a pro contract, but he had already begun to suffer severe back pain and rarely again attained the force of his earlier years. He played spasmodically into the Open Era and faded out in the early 1970s.

YEVGENY KAFELNIKOV (RUS)

After Andre Agassi, Kafelnikov is the only winner of the French Open in the last ten years who has also been able to win a Slam title on another surface. His talent has been tested more than his consistency. The busiest player on the circuit, from 1994-2001 Kafelnikov was never ranked lower than No. 12, reaching No. 1 in 1999.

Born: Sochi, Russia, February 18, 1974.
Grand Slam titles: Australian Open 1999. French Open 1996. Three doubles titles.
Olympics: Gold medal 2000.

Still the most successful Russian player in the history of tennis, Yevgeny Kafelnikov was an indefatigable competitor who played more matches, in singles and doubles, than anyone else on the ATP circuit in the 1990s. His total of 26 singles and 24 doubles titles, accumulated over a professional career beginning in 1992, was a testament to his busy and fruitful activity, although it has to be said that Kafelnikov's effort level varied from week to week.

He was a thoroughly modern player, his game characterised by hard hitting from the baseline (double-handed on the backhand), a powerful serve and a competent volleying ability, as evidenced by his success in doubles. Kafelnikov won titles on all four surfaces, although his record at Wimbledon, where he only once reached the quarterfinals, was far inferior to his showing in the other three Grand Slam events.

He was the first of a new generation of Russian players to benefit from the fall of communism. Under the Soviet regime, athletes' movements were controlled and their prizemoney forfeited to the government. Kafelnikov was able to enjoy unrestricted travel (although he continued to live in the Black Sea resort where he was born) and the lifestyle of a multi-millionaire, having earned over $22 million from the sport. He was staunchly patriotic and extended his career in order to achieve his final ambition – to win the Davis Cup for Russia. This was accomplished in 2002, and he carried on playing for one more year before retiring.

In 1996 he won both the singles and doubles (with Daniel Vacek) at the French Open, the first man to do so since Ken Rosewall in 1968, and made the top five of both singles and doubles rankings. His 1997 was less successful, the highlights being the French and US Open doubles titles (with Vacek) and reaching the final of the ATP World Championship, where he lost to Sampras.

After a poor year in 1998, when he dropped out of the top ten, Kafelnikov stormed back to top form at the 1999 Australian Open, beating Thomas Enqvist in a four set final. Soon afterwards he reached No.1 in the world and held this position for 16 weeks. He reached the final at Melbourne the following year but found Andre Agassi in irresistible mood. Apart from the Olympic title in 2000 and a US Open semifinal in 2001, the Russian shone less brightly in major events in later years.

JAN KODES (CZE)

Won Wimbledon the year of the boycott in 1973, but there was a stronger field when he won the French in 1970 and 1971 and reached the final of the 1971 US Open.

Born: Prague, Czechoslovakia, March 1, 1945.
Grand Slam titles: French Open 1970-71. Wimbledon 1973.

Some people might say that Jan Kodes was a 'lucky' Wimbledon champion in that the year he won, 1973, 79 of the world's top players boycotted the tournament in protest at the ITF's suspension of Yugoslavia's Nikki Pilic for missing a Davis Cup tie in order to honour a commitment to take part in a non-ITF event. In the admittedly second rate field that remained, Kodes came through to win a unique all-East European final against the USSR's Alex Metreveli.

But Kodes, a slightly-built but dogged baseliner who could also volley effectively, had already established a grass court pedigree by reaching the final of the US Open in 1971. At the West Side Club in Forest Hills, New York, the Czech stunned the three-time Wimbledon champion and top seed, John Newcombe, in the first round and the third seeded Arthur Ashe in the semifinals, only submitting to second seed Stan Smith in a four-set final. Then, in the 1973 US Open he once more reached the final, taking out Smith in a five set semi and losing to Newcombe only after five more hard fought sets.

Few players who showed an avowed preference for continental clay, the surface on which Kodes learned the game, ever adapted so effectively to grass, upon which three of the four Grand Slam championships were played until the US Open switched to clay in 1975. He won back-to-back French Open titles in 1970 and 1971, although in the former year he was, as at Wimbledon in 1973, the beneficiary of a weakened field. World Championship Tennis (WCT), a rival tour to the official ITF Grand Prix, had many of the world's top players under contract and they were all withdrawn from Roland Garros because of the French Federation's refusal to pay appearance fees. Kodes, seeded seventh, easily beat Yugoslavia's Zelijko Franulovic in the final. The following year, from an only slightly stronger entry, he overcame Nastase in four sets to retain the title. At Wimbledon in 1973 he survived both his quarterfinal, against Vijay Amritraj, and his semifinal, against Roger Taylor, by the narrow margin of 75 in the fifth set.

Unlike his compatriots Jaroslav Drobny, Martina Navratilova, Hana Mandlikova and Ivan Lendl, he never left his native Czechoslovakia and appeared in the Davis Cup every year from 1966 to 1980.

The Greatest – Men (continued)

JACK KRAMER (USA)
Nobody has dominated tennis like he did in 1946-47. In 1947 he won Wimbledon for the loss of only 37 games in seven matches, a record.

Born: Las Vegas, USA, August 5, 1921.
Grand Slam titles: Wimbledon 1947. United States 1946-47. Six men's doubles titles, one mixed doubles title.
Davis Cup winning teams: USA 1946-47.

Jack Kramer was a principal player on the amateur circuit for just two years, yet his influence on the game was greater than just about anyone else for almost 40 years. He was indisputably the world's top amateur in 1947, then he dominated the professional tour for five seasons. Even before his enforced retirement as a player because of an arthritic back he had taken over as the pro tour's promoter and was responsible for arranging the tour and recruiting its star performers into the 1960s. He worked tirelessly to help bring about Open tennis in 1968, which brought all the world's best players – professional and amateur – into the same events. He devised the Grand Prix – a points-linked system which was the precursor of today's ATP tour, and was instrumental in forming the Association of Tennis Professionals, which eventually took over the running of the top level of men's tennis. He was the world's leading television commentator. And by striking a deal with Wilson Sporting Goods in 1947 his name was perpetuated on the world's top-selling racket, earning himself a fortune in the process.

Kramer is credited with inventing 'The Big Game' – a style of play that was adopted by the vast majority of players who won Grand Slam titles on grass (which in those days excluded only the French Championships) until tennis began to move back to the baseline in the 1970s. The Big Game comprised a blistering serve and a decisive first volley, while returns consisted of a chip-and-charge strategy to gain the net. Kramer perfected this style on the high-bouncing cement courts of California and readily adapted it to grass, on which he was virtually unbeatable.

He made his international debut in the 1939 Davis Cup Challenge Round when he was selected to play doubles at the age of 18. Because of World War II, during which he served in the US Coastguards and played a restricted schedule, Kramer had to wait until 1946 for his Wimbledon debut. Suffering from severe blisters on his racket hand, he lost in the fourth round to Jaroslav Drobny, but the following year he won for the loss of only 37 games in seven rounds – a record. He finished his amateur career with a flourish, retaining the US title and the Davis Cup for Uncle Sam.

RENE LACOSTE (FRA)
Physical problems shortened his career and forced him to retire in 1929 having won seven Grand Slam titles and two Davis Cup championships as part of the French team.

Born: Paris, France, July 2, 1904.
Died: St Jean de Luz, France, October 12, 1996.
Grand Slam titles: French 1925, 1927, 1929. Wimbledon 1925, 1928. United States 1926-27. Three men's doubles titles.
Davis Cup winning teams: France 1927-28.

Chemise Lacoste is a brand name as famous as Fred Perry and Sergio Tacchini, and its logo, the crocodile, was adopted from its founder, Rene Lacoste, so nicknamed because he tended to gobble up his opponents. He was a self-made champion who did not take up tennis until he was 15, but by working assiduously on his game he made up for lost time and was a champion by the time he was 21. A slight man with pronounced Gallic features, Lacoste was frail of physique and did not suffer good health, but his determination compensated for these shortcomings. He played chiefly from the baseline and was a master of strategy, hitting to an impeccable length, rarely making an error, in order to wait for a mistake from his opponent or to score with a lob or passing shot.

In 1924 he reached the reached the Wimbledon final and was included in the French Davis Cup team. In 1925 he won Wimbledon, avenging his loss to Jean Borotra in the previous year's final, and also triumphed in the French championship, trouncing Borotra in straight sets. He would win a total of two Wimbledon and three French singles titles during his brief career, but it was his achievement in taking back-to-back US championships in 1926-27 that established him as the top player in the world. No non-American had ever won the title, which for six consecutive years had been the personal property of the great Bill Tilden. With Tilden losing early in the 1926 championship Lacoste swept to the title, brushing aside Borotra 64 60 64 after a much harder five set defeat of the third great Frenchman, Henri Cochet. The following year Lacoste met Tilden in the final and again came through, 119 63 119.

Even more sensationally, he beat Tilden on the latter's home court in Philadelphia to help win the Davis Cup for France for the first time. When the French defended the trophy at the newly-built Stade Roland Garros in 1928 Lacoste lost to Tilden but clinched the tie by overcoming John Hennessy.

Sadly, after winning the French title for the third time in 1929 his health began to deteriorate and he abruptly retired. But he would live on another 67 years, make his clothing brand one of the most famous in sport, and outlive the other three Musketeers.

ROD LAVER (AUS)

How many Grand Slam titles would he have won if had not been ruled out of competition as a professional for the best five years of his life? Won 31 consecutive matches at Wimbledon between 1961 and 1970.

Born: Rockhampton, Queensland, Australia, August 9, 1938.
Grand Slam titles: Australian 1960, 1962, 1969. French 1962, 1969. Wimbledon 1961-62, 1968-69. United States 1962, 1969. Six men's doubles titles, three mixed doubles titles.
Davis Cup winning teams: Australia 1959-62, 1973.

Rod Laver stands joint third with Bjorn Borg in the all-time pantheon of men's Grand Slam champions with 11 titles, behind Pete Sampras (13) and Roy Emerson (12) but many experts rate him the greatest player of all. His career spanned the final years of the pre-Open Era, when contract professionals were barred from the traditional championships, and the first few years of the Open game, after which he was able to return to the major arenas and take up where he had left off. Who knows how many more top titles he would have won if he had been able to compete in the events he was denied access to between 1963 and 1967, when he dominated the pro tour?

Laver did not cut an imposing figure, but his left arm produced the most magnificent tennis ever seen. He had a complete game, with a devastating serve, penetrating ground strokes, beautifully timed volleys, a decisive smash and exquisite half-volleys. His topspin backhand, a shot rarely seen before but later adopted by such champions as Borg (albeit with two hands) and Guillermo Vilas, drew gasps from observers and sighs of despair from opponents.

Laver stands alone as the only tennis player – male or female – to achieve the Grand Slam twice. He did so in 1962, as an amateur, and in 1969 as a professional. Born just before Don Budge became the first Slammer in 1938, 'Rocket' took time to mature as a champion. He reached his first major final at Wimbledon in 1959, losing to Alex Olmedo, and would fail again at the same stage in 1960 at the hands of Neale Fraser. But by this time he had beaten Fraser for the Australian title and was on his way to the pinnacle of the sport.

He won his first Wimbledon singles title in 1961, crushing Chuck McKinley for the loss of eight games, and would never lose again there until 1970, when he lost in the fourth round to Britain's Roger Taylor. The greatest threat to his 1962 Slam came in Paris, where he was match point down to Australia's Martin Mulligan, but he more easily beat the same player to retain his Wimbledon crown. His toughest match during the 1969 campaign was a 90-game marathon against Tony Roche at the Australian Open. He won no more major titles after 1969 but played on at a high level until 1977.

IVAN LENDL (CZE/USA)

Hard-working with obsessive, methodic preparation. He played eight consecutive finals at the US Open and won there three times in a row, losing only three of 66 sets played.

Born: Ostrava, Czechoslovakia, March 7, 1960.
Grand Slam titles: Australian Open 1989-90. French Open 1984, 1986-87. US Open 1985-87.
Davis Cup winning team: Czechoslovakia 1980.

Ivan Lendl introduced a brand of tennis which is very much still with us now: a strong, deep serve and extremely powerful ground strokes, struck like missiles. In his time the grass court season shrank to a few weeks around Wimbledon and for a few years he didn't bother to play there, but when he made a serious bid to compete at Wimbledon he never quite got to grips with the need to volley and did not succeed despite twice reaching the final. He was tall, well built and super fit, and his heavy forehand reaped a huge reward on all surfaces other than grass (although he did win at Queen's Club in 1989).

His first big success was in the 1980 Davis Cup, when he won all three of his rubbers against Italy to secure Czechoslovakia's sole triumph in the competition. For the next three years he readily gathered minor titles but seemed to waver on the brink of Grand Slam success. Lendl's most remarkable feat was reaching the final of the US Open eight years in succession – a record he shares with Bill Tilden. He lost the first three in 1982-84, but took the next three in a row against John McEnroe, Miroslav Mecir and Mats Wilander. Then he lost to Wilander in 1988 and to Boris Becker in 1989. His first Grand Slam title was in Paris in 1984, when he recovered from two sets down to defeat McEnroe, then the undisputed world No. 1. Lendl had himself achieved the No. 1 ranking in February 1983 despite his lack of Grand Slam titles at that stage and would eventually become the longest incumbent in that position, with 270 weeks at the top, until Pete Sampras overtook him for this record in 1999.

He lost to Wilander in the 1985 French final but won it back in 1986 over Mikael Perfors and over Wilander in 1987. Having lost to Wilander in the 1983 Australian final, when it was still played on grass, he captured the title Down Under on hard courts over Mecir (1989) and Stefan Edberg (1990). He surrendered the title in the 1991 final to Becker. He failed to win a set in either of his Wimbledon finals, crashing to Becker in 1986 and to Pat Cash in 1987.

Lendl moved to the US in 1984 and became a US citizen in 1992. A chronic back injury obliged him to retire in 1994.

The Greatest – Men (continued)

JOHN MCENROE (USA)
Greatest artist to ever play the game. His talent made everybody forgive his outrageous behaviour on court.

Born: Wiesbaden, Germany, February 16, 1959.
Grand Slam titles: Wimbledon 1981, 1983-84. US Open: 1979-81, 1984. Nine men's doubles titles, one mixed doubles title.
Davis Cup winning teams: USA 1978-79, 1981-82, 1992.

John McEnroe is probably the most naturally gifted player ever to step onto a tennis court, and the most controversial. Crowds gasped with admiration at the sheer brilliance of his shotmaking and were appalled by the extremes of his behaviour. He waged a one man war against the tennis establishment for most of his turbulent career and came close to being thrown out of the sport long before he was finally disqualified at the Australian Open in 1990. But he never shirked his responsibilities in the Davis Cup and played with great distinction for 12 years, five times on the winning team. He always said that he did not need to practise very much because he played as much doubles as singles, ending his career with 78 singles and 78 doubles titles on his record. He won 10 Grand Slam doubles championships, including eight with his fellow-American Peter Fleming.

The foundation of his game was a left-handed service that he could vary as required, whether a swinging slice that drew his opponent well out of the court or a fast missile down the middle. He could play awesome volleys, struck hard or with feather-like touch, at breathtaking angles. And when he lost his temper with umpires and line judges he usually played even better. His matches were often stormy – most notably the 1982 Wimbledon final, which he lost to Jimmy Connors in deplorable circumstances. But with his other great rival, Bjorn Borg, whom he played in two classic Wimbledon finals in 1980 and 1981, there was a strong mutual respect.

He burst onto the scene in 1977, when he reached the semifinal at his first Wimbledon as an 18-year-old qualifier. The following year he made his Davis Cup debut in the final against Great Britain, winning both of his rubbers. He won his first US Open in 1979 and his first Wimbledon in 1981, reversing the previous year's titanic battle against Borg. His greatest year was 1984, when he came within a few games of winning the French Open (ultimately submitting to Ivan Lendl) and won Wimbledon for the third time. In the final against Connors he gave one of the most devastatingly ruthless displays ever seen on the Centre Court, destroying the former champion 61 61 62 in 80 minutes. McEnroe retired in 1992 after reaching the semifinals at Wimbledon and winning the doubles with Michael Stich.

ILIE NASTASE (ROM)
Won many less titles than he should, but his style on court will never be equalled. Played an unpredictable, new style of tennis.

Born: Bucharest, Romania, July 19, 1946.
Grand Slam titles: French Open 1973, US Open 1972. Three men's doubles titles, two mixed doubles titles.

Ilie Nastase was a supremely talented artist who could dazzle galleries with his skills and showmanship, but he could never resist the temptation to show off, create a diversion and infuriate an opponent with mischievous pranks. As a result he fell short of fulfilling his potential – he should have won many more major titles and lifted the Davis Cup for his country. Nastase had the ability to play every shot in the book to perfection, and he was an innovator, always coming up with the unexpected and toying with an opponent before delivering the coup de grace. But his temperament was fragile, and he would waste energy arguing with officials and performing outrageous antics that delighted crowds but derailed his own aims.

A stalwart in the Davis Cup – he played more rubbers than any other player except Italy's Nicola Pietrangeli – Nastase and his mentor Ion Tiriac took Romania to the Challenge Round in the United States in 1969 and 1971, then in the first year of the Final, in 1972, missed a golden opportunity to win the trophy on home soil. Overwhelmed with nerves, Nastase lost in straight sets to Stan Smith in the opening rubber and the chance was gone.

In individual play he was top-seeded in the 1970 French Open but flopped against America's Cliff Richey in the quarterfinals, and at 1973 Wimbledon, the year of the ATP boycott, he was the strong favourite but crashed out to another American, Sandy Mayer, in the fourth round. He narrowly lost to Smith in a magnificent Wimbledon final in 1972 but at the same stage four years later was outplayed by Bjorn Borg in straight sets.

Against those failures, Nastase had a spectacular success at the 1972 US Open, where he recovered from two sets to one and 4-2 down in the fourth to beat Arthur Ashe for the title. The following year he won the French Open without dropping a set and became the first man to be ranked No. 1 when the ATP introduced its computerised world ranking list. Apart from these two Grand Slam titles he was four times the winner of the Grand Prix Masters (precursor of today's Tennis Masters Cup) and won two Italian Opens. During a playing career that lasted from 1966 to 1985 he had 57 singles and 51 doubles tournament victories.

JOHN NEWCOMBE (AUS)

He never won the French, but in Rome they will never forget the way he played and won the Italian Open in 1969, beating Jan Kodes in five sets in the semis and Tony Roche in the finals.

Born:	Sydney, Australia, May 23, 1944.
Grand Slam titles:	Australian Open 1973, 1975. Wimbledon 1967, 1970-71. United States 1967, 1973. 17 men's doubles titles, one mixed doubles title.
Davis Cup winning teams:	Australia 1965-67, 1973.

John Newcombe was the last of the line of great Australian champions who ruled tennis throughout the 1950s and 1960s, and he was the last amateur champion of Wimbledon, easily defeating Germany's Wilhelm Bungert 63 61 61 in a final that lasted only 71 minutes. Open tennis came at exactly the right time for him – he was 23 and the clear world No. 1 when he turned professional at the end of 1967, when the signs were that the distinction between amateurs and pros was about to be abolished.

Even with the pros on the scene he was good enough to reach the Wimbledon final in 1969, where he had to settle for a supporting role in Rod Laver's Grand Slam victory parade, but he regained the title in 1970 over another veteran Aussie, Ken Rosewall, and held onto it the following year against a determined challenge from America's Stan Smith.

Newcombe was an all-out, no-frills attacking player whose aim was always to deliver a fast, swinging first serve, get straight into the net and put away the volley. He was devastating in the air and overhead, and his game was ideally suited to grass, on which he won all his major titles. But he was so fit and ready to run that he achieved some success on clay as well, winning the German Open in 1968 and the Italian in 1969. He made few attempts on the French Open, where his best result was a 1969 quarterfinal.

His two United States championships – one as an amateur and one as a pro – were six years apart and widely differing in the manner of their achievement. In 1967 he dropped only three sets in six rounds, while in 1973 he was pushed all the way in the final by Jan Kodes, who beat him in the first round in 1971. He won his first Australian Open in a fairly weak field, because the event was staged between Christmas and the New Year, beating New Zealander Onny Parun in a four set final, and he took the title back from Jimmy Connors in the 1975 decider.

He was even more successful in doubles, winning 12 Grand Slam championships with Tony Roche and a grand total of 25 Slam trophies in singles, doubles and mixed – more than any other man except Roy Emerson. His top class playing career lasted from 1963 to 1978.

BUDGE PATTY (USA)

The most European of the Americans of his generation. An artist at the net. Won the French and Wimbledon in 1950.

Born:	Fort Smith, Arkansas, USA, February 11, 1924.
Grand Slam titles:	French 1950, Wimbledon 1950. One men's doubles title, one mixed doubles titles.

An American who has lived in Switzerland for many years, John Edward Patty was nicknamed 'Budge' by his elder brother because he was a lazy child. Patty went half way towards achieving the Grand Slam when he won the French Championship and Wimbledon within a month in 1950 – one of only a handful of men to do so. Despite his American nationality, Patty identified strongly with Europe and he developed his game on clay courts. He was a great stylist and had elegant ground strokes but his match-winning shot was a thunderous forehand volley.

He established himself as one of the world's leading players immediately after the war and reached the semifinals at Wimbledon in 1947, when he lost to Tom Brown, the semifinals of Roland Garros in 1948 (losing to Jaroslav Drobny) and the final in 1949, beating Pancho Gonzales and submitting to another American, Frank Parker.

At the start of 1950 he had made a big effort to improve his fitness. He gave up smoking and got into perfect physical condition. He won the French Championship with two gruelling victories in the last two rounds – 1311 in the fifth against Bill Talbert and 75 in the fifth against Drobny. At Wimbledon he battled past Talbert, Vic Seixas and Frank Sedgman to take the title. His superb forehand volley, considered one of the best of all time, and his perfect topspin lobs, which thwarted Sedgman's net attack, were the decisive factors in his victory.

In 1953 he clashed with Drobny in the third round and lost (at that time) Wimbledon's longest ever match – a 93-game classic that ended late in the evening. This was the most celebrated of a long series of epic matches between the two friends. He was also a semifinalist in 1954, losing to Drobny, and in 1955, when he fell to Tony Trabert. In 1957 he won the doubles with the 43-year-old American, Gardnar Mulloy, beating Neale Fraser and Lew Hoad in the final. With a combined age of 76, Patty and Mulloy are the oldest pair to win a post-war Grand Slam doubles title. He was also three times a quarterfinalist at Forest Hills and the Italian champion of 1954. His last notable match was in Paris in 1958, when he lost in the fourth round to Robert Haillet after leading 50 40-0 in the final set.

The Greatest – Men (continued)

FRED PERRY (GBR)

Everybody knows (especially Tim Henman) that he was the last British player to win Wimbledon, in 1936. He was also the last one to win any Grand Slam tournament.

Born:	Stockport, Cheshire, England, May 18, 1909.
Died:	Melbourne, Australia, February 2, 1995.
Grand Slam titles:	Australian 1934. French 1935. Wimbledon 1934-36. United States 1933-34, 1936. Two men's doubles titles, four mixed doubles titles.
Davis Cup winning teams:	Great Britain 1933-36.

Fred Perry was the greatest British player of all time and the last to date to win any Grand Slam men's singles titles. He was the first player to win all four majors (although not all in the same year) and his name is universally known today not only because he was such a successful player but through the sports clothes company he founded and which is still a prestigious brand. He became a world champion at two sports – at table tennis, whose world championship he won in 1929, and at tennis, at which he was the dominant player from 1934 to 1936.

He was a supremely confident and self-assured person and had the iron willpower and determination, that all champions need, in abundance. Considering that he did not take up tennis until he was 18, he mastered the game extraordinarily quickly. Benefiting from the competitive edge he had already acquired as a top table tennis player, Perry assembled a formidable array of shots, the best of which was his running forehand, hit early with a continental grip, which overwhelmed his opponents because he struck the ball as soon as it rose from the court.

He was good enough to make the world's top ten in 1931, just four years after he had taken up the game, and reached the semifinals at Wimbledon that year. In 1933 he spearheaded Great Britain's first triumph in the Davis Cup for 21 years, beating Wilmer Allison and Ellsworth Vines of the USA in the Inter-Zone Final and Henri Cochet and Andre Merlin of France in the Challenge Round. Both of these ties were on clay in Paris. Later that summer he won the United States Championship, overcoming Allison 86 in the fifth set of the final.

At Wimbledon he won three consecutive finals in straight sets – against Jack Crawford in 1934 and Gottfried von Cramm in 1935 and 1936. He beat Crawford again for the 1934 Australian title and von Cramm in the 1935 Roland Garros final. He played a pivotal role in retaining the Davis Cup for Britain in 1934-36, winning all his Challenge Round rubbers. In taking his third US crown he defeated Don Budge, who took over as world No. 1 when Perry turned professional at the end of 1936. Perry also won the US pro championship in 1938 and 1941.

BOBBY RIGGS (USA)

Known mostly for the match he lost to Billie Jean King in 1973 but don't forget that he won Wimbledon and the US Championships just before the outbreak of the war in 1939.

Born:	Los Angeles, USA, February 25, 1918.
Died:	Luecadia, California, USA, October 25, 1995.
Grand Slam titles:	Wimbledon 1939. United States 1939, 1941, One men's doubles titles, two mixed doubles titles.
Davis Cup winning team:	USA 1938.

Although Bobby Riggs has the rare distinction of winning all three titles open to him – singles, doubles and mixed – at his one and only attempt, in his appearance at Wimbledon in 1939, he is best remembered as the self-appointed 'Male Chauvinist Pig' of 1973 who played two highly publicised mixed singles matches against Margaret Court and Billie Jean King. The latter encounter, at the Houston Astradome, attracted more spectators (30,472) and a bigger television audience (50 million) than any other match in the history of tennis.

Riggs, an inveterate gambler who made a fortune by betting on his matches and arranging bizarre gimmick events, placed a wager with a London bookmaker before his Wimbledon campaign, backing himself at very long odds to win the triple crown. As he had just lost the final of the Queen's Club tournament 61 60 to Gottfried von Cramm, the likelihood of his losing his stake seemed great. But he went on to win the singles, beating his fellow-American Elwood Cooke in a five set singles final, joining Cooke to defeat Charles Hare and Frank Wilde for the men's doubles title, and taking the mixed doubles with Alice Marble over Wilde and Nina Brown. From his stake of £100 he netted £21,600 – a considerable sum in those days.

He didn't hit with great power, but he was a very clever strategist who could outmanoeuvre big hitters with subtlety and cunning. His lobs and drop shots were well disguised and uncannily accurate. Add to these qualities a boundless self-confidence and you have a very capable player, able to make the most of his opportunities. When Don Budge turned professional at the end of 1938 Riggs was ready to take over the amateur game. With war looming he followed up his Wimbledon victory by taking the United States title, demolishing Welby Van Horn in a straight set final. He lost the title to Don McNeill in 1940 but regained it the following year over Frank Kovacs.

He enjoyed a successful career as a pro throughout the 1940s, becoming a promoter at the end of the decade. Then over 20 years later he emerged from obscurity in the age of Women's Lib to challenge first Court, whom he beat 61 62 and then King, who made him look his age, winning 64 63 63. But he was believed to have made $1 million out of it.

TONY ROCHE (AUS)

On grass, his best surface, he always found Rod Laver or John Newcombe in his path, but he did win the French Open on clay. One of the best doubles players ever.

Born: Wagga Wagga, New South Wales, Australia, May 17, 1945.
Grand Slam titles: French 1966. 12 men's doubles titles, two mixed doubles titles.
Davis Cup winning teams: Australia 1965-67, 1977.

For a player who had a formidable left-handed serve and volleying skills second to none, it was a strange quirk of fate that Tony Roche never won a major singles title on grass. He was runner-up to Rod Laver at Wimbledon in 1968 and at Forest Hills in 1969, and to Ken Rosewall at Forest Hills in 1970. Then he won 14 Grand Slam doubles and mixed doubles titles during an 11-year stretch. But his only big singles victory was at the French Championships in 1966, a few weeks after he had lifted the next most important clay court title, the Italian. He won both the semifinal (against Francois Jauffret) and the final at Roland Garros (against Istvan Gulyas) in straight sets, tempering the power of his serve and volley game with well-struck, accurate ground strokes.

At the end of 1967 he turned professional a few months before the arrival of Open tennis. At Wimbledon 1968 he swept past the second seeded Rosewall on his way to the final, but once there he was no match for Laver. In 1969 at Forest Hills he defeated John Newcombe 8-6 in the fifth set of a thrilling semifinal, but could only play a supporting role in Laver's historic progress to a second Grand Slam. And in 1970 he could not prevent Rosewall from turning back the years to win the US Open 14 years after his previous triumph.

Not long afterwards, Roche began to suffer from shoulder trouble and tennis elbow. He tried numerous cures, eventually turning to a faith healer in the Philippines in 1974 who performed an operation by acupuncture. Although he never completely recovered from the injury he was able to resume competition and continued to acquire major doubles titles. His partnership with Newcombe garnered five Wimbledon championships – a record in the post-World War I period until overtaken by Todd Woodbridge and Mark Woodforde in 2000.

Roche was included in the Australian Davis Cup team for nine years between 1964 and 1978 and had his finest hour in 1977 when he was selected to play singles in the final against Italy in Sydney and beat Adriano Panatta in the opening rubber. He retired in 1979 and would later coach Ivan Lendl and Patrick Rafter, as well as coaching the Australian Davis Cup team from 1997 to 2000.

KEN ROSEWALL (AUS)

Both the youngest and the oldest winner of the Australian Championships. Won his two titles there 19 years apart and appeared in Wimbledon finals 20 years apart.

Born: Sydney, Australia, November 2, 1934.
Grand Slam titles: Australian 1953, 1955, 1971-72. French 1953, 1968. United States 1956, 1970. Nine men's doubles titles, one mixed doubles title.
Davis Cup winning teams: Australia, 1953, 1955-56.

Ken Rosewall is the ultimate long haul tennis champion: his international playing career lasted an amazing 25 years, from 1952 to 1977, and he won Grand Slam titles over a span of 17 years. He played his last Wimbledon final 20 years after his first, making him the oldest Grand Slam finalist in the post-war era. Ironically nicknamed 'Muscles', Rosewall was slight for a phenomenal athlete at only 5ft 7in tall and 135 pounds. He could not generate the power of his stablemate Lew Hoad, with whom he took the world by storm as a 17-year-old in 1952, but he used his brain and a matchless array of wonderful strokes to stay amongst the world's best 20 players for all of his quarter-century in the world class game.

Rosewall was, perhaps more than any other player, equally good on any surface. He could play the serve and volley game with magnificent panache because his serve, though not especially strong, was well placed and delivered with admirable technique. His net game was exemplary and his agility second to none. Similarly, he had such fine groundstrokes – including possibly the most beautifully hit backhand the world has ever seen – that he was as much a master on clay as grass. Blessed with an unflappable temperament and impeccable sportsmanship, you can understand the world's dismay that he never won Wimbledon despite reaching the final four times.

His career falls into three phases. From 1952 to 1956 he was one of the top amateurs, winning two Australian, one French and one US championship (plus the doubles at all four Grand Slams) and losing two Wimbledon finals – to Jaroslav Drobny in 1954 and to Hoad in 1956. Then he turned professional, and spent the next 12 years barred from the traditional events. When Open tennis arrived in 1968 he was 33 but still the world's No. 2 player, and for 10 more years he regularly won big titles, taking two more Australian, one French and one US Open.

He won the first ever Open tournament, beating Rod Laver in the final at Bournemouth, but his most remarkable feat was reaching the finals both at Wimbledon and Forest Hills in 1974 at the age of 39. Sadly, he was humiliated in both matches by Jimmy Connors, 18 years his junior. He also took part in the Davis Cup in years as far apart as 1953 and 1975.

Manuel Santana (ESP) received the 2004 ITF/ITHF Davis Cup Award of Excellence

PETE SAMPRAS (USA)

They shouldn't wait five years for his induction into the International Tennis Hall of Fame. Seven Wimbledons and seven other Grand Slam titles make up for the one he has not claimed in Paris.

Born: Washington DC, USA, August 12, 1971.
Grand Slam titles: Australian Open 1994, 1997. Wimbledon 1993-95, 1997-2000. US Open 1990, 1993, 1995-96, 2002.
Davis Cup winning teams: USA 1992, 1995.

With 14 Grand Slam titles to his name, Sampras is the all-time No. 1 men's Grand Slam champion, including two Australian and five US Opens in his tally. But those who argue that Rod Laver, with two calendar Slams was the greater player, point to an inescapable blemish on Sampras's record. He never, in 13 attempts, managed to take the French Open, and on only one occasion went further than the quarterfinals. Although he won the Italian Open on clay in 1994, Sampras always found the demands of the red clay Grand Slam event beyond his ability to conquer.

This great champion, regarded with awe and respect by all his fellow-players, proved himself over and over again on all surfaces other than clay by his peerless command of the game. A dynamic, beautifully constructed service action, crunching forehand, precision volleys and, above all, his famous 'slam dunk' jumping smash made him the winner of 64 career singles titles and a supreme status at No. 1 on the ATP rankings for 286 weeks, including a record six consecutive year-end finishes in pole position. This achievement is the one cited by those who insist he was better than Laver, disregarding the fact that Laver's career spanned the pre-Open and Open Eras, with all-player rankings impossible to determine before 1968. Against that, it must be acknowledged that the overall quality of the sport was much weaker in Laver's day.

Sampras became the youngest-ever US Open champion in 1990, when he was 19, and his unparalleled run of success at Wimbledon between 1993 and 2000 was broken only by a quarterfinal defeat by Richard Krajicek in 1996. At Flushing Meadows he was runner-up in 1992 (to Stefan Edberg), in 2000 (to Marat Safin) and in 2001 (to Lleyton Hewitt). Winning the 2002 US Open delivering a resounding response to those who had said his career was over. He defeated old rival Andre Agassi in a high-quality final, claiming his first title in 34 tournaments and winning his first event since claiming his record breaking 13th Grand Slam title at Wimbledon in 2000. The US Open win turned out to be his last professional match. After taking time off for the birth of his first child with his actress wife Bridgette Wilson, a son born in November 2002, Sampras officially announced his retirement a year later at the 2003 US Open.

MANUEL SANTANA (ESP)

The only Spanish player to win a Grand Slam title on grass, and he did it twice – at the US Championships in 1965 and at Wimbledon a year later. He introduced the passing lifted lob to tennis.

Born: Madrid, Spain, May 10, 1938.
Grand Slam titles: French 1961, 1964. Wimbledon 1966. United States 1965. One men's doubles title.

Manuel Santana remains the greatest Spanish player in the history of tennis despite the recent resurgence of the game in his country. Not only did he twice win the French championship on clay, the surface on which he learnt the game, but he captured two Grand Slam titles on grass, at Forest Hills and Wimbledon. A cheerful and popular character with a trademark gap-tooth smile, Santana was an impeccably good-mannered player and a consummate stylist. Not only did he hit the ball with both power and touch, but his exceptional racket control enabled him to produce amazing winners when least expected. This magician could improvise and dig himself out of seemingly impossible situations with clever drop shots, topspin lobs and half-volleys. During his career his rivalry with Roy Emerson enthralled galleries with the contrast between the irresistible force of the net-rushing Australian and the immovable object of the ever-resourceful Spaniard.

Santana reached the quarterfinals of the French Championship in 1960 and first won it the following year, scoring five-set victories over Rod Laver and Nicola Pietrangeli in the last two rounds. In 1962 and 1963 he was a semifinalist, losing to Emerson and Pierre Darmon, but he was champion again in 1964, avenging the previous year's defeat by Darmon in the semis and repeating his 1961 final victory over Pietrangeli. He also won the doubles in 1963 with Emerson. At Forest Hills he never made the later stages before 1965, when he overcame Arthur Ashe in the semis and Cliff Drysdale in the final. The following year he succumbed in the semis to John Newcombe. At Wimbledon he was in the last eight of 1962 and the last four of 1963, when he failed to win a set against Fred Stolle, but in 1966, seeded fourth, he was in the best form of his career. Santana survived two five set epics against Ken Fletcher in the quarters and Owen Davidson in the semis, both at 75 in the fifth, before outmanoeuvring Dennis Ralston 64 119 64 for the title.

In 1967 he became the only men's champion at Wimbledon ever to surrender his title in the first round, at the hands of Charlie Pasarell. He led Spain to two Davis Cup Challenge Rounds (1965, 1967) and between 1958 and 1973 played more times in the event than anyone in history except Pietrangeli and Ilie Nastase.

The Greatest – Men (continued)

TED SCHROEDER (USA)
Won Wimbledon the only time he played the tournament. Despite a limited schedule he was ranked in the top six for six years in a row.

Born: Newark, New Jersey, USA, July 20, 1921.
Grand Slam titles: Wimbledon 1949. United States 1942. Three men's doubles titles, one mixed doubles title.
Davis Cup winning teams: USA 1946-49.

Ted Schroeder is one of an elite group of four players who won Wimbledon at their sole attempt. (The others are Patrick Hadow, 1878, Bobby Riggs, 1939 and Pauline Betz, 1946.) He was the first champion to be presented with the trophy on court (before this, singles winners went up to the Royal Box for the presentation, like doubles champions still do today). And he is one of eight men's champions to win the title from match point down. A jovial, pipe-smoking American who walked with a rolling gait, Schroeder was also one of the few champions for whom tennis was never his number one priority. As an engineer his competitive outings were strictly limited, and this is why his overseas trips were so few: apart from the one Wimbledon appearance in 1949, his only other travels were as part of the US Davis Cup squad.

Schroeder was a formidable player whose major weapon was a fatally good volley. As a student at Stanford University he was one of only two players (the other was Don McNeill in 1940) to win both the US Intercollegiate title and the National Championship at Forest Hills in the same year, 1942. He had an uncanny knack of rising to the occasion and producing his best form at major events, and this was why, for six consecutive years, he was selected for the Davis Cup over players with far more matchplay under their belts. He justified these selections by compiling an 11-3 winning record in singles rubbers.

His Forest Hills record was impressive, beginning with the men's doubles in 1940 with his great friend Jack Kramer. The following year he reached the semifinal of the singles, pushing Riggs all the way before losing 75 in the fifth set. In his winning year of 1942 he eked out a five set victory over Frank Parker in the championship round. For the next three years he played little tennis because he was serving in the US Navy.

Apart from his Davis Cup outings he scarcely figured again until 1949, when he won Wimbledon after being match point down to Frank Sedgman in the quarterfinals and led Pancho Gonzales two sets to love before fading in the US final. Schroeder won three US men's doubles titles with Kramer and one mixed doubles with Louise Brough.

FRANK SEDGMAN (AUS)
The best player in the most difficult zone of the court – between the service line and the baseline – giving him spectacular coverage. Turned professional at 25 after winning five Grand Slam titles and three Davis Cups for Australia.

Born: Mount Albert, Victoria, Australia, October 29, 1927.
Grand Slam titles: Australian 1949-50. Wimbledon 1952. United States 1951-52. Nine men's doubles titles, eight mixed doubles titles.
Davis Cup winning teams: Australia 1950-52.

No other player ever accumulated so many Grand Slam singles, doubles and mixed doubles titles within a four year period as Frank Sedgman, who totted up 22 between 1949 and 1952, placing him third in the all-time men's list behind Roy Emerson (28) and John Newcombe (25). Who knows how many more Sedgman would have won had he not turned professional at the age of 25 and ruled himself out of contention. Sedgman was the first of a long line of Australian champions who ruled the game for 25 years. A fitness fanatic, he worked assiduously in the gym and in outdoor training to build up an enviable athletic physique and reserves of stamina that enabled him to compete, week after week, at tournaments around the world. He was a staunch disciple of the serve and volley game, and lived at the net, from whence he rarely needed to play a second volley.

His five singles, nine men's doubles and eight mixed doubles Grand Slam titles are a testament to his desire to compete to the full. He was the third and last man to win the triple crown at Wimbledon (Don Budge and Bobby Riggs were the others) and with fellow-Australian Ken McGregor he achieved the only Grand Slam in men's doubles in 1951. (They came within a whisker of repeating the sweep the following year but lost 86 in the fifth set of the US final to Mervyn Rose and Vic Seixas.)

Sedgman began his international career in 1947, and in 1949 he won the Australian championship, battering his more experienced compatriot John Bromwich in straight sets. The following year he overcame McGregor in four sets for the title. In the French singles, the only one of the 12 Grand Slam titles (including doubles) to elude him, he was runner-up to Jaroslav Drobny in 1952. At Wimbledon he lost the 1950 final to Budge Patty but won in 1952, avenging his Roland Garros loss to Drobny. He won the US championships in 1951 and 1952, against Seixas and Gardnar Mulloy.

He embarked on a glorious professional career at the end of 1952 and kept himself in such great shape that he was able to return to Wimbledon and the other traditional events after tennis went Open. Even in his mid-forties he was good enough to reach the third round at Wimbledon in 1971 and at Melbourne in 1972.

VIC SEIXAS (USA)

A great competitor. Won Wimbledon in 1953 and the US Championships in 1954, finishing that year with a great victory over Ken Rosewall in the Davis Cup Final in White City.

Born: Philadelphia, USA, August 30, 1923.
Grand Slam titles: Wimbledon 1953. United States 1954. Five men's doubles titles, eight mixed doubles titles.
Davis Cup winning team: USA 1954.

During the 1950s, nine men won the Wimbledon singles title – more than in any other decade. Only Lew Hoad won it twice. There are two reasons for such a wide distribution of victories: firstly, it was an era when no one man (apart from Hoad) got into a dominating position; and secondly it was a time when Wimbledon champions usually turned professional as soon as they had won the world's biggest title – a vital bargaining counter towards securing a lucrative contract. Vic Seixas, who won Wimbledon in 1953, was a one-time champion, but he preferred to keep his amateur status because he was already comfortably off. In fact, such was his love of the game that he carried on competing for years after his peak and last appeared at Wimbledon in the men's doubles of 1973, partnering another veteran, Frank Sedgman.

He wasn't an exceptionally talented player, but he had a superb match temperament and volleying skills that earned him 13 Grand Slam doubles and mixed doubles titles in addition to his two major singles championships. He served as a pilot in the US Air Force during World War II and graduated from the University of North Carolina, and his international tennis career began in earnest in 1950, when he reached the quarterfinals at Roland Garros and the semifinals at Wimbledon. His Wimbledon victory was marked by tough five-setters against Hoad in the quarterfinals and Mervyn Rose in the semis, but he dismissed the unseeded Dane, Kurt Nielsen, in straight sets in the final. He played three finals at Forest Hills, losing to Sedgman in 1951 and Tony Trabert in 1953, but won the following year over Rex Hartwig. He was also runner-up to Ken Rosewall in the 1953 French final. In the Davis Cup Seixas played every year from 1951 to 1957, and was on the winning team in 1954, when he beat Rosewall and won the doubles with Trabert. He won four consecutive mixed doubles titles from 1953 to 1956 – the first three with Doris Hart and the last with Shirley Fry.

He carried on playing throughout the 1960s. In 1966, when he was 42, Seixas won the fifth longest singles match in history – a 32 34 64 10 8 epic against Bill Bowrey at the Pennsylvania Grass Court Championships. And in 1973, when he was 50, he finally turned pro to compete on the Grand Masters circuit.

FRED STOLLE (AUS)

Lost three Wimbledon finals in a row but won the French and the US titles, the latter unseeded in 1966. He was a great doubles player.

Born: Hornsby, New South Wales, Australia, October 8, 1938.
Grand Slam titles: French 1965. United States 1966. Ten men's doubles titles, six mixed doubles titles.
Davis Cup winning teams: Australia 1964-66.

Such was the plethora of tennis talent that came out of Australia in the 1950s and 1960s that Fred Stolle tends to be overshadowed by the likes of Rod Laver, Ken Rosewall, Roy Emerson and John Newcombe. But he was a highly successful player, reaching the finals of all four Grand Slam events and winning all four doubles titles at these championships. He stands tenth in the all-time list of multiple Grand Slam champions, with a total of 18 titles – two singles, 10 men's doubles and six mixed doubles. A tall (6ft 3in) and rangy player, Stolle had an impressive serve and volley style but an excellent baseline game as well, enabling him to win the French and German titles on continental clay. Although he played in the Davis Cup for only three seasons he was on the winning team all three times and managed a commanding 13-3 win-loss record in the competition.

His singles record is one of enviable consistency over a long period, although he never reached the very pinnacle of the sport and his best world ranking was No. 2 for 1964 and 1966. His two Grand Slam singles titles came shortly before the arrival of Open tennis, and because he turned professional at the beginning of 1967 he missed only one year of traditional competition.

At the French Championships in 1965 he beat Cliff Drysdale in five sets in the semifinals and Tony Roche in four sets in the final. He also reached the last eight at Roland Garros in 1966 and 1969. In the Australian Championships he lost to Emerson in the finals of 1964 and 1965 – the first time easily and the second in five gruelling sets. At Wimbledon he had the misfortune to lose three consecutive finals – against Chuck McKinley in 1963 and against Emerson in 1964 and 1965. His finest hour came at Forest Hills in 1966. Despite having lost to Emerson in the 1964 final and having just won the German championship, he found himself unseeded and, stung by the slight, proceeded to win the title. At last he beat his old nemesis, Emerson, in a stunningly one-sided 64 61 61 semifinal and got the better of Newcombe, also unseeded, in a tough 46 12 10 63 64 final.

He also reached the quarterfinals at the US Open in 1969 and 1972, when at the age of 33 he beat Emerson, Newcombe and Drysdale before submitting to Ilie Nastase in four sets.

The Greatest – Men (continued)

BILL TILDEN (USA)

A legend. Old-time experts considered him the best ever, but the success of the Four Musketeers against him puts a question mark over that. Won his first and last Wimbledon title ten years apart, in 1920 and 1930.

Born:	Germantown, Pennsylvania, USA, February 10, 1893.
Died:	Los Angeles, USA, June 5, 1953.
Grand Slam titles:	Wimbledon 1920-21, 1930. United States 1920-25, 1929. Six men's doubles titles, five mixed doubles titles.
Davis Cup winning teams:	USA 1920-26.

Historians generally agree that Bill Tilden was one of the three greatest players of all time, along with Rod Laver and Pete Sampras. He was virtually unbeatable between 1920 and 1926, and achieved a level of dominance unsurpassed by any other man. He won seven US and three Wimbledon singles titles, the third 10 years after the first, and at 37 he was one of the oldest champions. With a total of 21 Grand Slam singles, doubles and mixed titles he stands fourth in the men's all-time table. An imposing figure at over 6ft tall with broad shoulders, Tilden was a master of every shot in the game, with a cannonball first serve and vicious, kicking American twist second serve, an extraordinary deployment of spin, slice and chop and devastatingly effective drop shots. He played chiefly from the back of the court and operated his matches like a game of chess, using innovative strategies to confound all but the most able of opponents.

Tilden lost half of one of his fingers in an accident early in his career but modified his grip and the handicap never affected him. There are stories of poor personal hygiene and homosexuality, which later caused him to be ostracised in tennis circles, but he had a very forceful personality, coloured by strong likes and dislikes. He was also constantly at loggerheads with his national association.

Tilden lost his first two US finals in 1918 and 1919 but began his reign as champion in 1920 when he won the first of six consecutive finals against his compatriot Bill Johnston. Also in 1920 he made his first appearance at Wimbledon and defeated the holder, Gerald Patterson, in the Challenge Round. In defending the title in 1921 he saved a match point against the young South African, Brian Norton. In the late 1920s he was eclipsed by the Frenchmen Henri Cochet and Rene Lacoste at major championships but in 1930 at Wimbledon he squeezed past Jean Borotra in the last four and regained the title against Wilmer Allison in the final.

At Forest Hills he won for the last time in 1929, over Frank Hunter. Tilden was twice runner-up for the French Championship and won 13 consecutive rubbers in the Challenge Round of the Davis Cup between 1920 and 1927. He turned professional in 1931 and continued playing right up to his death at the age of 60.

TONY TRABERT (USA)

Won five Grand Slam titles, three of them without losing a single set. He turned professional in 1955 at the age of 25.

Born:	Cincinnati, USA, August 16, 1930.
Grand Slam titles:	French 1954-55. Wimbledon 1955. United States 1953, 1955. Five men's doubles titles.
Davis Cup winning team:	USA 1954.

Tony Trabert, the archetypal 1950s American athlete with a strong physique, crewcut and pugnacious personality, is known to tennis fans today as former tournament director of the US Open, and he still introduces the finalists for the trophy presentations in Arthur Ashe Stadium. But in 1955 he achieved a stranglehold over men's tennis, winning three of the four Grand Slam championships and capturing 18 singles and 12 doubles titles at the 23 tournaments he entered. Unusually for a player in that era he was equally good on all surfaces, because in addition to an attacking game with firm volleys he owned superb ground strokes – particularly on the backhand. Between 1950, when he won the French doubles, and his annus mirabilis of 1955, he was a stalwart of the US Davis Cup team, joining Vic Seixas in his country's only victory over Australia in an eight year stretch in 1954.

His Grand Slam singles parade began in 1953, when he won his first US title without losing a set, brushing aside French champion Ken Rosewall in the last four and finishing with a decisive 64 61 61 victory over Seixas, the reigning Wimbledon champion. In 1954 and 1955 he was unbeaten at Roland Garros, trouncing Art Larsen and Sven Davidson in the two finals. No other American won the title until Michael Chang in 1989.

Trabert went on to win Wimbledon in 1955 without dropping a set, taking out Jaroslav Drobny, the holder, in the quarterfinals, Budge Patty, the 1950 champion, in the semifinals and crushing Kurt Nielsen 63 75 61 in the final. He repeated the feat at Forest Hills, allowing Lew Hoad only seven games in the semifinals and avenging his one blemish of the year against Ken Rosewall in the title round. Rosewall had wrecked Trabert's chances of winning the Grand Slam in the semifinals of the Australian Championships.

Trabert also had a strong doubles record. Partnering Seixas, he won the Australian title in 1955, the French in 1954 and 1955 and the US Nationals at Boston in 1954 as well as the 1950 French with Bill Talbert. He turned professional in 1956 but was unable to match the skills of Pancho Gonzales, then at the height of his powers. When his playing career ended in the early 1960s he became a coach and a television commentator and served as the US Davis Cup captain in 1978 and 1979, leading the team to victory both times.

GUILLERMO VILAS (ARG)

A clay court specialist who was able to win the Australian Open twice on grass. The only man from Argentina to have won a Grand Slam title.

Born: Mar del Plata, Argentina, August 17, 1952.
Grand Slam titles: Australian Open 1978-79. French Open 1977. US Open 1977.

South America has produced a string of fine male players over the years, but none has had as much success as Argentina's Guillermo Vilas, a relentless winning machine who achieved an Open Era record of 50 consecutive match wins and claimed two Grand Slam titles in his best year, 1977. A thick-set, muscular athlete with thighs like tree trunks, Vilas was a distinctive, head-banded figure with flowing brown hair and the strength of an ox. A left-hander with a dangerous, swinging serve, he could rally for ever with heavy, topspun ground strokes on both sides and a heartbreakingly cruel lob. But though his game was ideally suited to clay he proved his versatility by winning three major titles on grass at Melbourne. He also had a social conscience. He wore two bracelets that once belonged to unidentified American soldiers killed in the Vietnam War, and he composed poetry which indicated a sensitivity towards the world beyond the existence of the touring tennis professional.

Although his main tour career lasted from 1970 to 1989, the most productive stage was from 1973 to 1983, during which time he gathered 62 titles. Given the clear suitability of his game for clay, it was an extraordinary surprise that he won his first big title, the Grand Prix Masters, on grass. He beat John Newcombe, Bjorn Borg and Onny Parun in his group, then Raul Ramirez in the semifinals and Ilie Nastase in the final. He returned to Melbourne in 1977 and lost the Australian Open final to Roscoe Tanner, but he took the title in 1978 over John Marks and in 1979 over John Sadri.

But Vilas's forte was really on clay, and his monumental run in 1977 included victory at Roland Garros, where he destroyed Brian Gottfried 60 63 60 in the shortest final on record, and at Forest Hills, in the US Open's third staging on clay and last time at the West Side Club. He beat holder Jimmy Connors in a thrilling four set final and by rights should have overtaken the American as No. 1 in the world. However, the ATP's computer never raised him higher than No. 2. Vilas's last big final was at the 1982 French Open, where he lost to Mats Wilander, and in the Davis Cup he and Jose Luis Clerc took Argentina to the 1981 final but could not overcome the United States.

ELLSWORTH VINES (USA)

In 1933 he lost one of the best Wimbledon finals ever to Jack Crawford. He turned professional at the age of 22.

Born: Los Angeles, USA, September 28, 1911.
Died: La Quinta, California, USA, March 17, 1994.
Grand Slam titles: Wimbledon 1932. United States 1931-32. Two men's doubles titles, one mixed doubles title.

Nicknamed "The Californian Comet", Henry Ellsworth Vines Jr appeared at Wimbledon for the first time in 1932 and blazed to the title, losing just one set in seven matches. He briefly lost his way against Iwao Aoki of Japan in the fourth round, but then demolished Enrique Maier of Spain 62 63 62, Jack Crawford of Australia 62 61 63 and, in the final, Britain's Bunny Austin 64 62 60 in a devastating 50 minutes. His winning shot, an ace, was so fast that Austin never even saw it.

Vines was less overwhelming at Forest Hills, where he won in 1931 by overcoming Fred Perry in five sets in the semifinals and George Lott in a tough 79 63 97 75 final. He retained the title with even more difficulty, extended to 46 810 1210 108 61 by Charles Sutter in the semis and Henri Cochet 64 64 64 in the final. But the Comet really lived up to his name. In 1933 he lost both to Perry and Austin in the Davis Cup, was outmanoeuvred by the wily Crawford in the Wimbledon final and stunned by a less exalted American, Bitsy Grant, in the fourth round at Forest Hills. Shortly afterwards, at the age of only 22, he turned professional and won a series against Bill Tilden, but by the end of the 1930s he had lost interest in tennis and turned to golf, at which sport he became good enough to reach the semifinals of the 1951 US PGA Championship.

What made this phenomenal talent so good for such a short space of time? Vines had a thunderbolt serve, probably the fastest struck by any player in the wooden racket era, with very little spin, a fast and no holds barred forehand, deadly volleys and a smash that never came back. He had little margin for error, going for broke on everything, so that when he was on song he was unplayable, but if his timing was off he would perpetrate suicidal errors.

Vines's amateur career was so short – he first played Forest Hills as an 18-year-old in 1929 and turned pro just four years later – that it is difficult to assess his standing among the all-time greats. But Jack Kramer rated Vines the second greatest player he ever saw, after Don Budge. "On his best days, Vines played the best tennis ever," he wrote. "Hell, when Elly was on, you'd be lucky to get your racket on the ball once you served it."

The Greatest – Men (continued)

MATS WILANDER (SWE)

Shook the tennis world by winning the French Open age 17 in 1982. In 1988 won three of the four Grand Slam titles, finishing the year as No. 1.

Born:	Vaxjo, Sweden, August 22, 1964.
Grand Slam titles:	Australian Open 1983-84, 1988. French Open 1982, 1985, 1988. US Open 1988. One men's doubles title.
Davis Cup winning teams:	Sweden 1984-85, 1987.

A baseline metronome who won 33 professional titles during a 15-year pro career, Mats Wilander was often criticised for being dull and unenterprising. But he developed his game from simply grinding out endless backcourt rallies with his relentless topspinning ground strokes, double-handed on the backhand, to an all-court attacking mode which gained him two Australian singles titles on grass and the Wimbledon doubles crown with his fellow Swede, Joakim Nystrom.

Nobody ever made such a huge leap from the juniors to the pros as Wilander, who won the boys' singles at Roland Garros in 1981 and the men's singles the following year. He was only 17 years and nine months old at the time, and it was his first professional title. In an extraordinary series of upsets the skinny boy wonder took out Ivan Lendl, Vitas Gerulaitis, Jose Luis Clerc and Guillermo Vilas and made a mockery of the theory that the French Open is the most difficult title to win and requires the most experience.

Wilander had infinite patience and was always prepared to keep on slugging away until his opponents capitulated. It took him 4 hours, 42 minutes to outlast the similarly indefatigable Vilas, and in two Davis Cup rubbers the Swede battled for over six hours against John McEnroe (in 1982) and Austria's Horst Skoff in 1989 (though he lost both of these). He won two Australian Opens on grass, subduing Lendl in 1983 and Kevin Curren in 1984, and he vanquished Lendl to win again in Paris in 1985. But his great year was 1988, when he won three of the four Grand Slams and took over the No. 1 ranking for 20 weeks. He defeated Pat Cash at Melbourne, Henri Leconte in Paris and Lendl at Flushing Meadows, although at Wimbledon he never got further than the quarterfinals. He played in every Davis Cup from 1981 to 1990, finishing on the winning team three times.

After 1988 he lost motivation and slid down the rankings, taking a long break from the tour between June 1991 and May 1993. His last four years in competition were undistinguished compared with his performances throughout the 1980s and he did not get further than the last 16 at Melbourne and the low 40s in the rankings. Since then however, he has carved out a career as a coach, including a stint with Marat Safin, and in 2002 he was appointed Sweden's Davis Cup captain.

TODD WOODBRIDGE (AUS)

The younger member of the fantastically successful Woodies, he has gone on to further victories with the Swede, Jonas Bjorkman.

Born:	Sydney, New South Wales, Australia, April 2, 1971.
Grand Slam titles:	16 men's doubles, six mixed doubles titles.
Olympics:	Gold medal, doubles: 1996. Silver medal, doubles: 2000.
Davis Cup winning team:	Australia 1999, 2003.

Woodbridge is the younger, still active half of the famous 'Woodies' – the most successful men's doubles partnership of the open era and possibly of all time. Woodbridge and Mark Woodforde won a record 61 pro titles together, which is four more than Peter Fleming/John McEnroe and Bob Hewitt/Frew McMillan. During their 10 years in partnership they won every major title in the game. They shared 11 Grand Slam titles, which is one less than another Australian pair, John Newcombe and Tony Roche. They played together in 16 Davis Cup ties and lost only twice; they were in the winning team of 1999. And they landed two ATP Tour World Championships. Perhaps their only major disappointment was their very last match, the Sydney Olympic final of 2000, when they failed to retain the gold medal against Canadians Sebastien Lareau and Daniel Nestor.

The son of a policeman, Woodbridge took up tennis at the age of four and was coached by Ray Ruffels. He had an outstanding junior career, reaching the final of the Australian boys' singles in 1987 and 1989 and the Wimbledon boys' singles in 1989. He won seven junior Grand Slam doubles titles. He had already earned an ATP ranking at the age of 15 and was playing in the main draws of Grand Slam men's singles events at 17.

Although comparatively short for a tennis pro (5ft 10ins), Woodbridge has always been a fit, dedicated and highly competitive player. In 1989 he beat Pete Sampras at Wimbledon and in 1997 he reached the semifinals at the same event, beating Michael Chang and Patrick Rafter. But like Woodforde, this was the only time he survived beyond the last 16 at a Grand Slam singles event. He won two ATP singles titles (Coral Springs 1995 and Adelaide 1997) and he was runner-up at Toronto, a Super Nine (now Masters Series) event in 1996.

Since Woodforde's retirement Woodbridge has formed a highly fruitful partnership with Sweden's Jonas Bjorkman. They have gathered five Grand Slam titles together, the last at Wimbledon in 2004 when the victory gave Woodbridge a record ninth crown at the grass court event, breaking a 99-year-old record held by Laurie and Reggie Doherty, who won their eighth title in 1905. It was also with Bjorkman that Woodbridge broke Tom Okker's open era record of 78 doubles titles. The pair have amassed 14 titles with the Australian's now holding a record 82 in all. Woodbridge continues to play Davis Cup for Australia and has formed an effective partnership with Wayne Arthurs: they hold a 5-3 win-loss record since 2001.

MARK WOODFORDE (AUS)

Red-headed left-hander whose doubles partnership with Todd Woodbridge was one of the most successful of all time.

Born:	Adelaide, South Australia, September 23, 1965.
Grand Slam titles:	12 men's doubles, five mixed doubles titles.
Olympics:	Gold medal, doubles: 1996. Silver medal, doubles: 2000.
Davis Cup winning team:	Australia 1999.

Mark Woodforde is the older of the Woodies by six years. As a youngster, the Adelaide left-hander was coached by Barry Phillips-Moore, an old friend of his father. He turned pro in 1983, the year he earned his first world ranking, but took several years to work his way through the Satellite and Challenger circuits, winning his first ATP Tour singles at Auckland in 1986, when he was 20. In 1987 he reached the fourth round at the US Open and established a place in the top 100, a level at which he stayed inside, or very close to, for the next 11 years.

In the early part of his career Woodforde was equally successful in singles and doubles. He memorably beat John McEnroe in consecutive events (Toronto, US Open) in 1988 and won three more Tour singles titles – Adelaide (1988-89) and Philadelphia (1993). But in a Grand Slam singles career that stretched from 1985 to 2000 he only once got further than the fourth round – as a semifinalist at the 1996 Australian Open, where he beat Mark Philippoussis and Thomas Enqvist before falling to Boris Becker.

Before forming his doubles partnership with Woodbridge, Woodforde successfully played with a number of different partners, including John McEnroe, with whom he won the 1989 US Open, and Thomas Smid, fellow-winner at the 1989 Monte Carlo Open.

His doubles partnership with Woodbridge, which began in 1991 and was virtually constant until the end of 2000 (they occasionally partnered other players in Davis Cup ties) was probably the greatest of all time. Before the open era, many top players enjoyed successful careers in singles and doubles, but since John McEnroe, very few headlining stars have regularly taken part in both disciplines. The Woodies won five consecutive doubles titles at Wimbledon – a unique feat since the abolition of the Challenge Round in 1922 (only the Doherty brothers, who did not have to play through, had won it that many times consecutively). After years of disappointment, the two Australians completed a full set of Grand Slam titles when they won the French in 2000, Woodforde's farewell season.

Since retiring from competitive tennis at the end of 2000 Woodforde has become a television commentator and coach to the Australian Fed Cup team.

Todd Woodbridge (AUS) broke more records in 2004

The Women

TRACY AUSTIN (USA)

Set a host of age records in the 1970s. Renowned for relentless double-handed driving from the baseline, she became the youngest winner of the US Open and one year later the first player to win $1million prize money.

Born:	Palos Verdes, California, USA, December 12, 1962.
Grand Slam titles:	US Open 1979, 1981. One mixed doubles title.
Fed Cup winning teams:	USA 1978-80.

At 16, Tracy Austin became the youngest player ever to win the US Open and, until she was supplanted by Monica Seles, the youngest to be ranked No. 1 in the world at 17 years four months. An iron-willed, aggressive baseliner who had no weaknesses except for a rather effete serve, she was the first tennis player, male or female, ever to win $1 million in one season. But a chronic back injury robbed her of a long career in the game. She is cited as the first of the teenage 'burn-outs' – girls who played too much, too soon, and damaged their bodies before they had physically matured.

From a strong tennis-playing family – three of her elder siblings were also pros – Austin won 21 US junior titles and took her first professional title, at Portland, Oregon, when she was only just 14 in January 1977. She first appeared at Wimbledon that year, and though soundly beaten 61 61 by Chris Evert in the third round, attracted enormous interest. She looked even younger than her age – which was accentuated by her pinafore dresses, hair in bunches and the braces on her teeth – but her game was deadly, with hard, accurate ground strokes, double-handed on the backhand. Although she rarely volleyed, she was just as strong in the air as she was off the ground. Above all, her mental strength marked her as a great champion of the future.

She was a quarterfinalist at Forest Hills that year, and in 1978 she won a big tournament at Filderstadt, Germany. In 1979 she snapped Evert's six year unbeaten run on clay in the final of the Italian Open, and that autumn she beat Evert again to win the US Open. Although Austin achieved the No. 1 ranking in 1980 and won the year-end Toyota Series Championship over Martina Navratilova she was thwarted that year in the Grand Slams, losing at the semifinal stage of Wimbledon to Evonne Cawley and at Flushing Meadows to Evert. (She had the consolation of winning the Wimbledon mixed doubles with her brother John). But in 1981 she recaptured the US Open, edging Navratilova in a final set tiebreak.

In 1982 she began to suffer from sciatica in her back, and after lengthy lay-offs retired in 1984. An attempted comeback in 1989 was wrecked by a car accident, and another in 1993-94 only showed that she had lost too much time.

BLANCHE BINGLEY HILLYARD (GBR)

Won the third women's singles event at Wimbledon in 1886. Won another five Wimbledon singles titles in a remarkable span of 14 years. Even reached the semifinals when she competed in 1912 aged 48.

Born:	Greenford, England, November 3, 1863.
Died:	Pulborough, England, August 6, 1946.
Grand Slam titles:	Wimbledon 1886, 1889, 1894, 1897, 1899, 1900.

Blanche Bingley played in the very first Wimbledon women's singles championship in 1884 and competed 24 times until 1913, when she was 49 years old. She married Commander George Hillyard, Secretary of the All England Club from 1907 to 1925, in 1887 and is one of only four mothers to have won the championship. This indefatigable competitor never played outside Europe, and the French Championships were not open to foreigners in her day, but she was twice champion of Germany (1897, 1900), three times champion of Ireland (1888, 1894, 1897) and she won the South of England Championships at Eastbourne 11 times between 1885 and 1905.

As six times champion of Wimbledon she is surpassed only by Martina Navratilova, Helen Wills Moody, Dorothea Lambert Chambers and Steffi Graf, but in terms of featuring in the later stages she exceeds them all. She was runner-up seven times and a semifinalist on four occasions. Always wearing white gloves, she was active throughout the first phase of women's lawn tennis, between the first championship in 1884 and World War I. The size of entries in those early Wimbledons did not number more than 16 until 1898, although by the time she last played in 1913 it had grown to 42.

Hillyard was unusual for her time in that she served overarm, although according to a secretary of the LTA, Herbert Chipp, her service "possesses no great virtue". She rarely volleyed, and her smash, said Chipp, was "absolutely deficient". Her main strengths were her ground strokes, which she hit to an impeccable length, and her lobbing ability.

The best story about Blanche Hillyard concerns her preparation for her 1905 semifinal against Constance Wilson. Because of rain, Hillyard was told by the referee that she would not be needed to play that day. She went to the tea tent and consumed two Bath buns, seven slices of bread and butter, four cups of tea, seven biscuits, three slices of cake and three plates of strawberries. Then, to her horror, the rain stopped and she was asked to play. She lost, 75 911 62.

LOUISE BROUGH (USA)

For three years she dominated Wimbledon more completely than any player before or since by reaching nine finals and winning eight of them. In 1949 she played the singles, doubles and mixed doubles finals on the same day, playing 117 games in eight sets.

Born: Oklahoma City, USA, March 11, 1923.
Grand Slam titles: Australian 1950. Wimbledon 1948-50, 1955. United States 1947. 21 women's doubles titles, eight mixed doubles titles.

As a multiple title winner, Louise Brough was the fifth most successful woman tennis player of all time. She won a remarkable 35 Grand Slam titles – six singles, 21 women's doubles and eight mixed doubles – during a stretch of 16 years, 1942-1957. This indefatigable champion, who also had an unblemished 22-0 win-loss record in the Wightman Cup, was a disciple of the serve and volley game pioneered amongst women by Alice Marble. She had a strong, kicking serve and splendid hands for volleying. Her style was always to get to the net at every opportunity, which was ideal for grass but less so on clay – a surface that proved fairly barren ground for her.

Strong and successful though she was, Brough would have been even more prominent in the history of the game had her career not coincided with the golden age of American women's tennis. Whilst competitive tennis ground to a halt in Europe during the war, it continued in the USA, and a legion of amazons emerged to dominate the sport for the first decade after hostilities ceased. In addition to Brough, there was Pauline Betz, Margaret Osborne DuPont, Doris Hart, Shirley Fry, Maureen Connolly, Pat Todd and Althea Gibson – all exceptional players and all Grand Slam singles champions between 1946 and 1958.

Of all these champions, Brough gathered the most titles. Early on, she was regularly thwarted by Betz, who beat her in two US finals (1942, 1943) and at Wimbledon in 1946. She defeated Osborne for the US title in 1947 and then won three consecutive Wimbledons – over Hart in 1948 and over DuPont in 1949 and 1950. She also beat Hart for the 1950 Australian title. The arrival of the near-invincible Connolly put her singles ambitions on hold for three years in the early Fifties, but after Connolly's retirement she took one last Wimbledon in 1955, over Beverly Fleitz. In the women's doubles Brough was even more prolific. Her partnership with DuPont was one of the best of all time. They won 20 major titles together, including 12 US Championships.

At Wimbledon in 1948-1950 she won eight of the nine titles available to her. During the course of finals day in 1949 she played a record 117 games, winning the singles over DuPont 108 16 108, joining DuPont to beat Gussie Moran and Pat Todd 86 75, and with John Bromwich narrowly failing against Eric Sturgess and Sheila Summers of South Africa 97 911 75.

MARIA BUENO (BRA)

Between 1958-1967, the Brazilian with rare grace and artistry won 115 matches at Wimbledon, including 49 in singles, winning the title three times. Won the US singles four times before illness and injury prematurely ended her career.

Born: Sao Paulo, Brazil, October 11, 1939.
Grand Slam titles: Wimbledon 1959-60, 1964. United States 1959, 1963-64, 1966. 11 women's doubles titles, one mixed doubles title.

The best female player ever to come out of Latin America, Maria Bueno lit up the tennis scene and enthralled audiences around the world with her graceful, artistic and attacking style of tennis. She was an entirely natural player whose appeal was as much due to her decorative and exotic appearance as her arsenal of lovely shots. Although she learned the game on clay she was at her best on grass, with an elegant, fluid service and daring, penetrating volleys. Safe shots were not for her: she loved to take risks and dazzle the gallery with exquisitely constructed winners. When on form, she was magnificent. But she had little margin for error.

Bueno made her first European tour in 1958 and made an immediate impact, winning the Italian championship and the Wimbledon doubles with Althea Gibson. The following year she swept through Wimbledon, outclassing US No. 1 Darlene Hard 64 63 in the final. She added the US championship, dismissing Hard and Christine Truman in identical 61 64 scorelines in the last two rounds.

She retained the Wimbledon title in 1960 and came within a match point of the triple crown, although she lost in the quarterfinals of the Australian championship to the teenage sensation Margaret Smith, and to Hard in Paris (semis) and Forest Hills (final).

Then things began to turn sour for the balletic Brazilian. She missed most of the 1961 season because of hepatitis, and for the rest of her career she was afflicted with a variety of ailments, including jaundice, shoulder trouble and acute tennis elbow. She did not regain her best form until 1963, when she beat Smith for the US title, and then enjoyed a fine 1964, losing to Smith in a three set French final, gaining revenge in a marvellous final at Wimbledon and humiliating Carole Graebner 61 60 for a third US championship.

Bueno lost the 1965 US final to Smith and the 1966 Wimbledon decider to Billie Jean King but claimed one last Forest Hills crown in 1966, over Nancy Richey. After that her injuries and poor health reduced her effectiveness and she retired in early 1969. But she made a comeback in the mid-1970s, winning the Japan Open in 1974 and reaching the fourth round at Wimbledon in 1976. She was a superb doubles player, netting 11 Grand Slam titles in women's doubles and her partnership with Hard was one of the best in tennis history.

The Greatest – Women (continued)

JENNIFER CAPRIATI (USA)

Age 13, she won her first match for the United States in Wightman Cup. At 14 became the youngest to reach the top ten; at 15, the youngest Wimbledon semifinalist. In 2001, her rehabilitation complete, she won the Australian and French Open titles and gained the No. 1 ranking.

Born:	New York, USA, March 29, 1976.
Grand Slam titles:	Australian Open 2001-02. French Open 2001.
Olympics:	Gold medal, singles, 1992.
Fed Cup winning teams:	USA 1990, 2000.

Jennifer Capriati holds a unique place in tennis history. In an era of teenage prodigies she was the youngest achiever, reaching the semifinals of her first French Open at the age of 14. At 18 she was branded a victim of 'burn-out', had several brushes with the law and underwent rehabilitation for drug abuse. At 20 she returned to tennis but struggled to regain her early form. Then in 2001 she had a glorious year, winning two Grand Slam titles and reaching the No. 1 spot for the first time. Like most champions of the new millennium, Capriati is a baseline power-hitter, armed with a strong serve, bullet-like ground strokes (double-handed on the backhand) and the well-toned physique of a champion athlete.

As a 13-year-old winner of the French and US Open junior titles in 1989 she was selected to play for the United States in the last Wightman Cup. In 1990 she reached the final of her first pro tournament, at Boca Raton, Florida, and became the first 14 year-old to claim a place in the world's top ten.

Capriati marched on, reaching the semifinals at Wimbledon and the US Open in 1991, and in 1992 she dethroned Steffi Graf in the final of the Olympics at Barcelona. But there was trouble at home: her parents separated and she began to perform listlessly. After a disastrous first round loss to Leila Meshki at Flushing Meadows she walked away from the game. She continued to make headlines, but for the wrong reasons, and did not return to tennis until 1996.

She finally won a title in Strasbourg in 1999, six years after her last success, and in 2000 she reached the semifinals at the Australian Open. Then came the fulfilment of her talent. She won the 2001 Australian Open and at Paris she battled past Kim Clijsters 16 64 119 in a thrilling final. The following year, in 2002, Capriati defended her Australian Open title, fighting off four match points to beat three-time champ Martina Hingis in the final. Back down under in 2003 Capriati became the first defending champion to lose in the opening round in the open era. Later that year she narrowly missed out in the US Open semifinals, losing to eventual champion Justine Henin-Hardenne in an epic match that lasted just over three hours, and having served for the match in the second and third sets. History repeated itself in the following year, when Capriati again served for a place in the US Open final before succumbing to Svetlana Kuznetsova. Also in 2004 she reached the semifinal at Roland Garros.

MAUREEN CONNOLLY (USA)

2003 marks the 50th anniversary of her achievement in becoming the first woman to complete the Grand Slam in 1953. This natural left-hander, who was persuaded to play tennis right-handed, was forced to retire after an accident just before her 20 birthday..

Born:	San Diego, USA, September 17, 1934.
Died:	Dallas, USA, June 21, 1969.
Grand Slam titles:	Australian 1953. French 1953-54. Wimbledon 1952-54. United States 1951-53. Two women's doubles titles, one mixed doubles title.

Maureen Connolly ranks among the elite of women's tennis champions, although her career lasted no longer than her teenage years, and she died at an age when she might have still been playing. Compact and diminutive at a mere 5ft 5in tall, she was an implacable baseliner, pounding deep, penetrating ground strokes to an impeccable length and humbling the regiment of amazon-like warriors that faced her with merciless precision. Her serve was average and she rarely volleyed, but when attacked by net-rushers she had the perfect solution: razor-sharp passing shots that hardly ever missed. Blessed with astonishing determination and concentration, Connolly ruled because she never gave an opponent a weak return to exploit.

Guided by Eleanor 'Teach' Tennant, who had also coached Alice Marble, Connolly was left-handed but advised to switch to the right. She won the US girls' championship in 1949 and 1950 and made her debut in the Nationals at Forest Hills in the latter year. Her loss there was the only Grand Slam singles defeat of her career. In 1951 she became the youngest (to that time) winner of the title at 16 years, 11 months.

In 1952 she won Wimbledon, escaping seemingly certain defeat against a British player, Susan Partridge, in the fourth round but thereafter not losing a set. She defeated the four-time champion Louise Brough for the title. At Forest Hills she beat Hart for her second US championship. In 1953 she became the first woman to win the Grand Slam, dropping only one set in 20 matches played (in Paris, again to Partridge). Hart was her victim in three of the four finals.

In 1954 she retained the French and Wimbledon crowns but shortly before the US Championships, whilst out riding, her horse was hit by a truck and her leg was badly injured. It ended her competitive career. In four years on the circuit she was beaten just four times – twice by Hart, once by Fry and once by Beverly Baker. She had a 9-0 record in the Wightman Cup. Maureen Connolly married Norman Brinker, an Olympic showjumper, in 1955 and had two daughters. She died of ovarian cancer at the age of 34 in 1969.

MARGARET COURT (AUS)

It is doubtful whether her haul of 62 Grand Slam titles will ever be surpassed. The first woman to complete the Grand Slam in Open tennis, she was regarded as one of the hardest hitters the game had ever seen.

Born: Albury, New South Wales, Australia, July 16, 1942.
Grand Slam titles: Australian 1960-66, 1969-71, 1973. French 1962, 1964, 1969-70, 1973. Wimbledon 1963, 1965, 1970. United States 1962, 1965, 1969-70, 1973. 19 women's doubles titles, 19 mixed doubles titles.
Fed Cup winning teams: Australia 1964-65, 1968-69, 1971.

Margaret Court (who was Margaret Smith until her marriage in 1967) is the all-time supreme winner in tennis, with 62 Grand Slam titles – 24 in singles, 19 in women's doubles and 19 in mixed doubles. She won two calendar Grand Slams – in singles in 1970 and in mixed doubles (with Ken Fletcher) in 1963, took three of the four Slams in four other years and was ranked No. 1 seven times – yet few experts would judge her the greatest player in history. The reason for this is because, despite her unsurpassed record over 14 years of international competition, she was sometimes prone to nerves, and would then play badly. She never enjoyed invincible runs like Suzanne Lenglen, Helen Wills Moody, Maureen Connolly and Martina Navratilova, and defeats by more inspired rivals like Maria Bueno and Billie Jean King when she was at the height of her powers marred her reputation. Even in 1970, when she won 21 tournaments, she lost six times, including defeats by such lesser players as Joyce Williams, Patti Hogan and the then 15-year-old Chris Evert. Worst of all, she allowed herself to be totally intimidated by Bobby Riggs in their 1973 Battle of the Sexes, although Riggs was subsequently humiliated by King.

Nevertheless, at her best Court was a majestic and awesome performer. The first woman tennis player to train in the gym, she was tall, strong and athletic, with exceptionally long arms, giving her great reach at the net. She could play all the shots and was equally good on all surfaces. In mixed doubles opponents faced a woman who could play as well as half of a men's doubles partnership.

Her 11 Australian singles titles – a record for any Grand Slam event – were achieved over a period of 15 years, but in the majority of those the field she overcame was predominantly Australian. She suffered the indignity of becoming the first female top seed at a Grand Slam event to lose in her opening match at Wimbledon in 1962, when she was beaten by Billie Jean Moffitt, but she avenged this the following year in the final. Moffitt (later Mrs King) was the principal adversary of her career, and Court would get the better of their duel with a 22-10 head-to-head record. Their greatest battle was in the 1970 Wimbledon final, when, with both players injured, Court won a tremendous encounter 1412 119 – the longest women's final ever in that championship.

LINDSAY DAVENPORT (USA)

Holder of three Grand Slam titles, her successes made this tall and powerful player the first American-born Grand Slam champion since Chris Evert.

Born: Palos Verdes, California, USA, June 8, 1976.
Grand Slam titles: US Open 1998. Wimbledon 1999. Australian Open 2000. Three women's doubles titles.
Olympics: Gold medal, singles, 1996.
Fed Cup winning teams: USA 1996, 1999, 2000.

In an era when top professional athletes often seem aloof, distant and over-protected, Lindsay Davenport has no wish to be a celebrity and is well known as one of the friendliest and most approachable players on the WTA Tour.

One of the tallest and strongest players on the women's tour, Davenport has been ranked in, or just outside, the top ten for the past 11 years, but her ascent to the pinnacle of the sport was steady rather than meteoric. Apart from one notable early success, when she won the Olympic Gold in Atlanta at the age of 20, she was considered an underachiever. She broke into the top ten in June 1994 and had already won 13 tour singles titles before she reached her first Grand Slam semifinal at the 1997 US Open.

One of the reasons for this delay in her reaching the highest level was a lack of discipline when it came to fitness and training. She was always a powerful, commanding player, who hit the ball harder than almost anyone else on the tour, but she was overweight and comparatively slow.

In 1997 Davenport adopted a rigorous training regime, shed her excess weight and transformed herself from a top ten player into a Grand Slam champion. She won the US Open in 1998, outclassing Venus Williams in the semis and Martina Hingis 63 75 in the final. Soon afterwards she reached No. 1 in the world rankings. The following year she won Wimbledon, avenging a French Open loss to Steffi Graf and bringing down the curtain on the German's fabulous career. A third Slam success came in Australia in 2000, when she battered Hingis into submission, 61 75. In fact, she did not drop a set en route to any of her three Grand Slam triumphs.

Davenport regained the No. 1 ranking at the end of 2001 after taking seven Tour titles, although a second major injury on her right knee took her out of competition for the next eight months. She did not return until July 2002, but she did well enough to qualify for the end-of-season Tour Championships. After a steady 2003 surgery on a long-standing left foot injury ended her season in October. Despite considering retirement throughout 2004 Davenport had her best season for three years. She clinched seven titles, including a run of US Open Series titles before her 22-match winning streak ended in the US Open semifinals. She regained the No. 1 ranking for the sixth time in her career in October, and finished the year on top for the third time. Davenport married Jon Leach, the brother of her former coach in April 2003.

Lindsay Davenport (USA)

LOTTIE DOD (GBR)

No-one has yet beaten Charlotte (Lottie) Dod's record as the youngest Grand Slam singles champion, man or women. She was 15 years 285 days old when she won the Wimbledon title for the first of five times in 1887.

Born:	Bebington, England, June 8, 1871.
Died:	Sway, England, June 27, 1960.
Grand Slam titles:	Wimbledon 1887-88, 1891-93.

Lottie Dod was the youngest ever Wimbledon singles champion, winning the title at the age of 15 years, 285 days in 1887, although Martina Hingis took the women's doubles at 15 years, 282 days in 1996. But Dod was also unbeaten in five appearances at the championships and was probably the greatest all-round sportswoman the world has ever seen, reaching the highest level of ice-skating, archery, field hockey and golf as well. In an age when female tennis players were restricted by tight collars, cuffs, stays and petticoats, because of her tender years she was allowed to play in shorter skirts, giving her greater freedom of movement than her opponents. She served underarm, as did most women in the nineteenth century, but she had a powerful forehand drive, could volley capably and had a forceful smash.

Her first notable victory was over the first Wimbledon champion, Maud Watson, at Bath in 1886. Watson had won 55 consecutive matches dating back to the Edgbaston tournament in 1881, but she was disconcerted by the way her 15-year-old opponent ran to the net to volley whenever possible. In 1887 Dod made her debut at Wimbledon, where the entry numbered just five women. After a bye she beat Miss James 61 61 in the semifinals and Edith Cole 62 63 in the allcomers' final. Then she trounced the holder, Blanche Bingley 62 60 in the Challenge Round. As champion, Dod was not required to play through the following year. Despite the lack of matchplay she again beat Mrs Hillyard 63 63 to retain the title.

Because of her other sporting interests, Dod didn't bother to enter in either 1889 or 1890, when she was representing Britain in hockey and doing a spot of yachting, but she returned in 1891. She beat Mrs Parsons 60 60, Miss Steedman 63 61 and Mrs Hillyard 62 61, then regained the title because the holder, Helena Rice, did not defend it. In 1892 she once again sent Hillyard packing, 61 61 in the Challenge Round, and in 1893 Hillyard came through and this time actually managed to wrest a set before going down 68 61 64.

After this, at the grand old age of 20, Dod decided there was nothing left for her to achieve in tennis. (She had also won the Irish title in 1887). Deserting the sport for good, she conquered golf, winning the British women's championship at Troon in 1904, and won an Olympic silver medal at archery in 1908.

DOROTHEA DOUGLASS LAMBERT CHAMBERS (GBR)

Won the first of her seven Wimbledon titles in 1903 when she was also the All-England badminton champion. Dominated with her tenacity and wide variety of shots.

Born:	Ealing, England, September 3, 1878.
Died:	London, England, January 7, 1960.
Grand Slam titles:	Wimbledon singles 1903-04, 1906, 1910-11, 1913-14.

Dorothea Douglass, who married Robert Lambert Chambers in 1907, was the greatest female player before World War I, but it was as a veteran that she achieved her most remarkable feats. She played at all but two Wimbledons between 1900 and 1927 and her career spanned both the Edwardian era and the Roaring Twenties. The daughter of a clergyman who grew up in the leafy West London suburb of Ealing, Douglass began her tennis as a little girl by lining up her dolls on the vicarage court and pretending to beat them. Later on, as she swept to seven Wimbledon singles titles, her dream would be realised and she was for many years virtually invincible. Like a later British champion, Kitty McKane Godfree, Douglass also won the All England Badminton Championship the same year as her first Wimbledon triumph.

Douglass was a mighty competitor, armed with hard, well-struck ground strokes, a cruelly accurate lob and a teasing drop shot. But she was a relatively late developer, not playing her first Wimbledon until she was 21 and winning her first title at 24. She won the Challenge Round by default against Muriel Robb and ably defended it in 1904 against an old foe, Charlotte Sterry, herself a four-time champion. In 1905 Douglass lost to the American, May Sutton, and their duel for supremacy in women's tennis was a feature of three consecutive Challenge Rounds. Douglass won in 1906, Sutton in 1907, while in 1908 Douglass (by now Mrs Chambers) lost in the quarterfinals to Sterry.

Although by now in her thirties, Chambers was invincible for the rest of the pre-war period. She did not play in 1909 or 1912, when she was having babies, but she won all the other years. In 1911 she achieved Wimbledon's only 60 60 singles final, ruthlessly outplaying Dora Boothby, the 1909 champion. With the war, competition was suspended between 1915 and 1918, but Chambers was back to defend the title in 1919 against the phenomenal Frenchwoman, Suzanne Lenglen. She was 40 and Lenglen was just 20. It was possibly the most exciting of all Wimbledon finals and Lenglen won 108 46 97 after saving two match points.

Chambers was routed 63 60 by Lenglen in the 1920 final but she continued to play. In 1925, at the age of 47, she won a singles and a doubles to help Great Britain defeat the United States in the third Wightman Cup match at Forest Hills.

The Greatest – Women (continued)

CHRIS EVERT (USA)

Won at least one Grand Slam title every year between 1974 and 1986, and inspired a whole generation of youngsters to play with a double-handed backhand. Supreme in dictating the pattern of matches from the back of the court.

Born:	Fort Lauderdale, Florida, USA, December 21, 1954.
Grand Slam titles:	Australian Open 1982, 1984. French Open 1974-75, 1979-80, 1983, 1985-86. Wimbledon 1974, 1976, 1981. US Open 1975-78, 1980, 1982. Three women's doubles titles.
Fed Cup winning teams:	USA 1977-82, 1986, 1989.

Chris Evert won at least one Grand Slam title for 13 consecutive years – a record – and in 57 Grand Slam title attempts over 18 years she only four times failed to reach the semifinals. No other player in history has performed so constantly and consistently over such a long period. From September 1970, when as a 15-year-old she stunned Margaret Court in her Grand Slam year at Charlotte, North Carolina, until October 1989, when she was unbeaten in her swansong at the Federation Cup in Tokyo, Evert was a winner. She was ranked No. 1 in the world for five years, won a total of 157 professional singles titles and was runner-up for 72 more, reaching the final at 76 per cent of the 303 tournaments she entered. Evert, who was married to British player John Lloyd from 1979 to 1987, gained a total of 21 Grand Slam titles, including three in doubles.

Between 1973 and 1979 she won 125 consecutive matches on clay, her formative and best surface, including the three years that the US Open was a clay court event. Nevertheless, such was her control and accuracy that she was equally strong on grass, carpet and hard courts. She changed the course of the sport inasmuch as at the time she came to the fore, top class women's tennis was mainly played from the net. Evert's metronomic consistency from the back of the court, her crushing forehands and line-splitting double-handed backhands, allied to devastating finesse on drop shots and lobs, broke the mould and spawned a generation of imitators. Although she did not hit the ball as hard as some players, Evert had an acutely shrewd brain and her mental strength was her greatest asset.

She was also the perfect professional – immaculate in appearance and demeanour, always sporting and respected by all with whom she came into contact. Early on, Wimbledon crowds found her less appealing than her sunnier rival, Evonne Goolagong, but eventually she became as popular there and elsewhere as she always was in America. She won 55 consecutive matches in 1974, taking in the Italian, French and Wimbledon titles, but perhaps her greatest triumphs were in 1985 and 1986, when she beat Martina Navratilova in two classic French Open finals. Her rivalry with Navratilova was one of the greatest in sport. They played 80 times between 1973 and 1988, with Navratilova gaining the edge 43-37.

ALTHEA GIBSON (USA)

Overcame racial barriers to become the first black woman to achieve major success, winning five Grand Slam titles. She won the Wimbledon singles twice; the doubles three times plus the French Championship once and US title twice. Tall, hard hitter.

Born:	Silver, South Carolina, USA, August 25, 1927.
Died:	New Jersey, USA, September 28, 2003.
Grand Slam titles:	French 1956. Wimbledon 1957-58. United States 1957-58. Five women's doubles titles, one mixed doubles title.

Renowned as the first black player of either sex to win a major title, Althea Gibson rose from the humblest of origins and overcame the most disadvantaged of circumstances to reach the pinnacle of the sport when she was 30 years old. The child of poverty-stricken sharecroppers in the Deep South, Gibson moved with her family to Harlem when she was three years old. Abused by a brutal father, she ran away from home at 11 and lived in a hostel, surviving on a series of menial jobs. At 13 she was spotted playing paddle tennis by Buddy Walker, director of the Harlem Society Orchestra, who bought her a tennis racket and paid for her to have lessons at a New York club. At 18 she came under the patronage of Dr Walter Johnson, who was later to help Arthur Ashe, who took her into his home in Wilmington, North Carolina, and helped her develop her evident talent for tennis.

Gibson was a formidably tall and athletic performer who used her height to pound down powerful serves and volleys, but she played mainly from the back of the court. In 1950 she won the American Tennis Association's championship for black players and was grudgingly allowed to become the first player of African-American race ever to take part in the National Championships at Forest Hills. She nearly caused a sensational upset, leading Wimbledon champion Louise Brough 76 in the final set before the No. 3 seed profited from a rain break to escape.

Gibson had to endure endless obstacles, but she overcame massive prejudice to persevere in the white-dominated sport and make her first European tour in 1956, when she won the Italian and French championships and the French and Wimbledon doubles with a British player, Angela Buxton. She was also runner-up to Shirley Fry at Forest Hills. In 1957 she won the Wimbledon singles title without dropping a set, plus the doubles with Darlene Hard, then she went to Forest Hills and routed Brough 63 62 for the title and added the mixed doubles with Kurt Nielsen.

In 1958 she retained her Wimbledon singles and doubles (with Maria Bueno) and her US singles, beating Hard. After this she turned professional but there was little opposition in that field and she soon turned to golf, at which sport she played fairly successfully from 1963 to 1977.

EVONNE GOOLAGONG CAWLEY (AUS)

Few players radiated greater joy and enchantment even when she went 'walkabout' mentally. Won the French on her first visit in 1971 and four weeks later beat Billie Jean King and Margaret Court to win her first of two Wimbledon crowns.

Born: Griffith, New South Wales, Australia, July 31, 1951.
Grand Slam titles: Australian Open 1974-77. French Open 1971. Wimbledon 1971, 1980. Five women's doubles titles, one mixed doubles title.
Fed Cup winning teams: Australia 1971, 1973-74.

The only tennis player of Aboriginal extraction to reach greatness in the sport, Evonne Goolagong (who married Englishman Roger Cawley in 1975) was also unique in that she brought a freshness, joie de vivre and effortless talent that had never been seen before. She entranced Wimbledon by gliding to victory in 1971 at only her second attempt, and nine years later she won again – the first mother to win the title since Dorothea Lambert Chambers in 1914. Spectators were enchanted by the sight of this happy girl who weaved a gossamer web of magic on the Centre Court, delighting them with glorious winners and delicate touch shots, then laughing off careless mistakes.

Goolagong began life on a sheep farm in the Australian outback and only took up tennis when a local resident saw her peering through the fence at local courts and encouraged her to play. Her extraordinary natural ability was reported to a Sydney coach, Vic Edwards, who took her into his home and coached her to international standard. A serve and volleyer who caressed rather than pounded the ball, she made a strong impact on her first overseas tour in 1970, and after helping Australia to win the Federation Cup in Perth in December of that year she swiftly moved into the top stratum. She won the French Open in 1971, defeating her compatriot, Helen Gourlay, and then conquered Wimbledon, stunning the two best players in the world, Billie Jean King and Margaret Court, in straight sets in the last two rounds.

For the next seven years (plus one year out to have her first child) Goolagong lost some of her inspiration and became inconsistent. She lost two Wimbledon finals to King (after winning a dramatic first meeting against her principal career rival, Chris Evert, in 1972 and a semifinal against Court in 1975). And she was losing finalist at Forest Hills for four consecutive years – against Court in 1973, King in 1974 and Evert in 1975 and 1976. Her four Australian titles in weaker fields were small consolation. But in 1980 she rolled back the years and regained her Wimbledon title, overcoming Evert in the only final to end in a tiebreak. She retired in 1983 with 43 singles and nine doubles titles to her credit. She won five Grand Slam women's doubles championships including Wimbledon with Peggy Michel in 1974.

STEFFI GRAF (GER)

The blonde German with a sledgehammer forehand won all four Grand Slam titles and the singles gold medal in Seoul in 1988 when tennis returned to the Olympic Games as a full medal sport.

Born: Neckarau, Germany, June 14, 1969.
Grand Slam titles: Australian Open 1988-90, 1994. French Open: 1987-88, 1993, 1995-96, 1999. Wimbledon: 1988-89, 1991-93, 1995-96. US Open: 1988-89, 1993, 1995-96. One women's doubles title.
Olympics: Gold medal, singles, 1984, 1988. Silver medal, singles, 1992.
Fed Cup winning teams: Germany 1987, 1992.

A player of the highest stature in the game, Stefanie Maria Graf is regarded by many as a champion without equal. She won a unique Golden Slam of all four majors plus the Olympic gold medal in 1988 and is the only player of either sex to win all four Grand Slam titles at least four times. Graf introduced a new style of play that has been imitated but never bettered. A splendid athlete who once ran an Olympic qualifying time for the 800 metres, she could cover the court with amazing speed and intimidate her opponents with her rushing, impatient eagerness. Her service toss was unusually high, but the stroke was well hit, and although she seldom ventured to the net her volleys and overheads were effective. But it was from the baseline that this aggressive player really scored. Her sledgehammer forehand drive was probably the finest the game has ever seen, and her single-fisted backhand was sure when sliced – as it usually was – and devastating when hit with topspin.

Graf secured a WTA ranking at the age of 13 and was a precocious star, winning the exhibition Los Angeles Olympic Gold medal (restricted to players aged 20 and under) at 15. She made the world's top ten in 1985 and reached the top in August 1987. She held the premier spot for a record 377 weeks, including 187 consecutive weeks between 1987 and 1991. She rose to her zenith at the same time that Martina Navratilova and Chris Evert were beginning to wane, and she beat them both to win her first big title, the Lipton at Key Biscayne, in March 1987. She won her first Grand Slam title, the French Open, over Navratilova in June 1987 and established an edge over the same player to take her first Wimbledon in 1988. But her dominance was eventually usurped by a new star, Monica Seles, who overtook her in the rankings in 1991.

With Seles out of the game after being stabbed in 1993, Graf regained her pre-eminence in the mid-Nineties, but a succession of serious injuries forced her into a long time-out in 1997-1998. She returned falteringly, but in 1999 had her last and perhaps greatest triumph – a dramatic victory over Martina Hingis for the French title. Graf retired in July 1999 after losing to Lindsay Davenport in only her second unsuccessful Wimbledon final. She married Andre Agassi in October 2001 and has two children, Jaden Gil (born October 2001) and Jaz Elle (born October 2003).

The Greatest – Women (continued)

DORIS HART (USA)

Took up tennis aged six as a remedial exercise for an illness which might have crippled her. Won the triple crown at Wimbledon in 1951 and was twice singles champion in France and the United States.

Born: St Louis, Missouri, USA, June 20, 1925.
Grand Slam titles: Australian 1949. French 1950, 1952. Wimbledon 1951. United States 1954-55.14 women's doubles titles, 15 mixed doubles titles.

Doris Hart is the only player apart from Margaret Court to win the singles, doubles and mixed doubles at all four Grand Slam championships, and her total of 35 majors ties her at fifth with Louise Brough in the all-time list, behind Margaret Court, Martina Navratilova, Billie Jean King and Margaret DuPont. Hart was a swift and graceful player, equally at home at the back of the court and at the net, and was unfailingly gracious and sporting. She was even more successful at doubles than singles. Her seven-year partnership with her fellow-American Shirley Fry amassed 12 Grand Slam titles, and their rivalry with Brough and DuPont was a feature of many exciting finals. The most notable was in the 1953 US Championships at Boston when Fry and Hart recovered from 25 and two match points down in the third set to win 62 79 97. In the same year they crushed Maureen Connolly and Julie Sampson 60 60 in Wimbledon's only 'double bagel' doubles final.

Hart's athleticism and fluidity of movement was all the more remarkable because as a child she almost died from an infected knee and took up tennis as a form of therapy. She recovered so well that her legs, albeit thin and bowed, carried her surely around the court to despatch stylish winners. She also had no lack of stamina, reaching the finals of all three events at tournaments on many occasions and taking the triple crown at Wimbledon in 1951. In doing so, she dropped only one set in 17 matches – in the mixed with Frank Sedgman. In the singles final she overwhelmed Shirley Fry 61 60 in 35 minutes, giving possibly the most devastating display of attacking tennis ever seen from a woman on the Centre Court. Only a month before, Fry had beaten her in the French final.

She was ranked in the world's top four each year she competed on the international circuit (1946 to 1955). Her highest position was No. 1, in 1951. Her six Grand Slam singles titles were scant reward for such consistency, but she played in an era of exceptional quality. She was runner-up in one Australian, three French, three Wimbledon and five US championships. Hart retired to become a coach in 1955, but returned to Forest Hills in 1969 to reach the quarterfinals of the mixed doubles with her former co-champion, Vic Seixas.

JUSTINE HENIN-HARDENNE (BEL)

Though slight in stature, she has rightly earned the reputation as one of the sternest competitors in women's tennis who already has three Grand Slam titles and an Olympic Gold medal.

Born: Liege, Belgium, June 1, 1982.
Grand Slam titles: Australian Open 2004, French Open 2003, US Open 2003.
Olympics: Gold medal, singles, 2004
Fed Cup winning team: Belgium 2001.

The arrival of not one but two Belgians at the top of women's tennis is something that could never have been predicted. But the simultaneous rise of two Belgian players – one Flemish, the other Walloon, and only a year apart in age, has been the most striking feature of the sport in the early years of the 21st century.

Justine Henin-Hardenne, who is a year older than her compatriot Kim Clijsters, is physically very slight (5ft 5ins tall and 126 lbs) and is dwarfed by most of the other women on the tour. But she possesses exceptional drive, dedication and determination. She has a single-handed backhand drive that is generally agreed to be one of the best the sport has ever seen, and she has worked very hard at building up her strength and fitness during the off-season.

She has had a meteoric rse in the game. In 1999, aged 17, she received a wild card into the WTA Tour event in Antwerp and won the title. Soon after, as qualifier, she gave No. 2 seed Lindsay Davenport a fright before the American won their second round French Open match 63 26 75.

After a largely inactive 2000, during which she suffered a variety of injuries, Henin came storming back in 2001 and improved her world ranking from 18 to No. 7. During the course of the year she reached the semifinals at Roland Garros and the final at Wimbledon.

There was a less spectacular 2002, in which her highlight was the Wimbledon semifinals, but in 2003 Henin, by now married to Pierre-Yves Hardenne, was treading on Clijsters' heals every step of the way as the two Belgians took over leadership of the game from the ailing Williams sisters. Henin-Hardenne got the better of Serena in a dramatic semifinal at Roland Garros, then overwhelmed Clijsters in a historic first all-Belgian Grand Slam final. The Williams temporarily restored their pre-eminence at Wimbledon, but at Flushing Meadow there wasn't a Williams in sight and in another Belgian battle the Walloon once again triumphed. After holding the World No. 1 ranking for just one week in October 2003, Henin-Hardenne regained the top position for the end of the year. 2004 started as the previous year had finished, with a Grand Slam all-Belgian final, at the Australian Open Henin-Hardenne again triumphed over her compatriot. A lingering viral illness interrupted much of the rest of the year but she recovered enough to take Belgian's first tennis medal in singles when she beat Amelie Mauresmo for Gold at the Athens Olympic Games.

MARTINA HINGIS (SUI)

The youngest player ever to reach No.1 in the world, Hingis dominated the sport as a teenager but failed to fend off the challenge of stronger players like the Williams sisters.

Born:	Kosice, Czechoslovakia, September 30, 1980.
Grand Slam titles:	Australian Open 1997-99. Wimbledon 1997. US Open 1997. Nine women's doubles titles.

Martina Hingis was a truly exceptional champion in that she reached the peak of her career whilst still technically a junior. Having dominated women's tennis as a 16-year-old, she remained at the top of the rankings for most of the next four years but was unable to resist the advancing threat of more powerful rivals.

Like the Williams sisters, Hingis was bred to be a champion. Her mother, Melanie Molitor – herself a top 20 Czech player in the 1970s – named Martina after the great Navratilova and introduced her to tennis when she was two years old. Hingis spent her first eight years in what is now the Slovak Republic, but when her parents divorced and her mother married a Swiss, Andreas Zog, she moved with Melanie to Trubbach in Switzerland.

As a child, Hingis was a phenomenally precocious player. She won the French Open junior title at the age of 12 in 1993 and won her first professional title, a $10,000 event in Langenthal, Switzerland, the same year. In October 1994 she won her first match at a WTA Tour event in Zurich. Her progress in pro tennis was meteoric: first WTA final (Hamburg) in May 1995; the Wimbledon doubles title (with Helena Sukova) in 1996, making her the youngest player ever to win a Grand Slam title, and her first major singles title, the Australian Open, in January 1997.

Hingis did not succeed in tennis by hitting the ball harder than anyone else. She was better than anyone else at anticipating where her opponent was going to hit the ball, and finding a place from whence the opponent was least likely to return it. She possessed an amazingly mature brain for someone so young, but she would occasionally explode – most memorably in the 1999 French Open final which she lost to Steffi Graf after serving for the match. Roland Garros remained the one Grand Slam singles event she never won.

She won three of the four majors in 1997 and achieved the top spot in the world ranking three months into that year. She was only 16 and a half at the time and remains the youngest ever No.1. She won the Australian Open singles and doubles three years running and the Grand Slam of women's doubles in 1998, but as the new Millennium dawned, her best was behind her. She was gradually overpowered and overtaken by the Williams sisters and Jennifer Capriati and was also troubled by ankle injuries which she blamed on her footwear manufacturer.

Hingis announced her retirement from tennis in January 2003, but she retains a high profile as an ambassador for the World Health Organisation and a television presenter.

HELEN JACOBS (USA)

So often overshadowed by Helen Wills Moody but she won the US title four consecutive years. She also won the US doubles three times and the Wimbledon singles title in 1936.

Born:	Globe, Arizona, USA, August 6, 1908.
Died:	Easthampton, New York, USA, June 2, 1997.
Grand Slam titles:	Wimbledon 1936. United States 1932-35. Four women's doubles titles, one mixed doubles title.

Helen Jacobs' name is inextricably linked with that of another Helen – Wills Moody – whom she played in one French, four Wimbledon and two United States finals. Moody won each time except the 1933 US showdown, when she retired at 03 in the final set. The media built up a feud between them that was probably exaggerated, but they were certainly not friends. This despite the fact that they lived on the same street in Berkeley, California, played at the same club and had the same coach.

The two Helens contrasted in personality and playing style. Whereas Moody was reserved and aloof, Jacobs was cheerful, outgoing and generous. When Moody told the umpire in that 1933 Forest Hills final that she was in pain, Jacobs tried to comfort her but was rebuffed. When they met again in the 1938 Wimbledon final Jacobs was almost lame with an Achilles tendon injury, but Moody ignored her plight. Their most dramatic showdown came in the 1935 Wimbledon final. Jacobs had all but completed the job when she led Moody 52 and match point in the final set. Presented with an easy smash, a gust of wind deflected the ball and Jacobs netted it. The chance was gone.

Jacobs did not hit the ball as hard as Moody, but she had a tremendous competitive instinct and always fought to the last ditch. She had a poor forehand and adopted a slice which was merely defensive, but her backhand was positive and aggressive, and she had exceptional volleying skills. She was a Grand Slam finalist more often than a winner, and all her major titles were achieved (with the exception of her 1933 US victory) in the absence of Moody. She lost two French, five Wimbledon and four Forest Hills finals in a span from 1928 to 1940. But her four consecutive US titles, from 1932 to 1935, and her one Wimbledon in 1936 were just reward for years of enthusiastic application. In Moody's absence at the 1936 Wimbledon, Jacobs won through a strong field to beat Germany's Hilde Sperling (the reigning French champion) 62 46 75 in a desperately close final.

Jacobs won three US doubles titles, with Sarah Palfrey Fabian, in 1932, 1934 and 1935, and the 1934 mixed doubles with George Lott, thereby taking the triple crown. She played in 12 Wightman Cup matches, every year between 1927 and 1939 except 1938, and had a 19-11 winning record.

The Greatest – Women (continued)

ANN JONES (GBR)

A semifinalist at Wimbledon seven times, Jones at last won the title in 1969 – a fresh climax to a sporting career which began with her reaching five finals in the world table tennis championships.

Born: Birmingham, England, October 7, 1938.
Grand Slam titles: French 1961, 1966. Wimbledon 1969. Three women's doubles title, one mixed doubles title.

The most successful and enduring of a strong group of British players that emerged in the late 1950s, Ann Haydon (who married Pip Jones in 1962) was the first left-handed woman to win Wimbledon (the only other to date is Martina Navratilova) and one of the few players to raise their game to greater heights as a professional. In the early part of her career she combined top class tennis with table tennis, at which sport she was runner-up in five world championship finals. The influence of table tennis was evident in her tennis style – she had a stalwart baseline game with a strong topspin forehand and a defensive backhand. She was especially feared on clay because of her ability to rally interminably. These virtues brought her two French titles and one Italian, whilst on grass she reached a level just below the highest, with six Wimbledon semifinals between 1958 and 1968, Forest Hills semifinals in 1963 and 1968, and finals at Forest Hills in 1961 and 1967 and Wimbledon in 1967.

The factor that propelled her to the pinnacle was turning professional in 1968, just before tennis went Open. By practising with legendary men in her troupe such as Rod Laver, Ken Rosewall and Pancho Gonzales, Jones strengthened her net game and vastly improved her backhand. She also benefited by switching from a wooden to a steel-framed racket, which increased her power. Brought into close proximity with Billie Jean King, the dominant player at the time, and regularly playing against her, Jones transformed herself from a primarily defensive player into an attacking one. Her long years of being a bridesmaid at Wimbledon ended in 1969, when she beat three of the game's elite – Nancy Richey, Margaret Court and King – in the last three rounds. Her victory over Court, by 1012 63 62, was especially significant as the Australian won all three of the other Grand Slam titles that year.

Jones won three French women's doubles titles – with Renée Schuurman in 1963 and with Francoise Durr in 1968 and 1969 – and the mixed doubles at Wimbledon with Fred Stolle in 1969. She was also twice runner-up in the singles at Roland Garros – to Richey in 1968 and to Court in 1989. She played a low-key schedule in 1970, avoiding the Grand Slam events, and retired in 1971, although she made her 13th and last appearance in the Wightman Cup in 1975.

BILLIE JEAN KING (USA)

Few have contributed more to the popularity and growth of women's tennis. Best known for her exuberant serve and volley style. Won singles titles at all four Slams and her 'Battle of the Sexes' victory over Bobby Riggs drew a world record crowd of 30,000.

Born: Long Beach, California, USA, November 22, 1943.
Grand Slam titles: Australian 1968. French 1972. Wimbledon 1966-68, 1972-73, 1975. United States 1967, 1971-72, 1974. 16 women's doubles titles, 11 mixed doubles titles.
Fed Cup winning teams: USA 1963, 1966-67, 1976-79.

Probably the most important individual in the history of women's tennis, Billie Jean Moffitt (who married Larry King in 1965) competed valiantly on the world circuit from 1961 to 1983, amassing an all-time third best 39 Grand Slam titles, and fought ferociously for the women's professional game. Feisty, uncompromising and sometimes controversial, she rebelled against the amateur establishment to improve the lot of female players. As a player, King was one of the most accomplished serve-volleyers ever. No woman was ever technically better or hit a superior backhand drive, volley and half-volley, and although her game was markedly suited to fast surfaces she improved her baseline game to succeed on clay as well.

She won a record 20 Wimbledon titles – six singles, ten doubles and four mixed doubles – and appeared in a total of 28 finals. She was triple champion in 1967 and 1973, and her partners on both occasions were Rosie Casals and Owen Davidson. Her greatest rivalry was with Margaret Court, to whom she lost in the 1963 and 1970 finals but beat in the second round in 1962 and the semifinals in 1966. After Court had been trounced by Bobby Riggs in a battle of the sexes in 1973, King agreed to play Riggs and won, resoundingly, 64 63 63 at Houston.

Having established herself as world No. 1 in 1967, when she triumphed both at Wimbledon and Forest Hills, King entered the Open era as one of four women professionals (the others were Casals, Ann Jones and Francoise Durr). In the early years of Open tennis there was a huge disparity in prize money between men and women, and in 1970 King was in the forefront of a campaign to set up an independent women's tour, offering more appropriate rewards. In 1971 she spearheaded the Virginia Slims tour and became the first female athlete to win more than £100,000 in prize money in a single year.

King was also a magnificent team player. She was a forceful member of seven winning Federation Cup teams and of nine successful Wightman Cup sides between 1961 and 1978. Towards the end of her career, when she was a Wimbledon semifinalist at 39, King was sued for 'palimony' by a former female lover but achieved worldwide respect for the dignified way she endured the ordeal. She is currently captain of the United States Fed Cup team.

SUZANNE LENGLEN (FRA)

Won a staggering 81 singles titles, 73 in doubles and 87 in mixed. Three times she won the triple crown at Wimbledon. It was her success and notoriety – generated by her fiery temper and choice of dress – which prompted Wimbledon's move to a larger site.

Born:	Paris, France, May 24, 1899.
Died:	Paris, France, July 4, 1938.
Grand Slam titles:	French 1920-23, 1925-26. Wimbledon 1919, 1920-23, 1925. Eight women's doubles titles, five mixed doubles titles.
Olympics:	Gold medals, singles and mixed doubles, 1920.

Suzanne Lenglen achieved a greater degree of invincibility than any other player in the history of tennis. During a top class career that spanned nine seasons she suffered only two singles defeats. The first, against her compatriot Marguerite Broquedis, in the 1914 French Championship, was when she was 15 years old. The second, her only competitive match in the United States, in 1921, was when she was ill and retired after losing the first set against Molla Mallory. Despite suffering chronic ill-health, Lenglen had a unique talent for the game, and her uncanny powers of anticipation enabled her to prepare for her opponents' shots almost before they had been struck. She was one of the first women to play an all-court game, able to reach seemingly impossible volleys and to smash with unanswerable finality. She moved like a ballerina and had enormous charisma. Lenglen was also a pioneer of modern tennis clothing. Until she arrived on the scene, female players wore long skirts, long-sleeved blouses fastened at the neck, and stays; Lenglen turned out in loose, one-piece dresses that reached just below her knees.

She won a total of 241 titles, including 81 in singles, 73 in women's doubles and 87 in mixed. Her partnership with Elizabeth Ryan was undefeated. Having won her first major title, the World Hard Court Championship, in Paris in 1914, Lenglen was obliged to sit out the war before launching her international career in 1919. At her first Wimbledon she won one of the greatest finals of all time – a 10 8 4 6 9 7 classic against the 40-year-old holder, Dorothea Lambert Chambers, saving two match points. The Wimbledon spectators were thrilled by her skills, her flamboyance and her dramatic personality, and her popularity attracted far greater crowds than ever before, necessitating a move by the All England Club to larger grounds at Church Road in 1922.

In 1926 she pulled out of Wimbledon in a state of distress because of a misunderstanding over scheduling, and shortly afterwards she turned professional. Earlier that year she won her only meeting with the other great player of her time, Helen Wills, at Cannes. She died of Leukaemia at the age of 39 in 1938.

HANA MANDLIKOVA (CZE/AUS)

A superb athlete, she progressed from being world junior champion to winning three of the four Grand Slam singles titles and probably would have amassed rather more had her career not coincided with that of Chris Evert and Martina Navratilova.

Born:	Prague, Czechoslovakia, February 19, 1962.
Grand Slam titles:	Australian Open 1980, 1987. French Open 1981. US Open 1985. One women's doubles title.
Fed Cup winning teams:	Czechoslovakia 1983-85.

During the long reigns of Chris Evert and Martina Navratilova as joint queens of the game between 1978 and 1987, three players made incursions into their duopoly: Tracy Austin, Hana Mandlikova and Steffi Graf. Mandlikova, who memorably beat both Evert and Navratilova to win the 1985 US Open, was snapping at their heels for a long time, but never managed to lift herself above them in the world rankings. A richly talented player, she was a consistently successful competitor throughout the 1980s but her form fell away sharply in the last year of the decade.

Her father was an Olympic sprinter, and Mandlikova herself was a superb athlete, able to cover the court with lightning speed and superb footwork. She had an aggressive all-court game and had tremendous flair both off the ground and in the air. At the age of 16 she became the ITF's first World Junior Champion, winning the Italian and French girls' titles and losing the Wimbledon girls' final to Tracy Austin. She wasted no time in making an impact on the senior game, and in 1980 she won the Australian Open, trouncing Wendy Turnbull 6 0 7 5 in the final, and reaching the last round of the US Open, where she beat Navratilova and Andrea Jaeger before submitting in three sets to Evert.

In 1981 she rose to No. 4 in the world, winning the French Open with a straight sets victory over Evert in the semifinals, followed by an easy 6 2 6 4 verdict over Germany's Sylvia Hanika. Her march continued as far as the final at Wimbledon, where she outvolleyed Navratilova in the semis but flopped against Evert, who won 6 2 6 2. Instead of building on her already impressive record, the Czech faltered and did not reach another Grand Slam final until the 1982 US Open, where once again she gleaned but four games from Evert. Her apotheosis at Flushing Meadows in 1985, another Wimbledon final in 1986, when she beat Evert and lost to Navratilova, and a final Grand Slam title in Melbourne in 1987, where she snapped a 56-match streak by Navratilova, were the other highpoints in her career.

Mandlikova led Czechoslovakia to three consecutive Federation Cup wins (1983-85) but married an Australian of Czech origin, Jan Sedlak, in 1986 and became an Australian citizen in 1988. In 2001, her marriage long over, she gave birth to twins which were biologically fathered by a male friend but would be brought up by Mandlikova with her female partner, Liz Resseguie.

The Greatest – Women (continued)

ALICE MARBLE (USA)
Despite her trim figure, she was one of the most aggressive American players before the Second World War as she took serve and volley tennis to new heights. Recovered from tuberculosis to win the US title in 1936 and Wimbledon three years later.

Born:	Plumas, California, USA, September 28, 1913.
Died:	Palm Springs, California, USA, December 13, 1990.
Grand Slam titles:	Wimbledon 1939. United States 1936, 1938-40. Six women's doubles titles, seven mixed doubles titles.

A trim, pretty blonde who always sported shorts and a peaked cap, Alice Marble was a dynamic and well-loved champion who, but for a life-threatening illness in mid-career and the advent of World War II, might have won many more major titles. She is credited with being the first exponent of the 'big game' among women, playing the same way as such aggressive male players as Ellsworth Vines, Donald Budge and Jack Kramer to dominate from the net. Marble, born into a family of modest means from a rural part of Northern California, moved to San Francisco as a child and her abundant talent at racket sports was quickly noticed. Something of a tomboy, she developed her skills by frequently practising and playing with men, and this was how she perfected her exceptionally strong American twist serve – a shot few other women ever attempted. Taking the ball on the rise, her ground strokes were risky, with a short backswing, but her momentum was always to reach the net, and from there her volleying ability was sensational.

Already a US top ten player by the time she was 19, Marble had to play four matches in one day at a tournament in East Hampton, New York, in 1933. After playing 108 games in scorching heat she collapsed. The following year she was again taken ill when playing in Paris and was diagnosed first with pleurisy, then with tuberculosis. She was desperately ill and was unable to play again until late in 1935. Helped and inspired by her coach, Eleanor 'Teach' Tennant, who would later guide Maureen Connolly, Marble ended Helen Jacobs' four year reign as champion at Forest Hills in 1936.

She lost in the quarterfinals there in 1937 but won three more US titles in 1938, 1939 and 1940, overcoming Australia's Nancy Wynne in the first and Jacobs in the other two finals. At Wimbledon in 1939 she swept to the triple crown, taking the singles without losing a set and demolishing Britain's Kay Stammers 62 60 in the final and adding the women's doubles with Sarah Fabyan and the mixed with Bobby Riggs. She did not lose a match of any importance in either 1939 or 1940, after which she retired, turned professional and toured with Budge, Bill Tilden and Mary Hardwick. During World War II she served in US military intelligence.

MARTINA NAVRATILOVA (USA)
The finest female player in the game's history. She has won 58 Grand Slam titles – including two in 2003, at the age of 46 – and is the all-time Wimbledon record-holder. During her extraordinary career she has inspired moves towards added power and greater athleticism in women's tennis.

Born:	Prague, Czechoslovakia, October 18, 1956.
Grand Slam titles:	Australian Open 1981, 1983, 1985. French Open: 1982, 1984. Wimbledon 1978-79, 1982-87, 1990. US Open: 1983-84, 1986-87. 31 women's doubles titles, nine mixed doubles titles.

Martina Navratilova achieved more success than any other player in history during the main part of her career, which lasted from 1973 to 1994. But in 2003, in the fourth year of a doubles-only comeback career on the professional tour, the Czech-born American extended her record with two more Grand Slam mixed doubles titles and seven WTA doubles titles – although she was in her late forties.

With her 58 Grand Slam titles, Navratilova is still three short of the record held by Margaret Court, but in every other respect she should be regarded as the greatest female player in the history of the sport. In 2003 she equalled Billie Jean King's record of 20 Wimbledon titles, she also became the oldest player of either sex to win a Grand Slam title, beating a mark set by Margaret DuPont 41 years earlier. Navratilova competed in her first Olympic Games in 2004 and continued her Fed Cup career, suffering her first loss in 41 matches.

But more than any of these magnificent achievements, Navratilova will be remembered for her heyday in the 1980s when she won six consecutive Wimbledon singles titles (her total of nine is the most achieved by any player) and for several years made herself almost unbeatable. She was defeated only once in the whole of 1983, and in 1984 she went for 74 matches without loss. (Her doubles partnership with Pam Shriver at the same time was also invincible.)

Her abundant natural talent, nurtured on clay in her native Czechoslovakia, enabled Navratilova to enjoy sporadic success in her early years on the tour, but a realisation that she could turn herself into the best tennis player the world had ever seen raised her to levels never previously achieved. She worked intensively on her fitness, technique and nutrition and made herself into the complete player. This gave other women players a model to emulate and overall increased standards of playing and athleticism.

Her rivalry with Chris Evert was one of the greatest ever seen in sport, and their finals at Wimbledon and the French Open are regarded as classics of the women's game.

JANA NOVOTNA (CZE)

For so long this stylish player, one of the last natural serve and volleyers with exquisite touch at the net, was known as 'the nearly woman'. First her nerve deserted her in the 1993 Wimbledon final; then injury struck four years later before the prize was hers in 1998.

Born: Brno, Czechoslovakia, October 2, 1968.
Grand Slam titles: Wimbledon 1998. 12 women's doubles titles, four mixed doubles titles.
Olympics: Silver medals, doubles,1988, 1996. Bronze medal, singles, 1996.
Fed Cup winning team: Czechoslovakia 1988.

An exciting and popular player who could play glorious, aggressive tennis but suffered from fragile nerves, Jana Novotna captured 17 Grand Slam titles during her 13-year professional career. She will be best remembered not for a match she won but one she lost. In the first of her three Wimbledon singles finals in 1993, she had Steffi Graf on the ropes, leading 41 40 30 in the final set. But the Czech lost confidence and folded, allowing a grateful Graf to retain her title, 76 16 64. The image of a distressed Novotna sobbing on the shoulder of the Duchess of Kent is one that tennis fans will never forget.

It wasn't the only time Novotna suffered an horrendous choke: in the 1995 French Open she managed to lose to Chanda Rubin from a lead of 50 40-0 in the final set. In the 1997 Wimbledon final she won the first set 62 against Martina Hingis and watched the match slip away. But in 1998 she exorcised her demons, and having removed Hingis in the semifinals, overcame Nathalie Tauziat for the one title she wanted the most. Novotna was the last leading female player who was an out-and-out exponent of the serve and volley game. Although her high service toss sometimes gave her problems with timing, and her forehand, which had a big swing, was prone to be erratic, her backhand was sound whether sliced or topped, and she had sweet volleys.

Novotna spent most of the 1990s in the top ten, peaking at No. 2 in 1997. She was fairly consistent at the majors, with one Australian final (1991), two French semifinals (1990, 1996) and two US Open semifinals (1994, 1998). At Wimbledon she was a quarterfinalist or better seven years running (1993-99). She won the WTA Tour Championship in singles (1997) and doubles (1995, 1997) and a total of 24 singles and 76 tour doubles titles.

Her doubles record was magnificent, with multiple titles at all four majors, and she won three of the four Grand Slam women's doubles events in 1990 (with Helena Sukova) and 1998 (with Hingis). The only mixed doubles title to elude her was the French. Novotna played in the Fed Cup for 11 years and was on the winning team in 1988. She also took part in three Olympics (1988, 1992 and 1996) and won medals at Seoul and Atlanta.

MARGARET OSBORNE DUPONT (USA)

A regular title winner before the days of Open tennis, she accumulated 37 Grand Slam wins in singles, doubles and mixed. Outstanding in doubles, she and Louise Brough won 20 major titles.

Born: Joseph, Oregon, USA, March 4, 1918.
Grand Slam titles: French 1946, 1949. Wimbledon 1947. United States 1948-50. 21 women's doubles titles, 10 mixed doubles titles.

A prolific collector of major titles whose top class career lasted a remarkable 24 years, from 1938 to 1962, Margaret Osborne (who married William DuPont, from the multinational industrial dynasty, in 1947) was a class act in an era of strong female players. Although her contemporaries Pauline Betz, Louise Brough and Doris Hart are generally regarded as superior players, DuPont was ranked No. 1 in the world for four straight years from 1947 to 1950. She used guile and skill rather than power to win 37 titles in three of the four Grand Slam championships (she never travelled to Australia). She had a good serve and crisp volleys, whilst her forehand drive, hit with a heavy chop, and a lethal cocktail of spins and slices on both sides, bamboozled opponents and negated their efforts to overpower her with pace. Her fabulous doubles partnership with Brough racked up 12 American, five Wimbledon and three French titles, while in mixed doubles she assembled nine US championships playing with Bill Talbert, Ken McGregor, Ken Rosewall and Neale Fraser. Always taking the right court, DuPont was the mistress of doubles arts, and age did not wither her effectiveness. By winning the 1962 Wimbledon mixed doubles with Fraser she became the oldest ever women's Grand Slam champion at 44 (she has since been overtaken by Martina Navratilova).

Her singles title haul was not quite so fruitful, but during her peak years she was a vigorous and resolute competitor. She reached the first of her five Forest Hills finals in 1944, when she was beaten by Betz, and then succumbed to Brough at the same stage in 1947. The following year she turned the tables on her close friend and doubles partner, winning a titanic battle 46 64 1513. She retained the title in both 1949 and 1950 in straight sets against Hart.

At Wimbledon, DuPont was champion in 1947, defeating Hart, and she lost the 1949 and 1950 finals to Brough. On the former occasion they played out a marathon 108 16 108 before teaming up to retain the doubles. She won twice at Roland Garros, a shock 16 86 75 winner over Betz, at the time the world's dominant player, in 1946, and again in 1949 over Frenchwoman Nelly Adamson. Although she reached no more major singles finals after 1950, DuPont remained a redoubtable force in doubles for another dozen years (albeit interrupting her career in 1952 to have a son). In nine Wightman Cup matches between 1946 and 1962 she was never beaten, winning 10 singles and nine doubles rubbers.

The Greatest – Women (continued)

ELIZABETH RYAN (USA)

Probably the best woman player never to win a Grand Slam singles title. In doubles she collected 26, including a record 19 at Wimbledon, during a career spanning 22 years. Her insatiable love of tennis flourished especially in 1924 when she won 75 singles and doubles titles.

Born: Anaheim, California, USA, February 8, 1892.
Died: London, England, July 8, 1979.
Grand Slam titles: 17 women's doubles titles, nine mixed doubles titles.

Elizabeth Ryan, always known as 'Bunny', was probably the best woman player never to win a Grand Slam singles title, and with 26 major championships in doubles and mixed doubles won over 22 years she was perhaps the outstanding doubles player of all time.

Although American by nationality she settled in England before World War I and seldom returned to the US. Ryan was tirelessly active in tournaments from 1912 to 1914 and, when competition resumed in Europe, from 1919 to 1934. During the playing season she was constantly engaged in singles, doubles and mixed tournament draws and is estimated to have won a total of 659 titles. In her peak year of 1924 she was successful in 75 events.

Ryan, who won the majority of her titles in her thirties, was perhaps a little too stout and slow to challenge the top players of her time, who included Suzanne Lenglen and Helen Wills Moody. She had a trademark chopped forehand, a wicked drop shot and the most reliable of volleys, and in doubles her tactical ability was unparalleled. Her first notable singles title was the Russian Championship in 1914, and she went on to win the British Covered Courts in 1920, the British Hard Courts in 1924-25, the Irish in 1919-23, the Italian in 1933, Beckenham seven times between 1919 and 1928, the Welsh in 1924 and Queen's in 1923-25 and 1929. She was runner-up at Wimbledon in 1921 and 1930, and at Forest Hills in 1926, when she led 42-year-old Molla Mallory 40 in the final set and had a match point at 76 only to lose 46 64 97.

Perhaps her nearest miss at Wimbledon came in 1924, when she became the first player to wrest a set from Lenglen in five years and lost a desperately close quarterfinal 62 68 64 only for Lenglen to scratch in the following round. In doubles, however, Ryan was supreme, and her greatest partnership, with Lenglen, was invincible. They won Wimbledon six times, and when the French Federation insisted on Lenglen partnering another Frenchwoman, Didi Vlasto, in 1926, Ryan and Mary K. Browne beat Lenglen and Vlasto 36 97 62, saving two match points.

Ryan won her other Wimbledon doubles titles with Agnes Morton, Browne, Wills Moody and Simone Mathieu. Her total of 19 Wimbledon titles was a record until overtaken by Billie Jean King in 1979. Ryan collapsed and died at Wimbledon the day before her record fell.

GABRIELA SABATINI (ARG)

World junior champion at 13, Olympic silver medallist in Seoul at 18, her spectacularly exciting, all-court tennis was never better illustrated than in her victory over Steffi Graf at the 1990 US Open, yet her face and figure earned her even more than her tennis.

Born: Buenos Aires, Argentina, May 16, 1970.
Grand Slam titles: US Open 1990. One women's doubles title.
Olympics: Silver medal, singles, 1988.

South America's finest player after Maria Bueno, Gabriela Sabatini was the world's most photographed athlete until Anna Kournikova. Although she earned nearly $9 million in prize money during her 12-year professional career, she made many times that figure in product endorsements. Sabatini was striking in appearance, with arresting Latin features, a perfect physique and exceptional glamour. Despite her reserved personality she became a huge celebrity and was the top box office draw in the sport, adored by millions all over the world. The essence of Sabatini's tennis game was her powerful topspin driving. Her forehand was deep and solid, while her rolled backhand, struck single-handed, was a winning shot both crosscourt and down the line. Against this, her service was at best adequate and at worst a liability. In later years her tendency to double-fault was her downfall.

She was an exceptional junior, winning the French Open girls' title and the Orange Bowl 18 and under singles in 1984, when she was only 14. She was a semifinalist at Roland Garros at 15 and at Wimbledon at 16. Sabatini was a year younger than Steffi Graf, and the German had the edge in the early stage of their meetings, beating her in the US Open and Olympic finals of 1988. The two briefly paired up in doubles and won the 1988 Wimbledon doubles final over Larisa Savchenko and Natasha Zvereva, 63 16 1210.

In 1990 Sabatini sacked her coach, Angel Gimenez, and began to work with Carlos Kirmayr and sports psychologist Jim Loehr. Kirmayr taught her to play an effective serve and volley game and Loehr instilled in her a self-belief that had been hitherto lacking. Armed with these new assets, she had her finest hour at the US Open when she beat Graf 62 76 to win her only Grand Slam singles title.

She won five consecutive matches against Graf until the 1991 Wimbledon final, when she twice served for the match but lost 64 36 86. After this she was never better than a semifinalist in a Grand Slam event, although she won four Italian Open titles between 1988 and 1992 and the Virginia Slims Championship in 1988 and 1994. The later stages of her career were marred by injuries and a devastating loss of confidence after she squandered a lead of 61 5-1 against Mary Joe Fernandez in the quarterfinals of the 1993 French Open, double-faulting on match point.

ARANTXA SANCHEZ-VICARIO (ESP)

Between 1989-1999, this diminutive but always doughty competitor never dropped out of the world top ten. Her competitive longevity was underlined by the way her three triumphs at the French Open also spanned ten years, while she also won the US Open and was runner-up at eight other Grand Slam tournaments.

Born:	Barcelona, Spain, December 18, 1971.
Grand Slam titles:	French Open 1989, 1994, 1998. US Open 1994. Six women's doubles titles and four mixed doubles titles.
Olympics:	Silver medals, singles: 1996, doubles: 1992. Bronze medals, singles: 1992, doubles: 1996.
Fed Cup winning team:	Spain 1991, 1993-95, 1998.

Arantxa Sanchez-Vicario is the most successful woman player ever produced by Spain and the only one of her nationality to be ranked No.1 in the world. From a family of tennis achievers – her brothers Emilio and Javier were both Davis Cup players – she reached her peak in the mid-1990s. This was, admittedly, a time when women's tennis was in a slight trough. Monica Seles took two and a half years to recover from her stabbing, Jennifer Capriati was also out of the game and Davenport, Hingis and the Williams sisters had yet to emerge. Sanchez-Vicario was not a powerful player but she was strong (both mentally and physically) and very persistent. She was capable of running down most balls that would be winners against most other players and any opponent would expect to be involved in long, uncompromising rallies.

The 'Barcelona Bumblebee' (so dubbed by tennis writer Bud Collins) became the youngest player to win the French Open at 17 years, five months in 1989 when she shocked reigning Golden Slammer Steffi Graf 76(6) 36 75 in a compelling final. (Her record was broken the following year by the even younger Seles.) It would be another five years until the sizzling senorita would strike again. This time, also at Roland Garros, she stunned Mary Pierce and 15,000 French spectators by winning her second major and made her final assault on the WTA's No.1 ranking. Adding the US Open, with another battling victory over Graf, the top position was hers by February 1995. She held it for a total of 12 weeks.

Sanchez-Vicario's last great achievement was a third French Open title in 1998, when she surprised everyone to deny Seles the title after the American had easily dispatched Hingis in the semifinals. She was also a finalist at the Australian Open (1994-95) and Wimbledon (1995-96). There were two near misses in major finals against Graf: at Wimbledon, Sanchez Vicario lost by a whisker to the German in 1995 and at Roland Garros in 1996 she served for the match at 5-4 in the final set, only to lose an epic encounter 63 67(4)108.

With her compatriot Conchita Martinez, Sanchez-Vicario won the Fed Cup for Spain five times and reached a further five finals. One of the most active players in history, she accumulated 29 singles and 67 doubles titles during her 15-year professional career.

MONICA SELES (YUG/USA)

Until she was stabbed by a crazed spectator in Hamburg in 1993, she was firmly established as world No. 1, with many predicting she could be the best ever. Her powerful double-handed drives off both flanks had won her eight of the previous nine Grand Slams.

Born:	Novi Sad, Yugoslavia, December 2, 1973.
Grand Slam titles:	Australian Open 1991-93, 1996. French Open 1990-92. US Open 1991-92.
Olympics:	Bronze medal, singles, 2000.
Fed Cup winning teams:	USA 1996, 2000.

Monica Seles is almost indisputably the greatest female player not to have won Wimbledon. She captured the other three Grand Slam titles in both 1991 and 1992 and during her peak years she was almost unbeatable. In her only Wimbledon final – 1992 – she was trounced 62 61 by Steffi Graf after a concerted media campaign against her loud exhalation of air every time she hit the ball.

There is no question that Seles could have established herself as the most dominant player of all time had she not been stabbed in the back by a crazed spectator at Hamburg on April 30, 1993. At that point she was the queen of the courts, having overtaken Graf as world No. 1 in March 1991. The physical damage was slight, but the psychological impact on Seles was devastating: she did not return to competition for two and a half years. When she reappeared in the late summer of 1995 she lost to Graf in a spellbinding US Open final and won the following year's Australian Open, but this remains her only Grand Slam success since her tragic hiatus.

A left-hander, Seles plays double-handed on both sides. Taking the ball on the rise, she hits with tremendous power and penetration. Her serve is also an effective weapon, but since her return she has had to contend with weight and fitness problems and a succession of injuries. Also, whereas in the early part of her career she had no real rival except Graf, she has struggled to keep pace with the guile of Martina Hingis and the brutal power of the Williams sisters and Lindsay Davenport.

Born in Yugoslavia but resident in Florida from an early age (a US citizen since 1994), Seles exploded onto the tour as a 15-year-old in 1989, when she beat Chris Evert to win her first pro title in Houston. She was a semifinalist at Roland Garros in 1989 and became the youngest ever French Open champion at 16 years, 6 months in 1990. Between the 1990 and 1995 US Opens her 1992 loss to Graf at Wimbledon was her only defeat in eight Grand Slam appearances. Having lost to Graf in the US Open finals of 1995 and 1996 her only subsequent Grand Slam final has been at Roland Garros in 1998, when after beating Hingis in the semifinals she lost to Arantxa Sanchez-Vicario.

The Greatest – Women (continued)

VIRGINIA WADE (GBR)

Won the very first Open tournament at Bournemouth in 1968, a few months before claiming the US Open title. An attacking player, who won titles all round the world, she added Wimbledon to the list at her 16th attempt during the Championship's emotional centenary year.

Born: Bournemouth, England, July 10, 1945.
Grand Slam titles: Australian Open 1972. Wimbledon 1977. US Open 1968. Four women's doubles titles.

A passionate, dramatic and exciting player, Virginia Wade was arguably the most successful of all British women in tennis – certainly in the Open era. In addition to three Grand Slam singles titles she won four doubles championships – all with Margaret Court – the Australian and French in 1973 and the US Open in 1973 and 1975. She was in the world's top ten for 13 consecutive years – 1967 to 1979 – and reached No. 2 in 1968 and 1975. Moreover, she played more Wightman Cup and Federation Cup rubbers than any other player.

Wade was a fiery and aggressive player who had one of the best serves in women's tennis, a heavily sliced but effective backhand, strong forehand and fine volley and overhead. Over an exceptionally long top class career – 23 years from 1962 to 1985 – she tottered for years on a rollercoaster ranging between glorious victories and ignominious defeats. It was only from the mid-1970s, when she placed her destiny in the hands of an American coach, Jerry Teeguarden, that she largely eradicated her technical deficiencies and formulated a strategic sense that had hitherto been missing.

Winner of the world's first Open tournament at Bournemouth in 1968, Wade achieved an early career milestone in the same year when she trounced world No. 1 Billie Jean King 64 62 in the final of the first US Open. She achieved other successes, in the 1971 Italian Open and the 1972 Australian Open, but at Wimbledon, where the crowds were desperate for her to do justice to her undoubted talent, she suffered a succession of early shock defeats. In 1974 she at last made the semifinals but crashed out 16 75 64 after looking certain to beat Russia's Olga Morozova.

In 1977, days short of her 32nd birthday, Wade chose a unique occasion – the centenary Wimbledon championships, coinciding with the Queen's Silver Jubilee – to finally take the title. She played the match of her life to dethrone Chris Evert 62 46 61 in the semifinals and then willed herself to beat Betty Stove 46 63 61 in the final. To the accompaniment of deafening applause, she received the trophy from the Queen (a rare visitor to Wimbledon) and made herself the heroine of the tournament's greatest patriotic spectacle since the British glory days of the 1930s. Wade battled on and reached the Wimbledon quarterfinals as late as 1983, when she was nearly 38.

SERENA WILLIAMS (USA)

Just as her father Richard predicted, Serena has become even more successful than older sister Venus, sweeping to No. 1 during 2002 when she won the French, Wimbledon and US Open titles.

Born: Saginaw, Michigan, USA, September 26, 1981.
Grand Slam titles: Australian Open 2003, French Open 2002, Wimbledon 2002-03, US Open 1999, 2002.
Six women's doubles titles, two mixed doubles titles.
Olympics: Gold medal, doubles, 2000.
Fed Cup winning team: USA 1999.

The younger of the two sensational sisters, Serena surged to the top of the sport in 2002, winning three out of the four Grand Slam championships and five other titles. The 21 year-old set a notable record, rising from No. 9 in the world in March to No. 1 in July – a feat unsurpassed since the WTA Tour rankings began in 1975. Serena is unquestionably one of the strongest women's champions in physical terms. Although her height (5ft 8ins) and weight (130 lbs) are average among professional women tennis players, she has a highly-toned physique and muscle bulk of a track and field athlete. This is reflected in her game, which is extremely powerful. She has one of the best serves in the game and plays chiefly from the baseline, although her volleying ability is considerable.

Like her elder sister Venus, Serena was withdrawn from junior competition by her father and coach, Richard Williams. Apart from a one-off appearance as a 14-year-old in qualifying at Quebec City in the autumn of 1995, she made her debut on the WTA Tour in October 1997. In only her second tournament, at Chicago, she beat two seeds to reach the semifinals. This launched her very swift rise to the upper levels of the game. Her first Grand Slam singles title came in 1999, when she won the US Open. Few would have expected Serena to win a Grand Slam crown before Venus. She won four other titles that year and ended the season at No. 4 in the rankings.

Serena might have reached the very top sooner had she not suffered a series of niggling injuries in 2000 and 2001. During those two years she reached only one Grand Slam final – the 2001 US Open, losing to Venus.

In 2002, after missing the Australian Open because of an ankle injury, she took off on a procession of victories, gathering the French, Wimbledon and US Open titles (beating Venus in all three finals) and suffering only five defeats in 61 matches. Her first Australian Open title came at the start of 2003 when she became the fifth woman of all-time to hold all four Grand Slam titles at once. Also that year she partnered James Blake to the Hopman Cup title and successfully defended her Wimbledon crown, both 2003 Grand Slam finals were contested against her sister. Wimbledon turned out to be her last tournament of the season when a left knee injury required surgery and a long rehabilitation. 2004 was another injury plagued season, she lost her Wimbledon crown when beaten in the final by Maria Sharapova.

VENUS WILLIAMS (USA)

Capped a memorable year in 2000 by winning Wimbledon, the US Open and Olympic gold in singles and doubles (with sister Serena). Tall and powerful, she hits serves harder than many men and her forehand is also a ruthless matchwinner.

Born: Lynwood, California, USA, June 17, 1980.
Grand Slam titles: Wimbledon 2000-01, US Open 2000-01. Six women's doubles titles, two mixed doubles titles.
Olympics: Gold medals, singles and doubles, 2000.
Fed Cup winning team: USA 1999.

Venus Williams has been one of the most successful woman players of the new Millennium. In 2000 and 2001 she blazed a trail of success across the globe with barely a serious challenger in sight. Then her younger sister Serena, previously rather in her shadow, burst through in 2002 and supplanted her sibling at the top of the world rankings. They played in four consecutive Grand Slam finals starting at the 2002 French Open, Serena got the better of her sister on each occasion. Because, understandably, the sisters prefer not to face each other in singles match, the only tournaments they both enter are the very biggest – the Grand Slams and other top events such as Miami and the WTA Tour Championships.

Venus, a tall, athletic player who hits with great power and has the strongest (although not the most consistent) service in the women's game, made an immediate impact. She reached the final of the US Open the first time she played (1997) and ended her debut season just outside the top 20. The following year she won in Miami, defeating Martina Hingis and Anna Kournikova in the last two rounds. She retained this title in 1999, beating Serena in the first major final between sisters for 115 years, and was also successful in Hamburg and Rome.

Suffering from tendonitis in both wrists, Venus did not play at all between November 1999 and May 2000 but after a shaky start to her season she hit a 35-match winning streak, taking in Wimbledon, US Open, Sydney Olympics and three other tournaments. In 2001 she regained the Miami title and held on to both Wimbledon and the US Open. Mainly due to insufficient activity she did not attain the world No. 1 ranking until February 2002. She held it for a total of nine weeks until Serena took over after Wimbledon. Even so, Venus picked up seven titles during the year. An abdominal strain in 2003 put Venus out for the rest of the year after losing the Wimbledon final to her sister. She struggled to regain her form in 2004, capturing two titles but failing to reach the semifinals or further of any Grand Slam.

HELEN WILLS MOODY (USA)

This hard-hitting Californian, famous for wearing a white eyeshade and known as 'Little Miss Poker Face' because of her total focus, won 19 Grand Slam singles titles including eight at Wimbledon in only nine visits.

Born: Centerville, California, USA, October 6, 1905.
Died: Carmel, California, USA, January 1, 1998.
Grand Slam titles: French 1928-30, 1932. Wimbledon 1927-30, 1932-33, 1935, 1938. United States 1923-25, 1927-29, 1931. Nine women's doubles titles, three mixed doubles titles.
Olympics: Gold medals, singles and doubles, 1924.

Famously dubbed with such epithets as 'Little Miss Poker Face' and 'Venus with a headache', Helen Wills (who married Freddie Moody in 1929 and Aiden Roark in 1939, but divorced twice) was the undisputed queen of tennis from 1927 to 1933, when she did not yield a single set. Apart from a retirement, she was unbeaten for eight years. No other player, male or female, has ever achieved such dominance. Her total of 19 Grand Slam singles titles is bettered only by Margaret Court, and her eight Wimbledon crowns stood as a record until overtaken by Martina Navratilova in 1990. A strikingly beautiful woman who shunned the company of fellow-players and socialised with the rich and famous, she was a notable painter and writer as well as an exceptionally gifted tennis player. Her success was borne of iron determination, extreme mental strength and utter concentration. Inscrutable under a white eyeshade, Moody never showed any emotion on court, and because of her icy demeanour crowds never warmed to her.

Technically, her game was sound and as free from error as anyone who has ever played. Having practised against men in her native California she hit with great power and penetration, concentrating on hard, accurate ground strokes but able to volley and smash when necessary. Her sliced serve broke wide, pulling the receiver out of the court. Her only weakness was poor footwork, but such was the remorseless strength of her driving that this was hardly a handicap.

Over a long career, stretching from 1919 to 1938, she won 52 of 92 tournaments, but at her peak she was totally invincible. She lost only once at Wimbledon, to Britain's Kitty McKane in the 1924 final, from 41 in the final set, and was beaten 63 86 in her only meeting with Suzanne Lenglen, at Cannes in 1926. At Forest Hills she won seven times, but in the 1933 final she retired against Helen Jacobs at 03 in the final set – her only technical defeat against the other Helen in 11 encounters. She missed several Wimbledons due to illness or injury, but in five of her victories there she did not drop a set. Her doubles titles included four with Elizabeth Ryan and three with Hazel Wightman.

Davis Cup

Established in 1900. Until 1971 the defending champion did not play through, meeting the winner of a knock-out competition in the Challenge Round to decide the title, and having choice of venue. In 1972 the Challenge Round was abolished, the defending champion having to play the whole competition for a chance to reach the Final Round. The 16-nation World Group was introduced in 1981.

Challenge Round

1900 USA d. British Isles 3-0, Longwood Cricket Club, Boston, MA, USA (Grass)
(Winning Captain: Dwight Davis, losing Captain: Arthur Gore) M. Whitman (USA) d. A. Gore (GBR) 61 63 62; D. Davis (USA) d. E. Black (GBR) 46 62 64 64; D. Davis/H. Ward (USA) d. E. Black/H. Barrett (GBR) 64 64 64; D. Davis (USA) vs. A. Gore (GBR) 97 99 unfinished.

1901 Not held

1902 USA d. British Isles 3-2, Crescent Athletic Club, Brooklyn, NY, USA (Grass)
(Winning Captain: Malcolm Whitman, losing Captain: William Collins) R. Doherty (GBR) d. W. Larned (USA) 26 36 63 64 64; M. Whitman (USA) d. J. Pim (GBR) 61 61 16 60; R. Doherty/L. Doherty (GBR) d. D. Davis/H. Ward (USA) 36 108 63 64; W. Larned (USA) d. J. Pim (GBR) 63 62 63; M. Whitman (USA) d. R. Doherty (GBR) 61 75 64.

1903 British Isles d. USA 4-1, Longwood Cricket Club, Boston, MA, USA (Grass)
(Winning Captain: William Collins, losing Captain: William Larned) L. Doherty (GBR) d. R. Wrenn (USA) 60 63 64; W. Larned (USA) d. R. Doherty (GBR) ret; R. Doherty/L. Doherty (GBR) d. R. Wrenn/G. Wrenn (USA) 75 97 26 63; L. Doherty (GBR) d. W. Larned (USA) 63 68 60 26 75; R. Doherty (GBR) d. R. Wrenn (USA) 64 36 63 68 64.

1904 British Isles d. Belgium 5-0, Worple Road, Wimbledon, London, England (Grass)
(Winning Captain: William Collins, losing Captain: Paul de Borman) L. Doherty (GBR) d. L. de Borman (BEL) 64 61 61; F. Riseley (GBR) d. W. Lemaire de Warzee (BEL) 61 64 62; R. Doherty/L. Doherty (GBR) d. L. de Borman/W. Lemaire de Warzee (BEL) 60 61 63; L. Doherty (GBR) d. W. Lemaire de Warzee (BEL) w/o; F. Riseley (GBR) d. L. de Borman (BEL) 46 62 86 75.

1905 British Isles d. USA 5-0, Worple Road, Wimbledon, London, England (Grass)
(Winning Captain: William Collins, losing Captain: Paul Dashiel) L. Doherty (GBR) d. H. Ward (USA) 79 46 61 62 60; S. Smith (GBR) d. W. Larned (USA) 64 64 57 64; R. Doherty/L. Doherty (GBR) d. H. Ward/B. Wright (USA) 810 62 62 46 86; S. Smith (GBR) d. W. Clothier (USA) 46 61 64 63; L. Doherty (GBR) d. W. Larned (USA) 64 26 68 64 62.

1906 British Isles d. USA 5-0, Worple Road, Wimbledon, London, England (Grass)
(Winning Captain: William Collins, losing Captain: Beals Wright) S. Smith (GBR) d. R. Little (USA) 64 64 61; L. Doherty (GBR) d. H. Ward (USA) 62 86 63; R. Doherty/L. Doherty (GBR) d. R. Little/H. Ward (USA) 36 119 97 61; S. Smith (GBR) d. H. Ward (USA) 61 60 64; L. Doherty (GBR) d. R. Little (USA) 36 63 68 61 63.

1907 Australasia d. British Isles 3-2, Worple Road, Wimbledon, London, England (Grass)
(Winning Captain: Norman Brookes, losing Captain: Alfred Hickson) N. Brookes (AUS) d. A. Gore (GBR) 75 61 75; A. Wilding (AUS) d. H. Barrett (GBR) 16 64 63 75; A. Gore/H. Barrett (GBR) d. N. Brookes/A. Wilding (AUS) 36 46 75 62 1311; A. Gore (GBR) d. A. Wilding (AUS) 36 63 75 62; N. Brookes (AUS) d. H. Barrett (GBR) 62 60 63.

1908 Australasia d. USA 3-2, Albert Ground, Melbourne, VIC, Australia (Grass)
(Winning Captain: Norman Brookes, losing Captain: Beals Wright) N. Brookes (AUS) d. F. Alexander (USA) 57 97 62 46 63; B. Wright (USA) d. A. Wilding (AUS) 36 75 63 61; N. Brookes/A. Wilding (AUS) d. F. Alexander/B. Wright (USA) 64 62 57 16 64; B. Wright (USA) d. N. Brookes (AUS) 06 36 75 62 1210; A. Wilding (AUS) d. F. Alexander (USA) 63 64 61.

1909 Australasia d. USA 5-0, Double Bay Grounds, Sydney, NSW, Australia (Grass)
(Winning Captain: Norman Brookes, losing Captain: Maurice McLoughlin) N. Brookes (AUS) d. M. McLoughlin (USA) 62 62 64; A. Wilding (AUS) d. M. Long (USA) 62 75 61; N. Brookes/A. Wilding (AUS) d. M. Long/M. McLoughlin (USA) 1210 97 63; N. Brookes (AUS) d. M. Long (USA) 64 75 86; A. Wilding (AUS) d. M. McLoughlin (USA) 36 86 62 63.

1910 Not held

1911 Australasia d. USA 5-0, Hagley Park, Christchurch, New Zealand (Grass)
(Winning Captain: Norman Brookes, losing Captain: William Larned) N. Brookes (AUS) d. B. Wright (USA) 64 26 63 63; R. Heath (AUS) d. W. Larned (USA) 26 61 75 62; N. Brookes/A. Dunlop (AUS) d. B. Wright/M. McLoughlin (USA) 64 57 75 64; N. Brookes (AUS) d. M. McLoughlin (USA) 64 36 46 63 64; R. Heath (AUS) d. B. Wright (USA) w/o.

1912 British Isles d. Australasia 3-2, Albert Ground, Melbourne, VIC, Australia (Grass)
(Winning Captain: Charles Dixon, losing Captain: Norman Brookes) J. Parke (GBR) d. N. Brookes (AUS) 86 63 57 62; C. Dixon (GBR) d. R. Heath (AUS) 57 64 64 64; N. Brookes/A. Dunlop (AUS) d. A. Beamish/J. Parke (GBR) 64 61 57; N. Brookes (AUS) d. C. Dixon (GBR) 62 64 64; J. Parke (GBR) d. R. Heath (AUS) 62 64 64.

1913 USA d. British Isles 3-2, Worple Road, Wimbledon, London, England (Grass)
(Winning Captain: Harold Hackett, losing Captain: Roger McNair) J. Parke (GBR) d. M. McLoughlin (USA) 810 75 64 16 75; R. Williams (USA) d. C. Dixon (GBR) 86 36 62 16 75; H. Hackett/M. McLoughlin (USA) d. C. Dixon/H. Barrett (GBR) 57 61 26 75 64; M. McLoughlin (USA) d. C. Dixon (GBR) 86 63 62; J. Parke (GBR) d. R. Williams (USA) 62 57 57 64 62.

1914 Australasia d. USA 3-2, West Side Tennis Club, New York, NY, USA (Grass)
(Winning Captain: Norman Brookes, losing Captain: Maurice McLoughlin) A. Wilding (AUS) d. R. Williams (USA) 75 62 63; M. McLoughlin (USA) d. N. Brookes (AUS) 1715 63 63; N. Brookes/A. Wilding (AUS) d. T. Bundy/M. McLoughlin (USA) 63 86 97; N. Brookes (AUS) d. R. Williams (USA) 61 62 810 63; M. McLoughlin (USA) d. A. Wilding (AUS) 62 63 26 62.

1915-18 Not held

1919 Australasia d. British Isles 4-1, Double Bay Grounds, Sydney, NSW, Australia (Grass)
(Winning Captain: Norman Brookes, losing Captain: Algernon Kingscote) G. Patterson (AUS) d. A. Lowe (GBR) 64 63 26 63; A. Kingscote (GBR) d. J. Anderson (AUS) 75 62 64; N. Brookes/G. Patterson (AUS) d. A. Beamish/A. Kingscote (GBR) 60 60 62; G. Patterson (AUS) d. A. Kingscote (GBR) 64 64 86; J. Anderson (AUS) d. A. Lowe (GBR) 64 57 63 46 1210.

1920 USA d. Australasia 5-0, Domain Cricket Club, Auckland, New Zealand (Grass)
(Winning Captain: Sam Hardy, losing Captain: Norman Brookes) B. Tilden (USA) d. N. Brookes (AUS) 108 64 16 64; W. Johnston (USA) d. G. Patterson (AUS) 63 61 61; W. Johnston/B. Tilden (USA) d. N. Brookes/G. Patterson (AUS) 46 64 60 64; W. Johnston (USA) d. N. Brookes (AUS) 57 75 63; B. Tilden (USA) d. G. Patterson (AUS) 57 62 63 63.

1921 USA d. Japan 5-0, West Side Tennis Club, New York, NY, USA (Grass)
(Winning Captain: Norris Williams, losing Captain: Ichiya Kumagae) W. Johnston (USA) d. I. Kumagai (JPN) 62 64 62; B. Tilden (USA) d. Z. Shimizu (JPN) 57 46 75 62 61; W. Washburn/R. Williams (USA) d. I. Kumagai/Z. Shimizu (JPN) 62 75 46 75; B. Tilden (USA) d. I. K. (JPN) 97 64 61; W. Johnston (USA) d. Z. Shimizu (JPN) 63 57 62 64.

1922 USA d. Australasia 4-1, West Side Tennis Club, New York, NY, USA (Grass)
(Winning Captain: Norris Williams, losing Captain: James Anderson) B. Tilden (USA) d. G. Patterson (AUS) 75 108 60; W. Johnston (USA) d. J. Anderson (AUS) 61 62 63; P. O'Hara-Wood/G. Patterson (AUS) d. V. Richards/B. Tilden (USA) 64 60 63; W. Johnston (USA) d. G. Patterson (AUS) 62 62 61; B. Tilden (USA) d. J. Anderson (AUS) 64 57 36 64 62.

1923 USA d. Australia 4-1, West Side Tennis Club, Forest Hills, NY, USA (Grass)
(Winning Captain: Norris Williams, losing Captain: Gerald Patterson) J. Anderson (AUS) d. W. Johnston (USA) 46 62 26 75 62; B. Tilden (USA) d. J. Hawkes (AUS) 64 62 61; B. Tilden/R. Williams (USA) d. J. Anderson/J. Hawkes (AUS) 1715 1113 26 63 62; W. Johnston (USA) d. J. Hawkes (AUS) 60 62 61; B. Tilden (USA) d. J. Anderson (AUS) 62 63 16 75.

1924 USA d. Australia 5-0, Germantown Cricket Club, Philadelphia, PA, USA (Grass)
(Winning Captain: Norris Williams, losing Captain: Gerald Patterson) B. Tilden (USA) d. G. Patterson (AUS) 64 62 63; V. Richards (USA) d. P. O'Hara-Wood (AUS) 63 62 64; W. Johnston/B. Tilden (USA) d. P. O'Hara-Wood/G. Patterson (AUS) 57 63 64 61; B. Tilden (USA) d. P. O'Hara-Wood (AUS) 62 61 61; V. Richards (USA) d. G. Patterson (AUS) 63 75 64.

1925 USA d. France 5-0, Germantown Cricket Club, Philadelphia, PA, USA (Grass)
(Winning Captain: Norris Williams, losing Captain: Max Decugis) B. Tilden (USA) d. J. Borotra (FRA) 46 60 26 97 64; W. Johnston (USA) d. R. Lacoste (FRA) 61 61 68 63; V. Richards/R. Williams (USA) d. J. Borotra/R. Lacoste (FRA) 64 63 63; B. Tilden (USA) d. R. Lacoste (FRA) 36 1012 86 75 62; W. Johnston (USA) d. J. Borotra (FRA) 61 64 60.

Davis Cup (continued)

1926 USA d. France 4-1, Germantown Cricket Club, Philadelphia, PA, USA (Grass)
(Winning Captain: Norris Williams, losing Captain: Pierre Gillou) W. Johnston (USA) d. R. Lacoste (FRA) 60 64 06 60; B. Tilden (USA) d. J. Borotra (FRA) 62 63 63; V. Richards/R. Williams (USA) d. J. Brugnon/H. Cochet (FRA) 64 64 62; W. Johnston (USA) d. J. Borotra (FRA) 86 64 97; R. Lacoste (FRA) d. B. Tilden (USA) 46 64 86 86.

1927 France d. USA 3-2, Germantown Cricket Club, Philadelphia, PA, USA (Grass)
(Winning Captain: Pierre Gillou, losing Captain: Charles Garland) R. Lacoste (FRA) d. W. Johnston (USA) 63 62 62; B. Tilden (USA) d. H. Cochet (FRA) 64 26 62 86; F. Hunter/B. Tilden (USA) d. J. Borotra/J. Brugnon (FRA) 36 63 63 46 60; R. Lacoste (FRA) d. B. Tilden (USA) 64 46 63 63; H. Cochet (FRA) d. W. Johnston (USA) 64 46 62 64.

1928 France d. USA 4-1, Stade Roland Garros, Paris, France (Red Clay)
(Winning Captain: Pierre Gillou, losing Captain: Joseph Wear) B. Tilden (USA) d. R. Lacoste (FRA) 16 64 64 26 63; H. Cochet (FRA) d. J. Hennessey (USA) 57 97 63 60; J. Borotra/H. Cochet (FRA) d. F. Hunter/B. Tilden (USA) 64 68 75 46 62; R. Lacoste (FRA) d. J. Hennessey (USA) 46 61 75 63; H. Cochet (FRA) d. B. Tilden (USA) 97 86 64.

1929 France d. USA 3-2, Stade Roland Garros, Paris, France (Red Clay)
(Winning Captain: Pierre Gillou, losing Captain: Fitz-Eugene Dixon) H. Cochet (FRA) d. B. Tilden (USA) 63 61 62; J. Borotra (FRA) d. G. Lott (USA) 61 36 64 75; W. Allison/J. Van Ryn (USA) d. J. Borotra/H. Cochet (FRA) 61 86 64; H. Cochet (FRA) d. G. Lott (USA) 61 36 60 63; B. Tilden (USA) d. J. Borotra (FRA) 46 61 64 75.

1930 France d. USA 4-1, Stade Roland Garros, Paris, France (Red Clay)
(Winning Captain: Pierre Gillou, losing Captain: Fitz-Eugene Dixon) B. Tilden (USA) d. J. Borotra (FRA) 26 75 64 75; H. Cochet (FRA) d. G. Lott (USA) 64 62 62; J. Brugnon/H. Cochet (FRA) d. W. Allison/J. Van Ryn (USA) 63 75 16 62; J. Borotra (FRA) d. G. Lott (USA) 57 63 26 62 86; H. Cochet (FRA) d. B. Tilden (USA) 46 63 61 75.

1931 France d. Great Britain 3-2, Stade Roland Garros, Paris, France (Red Clay)
(Winning Captain: Rene Lacoste, losing Captain: Herbert Barrett) H. Cochet (FRA) d. B. Austin (GBR) 36 119 62 64; F. Perry (GBR) d. J. Borotra (FRA) 46 108 60 46 64; J. Brugnon/H. Cochet (FRA) d. P. Hughes/C. Kingsley (GBR) 61 57 63 86; H. Cochet (FRA) d. F. Perry (GBR) 64 16 97 63; B. Austin (GBR) d. J. Borotra (FRA) 75 63 36 75.

1932 France d. USA 3-2, Stade Roland Garros, Paris, France (Red Clay)
(Winning Captain: Rene Lacoste, losing Captain: Bernon Prentice) H. Cochet (FRA) d. W. Allison (USA) 57 75 36 75 62; J. Borotra (FRA) d. E. Vines (USA) 64 62 26 64; W. Allison/J. Van Ryn (USA) d. J. Brugnon/H. Cochet (FRA) 63 1113 75 46 64; J. Borotra (FRA) d. W. Allison (USA) 16 36 64 62 75; E. Vines (USA) d. H. Cochet (FRA) 46 06 75 86 62.

1933 Great Britain d. France 3-2, Stade Roland Garros, Paris, France (Red Clay)
(Winning Captain: Herbert Barrett, losing Captain: Rene Lacoste) B. Austin (GBR) d. A. Merlin (FRA) 63 64 60; F. Perry (GBR) d. H. Cochet (FRA) 810 64 86 36 61; J. Borotra/J. Brugnon (FRA) d. P. Hughes/H. Lee (GBR) 63 86 62; H. Cochet (FRA) d. B. Austin (GBR) 57 64 46 64 64; F. Perry (GBR) d. A. Merlin (FRA) 46 86 62 75.

1934 Great Britain d. USA 4-1, Centre Court, Wimbledon, London, England (Grass)
(Winning Captain: Herbert Barrett, losing Captain: Norris Williams) F. Perry (GBR) d. S. Wood (USA) 61 46 57 60 63; B. Austin (GBR) d. F. Shields (USA) 64 64 61; G. Lott/L. Stoefen (USA) d. P. Hughes/H. Lee (GBR) 75 60 46 97; F. Perry (GBR) d. F. Shields (USA) 64 46 62 1513; B. Austin (GBR) d. S. Wood (USA) 64 60 68 63.

1935 Great Britain d. USA 5-0, Centre Court, Wimbledon, London, England (Grass)
Winning Captain: Herbert Barrett, losing Captain: Joseph Wear) F. Perry (GBR) d. D. Budge (USA) 60 68 63 64; B. Austin (GBR) d. W. Allison (USA) 62 26 46 63 75; P. Hughes/R. Tuckey (GBR) d. W. Allison/J. Van Ryn (USA) 62 16 68 63 63; F. Perry (GBR) d. W. Allison (USA) 46 64 75 63; B. Austin (GBR) d. D. Budge (USA) 62 64 68 75.

1936 Great Britain d. Australia 3-2, Centre Court, Wimbledon, London, England (Grass)
(Winning Captain: Herbert Barrett, losing Captain: Cliff Sproule) B. Austin (GBR) d. J. Crawford (AUS) 46 63 61 61; F. Perry (GBR) d. A. Quist (AUS) 61 46 75 62; J. Crawford/A. Quist (AUS) d. P. Hughes/R. Tuckey (GBR) 64 26 75 108; A. Quist (AUS) d. B. Austin (GBR) 64 36 75 62; F. Perry (GBR) d. J. Crawford (AUS) 62 63 63.

1937 USA d. Great Britain 4-1, Centre Court, Wimbledon, London, England (Grass)
(Winning Captain: Walter Pate, losing Captain: Herbert Barrett) B. Austin (GBR) d. F. Parker (USA) 63 62 75; D. Budge (USA) d. C. Hare (GBR) 1513 61 62; D. Budge/G. Mako (USA) d. R. Tuckey/F. Wilde (GBR) 63 75 79 1210; F. Parker (USA) d. C. Hare (GBR) 62 64 62; D. Budge (USA) d. B. Austin (GBR) 86 36 64 63.

1938 USA d. Australia 3-2, Germantown Cricket Club, Philadelphia, PA, USA (Grass)
(Winning Captain: Walter Pate, losing Captain: Harry Hopman) B. Riggs (USA) d. A. Quist (AUS) 46 60 86 61; D. Budge (USA) d. J. Bromwich (AUS) 62 63 46 75; J. Bromwich/A. Quist (AUS) d. D. Budge/G. Mako (USA) 06 63 64 62; D. Budge (USA) d. A. Quist (AUS) 86 61 62; J. Bromwich (AUS) d. B. Riggs (USA) 64 46 60 62.

1939 Australia d. USA 3-2, Merion Cricket Club, Haverford, PA, USA (Grass)
(Winning Captain: Harry Hopman, losing Captain: Walter Pate) B. Riggs (USA) d. J. Bromwich (AUS) 64 60 75; F. Parker (USA) d. A. Quist (AUS) 63 26 64 16 75; J. Bromwich/A. Quist (AUS) d. J. Hunt/J. Kramer (USA) 57 62 75 62; A. Quist (AUS) d. B. Riggs (USA) 61 64 36 36 64; J. Bromwich (AUS) d. F. Parker (USA) 60 63 61.

1940-45 Not held

1946 USA d. Australia 5-0, Kooyong Stadium, Melbourne, VIC, Australia (Grass)
(Winning Captain: Walter Pate, losing Captain: Gerald Patterson) T. Schroeder (USA) d. J. Bromwich (AUS) 36 61 62 06 63; J. Kramer (USA) d. D. Pails (AUS) 86 62 97; J. Kramer/T. Schroeder (USA) d. J. Bromwich/A. Quist (AUS) 62 75 64; J. Kramer (USA) d. J. Bromwich (AUS) 86 64 62 64; G. Mulloy (USA) d. D. Pails (AUS) 63 63 64.

1947 USA d. Australia 4-1, West Side Tennis Club, Forest Hills, NY, USA (Grass
(Winning Captain: Alrick Man, losing Captain: Roy Cowling) J. Kramer (USA) d. D. Pails (AUS) 62 61 62; T. Schroeder (USA) d. J. Bromwich (AUS) 64 57 63 63; J. Bromwich/C. Long (AUS) d. J. Kramer/T. Schroeder (USA) 64 26 62 64; T. Schroeder (USA) d. D. Pails (AUS) 63 86 46 911 108; J. Kramer (USA) d. J. Bromwich (AUS) 63 62 62.

1948 USA d. Australia 5-0, West Side Tennis Club, Forest Hills, NY, USA (Grass)
(Winning Captain: Alrick Man, losing Captain: Adrian Quist) F. Parker (USA) d. B. Sidwell (AUS) 64 64 64; T. Schroeder (USA) d. A. Quist (AUS) 63 46 60 60; G. Mulloy/B. Talbert (USA) d. C. Long/B. Sidwell (AUS) 86 97 26 75; F. Parker (USA) d. A. Quist (AUS) 62 62 63; T. Schroeder (USA) d. B. Sidwell (AUS) 62 61 61.

1949 USA d. Australia 4-1, West Side Tennis Club, Forest Hills, NY, USA (Grass)
(Winning Captain: Alrick Man, losing Captain: John Bromwich) T. Schroeder (USA) d. B. Sidwell (AUS) 61 57 46 62 63; P. Gonzales (USA) d. F. Sedgman (AUS) 86 64 97; J. Bromwich/B. Sidwell (AUS) d. G. Mulloy/B. Talbert (USA) 36 46 108 97 97; T. Schroeder (USA) d. F. Sedgman (AUS) 64 63 63; P. Gonzales (USA) d. B. Sidwell (AUS) 61 63 63.

1950 Australia d. USA 4-1, West Side Tennis Club, Forest Hills, NY, USA (Grass)
(Winning Captain: Harry Hopman, losing Captain: Alrick Man) F. Sedgman (AUS) d. T. Brown (USA) 60 86 97; K. McGregor (AUS) d. T. Schroeder (USA) 1311 63 64; J. Bromwich/F. Sedgman (AUS) d. G. Mulloy/T. Schroeder (USA) 46 64 62 46 64; F. Sedgman (AUS) d. T. Schroeder (USA) 62 62 62; T. Brown (USA) d. K. McGregor (AUS) 911 810 119 61 64.

1951 Australia d. USA 3-2, White City Stadium, Sydney, NSW, Australia (Grass)
(Winning Captain: Harry Hopman, losing Captain: Frank Shields) V. Seixas (USA) d. M. Rose (AUS) 63 64 97; F. Sedgman (AUS) d. T. Schroeder (USA) 64 63 46 64; K. McGregor/F. Sedgman (AUS) d. T. Schroeder/T. Trabert (USA) 62 97 63; T. Schroeder (USA) d. M. Rose (AUS) 64 1311 75; F. Sedgman (AUS) d. V. Seixas (USA) 64 62 62.

1952 Australia d. USA 4-1, Memorial Drive, Adelaide, SA, Australia (Grass)
(Winning Captain: Harry Hopman, losing Captain: Vic Seixas) F. Sedgman (AUS) d. V. Seixas (USA) 63 64 63; K. McGregor (AUS) d. T. Trabert (USA) 119 64 61; K. McGregor/F. Sedgman (AUS) d. V. Seixas/T. Trabert (USA) 63 64 16 63; F. Sedgman (AUS) d. T. Trabert (USA) 75 64 108; V. Seixas (USA) d. K. McGregor (AUS) 63 86 68 63.

1953 Australia d. USA 3-2, Kooyong Stadium, Melbourne, VIC, Australia (Grass)
(Winning Captain: Harry Hopman, losing Captain: Bill Talbert) L. Hoad (AUS) d. V. Seixas (USA) 64 62 63; T. Trabert (USA) d. K. Rosewall (AUS) 63 64 64; V. Seixas/T. Trabert (USA) d. R. Hartwig/L. Hoad (AUS) 62 64 64; L. Hoad (AUS) d. T. Trabert (USA) 1311 63 26 36 75; K. Rosewall (AUS) d. V. Seixas (USA) 62 26 63 64.

Davis Cup (continued)

1954 USA d. Australia 3-2, White City Stadium, Sydney, NSW, Australia (Grass)
(Winning Captain: Bill Talbert, losing Captain: Harry Hopman) T. Trabert (USA) d. L. Hoad (AUS) 64 26 1210 63; V. Seixas (USA) d. K. Rosewall (AUS) 86 68 64 63; V. Seixas/T. Trabert (USA) d. L. Hoad/K. Rosewall (AUS) 62 46 62 108; K. Rosewall (AUS) d. T. Trabert (USA) 97 75 63; R. Hartwig (AUS) d. V. Seixas (USA) 46 63 62 63.

1955 Australia d. USA 5-0, West Side Tennis Club, Forest Hills, NY, USA (Grass)
(Winning Captain: Harry Hopman, losing Captain: Bill Talbert) K. Rosewall (AUS) d. V. Seixas (USA) 63 108 46 62; L. Hoad (AUS) d. T. Trabert (USA) 46 63 63 86; R. Hartwig/L. Hoad (AUS) d. V. Seixas/T. Trabert (USA) 1214 64 63 36 75; K. Rosewall (AUS) d. H. Richardson (USA) 64 36 61 64; L. Hoad (AUS) d. V. Seixas (USA) 79 61 64 64.

1956 Australia d. USA 5-0, Memorial Drive, Adelaide, SA, Australia (Grass)
(Winning Captain: Harry Hopman, losing Captain: Bill Talbert) L. Hoad (AUS) d. H. Flam (USA) 62 63 63; K. Rosewall (AUS) d. V. Seixas (USA) 62 75 63; L. Hoad/K. Rosewall (AUS) d. S. Giammalva/V. Seixas (USA) 16 61 75 64; L. Hoad (AUS) d. V. Seixas (USA) 62 75 63; K. Rosewall (AUS) d. S. Giammalva (USA) 46 61 86 75.

1957 Australia d. USA 3-2, Kooyong Stadium, Melbourne, VIC, Australia (Grass)
(Winning Captain: Harry Hopman, losing Captain: Bill Talbert) A. Cooper (AUS) d. V. Seixas (USA) 36 75 61 16 63; M. Anderson (AUS) d. B. MacKay (USA) 63 75 36 79 63; M. Anderson/M. Rose (AUS) d. B. MacKay/V. Seixas (USA) 64 64 86; B. MacKay (USA) d. A. Cooper (AUS) 64 16 46 64 63; V. Seixas (USA) d. M. Anderson (AUS) 63 46 63 06 1311.

1958 USA d. Australia 3-2, Milton Courts, Brisbane, QLD, Australia (Grass)
(Winning Captain: Perry Jones, losing Captain: Harry Hopman) A. Olmedo (USA) d. M. Anderson (AUS) 86 26 97 86; A. Cooper (AUS) d. B. MacKay (USA) 46 63 62 64; A. Olmedo/H. Richardson (USA) d. M. Anderson/N. Fraser (AUS) 1012 36 1614 63 75; A. Olmedo (USA) d. A. Cooper (AUS) 63 46 64 86; M. Anderson (AUS) d. B. MacKay (USA) 75 1311 119.

1959 Australia d. USA 3-2, West Side Tennis Club, Forest Hills, NY, USA (Grass)
(Winning Captain: Harry Hopman, losing Captain: Perry Jones) N. Fraser (AUS) d. A. Olmedo (USA) 86 68 64 86; B. MacKay (USA) d. Rod Laver (AUS) 75 64 61; R. Emerson/N. Fraser (AUS) d. B. Buchholz/A. Olmedo (USA) 75 75 64; A. Olmedo (USA) d. R. Laver (AUS) 97 46 108 1210; N. Fraser (AUS) d. B. MacKay (USA) 86 36 62 64.

1960 Australia d. Italy 4-1, White City Stadium, Sydney, NSW, Australia (Grass)
(Winning Captain: Harry Hopman, losing Captain: Vanni Canapele) N. Fraser (AUS) d. O. Sirola (ITA) 46 63 63 63; R. Laver (AUS) d. N. Pietrangeli (ITA) 86 64 63; R. Emerson/N. Fraser (AUS) d. N. Pietrangeli/O. Sirola (ITA) 108 57 63 64; R. Laver (AUS) d. O. Sirola (ITA) 97 62 63; N. Pietrangeli (ITA) d. N. Fraser (AUS) 119 63 16 62.

1961 Australia d. Italy 5-0, Kooyong Stadium, Melbourne, VIC, Australia (Grass)
(Winning Captain: Harry Hopman, losing Captain: Vanni Canapele) R. Emerson (AUS) d. N. Pietrangeli (ITA) 86 64 60; R. Laver (AUS) d. O. Sirola (ITA) 61 64 63; R. Emerson/N. Fraser (AUS) d. N. Pietrangeli/O. Sirola (ITA) 62 63 64; R. Emerson (AUS) d. O. Sirola (ITA) 62 63 46 62; R. Laver (AUS) d. N. Pietrangeli (ITA) 63 36 46 63 86.

1962 Australia d. Mexico 5-0, Milton Courts, Brisbane, QLD, Australia (Grass)
(Winning Captain: Harry Hopman, losing Captain: Francisco Contreras) N. Fraser (AUS) d. T. Palafox (MEX) 79 63 64 119; R. Laver (AUS) d. R. Osuna (MEX) 62 61 75; R. Emerson/R. Laver (AUS) d. R. Osuna/T. Palafox (MEX) 75 62 64; N. Fraser (AUS) d. R. Osuna (MEX) 36 119 61 36 64; R. Laver (AUS) d. T. Palafox (MEX) 61 46 64 86.

1963 USA d. Australia 3-2, Memorial Drive, Adelaide, SA, Australia (Grass)
(Winning Captain: Robert Kelleher, losing Captain: Harry Hopman) D. Ralston (USA) d. J. Newcombe (AUS) 64 61 36 46 75; R. Emerson (AUS) d. C. McKinley (USA) 63 36 75 75; C. McKinley/D. Ralston (USA) d. R. Emerson/N. Fraser (AUS) 63 46 119 119; R. Emerson (AUS) d. D. Ralston (USA) 62 63 36 62; C. McKinley (USA) d. J. Newcombe (AUS) 1012 62 97 62.

1964 Australia d. USA 3-2, Harold Clark Courts, Cleveland, OH, USA (Clay)
(Winning Captain: Harry Hopman, losing Captain: Vic Seixas) C. McKinley (USA) d. F. Stolle (AUS) 61 97 46 62; R. Emerson (AUS) d. D. Ralston (USA) 63 61 63; C. McKinley/D. Ralston (USA) d. R. Emerson/F. Stolle (AUS) 64 46 46 63 64; F. Stolle (AUS) d. D. Ralston (USA) 75 63 36 911 64; R. Emerson (AUS) d. C. McKinley (USA) 36 62 64 64.

1965 Australia d. Spain 4-1, White City Stadium, Sydney, NSW, Australia (Grass)
(Winning Captain: Harry Hopman, losing Captain: Jaime Bartroli) F. Stolle (AUS) d. M. Santana (ESP) 1012 36 61 64 75; R. Emerson (AUS) d. J. Gisbert (ESP) 63 62 62; J. Newcombe/T. Roche (AUS) d. J. Arilla/M. Santana (ESP) 63 46 75 62; M. Santana (ESP) d. R. Emerson (AUS) 26 63 64 1513; F. Stolle (AUS) d. J. Gisbert (ESP) 62 64 86.

1966 Australia d. India 4-1, Kooyong Stadium, Melbourne, VIC, Australia (Grass)
(Winning Captain: Harry Hopman, losing Captain: Raj Khanna) F. Stolle (AUS) d. R. Krishnan (IND) 63 62 64; R. Emerson (AUS) d. J. Mukerjea (IND) 75 64 62; R. Krishnan/J. Mukerjea (IND) d. J. Newcombe/T. Roche (AUS) 46 75 64 64; R. Emerson (AUS) d. R. Krishnan (IND) 60 62 108; F. Stolle (AUS) d. J. Mukerjea (IND) 75 68 63 57 63.

1967 Australia d. Spain 4-1, Milton Courts, Brisbane, QLD, Australia (Grass)
(Winning Captain: Harry Hopman, losing Captain: Jaime Bartroli) R. Emerson (AUS) d. M. Santana (ESP) 64 61 61; J. Newcombe (AUS) d. M. Orantes (ESP) 63 63 62; J. Newcombe/T. Roche (AUS) d. M. Orantes/M. Santana (ESP) 64 64 64; M. Santana (ESP) d. J. Newcombe (AUS) 75 64 62; R. Emerson (AUS) d. M. Orantes (ESP) 61 61 26 64.

1968 USA d. Australia 4-1, Memorial Drive, Adelaide, SA, Australia (Grass)
(Winning Captain: Donald Dell, losing Captain: Harry Hopman) C. Graebner (USA) d. B. Bowrey (AUS) 810 64 86 36 61; A. Ashe (USA) d. R. Ruffels (AUS) 68 75 63 63; B. Lutz/S. Smith (USA) d. J. Alexander/R. Ruffels (AUS) 64 64 62; C. Graebner (USA) d. R. Ruffels (AUS) 36 86 26 63 61; B. Bowrey (AUS) d. A. Ashe (USA) 26 63 119 86.

1969 USA d. Romania 5-0, Harold Clark Courts, Cleveland, OH, USA (Hard)
(Winning Captain: Donald Dell, losing Captain: Georgy Cobzucs) A. Ashe (USA) d. I. Nastase (ROM) 62 1513 75; S. Smith (USA) d. I. Tiriac (ROM) 68 63 57 64 64; B. Lutz/S. Smith (USA) d. I. Nastase/I. Tiriac (ROM) 86 61 119; S. Smith (USA) d. I. Nastase (ROM) 46 46 64 61 119; A. Ashe (USA) d. I. Tiriac (ROM) 63 86 36 40 ret.

1970 USA d. West Germany 5-0, Harold Clark Courts, Cleveland, OH, USA (Hard)
(Winning Captain: Edward Turville, losing Captain: Ferdinand Henkel) A. Ashe (USA) d. W. Bungert (GER) 62 108 62; C. Richey (USA) d. C. Kuhnke (GER) 63 64 62; B. Lutz/S. Smith (USA) d. W. Bungert/C. Kuhnke (GER) 63 75 64; C. Richey (USA) d. W. Bungert (GER) 64 64 75; A. Ashe (USA) d. C. Kuhnke (GER) 68 1012 97 1311 64.

1971 USA d. Romania 3-2, Olde Providence Racquet Club, Charlotte, NC, USA (Hard)
(Winning Captain: Edward Turville, losing Captain: Stefan Georgescu) S. Smith (USA) d. I. Nastase (ROM) 75 63 61; F. Froehling (USA) d. I. Tiriac (ROM) 36 16 61 63 86; I. Nastase/I. Tiriac (ROM) d. S. Smith/E. Van Dillen (USA) 75 64 86; S. Smith (USA) d. I. Tiriac (ROM) 86 63 60; I. Nastase (ROM) d. F. Froehling (USA) 63 61 16 61.

Final Round

1972 USA d. Romania 3-2, Progresul Club, Bucharest, Romania (Red Clay)
(Winning Captain: Dennis Ralston, losing Captain: Stefan Georgescu) S. Smith (USA) d. I. Nastase (ROM) 119 62 63; I. Tiriac (ROM) d. T. Gorman (USA) 46 26 64 63 62; S. Smith/E. Van Dillen (USA) d. I. Nastase/I. Tiriac (ROM) 62 60 63; S. Smith (USA) d. I. Tiriac (ROM) 46 62 64 26 60; I. Nastase (ROM) d. T. Gorman (USA) 61 62 57 108.

1973 Australia d. USA 5-0, Public Auditorium, Cleveland, OH, USA (Carpet)
(Winning Captain: Neale Fraser, losing Captain: Dennis Ralston) J. Newcombe (AUS) d. S. Smith (USA) 61 36 63 36 64; R. Laver (AUS) d. T. Gorman (USA) 810 86 68 63 61; R. Laver/J. Newcombe (AUS) d. S. Smith/E. Van Dillen (USA) 61 62 64; J. Newcombe (AUS) d. T. Gorman (USA) 62 61 63; R. Laver (AUS) d. S. Smith (USA) 63 64 36 62.

1974 South Africa d. India w/o.

1975 Sweden d. Czechoslovakia 3-2, Kungliga Tennishallen, Stockholm, Sweden (Carpet)
(Winning Captain: Lennart Bergelin, losing Captain: Antonin Bolardt) J. Kodes (TCH) d. O. Bengtsson (SWE) 64 26 75 64; B. Borg (SWE) d. J. Hrebec (TCH) 61 63 60; O. Bengtsson/B. Borg (SWE) d. J. Kodes/V. Zednik (TCH) 64 64 64; B. Borg (SWE) d. J. Kodes (TCH) 64 62 62; J. Hrebec (TCH) d. O. Bengtsson (SWE) 16 63 61 64.

Davis Cup (continued)

1976 Italy d. Chile 4-1, Estadio Nacional, Santiago, Chile (Red Clay)
(Winning Captain: Nicola Pietrangeli, losing Captain: Luis Ayala) C. Barazzutti (ITA) d. J. Fillol (CHI) 75 46 75 61; A. Panatta (ITA) d. P. Cornejo (CHI) 63 61 63; P. Bertolucci/A. Panatta (ITA) d.. P. Cornejo/J. Fillol (CHI) 36 62 97 63; A. Panatta (ITA) d. J. Fillol (CHI) 86 64 36 108; B. Prajoux (CHI) d. A. Zugarelli (ITA) 64 64 62.

1977 Australia d. Italy 3-1, White City Stadium, Sydney, NSW, Australia (Grass)
(Winning Captain: Neale Fraser, losing Captain: Nicola Pietrangeli) T. Roche (AUS) d. A. Panatta (ITA) 63 64 64; J. Alexander (AUS) d. C. Barazzutti (ITA) 62 86 46 62; P. Bertolucci/A. Panatta (ITA) d. J. Alexander/P. Dent (AUS) 64 64 75; J. Alexander (AUS) d. A. Panatta (ITA) 64 46 26 86 119; T. Roche (AUS) vs. C. Barazzutti (ITA) 1212 unfinished.

1978 USA d. Great Britain 4-1, Mission Hills C.C., Rancho Mirage, CA, USA (Hard)
(Winning Captain: Tony Trabert, losing Captain: Paul Hutchins) J. McEnroe (USA) d. J. Lloyd (GBR) 61 62 62; B. Mottram (GBR) d. B. Gottfried (USA) 46 26 108 64 63; B. Lutz/S. Smith (USA) d. M. Cox/D. Lloyd (GBR) 62 62 63; J. McEnroe (USA) d. B. Mottram (GBR) 62 62 61; B. Gottfried (USA) d. J. Lloyd (GBR) 61 62 64.

1979 USA d. Italy 5-0, Civic Auditorium, San Francisco, CA, USA (Carpet)
(Winning Captain: Tony Trabert, losing Captain: Vittorio Crotta) V. Gerulaitis (USA) d. C. Barazzutti (ITA) 63 32 ret; J. McEnroe (USA) d. A. Panatta (ITA) 62 63 64; B. Lutz/S. Smith (USA) d. P. Bertolucci/A. Panatta (ITA) 64 1210 62; J. McEnroe (USA) d. A. Zugarelli (ITA) 64 63 61; V. Gerulaitis (USA) d. A. Panatta (ITA) 61 63 63.

1980 Czechoslovakia d. Italy 4-1, Sportovni Hala, Prague, Czechoslovakia (Carpet)
(Winning Captain: Antonin Bolardt, losing Captain: Vittorio Crotta) T. Smid (TCH) d. A. Panatta (ITA) 36 36 63 64 64; I. Lendl (TCH) d. C. Barazzutti (ITA) 46 61 61 62; I. Lendl/T. Smid (TCH) d. P. Bertolucci/A. Panatta (ITA) 36 63 36 63 64; C. Barazzutti (ITA) d. T. Smid (TCH) 36 63 62; I. Lendl (TCH) d. G. Ocleppo (ITA) 63 63.

World Group Final Round

1981 USA d. Argentina 3-1, Riverfront Coliseum, Cincinnati, OH, USA (Carpet)
(Winning Captain: Arthur Ashe, losing Captain: Carlos Junquet) J. McEnroe (USA) d. G. Vilas (ARG) 63 62 62; J. Clerc (ARG) d. R. Tanner (USA) 75 63 86; P. Fleming/J. McEnroe (USA) d. J. Clerc/G. Vilas (ARG) 63 46 64 46 119; J. McEnroe (USA) d. J. Clerc (ARG) 75 57 63 36 63; R. Tanner (USA) vs. G. Vilas (ARG) 1110 unfinished.

1982 USA d. France 4-1, Palais des Sports, Grenoble, France (Red Clay)
(Winning Captain: Arthur Ashe, losing Captain: Jean-Paul Loth) J. McEnroe (USA) d. Y. Noah (FRA) 1210 16 36 62 63; G. Mayer (USA) d. H. Leconte (FRA) 62 62 79 64; P. Fleming/J. McEnroe (USA) d. H. Leconte/Y. Noah (FRA) 63 64 97; Y. Noah (FRA) d. G. Mayer (USA) 61 60; J. McEnroe (USA) d. H. Leconte (FRA) 62 63.

1983 Australia d. Sweden 3-2, Kooyong Stadium, Melbourne, VIC, Australia (Grass)
(Winning Captain: Neale Fraser, losing Captain: Hans Olsson) M. Wilander (SWE) d. P. Cash (AUS) 63 46 97 63; J. Fitzgerald (AUS) d. J. Nystrom (SWE) 64 62 46 64; M. Edmondson/P. McNamee (AUS) d. A. Jarryd/H. Simonsson (SWE) 64 64 62; P. Cash (AUS) d. J. Nystrom (SWE) 64 61 61; M. Wilander (SWE) d. J. Fitzgerald (AUS) 68 60 61.

1984 Sweden d. USA 4-1, The Scandinavium, Gothenburg, Sweden (Red Clay)
(Winning Captain: Hans Olsson, losing Captain: Arthur Ashe) M. Wilander (SWE)] d. J. Connors (USA) 61 63 63; H. Sundstrom (SWE) d. J. McEnroe (USA) 1311 64 63; S. Edberg/A. Jarryd (SWE) d. P. Fleming/J. McEnroe (USA) 75 57 62 75; J. McEnroe (USA) d. M. Wilander (SWE) 63 67 63; H. Sundstrom (SWE) d. J. Arias (USA) 36 86 63.

1985 Sweden d. West Germany 3-2, Olympiahalle, Munich, Germany (Carpet)
(Winning Captain: Hans Olsson, losing Captain: Wilhelm Bungert) M. Wilander (SWE) d. M. Westphal (GER) 63 64 108; B. Becker (GER) d. S. Edberg (SWE) 63 36 75 86; M. Wilander/J. Nystrom (SWE) d. B. Becker/A. Maurer (GER) 64 62 61; B. Becker (GER) d. M. Wilander (SWE) 63 26 63 36; S. Edberg (SWE) d. M. Westphal (GER) 36 75 64 63.

1986 Australia d. Sweden 3-2, Kooyong Stadium, Melbourne, VIC, Australia (Grass)
(Winning Captain: Neale Fraser, losing Captain: Hans Olsson) P. Cash (AUS) d. S. Edberg (SWE) 1311 1311 64; M. Pernfors (SWE) d. P. McNamee (AUS) 63 61 63; P. Cash/J. Fitzgerald (AUS) d. S. Edberg/A. Jarryd (SWE) 63 64 46 61; P. Cash (AUS) d. M. Pernfors (SWE) 26 46 63 64 63; S. Edberg (SWE) d. P. McNamee (AUS) 108 64.

1987 Sweden d. India 5-0, The Scandinavium, Gothenburg, Sweden (Red Clay)
(Winning Captain: Hans Olsson, losing Captain: Vijay Amritraj) M. Wilander (SWE) d. R. Krishnan (IND) 64 61 63; A. Jarryd (SWE) d. V. Amritraj (IND) 63 63 61; M. Wilander/J. Nystrom (SWE) d. A. Amritraj/V. Amritraj (IND) 62 36 61 62; A. Jarryd (SWE) d. R. Krishnan (IND) 64 63; M. Wilander (SWE) d. V. Amritraj (IND) 62 60.

1988 West Germany d. Sweden 4-1, The Scandinavium, Gothenburg, Sweden (Red Clay)
(Winning Captain: Niki Pilic, losing Captain: Hans Olsson) C. Steeb (GER) d. M. Wilander (SWE) 810 16 62 64 86; B. Becker (GER) d. S. Edberg (SWE) 63 61 64; B. Becker/E. Jelen (GER) d. S. Edberg/A. Jarryd (SWE) 36 26 75 63 62; S. Edberg (SWE) d. C. Steeb (GER) 64 86; P. Kuhnen (GER) d. K. Carlsson (SWE) w/o.

1989 West Germany d. Sweden 3-2, Schleyer Halle, Stuttgart, Germany (Carpet)
(Winning Captain: Niki Pilic, losing Captain: John-Anders Sjogren) M.Wilander (SWE) d. C. Steeb (GER) 57 76 67 62 63; B. Becker (GER) d. S. Edberg (SWE) 62 62 64; B. Becker/E. Jelen (GER) d. A. Jarryd/J. Gunnarsson (SWE) 76 64 36 67 64; B. Becker (GER) d. M. Wilander (SWE) 62 60 62; S. Edberg (SWE) d. C. Steeb (GER) 62 64.

1990 USA d. Australia 3-2, Suncoast Dome, St. Petersburg, FL, USA (Red Clay)
(Winning Captain: Tom Gorman, losing Captain: Neale Fraser) A. Agassi (USA) d. R. Fromberg (AUS) 46 62 46 62 64; M. Chang (USA) d. D. Cahill (AUS) 62 76 60; R. Leach/J. Pugh (USA) d. P. Cash/J. Fitzgerald (AUS) 64 62 36 76; D. Cahill (AUS) d. A. Agassi (USA) 64 46 ret; R. Fromberg (AUS) d. M. Chang (USA) 75 26 63.

1991 France d. USA 3-1, Palais des Sports Gerland, Lyon, France (Carpet)
(Winning Captain: Yannick Noah, losing Captain: Tom Gorman) A. Agassi (USA) d. G. Forget (FRA) 67 62 61 62; H. Leconte (FRA) d. P. Sampras (USA) 64 75 64; G. Forget/H. Leconte (FRA) d. K. Flach/R. Seguso (USA) 61 64 46 62; G. Forget (FRA) d. P. Sampras (USA) 76 36 63 64; H. Leconte (FRA) vs. A. Agassi (USA) not played.

1992 USA d. Switzerland 3-1, Tarrant County Center, Ft. Worth, TX, USA (Hard)
(Winning Captain: Tom Gorman, losing Captain: Dimitri Sturdza) A. Agassi (USA) d. J. Hlasek (SUI) 61 62 62; M. Rosset (SUI) d. J. Courier (USA) 63 67 36 64 64; J. McEnroe/P. Sampras (USA) d. J. Hlasek/M. Rosset (SUI) 67 67 75 61 62; J. Courier (USA) d. J. Hlasek (SUI) 63 36 63 64; A. Agassi (USA) vs. M. Rosset (SUI) not played.

1993 Germany d. Australia 4-1, Messe Dusseldorf, Dusseldorf, Germany (Clay)
(Winning Captain: Niki Pilic, losing Captain: Neale Fraser) M. Stich (GER) d. J. Stoltenberg (AUS) 67 63 61 46 63; R. Fromberg (AUS) d. M. Goellner (GER) 36 57 76 62 97; P. Kuhnen/M. Stich (GER) d. T. Woodbridge/M. Woodforde (AUS) 76 46 63 76; M. Stich (GER) d. R. Fromberg (AUS) 64 62 62; M. Goellner (GER) d. J. Stoltenberg (AUS) 61 67 76.

1994 Sweden d. Russia 4-1, Olympic Stadium, Moscow, Russia (Carpet)
(Winning Captain: John-Anders Sjogren, losing Captain: Vadim Borisov) S. Edberg (SWE) d. A. Volkov (RUS) 64 62 67 06 86; M. Larsson (SWE) d. Y. Kafelnikov (RUS) 60 62 36 26 63; J. Apell/J. Bjorkman (SWE) d. Y. Kafelnikov/A. Olhovskiy(RUS) 67 62 63 16 86; Y. Kafelnikov (RUS) d. S. Edberg (SWE) 46 64 60; M. Larsson (SWE) d. A. Volkov (RUS) 76 64.

1995 USA d. Russia 3-2, Olympic Stadium, Moscow, Russia (Red Clay)
(Winning Captain: Tom Gullikson, losing Captain: Anatoly Lepeshin) P. Sampras (USA) d. A. Chesnokov (RUS) 36 64 63 67 64; Y. Kafelnikov (RUS) d. J. Courier (USA) 76 75 63; T. Martin/P. Sampras (USA) d. Y. Kafelnikov/A. Olhovskiy (RUS) 75 64 63; P. Sampras (USA) d. Y. Kafelnikov (RUS) 62 64 76; A. Chesnokov (RUS) d. J. Courier (USA) 67 75 60.

1996 France d. Sweden 3-2, Malmomassan, Malmo, Sweden (Hard)
(Winning Captain: Yannick Noah, losing Captain: Carl-Axel Hageskog) C. Pioline (FRA) d. S. Edberg (SWE) 63 64 63; T. Enqvist (SWE) d. A. Boetsch (FRA) 64 63 76; G. Forget/G. Raoux (FRA) d. J. Bjorkman/N. Kulti (SWE) 63 16 63 63; T. Enqvist (SWE) d. C. Pioline (FRA) 36 67 64 64 97; A. Boetsch (FRA) d. N. Kulti (SWE) 76 26 46 76 108.

1997 Sweden d. USA 5-0, The Scandinavium, Gothenburg, Sweden (Carpet)
(Winning Captain: Carl-Axel Hageskog, losing Captain: Tom Gullikson) J. Bjorkman (SWE) d. M. Chang (USA) 75 16 63 63; M. Larsson (SWE) d. P. Sampras (USA) 36 76 21 ret; J. Bjorkman/N. Kulti (SWE) d. T. Martin/J. Stark (USA) 64 64 64; J. Bjorkman (SWE) d. J. Stark (USA) 61 61; M. Larsson (SWE) d. M. Chang (USA) 76 67 64.

1998 Sweden d. Italy 4-1, The Forum, Milan, Italy (Red Clay)
(Winning Captain: Carl-Axel Hageskog, losing Captain: Paolo Bertolucci) M. Norman (SWE) d. A. Gaudenzi (ITA) 67 76 46 63 66 ret; M. Gustafsson (SWE) d. D. Sanguinetti (ITA) 61 64 60; J. Bjorkman/Nicklas Kulti (SWE) d. D. Nargiso/D. Sanguinetti (ITA) 76 61 63; M. Gustafsson (SWE) d. G. Pozzi (ITA) 64 62; D. Nargiso (ITA) d. M. Norman (SWE) 62 63.

1999 Australia d. France 3-2, Nice Acropolis, Nice, France (Red Clay)
(Winning Captain: John Newcombe, losing Captain: Guy Forget) M. Philippoussis (AUS) d. S. Grosjean (FRA) 64 62 64; C. Pioline (FRA) d. L. Hewitt (AUS) 76 76 75; T. Woodbridge/M. Woodforde (AUS) d. O. Delaitre/F. Santoro (FRA) 26 75 62 62; M. Philippoussis (AUS) d. C. Pioline (FRA) 63 57 61 62; S. Grosjean (FRA) d. L. Hewitt (AUS) 64 63.

2000 Spain d. Australia 3-1, Palau Sant Jordi, Barcelona, Spain (Red Clay)
(Winning Captain: Javier Duarte, losing Captain: John Newcombe) L. Hewitt (AUS) d. A. Costa (ESP) 36 61 26 64 64; J. Ferrero (ESP) d. P. Rafter (AUS) 67 76 62 31 ret; J. Barcells/A. Corretja (ESP) d. S. Stolle/M. Woodforde (AUS) 64 64 64; J. Ferrero (ESP) d. L. Hewitt (AUS) 62 76 46 64; A. Corretja (ESP) vs. P. Rafter (AUS) not played.

2001 France d. Australia 3.2 Melbourne Park, Melbourne, VIC, Australia (Grass)
(Winning Captain: Guy Forget, losing Captain: John Fitzgerald) N. Escude (FRA) d. L Hewitt (AUS) 46 63 36 63 64; P. Rafter (AUS) d. S. Grosjean (FRA) 63 76 75; C. Pioline/F. Santoro (FRA) d. L. Hewitt/P. Rafter (AUS) 26 63 76 61; L. Hewitt (AUS) d. S Grosjean (FRA) 63 62 63; N. Escude (FRA) d. W. Arthurs (AUS) 76 67 63 63.

2002 Russia d. France 3-2, Palais Omnisports Paris Bercy, Paris, France (Red Clay)
(Winning Captain: Shamil Tarpischev, losing Captain: Guy Forget) M. Safin (RUS) d. P. Mathieu (FRA) 64 36 61 64; S. Grosjean (FRA) d. Y. Kafelnikov (RUS) 76 63 60; N. Escude/F. Santoro (FRA) d. Y. Kafelnikov/M. Safin (RUS) 63 36 57 63 64; M. Safin (RUS) d. S. Grosjean (FRA) 63 62 76; M. Youzhny (RUS) d. P. Mathieu (FRA) 36 26 63 75 64.

2003 Australia d. Spain 3-1, Melbourne Park, Melbourne, VIC, Australia, (Grass)
(Winning Captain: John Fitzgerald, losing Captain: Jordi Arrese) L. Hewitt (AUS) d. J. Ferrero (ESP) 36 63 36 76 62; C. Moya (ESP) d. M. Philippoussis (AUS) 64 64 46 76; W. Arthurs/T. Woodbridge (AUS) d. A. Corretja/F. Lopez (ESP) 63 61 63; M. Philippoussis (AUS) d. J. Ferrero (ESP) 75 63 16 26 60; L. Hewitt (AUS) vs. C. Moya (ESP) not played.

2004 Spain d. USA 3-2, Estadio Olimpico de Sevilla, Seville, Spain (Red Clay)
(Winning Captain: Jordi Arrese, losing Captain: Patrick McEnroe) C. Moya (ESP) d. M. Fish (USA) 64 62 63; R. Nadal (ESP) d. A. Roddick (USA) 67 62 76 62; B. Bryan/M. Bryan (USA) d. J. Ferrero/T. Robredo (ESP) 60 63 62; C. Moya (ESP) d. A. Roddick (USA) 62 76 76; M. Fish (USA) d. T. Robredo (ESP) 76 62.

Fed Cup

Launched in 1963 as The Federation Cup. Renamed the Fed Cup in 1995.

1963 USA d. Australia 2-1, Queen's Club, London, England (Grass)
(Winning Captain: William Kellogg, losing Captain: Nell Hopman) M. Smith (AUS) d. D. Hard (USA) 63 60; B. Moffitt (USA) d. L. Turner (AUS) 57 60 63; D. Hard/B. Moffitt (USA) d. M. Smith/L. Turner (USA) 36 1311 63.

1964 Australia d. USA 2-1, Germantown Cricket Club, Philadelphia, PA, USA (Grass)
(Winning Captain: Brian Tobin, losing Captain: Madge Vosters) M. Smith (AUS) d. B. Moffitt (USA) 62 63; L. Turner (AUS) d. N. Richey (USA) 75 61; B. Moffitt/K. Hantze Susman (USA) d. M. Smith/L. Turner (AUS) 46 75 61.

1965 Australia d. USA 2-1, Kooyong Tennis Club, Melbourne, VIC, Australia (Grass)
(Winning Captain: Margaret Smith, losing Captain: Billie Jean Moffitt) L. Turner (AUS) d. C. Graebner (USA) 63 26 63; M. Smith (AUS) d. B. Moffitt (USA) 64 86; B. Moffitt/C. Graebner (USA) d. M. Smith/J. Tegart (AUS) 75 46 64.

1966 USA d. Germany 3-0, Press Sporting Club, Turin, Italy (Clay)
(Winning Captain: Ros Greenwood, losing Captain: Edda Buding) J. Heldman (USA) d. H. Niessen (GER) 46 75 61; B. King (USA) d. E. Buding (GER) 63 36 61; C. Graebner/B. King (USA) d. E. Buding/H. Schulz (GER) 64 62.

1967 USA d. Great Britain 2-0, Blau Weiss Club, Berlin, Germany (Clay)
(Winning Captain: Donna Fales, losing Captain: Angela Mortimer Barrett) R. Casals (USA) d. V. Wade (GBR) 97 86; B. King (USA) d. A. Haydon Jones (GBR) 63 64; doubles match called at one-set all.

1968 Australia d. Netherlands 3-0, Stade Roland Garros, Paris, France (Clay)
(Winning Captain: Margaret Court, losing Captain: Jenny Ridderhof) K. Melville (AUS) d. M. Jansen (NED) 46 75 63; M. Court (AUS) d. A. Suurbeek (NED) 61 63; M. Court/K. Melville (AUS) d. A. Suurbeek/L. Jansen Venneboer (NED) 63 68 75.

1969 USA d. Australia 2-1, Athens Tennis Club, Athens, Greece
(Winning Captain: Donna Fales, losing Captain: Wayne Reid) N. Richey (USA) d. K. Melville (AUS) 64 63; M. Court (AUS) d. J. Heldman (USA) 61 86; P. Bartkowicz/N. Richey (USA) d. M. Court/J. Tegart (AUS) 64 64.

1970 Australia d. Germany 3-0, Freiburg Tennis Club, Freiburg, Germany (Clay)
(Winning Captain: Alf Chave, losing Captain: Edward Dorrenberg) K. Krantzcke (AUS) d. H. Schultz Hoesl (GER) 62 63; J. Dalton (AUS) d. H. Niessen (GER) 46 63 63; K. Krantzcke/J. Dalton (AUS) d. H. Schultz Hoesl/H. Niessen (GER) 62 75.

1971 Australia d. Great Britain 3-0, Royal King's Park Tennis Club, Perth, Australia (Grass)
(Winning Captain: Margaret Court, losing Captain: Ann Haydon Jones) M. Court (AUS) d. A. Haydon Jones (GBR) 68 63 62; E. Goolagong (AUS) d. V. Wade (GBR) 64 61; M. Court/L. Hunt (AUS) d. W. Shaw/V. Wade (GBR) 64 64.

1972 South Africa d. Great Britain 2-1, Ellis Park, Johannesburg, South Africa (Grass)
(Winning Captain: Dr. Jackie Du Toit, losing Captain: Virginia Wade) V. Wade (GBR) d. P. Waldken Pretorius (RSA) 63 62; B. Kirk (RSA) d. W. Shaw (GBR) 46 75 60; B. Kirk/P. Waldken Pretorius (RSA) d. V. Wade/J. Williams (GBR) 61 75.

1973 Australia d. South Africa 3-0, Bad Homburg Tennis Club, Bad Homburg, Germany (Clay)
(Winning Captain: Vic Edwards, losing Captain: Dr. Jackie Du Toit) E. Goolagong (AUS) d. P. Waldken Pretorius (RSA) 60 62; P. Coleman (AUS) d. B. Kirk (RSA) 108 60; E. Goolagong/J. Young (AUS) d. B. Kirk/P. Waldken Pretorius (RSA) 61 62.

1974 Australia d. USA 2-1, Tennis Club of Naples, Naples, Italy (Clay)
(Winning Captain: Vic Edwards, losing Captain: Donna Fales) E. Goolagong (AUS) d. J. Heldman (USA) 61 75; J. Evert (USA) d. D. Fromholtz (AUS) 26 75 64; E. Goolagong/J. Young (AUS) d. J. Heldman/S. Walsh (USA) 75 86.

1975 Czechoslovakia d. Australia 3-0, Aixoise Country Club, Aix-en-Provence, France (Clay)
(Winning Captain: Vera Sukova, losing Captain: Vic Edwards) M. Navratilova (TCH) d. E. Goolagong (AUS) 63 64; R. Tomanova (TCH) d. H. Gourlay (AUS) 64 62; M. Navratilova/R. Tomanova (TCH) d. D. Fromholtz/H. Gourlay (AUS) 63 61.

1976 USA d. Australia 2-1, The Spectrum, Philadelphia, PA, USA (Carpet)
(Winning Captain: Billie Jean King, losing Captain: Neale Fraser) K. Reid (AUS) d. R. Casals (USA) 16 63 75; B. King (USA) d. E. Goolagong (AUS) 76 64; R. Casals/B. King (USA) d. E. Goolagong/K. Reid (AUS) 75 63.

1977 USA d. Australia 2-1, Devonshire Park, Eastbourne, England (Grass)
(Winning Captain: Vicky Berner, losing Captain: Neale Fraser) B. King (USA) d. D. Fromholtz (AUS) 61 26 62; C. Evert (USA) d. K. Reid (AUS) 75 63; K. Reid/W. Turnbull (AUS) d. R. Casals/C. Evert (USA) 63 63.

1978 USA d. Australia 2-1, Kooyong Stadium, Melbourne, VIC, Australia (Grass)
(Winning Captain: Vicky Berner, losing Captain: Neale Fraser) K. Reid (AUS) d. T. Austin (USA) 63 63; C. Evert (USA) d. W. Turnbull (AUS) 36 61 61; C. Evert/B. King (USA) d. K. Reid/W. Turnbull (AUS) 46 61 64.

1979 USA d. Australia 3-0, R.S.H.E. Club de Campo, Madrid, Spain (Clay)
(Winning Captain: Vicky Berner, losing Captain: Neale Fraser) T. Austin (USA) d. K. Reid (AUS) 63 60; C. Evert (USA) d. D. Fromholtz (AUS) 26 63 86; R. Casals/B. King (USA) d. K. Reid/W. Turnbull (AUS) 36 63 86.

Fed Cup (continued)

1980 USA d. Australia 3-0, Rot-Weiss Tennis Club, Berlin, Germany (Clay)
(Winning Captain: Vicky Berner, losing Captain: Mary Hawton) C. Evert (USA) d. D. Fromholtz (AUS) 46 61 61; T. Austin (USA) d. W. Turnbull (AUS) 62 63; R. Casals/K. Jordan (USA) d. D. Fromholtz/S. Leo (AUS) 26 64 64.

1981 USA d. Great Britain 3-0, Tamagawa-en Racquet Club, Tokyo, Japan (Clay)
(Winning Captain: Chris Evert, losing Captain: Sue Mappin) C. Evert (USA) d. S. Barker (GBR) 62 61; A. Jaeger (USA) d. V. Wade (GBR) 63 61; R. Casals/K. Jordan (USA) d. S. Barker/V. Wade (GBR) 64 75.

1982 USA d. Germany 3-0, Decathlon Club, Santa Clara, CA, USA (Hard)
(Winning Captain: Judy Dalton, losing Captain: Klaus Hofsass) C. Evert (USA) d. C. Kohde (GER) 26 61 63; M. Navratilova (USA) d. B. Bunge (GER) 64 64; C. Evert/M. Navratilova (USA) d. B. Bunge/C. Kohde (GER) 36 61 62.

1983 Czechoslovakia d. Germany 2-1, Albisguetli Tennis Complex, Zurich, Switzerland (Clay)
(Winning Captain: Jan Kukal, losing Captain: Klaus Hofsass) H. Sukova (TCH) d. C. Kohde (GER) 64 26 62; H. Mandlikova (TCH) d. B. Bunge (GER) 62 30 ret; C. Kohde/E. Pfaff (GER) d. I. Budarova/M. Skuherska (TCH) 36 62 61.

1984 Czechoslovakia d. Australia 2-1, Esporte Clube Pinheiros, Sao Paulo, Brazil (Clay)
(Winning Captain: Jan Kukal, losing Captain: Judy Dalton) A. Minter (AUS) d. H. Sukova (TCH) 75 75; H. Mandlikova (TCH) d. E. Sayers (AUS) 61 60; H. Mandlikova/H. Sukova (TCH) d. E. Sayers/W. Turnbull (AUS) 62 62.

1985 Czechoslovakia d. USA 2-1, Nagoya Green Tennis Club, Nagoya, Japan (Hard)
(Winning Captain: Jiri Medonos, losing Captain: Tom Gorman) H. Mandlikova (TCH) d. K. Jordan (USA) 75 61; H. Sukova (TCH) d. E. Burgin (USA) 63 67 64; E. Burgin/S. Walsh (USA) d. A. Holikova/R. Marsikova (TCH) 62 63.

1986 USA d. Czechoslovakia 3-0, Stvanice Stadium, Prague, Czechoslovakia (Clay)
(Winning Captain: Marty Riessen, losing Captain: Jiri Medonos) C. Evert (USA) d. H. Sukova (TCH) 75 76; M. Navratilova (USA) d. H. Mandlikova (TCH) 75 61; M. Navratilova/P. Shriver (USA) d. H. Mandlikova/H. Sukova (TCH) 64 62.

1987 Germany d. USA 2-1, Hollyburn Country Club, Vancouver, Canada (Hard)
(Winning Captain: Klaus Hofsass, losing Captain: Marty Riessen) P. Shriver (USA) d. C. Kohde-Kilsch (GER) 60 76; S. Graf (GER) d. C. Evert (USA) 62 61; S. Graf/C. Kohde-Kilsch (GER) d. C. Evert/P. Shriver (USA) 16 75 64.

1988 Czechoslovakia d. USSR 2-1, Flinders Park, Melbourne, VIC, Australia (Hard)
(Winning Captain: Jiri Medonos, losing Captain: Olga Morozova) R. Zrubakova (TCH) d. L. Savchenko (URS) 61 76; H. Sukova (TCH) d. N. Zvereva (URS) 63 64; L. Savchenko/N. Zvereva (URS) d. J. Novotna/J. Pospisilova (TCH) 76 75.

1989 USA d. Spain 3-0, Ariake Tennis Centre, Tokyo, Japan (Hard)
(Winning Captain: Marty Riessen, losing Captain: Juan Alvarino) C. Evert (USA) d. C. Martinez (ESP) 63 62; M. Navratilova (USA) d. A. Sanchez Vicario (ESP) 06 63 64; Z. Garrison/P. Shriver (USA) d. C. Martinez/A. Sanchez Vicario (ESP) 75 61.

1990 USA d. USSR 2-1, Peachtree World of Tennis, Atlanta, GA, USA (Hard)
(Winning Captain: Marty Riessen, losing Captain: Olga Morozova) J. Capriati (USA) d. L. Meskhi (URS) 76 62; N. Zvereva (URS) d. Z. Garrison (USA) 63 75; G. Fernandez/Z. Garrison (USA) d. L. Savchenko/N. Zvereva (URS) 64 63.

1991 Spain d. USA 2-1, City of Nottingham Tennis Centre, Nottingham, England (Hard)
(Winning Captain: Juan Alvarino, losing Captain: Marty Riessen) J. Capriati (USA) d. C. Martinez (ESP) 46 76 61; A. Sanchez Vicario (ESP) d. M. Fernandez 63 64; C. Martinez/A. Sanchez Vicario (ESP) d. G. Fernandez/Z. Garrison (USA) 36 61 61.

1992 Germany d. Spain 2-1, Waldstadion, Frankfurt, Germany (Clay)
(Winning Captain: Klaus Hofsass, losing Captain: Juan Alvarino) A. Huber (GER) d. C. Martinez (ESP) 63 67 61; S. Graf (GER) d. A. Sanchez Vicario (ESP) 64 62; C. Martinez/A. Sanchez Vicario (ESP) d. A. Huber/B. Rittner (GER) 61 62.

1993 Spain d. Australia 3-0, Waldstadion, Frankfurt, Germany (Clay)
(Winning Captain: Miguel Margets, losing Captain: Wendy Turnbull) C. Martinez (ESP) d. M. Jaggard-Lai (AUS) 60 62; A. Sanchez Vicario (ESP) d. N. Provis (AUS) 62 63; C. Martinez/A. Sanchez Vicario (ESP) d. L. Smylie/R. Stubbs (AUS) 36 61 63.

1994 Spain d. USA 3-0, Waldstadion, Frankfurt, Germany (Clay)
(Winning Captain: Miguel Margets, losing Captain: Marty Riessen) C. Martinez (ESP) d. M. Fernandez (USA) 62 62; A. Sanchez Vicario (ESP) d. L. Davenport (USA) 62 61; C. Martinez/A. Sanchez Vicario (ESP) d. G. Fernandez/M. Fernandez (USA) 63 64.

1995 Spain d. USA 3-2, Club Tenis de Valencia, Valencia, Spain (Clay)
(Winning Captain: Miguel Margets, losing Captain: Billie Jean King) C. Martinez (ESP) d. C. Rubin (USA) 75 76; A. Sanchez Vicario (ESP) d. M. Fernandez 63 62; C. Martinez (ESP) d. M. Fernandez (USA) 63 64; C. Rubin (USA) d. A. Sanchez Vicario (ESP) 16 64 64; L. Davenport/ G. Fernandez (USA) d. V. Ruano Pascual/M. Sanchez Lorenzo (ESP) 63 76.

1996 USA d. Spain 5-0, Atlantic City Convention Center, Atlantic City, NJ, USA (Carpet)
(Winning Captain: Billie Jean King, losing Captain: Miguel Margets) M. Seles (USA) d. C. Martinez (ESP) 62 64; L. Davenport (USA) d. A. Sanchez Vicario (ESP) 75 61; M. Seles (USA) d. A. Sanchez Vicario (ESP) 36 63 61; L. Davenport (USA) d. G. Leon Garcia (ESP) 75 62; M. Fernandez/L. Wild (USA) d. G. Leon Garcia/V. Ruano Pascual (ESP) 61 64.

1997 France d. Netherlands 4-1, Brabanthallen, s'Hertogenbosch, Netherlands (Carpet)
(Winning Captain: Yannick Noah, losing Captain: Fred Hemmes) S. Testud (FRA) d B. Schultz-McCarthy (NED) 64 46 63; M. Pierce (FRA) d M. Oremans (NED) 64 61; B. Schultz-McCarthy (NED) d M. Pierce (FRA) 46 63 64; S. Testud (FRA) d M. Oremans (NED) 06 63 63; A. Fusai/ N. Tauziat (FRA) d M. Bollegraf/C. Vis (NED) 63 64.

1998 Spain d. Switzerland 3-2, Palexpo Hall, Geneva, Switzerland (Hard)
(Winning Captain: Miguel Margets, losing Captain: Melanie Molitor) A. Sanchez-Vicario (ESP) d. P. Schnyder (SUI) 62 36 62; M. Hingis (SUI) d. C. Martinez (ESP) 64 64; M. Hingis (SUI) d. A. Sanchez-Vicario (ESP) 76(5) 63; C. Martinez (ESP) d. P. Schnyder (SUI) 63 26 97; C. Martinez/A. Sanchez-Vicario (ESP) d. M. Hingis/P. Schnyder (SUI) 60 62.

1999 USA d. Russia 4-1, Taube Tennis Stadium, Stanford, CA, USA (Hard)
(Winning Captain: Billie Jean King, losing Captain: Konstantin Bogoroditsky) V. Williams (USA) d. E. Likhovtseva (RUS) 63 64; L. Davenport (USA) d. E. Dementieva (RUS) 64 60; L. Davenport (USA) d. E. Likhovtseva (RUS) 64 64; E. Dementieva (RUS) d. V. Williams (USA) 16 63 76; S. Williams/V. Williams (USA) d. E. Dementieva/E. Makarova (RUS) 62 61.

2000 USA d. Spain 5-0, Mandalay Bay Resort, Las Vegas, NV, USA (Carpet)
(Winning Captain: Billie Jean King, losing Captain: Miguel Margets) M. Seles (USA) d. C. Martinez (ESP) 62 63; L. Davenport (USA) d. A. Sanchez-Vicario (ESP) 62 16 63; L. Davenport (USA) d. C. Martinez (ESP) 61 62; J. Capriati (USA) d. A. Sanchez-Vicario (ESP) 61 10 ret; J. Capriati/L. Raymond (USA) d. V. Ruano Pascual/M. Serna (ESP) 46 64 62.

2001 Belgium d. Russia 2-1, Parque Ferial Juan Carlos I, Madrid, Spain (Clay)
(Winning Captain: Ivo Van Aken, losing Captain: Shamil Tarpishev) J. Henin (BEL) d. N. Petrova (RUS) 60 63; K. Clijsters (BEL) d. E. Dementieva (RUS) 60 64; E. Likhovtseva/N. Petrova (RUS) d. E. Callens/L. Courtois (BEL) 75 76.

2002 Slovak Republic d. Spain 3-1, Palacio de Congresos de Maspalomas, Maspalomas, Gran Canaria (Hard)
(Winning Captain: Tomas Malik, losing Captain: Miguel Margets) C. Martinez (ESP) d. J. Husarova (SVK) 64 76; D. Hantuchova (SVK) d. M. Serna (ESP) 62 61; D. Hantuchova (SVK) d. C. Martinez (ESP) 67 75 64; J. Husarova (SVK) d. A. Sanchez-Vicario (ESP) 60 62; doubles not played.

2003 France d. USA 4-1, Olympic Stadium, Moscow, Russia (Carpet)
(Winning Captain: Guy Forget, losing Captain: Billie Jean King) A. Mauresmo (FRA) d. L. Raymond (USA) 64 63; M. Pierce (FRA) d. M. Shaughnessy (USA) 63 36 86; A. Mauresmo (FRA) d. M. Shaughnessy (USA) 62 61; E. Loit (FRA) d. A. Stevenson (USA) 64 62; M. Navratilova/ L. Raymond (USA) d. S. Cohen-Aloro/E. Loit (FRA) 64 60.

2004 Russia d. France 3-2, Ice Stadium "Krylatskoe", Moscow, Russia (Carpet)
(Winning Captain: Shamil Tarpischev, losing Captain: Guy Forget) N. Dechy (FRA) d. S. Kuznetsova (RUS) 36 76 86; A. Myskina (RUS) d. T. Golovin (FRA) 64 76; A. Myskina (RUS) d. N. Dechy (FRA) 63 64; T. Golovin (FRA) d. S. Kuznetsova (RUS) 64 61; A. Myskina/V. Zvonareva (RUS) d. M. Bartoli/E. Loit (FRA) 76 75.

Carole Caldwell is also Carole Graebner
Evonne Goolagong is also Evonne Cawley
Claudia Kohde is also Claudia Kohde-Kilsch
Kerry Melville is also Kerry Reid

Billie Jean Moffitt is also Billie Jean King
Margaret Smith is also Margaret Court
Judy Tegart is also Judy Dalton.

Hopman Cup

A mixed team event first played in 1989, Hopman Cup has been an official event of the ITF since 1997. It is played every January in Perth, Australia.

1989 Czechoslovakia d. Australia 2-0: H. Sukova (TCH) d. H. Mandlikova (AUS) 64 63; M. Mecir/H. Sukova (TCH) d. P. Cash/H. Mandlikova (AUS) 62 64.

1990 Spain d. USA 2-1: E. Sanchez (ESP) d. J. McEnroe (USA) 57 75 75; J. McEnroe/P. Shriver (USA) d. E. Sanchez/A. Sanchez-Vicario (ESP) 63 62; A. Sanchez-Vicario (ESP) d. P. Shriver (USA) 63 63.

1991 Yugoslavia d. USA 3-0: M. Seles (YUG) d. Z. Garrison (USA) 61 61; G. Prpic (YUG) d. D. Wheaton (USA) 46 63 75; G. Prpic/M. Seles (YUG) d. D. Wheaton/Z. Garrison (USA) 83 (pro set).

1992 Switzerland d. Czechoslovakia 2-1: M. Maleeva-Fragniere (SUI) d. H. Sukova (TCH) 62 64; J. Hlasek (SUI) d. K. Novacek (TCH) 64 64; K. Novacek/H. Sukova (TCH) d. J. Hlasek/M. Maleeva-Fragniere (SUI) 84 (pro set).

1993 Germany d. Spain 2-1: S. Graf (GER) d. A. Sanchez-Vicario (ESP) 64 63; M. Stich (GER) d. E. Sanchez (ESP) 75 63; E. Sanchez/A. Sanchez-Vicario (ESP) d. M. Stich/S. Graf (GER) w/o.

1994 Czech Republic d. Germany 2-1: J. Novotna (CZE) d. A. Huber (GER) 16 64 63; P. Korda (CZE) d. B. Karbacher (GER) 63 63; B. Karbacher/A. Huber (GER) d. P. Korda/J. Novotna (CZE) 83 (pro set).

1995 Germany d. Ukraine 3-0: A. Huber (GER) d. N. Medvedeva (UKR) 64 36 64; B. Becker (GER) d. A. Medvedev (UKR) 63 67 63; B. Becker/A. Huber (GER) d. A. Medvedev/N. Medvedeva (UKR) w/o.

1996 Croatia d. Switzerland 2-1: M. Hingis (SUI) d. I. Majoli (CRO) 63 60; G. Ivanisevic (CRO) d. M. Rosset (SUI) 76 75; G. Ivanisevic/I. Majoli (CRO) d. M. Rosset/M. Hingis (SUI) 36 76 55 ret.

1997 USA d. South Africa 2-1: C. Rubin (USA) d. A. Coetzer (RSA) 75 62; W. Ferreira (RSA) d. J. Gimelstob (USA) 64 76; J. Gimelstob/C. Rubin (USA) d. W. Ferreira/A. Coetzer (RSA) 36 62 75.

1998 Slovak Republic d. France 2-1: M. Pierce (FRA) d. K. Habsudova (SVK) 64 75; K. Kucera (SVK) d. C. Pioline (FRA) 76 64; K. Kucera/K. Habsudova (SVK) d. C. Pioline/M. Pierce (FRA) 63 64.

1999 Australia d. Sweden 2-1: J. Dokic (AUS) d. A. Carlsson (SWE) 62 76; M. Philippoussis (AUS) d. J. Bjorkman (SWE) 63 76; J. Bjorkman/A. Carlsson (SWE) d. M. Philippoussis/J. Dokic (AUS) 86 (pro set).

2000 South Africa d. Thailand 3-0: A. Coetzer (RSA) d. T. Tanasugarn (THA) 36 64 64; W. Ferreira (RSA) d. P. Srichaphan (THA) 76 63; W. Ferreira/A. Coetzer (RSA) d. P. Srichaphan/T. Tanasugarn (THA) 81 (pro set).

2001 Switzerland d. USA 2-1: M. Hingis (SUI) d. M. Seles (USA) 75 64; R. Federer (SUI) d. J. Gambill (USA) 64 63; J. Gambill/M. Seles (USA) d. R. Federer/M. Hingis (SUI) 26 64 76.

2002 Spain d. USA 2-1: M. Seles (USA) d. A. Sanchez-Vicario (ESP) 61 76; T. Robredo (ESP) d. J. Gambill (USA) 63 26 76; T. Robredo/A. Sanchez-Vicario (ESP) d. J. Gambill/M. Seles (USA) 64 62.

2003 USA d. Australia 3-0: S. Williams (USA) d. A. Molik (AUS) 62 63; J. Blake (USA) d. L. Hewitt (AUS) 63 64; J. Blake/S.Williams (USA) d. L. Hewitt/A. Molik ((AUS) 63 62.

2004 USA d. Slovak Republic 2-1: L. Davenport (USA) d. D. Hantuchova (SVK) 63 61; K. Kucera (SVK) d. J. Blake (USA) 46 64 76; J. Blake/L. Davenport (USA) d. K. Kucera/D. Hantuchova (SVK) 62 63.

Olympic Tennis Event

Tennis was one of the original sports at the first modern Olympiad in Athens in 1896, but was withdrawn after the 1924 Paris Games. It returned as a full medal sport at Seoul in 1988.

Year/Venue	Event	Gold	Silver	Bronze
1896 Athens, Greece	Men's Singles	John Boland (IRL)	Dionysios Kasdaglis (GRE)	Konstantinos Paspatis (GRE) Momcilo Tapavica (HUN)
	Men's Doubles	John Boland (IRL)/ Friedrich Traun (GER)	Dionysios Kasdaglis/ Dimitrios Petrokokkinos (GRE)	A. Akratopoulos/ K. Akratopoulos (GRE) Edwin Flack (AUS)/ George Robertson (GBR)
1900 Paris, France	Men's Singles	Laurence Doherty (GBR)	Harold Mahony (IRL)	Reginald Doherty (GBR) Arthur Norris (GBR)
	Men's Doubles	Laurence Doherty/ Reginald Doherty (GBR)	Maxime Decugis (FRA)/ Basil De Garmendia (USA)	Georges De La Chapelle/ Andre Prevost (FRA) Harold Mahony (IRL)/ Arthur Norris (GBR)
	Women's Singles	Charlotte Cooper (GBR)	Helene Prevost (FRA)	Marion Jones (USA) Hedwig Rosenbaum (BOH)
	Mixed Doubles	Reginald Doherty/ Charlotte Cooper (GBR)	Harold Mahony (IRL)/ Helene Prevost (FRA)	Laurence Doherty (GBR)/ Marion Jones (USA) Archibald Warden (GBR)/ Hedwig Rosenbaum (BOH)
1904 St. Louis, USA	Men's Singles	Beals Wright (USA)	Robert Le Roy (USA)	Alphonzo Bell (USA) Edgar Leonard (USA)
	Men's Doubles	Edgar Leonard/ Beals Wright (USA)	Alphonzo Bell/ Robert Le Roy (USA)	Clarence Gamble/ Arthur Wear (USA) Joseph Wear/ Allen West (USA)
1906 Athens, Greece (Demonstration)	Men's Singles	Maxime Decugis (FRA)	Maurice Germot (FRA)	Zdenek Zemla (BOH)
	Men's Doubles	Maxime Decugis/ Maurice Germot (FRA)	Joannis Ballis/ Xenophon Kasdaglis (GRE)	Ladislav Zemla/ Zdenek Zemla (BOH)
	Women's Singles	Esmee Simirioti (GRE)	Sophia Marinou (GRE)	Euphrosine Paspati (GRE)
	Mixed Doubles	Maxime Decugis/ Marie Decugis (FRA)	Georgios Simiriotis/ Sophia Marinou (GRE)	Xenophon Kasdaglis/ Aspasia Matsa (GRE)
1908 London Indoor, England	Men's Singles	Arthur Gore (GBR)	George Caridia (GBR)	Josiah Ritchie (GBR)
	Mixed Doubles	Herbert Roper Barrett/ Arthur Gore (GBR)	George Caridia/ George Simond (GBR)	Wollmar Bostrom/ Gunnar Setterwall (SWE)
	Women's Singles	Gladys Eastlake-Smith (GBR)	Alice Greene (GBR)	Martha Adlerstrahle (SWE)
1908 London Outdoor, England	Men's Singles	Josiah Ritchie (GBR)	Otto Froitzheim (GBR)	Wilberforce Eaves (GBR)
	Men's Doubles	Reginald Doherty/ George Hillyard (GBR)	James Parke (IRL)/ Josiah Ritchie (GBR)	Clement Cazalet/ Charles Dixon (GBR)
	Women's Singles	Dorothea Lambert-Chambers (GBR)	Dora Boothby (GBR)	Ruth Winch (GBR)
1912 Stockholm Indoor, Sweden	Men's Singles	Andre Gobert (FRA)	Charles Dixon (GBR)	Anthony Wilding (NZL)
	Men's Doubles	Maurice Germot/ Andre Gobert (FRA)	Carl Kempe/ Gunnar Setterwall (SWE)	Alfred Beamish/ Charles Dixon (GBR)
	Women's Singles	Edith Hannam (GBR)	Sofie Castenschiold (DEN)	Mabel Parton (GBR)
	Mixed Doubles	Charles Dixon/ Edith Hannam (GBR)	Herbert Roper Barrett/ Helen Aitchison (GBR)	Gunnar Setterwall/ Sigrid Fick (SWE)

Olympic Tennis Event (continued)

Year/Venue	Event	Gold	Silver	Bronze
1912 Stockholm Outdoor, Sweden	Men's Singles	Charles Winslow (RSA)	Harold Kitson (RSA)	Oskar Kreuzer (GER)
	Men's Doubles	Harold Kitson/ Charles Winslow (RSA)	Felix Pipes/ Arthur Zborzil (AUT)	Albert Canet/ Eduard Meny De Marangue (FRA)
	Women's Singles	Marguerite Broquedis (FRA)	Dorothea Koring (GER)	Margrethe Bjurstedt (NOR)
	Mixed Doubles	Heinrich Schomburgk/ Dorothea Koring (GER)	Gunnar Setterwall/ Sigrid Fick (SWE)	Albert Canet/ Marguerite Broquedis (FRA)
1920 Antwerp, Belgium	Men's Singles	Louis Raymond (RSA)	Ichiya Kumagai (JPN)	Charles Winslow (RSA)
	Men's Doubles	Noel Turnbull/ Maxwell Woosnam (GBR)	Seiichiro Kashio/ Ichiya Kumagai (JPN)	Pierre Albarran/ Maxime Decugis (FRA)
	Women's Singles	Suzanne Lenglen (FRA)	Dorothy Holman (GBR)	Kathleen McKane (GBR)
	Women's Doubles	Kathleen McKane/ Winifred McNair (GBR)	Geraldine Beamish/ Dorothy Holman (GBR)	Elisabeth D'Ayen/ Suzanne Lenglen (FRA)
	Mixed Doubles	Maxime Decugis/ Suzanne Lenglen (FRA)	Maxwell Woosnam/ Kathleen McKane (GBR)	Ladislav Zemla/ Milada Skrobkova (TCH)
1924 Paris, France	Men's Singles	Vincent Richards (USA)	Henri Cochet (FRA)	Umberto De Morpurgo (ITA)
	Men's Doubles	Francis Hunter/ Vincent Richards (USA)	Jacques Brugnon/ Henri Cochet (FRA)	Jean Borotra/ Rene Lacoste (FRA)
	Women's Singles	Helen Wills (USA)	Julie Vlasto (FRA)	Kathleen McKane (GBR)
	Women's Doubles	Hazel Wightman/ Helen Wills (USA)	Phyllis Covell/ Kathleen McKane (GBR)	Evelyn Colyer/ Dorothy Shepherd-Barron (GBR)
	Mixed Doubles	Richard Williams/ Hazel Wightman (USA)	Vincent Richards/ Marion Jessup (USA)	Hendrik Timmer/ Kornelia Bouman (NED)
1968 Guadalajara, Mexico (Demonstration)	Men's Singles	Manuel Santana (ESP)	Manuel Orantes (ESP)	Herbert Fitzgibbon (USA)
	Men's Doubles	Rafael Osuna/ Vicente Zarazua (MEX)	Juan Gisbert/ Manuel Santana (ESP)	Pierre Darmon (FRA)/ Joaquin Loyo-Mayo (MEX)
	Women's Singles	Helga Niessen (FRG)	Jane Bartkowicz (USA)	Julie Heldman (USA)
	Women's Doubles	Edda Buding/ Helga Niessen (FRG)	Rosa-Maria Darmon (FRA)/ Julie Heldman (USA)	Jane Bartkowicz/ Valerie Ziegenfuss (USA)
	Mixed Doubles	Herbert Fitzgibbon/ Julie Heldman (USA)	Jurgen Fassbender/ Helga Niessen (FRG)	James Osborne/ Jane Bartkowicz (USA)
1968 Mexico City, Mexico (Exhibition)	Men's Singles	Rafael Osuna (MEX)	Inge Buding (FRG)	Vladimir Korotkov (URS) Nicola Pietrangeli (ITA)
	Men's Doubles	Rafael Osuna/ Vicente Zarazua (MEX)	Pierre Darmon (FRA)/ Joaquin Loyo-Mayo (MEX)	Francisco Guzman (ECU)/ Teimuraz Kakulia (URS) Vladimir Korotkov/ Anatoly Volkov (URS)
	Women's Singles	Jane Bartkowicz (USA)	Julie Heldman (USA)	Maria-Eugenia Guzman (ECU) Suzana Petersen (BRA)
	Women's Doubles	Rosa-Maria Darmon (FRA)/ Julie Heldman (USA)	Jane Bartkowicz/ Valerie Ziegenfuss (USA)	Maria-Eugenia Guzman (ECU)/ Suzana Petersen (BRA) Cecilia Rosado (MEX)/ Zaiga Yansone (URS)
	Mixed Doubles	Vladimir Korotkov/ Zaiga Yansone (URS)	Inge Buding (FRG)/ Jane Bartkowicz (USA)	Pierre Darmon/ Rosa-Maria Darmon (FRA) Teimuraz Kakulia (URS)/ Suzana Petersen (BRA)
1984 Los Angeles, USA (Demonstration)	Men's Singles	Stefan Edberg (SWE)	Francisco Maciel (MEX)	James Arias (USA) Paolo Cane (ITA)
	Women's Singles	Steffi Graf (FRG)	Sabrina Goles (YUG)	Raffaella Reggi (ITA) Catherine Tanvier (FRA)

Year/Venue	Event	Gold	Silver	Bronze
1988 Seoul, Korea	Men's Singles	Miloslav Mecir (TCH)	Timothy Mayotte (USA)	Stefan Edberg (SWE) Brad Gilbert (USA)
	Men's Doubles	Ken Flach/ Robert Seguso (USA)	Sergio Casal/ Emilio Sanchez (ESP)	Stefan Edberg/ Anders Jarryd (SWE) Miloslav Mecir Milan Srejber (TCH)
	Women's Singles	Steffi Graf (FRG)	Gabriela Sabatini (ARG)	Zina Garrison (USA) Manuela Maleeva (BUL)
	Women's Doubles	Zina Garrison/ Pamela Shriver (USA)	Jana Novotna/ Helena Sukova (TCH)	Steffi Graf/ Claudia Kohde-Kilsch (FRG) Elizabeth Smylie/ Wendy Turnbull (AUS)
1992 Barcelona, Spain	Men's Singles	Marc Rosset (SUI)	Jordi Arrese (ESP)	Andrei Cherkasov (EUN) Goran Ivanisevic (CRO)
	Men's Doubles	Boris Becker/ Michael Stich (GER)	Wayne Ferreira/ Piet Norval (RSA)	Javier Frana/ Cristian Miniussi (ARG) Goran Ivanisevic/ Goran Prpic (CRO)
	Women's Singles	Jennifer Capriati (USA)	Steffi Graf (GER)	Mary Joe Fernandez (USA) Arantxa Sanchez-Vicario (ESP)
	Women's Doubles	Gigi Fernandez/ Mary Joe Fernandez (USA)	Conchita Martinez/ A. Sanchez-Vicario (ESP)	Rachel McQuillan/ Nicole Provis (AUS) Leila Meskhi/ Natalia Zvereva (EUN)
1996 Atlanta, USA	Men's Singles	Andre Agassi (USA)	Sergio Bruguera (ESP)	Leander Paes (IND)
	Men's Doubles	Todd Woodbridge/ Mark Woodforde (AUS)	Neil Broad/ Tim Henman (GBR)	Marc-Kevin Goellner/ David Prinosil (GER)
	Women's Singles	Lindsay Davenport (USA)	A. Sanchez-Vicario (ESP)	Jana Novotna (CZE)
	Women's Doubles	Gigi Fernandez/ Mary Joe Fernandez (USA)	Jana Novotna/ Helena Sukova (CZE)	Conchita Martinez/ Arantxa Sanchez-Vicario (ESP)
2000 Sydney, Australia	Men's Singles	Yevgeny Kafelnikov (RUS)	Tommy Haas (GER)	Arnaud Di Pasquale (FRA)
	Men's Doubles	Sebastien Lareau/ Daniel Nestor (CAN)	Tood Woodbridge/ Mark Woodforde (AUS)	Alex Corretja/ Albert Costa (ESP)
	Women's Singles	Venus Williams (USA)	Elena Dementieva (RUS)	Monica Seles (USA)
	Women's Doubles	Serena Williams/ Venus Williams (USA)	Kristie Boogert/ Miriam Oremans (NED)	Els Callens/ Dominique Van Roost (BEL)
2004 Athens, Greece	Men's Singles	Nicolas Massu (CHI)	Mardy Fish (USA)	Fernando Gonzalez (CHI)
	Men's Doubles	Fernando Gonzalez/ Nicolas Massu (CHI)	Nicolas Kiefer/ Rainer Schuettler (GER)	Mario Ancic/ Ivan Ljubicic (CRO)
	Women's Singles	Justine Henin-Hardenne (BEL)	Amelie Mauresmo (FRA)	Alicia Molik (AUS)
	Women's Doubles	Ting Li/ Tian Tian Sun (CHN)	Conchita Martinez/ Virginia Ruano Pascual (ESP)	Paola Suarez/ Patricia Tarabini (ARG)

Lleyton Hewitt (AUS)

Australian Championships

Men's Singles

Year	Champion	Runner-up	Score
1905	R. Heath (AUS)	A. Curtis (AUS)	46 63 64 64
1906	A. Wilding (NZL)	F. Fisher (AUS)	60 64 64
1907	H. Rice (AUS)	H. Parker (AUS)	63 64 64
1908	F. Alexander (USA)	A. Dunlop (AUS)	36 36 60 62 63
1909	A. Wilding (NZL)	E. Parker (AUS)	61 75 62
1910	R. Heath (AUS)	H. Rice (AUS)	64 63 62
1911	N. Brookes (AUS)	H. Rice (AUS)	61 62 63
1912	J. Parke (GBR)	A. E. Beamish (AUS)	36 63 16 61 75
1913	E. Parker (AUS)	H. Parker (AUS)	26 61 63 62
1914	A. O'Hara Wood (AUS)	G. Patterson (AUS)	64 63 57 61
1915	G. Lowe (GBR)	H. Rice (AUS)	46 61 61 64
1916-18 not played			
1919	A. Kingscote (GBR)	E. Pockley (AUS)	64 60 63
1920	P. O'Hara Wood (AUS)	R. Thomas (AUS)	63 46 68 61 63
1921	R. Gemmell (AUS)	A. Hedeman (AUS)	75 61 64
1922	J. Anderson (AUS)	G. Patterson (AUS)	60 36 36 63 62
1923	P. O'Hara Wood (AUS)	C. St John (AUS)	61 61 63
1924	J. Anderson (AUS)	R. Schlesinger (AUS)	63 64 36 57 63
1925	J. Anderson (AUS)	G. Patterson (AUS)	119 26 62 63
1926	J. Hawkes (AUS)	J. Willard (AUS)	61 63 61
1927	G. Patterson (AUS)	J. Hawkes (AUS)	36 64 36 1816 63
1928	J. Borotra (FRA)	R. Cummings (AUS)	64 61 46 57 63
1929	J. Gregory (GBR)	R. Schlesinger (AUS)	62 62 57 75
1930	E. Moon (AUS)	H. Hopman (AUS)	63 61 63
1931	J. Crawford (AUS)	H. Hopman (AUS)	64 62 26 61
1932	J. Crawford (AUS)	H. Hopman (AUS)	46 63 36 63 61
1933	J. Crawford (AUS)	K. Gledhill (AUS)	26 75 63 62
1934	F. Perry (GBR)	J. Crawford (AUS)	63 75 61
1935	J. Crawford (AUS)	F. Perry (GBR)	26 64 64 64
1936	A. Quist (AUS)	J. Crawford (AUS)	62 63 46 36 97
1937	V. McGrath (AUS)	J. Bromwich (AUS)	63 16 60 26 61
1938	D. Budge (USA)	J. Bromwich (AUS)	64 62 61
1939	J. Bromwich (AUS)	A. Quist (AUS)	64 61 63
1940	A. Quist (AUS)	J. Crawford (AUS)	63 61 62
1941-45 not played			
1946	J. Bromwich (AUS)	D. Pails (AUS)	57 63 75 36 62
1947	D. Pails (AUS)	J. Bromwich (AUS)	46 64 36 75 86
1948	A. Quist (AUS)	J. Bromwich (AUS)	64 36 63 26 63
1949	F. Sedgman (AUS)	J. Bromwich (AUS)	63 62 62
1950	F. Sedgman (AUS)	K. McGregor (AUS)	63 64 46 61
1951	D. Savitt (USA)	K. McGregor (AUS)	63 26 63 61
1952	K. McGregor (AUS)	F. Sedgman (AUS)	75 1210 26 62
1953	K. Rosewall (AUS)	M. Rose (AUS)	60 63 64
1954	M. Rose (AUS)	R. Hartwig (AUS)	62 06 64 62
1955	K. Rosewall (AUS)	L. Hoad (AUS)	97 64 64
1956	L. Hoad (AUS)	K. Rosewall (AUS)	64 36 64 75
1957	A. Cooper (AUS)	N. Fraser (AUS)	63 911 64 62
1958	A. Cooper (AUS)	M. Anderson (AUS)	75 63 64
1959	A. Olmedo (USA)	N. Fraser (AUS)	61 62 36 63
1960	R. Laver (AUS)	N. Fraser (AUS)	57 36 63 86 86
1961	R. Emerson (AUS)	R. Laver (AUS)	16 63 75 64
1962	R. Laver (AUS)	R. Emerson (AUS)	86 06 64 64
1963	R. Emerson (AUS)	K. Fletcher (AUS)	63 63 61
1964	R. Emerson (AUS)	F. Stolle (AUS)	63 64 62

Australian Championships (continued)

Year	Champion	Runner-up	Score
1965	R. Emerson (AUS)	F. Stolle (AUS)	79 26 64 75 61
1966	R. Emerson (AUS)	A. Ashe (USA)	64 68 62 63
1967	R. Emerson (AUS)	A. Ashe (USA)	64 61 64
1968	W. Bowrey (AUS)	J. Gisbert (ESP)	75 26 97 64
1969	R. Laver (AUS)	A. Gimeno (ESP)	63 64 75
1970	A. Ashe (USA)	R. Crealy (AUS)	64 97 62
1971	K. Rosewall (AUS)	A. Ashe (USA)	61 75 63
1972	K. Rosewall (AUS)	M. Anderson (AUS)	76 63 75
1973	J. Newcombe (AUS)	O. Parun (NZL)	63 67 75 61
1974	J. Connors (USA)	P. Dent (AUS)	76 64 46 63
1975	J. Newcombe (AUS)	J. Connors (USA)	75 36 64 76
1976	M. Edmondson (AUS)	J. Newcombe (AUS)	67 63 76 61
1977 (Jan)	R. Tanner (USA)	G. Vilas (ARG)	63 63 63
1977 (Dec)	V. Gerulaitis (USA)	J. Lloyd (GBR)	63 76 57 36 62
1978	G. Vilas (ARG)	J. Marks (AUS)	64 64 36 63
1979	G. Vilas (ARG)	J. Sadri (USA)	76 63 62
1980	B. Teacher (USA)	K. Warwick (AUS)	75 76 63
1981	J. Kriek (RSA)	S. Denton (USA)	62 76 67 64
1982	J. Kriek (USA)	S. Denton (USA)	63 63 62
1983	M. Wilander (SWE)	I. Lendl (TCH)	61 64 64
1984	M. Wilander (SWE)	K. Curren (RSA)	67 64 76 62
1985 (Nov)	S. Edberg (SWE)	M. Wilander (SWE)	64 63 63
1986 not played			
1987 (Jan)	S. Edberg (SWE)	P. Cash (AUS)	63 64 36 57 63
1988	M. Wilander (SWE)	P. Cash (AUS)	63 67 36 61 86
1989	I. Lendl (TCH)	M. Mecir (TCH)	62 62 62
1990	I. Lendl (TCH)	S. Edberg (SWE)	46 76 52 ret.
1991	B. Becker (GER)	I. Lendl (TCH)	16 64 64 64
1992	J. Courier (USA)	S. Edberg (SWE)	63 36 64 62
1993	J. Courier (USA)	S. Edberg (SWE)	62 61 26 75
1994	P. Sampras (USA)	T. Martin (USA)	76 64 64
1995	A. Agassi (USA)	P. Sampras (USA)	46 61 76 64
1996	B. Becker (GER)	M. Chang (USA)	62 64 26 62
1997	P. Sampras (USA)	C. Moya (ESP)	62 63 63
1998	P. Korda (CZE)	M. Rios (CHI)	62 62 62
1999	Y. Kafelnikov (RUS)	T. Enqvist (SWE)	46 60 63 76
2000	A. Agassi (USA)	Y. Kafelnikov (RUS)	36 63 62 64
2001	A. Agassi (USA)	A. Clement (FRA)	64 62 62
2002	T. Johansson (SWE)	M. Safin (RUS)	36 64 64 76
2003	A. Agassi (USA)	R. Schuettler (GER)	62 62 61
2004	R. Federer (SUI)	M. Safin (RUS)	76 64 62

Women's Singles

Year	Champion	Runner-up	Score
1922	Mrs M. Molesworth (AUS)	E. Boyd (AUS)	63 108
1923	Mrs M. Molesworth (AUS)	E. Boyd (AUS)	61 75
1924	S. Lance (AUS)	E. Boyd (AUS)	63 36 86
1925	D. Akhurst (AUS)	E. Boyd (AUS)	16 86 64
1926	D. Akhurst (AUS)	E. Boyd (AUS)	61 63
1927	E. Boyd (AUS)	Mrs S. Harper (AUS)	57 61 62
1928	D. Akhurst (AUS)	E. Boyd (AUS)	75 62
1929	D. Akhurst (AUS)	L. Bickerton (AUS)	61 57 62
1930	D. Akhurst (AUS)	S. Harper (AUS)	108 26 75
1931	Mrs C. Buttsworth (AUS)	M. Crawford (AUS)	16 63 64
1932	Mrs C. Buttsworth (AUS)	K. Le Mesurier (AUS)	97 64

Year	Champion	Runner-up	Score
1933	J. Hartigan (AUS)	Mrs C. Buttsworth (AUS)	64 63
1934	J. Hartigan (AUS)	Mrs M. Molesworth (AUS)	61 64
1935	D. Round (GBR)	N. Lyle (AUS)	16 61 63
1936	J. Hartigan (AUS)	N. Wynne (AUS)	64 64
1937	N. Wynne (AUS)	E. Westacott (AUS)	63 57 64
1938	D. Bundy (USA)	D. Stevenson (AUS)	63 62
1939	E. Westacott (AUS)	N. Hopman (AUS)	61 62
1940	N. Bolton (AUS)	T. Coyne (AUS)	57 64 60
1941-45 not played			
1946	N. Bolton (AUS)	J. Fitch (AUS)	64 64
1947	N. Bolton (AUS)	N. Hopman (AUS)	63 62
1948	N. Bolton (AUS)	M. Toomey (AUS)	63 61
1949	D. Hart (USA)	N. Bolton (AUS)	63 64
1950	L. Brough (USA)	D. Hart (USA)	64 36 64
1951	N. Bolton (AUS)	T. Long (AUS)	61 75
1952	T. Long (AUS)	H. Angwin (AUS)	62 63
1953	M. Connolly (USA)	J. Sampson (USA)	63 62
1954	T. Long (AUS)	J. Staley (AUS)	63 64
1955	B. Penrose (AUS)	T. Long (AUS)	64 63
1956	M. Carter (AUS)	T. Long (AUS)	36 62 97
1957	S. Fry (USA)	A. Gibson (USA)	63 63
1958	A. Mortimer (GBR)	L. Coghlan (AUS)	63 64
1959	M. Reitano (AUS)	R. Schuurman (RSA)	62 63
1960	M. Smith (AUS)	J. Lehane (AUS)	75 62
1961	M. Smith (AUS)	J. Lehane (AUS)	61 64
1962	M. Smith (AUS)	J. Lehane (AUS)	60 62
1963	M. Smith (AUS)	J. Lehane (AUS)	62 62
1964	M. Smith (AUS)	L. Turner (AUS)	63 62
1965	M. Smith (AUS)	M. Bueno (BRA)	57 64 52 ret.
1966	M. Smith (AUS)	N. Richey (USA)	w/o
1967	N. Richey (USA)	L. Turner (AUS)	61 64
1968	B. King (USA)	M. Court (AUS)	61 62
1969	M. Court (AUS)	B. King (USA)	64 61
1970	M. Court (AUS)	K. Melville (AUS)	63 61
1971	M. Court (AUS)	E. Goolagong (AUS)	26 76 75
1972	V. Wade (GBR)	E. Goolagong (AUS)	64 64
1973	M. Court (AUS)	E. Goolagong (AUS)	64 75
1974	E. Goolagong (AUS)	C. Evert (USA)	76 46 60
1975	E. Goolagong (AUS)	M. Navratilova (TCH)	63 62
1976	E. Goolagong Cawley (AUS)	R. Tomanova (TCH)	62 62
1977 (Jan)	K. Reid (AUS)	D. Balestrat (AUS)	75 62
1977 (Dec)	E. Goolagong Cawley (AUS)	H. Gourlay (AUS)	63 60
1978	C. O'Neil (AUS)	B. Nagelsen (USA)	63 76
1979	B. Jordan (USA)	S. Walsh (USA)	63 63
1980	H. Mandlikova (TCH)	W. Turnbull (AUS)	60 75
1981	M. Navratilova (USA)	C. Evert Lloyd (USA)	67 64 75
1982	C. Evert Lloyd (USA)	M. Navratilova (USA)	63 26 63
1983	M. Navratilova (USA)	K. Jordan (USA)	62 76
1984	C. Evert Lloyd (USA)	H. Sukova (TCH)	67 61 63
1985 (Nov)	M. Navratilova (USA)	C. Evert Lloyd (USA)	62 46 62
1986 not played			
1987 (Jan)	H. Mandlikova (TCH)	M. Navratilova (USA)	75 76
1988	S. Graf (GER)	C. Evert (USA)	61 76
1989	S. Graf (GER)	H. Sukova (TCH)	64 64
1990	S. Graf (GER)	M. Fernandez (USA)	63 64

Australian Championships (continued)

Year	Champion	Runner-up	Score
1991	M. Seles (YUG)	J. Novotna (TCH)	57 63 61
1992	M. Seles (YUG)	M. Fernandez (USA)	62 63
1993	M. Seles (YUG)	S. Graf (GER)	46 63 62
1994	S. Graf (GER)	A. Sanchez-Vicario (ESP)	60 62
1995	M. Pierce (FRA)	A. Sanchez-Vicario (ESP)	63 62
1996	M. Seles (USA)	A. Huber (GER)	64 61
1997	M. Hingis (SUI)	M. Pierce (FRA)	62 62
1998	M. Hingis (SUI)	C. Martinez (ESP)	63 63
1999	M. Hingis (SUI)	A. Mauresmo (FRA)	62 63
2000	L. Davenport (USA)	M. Hingis (SUI)	61 75
2001	J. Capriati (USA)	M. Hingis (SUI)	64 63
2002	J. Capriati (USA)	M. Hingis (SUI)	46 76 62
2003	S. Williams (USA)	V. Williams (USA)	76 36 64
2004	J. Henin-Hardenne (BEL)	K. Clijsters (BEL)	62 76

Year	Men's Doubles Champions	Women's Doubles Champions	Mixed Doubles Champions
1905	R. Lycett/T. Tachell		
1906	R. Heath/A. Wilding		
1907	W. Gregg/H. Parker		
1908	F. Alexander/A. Dunlop		
1909	J. Keane/E. Parker		
1910	A. Campbell/H. Rice		
1911	R. Heath/R. Lycett		
1912	C. Dixon/J. Parke		
1913	A. Hedemann/E. Parker		
1914	A. Campbell/G. Patterson		
1915	H. Rice/C. Todd		
1916-1918 not played			
1919	P. O'Hara Wood/R. Thomas		
1920	P. O'Hara Wood/R. Thomas		
1921	S. Eaton/R. Gemmell		
1922	J. Hawkes/G. Patterson	E. Boyd/M. Mountain	J. Hawkes/E. Boyd
1923	P. O'Hara Wood/C. St John	E. Boyd/S. Lance	H. Rice/S. Lance
1924	J. Anderson/N. Brookes	D. Akhurst/S. Lance	J. Willard/D. Akhurst
1925	P. O'Hara Wood/G. Patterson	D. Akhurst/R. Harper	J. Willard/D. Akhurst
1926	J. Hawkes/G. Patterson	E. Boyd/M. O'Hara Wood	J. Hawkes/E. Boyd
1927	J. Hawkes/G. Patterson	L. Bickerton/M. O'Hara Wood	J. Hawkes/E. Boyd
1928	J. Borotra/J. Brugnon	D. Akhurst/E. Boyd	J. Borotra/D. Akhurst
1929	J. Crawford/H. Hopman	D. Akhurst/L. Bickerton	E. Moon/D. Akhurst
1930	J. Crawford/H. Hopman	E. Hood/Mrs M. Molesworth	H. Hopman/N. Hall
1931	C. Donohoe/R. Dunlop	L. Bickerton/R. Cozens	J. Crawford/M. Crawford
1932	J. Crawford/E. Moon	Mrs C. Buttsworth/M. Crawford	J. Crawford/M. Crawford
1933	K. Gledhill/E. Vines	Mrs M. Molesworth/E. Westacott	J. Crawford/M. Crawford
1934	G. Hughes/F. Perry	Mrs M. Molesworth/E. Westacott	E. Moon/J. Hartigan
1935	J. Crawford/V. McGrath	E. Dearman/N. Lyle	C. Boussus/L. Bickerton
1936	A. Quist/P. Turnbull	T. Coyne/N. Wynne	H. Hopman/N. Hopman
1937	A. Quist/P. Turnbull	T. Coyne/N. Wynne	H. Hopman/N. Hopman
1938	J. Bromwich/A. Quist	T. Coyne/N. Wynne	J. Bromwich/J. Wilson
1939	J. Bromwich/A. Quist	T. Coyne/N. Wynne	H. Hopman/N. Hopman
1940	J. Bromwich/A. Quist	T. Coyne/N. Bolton	C. Long/N. Bolton
1941-1945 not played			
1946	J. Bromwich/A. Quist	M. Bevis/J. Fitch	C. Long/N. Bolton
1947	J. Bromwich/A. Quist	N. Bolton/T. Long	C. Long/N. Bolton
1948	J. Bromwich/A. Quist	N. Bolton/T. Long	C. Long/N. Bolton

Reference Section: Roll of Honour: Australian Championships

Year	Champions	Champions	Champions
1949	J. Bromwich/A. Quist	N. Bolton/T. Long	F. Sedgman/D. Hart
1950	J. Bromwich/A. Quist	L. Brough/J. Hart	F. Sedgman/D. Hart
1951	K. McGregor/F. Sedgman	N. Bolton/T. Long	G. Worthington/T. Long
1952	K. McGregor/F. Sedgman	N. Bolton/T. Long	G. Worthington/T. Long
1953	L. Hoad/K. Rosewall	M. Connolly/J. Sampson	R. Hartwig/J. Sampson
1954	R. Hartwig/M. Rose	M. Hawton/B. Penrose	R. Hartwig/T. Long
1955	V. Seixas/T. Trabert	M. Hawton/B. Penrose	G. Worthington/T. Long
1956	L. Hoad/K. Rosewall	M. Hawton/T. Long	N. Fraser/B. Penrose
1957	N. Fraser/L. Hoad	S. Fry/A. Gibson	M. Anderson/F. Muller
1958	A. Cooper/N. Fraser	M. Hawton/T. Long	R. Howe/Mrs M. Hawton
1959	R. Laver/R. Mark	S. Reynolds/R. Schuurman	R. Mark/S. Reynolds
1960	R. Laver/R. Mark	M. Bueno/C. Truman	T. Fancutt/J. Lehane
1961	R. Laver/R. Mark	M. Reitano/M. Smith	R. Hewitt/J. Lehane
1962	R. Emerson/N. Fraser	R. Ebbern/M. Smith	F. Stolle/L. Turner
1963	R. Hewitt/F. Stolle	R. Ebbern/M. Smith	K. Fletcher/M. Smith
1964	R. Hewitt/F. Stolle	J. Tegart/L. Turner	K. Fletcher/M. Smith
1965	J. Newcombe/T. Roche	M. Smith/L. Turner	J. Newcombe/M. Smith & O. Davidson/R. Ebbern
1966	R. Emerson/F. Stolle	C. Graebner/N. Richey	A. Roche/J. Tegart
1967	J. Newcombe/T. Roche	J. Tegart/L. Turner	O. Davidson/L. Turner
1968	R. Crealy/A. Stone	K. Krantzcke/K. Melville	R. Crealy/B. King
1969	R. Emerson/R. Laver	M. Court/A. Tegart	M. Riessen/M. Court & F. Stolle/A. Jones
1970	R. Lutz/S. Smith	M. Court/J. Dalton	1970-1986 not played
1971	J. Newcombe/T. Roche	M. Court/E. Goolagong	
1972	O. Davidson/K. Rosewall	H. Gourlay/K. Harris	
1973	M. Anderson/J. Newcombe	M. Court/V. Wade	
1974	R. Case/G. Masters	E. Goolagong/M. Michel	
1975	J. Alexander/P. Dent	E. Goolagong/M. Michel	
1976	J. Newcombe/T. Roche	E. Goolagong Cawley/H. Gourlay	
1977 (Jan)	A. Ashe/T. Roche	D. Fromholtz/H. Gourlay	
1977 (Dec)	A. Stone/R. Ruffels	E. Goolagong Cawley/H. Gourlay	
1978	W. Fibak/K. Warwick	B. Nagelsen/R. Tomanova	
1979	P. McNamara/P. McNamee	J. Chaloner/R. Evers	
1980	M. Edmondson/K. Warwick	B. Nagelsen/M. Navratilova	
1981	M. Edmondson/K. Warwick	K. Jordan/A. Smith	
1982	J. Alexander/J. Fitzgerald	M. Navratilova/P. Shriver	
1983	M. Edmondson/P. McNamee	M. Navratilova/P. Shriver	
1984	M. Edmondson/S. Stewart	M. Navratilova/P. Shriver	
1985 (Nov)	P. Annacone/C. Van Rensburg	M. Navratilova/P. Shriver	
1986 not played			
1987 (Jan)	S. Edberg/A. Jarryd	M. Navratilova/P. Shriver	S. Stewart/Z. Garrison
1988	R. Leach/J. Pugh	M. Navratilova/P. Shriver	J. Pugh/J. Novotna
1989	R. Leach/J. Pugh	M. Navratilova/P. Shriver	J. Pugh/J. Novotna
1990	P. Aldrich/D. Visser	J. Novotna/H. Sukova	J. Pugh/N. Zvereva
1991	S. Davis/D. Pate	P. Fendick/M. Fernandez	J. Bates/J. Durie
1992	T. Woodbridge/M. Woodforde	A. Sanchez-Vicario/H. Sukova	M. Woodforde/N. Provis
1993	D. Visser/L. Warder	G. Fernandez/N. Zvereva	T. Woodbridge/A. Sanchez-Vicario
1994	J. Eltingh/P. Haarhuis	G. Fernandez/N. Zvereva	A. Olhovskiy/L. Neiland
1995	J. Palmer/R. Reneberg	J. Novotna/A. Sanchez-Vicario	R. Leach/N. Zvereva
1996	S. Edberg/P. Korda	C. Rubin/A. Sanchez-Vicario	M. Woodforde/L. Neiland
1997	T. Woodbridge/M. Woodforde	M. Hingis/N. Zvereva	R. Leach/M. Bollegraf
1998	J. Bjorkman/J. Eltingh	M. Hingis/M. Lucic	J. Gimelstob/V. Williams
1999	J. Bjorkman/P. Rafter	M. Hingis/A. Kournikova	D. Adams/M. De Swardt
2000	W. Ferreira/R. Leach	L. Raymond/R. Stubbs	J. Palmer/R. Stubbs
2001	J. Bjorkman/T. Woodbridge	S. Williams/V. Williams	E. Ferreira/C. Morariu
2002	M. Knowles/D. Nestor	M. Hingis/A. Kournikova	K. Ullyett/D. Hantuchova

Australian Championships (continued)

Year	Champions	Champions	Champions
2003	M. Llodra/F. Santoro	S. Williams/V. Williams	L. Paes/M. Navratilova
2004	M. Llodra/F. Santoro	V. Ruano Pascual/P. Suarez	N. Zimonjic/E. Bovina

French Championships Roland Garros

Men's Singles

Year	Champion	Runner-up	Score
1891	H. Briggs (GBR)	P. Baigneres (FRA)	63 64
1892	J. Schopfer (FRA)	Fassitt (GBR)	62 16 62
1893	L. Riboulet (FRA)	J. Schopfer (FRA)	63 63
1894	A. Vacherot (FRA)	G. Brosselin (FRA)	16 63 63
1895	A. Vacherot (FRA)	L. Riboulet (FRA)	97 62
1896	A. Vacherot (FRA)	G. Brosselin (FRA)	61 75
1897	P. Ayme (FRA)	F. Wardan (GBR)	46 64 62
1898	P. Ayme (FRA)	P. Lebreton (FRA)	
1899	P. Ayme (FRA)	P. Lebreton (FRA)	
1900	P. Ayme (FRA)	A. Prevost (FRA)	
1901	A. Vacherot (FRA)	P. Lebreton (FRA)	
1902	M. Vacherot (FRA)	M. Decugis (FRA)	64 62
1903	M. Decugis (FRA)	A. Vacherot (FRA)	62 86 810 61
1904	M. Decugis (FRA)	A. Vacherot (FRA)	61 97 68 61
1905	M. Germot (FRA)	A. Vacherot (FRA)	
1906	M. Germot (FRA)	M. Decugis (FRA)	
1907	M. Decugis (FRA)	R. Wallet (FRA)	60 63 61
1908	M. Decugis (FRA)	M. Germot (FRA)	62 61 36 108
1909	M. Decugis (FRA)	M. Germot (FRA)	36 26 64 64 64
1910	M. Germot (FRA)	F. Blanchy (FRA)	61 63 46 63
1911	A. Gobert (FRA)	M. Germot (FRA)	61 86 75
1912	M. Decugis (FRA)	A. Gobert (FRA)	61 75 60
1913	M. Decugis (FRA)	G. Gault (FRA)	
1914	M. Decugis (FRA)	J. Samazeuilh (FRA)	36 61 64 64
1915-1919 not played			
1920	A. Gobert (FRA)	M. Decugis (FRA)	63 36 16 62 63
1921	J. Samazeuilh (FRA)	A. Gobert (FRA)	63 63 26 75
1922	H. Cochet (FRA)	J. Samazeuilh (FRA)	86 63 75
1923	F. Blanchy (FRA)	M. Decugis (FRA)	16 62 60 62
1924	J. Borotra (FRA)	R. Lacoste (FRA)	75 64 06 57 62
1925	R. Lacoste (FRA)	J. Borotra (FRA)	75 61 64
1926	H. Cochet (FRA)	R. Lacoste (FRA)	62 64 63
1927	R. Lacoste (FRA)	W. Tilden (USA)	64 46 57 63 119
1928	H. Cochet (FRA)	R. Lacoste (FRA)	57 63 61 63
1929	R. Lacoste (FRA)	J. Borotra (FRA)	63 26 60 26 86
1930	H. Cochet (FRA)	W. Tilden (USA)	36 86 63 61
1931	J. Borotra (FRA)	C. Boussus (FRA)	26 64 75 64
1932	H. Cochet (FRA)	G. De Stefani (ITA)	60 64 46 63
1933	J. Crawford (AUS)	H. Cochet (FRA)	86 61 63
1934	G. Von Cramm (GER)	J. Crawford (AUS)	64 79 36 75 63
1935	F. Perry (GBR)	G. Von Cramm (GER)	63 36 61 63
1936	G. Von Cramm (GER)	F. Perry (GBR)	60 26 62 26 60
1937	H. Henkel (GER)	H. Austin (USA)	61 64 63
1938	D. Budge (USA)	R. Menzel (TCH)	63 62 64
1939	W. McNeill (USA)	R. Riggs (USA)	75 60 63
1940-1945 not played			
1946	M. Bernard (FRA)	J. Drobny (TCH)	36 26 61 64 63

Year	Champion	Runner-up	Score
1947	J. Asboth (HUN)	E. Sturgess (RSA)	86 75 64
1948	F. Parker (USA)	J. Drobny (TCH)	64 75 57 86
1949	F. Parker (USA)	B. Patty (USA)	63 16 61 64
1950	B. Patty (USA)	J. Drobny (CZE)	61 62 36 57 75
1951	J. Drobny (TCH)	E. Sturgess (RSA)	63 63 63
1952	J. Drobny (TCH)	F. Sedgman (AUS)	62 60 36 64
1953	K. Rosewall (AUS)	V. Seixas (USA)	63 64 16 62
1954	T. Trabert (USA)	A. Larsen (USA)	64 75 61
1955	T. Trabert (USA)	S. Davidson (SWE)	26 61 64 62
1956	L. Hoad (AUS)	S. Davidson (SWE)	64 86 63
1957	S. Davidson (SWE)	H. Flam (USA)	63 64 64
1958	M. Rose (AUS)	L. Ayala (CHI)	63 64 64
1959	N. Pietrangeli (ITA)	I. Vermaak (RSA)	36 63 64 61
1960	N. Pietrangeli (ITA)	L. Ayala (CHI)	36 63 64 46 63
1961	M. Santana (ESP)	N. Pietrangeli (ITA)	46 61 36 60 62
1962	R. Laver (AUS)	R. Emerson (AUS)	36 26 63 97 62
1963	R. Emerson (AUS)	P. Darmon (FRA)	36 61 64 64
1964	M. Santana (ESP)	N. Pietrangeli (ITA)	63 61 46 75
1965	F. Stolle (AUS)	T. Roche (AUS)	36 60 62 63
1966	T. Roche (AUS)	I. Gulyas (HUN)	61 64 75
1967	R. Emerson (AUS)	T. Roche (AUS)	61 64 26 62
1968	K. Rosewall (AUS)	R. Laver (AUS)	63 61 26 62
1969	R. Laver (AUS)	K. Rosewall (AUS)	64 63 64
1970	J. Kodes (TCH)	Z. Franulovic (YUG)	62 64 60
1971	J. Kodes (TCH)	I. Nastase (ROM)	86 62 26 75
1972	A. Gimeno (ESP)	P. Proisy (FRA)	46 63 61 61
1973	I. Nastase (ROM)	N. Pilic (YUG)	63 63 60
1974	B. Borg (SWE)	M. Orantes (ESP)	26 67 60 61 61
1975	B. Borg (SWE)	G. Vilas (ARG)	62 63 64
1976	A. Panatta (ITA)	H. Solomon (USA)	61 64 46 76
1977	G. Vilas (ARG)	B. Gottfried (USA)	60 63 60
1978	B. Borg (SWE)	G. Vilas (ARG)	61 61 63
1979	B. Borg (SWE)	V. Pecci (PAR)	63 61 67 64
1980	B. Borg (SWE)	V. Gerulaitis (USA)	64 61 62
1981	B. Borg (SWE)	I. Lendl (TCH)	61 46 62 36 61
1982	M. Wilander (SWE)	G. Vilas (ARG)	16 76 60 64
1983	Y. Noah (FRA)	M. Wilander (SWE)	62 75 76
1984	I. Lendl (TCH)	J. McEnroe (USA)	36 26 64 75 75
1985	M. Wilander (SWE)	I. Lendl (TCH)	36 64 62 62
1986	I. Lendl (TCH)	M. Pernfors (SWE)	63 62 64
1987	I. Lendl (TCH)	M. Wilander (SWE)	75 62 36 76
1988	M. Wilander (SWE)	H. Leconte (FRA)	75 62 61
1989	M. Chang (USA)	S. Edberg (SWE)	61 36 46 64 62
1990	A. Gomez (ECU)	A. Agassi (USA)	63 26 64 64
1991	J. Courier (USA)	A. Agassi (USA)	36 64 26 61 64
1992	J. Courier (USA)	P. Korda (TCH)	75 62 61
1993	S. Bruguera (ESP)	J. Courier (USA)	64 26 62 36 63
1994	S. Bruguera (ESP)	A. Berasategui (ESP)	63 75 26 61
1995	T. Muster (AUT)	M. Chang (USA)	75 62 64
1996	Y. Kafelnikov (RUS)	M. Stich (GER)	76 75 76
1997	G. Kuerten (BRA)	S. Bruguera (ESP)	63 64 62
1998	C. Moya (ESP)	A. Corretja (ESP)	63 75 63
1999	A. Agassi (USA)	A. Medvedev (UKR)	16 26 64 63 64
2000	G. Kuerten (BRA)	M. Norman (SWE)	62 63 26 76
2001	G. Kuerten (BRA)	A. Corretja (ESP)	67 75 62 60

French Championships Roland Garros (continued)

Year	Champion	Runner-up	Score
2002	A. Costa (ESP)	J. Ferrero (ESP)	61 60 46 63
2003	J. Ferrero (ESP)	M. Verkerk (NED)	61 63 62
2004	G. Gaudio (ARG)	G. Coria (ARG)	06 36 64 61 86

Women's Singles

Year	Champion	Runner-up	Score
1897	F. Masson (FRA)	P. Girod (FRA)	63 61
1898	F. Masson (FRA)		
1899	F. Masson (FRA)		
1900	Y. Prevost (FRA)		
1901	P. Girod (FRA)	Leroux (FRA)	61 61
1902	F. Masson (FRA)	P. Girod (FRA)	60 61
1903	F. Masson (FRA)	K. Gillou (FRA)	60 68 60
1904	K. Gillou (FRA)	F. Masson (FRA)	
1905	K. Gillou (FRA)	Y. De Pfooffel (FRA)	63 119
1906	K. Gillou-Fenwick (FRA)	M. Veagh (GBR)	
1907	C. De Kermel (FRA)	D'Elva (FRA)	w/o
1908	K. Gillou-Fenwick (FRA)	A. Pean (FRA)	62 62
1909	J. Matthey (FRA)	Gallay (FRA)	108 64
1910	J. Matthey (FRA)	G. Regnier (FRA)	16 61 97
1911	J. Matthey (FRA)	M. Broquedis (FRA)	62 75
1912	J. Matthey (FRA)	M. Danet (FRA)	62 75
1913	M. Broquedis (FRA)	J. Matthey (FRA)	
1914	M. Broquedis (FRA)	S. Lenglen (FRA)	57 64 63

1915-1919 not played

Year	Champion	Runner-up	Score
1920	S. Lenglen (FRA)	M. Broquedis-Billout (FRA)	61 75
1921	S. Lenglen (FRA)	G. Golding (GBR)	w/o
1922	S. Lenglen (FRA)	G. Golding (GBR)	64 60
1923	S. Lenglen (FRA)	G. Golding (GBR)	61 64
1924	D. Vlasto (FRA)	J. Vaussard (FRA)	62 63
1925	S. Lenglen (FRA)	K. McKane (GBR)	61 62
1926	S. Lenglen (FRA)	M. Browne (USA)	61 60
1927	K. Bouman (NED)	I. Peacock (RSA)	62 64
1928	H. Wills (USA)	E. Bennett (GBR)	61 62
1929	H. Wills (USA)	S. Mathieu (FRA)	63 64
1930	H. Wills Moody (USA)	H. Jacobs (USA)	62 61
1931	C. Aussem (GER)	B. Nuthall (GBR)	86 61
1932	H. Wills Moody (USA)	S. Mathieu (FRA)	75 61
1933	M. Scriven (GBR)	S. Mathieu (FRA)	62 46 64
1934	M. Scriven (GBR)	H. Jacobs (USA)	75 46 61
1935	H. Sperling (GER)	S. Mathieu (FRA)	62 61
1936	H. Sperling (GER)	S. Mathieu (FRA)	63 64
1937	H. Sperling (GER)	S. Mathieu (FRA)	62 64
1938	S. Mathieu (FRA)	N. Landry (FRA)	60 63
1939	S. Mathieu (FRA)	J. Jedrzejowska (POL)	63 86

1940-1945 not played

Year	Champion	Runner-up	Score
1946	M. Osborne (USA)	P. Betz (USA)	16 86 75
1947	P. Todd (USA)	D. Hart (USA)	63 36 64
1948	N. Landry (FRA)	S. Fry (USA)	62 06 60
1949	M. Osborne DuPont (USA)	N. Adamson-Landry (FRA)	75 62
1950	D. Hart (USA)	P. Todd (USA)	64 46 62
1951	S. Fry (USA)	D. Hart (USA)	63 36 63
1952	D. Hart (USA)	S. Fry (USA)	64 64
1953	M. Connolly (USA)	D. Hart (USA)	62 64
1954	M. Connolly (USA)	G. Bucaille (FRA)	64 61

Year	Champion	Runner-up	Score
1955	A. Mortimer (GBR)	D. Knode (USA)	26 75 108
1956	A. Gibson (USA)	A. Mortimer (GBR)	60 1210
1957	S. Bloomer (GBR)	D. Knode (USA)	61 63
1958	Z. Kormoczy (HUN)	S. Bloomer (GBR)	64 16 62
1959	C. Truman (GBR)	Z. Kormoczy (HUN)	64 75
1960	D. Hard (USA)	Y. Ramirez (MEX)	63 64
1961	A. Haydon (GBR)	Y. Ramirez (MEX)	62 61
1962	M. Smith (AUS)	L. Turner (AUS)	63 36 75
1963	L. Turner (AUS)	A. Haydon Jones (GBR)	26 63 75
1964	M. Smith (AUS)	M. Bueno (BRA)	57 61 62
1965	L. Turner (AUS)	M. Smith (AUS)	63 64
1966	A. Haydon Jones (GBR)	Nancy Richey (USA)	63 61
1967	F. Durr (FRA)	L. Turner (AUS)	46 63 64
1968	N. Richey (USA)	A. Haydon Jones (GBR)	57 64 61
1969	M. Smith Court (AUS)	A. Haydon Jones (GBR)	61 46 63
1970	M. Smith Court (AUS)	H. Niessen (GER)	62 64
1971	E. Goolagong (AUS)	H. Gourlay (AUS)	63 75
1972	B. King (USA)	E. Goolagong (AUS)	63 63
1973	M. Smith Court (AUS)	C. Evert (USA)	67 76 64
1974	C. Evert (USA)	O. Morozova (URS)	61 62
1975	C. Evert (USA)	M. Navratilova (TCH)	26 62 61
1976	S. Barker (GBR)	R. Tomanova (TCH)	62 06 62
1977	M. Jausovec (YUG)	F. Mihai (ROM)	62 67 61
1978	V. Ruzici (ROM)	M. Jausovec (YUG)	62 62
1979	C. Evert Lloyd (USA)	W. Turnbull (AUS)	62 60
1980	C. Evert Lloyd (USA)	V. Ruzici (ROM)	60 63
1981	H. Mandlikova (TCH)	S. Hanika (GER)	62 64
1982	M. Navratilova (USA)	A. Jaeger (USA)	76 61
1983	C. Evert Lloyd (USA)	M. Jausovec (YUG)	61 62
1984	M. Navratilova (USA)	C. Evert Lloyd (USA)	63 61
1985	C. Evert Lloyd (USA)	M. Navratilova (USA)	63 67 75
1986	C. Evert Lloyd (USA)	M. Navratilova (USA)	26 63 63
1987	S. Graf (GER)	M. Navratilova (USA)	64 46 86
1988	S. Graf (GER)	N. Zvereva (URS)	60 60
1989	A. Sanchez (ESP)	S. Graf (GER)	76 36 75
1990	M. Seles (YUG)	S. Graf (GER)	76 64
1991	M. Seles (YUG)	A. Sanchez-Vicario (ESP)	63 64
1992	M. Seles (YUG)	S. Graf (GER)	62 36 108
1993	S. Graf (GER)	M. Fernandez (USA)	46 62 64
1994	A. Sanchez-Vicario (ESP)	M. Pierce (FRA)	64 64
1995	S. Graf (GER)	A. Sanchez-Vicario (ESP)	75 46 60
1996	S. Graf (GER)	A. Sanchez-Vicario (ESP)	63 67 108
1997	I. Majoli (CRO)	M. Hingis (SUI)	64 62
1998	A. Sanchez-Vicario (ESP)	M. Seles (USA)	76 06 62
1999	S. Graf (GER)	M. Hingis (SUI)	46 75 62
2000	M. Pierce (FRA)	C. Martinez (ESP)	62 75
2001	J. Capriati (USA)	K. Clijsters (BEL)	16 64 1210
2002	S. Williams (USA)	V. Williams (USA)	75 63
2003	J. Henin-Hardenne (BEL)	K. Clijsters (BEL)	60 64
2004	A. Myskina (RUS)	E. Dementieva (RUS)	61 62

	Men's Doubles	**Women's Doubles**	**Mixed Doubles**
Year	Champions	Champions	Champions
1891	B. Desjoyau/T. Legrand		
1892	J. Havet/D. Albertini		

French Championships Roland Garros (continued)

Year	Champions	Champions	Champions
1893	J. Schopfer/Goldsmith		
1894	G. Brosselin/Lesage		
1895	A. Vacherot/G. Winzer		
1896	F. Warden/Wynes		
1897	P. Ayme/P. Lebreton		
1898	M. Vacherot/X. Casdagli		
1899	P. Ayme/P. Lebreton		
1900	P. Ayme/P. Lebreton		
1901	A. Vacherot/M. Vacherot		
1902	M. Decugis/J. Worth		R. Forbes/Y. Prevost
1903	M. Decugis/J. Worth		R. Forbes/Y. Prevost
1904	M. Decugis/M. Germot		M. Decugis/K. Gillou
1905	M. Decugis/J. Worth		M. Decugis/Y. De Pfoeffel
1906	M. Decugis/M. Germot		M. Decugis/Y. De Pfoeffel
1907	M. Decugis/M. Germot	F. Masson/Y. De Pfoeffel	R. Wallet/A. Pean
1908	M. Decugis/M. Germot	K. Fenwick/C. Matthey	M. Decugis/K. Gillou Fenwick
1909	M. Decugis/M. Germot	J. Matthey/D. Speranza	M. Decugis/J. Matthey
1910	M. Dupont/M. Germot	J. Matthey/D. Speranza	M. Meny/M. Meny
1911	M. Decugis/M. Germot	J. Matthey/D. Speranza	A. Gobert/M. Broquedis
1912	M. Decugis/M. Germot	J. Matthey/D. Speranza	W. Laurentz/D. Speranza
1913	M. Decugis/M. Germot	B. Amblard/S. Amblard	W. Laurentz/D. Speranza
1914	M. Decugis/M. Germot	B. Amblard/S. Amblard	M. Decugis/S. Lenglen
1915-1919 not played			
1920	M. Decugis/M. Germot	E. d'Ayen/S. Lenglen	M. Decugis/S. Lenglen
1921	A. Gobert/W. Laurentz	S. Lenglen/F. Pigueron	J. Brugnon/S. Lenglen
1922	J. Brugnon/M. Dupont	S. Lenglen/F. Pigueron	J. Brugnon/S. Lenglen
1923	F. Blanchy/J. Samazeuilh	S. Lenglen/D. Vlasto	J. Brugnon/S. Lenglen
1924	J. Borotra/R. Lacoste	M. Billout/Y. Bourgeois	J. Borotra/M. Broquedis
1925	J. Borotra/R. Lacoste	S. Lenglen/D. Vlasto	J. Brugnon/S. Lenglen
1926	H. Kinsey/V. Richards	S. Lenglen/D. Vlasto	J. Brugnon/S. Lenglen
1927	J. Brugnon/H. Cochet	B. Heine/I. Peacock	J. Borotra/M. Broquedis
1928	J. Borotra/J. Brugnon	E. Bennett/P. Watson	H. Cochet/E. Bennett
1929	J. Borotra/R. Lacoste	L. De Alvarez/K. Bouman	H. Cochet/E. Bennett
1930	J. Brugnon/H. Cochet	H. Moody/E. Ryan	W. Tilden/C. Aussem
1931	G. Lott/J. Van Ryn	B. Nuthall/E. Bennett-Whittingstall	P. Spense/B. Nuthall
1932	J. Brugnon/H. Cochet	H. Moody/E. Ryan	F. Perry/B. Nuthall
1933	P. Hughes/F. Perry	S. Mathieu/E. Ryan	J. Crawford/M. Scriven
1934	J. Borotra/J. Brugnon	S. Mathieu/E. Ryan	J. Borotra/C. Rosambert
1935	J. Crawford/A. Quist	M. Scriven/K. Stammers	M. Bernard/L. Payot
1936	M. Bernard/J. Borotra	S. Mathieu/A. Yorke	M. Bernard/A. Yorke
1937	G. Von Cramm/H. Henkel	S. Mathieu/A. Yorke	Y. Petra/S. Mathieu
1938	B. Destremau/Y. Petra	S. Mathieu/A. Yorke	D. Mitic/S. Mathieu
1939	C. Harris/W. McNeill	J. Jedrzejowska/S. Mathieu	E. Cooke/S. Fabyan
1940-1945 not played			
1946	M. Bernard/Y. Petra	L. Brough/M. Osborne	B. Patty/P. Betz
1947	E. Fannin/E. Sturgess	L. Brough/M. Osborne	E. Sturgess/S. Summers
1948	L. Bergelin/J. Drobny	D. Hart/P. Todd	J. Drobny/P. Todd
1949	R. Gonzales/F. Parker	L. Brough/M. Osborne DuPont	E. Sturgess/S. Summers
1950	W. Talbert/T. Trabert	S. Fry/D. Hart	E. Morea/B. Scofield
1951	K. McGregor/F. Sedgman	S. Fry/D. Hart	F. Sedgman/D. Hart
1952	K. McGregor/F. Sedgman	S. Fry/D. Hart	F. Sedgman/D. Hart
1953	L. Hoad/K. Rosewall	S. Fry/D. Hart	V. Seixas/D. Hart
1954	V. Seixas/T. Trabert	M. Connolly/N. Hopman	L. Hoad/M. Connolly
1955	V. Seixas/T. Trabert	B. Fleitz/D. Hard	G. Forbes/D. Hard
1956	D. Candy/R. Perry	A. Buxton/A. Gibson	L. Ayala/T. Long

Year	Champions	Champions	Champions
1957	M. Anderson/A. Cooper	S. Bloomer/D. Hard	J. Javorsky/V. Puzejova
1958	A. Cooper/N. Fraser	Y. Ramirez/R. Reyes	N. Pietrangeli/S. Bloomer
1959	N. Pietrangeli/O. Sirola	S. Reynolds/R. Schuurman	W. Knight/Y. Ramirez
1960	R. Emerson/N. Fraser	M. Bueno/D. Hard	R. Howe/M. Bueno
1961	R. Emerson/R. Laver	S. Reynolds/R. Schuurman	R. Laver/D. Hard
1962	R. Emerson/N. Fraser	S. Reynolds/R. Schuurman	R. Howe/R. Schuurmann
1963	R. Emerson/M. Santana	A. Jones/R. Schuurman	K. Fletcher/M. Smith
1964	R. Emerson/K. Fletcher	M. Smith/L. Turner	K. Fletcher/M. Smith
1965	R. Emerson/F. Stolle	M. Smith/L. Turner	K. Fletcher/M. Smith
1966	C. Graebner/D. Ralston	M. Smith/J. Tegart	F. McMillan/A. Van Zyl
1967	J. Newcombe/T. Roche	F. Durr/G. Sheriff	O. Davidson/B. King
1968	K. Rosewall/F. Stolle	F. Durr/A. Jones	J. Barclay/F. Durr
1969	J. Newcombe/T. Roche	F. Durr/A. Jones	M. Riessen/M. Smith Court
1970	I. Nastase/I. Tiriac	G. Sheriff Chanfreau/F. Durr	R. Hewitt/B. King
1971	A. Ashe/M. Riessen	G. Sheriff Chanfreau/F. Durr	J. Barclay/F. Durr
1972	R. Hewitt/F. McMillan	B. King/B. Stove	K. Warwick/E. Goolagong
1973	J. Newcombe/T. Okker	M. Smith Court/V. Wade	J. Barclay/F. Durr
1974	R. Crealy/O. Parun	C. Evert/O. Morozova	I. Molina/M. Navratilova
1975	B. Gottfried/R. Ramirez	C. Evert/M. Navratilova	T. Koch/F. Bonicelli
1976	F. McNair/S. Stewart	F. Bonicelli/G. Sheriff Lovera	K. Warwick/I. Kloss
1977	B. Gottfried/R. Ramirez	R. Marsikova/P. Teeguarden	J. McEnroe/M. Carillo
1978	G. Mayer/H. Pfister	M. Jausovec/V. Ruzici	P. Slozil/R. Tomanova
1979	S. Mayer/G. Mayer	B. Stove/W. Turnbull	R. Hewitt/W. Turnbull
1980	V. Amaya/H. Pfister	K. Jordan/A. Smith	W. Martin/A. Smith
1981	H. Gunthardt/B. Taroczy	R. Fairbank/T. Harford	J. Arias/A. Jaeger
1982	S. Stewart/F. Taygan	M. Navratilova/A. Smith	J. Lloyd/W. Turnbull
1983	A. Jarryd/H. Simonsson	R. Fairbank/C. Reynolds	E. Teltscher/B. Jordan
1984	Y. Noah/H. Leconte	M. Navratilova/P. Shriver	D. Stockton/A. Smith
1985	M. Edmondson/K. Warwick	M. Navratilova/P. Shriver	H. Gunthardt/M. Navratilova
1986	J. Fitzgerald/T. Smid	M. Navratilova/A. Temesvari	K. Flach/K. Jordan
1987	A. Jarryd/R. Seguso	M. Navratilova/P. Shriver	E. Sanchez/P. Shriver
1988	A. Gomez/E. Sanchez	M. Navratilova/P. Shriver	J. Lozano/L. McNeil
1989	J. Grabb/P. McEnroe	L. Savchenko/N. Zvereva	T. Nijssen/M. Bollegraf
1990	S. Casal/E. Sanchez	J. Novotna/H. Sukova	J. Lozano/A. Sanchez
1991	J. Fitzgerald/A. Jarryd	G. Fernandez/J. Novotna	C. Suk/H. Sukova
1992	J. Hlasek/M. Rosset	G. Fernandez/N. Zvereva	T. Woodbridge/A. Sanchez
1993	L. Jensen/M. Jensen	G. Fernandez/N. Zvereva	A. Olhovskiy/E. Maniokova
1994	B. Black/J. Stark	G. Fernandez/N. Zvereva	M. Oosting/K. Boogert
1995	J. Eltingh/P. Haarhuis	G. Fernandez/N. Zvereva	M. Woodforde/L. Neiland
1996	Y. Kafelnikov/D. Vacek	L. Davenport/M. Fernandez	J. Frana/P. Tarabini
1997	Y. Kafelnikov/D. Vacek	G. Fernandez/N. Zvereva	M. Bhupathi/R. Hiraki
1998	J. Eltingh/P. Haarhuis	M. Hingis/J. Novotna	J. Gimelstob/V. Williams
1999	M. Bhupathi/L. Paes	V. Williams/S. Williams	P. Norval/K. Srebotnik
2000	M. Woodforde/T. Woodbridge	M. Hingis/M. Pierce	D. Adams/M. De Swardt
2001	M. Bhupathi/L. Paes	V. Ruano Pascual/P. Suarez	T. Carbonell/V. Ruano Pascual
2002	P. Haarhuis/Y. Kafelnikov	V. Ruano Pascual/P. Suarez	W. Black/C. Black
2003	B. Bryan/M. Bryan	K. Clijsters/A. Sugiyama	M. Bryan/L. Raymond
2004	X. Malisse/O. Rochus	V. Ruano Pascual/P. Suarez	R. Gasquet/T. Golovin

The Championships, Wimbledon

Men's Singles

Year	Champion	Runner-up	Score
1877	S. Gore (GBR)	W. Marshall (GBR)	61 62 64
1878	P. Hadow (GBR)	S. Gore (GBR)	75 61 97
1879	J. Hartley (GBR)	V. St L. Goold (GBR)	62 64 62
1880	J. Hartley (GBR)	H. Lawford (GBR)	63 62 26 63
1881	W. Renshaw (GBR)	J. Hartley (GBR)	60 61 61
1882	W. Renshaw (GBR)	E. Renshaw (GBR)	61 26 46 62 62
1883	W. Renshaw (GBR)	E. Renshaw (GBR)	26 63 63 46 63
1884	W. Renshaw (GBR)	H. Lawford (GBR)	60 64 97
1885	W. Renshaw (GBR)	H. Lawford (GBR)	75 62 46 75
1886	W. Renshaw (GBR)	H. Lawford (GBR)	60 57 63 64
1887	H. Lawford (GBR)	E. Renshaw (GBR)	16 63 36 64 64
1888	E. Renshaw (GBR)	H. Lawford (GBR)	63 75 60
1889	W. Renshaw (GBR)	E. Renshaw (GBR)	64 61 36 60
1890	W. Hamilton (GBR)	W. Renshaw (GBR)	68 62 36 61 61
1891	W. Baddeley (GBR)	J. Pim (GBR)	64 16 75 60
1892	W. Baddeley (GBR)	J. Pim (GBR)	46 63 63 62
1893	J. Pim (GBR)	W. Baddeley (GBR)	36 61 63 62
1894	J. Pim (GBR)	W. Baddeley (GBR)	108 62 86
1895	W. Baddeley (GBR)	W. Eaves (GBR)	46 26 86 62 63
1896	H. Mahony (GBR)	W. Baddeley (GBR)	62 68 57 86 63
1897	R. Doherty (GBR)	H. Mahony (GBR)	64 64 63
1898	R. Doherty (GBR)	H. Doherty (GBR)	63 63 26 57 61
1899	R. Doherty (GBR)	A. Gore (GBR)	16 46 63 63 63
1900	R. Doherty (GBR)	S. Smith (GBR)	68 63 61 62
1901	A. Gore (GBR)	R. Doherty (GBR)	46 75 64 64
1902	H. Doherty (GBR)	A. Gore (GBR)	64 63 36 60
1903	H. Doherty (GBR)	F. Riseley (GBR)	75 63 60
1904	H. Doherty (GBR)	F. Riseley (GBR)	61 75 86
1905	H. Doherty (GBR)	N. Brookes (AUS)	86 62 64
1906	H. Doherty (GBR)	F. Riseley (GBR)	64 46 62 63
1907	N. Brookes (AUS)	A. Gore (GBR)	64 62 62
1908	A. Gore (GBR)	H. Roper Barrett (GBR)	63 62 46 36 64
1909	A. Gore (GBR)	M. Ritchie (GBR)	68 16 62 62 62
1910	A. Wilding (NZL)	A. Gore (GBR)	64 75 46 62
1911	A. Wilding (NZL)	H. Roper Barrett (GBR)	64 46 26 62 ret.
1912	A. Wilding (NZL)	A. Gore (GBR)	64 64 46 64
1913	A. Wilding (NZL)	M. McLoughlin (USA)	86 63 108
1914	N. Brookes (AUS)	A. Wilding (NZL)	64 64 75
1915-18 not played			
1919	G. Patterson (AUS)	N. Brookes (AUS)	63 75 62
1920	W. Tilden (USA)	G. Patterson (AUS)	26 62 62 64
1921	W. Tilden (USA)	B. Norton (RSA)	46 26 61 60 75
1922	G. Patterson (AUS)	R. Lycett (GBR)	63 64 62
1923	W. Johnston (USA)	F. Hunter (USA)	60 63 61
1924	J. Borotra (FRA)	R. Lacoste (FRA)	61 36 61 36 64
1925	R. Lacoste (FRA)	J. Borotra (FRA)	63 63 46 86
1926	J. Borotra (FRA)	H. Kinsey (USA)	86 61 63
1927	H. Cochet (FRA)	J. Borotra (FRA)	46 46 63 64 75
1928	R. Lacoste (FRA)	H. Cochet (FRA)	61 46 64 62
1929	H. Cochet (FRA)	J. Borotra (FRA)	64 63 64
1930	W. Tilden (USA)	W. Allison (USA)	63 97 64
1931	S. Wood (USA)	F. Shields (USA)	w/o
1932	E. Vines (USA)	H. Austin (GBR)	62 62 60
1933	J. Crawford (AUS)	E. Vines (USA)	46 119 62 26 64

Year	Champion	Runner-up	Score
1934	F. Perry (GBR)	J. Crawford (AUS)	63 60 75
1935	F. Perry (GBR)	G. Von Cramm (GER)	62 64 64
1936	F. Perry (GBR)	G. Von Cramm (GER)	61 61 60
1937	D. Budge (USA)	G. Von Cramm (GER)	63 64 62
1938	D. Budge (USA)	H. Austin (GBR)	61 60 63
1939	R. Riggs (USA)	E. Cooke (USA)	26 86 36 63 62
1940-45 not played			
1946	Y. Petra (FRA)	G. Brown (AUS)	62 64 79 57 64
1947	J. Kramer (USA)	T. Brown (USA)	61 63 62
1948	R. Falkenburg (USA)	J. Bromwich (AUS)	75 06 62 36 75
1949	F. Schroeder (USA)	J. Drobny (TCH)	36 60 63 46 64
1950	B. Patty (USA)	F. Sedgman (AUS)	61 810 62 63
1951	R. Savitt (USA)	K. McGregor (AUS)	64 64 64
1952	F. Sedgman (AUS)	J. Drobny (EGY)	46 62 63 62
1953	V. Seixas (USA)	K. Nielsen (DEN)	97 63 64
1954	J. Drobny (EGY)	K. Rosewall (AUS)	1311 46 62 97
1955	T. Trabert (USA)	K. Nielsen (DEN)	63 75 61
1956	L. Hoad (AUS)	K. Rosewall (AUS)	62 46 75 64
1957	L. Hoad (AUS)	A. Cooper (AUS)	62 61 62
1958	A. Cooper (AUS)	N. Fraser (AUS)	36 63 64 1311
1959	A. Olmedo (USA)	R. Laver (AUS)	64 63 64
1960	N. Fraser (AUS)	R. Laver (AUS)	64 36 97 75
1961	R. Laver (AUS)	C. McKinley (USA)	63 61 64
1962	R. Laver (AUS)	M. Mulligan (AUS)	62 62 61
1963	C. McKinley (USA)	F. Stolle (AUS)	97 61 64
1964	R. Emerson (AUS)	F. Stolle (AUS)	64 1210 46 63
1965	R. Emerson (AUS)	F. Stolle (AUS)	62 64 64
1966	M. Santana (ESP)	R. Ralston (USA)	64 119 64
1967	J. Newcombe (AUS)	W. Bungert (GER)	63 61 61
1968	R. Laver (AUS)	T. Roche (AUS)	63 64 62
1969	R. Laver (AUS)	J. Newcombe (AUS)	64 57 64 64
1970	J. Newcombe (AUS)	K. Rosewall (AUS)	57 63 62 36 61
1971	J. Newcombe (AUS)	S. Smith (USA)	63 57 26 64 64
1972	S. Smith (USA)	I. Nastase (ROM)	46 63 63 46 75
1973	J. Kodes (TCH)	A. Metreveli (URS)	61 98 63
1974	J. Connors (USA)	K. Rosewall (AUS)	61 61 64
1975	A. Ashe (USA)	J. Connors (USA)	61 61 57 64
1976	B. Borg (SWE)	I. Nastase (ROM)	64 62 97
1977	B. Borg (SWE)	J. Connors (USA)	36 62 61 57 64
1978	B. Borg (SWE)	J. Connors (USA)	62 62 63
1979	B. Borg (SWE)	R. Tanner (USA)	67 61 36 63 64
1980	B. Borg (SWE)	J. McEnroe (USA)	16 75 63 67 86
1981	J. McEnroe (USA)	B. Borg (SWE)	46 76 76 64
1982	J. Connors (USA)	J. McEnroe (USA)	36 63 67 76 64
1983	J. McEnroe (USA)	C. Lewis (NZL)	62 62 62
1984	J. McEnroe (USA)	J. Connors (USA)	61 61 62
1985	B. Becker (GER)	K. Curren (USA)	63 67 76 64
1986	B. Becker (GER)	I. Lendl (TCH)	64 63 75
1987	P. Cash (AUS)	I. Lendl (TCH)	76 62 75
1988	S. Edberg (SWE)	B. Becker (GER)	46 76 64 62
1989	B. Becker (GER)	S. Edberg (SWE)	60 76 64
1990	S. Edberg (SWE)	B. Becker (GER)	62 62 36 36 64
1991	M. Stich (GER)	B. Becker (GER)	64 76 64
1992	A. Agassi (USA)	G. Ivanisevic (CRO)	67 64 64 16 64
1993	P. Sampras (USA)	J. Courier (USA)	76 76 36 63

The Championships, Wimbledon (continued)

Year	Champion	Runner-up	Score
1994	P. Sampras (USA)	G. Ivanisevic (CRO)	76 76 60
1995	P. Sampras (USA)	B. Becker (GER)	67 62 64 62
1996	R. Krajicek (NED)	M. Washington (USA)	63 64 63
1997	P. Sampras (USA)	C. Pioline (FRA)	64 62 64
1998	P. Sampras (USA)	G. Ivanisevic (CRO)	67 76 64 36 62
1999	P. Sampras (USA)	A. Agassi (USA)	63 64 75
2000	P. Sampras (USA)	P. Rafter (AUS)	67 76 64 62
2001	G. Ivanisevic (CRO)	P. Rafter (AUS)	63 36 63 26 97
2002	L. Hewitt (AUS)	D. Nalbandian (ARG)	61 63 62
2003	R. Federer (SUI)	M. Philippoussis (AUS)	76 62 76
2004	R. Federer (SUI)	A. Roddick (USA)	46 75 76 64

Women's Singles

Year	Champion	Runner-up	Score
1884	M. Watson (GBR)	L. Watson (GBR)	68 63 63
1885	M. Watson (GBR)	B. Bingley (GBR)	61 75
1886	B. Bingley (GBR)	M. Watson (GBR)	63 63
1887	C. Dod (GBR)	B. Bingley (GBR)	62 60
1888	C. Dod (GBR)	B. Bingley Hillyard (GBR)	63 63
1889	B. Bingley Hillyard (GBR)	H. Rice (GBR)	46 86 64
1890	H. Rice (GBR)	M. Jacks (GBR)	64 61
1891	C. Dod (GBR)	B. Bingley Hillyard (GBR)	62 61
1892	C. Dod (GBR)	B. Bingley Hillyard (GBR)	61 61
1893	C. Dod (GBR)	B. Bingley Hillyard (GBR)	68 61 64
1894	B. Bingley Hillyard (GBR)	L. Austin (GBR)	61 61
1895	C. Cooper (GBR)	H. Jackson (GBR)	75 86
1896	C. Cooper (GBR)	Mrs W. Pickering (GBR)	62 63
1897	B. Bingley Hillyard (GBR)	C. Cooper (GBR)	57 75 62
1898	C. Cooper (GBR)	L. Martin (GBR)	64 64
1899	B. Bingley Hillyard (GBR)	C. Cooper (GBR)	62 63
1900	B. Bingley Hillyard (GBR)	C. Cooper (GBR)	46 64 64
1901	C. Sterry (GBR)	B. Bingley Hillyard (GBR)	62 62
1902	M. Robb (GBR)	C. Sterry (GBR)	75 61
1903	D. Douglass (GBR)	E. Thomson (GBR)	46 64 62
1904	D. Douglass (GBR)	C. Sterry (GBR)	60 63
1905	M. Sutton (USA)	D. Douglass (GBR)	63 64
1906	D. Douglass (GBR)	M. Sutton (USA)	63 97
1907	M. Sutton (USA)	D. Douglass Lambert Chambers (GBR)	61 64
1908	C. Sterry (GBR)	A. Morton (GBR)	64 64
1909	D. Boothby (GBR)	A. Morton (GBR)	64 46 86
1910	D. Douglass Lambert Chambers (GBR)	D. Boothby (GBR)	62 62
1911	D. Douglass Lambert Chambers (GBR)	D. Boothby (GBR)	60 60
1912	Mrs D. Larcombe (GBR)	C. Sterry (GBR)	63 61
1913	D. Douglass Lambert Chambers (GBR)	Mrs R. McNair (GBR)	60 64
1914	D. Douglass Lambert Chambers (GBR)	E. Larcombe (GBR)	75 64
1915-18 not played			
1919	S. Lenglen (FRA)	D. Douglass Lambert Chambers (GBR)	108 46 97
1920	S. Lenglen (FRA)	D. Douglass Lambert Chambers (GBR)	63 60
1921	S. Lenglen (FRA)	E. Ryan (USA)	62 60
1922	S. Lenglen (FRA)	M. Mallory (USA)	62 60
1923	S. Lenglen (FRA)	K. McKane (GBR)	62 62
1924	K. McKane (GBR)	H. Wills (USA)	46 64 64
1925	S. Lenglen (FRA)	J. Fry (GBR)	62 60
1926	K. McKane Godfree (GBR)	E. De Alvarez (ESP)	62 46 63
1927	H. Wills (USA)	E. De Alvarez (ESP)	62 64

Year	Champion	Runner-up	Score
1928	H. Wills (USA)	E. De Alvarez (ESP)	62 63
1929	H. Wills (USA)	H. Jacobs (USA)	61 62
1930	H. Wills Moody (USA)	E. Ryan (USA)	62 62
1931	C. Aussem (GER)	H. Krahwinkel (GER)	62 75
1932	H. Wills Moody (USA)	H. Jacobs (USA)	63 61
1933	H. Wills Moody (USA)	D. Round (GBR)	64 68 63
1934	D. Round (GBR)	H. Jacobs (USA)	62 57 63
1935	H. Wills Moody (USA)	H. Jacobs (USA)	63 36 75
1936	H. Jacobs (USA)	H. Sperling (GER)	62 46 75
1937	D. Round (GBR)	J. Jedrzejowska (POL)	62 26 75
1938	H. Wills Moody (USA)	H. Jacobs (USA)	64 60
1939	A. Marble (USA)	K. Stammers (GBR)	62 60
1940-45 not played			
1946	P. Betz (USA)	L. Brough (USA)	62 64
1947	M. Osborne (USA)	D. Hart (USA)	62 64
1948	L. Brough (USA)	D. Hart (USA)	63 86
1949	L. Brough (USA)	M. Osborne DuPont (USA)	108 16 108
1950	L. Brough (USA)	M. Osborne DuPont (USA)	61 36 61
1951	D. Hart (USA)	S. Fry (USA)	61 60
1952	M. Connolly (USA)	L. Brough (USA)	75 63
1953	M. Connolly (USA)	D. Hart (USA)	86 75
1954	M. Connolly (USA)	L. Brough (USA)	62 75
1955	L. Brough (USA)	B. Fleitz (USA)	75 86
1956	S. Fry (USA)	A. Buxton (GBR)	63 61
1957	A. Gibson (USA)	D. Hard (USA)	63 62
1958	A. Gibson (USA)	A. Mortimer (GBR)	86 62
1959	M. Bueno (BRA)	D. Hard (USA)	64 63
1960	M. Bueno (BRA)	S. Reynolds (RSA)	86 60
1961	A. Mortimer (GBR)	C. Truman (GBR)	46 64 75
1962	K. Susman (USA)	V. Sukova (TCH)	64 64
1963	M. Smith (AUS)	B. Moffitt (USA)	63 64
1964	M. Bueno (BRA)	M. Smith (AUS)	64 79 63
1965	M. Smith (AUS)	M. Bueno (BRA)	64 75
1966	B. King (USA)	M. Bueno (BRA)	63 36 61
1967	B. King (USA)	A. Jones (GBR)	63 64
1968	B. King (USA)	J. Tegart (AUS)	97 75
1969	A. Jones (GBR)	B. King (USA)	36 63 62
1970	M. Smith Court (AUS)	B. King (USA)	1412 119
1971	E. Goolagong (AUS)	M. Smith Court (AUS)	64 61
1972	B. King (USA)	E. Goolagong (AUS)	63 63
1973	B. King (USA)	C. Evert (USA)	60 75
1974	C. Evert (USA)	O. Morozova (URS)	60 64
1975	B. King (USA)	E. Goolagong Cawley (AUS)	60 61
1976	C. Evert (USA)	E. Goolagong Cawley (AUS)	63 46 86
1977	V. Wade (GBR)	B. Stove (NED)	46 63 61
1978	M. Navratilova (USA)	C. Evert (USA)	26 64 75
1979	M. Navratilova (USA)	C. Evert Lloyd (USA)	64 64
1980	E. Goolagong Cawley (AUS)	C. Evert Lloyd (USA)	61 76
1981	C. Evert Lloyd (USA)	H. Mandlikova (TCH)	62 62
1982	M. Navratilova (USA)	C. Evert Lloyd (USA)	61 36 62
1983	M. Navratilova (USA)	A. Jaeger (USA)	60 63
1984	M. Navratilova (USA)	C. Evert Lloyd (USA)	76 62
1985	M. Navratilova (USA)	C. Evert Lloyd (USA)	46 63 62
1986	M. Navratilova (USA)	H. Mandlikova (TCH)	76 63
1987	M. Navratilova (USA)	S. Graf (GER)	75 63

The Championships, Wimbledon (continued)

Year	Champion	Runner-up	Score
1988	S. Graf (GER)	M. Navratilova (USA)	57 62 61
1989	S. Graf (GER)	M. Navratilova (USA)	62 67 61
1990	M. Navratilova (USA)	Z. Garrison (USA)	64 61
1991	S. Graf (GER)	G. Sabatini (ARG)	64 36 86
1992	S. Graf (GER)	M. Seles (YUG)	62 61
1993	S. Graf (GER)	J. Novotna (CZE)	76 16 64
1994	C. Martinez (ESP)	M. Navratilova (USA)	64 36 63
1995	S. Graf (GER)	A. Sanchez-Vicario (ESP)	46 61 75
1996	S. Graf (GER)	A. Sanchez-Vicario (ESP)	63 75
1997	M. Hingis (SUI)	J. Novotna (CZE)	26 63 63
1998	J. Novotna (CZE)	N. Tauziat (FRA)	64 76
1999	L. Davenport (USA)	S. Graf (GER)	64 75
2000	V. Williams (USA)	L. Davenport (USA)	63 76
2001	V. Williams (USA)	J. Henin (BEL)	61 36 60
2002	S. Williams (USA)	V. Williams (USA)	76 63
2003	S. Williams (USA)	V. Williams (USA)	46 64 62
2004	M. Sharapova (RUS)	S. Williams (USA)	61 64

Year	Men's Doubles Champions	Women's Doubles Champions	Mixed Doubles Champions
1884	E. Renshaw/W. Renshaw		
1885	E. Renshaw/W. Renshaw		
1886	E. Renshaw/W. Renshaw		
1887	P. Lyon/W. Wilberforce		
1888	E. Renshaw/W. Renshaw		
1889	E. Renshaw/W. Renshaw		
1890	J. Pim/F. Stoker		
1891	H. Baddeley/W. Baddeley		
1892	H. Barlow/E. Lewis		
1893	J. Pim/F. Stoker		
1894	H. Baddeley/W. Baddeley		
1895	H. Baddeley/W. Baddeley		
1896	H. Baddeley/W. Baddeley		
1897	H. Doherty/R. Doherty		
1898	H. Doherty/R. Doherty		
1899	H. Doherty/R. Doherty		
1900	H. Doherty/R. Doherty		
1901	H. Doherty/R. Doherty		
1902	F. Riseley/S. Smith		
1903	H. Doherty/R. Doherty		
1904	H. Doherty/R. Doherty		
1905	H. Doherty/R. Doherty		
1906	F. Riseley/S. Smith		
1907	N. Brookes/A. Wilding		
1908	M. Ritchie/A. Wilding		
1909	A. Gore/H. Roper Barrett		
1910	M. Ritchie/A. Wilding		
1911	M. Decugis/A. Gobert		
1912	C. Dixon/H. Roper Barrett		
1913	C. Dixon/H. Roper Barrett	P. Boothby/Mrs R. McNair	H. Crisp/Mrs C. Tuckey
1914	N. Brookes/A. Wilding	A. Morton/E. Ryan	J. Parke/E. Larcombe
1915-1918 not played			
1919	P. O'Hara Wood/R. Thomas	S. Lenglen/E. Ryan	R. Lycett/E. Ryan
1920	C. Garland/R. Williams	S. Lenglen/E. Ryan	G. Patterson/S. Lenglen
1921	R. Lycett/M. Woosnam	S. Lenglen/E. Ryan	R. Lycett/E. Ryan

Year	Champions	Champions	Champions
1922	J. Anderson/R. Lycett	S. Lenglen/E. Ryan	P. O'Hara Wood/S. Lenglen
1923	L. Godfree/R. Lycett	S. Lenglen/E. Ryan	R. Lycett/E. Ryan
1924	F. Hunter/V. Richards	H. Hotchkiss Wightman/H. Wills	J. Gilbert/K. McKane
1925	J. Borotra/R. Lacoste	S. Lenglen/E. Ryan	J. Borotra/S. Lenglen
1926	J. Brugnon/H. Cochet	M. Browne/E. Ryan	L. Godfree/K. McKane Godfree
1927	F. Hunter/W. Tilden	E. Ryan/H. Wills	F. Hunter/E. Ryan
1928	J. Brugnon/H. Cochet	M. Saunders/P. Watson	P. Spence/E. Ryan
1929	W. Allison/J. Van Ryn	M. Mitchell/P. Watson	F. Hunter/H. Wills
1930	W. Allison/J. Van Ryn	H. Wills Moody/E. Ryan	J. Crawford/E. Ryan
1931	G. Lott/J. Van Ryn	P. Mudford/Mrs W. Shepherd-Barron	G. Lott/Mrs L. Harper
1932	J. Borotra/J. Brugnon	D. Metaxa/J. Sigart	E. Maier/E. Ryan
1933	J. Borotra/J. Brugnon	S. Mathieu/E. Ryan	G. Von Cramm/H. Krahwinkel
1934	G. Lott/L. Stoefen	S. Mathieu/E. Ryan	R. Miki/D. Round
1935	J. Crawford/A. Quist	W. James/K. Stammers	F. Perry/D. Round
1936	G. Hughes/C. Tuckey	W. James/K. Stammers	F. Perry/D. Round
1937	D. Budge/G. Mako	S. Mathieu/A. Yorke	D. Budge/A. Marble
1938	D. Budge/G. Mako	S. Fabyan/A. Marble	D. Budge/A. Marble
1939	E. Cooke/R. Riggs	S. Fabyan/A. Marble	R. Riggs/A. Marble
1940-45 not played			
1946	T. Brown/J. Kramer	L. Brough/M. Osborne	T. Brown/L. Brough
1947	R. Falkenburg/J. Kramer	D. Hart/P. Todd	J. Bromwich/L. Brough
1948	J. Bromwich/F. Sedgman	L. Brough/M. Osborne DuPont	J. Bromwich/L. Brough
1949	R. Gonzales/F. Parker	L. Brough/M. Osborne DuPont	E. Sturgess/Mrs R. Summers
1950	J. Bromwich/A. Quist	L. Brough/M. Osborne DuPont	E. Sturgess/L. Brough
1951	K. McGregor/F. Sedgman	S. Fry/D. Hart	F. Sedgman/D. Hart
1952	K. McGregor/F. Sedgman	S. Fry/D. Hart	F. Sedgman/D. Hart
1953	L. Hoad/K. Rosewall	S. Fry/D. Hart	V. Seixas/D. Hart
1954	R. Hartwig/M. Rose	L. Brough/M. Osborne DuPont	V. Seixas/D. Hart
1955	R. Hartwig/L. Hoad	A. Mortimer/J. Shilcock	V. Seixas/D. Hart
1956	L. Hoad/K. Rosewall	A. Buxton/A. Gibson	V. Seixas/S. Fry
1957	G. Mulloy/J. Patty	A. Gibson/D. Hard	M. Rose/D. Hard
1958	S. Davidson/U. Schmidt	M. Bueno/A. Gibson	R. Howe/L. Coghlan
1959	R. Emerson/N. Fraser	J. Arth/D. Hard	R. Laver/D. Hard
1960	R. Osuna/R. Ralston	M. Bueno/D. Hard	R. Laver/D. Hard
1961	R. Emerson/N. Fraser	K. Hantze/B. Moffitt	F. Stolle/L. Turner
1962	R. Hewitt/F. Stolle	B. Moffitt/K. Susman	N. Fraser/M. Osborne DuPont
1963	R. Osuna/A. Palafox	M. Bueno/D. Hard	K. Fletcher/M. Smith
1964	R. Hewitt/F. Stolle	M. Smith/L. Turner	F. Stolle/L. Turner
1965	J. Newcombe/T. Roche	M. Bueno/B. Moffitt	K. Fletcher/M. Smith
1966	K. Fletcher/J. Newcombe	M. Bueno/N. Richey	K. Fletcher/M. Smith
1967	R. Hewitt/F. McMillan	R. Casals/B. King	O. Davidson/B. King
1968	J. Newcombe/T. Roche	R. Casals/B. King	K. Fletcher/M. Smith Court
1969	J. Newcombe/T. Roche	M. Smith Court/J. Tegart	F. Stolle/A. Jones
1970	J. Newcombe/T. Roche	R. Casals/B. King	I. Nastase/R. Casals
1971	R. Emerson/R. Laver	R. Casals/B. King	O. Davidson/B. King
1972	R. Hewitt/F. McMillan	B. King/B. Stove	I. Nastase/R. Casals
1973	J. Connors/I. Nastase	R. Casals/B. King	O. Davidson/B. King
1974	J. Newcombe/T. Roche	E. Goolagong/M. Michel	O. Davidson/B. King
1975	V. Gerulaitis/A. Mayer	A. Kiyomura/K. Sawamatsu	M. Riessen/M. Smith Court
1976	B. Gottfried/R. Ramirez	C. Evert/M. Navratilova	T. Roche/F. Durr
1977	R. Case/G. Masters	E. Goolagong Cawley/J. Russell	R. Hewitt/G. Stevens
1978	R. Hewitt/F. McMillan	Mrs G. Reid/W. Turnbull	F. McMillan/B. Stove
1979	P. Fleming/J. McEnroe	B. King/M. Navratilova	R. Hewitt/G. Stevens
1980	P. McNamara/P. McNamee	K. Jordan/A. Smith	J. Austin/T. Austin
1981	P. Fleming/J. McEnroe	M. Navratilova/P. Shriver	F. McMillan/B. Stove

The Championships, Wimbledon (continued)

Year	Champions	Champions	Champions
1982	P. McNamara/P. McNamee	M. Navratilova/P. Shriver	K. Curren/A. Smith
1983	P. Fleming/J. McEnroe	M. Navratilova/P. Shriver	J. Lloyd/W. Turnbull
1984	P. Fleming/J. McEnroe	M. Navratilova/P. Shriver	J. Lloyd/W. Turnbull
1985	H. Gunthardt/B. Taroczy	K. Jordan/L. Smylie	P. McNamee/M. Navratilova
1986	J. Nystrom/M. Wilander	M. Navratilova/P. Shriver	K. Flach/K. Jordan
1987	K. Flach/R. Seguso	C. Kohde-Kilsch/H. Sukova	J. Bates/J. Durie
1988	K. Flach/R. Seguso	S. Graf/G. Sabatini	S. Stewart/Z. Garrison
1989	J. Fitzgerald/A. Jarryd	J. Novotna/H. Sukova	J. Pugh/J. Novotna
1990	R. Leach/J. Pugh	J. Novotna/H. Sukova	R. Leach/Z. Garrison
1991	J. Fitzgerald/A. Jarryd	L. Savchenko/N. Zvereva	J. Fitzgerald/L. Smylie
1992	J. McEnroe/M. Stich	G. Fernandez/N. Zvereva	C. Suk/L. Neiland
1993	T. Woodbridge/M. Woodforde	G. Fernandez/N. Zvereva	M. Woodforde/M. Navratilova
1994	T. Woodbridge/M. Woodforde	G. Fernandez/N. Zvereva	T. Woodbridge/H. Sukova
1995	T. Woodbridge/M. Woodforde	J. Novotna/A. Sanchez-Vicario	J. Stark/M. Navratilova
1996	T. Woodbridge/M. Woodforde	M. Hingis/H. Sukova	C. Suk/H. Sukova
1997	T. Woodbridge/M. Woodforde	G. Fernandez/N. Zvereva	C. Suk/H. Sukova
1998	J. Eltingh/P. Haarhuis	M. Hingis/J. Novotna	M. Miryni/S. Williams
1999	M. Bhupathi/L. Paes	L. Davenport/C. Morariu	L. Paes/L. Raymond
2000	T. Woodbridge/M. Woodforde	S. Williams/V. Williams	D. Johnson/K. Po
2001	D. Johnson/J. Palmer	L. Raymond/R. Stubbs	L. Friedl/D. Hantuchova
2002	J. Bjorkman/T. Woodbridge	S. Williams/V. Williams	M. Bhupathi/E. Likhovtseva
2003	J. Bjorkman/T. Woodbridge	K. Clijsters/A. Sugiyama	L. Paes/M. Navratilova
2004	J. Bjorkman/T. Woodbridge	C. Black/R. Stubbs	W. Black/C. Black

US Championships

Men's Singles

Year	Champion	Runner-up	Score
1881	R. Sears (USA)	W. Glyn (USA)	60 63 62
1882	R. Sears (USA)	C. Clark (USA)	61 64 60
1883	R. Sears (USA)	J. Dwight (USA)	62 60 97
1884	R. Sears (USA)	H. Taylor (USA)	60 16 60 62
1885	R. Sears (USA)	G. Brinley (USA)	63 46 60 63
1886	R. Sears (USA)	L. Beeckman (USA)	46 61 63 64
1887	R. Sears (USA)	H. Slocum (USA)	61 63 62
1888	H. Slocum (USA)	H. Taylor (USA)	64 61 60
1889	H. Slocum (USA)	Q. Shaw (USA)	63 61 46 62
1890	O. Campbell (USA)	H. Slocum (USA)	62 46 63 61
1891	O. Campbell (USA)	C. Hobart (USA)	26 75 79 61 62
1892	O. Campbell (USA)	F. Hovey (USA)	75 36 63 75
1893	R. Wrenn (USA)	F. Hovey (USA)	64 36 64 64
1894	R. Wrenn (USA)	M. Goodbody (GBR)	68 61 64 64
1895	F. Hovey (USA)	R. Wrenn (USA)	63 62 64
1896	R. Wrenn (USA)	F. Hovey (USA)	75 36 60 16 61
1897	R. Wrenn (USA)	W. Eaves (GBR)	46 86 63 26 62
1898	M. Whitman (USA)	D. Davis (USA)	36 62 62 61
1899	M. Whitman (USA)	P. Paret (USA)	61 62 36 75
1900	M. Whitman (USA)	W. Larned (USA)	64 16 62 62
1901	W. Larned (USA)	B. Wright (USA)	62 68 64 64
1902	W. Larned (USA)	R. Doherty (GBR)	46 62 64 86
1903	H. Doherty (GBR)	W. Larned (USA)	60 63 108
1904	H. Ward (USA)	W. Clothier (USA)	108 64 97
1905	B. Wright (USA)	H. Ward (USA)	62 61 119
1906	W. Clothier (USA)	B. Wright (USA)	63 60 64

Year	Champion	Runner-up	Score
1907	W. Larned (USA)	R. LeRoy (USA)	62 62 64
1908	W. Larned (USA)	B. Wright (USA)	61 62 86
1909	W. Larned (USA)	W. Clothier (USA)	61 62 57 16 61
1910	W. Larned (USA)	T. Bundy (USA)	61 57 60 68 61
1911	W. Larned (USA)	M. McLoughlin (USA)	64 64 62
1912	M. McLoughlin (USA)	W. Johnson (USA)	36 26 62 64 62
1913	M. McLoughlin (USA)	R. Williams (USA)	64 57 63 61
1914	R. Williams (USA)	M. McLoughlin (USA)	63 86 108
1915	W. Johnston (USA)	M. McLoughlin (USA)	16 60 75 108
1916	R. Williams (USA)	W. Johnston (USA)	46 64 06 62 64
1917	L. Murray (USA)	N. Niles (USA)	57 86 63 63
1918	L. Murray (USA)	W. Tilden (USA)	63 61 75
1919	W. Johnston (USA)	W. Tilden (USA)	64 64 63
1920	W. Tilden (USA)	W. Johnston (USA)	61 16 75 57 63
1921	W. Tilden (USA)	W. Johnston (USA)	61 63 61
1922	W. Tilden (USA)	W. Johnston (USA)	46 36 62 63 64
1923	W. Tilden (USA)	W. Johnston (USA)	64 61 64
1924	W. Tilden (USA)	W. Johnston (USA)	61 97 62
1925	W. Tilden (USA)	W. Johnston (USA)	46 119 63 46 63
1926	R. Lacoste (FRA)	J. Borotra (FRA)	64 60 64
1927	R. Lacoste (FRA)	W. Tilden (USA)	119 63 119
1928	H. Cochet (FRA)	F. Hunter (USA)	46 64 36 75 63
1929	W. Tilden (USA)	F. Hunter (USA)	36 63 46 62 64
1930	J. Doeg (USA)	F. Shields (USA)	108 16 64 1614
1931	E. Vines (USA)	G. Lott (USA)	79 63 97 75
1932	E. Vines (USA)	H. Cochet (FRA)	64 64 64
1933	F. Perry (GBR)	J. Crawford (AUS)	63 1113 46 60 61
1934	F. Perry (GBR)	W. Allison (USA)	64 63 16 86
1935	W. Allison (USA)	S. Wood (USA)	62 62 63
1936	F. Perry (GBR)	D. Budge (USA)	26 62 86 16 108
1937	D. Budge (USA)	G. Von Cramm (GER)	61 79 61 36 61
1938	D. Budge (USA)	G. Mako (USA)	63 68 62 61
1939	R. Riggs (USA)	S. Van Horn (USA)	64 62 64
1940	D. McNeill (USA)	R. Riggs (USA)	46 68 63 63 75
1941	R. Riggs (USA)	F. Kovacs (USA)	57 61 63 63
1942	F. Schroeder (USA)	F. Parker (USA)	86 75 36 46 62
1943	J. Hunt (USA)	J. Kramer (USA)	63 68 108 60
1944	F. Parker (USA)	W. Talbert (USA)	64 36 63 63
1945	F. Parker (USA)	W. Talbert (USA)	1412 61 62
1946	J. Kramer (USA)	T. Brown (USA)	97 63 60
1947	J. Kramer (USA)	F. Parker (USA)	46 26 61 60 63
1948	R. Gonzales (USA)	E. Sturgess (RSA)	62 63 1412
1949	R. Gonzales (USA)	F. Schroeder (USA)	1618 26 61 62 64
1950	A. Larsen (USA)	H. Flam (USA)	63 46 57 64 63
1951	F. Sedgman (AUS)	V. Seixas (USA)	64 61 61
1952	F. Sedgman (AUS)	G. Mulloy (USA)	61 62 63
1953	T. Trabert (USA)	V. Seixas (USA)	63 62 63
1954	V. Seixas (USA)	R. Hartwig (AUS)	36 62 64 64
1955	T. Trabert (USA)	K. Rosewall (AUS)	97 63 63
1956	K. Rosewall (AUS)	L. Hoad (AUS)	46 62 63 63
1957	M. Anderson (AUS)	A. Cooper (AUS)	108 75 64
1958	A. Cooper (AUS)	M. Anderson (AUS)	62 36 46 108 86
1959	N. Fraser (AUS)	A. Olmedo (PER)	63 57 62 64
1960	N. Fraser (AUS)	R. Laver (AUS)	64 64 97
1961	R. Emerson (AUS)	R. Laver (AUS)	75 63 62

US Championships (continued)

Year	Champion	Runner-up	Score
1962	R. Laver (AUS)	R. Emerson (AUS)	62 64 57 64
1963	R. Osuna (MEX)	F. Froehling (USA)	75 64 62
1964	R. Emerson (AUS)	F. Stolle (AUS)	64 62 64
1965	M. Santana (ESP)	C. Drysdale (RSA)	62 79 75 61
1966	F. Stolle (AUS)	J. Newcombe (AUS)	46 1210 63 64
1967	J. Newcombe (AUS)	C. Graebner (USA)	64 64 86
1968	A. Ashe (USA)	T. Okker (NED)	1412 57 63 36 63
1969	R. Laver (AUS)	T. Roche (AUS)	79 61 62 62
1970	K. Rosewall (AUS)	T. Roche (AUS)	26 64 76 63
1971	S. Smith (USA)	J. Kodes (TCH)	36 63 62 76
1972	I. Nastase (ROM)	A. Ashe (USA)	36 63 67 64 63
1973	J. Newcombe (AUS)	J. Kodes (TCH)	64 16 46 62 62
1974	J. Connors (USA)	K. Rosewall (AUS)	61 60 61
1975	M. Orantes (ESP)	J. Connors (USA)	64 63 63
1976	J. Connors (USA)	B. Borg (SWE)	64 36 76 64
1977	G. Vilas (ARG)	J. Connors (USA)	26 63 75 60
1978	J. Connors (USA)	B. Borg (SWE)	64 62 62
1979	J. McEnroe (USA)	V. Gerulaitis (USA)	75 63 63
1980	J. McEnroe (USA)	B. Borg (SWE)	76 61 67 57 64
1981	J. McEnroe (USA)	B. Borg (SWE)	46 62 64 63
1982	J. Connors (USA)	I. Lendl (TCH)	63 62 46 64
1983	J. Connors (USA)	I. Lendl (TCH)	63 67 75 60
1984	J. McEnroe (USA)	I. Lendl (TCH)	63 64 61
1985	I. Lendl (TCH)	J. McEnroe (USA)	76 63 64
1986	I. Lendl (TCH)	M. Mecir (TCH)	64 62 60
1987	I. Lendl (TCH)	M. Wilander (SWE)	67 60 76 64
1988	M. Wilander (SWE)	I. Lendl (TCH)	64 46 63 57 64
1989	B. Becker (GER)	I. Lendl (TCH)	76 16 63 76
1990	P. Sampras (USA)	A. Agassi (USA)	64 63 62
1991	S. Edberg (SWE)	J. Courier (USA)	62 64 60
1992	S. Edberg (SWE)	P. Sampras (USA)	36 64 76 62
1993	P. Sampras (USA)	C. Pioline (FRA)	64 64 63
1994	A. Agassi (USA)	M. Stich (GER)	61 76 75
1995	P. Sampras (USA)	A. Agassi (USA)	64 63 46 75
1996	P. Sampras (USA)	M. Chang (USA)	61 64 76
1997	P. Rafter (AUS)	G. Rusedski (GBR)	63 62 46 75
1998	P. Rafter (AUS)	M. Philippoussis (AUS)	63 36 62 60
1999	A. Agassi (USA)	T. Martin (USA)	64 67 67 63 62
2000	M. Safin (RUS)	P. Sampras (USA)	64 63 63
2001	L. Hewitt (AUS)	P. Sampras (USA)	76 61 61
2002	P. Sampras (USA)	A. Agassi (USA)	63 64 57 64
2003	A. Roddick (USA)	J. Ferrero (ESP)	63 76 63
2004	R. Federer (SUI)	L. Hewitt (AUS)	60 76 60

Women's Singles

Year	Champion	Runner-up	Score
1887	E. Hansell (USA)	L. Knight (USA)	61 60
1888	B. Townsend (USA)	E. Hansell (USA)	63 65
1889	B. Townsend (USA)	L. Voorhes (USA)	75 62
1890	E. Roosevelt (USA)	B. Townsend (USA)	62 62
1891	M. Cahill (USA)	E. Roosevelt (USA)	64 61 46 63
1892	M. Cahill (USA)	E. Moore (USA)	57 63 64 46 62
1893	A. Terry (USA)	A. Schultz (USA)	61 63
1894	H. Hellwig (USA)	A. Terry (USA)	75 36 60 36 63
1895	J. Atkinson (USA)	H. Hellwig (USA)	64 62 61

Reference Section: Roll of Honour: US Championships

Year	Champion	Runner-up	Score
1896	E. Moore (USA)	J. Atkinson (USA)	64 46 62 62
1897	J. Atkinson (USA)	E. Moore (USA)	63 63 46 36 63
1898	J. Atkinson (USA)	M. Jones (USA)	63 57 64 26 75
1899	M. Jones (USA)	M. Banks (USA)	61 61 75
1900	M. McAteer (USA)	E. Parker (USA)	62 62 60
1901	E. Moore (USA)	M. McAteer (USA)	64 36 75 26 62
1902	M. Jones (USA)	E. Moore (USA)	61 10 ret.
1903	E. Moore (USA)	M. Jones (USA)	75 86
1904	M. Sutton (USA)	E. Moore (USA)	61 62
1905	E. Moore (USA)	H. Homans (USA)	64 57 61
1906	H. Homans (USA)	M. Barger-Wallach (USA)	64 63
1907	E. Sears (USA)	C. Neely (USA)	63 62
1908	M. Barger-Wallach (USA)	E. Sears (USA)	63 16 63
1909	H. Hotchkiss (USA)	M. Barger-Wallach (USA)	60 61
1910	H. Hotchkiss (USA)	L. Hammond (USA)	64 62
1911	H. Hotchkiss (USA)	F. Sutton (USA)	810 61 97
1912	M. Browne (USA)	E. Sears (USA)	64 62
1913	M. Browne (USA)	D. Green (USA)	62 75
1914	M. Browne (USA)	M. Wagner (USA)	62 16 61
1915	M. Bjurstedt (NOR)	H. Hotchkiss Wightman (USA)	46 62 60
1916	M. Bjurstedt (NOR)	L. Hammond Raymond (USA)	60 61
1917	M. Bjurstedt (NOR)	M. Vanderhoef (USA)	46 60 62
1918	M. Bjurstedt (NOR)	E. Goss (USA)	64 63
1919	H. Hotchkiss Wightman (USA)	M. Zinderstein (USA)	61 62
1920	M. Mallory (USA)	M. Zinderstein (USA)	63 61
1921	M. Mallory (USA)	M. Browne (USA)	46 64 62
1922	M. Mallory (USA)	H. Wills (USA)	63 61
1923	H. Wills (USA)	M. Mallory (USA)	62 61
1924	H. Wills (USA)	M. Mallory (USA)	61 63
1925	H. Wills (USA)	K. McKane (GBR)	36 60 62
1926	M. Mallory (USA)	E. Ryan (USA)	46 64 97
1927	H. Wills (USA)	B. Nuthall (GBR)	61 64
1928	H. Wills (USA)	H. Jacobs (USA)	62 61
1929	H. Wills (USA)	P. Holcroft Watson (GBR)	64 62
1930	B. Nuthall (GBR)	A. McCune Harper (USA)	61 64
1931	H. Wills Moody (USA)	E. Bennett Whittingstall (GBR)	64 61
1932	H. Jacobs (USA)	C. Babcock (USA)	62 62
1933	H. Jacobs (USA)	H. Wills Moody (USA)	86 36 30 ret.
1934	H. Jacobs (USA)	S. Palfrey (USA)	61 64
1935	H. Jacobs (USA)	S. Palfrey Fabyan (USA)	62 64
1936	A. Marble (USA)	H. Jacobs (USA)	46 63 62
1937	A. Lizana (CHI)	J. Jedrzejowska (POL)	64 62
1938	A. Marble (USA)	N. Wynne (AUS)	60 63
1939	A. Marble (USA)	H. Jacobs (USA)	60 810 64
1940	A. Marble (USA)	H. Jacobs (USA)	62 63
1941	S. Palfrey Cooke (USA)	P. Betz (USA)	75 62
1942	P. Betz (USA)	L. Brough (USA)	46 61 64
1943	P. Betz (USA)	L. Brough (USA)	63 57 63
1944	P. Betz (USA)	M. Osborne (USA)	63 86
1945	S. Palfrey Cooke (USA)	P. Betz (USA)	36 86 64
1946	P. Betz (USA)	D. Hart (USA)	119 63
1947	L. Brough (USA)	M. Osborne (USA)	86 46 61
1948	M. Osborne DuPont (USA)	L. Brough (USA)	46 64 1513
1949	M. Osborne DuPont (USA)	D. Hart (USA)	64 61
1950	M. Osborne DuPont (USA)	D. Hart (USA)	63 63

325

US Championships (continued)

Year	Champion	Runner-up	Score
1951	M. Connolly (USA)	S. Fry (USA)	63 16 64
1952	M. Connolly (USA)	D. Hart (USA)	63 75
1953	M. Connolly (USA)	D. Hart (USA)	62 64
1954	D. Hart (USA)	L. Brough (USA)	68 61 86
1955	D. Hart (USA)	P. Ward (GBR)	64 62
1956	S. Fry (USA)	A. Gibson (USA)	63 64
1957	A. Gibson (USA)	L. Brough (USA)	63 62
1958	A. Gibson (USA)	D. Hard (USA)	36 61 62
1959	M. Bueno (BRA)	C. Truman (GBR)	61 64
1960	D. Hard (USA)	M. Bueno (BRA)	64 1012 64
1961	D. Hard (USA)	A. Haydon (GBR)	63 64
1962	M. Smith (AUS)	D. Hard (USA)	97 64
1963	M. Bueno (BRA)	M. Smith (AUS)	75 64
1964	M. Bueno (BRA)	C. Caldwell Graebner (USA)	61 60
1965	M. Smith (AUS)	B. Moffitt (USA)	86 75
1966	M. Bueno (BRA)	N. Richey (USA)	63 61
1967	B. King (USA)	A. Haydon Jones (GBR)	119 64
1968	V. Wade (GBR)	B. King (USA)	64 64
1969	M. Smith Court (AUS)	N. Richey (USA)	62 62
1970	M. Smith Court (AUS)	R. Casals (USA)	62 26 61
1971	B. King (USA)	R. Casals (USA)	64 76
1972	B. King (USA)	K. Melville (AUS)	63 75
1973	M. Smith Court (AUS)	E. Goolagong (AUS)	76 57 62
1974	B. King (USA)	E. Goolagong (AUS)	36 63 75
1975	C. Evert (USA)	E. Goolagong Cawley (AUS)	57 64 62
1976	C. Evert (USA)	E. Goolagong Cawley (AUS)	63 60
1977	C. Evert (USA)	W. Turnbull (AUS)	76 62
1978	C. Evert (USA)	P. Shriver (USA)	75 64
1979	T. Austin (USA)	C. Evert Lloyd (USA)	64 63
1980	C. Evert Lloyd (USA)	H. Mandlikova (TCH)	57 61 61
1981	T. Austin (USA)	M. Navratilova (USA)	16 76 76
1982	C. Evert Lloyd (USA)	H. Mandlikova (TCH)	63 61
1983	M. Navratilova (USA)	C. Evert Lloyd (USA)	61 63
1984	M. Navratilova (USA)	C. Evert Lloyd (USA)	46 64 64
1985	H. Mandlikova (TCH)	M. Navratilova (USA)	76 16 76
1986	M. Navratilova (USA)	H. Sukova (TCH)	63 62
1987	M. Navratilova (USA)	S. Graf (GER)	76 61
1988	S. Graf (GER)	G. Sabatini (ARG)	63 36 61
1989	S. Graf (GER)	M. Navratilova (USA)	36 75 61
1990	G. Sabatini (ARG)	S. Graf (GER)	62 76
1991	M. Seles (YUG)	M. Navratilova (USA)	76 61
1992	M. Seles (YUG)	A. Sanchez-Vicario (ESP)	63 63
1993	S. Graf (GER)	H. Sukova (CZE)	63 63
1994	A. Sanchez-Vicario (ESP)	S. Graf (GER)	16 76 64
1995	S. Graf (GER)	M. Seles (USA)	76 06 63
1996	S. Graf (GER)	M. Seles (USA)	75 64
1997	M. Hingis (SUI)	V. Williams (USA)	60 64
1998	L. Davenport (USA)	M. Hingis (SUI)	63 75
1999	S. Williams (USA)	M. Hingis (SUI)	63 76
2000	V. Williams (USA)	L. Davenport (USA)	64 75
2001	V. Williams (USA)	S. Williams (USA)	62 64
2002	S. Williams (USA)	V. Williams (USA)	64 63
2003	J. Henin-Hardenne (BEL)	K. Clijsters (BEL)	75 61
2004	S. Kuznetsova (RUS)	E. Dementieva (RUS)	63 75

Year	Men's Doubles Champions	Women's Doubles Champions	Mixed Doubles Champions
1881	C. Clark/F. Taylor		
1882	J. Dwight/R. Sears		
1883	J. Dwight/R. Sears		
1884	J. Dwight/R. Sears		
1885	J. Clark/R. Sears		
1886	J. Dwight/R. Sears		
1887	J. Dwight/R. Sears		
1888	O. Campbell/V. Hall		
1889	H. Slocum/H. Taylor	M. Ballard/B. Townsend	
1890	V. Hall/C. Hobart	E. Roosevelt/G. Roosevelt	
1891	O. Campbell/R. Huntington	M. Cahill/Mrs W. Fellowes Morgan	
1892	O. Campbell/R. Huntington	M. Cahill/A. McKinlay	C. Hobart/M. Cahill
1893	C. Hobart/F. Hovey	H. Butler/A. Terry	C. Hobart/E. Roosevelt
1894	C. Hobart/F. Hovey	J. Atkinson/H. Hellwig	E. Fischer/J. Atkinson
1895	M. Chace/R. Wrenn	J. Atkinson/H. Hellwig	E. Fischer/J. Atkinson
1896	C. Neel/G. Sheldon	J. Atkinson/E. Moore	E. Fischer/J. Atkinson
1897	G. Sheldon/L. Ware	J. Atkinson/K. Atkinson	D. Magruder/L. Henson
1898	G. Sheldon/L. Ware	J. Atkinson/K. Atkinson	E. Fischer/C. Neely
1899	D. Davis/H. Ward	J. Craven/M. McAteer	A. Hoskins/E. Rastall
1900	D. Davis/H. Ward	H. Champlin/E. Parker	A. Codman/M. Hunnewell
1901	D. Davis/H. Ward	J. Atkinson/M. McAteer	R. Little/M. Jones
1902	H. Doherty/R. Doherty	J. Atkinson/M. Jones	W. Grant/E. Moore
1903	H. Doherty/R. Doherty	E. Moore/C. Neely	H. Allen/H. Chapman
1904	H. Ward/B. Wright	M. Hall/M. Sutton	W. Grant/E. Moore
1905	H. Ward/B. Wright	H. Homans/C. Neely	C. Hobart/Mrs A. Hobart
1906	H. Ward/B. Wright	Mrs L. Coe/Mrs D. Platt	E. Dewhurst/S. Coffin
1907	F. Alexander/H. Hackett	C. Neely/M. Wimer	W. Johnson/M. Sayres
1908	F. Alexander/H. Hackett	M. Curtis/E. Sears	N. Niles/E. Rotch
1909	F. Alexander/H. Hackett	H. Hotchkiss/E. Rotch	W. Johnson/H. Hotchkiss
1910	F. Alexander/H Hackett	H. Hotchkiss/E. Rotch	J. Carpenter/H. Hotchkiss
1911	R. Little/G. Touchard	H. Hotchikss/E. Sears	W. Johnson/H. Hotchkiss
1912	T. Bundy/M. McLoughlin	M. Browne/D. Green	R. Williams/M. Browne
1913	T. Bundy/M. McLoughlin	M. Browne/Mrs. R. Williams	W. Tilden/M. Browne
1914	T. Bundy/M. McLoughlin	M. Browne/Mrs. R. Williams	W. Tilden/M. Browne
1915	C. Griffin/W. Johnston	H. Hotchkiss Wightman/E. Sears	H. Johnson/H. Wightman
1916	C. Griffin/W. Johnston	M. Bjurstedt/E. Sears	W. Davis/E. Sears
1917	F. Alexander/H. Throckmorton	M. Bjurstedt/E. Sears	I. Wright/M. Bjurstedt
1918	V. Richards/W. Tilden	E. Goss/M. Zinderstein	I. Wright/H. Wightman
1919	N. Brookes/G. Patterson	E. Goss/M. Zinderstein	V. Richards/M. Zinderstein
1920	C. Griffin/W. Johnston	E. Goss/M. Zinderstein	W. Johnson/H. Wightman
1921	V. Richards/W. Tilden	M. Browne/Mrs. R. Williams	W. Johnston/M. Browne
1922	V. Richards/W. Tilden	M. Jessup/H. Wills	W. Tilden/M. Browne
1923	B. Norton/W. Tilden	P. Covell/K. McKane	W. Tilden/M. Mallory
1924	H. Kinsey/R. Kinsey	H. Hotchkiss Wightman/H. Wills	V. Richards/H. Wills
1925	V. Richards/R. Williams	M. Browne/H. Wills	J. Hawkes/K. McKane
1926	V. Richards/R. Williams	E. Goss/E. Ryan	J. Borotra/E. Ryan
1927	F. Hunter/W. Tilden	K. Godfree/E. Harvey	H. Cochet/E. Bennett
1928	J. Doeg/G. Lott	H. Hotchkiss Wightman/H. Wills	J. Hawkes/H. Wills
1929	J. Doeg/G. Lott	P. Mitchell/P. Watson	G. Lott/B. Nuthall
1930	J. Doeg/G. Lott	B. Nuthall/S.Palfrey	W. Allison/E. Cross
1931	W. Allison/J. Van Ryn	B. Nuthall/E. Whitingstall	G. Lott/B. Nuthall
1932	K. Gledhill/E. Vines	H. Jacobs/S. Palfrey	F. Perry/S. Palfrey
1933	G. Lott/L. Stoefen	F. James/B. Nuthall	E. Vines/E. Ryan
1934	G. Lott/L. Stoefen	H. Jacobs/S. Palfrey	G. Lott/H. Jacobs

US Championships (continued)

Year	Champions	Champions	Champions
1935	W. Allison/J. Van Ryn	H. Jacobs/S. Palfrey Fabyan	E. Maier/S. Palfrey
1936	J. Budge/G. Mako	C. Babcock/M. Van Ryn	G. Mako/A. Marble
1937	G. Von Cramm/H. Henkel	A. Marble/S. Palfrey Fabyan	D. Budge/S. Palfrey Fabyan
1938	D. Budge/G. Mako	A. Marble/S. Palfrey Fabyan	D. Budge/A. Marble
1939	J. Bromwich/A. Quist	A. Marble/S. Palfrey Fabyan	H. Hopman/A. Marble
1940	J. Kramer/F. Schroeder	A. Marble/S. Palfrey Fabyan	R. Riggs/A. Marble
1941	J. Kramer/F. Schroeder	M. Osborne/S. Palfrey Fabyan	J. Kramer/S. Palfrey Cooke
1942	G. Mulloy/W. Talbert	L. Brough/M. Osborne	F. Schroeder/L. Brough
1943	J. Kramer/F. Parker	L. Brough/M. Osborne	W. Talbert/M. Osborne
1944	R. Falkenburg/D. McNeill	L. Brough/M. Osborne	W. Talbert/M. Osborne
1945	G. Mulloy/W. Talbert	L. Brough/M. Osborne	W. Talbert/M. Osborne
1946	G. Mulloy/W. Talbert	L. Brough/M. Osborne	W. Talbert/M. Osborne
1947	J. Kramer/F. Schroeder	L. Brough/M. Osborne	J. Bromwich/L. Brough
1948	G. Mulloy/W. Talbert	L. Brough/M. Osborne	T. Brown/L. Brough
1949	J. Bromwich/W. Sidwell	L. Brough/M. Osborne	E. Sturgess/L. Brough
1950	J. Bromwich/F. Sedgman	L. Brough/M. Osborne	K. McGregor/M. Osborne DuPont
1951	K. McGregor/F. Sedgman	S. Fry/D. Hart	F. Sedgman/D. Hart
1952	M. Rose/V. Seixas	S. Fry/D. Hart	F. Sedgman/D. Hart
1953	R. Hartwig/M. Rose	S. Fry/D. Hart	V. Seixas/D. Hart
1954	V. Seixas/T. Trabert	S. Fry/D. Hart	V. Seixas/D. Hart
1955	K. Kamo/A. Miyagi	L. Brough/M. Osborne DuPont	V. Seixas/D. Hart
1956	L. Hoad/K. Rosewall	L. Brough/M. Osborne DuPont	K. Rosewell/M. Osborne DuPont
1957	A. Cooper/N. Fraser	L. Brough/M. Osborne DuPont	K. Nelson/A. Gibson
1958	A. Ulmedo/H. Richardson	J. Arth/D. Hard	N. Fraser/M. Osborne DuPont
1959	R. Emerson/N. Fraser	J. Arth/D. Hard	N. Fraser/M. Osborne DuPont
1960	R. Emerson/N. Fraser	M. Bueno/D. Hard	N. Fraser/M. Osborne DuPont
1961	C. McKinley/D. Ralston	D. Hard/L. Turner	R. Mark/M. Smith
1962	R. Osuna/A. Palafox	M. Bueno/D. Hard	F. Stolle/M. Smith
1963	C. McKinley/D. Ralston	R. Ebbern/M. Smith	K. Fletcher/M. Smith
1964	C. McKinley/D. Ralston	B. Moffitt/K. Susman	J. Newcombe/M. Smith
1965	R. Emerson/F. Stolle	C. Caldwell Graebner/N. Richey	F. Stolle/M. Smith
1966	R. Emerson/F. Stolle	M. Bueno/N. Richey	O. Davidson/D. Floyd Fales
1967	J. Newcombe/T. Roche	R. Casals/B. King	O. Davidson/B. King
1968	R. Lutz/S. Smith	M. Bueno/M. Smith Court	Not held
1969	K. Rosewall/F. Stolle	F. Durr/D. Hard	M. Riessen/M. Smith Court
1970	P. Barthes/N. Pilic	M. Smith Court/J. Tegart Dalton	M. Riessen/M. Smith Court
1971	J. Newcombe/R. Taylor	R. Casals/J. Tegart Dalton	O. Davidson/B. King
1972	C. Drysdale/R. Taylor	F. Durr/B. Stove	M. Riessen/M. Smith Court
1973	O. Davidson/J. Newcombe	M. Smith Court/V. Wade	O. Davidson/B. King
1974	R. Lutz/S. Smith	R. Casals/B. King	G. Masters/P. Teeguarden
1975	J. Connors/I. Nastase	M. Smith Court/V. Wade	R. Stockton/R. Casals
1976	T. Okker/M. Riessen	D. Boshoff/I. Kloss	P. Dent/B. King
1977	R. Hewitt/F. McMillan	M. Navratilova/B. Stove	F. McMillan/B. Stove
1978	R. Lutz/S. Smith	B. King/M. Navratilova	F. McMillan/B. Stove
1979	P. Fleming/J. McEnroe	B. Stove/W. Turnbull	R. Hewitt/G. Stevens
1980	R. Lutz/S. Smith	B. King/M. Navratilova	M. Riessen/W. Turnbull
1981	P. Fleming/J. McEnroe	K. Jordan/A. Smith	K. Curren/A. Smith
1982	K. Curren/S. Denton	R. Casals/W. Turnbull	K. Curren/A. Smith
1983	P. Fleming/J. McEnroe	M. Navratilova/P. Shriver	J. Fitzgerald/E. Sayers
1984	J. Fitzgerald/T. Smid	M. Navratilova/P. Shriver	T. Gullikson/M. Maleeva
1985	K. Flach/R. Seguso	C. Kohde-Kilsch/H. Sukova	H. Gunthardt/M. Navratilova
1986	A. Gomez/S. Zivojinovic	M. Navratilova/P. Shriver	S. Casal/R. Reggi
1987	S. Edberg/A. Jarryd	M. Navratilova/P. Shriver	E. Sanchez/M. Navratilova
1988	S. Casal/E. Sanchez	G. Fernandez/R. White	J. Pugh/J. Novotna
1989	J. McEnroe/M. Woodforde	H. Mandlikova/M. Navratilova	S. Cannon/R. White

Year	Champions	Champions	Champions
1990	P. Aldrich/D. Visser	G. Fernandez/M. Navratilova	T. Woodbridge/E. Smylie
1991	J. Fitzgerald/A. Jarryd	P. Shriver/N. Zvereva	T. Nijssen/M. Bollegraf
1992	J. Grabb/R. Reneberg	G. Fernandez/N. Zvereva	M. Woodforde/N. Provis
1993	K. Flach/R. Leach	A. Sanchez-Vicario/H. Sukova	T. Woodbridge/H. Sukova
1994	J. Eltingh/P. Haarhuis	J. Novotna/A. Sanchez-Vicario	E. Reinach/P. Galbraith
1995	T. Woodbridge/M. Woodforde	G. Fernandez/N. Zvereva	M. Lucena/M. McGrath
1996	T. Woodbridge/M. Woodforde	G. Fernandez/N. Zvereva	P. Galbraith/L. Raymond
1997	Y. Kafelnikov/D. Vacek	L. Davenport/J. Novotna	R. Leach/M. Bollegraf
1998	S. Stolle/C. Suk	M. Hingis/J. Novotna	M. Mirnyi/S. Williams
1999	S. Lareau/A. O'Brien	S. Williams/V. Williams	M. Bhupathi/A. Sugiyama
2000	L. Hewitt/M. Mirnyi	J. Halard-Decugis/A. Sugiyama	J. Palmer/A. Sanchez-Vicario
2001	W. Black/K. Ullyett	L. Raymond/R. Stubbs	T. Woodbridge/R. Stubbs
2002	M. Bhupathi/M. Mirnyi	V. Ruano Pascual/P. Suarez	M. Bryan/L. Raymond
2003	J. Bjorkman/T. Woodbridge	V. Ruano Pascual/P. Suarez	B. Bryan/K. Srebotnik
2004	M. Knowles/D. Nestor	V. Ruano Pascual/P. Suarez	B. Bryan/V. Zvonareva

ITF

ITFTENNIS.COM IS YOUR GATEWAY TO ALL THAT MATTERS IN TENNIS. AS WELL AS LIVE SCORING AND ALL THE LATEST NEWS AND PHOTOS, WE'LL ALSO GIVE YOU ACCESS TO THE MOST COMPREHENSIVE RANGE OF TENNIS STATISTICS AND FACTUAL INFORMATION AVAILABLE.

USE THE NET TO ITS FULL ADVANTAGE

WWW.ITFTENNIS.COM

WWW.DAVISCUP.COM

WWW.FEDCUP.COM

WWW.ITFWHEELCHAIRTENNIS.COM

DAVIS CUP by BNP PARIBAS

FedCup

The Grand Slam

To achieve the Grand Slam, a player must win the Australian, French, Wimbledon and US Championships in the same calendar year.

Men's Singles
1938	Donald Budge (USA)
1962	Rod Laver (AUS)
1969	Rod Laver (AUS)

Women's Singles
1953	Maureen Connolly (USA)	
1970	Margaret Court (AUS)	
1988	Steffi Graf (GER)*	*Achieved a unique 'Golden Slam', also winning gold at the 1988 Olympics in Seoul

Men's Doubles
1951	Ken McGregor/Frank Sedgman (AUS)

Women's Doubles
1960	Maria Bueno (BRA)	Australian with Christine Truman (GBR)
		French, Wimbledon and US Championships with Darlene Hard (USA)
1984	Martina Navratilova	Pam Shriver (USA)
1998	Martina Hingis (SUI)	Australian with Mirjana Lucic (CRO)
		French, Wimbledon and US Championships with Jana Novotna (CZE)

Mixed Doubles
1963	Ken Fletcher	Margaret Smith (AUS)
1967	Owen Davidson (AUS)	Australian with Lesley Turner (AUS)
		French, Wimbledon and US Championships with Billie Jean King (USA)

Juniors
1983	Stefan Edberg (SWE)

Tennis Masters Cup

The end of season men's event, jointly owned by the ATP, ITF and the Grand Slams tournaments, began in 2000 and replaced the ATP Tour World Championship and the Grand Slam Cup. Records of both previous events are shown.

Singles
Year	Venue	Champion	Runner-up	Score
2000	Lisbon, Portugal	G. Kuerten (BRA)	A. Agassi (USA)	64 64 64
2001	Sydney, Australia	L. Hewitt (AUS)	S. Grosjean (FRA)	63 63 64
2002	Shanghai, China	L. Hewitt (AUS)	J. Ferrero (ESP)	75 75 26 26 64
2003	Houston, TX, USA	R. Federer (SUI)	A. Agassi (USA)	63 60 64
2004	Houston, TX, USA	R. Federer (SUI)	L. Hewitt (AUS)	63 62

Doubles
Year	Venue	Champion	Runner-up	Score
2003	Houston, TX, USA	B. Bryan/M. Bryan (USA)	M. Llodra/F. Santoro (FRA)	67 63 36 76 64
2004	Houston, TX, USA	B. Bryan/M. Bryan (USA)	W. Black/K. Ullyett (ZIM)	46 75 64 62

WTA Tour Championships

Singles

Year	Venue	Champion	Runner-up	Score
1972	Boca Raton, FL, USA	C. Evert (USA)	K. Melville (AUS)	75 64
1973	Boca Raton, FL, USA	C. Evert (USA)	N. Richey (USA)	63 63
1974	Los Angeles, CA, USA	E. Goolagong (AUS)	C. Evert (USA)	63 64
1975	Los Angeles, CA, USA	C. Evert (USA)	M. Navratilova (TCH)	64 62
1976	Los Angeles, CA, USA	E. Goolagong Cawley (AUS)	C. Evert (USA)	63 57 63
1977	New York, NY, USA	C. Evert (USA)	S. Barker (GBR)	26 61 61
1978	Oakland, CA, USA	M. Navratilova (TCH)	E. Goolagong Cawley (AUS)	76 64
1979	New York, NY, USA	M. Navratilova (TCH)	T. Austin (USA)	63 36 62
1980	New York, NY, USA	T. Austin (USA)	M. Navratilova (TCH)	62 26 62
1981	New York, NY, USA	M. Navratilova (USA)	A. Jaeger (USA)	63 76
1982	New York, NY, USA	S. Hanika (GER)	M. Navratilova (USA)	16 63 64
1983	New York, NY, USA	M. Navratilova (USA)	C. Evert (USA)	62 60
1984	New York, NY, USA	M. Navratilova (USA)	C. Evert (USA)	63 75 61
1985	New York, NY, USA	M. Navratilova (USA)	H. Sukova (TCH)	63 75 64
1986 (Mar)	New York, NY, USA	M. Navratilova (USA)	H. Mandlikova (TCH)	62 60 36 61
1986 (Nov)	New York, NY, USA	M. Navratilova (USA)	S. Graf (GER)	76 63 62
1987	New York, NY, USA	S. Graf (GER)	G. Sabatini (ARG)	46 64 60 64
1988	New York, NY, USA	G. Sabatini (ARG)	P. Shriver (USA)	75 62 62
1989	New York, NY, USA	S. Graf (GER)	M. Navratilova (USA)	64 75 26 62
1990	New York, NY, USA	M. Seles (YUG)	G. Sabatini (ARG)	64 57 36 64 62
1991	New York, NY, USA	M. Seles (YUG)	M. Navratilova (USA)	64 36 75 60
1992	New York, NY, USA	M. Seles (YUG)	M. Navratilova (USA)	75 63 61
1993	New York, NY, USA	S. Graf (GER)	A. Sanchez-Vicario (ESP)	61 64 36 61
1994	New York, NY, USA	G. Sabatini (ARG)	L. Davenport (USA)	63 62 64
1995	New York, NY, USA	S. Graf (GER)	A. Huber (GER)	61 26 61 46 63
1996	New York, NY, USA	S. Graf (GER)	M. Hingis (SUI)	63 46 60 46 60
1997	New York, NY, USA	J. Novotna (CZE)	M. Pierce (FRA)	76 62 63
1998	New York, NY, USA	M. Hingis (SUI)	L. Davenport (USA)	75 64 46 62
1999	New York, NY, USA	L. Davenport (USA)	M. Hingis (SUI)	64 62
2000	New York, NY, USA	M. Hingis (SUI)	M. Seles (USA)	67 64 64
2001	Munich, GER	S. Williams (USA)	L. Davenport (USA)	w/o
2002	Los Angeles, CA, USA	K. Clijsters (BEL)	S. Williams (USA)	75 63
2003	Los Angeles, CA, USA	K. Clijsters (BEL)	A. Mauresmo (FRA)	62 60
2004	Los Angeles, CA, USA	M. Sharapova (RUS)	S. Williams (USA)	46 62 64

Doubles

Year	Venue	Champion	Runner-up	Score
1973	Boca Raton, FL, USA	R. Casals (USA)/M. Court (AUS)	F. Durr (FRA)/B. Stove (NED)	62 64
1974	Los Angeles, CA, USA	B. King/R. Casals (USA)	F. Durr (FRA)/B. Stove (NED)	61 67 75
1975-78 not played				
1979	New York, NY, USA	F. Durr (FRA)/B. Stove (NED)	S. Barker (GBR)/A. Kiyomura (USA)	64 62
1980	New York, NY, USA	B. King (USA)/M. Navratilova (TCH)	R. Casals (USA)/W. Turnbull (AUS)	63 46 63
1981	New York, NY, USA	M. Navratilova/P. Shriver (USA)	B. Potter/S. Walsh (USA)	60 76
1982	New York, NY, USA	M. Navratilova/P. Shriver (USA)	K. Jordan/A. Smith (USA)	64 63
1983	New York, NY, USA	M. Navratilova/P. Shriver (USA)	C. Kohde-Kilsch/E. Pfaff (GER)	75 62
1984	New York, NY, USA	M. Navratilova/P. Shriver (USA)	J. Durie (GBR)/A. Kiyomura (USA)	63 61
1985	New York, NY, USA	M. Navratilova/P. Shriver (USA)	C. Kohde-Kilsch (GER)/H. Sukova (TCH)	67 64 76
1986 (Mar)	New York, NY, USA	H. Mandlikova (TCH)/W. Turnbull (AUS)	C. Kohde-Kilsch (GER)/H. Sukova (TCH)	64 67 63
1986 (Nov)	New York, NY, USA	M. Navratilova/P. Shriver (USA)	C. Kohde-Kilsch (GER)/H. Sukova (TCH)	76 63
1987	New York, NY, USA	M. Navratilova/P. Shriver (USA)	C. Kohde-Kilsch (GER)/H. Sukova (TCH)	61 61
1988	New York, NY, USA	M. Navratilova/P. Shriver (USA)	L. Neiland/N. Zvereva (URS)	63 64
1989	New York, NY, USA	M. Navratilova/P. Shriver (USA)	L. Neiland/N. Zvereva (URS)	63 62
1990	New York, NY, USA	K. Jordan (USA)/E. Smylie (AUS)	M. Paz (ARG)/A. Sanchez-Vicario (ESP)	76 64
1991	New York, NY, USA	M. Navratilova/P. Shriver (USA)	G. Fernandez (USA)/J. Novotna (TCH)	46 75 64

Year	Venue	Champion	Runner-up	Score
1992	New York, NY, USA	A. Sanchez-Vicario (ESP)/H. Sukova (TCH)	L. Neiland (URS)/J. Novotna (TCH)	76 61
1993	New York, NY, USA	G. Fernandez (USA)/N. Zvereva (BLR)	L. Neiland (LAT)/J. Novotna (CZE)	63 75
1994	New York, NY, USA	G. Fernandez (USA)/N. Zvereva (BLR)	J. Novotna (CZE)/A. Sanchez-Vicario (ESP)	63 67 63
1995	New York, NY, USA	J. Novotna (CZE)/A. Sanchez-Vicario (ESP)	G. Fernandez (USA)/N. Zvereva (BLR)	62 61
1996	New York, NY, USA	L. Davenport/M. Fernandez (USA)	J. Novotna (CZE)/A. Sanchez-Vicario (ESP)	63 62
1997	New York, NY, USA	L. Davenport (USA)/J. Novotna (CZE)	A. Fusai/N. Tauziat (FRA)	67 63 62
1998	New York, NY, USA	L. Davenport (USA)/N. Zvereva (BLR)	A. Fusai/N. Tauziat (FRA)	67 75 63
1999	New York, NY, USA	M. Hingis (SUI)/A. Kournikova (RUS)	L. Neiland (LAT)/A. Sanchez-Vicario (ESP)	64 64
2000	New York, NY, USA	M. Hingis (SUI)/A. Kournikova (RUS)	N. Arendt (USA)/M. Bollegraf (NED)	62 63
2001	Munich, GER	L. Raymond (USA)/R. Stubbs (AUS)	C. Black (ZIM)/E. Likhovtseva (RUS)	75 36 63
2002	Los Angeles, CA, USA	E. Dementieva (RUS)/J. Husarova (SVK)	C. Black (ZIM)/E. Likhovtseva (RUS)	46 64 63
2003	Los Angeles, CA, USA	V. Ruano Pascual (ESP)/P. Suarez (ARG)	K. Clijsters (BEL)/A. Sugiyama (JPN)	64 36 63
2004	Los Angeles, CA, USA	N. Petrova (RUS)/M. Shaughnessy (USA)	C. Black (ZIM)/R. Stubbs (AUS)	75 62

ATP Tour World Championships

Held 1970-1999.

Year	Venue	Champion	Runner-up	Score
1970	Tokyo, Japan	S. Smith (USA)	R. Laver (AUS)	Round robin
1971	Paris, France	I. Nastase (ROM)	S. Smith (USA)	Round robin
1972	Barcelona, Spain	I. Nastase (ROM)	S. Smith (USA)	63 62 36 26 63
1973	Boston, MA, USA	I. Nastase (ROM)	T. Okker (NED)	63 75 46 63
1974	Melbourne, Australia	G. Vilas (ARG)	I. Nastase (ROM)	76 62 36 36 64
1975	Stockholm, Sweden	I. Nastase (ROM)	B. Borg (SWE)	62 62 61
1976	Houston, TX, USA	M. Orantes (ESP)	W. Fibak (POL)	57 62 06 76 61
1977	New York, NY, USA	J. Connors (USA)	B. Borg (SWE)	64 16 64
1978	New York, NY, USA	J. McEnroe (USA)	A. Ashe (USA)	67 63 75
1979	New York, NY, USA	B. Borg (SWE)	V. Gerulaitis (USA)	62 62
1980	New York, NY, USA	B. Borg (SWE)	I. Lendl (TCH)	64 62 62
1981	New York, NY, USA	I. Lendl (TCH)	V. Gerulaitis (USA)	67 26 76 62 64
1982	New York, NY, USA	I. Lendl (TCH)	J. McEnroe (USA)	64 64 62
1983	New York, NY, USA	J. McEnroe (USA)	I. Lendl (TCH)	63 64 64
1984	New York, NY, USA	J. McEnroe (USA)	I. Lendl (TCH)	75 60 64
1985	New York, NY, USA	I. Lendl (TCH)	B. Becker (GER)	62 76 63
1986	New York, NY, USA	I. Lendl (TCH)	B. Becker (GER)	64 64 64
1987	New York, NY, USA	I. Lendl (TCH)	M. Wilander (SWE)	62 62 63
1988	New York, NY, USA	B. Becker (GER)	I. Lendl (TCH)	57 76 36 62 76
1989	New York, NY, USA	S. Edberg (SWE)	B. Becker (GER)	46 76 63 61
1990	Frankfurt, Germany	A. Agassi (USA)	S. Edberg (SWE)	57 76 75 62
1991	Frankfurt, Germany	P. Sampras (USA)	J. Courier (USA)	36 76 63 64
1992	Frankfurt, Germany	B. Becker (GER)	J. Courier (USA)	64 63 75
1993	Frankfurt, Germany	M. Stich (GER)	P. Sampras (USA)	76 26 76 62
1994	Frankfurt, Germany	P. Sampras (USA)	B. Becker (GER)	46 63 75 64
1995	Frankfurt, Germany	B. Becker (GER)	M. Chang (USA)	76 60 76
1996	Hannover, Germany	P. Sampras (USA)	B. Becker (GER)	36 76 76 67 64
1997	Hannover, Germany	P. Sampras (USA)	Y. Kafelnikov (RUS)	63 62 62
1998	Hannover, Germany	A. Corretja (ESP)	C. Moya (ESP)	36 36 75 63 75
1999	Hannover, Germany	P. Sampras (USA)	A. Agassi (USA)	61 75 64

Grand Slam Cup

Held 1990-1999 in Munich, Germany. A women's event was added for the last two years.

Men

Year	Champion	Runner-up	Score
1990	P. Sampras (USA)	B. Gilbert (USA)	63 64 62
1991	D. Wheaton (USA)	M. Chang (USA)	75 62 64
1992	M. Stich (GER)	M. Chang (USA)	62 63 62
1993	P. Korda (TCH)	M. Stich (GER)	26 64 76 26 119
1994	M. Larsson (SWE)	P. Sampras (USA)	76 46 76 64
1995	G. Ivanisevic (CRO)	T. Martin (USA)	76 63 64
1996	B. Becker (GER)	G. Ivanisevic (CRO)	63 64 64
1997	P. Sampras (USA)	P. Rafter (AUS)	62 64 75
1998	M. Rios (CHI)	A. Agassi (USA)	64 26 76 57 63
1999	G. Rusedski (GBR)	T. Haas (GER)	63 64 67 76

Women

Year	Champion	Runner-up	Score
1998	V. Williams (USA)	P. Schnyder (SUI)	62 36 62
1999	S. Williams (USA)	V. Williams (USA)	61 36 63

Australian Junior Championships

Boys' Singles

Year	Champion	Runner-up	Score
1922	A. Yeldham (AUS)		
1923	L. Cryle (AUS)		
1924	H. Coldham (AUS)		
1925	H. Coldham (AUS)		
1926	J. Crawford (AUS)		
1927	J. Crawford (AUS)		
1928	J. Crawford (AUS)		
1929	J. Crawford (AUS)		
1930	D. Turnbull (AUS)		
1931	B. Moore (AUS)		
1932	V. McGrath (AUS)		
1933	A. Quist (AUS)		
1934	N. Ennis (AUS)		
1935	J. Bromwich (AUS)		
1936	J. Bromwich (AUS)		
1937	J. Bromwich (AUS)		
1938	M. Newcombe (AUS)		
1939	W. Sidwell (AUS)		
1940	D. Pails (AUS)		
1941-45 not played			
1946	F. Sedgman (AUS)		
1947	D. Candy (AUS)		
1948	K. McGregor (AUS)	K. Johnstone (AUS)	60 61
1949	C. Wilderspin (AUS)		
1950	K. Rosewall (AUS)	P. Cawthorn (AUS)	64 46 75
1951	L. Hoad (AUS)	K. Rosewall (AUS)	63 62
1952	K. Rosewall (AUS)	L. Hoad (AUS)	108 62
1953	W. Gilmour (AUS)		
1954	W. Knight (GBR)	R. Emerson (AUS)	63 61
1955	G. Moss (USA)	M. Green (USA)	108 62
1956	R. Mark (AUS)	M. Collins (AUS)	63 86
1957	R. Laver (AUS)	J. Pearce (AUS)	11 13 75 62
1958	M. Mulligan (AUS)	R. Hewitt (AUS)	64 63
1959	E. Buchholz (USA)	M. Mulligan (AUS)	36 63 63
1960	W. Coghlan (AUS)	G. Pares (AUS)	64 61
1961	J. Newcombe (AUS)	G. Pollard (AUS)	63 63
1962	J. Newcombe (AUS)	O. Davidson (AUS)	61 46 64
1963	J. Newcombe (AUS)	G. Stilwell (GBR)	64 64
1964	A. Roche (AUS)	G. Stilwell (GBR)	1210 63
1965	G. Goven (FRA)	J. Walker (AUS)	75 26 63
1966	K. Coombes (AUS)	G. Olsson (AUS)	64 46 86
1967	B. Fairlie (NZL)	D. Smith (AUS)	60 63
1968	P. Dent (AUS)	R. Giltinan (AUS)	62 64
1969	A. McDonald (AUS)	A. Wijono (INA)	60 61
1970	J. Alexander (AUS)	P. Dent (AUS)	46 63 86
1971	C. Letcher (AUS)		
1972	P. Kronk (AUS)		
1973	P. McNamee (AUS)		
1974	H. Brittain (AUS)	J. Haillet (FRA)	108 75
1975	B. Drewett (AUS)		
1976	R. Kelly (AUS)	J. Dilouie (USA)	62 64
1977 (Jan)	B. Drewett (AUS)	T. Wilkison (USA)	64 76
1977 (Dec)	R. Kelly (AUS)		
1978	P. Serrett (AUS)	C. Johnstone (AUS)	64 63

Australian Junior Championships (continued)

Year	Champion	Runner-up	Score
1979	G. Whitecross (AUS)	C. Miller (AUS)	64 63
1980	C. Miller (AUS)	W. Masur (AUS)	76 62
1981	J. Windahl (SWE)	P. Cash (AUS)	64 64
1982	M. Kratzmann (AUS)	S. Youl (AUS)	63 75
1983	S. Edberg (SWE)	S. Youl (AUS)	64 64
1984	M. Kratzmann (AUS)	P. Flyn (AUS)	64 61
1985 (Nov)	S. Barr (AUS)	S. Furlong (AUS)	76 67 63
1986 not played			
1987 (Jan)	J. Stoltenberg (AUS)	T. Woodbridge (AUS)	62 76
1988	J. Anderson (AUS)	A. Florent (AUS)	75 76
1989	N. Kulti (SWE)	T. Woodbridge (AUS)	62 60
1990	D. Dier (GER)	L. Paes (IND)	64 76
1991	T. Enqvist (SWE)	S. Gleeson (AUS)	76 67 61
1992	G. Doyle (AUS)	B. Dunn (USA)	62 60
1993	J. Baily (GBR)	S. Downs (NZL)	63 62
1994	B. Ellwood (AUS)	A. Ilie (AUS)	57 63 63
1995	N. Kiefer (GER)	J. Lee (KOR)	64 64
1996	B. Rehnqvist (SWE)	M. Hellstrom (SWE)	26 62 75
1997	D. Elsner (GER)	W. Whitehouse (RSA)	76 62
1998	J. Jeanpierre (FRA)	A. Vinciguerra (SWE)	46 64 63
1999	K. Pless (DEN)	M. Youzhny (RUS)	64 63
2000	A. Roddick (USA)	M. Ancic (CRO)	76 63
2001	J. Tipsarevic (YUG)	Y. Wang (TPE)	36 75 60
2002	C. Morel (FRA)	T. Roid (AUS)	64 64
2003	M. Baghdatis (CYP)	F. Mergea (ROM)	64 64
2004	G. Monfils (FRA)	J. Ouanna (FRA)	60 63

Girls' Singles

Year	Champion	Runner-up	Score
1930	E. Hood (AUS)	N. Hall (AUS)	64 57 119
1931	J. Hartigan (AUS)		
1932	N. Lewis (AUS)		
1933	N. Lewis (AUS)		
1934	M. Blick (AUS)		
1935	T. Coyne (AUS)		
1936	T. Coyne (AUS)		
1937	M. Wilson (AUS)		
1938	J. Wood (AUS)		
1939	J. Wood (AUS)		
1940	J. Wood (AUS)		
1941-45 not played			
1946	S. Grant (AUS)		
1947	J. Tuckfield (AUS)		
1948	B. Penrose (AUS)		
1949	J. Warnock (AUS)		
1950	B. McIntyre (AUS)	H. Angwin (AUS)	46 64 64
1951	M. Carter (AUS)	H. Astley (AUS)	36 64 64
1952	M. Carter (AUS)		
1953	J. Staley (AUS)	M. Carter (AUS)	61 64
1954	E. Orton (AUS)	M. McCalman (AUS)	63 64
1955	E. Orton (AUS)	M. Hellyer (AUS)	60 75
1956	L. Coghlan (AUS)	M. Hellyer (AUS)	60 75
1957	M. Rayson (AUS)	J. Lehane (AUS)	57 62 62
1958	J. Lehane (AUS)	B. Holstein (AUS)	75 61
1959	J. Lehane (AUS)	M. Smith (AUS)	60 61

Year	Champion	Runner-up	Score
1960	L. Turner (AUS)	M. Smith (AUS)	26 62 62
1961	R. Ebbern (AUS)	F. Toyne (AUS)	46 86 60
1962	R. Ebbern (AUS)	M. Schacht (AUS)	64 63
1963	R. Ebbern (AUS)	K. Dening (AUS)	75 63
1964	K. Dening (AUS)	K. Melville (AUS)	26 63 97
1965	K. Melville (AUS)	H. Gourlay (AUS)	61 61
1966	A. Krantzcke (AUS)	K. Melville (AUS)	63 63
1967	A. Kenny (AUS)	J. Young (AUS)	63 46 61
1968	L. Hunt (AUS)	K. Harris (AUS)	26 63 86
1969	L. Hunt (AUS)	J. Young (AUS)	46 61 75
1970	E. Goolagong (AUS)	J. Young (AUS)	61 61
1971	P. Coleman (AUS)		
1972	P. Coleman (AUS)		
1973	C. O'Neill (AUS)	J. Walker (AUS)	26 62 86
1974	J. Walker (AUS)		
1975	S. Barker (GBR)	C. O'Neill (AUS)	62 76
1976	S. Saliba (AUS)	J. Fenwick (AUS)	26 63 64
1977 (Jan)	P. Bailey (AUS)	A. Tobin (AUS)	62 63
1977 (Dec)	A. Tobin (AUS)	L. Harrison (AUS)	61 62
1978	E. Little (AUS)	S. Leo (AUS)	61 62
1979	A. Minter (AUS)	S. Leo (AUS)	64 63
1980	A. Minter (AUS)	E. Sayers (AUS)	64 62
1981	A. Minter (AUS)	C. Vanier (FRA)	64 62
1982	A. Brown (GBR)	P. Paradis (FRA)	63 64
1983	A. Brown (GBR)	B. Randall (AUS)	76 63
1984	A. Croft (GBR)	H. Dahlstrom (SWE)	60 61
1985	J. Byrne (AUS)	L. Field (AUS)	61 63
1986 not played			
1987	M. Jaggard (AUS)	N. Provis (AUS)	62 64
1988	J. Faull (AUS)	E. Derly (FRA)	64 64
1989	J. Kessaris (AUS)	A. Farley (USA)	61 62
1990	M. Maleeva (BUL)	L. Stacey (AUS)	75 67 61
1991	N. Pratt (AUS)	K. Godridge (AUS)	64 63
1992	J. Limmer (AUS)	L. Davenport (USA)	75 62
1993	H. Rusch (GER)	A. Glass (GER)	61 62
1994	T. Musgrave (AUS)	B. Schett (AUT)	46 64 62
1995	S. Drake-Brockman (AUS)	A. Elwood (AUS)	63 46 75
1996	M. Grzybowska (POL)	N. Dechy (FRA)	61 46 61
1997	M. Lucic (CRO)	M. Weingartner (GER)	62 62
1998	J. Kostanic (CRO)	W. Prakusya (INA)	60 75
1999	V. Razzano (FRA)	K. Basternakova (SVK)	61 61
2000	A. Kapros (HUN)	M. Martinez (ESP)	62 36 62
2001	J. Jankovic (YUG)	S. Arvidsson (SWE)	62 61
2002	B. Strycova (CZE)	M. Sharapova (RUS)	60 75
2003	B. Strycova (CZE)	V. Kutuzova (UKR)	06 62 62
2004	S. Peer (ISR)	N. Vaidisova (CZE)	61 64

	Boys' Doubles	**Girls' Doubles**
Year	Champions	Champions
1922	C. Grogan/L. Roche	
1923	E. Moon/L. Roche	
1924	A. Berckelman/R. Dunlop	
1925	J. Crawford/H. Hopman	
1926	J. Crawford/H.Hopman	
1927	J. Crawford/H. Hopman	

Australian Junior Championships (continued)

Year	Champions	Champions
1928	J. Crawford/C. Whiteman	
1929	C. Cropper/W. Walker	
1930	A. Quist/D. Turnbull	N. Hall/E. Hood (AUS)
1931	J. Purcell/B. Tonkin	S. Moon/E. Westacott (AUS)
1932	A. Quist/L. Schwartz	F. Francisco/J. Williams (AUS)
1933	J. Purcell/B. Tonkin	D. Stevenson/G. Stevenson (AUS)
1934	N. Ennis/C. McKenzie	E. Chrystal/E. McColl (AUS)
1935	J. Bromwich/A. Huxley	D. Stevenson/N. Wynne (AUS)
1936	J. Gilchrist/H. Lindo (AUS)	M. Carter/M. Wilson (AUS)
1937	J. Bromwich/D. Pails (AUS)	J. Prior/I. Webb (AUS)
1938	D. Pails/W. Sidwell (AUS)	A. Burton/J. Wood (AUS)
1939	R. Felan/H. Impey (AUS)	A. Burton/J. Wood (AUS)
1940	W. Edwards/D. Pails (AUS)	A. Burton/J. Wood (AUS)
1941-45 not played		
1946	F. Herringe/G. Worthington (AUS)	N. Reid/H. Utz (AUS)
1947	R. Hartwig/A. Kendall (AUS)	S. Jackson/V. Linehan (AUS)
1948	D. Candy/K. McGregor (AUS)	G. Blair/B. Bligh (AUS)
1949	J. Blacklock/C. Wilderspin (AUS)	B. Penrose/J. Robbins (AUS)
1950	L. Hoad/K. Rosewall (AUS)	C. Borelli/P. Southcombe (AUS)
1951	L. Hoad/K. Rosewall (AUS)	J. Staley/M. Wallis (AUS)
1952	L. Hoad/K. Rosewall (AUS)	M. Carter/B. Holstein (AUS)
1953	W. Gilmore/W. Woodcock (AUS)	M. Carter/B. Warby (AUS)
1954	M. Anderson/R. Emerson (AUS)	B. Holstein/B. Jones (AUS)
1955	M. Green/C. Moss (USA)	F. Orton/P. Parmenter (AUS)
1956	P. Hearnden/B. Mark (AUS)	S. Armstrong (GBR)/L. Coghlan (AUS)
1957	F. Gorman/R. Laver (AUS)	M. Rayson/V. Roberts (AUS)
1958	R. Hewitt/M. Mulligan (AUS)	B. Holstein/J. Lehane (AUS)
1959	J. Arilla (ESP)/B. Buchholz (AUS)	J. Lehane/D. Robberds (AUS)
1960	G. Hughes/J. Shepherd (AUS)	D. Robberds/L. Turner (AUS)
1961	R. Brent/J. Newcombe (AUS)	R. Ebbern/M. Schacht (AUS)
1962	W. Bowrey/G. Knox (AUS)	H. Ross/J. Star (AUS)
1963	R. Brien/J. Cotterill (AUS)	P. McClenaughan/G. Sherriff (AUS)
1964	S. Matthews/G. Stilwell (GBR)	K. Dening/H. Gourlay (AUS)
1965	T. Musgrave/J. Walker (AUS)	H. Gourlay/K. Melville (AUS)
1966	R. Layton/P. McCumstie (AUS)	K. Krantzcke/P. Turner (AUS)
1967	J. Bartlett (AUS)/S. Ginman (SWE)	S. Alexander/C. Cooper (AUS)
1968	P. Dent/W. Lloyd (AUS)	L. Hunt/V. Lancaster (AUS)
1969	N. Higgins/J. James (AUS)	P. Edwards/E. Goolagong (AUS)
1970	A. McDonald/G. Perkins (AUS)	J. Fallis/J. Young (AUS)
1971	S. Marks/M. Phillips (AUS)	P. Edwards/J. Whyte (AUS)
1972	W. Durham/S. Myers (AUS)	S. Irvine/P. Whytcross (AUS)
1973	T. Saunders/G. Thoroughgood (AUS)	J. Dimond/D. Fromholtz (AUS)
1974	D. Carter/T. Little (AUS)	N. Gregory/J. Hanrahan (AUS)
1975	G. Busby/W. Maher (AUS)	D. Evers/N. Gregory (AUS)
1976	C. Fancutt/P. McCarthy (AUS)	J. Morton/J. Wilton (AUS)
1977 (Jan)	P. Davies/P. Smylie (AUS)	K. Pratt/A. Tobin (AUS)
1977 (Dec)	R. Kelly/G. Thams (AUS)	K. Pratt/A. Tobin (AUS)
1978	M. Fancutt/W. Gilmour (AUS)	D. Freeman/K. Mantle (AUS)
1979	M. Fancutt/G. Whitecross (AUS)	L. Cassell/S. Leo (AUS)
1980	C. Miller/W. Masur (AUS)	A. Minter/M. Yates (AUS)
1981	D. Lewis (NZL)/T. Withers (AUS)	M. Booth/S. Hodgk (AUS)
1982	B. Burke/M. Hartnett (AUS)	A. Gulley/K. Staunton (AUS)
1983	J. Harty/D. Tyson (AUS)	B. Randall/K. Staunton (AUS)
1984	M. Baroch/M. Kratzmann (AUS)	L. Field (AUS)/L. Savchenko (URS)
1985	B. Custer/D. Macpherson (AUS)	J. Byrne/J. Thompson (AUS)

Year	Champions	Champions
1986 not played		
1987	J. Stoltenberg/T. Woodbridge (AUS)	A. Devries (BEL)/N. Provis (AUS)
1988	J. Stoltenberg/T. Woodbridge (AUS)	J. Faull/R. McQuillan (AUS)
1989	J. Anderson/T. Woodbridge (AUS)	A. Strnadova/E. Sviglerova (TCH)
1990	R. Petterson/M. Renstroem (SWE)	R. Mayer/L. Zaltz (ISR)
1991	G. Doyle/J. Eagle (AUS)	K. Habsudova (TCH)/B. Ritter (GER)
1992	G. Doyle/B. Sceney (AUS)	L. Davenport/N. London (USA)
1993	L. Rehmann/C. Tambue (GER)	J. Manta (SUI)/L. Richterova (TCH)
1994	B. Ellwood/M. Philippoussis (AUS)	C. Morariu (USA)/L. Varmuzova (CZE)
1995	L. Bourgeois (AUS)/J. Lee (KOR)	C. Morariu (USA)/L. Varmuzova (CZE)
1996	D. Bracciali (ITA)/J. Robichaud (CAN)	M. Pastikova/J. Schonfeldova (CZE)
1997	D. Sherwood/J. Trotman (GBR)	M. Lucic (CRO)/J. Wohr (GER)
1998	J. Haehnel/J. Jeanpierre (FRA)	E. Dominikovic/A. Molik (AUS)
1999	J. Melzer (AUT)/K. Pless (DEN)	E. Daniilidou (GRE)/V. Razzano (FRA)
2000	N. Mahut (FRA)/T. Robredo (ESP)	A. Kapros (HUN)/C. Wheeler (AUS)
2001	Y. Abougzir (USA)/L. Vitullo (ARG)	P. Cetkovska/B. Strycova (CZE)
2002	R. Henry/T. Reid (AUS)	G. Dulko (ARG)/A. Widjaja (INA)
2003	S. Oudsema/P. Simmonds (USA)	C. Dell'Acqua/A. Szili (AUS)
2004	B. Evans/S. Oudsema (USA)	Y. Chan (TPE)/S. Sun (CHN)

French Junior Championships – Roland Garros

Boys' Singles

Year	Champion	Runner-up	Score
1947	J. Brichant (BEL)	A. Roberts (GBR)	63 46 75
1948	K. Nielsen (DEN)	J. Brichant (BEL)	36 63 64
1949	J. Molinari (FRA)	R. Haillet (FRA)	62 79 86
1950	R. Dubuisson (FRA)	G. Pilet (FRA)	1012 61 63
1951	H. Richardson (USA)	G. Mezzi (BEL)	63 62
1952	K. Rosewall (AUS)	J. Grinda (FRA)	62 62
1953	J. Grinda (FRA)	F. Andries (BEL)	61 62
1954	R. Emerson (AUS)	J. Grinda (FRA)	61 68 64
1955	A. Gimeno (ESP)	M. Belkhodja (TUN)	62 46 75
1956	M. Belkhodja (TUN)	R. Laver (AUS)	46 64 63
1957	A. Arilla (ESP)	J. Renavand (FRA)	68 63 64
1958	B. Buchholz (USA)	A. Bresson (FRA)	68 64 62
1959	I. Buding (GER)	E. Mandarino (BRA)	60 06 64
1960	I. Buding (GER)	J. Gisbert (ESP)	63 86
1961	J. Newcombe (AUS)	D. Contet (FRA)	67 15-15 ret
1962	J. Newcombe (AUS)	T. Koch (BRA)	46 64 86
1963	N. Kalogeropoulos (GRE)	T. Koch (BRA)	26 97 63
1964	C. Richey (USA)	G. Goven (FRA)	64 62
1965	G. Battrick (GBR)	G. Goven (FRA)	75 64
1966	V. Korotkov (URS)	J. Guerrero (ESP)	63 62
1967	P. Proisy (FRA)	J. Tavares (BRA)	63 86
1968	P. Dent (AUS)	J. Alexander (AUS)	63 36 75
1969	A. Munoz (ESP)	J. Thamin (FRA)	62 46 64
1970	J. Herrera (ESP)	J. Thamin (FRA)	46 62 64
1971	C. Barazzutti (ITA)	S. Warboys (GBR)	26 63 61
1972	C. Mottram (GBR)	U. Pinner (GER)	62 26 75
1973	V. Pecci (PAR)	P. Slozil (TCH)	64 64
1974	C. Casa (FRA)	U. Marten (GER)	16 64 61
1975	C. Roger-Vasselin (FRA)	P. Elter (GER)	61 62
1976	H. Gunthardt (SUI)	J. Clerc (ARG)	46 76 64

French Junior Championships – Roland Garros (continued)

Year	Champion	Runner-up	Score
1977	J. McEnroe (USA)	R. Kelly (AUS)	61 61
1978	I. Lendl (TCH)	P. Hjertquist (SWE)	76 64
1979	R. Krishnan (IND)	B. Testerman (USA)	26 61 60
1980	H. Leconte (FRA)	A. Tous (ESP)	76 63
1981	M. Wilander (SWE)	J. Brown (USA)	75 61
1982	T. Benhabiles (FRA)	L. Courteau (FRA)	76 62
1983	S. Edberg (SWE)	F. Fevrier (FRA)	26 62 61
1984	K. Carlsson (SWE)	M. Kratzmann (AUS)	63 63
1985	J. Yzaga (PER)	T. Muster (AUT)	26 63 60
1986	G. Perez-Roldan (ARG)	S. Grenier (FRA)	46 63 62
1987	G. Perez-Roldan (ARG)	J. Stoltenberg (AUS)	63 36 61
1988	N. Pereira (VEN)	M. Larsson (SWE)	76 63
1989	F. Santoro (FRA)	J. Palmer (USA)	63 36 97
1990	A. Gaudenzi (ITA)	T. Enqvist (SWE)	26 76 64
1991	A. Medvedev (UKR)	T. Enqvist (SWE)	64 76
1992	A. Pavel (ROM)	M. Navarra (ITA)	61 36 63
1993	R. Carretero (ESP)	A. Costa (ESP)	60 76
1994	J. Diaz (ESP)	G. Galimberti (ITA)	63 76
1995	M. Zabaleta (ARG)	M. Puerta (ARG)	62 63
1996	A. Martin (ESP)	B. Rehnquist (SWE)	63 76
1997	D. Elsner (GER)	L. Horna (PER)	64 64
1998	F. Gonzalez (CHI)	J. Ferrero (ESP)	46 64 63
1999	G. Coria (ARG)	D. Nalbandian (ARG)	64 63
2000	P. Mathieu (FRA)	T. Robredo (ESP)	36 76 62
2001	C. Cuadrado (ESP)	B. Dabul (ARG)	61 60
2002	R. Gasquet (FRA)	L. Recouderc (FRA)	60 61
2003	S. Wawrinka (SUI)	B. Baker (USA)	75 46 63
2004	G. Monfils (FRA)	A. Kuznetsov (USA)	62 62

Girls' Singles

Year	Champion	Runner-up	Score
1953	C. Brunon (FRA)	B. De Chambure (FRA)	26 62 60
1954	B. De Chambure (FRA)	C. Monnot (FRA)	64 86
1955	M. Reidl (ITA)	C. Baumgarten (FRA)	64 60
1956	E. Launay (FRA)	J. Lieffrig (FRA)	61 64
1957	I. Buding (GER)	C. Seghers (FRA)	62 75
1958	F. Gordigiani (ITA)	S. Galtier (FRA)	63 26 62
1959	J. Cross (RSA)	M. Rucquoy (BEL)	61 64
1960	F. Durr (FRA)	M. Rucquoy (BEL)	60 61
1961	R. Ebbern (AUS)	F. Courteix (FRA)	61 63
1962	K. Dening (AUS)	R. Ebbern (AUS)	16 61 63
1963	M. Salfati (FRA)	A. Van Zyl (RSA)	62 46 61
1964	N. Seghers (FRA)	E. Subirats (MEX)	63 63
1965	E. Emanuel (RSA)	E. Subirats (MEX)	64 62
1966	O. De Roubin (FRA)	M. Cristiani (FRA)	64 63
1967	C. Molesworth (GBR)	P. Montano (MEX)	36 64 64
1968	L. Hunt (AUS)	E. Izopajtyse (URS)	64 62
1969	K. Sawamatsu (JPN)	A. Cassaigne (FRA)	62 60
1970	V. Burton (GBR)	R. Tomanova (TCH)	64 64
1971	E. Granatourova (URS)	F. Guedy (FRA)	26 64 75
1972	R. Tomanova (TCH)	M. Jausovec (YUG)	62 63
1973	M. Jausovec (YUG)	R. Marsikova (TCH)	63 62
1974	M. Simionescu (ROM)	S. Barker (GBR)	63 63
1975	R. Marsikova (TCH)	L. Mottram (GBR)	63 57 62
1976	M. Tyler (GBR)	M. Zoni (ITA)	61 63

Girls' Singles

Year	Champion	Runner-up	Score
1977	A. Smith (USA)	H. Strachonova (TCH)	63 76
1978	H. Mandlikova (TCH)	M. Rothschild (USA)	60 61
1979	L. Sandin (SWE)	M. Piatek (USA)	63 61
1980	K. Horvath (USA)	K. Henry (USA)	62 62
1981	B. Gadusek (USA)	H. Sukova (TCH)	67 61 64
1982	M. Maleeva (BUL)	P. Barg (USA)	75 62
1983	P. Paradis (FRA)	D. Spence (USA)	76 63
1984	G. Sabatini (ARG)	K. Maleeva (BUL)	63 57 63
1985	L. Garrone (ITA)	D. Van Rensburg (RSA)	61 63
1986	P. Tarabini (ARG)	N. Provis (AUS)	63 63
1987	N. Zvereva (URS)	J. Pospisilova (TCH)	61 60
1988	J. Halard (FRA)	A. Farley (USA)	62 46 75
1989	J. Capriati (USA)	E. Sviglerova (TCH)	64 60
1990	M. Maleeva (BUL)	T. Ignatieva (URS)	62 63
1991	A. Smashnova (ISR)	I. Gorrochategui (ARG)	26 75 61
1992	R. De Los Rios (PAR)	P. Suarez (ARG)	64 60
1993	M. Hingis (SUI)	L. Courtois (BEL)	75 75
1994	M. Hingis (SUI)	S. Jeyaseelan (CAN)	63 61
1995	A. Cocheteux (FRA)	M. Weingartner (GER)	75 64
1996	A. Mauresmo (FRA)	M. Shaughnessy (USA)	60 64
1997	J. Henin (BEL)	C. Black (ZIM)	46 64 64
1998	N. Petrova (RUS)	J. Dokic (AUS)	63 63
1999	L. Dominguez Lino (ESP)	S. Foretz (FRA)	64 64
2000	V. Razzano (FRA)	M. Salerni (ARG)	57 64 86
2001	K. Kanepi (EST)	S. Kuznetsova (RUS)	63 16 62
2002	A. Widjaja (INA)	A. Harkleroad (USA)	36 61 64
2003	A-L. Groenefeld (GER)	V. Douchevina	64 64
2004	S. Karatantcheva (BUL)	M Gojnea (ROM)	64 60

Boys' Doubles / Girls' Doubles

Year	Boys' Doubles Champions	Girls' Doubles Champions
1981	B. Moir/M. Robertson (RSA)	S. Amiach/C. Vanier (FRA)
1982	P. Cash/J. Frawley (AUS)	B. Herr/J. Lagasse (USA)
1983	M. Kratzmann/S. Youl (AUS)	C. Anderholm/H. Olsson (SWE)
1984	L. Jensen/P. McEnroe (USA)	D. Ketelaar/S. Schilder (NED)
1985	P. Korda/C. Suk (TCH)	M. Perez-Roldan/P. Tarabini (ARG)
1986	F. Davin/G. Perez-Roldan (ARG)	L. Meskhi/N. Zvereva (URS)
1987	J. Courier/J. Stark (USA)	N. Medvedeva/N. Zvereva (URS)
1988	J. Stoltenberg/T. Woodbridge (AUS)	A. Dechaume/E. Derly (FRA)
1989	J. Anderson/T. Woodbridge (AUS)	N. Pratt (AUS)/S. Wang (TPE)
1990	S. Leblanc/S. Lareau (CAN)	R. Dragomir/I. Spirlea (ROM)
1991	T. Enqvist/M. Martinelle (SWE)	E. Bes (ESP)/I. Gorrochategui (ARG)
1992	E. Abaroa (MEX)/G. Doyle (AUS)	L. Courtois/N. Feber (BEL)
1993	S. Downs/J. Greenhalgh (NZL)	L. Courtois/N. Feber (BEL)
1994	G. Kuerten (BRA)/N. Lapentti (ECU)	M. Hingis (SUI)/H. Nagyova (SVK)
1995	R. Sluiter/P. Wessels (NED)	C. Morariu (USA)/L. Varmuzova (CZE)
1996	S. Grosjean/O. Mutis (FRA)	A. Canepa/G. Casoni (ITA)
1997	J. de Armas (VEN)/L. Horna (PER)	C. Black (ZIM)/I. Selyutina (KAZ)
1998	J. de Armas (VEN)/F. Gonzalez (CHI)	K. Clijsters (BEL)/J. Dokic (AUS)
1999	I. Labadze (GEO)/L. Zovko (CRO)	F. Pennetta/R. Vinci (ITA)
2000	M. Lopez/T. Robredo (ESP)	M. Martinez/A. Medina (ESP)
2001	A. Falla/C. Salamanca (COL)	P. Cetkovska/R. Voracova (CZE)
2002	M. Bayer/P. Petzschner (GER)	A. Groenefeld (GER)/B. Strycova (CZE)
2003	G. Balazs (HUN)/D. Sela (ISR)	M. Fraga-Perez/A. Gonzalez-Penas (ESP)
2004	P. Andujar-Alba/M. Granollers-Pujol (ESP)	K. Bohmova (CZE)/M. Krajicek (NED)

The Junior Championships, Wimbledon

Boys' Singles

Year	Champion	Runner-up	Score
1947	K. Nielsen (DEN)	S. Davidson (SWE)	86 61 97
1948	S. Stockenberg (SWE)	D. Vad (HUN)	60 68 57 64 62
1949	S. Stockenberg (SWE)	J. Horn (GBR)	62 61
1950	J. Horn (GBR)	K. Mobarek (EGY)	60 62
1951	J. Kupferburger (RSA)	K. Mobarek (EGY)	86 64
1952	B. Wilson (GBR)	T. Fancutt (RSA)	63 63
1953	B. Knight (GBR)	R. Krishnan (IND)	75 64
1954	R. Krishnan (IND)	A. Cooper (AUS)	62 75
1955	M. Hann (GBR)	J. Lundquist (SWE)	60 119
1956	R. Holmberg (USA)	R. Laver (AUS)	61 61
1957	J. Tattershall (GBR)	I. Ribeiro (BRA)	62 61
1958	B. Buchholz (USA)	P. Lall (IND)	61 63
1959	T. Lejus (URS)	R. Barnes (BRA)	62 64
1960	R. Mandelstam (RSA)	J. Mukerjea (IND)	16 86 64
1961	C. Graebner (USA)	E. Blanke (AUT)	63 97
1962	S. Matthews (GBR)	A. Metreveli (URS)	108 36 64
1963	N. Kalogeropoulos (GRE)	I. El Shafei (EGY)	64 63
1964	I. El Shafei (EGY)	V. Korotkov (URS)	62 63
1965	V. Korotkov (URS)	G. Goven (FRA)	62 36 63
1966	V. Korotkov (URS)	B. Fairlie (NZL)	63 119
1967	M. Orantes (ESP)	M. Estep (USA)	62 60
1968	J. Alexander (AUS)	J. Thamin (FRA)	61 62
1969	B. Bertram (RSA)	J. Alexander (AUS)	75 57 64
1970	B. Bertram (RSA)	F. Gebert (GER)	60 63
1971	R. Kreiss (USA)	S. Warboys (GBR)	26 64 63
1972	B. Borg (SWE)	C. Mottram (GBR)	63 46 75
1973	B. Martin (USA)	C. Dowdeswell (RHO)	62 64
1974	B. Martin (USA)	A. Amritraj (IND)	62 61
1975	C. Lewis (NZL)	R. Ycaza (ECU)	61 64
1976	H. Gunthardt (SUI)	P. Elter (GER)	64 75
1977	V. Winitsky (USA)	T. Teltscher (USA)	61 16 86
1978	I. Lendl (TCH)	J. Turpin (USA)	63 64
1979	R. Krishnan (IND)	D. Siegler (USA)	60 62
1980	T. Tulasne (FRA)	H. Beutel (GER)	64 36 64
1981	M. Anger (USA)	P. Cash (AUS)	76 75
1982	P. Cash (AUS)	H. Sundstrom (SWE)	64 67 63
1983	S. Edberg (SWE)	J. Frawley (AUS)	63 76
1984	M. Kratzmann (AUS)	S. Kruger (RSA)	64 46 63
1985	L. Lavalle (MEX)	E. Velez (MEX)	64 64
1986	E. Velez (MEX)	J. Sanchez (ESP)	63 75
1987	D. Nargiso (ITA)	J. Stoltenberg (AUS)	76 64
1988	N. Pereira (VEN)	G. Raoux (FRA)	76 62
1989	N. Kulti (SWE)	T. Woodbridge (AUS)	64 63
1990	L. Paes (IND)	M. Ondruska (RSA)	75 26 64
1991	T. Enqvist (SWE)	M. Joyce (USA)	64 63
1992	D. Skoch (TCH)	B. Dunn (USA)	64 63
1993	R. Sabau (ROM)	J. Szymanski (VEN)	61 63
1994	S. Humphries (USA)	M. Philippoussis (AUS)	76 36 64
1995	O. Mutis (FRA)	N. Kiefer (GER)	62 62
1996	V. Voltchkov (BLR)	I. Ljubicic (CRO)	36 62 63
1997	W. Whitehouse (RSA)	D. Elsner (GER)	63 76
1998	R. Federer (SUI)	I. Labadze (GEO)	64 64
1999	J. Melzer (AUT)	K. Pless (DEN)	76 63
2000	N. Mahut (FRA)	M Ancic (CRO)	36 63 75

Year	Champion	Runner-up	Score
2001	R. Valent (SUI)	G. Muller (LUX)	36 75 63
2002	T. Reid (AUS)	L. Ouahab (ALG)	76 64
2003	F. Mergea (ROM)	C. Guccione (AUS)	62 76
2004	G. Monfils (FRA)	M. Kasiri (GBR)	75 76

Girls' Singles

Year	Champion	Runner-up	Score
1947	G. Domken (BEL)	B. Wallen (SWE)	61 64
1948	O. Miskova (TCH)	V. Rigollet (SUI)	64 62
1949	C. Mercelis (BEL)	J. Partridge (GBR)	64 62
1950	L. Cornell (GBR)	A. Winter (NOR)	62 64
1951	L. Cornell (GBR)	S. Lazzarino (ITA)	63 64
1952	F. ten Bosch (NED)	R. Davar (IND)	57 61 75
1953	D. Killan (RSA)	V. Pitt (GBR)	64 46 61
1954	V. Pitt (GBR)	C. Monnot (FRA)	57 63 62
1955	S. Armstrong (GBR)	B. De Chambure (FRA)	62 64
1956	A. Haydon (GBR)	I. Buding (GER)	63 64
1957	M. Arnold (USA)	E. Reyes (MEX)	86 62
1958	S. Moore (USA)	A. Dmitrieva (URS)	62 64
1959	J. Cross (RSA)	D. Schuster (AUT)	61 61
1960	K. Hantze (USA)	L. Hutchings (RSA)	64 64
1961	G. Baksheeva (URS)	K. Chabot (USA)	64 86
1962	G. Baksheeva (URS)	E. Terry (NZL)	64 62
1963	M. Salfati (FRA)	K. Dening (AUS)	64 61
1964	P. Bartkowicz (USA)	E. Subirats (MEX)	63 61
1965	O. Morozova (URS)	R. Giscafre (ARG)	63 63
1966	B. Lindstrom (FIN)	J. Congdon (GBR)	75 63
1967	J. Salome (NED)	E. Strandberg (SWE)	64 62
1968	K. Pigeon (USA)	L. Hunt (AUS)	64 63
1969	K. Sawamatsu (JPN)	B. Kirk (RSA)	61 16 75
1970	S. Walsh (USA)	M. Kroshina (URS)	86 64
1971	M. Kroshina (URS)	S. Minford (GBR)	64 64
1972	I. Kloss (RSA)	G. Coles (GBR)	64 46 64
1973	A. Kiyomura (USA)	M. Navratilova (TCH)	64 75
1974	M. Jausovec (YUG)	M. Simionescu (ROM)	75 64
1975	N. Chmyreva (URS)	R. Marsikova (TCH)	64 63
1976	N. Chmyreva (URS)	M. Kruger (RSA)	63 26 61
1977	L. Antonoplis (USA)	M. Louie (USA)	75 61
1978	T. Austin (USA)	H. Mandlikova (TCH)	60 36 64
1979	M. Piatek (USA)	A. Moulton (USA)	61 63
1980	D. Freeman (AUS)	S. Leo (AUS)	76 75
1981	Z. Garrison (USA)	R. Uys (RSA)	64 36 60
1982	C. Tanvier (FRA)	H. Sukova (TCH)	62 75
1983	P. Paradis (FRA)	P. Hy (HKG)	62 61
1984	A. Croft (GBR)	E. Reinach (RSA)	36 63 62
1985	A. Holikova (TCH)	J. Byrne (AUS)	75 61
1986	N. Zvereva (URS)	L. Meskhi (URS)	26 62 97
1987	N. Zvereva (URS)	J. Halard (FRA)	64 64
1988	B. Schultz (NED)	E. Derly (FRA)	76 61
1989	A. Strnadova (TCH)	M. McGrath (USA)	62 63
1990	A. Strnadova (TCH)	K. Sharpe (AUS)	62 64
1991	B. Rittner (GER)	E. Makarova (URS)	67 62 63
1992	C. Rubin (USA)	L. Courtois (BEL)	62 75
1993	N. Feber (BEL)	R. Grande (ITA)	76 16 62
1994	M. Hingis (SUI)	M. Jeon (KOR)	75 64

The Junior Championships, Wimbledon (continued)

Year	Champion	Runner-up	Score
1995	A. Olsza (POL)	T. Tanasugarn (THA)	75 76
1996	A. Mauresmo (FRA)	M. Serna (ESP)	46 63 64
1997	C. Black (ZIM)	A. Rippner (USA)	63 75
1998	K. Srebotnik (SLO)	K. Clijsters (BEL)	76 63
1999	I. Tulyaganova (UZB)	L. Krasnoroutskaya (RUS)	76 64
2000	M. Salerni (ARG)	T. Perebiynis (UKR)	64 75
2001	A. Widjaja (INA)	D. Safina (RUS)	64 06 75
2002	V. Douchevina (RUS)	M. Sharapova (RUS)	46 61 62
2003	K. Flipkens (BEL)	A. Tchakvetadze (RUS)	64 36 63
2004	K. Bondarenko (UKR)	A. Ivanovic (SCG)	64 67 62

Boys' Doubles / Girls' Doubles

Year	Boys' Doubles Champions	Girls' Doubles Champions
1982	P. Cash/J. Frawley (AUS)	P. Barg/B. Herr (USA)
1983	M. Kratzmann/S. Youl (AUS)	P. Fendick (USA)/P. Hy (HKG)
1984	R. Brown/R. Weiss (USA)	C. Kuhlman/S. Rehe (USA)
1985	A. Moreno (MEX)/J. Yzaga (PER)	L. Field/J. Thompson (AUS)
1986	T. Carbonell (ESP)/P. Korda (TCH)	M. Jaggard/L. O'Neill (AUS)
1987	J. Stoltenberg/T. Woodbridge (AUS)	N. Medvedeva/N. Zvereva (URS)
1988	J. Stoltenberg/T. Woodbridge (AUS)	J. Faull/R. McQuillan (AUS)
1989	J. Palmer/J. Stark (USA)	J. Capriati/M. McGrath (USA)
1990	S. Lareau/S. Leblanc (CAN)	K. Habsudova/A. Strnadova (TCH)
1991	K. Alami (MAR)/G. Rusedski (CAN)	C. Barclay (AUS)/L. Zaltz (ISR)
1992	S. Baldas/S. Draper (AUS)	M. Avotins/L. McShea (AUS)
1993	S. Downs/J. Greenhalgh (NZL)	L. Courtois/N. Feber (BEL)
1994	B. Ellwood/M. Philippoussis (AUS)	E. DeVilliers (RSA)/E. Jelfs (GBR)
1995	M. Lee/J. Trotman (GBR)	C. Black (ZIM)/A. Olsza (POL)
1996	D. Bracciali (ITA)/J. Robichaud (CAN)	O. Barabanschikova (BLR)/A. Mauresmo (FRA)
1997	L. Horna (PER)/N. Massu (CHI)	C. Black (ZIM)/I. Selyutina (KAZ)
1998	R. Federer (SUI)/O. Rochus (BEL)	E. Dyrberg (DEN)/J. Kostanic (CRO)
1999	G. Coria/D. Nalbandian (ARG)	D. Bedanova (CZE)/M. Salerni (ARG)
2000	D. Coene/K. Vliegen (BEL)	I. Gaspar (ROM)/T. Perebiynis (UKR)
2001	F. Dancevic (CAN)/G. Lapentti (ECU)	G. Dulko (ARG)/A. Harkleroad (USA)
2002	F. Mergea/H. Tecau (ROM)	E. Clijsters (BEL)/B. Strycova (CZE)
2003	F. Mergea/H. Tecau (ROM)	A. Kleybanova (RUS)/S. Mirza (IND)
2004	B. Evans/S. Oudsema (USA)	V. Azarenka/V. Havartsova (BLR)

US Junior Championships

Boys' Singles

Year	Champion	Runner-up	Score
1973	B. Martin (USA)	C. Dowdeswell (RHO)	46 63 63
1974	B. Martin (USA)	F. Taygan (USA)	64 62
1975	H. Schoenfield (USA)	C. Lewis (NZL)	64 63
1976	R. Ycaza (ECU)	J. Clerc (ARG)	64 57 60
1977	V. Winitsky (USA)	E. Teltscher (USA)	64 64
1978	P. Hjertquist (SWE)	S. Simonsson (SWE)	76 16 76
1979	S. Davis (USA)	J. Gunnarsson (SWE)	63 61
1980	M. Falberg (USA)	E. Wilborts (NED)	67 63 63
1981	T. Hogstedt (SWE)	H. Schwaier (GER)	75 63
1982	P. Cash (AUS)	G. Forget (FRA)	63 63
1983	S. Edberg (SWE)	S. Youl (AUS)	62 64
1984	M. Kratzmann (AUS)	B. Becker (GER)	63 76
1985	T. Trigueiro (USA)	J. Blake (USA)	62 63

Boys' Singles

Year	Champion	Runner-up	Score
1986	J. Sanchez (ESP)	F. Davin (ARG)	62 62
1987	D. Wheaton (USA)	A. Cherkasov (URS)	76 60
1988	N. Pereira (VEN)	N. Kulti (SWE)	61 62
1989	J. Stark (USA)	N. Kulti (SWE)	64 61
1990	A. Gaudenzi (ITA)	M. Tillstroem (SWE)	62 46 76
1991	L. Paes (IND)	K. Alami (MAR)	64 64
1992	B. Dunn (USA)	N. Behr (ISR)	75 62
1993	M. Rios (CHI)	S. Downs (NZL)	76 63
1994	S. Schalken (NED)	M. Tahiri (MAR)	62 76
1995	N. Kiefer (GER)	U. Seetzen (GER)	63 64
1996	D. Elsner (GER)	M. Hipfl (AUT)	63 62
1997	A. Di Pasquale (FRA)	W. Whitehouse (RSA)	67 64 61
1998	D. Nalbandian (ARG)	R. Federer (SUI)	63 75
1999	J. Nieminen (FIN)	K. Pless (DEN)	67 63 64
2000	A. Roddick (USA)	R. Ginepri (USA)	61 63
2001	G. Muller (LUX)	Y. Wang (TPE)	76 62
2002	R. Gasquet (FRA)	M. Baghdatis (CYP)	75 62
2003	J. Tsonga (FRA)	M. Baghdatis (CYP)	76 63
2004	A. Murray (GBR)	S. Stakhovsky (UKR)	64 62

Girls' Singles

Year	Champion	Runner-up	Score
1974	I. Kloss (RSA)	M. Jausovec (YUG)	64 63
1975	N. Chmyeva (URS)	G. Stevens (RSA)	67 62 62
1976	M. Kruger (RSA)	L. Romanov (ROM)	63 75
1977	C. Casabianca (ARG)	L. Antonoplis (USA)	63 26 62
1978	L. Siegel (USA)	I. Madruga (ARG)	64 64
1979	A. Moulton (USA)	M. Piatek (USA)	76 76
1980	S. Mascarin (USA)	K. Keil (USA)	63 64
1981	Z. Garrison (USA)	K. Gompert (USA)	60 63
1982	B. Herr (USA)	G. Rush (USA)	63 61
1983	E. Minter (AUS)	M. Werdel (USA)	63 75
1984	K. Maleeva (BUL)	N. Sodupe (USA)	61 62
1985	L. Garrone (ITA)	A. Holikova (TCH)	62 76
1986	E. Hakami (USA)	S. Stafford (USA)	62 61
1987	N. Zvereva (URS)	S. Birch (USA)	60 63
1988	C. Cunningham (USA)	R. McQuillan (AUS)	75 63
1989	J. Capriati (USA)	R. McQuillan (AUS)	62 63
1990	M. Maleeva (BUL)	N. Van Lottum (FRA)	75 62
1991	K. Habsudova (TCH)	A. Mall (USA)	61 63
1992	L. Davenport (USA)	J. Steven (USA)	62 62
1993	M. Francesca Bentivoglio (ITA)	Y. Yoshida (JPN)	76 64
1994	M. Tu (USA)	M. Hingis (SUI)	62 64
1995	T. Snyder (USA)	A. Ellwood (AUS)	64 46 62
1996	M. Lucic (CRO)	M. Weingartner (GER)	62 61
1997	C. Black (ZIM)	K. Chevalier (FRA)	67 61 63
1998	J. Dokic (AUS)	K. Srebotnik (SLO)	64 62
1999	L. Krasnoroutskaia (RUS)	N. Petrova (RUS)	63 62
2000	M. Salerni (ARG)	T. Perebiynis (UKR)	63 64
2001	M. Bartoli (FRA)	S. Kuznetsova (RUS)	46 63 64
2002	M. Kirilenko (RUS)	B. Strycova (CZE)	64 64
2003	K. Flipkens (BEL)	M. Krajicek (NED)	63 75
2004	M. Krajicek (NED)	J. Kirkland (USA)	61 61

US Junior Championships (continued)

Year	Boys' Doubles Champions	Girls' Doubles Champions
1982	J. Canter/M. Kures (USA)	P. Barg/B. Herr (USA)
1983	M. Kratzmann/S. Youl (AUS)	A. Hulbert (USA)/B. Randall (AUS)
1984	L. Lavalle (MEX)/M. Nastase (ROM)	M. Paz/G. Sabatini (ARG)
1985	J. Blake/D. Yates (USA)	A. Holikova/R. Zrubakova (TCH)
1986	T. Carbonell/J. Sanchez (ESP)	J. Novotna/R. Zrubakova (TCH)
1987	G. Ivanisevic (YUG)/D. Nargiso (ITA)	M. McGrath/K. Po (USA)
1988	J. Stark/J. Yancey (USA)	M. McGrath/K. Po (USA)
1989	W. Ferreira/G. Stafford (RSA)	J. Capriati/M. McGrath (USA)
1990	M. Renstrom/M. Tillstrom (SWE)	K. Godridge/N. Pratt (AUS)
1991	K. Alami (MAR)/J. De Jager (USA)	K. Godridge/K. Sharpe (AUS)
1992	J. Jackson/E. Taino (USA)	L. Davenport/N. London (USA)
1993	N. Godwin/G. Williams (RSA)	N. London/J. Steven (USA)
1994	B. Ellwood (AUS)/N. Lapentti (ECU)	S. De Beer (RSA)/C. Reuter (NED)
1995	J. Lee (KOR)/J. Robichaud (CAN)	C. Morariu (USA)/L. Varmuzova (CZE)
1996	B. Bryan/M. Bryan (USA)	S. De Beer/J. Steck (RSA)
1997	F. Gonzalez/N. Massu (CHI)	M. Irvin/A. Stevenson (USA)
1998	K. Hippensteel/D. Martin (USA)	K. Clijsters (BEL)/E. Dyrberg (DEN)
1999	J. Benneteau/N. Mahut (FRA)	D. Bedanova (CZE)/I. Tulyaganova (UZB)
2000	L. Childs/J. Nelson (GBR)	G. Dulko/M. Salerni (ARG)
2001	T. Berdych (CZE)/S. Bohli (SUI)	G. Fokina/S. Kuznetsova (RUS)
2002	M. Koning/B. Van Der Valk (NED)	E. Clijsters/K. Flipkens (BEL)
2003 not played		
2004	R. Evans/S. Oudsema (USA)	M. Erakovic (NZL)/M. Krajicek (NED)

World Junior Tennis

International Team Competition for players aged 14 and under, launched by the ITF in 1991. Sixteen boys' teams and 16 girls' teams qualify for a place in the final, held at one venue over a week.

Boys' Championships

1991 Final: Spain d. Italy 2-1, Yamanakako, Japan: J. Saiz (ESP) d. P. Tabini (ITA) 62 61; A. Martin (ESP) d. C. Zoppi (ITA) 62 76; A. Ciceroni/P. Tabini (ITA) d. A. Martin/J. Vicente (ESP) 57 64 86.

1992 Final: Austria d. USA 2-1, Yamanakako, Japan: C. Trimmel (AUT) d. K. Brill (USA) 46 62 62; M. Hipfl (AUT) d. G. Abrams (USA) 64 60; G. Abrams/B. Bryan (USA) d. M. Hipfl/C. Trimmel (AUT) 61 63.

1993 Final: France d. Slovenia 2-1, Yamanakako, Japan: J. Lisnard (FRA) d. A. Krasevec (SLO) 76 63; A. Di Pasquale (FRA) d. M. Gregorc (SLO) 61 61; M. Gregorc/A. Krasevec (SLO) d. A. Di Pasquale/V. Lavergne (FRA) 75 75.

1994 Final: Italy d. Belgium 2-1, Yamanakako, Japan: O. Rochus (BEL) d. N. Fracassi (ITA) 76 36 63; F. Luzzi (ITA) d. X. Malisse (BEL) 63 76; N. Fracassi/F. Luzzi (ITA) d. X. Malisse/O. Rochus (BEL) 64 16 63.

1995 Final: Great Britain d. Germany 3-0, Yamanakako, Japan: M. Hilton (GBR) d. P. Hammer (GER) 63 46 64; S. Dickson (GBR) d. B. Bachert (GER) 75 62; S. Dickson/A. Mackin (GBR) d. B. Bachert/R. Neurohr (GER) 75 61.

1996 Final: Argentina d. Sweden 3-0, Nagoya, Japan: G. Coria (ARG) d. F. Prpic (SWE) 61 61; D. Nalbandian (ARG) d. J. Johansson (SWE) 63 63; G. Coria/A. Pastorino (ARG) d. J. Johansson/F. Prpic (SWE) 61 63.

1997 Final: South Africa d. Czech Republic 2-1, Nagoya, Japan: A. Anderson (RSA) d. M. Kokta (CZE) 75 64; D. Stegmann (RSA) d. J. Masik (CZE) 63 60; D. Karol/J. Masik (CZE) d. A. Anderson/R. Blair (RSA) 61 60.

1998 Final: Austria d. Argentina 3-0, Nagoya, Japan: J. Ager (AUT) d. J. Monaco (ARG) 64 64; S. Wiespeiner (AUT) d. B. Dabul (ARG) 46 64 61; J. Ager/C. Polessnig (AUT) d. B. Dabul/J. Ottabiani (ARG) 64 75.

1999 Final: France d. Chile 2-1, Prostejov, Czech Republic: J. Tsonga (FRA) d. G. Hormazabal (CHI) 64 63; R. Gasquet (FRA) d. J. Aguilar (CHI) 76 36 64; J. Aguilar/G. Hormazabal (CHI) d. J. Robin/J. Tsonga (FRA) 75 63.

2000 Final: Spain d. Russia 3-0, Prostejov, Czech Republic: B. Salva (ESP) d. A. Sitak (RUS) 63 63; R. Nadal (ESP) d. N. Soloviev (RUS) 63 62; M. Granollers/R. Nadal (ESP) d. D. Matsoukevitch/A. Sitak (RUS) 46 61 64.

2001 Final: Germany d. Yugoslavia 2-0, Prostejov, Czech Republic: J. Schottler (GER) d. D. Bejtulahi (YUG) 36 61 63; A. Thron (GER) d. N. Djokovic (YUG) 64 06 62; doubles not played.

2002 Final: USA d. Spain 2-1, Prostejov, Czech Republic: J. Garrapiz (ESP) d. D. Arnould (USA) 62 62; M. Fugate (USA) d. R. Bautista (ESP) 61 64; D. Arnould/M. Fugate (USA) d. R. Bautista/J. Ramos (ESP) 64 63.

2003 Final: USA d. Japan 2-1, Prostejov, Czech Republic: K. Nishikori (JPN) d. L. Rosenberg (USA) 76 26 62; D. Young (USA) d. F. Kita (JPN) 62 63; L. Rosenberg/D. Young (USA) d. F. Kita/K. Nishikori (JPN) 61 61.

2004 Final: Great Britain d. Czech Republic 2-0, Prostejov, Czech Republic: L. Barnes (GBR) d. J. Trocil (CZE) 63 75; D. Cox (GBR) d. E. Rehola (CZE) 75 76; doubles not played.

Girls' Championships

1991 Final: Czechoslovakia d. Australia 3-0, Yamanakako, Japan: A. Havrlikova (TCH) d. A. Venkatesan (AUS) 61 62; L. Cenkova (TCH) d. A. Ellwood (AUS) 75 62; L. Cenkova/A. Havrlikova (TCH) d. A. Ellwood/E. Knox (AUS) 62 76.

1992 Final: USA d. Australia 3-0, Yamanakako, Japan: A. Basica (USA) d. R. Reid (AUS) 36 76 64; M. Tu (USA) d. A. Ellwood (AUS) 64 64; A. Augustus/A. Basica (USA) d. S. Drake-Brockman/R. Reid (AUS) 62 75.

World Junior Tennis (continued)

1993 Final: Germany d. USA 2-1, Yamanakako, Japan: S. Halsell (USA) d. C. Christian (GER) 60 63; S. Klosel (GER) d. K. Gates (USA) 64 76; C. Christian/S. Klosel (GER) d. K. Gates/S. Halsell (USA) 36 63 75.

1994 Final: Germany d. Czech Republic 2-1, Yamanakako, Japan: J. Wohr (GER) d. J. Schonfeldova (CZE) 75 60; S. Kovacic (GER) d. M. Pastikova (CZE) 62 75; M. Pastikova/J. Schonfeldova (CZE) d. S. Losel/Wohr (GER) 64 61.

1995 Final: Slovenia d. Hungary 2-1, Yamanakako, Japan: T. Pisnik (SLO) d. S. Szegedi (HUN) 76 63; Z. Gubacsi (HUN) d. K. Srebotnik (SLO) 46 63 64; T. Pisnik/K. Srebotnik (SLO) d. Z. Gubacsi/I. Szalai (HUN) 63 63.

1996 Final: Slovak Republic d. Great Britain 3-0, Nagoya, Japan: S. Hrozenska (SVK) d. S. Gregg (GBR) 61 62; K. Basternakova (SVK) d. H. Collin (GBR) 63 61; S. Hrozenska/Z. Kucova (SVK) d. H. Collin/H. Reesby (GBR) 64 62.

1997 Final: Russia d. Slovak Republic 2-1, Nagoya, Japan: L. Krasnoroutskaia (RUS) d. D. Hantuchova (SVK) 62 64; E. Bovina (RUS) d. M. Babakova (SVK) 64 61; D. Hantuchova/L. Kurhajcova (SVK) d. G. Fokina/L. Krasnoroutskaia (RUS) 62 26 62.

1998 Final: Czech Republic d. Russia 2-1, Nagoya, Japan: E. Birnerova (CZE) d. V. Zvonareva (RUS) 63 64; P. Cetkovska (CZE) d. G. Fokina (RUS) 62 26 64; E. Birnerova/P. Cetkovska (CZE) d. G. Fokina/R. Gourevitch (RUS) 75 16 63.

1999 Final: Russia d. Slovak Republic 2-1, Prostejov, Czech Republic: D. Safin (RUS) d. M. Zivcicova (SVK) 63 61; A. Bastrikova (RUS) d. K. Kachlikova (SVK) 63 62; L. Smolenakova/M. Zivcicova (SVK) d. A. Bastrikova/N. Brattchikova (RUS) 63 64.

2000 Final: Russia d. Czech Republic 3-0, Prostejov, Czech Republic: D. Tchemarda (RUS) d. L. Safarova (CZE) 76 62; V. Douchevina (RUS) d. B. Strycova (CZE) 46 61 62; I. Kotkina/D. Tchemarda (RUS) d. N. Freislerova/L. Safarova (CZE) 64 60.

2001 Final: Czech Republic d. Russia 2-1, Prostejov, Czech Republic: A. Tchakvetadze (RUS) d. R. Kucerkova (CZE) 61 60; L. Safarova (CZE) d. M. Kirilenko (RUS) 61 75; R. Kucerkova/L. Safarova (CZE) d. M. Kirilenko/E. Kiriyanova (RUS) 64 64.

2002 Final: Netherlands d. Poland 3-0, Prostejov, Czech Republic: B. Schoofs (NED) d. M. Lesniak (POL) 75 63; M. Krajicek (NED) d. M. Kiszczynska (POL) 61 61; M. Krajicek/B. Schoofs (NED) d. M. Kiszczynska/M. Lesniak (POL) 64 36 62.

2003 Final: Czech Republic d. Russia 2-1, Prostejov, Czech Republic: R. Kulikova (RUS) d. S. Novakova (CZE) 62 61; N. Vaidisova (CZE) d. E. Rodina (RUS) 61 61; E. Kadlecova/N. Vaidisova (CZE) d. R. Kulikova/E. Rodina (RUS) 64 76.

2004 Final: Belarus d. Austria 2-1, Prostejov, Czech Republic: M. Klaffner (AUT) d. I. Bohush (BLR) 76 75; K. Milevskaya (BLR) d. N. Hofmanova (AUT) 61 75; I. Bohush/K. Milevskaya (BLR) d. N. Hofmanova/M. Klaffner (AUT) 60 61.

Junior Davis Cup

International Team Competition for boys aged 16 and under. Launched by the ITF in 1985 as the World Youth Cup, renamed the Junior Davis Cup by BNP Paribas in 2002. Sixteen boys' teams qualify for a place in the final, held at one venue over a week.

1985 Final: Australia d. USA 2-1, Kobe, Japan: F. Montana (USA) d. R. Fromberg (AUS) 62 62; S. Barr (AUS) d. J. Falbo (USA) 64 64; S. Barr/J. Stoltenberg (AUS) d. J. Falbo/F. Montana (USA) 46 76 75.

1986 Final: Australia d. USA 2-1, Tokyo, Japan: M. Chang (USA) d. R. Fromberg (AUS) 64 64; J. Stoltenberg (AUS) d. J. Courier (USA) 62 64; J. Stoltenberg/T. Woodbridge (AUS) d. J. Courier/D. Kass (USA) 76 62.

1987 Final: Australia d. Netherlands 3-0, Freiburg, West Germany: J. Anderson (AUS) d. F. Wibier (NED) 60 61; T. Woodbridge (AUS) d. P. Dogger (NED) 75 36 62; J. Morgan/T. Woodbridge (AUS) d. P. Dogger/F. Wibier (NED) 63 62.

1988 Final: Czechoslovakia d. USA 2-1, Perth, Australia: J. Kodes (TCH) d. R. Leach (USA) 76 62; M. Damm (TCH) d. B. MacPhie (USA) 62 67 64; W. Bull/R. Leach (USA) d. M. Damm/L. Hovorka (TCH) 64 64.

1989 Final: West Germany d. Czechoslovakia 2-1, Asuncion, Paraguay: G. Paul (FRG) d. P. Gazda (TCH) 64 64; L. Thomas (TCH) d. S. Gessner (FRG) 75 75; D. Prinosil/P. Prinosil (FRG) d. P. Gazda/L. Thomas (TCH) 75 61.

Pere Riba led Spain to victory in the Junior Davis Cup by BNP Paribas

Junior Davis Cup (continued)

1990 Final: USSR d. Australia 2-1, Rotterdam, Netherlands: D. Tomashevich (URS) d. T. Vasiliadis (AUS) 63 62; G. Doyle (AUS) d. A. Medvedev (URS) 06 64 75; Y. Kafelnikov/A. Medvedev (URS) d. G. Doyle/B. Sceney (AUS) 76 63.

1991 Final: Spain d. Czechoslovakia 2-1, Barcelona, Spain: G. Corrales (ESP) d. D. Skoch (TCH) 75 75; F. Kascak (TCH) d. A. Costa (ESP) 64 75; G. Corrales/A. Costa (ESP) d. F. Kascak/D. Skoch (TCH) 64 62.

1992 Final: France d. Germany 2-1, Castelldefels, Spain: R. Nicklisch (GER) d. N. Escude (FRA) 26 63 63; M. Boye (FRA) d. A. Nickel (GER) 75 06 63; M. Boye/N. Escude (FRA) d. A. Nickel/R. Nicklisch (GER) 67 60 63.

1993 Final: France d. New Zealand 2-1, Wellington, New Zealand: T. Susnjak (NZL) d. O. Mutis (FRA) 61 16 63; J. Bachelot (FRA) d. S. Clark (NZL) 46 64 64; O. Mutis/J. Potron (FRA) d. S. Clark/M. Nielsen (NZL) 63 64.

1994 Final: Netherlands d. Austria 2-1, Tucson, AZ, USA: C. Trimmel (AUT) d. P. Wessels (NED) 46 63 75; R. Sluiter (NED) d. M. Hipfl (AUT) 76 61; R. Sluiter/P. Wessels (NED) d. M. Hipfl/C. Trimmel (AUT) 63 64.

1995 Final: Germany d. Czech Republic 3-0, Essen, Germany: T. Messmer (GER) d. P. Kralert (CZE) 63 75; D. Elsner (GER) d. M. Tabara (CZE) 63 64; D. Elsner/T. Zivnicek (GER) d. P. Kralert/P. Riha (CZE) 67 64 64.

1996 Final: France d. Australia 2-1, Zurich, Switzerland: J. Haehnel (FRA) d. N. Healey (AUS) 64 62; J. Jean-Pierre (FRA) d. L. Hewitt (AUS) 63 75; N. Healey/L. Hewitt (AUS) d. J. Haehnel/O. Patience (FRA) 75 46 76.

1997 Final: Czech Republic d. Venezuela 2-0, Vancouver, Canada: J. Levinsky (CZE) d. E. Nastari (VEN) 60 62; L. Chramosta (CZE) d. J. De Armas (VEN) 76 62; doubles not played.

1998 Final: Spain d. Croatia 2-1, Cuneo, Italy: M. Lopez (ESP) d. R. Karanusic (CRO) 63 36 36; T. Robredo (ESP) d. M. Radic (CRO) 64 64; M. Lopez/T. Robredo (ESP) d. R. Karanusic/M. Radic (CRO) 64 62.

1999 Final: USA d. Croatia 3-0, Perth, Australia: R. Redondo (USA) d. I. Stelko (CRO) 76 64; A. Bogomolov (USA) d. M. Ancic (CRO) 76 63; R. Redondo/T. Rettenmaier (USA) d. M. Ancic/T. Peric (CRO) 76 76.

2000 Final: Australia d. Austria 2-0, Hiroshima, Japan: R. Henry (AUS) d. S. Wiespeiner (AUT) 57 64 86; T. Reid (AUS) d. J. Ager (AUT) 64 75; R. Henry/T. Reid (AUS) d. J. Ager/S. Wiespeiner (AUT); doubles not played.

2001 Final: Chile d. Germany 3-0, Santiago, Chile: G. Hormazabal (CHI) d. S. Klor (GER) 62 64; J. Aguilar (CHI) d. M. Zimmermann (GER) 60 61; G. Hormazabal/C. Rios (CHI) d. B. Koch/M. Zimmermann (GER) 62 16 76.

2002 Final: Spain d. USA 3-0, La Baule, France: T. Salva (ESP) d. P. Simmonds (USA) 62 63; R. Nadal (ESP) d. B. Evans (USA) 62 62; M. Granollers/R. Nadal (ESP) d. S. Oudsema/P. Simmonds (USA) 76 63.

2003 Final: Germany d. France 2-1, Essen, Germany: M. Dehaine (FRA) d. M. Bachinger (GER) 76 26 63; M. Zverev (GER) d. J. Chardy (FRA) 63 64; M. Bachinger/M. Zverev (GER) d. J. Chardy/J. Drean (FRA) 62 61.

2004 Final: Spain d. Czech Republic 2-1, Barcelona, Spain: M. Navratil (CZE) d. R. Bautista (ESP) 61 64; P. Riba (ESP) d. D. Lojda (CZE) 61 64; R. Bautista/P. Riba (ESP) d. D. Lojda/F. Zeman (CZE) 63 64.

Junior Fed Cup

International Team Competition for girls aged 16 and under. Launched by the ITF in 1985 as the World Youth Cup, renamed the Junior Fed Cup in 2002. Sixteen girls' teams qualify for a place in the final, held at one venue over a week.

1985 Final: Czechoslovakia d. Australia 3-0, Kobe, Japan: J. Pospisilova (TCH) d. S. McCann (AUS) 64 64; R. Zrubakova (TCH) d. N. Provis (AUS) 76 75; J. Pospisilova/R. Zrubakova (TCH) d. W. Frazer/N. Provis (AUS) 75 64.

1986 Final: Belgium d. Czechoslovakia 2-1, Tokyo, Japan: S. Wasserman (BEL) d. P. Langrova (TCH) 64 75; A. Devries (BEL) d. R. Zrubakova (TCH) 63 64; P. Langrova/R. Zrubakova (TCH) d. A. Devries/C. Neuprez (BEL) 64 62.

1987 Final: Australia d. USSR 2-1, Freiburg, West Germany: R. McQuillan (AUS) d. E. Brioukhovets (URS) 36 62 63; N. Medvedeva (URS) d. J. Faull (AUS) 46 62 62; J. Faull/R. McQuillan (AUS) d. E. Brioukhovets/N. Medvedeva (URS) 63 61.

1988 Final: Australia d. Argentina 3-0, Perth, Australia: K. Guse (AUS) d. F. Haumuller (ARG) 76 64; L. Guse (AUS) d. C. Tessi (ARG) 76 16 62; K. Guse/K. Sharpe (AUS) d. I. Gorrochategui/C. Tessi (ARG) 60 62.

1989 Final: West Germany d. Czechoslovakia 2-1, Asuncion, Paraguay: M. Skulj-Zivec (FRG) d. K. Matouskova (TCH) 60 75; A. Huber (FRG) d. K. Habsudova (TCH) 60 63; K. Habsudova/P. Kucova (TCH) d. K. Duell/M. Skulj-Zivec (FRG) 63 60.

1990 Final: Netherlands d. USSR 2-1, Rotterdam, Netherlands: P. Kamstra (NED) d. I. Sukhova (URS) 61 76; T. Ignatieva (URS) d. L. Niemantsverdriet (NED) 60 16 64; P. Kamstra/L. Niemantsverdriet (NED) d. T. Ignatieva/I. Sukhova (URS) 63 46 61.

1991 Final: Germany d. Paraguay 2-1, Barcelona, Spain: L. Schaerer (PAR) d. H. Rusch (GER) 76 63; M. Kochta (GER) d. R. De Los Rios (PAR) 63 61; K. Freye/M. Kochta (GER) d. R. De Los Rios/L. Schaerer (PAR) 57 63 63.

1992 Final: Belgium d. Argentina 3-0, Castelldefels, Spain: L. Courtois (BEL) d. L. Montalvo (ARG) 61 63; N. Feber (BEL) d. M. Reynares (ARG) 16 64 61; L. Courtois/S. Deville (BEL) d. M. Diaz Oliva/L. Montalvo (ARG) 16 75 64.

1993 Final: Australia d. USA 2-1, Wellington, New Zealand: S. Drake-Brockman (AUS) d. S. Nickitas (USA) 62 57 62; A. Ellwood (AUS) d. A. Basica (USA) 62 61; C. Moros/S. Nickitas (USA) d. A. Ellwood/J. Richardson (AUS) 26 75 60.

1994 Final: South Africa d. France 3-0, Tucson, AZ, USA: J. Steck (RSA) d. A. Cocheteux (FRA) 75 63; S. De Beer (RSA) d. A. Castera (FRA) 64 63; doubles not played (walkover for South Africa).

1995 Final: France d. Germany 2-1, Essen, Germany: S. Kovacic (GER) d. K. Jagieniak (FRA) 64 63; A. Mauresmo (FRA) d. S. Klosel (GER) 60 63; K. Chevalier/A. Mauresmo (FRA) d. C. Christian/S. Kovacic (GER) 63 75.

1996 Final: Slovenia d. Germany 2-1, Zurich, Switzerland: K. Srebotnik (SLO) d. S. Kovacic (GER) 61 63; J. Wohr (GER) d. P. Rampre (SLO) 62 61; P. Rampre/K. Srebotnik (SLO) d. S. Kovacic/J. Wohr (GER) 61 64.

1997 Final: Russia d. France 2-0, Vancouver, Canada: A. Myskina (RUS) d. S. Schoeffel (FRA) 63 26 86; E. Dementieva (RUS) d. S. Rizzi (FRA) 62 46 64; doubles not played.

1998 Final: Italy d. Slovak Republic 2-1, Cuneo, Italy: R. Vinci (ITA) d. S. Hrozenska (SLO) 62 26 68; D. Hantuchova (SLO) d. M. Camerin (ITA) 64 62; F. Pennetta/R. Vinci (ITA) d. D. Hantuchova/S. Hrozenska (SLO) 64 61.

1999 Final: Argentina d. Slovak Republic 2-1, Perth, Australia: L. Dlhopolcova (SVK) d. G. Dulko (ARG) 63 63; M. Salerni (ARG) d. L. Kurhajcova (SVK) 63 64; E. Chialvo/M. Salerni (ARG) d. L. Dlhopolcova/L. Kurhajcova (SVK) 63 62.

2000 Final: Czech Republic d. Hungary 2-1, Hiroshima, Japan: E. Birnerova (CZE) d. D. Magas (HUN) 76 63; V. Nemeth (HUN) d. P. Cetkovska (CZE) 75 46 86; P. Cetkovska/E. Janaskova (CZE) d. D. Magas/V. Nemeth (HUN) 75 57 61.

2001 Final: Czech Republic d. Poland 3-0, Santiago, Chile: P. Cetkovska (CZE) d. O. Brozda (POL) 61 63; B. Strycova (CZE) d. M. Domachowska (POL) 62 62; P. Cetkovska/L. Safarova (CZE) d. M. Domachowska/A. Rosolska (POL) 63 62.

2002 Final: Belarus d. Czech Republic 3-0, La Baule, France: D. Kustava (BLR) d. A. Hlavackova (CZE) 63 61; A. Yakimava (BLR) d. K. Bohmova (CZE) 63 64; D. Kustava/A. Yakimava (BLR) d. K. Bohmova/A. Hlavackova (CZE) 62 63.

2003 Final: Netherlands d. Canada 2-1, Essen, Germany: E. Shulaeva (CAN) d. B. Schoofs (NED) 61 63; M. Krajicek (NED) d. A. Wozniak (POL) 60 75; M. Krajicek/B. Schoofs (NED) d. A. Wozniak/K. Zoricic (POL) 61 64.

2004 Final: Argentina d. Canada 2-0, Barcelona, Spain: B. Jozami (ARG) d. V. Tetreault (CAN) 61 63; F. Molinero (ARG) d. S. Fichman (CAN) 36 64 62; doubles not played.

ITF Sunshine Cup

International Team Competition for boys aged 18 and under. Established in 1958, the event was originally known as the Orange Bowl Junior Cup. The ITF took over its organisation in 1997.

Winning nations 1958-1990

1958 Brazil	1964 Australia	1970 USA	1976 USA	1982 France	1988 France
1959 Spain	1965 USA	1971 Spain	1977 France	1983 Spain	1989 Canada
1960 USA	1966 USA	1972 USA	1978 Spain	1984 USA	1990 USSR
1961 USA	1967 USA	1973 USA	1979 USA	1985 Argentina	
1962 USA	1968 Australia	1974 USA	1980 Sweden	1986 Spain	
1963 Mexico	1969 USA	1975 USA	1981 Sweden	1987 USSR	

1991 Final: Spain d. France 2-1, Weston, FL, USA: S. Matheu (FRA) d. J. Martinez (ESP) 64 16 63; A. Berasategui (ESP) d. L. Rioux (FRA) 64 76; A. Berasategui/J. Martinez (ESP) d. S. Matheu/L. Rioux (FRA) 62 76.

1992 Final: Spain d. USA 2-0, Delray Beach, FL, USA: A. Costa (ESP) d. V. Spadea (USA) 63 75; F. Mantilla (ESP) d. J. Jackson (USA) 61 63; doubles not played.

1993 Final: Brazil d. Chile 2-1, Delray Beach, FL, USA: M. Carlsson (BRA) d. J. Gamonal (CHI) 63 63; M. Rios (CHI) d. G. Kuerten (BRA) 61 64; M. Carlsson/G. Kuerten (BRA) d. J. Gamonal/M. Rios (CHI) 62 67 64.

1994 Final: Argentina d. Spain 2-1, Delray Beach, FL, USA: J. Diaz (ESP) d. M. Zabaleta (ARG) 63 61; F. Browne (ARG) d. C. Moya (ESP) 64 16 64; F. Browne/G. Cavallaro (ARG) d. C. Moya/F. Vicente (ESP) 46 76 61.

1995 Final: USA d. Argentina 2-1, Delray Beach, FL, USA: R. Wolters (USA) d. M. Puerta (ARG) 63 26 62; M. Zabaleta (ARG) d. J. Gimelstob (USA) 63 61; J. Gimelstob/R. Wolters (USA) d. G. Canas/M. Zabaleta (ARG) 75 46 76.

1996 Final: France d. Germany 2-0, Delray Beach, FL, USA: O. Mutis (FRA) d. T. Messmer (GER) 76 62; S. Grosjean (FRA) d. D. Elsner (GER) 61 62; doubles not played.

1997 Final: France d. Germany 2-1, Delray Beach, FL, USA: J. Jean-Pierre (FRA) d. T. Zivnicek (GER) 64 67 64; A. Di Pasquale (FRA) d. B. Phau (GER) 60 76; T. Messmer/B. Phau (GER) d. A. Di Pasquale/J. Jean-Pierre (FRA) w/o.

1998 Final: France d. Russia 3-0, Key Biscayne, FL, USA: J. Haehnel (FRA) d. I. Kounitsyn (RUS) 64 64; J. Jean-Pierre (FRA) d. K. Ivanov-Smolenski (RUS) 61 75; J. Haehnel/J. Jean-Pierre (FRA) d. A. Derepasko/I. Kounitsyn (RUS) 64 63.

1999 Final: France d. Argentina 2-0, Key Biscayne, FL, USA: J. Benneteau (FRA) d. J. Acasuso (ARG) 62 64; N. Mahut (FRA) d. G. Coria (ARG) 76 26 62; doubles not played.

2000 Final: USA d. Spain 2-0, Key Biscayne, FL, USA: R. Ginepri (USA) d. C. Cuadrado (ESP) 61 62; A. Roddick (USA) d. M. Lopez (ESP) 64 67 64; doubles not played.

2001 Final: Russia d. Argentina 2-0, Key Biscayne, FL, USA: I. Andreev (RUS) d. L. Vitullo (ARG) 36 62 40 ret; P. Ivanov (RUS) d. B. Dabul (ARG) 61 76(4); doubles not played.

2002: Competition not played.

2003: Competition not played.

2004: Competition not played.

ITF Connolly Continental Cup

International Team Competition for girls aged 18 and under. Established in 1976, the event was originally known as the Maureen Connolly Brinker Continental Players Cup. The ITF took over its running in 1997.

Winning nations 1976-1990

1976 USA	1979 Peru	1982 Italy	1985 Argentina	1988 Argentina
1977 USA	1980 USA	1983 USA	1986 Czechoslovakia	1989 USA
1978 USA	1981 USA	1984 USA	1987 USSR	1990 Spain

1991 Final: USA d. Spain 2-0, Plantation, FL, USA: P. Nelson (USA) d. L. Bitter (NED) 62 75; L. Davenport (USA) d. L. Niemantsverdriet (NED) 62 64; doubles not played.

1992 Final: USA d. Italy 2-1, Delray Beach, FL, USA: J. Stevens (USA) d. R. Grande (ITA) 64 36 62; F. Bentivoglio (ITA) d. N. London (USA) 63 63; N. London/J. Stevens (USA) d. F. Bentivoglio/R. Grande (ITA) 76 60.

1993 Final: Argentina d. Poland 3-0, Delray Beach, FL, USA: M. Diaz-Oliva (ARG) d. K. Bulat (POL) 61 61; L. Montalvo (ARG) d. K. Malec (POL) 63 62; M. Landa/L. Montalvo d. M. Grzybowska/K. Malec (POL) 85.

1994 Final: Italy d. Hungary 2-1, Delray Beach, FL, USA: K. Nagy (HUN) d. A. Canepa (ITA) 62 62; F. Lubiani (ITA) d. P. Mandula (HUN) 46 62 63; A. Canepa/F. Lubiani (ITA) d. P. Mandula/K. Marosi (HUN) 76 62.

1995 Final: Russia d. Spain 2-1, Boca Raton, FL, USA: A. Alcazar (ESP) d. E. Koulkikovskaia (RUS) 64 63; A. Kournikova (RUS) d. P. Hermida (ESP) 75 64; E. Koulkikovskaia/A. Kournikova (RUS) d. A. Alcazar/P. Hermida (ESP) 64 64.

1996 Final: Spain d. USA 3-0, Boca Raton, FL, USA: L. Pena (ESP) d. L. Osterloh (USA) 57 63 76; A. Alcazar (ESP) d. C. Morariu (USA) 76 63; A. Alcazar/L. Pena (ESP) d. L. Osterloh/T. Singian (USA) 60 ret.

1997 Final: Slovenia d. Russia 2-1, Delray Beach, FL, USA: T. Pisnik (SLO) d. E. Dementieva (RUS) 63 75; K. Srebotnik (SLO) d. E. Syssoeva (RUS) 36 64 63; E. Dementieva/A. Myskina (RUS) d. M. Matevzic/T. Pisnik (SLO) 64 61.

1998 Final: Russia d. Spain 2-1, Key Biscayne, FL, USA: M. Marrero (ESP) d. A. Myskina (RUS) 36 76 62; E. Dementieva (RUS) d. L. Dominguez (ESP) 76 76; E. Dementieva/A. Myskina (RUS) d. M. Marrero/M. Martinez (ESP) 36 63 61.

1999 Final: Russia d. Spain 2-0, Key Biscayne, FL, USA: N. Petrova (RUS) d. M. Martinez (ESP) 64 61; L. Krasnoroutskaia (RUS) d. A. Medina (ESP) 76 63; doubles not played.

2000 Final: USA d. Estonia 2-1, Key Biscayne, FL, USA: A. Harkleroad (USA) d. M. Ani (EST) 64 76; K. Kanepi (EST) d. M. Middleton (USA) 62 64; A. Harkleroad/B. Mattek (USA) d. M. Ani/K. Kanepi (EST) 76 64.

2001 Final: Russia d. Croatia 2-0, Key Biscayne, FL, USA: V. Zvonareva (RUS) d. K. Sprem (CRO) 75 62; S. Kuznetsova (RUS) d. M. Mezak (CRO) 36 75 75; doubles not played.

2002: Competition not played.

2003: Competition not played.

2004: Competition not played.

Wheelchair Tennis Masters

The premier event on the ITF's wheelchair tennis circuit, this tournament invites only the top eight men and women, and four quad players to participate. Played every year in Eindhoven, Netherlands, until 1999, the event moved to Amersfoort, Netherlands, in 2000, and a doubles tournament was added.

Singles

Year	Event	Champion	Runner-up	Score
1994	Men	R. Snow (USA)	S. Welch (USA)	62 64
	Women	M. Kalkman (NED)	C. Vandierendonck (NED)	61 64
1995	Men	L. Giammartini (FRA)	R. Snow (USA)	75 46 64
	Women	M. Kalkman (NED)	C. Vandierendonck (NED)	61 62
1996	Men	S. Welch (USA)	L. Giammartini (FRA)	64 26 64
	Women	C. Vandierendonck (NED)	D. Di Toro (AUS)	64 63
1997	Men	K. Schrameyer (GER)	S. Welch (USA)	46 75 60
	Women	M. Smit (NED)	M. Kalkman (NED)	63 46 75
1998	Men	R. Molier (NED)	L. Giammartini (FRA)	75 75
	Women	E. Vergeer (NED)	M. Smit (NED)	60 76
1999	Men	R. Ammerlaan (NED)	M. Legner (AUT)	75 61
	Women	E. Vergeer (NED)	M. Smit (NED)	60 61
2000	Men	R. Ammerlaan (NED)	R. Molier (NED)	76 61
	Women	E. Vergeer (NED)	D. Van Marum (NED)	61 63
2001	Men	R. Molier (NED)	R. Ammerlaan (NED)	60 67 61
	Women	E. Vergeer (NED)	M. Smit (NED)	62 63
2002	Men	D. Hall (AUS)	R. Ammerlaan (NED)	26 63 64
	Women	E. Vergeer (NED)	S. Peters (NED)	46 64 76
2003	Men	R. Ammerlaan (NED)	S. Welch (USA)	63 64
	Women	E. Vergeer (NED)	S. Walraven (NED)	61 63
2004	Men	D. Hall (AUS)	M. Jeremiasz (FRA)	62 64
	Women	E. Vergeer (NED)	J. Griffioen (NED)	62 60
	Quad	D. Wagner (USA)	B. Van Erp (NED)	63 62

Doubles

Year	Event	Champions	Runners-up	Score
2000	Men	R. Molier (NED)/S. Welch (USA)	R. Ammerlaan/E. Stuurman (NED)	63 62
	Women	D. Di Toro (AUS)/M. Smit (NED)	E. Vergeer/S. Peters (NED)	64 64
2001	Men	M. Brychta (CZE)/M. Legner (AUT)	T. Kruszelnicki (POL)/J. Mistry (GBR)	63 62
	Women	E. Vergeer/M. Smit (NED)	B. Klave/D. Van Marum (NED)	75 75
2002	Men	K. Schrameyer (GER)/S. Welch (USA)	M. Legner (AUT)/S. Saida (JPN)	26 63 62
	Women	M. Smit/E. Vergeer (NED)	B. Klave/D. Van Marum (NED)	76 63
2003	Men	M. Legner (AUT)/S. Saida (JPN)	M. Jeremiasz (FRA)/J. Mistry (GBR)	63 76
	Women	M. Smit/E. Vergeer (NED)	J. Griffioen/S. Walraven (NED)	62 62
	Quad	P. Norfolk (GBR)/S. Hunter (CAN)	R. Draney/D. Wagner (USA)	64 61
2004	Men	M. Legner (AUT)/S. Saida (JPN)	M. Jeremiasz (FRA)/J. Mistry (GBR)	61 36 63
	Women	J. Griffioen/K. Homan (NED)	B. Ameryckx (BEL)/S. Walraven (NED)	64 62
	Quad	S. Hunter (CAN)/P. Norfolk (GBR)	G. Polidori/A. Raffaele (ITA)	61 63

World Team Cup

The official ITF wheelchair tennis team event. Men and women play on a knock-out principle, with a playoff system to determine the ranking of all participating teams. Quads and Junior events, added in recent years, are played in a round robin format. Winning nations in each category are listed.

Year	Venue	Men	Women	Quads	Juniors
1985	Irvine, CA, USA	USA			
1986	Irvine, CA, USA	USA	NED		
1987	Irvine, CA, USA	USA	NED		
1988	Irvine, CA, USA	USA	NED		

Year	Venue	Men	Women	Quads	Juniors
1989	Irvine, CA, USA	USA	NED		
1990	Irvine, CA, USA	USA	NED		
1991	Irvine, CA, USA	USA	NED		
1992	Brussels, Belgium	FRA	NED		
1993	Villach, Austria	FRA	NED		
1994	Nottingham, Great Britain	AUS	USA		
1995	Roermond, Netherlands	USA	NED		
1996	Melbourne, VIC, Australia	AUS	NED		
1997	Nottingham, Great Britain	USA	NED		
1998	Barcelona, Spain	GER	NED	USA	
1999	New York, NY, USA	NED	AUS	ISR	
2000	Paris, France	AUS	NED	ISR	USA
2001	Sion, Switzerland	NED	NED	GBR	NED
2002	Tremosine, Italy	AUS	NED	GBR	NED
2003	Sopot, Poland	JPN	NED	USA	SWE
2004	Christchurch, New Zealand	NED	NED	ISR	NED

Paralympic Wheelchair Tennis Event

Wheelchair tennis has been a medal sport at the Paralympic Games since 1992.

1992 Barcelona, Spain

Men's Singles	Gold:	Randy Snow (USA)
	Silver:	Kai Schrameyer (GER)
	Bronze:	Laurent Giammartini (FRA)
Women's Singles	Gold:	Monique van den Bosch (NED)
	Silver:	Chantal Vandierendonck (NED)
	Bronze:	Regina Isecke (GER)
Men's Doubles	Gold:	Randy Snow/Brad Parks (USA)
	Silver:	Laurent Giammartinin/Thierry Caillier (FRA)
	Bronze:	Kai Schrameyer/Stefan Bitterauf (GER)
Women's Doubles	Gold:	Monique van den Bosch/Chantal Vandierendonck (NED)
	Silver:	Nancy Olson/Lynn Seidemann (USA)
	Bronze:	Oristelle Marx/Arlette Racineux (FRA)

1996 Atlanta, GA, USA

Men's Singles	Gold:	Ricky Molier (NED)
	Silver:	Stephen Welch (USA)
	Bronze:	David Hall (AUS)
Women's Singles	Gold:	Maaike Smit (NED)
	Silver:	Monique Kalkman* (NED)
	Bronze:	Chantal Vandierendonck (NED)
Men's Doubles	Gold:	Stephen Welch/Chip Parmelly (USA)
	Silver:	David Hall/Mick Connell (AUS)
	Bronze:	Ricky Molier/Eric Stuurman (NED)
Women's Doubles	Gold:	Monique Kalkman*/Chantal Vandierendonck (NED)
	Silver:	Nancy Olson/Hope Lewellen (USA)
	Bronze:	Oristelle Marx/Arlette Racineux (FRA)

* Née Monique van den Bosch

Paralympic Wheelchair Tennis Event (continued)

2000 Sydney, NSW, Australia

Men's Singles	Gold:	David Hall (AUS)
	Silver:	Stephen Welch (USA)
	Bronze:	Kai Schrameyer (GER)
Women's Singles	Gold:	Esther Vergeer (NED)
	Silver:	Sharon Walraven (NED)
	Bronze:	Maaike Smit (NED)
Men's Doubles	Gold:	Ricky Molier/Robin Ammerlaan (NED)
	Silver:	David Hall/David Johnson (AUS)
	Bronze:	Stephen Welch/Scott Douglas (USA)
Women's Doubles	Gold:	Esther Vergeer/Maaike Smit (NED)
	Silver:	Daniela Di Toro/Branka Pupovac (AUS)
	Bronze:	Petra Sax-Scharl/Christine Otterbach (GER)

2004 Athens, Greece

Men's Singles	Gold:	Robin Ammerlaan (NED)
	Silver:	David Hall (AUS)
	Bronze:	Michael Jeremiasz (FRA)
Women's Singles	Gold:	Esther Vergeer (NED)
	Silver:	Sonja Peters (NED)
	Bronze:	Daniela Di Toro (AUS)
Men's Doubles	Gold:	Shingo Kunieda/Satoshi Saida (JPN)
	Silver:	Michael Jeremiasz/Lahcen Majdi (FRA)
	Bronze:	Anthony Bonaccurso/David Hall (AUS)
Women's Doubles	Gold:	Esther Vergeer/Maaike Smith (NED)
	Silver:	Sakhorn Khanthasit/Ratana Techamaneewat (THA)
	Bronze:	Sandra Kalt/Karin Suter-Erath (SUI)
Quad Singles	Gold:	Peter Norfolk (GBR)
	Silver:	David Wagner (USA)
	Bronze:	Bas Van Erp (NED)
Quad Doubles	Gold:	Nick Taylor/David Wagner (USA)
	Silver:	Mark Eccleston/Peter Norfolk (GBR)
	Bronze:	Monique De Beer/Bas Van Erp (NED)

ITF Seniors and Super-Seniors World Individual Championships

The International Vets World Championships were renamed ITF Seniors World Championships (formerly Group A) and ITF Super-Seniors World Individual Championships (formerly Group B) in 2004. The winner of each category is shown below:

1981 Sao Paulo, Brazil

Men

45 Singles	Sven Davidson (SWE)
45 Doubles	Sven Davidson (SWE)/Hugh Stewart (USA)
55 Singles	Straight Clark (USA)
55 Doubles	Straight Clark (USA)/Torsten Johansson (SWE)

Women

40 Singles	Estrella de Molina (ARG)
40 Doubles	Nancy Reed (USA)/M. A. Plante (USA)
50 Singles	Amelia Cury (BRA)

1982 Portschach, Austria

Men

45 Singles	Istvan Gulyas (HUN)
45 Doubles	Jason Morton (USA)/Jim Nelson (USA)
55 Singles	Robert McCarthy (AUS)
55 Doubles	Adi Hussmeller (GER)/Laci Legenstein (AUT)
60 Singles	Torsten Johansson (SWE)
60 Doubles	Torsten Johansson (SWE)/Albert Ritzenberg (USA)
65 Singles	Fritz Klein (USA)
65 Doubles	Fritz Klein (USA)/Jean Becker (FRA)

Women

40 Singles	Renate Drisaldi (GER)
40 Doubles	Charleen Hillebrand (USA)/Nancy Reed (USA)
50 Singles	Eva Sluytermann (GER)
50 Doubles	Eva Sluytermann (GER)/I. Burmester (GER)

1983 Bahia, Brazil

Men

45 Singles	Istvan Gulyas (HUN)
45 Doubles	Klaus Fuhrmann (GER)/Folker Seemann (GER)
55 Singles	Robert McCarthy (AUS)
55 Doubles	Laci Legenstein (AUT)/Adi Hussmuller (GER)
65 Singles	Ricardo San Martin (CHI)
65 Doubles	Federico Barboza (ARG)/Hector Hugo Pizani (ARG)

Women

40 Singles	Helga Masthoff (GER)
40 Doubles	Helga Masthoff (GER)/Heide Orth (GER)
50 Singles	Ines de Pla (ARG)
50 Doubles	Gladys Barbosa (ARG)/Julia Borzone (ARG)

1984 Cervia, Italy

Men

35 Singles	Juergen Fassbender (GER)
35 Doubles	Gene Malin (USA)/Armistead Neely (USA)
45 Singles	Istvan Gulyas (HUN)
45 Doubles	Klaus Fuhrmann (GER)/Folker Seemann (GER)
55 Singles	Giuseppe Merlo (ITA)
55 Doubles	Jason Morton (USA)/Hugh Stewart (USA)
65 Singles	Gardnar Mulloy (USA)
65 Doubles	Gardnar Mulloy (USA)/Fritz Klein (USA)

Women

40 Singles	Helga Masthoff (GER)
40 Doubles	Helga Masthoff (GER)/Heide Orth (GER)
50 Singles	Clelia Mazzoleni (ITA)
50 Doubles	Hana Brabenec (CAN)/Pam Warne (AUS)

1985 Melbourne, VIC, Australia

Men

35 Singles	Juergen Fassbender (GER)
35 Doubles	Juergen Fassbender (GER)/Federico Gadoni (ITA)
45 Singles	Ian Barclay (AUS)
45 Doubles	Bob Duesler (USA)/Jim Nelson (USA)
55 Singles	Hugh Stewart (USA)
55 Doubles	Hugh Stewart (USA)/Jason Morton (USA)
65 Singles	Jim Gilchrist (AUS)
65 Doubles	Fritz Klein (USA)/Albert Ritzenberg (USA)

Women

40 Singles	Heide Orth (GER)
40 Doubles	Heide Orth (GER)/Judy Dalton (AUS)
50 Singles	Ilse Michael (GER)
50 Doubles	Ann Fotheringham (AUS)/Helen Polkinghorne (AUS)

ITF Seniors and Super-Seniors World Individual Championships (continued)

1986 Portschach, Austria

Men
35 Singles	Robert Machan (HUN)
35 Doubles	Juergen Fassbender (GER)/Hans-Joachim Ploetz (GER)
45 Singles	Jorge Lemann (BRA)
45 Doubles	Jorge Lemann (BRA)/Ivo Ribeiro (BRA)
55 Singles	Lorne Main (CAN)
55 Doubles	Bob Howe (AUS)/Russell Seymour (USA)
65 Singles	Torsten Johansson (USA)
65 Doubles	Gardnar Mulloy (USA)/Verne Hughes (USA)

Women
40 Singles	Helga Masthoff (GER)
40 Doubles	Helga Masthoff (GER)/Heide Orth (GER)
50 Singles	Shirley Brasher (GBR)
50 Doubles	Shirley Brasher (GBR)/Lorna Cawthorn (GBR)

1987 Garmisch-Partenkirchen, Germany

Men
35 Singles	Robert Machan (HUN)
35 Doubles	Robert Machan (HUN)/Jurgen Fassbender (GER)
45 Singles	Giorgio Rohrich (ITA)
45 Doubles	Hans Gradischnig (AUT)/Peter Pokorny (AUT)
55 Singles	Istvan Gulyas (HUN)
55 Doubles	Istvan Gulyas (HUN)/Hugh Stewart (USA)
60 Singles	Bob Howe (AUS)
60 Doubles	Andreas Stolpa (GER)/Laci Legenstein (AUT)
65 Singles	Alex Swetka (USA)
65 Doubles	Bernhard Kempa (GER)/Walter Kessler (GER)
70 Singles	Fritz Klein (USA)
70 Doubles	Gardnar Mulloy (USA)/Verne Hughes (USA)

Women
40 Singles	Marie Pinterova (HUN)
40 Doubles	Marie Pinterova (HUN)/Gail Lovera (FRA)
50 Singles	Shirley Brasher (GBR)
50 Doubles	Shirley Brasher (GBR)/Lorna Cawthorn (GBR)
60 Singles	Dorothy Cheney (USA)
60 Doubles	Dorothy Cheney (USA)/Cortez Murdock (USA)

1988 Huntingdon Beach, CA, USA

Men
35 Singles	Alvin Gardiner (USA)
35 Doubles	Lajos Levai (GER)/Robert Machan (HUN)
45 Singles	Keith Diepram (USA)
45 Doubles	Friedhelm Krauss (GER)/Gunter Krauss (GER)
55 Singles	Istvan Gulyas (HUN)
55 Doubles	Sven Davidson (SWE)/Hugh Stewart (USA)
60 Singles	Robert McCarthy (AUS)
60 Doubles	Robert McCarthy (AUS)/Bob Howe (AUS)
65 Singles	Tom Brown (USA)
65 Doubles	Lee Hammel (USA)/Bob Sherman (USA)
70 Singles	Fritz Klein (USA)
70 Doubles	Glen Hippenstiel (USA)/Geoff Young (USA)

Women
40 Singles	Marie Pinterova (HUN)
40 Doubles	Rosie Darmon (FRA)/Gail Lovera (FRA)
50 Singles	Dorothy Matthiessen (USA)
50 Doubles	Dorothy Matthiessen (USA)/Jane Crofford (USA)
60 Singles	Virginia Glass (USA)
60 Doubles	Dorothy Cheney (USA)/Cortez Murdock (USA)

1989 Vina del Mar, Chile

Men

35 Singles	Alvaro Fillol (CHI)
35 Doubles	Robert Machan (GER)/Lajos Levai (GER)
45 Singles	Harold Elschenbroich (GER)
45 Doubles	Bodo Nitsche (GER)/Gunter Krauss (GER)
55 Singles	Istvan Gulyas (HUN)
55 Doubles	Chuck de Voe (USA)/John Powless (USA)
60 Singles	Robert McCarthy (AUS)
60 Doubles	Robert McCarthy (AUS)/Bob Howe (AUS)
65 Singles	Armando Vieira (BRA)
65 Doubles	Armando Vieira (BRA)/Sergio Verrati (FRA)
70 Singles	Albert Ritzenberg (USA)
70 Doubles	Albert Ritzenberg (USA)/Fritz Klein (USA)

Women

40 Singles	Marie Pinterova (HUN)
40 Doubles	Marie Pinterova (HUN)/Heide Orth (GER)
50 Singles	Ilse Michael (GER)
50 Doubles	Nancy Reed USA)/Barbel Allendorf (GER)
60 Singles	Betty Pratt (USA)
60 Doubles	Dorothy Cheney (USA)/Cortez Murdock (USA)

1990 Umag, Yugoslavia

Men

35 Singles	Robert Machan (HUN)
35 Doubles	Robert Machan (HUN)/Lajos Levai (GER)
45 Singles	Harald Elschenbroich (GER)
45 Doubles	Dick Johnson (USA)/Jim Parker (USA)
55 Singles	Istvan Gulyas (HUN)
55 Doubles	Ken Sinclair (CAN)/Lorne Main (CAN)
60 Singles	Sven Davidson (SWE)
60 Doubles	Sven Davidson (SWE)/Hugh Stewart (USA)
65 Singles	Robert McCarthy (AUS)
65 Doubles	Oskar Jirkovsky (AUT)/Josef Karlhofer (AUT)
70 Singles	William Parsons (USA)
70 Doubles	Alex Swetka (USA)/Albert Ritzenberg (USA)

Women

40 Singles	Marie Pinterova (HUN)
40 Doubles	Barbara Mueller (USA)/Louise Cash (USA)
50 Singles	Margit Schultze (ESP)
50 Doubles	Kay Schiavinato (AUS)/Jan Blackshaw (AUS)
60 Singles	Louise Owen (USA)
60 Doubles	Lurline Stock (AUS)/Dulcie Young (AUS)

1991 Perth, Australia

Men

35 Singles	Paul Torre (FRA)
35 Doubles	Yestedjo Traik (INA)/Atet Wijono (INA)
45 Singles	Don McCormick (CAN)
45 Doubles	Bruce Burns (AUS)/John Weaver (AUS)
55 Singles	Peter Froelich (AUS)
55 Doubles	Gordon Davis (USA)/Herman Ahlers (USA)
60 Singles	Lorne Main (CAN)
60 Doubles	Frank Sedgman (AUS)/Clive Wilderspin (AUS)
65 Singles	Robert McCarthy (AUS)
65 Doubles	Robert McCarthy (AUS)/Bob Howe (AUS)
70 Singles	Robert Sherman (USA)
70 Doubles	Verne Hughes (USA)/Merwin Miller (USA)

Women

40 Singles	Carol Bailey (USA)
40 Doubles	Carol Bailey (USA)/Barbara Mueller (USA)
50 Singles	Charleen Hillebrand (USA)
50 Doubles	Betty Whitelaw (AUS)/Jan Blackshaw (AUS)
55 Singles	Carol Wood (USA)
55 Doubles	Carol Wood (USA)/Margaret Kohler (USA)
60 Singles	Betty Pratt (USA)
60 Doubles	Ruth Illingworth (GBR)/Ann Williams (GBR)

ITF Seniors and Super-Seniors World Individual Championships (continued)

1992 Palermo, Sicily

Men

35 Singles	Ferrante Rocchi-Landir (ITA)
35 Doubles	Paul French (GBR)/Stanislav Birner (CZE)
45 Singles	Rolf Staguhn (GER)
45 Doubles	Gary Penberthy (AUS)/Ben de Jell (NED)
50 Singles	Jorge Lemann (BRA)
50 Doubles	Gerhard Schelch (AUT)/Peter Fuchs (AUT)
55 Singles	Klaus Fuhrmann (GER)
55 Doubles	Hugh Stewart (USA)/Les Dodson (USA)
60 Singles	Werner Mertins (GER)
60 Doubles	Ken Sinclair (CAN)/Lorne Main (CAN)
65 Singles	Robert McCarthy (AUS)
65 Doubles	Robert McCarthy (AUS)/Bob Howe (AUS)
70 Singles	Robert Sherman (USA)
70 Doubles	Robert Sherman (USA)/Mario Isidori (ITA)
75 Singles	Gaetano Longo (ITA)
75 Doubles	Tiverio de Grad (ROM)/Georg Hunger (GER)

Women

35 Singles	Sally Freeman (GBR)
35 Doubles	Luisa Figueroa (ARG)/Oliveira Villani (BRA)
40 Singles	Marilyn Rasmussen (AUS)
40 Doubles	Marilyn Rasmussen (AUS)/Lesley Charles (GBR)
45 Singles	Marie Pinterova (HUN)
45 Doubles	Marie Pinterova (HUN)/Shirley Brasher (GBR)
50 Singles	Charleen Hillebrand (USA)
50 Doubles	Charleen Hillebrand (USA)/Jacqueline Boothman (GBR)
55 Singles	Nancy Reed (USA)
55 Doubles	Nancy Reed (USA)/Belmar Gunderson (USA)
60 Singles	Beverley Rae (AUS)
60 Doubles	Beverley Rae (AUS)/Astri Hobson (AUS)

1993 Barcelona, Spain

Men

35 Singles	Fernando Luna (ESP)
35 Doubles	Steven Packham (AUS)/Tony Luttrell (AUS)
45 Singles	Robert Machan (HUN)
45 Doubles	Robert Machan (HUN)/Miodrag Mijuca (GER)
50 Singles	Jorge Lemann (BRA)
50 Doubles	Jim Parker (USA)/Ken Robinson (USA)
55 Singles	King Van Nostrand (USA)
55 Doubles	King Van Nostrand (USA)/Juan Manuel Couder (ESP)
60 Singles	Lorne Main (CAN)
60 Doubles	Lorne Main (CAN)/Ken Sinclair (CAN)
65 Singles	Jason Morton (USA)
65 Doubles	Laci Legenstein (AUT)/Hugh Stewart (USA)
70 Singles	Tom Brown (USA)
70 Doubles	Tom Brown (USA)/Buck Archer (USA)
75 Singles	Gordon Henley (AUS)
75 Doubles	Albert Ritzenberg (USA)/Mirek Kizlink (GBR)

Women

35 Singles	Jutta Fahlbusch (GER)
35 Doubles	Jutta Fahlbusch (GER)/Dagmar Anwar (GER)
40 Singles	Maria Geyer (AUT)
40 Doubles	Elizabeth Craig (AUS)/Carol Campling (AUS)
45 Singles	Marie Pinterova (HUN)
45 Doubles	Marie Pinterova (HUN)/Tuija Hannuakainen (FIN)
50 Singles	Cathie Anderson (USA)
50 Doubles	Brigitte Hoffmann (GER)/Siegrun Fuhrmann (GER)
55 Singles	Roberta Beltrame (ITA)
55 Doubles	Belmar Gunderson (USA)/Nancy Reed (USA)
60 Singles	Nancy Reed (USA)
60 Doubles	Marta Pombo (ESP)/Ana Maria Estalella (ESP)
65 Singles	Betty Pratt (USA)
65 Doubles	Betty Pratt (USA)/Betty Cookson (USA)

1994 (Group A) Buenos Aires, Argentina

Men

35 Singles	Jose Luis Clerc (ARG)
35 Doubles	Jose Luis Clerc (ARG)/Victor Pecci (PAR)
45 Singles	Jairo Velasco (ESP)
45 Doubles	Jairo Velasco (ESP)/Thomaz Koch (BRA)
50 Singles	Jimmy Parker (USA)
50 Doubles	Jimmy Parker (USA)/Ken Robinson (USA)

Women

35 Singles	Jutta Fahlbusch (GER)
35 Doubles	Marcela de Gregorio (ARG)/Beatriz Villaverde (ARG)
40 Singles	Renata Vojtischek (GER)
40 Doubles	Tina Karwasky (USA)/Susan Stone (CAN)
45 Singles	Louise Cash (USA)
45 Doubles	Carol Campling (AUS)/Elizabeth Craig (AUS)

1994 (Group B) Los Gatos, CA, USA

Men

55 Singles	Gil Howard (USA)
55 Doubles	Klaus Fuhrmann (GER)/Leslie Dodson (USA)
60 Singles	King Van Nostrand (USA)
60 Doubles	Russell Seymour (USA)/Whitney Reed (USA)
65 Singles	Jason Morton (USA)
65 Doubles	Jason Morton (USA)/William Davis (USA)
70 Singles	Oskar Jirkovsky (AUT)
70 Doubles	Francis Bushmann (USA)/Vincent Fotre (USA)
75 Singles	Alex Swetka (USA)
75 Doubles	Dan Walker (USA)/Verne Hughes (USA)

Women

50 Singles	Petro Kruger (RSA)
50 Doubles	Ellen Bryant (USA)/Barbara Mueller (USA)
55 Singles	Rosie Darmon (FRA)
55 Doubles	Dorothy Matthiessen (USA)/Lynn Little (USA)
60 Singles	Ilse Michael (GER)
60 Doubles	Nancy Reed (USA)/Belmar Gunderson (USA)
65 Singles	Louise Owen (USA)
65 Doubles	Louise Owen (USA)/Liz Harper (USA)

1995 (Group A) Bad Neuenahr, Germany

Men

35 Singles	Thibaut Kuentz (FRA)
35 Doubles	Thibaut Kuentz (FRA)/Stephan Medem (GER)
45 Singles	Robert Machan (HUN)
45 Doubles	Armistead Neely (USA)/Larry Turville (USA)
50 Singles	Giorgio Rohrich (ITA)
50 Doubles	Jody Rush (USA)/Richard Johnson (USA)

Women

35 Singles	Regina Marsikova (CZE)
40 Singles	Renata Vojtischek (GER)
40 Doubles	Renata Vojtischek (GER)/Tina Karwasky (USA)
45 Singles	Marie Pinterova (HUN)
45 Doubles	Carol Campling (AUS)/Elizabeth Craig-Allan (AUS)

1995 (Group B) Nottingham, Great Britain

Men

55 Singles	Len Saputo (USA)
55 Doubles	Leslie Dodson (USA)/Klaus Fuhrmann (GER)
60 Singles	James Nelson (USA)
60 Doubles	James Nelson (USA)/Leonard Lindborg (USA)
65 Singles	Lorne Main (CAN)
65 Doubles	Lorne Main (CAN)/Ken Sinclair (CAN)
70 Singles	Oskar Jirkovsky (AUT)
70 Doubles	Brian Hurley (AUS)/Neale Hook (AUS)
75 Singles	Robert Sherman (USA)
75 Doubles	Mirek Kizlink (GBR)/Tony Starling (GBR)

Women

50 Singles	Charleen Hillebrand (USA)
50 Doubles	Elly Blomberg (NED)/Jacqueline Boothman (GBR)
55 Singles	Renate Mayer-Zdralek (GER)
55 Doubles	Carol Wood (USA)/Sinclair Bill (USA)
60 Singles	Jennifer Hoad (ESP)
60 Doubles	Rita Lauder (GBR)/Ruth Illingworth (GBR)
65 Singles	Betty Pratt (USA)
65 Doubles	Louise Owen (USA)/Elaine Mason (USA)

1996 (Group A) Velden, Austria

Men

35 Singles	Greg Neuhart (USA)
35 Doubles	Greg Neuhart (USA)/Mike Fedderly (USA)
40 SIngles	Julio Goes (BRA)
40 Doubles	Julio Goes (BRA)/Harry Ufer (BRA)
45 Singles	Jairo Velasco (ESP)
45 Doubles	Jairo Velsco (ESP)/Robert Machan (HUN)
50 Singles	Peter Pokorny (AUT)
50 Doubles	Ted Hoehn (USA)/Richard Johnson (USA)

Women

35 Singles	Regina Marsikova (CZE)
35 Doubles	Regina Marsikova (CZE)/Jutta Fahlbusch (GER)
40 Singles	Renata Vojtischek (GER)
40 Doubles	Renata Vojtischek (GER)/Tina Karwasky (USA)
45 Singles	Marie Pinterova (HUN)
45 Doubles	Marie Pinterova (HUN)/Heide Orth (GER)
50 Singles	Eva Szabo (HUN)
50 Doubles	Carol Campling (AUS)/Elizabeth Craig-Allan (AUS)

ITF Seniors and Super-Seniors World Individual Championships (continued)

1996 (Group B), Vienna, Austria

Men

55 Singles	Giorgio Rohrich (ITA)
55 Doubles	Peter Pokorny (AUT)/Hans Gradischnig (AUT)
60 Singles	King Van Nostrand (USA)
60 Doubles	Jim Nelson (USA)/Bob Duesler (USA)
65 Singles	Lorne Main (CAN)
65 Doubles	Lorne Main (CAN)/Ken Sinclair (CAN)
70 Singles	Fred Kovaleski (USA)
70 Doubles	Fred Kovaleski (USA)/Bob Howe (USA)
75 Singles	Robert Sherman (USA)
75 Doubles	Merwin Miller (USA)/Verne Hughes (USA)
80 Singles	Dan Miller (USA)
80 Doubles	Dan Miller (USA)/Irving Converse (USA)

Women

55 Singles	Charleen Hillebrand (USA)
55 Doubles	Dorothy Mattiessen (USA)/Sinclair Bill (USA)
60 Singles	Ilse Michael (GER)
60 Doubles	Inge Weber (CAN)/Nancy Reed (USA)
65 Singles	Ines de Pla (ARG)
65 Doubles	Ruth Illingworth (GBR)/Rita Lauder (GBR)
70 Singles	Betty Pratt (USA)
70 Doubles	Betty Pratt (USA)/Elaine Mason (USA)

1997 (Group A) Johannesburg, South Africa

Men

35 Singles	Greg Neuhart (USA)
35 Doubles	Chris Loock (RSA)/Kobus Visagie (RSA)
40 Singles	Pierre Godfroid (BEL)
40 Doubles	Pierre Godfroid (BEL)/Bruce Osborne (AUS)
45 Singles	Frank Puncec (RSA)
45 Doubles	Max Bates (AUS)/Andrew Rae (AUS)
50 Singles	Jairo Velasco (ESP)
50 Doubles	Jairo Velasco (ESP)/Luis Flor (ESP)

Women

35 Singles	Tracy Houk (USA)
35 Doubles	Alexi Beggs (USA)/Vikki Beggs (USA)
40 Singles	Renata Vojtischek (GER)
40 Doubles	Sherri Bronson (USA)/Helle Viragh (USA)
45 Singles	Rita Theron (RSA)
45 Doubles	Kerry Ballard (AUS)/Wendy Gilchrist (AUS)
50 Singles	Marie Pinterova (HUN)
50 Doubles	Carol Campling (AUS)/Elizabeth Craig-Allan (AUS)

1997 (Group B) Newcastle, NSW, Australia

Men

55 Singles	Bob Howes (AUS)
55 Doubles	Maurince Broom (AUS)/Max Senior (AUS)
60 Singles	Klaus Fuhrmann (GER)
60 Doubles	Robert Duesler (USA)/Jim Nelson (USA)
65 Singles	Russell Seymour (USA)
65 Doubles	William Davis (USA)/Chuck de Voe (USA)
70 Singles	Laci Legenstein (AUT)
70 Doubles	Laci Legenstein (AUT)/Fred Kovaleski (USA)
75 Singles	Robert Sherman (USA)
75 Doubles	Robert Sherman (USA)/Ellis Williamson (USA)
80 Singles	Alex Swetka (USA)
80 Doubles	Alex Swetka (USA)/Gordon Henley (AUS)

Women

55 Singles	Heide Orth (GER)
55 Doubles	Lyn Wayte (AUS)/Margaret Wayte (AUS)
60 Singles	Judith Dalton (AUS)
60 Doubles	Lorice Forbes (AUS)/Peg Hoysted (AUS)
65 Singles	Beverley Rae (AUS)
65 Doubles	Ruth Illingworth (GBR)/Rita Lauder (GBR)
70 Singles	Twinx Rogers (RSA)
70 Doubles	Deedy Krebs (USA)/Elaine Mason (USA)

1998 (Group A) Nottingham, Great Britain

Men

35 Singles	Nick Fulwood (GBR)
35 Doubles	Nick Fulwood (GBR)/Brad Properjohn (AUS)
40 Singles	Pierre Godfroid (BEL)
40 Doubles	Pierre Godfroid (BEL)/Bruce Osborne (AUS)
45 Singles	Wayne Cowley (AUS)
45 Doubles	Benson Greatrex (GBR)/Philip Siviter (GBR)
50 Singles	Frank Briscoe (RSA)
50 Doubles	Keith Bland (GBR)/Richard Tutt (GBR)

Women

35 Singles	Tracy Houk (USA)
35 Doubles	Susanne Turi (HUN)/Kathy Vick (USA)
40 Singles	Ros Balodis (AUS)
40 Doubles	Ros Balodis (AUS)/Kaye Nealon (AUS)
45 Singles	Marlie Buehler (USA)
45 Doubles	Elizabeth Boyle (GBR)/Pauline Fisher (GBR)
50 Singles	Marie Pinterova (HUN)
50 Doubles	Carol Campling (AUS)/Elizabeth Craig-Allan (AUS)

1998 (Group B) Palm Beach Gdns, FL, USA

Men
55 Singles	Bob Howes (AUS)
55 Doubles	Stasys Labanauskas (LTU)/Peter Pokorny (AUT)
60 Singles	Bodo Nitsche (GER)
60 Doubles	Henry Leichtfried (USA)/Leonard Lindborg (USA)
65 Singles	Jim Perley (USA)
65 Doubles	Lorne Main (CAN)/Kenneth Sinclair (CAN)
70 Singles	Jason Morton (USA)
70 Doubles	Jason Morton (USA)/Fred Kovaleski (USA)
75 Singles	Robert Sherman (USA)
75 Doubles	Fran Bushmann (USA)/George Druliner (USA)
80 Singles	Alex Swetka (USA)
80 Doubles	Irving Converse (USA)/Dan Miller (USA)

Women
55 Singles	Heide Orth (GER)
55 Doubles	Heide Orth (GER)/Rosie Darmon (FRA)
60 Singles	Judith Dalton (AUS)
60 Doubles	Belmar Gunderson (USA)/Katie Koontz (USA)
65 Singles	Clelia Mazzoleni (ITA)
65 Doubles	Lorice Forbes (AUS)/Peg Hoysted (AUS)
70 Singles	Betty Eisenstein (USA)
70 Doubles	Phyllis Adler (USA)/Elaine Mason (USA)

1999 (Group A) Amsterdam, Netherlands

Men
35 Singles	Ned Caswell (USA)
35 Doubles	Ned Caswell (USA)/Mike Fedderly (USA)
40 Singles	Maris Rozentals (LAT)
40 Doubles	Pierre Godfroid (BEL)/Maris Rozentals (BEL)
45 Singles	Andrew Rae (AUS)
45 Doubles	Andrew Rae (AUS)/Rob Prouse (AUS)
50 Singles	Lito Alvarez (AUS)
50 Doubles	Lito Alvarez (AUS)/Peter Rigg (AUS)

Women
35 Singles	Klaartje van Baarle (BEL)
35 Doubles	Jackie Reardon (GBR)/Jackie van Wijk (NED)
40 Singles	Anna Iuale (ITA)
40 Doubles	Gerda Preissing (GER)/Beatriz Villaverde (ARG)
45 Singles	Renata Vojtischek (GER)
45 Doubles	Mary Ginnard (USA)/Lilian Peltz-Petow (USA)
50 Singles	Maria Pinterova (HUN)
50 Doubles	Carol Campling (AUS)/Elizabeth Craig-Allan (AUS)

1999 (Group B) Barcelona, Spain

Men
55 Singles	Giorgio Rohrich (ITA)
55 Doubles	Giorgio Rohrich (ITA)/Bepi Zambon (ITA)
60 Singles	Roberto Aubone (ARG)
60 Doubles	Bob Duesler (USA)/Henry Leichtfried (USA)
65 Singles	Jim Perley (USA)
65 Doubles	Lorne Main (CAN)/Kenneth Sinclair (CAN)
70 Singles	William Davis (USA)
70 Doubles	Kingman Lambert (USA)/Jason Morton (USA)
75 Singles	Oskar Jirkovsky (AUT)
75 Doubles	Francis Bushman (USA)/Newton Meade (USA)
80 Singles	Alex Swetka (USA)
80 Doubles	Nehemiah Atkinson (USA)/Gardnar Mulloy (USA)
85 Singles	Gardnar Mulloy (USA)
85 Doubles	Edward Baumer (USA)/David Carey (USA)

Women
55 Singles	Heide Orth (GER)
55 Doubles	Petro Kruger (RSA)/Marietjie Viljoen (RSA)
60 Singles	Jan Blackshaw (AUS)
60 Doubles	Jan Blackshaw (AUS)/Mary Gordon (AUS)
65 Singles	Nancy Reed (USA)
65 Doubles	Belmar Gunderson (USA)/Nancy Reed (USA)
70 Singles	Ines de Pla (ARG)
70 Doubles	Amelia Cury (BRA)/Ines de Pla (ARG)
75 Singles	Dorothy Cheney (USA)
75 Doubles	Julia Borzone (ARG)/Carmen Fernandez (MEX)

2000 (Group A) Buenos Aires, Argentina

Men
35 Singles	Jaroslav Bulant (CZE)
35 Doubles	Ricardo Rivera (ARG)/Gustavo Tibert (ARG)
40 Singles	Patrick Serrett (AUS)
40 Doubles	Mike Fedderly (USA)/Paul Smith (USA)
45 Singles	Victor Pecci (PAR)
45 Doubles	Michael Collins (AUS)/Wayne Pascoe (AUS)
50 Singles	Bruno Renoult (FRA)
50 Doubles	Max Bates (AUS)/Xavier Lemoine (FRA)

Women
35 Singles	Raquel Contreras (MEX)
35 Doubles	Beatrix Mezger-Reboul (GER)/Cora Salimei (ARG)
40 Singles	Gabriela Groell-Dinu (GER)
40 Doubles	Ros Balodis (AUS)/Kaye Nealon (AUS)
45 Singles	Elly Appel (NED)
45 Doubles	Ann Brown (GBR)/Pauline Fisher (GBR)
50 Singles	Heidi Eisterlehner (GER)
50 Doubles	Carol Campling (AUS)/Elizabeth Craig-Allan (AUS)

ITF Seniors and Super-Seniors World Individual Championships (continued)

2000 (Group B) Cape Town, South Africa

Men
55 Singles	Hugh Thomson (USA)
55 Doubles	Ben de Jel (NED)/ Hans-Joachim Ploetz (GER)
60 Singles	Robert Howes (AUS)
60 Doubles	Bodo Nitsche (GER)/Peter Pokorny (AUT)
65 Singles	Joseph Mateo (FRA)
65 Doubles	Abie Nothnagel (RSA)/Neville Whitfield (RSA)
70 Singles	Lorne Main (CAN)
70 Doubles	Lorne Main (CAN)/Kenneth Sinclair (CAN)
75 Singles	Vincent Fotre (USA)
75 Doubles	Neale Hook (AUS)/Brian Hurley (AUS)
80 Singles	Robert Sherman (USA)
80 Doubles	Nehemiah Atkinson (USA)/Alex Swetka (USA)
85 Singles	David Carey (CAN)
85 Doubles	David Carey (CAN)/Edward Baumer (USA)

Women
55 Singles	Ellie Krocke (NED)
55 Doubles	Charleen Hillebrand (USA)/Suella Steel (USA)
60 Singles	Rosie Darmon (FRA)
60 Doubles	Sinclair Bill (USA)/Rosie Darmon (FRA)
65 Singles	Lee Burling (USA)
65 Doubles	Patricia Bruorton (RSA)/Jackie Zylstra (RSA)
70 Singles	Louise Owen (USA)
70 Doubles	Louise Owen (USA)/Louise Russ (USA)
75 Singles	Elaine Mason (USA)
75 Doubles	Twinx Rogers (RSA)/Amy Wilmot (RSA)

2001 (Group A) Velden, Austria

Men
35 Singles	Jeff Greenwald (USA)
35 Doubles	Stefan Fasthoff (GER)/Stefan Heckmanns (GER)
40 Singles	Patrick Serret (AUS)
40 Doubles	Mike Fedderly (USA)/Patrick Serret (AUS)
45 Singles	Trevor Allan (FRA)
45 Doubles	Sal Castillo (USA)/Ferrante Rocchi Lonoir (ITA)
50 Singles	Andrew Rae (AUS)
50 Doubles	Max Bates (AUS)/Andrew Rae (AUS)

Women
35 Singles	Klaartje Van Baarle (BEL)
35 Doubles	Olga Shaposhnikova (RUS)/Klaartje Van Baarle (BEL)
40 Singles	Ingrid Resch (AUT)
40 Doubles	Gerda Preissing (GER)/Beatriz Villaverde (ARG)
45 Singles	Patricia Medrado (BRA)
45 Doubles	Patricia Medrado (BRA)/Carmen Perea Alcala (ESP)
50 Singles	Elizabeth Craig-Allan (AUS)
50 Doubles	Kerry Ballard (AUS)/Elizabeth Craig-Allan (AUS)

2001 (Group B) Perth, Australia

Men
55 Singles	Hans-Joachim Ploetz (GER)
55 Doubles*	Jerry Kirk (USA)/Hugh Thomson (USA) Keith Bland (GBR)/Richard Tutt (GBR)
60 Singles	Len Saputo (USA)
60 Doubles	Derek Arthurs (AUS)/Bob Howes (AUS)
65 Singles	Peter Froelich (AUS)
65 Doubles*	Peter Froelich (AUS)/King Van Nostrand (USA) Ross Jones (AUS)/John Whittaker (AUS)
70 Singles	Lorne Main (CAN)
70 Doubles	Charles Devoe (USA)/ Russell Seymour (USA)
75 Singles	Laci Legenstein (AUT)
75 Doubles	Oskar Jirkovsky (AUS)/Laci Legenstein (AUT)
80 Singles	Nehemiah Atkinson (USA)
80 Doubles	John Benn (USA)/Charles Roe (AUS)
85 Singles	Gardnar Mulloy (USA)
85 Doubles	David Carey (USA)/Gardnar Mulloy (USA)

Women
55 Singles	Trish Faulkner (USA)
55 Doubles	Carol Campling (AUS)/ Frances Taylor (GBR)
60 Singles	Heather Mckay (AUS)
60 Doubles	Rosie Darmon (FRA)/Suella Steel (USA)
65 Singles	Dorothy Matthiessen (USA)
65 Doubles	Ann Fotheringham (AUS)/ Margaret Robinson (AUS)
70 Singles	Ruth Illingworth (GBR)
70 Doubles*	Louise Owen (USA)/Louise Russ (USA) Ruth Illingworth (GBR)/Rita Lauder (GBR)
75 Singles	Elaine Mason (USA)
75 Doubles	Elaine Mason (USA)/Virginia Nichols (USA)

* not played due to rain – two winning pairs

2002 (Group A) Fort Lauderdale, FL, USA

Men

35 Singles	Franck Fevrier (FRA)
35 Doubles	Ned Caswell (USA)/Orlando Lourenco (USA)
40 Singles	Pablo Arraya (PER)
40 Doubles	Peter Doohan (AUS)/Patrick Serret (AUS)
45 Singles	Harold Solomon (USA)
45 Doubles	Sal Castillo (USA)/Larry Schnall (USA)
50 Singles	Andrew Rae (AUS)
50 Doubles	Tom Smith (USA)/Hugh Thomson (USA)

Women

35 Singles	Rene Simpson (CAN)
35 Doubles	Suzanne Hatch (CAN)/Rene Simpson (CAN)
40 Singles	Ros Balodis (AUS)
40 Doubles	Ros Balodis (AUS)/Brenda Foster (AUS)
45 Singles	Diane Fishburne (USA)
45 Doubles	Vicki Collins (AUS)/Kaye Nealon (AUS)
50 Singles	Elisabeth Appel (NED)
50 Doubles	Kerry Ballard (AUS)/Elizabeth Craig-Allan (AUS)

2002 (Group B) Velden, Austria

Men

55 Singles	Hugh Thomson (USA)
55 Doubles	Peter Blaas (NED)/Nico Welschen (NED)
60 Singles	Peter Pokorny (AUT)
60 Doubles	Alan Carter (USA)/Geoff Grant (USA)
65 Singles	Klaus Fuhrmann (GER)
65 Doubles	Peter Froelich (AUS)/King Van Nostrand (USA)
70 Singles	Kenneth Sinclair (CAN)
70 Doubles	Lorne Main (CAN)/Kenneth Sinclair (CAN)
75 Singles	William Tully (USA)
75 Doubles	Douglas Corbett (AUS)/Harward Hillier (AUS)
80 Singles	Cornelis Marre (NED)
80 Doubles	Bernhard Kempa (GER)/Hans Wendschoff (GER)
85 Singles	Alex Swetka (USA)
85 Doubles	Donal Barnes (RSA)/Alex Swetka (USA)

Women

55 Singles	Carol Campling (AUS)
55 Doubles	Carol Campling (AUS)/Frances Taylor (GBR)
60 Singles	Heide Orth (GER)
60 Doubles	Charleen Hillebrand (USA)/Suella Steel (USA)
65 Singles	Dorothy Matthiessen (USA)
65 Doubles	Dori de Vries (USA)/Belmar Gunderson (USA)
70 Singles	Louise Russ (USA)
70 Doubles	Mary Boswell (USA)/Louise Russ (USA)
75 Singles	Elaine Mason (USA)
75 Doubles	Elsie Crowe (AUS)/June Farrar (AUS)

2003 (Group A) Hannover, Germany

Men

35 Singles	Guido Van Rompaey (BEL)
35 Doubles	Girts Dzelde (LAT)/Torben Theine (GER)
40 Singles	Anders Jarryd (SWE)
40 Doubles	Tom Coulton (USA)/Anders Jarryd (SWE)
45 Singles	Fernando Luna (ESP)
45 Doubles	Pierre Godfroid (BEL)/Heiner Seuss (GER)
50 Singles	Radovan Cizek (CZE)
50 Doubles	Max Bates (AUS)/Andrew Rae (AUS)

Women

35 Singles	Rene Simpson (CAN)
35 Doubles	Heike Thoms (GER)/Lucie Zelinka (AUT)
40 Singles	Regina Marsikova (CZE)
40 Doubles	Mary Dailey (USA)/Diane Fishburne (USA)
45 Singles	Patricia Medrado (BRA)
45 Doubles	Ros Balodis (AUS)/Vicki Collins (AUS)
50 Singles	Eugenia Birukova (ITA)
50 Doubles	Kerry Ballard (AUS)/Elizabeth Craig-Allan (AUS)

ITF Seniors and Super-Seniors World Individual Championships (continued)

2003 (Group B) Antalya, Turkey

Men

55 Singles	Jiri Marik (CZE)
55 Doubles	Lito Alvarez (AUS)/Peter Rigg (AUS)
60 Singles	Peter Pokorny (AUT)
60 Doubles	Stasys Labanauskas (LTU)/Peter Pokorny (AUT)
65 Singles	Bodo Nitsche (GER)
65 Doubles	Robert Duesler (USA)/Jim Nelson (USA)
70 Singles	Lorne Main (CAN)
70 Doubles	Donald Dippold (USA)/James Perley (USA)
75 Singles	Clement Hopp (USA)
75 Doubles	Jack Dunn (USA)/Graydon Nichols (USA)
80 Singles	Robert Sherman (USA)
80 Doubles	Neville Halligan (AUS)/Frank Pitt (AUS)
85 Singles	Federico Barboza (ARG)

Women

55 Singles	Carol Campling (AUS)
55 Doubles	Carol Campling (AUS)/Frances Taylor (GBR)
60 Singles	Heide Orth (GER)
60 Doubles	Charleen Hillebrand (USA)/Suella Steel (USA)
65 Singles	Jeannine Lieffrig (RSA)
65 Doubles	Lynn Little (USA)/Dorothy Matthiessen (USA)
70 Singles	Margaret Robinson (AUS)
70 Doubles	Mary Boswell (USA)/Louise Russ (USA)
75 Singles	Elaine Mason (USA)
75 Doubles	Olga Mahaney (USA)/Elaine Mason (USA)

2004 (Seniors) Antalya, Turkey

Men

35 Singles	Sander Groen (NED)
35 Doubles	Hubert Karrasch (CAN)/Pete Peterson (USA)
40 Singles	Marcos Gorriz (ESP)
40 Doubles	Egan Adams (USA)/Tom Coulton (USA)
45 Singles	Vallis Wilder (USA)
45 Doubles	Mike Fedderly (USA)/Paul Smith (NZL)
50 Singles	Radovan Cizek (CZE)
50 Doubles	Michael Collins (AUS)/Andrew Rae (AUS)

Women

35 Singles	Lucie Zelinka (AUT)
35 Doubles	Karim Strohmeier (PER)/Lucie Zelinka (AUT)
40 Singles	Klaartje Van Baarle (BEL)
40 Doubles	Brenda Foster (AUS)/Sylvie Mattel (FRA)
45 Singles	Diane Fishburne (USA)
45 Doubles	Susana Villaverde (SUI)/Beatriz Villaverde (ARG)
50 Singles	Sherri Bronson (USA)
50 Doubles	Lynette Mortimer (AUS)/Susanne Walter (AUS)

2004 (Super-Seniors) Philadelphia, USA

Men

55 Singles	Tomas Koch (BRA)
55 Doubles	Neal Newman (USA)/Larry Turville (USA)
60 Singles	Jimmy Parker (USA)
60 Doubles	Peter Adrigan (GER)/Hans-Joachim Plötz (GER)
65 Singles	Gene Scott (USA)
65 Doubles	Henry Leichtfried (USA)/George Sarantos (USA)
70 Singles	King Van Nostrand (USA)
70 Doubles	Richard Doss (USA)/John Powless (USA)
75 Singles	Jason Morton (USA)
75 Doubles	William Davis (USA)/Edward Kauder (USA)
80 Singles	Fred Kovaleski (USA)
80 Doubles	Fred Kovaleski (USA)/Robert Sherman (USA)
85 Singles	Alex Swetka (USA)
85 Doubles	Irving Converse (USA)/Howard Kuntz (USA)

Women

55 Singles	Anne Guerrant (USA)
55 Doubles	Kerry Ballard (AUS)/Elizabeth Craig-Allen (AUS)
60 Singles	Heide Orth (GER)
60 Doubles	Susan Hill (GBR)/Jenny Waggott (GBR)
65 Singles	Rosie Darmon (FRA)
65 Doubles	Janine Lieffrig (RSA)/Audrey Van Coller (RSA)
70 Singles	Yvonne Van Nostrand (USA)
70 Doubles	Mary Boswell (USA)/Belmar Gunderson (USA)
75 Singles	Louise Russ (USA)
75 Doubles	Louise Owen (USA)/Louise Russ (USA)

ITF Seniors and Super-Seniors World Team Championships

The International Vets World Team Championships were renamed ITF Seniors World Team Championships (formerly Group A) and ITF Super-Seniors World Team Championships (formerly Group B) in 2004.

Suzanne Lenglen Cup (Women's 35)

Year	Venue	Winner	Runner-up	Score
2001	Velden, Austria	GER	FRA	2-1
2002	Naples, FL, USA	NED	USA	2-1
2003	Hamburg, Germany	GER	FRA	2-1
2004	Manavgat, Turkey	USA	NED	3-0

Young Cup (Women's 40)

Year	Venue	Winner	Runner-up	Score
1977	Malmo, Sweden	ARG	GER	3-0
1978	Ancona, Italy	ITA	GER	3-0
1979	Cannes, France	GER	USA	3-0
1980	Bad Wiessee, Germany	GER	ITA	3-0
1981	Bad Wiessee, Germany	FRA	ITA	2-1
1982	Brand, Austria	FRA	ITA	3-0
1983	Cervia, Italy	GER	FRA	2-1
1984	Cervia, Italy	USA	FRA	3-0
1985	Portschach, Austria	GER	FRA	3-0
1986	Brand, Austria	GER	USA	2-1
1987	Venice, Italy	FRA	USA	2-1
1988	Bagnoles de l'Orne, France	GBR	GER	3-0
1989	Portschach, Austria	FRA	GER	3-0
1990	Keszthely, Hungary	FRA	USA	3-0
1991	Brisbane, QLD, Australia	AUS	GER	2-1
1992	Malahide, Ireland	GBR	AUS	2-1
1993	Bournemouth, Great Britain	USA	GBR	2-1
1994	Montevideo, Uruguay	USA	GER	2-1
1995	Dortmund, Germany	USA	GER	2-1
1996	Bad Hofgastein, Austria	USA	GER	2-1
1997	Pretoria, South Africa	USA	GER	3-0
1998	RAF Halton, Great Britain	USA	RSA	3-0
1999	Gladbeck, Germany	USA	ARG	3-0
2000	Mar del Plata, Argentina	GER	ARG	2-0
2001	Velden, Austria	FRA	ITA	2-1
2002	Naples, FL, USA	AUS	FRA	2-1
2003	Gladbeck, Germany	USA	NED	2-0
2004	Manavgat, Turkey	AUS	GER	2-1

Margaret Court Cup (Women's 45)

Year	Venue	Winner	Runner-up	Score
1994	Perth, WA, Australia	FRA	USA	2-1
1995	Gladbeck, Germany	USA	AUS	3-0
1996	Seeboden, Austria	USA	RSA	3-0
1997	Pretoria, South Africa	USA	FRA	3-0
1998	Warwick, Great Britain	USA	RSA	2-1
1999	Hoofddorp, Netherlands	GER	AUT	3-0
2000	Montevideo, Uruguay	USA	NED	3-0
2001	Bad Hofgastein, Austria	AUT	NED	2-1
2002	Ballenisles, FL, USA	USA	BRA	2-0
2003	Erfurt, Germany	AUS	USA	2-0
2004	Manavgat, Turkey	USA	FRA	2-1

ITF Seniors and Super-Seniors World Team Championships (continued)

Maria Esther Bueno Cup (Women's 50)

Year	Venue	Winner	Runner-up	Score
1983	Portschach, Austria	GBR	USA	2-1
1984	Le Touquet, France	USA	GBR	2-1
1985	Bremen, Germany	USA	GBR	3-0
1986	Brand, Austria	USA	GBR	2-1
1987	Helsinki, Finland	USA	GBR	2-1
1988	Itaparica, Bahia, Brazil	USA	CAN	2-1
1989	Bournemouth, Great Britain	USA	GBR	2-1
1990	Barcelona, Spain	AUS	ESP	2-1
1991	Perth, WA, Australia	USA	FRA	2-1
1992	Bagnoles de L'Orne, France	USA	FRA	2-1
1993	Barcelona, Spain	USA	GER	2-1
1994	San Francisco, CA, USA	USA	GER	3-0
1995	Velden, Austria	NED	USA	2-1
1996	St Kanzian, Austria	AUS	GER	2-1
1997	Pretoria, South Africa	AUS	GER	2-1
1998	Dublin, Ireland	USA	AUS	2-1
1999	Hoofddorp, Netherlands	USA	GER	3-0
2000	Sao Paulo, Brazil	FRA	USA	2-1
2001	Bad Waltersdorf, Austria	GER	USA	2-1
2002	Ballenisles, FL, USA	GER	FRA	2-1
2003	Eisenach, Germany	USA	AUT	3-0
2004	Manavgat, Turkey	USA	NED	2-1

Maureen Connolly Cup (Women's 55)

Year	Venue	Winner	Runner-up	Score
1992	Tyler, USA	AUS	GBR	2-1
1993	Corsica, France	USA	FRA	3-0
1994	Carmel, CA, USA	USA	FRA	2-1
1995	Le Touquet, France	FRA	RSA	2-1
1996	Eugendorf, Austria	FRA	USA	2-1
1997	Canberra, ACT, Australia	USA	FRA	3-0
1998	Pompano Beach, FL, USA	GER	GBR	3-0
1999	Murcia, Spain	USA	NED	3-0
2000	Durban, South Africa	RSA	USA	2-1
2001	Perth, WA, Australia	USA	GER	2-1
2002	Vienna, Austria	HUN	AUS	2-1
2003	Belek, Turkey	USA	GER	3-0
2004	Philadelphia, USA	AUS	USA	2-1

Alice Marble Cup (Women's 60)

Year	Venue	Winner	Runner-up	Score
1988	Portschach, Austria	USA	GER	3-0
1989	Brand, Austria	USA	GER	2-1
1990	Paderborn, Germany	USA	GER	2-1
1991	Perth, WA, Australia	USA	GER	3-0
1992	Keszthely, Hungary	GBR	USA	2-1
1993	Portschach, Austria	USA	GBR	2-1
1994	Carmel, CA, USA	USA	GBR	2-1
1995	Worthing, Great Britain	USA	ESP	2-1
1996	Bad Hofgastein, Austria	USA	ESP	3-0
1997	Adelaide, SA, Australia	USA	CAN	3-0
1998	Boca Raton, FL, USA	AUS	USA	2-1
1999	Sabadell, Spain	FRA	RSA	2-0
2000	Sun City, South Africa	AUS	RSA	2-1

Year	Venue	Winner	Runner-up	Score
2001	Adelaide, SA, Australia	AUS	RSA	3-0
2002	Bad Hofgastein, SA, Austria	FRA	USA	2-1
2003	Manavgat, Turkey	GER	FRA	3-0
2004	Philadelphia, USA	GBR	AUS	2-1

Kitty Godfree Cup (Women's 65)

Year	Venue	Winner	Runner-up	Score
1995	Bournemouth, Great Britain	USA	CAN	2-1
1996	Brand, Austria	GBR	USA	2-1
1997	Melbourne, VIC, Australia	GBR	USA	2-1
1998	Ft. Lauderdale, FL, USA	GBR	USA	2-1
1999	Palafrugell, Spain	USA	GBR	2-0
2000	Cape Town, South Africa	USA	RSA	2-1
2001	Perth, WA, Australia	USA	CAN	2-1
2002	Velden, Austria	USA	CAN	2-1
2003	Belek, Turkey	RSA	USA	2-1
2004	Philadelphia, USA	FRA	AUS	2-0

Althea Gibson Cup (Women's 70)

Year	Venue	Winner	Runner-up	Score
1998	Palm Beach Gardens, FL, USA	USA	GER	Round Robin
1999	Barcelona, Spain	GBR	USA	2-1
2000	Cape Town, South Africa	USA	RSA	2-1
2001	Melbourne, VIC, Australia	GBR	NZL	2-0
2002	Portschach, Austria	USA	GBR	2-1
2003	Manavgat, Turkey	USA	GBR	2-0
2004	Philadelphia, USA	AUS	USA	2-0

Queen's Cup (Women's 75)

Year	Venue	Winner		Score
2002	St Kanzian, Austria	USA		Round Robin
2003	Manavgat, Turkey	USA		Round Robin
2004	Philadelphia, USA	USA	GBR	3-0

Italia Cup (Men's 35)

Year	Venue	Winner	Runner-up	Score
1982	Cervia, Italy	ITA	USA	2-1
1983	Cervia, Italy	GER	USA	2-1
1984	Brand, Austria	GER	FRA	2-1
1985	Reggio Calabria, Italy	USA	ITA	2-0
1986	Bagnoles de L'Orne, France	GER	USA	3-0
1987	Grado, Italy	USA	AUT	2-1
1988	Bol, Yugoslavia	GER	USA	3-0
1989	Mainz, Germany	GER	USA	3-0
1990	Glasgow, Great Britain	ESP	AUS	2-1
1991	Melbourne, VIC, Australia	AUS	ESP	3-0
1992	Ancona, Italy	ITA	FRA	2-1
1993	Barcelona, Spain	ESP	FRA	2-1
1994	Rosario, Argentina	GER	USA	2-1
1995	Dormagen, Germany	GER	USA	2-1
1996	Rome, Italy	USA	ITA	2-1
1997	Johannesburg, South Africa	USA	GBR	2-1
1998	Winchester, Great Britain	GBR	ITA	2-1
1999	Velbert, Germany	GBR	GER	2-1
2000	Buenos Aires, Argentina	GER	USA	3-0

ITF Seniors and Super-Seniors World Team Championships (continued)

Year	Venue	Winner	Runner-up	Score
2001	Portschach, Austria	FRA	USA	3-0
2002	Hallandale, FL, USA	GBR	GER	2-1
2003	Berlin, Germany	GER	FRA	3-0
2004	Manavgat, Turkey	GER	FRA	2-1

Tony Trabert Cup (Men's 40)

Year	Venue	Winner	Runner-up	Score
2000	Santa Cruz, Bolivia	USA	GER	3-0
2001	St Kanzian, Austria	GER	USA	2-0
2002	Naples, FL, USA	USA	GBR	3-0
2003	Hamburg, Germany	GER	USA	3-0
2004	Manavgat, Turkey	ESP	AUT	3-0

Dubler Cup (Men's 45)

Year	Venue	Winner	Runner-up	Score
1958	Monte Carlo, Monaco	ITA	GER	3-1
1959	Bad Ischl, Austria	SUI	ITA	4-1
1960	Bad Gastain, Austria	ITA	SUI	5-0
1961	Ancona, Italy	ITA	AUT	4-1
1962	Merrano, Italy	ITA	FRA	3-2
1963	Merrano, Italy	ITA	BEL	4-1
1964	Merrano, Italy	ITA	GER	5-0
1965	Merrano, Italy	ITA	SWE	3-0
1966	Florence, Italy	SWE	ITA	4-1
1967	Avesta, Sweden	FRA	SWE	3-2
1968	Paris, France	USA	FRA	5-0
1969	St. Louis, MO, USA	USA	SWE	4-1
1970	Cleveland, OH, USA	USA	SWE	4-1
1971	Le Touquet, France	USA	FRA	4-1
1972	Le Touquet, France	USA	FRA	4-1
1973	London, Great Britain	AUS	USA	3-1
1974	New York, USA	USA	AUS	3-2
1975	London, Great Britain	AUS	USA	5-0
1976	Alassio, Italy	ITA	CAN	3-2
1977	Barcelona, Spain	USA	FRA	4-1
1978	Le Touquet, France	USA	AUS	4-1
1979	Vienna, Italy	AUT	USA	3-2
1980	Cervia, Italy	SWE	AUT	2-1
1981	Buenos Aires, Argentina	USA	GBR	2-1
1982	Athens, Greece	USA	GBR	2-1
1983	New York, USA	USA	GER	2-1
1984	Bastad, Sweden	GER	USA	3-0
1985	Perth, WA, Australia	GER	AUS	2-1
1986	Berlin, Germany	GER	SUI	3-0
1987	Portschach, Austria	ITA	AUT	2-1
1988	Huntingdon Beach, CA, USA	USA	GER	3-0
1989	Montevideo, Uruguay	USA	GER	2-1
1990	Bol, Yugoslavia	GER	USA	2-1
1991	Sydney, NSW, Australia	USA	GER	3-0
1992	Portschach, Austria	GER	ESP	2-1
1993	Barcelona, Spain	ESP	FRA	2-1
1994	Santiago, Chile	USA	CHI	2-1
1995	Saarbrucken, Germany	USA	GER	2-1
1996	Velden, Austria	USA	AUS	3-0
1997	Pretoria, South Africa	AUS	RSA	2-1
1998	Dublin, Ireland	USA	ESP	2-1

Year	Venue	Winner	Runner-up	Score
1999	Arquebusiers, Luxembourg	BRA	ESP	2-1
2000	Asuncion, Paraguay	USA	FRA	2-1
2001	Vienna, Austria	FRA	USA	3-0
2002	Ballenisles, FL, USA	FRA	USA	2-1
2003	Bielefeld, Germany	GER	FRA	3-0
2004	Manavgat, Turkey	USA	GER	3-0

Fred Perry Cup (Men's 50)

Year	Venue	Winner	Runner-up	Score
1991	Bournemouth, Great Britain	GER	GBR	3-0
1992	Berlin, Germany	GER	USA	3-0
1993	Royan, Germany	GER	USA	2-1
1994	Buenos Aires, Argentina	FRA	USA	2-1
1995	Luchow, Germany	FRA	GER	2-1
1996	Portschach, Austria	GER	AUT	3-0
1997	Sun City, South Africa	ESP	GER	2-1
1998	Glasgow, Great Britain	USA	ESP	2-1
1999	Amstelveen, Netherlands	USA	ESP	3-0
2000	Santiago, Chile	USA	CHI	2-1
2001	Velden, Austria	USA	AUS	2-1
2002	Ballenisles, FL, USA	ESP	AUS	2-0
2003	Bielefeld, Germany	GER	AUS	2-1
2004	Manavgat, Turkey	AUS	USA	2-1

Austria Cup (Men's 55)

Year	Venue	Winner	Runner-up	Score
1977	Baden, Austria	GBR	AUT	2-1
1978	Brand, Austria	USA	SWE	2-1
1979	Brand, Austria	USA	SWE	3-0
1980	Brand, Austria	USA	SWE	2-1
1981	Portschach, Austria	USA	SWE	3-0
1982	Cervia, Italy	AUS	USA	2-1
1983	New York, USA	AUS	USA	2-1
1984	Portschach, Austria	USA	AUS	2-1
1985	Perth, WA, Austria	AUS	USA	3-0
1986	Portschach, Austria	AUS	CAN	2-1
1987	Umag, Yugoslavia	CAN	AUS	3-0
1988	Huntingdon Beach, CA, USA	CAN	GER	2-1
1989	Buenos Aires, Argentina	CAN	USA	2-1
1990	Portschach, Austria	CAN	USA	3-0
1991	Sydney, NSW, Australia	USA	AUS	3-0
1992	Monte Carlo, Monaco	GER	USA	2-1
1993	Murcia, Spain	USA	AUS	2-1
1994	Carmel, CA, USA	AUS	USA	2-1
1995	Dublin, Ireland	GER	AUT	2-1
1996	Portschach, Austria	AUT	USA	2-1
1997	Canberra, ACT, Australia	AUT	GER	2-1
1998	Naples, FL, USA	USA	NED	3-0
1999	Barcelona, Spain	FRA	GER	2-0
2000	Pietermaritzburg, South Africa	USA	FRA	2-1
2001	Perth, WA, Australia	FRA	AUS	2-1
2002	Vienna, Austria	ESP	FRA	3-0
2003	Belek, Turkey	USA	NED	2-1
2004	Philadelphia, USA	ESP	USA	2-1

Von Cramm Cup (Men's 60)

Year	Venue	Winner	Runner-up	Score
1989	Kempten, Germany	AUS	NZL	3-0
1990	Ontario, Canada	USA	AUT	2-1
1991	Adelaide, SA, Australia	USA	NZL	2-1
1992	Bournemouth, Great Britain	CAN	USA	2-1
1993	Aix les Bains, France	USA	FRA	3-0
1994	Burlingame, CA, USA	USA	GER	3-0
1995	Portschach, Austria	USA	GER	3-0
1996	Velden, Austria	USA	FRA	3-0
1997	Hamilton, New Zealand	USA	AUS	3-0
1998	Ft. Lauderdale, FL, USA	GER	USA	2-1
1999	Tarragona, Spain	FRA	GER	2-1
2000	Cape Town, South Africa	AUT	AUS	2-1
2001	Adelaide, SA, Australia	GER	USA	2-1
2002	St Kanzian, Austria	AUT	ITA	3-0
2003	Manavgat, Turkey	AUT	AUS	3-0
2004	Philadelphia, USA	USA	GER	2-0

Britannia Cup (Men's 65)

Year	Venue	Winner	Runner-up	Score
1979	London, Great Britain	USA	GBR	3-0
1980	Frinton-on-Sea, Great Britain	USA	SWE	3-0
1981	London, Great Britain	USA	SWE	3-0
1982	New York, USA	USA	CAN	3-0
1983	Portschach, Austria	USA	AUS	3-0
1984	Portschach, Austria	USA	AUS	3-0
1985	Portschach, Austria	USA	AUS	0-0
1986	Bournemouth, Great Britain	USA	NOR	3-0
1987	Bastad, Sweden	USA	SWE	2-1
1988	Huntingdon Beach, CA, USA	USA	FRA	3-0
1989	Umag, Yugoslavia	USA	FRA	3-0
1990	Bournemouth, Great Britain	USA	AUS	2-1
1991	Canberra, ACT, Australia	AUT	AUS	2-1
1992	Seefeld, Austria	AUS	AUT	2-1
1993	Le Touquet, France	USA	ITA	2-1
1994	Portola Valley, CA, USA	USA	AUT	2-1
1995	Glasgow, Great Britain	USA	CAN	2-1
1996	Warmbad Villach, Austria	USA	CAN	2-1
1997	Hamilton, New Zealand	USA	CAN	2-1
1998	Palm Beach Gardens, FL, USA	CAN	USA	3-0
1999	Palafrugell, Spain	USA	CAN	2-1
2000	Cape Town, South Africa	AUS	USA	2-1
2001	Perth, WA, Australia	USA	AUS	2-1
2002	Velden, Austria	USA	GER	3-0
2003	Belek, Turkey	GER	MEX	3-0
2004	Philadelphia, USA	USA	AUS	2-0

Jack Crawford Cup (Men's 70)

Year	Venue	Winner	Runner-up	Score
1983	Brand, Austria	USA	SWE	3-0
1984	Helsinki, Finland	USA	GBR	3-0
1985	Brand, Austria	USA	AUT	3-0
1986	Seefeld, Austria	USA	FRA	3-0
1987	Portschach, Austria	USA	GBR	3-0
1988	Keszthely, Hungary	USA	GBR	3-0
1989	Bol, Yugoslavia	USA	BRA	3-0
1990	Brand, Austria	USA	BRA	3-0

Year	Venue	Winner	Runner-up	Score
1991	Canberra, ACT, Australia	GER	USA	2-1
1992	Le Touquet, France	USA	GER	3-0
1993	Menorca, Spain	USA	FRA	3-0
1994	Oakland, CA, USA	AUS	FRA	2-1
1995	Aix les Bains, France	USA	AUS	2-1
1996	Seeboden, Austria	AUT	USA	2-1
1997	Adelaide, SA, Australia	AUT	USA	2-1
1998	Pompano Beach, FL, USA	USA	AUT	2-1
1999	Barcelona, Spain	USA	AUS	3-0
2000	Cape Town, South Africa	CAN	USA	2-1
2001	Melbourne, VIC, Australia	CAN	USA	2-0
2002	Portschach, Austria	CAN	USA	3-0
2003	Manavgat, Turkey	USA	CAN	2-1
2004	Philadelphia, USA	USA	JPN	3-0

Bitsy Grant Cup (Men's 75)

Year	Venue	Winner	Runner-up	Score
1994	Mill Valley, USA	USA	MEX	3-0
1995	Bournemouth, Great Britain	USA	SWE	3-0
1996	Bad Waltersdorf, Austria	USA	GER	3-0
1997	Hobart, TAS, Australia	USA	AUS	3-0
1998	Boca Raton, FL, USA	USA	AUS	3-0
1999	Barcelona, Spain	USA	MEX	3-0
2000	Cape Town, South Africa	USA	GBR	3-0
2001	Perth, WA, Australia	AUT	AUS	3-0
2002	Bad Waltersdorf, Austria	AUS	AUT	2-1
2003	Manavgat, Turkey	USA	FRA	3-0
2004	Philadelphia, USA	FRA	USA	2-1

Gardnar Mulloy Cup (Men's 80)

Year	Venue	Winner	Runner-up	Score
1996	Seefeld, Austria	USA	MEX	Round Robin
1997	Melbourne, VIC, Australia	USA	AUS	Round Robin
1998	Naples, FL, USA	USA	AUS	Round Robin
1999	Murcia, Spain	USA	AUS	3-0
2000	Cape Town, South Africa	USA	AUS	2-1
2001	Perth, WA, Australia	USA	GER	Round Robin
2002	St Kanzian, Austria	AUS	USA	3-0
2003	Manavgat, Turkey	USA	AUS	2-1
2004	Philadelphia, USA	USA	AUS	2-0

Nations Senior Cup

The ITF-sanctioned Nations Senior Cup was first held in 1999, and became the first nations senior tournament to bring together the most successful elite tennis players, retired from the ATP Tour and Davis Cup play.

Year	Champion
1999	Sweden
2000	France
2001	Spain
2003	**Spain d. Germany 2-1:** Carlos Costa (ESP) d. Patrik Kuhnen (GER) 64 63; Boris Becker (GER) d. Sergi Bruguera (ESP) 76 75; Emilio Sánchez/Carlos Costa (ESP) d. Michael Stich/Boris Becker (GER) 16 64 10(7).
2004	**Russia d. USA 2-1:** Andrei Cherkasov (RUS) d. Aaron Krickstein (USA) 76(4) 64; Jim Courier (USA) d. Andrei Chesnokov (RUS) 64 62; Andrei Cherkasov/Andrei Olhovskiy (RUS) d. Jim Courier/Jonathan Stark (USA) 63 46 119

National Associations

Correct as at 17 December 2004

INTERNATIONAL TENNIS FEDERATION (ITF)
Bank Lane
Roehampton
London SW15 5XZ
United Kingdom
President: Mr Francesco Ricci Bitti
Executive Vice President: Mr Juan Margets
Telephone: 44 20 8878 6464
Fax: 44 20 8878 7799
Email: reception@itftennis.com
Website: www.itftennis.com

Class B (Full) Members With Voting Rights (146)

ALGERIA – ALG
Fédération Algerienne de Tennis
CNOSAOS
Rue Ahmed Ouaked
Dely Ibrahim Alger, Algeria
President: Dr Mohamed Bouabdallah
Secretary: Mr Hakim Fateh
Telephone: 213 21 79 13 70/71
Fax: 213 21 79 13 71
Email: fatehkim@yahoo.fr
Website: www.multimania.com/tennisdz

ANDORRA – AND
Fed Andorrana de Tenis St. Antoni
C/Verge Del Pilar 5
3er Desp. No 10
Andorra La Vella, Andorra
President: Mr Antoni Ricart
Secretary: Mr Joan Grau
Telephone: 376 861 381
Fax: 376 868 381
Email: tennisfat@andorra.ad

ANGOLA – ANG
Federacao Angolana de Tenis
Cidadeia Desportive
PO Box 6533
Luanda, Angola
President: Mr Luis Rosa Lopes
Secretary: Mr M N Joao
Telephone: 244 2 261 494
Fax: 244 2 261 496/265 711
Email: luisrosa.lopes@snet.co.ao

ANTIGUA & BARBUDA – ANT
Antigua & Barbuda Tennis Association
PO Box 2758
St John's, Antigua & Barbuda
President: Mr Cordell Williams
Secretary: Mr Derald Williams
Telephone: 1 268 460 5573
Fax: 1 268 462 4658
Email: a_btennis@hotmail.com

ARGENTINA – ARG
Asociacion Argentina de Tenis
Maipu 471 – 3er piso
1376 Capital Federal
Buenos Aires, Argentina
President: Mr Enrique Morea
Secretary: Mr Roberto Fernandez
Telephone: 54 11 4322 0059
Fax: 54 11 4328 9124/9145
Email: secconsejo@aat.com.ar
Website: www.aat.com.ar

ARMENIA – ARM
Armenian Tennis Association
Hrazdan Sport Complex
Tennis School
Kilikia 375082
Yerevan, Armenia
President: Mr Harutyun Pambukian
Secretary: Mr George Karamanukyan
Telephone: 3741 529 429
Fax: 3741 529 429
Email: tennisarmenia@mail.com

AUSTRALIA – AUS
Tennis Australia
Private Bag 6060
Richmond South
Victoria 3121, Australia
President: Mr Geoff Pollard
Secretary: Mr David Roberts
Telephone: 61 392 861 177
Fax: 61 396 502 743
Email: tennis@tennisaustralia.com.au
Website: www.tennisaustralia.com.au

AUSTRIA – AUT
Osterreichischer Tennisverband
Eisgrubengasse 2 – 6
2331 Vösendorf, Austria
President: Dr Ernst Wolner
Secretary: Mr Martin Reiter
Telephone: 43 1 865 4506 0
Fax: 43 1 865 45 06 85
Email: info@tennisaustria.at
Website: www.asn.or.at/oetv/

AZERBAIJAN – AZE
Azerbaijan Tennis Federation
67 Tbilisi Ave – ap. 206
Baku 1012, Azerbaijan
President: Mr Oktay Asadov
Secretary: Mr Ilham Kuliyev
Telephone: 99 412 314767
Fax: 99 412 313355
Email: tennisfed@azeronline.com

BAHAMAS – BAH
The Bahamas Lawn Tennis Association
National Tennis Centre
QE Sports Centre
PO Box N-10169
Nassau, Bahamas
President: Mrs Mary Shelley
Secretary: Mr Kevin Major
Telephone: 1 242 323 3933
Fax: 1 242 323 3934
Email: bltatennis@speedwayinternet.com

BAHRAIN – BRN
Bahrain Tennis Federation
PO Box 26985, Bahrain
President: H H Shaikh Ahmed Al Khalifa
Secretary: Mr Matter Yousuf Matter
Telephone: 973 17 687 236
Fax: 973 17 781 533
Email: btennisf@batelco.com.bh

BANGLADESH – BAN
Bangladesh Tennis Federation
Tennis Complex
Ramna Green
Dhaka 1000, Bangladesh
President: Mr Toufiq M Seraj
Secretary: Mr Nurul Hoque Prodhan
Telephone: 880 2 862 6287
Fax: 880 2 966 2711
Email: btf@bttb.net.bd

BARBADOS – BAR
Barbados Lawn Tennis Association
PO Box 615C
Bridgetown, Barbados
President: Dr Raymond Forde
Secretary: Mrs Eleanor Brown
Telephone: 1 246 426 6453
Fax: 1 246 429 3342
Email: blta@sunbeach.net

BELARUS – BLR
Belarus Tennis Association
63 Masherov Avenue
Minsk 220035
Belarus
President: Mr Mikhail Pavlov
Secretary: Mr Simon Kagan
Telephone: 375 17 226 9374
Fax: 375 172 269 823
Email: beltennis@yahoo.com

BELGIUM – BEL
Fédération Royale Belge de Tennis
Galerie de la Porte Louise 203/3
1050 Bruxelles, Belgium
President: Mr Yves Freson
Secretary: Mr Franz Lemaire
Telephone: 32 2 548 0304/513 2920
Fax: 32 2 548 0303
Email: info@rbtf.be
Website: www.rbtf.be

BENIN – BEN
Fédération Beninoise de Lawn Tennis
BP 2709
Cotonou I, Benin
President: Mr Gustave Gazard
Secretary: Mr Ladami Gafari
Telephone: 229 315 153
Fax: 229 311 252
Email: fbtennis@netcourrier.com

BERMUDA – BER
Bermuda Lawn Tennis Association
PO Box HM 341
Hamilton HM BX, Bermuda
President: Mr David Lambert
Secretary: Ms Zoe Mulholland
Telephone: 1 441 296 0834
Fax: 1 441 295 3056
Email: blta@northrock.bm
Website: www.blta.bm

BOLIVIA – BOL
Federación Boliviana De Tennis
Calle Sucre 551
Santa Cruz, Bolivia
President: Mr Edmundo Rodriguez
Secretary: Ms Maria Eugenia Oporto
Telephone: 5913 332 9244
Fax: 5913 336 8625
Email: secfbt@fbtenis.org.bo
Website: www.fbtenis.org.bo

BOSNIA HERZEGOVINA – BIH
Tennis Assn. of Bosnia & Herzegovina
Bulevar Kulina Bana 30
Zenica, Bosnia Herzegovina
President: Mr Zoran Djeric
Secretary: Mr Milenko Rimac
Telephone: 387 32 409 161
Fax: 387 32 411 077
Email: tsbih@yahoo.com

BOTSWANA – BOT
Botswana Tennis Association
PO Box 1174
Gaborone, Botswana
President: Mr Judge Mookodi
Secretary: Mr Nelson Amanze
Telephone: 267 3973 193
Fax: 267 3973 193
Email: bta@it.bw

BRAZIL – BRA
Confederacao Brasileira de Tenis
Av Paulista Nr. 326, 16o Andar
CEP 01310-902
Sao Paulo/SP, Brazil
President: Mr Nelson Nastas
Secretary: Mr Carlos Alberto Martelotte
Telephone: 55 11 3 283 1046
Fax: 55 11 3 283 0768
Email: cbt@cbtenis.com.br
Website: www.cbtenis.com.br

BRUNEI – BRU
Brunei Darussalam Tennis Association
Hassanal Bolkiah Sports Complex
PO Box 859, Gadong Post Office
Bandar Seri Begawan
Negara BE 3978
Brunei
President: Mr. Pg Kamaruddin Pg Hj Radin
Secretary: Mr Hj Zuraimi Hj Abd Sani
Telephone: 673 2 381 205
Fax: 673 2 381 205
Email: bdta@brunet.bn

BULGARIA – BUL
Bulgarian Tennis Federation
Bul. Vasil Levski 75
Sofia 1040, Bulgaria
President: Mr. Pg Kamaruddin Pg Hj Radin
Secretary: Mr Hj Zuraimi Hj Abd Sani
Telephone: 673 2 381 205
Fax: 673 2 381 205
Email: bdta@brunet.bn

BURKINA FASO – BUR
Fédération Burkinabe De Tennis
01 BP 45
Ouagadougou 1, Burkina Faso
President: Mr Zambo Martin Zongo
Secretary: Wenceslas Zagre
Telephone: 226 5030 4031
Fax: 226 5030 4031
Email: cemagn@fasonet.bf

National Associations (continued)

CAMEROON – CMR
Fédération Camerounaise de Tennis
BP 1121
Yaounde, Cameroon
President: Mr Paul Kemadjou
Secretary: Mr Eko Bikele
Fax: 237 222 4694
Email: fecat-yao@caramail.com

CANADA – CAN
Tennis Canada
1 Shoreham Drive
Toronto, Ontario
M3N 1S4, Canada
President: Mr Michael Downey
Secretary: Ms. Kim Ali
Telephone: 1 416 665 9777
Fax: 1 416 665 9017
Email: compcoord@tenniscanada.com
Website: www.tenniscanada.com

CHILE – CHI
Federacion de Tenis de Chile
Jose Joaquin Prieto No. 4040
San Miguel
Santiago, Chile
President: Mr Andres Fazio Molina
Secretary: Mr Patricio Stevens Diaz
Telephone: 56 2 554 0068/0154
Fax: 56 2 554 1078
Email: ftch@tie.cl
Website: www.ftch.cl

HONG KONG, CHINA – HKG
Hong Kong Tennis Association Ltd
Room 1021, Sports House
1 Stadium Path
So Kon Po, Causeway Bay
Hong Kong, China
President: Mr Kenneth Tsui
Secretary: Mr General Secretary
Telephone: 852 2 504 8266
Fax: 852 2 894 8704
Email: info@tennishk.org

CHINA, PEOPLE'S REPUBLIC OF – CHN
Chinese Tennis Association
5' Tiyuguan Road
Beijing 100763
China, People's Republic Of
President: Mr Lu Zhenchao
Secretary: Ms Sun Jin Fang
Telephone: 86 10 67180176
Fax: 86 10 6711 4096
Email: cta@tennis.org.cn

CHINESE TAIPEI – TPE
Chinese Taipei Tennis Association
Room 705, 7th Floor
No. 20, Chu-Lun Street
Taiwan, R.O.C. 104
Chinese Taipei
President: Mr Chen-Yen Yeh
Secretary: Mr Jesse Wu
Telephone: 886 2 2772 0298
Fax: 886 2 2771 1696
Email: ctta@gcn.net.tw
Website: www.cttatennis.org.tw

COLOMBIA – COL
Federacion Colombiana de Tenis
Centro De Alto Rendimiento
Calle 63 No 47-06
Bogota D.C., Colombia
President: Dr Gabriel Sanchez Sierra
Secretary: Mr Armando Gonzalez
Telephone: 571 314 3885
Fax: 571 660 4234
Email: fct@etb.net.co
Website: www.fedetenis.com

CONGO – CGO
Fédération Congolaise de Lawn Tennis
BP 550
Brazzaville, Congo
President: Mr Germain Ickonga Akindou
Secretary: Mr Antoine Ouabonzi
Telephone: 242 411 222
Fax: 242 810 330
Email: g_ickonga_akindou@hotmail.com

COSTA RICA – CRC
Federación Costarricense de Tenis
Apartado 575 1000
San José, Costa Rica
President: Mr Ricardo Castro
Secretary: Mr Jurgen G Nanne-Koberg
Telephone: 506 524 2400
Fax: 506 524 2433
Email: fedtenis@racsa.co.cr
Website: www.fctenis.com

COTE D'IVOIRE – CIV
Fédération Ivoirienne de Tennis
01 BPV 273
Abidjan 01, Cote D'ivoire
President: Mr Georges N'Goan
Secretary: Mr Athanase Kakou
Telephone: 225 22 441 354
Fax: 225 22 442 707
Email: fede_ivoirtennis@yahoo.fr

CROATIA – CRO
Croatian Tennis Association
HR-10 000 Zagreb
Gundulieeva 3, Croatia
President: Mr Radimir Cacic
Secretary: Miss Suzana Knezevic
Telephone: 385 1 4830 756
Fax: 385 1 4830 720
Email: hts@hts.hr
Website: www.hts.hr

CUBA – CUB
Federacion Cubana de Tenis de Campo
Calle 13 Nr 601 Esq Ac
Vedado Habana 4, Cuba
President: Mr Rolando Martínez Pérez
Secretary: Mr Juan Baez
Telephone: 53 7 951694/973011
Fax: 53 7 952 121
Email: fctennis@inder.co.cu

CYPRUS – CYP
Cyprus Tennis Federation
Ionos Str. 20
PO Box 3931
Nicosia 1687, Cyprus
President: Mr Philios Christodoulou
Secretary: Mr Stavros Ioannou
Telephone: 357 22 666 822
Fax: 357 22 668 016
Email: cytennis@spidernet.com.cy

CZECH REPUBLIC – CZE
Czech Tenisova Asociace
Ostrov Stvanice 38
170 00 Prague 7, Czech Republic
President: Mr Ivo Kaderka
Secretary: Mr Josef Nechutny
Telephone: 420 222 333 444
Fax: 420 222 311 327
Email: cts@cta.cz
Website: www.cztenis.cz

DENMARK – DEN
Dansk Tennis Forbund
Idraettens Hus
Broendby Stadion 20
DK-2605 Broendby, Denmark
President: Mr Henrik Klitvad
Secretary: Mr Niels Persson
Telephone: 45 43 262 660
Fax: 45 43 262 670
Email: dtf@dtftennis.dk
Website: www.dtftennis.dk

DJIBOUTI – DJI
Fédération Djiboutienne de Tennis
BP 728, Djibouti
President: Mr Houmed Houssein
Secretary: Mr Ibrahim Ali
Telephone: 253 352 536
Fax: 253 352 536
Email: oned@intnet.dj

DOMINICAN REPUBLIC – DOM
Federacion Dominicana de Tenis
Club Deportivo Naco
Calle Central
Ens Naco, Santo Domingo
Dominican Republic
President: Mr Mario Emilio Guerrero
Secretary: Mr J Ravelo
Telephone: 1 809 483 8883
Fax: 1 809 483 8882
Email: fedotenis@hotmail.com

ECUADOR – ECU
Federacion Ecuatoriana de Tenis
Edificio de la FET
Lomas de Urdesa
Tres Cerritos
Guayaquil, Ecuador
President: Mr Manuel Carrera del Rio
Secretary: Mr Jorge Enderica
Telephone: 593 42 610 467
Fax: 593 42 610 466
Email: fetenis@gye.satnet.net

EGYPT – EGY
Egyptian Tennis Federation
13 Kasr El Nile Street
Cairo, Egypt
President: Mr Mohamed Halawa
Secretary: Mr Motaz Sonbol
Telephone: 202 576 3522
Fax: 202 575 3235
Email: etf@urgentmail.com

EL SALVADOR – ESA
Federacion Salvadorena de Tenis
Apartado Postal (01) 110
San Salvador, El Salvador
President: Mr Enrique Molins Rubio
Secretary: Mr Miguel Irigoyen
Telephone: 503 278 3275/3276
Fax: 503 278 8087
Email: fedetenis_esa@integra.com.sv

ESTONIA – EST
Estonian Tennis Association
1-5P Regati Ave
11911 Tallinn, Estonia
President: Mr Jaanus Otsa
Secretary: Ms Ilona Poljakova
Telephone: 372 6 398 637
Fax: 372 6 398 635
Email: estonian.tennis@tennis.ee

ETHIOPIA – ETH
Ethiopian Tennis Federation
PO Box 3241
Addis Ababa, Ethiopia
President: Mr Bezuayehu Tesfaye
Secretary: Mrs Werkeye Ferede
Telephone: 251 1 639170 or 186009
Fax: 251 1 513 345
Email: werkeyeetftennis.com

FIJI – FIJ
Fiji Tennis Association
P O Box 63
Lautoka, Fiji
President: Mr John Shannon
Secretary: Mr Paras Naidu
Telephone: 679 662 525
Fax: 679 668 837
Email: john@fsc.com.fj

FINLAND – FIN
Suomen Tennisliitto
Varikkotie 4
SF – 00900 Helsinki, Finland
President: Mr Jukka Roiha
Secretary: Mr Mika Bono
Telephone: 358 9 3417 1533
Fax: 358 9 323 1105
Email: mika.bono@tennis.fi
Website: www.tennis.fi

FRANCE – FRA
Fédération Française de Tennis
Stade Roland Garros
2 Avenue Gordon Bennett
75016 Paris, France
President: Mr Christian Bimes
Secretary: Mr J Dupre
Telephone: 33 1 4743 4800
Fax: 33 1 4743 0494
Email: fft@fft.fr
Website: www.fft.fr

GABON – GAB
Fédération Gabonaise de Tennis
PO Box 4241
Libreville, Gabon
President: Mr Samuel Minko Mindong
Secretary: Mr Marcel Desire Mebale
Telephone: 241 247 344
Fax: 241 703 190
Email: minkomindo@yahoo.fr
Website: rdd.rdd-gabon.gouv.ga.fegaten

GEORGIA – GEO
Georgian Tennis Federation
K Marjanishvili St 29
Tbilisi, Georgia
President: Ms Leila Meskhi
Secretary: Mr Zurab Katsarava
Telephone: 995 32 952 781
Fax: 995 32 953 829
Email: gtf@gol.ge

GERMANY – GER
Deutscher Tennis Bund EV
Hallerstrasse 89
Hamburg 20149
Germany
President: Dr Georg von Waldenfels
Secretary: Mr Reimund Schneider
Telephone: 49 40 411 782 60
Fax: 49 40 411 782 33
Email: dtb@dtb-tennis.de
Website: www.dtb-tennis.de

GHANA – GHA
Ghana Tennis Association
PO Box T-95
Sports Stadium Post Office
Accra, Ghana
President: Mr Jeffrey Abeasi
Secretary: Mr Charles Kudzo Attah
Telephone: 233 21 667 267
Fax: 233 21 236 788
Email: gtennis@africaonline.com.gh

GREAT BRITAIN – GBR
The Lawn Tennis Association
The Queen's Club
Palliser Road
London W14 9EG, Great Britain
President: Mr Charles Trippe
Secretary: Mr Bruce Mellstrom
Telephone: 44 20 7381 7000
Fax: 44 20 7381 5965
Email: info@lta.org.uk
Website: www.lta.org.uk

National Associations (continued)

GREECE – GRE
Hellenic Tennis Federation
267 Imitou Street
11631 Pagrati
Athens, Greece
President: Mr Spyros Zannias
Secretary: Mr Dimitris Stamatiadis
Telephone: 30 210 756 3170/1/2
Fax: 30 210 756 3173
Email: efoa@otenet.gr

GUATEMALA – GUA
Fed. Nacional de Tenis de Guatemala
Section 1551
PO Box 02-5339
Miami, Florida 33102-5339
USA
President: Ms Marissa Maselli de Gabriel
Secretary: Mr Mario España Estrada
Telephone: 502 2385 1224
Fax: 502 2331 0261
Email: fedtenis@terra.com.gt

HAITI – HAI
Fédération Haitienne de Tennis
PO Box 1442
Port Au Prince, Haiti
President: Mr Frantz Liautaud
Secretary: Mr Hulzer Adolphe
Telephone: 509 45 1461/46 2544
Fax: 509 49 1233/46 1259
Email: tennis_haiti@abhardware.com

HONDURAS – HON
Federacion Hondurena de Tenis
P.O. Box 30152
Toncontin
Tegueigalpa MDC, Honduras
President: Mr Humberto Rodriguez
Secretary: Mr Rodulio Perdomo
Telephone: 504 2 396 890
Fax: 504 2 396 889
Email: fedtenishon@123.hn

HUNGARY – HUN
Magyar Tenisz Szovetseg
Dozsa Gyorgy UT 1-3
Budapest 1143
Hungary
President: Dr Janos Berenyi
Secretary: Mr Attila Deak
Telephone: 36 1 252 6687
Fax: 36 1 251 0107
Email: tennis@interware.hu
Website: www.tennis.hu

ICELAND – ISL
Icelandic Tennis Association
Engjavegur 6
104 Reykjavik, Iceland
President: Mr Skjoldur Vatnar Bjornsson
Secretary: Mr Jón Gunnar Grjetarsson
Telephone: 354 514 4000
Fax: 354 514 4001
Email: jongg@ruv.is
Website: www.isisport.is/tennis/

INDIA – IND
All India Tennis Association
R K Khanna Tennis Stadium
Africa Avenue
110029 New Delhi, India
President: Mr Yashwant Sinha
Secretary: Mr Anil Khanna
Telephone: 91 11 2617 9062
Fax: 91 11 2617 3159
Email: aita@aitatennis.com
Website: www.aitatennis.com

INDONESIA – INA
Indonesian Tennis Association
Gelora Senayan Tennis Stadium
Jakarta 10270, Indonesia
President: Mrs Martina Widjaja
Secretary: Mr Soebronto Laras
Telephone: 62 21 571 0298
Fax: 62 21 570 0157
Email: pelti@vision.net.id

IRAN, ISLAMIC REPUBLIC OF – IRI
Tennis Fed. of Islamic Republic of Iran
PO Box 15815 – 1881
Tehran
Iran, Islamic Republic Of
President: Mr Abbas Khazei
Secretary: Mr Issa Khodaei
Telephone: 98 21 884 1620/4731
Fax: 98 21 884 1620/4731
Email: info@tennisiran.org

IRAQ – IRQ
Iraqi Tennis Federation
P O Box 440
Baghdad, Iraq
President: Mr Ghazi Al-Shaya'a Hamel
Secretary: Mr Khalid Saeed Al-Sultani
Telephone: 964 1 774 8261
Fax: 964 1 772 8424
Email: Iraqitenfed2003@yahoo.com

IRELAND – IRL
Tennis Ireland
Dublin City University
Glasnevin
Dublin 9, Ireland
President: Mr David Nathan
Secretary: Mrs Jan Singleton
Telephone: 353 1 8844 010
Fax: 353 1 8844 013
Email: info@tennisireland.ie
Website: www.tennisireland.ie

ISRAEL – ISR
Israel Tennis Association
2 Shitrit Street
Hader Yosef
69482 Tel Aviv, Israel
President: Dr Ian Froman
Secretary: Mr Yoram Baron
Telephone: 972 36 499 440
Fax: 972 36 499 144
Email: igutenis@netvision.net.il

ITALY – ITA
Federazione Italiana Tennis
Violo Tiziann 74
00196 Rome, Italy
President: Mr Angelo Binaghi
Secretary: Mrs Felicetta Rossitto
Telephone: 390 636 858 406
Fax: 390 636 858 166
Email: segreteria@federtennis.it
Website: www.federtennis.it/

JAMAICA – JAM
Tennis Jamaica
68 Lady Musgrave Road
Kingston 10, Jamaica
President: Mr Ken Morgan
Secretary: Mrs. Joycelin Morgan
Telephone: 1 876 927 9466
Fax: 1 876 927 9436
Email: tennisjam@cwjamaica.com

JAPAN – JPN
Japan Tennis Association
C/o Kishi Memorial Hall
1-1-1 Jinnan, Shibuya-ku
Tokyo 150-8050
Japan
President: Mr Masaaki Morita
Secretary: Mr Hiroshi Suzuki
Telephone: 81 33 481 2321
Fax: 81 33 467 5192
Email: office@jta-tennis.or.jp
Website: www.tennis.or.jp

JORDAN – JOR
Jordan Tennis Federation
Sport City
Gate 4 or 5
PO Box 961046
11196 Amman, Jordan
President: Mr Saad Hijjawi
Secretary: Ms Tamara Qunash
Telephone: 962 6 568 2796
Fax: 962 6 568 2796
Email: tennisfed@tennisfed.org.jo

KAZAKHSTAN – KAZ
Kazakhstan Tennis Federation
Central Sports Club
Of The Army
480051 Almaty, Kazakhstan
President: Mr Pavel Novikov
Secretary: Mr Valery Kovalev
Telephone: 7 3272 640 469
Fax: 7 3272 640 469
Email: kovalev2001@pochtamt.ru

KENYA – KEN
Kenya Lawn Tennis Association
PO Box 48620 – 00100
Nairobi, Kenya
President: Mr Francis Mutuku
Secretary: Mr Baldev Aggarwal
Telephone: 254 20 582646
Fax: 254 20 583500
Email: baggarwal@inteluni.ac.ke

KOREA, REPUBLIC OF – KOR
Korea Tennis Association
Room 108, Olympic Gym No. 2
88-2 Oryun-Dong, Songpa-Gu
Seoul 138-151
Korea, Republic of
President: Mr Dong-Kil Cho
Secretary: Mr Yeong-Moo Huh
Telephone: 82 2 420 4285
Fax: 82 2 420 4284
Email: kortennis@hanmail.net

KUWAIT – KUW
Kuwait Tennis Federation
PO Box 1462
Hawalli 32015, Kuwait
President: Sheik Ahmed Al-Sabah
Secretary: Mr Abdul-Ridha Ghareeb
Telephone: 965 539 7261
Fax: 965 539 0617
Email: info@kuwaittennis.com
Website: www.kuwaittennis.com

KYRGYZSTAN – KGZ
Kyrgyzstan Tennis Federation
Moskovskey Str 121/58
Bishkek 720000, Kyrgyzstan
President: Mr Tanaev Nikolai Tanaev
Secretary: Mr Valentin Akinshin
Telephone: 996 312 664 713
Fax: 996 312 664 713
Email: tfkr@elcat.kg

LATVIA – LAT
Latvian Tennis Union
Oskara Kalpaka Pr.16
LV 2010 Jurmala, Latvia
President: Mr Juris Savickis
Secretary: Mr Janis Pliens
Telephone: 371 775 2121
Fax: 371 775 5021
Email: teniss@parks.lv

LEBANON – LIB
Fédération Libanaise de Tennis
1st Floor – Beirut-Lebanon &
Kuwait Building
Dora Main Street
Beirut, Lebanon
President: Mr Riad Haddad
Secretary: Mr Nohad V Schoucair
Telephone: 961 1 879 288
Fax: 961 1 879 277
Email: lbtf@elbarid.net

LESOTHO – LES
Lesotho Lawn Tennis Association
PO Box 156
Maseru 100, Lesotho
President: Mr Khoai Matete
Secretary: Mr Mokhali Lithebe
Telephone: 266 22 321 543
Fax: 266 22 321 543
Email: tennis@ilesotho.com

LIBYA – LBA
Libyan Arab Tennis & Squash
Federation
PO Box 879 – 2729
Tripoli, Libya
President: Mr Abdulssalem A Bellel
Secretary: Mr Mourad H Helal
Telephone: 218 21 333 9150
Fax: 218 21 333 9150
Email: libyan_tennis_fed@hotmail.com

LIECHTENSTEIN – LIE
Liechtensteiner Tennisverband
Rheingau 15
9495 Triesen, Liechtenstein
President: Mr Daniel Kieber
Secretary: Ms Vanessa Schurte
Telephone: 423 392 4440
Fax: 423 392 4418
Email: tsv@strub.lol.li
Website: www.ltv.li

LITHUANIA – LTU
Lithuanian Tennis Association
Pasiles 39a
LT-3031 Kaunas, Lithuania
President: Mr Liutauras Radzevicius
Secretary: Ms Edita Liachoviciute
Telephone: 370 680 23868
Fax: 370 5246 0829
Email: LTS@TAKAS.LT
Website: www.tenisosajunga.lt

LUXEMBOURG – LUX
Fédération Luxembourgeoise de Tennis
Boite Postale 134
L-4002 Esch-sur-Alzette, Luxembourg
President: Mr Yves Kemp
Secretary: Mr Francois Dahm
Telephone: 352 574 470
Fax: 352 574 473
Email: fltennis@pt.lu
Website: www.flt.lu

MACEDONIA, F. Y. R. – MKD
Macedonian Tennis Association
Gradski Park Bb
91000 Skopje
Macedonia, F. Y. R.
President: Mr George Gurkovic
Secretary: Mr Ljubomir Davidovic
Telephone: 389 2 3131 361
Fax: 389 2 3131 361
Email: mta@unet.com.mk

MADAGASCAR – MAD
Fédération Malgache de Tennis
BP 200
Antananarivo (101), Madagascar
President: Mr Serge Ramiandrasoa
Secretary: Ms Emma Lisiarisoa
Rabodomalala
Telephone: 261 20 22 200 31
Fax: 261 20 22 338 06
Email: fmt@freenet.mg

National Associations (continued)

MALAYSIA – MAS
Lawn Tennis Association of Malaysia
National Tennis Centre
Jalan Duta
50480 Kuala Lumpur, Malaysia
President: Tan Sri Sallehuddin Mohamed
Secretary: Mr Musaladin Dahalan
Telephone: 603 620 161 73
Fax: 603 620 161 67
Email: ltam@first.net.my

MALI – MLI
Fédération Malienne de Tennis
IFA-BACO
425, Avenue de L'Yser
Quartier du Fleuve
Bamako, Mali
President: Mr Mohamed Traore
Secretary: General Secretary
Telephone: 223 222 48 05
Fax: 223 222 23 24
Email: ifabaco@cefib.com

MALTA – MLT
Malta Tennis Federation
P O Box 50
Sliema, Malta
President: Mr Anthony Cilia Pisani
Secretary: Dr David Faruggia Sacco
Telephone: 356 9942 3049
Email: davidfs@maltanet.net

MAURITIUS – MRI
Mauritius Tennis Federation
National Tennis Center
Petit Camp
Phoenix, Mauritius
President: Mr Jean-Michel Giraud
Secretary: Mr Akhtar Toorawa
Telephone: 230 686 3214
Fax: 230 686 3231
Email: mltate@intnet.mu

MEXICO – MEX
Federacion Mexicana de Tenis
Miguel Angel de Quevedo 953
Mexico City 04330 DF, Mexico
President: Mr Francisco Maciel
Secretary: Mr Antonio Vargas
Telephone: 52 55 5689 9733
Fax: 52 55 5689 6307
Email: direcciongeneral@fmt.com.mx
Website: www.fmttenis.com

MOLDOVA – MDA
Moldova Republic Tennis Federation
11 Tiraspol Str.
Chisinau, Moldova
President: Mr Sergei Sava
Secretary: Ms Larisa Mitrofanova
Telephone: 37322 72123
Fax: 37322 568 312
Email: ftenis@mdl.net
Website: www.angelfire.com/vt/mtennis

MONACO – MON
Fédération Monegasque de Lawn Tennis
BP No 253
98005 Monaco Cedex, Monaco
President: Mrs Elisabeth De Massy
Secretary: Mr Alain Manigley
Telephone: 377 93 255 574
Fax: 377 93 305 482
Email: info@monaco-tennis.com

MONGOLIA – MGL
Mongolian Tennis Association
P O Box 522
Ulaanbaatar 44, Mongolia
President: Mr Ch. Ganzorig
Secretary: Mr Janchiv Batjargal
Telephone: 976 11 350 071
Fax: 976 11 343 611
Email: mta@magicnet.mn

MOROCCO – MAR
Fédération Royale Marocaine de Tennis
BP 50171
Casa Ghandi
Casablanca 20007
Morocco
President: Mr Mohamed M'Jid
Secretary: Mr Hachem Kacimi My
Telephone: 212 22 981 266 or 262
Fax: 212 22 981 265
Email: frmt@casanet.net.ma
Website: www.frmtennis.com

MYANMAR – MYA
Tennis Federation of Myanmar
Thien Byu Tennis Plaza
Mingalar Taung Nyunt
Yangon, Myanmar
President: Mr U Zaw Zaw
Secretary: Mr Tin Aung Lynn
Telephone: 951 372 360 or 951 513 009
Fax: 951 527 797
Email: reservation@maxmyanmar.com.mm

NAMIBIA – NAM
Namibia Tennis Association
PO Box 479
Windhoek 9000
Namibia
President: Mr Bob Mould
Secretary: Ms Birgit Hacker
Telephone: 264 61 244 495
Fax: 264 61 251 718
Email: Birgit@mweb.com.na

NETHERLANDS – NED
Koninklijke Nederlandse
Lawn Tennis Bond
PO Box 1617
3800 BP Amersfoort, Netherlands
President: Mr Klaas Rijpma
Secretary: Mr Evert-Jan Hulshof
Telephone: 31 33 454 26 00
Fax: 31 33 454 26 45
Email: knltb@knltb.nl
Website: www.knltb.nl

NETHERLANDS ANTILLES – AHO
Netherlands Antilles Tennis Assn.
PO Box 3644
Willemstad
Curacao, Netherlands Antilles
President: Mr. Kenneth Hennep
Secretary: Ms Shariselle Gonet
Telephone: 599 9 737 8086
Fax: 599 9 738 3486
Email: president@natf.an
Website: www.natf.an

NEW ZEALAND – NZL
Tennis New Zealand
P O Box 18 308
Vodafone Tennis Park
69 Merton Road, Glen Innes
Auckland, New Zealand
President: Mr Jim Martin
Secretary: Mr Don Turner
Telephone: 64 9 528 5428
Fax: 64 9 528 5789
Email: info@tennisnz.com
Website: www.tennisnz.com

NIGERIA – NGR
Nigeria Tennis Federation
National Stadium Complex
PO Box 7956
Surulere, Lagos
Nigeria
President: Mr Sanni Ndanusa
Secretary: Mr Segun Oguntade
Telephone: 234 1 472 2006
Fax: 234 1 585 0530
Email: nigtennisfederation@yahoo.com

NORWAY – NOR
Norges Tennisforbund
Haslevangen 33
PO Box 287 – Okern
0511 Oslo, Norway
President: Mr Per Wright
Secretary: Mr Jarle Aambo
Telephone: 47 22 72 70 00
Fax: 47 22 72 70 01
Email: tennis@nif.idrett.no
Website: www.nif.idrett.no/tennis/

OMAN – OMA
Oman Tennis Association
PO Box 2226
Ruwi, Postal Code 112, Oman
President:
Mr Yahya Bin Nacir Bin Khamis Al Fahdi
Secretary:
Mr Aqeel Bin Salem Bin Md Al Sherif
Telephone: 968 751 402
Fax: 968 751 394

PAKISTAN – PAK
Pakistan Tennis Federation
39-A Jinnah Stadium
Kashmir Highway
Islamabad, Pakistan
President: Mr Syed Dilawar Abbas
Secretary: Major Abdul Rashid Khan
Telephone: 92 519 212 846
Fax: 92 519 212 846
Email: pktenfed@isb.comsats.net.pk

PANAMA – PAN
Federacion Panamena de Tenis
Apartado 55-0333
Panama City, Panama
President: Mr Michael Bettsak
Secretary: Mr Juan B Quintero
Telephone: 507 263 6422
Fax: 507 263 7590
Email: bal43cl@ventas.net

PARAGUAY – PAR
Asociacion Paraguaya de Tenis
Centro Nacional de Tenis
Direccion Gral. de Deportes
Avda Eusebio Ayala km 4 y 1/2
Asuncion, Paraguay
President: Dr Ruben Meilicke
Secretary: Mr Atilio Pereira
Telephone: 595 21 446 855
Fax: 595 21 524 880
Email: apt@pla.net.py
Website: www.apt.com.py

PERU – PER
Federacion de Tenis de Peru
Cercado Campo de Marte S/N
Casilla Nro. 11-0488
Lima 11, Peru
President: Mr Edmundo Jaramillo
Secretary: Mr Javier Tori Guerrero
Telephone: 511 424 9979
Fax: 511 431 0533
Email: tenisperu@terra.com.pe
Website: www.perutenis.com.pe

PHILIPPINES – PHI
Philippine Tennis Association
Rizal Memorial Sports Complex
Pablo Ocampo Sr. Street
Manila, Philippines
President: Colonel Salvador H Andrada
Secretary: Mr Romeo Magat
Telephone: 63 2 525 6434
Fax: 63 2 525 2016
Email: philta@info.com.ph

POLAND – POL
Polski Zwiazek Tenisowy
Ul. Marszalkowska 2
3rd Floor
00-581 Warsaw, Poland
President: Mr Waldemar Dubaniowski
Secretary: Mr Stefan Makarczyk
Telephone: 48 22 629 2621
Fax: 48 22 621 8001
Email: pzt@pzt.pl

PORTUGAL – POR
Federacao Portuguesa de Tenis
Rua Actor Chaby Pinheiro, 7A
2795-060 Linda-a-Velha, Portugal
President: Mr Manuel Valle-Domingues
Secretary: Mr Jose Costa
Telephone: 351 21 415 1356
Fax: 351 21 414 1520
Email: fptenis@mail.telepac.pt
Website: www.fptenis.pt

PUERTO RICO – PUR
Associacion de Tenis de Puerto Rico
1611 Fernandez Juncos Avenue
Santurce
PR 00909, Puerto Rico
President: Dr Pedro Beauchamp
Secretary: Mr Fernando Figueroa
Telephone: 1 787 982 7782
Fax: 1 787 982 7783
Email: rodriguez@cta.usta.com

QATAR – QAT
Qatar Tennis Federation
Khalifa Int. Tennis Complex
Majlis Al – Taawon St
Al Dafna – PO Box 4959
Doha, Qatar
President:
Sheikh Mohammad Bin Faleh Al-Thani
Secretary: Mr Tariq A Al-Siddiqi
Telephone: 974 4 409 666
Fax: 974 4 832 990
Email: qatartennis@qatartennis.org

ROMANIA – ROM
Federatia Romana de Tennis
Bd. Pierre de Coubertin 11
Sector 2
70139 Bucharest, Romania
President: Mr Ilie Nastase
Secretary: Mr Dimitru Haradau
Telephone: 4021 324 5330
Fax: 4021 324 5329
Email: frtenis@mcit.ro

RUSSIA – RUS
Russian Tennis Federation
Lutzhnetskaya Nab 8
119871 Moscow, Russia
President: Mr Shamil Tarpischev
Secretary: Mr Barazby Sabanchiev
Telephone: 7 095 923 21 37
Fax: 7 095 924 6427
Email: arta@russport.ru

National Associations (continued)

RWANDA – RWA
Fédération Rwandaise de Tennis
Stade National Amahoro
BP 3321, Kigali, Rwanda
President: Dr Charles Ruadkubana
Secretary: Mr Freddy Somayire Rubona
Telephone: 250 574521
Fax: 250 574074
Email: ntwalit@hotmail.com
or frttennis@yahoo.fr

SAINT LUCIA – LCA
St Lucia Lawn Tennis Association
PO Box 189
20 Micoud Street
Castries, Saint Lucia
President: Mr Stephen Mcnamara
Secretary: Mrs Pauline Erlinger-Ford
Telephone: 1 758 452 2662
Fax: 1 758 452 3885
Email: mcnmara.co@candw.lc

SAN MARINO – SMR
San Marino Tennis Federation
Parco di Montecchio 1
47890 San Marino, San Marino
President: Mr Christian Forcellini
Secretary: Mr Marino Guardigli
Telephone: 378 0549 990 578
Fax: 378 0549 990 584
Email: fst@omniway.sm
Website: www.fst.sm

SAUDI ARABIA, KINGDOM OF – KSA
Saudi Arabian Tennis Federation
Saudi Olympic Complex
PO Box 29454
Riyadh 11457
Saudi Arabia, Kingdom Of
President: Dr Ahmad Al Senany
Secretary: Mr Rasheed Abu Rasheed
Telephone: 966 1 482 0188
Fax: 966 1 482 2829
Email: sf@sauditenfed.gov.sa
Website: www.sauditennis.com

SENEGAL – SEN
Fédération Senegalaise de Tennis
km 7,5 Boulevard du Centenaire
de la Commune
BP 510, Dakar, Senegal
President: Mr Issa Mboup
Secretary: Mr Ousseynou Kama
Telephone: 221 832 0267
Fax: 221 832 0496
Email: fst@arc.sn

SERBIA AND MONTENEGRO – SCG
Serbia & Montenegro Tennis Federation
Aleksandra Stanboliskog 26
11000 Beograd
Serbia and Montenegro
President: Mr Predrag Mitrovic
Secretary: Mr Dusan Orlandic
Telephone: 381 11 367 0787
Fax: 381 11 367 0509
Email: yugtenis@verat.net.

SINGAPORE – SIN
Singapore Tennis Association
Unit 10 National Stadium
15 Stadium Road
397718, Singapore
President: Mr Edwin Lee
Secretary: Mr Philip Phang
Telephone: 65 6348 0124
Fax: 65 6348 2414
Email: slta@pacific.net.sg

SLOVAK REPUBLIC – SVK
Slovak Tennis Association
Prikopova 6
831 03 Bratislava, Slovak Republic
President: Mr Tibor Macko
Secretary: Mr Igor Moska
Telephone: 421 2 49209 877
Fax: 421 2 49209 879
Email: stz@stz.sk
Website: www.stz.sk

SLOVENIA – SLO
Slovene Tennis Association
Vurnikova 2/vi
1000 Ljubljana, Slovenia
President: Mr Andrej Polenec
Secretary: Mrs Marjeta Smodis
Telephone: 386 1 430 63 70
Fax: 386 1 430 66 95
Email: info@teniska-zveza.si
Website: slotenis.megahit.si

SOUTH AFRICA, REPUBLIC OF – RSA
South African Tennis Association
P O Box 10012
Centurion 00 46
South Africa, Republic Of
President: Mr Johann Koorts
Secretary: Mrs Sandra Delport
Telephone: 27 11 442 0500/01
Fax: 27 11 442 0503
Email: satennis@mweb.co.za
Website: www.supertennis.co.za

SPAIN – ESP
Real Federación Española de Tenis
Avda Diagonal 618 2-B
08021 Barcelona, Spain
President: Mr Agustin Pujol Niubo
Secretary: Mr Victor Barreira
Telephone: 34 93 200 5355
Fax: 34 93 202 1279
Email: riba@rfet.es
Website: www.rfet.es

SRI LANKA – SRI
Sri Lanka Tennis Association
45 Sir Marcus Fernando Mawatha
Colombo 7, Sri Lanka
President: Mr Suresh Subramaniam
Secretary: Mr Maxwell de Silva
Telephone: 94 11 533 7161
Fax: 94 11 268 6174
Email: sltennis@sltnet.lk

SUDAN – SUD
Sudan Lawn Tennis Association
PO Box 3792
Africa House
Khartoum, Sudan
President: Mr Khalid Talaat Farid
Secretary: Mr Ahmed Abuelgasim Hasim
Telephone: 249 1 837 95473
Fax: 249 1 837 70246

SWEDEN – SWE
The Swedish Tennis Association
Box 1064
269 21 Bastad, Sweden
President: Mr Jan Carlzon
Secretary: Mr Tony Wiréhn
Telephone: +46 431 783 90
Fax: +46 431 756 84
Email: info@tennis.se
Website: www.tennis.se

SWITZERLAND – SUI
Swiss Tennis
Solothurnstrasse 112
2501 Biel, Switzerland
President: Mrs Christine Ungricht
Secretary: Mr Daniel Monnin
Telephone: 41 32 344 0707
Fax: 41 32 344 0700
Email: daniel.monnin@swisstennis.com
Website: www.myTennis.ch

SYRIA – SYR
Syrian Arab Tennis Federation
P O Box 421, 967
Baramke
Damascus, Syria
President: Mr Samer Mourad
Secretary: Miss Safa Sarakbi
Telephone: 963 11 441 1972
Fax: 963 11 441 1972
Email: Syria@AsianTennis.com

TAJIKISTAN – TJK
National Tennis Federation of Republic of Tajikistan
Tennis Palace
A/b 308
Dushanbe 734001, Tajikistan
President: Mr Amircul Azimov
Secretary: Mr Vazirbek Nazirov
Telephone: 992 372 246342
Fax: 992 372 246342
Email: ttf@tojikiston.com

THAILAND – THA
Lawn Tennis Association of Thailand
327 Chartpattana Party Building
Sukhothai Road
Dusit District
Bangkok 10300, Thailand
President: H.E. Suwat Liptapanlop
Secretary: Admiral Banawit Kengrian
Telephone: 662 668 7624
Fax: 662 668 7435
Email: ltat@ksc.th.com
Website: www.ltat.org

TOGO – TOG
Fédération Togolaise de Tennis
BP 7160
Lome, Togo
President: Mr Kouassi Luc Dofontien
Secretary: Mr Koffi Galokpo
Telephone: 228 227 43 53
Fax: 228 222 02 72
Email: fttennis@togo-imet.com

TRINIDAD AND TOBAGO – TRI
Tennis Assn. of Trinidad & Tobago
21 Taylor Street
Woodbrook
Port of Spain, Trinidad and Tobago
President: Mr Dave James
Secretary: Mrs Christine Alexis
Telephone: 1 868 628 0783
Fax: 1 868 628 0783
Email: tatt@tstt.net.tt

TUNISIA – TUN
Fédération Tunisienne de Tennis
B.P. 350
Cite Nationale Sportive
El Menzah
1004 Tunis, Tunisia
President: Mr Tarak Cherif
Secretary: Mr Moez Snoussi
Telephone: 216 71 844 144
Fax: 216 71 798 844
Email: ftt@ati.tn

TURKEY – TUR
Turkiye Tenis Federasyonu
Ulus Is Hani
Ankara, Turkey
President: Mr Azmi Kumova
Secretary: Mr Naci Dumanoglu
Telephone: 90 312 310 7345
Fax: 90 312 3107345
Email: tenis@ttf.org.tr
Website: www.ttf.org.tr

TURKMENISTAN – TKM
Turkmenistan Tennis Association
Azadi Str, 44/app 4
744000 Ashgabat, Turkmenistan
President: Mr Berdimurad Redjepov
Secretary: Mr Bjashimov Serdar
Telephone: 993 12 35 1819
Fax: 993 12 35 1819
Email: olimpya@online.tm

UGANDA – UGA
Uganda Tennis Association
PO Box 506
Jingi, Uganda
President: Dr Ben Mbonye
Secretary: Mr Cedric Babu
Telephone: 256 41 236 688
Fax: 256 43 123 200
Email: cedricb@iconafrica.com

UKRAINE – UKR
Ukrainian Tennis Federation
A/C B-2
PO 252001
Kiev, Ukraine
President: Mr German Benyaminov
Secretary: Mr Andriy Medvedev
Telephone: 38 044 224 8782
Fax: 38 044 234 8782
Email: ftu@rql.net.ua

UNITED ARAB EMIRATES – UAE
United Arab Emirates Tennis Association
PO Box 22466
Dubai, United Arab Emirates
President: Sheikh Hasher Al-Maktoum
Secretary: Mr Mohammed Al-Merry
Telephone: 971 4 269 0393
Fax: 971 4 266 9390
Email: tennis@emirates.net.ae

UNITED STATES OF AMERICA – USA
United States Tennis Association
70 West Red Oak Lane
White Plains – New York
N.Y. 10604-3602
USA
President: Mr Alan G Schwartz
Secretary: Mr Lee Hamilton
Telephone: 1 914 696 7000
Fax: 1 914 696 7167
Website: www.usta.com

UNITED STATES VIRGIN ISLANDS – ISV
Virgin Islands Tennis Association
P.O. Box 303408
St Thomas, USVI 00803
US Virgin Islands
President: Mr William F McComb
Secretary: Ms Deborah Davis
Telephone: 1 340 774 8547
Fax: 1 340 776 1558
Email: wfmccomb.eng@attglobal.net

URUGUAY – URU
Asociacion Uruguaya de Tenis
Galicia 1392
CP 11.200
Montevideo, Uruguay
President: Sr Gilberto Saenz
Secretary: Mr Elbio Arias
Telephone: 598 2 902 9391
Fax: 598 2 902 1809
Email: aut@montevideo.com.uy

UZBEKISTAN – UZB
Uzbekistan Tennis Federation
1 Assaka Pereulok
House 14
Tashkent 700035, Uzbekistan
President: Mr R Inoyatov
Secretary: Mr I Shepelev
Telephone: 99 871 137 2554
Fax: 99 871 133 5503
Email: uztennis@intal.uz
Website: www.uzbektennis.uz

National Associations (continued)

VENEZUELA – VEN
Federacion Venezolana de Tenis
Complejo Nacional de Tenis
Calle A – Apartado 70539
Urb Santa Rosa de Lima
Caracas 1070-A, Venezuela
President: Mr Rene Herrera
Secretary: Mr Deva de Gonzalez
Telephone: 58 212 979 2421
Fax: 58 212 979 2694 or 7462
Email: gerencia@fvtenis.com
Website: www.fvtenis.com

VIETNAM – VIE
Vietnam Tennis Federation
175 Nguyen Thai Hoc Street
Ba Dinh District
Hanoi, Vietnam
President: Mr Dang Huu Hai
Secretary: Mr Tran Ngoc Linh
Telephone: 844 733 0036
Fax: 844 733 0036
Email: vtf@fpt.vn

ZAMBIA – ZAM
Zambia Lawn Tennis Association
c/o Mopani Copper Mines plc
P O Box 40499
Mufulira, Zambia
President: Mr John Mupeta
Secretary: Mr Masauso Zimba
Telephone: 260 2 441 832/45
Fax: 260 2 447 005
Email: maszimba@mopani.com.zm

ZIMBABWE – ZIM
Tennis Zimbabwe
PO Box A575
Avondale
Harare, Zimbabwe
President: Mr Cecil Gombera
Secretary: Ms Patricia Mavunduke
Telephone: 2634 740 509
Fax: 2634 740 351/753 992
Email: teniszim@africaonline.co.zw

Class C (Associate) Members Without Voting Rights (56)

AFGHANISTAN – AFG
Afghanistan Tennis Federation
c/o Ahmad Shaheer
British Embassy
Kabul, Afghanistan
President: Mr Abdul Azim Niazi
Secretary: Mr Ahmad Shaheer Shahriar
Telephone: 93 70 274 772
Email: shaheerahmad@hotmail.com

ALBANIA – ALB
Albanian Tennis Federation
Rruga Myslym Shyri
Pallati 46, Ap.10/1
Tirana, Albania
President: Mr Avni Ponari
Secretary: Mr Tonin Mema
Telephone: 355 42 74 361
Fax: 355 42 74 361
Email: albanian_tennis_federation@yahoo.com

AMERICAN SAMOA – ASA
American Samoa Tennis Association
PO Box 2070
Pago Pago
AS 96799 USA, American Samoa
President: Mr Dave Godinet
Secretary: Ms Elena Dworsky
Telephone: 684 699 9512
Fax: 684 699 2105

ARUBA – ARU
Aruba Lawn Tennis Bond
Fergusonstraat Nr 40-a
PO Box 1151
Oranjestad, Aruba
President: Mr Ling Wong
Secretary: Mrs Bernadetta Henriquez-Every
Telephone: 297 5 833 506
Fax: 297 5 887 184
Email: arubalawntennis@hotmail.com

BELIZE – BIZ
Belize Tennis Association
P O Box 365
Belize City, Belize
President: Mr Edward Nabil Musa Sr
Secretary: Mr Clement Usher
Telephone: 501 22 77070
Fax: 501 22 75593

BHUTAN – BHU
Bhutan Tennis Federation
PO Box 838
Thimphu, Bhutan
President: Mr Lyonpo Ugen Tschering
Secretary: Mr Chencho Norbu
Telephone: 975 232 2138
Fax: 975 232 6768
Email: btftennis@druknet.bt

BRITISH VIRGIN ISLANDS – IVB
British Virgin Islands LTA
P O Box 3169
PMB 259
Road Town
Tortola, British Virgin Islands
President: Mr Henry Creque
Secretary: Mr Clive Gumbs
Telephone: 1 284 494 9225
Fax: 1 284 494 4291

BURUNDI – BDI
Fédération de Tennis du Burundi
BP 2221
Bujumbura, Burundi
President: Mr Salvator Matata
Secretary: General Secretary
Telephone: 257 242 443
Fax: 257 222 247
Email: salmatfr@yahoo.fr or domini@yahoo.fr

CAPE VERDE ISLANDS – CPV
Federação Cabo Verdiana de Ténis
Pavilhão Desportivo Váva Duarte
Chã de Areia – B.P. 584
Praia – Cabo Verde (Island)
Cape Verde Islands
President: Mr Hugo Almeida
Secretary: Mr General Secretary
Telephone: 238 2 613 309
Fax: 238 2 613 309
Email: fedcabtenis@cvtelecom.cv

CAYMAN ISLANDS – CAY
Tennis Fed. of the Cayman Islands
P O Box 2499
Strathvale House
Grand Cayman, Cayman Islands
President: Mr Chris Johnson
Secretary: Mr John Smith
Telephone: 1 345 946 0820
Fax: 1 345 946 0864
Email: chrisjohnson@candw.ky

CENTRAL AFRICAN REPUBLIC – CAF
Fédération Centrafricaine de Tennis
S/c Dameca
B P 804
Bangui, Central African Republic
President: Mr I Kamach
Secretary: Mr Jean Ombi
Telephone: 236 61 18 05
Fax: 236 61 56 60
Email: fcat_cf@yahoo.fr

CONGO, DEMOCRATIC REPUBLIC OF – COD
Fédération Congolaise Démocratique de Lawn Tennis
BP 11 497 KIN 1
Kinshasa
Congo, Democratic Republic Of
President: Mr Ndombe Jacob
Secretary: Mr Georges Koshi
Telephone: 243 884 3469
Fax: 243 880 1625
Email: fecodelat@yahoo.fr or ndombepres@yahoo.fr

COOK ISLANDS – COK
Tennis Cook Islands
PO Box 806
Rarotonga, Cook Islands
President: Mr Brian Baudinet
Secretary: Mr Brendan Stone
Telephone: 682 26027
Fax: 682 26027
Email: brian@baudinet.co.ck
Website: www.baudinet.com

DOMINICA – DMA
Dominica Lawn Tennis Association
PO Box 138
Roseau, Dominica
President: Mr Thomas Dorsett
Secretary: Mr Simon Butler
Telephone: 1 767 448 8367
Fax: 1 767 448 7010
Email: tomd@cwdom.dm

EQUATORIAL GUINEA – GEQ
Equatorial Guinea Tennis Federation
PO Box 980 BN
Malabo, Equatorial Guinea
President: Mr Enrique Mercader Costa
Secretary: Mr Francisco Sibita
Telephone: 240 09 2866
Fax: 240 09 3313

ERITREA – ERI
Eritrean Tennis Federation
C/o Eritrean Olympic Committee
PO Box 3665
Asmara, Eritrea
President: Mr Fessahaie Haile
Secretary: Dr General Secretary
Telephone: 291 1 121 533
Fax: 291 1 120 967
Email: tesat@tse.com.er

GAMBIA – GAM
Gambia Lawn Tennis Association
PMB 664
Serrekunda, Gambia
President: Mr Sheriff Jammeh
Secretary: Mr Tunde Taylor-Thomas
Telephone: 220 4495 946
Fax: 220 4378 894
Email: jakes_r@hotmail.com

GRENADA – GRN
Grenada Tennis Association
PO Box 514
St George's, Grenada
President: Mr Ricardo Charles
Secretary: Ms Aarona Moses
Telephone: 1 473 440 1977
Fax: 1 473 440 1977

GUAM – GUM
Guam National Tennis Federation
PO Box 4379
Hagatna 96932
Guam
President: Mr Rick Ninete
Secretary: Ms Jane Aguon
Telephone: 1 671 472 6270
Fax: 1 671 472 0997
Email: ricn@ite.net

GUINEA-BISSAU – GBS
Fédération deTennis de la Guinee-Bissau
Caixa Postal 387
Bissau, Guinea-Bissau
President: Mr Jose Rodrigues-Santy
Secretary: General Secretary
Telephone: 245 720 6030

GUINEE CONAKRY – GUI
Fédération Guineenne de Tennis
B P 4897
Conakry, Guinee Conakry
President: Mr Kiridi Bangoura
Secretary: Mr Abdoulaye Conte
Telephone: 224 44 40 19
Fax: 224 41 19 26

GUYANA – GUY
Guyana Lawn Tennis Association
PO Box 10205
Olympic House
Church & Peter Rose Streets
Georgetown, Guyana
President: Mr Wilfred Lee
Secretary: Ms Grace McCalman
Telephone: 592 2 2 75501
Fax: 592 2 2 55865
Email: glta18@yahoo.com

KIRIBATI – KIR
Kiribati Tennis Association
P O Box 245
Tarawa, Kiribati
President: Dr Komeri Onorio
Secretary: Mr Ahling Onorio
Telephone: 686 26541
Fax: 686 26606
Email: komeri@tskl.net.ki

KOREA, DEMOCRATIC PEOPLE'S REPUBLIC OF – PRK
Tennis Assocation of DPR of Korea
Kumsong
Mangyongdae Dist
Pyongyang
North Korea
Korea, Democratic People's Republic of
President: Mr Kim Su Ik
Secretary: Mr Ko Yong Su
Telephone: 850 218 111 Ext. 8164
Fax: 850 2381 4403

National Associations (continued)

LAO, DEMOCRATIC PEOPLE'S REPUBLIC – LAO
Lao Tennis Federation
PO Box 6280
Vientiane
Lao, Democratic People's Republic
President: Mr Kikham Vongsay
Secretary: Mr Phoukhong Niraxay
Telephone: 856 21 218956
Fax: 856 21 218956
Email: gcdnl@laopdr.com

LIBERIA – LBR
Liberia Tennis Association
PO Box 1742
Randall Street
Monrovia, Liberia
President: Cllr. Lloyd Kennedy
Secretary: Mr Manfred Jones
Telephone: 231 225 626
Fax: 231 226 253/225
Email: clemenceauurey@yahoo.com

MALAWI – MAW
Lawn Tennis Association of Malawi
c/o Wellcome Trust Research Labs.
P O Box 30096
Blantyre 3, Malawi
President: Mr Steve Graham
Secretary: Ms Barbara Halse
Telephone: 265 1 676 444
Fax: 265 1 675 774

MALDIVES – MDV
Tennis Association of the Maldives
P O Box 20175
Chaandhanee Magu
Male, Maldives
President: Mr Maizan Ali Manik
Secretary: Ms Fazna Mansoor
Telephone: 960 317 018
Fax: 960 310 325
Email: tennismaldives@avasmail.com.mv

MARSHALL ISLANDS – MSH
Marshall Islands Tennis Federation
PO Box 197
Marjuro
MH96960, Marshall Islands
President: Mr Wally Milne
Secretary: Mr Dwight Heine
Telephone: 692 625 5275
Fax: 692 625 3655
Email: wally@ntamar.com

MAURITANIA – MTN
Fédération Mauritanienne de Tennis
Office du Complexe Olympique
BP 3128
Nouakchott., Mauritania
President: Mr Isaac Ould Ragel
Secretary: Mr Cheickh Ould Horomtala
Telephone: 222 641 2092
Fax: 222 525 3787
Email: rimtennis2002@yahoo.fr

MICRONESIA, FEDERATED STATES OF – FSM
Federated States of Micronesia LTA
PO Box PS319
Paliker
Pohnpei
FM 96941
Micronesia, Federated States Of
President: Mr Sterling Skilling
Secretary: Mr Simao Ieshi
Telephone: 691 320 619
Fax: 691 320 8915
Email: fsmnoc@mail.fm

MOZAMBIQUE – MOZ
Federacao Mocambicana de Tenis
Caixa Postal 4351
Maputo, Mozambique
President: Mr Arao Nhancale
Secretary: Mr Armindo Nhavene
Telephone: 258 1 427 027
Fax: 258 1 303 665
Email: FMTenis@hotmail.com

NAURU – NRU
Nauru Tennis Association
PO Box 274
Aiwo District, Nauru
President: Chief Paul Aingimea
Secretary: Mr Preston Itaia
Telephone: 674 444 3118
Fax: 674 444 3231
Email: naurutennis@yahoo.com

NEPAL – NEP
All Nepal Tennis Association
PO Box 3943
Kathmandu, Nepal
President: Mr Siddheshwar K Singh
Secretary: Mr Ramji Thapa
Telephone: 977 1 426 002
Fax: 977 1 416 427
Email: anlta@mos.com.np

NICARAGUA – NCA
Federacion Nicaraguense de Tenis
Apartado Postal C-119
Managua, Nicaragua
President: Mr Ramon Sevilla
Secretary: Mr J Camilo Munoz
Telephone: 505 276 1954
Fax: 505 276 0948
Email: rsevilla@cablenet.com.ni

NIGER – NIG
Fédération Nigerienne de Tennis
Stade du 29 juillet 1991
Avenue du Zarmaganda
BP 10 788 Niamey, Niger
President: Mr Ahmed Ousman Diallo
Secretary: Mr Boubacar Djibo
Telephone: 227 735 893/734 286
Fax: 227 732 876
Email: nigerautennis@hotmail.com

NORFOLK ISLANDS – NFK
Norfolk Islands Tennis Association
Queen Elizabeth Avenue
PO Box 283 – 2899
South Pacific, Norfolk Islands
President: Mr John Henderson
Secretary: Ms Julie South
Telephone: 6723 229 66
Fax: 6723 232 26
Email: tennis@norfolk.net.nf

NORTHERN MARIANA ISLANDS – NMI
Northern Mariana Islands Tennis Assn.
P O Box 10,000
Saipan
MP 96950-9504, Northern Mariana Islands
President: Mr Jeff Race
Secretary: Mr Ed Johnson
Telephone: 1 670 234 8438
Fax: 1 670 234 5545
Email: race@saipan.com

PALAU, DEMOCRATIC REPUBLIC OF – PAL
Palau Tennis Federation
PO Box 44
Koror 96940
Palau, Democratic Republic Of
President: Ms Christina Michelsen
Secretary: Ms Annabel Lyman
Telephone: 680 488 6267
Fax: 680 488 6271
Email: cmichelsen@boh.com

PALESTINE – PLE
Palestinian Tennis Association
Beit Sahour
PO Box 131, Palestine
President: Mr Issa Rishmawi
Secretary: Mrs Samar Mousa Araj
Telephone: 972 2 277 2833/4
Fax: 972 2 277 4677
Email: pta@p-ol.com
Website: www.paltennis.org

PAPUA NEW GUINEA – PNG
Papua New Guinea Lawn Tennis Association
P O Box 1230
Boroko, NCD
Papua New Guinea
President: Mr David Toua
Secretary: Mr John Vince
Telephone: 675 325 1421
Fax: 675 325 1421
Email: jvince@datec.net.pg

SAINT KITTS & NEVIS – SKN
St Kitts Lawn Tennis Association
Cayon Street
Basseterre, Saint Kitts & Nevis
President: Mr Raphael Jenkins
Secretary: Ms Connie Marsham
Telephone: 1 869 465 6809
Fax: 1 869 465 1190

SAINT VINCENT & THE GRENADINES – VIN
St Vincent & The Grenadines LTA
PO Box 1749
Kingstown
Saint Vincent & The Grenadines
President: Mr Orville B Haslam
Secretary: Mr Sonny Williams
Telephone: 1 784 457 9847
Fax: 1 784 457 2908
Email: tinkerbell@caribsurf.com

SAMOA – SAM
Tennis Samoa Inc
P O Box 6402
Apia, Samoa
President: Mr Waikaremoana Soonalole
Secretary: Miss Fiaapia Devoe
Telephone: 685 22 115
Fax: 685 21 145
Email: lwsoonal@ipasifika.net

SEYCHELLES – SEY
Seychelles Tennis Association
PO Box 580
Mahe
Victoria, Seychelles
President: Mr John Adam
Secretary: Mr Stephen Ah-Moye
Telephone: 248 323 908
Fax: 248 324 066
Email: johnladam@hotmail.com or tennisey@seychelles.net

SIERRA LEONE – SLE
Sierra Leone Lawn Tennis Association
National Sports Council
PO Box 1181
Freetown, Sierra Leone
President: Mr John Benjamin
Secretary: Mr E T Ngandi
Telephone: 232 22 226 874
Fax: 232 22 229 083
Email: johnben@sierratel.sl

SOLOMON ISLANDS – SOL
Solomon Islands Tennis Association
PO Box 111
Honiara, Solomon Islands
President: Mr Ranjit Hewagama
Secretary: Mr Selwyn Miduku
Telephone: 677 27354
Fax: 677 25 686
Email: tennis@solomon.com.sb

SOMALIA – SOM
The Somali Tennis Association
C/o 5 Gabalaya Street
11567 El Borg
Cairo, Egypt
President: Mr Osman Mohiadin Moallim
Secretary: Mr Farah Ali Moallin
Telephone: 252 1 215 639
Fax: 252 1 216 516
Email: osmanmoallim@yahoo.com

SURINAM – SUR
Surinaamse Tennisbond
P O Box 2087
Paramaribo-Zuid, Surinam
President: Mr Manodj Hindori
Secretary: Ms Yolande D'Hamecourt
Telephone: 597 452 545
Fax: 597 471 047
Email: stb@cq-link.sr

SWAZILAND – SWZ
Swaziland National Tennis Union
PO Box 2397
Manzini, Swaziland
President: Mr L Nxumalo
Secretary: Mr J Mazibuko
Telephone: 268 408 2329
Fax: 268 505 8903
Email: tennisswaziland@realnet.co.sz

TANZANIA – TAN
Tanzania Lawn Tennis Association
c/o Royal Norwegian Embassy
PO Box 2646
Dar Es Salaam, Tanzania
President: Mr Dennis Makoi
Secretary: Mrs Inger Johanne Njau
Telephone: 255 22 741 291 864
Fax: 255 22 211 6564
Email: ijn@norad.no

TONGA – TGA
Tonga Tennis Association
PO Box 816
Nuku'alofa, Tonga
President: Mr Fuka Kitekeiaho
Secretary: Ms Kiu Tatafu
Telephone: 676 23933
Fax: 676 24127

TURKS & CAICOS ISLANDS – TKS
Turks & Caicos Tennis Association
P O Box 205
Providenciales
British West Indies
Turks & Caicos Islands
President: Mr Robert Smith
Secretary: Mrs Tanis Wake-Forbes
Telephone: 649 946 5918
Email: tcinoc@hotmail.com

TUVALU – TUV
Tuvalu Tennis Association
Private Mail Bag
Vaiaku
Funafuti, Tuvalu
President: Mr Levi Telli
Secretary: Mr Molotii General Secretary
Fax: 688 20 304
Email: levi@tuvalu.tv

National Associations (continued)

VANUATU – VAN
Fédération de Tennis de Vanuatu
B P 895
Port Vila, Vanuatu
President: Mme Evelyne Jacobe
Secretary: Mr Michel Mainguy
Telephone: 678 24817
Fax: 678 26133 or 24817
Email: evyvallette@vanuatu.com.vu

YEMEN – YEM
Yemen Tennis Federation
P O Box 19816
Sana'a, Yemen
President: Dr Rashad Al-Alimi
Secretary: Mr Ahmed Al-Sadiq
Telephone: 967 1 271 857
Fax: 967 1 271 857
Email: ytf@y.net.ye

Regional Associations

ASIAN TENNIS FEDERATION (ATF)
12F Manulife Tower
169 Electric Road
North Point
Hong Kong, China
President: Mr Salvador H Andrada
Secretary: Mr Anil Khanna
Telephone: 852 2512 8226
Fax: 852 2512 8649
Email: atf@i-wave.net.hk
Website: www.asiantennis.com

CONFEDERACION SUDAMERICANA DE TENIS (COSAT)
Calle Mexico Nº 1638
La Paz
Casilla 14752
Bolivia
President: Mr Vicente Calderon Zeballos
Secretary: Mr Miguel Carrizosa Galiano
Telephone: 591 2 2313310 or 2313334
Fax: 5912 2313 323
Email: seccosat@entelnet.bo
Website: www.cosat.org

CONFEDERATION OF AFRICAN TENNIS (CAT)
c/o International Tennis Federation
Bank Lane
Roehampton
London SW15 5XZ
Great Britain
President: Mr Tarak Cherif
Telephone: 44 20 8878 6464
Fax: 44 20 8392 4742
Email: catennis@itftennis.com
Website: www.cat.sn

COTECC
C/O Federacion Salvadorena
Apartado Postal (01) 110
San Salvador
El Salvador
President: Mr Enrique Molins
Secretary: Mr Frank Liautaud
Telephone: 503 278 8850
Fax: 503 278 8087
Email: cotecc@telesal.net

OCEANIA TENNIS FEDERATION (OTF)
P O Box 13759
Johnsonville
Wellington
New Zealand
President: Mr Geoff Pollard
Secretary: Mr Patrick O'Rourke
Telephone: 64 4 478 0465
Fax: 64 4 477 0465
Email: patrick@oceaniatennis.com
Website: www.oceaniatennis.com

TENNIS EUROPE
Seltisbergerstrasse 6
4059 Basel
Switzerland
President: Mr John James
Secretary: Mrs Charlotte Ferrari
Telephone: 41 61 331 76 75
Fax: 41 61 331 72 53
Email: info@tenniseurope.org
Website: www.tenniseurope.org

ITF Recognised Organisations

The ITF recognises and works closely with the following three organisations.

International Tennis Hall of Fame

Officially sanctioned by the United States Tennis Association in 1954, the International Tennis Hall of Fame (ITHF) was recognised by the ITF in 1986. Situated at the historic Newport Casino, the site of the first US National Championships in 1881, the ITHF was founded by James Van Alen in 1954 as a tribute to the ideals of the game. It is a non-profit institution committed to preserving the history of the sport, enshrining tennis heroes and heroines, inspiring and encouraging junior tennis development, and providing a landmark for tennis enthusiasts worldwide. The ITHF is the world's largest tennis museum and owns the world's largest collection of tennis memorabilia. Since 1955, 183 people have been elected to the ITHF as a tribute to their outstanding contribution to the game. See the full list of the ITHF Enshrinees which follow.

In 2001 the ITHF and the ITF unveiled a new Award of Excellence for Davis Cup and Fed Cup. It was decided that, where possible, the candidate should come from the nation or region in which the host nation for the semifinals/final is located.

Contact details:
International Tennis Hall of Fame
194 Bellevue Avenue
Newport, Rhode Island 02840, USA
Telephone: 1 401 849 3990 Fax: 1 401 849 8780
Email: newport@tennisfame.com
Website: www.tennisfame.com

The International Club

The concept of a series of International Clubs was the idea of British tennis correspondent A. Wallis Myers in 1924. He said "We are seeking to cement the ties that bind us to all international players, to exchange greetings with them from time to time, to offer them hospitality when they come in our midst. Hands across the net, in fact, means hands across the ocean."

Membership of the clubs is limited to those who have played representative international tennis overseas. As a result many former Davis and Fed Cup players participate in competitive events and friendly matches arranged by individual clubs.

In 2003, 34 countries had International Clubs, reflecting the increasing globalisation of tennis. While the IC's traditional ideals remain relevant, Clubs are encouraging junior membership by holding junior competitions.

Contact details:

Chairman – Barry Weatherill
Council of International Lawn Tennis Clubs
16 Bedford Street, London WC2E 9HF
Telephone: 44 20 7395 3000 Fax: 44 20 7240 7316
Website: www.ic-tennis.org

Honorary Secretary – Peter McQuibban
20 Roskeen Court, 45 Arterberry Road
Wimbledon, London SW20 8AU
Tel: 44 20 8947 1578 Fax: 44 20 9847 2730
Email: iccouncil@hotmail.com

The Association of Centenary Clubs

In 1995 Juan-Maria Tintore, President du Real Club de Tenis Barcelona, had the idea of bringing together tennis clubs with over a hundred years of history. Since well over 300 clubs throughout the world are eligible to join the Association, it is hoped that the Association will expand gradually for the benefit of the game. Eligible clubs include 60 in Germany, 90 in the United Kingdom, 13 in Denmark, nine in France and Italy, six in the Netherlands, not to mention 50 in the US and 16 in Australia.

Recognised by the International Olympic Committee (IOC), the Association of Centenary Tennis Clubs headquarters is at the Olympic Museum in Lausanne. Founded on 11 June 1996 by eight European clubs, the aim of the Centenary Club is to continue the traditions of tennis through the activities of its members by staging sporting and cultural reunions, tennis meetings and by maintaining the spirit of fair play inherent in sport.

Contact details:
Juan M. Tintore, President, Real Club de Tenis Barcelona 1899
President, Centenary Tennis Clubs Association or/and
Carlos Merce General Manager, Real Club de Tenis Barcelona 1899
Secretary, Centenary Tennis Clubs Association
Bosch i Gimpera, 5-13, 08034 Barcelona/Spain
Telephone: 34 93 2037852 Fax: 34 93 2045010
Email: info@centenarytennisclubs.com
www.centenarytennisclubs.com

Official Tennis Championships Recognised by the ITF

a) The ITF officially recognises the following Championships know as "Official Tennis Championships of the International Tennis Federation:

i) Championships organised by National Associations or bodies associated with them
The Lawn Tennis Championships (Wimbledon)
The United States Open
The French Championships
The Australian Championships
(known as "The Grand Slam")

The Japan Open
The Italian Open Championships
The International Championships of Spain

ii) Championships organised by the ITF
Olympic Tennis Event
ITF Seniors World Individual Championships
ITF Super Seniors World Individual Championships
The Wheelchair Tennis Masters

b) The ITF is a partner with other constituencies in the organisation of the following championships:
Tennis Masters Cup
WTA Tour Championships

Roger Federer (SUI) won three Grand Slams in 2004

International Tennis Hall of Fame Enshrinees

Over 186 individuals have been enshrined into the International Tennis Hall of Fame representing 18 countries worldwide.

Name	Year
*# Adee, George – USA	1964
# Alexander, Fred – USA	1961
# Allison, Wilmer – USA	1963
# Alonso, Manuel – ESP	1977
Anderson, Malcolm – AUS	2000
# Ashe, Arthur – USA	1985
# Atkinson, Juliette – USA	1974
# Austin, H.W. 'Bunny' – GBR	1997
Austin, Tracy – USA	1992
*# Baker, Lawrence, Sr. – USA	1975
# Barger-Wallach, Maud – USA	1958
Becker, Boris – GER	2003
# Behr, Karl – USA	1969
Betz Addie, Pauline – USA	1965
# Bjurstedt Mallory, Molla – USA	1958
Borg, Bjorn – SWE	1987
# Borotra, Jean – FRA	1976
Bowrey, Lesley Turner – AUS	1997
# Bromwich, John – AUS	1984
# Brookes, Norman – AUS	1977
Brough Clapp, Louise – USA	1967
# Browne, Mary K. – USA	1957
# Brugnon, Jacques – FRA	1976
# Budge, Don – USA	1964
Bueno, Maria – BRA	1978
# Cahill, Mabel – IRL	1976
# Campbell, Oliver – USA	1955
Casals, Rosie – USA	1996
# Chace, Malcolm – USA	1961
*# Chatrier, Philippe – FRA	1992
Cheney, Dorothy 'Dodo' – USA	2004
# Clark, Clarence – USA	1983
# Clark, Joseph – USA	1955
# Clothier, William – USA	1956
# Cochet, Henri – FRA	1976
* Collins, Arthur W. 'Bud', Jr. – USA	1994
# Connolly Brinker, Maureen – USA	1968
Connors, Jimmy – USA	1998
Cooper, Ashley – AUS	1991
Court, Margaret Smith – AUS	1979
# Crawford, Jack – AUS	1979
*# Cullman, Joseph F., 3rd – USA	1990
*# Danzig, Allison – USA	1968
*# David, Herman – GBR	1998
# Davis, Dwight – USA	1956
# Dod, Lottie – GBR	1983
# Doeg, John – USA	1962
# Doherty, Lawrence – GBR	1980
# Doherty, Reginald – GBR	1980

Name	Year
# Douglass Chambers, Dorothea – GBR	1981
# Drobny, Jaroslav – GBR	1983
duPont, Margaret Osborne – USA	1967
Durr, Francoise – FRA	2003
# Dwight, James – USA	1955
Edberg, Stefan – SWE	2004
Emerson, Roy – AUS	1982
+# Etchebaster, Pierre – FRA	1978
Evert, Chris – USA	1995
Falkenburg, Bob – USA and BRA	1974
Fraser, Neale – AUS	1984
Fry-Irvin, Shirley – USA	1970
# Garland, Chuck – USA	1969
# Gibson, Althea – USA	1971
# Gonzalez, Pancho – USA	1968
Goolagong Cawley, Evonne – AUS	1988
Graf, Steffi – GER	2004
# Grant, Bryan 'Bitsy' – USA	1972
*# Gray, David – GBR	1985
# Griffin, Clarence – USA	1970
*# Gustav V, King of Sweden – SWE	1980
# Hackett, Harold – USA	1961
# Hansell, Ellen – USA	1965
Hard, Darlene – USA	1973
Hart, Doris – USA	1969
Haydon Jones, Ann – GBR	1985
*# Heldman, Gladys – USA	1979
*# Hester, W.E. 'Slew' – USA	1981
Hewitt, Bob – AUS and RSA	1992
# Hoad, Lew – AUS	1980
# Hopman, Harry – AUS	1978
# Hotchkiss Wightman, Hazel – USA	1957
# Hovey, Fred – USA	1974
# Hunt, Joe – USA	1966
* Hunt, Lamar – USA	1993
# Hunter, Frank – USA	1961
# Jacobs, Helen Hull – USA	1962
# Johnston, Bill – USA	1958
*# Jones, Perry – USA	1970
* Kelleher, Robert – USA	2000
King, Billie Jean – USA	1987
Kodes, Jan – TCH	1990
Kramer, Jack – USA	1968
# Lacoste, Rene – FRA	1976
*# Laney, Al – USA	1979

Name	Year
# Larned, William – USA	1956
Larsen, Art – USA	1969
Laver, Rod – AUS	1981
Lendl, Ivan – USA	2001
# Lenglen, Suzanne – FRA	1978
# Lott, George – USA	1964
Mako, Gene – USA	1973
Mandlikova, Hana – AUS and TCH	1994
# Marble, Alice – USA	1964
* Martin, Alastair – USA	1973
*# Martin, William McChesney – USA	1982
*# Maskell, Dan – GBR	1996
McEnroe, John – USA	1999
McGregor, Ken – AUS	1999
# McKane Godfree, Kathleen – GBR	1978
# McKinley, Chuck – USA	1986
# McLoughlin, Maurice – USA	1957
McMillan, Frew – RSA	1992
# McNeill, Don – USA	1965
# Moore, Elisabeth – USA	1971
Mortimer Barrett, Angela – GBR	1993
Mulloy, Gardnar – USA	1972
# Murray, R. Lindley – USA	1958
*# Myrick, Julian – USA	1963
Nastase, Ilie – ROM	1991
Navratilova, Martina – USA	2000
Newcombe, John – AUS	1986
*# Nielsen, Arthur – USA	1971
# Nuthall Shoemaker, Betty – GBR	1977
Olmedo, Alex – PER	1987
# Osuna, Rafael – MEX	1979
*# Outerbridge, Mary – USA	1981
# Palfrey Danzig, Sarah – USA	1963
# Parker, Frank – USA	1966
# Patterson, Gerald – AUS	1989
Patty, Budge – USA	1977
# Pell, Theodore – USA	1966
# Perry, Fred – GBR	1975
+# Pettitt, Tom – GBR	1982
Pietrangeli, Nicola – ITA	1986
# Quist, Adrian – AUS	1984
Ralston, Dennis – USA	1987
# Renshaw, Ernest – GBR	1983
# Renshaw, William – GBR	1983
# Richards, Vincent – USA	1961
Richey, Nancy – USA	2003

International Tennis Hall of Fame Enshrinees (continued)

Name	Year
#Riggs, Bobby – USA	1967
Roche, Tony – AUS	1986
#Roosevelt, Ellen – USA	1975
Rose, Mervyn – AUS	2001
Rosewall, Ken – AUS	1980
#Round Little, Dorothy – GBR	1986
#Ryan, Elizabeth – USA	1972
Santana, Manuel – ESP	1984
Savitt, Dick – USA	1976
Schroeder, Ted – USA	1966
#Sears, Eleonora – USA	1968
#Sears, Richard – USA	1955
Sedgman, Frank – AUS	1979
Segura, Pancho – ECU	1984
Seixas, Vic – USA	1971
#Shields, Frank – USA	1964
Shriver, Pam – USA	2002
#Slocum, Henry – USA	1955
Smith, Stan – USA	1987

Name	Year
Stolle, Fred – AUS	1985
#Sutton Bundy, May – USA	1956
#Talbert, Bill – USA	1967
#Tilden, Bill – USA	1959
*#Tingay, Lance – GBR	1982
*#Tinling, Ted – GBR	1986
* Tobin, Brian – AUS	2003
#Townsend Toulmin, Bertha – USA	1974
Trabert, Tony – USA	1970
*#Van Alen, James – USA	1965
#Van Ryn, John – USA	1963
Vilas, Guillermo – ARG	1991
#Vines, Ellsworth – USA	1962
#von Cramm, Gottfried – GER	1977
Wade, Virginia – GBR	1989
#Wagner, Marie – USA	1969
#Ward, Holcombe – USA	1956

Name	Year
#Washburn, Watson – USA	1965
#Whitman, Malcolm – USA	1955
Wilander, Mats – SWE	2002
#Wilding, Anthony – NZL	1978
#Williams, Richard, 2nd – USA	1957
#Wills Moody Roark, Helen – USA	1959
*#Wingfield, Major Walter Clopton – GBR	1997
Wood, Sidney – USA	1964
#Wrenn, Robert – USA	1955
#Wright, Beals – USA	1956

Key
\# Deceased
* Enshrined for Contributions to Tennis
\+ Enshrined as a Royal Tennis Player

Eligibility was extended to include candidates worldwide in 1975

Golden Achievers
This award was first instituted in 1999 to recognise people, in addition to tennis players, who were contributing significantly to tennis worldwide.

Brian Tobin, ITF President 1991-99	1999
Gil de Kermadec	2000
Pablo Llorens Renaga	2001
Enrique Morea	2002
J. Howard "Bumpy" Frazer	2003
John Curry	2004

ITF/ITHF Davis Cup Award of Excellence

Neale Fraser (AUS)	2001
Pierre Darmon (FRA)	2002
John Newcombe (AUS)	2003
Manuel Santana (ESP)	2004

ITF/ITHF Fed Cup Award of Excellence

Arantxa Sanchez-Vicario and Conchita Martinez (ESP)	2001
Virginia Wade (GBR)	2002
Larisa Savchenko-Neiland (LAT)	2003
Olga Morozova (RUS)	2004

Obituaries

JOSEPH CULLMAN
Former International Tennis Hall of Fame President and Chairman Joseph Cullman died age 92 on 30 April in New York. Cullman was one of the pioneers of women's tennis, assisting in the implementation of the women's professional tour, the Virginia Slims Circuit, in 1970. He was President/Chairman and CEO of Philip Morris Co. from 1957 to 1978, and served as US Open Tournament Chairman 1969-70 during the transition to Open Era tennis. Cullman was President of the International Hall of Fame in 1982, and served as Chairman from 1985 to 1988. In 1988, he was designated Chairman Emeritus and appointed Chairman of the Executive Committee, before being inducted into the Hall of Fame in 1990.

DWIGHT DAVIS III
Dwight Davis III, grandson of Dwight Davis the founder of the Davis Cup competition, passed away on 7 May 2004 in New York City aged 68. Davis was an active member of the USTA Tennis & Education Foundation Board of Directors. Four years ago, he endowed a Foundation scholarship in his grandfather's name, designed to enable young people demonstrating an ability in tennis, academics and good character to attend college.

BOB HOWE
Former Australian professional Bob Howe died in Los Angeles on 30 November 2004 aged 79. During the late 1950's/early 1960's Howe won a number of mixed doubles titles at the Australian Open, Roland Garros and Wimbledon. After his retirement from professional tennis he became Deputy Referee of the US Open before taking over as Referee from 1983 to 1985. He also presided over 22 Davis Cup ties including the 1982 Final.

FRED HOYLES
Fred Hoyles, who served as referee at The Championships, Wimbledon between 1976 and 1982, died on 25 March. After retiring from Wimbledon, Hoyles took charge of several international matches, including the 1986 Davis Cup Final between Australia and Sweden and the qualifying rounds for the 1988 Seoul Olympics.

FINN KALHAUGE
The President of the Danish Tennis Federation (DTF), Finn Kalhauge, died suddenly in Paris on 1 June, he was 59 years old. Kalhauge was elected to the DTF Committee in 1989, where he did comprehensive work for junior tennis. He was Tournament Director of the Copenhagen Open for five years, and after serving as acting president of the DTF for two months, he was unanimously elected President in March 2003.

GORDON MARTIN
Gordon U.A. Martin passed away on 31 March 2004 at the age of 76, after a long career of promoting and supporting tennis in Asia. Martin was an advisor to the Lawn Tennis Association of Thailand between 1979 and 1992 and was Tournament Director for numerous ITF tournaments for juniors, men, women and vets, and founded many others throughout Asia and in particular Thailand. He was also the author of the Encyclopedia of Asian Tennis.

JOHN PARSONS
John Parsons, or JP as he was known, died in Miami, Florida on 26 April aged 66. He had been admitted to hospital while covering the NASDAQ-100 tournament. Parsons began his journalistic career at the Oxford Mail in 1956, he joined the Daily Mail in 1964 and had been the Daily Telegraph's lawn tennis correspondent since 1981. He first covered Wimbledon professionally in 1960 and won awards for his contribution to the sport from the ITF, LTA, WTA and ATP. Parsons was awarded the Ron Bookman Media Excellence Award for his life-long service to the sport in the 2003 ATP Awards. He was a former Chairman of The Lawn Tennis Writers Association and a member of the ITF Media Commission.

AUDRENE SNYDER
Audrene Snyder passed away on 31 December after a long illness. She was a long-time USTA volunteer and was first lady of the USTA when her husband, Lester M Snyder, served as USTA president in 1995-96. He also held a place on the ITF Board of Directors from 1995 to 1997. Mrs Snyder was a loyal USTA volunteer with many years of service on several committees.

Obituaries (continued)

ERIC STURGESS
South Africa's Eric Sturgess, winner of six Grand Slam doubles titles, died after a short illness on 14 January at the age of 83. Sturgess won the men's doubles title at the French Championships in 1947 and five more Grand Slam mixed doubles titles. In singles he reached three Grand Slam finals and represented South Africa in Davis Cup in six ties.

TORSTEN JOHANSSON
Former Swedish tennis player, Torsten Johansson died aged 84 on 14 May. Johansson played Davis Cup for Sweden for 16 years, retiring in 1962. He and Lennart Bergelin turned Sweden into a tennis power after World War II. Johansson holds a record at Wimbledon for being the only player to have produced two consecutive 60 60 60 victories at The Championships, a record that has held since 1947.

JOHN WARAMBO
The President of the Kenya Lawn Tennis Association, John Warambo, died suddenly on 2 March.

Country Abbreviations

AFG	Afghanistan		ECA	East Caribbean States
AHO	Netherlands Antilles		ECU	Ecuador
ALB	Albania		EGY	Egypt
ALG	Algeria		ERI	Eritrea
AND	Andorra		ESA	El Salvador
ANG	Angola		ESP	Spain
ANT	Antigua and Barbuda		EST	Estonia
ARG	Argentina		ETH	Ethiopia
ARM	Armenia		FIJ	Fiji
ARU	Aruba		FIN	Finland
ASA	American Samoa		FRA	France
AUS	Australia		FSM	Micronesia
AUT	Austria		GAB	Gabon
AZE	Azerbaijan		GAM	Gambia
BAH	Bahamas		GBR	Great Britain
BAN	Bangladesh		GBS	Guinea-Bissau
BAR	Barbados		GEO	Georgia
BDI	Burundi		GEQ	Equatorial Guinea
BEL	Belgium		GER	Germany
BEN	Benin		GHA	Ghana
BER	Bermuda		GRE	Greece
BHU	Bhutan		GRN	Grenada
BIH	Bosnia/Herzegovina		GUA	Guatemala
BIZ	Belize		GUI	Guinee Conakry
BLR	Belarus		GUM	Guam
BOL	Bolivia		GUY	Guyana
BOT	Botswana		HAI	Haiti
BRA	Brazil		HKG	Hong Kong, China
BRN	Bahrain		HON	Honduras
BRU	Brunei Darussalam		HUN	Hungary
BUL	Bulgaria		INA	Indonesia
BUR	Burkina Faso		IND	India
CAF	Central African Republic		IRI	Iran
CAM	Cambodia		IRL	Ireland
CAN	Canada		IRQ	Iraq
CAY	Cayman Islands		ISL	Iceland
CGO	Congo		ISR	Israel
CHA	Chad		ISV	US Virgin Islands
CHI	Chile		ITA	Italy
CHN	China, People's Rep. of		IVB	British Virgin Islands
CIV	Cote d'Ivoire		JAM	Jamaica
CMR	Cameroon		JOR	Jordan
COD	Congo, Democratic Rep. of (Zaire)		JPN	Japan
COK	Cook Islands		KAZ	Kazakhstan
COL	Colombia		KEN	Kenya
COM	Comoros		KGZ	Kyrgyzstan
CPV	Cape Verde Islands		KIR	Kiribati
CRC	Costa Rica		KOR	Korea, Rep. of
CRO	Croatia		KSA	Saudi Arabia
CUB	Cuba		KUW	Kuwait
CYP	Cyprus		LAO	Laos
CZE	Czech Republic		LAT	Latvia
DEN	Denmark		LBA	Libya
DJI	Djibouti		LBR	Liberia
DMA	Dominica		LCA	St Lucia
DOM	Dominican Republic		LES	Lesotho

Country Abbreviations (continued)

LIB	Lebanon	**SKN**	Saint Kitts & Nevis
LIE	Liechtenstein	**SLE**	Sierra Leone
LTU	Lithuania	**SLO**	Slovenia
LUX	Luxembourg	**SMR**	San Marino
MAD	Madagascar	**SOL**	Solomon Islands
MAR	Morocco	**SOM**	Somalia
MAS	Malaysia	**SRI**	Sri Lanka
MAW	Malawi	**STP**	Sao Tome and Principe
MDA	Moldova	**SUD**	Sudan
MDV	Maldives	**SUI**	Switzerland
MEX	Mexico	**SUR**	Surinam
MGL	Mongolia	**SVK**	Slovak Republic
MKD	Macedonia, Former Yugoslavian Rep. of	**SWE**	Sweden
MLI	Mali	**SWZ**	Swaziland
MLT	Malta	**SYR**	Syria
MON	Monaco	**TAN**	Tanzania
MOZ	Mozambique	**TGA**	Tonga
MRI	Mauritius	**THA**	Thailand
MSH	Marshall Islands	**TJK**	Tajikistan
MTN	Mauritania	**TKM**	Turkmenistan
MYA	Myanmar (Burma)	**TLS**	Timor-Leste
NAM	Namibia	**TOG**	Togo
NCA	Nicaragua	**TPE**	Chinese Taipei
NED	Netherlands	**TRI**	Trinidad & Tobago
NEP	Nepal	**TUN**	Tunisia
NFK	Norfolk Islands	**TUR**	Turkey
NGR	Nigeria	**UAE**	United Arab Emirates
NIG	Niger	**UGA**	Uganda
NMI	Northern Mariana Islands	**UKR**	Ukraine
NOR	Norway	**URU**	Uruguay
NRU	Nauru	**USA**	United States
NZL	New Zealand	**UZB**	Uzbekistan
OMA	Oman	**VAN**	Vanuatu
PAK	Pakistan	**VEN**	Venezuela
PAN	Panama	**VIE**	Vietnam
PAR	Paraguay	**VIN**	Saint Vincent & Grenadines
PER	Peru	**YEM**	Yemen
PHI	Philippines	**ZAM**	Zambia
PLE	Palestine	**ZIM**	Zimbabwe
PLW	Palau		
PNG	Papua New Guinea		
POC	Pacific Oceania		
POL	Poland		
POR	Portugal		
PRK	Korea, Democratic People's Rep. of		
PUR	Puerto Rico		
QAT	Qatar		
ROM	Romania		
RSA	South Africa		
RUS	Russia		
RWA	Rwanda		
SAM	Samoa		
SCG	Serbia and Montenegro		
SEN	Senegal		
SEY	Seychelles		
SIN	Singapore		

Historical Country Codes

FRG	Germany FR (GER since 1990)
GDR	Germany DR (GER since 1990)
BOH	Bohemia (TCH from 1920)
TCH	Czechoslovakia (SVK or CZE since 1994)
URS	USSR (former Soviet Union)
EUN	Unified Team (ex USSR)
RHO	Rhodesia (Zimbabwe from 1968)
YUG	Yugoslavia (Serbia and Montenegro from 2004)